Praise for *A World on Fire*

"Ms. Foreman is such an engaging writer that readers may find this 958-page volume too short." —MICHAEL BURLINGAME, *The Wall Street Journal*

"Foreman's descriptive gifts show especially well in bringing vividly to life the political and diplomatic worlds of Washington and London.... A brief review can only hint at the expansive scope, rich detail and pulsing energy of *A World on Fire*. Foreman succeeds admirably in evoking the British dimension of the great American crisis."

—*The Washington Post*

"This is an essential book, well-written and almost cinematic in sweep. As the historian Piers Brendon said about it, 'If her tome is hard to pick up, it is also hard to put down.'" —Newark *Star-Ledger*

"Meticulously researched, colorfully written and lavishly illustrated, Foreman's volume is a worthy addition to the Civil War sesquicentennial bookshelf." —Cleveland *Plain Dealer*

"[*A World on Fire*] is a tour de force, a work of extreme virtuosity both in the research and the telling." —Bloomberg.com

"[Foreman] is one of the more exciting historians I have encountered in years.... She has the knack of finding and using the quotations and descriptions that put vitality into her writing.... Five stars, at least."

—*The Washington Times*

"[Foreman's] book offers a brisk, compelling narrative that shows how important Britain was to the outcome of the war and how close the Union came to losing it." —*The Dallas Morning News*

"A splendid book...solidly grounded in a prodigious amount of research...[Foreman] breaks new ground in telling this vastly complicated story through the eyes of myriad characters."   —*The Wilson Quarterly*

"The contribution of *A World on Fire* lies in its richness of description, vivid writing, and focus on individual personalities....Some two hundred people figure with varying degrees of prominence in Foreman's story. And what a gripping story it is."

—JAMES McPHERSON, *The New York Review of Books*

"*A World on Fire* never flags. It is illuminated by the characters Foreman brings to life, and by the skill with which she describes the conflict itself. There are countless books on the Civil War, too many of them instantly forgettable, but this big book has something new to say, and says it with narrative brilliance."   —BERNARD CORNWELL, *The Mail on Sunday*

A World on Fire

BRITAIN'S CRUCIAL ROLE
IN THE AMERICAN CIVIL WAR

Amanda Foreman

RANDOM HOUSE TRADE PAPERBACKS

NEW YORK

2012 Random House Trade Paperback Edition

Published in the United States by Random House Trade Paperbacks,
an imprint of The Random House Publishing Group,
a division of Random House, Inc., New York.

RANDOM HOUSE TRADE PAPERBACKS and colophon are
trademarks of Random House, Inc.

Originally published in hardcover in the United States by Random House, an imprint of
The Random House Publishing Group, a division of Random House, Inc., in 2011.
Originally published in hardcover in the United Kingdom by Allen Lane, an imprint of
Penguin Press, a member of Penguin Group (U.K.) in 2010.

LIBRARY OF CONGRESS CATALOGING-IN-PUBLICATION DATA
Foreman, Amanda
A world on fire: Britain's crucial role in the American Civil War / Amanda Foreman.
p. cm.
Originally published: London: Allen Lane, 2010. Subtitle varies.
ISBN 978-0-375-75696-2
eBook ISBN 978-0-679-60397-9
1. United States—History—Civil War, 1861–1865—Participation, British.
2. United States—History—Civil War, 1861–1865—Foreign public opinion,
British. 3. United States—Foreign relations—Great Britain. 4. Great Britain—
Foreign relations—United States. 5. United States—Foreign relations—
1861–1865. 6. Great Britain—Foreign relations—1837–1901.
7. Public opinion—Great Britain—History—19th century. I. Title.
E469.F67   2011
973.7'2—dc22   2011003726

Printed in the United States of America

www.atrandom.com

2 4 6 8 9 7 5 3 1

Book design by Casey Hampton

For the children

Contents

List of Illustrations

The dates given in this list are the dates of first publication of the illustrations, not the dates on which the events they record took place.

List of Plates

Section Two

List of Maps

Preface

Some years ago, while researching the life of Georgiana, Duchess of Devonshire, I learned that her great-nephew, later the eighth Duke of Devonshire, had spent Christmas Day 1862 making eggnog for the Confederate cavalry officers of General Robert E. Lee's army. "I hope Freddy [his younger brother, Lord Frederick Cavendish] won't groan much over my rebel sympathies, but I can't help them," he wrote to his father three days later. "The people here are so much more earnest about the [war] than the North seems to be."

I was aware that the American Civil War had sharply polarized public opinion in Britain (my original doctoral thesis had examined attitudes toward race and color in pre-Victorian England), but it was still a shock to discover that the heir to the greatest Liberal peerage in England thought the slaveholding South had the moral advantage over the anti-slavery North. Understanding how the Confederacy had managed to achieve this ascendancy, not only with the duke but also with people who might generally be considered as belonging to the "progressive" classes in Britain—journalists, writers, university students, actors, social reformers, even the clergy—became one of the driving obsessions behind this book.

My original intention was to write a history of the British volunteers who fought in the Civil War. I had assumed that by examining their reasons for joining the Union or Confederate armies, I would gain an insight into the forces that had shaped public opinion. But once I began, the book refused to stay within its intended confines, especially as it became clear that these volunteers were part of an Anglo-American world that was far greater and more complex than I had ever imagined. It gradually became a biography of a relationship, or, more accurately, of the many relationships that together formed the British-American experience during the Civil War.

The war began on April 12, 1861, when Confederate troops fired on the Federal garrison at Fort Sumter in Charleston, South Carolina. The ensuing four-year struggle would lead to the freedom of 4 million slaves and cost the lives of more than 620,000 soldiers and 50,000 civilians. President Abraham Lincoln responded to the attack on Fort Sumter by calling for 75,000 volunteer soldiers and declaring a blockade of Southern ports. Across the Atlantic, however, Lord Palmerston's Liberal government was chiefly concerned with ensuring that Britain did not become embroiled in the conflict. There was too much at stake: the livelihoods of nearly a million workers depended on Southern cotton, while British investors held $444 million worth of U.S. stocks and securities. On May 13, reflecting a rare moment of unanimity between Parliament, the press, and the public, Queen Victoria issued a proclamation of neutrality, which recognized that a state of war existed between the Union and the Confederacy and forbade British subjects to take part. But this well-meaning act had precisely the opposite effect of what was intended. Each side accused Britain of favoring the other: the North threatened to invade Canada in retaliation, the South used every legal loophole to build its warships in British dockyards, and Britons ignored the injunction against interfering and volunteered by the thousands in the Union and Confederate armies. Twice in four years Britain and the North were on the brink of war: the first time, in December 1861, British troops were halfway to Canada by the time the two governments backed down.

Biography is a subset of history, yet it stands independently, too. The most obvious difference is that biographers delve deeply into individual lives and the influences that shaped them, whereas for historians it is the sum of individual experiences that is important. In *A World on Fire* I have tried to combine both approaches. I decided from the beginning to treat each of the significant figures in the story, and many of the lesser ones, as though he or she was the principal subject of the book, so that I could understand the antecedents of their motives and decisions during the

Civil War. This not only added several years to the project but also created the problem of how to construct a single narrative out of competing points of view within a time frame that encompassed multiple simultaneous events. The challenge seemed insurmountable, until one day I remembered having seen Trevor Nunn's 1980 *Nicholas Nickleby,* an extraordinary "theater-in-the-round" production that brought together a vast panoply of characters through a combination of three-dimensional staging, shifting scenes, and running narratives that created an all-enveloping experience for the audience. This memory became my guide and inspiration, and I set about writing a history-in-the-round in the hope of immersing the reader inside the British-American world of the Civil War. I was fortunate that many areas of this world had already been researched by Brian Jenkins, Howard Jones, R.J.M. Blackett, Charles Hubbard, D. P. Crook, Frank Merli, Warren F. Spencer, Norman Ferris, and others. My debt to their pioneering work cannot be overstated; any omissions or errors in the book are mine alone.

I am deeply grateful to Eve and Michael Williams-Jones, Hugh Dubrulle, Jonathan Foreman, Brian Jenkins, James McPherson, Christopher Mason, Michael Musick, Fredric Smoler, and Richard Snow for their help and criticisms of early versions of *A World on Fire.* The book took twelve years to complete, and I owe heartfelt thanks to Andrew Wylie, Sarah Chalfont, and Jeffrey Posternak of the Wylie Agency for their loyalty during all that time. True to the spirit of the book, *A World on Fire* was simultaneously edited by Susanna Porter at Random House in New York and Stuart Proffitt at Allen Lane in London; it has been a profoundly rewarding and intellectually satisfying process to work with them both. Over the years I have benefited enormously from the help and guidance provided by librarians and archivists all over the world, and they are thanked by name in the acknowledgments section. My family have been a tremendous support to me, but there is one person who, above all, made this book possible, and that is my husband: the center of *my* world.

Dramatis Personae

James Dunwoody Bulloch (1823–1901) CONFEDERATE—Chief Confederate secret service agent in England and architect of the Confederate naval acquisition program in Europe.

Clement Claiborne Clay (1789–1866) CONFEDERATE—U.S. senator from Alabama, 1853–61; Confederate senator from Alabama, 1862–64; Confederate commissioner in Canada, 1864–65.

George Mifflin Dallas (1792–1864) UNION—Minister at the U.S. legation in London, 1856–61.

William Lewis Dayton (1807–64) UNION—Minister at the U.S. legation in Paris, 1861–64.

Edwin De Leon (1818–91) CONFEDERATE—U.S. consul in Cairo, 1853–61; Confederate propagandist in England and France, 1862–64.

Thomas Haines Dudley (1819–93) UNION—U.S. consul in Liverpool, 1861–65; co-head of the U.S. secret service with Freeman H. Morse.

Ambrose Dudley Mann (1801–89) CONFEDERATE—U.S. assistant secretary of state, 1853–55; Confederate commissioner to Belgium, 1861–65.

William Maxwell Evarts (1818–1901) UNION—New York lawyer, sent to England to liaise with Crown prosecution lawyers in the *Alexandra* trial in 1863.

John Murray Forbes (1813–98) UNION—Influential businessman; sent to England to prevent the Confederacy from purchasing ships.

Rose O'Neal Greenhow (1817–64) CONFEDERATE—Washington society leader and Confederate spy.

James Holcombe (1820–73) CONFEDERATE—Confederate commissioner in Canada, 1864; former law professor at the University of Virginia.

Henry Hotze (1833–87) CONFEDERATE—Confederate propagandist, sent to England in 1862; editor of the pro-Southern *Index*.

Caleb Huse (1831–1905) CONFEDERATE—Purchasing agent for the Confederate army in England.

Colin McRae (1813–77) CONFEDERATE—Confederacy's chief financial agent in Europe, 1863–65.

James Murray Mason (1798–1871) CONFEDERATE—Senator from Virginia, 1847–61; Confederate commissioner in Britain, 1861–65; with Slidell, one of the two subjects of the *Trent* affair.

Benjamin Moran (1820–86) UNION—Assistant secretary at the U.S. legation in London, 1857–64, and secretary, 1864–74.

Freeman Harlow Morse (1807–91) UNION—U.S. consul in London, 1861–69; co-head with Thomas Haines Dudley of the U.S. secret service.

John Lothrop Motley (1814–77) UNION—Historian; U.S. minister to the Austrian Empire, 1861–67.

Pierre Adolphe Rost (1797–1868) CONFEDERATE—Confederate commissioner to France, 1861, and to Spain, 1862–65.

Henry Shelton Sanford (1823–91) UNION—Minister at the U.S. legation in Brussels; set up U.S. secret service operations in England and then in Belgium, 1862–65.

John Slidell (1793–1871) CONFEDERATE—Confederate commissioner to France; captured, with Mason, aboard the *Trent*.

Jacob Thompson (1810–85) CONFEDERATE—Colonel in Confederate army; head of clandestine operations in Canada.

Norman Walker (1831–1913) CONFEDERATE—Major in Confederate army; shipping agent in Bermuda; husband of Georgiana Walker.

Thurlow Weed (1797–1882) UNION—Adviser to Seward; unofficial envoy to France with Archbishop Hughes, Bishop McIlvaine, and General Winfield Scott, 1861.

Charles Wilson (1818–78) UNION—Illinois newspaper editor; secretary to the U.S. legation in London, 1861–64.

William Lowndes Yancey (1814–63) CONFEDERATE—Confederate commissioner to Britain and France, 1861–65.

Military

Nathaniel Prentice Banks (1816–94) UNION—Commander of the Department of the Gulf, 1862–64.

Braxton Bragg (1817–76) CONFEDERATE—Principal Confederate commander in the Western theater of the war; commander of the Department of Western Florida and the Army of Pensacola, 1861; commander of the Army of the Mississippi and the Army of Tennessee, 1862–63; chief military adviser to Jefferson Davis, 1864–65.

John Yates Beall (1835–65) CONFEDERATE—Confederate privateer.

Pierre Gustave Toutant Beauregard (1818–93) CONFEDERATE—First prominent general of the Confederacy, 1861–65; hero of Fort Sumter and First Battle of Bull Run; commander in the defense of Charleston.

Ambrose Everett Burnside (1824–81) UNION—Brigadier general and commander of the Army of the Potomac, 1861–63; commander of the Department of the Ohio, 1863–64; his prodigious whiskers allegedly inspired the word "sideburns."

Benjamin Franklin Butler (1818–93) UNION—Commander of Fort Monroe, 1861; administrator of the occupation of New Orleans; commander of the Department of Virginia and North Carolina, 1863, later designated the Army of the James, 1864.

Josiah Gorgas (1818–83) CONFEDERATE—Chief of the Confederate Ordnance Bureau.

Ulysses S. Grant (1822–85) UNION—Commander of the Army of the Tennessee, 1862–63, and the Military Division of the Mississippi, 1863–64; commanding general of the U.S. Army, 1864–69. Known as "Unconditional Surrender Grant" because of the terms he offered to the defeated Confederates at Fort Donelson.

Henry Wager Halleck (1815–72) UNION—Commander of the Department of the Missouri, 1861–62, and the Department of the Mississippi, 1862; general-in-chief of all Union armies, 1862–64; chief of staff, 1864–65; known as "Old Brains" for his treatise on military theory.

John William Headley (1841–1930) CONFEDERATE—Captain in General John Hunt Morgan's brigade; participated in the plot to bomb New York in 1864.

Thomas Henry Hines (1838–98) CONFEDERATE—Spy sent to Canada, via Chicago, to recruit propagandists and fighters for the South.

James Longstreet (1821–1904) CONFEDERATE—Commander of the Department of Virginia and North Carolina, 1863; commander of the Department of East Tennessee, 1863–64; principal subordinate to General Lee, who called him "Old War Horse." Also known as "Old Pete."

Thomas Jonathan "Stonewall" Jackson (1824–63) CONFEDERATE—Commander of the 1862 Shenandoah Valley campaign; corps commander in the Army of Northern Virginia under Robert E. Lee, 1862–63; nicknamed "Stonewall" after the First Battle of Bull Run.

Albert Sidney Johnston (1803–62) CONFEDERATE—Commander of the Western Department, 1861; led the Army of the Mississippi to defend Confederate lines from the Mississippi River to Kentucky and the Allegheny Mountains.

Joseph Eggleston Johnston (1807–91) CONFEDERATE—Commander of the Army of the Shenandoah, 1861; commander of the Army of the Potomac (later rechristened the Army of Northern Virginia), 1862; commander of the Department of the West, which gave him control over the Army of the Tennessee and the Department of Mississippi and East Louisiana.

Fitzhugh Lee (1835–1905) CONFEDERATE—Rose from lieutenant colonel of the 1st Virginia Cavalry to major general, 1861–65; nephew of Robert E. Lee.

Robert Edward Lee (1807–70) CONFEDERATE—Commander of the Army of Northern Virginia, 1862–65; general-in-chief of Confederate forces, 1865.

George Brinton McClellan (1826–85) UNION—Commander of the Department of the Ohio, 1861; commander of the Department of the Potomac, July 1861–November 1862; general-in-chief of the Union army, November 1861–March 1862.

Irvin McDowell (1818–85) UNION—Commander of the Army of Northeastern Virginia, 1861; commander of the Army of the Potomac, 1861–62.

George Gordon Meade (1815–72) UNION—Commander of the Army of the Potomac, 1863–65; defeated General Lee at the Battle of Gettysburg; nicknamed "The Old Snapping Turtle" for his hair-trigger temper.

George Washington Morgan (1820–93) UNION—Commander of the 7th Division of the Army of the Ohio, 1862–63; commander of the 3rd Division of the Union army's XIII Corps, 1863.

John Hunt Morgan (1825–64) CONFEDERATE—Colonel and brigadier general, 2nd Kentucky Cavalry Regiment, 1862–64; commander of the Trans-Allegheny Department, 1864; known for instigating "Morgan's raid."

John Singleton Mosby (1833–1916) CONFEDERATE—Commanded the 43rd Battalion, 1st Virginia Cavalry (known as the Partisan Rangers), 1863–65; nicknamed the "Gray Ghost."

John Pope (1822–92) UNION—Commander of the District of North and Central Missouri, 1861–62; commander of the Army of the Mississippi, 1862; commander of the Army of Virginia, 1862.

Winfield Scott (1786–1866) UNION—Commanding general of the U.S. Army, 1841–61.

Phillip Henry Sheridan (1831–88) UNION—Commander of the 3rd Division, XIV Corps, Army of the Cumberland, 1862–63; commander of the 2nd Division, IV Corps, Army of the Cumberland, 1863–64; commander of the Army of the Shenandoah, 1864–65.

William Tecumseh Sherman (1820–91) UNION—Brigadier general in the Army of the Tennessee, 1862; commander of the Department of the Tennessee, 1863–64; commander of the Military Division of the Mississippi, 1864–65.

James Ewell Brown ("Jeb") Stuart (1833–64) CONFEDERATE—Commander of the 1st Virginia Cavalry Regiment, 1861; commander of the Virginia Cavalry Brigade, 1861–62; commander of the Virginia Cavalry Division, 1862–63; commander of the Virginia Cavalry Corps, 1863–64.

Politicians

Judah Philip Benjamin (1811–84) CONFEDERATE—The second Jewish senator in U.S. history; Confederate attorney general, 1861; secretary of war, 1861–62; and secretary of state, 1862–65.

John Cabell Breckinridge (1821–75) CONFEDERATE—Confederate secretary of war, 1865.

Salmon Portland Chase (1808–73) UNION—U.S. secretary of the treasury, 1861–64.

Jefferson Davis (1808–89) CONFEDERATE—President of the Confederate States, 1861–65.

John Adams Dix (1798–1879) UNION—Military governor of New York.

Edward Everett (1794–1865)—U.S. secretary of state, 1852–53; U.S. senator from Massachusetts, 1853–54; celebrated educator and orator, famous for his two-hour speech before Lincoln's Gettysburg Address.

Abraham Lincoln (1809–65) UNION—First Republican president of the United States, 1861–65.

Stephen Russell Mallory (1813–73) CONFEDERATE—Confederate secretary of the navy, 1861–65.

James Alexander Seddon (1815–80) CONFEDERATE—Confederate secretary of war, 1862–65.

Frederick William Seward (1830–1915) UNION—U.S. assistant secretary of state, 1861–69 and 1877–79; son of William H. Seward.

William Henry Seward (1801–72) UNION—U.S. secretary of state, 1861–69.

Edwin Stanton (1814–69) UNION—U.S. secretary of war, 1862–65.

Charles Sumner (1811–74) UNION—U.S. senator from Massachusetts, 1851–74.

Robert Augustus Toombs (1810–85) CONFEDERATE—Confederate secretary of state, February–July 1861.

George Alfred Trenholm (1807–76) CONFEDERATE—Confederate secretary of the treasury 1864–65; founder of Fraser, Trenholm and Co.

Clement Laird Vallandigham (1820–71) UNION—U.S. House of Representatives, 3rd District Ohio, 1858–63; head of the Copperhead antiwar movement.

LeRoy Pope Walker (1817–84) CONFEDERATE—Confederate secretary of war, February–September 1861.

Gideon Welles (1802–78) UNION—U.S. secretary of the navy, 1861–69.

Pro-Northern Supporters

Edwin Thomas Booth (1833–93)—Actor; brother of John Wilkes Booth.

Frederick Douglass (1818–95)—Former slave; social reformer and abolition campaigner.

Horace Greeley (1811–72)—Editor of the *New York Herald.*

Sarah Parker Remond (1826–94)—Campaigner for abolition.

George Templeton Strong (1820–75)—Lawyer, co-founder, and treasurer of the U.S. Sanitary Commission.

Pro-Southern Supporters

Belle Boyd (1844–1900)—Confederate spy.

Mary Boykin Chesnut (1823–86)—South Carolinian diarist.

William Wilkins Glenn (1824–76)—Maryland journalist; conduit for British travelers entering the South.

John B. Jones (1810–66)—Virginian diarist; clerk in the War Department, Richmond, Virginia.

Charles Kuhn Prioleau (1827–87)—Head of Fraser, Trenholm and Co., Liverpool, England.

John R. Thompson (1828–73)—Poet, editor of the *Southern Literary Messenger*, 1847–59; contributor to the *Index*.

At Sea

David Glasgow Farragut (1801–70) UNION—Admiral on USS *Hartford*, 1862–66.

John Newland Maffitt (1819–86) CONFEDERATE—Captain of CSS *Florida*.

Matthew Fontaine Maury (1806–73) CONFEDERATE—Oceanographer; Confederate purchasing agent in Britain.

William Lewis Maury (1813–78) CONFEDERATE—Commander of CSS *Georgia*.

James Morris Morgan (1845–1928) CONFEDERATE—Lieutenant on CSS *Georgia*.

David Dixon Porter (1813–91) UNION—Commander of USS *Powhatan;* rear admiral of the Mississippi River Squadron.

Raphael Semmes (1809–77) CONFEDERATE—Commander of CSS *Sumter*, 1861–62; Captain of CSS *Alabama*, 1862–64.

Charles Wilkes (1798–1877) UNION—Captain of USS *San Jacinto;* instigator of the *Trent* affair.

John Ancrum Winslow (1811–73) UNION—Captain of USS *Kearsarge;* sank CSS *Alabama*.

BRITISH

Diplomats

Sir Edward Mortimer Archibald (1810–94)—British consul at New York, 1857–71.

Robert Bunch—British consul at Charleston, South Carolina, 1853–64.

Joseph Hume Burnley—Secretary of the British legation, Washington.

Richard Bickerton Pemell Lyons, 2nd Lord Lyons (1817–87)—Minister at the British legation, Washington, 1859–65.

Edward Baldwin Malet (1837–1908)—Attaché at the British legation, Washington, 1862–64.

Charles Stanley Monck, 4th Viscount Monck (1819–94)—Governor-general of Canada, 1867–69.

William Mure (1813–64)—British consul at New Orleans, Louisiana, 1843–57.

Francis Napier, 10th Lord Napier (1819–98)—Minister at the British legation, Washington, 1857–59.

Arthur H. Seymour—Third secretary of the British legation, Washington.

George Sheffield—Attaché at the British legation, Washington, 1859–64.

William Stuart (1824–96)—Secretary of the British legation, Washington, 1861–64.

Henry Wellesley, 1st Earl Cowley (1804–84)—British ambassador to France, 1852–67.

Journalists

John Chandler Bancroft Davis (1822–1907)—Pro-Northern correspondent, *The Times,* 1861.

Samuel Phillips Day—Pro-Southern correspondent, *Morning Herald,* 1861.

John Thadeus Delane (1817–79)—Editor of *The Times,* 1841–77.

Edward James Stephen Dicey (1832–1911)—Pro-Northern contributor, *Spectator.*

The Hon. Francis Charles Lawley (1825–1901)—Pro-Southern contributor, *The Times.*

Charles Mackay (1814–89)—Pro-Southern New York correspondent, *The Times,* 1862–65.

Harriet Martineau (1802–76)—Writer, social theorist, and contributor to the *Edinburgh Review* and the *Daily News,* 1852–68.

Mowbray Morris (1819–74)—Managing editor of *The Times.*

William Howard Russell (1820–1907)—Celebrated war reporter for *The Times.*

George Augustus Henry Sala (1828–95)—Novelist and pro-Southern contributor, *Daily Telegraph;* ghost writer for several pro-Southern memoirs.

Tom Taylor (1817–80)—Journalist and contributor to *Punch,* playwright, author of *Our American Cousin,* 1858.

Frank Vizetelly (1830–83)—War artist and correspondent, *Illustrated London News.*

Observers

Thomas Conolly (1823–76)—Member of Parliament for the County of Donegal.

Griffith Evans (1835–1935)—Veterinarian officer, Royal Artillery, British Army.

Arthur James Lyon Fremantle (1835–1901)—Lieutenant colonel, British Army; member of Her Majesty's Coldstream Regiment of Foot Guards; observer of the Battle of Gettysburg and the New York draft riots, April–July 1863.

Spencer Compton Cavendish, 8th Duke of Devonshire, Marquess of Hartington (1833–1908)—Civil Lord of the Admiralty, 1863; British undersecretary for war, 1863–66.

George Alfred Lawrence (1827–76)—British lawyer and novelist; author of *Guy Livingstone,* 1857.

Edward Fitzgerald Turton Ross (1835–?)—Captain, Austrian Hussars; Confederate propagandist and observer, 1863–64.

Lord Edward Percy St. Maur (1841–65)—Captain, volunteer cavalry, British Army; diplomat.

Edward Lyulph Stanley, 4th Baron Sheffield, 4th Baron Stanley of Alderly, and 3rd Baron Eddisbury (1839–1925)—British peer and member of Parliament for Oldham, 1880–85.

Leslie Stephen (1832–1904)—Author, literary critic, and editor of the *Dictionary of National Biography,* 1885–91.

Henry Yates Thompson (1838–1928)—Owner of the *Pall Mall Gazette,* 1878–92; observer of General Grant's victory at Chattanooga, 1863.

Garnet Wolseley, 1st Viscount Wolseley (1833–1913)—Field marshal, British Army; special service officer sent to Canada following the *Trent* affair, 1861; Pro-Southern observer, 1862–65.

Politicians

George John Douglas Campbell, 8th Duke of Argyll (1823–1900) LIBERAL—Lord Privy Seal, 1853–55, 1859–66, and 1880–81; postmaster general, 1855–58.

John Bright (1811–89) LIBERAL—Manufacturer; member of Parliament, and co-founder, with Richard Cobden, MP, of the Anti–Corn Law League, 1836.

George William Frederick Villiers, 4th Earl of Clarendon (1800–70) LIBERAL—Secretary of state for foreign affairs, 1853–58, 1865–66, and 1868–70.

Richard Cobden (1804–65) LIBERAL—Businessman, member of Parliament, and co-founder, with John Bright, of the Anti–Corn Law League, 1836; he and John Bright were known derisively in the House of Commons as "members for the United States."

Edward Smith Geoffrey Smith-Stanley, 14th Earl of Derby (1799–1869) CONSERVATIVE—Prime minister, February–December 1852, 1858–59, and 1866–68.

Benjamin Disraeli, 1st Earl of Beaconsfield (1804–81) CONSERVATIVE—Leader of the opposition in the House of Commons, 1851–52, 1852–58, 1859–66; chancellor of the exchequer, 1852, 1858–59, 1866–68; prime minister, 1868, 1874–80.

William Edward Forster (1818–86) LIBERAL—Industrialist; member of Parliament for Bradford, Yorkshire, 1861–85.

William Ewart Gladstone (1809–98) LIBERAL—chancellor of the exchequer, 1852–55, 1859–66; prime minister, 1868–74, 1880–85.

William Henry Gregory (1817–92) CONSERVATIVE—Pro-Southern member of Parliament for Dublin City, 1842–47, and County Galway, 1857–72.

Edmund Hammond, 1st and last Baron Hammond of Kirkella (1802–90) LIBERAL—Permanent undersecretary of Foreign Affairs, 1854–73.

John Laird (1805–74) CONSERVATIVE—Pro-Southern member of Parliament for Birkenhead, 1861–74; founder of John Laird, Sons and Co.

Sir Austen Henry Layard (1817–94) LIBERAL—Undersecretary of state for Foreign Affairs, January–February 1852, 1861–66.

Sir George Cornewall Lewis, 2nd Baronet (1806–63) LIBERAL—Chancellor of the exchequer, 1855–58; home secretary, 1859–61; secretary of state for war, 1861–63.

William Schaw Lindsay (1816–77) LIBERAL—Pro-Southern Scottish shipping magnate; founder and owner of W. S. Lindsay and Co., 1849–64; member of Parliament for Tynemouth and North Shields, 1854–59; member of Parliament for Sunderland, 1859–65.

Richard Monckton Milnes, 1st Baron Houghton (1809–85) CONSERVATIVE—Poet; member of Parliament for Pontefract, 1837–63; pro-Northern.

Henry Pelham-Clinton, 5th Duke of Newcastle (1811–64) LIBERAL—Secretary of state for war and the colonies, 1852–54; secretary of state for war, 1854–55; secretary of state for the colonies, 1859–64.

Roundell Palmer, 1st Earl of Selborne (1812–95) LIBERAL—Pro-Northern solicitor general, 1861–63; attorney general, 1863–66; Lord Chancellor, 1872–74 and 1880–85.

Henry John Temple, 3rd Viscount Palmerston, known as Lord Palmerston (1784–1865) LIBERAL—Secretary of state for foreign affairs, 1830–34, 1835–41, and 1846–51; home secretary, 1852–55; prime minister, 1855–58 and 1859–65.

John Arthur Roebuck (1802–79) LIBERAL—Member of Parliament for Bath, 1832–37 and 1841–47; member of Parliament for Sheffield, 1849–68 and 1874–79; pro-Southern.

John Russell, 1st Earl Russell (1792–1878) LIBERAL—Secretary of state for foreign affairs, 1852–53 and 1859–65; leader of the opposition, February–December 1852 and 1866–68; prime minister, 1846–52 and 1865–66.

Edward Adolphus Seymour (later St. Maur), 12th Duke of Somerset (1804 or 1805–85) LIBERAL—First commissioner of woods and forests, 1849–51; first commissioner of works, 1851–52; First Lord of the Admiralty, 1859–66.

Pro-Northern Supporters

Elizabeth Blackwell (1821–1910)—British-born doctor; first woman to earn a medical degree in the United States; first woman to be placed on the British Medical Register; founder of the New York Infirmary for Indigent Women and Children, 1857.

John Elliott Cairnes (1823–75)—Irish economist; Whatley Professor, Trinity College, Dublin, 1856–61; professor of jurisprudence and political economy at Queen's College Galway, 1859–70; author of *The Slave Power,* 1862.

Lord Frederick Charles Cavendish (1836–82)—Progressive politician; private secretary to Lord Granville, 1859–64; private secretary to Prime Minister Gladstone, 1872–73.

Thomas Hughes (1822–96)—Author of *Tom Brown's Schooldays,* 1857.

Fanny Kemble (1809–93)—Actress; author of *Journal of a Residence on a Georgian Plantation in 1838–1839,* 1863.

Peter Sinclair—Social reformer; author of *Freedom or Slavery in the United States: Being Fact and Testimonies for the Consideration of the British People,* 1863.

Goldwin Smith (1823–1910)—British Canadian historian and journalist; Regius Professor of Modern History at Oxford University, 1858–66.

Harriet Sutherland-Leveson-Gower, Duchess of Sutherland (1806–68)—Granddaughter of Georgiana, Duchess of Devonshire; a champion of the American antislavery movement.

Pro-Southern Supporters

Mary Sophia Hill (1819–1902)—Sister of Sam Hill, 6th Louisiana Volunteers; regimental nurse in the 6th Louisiana Volunteers; Federal prisoner of war, 1864.

Thomas Kershaw—British peace campaigner on behalf of the South.

James Spence (1816–1905)—Author of *The American Union,* 1862; Liverpool businessman; pro-Southern propagandist and lobbyist.

Francis William Tremlett (1821–1913)—Vicar of St. Peter's Church, Belsize Park; unofficial chaplain to the Confederate navy in England.

Edward Montagu Stuart Granville Montagu-Stuart-Wortley-Mackenzie, 3rd Baron Wharncliffe (1827–99)—President of the Manchester Southern Independence Association.

The War at Sea

Sir William Nathan Wrighte Hewett (1834–88)—Commander of HMS *Rinaldo*, 1861–62, and HMS *Basilisk*, 1865–69; commander of the ill-fated *Condor*, 1864.

The Hon. Augustus Charles Hobart-Hampden (1822–86)—Under the pseudonym "Captain Roberts" commanded the blockade runners *Don* and *Falcon* during the Civil War.

Sir Alexander Milne, 1st Baronet (1806–96)—Royal Navy commander-in-chief, North America and West Indies, 1860–64; First Naval Lord, 1866–68 and 1872–76.

Thomas Taylor (1841–?)—Supercargo on the blockade runners *Banshee, Will o' the Wisp, Wild Dayrell, Stormy Petrel,* and *Wild Rover;* author of *Running the Blockade,* 1896.

Volunteers

Bennet Graham Burley [also spelled Burleigh] (c. 1844–1914) CONFEDERATE—Scottish volunteer, Confederate navy; Federal prisoner of war, 1864; went on to become a notable war correspondent.

Charles Culverwell (1837–1919) UNION—Actor (stage name: Charles Wyndham); brigade surgeon in the Union army, 1862–64.

Leonard Douglas Hay Currie (1832–1907) UNION—Assistant adjutant general to Brigadier General W. F. Smith; colonel in the 133rd New York Volunteer Infantry.

Francis Warrington Dawson [né Austin John Reeks] (1840–89) CONFEDERATE—Common sailor, CSS *Nashville,* 1861; master's mate, CSS *Louisiana,* 1862; 1st lieutenant of artillery in the "Purcell Artillery" battalion, under the command of Captain William "Willy" Johnson Pegram.

John Fitzroy De Courcy, 31st Baron Kingsale (1821–90) UNION—Stipendiary magistrate of San Juan Island; colonel of the 16th Ohio Volunteer Infantry.

Frederick Farr (1844–64) UNION—Private, Company F, 7th Maine Infantry, 1863–64.

Henry Wemyss Feilden (1838–1921) CONFEDERATE—Private, 42nd (Royal Highland) Regiment of the Foot (also known as the Black Watch), 1857–60; assistant adjutant general in Charleston, Confederate army.

George St. Leger Grenfell (1808–68) CONFEDERATE—Assistant inspector general of the corps of cavalry of the Army of Tennessee, 1862; assistant inspector general of the corps of cavalry of the Army of Northern Virginia, 1863.

George Henry Herbert UNION—Lieutenant, 9th New York Volunteer Infantry ("Hawkins's Zouaves").

Henry George Hore (d. 1887) UNION—Aide-de-camp to Major General John Sedgwick.

James Horrocks UNION—Private, 5th Battery, New Jersey Volunteers.

Robert Moffat Livingstone (1846–64) UNION—3rd New Hampshire Infantry; son of the explorer Dr. David Livingstone.

Henry Ronald Douglas MacIver (1841–1907) CONFEDERATE—Lieutenant, variously as aide to Generals "Stonewall" Jackson, Jeb Stuart, and Edmund Kirby-Smith.

Charles Mayo (1837–77) UNION—Staff surgeon-major and medical inspector of the XIII Army Corps.

Robert Neve (1831–79) UNION—5th Kentucky Volunteers.

James Pendlebury (1841–97) UNION—Private, 69th New York Infantry.

Alfred Rubery CONFEDERATE—Would-be privateer.

Llewellyn Traherne Bassett Saunderson (1841–1913) CONFEDERATE—Staff officer to General Fitzhugh Lee.

Henry Morton Stanley [né John Rowlands] (1841–1904) CONFEDERATE—and Union "Dixie Grays," Company E, 6th Arkansas Regiment of Volunteers, Confederate army.

William Watson (1826–?) CONFEDERATE—Scottish businessman living in Louisiana; enlisted in the Confederate army in 1861 with the 3rd Louisiana Infantry; author of *Life in the Confederate Army*.

Ebenezer Wells UNION—Wagon master, 79th New York Highlanders.

Stephen Winthrop (1839–79) CONFEDERATE—Staff officer to General Alexander.

Sir Percy Wyndham (1833–79) UNION—Colonel of 1st New Jersey Cavaliers.

United States of America and the Confederate States of America

United States of America

Confederate States of America

Border States

WASHINGTON TERRITORY

Columbia R.

• Salem

OREGON

Snake R.

Missouri R.

UNORGANIZED TERRITORY

NEBRASKA TERRITORY

Sacramento

San Francisco

UTAH TERRITORY

Colorado R.

CALIFORNIA

KANSAS TERRITORY

Arka

COLORADO TERRITORY

Public land strip

The 1820 compromise

INDIAN TERRITO

Rio Grande R.

NEW MEXICO TERRITORY

TEXAS

Ft. Mason ▲

Pacific Ocean

Aus

San • Antonio

Rio Grande R.

MEXICO

Miles

0   100   200   300

CANADA

L. Superior

Ottawa R.

St. Lawrence R.

MAINE
Bangor

MINNESOTA

MICHIGAN

L. Huron

L. Ontario

NEW YORK

Montpelier
V.T.
N.H.
Concord

WISCONSIN

St. Paul

Mississippi R.

L. Michigan

Lansing

Detroit

Buffalo

West Point

Watervliet
Troy
Albany

MASS.

Boston
Providence

R.I.

IOWA

Madison

Freeport
Chicago

Cleveland

L. Erie

PENNSYLVANIA

Harrisburg
Lancaster

Gettysburg

Hartford
CONN.

New York

Trenton
Philadelphia

NEW JERSEY

Des Moines

ILLINOIS
Bloomington

INDIANA

OHIO

Pittsburgh

Baltimore
Annapolis

Dover

DELAWARE

Quincy
Springfield

Indianapolis

Dayton

Columbus

Harpers Ferry

Washington
D.C.

MARYLAND

Missouri R.

Alton

Ohio R.

Cincinnati

Ft. Leavenworth

Jefferson
City

St. Louis

Louisville
Frankfort
Lexington

VIRGINIA

Richmond

Ft. Monroe
Norfolk

Lecompton

KENTUCKY

Petersburg

Roanoke Island

Cairo

Cumberland

MISSOURI

30'

Tennessee R.

NORTH
CAROLINA

Raleigh

Ft. Macon

ARKANSAS

Nashville
Franklin

TENNESSEE

Wilmington

Memphis
Shiloh
Iuka

SOUTH
CAROLINA

Columbia

Little
Rock

Mississippi R.

MISSISSIPPI

Atlanta

Augusta

Charleston

Ft. Sumter

Red R.

ALABAMA

Milledgeville

Ft. Pulaski
Savannah

Atlantic
Ocean

LOUISIANA

Vicksburg
Jackson

Montgomery

GEORGIA

Bermuda

Mt. Vernon
Ft. Barrancas

Mobile

Pensacola

Tallahassee

Baton
Rouge

Biloxi

Ft. Pickens
Ft. McRee

FLORIDA

New Orleans

Ft. Gaines

Galveston

Ship Island

BAHAMAS ISLANDS

Gulf of Mexico

Ft. Taylor

Ft. Jefferson
Dry Tortugas

Key West

Virginia and the Washington Area

Cumberland

Potomac R.

Baltimore & Ohio R.R.

Romney

Clarksburg • Grafton

Philippi •

Cedar Creek
Strasbu
Fisher's Hill

Buckhannon •

W E S T

Beverly •

V I R G I N I A

Manassas Gap R.R.

Shenandoah R.

New Market ⚔

Lur

Elkwater •

Franklin •

Thornt
Gap

Harrisonburg •

Swift R
Gap

McDowell •

Cross Keys ⚔

Huntersville •

Port Republic ⚔

Brown's
Gap

Piedmont ⚔

Staunton •

Waynesboro ⚔

Rockfish
Gap

Charlottesvil

N

W ⚬ E

S

Clifton
Forge •

Lexington •

Blue Ridge Mountains

James R.

Miles

0   10   20   30   40   50

V I R G I

Appomattox
Court House

Lynchburg •

Farmvill

Roanoke •

Appomattox Sta.

Virginia & Tennessee R.R.

Roanoke R.

Mississippi River to Virginia

Gulf of Mexico

Miles
0   100   200

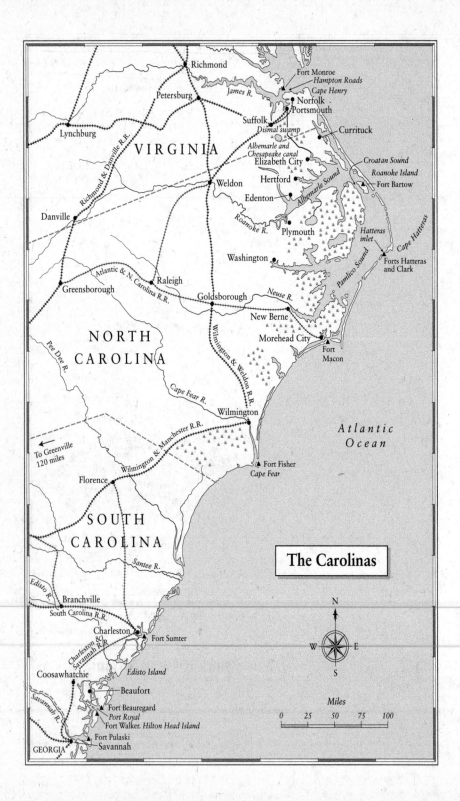

The Carolinas

A World on Fire

Prologue

Farewell to Lord Napier—Lord Lyons puzzles Washington society—Rocky relations between Britain and America

Washington society adored the Napiers. From the moment they had arrived at the British legation in 1857, Lord Napier was hailed as the friendliest and most sensible diplomat ever to set foot in the capital. For her part, Lady Napier soon won her own following as a hostess of unparalleled warmth and grace. "Her cozy at-homes were remarkable for their informality," recalled a Southerner after the war. Their presence was considered essential at any fashionable gathering. The legation was neutral territory and "one met there the talented and distinguished; heard good music, listened to the flow of wholesome wit; and enjoyed delectable repasts. . . . A feeling of universal regret spread over the capital when it became known that the Napiers were to return to England."[1]

Senator William Henry Seward of New York, Lord Napier's closest friend in Washington and the heir apparent to the Republican leadership, invited a small group of senators to join him in organizing a farewell ball. The committee had hoped to control the number of guests by charging $10 per person,* but the heady combination of popularity and power resulted in no fewer than 1,800 subscriptions for the gala. Only one venue other than the White House could accommodate so large a gathering:

---

* Equivalent to $1,700 in today's money.

Willard's Hotel on the corner of E and Fourteenth streets. *The New York Times* joked that a ticket to the Napier ball was harder to come by than a front row seat at the current Broadway hit comedy *Our American Cousin* by the British playwright Tom Taylor.[2]

On February 17, 1859, the grand ballroom at Willard's was specially decorated with an Anglo-American theme. Flags and mirrors lined the walls, and two large portraits, one of George Washington, the other of Queen Victoria, hung majestically from the ceiling. A representation of Saint George and the Dragon, made of sand, covered the floor. It was, however, the lavish banquet that created the most excitement. The chef had fashioned the Napiers' coat of arms out of spun sugar, as well as "dolphins in a sea of rock candy, and ices in every form, from a pair of turtle doves to a pillared temple."[3]

The Napiers made their appearance at 9:45 P.M. to the strains of "God Save the Queen" and were greeted with loud cheers and applause. Their evening dress was decidedly old-fashioned according to American tastes. Boldly resisting the trend among men for black evening attire, Lord Napier wore a royal blue jacket over a white waistcoat. Lady Napier's dress was also characteristically idiosyncratic: rather than trying to compete with her wealthy friends, she had chosen to wear a white silk gown decorated with tulle and edged in black lace. "You did not hear ladies say of her, as of so many others: 'What a splendid dress—how much did it cost!'" commented the *New York Times* reporter. "When will women learn that to beauty and perfection of attire, cost is but a small essential?" The gallant journalist was clearly ignorant of the sartorial revolution that had taken place during the previous year. On the inside, every woman of means was wearing one of W. S. Thompson's new steel crinoline cages; on the outside, they were experimenting with the new range of colors made possible by the invention of synthetic dye. (Even Queen Victoria was not immune to the changes in fashion and had worn mauve to the wedding of her eldest daughter, Princess Victoria, to Prince Frederick of Prussia in January 1858.) Lady Napier's elegant but austere dress reflected none of these developments and yet still managed to cause a sensation, not only on account of its simple design but also because amid the unavoidable clash of magentas and fuchsias the pure white cast all other colors in the shade.

The enmity that had begun to poison social life in Washington went into suspension during the ball. The crush was so great that dancing had to take place in relays, the guests jamming the bars and corridors while they waited their turn to enter the ballroom. Decorated veterans from the Mexican War chatted sociably with bankers from New York, and the broad vowels of Mississippi intermingled with the clipped tones of Massachusetts. The reigning queens of society made a rare collective appearance: Mrs. John Slidell and Mrs. Rose Greenhow rotated around each other like brilliant stars, their orbits passing close by but never quite touching. It was said by Mrs. Greenhow's rivals that she had adorned the British legation in much the same way as Lord Nelson's mistress, Lady Hamilton, had adorned his ship.[4]

Among the few who were missing from the ball was President Buchanan, who remained at home with a head cold. William Lowndes Yancey of Alabama was also indisposed; this was perhaps fortunate, since his booming voice could overpower a brass band—particularly when warming to his twin obsessions of slavery now and slavery forever. Charles Francis Adams, the congressman-elect from Massachusetts, had also stayed away, despite his family's long association with British-American diplomacy.* Adams despised small talk, hardly drank, and never danced. Not even the disappointment of his wife, Abigail, could overcome his reluctance to attend.

One of the highlights of the evening came when Lord Frederick Cavendish, second son of the seventh Duke of Devonshire, and the Hon. Evelyn Ashley, step-grandson of the former prime minister Viscount Palmerston, walked onto the dance floor. There were frissons among the debutantes as the two bachelors repaid many debts of hospitality accrued during their tour of America by dancing into the small hours of the morning. However, it was only in retrospect that the Napier ball became famous—not for its exalted guests or its lavish banquet, but as the last time Northerners and Southerners socialized together before the war.

———

Lord Napier's replacement as the senior British diplomat in America, Lord Lyons, arrived in Washington at the beginning of April 1859. Even by English standards, the forty-two-year-old Richard Bickerton Pemell

---

* Charles Francis Adams's grandfather, John Adams (the second president of the United States), and father, John Quincy Adams (the sixth president), had both served as ministers plenipotentiary to the Court of St. James's.

The Napier Ball at Willard's Hotel, Washington, D.C., February 17, 1859.

Lyons was an eccentric character. Any display of emotion—including his own—made him uncomfortable. Women and servants tended to suffer from an excess of it, in his opinion, which made him dread close contact with either. He was reluctant to look people in the eye and knew the shoes and stockings of his servants far better than their faces. Though not a killjoy, Lyons had never developed a taste for alcohol, and smoking made him ill; this was less of a handicap in Europe, where his witty and erudite conversation made him a favorite of hostesses.[5] But in Washington, his lack of interest in cigars and whiskey simply accentuated his strangeness. Napier did his best for Lyons during the short time they overlapped at the legation. With Congress in recess and mass departures from Washington already under way, he rushed to introduce Lyons to potential allies in the Senate before they scattered to their home states. But William Seward left Washington in late April to spend a couple of weeks with his family before embarking on an extended tour of Europe. Seward's early departure prevented Napier from fostering any meaningful understanding between his friend and his successor.

"Lord Napier has exerted himself very much to assist me in every way," wrote Lyons gratefully in mid-April, "and has done all that was possible to start me well both socially and politically."[6] Privately, he was relieved that his education in the complexities and nuances of American politics had begun during the quiet season. Lyons had never previously heard of the term "Mason-Dixon Line," yet every person he met described himself as living either above or below this boundary. Napier explained to him that it was the cultural as well as geographical divide between the North and South.* Although America was one country, Lyons would discover that it was two distinct regions whose ties were straining over the question of slavery. Above all else, warned Napier, a British minister must not become embroiled or be thought to take sides in this fractious debate.

Napier used the term "minister" because there were no ambassadors or embassies in Washington. In the mid-nineteenth century there were only three British embassies abroad: Paris, Vienna, and Constantinople. The rest of the world had to make do with second-tier "legations," which functioned in the same way, only with less pomp and a smaller budget. These were headed by a representative with the longwinded title of "British envoy extraordinary and minister plenipotentiary," or "minister" for short. Naturally, there was a hierarchy; the British minister to the United States ranked lower than his colleagues in Russia and Spain, but above those in Greece, Denmark, and Bavaria. Languishing below the legations were general consulates, which were reserved for countries of unproven stability in places like South America.[7]

The British legation was the largest and most important of the diplomatic missions in Washington. With the exception of the French legation, the other twenty-one were insignificant establishments. The nine Latin American ministers were too impoverished to receive visitors; the Austrian legation consisted of one minister living in a hotel, and the Italian minister loathed the capital so much that he lived in New York.[8] The burdens placed on the British minister were also greater than those faced by his foreign counterparts. Lyons was not only the conduit between London and Washington but also Her Majesty's guardian over the two and a half million British expatriates living in America.[9]

The tumultuous history between the two countries made every

---

* The line was originally drawn in 1767 by two British astronomers, Charles Mason and Jeremiah Dixon, who had been commissioned to settle a border dispute between Maryland and Pennsylvania. But by the mid-nineteenth century, "Mason-Dixon Line" had come to mean the separation between the "northern" state of Pennsylvania and the "southern" state of Maryland, and all the states above and below the 39th parallel.

British minister a soft target for American politicians. Lyons was sent to Washington with the same set of instructions and warnings that had accompanied each of his predecessors. He was to improve relations between the two countries and must be prepared to accept that the kindness bestowed on him in private would be matched by untrammeled hostility in public. Lyons was also to expect a regular whipping from the White House and Congress.[10]

Lyons was used to loneliness. "A trained diplomatist is reserved while appearing open," wrote a nineteenth-century journalist; "one who has the air of telling you everything, and yet tells you nothing; who seems to go with you all the way, yet advances never an inch beyond the line he has drawn for himself."[11] This described Lyons perfectly. He was tactful and discreet to the point of parody; outside his work he had few interests that could not be met by a comfortable chair and a warm fire. Many years later the Paris police compiled an intelligence report on Lyons that consisted of one line: *On ne lui connait pas de vice* ("He has no known vices").[12] His most regular female correspondents were his two sisters, particularly his youngest and favorite, Minna, who was married to the Duke of Norfolk. Lyons's horror of "scenes" made him so reticent that for years he put up with the same breakfast every morning rather than risk upsetting his valet with a request for something different.[13]

Lyons had hesitated to accept the Washington post for fear that he might prove to be a disappointment. Though the eldest of four children, he had always suffered in comparison to his younger brother, Edmund. Richard was portly, nonathletic, and incapable of stepping onto a boat without being sick. In contrast, Edmund was charismatic, adventurous, and loved the sea, like their father, the 1st Lord Lyons. The latter had forged a successful double career in the Royal Navy and the Foreign Office, which led to becoming a rear admiral in 1851 and receiving a peerage in 1856.

Richard Lyons had entered the diplomatic service in 1839 after graduating from Oxford with a fourth-class degree and no other prospects. For five years he worked as an unpaid attaché for his father, who was serving as the British minister in Athens. In his sixth year, he was promoted to paid attaché, but there he remained long after his father moved on to more interesting posts. For thirteen years Richard worked quietly and efficiently, hoping that the Foreign Office would take notice of him. Finally, he could no longer bear his life at the conflict-riven legation or put up with the humiliation of being the oldest attaché in the service, and in 1852 he announced his intention to resign. His protest resulted in a rapid transfer to Dresden, though with the same rank.

By 1857, Lyons was serving in the Florence legation, though still only ranked twenty-fourth out of the twenty-six secretaries in the service. This was a significant improvement in his fortunes, yet one that his father thought long overdue. Admiral Lyons's beloved Edmund had been killed in 1855, in the waning months of the Crimean War, while carrying out his father's order to attack the batteries of Sebastopol. The admiral's health declined rapidly after Edmund's death, but during his last years he continued to exert himself on Richard's behalf, arguing his merits to former colleagues.[14] His efforts were vindicated after Lyons surprised himself and others with his elegant resolution of a dispute between the Neapolitans and the Sardinians before it escalated into an international controversy. Overnight, he became the Foreign Office's preferred man for difficult situations. Admiral Lyons died in November 1858, a few days after learning of his son's promotion to the Washington legation.

Lord Lyons would have arrived in Washington much sooner had not the settlement of the will detained him in England until mid-February 1859. There was a further delay caused by the Foreign Office's parsimonious attitude to travel; Lyons had to cross the Atlantic on an inferior ship that burned through its coal halfway through the voyage. The crossing took a stomach-churning six weeks to complete instead of the usual ten days, sheer torture for a man who was terrified of water.[15]

Lyons's doubts about his fitness for his new post were shared by President James Buchanan, who resented the implication that Washington ranked next to Florence in importance—especially since 80 percent of Britain's cotton supply came from America. The textile industry was one of the most important in Britain, and the cotton trade translated into a business worth $600 million a year, providing employment and financial security in England for more than 5 million men and women. This alone, believed Buchanan, merited a "first-rate man whose character is known to this country."[16] Lord Lyons's courtesy call to the American legation in London before he sailed had unwittingly confirmed the U.S. administration's suspicion that the British Foreign Office was sending a nonentity. "Sensible," "unobtrusive," and "short" were the legation's chief impressions of Lyons.[17]

Buchanan's misgivings about the quality of his new British minister were mild compared to Lord Lyons's judgment of his new place of residence. Washington was not a city at all, in his opinion. "It is in fact little more than a large village," he wrote to Lord Malmesbury, the Conservative foreign secretary, a month after he arrived, "and when Congress is not sitting it is a deserted village."[18] The original political and strategic reasons for building the nation's capital by the Potomac River had been obsolete for decades. The War of 1812 between Britain and America had demonstrated that the city could be invaded just as easily as New York. The Potomac had seemed to promise a thriving water trade, but the river proved too shallow for modern transports. Washington had been the geographic center when the Union consisted of only thirteen states; the country's expansion to thirty-three now placed it on the periphery.

Washington lacked the literary salons, studios, universities, and conservatories that distinguished the capitals of Europe. The theaters relied on touring productions from New York; the shops were small and understocked. There was no commercial or manufacturing district such as those found in the new industrial cities, though the levels of violence, drunkenness, and corruption were not dissimilar. There were few cultural amenities save for the Smithsonian Institution, which had been established in 1846 with a bequest from the British scientist James Smithson. (Strangely, Smithson had never even visited the United States, let alone Washington.) The majority of the city's permanent residents were civil servants, lawyers, or saloon keepers. When Charles Dickens traveled to the capital in 1842, he thought the city had "Magnificent Intentions" but little else. It had "spacious avenues, that begin in nothing and lead to nowhere" and "streets [a] mile long, that only want houses, roads, and inhabitants."[19]

Fifteen years later, these intentions remained unfulfilled. "Most members of Congress live in hotels or furnished lodgings," wrote an English tourist. "In consequence, there is no style about the mode of living. . . . The whole place looks run up in a night, like the cardboard cities which Potemkin erected."[20] The boundaries of Washington were still ragged and ill defined. A disagreement between the government and a local landowner had stranded the unfinished Capitol on top of a steep hill at the edge of town, facing the wrong way. Washington's smart district lay two miles in the opposite direction, across marshland and noisome swamps that were breeding grounds for malaria in the summer. Elsewhere, the roads were still dirt tracks that frequently ended in piles of rubble or were interrupted by pastures. A pedestrian was in danger not only from one of the city's unregulated hackney cabs, but also from being run over by wandering livestock. "On nine days out of every ten, the climate of Washington is simply detestable," complained a British journalist. "When it rains, the streets are sloughs of liquid mud. In a couple of hours from the time the rain ceases, the same streets are enveloped in clouds of dust."[21]

The real political center of the city was Willard's Hotel. Just a five-minute walk from the White House, this was where the "wire pullers," the information seekers (and sellers), and those looking for employment seized the opportunity to mix with the temporary occupants of the Capitol. Here, on an average day, twenty-five hundred people passed through its doors. "Heavy persons, whom you have never seen before, with moist hands, eyes luminous with intoxicating beverages, break through the crowd and wildly shake your hand," observed an anonymous journalist. "They convict you of having met them before somewhere. You say you have been there, whereupon you are instantly saddled with an acquaintance who grasps your hand fifty times a day, and whom you heartily wish at the—Antipodes."[22] The hotel's regulars downed cocktails in one

The arrival of President Lincoln at Willard's Hotel, February 23, 1861.

of its many saloons or puffed themselves hoarse in the cigar bar, rendering real tourists appalled. "The tumult," complained one English traveler, "the miscellaneous nature of the company, the heated, muggy rooms," the revolting globs of tobacco spat on every surface, "despite a most liberal provision of spittoons," made it "by no means agreeable to a European."[23]

The British legation was established in Rush House at 1710 H Street, only a block from Lafayette Square, where the White House, the State Department, and many of Washington's grandest mansions were clustered. Rush House was large enough to accommodate the chancery, the business end of the legation, and was sufficiently imposing to impart an air of consequence to diplomatic functions. Lord Lyons's arrival created a stir similar to the excitement described by Jane Austen after the leasing of Netherfield Hall. "The gossips at once set about predicting that the newcomer would capitulate to the charms of some American woman, and speculation was already rife as to who would be the probable bride," wrote Mrs. Clay, the wife of Senator Clement C. Clay of Alabama.[24]

It was soon discovered, however, that Lyons, with his little round face and droopy eyes, was neither a Mr. Bingley nor a Mr. Darcy. Mrs. Clay received a "formidable card to the first Senatorial dinner given by the newly arrived diplomat" and decided this was her chance to collar him for a Southern belle. "I soon became emboldened to the point of suggesting to him the possibility of some lovely American consenting to become 'Lyonised.' His Lordship's prompt rejoinder and quizzical look quite abashed me, and brought me swiftly to the conclusion that I would best let this old lion alone."[25] Lyons had quoted *Tristram Shandy* at Mrs. Clay, but his arcane reference to Uncle Toby's habit of sleeping "slantindicularly" not only passed over her head but made her wonder whether the new British minister was quite sane.

Mrs. Clay's encounter with Lyons confirmed the general impression in Washington that he had replaced the Napiers but would never supplant them in the capital's affections. Varina Davis, the wife of Senator Jefferson Davis of Mississippi, wrote that people thought Lyons "very taciturn and very stupid."[26] Lord Napier gave his final speech in the United States on April 15, 1859. "I can never forget or requite the incessant kindness . . . offered to me by the American people," he told an emotional audience at Astor House in New York. The following day, the press commented on the coincidence that Britain's two most popular exports should make their farewells to America on the same night. The fifteenth also marked the last performance of the comedy *Our American Cousin*. It had run for 140 nights, a feat never before achieved in the history of American theater.

Lord Napier's popularity had proved his undoing at the Foreign Office. "Napier is much too frank and too yielding to the Yankees," the then prime minister, Lord Derby, had complained, "and they take advantage of him in every way."[27] Napier's friendship with Senator Seward was considered symptomatic of his mistaken priorities. The Foreign Office was not interested in having a minister who understood the Americans' point of view. The choice of Lord Lyons to replace the adored Lord Napier—a decision that seemed incomprehensible to Washington—made perfect sense to London. Lyons's views on America were generally in keeping with those of the Foreign Office: he was well disposed to its people, but he thought that democracy made the government weak and handed too much power to the violent and ignorant elements of society. If Lord Lyons were to feel concern over whether the Americans liked him, his superiors in London were confident such insecurities would be sublimated by his renowned sense of duty.

Lord Lyons soon realized that Napier had not been exaggerating when he described America as the "Castle Dangerous" of British diplomacy. His first request to the Foreign Office was for more staff; "considering . . . the very great importance of not giving offence and the extreme readiness of people here to take it, I think that few ministers abroad have so much need of a private secretary's help as I have."[28] Already it was apparent to him that the taking and giving of offense had become a reflexive habit in Anglo-American relations since the separation of 1775–83. For prudence's sake, he had decided to "gratify their vanity by treating them in matters of form as [a] great people . . . as if they were really a considerable military power."[29] But Lyons had made an error in assuming that he needed only to practice a little flattery to assuage America's suspicions about Britain. Relations between the two countries had been bent and twisted by eighty-three years of wars, disputes, and reconciliations. "I hate England," the American novelist Nathaniel Hawthorne had recently written from his consular post in Liverpool, "though I love some Englishmen, and like them generally."[30]

M St.

20th St.

19th St.

18th St.

Connecticut Avenue

17th St.

16th St.

15th St.

Vermont Avenue

14th St.

13th St.

12th St.

L St.

K St.

Pennsylvania Avenue

I St.

Secretary Stanton's house ■

St. John's Church

British legation Lord Lyons's house

Secretary Welles's house ■   ■   ■   ■

Edward Malet's house

Blair House ■

Lafayette Square

Secretary Seward's house

McClellan's headquarters ■   ■

■ New York Av Presbyterian Church

War Department ■

State Department ■

Navy Department ■

Treasury Department

White House

■ Newspaper Row

Grove Theat ■

Willard's Hotel ■

President's Park

Globe Hotel ■

New York Avenue

B St.

To Virginia

M

Potomac River

Washington Monument ■

Washington

11th St.

Massachusetts Ave.

New York Avenue

K St.

I St.

H St.

10th St.　9th St.　8th St.　7th St.　6th St.　5th St.　4th St.　3rd St.　2nd St.　1st St.

G St.

F St.

Patent
Office

Ford's
Theatre

Post Office
Department

Judiciary
Hospital

E St.

Kirkwood
House

Star Newspaper

D St.

Pennsylvania Avenue

Metropolitan
Hotel

C St.

B & O Train
Station

National
Hotel

New Jersey Ave.

U.S.
Capitol

L   L

War Memorial

Smithsonian Museum,
Library, and Lecture Hall

DC Armory

Maryland Ave.

To wharves—
Ferry to Virginia

N
W   E
S

PART I

COTTON IS KING

ONE

The Uneasy Cousins

Britain and America—Divisions over slavery—Lord Palmerston—Uncle Tom's Cabin and the Stafford House Address—Charles Dickens's disappointment—The caning of Charles Sumner

For seventy-five years after the War of Independence, the British approach to dealing with the Americans had boiled down to one simple tactic: to be "very civil, very firm, and to go our own way."[1] During the late 1850s, the prevailing view in London was that Washington could not be trusted. "These Yankees are most disagreeable Fellows to have to do anything about any American Question," the prime minister, Lord Palmerston, had complained in 1857 to Lord Clarendon, his foreign secretary, fourteen months before Lord Lyons's arrival in America. "They are on the Spot, strong . . . totally unscrupulous and dishonest and determined somehow or other to carry their Point."[2] It went without saying that the Foreign Office expected Lyons to be on guard against any American chicanery.

One of the legacies of the War of 1812 was a British fear that the United States might try to annex British North America (as Canada was then known), accompanied by a conviction among Americans that they should never stop trying. It was neither forgiven nor forgotten in England that precious ships and men had had to be diverted from the desperate war against Napoleon Bonaparte in order to defend Canada from three invasion attempts by the United States between 1812 and 1814. London regarded the burning of Washington and the White House by

British soldiers in August 1814 as a well-deserved retribution for the sacking of York (later called Toronto) by American troops.

Lyons soon discovered, as had each of his predecessors, that the War of 1812 had not only an entirely different meaning in the United States, but also a different outcome. In American histories, Britain had provoked the war by her arrogant and unreasonable behavior, first, by blockading all ports under Napoleonic rule, thereby stifling American trade, and second, by boarding American ships in search of deserters from the Royal Navy. The practice of "impressing" American sailors* into the navy was considered beyond the pale, especially when it took place off the coast of Virginia.³ Despite furious protests from Washington, the number of American citizens wrongly impressed had steadily increased over the years, and by 1812 the tally had reached over six thousand. But when the U.S. Congress declared war on June 8, 1812, it was to stop a practice that had already been disavowed by the English; just two days earlier, in London, the British government had agreed to stop impressment—too late to affect the outcome of the debates in Washington.

The peace treaty signed by Britain and America in 1814, the Treaty of Ghent, was based on the assumption that the war had been a draw since no territory was lost or gained by either side. However, news of the treaty had not yet reached the British and American armies facing each other in New Orleans, and a battle still took place on January 26. Though a small engagement compared to the great battles unfolding in Europe, it was a decisive American victory. General Andrew Jackson's force of four thousand men managed to defeat a British expedition almost three times its size. The fact that this stunning victory occurred after peace had been declared was later brushed aside in the telling. Two great American myths were born: that Andrew Jackson won the war, and that he had not only put the British in their place, but also crushed the army that had defeated Napoleon.

The failure of the United States to conquer Canada during the war had come as a great surprise to many Americans. Former president Thomas Jefferson wrote to a colleague in August 1812, "The acquisition of Canada this year, as far as the neighborhood of Quebec, will be a mere

---

* The term "impressment" meant the legal conscription of a civilian, usually a sailor, into the Royal Navy. The practice had been going on since the 1600s. It was rare for "landlubbers" to be impressed, but in time of war all kinds of injustices took place, which for the most part the authorities pretended not to notice.

matter of marching, and will give us experience for the attack of Halifax the next, and the final expulsion of England from the American continent."[4] Over the next few decades, politicians often expressed their desire to expel England from the "American continent." When small local rebellions broke out in Quebec and Toronto in 1837, it came as no surprise to the British to learn that President Martin Van Buren had ostentatiously invoked international law and declared U.S. neutrality, or that American sympathizers were providing arms and volunteers to the rebels. By announcing "neutrality," Van Buren elevated the uprising of a few hundred Canadians to the standard applied to an international war, giving hope to Americans who believed that a Canada free from British "shackles" would want to join the Union.[5]

———

That the original thirteen states would increase in number over the years had never been in doubt, but whether these new states would allow slavery was a question that had troubled Americans from the beginning. When the first Constitutional Convention met in Philadelphia in 1787, five of the thirteen*—Massachusetts, Pennsylvania, New Hampshire, Rhode Island, and Connecticut—had abolished slavery, and eight—New York, New Jersey, Delaware, Maryland, Virginia, North Carolina, South Carolina, and Georgia—had not. There had been slaves in America since 1619—one year before the arrival of the *Mayflower*. And at the time of independence, one in five of the 4 million ex-colonists were black. The Convention agreed on a compromise, the first of many that would be tried until the Civil War. Slavery was left alone, but the slave trade was given a twenty-one-year time limit. After 1808, the importation of slaves was to be banned.

The invention in 1793 of Eli Whitney's cotton gin (which separated the tough cotton fibers from their seeds, saving many hours of manual labor), however, meant that slavery not only continued but also even flourished in the Southern states. The demand for cotton by England's textile mills was apparently inexhaustible and within two years after Whitney's gin arrived in the South, shipments of cotton across the Atlantic had increased from roughly 130,000 pounds a year to more than 1.5 million. The rise of cotton

---

* Although slavery was abolished in Vermont in 1777, the former colony attempted to go it alone for the first fourteen years after independence, joining the Union only in 1791.

over rice, tobacco, or corn as *the* primary Southern crop coincided with the government's acquisition of the Louisiana territories from the French in 1803. The United States doubled in size as a result of the Louisiana Purchase, opening up to development and potential statehood more than 820,000 square miles from the Gulf of Mexico to the Canadian border. Instead of dying out, as some of the original framers of the Constitution had hoped, slavery was spreading north and west.

By 1819 the thirteen states had become twenty-two, evenly split between free and slave states. But in 1819 the territory of Missouri applied to join the Union, and the balance was suddenly upset. Missouri straddled the implied boundary established by the Mason-Dixon Line; both the Northern and Southern states claimed her as one of their own. Both feared what would happen to the balance of power in the Senate, where each state sent two senators regardless of size or population. By now, the two regions were developing separate though intertwined economies. The Northern states were hurtling toward industrialization, building factories, constructing cities, and developing financial institutions; the Southern states kept to their agricultural base, received fewer immigrants, and developed an alternative financial system based on the buying and selling of slaves and cotton.* The majority of Northerners could read and write; in the South, the literacy rate was less than half. The growing political, economic, and cultural differences between the North and South could not be easily reconciled. Finally, in 1820, Congress agreed to the "Missouri Compromise," which admitted Missouri as a new state to the Union, with slavery allowed. As a balance, however, Maine was admitted as a free state, and the future growth of slavery was confined to new states south of the Missouri border. The Southern states suddenly became deeply interested in the expansion of the United States into Mexico and Central America.

Britain could not help becoming entangled in these territorial disputes. In 1823, President James Monroe announced the "Monroe Doctrine," which essentially called for the Old World to stay on its side of the Atlantic and allow the New World to develop without interference. Since Britain had possessions and interests on both continents, this was

---

* Southerners referred to slavery (and by extension the cotton economy) as the "peculiar institution" not because it was strange, but because the mode of life was particular to the South and nowhere else.

neither desirable nor possible for her.* After a decade as foreign secretary, from 1830 to 1841, Lord Palmerston had become thoroughly exasperated by the continuous bickering between the two countries over Canada's borders. "It never answers to give way [to the Americans]," he wrote in January 1841, "because they always keep pushing on their own encroachments as far as they are permitted to do so; and what we dignify by the names of moderation and conciliation, they naturally enough call fear."[6] Palmerston followed his own advice in the case of a British subject named Alexander McLeod, who was being held in a New York prison on the charge of murder. McLeod had been arrested in November 1840 after he drunkenly boasted in a New York bar of killing an American sympathizer who had been on his way to take part in the Canadian revolts of 1837. Palmerston informed Washington that McLeod's execution "would produce war; war immediate and frightful in its character."[7] Hints from William H. Seward, the governor of New York, that he would pardon McLeod once the public outcry had petered out had no effect on Palmerston's determination to go to war unless the prisoner was released. Fortunately, a jury acquitted McLeod since there was no evidence against him except his own bibulous lies.[8]

Palmerston's approach to American issues was a reflection of his general attitude toward foreign policy: that Britain's interests should never be sacrificed to satisfy her friends or appease her enemies. His unapologetic nationalism made him widely disliked in Europe. According to legend, a Frenchman once complimented him by saying, "If I were not a Frenchman, I should wish to be an Englishman." To that Palmerston replied, "If I were not an Englishman, I should wish to be an Englishman." The Germans complained, *"Hat der Teufel einen Sohn, / So ist er sicher Palmerston"* ("If the Devil has a son, surely he must be Palmerston"). Palmerston's willingness to use the Royal Navy, which was the largest in the world, at the slightest provocation earned him the sobriquet "Lord Pumicestone" among his detractors. It was also noticed that Palmerston employed his gunboat diplomacy only against smaller nations such as Greece, while his manner toward the other Great Powers of Europe (France, Austria, Prussia, and Russia) was far more conciliatory.

---

* For the first half of the nineteenth century, the "Monroe Doctrine," when it was observed at all, was enforced by the Royal Navy, since it was in Britain's interest to prevent the Great Powers from interfering with the balance of power in South America.

Palmerston's attitudes had been formed in the age when wigs and rouge were worn by men as well as women. He had personally witnessed the first wave of violent revolutions in Europe as a child when his parents joined the retinue of friends and relations escorting Georgiana, Duchess of Devonshire, through France. The family's brief but terrifying experience at the hands of a citizens' committee in Paris left Palmerston with only tepid faith in the ability of the lower classes to make rational decisions. During the first half of his political career, Palmerston was better known for his womanizing (which won him his initial nickname of "Lord Cupid") than for his work at the War Office, where he toiled diligently for twenty years at the midlevel post of secretary for war. But apart from his enjoyment of female company—the more the better—Palmerston was in every other way a serious politician whose capacity for long hours and hard work almost incited a rebellion among the clerks when he became foreign secretary in 1830. It was a shame, Florence Nightingale remarked after she came to know the real Palmerston, that people accepted his jocular, almost flippant manner at face value, since "he was so much more in earnest than he appeared." Once his slumbering humanitarian instincts were aroused by a particular cause, he could act with unbounded zeal. The abolition of the slave trade became a lifelong obsession as Palmerston painstakingly attempted to create an impregnable web of international treaties that would allow the navy the right to search suspected slave ships in any part of the world.

One of the driving forces behind Palmerston's enmity toward the United States was its refusal to agree to a slave trade treaty. To his mind, the acts abolishing the slave trade in 1807 and then slavery throughout the British Empire in 1833 had joined such other events as the Glorious Revolution and Waterloo in the pantheon of great moments in the nation's history. For many Britons, the eradication of slavery around the globe was not simply an ideal but an inescapable moral duty, since no other country had the navy or the wealth to see it through. At the beginning of 1841, Palmerston had almost concluded the Quintuple Treaty, which would allow the Royal Navy to search the merchant ships of the Great Powers. "If we succeed," Palmerston told the House of Commons on April 15, 1841, "we shall have enlisted in this league . . . every state in Christendom which has a flag that sails on the ocean, with the single exception of the United States of North America."[9] The Quintuple Treaty was signed, but without the signature of the United States. As a consequence, the slave trade continued exclusively under the American flag. The one concession Britain did obtain—and this was not accomplished by Palmerston, who was out of government between 1841 and 1846—was the formation of joint patrols with the U.S. Navy off the West African coast.

Whether Palmerston was foreign secretary, however, made no difference to the constant wrangling or the relentless expansion of the Union over the lands of Native Americans as well as British-held territories. Three years later, in 1844, the presidential candidate of the Democratic Party, James Polk, ran on a platform that all of Britain's Oregon territories right up to Russian America should be annexed by the United States. "The only way to treat John Bull is to look him in the eye," Polk wrote in his diary. "If Congress falters or hesitates in their course, John Bull will immediately become arrogant and more grasping in his demands."[10] Polk's claim for all the land as far as what is now southern Alaska resulted in the popular slogan "Fifty-four Forty or Fight!" (meaning that the new boundary line should be drawn along the 54°40' parallel). But the expected fight never occurred; Texas joined the Union as a slave state in 1845, and a year later President Polk declared war on Mexico, a far less dangerous opponent. The British foreign secretary, Lord Aberdeen, who shied away from gunboat diplomacy, was willing to negotiate, and the Oregon Treaty was signed in June 1846, giving all of present-day Washington, Oregon, and Idaho to the United States.[11] Victory in the Mexican-American War in 1848 resulted in the United States acquiring a further 600 million acres, most of them below the Mason-Dixon Line. There were now thirty states in the Union, once again in an even split between slave and free.

In 1848, the discovery of gold in California led to a rush of settlers—more than eighty thousand of them in a matter of months—and the urgent need to accept the newly acquired territory as the thirty-first state so that law and order could be imposed. But the Southern states would not agree to the addition (since the Californians were demanding to be admitted as a free state) until they had secured a series of concessions. The most bitterly contested of these was the Fugitive Slave Act of 1850, which allowed "owners" to pursue and recapture their escaped "property" in whatever state he or she happened to be hiding. Graphic newspaper reports—of families torn apart, of law-abiding blacks dragged in chains back to their erstwhile masters—raised an outcry in the North. Several

Northern states passed personal liberty laws to try to circumvent the act; in some towns, there was violent resistance to the federal agents who arrived in search of fugitive slaves; and the "underground railroad," with its vast network of safe houses from Louisiana to the Canadian border, received many more volunteers.

———

The domestic and political turbulence during 1850 was one of the reasons why the United States' pavilion at the Great Exhibition in London in 1851 displayed so few objects compared to those of other nations. The suspicion among Americans that Britain had put on the exhibition simply to show off its status as the richest country in the world had also diminished enthusiasm for taking part. Yet even with a fraction of the exhibits presented by the Great Powers, the American pavilion still won 5 of the 170 Council medals (admittedly, France won 56). The American photography contingent, led by Mathew Brady, won first, second, and third prize.* The great number of American tourists and businessmen who visited the exhibition brought more contact between the citizens of the two countries than at any other time during the century. Britons now realized the extent to which the United States had developed separately from the mother country. Americans not only had different accents and wore different fashions; their choice of words and phrases sounded quite foreign. They said "I guess" instead of "I suppose," and "Let's skedaddle" instead of "Shall we go," and they called con men "shysters," an epithet entirely new to English ears.[12] It was their strange and different mannerisms that inspired Tom Taylor to compose *Our American Cousin*.

Taylor also wrote the popular 1852 stage version of the novel *Uncle Tom's Cabin* by Harriet Beecher Stowe. The English took to heart the story of the saintly slave whose goodness and humanity upstage a succession of masters until his murder by the evil Simon Legree. In 1852, its first year of publication, the book sold a million copies in Britain—compared to 300,000 in the United States.[13] Every respectable British household owned a copy. *Uncle Tom's Cabin* was allegedly the first novel Lord Palmerston had read in thirty years, and whether it was the effects of the long abstinence or the allure of the book, he read it from cover to cover

---

* Several objects, including the Singer sewing machine and the Colt .45-caliber single-action army revolver, were subsequently sent on a triumphant tour around Britain.

three times.[14] The depressing and grisly portrayal of slavery in *Uncle Tom's Cabin* articulated what the British had long suspected was the truth—despite the South's self-depiction as an agrarian paradise of courtly manners, charming plantations, and contented slaves. Few Britons had ever seen how slaves really lived, unlike the celebrated British actress Fanny Kemble, whose marriage to Pierce Butler, a Southern slave owner, fell apart after they moved to his Georgia plantation in 1838. They divorced acrimoniously in 1849, with Butler holding Fanny's daughters hostage until they turned twenty-one.

The publication of *Uncle Tom's Cabin* led to a renaissance of antislavery clubs in Britain, after they had tottered along in a state of earnest torpor since 1833. The public agitated for Britain "to do something." In November 1852, Harriet, Duchess of Sutherland, and the Earl of Shaftesbury drafted a petition to "the Women of the United States of America," urging them to "raise your voices" against slavery. More than half a million British women signed their names to the public letter, which was known as the Stafford House Address. Predictably, the American response was one of outrage.[15] Julia Tyler, the wife of former president John Tyler, led the barrage of scathing replies to "The Duchess of Sutherland and the Ladies of England." British labor conditions, rigid class structure, and lack of opportunity for self-betterment all came under attack. But it could not be denied that Britain possessed the moral high ground on the issue of slavery. American abolitionists who visited England were amazed to discover that British blacks enjoyed the same rights as their white peers. "We found none of that prejudice against color in England which is so inveterate among the American people," Elizabeth Cady Stanton had written about her honeymoon in Britain during the summer of 1840. "At my first dinner in England I found myself beside a gentleman from Jamaica, as black as the ace of spades."[16] Similarly, a former slave, the author Harriet Jacobs, recalled how her self-esteem had changed after visiting England. "For the first time in my life," she wrote, "I was in a place where I was treated according to my deportment, without reference to my complexion. I felt as if a great millstone had been lifted from my breast."[17]

The Stafford House Address had been doomed to fail no matter how good and sincere its intentions. The Anglophobia that was so often articulated in the U.S. Congress was no more than a reflection of public opinion. Alexis de Tocqueville commented in *Democracy in America* in

1835 that he had never encountered hatred more poisonous than that which Americans felt for England.[18] There were notable exceptions, of course. In the early 1840s the American minister in London told a wildly receptive audience that "the roots of our history run into the soil of England. . . . For every purpose but that of political jurisdiction we are one people."[19] But there had existed a deep-rooted prejudice since the War of Independence. The influx of a million Irish refugees during the potato famine merely added more venom to the mix. "Why," wrote a nineteenth-century American journalist, "does America hate England?" He answered: "Americans believe that England dreads their growing power, and is envious of their prosperity. They detest and hate England accordingly. They have 'licked' her twice and can 'lick' her again."[20]

Tocqueville attributed the hostility to fifty years of self-congratulatory propaganda. He thought Americans were convinced that their country was a beacon of light to the world; "that they are the only religious, enlightened, and free people . . . hence they conceive a high opinion of their superiority and are not very remote from believing themselves to be a distinct species of mankind." The more the English scoffed at this view, the more furious and resentful Americans became toward Britain. The most memorable attack on American exceptionalism was Sydney Smith's scornful comparison of the two cultures in 1820. "Who reads an American book?" he wrote in the *Edinburgh Review*:

> Or goes to an American play? Or looks at an American picture or statue? What does the world yet owe to American physicians or surgeons? Who drinks out of American glasses? Or eats from American plates? Or wears American coats or gowns? Or sleeps in American blankets? Finally, under which of the old tyrannical governments of Europe is every sixth man a slave whom his fellow-creatures may buy and sell and torture?[21]

A decade later, Fanny Trollope, the novelist and mother of Anthony Trollope, rekindled the impression that all Britons looked down their noses at the former colonists with her book *Domestic Manners of the Americans*. Mrs. Trollope had spent a brief and unhappy period in Ohio in the late 1820s, trying to build a commercial business, which had ended with the family becoming bankrupt and homeless. Her book was not meant to be a serious study of America, but a piece of entertainment to help solve

LIFE IN AN AMERICAN HOTEL?

Punch's view of American manners, 1856.

her family's financial difficulties. While not condemning all Americans in all areas of life, she portrayed the majority as too vulgar, violent, and vainglorious to be really likable. Her view of America inspired hundreds of English imitators, further souring cultural relations between the two countries.

Other British writers sneered that the self-styled "superior" United States was militarily weak, politically corrupt, and financially unsound.[22] America's markets were prone to panics; its people preached equality but practiced "mobocracy." English travelers who saw American democracy in action either condemned it outright or praised it halfheartedly as an evolving system. The greatest blow to American pride came from Charles Dickens. Until his visit to the country in 1842, Americans had considered the world's bestselling novelist to be almost an adopted son. His humble beginnings and liberal politics had fostered their assumption that the United States would be far more congenial to him than class-ridden England. Dickens had indeed wanted to admire America during his triumphant lecture tour. "Still it is of no use," he wrote dolefully to a friend during the tour. "I *am* disappointed. This is not the republic I came to see; this is not the republic of my imagination." He warmed to the friendliness and generosity of its people, and he admired the emphasis on education and public philanthropy. But he found American society as a whole utterly intolerant of dissenting views. "Freedom of opinion! Where is it?" he asked rhetorically after being warned not to discuss the slave mutiny on board the *Creole* outside abolitionist circles, even though the subject was dominating British-American relations.* If American democracy was simply a vehicle for majority rule, then, asserted Dickens, "I infinitely prefer a liberal monarchy."[23] He gave vent to his disenchantment in *American Notes,* published in 1842, and *Martin Chuzzlewit,* which followed the year after.

———

The great influx of immigrants into the United States after 1846 accelerated the rise of the harsh, strident politics that Dickens so deplored. In 1840 there had been 17 million people living in America; by 1850 there were 23 million, an increase of 35 percent. The altered political landscape—where ethnic identity and class affiliation translated into thousands of votes—demanded a new breed of politician, the kind exemplified by William Henry Seward, who was elected to one of the two New York Senate seats in 1849. While governor he had behaved with shameless opportunism, courting the state's large Irish vote with his vitriolic diatribes against England. The annexation of Canada was a constant theme in his speeches.[24] Though not a bigot himself, Seward was an expert at appealing to popular prejudice to shore up his power base. Once he realized that the Democratic and Whig parties were fragmenting into Northern and Southern, proslavery and antislavery factions, he abandoned the Whigs and became a Republican.† He subtly repositioned himself, raising his antislavery rhetoric and emphasizing his protection-

---

* In November 1841, the journey of the *Creole* from Virginia to Louisiana was interrupted when the slaves on board mutinied and took the ship to Nassau in the Bahamas. The British authorities refused to hand over the mutineers or return the slaves.

† Despite fronting four presidents, the Whig Party survived for less than twenty-five years and was more a collection of factions than a cohesive national party. By the time of its demise in the early 1850s, several new parties were forming, including the anti-immigrant Know-Nothing Party, so called because when questioned about their affiliation, its members were instructed to say "I know nothing."

ist credentials. This infuriated the free-trade South, but it endeared him to states that feared competition from European goods.

There were two different Sewards, according to his friend Henry Adams: the "political and the personal." But over time they had become so entwined "that no one could tell which was the mask and which the features." "I am an enigma, even to myself," Seward once quipped.[25] With his soft, husky voice and confiding manner, he exuded the air of a man who knew the foibles of humanity but did not sit over them in judgment. "You are at your ease with him at once," recorded an English admirer. "There is a frankness and bonhomie. In our English phrase, Mr. Seward is good company. A good cigar, a good glass of wine, and a good story, even if it is a little risqué, are the pleasures which he obviously enjoys keenly." His opposition to slavery was never in doubt, but his preference for pragmatism over principle meant that sometimes his ends became lost in the means. Shortly after his election to the Senate, Seward explained that one consideration governed all his political actions: "My duty is to promote the welfare, interest, and happiness of the people of the United States." But whether this view was a goal or a cover remained the subject of debate. His wife, Frances, became increasingly disillusioned by her husband's ability to temporize. She had once been a woman of strong political views, but her confidence had been crushed by prolonged exposure to Seward's ego. She preferred to live in seclusion in New York, pleading ill health, while Seward lived in Washington. It was almost as if Frances represented some part of his conscience: safely left at home but still accessible by post.

Seward had become the leader of the nascent Republican Party in the Senate when Senator Stephen Douglas, a Democrat from Illinois, proposed a bill in 1854 to admit two new territories, Kansas and Nebraska, into the Union. However, the provisions included a bombshell: the two territories would decide for themselves whether to be free or slave states. Douglas had proposed breaking the 1820 Missouri Compromise because it was the only way he could achieve his real aim of obtaining Southern support for a transcontinental railroad. But the result was catastrophic for the residents of Kansas. In theory, majority rule was going to decide the issue. In practice, pro- and antislavery settlers began to slaughter each other in cold blood. "Border Ruffians" based in Missouri charged over the border to join forces with Kansas slave owners, while New England abolitionists shipped caseloads of rifles to their western brethren. Each of the rival factions proclaimed its own legislature. Throughout 1855, American newspapers referred to "Bleeding Kansas."

Seward tried to find common ground with the Southern senators as a means to ending the violence in Kansas without endangering the Union. But the North and South each regarded the fate of Kansas as the key to slavery's future. There could be no compromise. In the spring of 1856, President Franklin Pierce gave his full support to a bill proposed by Senator Douglas to repeal the Missouri Compromise ban on slavery in territories north of the 36°30' parallel, which included Kansas. Seward responded on behalf of the Republican Party with a bill to admit Kansas as a free state. The Senate leader of the Free-Soil Party,* Charles Sumner, showed Seward the speech he was preparing to deliver on May 19. Entitled "The Crime Against Kansas," the speech was a devastating indictment of the South, her institutions, and the character of her most prominent politicians. Although Seward personally disliked Sumner—considering him far too priggish for a politician—he shuddered at his folly. Seward tried to persuade him to at least remove the personal attacks within his speech, but Sumner refused. After initially hailing Seward as a fellow soldier in the battle against slavery, the aristocratic Bostonian had come to regard him with disdain. According to a mutual friend, "The two men would have disliked each other by instinct had they lived in different planets."[26] Seward had brawled and clawed his way from New York to national prominence; by contrast, Sumner was a seventh-generation American, a Harvard man who spoke four languages and was an acknowledged authority in jurisprudence.

The forty-year-old Sumner had never held office before he took his Senate seat in 1851. Unlike Seward, who knew the inside of every back room between Buffalo and Brooklyn, Sumner had deliberately eschewed politics. Seward had been abroad only once, in 1833, and the New Yorker had returned with his prejudices against Britain confirmed. By contrast, Sumner had become something of a sensation when he visited England in 1838, prompting the essayist and historian Thomas Carlyle, who opposed abolition, to dub him sarcastically "Popularity Sumner." Although he lacked a sense of humor—a fatal disability for

---

* The East Coast–based Free-Soilers, whose slogan was "Free soil, free speech, free labor, and free men," initially competed with the Republican Party, which was born in the Midwest in 1854 and also opposed slavery, and then became absorbed by their newer rival.

most foreigners in Britain—Sumner exuded a charismatic earnestness combined with obvious brilliance. He knew more dukes and earls than most Englishmen, let alone any other American. But the most important friend he made during this time was Harriet, Duchess of Sutherland, whose views on abolition and social reform coincided with his own. After he returned to America, they maintained their friendship. She saw Sumner as he wished to see himself: as a proud and tireless advocate of society's victims.

Sumner's lack of experience or even understanding of basic political realities proved his undoing. In contrast to Seward, he was incapable of trimming his actions or modulating his speeches to suit political expediencies. Sumner abhorred compromise: "From the beginning of our history," he explained, "the country has been afflicted with compromise. It is by compromise that human rights have been abandoned." Sumner was prepared to make a last, defiant stand against the forces of accommodation, and did so at every opportunity. On May 19, 1856, he began a two-day marathon of invective in the Senate. Congress had just learned that the border town of Lawrence, Kansas—which had held out against slavery—was surrounded by a thousand Border Ruffians. The tension in the chamber added force to his words, which needed no extra help. Sumner was already a mesmerizing orator; his speeches were emotional to the point of being histrionic. Between damning the South to hell, he accused Senator Andrew Butler of South Carolina of being so attached to the idea of slavery that he was like an adulterer obsessed with his mistress. Then he scored some gratuitous blows by making fun of Butler's infirmities. He also insulted Senator Stephen Douglas, who responded, "That damn fool will get himself killed by some other damned fool."

Two days later, while Sumner was sitting at his desk in the nearly empty Senate chamber, one of the insulted Butler's nephews, Congressman Preston Brooks, silently approached him from behind. After speaking a few words, Brooks raised his arm and smashed his heavy cane on Sumner's head. Blinded by blood and in shock, Sumner struggled to get his long legs out from under his desk. He finally managed to stand up while Brooks continued beating him with increasing ferocity. According to horrified observers, Sumner tried to stagger away only to be grabbed by Brooks, who held his lapel with one hand while raining down blows with the other. By his own count, he struck Sumner about thirty times before his cane splintered. His mission completed, Brooks calmly walked away unmolested. Within a few minutes he was strolling down Pennsylvania Avenue as if nothing had happened.[27]

The House of Representatives failed to muster enough votes to expel Brooks, and, although he immediately resigned his seat, South Carolinians expressed their views by promptly reelecting him. To Southerners, infuriated by the constant moral and political tirades poured down on them by Northern abolitionists, Brooks was a hero. They had long felt beleaguered by the persistence of Northern attempts to curtail slavery. For many, Brooks had acted out their greatest fantasy against the abolitionists. Thousands of canes arrived at his house, some with gold or silver tips and one that bore the words "Hit Him Again."

Abolitionists, on the other hand, regarded Sumner's savage beating as a call to action. The terrible scene on the chamber floor, described in lurid detail by every newspaper, also served to unite the North. Rather than worrying about the activities of immigrants, or black preachers, or Freemasons, Northerners could finally agree on a common enemy. The Republican Party was overwhelmed with new members. But for Sumner, his martyrdom came at a terrible price. Even after his wounds healed, the psychological scars proved far more intractable. On March 7, 1857, the frail patient was gently conveyed onto a steamer bound for England. It was the beginning of three years of self-imposed exile. By his own estimation, his political career and possibly his life were concluded. Still, Sumner was not just popular abroad; he was now a bona fide hero. His English friends welcomed him as though he were a wounded general returning from war. Later, some would claim that his assault marked the beginning of the Civil War.[28]

The Duchess of Sutherland insisted that the wounded warrior recuperate at Stafford House. After his caning she had redoubled her efforts to arouse English sympathy against Southern slavery. One of her most successful events was a public reading of Uncle Tom's Cabin by the black American performer Mary Webb. The scene at Stafford House "would have caused considerable astonishment to any gentleman of the Southern States of America," reported the Illustrated London News. "A large audience was gathered together in that hall . . . to listen to a lady of color giving dramatic readings. . . . Our Southerner would have been confounded and disgusted at the sight of what he would call a 'tarnation nigger' being listened to with the most respectful attention by no inconsiderable number of the aristocracy of England."[29]

Among the new friends Sumner made during his stay at Stafford House were the Duchess of Sutherland's daughter, Elizabeth, and her husband, the Duke of Argyll. For the Argylls, it was the perfect meeting of minds. "He was a tall, good-looking man," recalled the duke in his memoirs, "very erect in attitude, with a genial smile and a very intellectual expression. I always found his conversation full of charm, not only from his devotion to one great cause, but from his wide and cultivated interest in literature and in art."[30] Like Sumner, the thirty-three-year-old duke was a striking figure, whose flaming red hair—which he wore shoulder length—and theatrical dress were considered emblematic of his idiosyncratic politics. His views were always logical and well thought out, and yet strangely angular, so that on any given subject it defied prediction whether they coincided with those of his own party or with those of the opposition. This trait, combined with his caustic and often dogmatic style of debating, meant that Argyll carried weight in politics but would never inspire a following. Both he and Sumner would always be forces in their own right, and yet also their own greatest impediments to power. For the future of British-American relations, however, the relationship between Argyll and Sumner would prove to be one of the most important friendships of the Civil War.

TWO

On the Best of Terms

The Dred Scott case—William Seward visits London—The Liberals come to power—John Brown's raid—The Prince of Wales tours America

Seward was delighted when many Southern newspapers suggested that he ought to be next in line for a caning. With Sumner recuperating in Europe, Seward hoped to appeal to radical antislavery voters in the Republican Party. His chance to shine came just two days after Sumner set sail and the Democrat James Buchanan was sworn in as president. On March 6, 1857, the Supreme Court handed down its opinion on the notorious Dred Scott case. Scott was a former slave who had been taken by his late master from Missouri, where slavery was legal, to Illinois, which had abolished slavery in 1818. Scott had sued for his freedom, but the Southern-dominated Court decided that the federal government had no right to decide matters pertaining to slavery in any part of the United States, whether free or unfree.

The Court's decision wrecked the thirty-seven-year-old Missouri Compromise, which had ensured that as more territories joined the Union there would always be an even balance between the slave and free-soil states. Worse still, the Court declared that black people were not citizens, and were "so far inferior that they had no rights which the white man was bound to respect." Blacks were no more entitled to citizenship than horses or sheep; they could not vote, own a passport, or apply to the courts. Seward denounced the Dred Scott decision at every opportunity, accusing President James Buchanan and Chief Justice Rodger B. Taney of having colluded over the ruling. Northern public opinion supported Seward's attacks, since it was widely believed above the Mason-Dixon Line that there was a slave-power conspiracy afoot to spread slavery throughout the United States.

In the fall of 1857, six months after the Dred Scott ruling, the collapse of the largest insurance company in the country sparked a catastrophic economic crisis throughout the North. During the financial panic that followed, prices on the New York Stock Exchange plunged by 45 percent, hundreds of banks failed, railroads went bankrupt, factories closed, and seemingly overnight there was mass unemployment running into the hundreds of thousands. The Panic of 1857 spread to Britain, too—where investors held, among other securities, £80 million worth of railroad stocks and bonds.[1] Only the Southern cotton-growing states escaped the panic largely unscathed, apparently vindicating the superiority of a slave system over the factory-based economy of the North. In a speech to the Senate on March 4, 1858, Senator James Hammond of South Carolina boasted that Southern cotton exports had saved the economy from total collapse during the 1857 panic, and for this reason the South had the right to dictate terms to the whole of the United States. "Cotton is King. . . . What would happen if no cotton was furnished for three years? England would topple headlong and carry the whole civilized world with her, save the South." Hammond and the other Southern senators fiercely resisted subsequent attempts by the Northern states to protect their domestic industrial base by imposing high tariffs on foreign imports.

Seward's language became increasingly violent whenever he discussed the differences between the two sections of the country. By the end of 1858 he was arguing that the Dred Scott case should mark the end of all Northern concessions to the South. During a speech on October 25, 1858, in Rochester, New York, he declared that the South had started "an irrepressible conflict" with the North: "The United States must . . . become either entirely a slave-holding nation or entirely a free-labor nation." A week earlier, while debating his Democratic opponent in the contest for one of Illinois's two seats in the United States Senate, the Republican candidate, a lawyer from Springfield, had made a similar-sounding statement: that "a house divided against itself cannot stand."* The lawyer, Abraham Lincoln, lost the election, but his speech won him national acclaim. Whereas Lincoln sounded as though he were giving a warning, Seward seemed to be laying down a challenge.[2] Seward later claimed that "irrepressible" was not the same as "unavoidable," but the damage could not be undone. The press dubbed him "Irrepressible Conflict Seward," fostering the sense that he was a divisive rather than a unifying figure and voiding three years of careful positioning by Seward to be perceived as the moderate alternative to Charles Sumner.

Seward's friend and political manager, Thurlow Weed, advised him to take a long trip abroad in the hope that the public would forget the unfortunate phrase. The presidential election would not be until November 1860, which was two years away. There was still sufficient time for Seward to repair his reputation. Weed was confident that the British would have no idea anything was amiss with Seward's presidential aspirations and would treat him with the respect afforded to the next leader of the Americans.

———

Seward's arrival in England on May 20, 1859, coincided with a recent improvement in Anglo-American relations. English outrage over U.S. support for the Russians during the Crimean War of 1854–56† had become less acute after the Indian Mutiny of 1857–58, when the Americans were firmly behind the British Army rather than the mutinous Indian soldiers known as Sepoys. Closer to home, Lord Napier's popularity in Washington had overcome some of the bad feelings on both sides of the Atlantic after his unlucky predecessor, John Crampton, was expelled by the U.S. government for participating in a secret scheme to recruit American volunteers to fight on the British side in the Crimean War. The perennial flashpoints between Britain and America—the right of the Royal Navy

---

* From the outset, Abraham Lincoln promoted himself as representing the middle ground. He believed that whites were superior to blacks, but that this did not give one human being the right to deprive another of his liberty. "As God made us separate, we can leave one another alone, and do one another much good thereby."

† The English were furious that U.S. sympathy for the Russians had extended to military aid, in the form of a steamship built for the Russian government by a private firm and revolvers supplied by Samuel Colt, as well as practical help from American doctors and engineers who volunteered their services.[3]

to search American ships suspected of transporting slaves from Africa or the Caribbean and the jostling over boundaries and territorial control in British North America and Central America—had threatened to ignite in 1858. However, these were contained by successful diplomacy in some instances, and by plain reluctance to go from words to something worse in others.[4] In his second annual address to Congress in December 1858, President Buchanan stressed the importance of peaceful relations between the two countries: "Any serious interruption of the commerce between the United States and Great Britain would be equally injurious to both. In fact, no two nations have ever existed on the face of the earth which could do each other so much good or so much harm."

When the two navies did meet at sea, on July 29, 1858, it was to perform the heroic maneuver of linking together the first transatlantic telegraph cable. An underwater cable had been laid in 1851 between Dover and Calais, but the raging storms of the Atlantic had twice defeated the combined efforts of British and American engineers. This time, the cable held strong as HMS *Agamemnon* and USS *Niagara* sailed toward their respective destinations flying specially designed flags that incorporated the stars of Old Glory with the stripes of the Union Jack. On August 16, 1858, the line was opened with the message "Glory to God in the highest; on earth, peace and goodwill to men." Queen Victoria followed with a cable of congratulations to President Buchanan and the people of the United States. Both countries celebrated in a "Festival of Connection," New York held a candlelight parade, newspapers printed special editions, the streets were decorated with flags, and shops displayed commemorative posters and ribbons.[5] Cyrus Field, the American investor behind the venture, was hailed as a genius and visionary. But the telegraph worked for only a month, and the disintegrating connection was destroyed in a clumsy repair attempt by one of the English engineers. The Atlantic cable would remain a dream for another eight years.

The Central American disputes were still under negotiation, however, when Seward arrived in London on May 20, 1859. The city had grown blacker, noisier, and more frantic since Seward's visit in his youth. Its population had increased from 900,000 to more than 3 million. Horse-drawn omnibuses, carriages, and wagons bumped and jostled one another and pedestrians on some of the most congested streets in the world; a thousand vehicles an hour crossed over London Bridge.[6] Nor was London the dirty, unregulated city of a generation before. The Great

Stink of 1858 (a mini–heat wave "cooked" the raw sewage in the Thames, sending noxious fumes through the city) had forced city planners to begin an ambitious sewer and water system for the capital. The squares and parks were just as Seward remembered, but these green spaces were now dwarfed by a new set of landmarks. The Gothic architecture of the rebuilt Houses of Parliament (after the great fire of 1834) seemed especially foreign to him compared to the neoclassical government buildings of Washington. This was a bold, even arrogant London that dared other cities to emulate its style.

As Weed predicted, Seward's arrival was eagerly anticipated by the denizens of Fleet Street and Westminster, who assumed that he was visiting England to cement his relationship with the country's leaders ahead of his election to the presidency. That it might be curiosity rather than admiration behind the scramble to make the acquaintance of the great Anglophobe never seemed to occur to Seward. He peppered his letters to his wife, Frances, with exclamations of excitement that so many famous figures wished to meet him. The morning after his first London ball, he boasted that he had "conversed with royalties and nobles, ad infinitum." There were "Princesses and Princes, and Dukes and Duchesses of the royal party, Indian Princes, and all the Diplomatic Corps. It was a thorough jam—like the Napier ball."[7]

Seward owed his initial entrée into London society to the Napiers, who had taken great pains to introduce him to their friends and relations. By the time the Season was in full swing, he was on nodding terms with every senior politician and fashionable hostess in London. Lord Napier also prepared Seward for his presentation to the Queen, sending him to his own tailor, shoemaker, and hatter. But as memorable as the occasion was for the unabashed republican, Seward was more star-struck by his visit to Stafford House to meet the Duke and Duchess of Sutherland. "The Duchess is the most accomplished lady in England. I could not tell you how kind and gracious she was to me," he wrote to his wife. "She detained me after the party had left, and we had a long, and most agreeable tete-a-tete." Believing Seward's abolitionism to be sincere, the duchess ordered her relations to show him the same hospitality; her daughter and son-in-law, the Duke and Duchess of Argyll, her brother, the Earl of Carlisle, and her cousin, the Duke of Devonshire, dutifully opened their houses to Seward, the last being anxious to repay him for the courtesy shown to his son, Lord Frederick Cavendish. By the beginning of June,

Seward was able to reel off the names and titles of society figures as though they had been his friends for years: "I dined with the Earl of Carlisle, and a large party of nobles and statesmen of the Liberal class. It would be tedious to recount [all] their names," he wrote to Frances in early June: "Lord Granville, Lord and Lady Shaftsbury [*sic*], Lord and Lady Palmerston, Lord John Russell, Mr. and Mrs. Gladstone, Mr. Delane, editor of *The Times,* and others. It was a most agreeable party."[8]

The polite conversations around the table were merely a façade; behind the scenes, intense political negotiations were taking place. Seward had arrived in London at an extraordinary moment in British politics. The liberal factions in Parliament were coming together to oust Lord Derby's Conservative government. Lord John Russell and Viscount Palmerston had reached a cordial understanding to form a new political party. Since Palmerston was on what could loosely be termed the "right" of liberal politics and Russell on the "left," between them they would be able to form a broad coalition.

On June 6, 1859, 274 MPs assembled in the ballroom of Willis's Rooms in St. James's and declared themselves the Liberal Party. Lord Palmerston and Lord John Russell shook hands, demonstrating forgiveness of all previous acts of treachery and rivalry toward each other during their previous stints as prime minister, agreeing to become the party's joint leaders. (It was noted that the seventy-five-year-old Palmerston sprang onto the dais while the sixty-nine-year-old Russell had to be helped up the steps.) Four days later, on June 10, the Liberals voted en masse in a motion of no confidence against Lord Derby's ministry, winning by a majority of thirteen votes. The Queen, who disliked both Russell and Palmerston, was annoyed with "those two terrible old men," as she called them. After considerable prevarication, she chose Palmerston as her new prime minister—much to Russell's disappointment. Russell became foreign secretary, a post that played to his weaknesses rather than his strengths.

Nothing had quite gone Russell's way since he achieved iconic status as the young man who ushered through the Great Reform Bill of 1832. That achievement had been all the more remarkable considering his lifelong poor health and nervous disposition, which had turned him into something of a self-absorbed eccentric.* Many of his ailments could be

---

* According to a well-known anecdote, Russell was chatting to the Duchess of Inverness at a party one winter evening when he suddenly stood up, went over to the

traced back to the fact that he had been born more than two months pre-
mature, and his survival was almost without precedent in the nineteenth
century. Throughout his life, Russell would be blessed and cursed in
equal measure. He enjoyed close relations with his family, particularly
his older brother, the Duke of Bedford, and yet he was never comfortable in society. Both of his marriages were reasonably happy; on the
other hand, the second Lady John never pretended that her love was of
the romantic kind. Nor was she capable of providing the support and
help that Palmerston received from his wife. Unlike Lady John, who
never entertained if she could help it, Lady Palmerston used all the
means in her power to assist her husband. They had been lovers for
many years until the death of her husband, Lord Cowper, enabled them
to marry. During their long political partnership, she had developed her
own skills and insights into human nature. According to one diplomat, a
morning call on her "was more instructive than studying the newspapers."[9] Lady Palmerston was adept at converting enemies and newspaper
editors into political allies, her most important conquest being John Delane, editor of *The Times.*

   Russell was one of the most cultured politicians of his generation, but
"Little Jonny," as he was called on account of his diminutive stature, was
desperately shy and stiff to the point of rudeness while also being overly
sensitive and demanding of others. Consequently, he was a dreadful
manager of men, incapable of fulfilling the most basic requirements of
leadership.[10] Although not exactly devious, he could be slippery with his
colleagues, who accused him of withholding information and of acting
without consultation or contrary to agreed plans. Sydney Smith once
said of him, "It is impossible to sleep soundly while Lord John has command of the watch."

   With all these talents and handicaps, Russell was driven by a lofty idealism for genuine political and social reform; but the failures of his career
had been catastrophic, not least his inability to come to grips with the
Irish Potato Famine in the 1840s. Russell ought to have retired from politics after the fall of his administration in 1852, as one of his biographers

---

far corner, and began a conversation with the Duchess of Sutherland. A short time
later, one of his friends asked him what on earth had happened. He had been sitting too close to the fire, Russell explained. "I hope," the friend remarked, "that
you told the Duchess of Inverness why you abandoned her." After a pause he
replied, "No, but I did tell the Duchess of Sutherland."

noted, "with his two and a half dozen bottles of Australian wine and his Colt's revolving firearm from the Great Exhibition."* Then he would have been remembered as a great but flawed leader.[11]

The new Liberal cabinet had fifteen members, a substantial number by the standards of the day, and included a broad cross section of views and personalities, from the flamboyant and combative Duke of Argyll (Lord Privy Seal) to the intellectual and moderately inclined Sir George Cornewall Lewis (home secretary).† The most surprising inclusion was William Gladstone as chancellor of the exchequer. Once hailed as the "rising hope of those stern unbending Tories," Gladstone had initially refused to show any interest in joining the Liberal Party, staying away from Willis's and voting with the Conservative government on June 10. What brought him into the fold was a case of mutual need. Gladstone could not bear the thought of four more years in the wilderness after his celebrated turn as chancellor from 1852 to 1855, and despite a personal antipathy toward him, Palmerston needed Gladstone's reputation and proven abilities as chancellor to give weight to his administration. Gladstone was by far the best orator in the House of Commons, which made him a hazard outside government. Moreover, there was one topic on which they both agreed: neither wanted Russell to succeed in enacting further political reform. It was not the most promising of partnerships. Gladstone always joked that he never attended a cabinet meeting without a letter of resignation in his pocket, while Palmerston liked to claim that he kept the fires stoked for just such an event.‡

In the matters of faith and the Church of England, Gladstone had few competitors. His rather ostentatious moral rectitude once led the Radical MP Henry Labouchere to complain that he did not object to Gladstone's always having the ace of trumps up his sleeve, only to his pretense that God had put it there. If Seward was an enigma, Gladstone was a man

---

* Small quantities of Australian wine were on display at the Great Exhibition of 1851.

† Lewis's sardonic humor is best remembered in his quip "Life would be tolerable were it not for its amusements."

‡ On hearing the news that Gladstone had joined the government, Charles Sumner claimed, with his customary humility, that he had always known Mr. Gladstone would join the Liberals. "Mr. Gladstone's fame seems constantly ascending," he wrote to the Duchess of Argyll. "When I first met him at Clifton, at a time when he was out of office and much abused, I predicted what has taken place, though I hardly thought it would come so soon."[12]

of complex contradictions. In contrast to Palmerston and Russell, whose political principles remained consistent, Gladstone's could and did change. He had begun his career as hostile to the abolition of slavery and cool on political reform. But the man who once said "I am a firm believer in the aristocratic principle—the rule of the best. I am an out-and-out inegalitarian" would develop a zeal for both causes during the 1860s, later becoming known as "the People's William."

————

Seward was conscious that there was no place in British society for a man like him, a professional politician with neither land nor personal wealth to sustain him. "I would not be an aristocrat here," he mused. "I could not be a plebeian."[13] He had received more kindness and respect from the English than he had ever expected, and never again would he feel abashed by Charles Sumner's casual references to his aristocratic friends. But his success in London had been rather more mixed than Sumner's.

Seward had failed to impress the assistant secretary at the American legation. Benjamin Moran had worked at the legation since 1853, starting as a temporary clerk and gradually moving up the ranks to assistant secretary in 1857. His wife died a few months after his promotion, leaving him to grieve in the basement of the legation, where, surrounded by mildewed records, broken lamps, and rusting trunks, he diligently copied out dispatches and reviewed documents. When the occasion arose, he also issued passports and performed minor services for American citizens. Moran was sympathetic to those who came begging for help, but his manner was a repellent combination of the insinuating and the supercilious. Although he could never understand why, every minister he served took pains to keep him in the basement and away from social functions. His diary became his best friend, a silent confidant with whom he could share his prejudices and disappointments. Moran yearned to be a popular man-about-town—a desire so entirely out of keeping with his manner and humble Pennsylvanian origins that if known, it would have provoked hoots of laughter. Yet he persisted in believing it an attainable goal, despite the cruel neglect of his superiors.

Moran was prepared to give Seward the benefit of the doubt at their first meeting on May 21, 1859. "He is a much smaller man than I thought him," noted Moran with a thrill of pleasure. His head, he noticed, was only a "little larger than mine" and he had "a pleasing manner."[14] His opinion altered, however, when Seward ignored him at the next occasion. "I met Seward at Fenton's [hotel] last night," recorded Moran on June 23, adding bitterly, "and found his head turned with the attention he has received from England's aristocracy."[15] Moran was consoled that his political heroes in Parliament, the Radical MPs Richard Cobden and John Bright, had shown little interest in cultivating Seward.[16] Known somewhat derisively as the "Members for the United States" (Bright's portrait hung in the American legation), their friendship with Charles Sumner was well known, and Moran had expected the same with Seward. The two British reformers were generally spoken of in the same breath, even though they did not always agree with each other. Cobden was the quieter, the more intellectual, and the better liked of the two. Bright, his onetime protégé, was a brilliant orator whose passion for denouncing the sins of the aristocracy made him a hero among the working class. Both MPs were exponents of the so-called Manchester School of politics: they believed in democracy, low taxation, universal education, no government regulation, no military expenditure unless in self-defense, and free trade. America had already achieved many of these goals, which in their view rendered its other faults far more excusable than any of the "great crimes" committed by Britain. Lord Palmerston angrily attacked the pair for being traitors and haters of all things English, for whom "everything that was hostile to England was right."[17]

Seward was unaware that Richard Cobden thought him a "light weight" who "wrote too much, and thought too little."[18] Seward had also disappointed Harriet Martineau, whose reputation as a woman of letters, social reformer, and commentator was almost as great in America as it was in England. Her study of the United States in 1837, *Society in America*—written after a ten-thousand-mile trek across the country that took two years—was considered by Americans to be one of the least obnoxious ever produced by an English writer. Seward had traveled to her home in the Lake District to pay court. "Miss Martineau . . . applied her ear trumpet; and we talked right on, an hour and a half, chiefly, of course, about the great American question." Seward was honest about the difficulty of forcing abolition on the country, perhaps too honest: "I gave her my own more practical views, and spoke, of course, hopefully. She betrayed, or rather confessed, an opinion, that I was a politician, rather than an abolitionist of her school." But Harriet Martineau's actual objection was not over his abolition principles per se but his lack of principles in general. She thought he was cynical and self-aggrandizing, especially after he revealed that he had supported the complaints against the Royal Navy's pursuit of suspected slave traders because "the more noise there is about war, the less probable war becomes; he always makes the utmost possible noise at the earliest moment," wrote Miss Martineau. "In truth I was aghast. 'You see,' said he, 'I am very candid.' "[19]

Lord Palmerston himself went even further in his condemnation of Seward. The American was a "vapouring, blustering, ignorant Man," whose overbearing egotism made him a danger to Anglo-American relations.[20] Palmerston had accepted his first ministerial post when Seward was seven years old, and by 1859 he had served as secretary for war, foreign secretary (three times), home secretary, and prime minister. He had been in politics long enough to recognize a fellow bluffer and opportunist. But having observed Seward's evident pleasure at his reception in England, Palmerston hoped that the good experience would translate into better diplomacy in the future.*

Seward was still abroad when the radical abolitionist John Brown led a raiding party of sixteen whites and five blacks in an attack on the federal armory at Harpers Ferry, Virginia, on October 16, 1859. The raid was meant to be the catalyst for a slave uprising. But rather than sparking a Santo Domingo–style revolution, the attempt ended in a bloody standoff against a company of U.S. Marines directed by Colonel Robert E. Lee. Brown was hanged for treason on December 2. The public's hysterical reaction to the raid, particularly in the South, frightened many abolitionists. Fearing arrest because of his known friendship with John Brown, the former slave and abolition campaigner Frederick Douglass gathered his family and fled to England.

Soon after his arrival, Douglass was invited to give a lecture in Paris. The visit required a passport, but Benjamin Moran refused to give him one, in accordance with the Dred Scott decision. Douglass felt it was beneath his dignity to protest and called upon the French embassy instead, which issued a passport without demur. In a separate incident on Novem-

---

* Shortly after Seward departed, a report arrived from China that the U.S. Navy commodore in command of the American squadron had come to the aid of the Royal Navy during a fierce battle to capture the Taku forts in northeastern China. The U.S. commodore explained his decision to join the fight by declaring "blood is thicker than water." This unexpected display of Anglo-American solidarity lent a rosy glow to Seward's visit. If the traditional enmity between the two navies could be overcome, then anything was possible—even a friendly White House under a Republican administration.

ber 21, Moran also shooed away Sarah Parker Remond, a black abolitionist from Boston who had become a popular public speaker since her arrival in England the previous February.[21] In his diary he claimed he would have issued a passport if she had sent the request by post, but Moran could not bear to be challenged, especially by a social inferior. Remond "was so impudent," he recorded, "that I had to order her out of the house."[22]

The following week, on November 28, 1859, Moran foiled Remond's attempt to gain a passport using a third party. This, he thought, was the end of the matter until he read about her "unjust" treatment in the newspapers. The *Morning Star,* which represented the views of Richard Cobden and John Bright, took the lead and attacked the legation for three days running. "This has fallen like a bomb-shell among the family," recorded Moran, referring to the American minister, George Dallas. Notwithstanding his Quakerism, Dallas was incensed at having his character impugned over a spat with a "negress" and talked wildly of teaching the English a lesson by closing down the legation.[23] He wrote an angry letter to Remond, who replied by reminding him that it was her taxes that paid his salary.[24] To the British, the passport episode exposed the United States as a racist and morally backward country whose treatment of nonwhites was reprehensible. "You may read the facts," wrote Remond in the Quaker journal the *British Friend,* "but no words can express the mental suffering we are obliged to bear because we happen to have a dark complexion. No language can give one an idea of the spirit of prejudice which exists in the States."[25]

Charles Sumner returned to Washington in time for the opening of Congress on December 5, 1859. By staying in Italy throughout May and June, Sumner had spared himself the spectacle of Seward being welcomed in London as though he were already the next president. Sumner had changed during his time abroad. He had always been prone to bombast and fanaticism and had always abhorred compromise. After his caning on the floor of the House, these qualities were joined by a lack of restraint that made him vain and capricious.

Washington was much the worse, Sumner complained to his friends in Europe.[26] He was not only more unpopular than ever in the South, but was also blamed in many quarters for inspiring John Brown's raid. The atmosphere in Washington was growing poisonous as Southerners sought to implicate leading Republicans in the supposed conspiracy behind the raid. Senator James Murray Mason was elected head of a Select Committee with powers to call witnesses to testify before Congress. One such witness was Seward, who received a summons as soon as he returned to America on December 28. He kept his cool while Mason, whose seat was next to his in the Senate, harangued him for being the moral, though not actual, instigator of the action. Again and again, Seward's unfortunate phrase "irrepressible conflict" was hurled back in his face. Democratic newspapers denounced him as the "arch agitator who is responsible for this insurrection." One Virginia newspaper even went so far as to put a price of $50,000 on his head; the governor of Virginia urged the South to demand Seward's exclusion from the presidency.[27]

The hysteria created by John Brown's raid led Louisiana and South Carolina to call for the imprisonment of free Negro sailors in December, while their ships were docked at port. "There are plans for the re-enslavement of all the emancipated Negroes, and for purging the South of all Whites suspected of abolition tendencies, and what not," Lord Lyons informed the Foreign Office.[28] But the minister was ready to fight "the Lynch Law Assassins," as he called them, and ordered the British consuls in the South to insist on "decent treatment for Coloured British Subjects" even if it meant defying local opinion.

Mason's Select Committee found no evidence of Republican connivance in Brown's raid.[29] This did not lessen Southern suspicions, however. "Our social lines were now strictly drawn between North and South," recalled Mrs. Roger Pryor, the Southern memoirist. "Names were dropped from visiting lists, occasions avoided on which we might expect to meet members of the party antagonistic to our own."[30] The few attempts to revive the old Washington life ended in failure. Shortly after Seward testified to the committee, he went to a large dinner party given by the Southern society hostess and wealthy widow Mrs. Rose Greenhow. His protégé, the newly elected congressional representative for Massachusetts, Charles Francis Adams, was also present, with his wife, Abigail. "An unfortunate allusion was made to some circumstances connected with the affair at Harpers Ferry, when Mrs. Adams launched out into a panegyric on John Brown," wrote Mrs. Greenhow, "calling him that 'holy saint and martyr,' turning her glance full upon me at the time—to which I replied, in a clear and audible voice—for it may be supposed that this conversation silenced all other—'I have no sympathy for John Brown: he was a traitor, and met a traitor's doom.' "[31] The rest of the company remained mute, including Charles Francis Adams, who was too mortified to put together a coherent sentence. He had expressly refrained from speaking about the raid in order to begin his congressional career "perfectly unencumbered."[32] Seward was the first to recover. He "aided me with great skill in directing [the conversation] into a new channel," Mrs. Greenhow continued. "A few days after I encountered Mr. Seward, and he approached me, saying, 'I have just been writing to our friend Lady Napier, and have told her that in all Washington you were the only person who had the independence to give a mixed dinner party.' " Mrs. Greenhow had not given the dinner party for the reasons Seward supposed. "Perhaps," she wrote, "had he fathomed my real object, he would not have been so grateful to me for the social countenance. At this early day I saw foreshadowed what was to follow, and I desired to obtain a thorough insight into the plans and schemes of those who were destined to become the prominent actors in the fearful drama, in order that I might turn it to the advantage of my country when the hour for action arrived."[33]

Abigail Adams's career as a Washington hostess was stillborn as a result of her faux pas at the dinner. She had never wholeheartedly embraced the idea anyway; it was Seward and Henry Adams, her third son, who had pushed her into the role. Henry had written to her from Germany, where he was studying, "Be ambitious, Mrs. A. You're young yet! I wish you could make your 'salons' the first in Washington . . . not on my own account, but as a family joint-stock affair." Papa needed her, Henry argued: "His weak point is just where you can fill it; he doesn't like the bother and fuss of entertaining and managing people who can't be reasoned with, and he won't take the trouble to acquire strength and influence that won't fall into his mouth."[34]

Henry's assessment of his father's social limitations was harsh but accurate. At fifty-three, Charles Francis Adams was a curious figure of a man; he managed to convey the impression of being not quite formed, that there were still untapped reserves of potential, while simultaneously appearing old and disillusioned with the world. Being the son and grandson of American presidents* had paradoxically both defined him and

---

*John Adams and John Quincy Adams, the second and sixth presidents of the United States, also served as minister to the Court of St. James's, from 1785 to 1788 and 1815 to 1817, respectively.

robbed him of ambition. He sought neither power nor attention. Small by American standards, he cultivated a professorial appearance, accentuated by a receding hairline that ended in fluffy wisps just above his ears. His face was kind, but it seemed more like a mask than a canvas for displaying emotion. It was as if at a young age Adams had entered internal exile and found the place congenial.

Adams's unsettled early life had no doubt impressed upon him a sense of being different from others. In 1814, after six years in Russia, his father became the American minister to the Court of St. James's, having helped negotiate peace with England. But for eight-year-old Charles it meant being transplanted from cosmopolitan St. Petersburg to a small country house in the village of Ealing, several miles west of London, which his father preferred to living in the city. It also meant leaving a friendly nation to go to one that had been, until a few months earlier, America's enemy.

It was the Adams legacy, however, rather than any particular childhood event, that cast the longest shadow over Charles's life. His father constantly invoked the family name as both praise and chastisement. If one of his children performed well, he was simply doing what was expected of an Adams; if he failed, the shame would follow him into the afterlife.[35] The treatment crushed Charles's elder brother, but in Charles it created a morbid sense of duty. When the family returned to Boston, Charles followed a well-trodden path, entering law, then politics, the occupations of an Adams, and taking up the family crusade to see slavery abolished.

Charles Francis Adams loathed the noisy, public side of politics. He admired Sumner and Seward precisely because they possessed the drive and bravado he lacked. He could never emulate Seward's theatrical embrace of working-class voters, and public speaking made him miserable. He also lacked Sumner's charisma and conversational ease. Adams was no more likely to frequent Willard's than was Lord Lyons. His greatest pleasures were the quiet concentration of historical research and the inner satisfaction of rock collecting. John Quincy Adams, who had become president at the age of fifty-eight—beating his own father by four years—would not have been impressed to learn that at fifty-one his son had only just managed to reach the House of Representatives.[36]

The price Adams paid for this determination to remain above, or at least away from, the fray was his failure to be considered for a place on any of the prestigious committees in Congress. Indeed, he was so reticent that the winter of 1860 passed without his having made his maiden speech. He did not even attempt to cultivate Lord Lyons, despite a family history that gave him a far greater claim to the minister's notice than Sumner, who stopped by the legation at every opportunity.

Lyons appreciated Sumner's visits. The senator happily shared with him the sort of insider political gossip that diplomats are required to know but find it hardest to obtain. Although Lyons was one of the only Washington figures whose standing had not been affected by the widening social chasm between the North and South, he was still as friendless as the day he arrived in the city. Ironically, his inability to make social inroads made it easier for President Buchanan to confide in him. On April 5, 1860, Lyons bumped into Buchanan while taking his constitutional around Lafayette Square. The president looked harassed and careworn. He felt helpless, he told Lyons, against the forces that were driving the country apart. The only area in which he still hoped to make a positive contribution was that of Anglo-American relations; here he still considered himself master of his own house. "He began by repeating an observation he often makes to me," reported Lyons after their meeting, "that it has been his great ambition to be able to say at the end of his administration that he had left no question with Great Britain unsettled; that for the first time since the Revolution 'the docket was clear.' " Yet even in this, Buchanan feared that events were conspiring against him.

Ten months earlier, in June 1859, a domestic pig on San Juan Island in the Straits of Juan de Fuca had wandered from its enclosure into the potato patch of a neighboring farm. The patch belonged to Lyman Cutlar, one of twenty-five Americans living on the rugged, tree-lined island. Cutlar was tired of having his potatoes raided by the pig, and he settled the matter for good with a bullet. The pig's owners happened to be British. They demanded compensation, and when Cutlar refused, they took their case to the governor of British Columbia. Unfortunately, it was unclear where the exact boundary lay between Washington State and the province of British Columbia. The arrival in July of a company from the 9th U.S. Infantry under Captain George Pickett appeared to settle the question, but then the British governor countered by dispatching a magistrate, Major John Fitzroy De Courcy, to the island. The major was a decorated veteran of the Crimean War, and fighting—rather than diplomacy—was his forte. He did not bother to hold a parley with Pickett, instead ordering him to leave the island or face arrest. Pickett refused and requested several hundred reinforcements. The governor sent several warships to reinforce De Courcy's authority. Pickett's men dug in, and the gunboats maneuvered into position.

Alarmed that the two nations could stumble into war over a dead pig, Lord Lyons and Secretary of State Lewis Cass immediately ordered the withdrawal of their respective troops. But the actual details surrounding the dispute were more difficult to resolve. Neither nation was willing to concede its right to the island. The best that Lyons and Cass could achieve was a compromise whereby each country would maintain a small company of soldiers on the island until the question was resolved.[37] President Buchanan confessed to Lyons that he could not see any way to end the matter. "The People of the West Coast were becoming very excited," he told Lyons, "and he really did not know what to do. He concluded by begging me to set my wits to work to devise some plan of coming to an amicable settlement." Lyons promised to try, though he privately doubted that anything he suggested would be acceptable to the inhabitants of the West Coast.[38]

Lyons was still considering the problem when the Democratic Party convened in Charleston on April 23, 1859. A total of 630 delegates from around the country descended on the city to select the party's presidential candidate for the election in November. The Southerners who openly advocated secession from the United States, known as the "Fire-eaters," were determined to force the slavery debate into the open. William Yancey of Alabama had sufficiently recovered from the illness that had kept him from Lord Napier's farewell ball to lead the way with his brilliant oratory. The Fire-eaters wanted the party to endorse a platform guaranteeing federal protection of slavery in all states and territories, including any new acquisitions such as Cuba or Honduras, but most Northern members of the party wanted to maintain the status quo. Yancey ostentatiously led a walkout of fifty delegates from the cotton states after the Northern majority voted down the proslavery platform. The convention ended in disarray, without a presidential nominee being selected.

It was obvious to all that the Fire-eaters were blackmailing the Democratic Party with the threat of a split unless their platform was adopted. The Southern Democrats in the Senate pleaded with Yancey and the others not to turn the election into a three-horse race. The Democrats' turmoil had naturally boosted the morale of the Republican Party by the time its delegates gathered in Chicago in mid-May to choose their presidential candidate. Seward was so certain of victory that he departed for his hometown of Auburn in upstate New York with his farewell speech to the Senate already prepared. But once the balloting began, his supporters realized they had made a tactical mistake in allowing the convention to take place in Illinois, Abraham Lincoln's home state, instead of in New York. Seward's campaign was outmaneuvered at every turn. Lincoln's supporters successfully portrayed their candidate as an American success story. Lincoln was "honest Abe," the humble rail splitter turned prominent lawyer, whose moderate views on slavery would do more to unite the country than Seward's radical rhetoric. Seward's campaign manager, Thurlow Weed, spent too much time doing deals and not enough assuaging the fears of the doubters. After a blazing start, Seward's camp began to lose supporters, and by the third ballot, Lincoln emerged as the clear winner.

Seward was crushed. He had refrained from running for the presidency in 1856 on Thurlow Weed's advice. Now he looked back and saw it as his squandered opportunity. His loss to Lincoln seemed inexplicable to anyone who had not attended the convention. "Seward went away from Washington a few days ago feeling perfectly certain of being named as the Candidate of the Republicans," Lyons reported on May 22, 1860. "I never heard Lincoln even mentioned by the heads of the Party here." Lyons could provide only scant details: "He is, I understand, a rough farmer who began life as a farm labourer and got on by a talent for stump speaking. Little more is known of him."[39] Charles Sumner sent a letter of commiseration to Seward expressing his shock at the surprise result, although he wrote to the Duchess of Argyll "that, while in England, I always expressed a doubt whether Seward could be nominated."[40]

The British government was pondering the meaning of Seward's defeat for Anglo-American relations when President Buchanan issued an invi-

tation for the Prince of Wales to tour the United States.* The president
had heard that Queen Victoria was sending the eighteen-year-old Prince
Edward to Canada, in fulfillment of a long-standing request from the
Canadians for a royal visit. Buchanan suggested that the prince's trip
could be extended by a further six weeks to include a stay at the White
House.

Although the Queen was initially doubtful whether her son was up to
the job, Prince Albert and the cabinet realized that Britain had been presented with a rare opportunity to improve the transatlantic relationship.
Lyons, who was awarded the daunting task of deciding the prince's itinerary, was delighted to have something other than the island of San Juan
to discuss with Buchanan. Together with the Queen and the Foreign Office, Lyons devised an arrangement whereby the prince would travel to
the United States in an unofficial capacity, as if on holiday, though accompanied by himself and the Duke of Newcastle at all times. There
were to be no official deputations, delegations, or ceremonies. This,
Lyons hoped, would dampen any attempts by Irish agitators to whip up
local Anglophobia. Furthermore, in a nod to republican sentiment, the
prince would use the least of all his titles, Baron Renfrew, allowing him
to be treated as an ordinary British subject while "incognito." Except for
a passing visit to Virginia, Lyons simply left the South off the prince's
itinerary.

Naturally, in all the cities on the prince's route, the request for
"Baron Renfrew" to be treated as a private citizen was ignored. Almost
every inhabitant of Detroit was at the docks when the royal party clambered off the ferry *Windsor* on September 20, 1860. The same was true at
the train station in Chicago. "Bertie," as his family called him, was taken
aback by the enthusiasm that greeted his arrival. The Americans seemed
to like him even more than the Canadians did. At his every stop there
were parades, fireworks, banquets, triumphant tours, and thousands
upon thousands of cheering spectators. For a young man who was used

---

* The biggest Anglo-American controversy in the early months of 1860 had been the
bare-knuckle prizefight between the Englishman Tom Sayers and the American
John Heenan on April 17. Billed as the world's first international boxing contest,
the match dragged on for thirty-seven rounds, until Heenan's supporters broke
into the ring. The contest was declared a draw, which led to the claim by furious
supporters of Sayers that he had been robbed of his victory.

to being treated as a great disappointment by his parents, this was an experience beyond fantasy.

By the time the royal entourage arrived at Washington in early October, Bertie had become an enthusiastic admirer of America; he even thought the unfinished capital was a fine place to visit. He spent a night at the White House, where President Buchanan and his niece, Miss Harriet Lane, made an exception for the young prince by allowing card games after dinner (although no dancing).[41] After being shown Congress, the Washington Monument, the Treasury, and a score of other public buildings, he informed his parents, "We might easily take some hints for our own buildings, which are so very bad."[42]

From Washington, Lyons accompanied Prince Edward to Mount Vernon, George Washington's estate on the banks of the Potomac River, sixteen miles from Washington, where the prince planted a tree at Washington's tomb. The British minister was just beginning to congratulate himself upon a splendid piece of organization when the visit threatened to unravel during the trip to Richmond, Virginia. The locals were furious because the prince's hosts had canceled a large slave auction, and a hostile crowd gathered outside his hotel. Lyons managed to avoid a public confrontation, but that afternoon, he and Newcastle encountered a second embarrassment when they discovered en route that the royal party was being taken to visit a slave plantation. Only with great difficulty did they convince their hosts that a tour of the mayor's office would be much more pleasurable.[43]

When "Baron Renfrew" arrived in New York on October 11, his guardians were beginning to fear that the good-natured prince's appetite for orphanages and parades had run its course. But Bertie absolutely loved New York. Some 300,000 people (out of a population of 800,000) lined the streets, climbing on rooftops, trees, and carriages, even hanging from streetlamps, to watch his carriage proceed up Broadway to his hotel. They cheered, threw flowers, and waved placards that said "Welcome, Victoria's Royal Son." "I never dreamed we would be received as we were," he wrote.[44]

The prince had never imagined such comforts, either. The Fifth Avenue Hotel was the newest and grandest addition to New York's already magnificent accommodations. Completed in 1859 on the "edge" of town at Twenty-fourth Street and Madison Square, the marble-clad six-story building had the latest conveniences including en suite bathrooms, communication tubes that allowed a guest to speak his request to room service, central heating, and, most exciting of all, a "perpendicular railway intersecting each floor." The American ideal of luxury was different from the European. The ornaments and objets d'art often taken for granted in English or French houses were missing, but "the rooms are so light and lofty; the passages are so well warmed; the doors slide backward in their grooves so easily and yet so tightly; the chairs are so luxurious; the beds are so elastic, and the linen so clean, and, let me add, the living so excellent," he wrote, "that I would never wish for better quarters. . . . All the domestic arrangements (to use a fine word for gas, hot water, and other comforts) are wonderfully perfect."[45]

For one night the prince was allowed to sample life as it was lived by New York's gilded "Four Hundred." On October 12, 1860, the entire entourage, including Lyons, traveled in a parade of open carriages to a grand ball at the Academy of Music on Fourteenth Street organized by New York's most distinguished citizen, Peter Cooper. Four thousand guests bribed, blackmailed, or otherwise insinuated their way into the most coveted social event of the decade. The danger that the prince would inadvertently start a stampede was so great that the entrances to

Grand torchlight parade of the New York firemen in honor of the Prince of Wales, passing the Fifth Avenue Hotel, October 13, 1860.

the supper rooms were guarded by prominent citizens, who admitted fifty guests at a time.[46] Even so, the ballroom floor partially collapsed beneath the dancers' weight and carpenters had to be called in during dinner. Bertie danced until five in the morning. Four hours later, he was dressed and dutifully touring P. T. Barnum's American Museum, where he saw the "Feejee Mermaid" and shook hands with Tom Thumb.

That night, five thousand men from the City Fire Brigade marched in a torchlight procession past his hotel. Each company let off fireworks as it went under the prince's balcony. "This is all for me! All for me!" he exclaimed.[47] He was exhausted, like the rest of his entourage, but also elated. The warmth of the American reception made it difficult to imagine that there had ever been open hostility between the two countries. Even the much-anticipated protests from Irish immigrants had been confined to a single incident, when the Irish-dominated 69th Regiment of the New York State Militia refused to march in the parade up Broadway.[48] Leaving New York with great regret, the prince traveled to Albany on October 15, 1860, for a grand dinner given by the governor of the state, Edwin Morgan.

Seward also attended Morgan's dinner. The past few months had been turbulent for him. His return to Washington following the Republican convention was one of the most humiliating episodes of his life. He told his wife that the house felt "sad and mournful" and that he missed the Napiers, whose engravings on the wall seemed "like pictures of the dead."[49] Seward could not decide which was worse, the complacent sympathy of Sumner or the exaggerated politeness of Mason and the other Senate Democrats.[50] The demeanor of both demonstrated that they considered his political career effectively at an end. Only the Adamses, wrote Seward, were as "generous, kind, faithful as ever." Adams took him to task with uncharacteristic force after he learned that Seward was contemplating his retirement from politics. Neither Adams nor Weed thought Lincoln capable of winning the election without Seward, let alone running the country. Thurlow Weed had met with Lincoln after the convention and offered his services for the upcoming campaign. His conversation had convinced him that if Lincoln were elected, which was beginning to look quite possible, the newcomer would never be a match for Seward. Lincoln might be president in name, but the real power would reside with Seward.

Weed's optimism about Seward's role stemmed from the Democrats' recent split into two camps. The Northern and Southern factions had decided to field their own candidates, Stephen Douglas for the North and John Breckinridge for the South, almost guaranteeing the defeat of both in favor of the Republicans. By early August, Weed had managed to drag Seward out of his despondency and into a sufficiently robust frame of mind to contemplate a tour through Northern and western states on Lincoln's behalf. Seward had to put up a brave front and conduct himself as a loyal party man; any other action would have given Lincoln an excuse to leave him out of his cabinet. Seward knew that Weed was right, but his wisdom did not make the effort any less painful.[51] The Republican message that Seward carried to the Northern states contained something for everyone: no expansion of slavery, a protective tariff for American industries, a homestead law giving away undeveloped federal land, and government aid to construct a transcontinental railroad.

Seward decided that he could not face the next leg of his tour unless he had sufficient company to keep him distracted. He set off in September with a large retinue that included a reluctant but loyal Adams and his twenty-five-year-old son, Charles Francis Jr.; the president of the New York City police board, General James Nye (and Nye's daughter); his biographer George Baker; and his daughter, Fanny. But even surrounded by friends and family, Seward had to wrestle with his emotions. The signs of his inner struggle were evident in the copious cigars and glasses of brandy that he consumed during the long train journeys. Charles Francis Jr. never saw Seward visibly drunk, but he was sometimes sufficiently inebriated to lose control "and set his tongue going with dangerous volubility." Throughout the northwestern states, thousands of people flocked to hear Seward speak. The public adulation heightened Seward's already febrile emotions; his speeches became coarser and more strident. In Michigan on September 4, he marred a strong antislavery speech with racist asides about the feebleness of the African race. In Minnesota on September 22, he declared that Canada was destined to become part of the United States.

Seward no doubt believed that it was more important to reach out to undecided voters with his populist message than to concern himself about the effect of his pronouncements in far-off places. The Prince of Wales's tour of Canada was in midswing when Seward made his speech about its future as a United States territory. The unfortunate timing prompted the Canadian and British press to give his speech much greater attention and credence than it merited. When he sauntered into Governor Morgan's house on the night of the dinner for the prince, Seward was apparently unaware of the huge offense he had caused. The occasion was already a difficult one for Seward; he had often discussed the idea of a royal visit with Lord Napier, but Seward had avoided the British legation after Napier's departure, and barely knew Lyons. He felt more comfortable talking to the Duke of Newcastle, who gratifyingly remembered him from his visit to England. Seward started well, until the same urge to drink and talk crept over him. By the end of the meal, the duke was reeling from the encounter. "He fairly told me he should make use of insults to England to secure his own position in the States, and that I must not suppose he meant war. On the contrary he did not wish war with England and he was confident we should never go to war with the States—we dared not and could not afford it," the duke reported later to the governor-general of Canada.

Outraged by Seward's effrontery, Newcastle did not mince his words in reply: "I then told him there was no fear of war except from a policy as he indicated, and that if he carried it out and touched our honor, he would, some fine morning, find he had embroiled his country in a disastrous conflict at the moment when he fancied he was bullying all before him."[52] Seward never gave another thought to the conversation. With the election less than a month away, all his energy was directed toward the campaign in New York.

The royal party proceeded to Boston for more banquets, balls, and celebrations, and finally to Maine for one last hurrah. "During [Prince Edward's] last day [in America] I was with the party & parted with him on the pier," wrote Charles Sumner to his friend Evelyn Denison, speaker of the House of Commons. "At every station on the railway there was an immense crowd, headed by the local authorities, while our national flags were blended together. I remarked to Dr. Acland [the Radcliffe librarian at Oxford] that it seemed as if a young heir long absent was returning to take possession. 'It is more than that,' said he, affected almost to tears."[53]

Sumner believed that the two countries had arrived at a turning point in their relations. The prince was "carrying home an unwritten Treaty of Alliance and Amity between two great nations."[54] A similar feeling was evident in England. After reading his New York correspondent's reports, Mowbray Morris, the managing editor of The Times, wrote that the royal tour "will do a great deal of good here. It will convince persons who know nothing of Americans except by very bad specimens, that Brother Jonathan [the United States] really has brotherly feelings towards John Bull [Britain]."[55]

It was only later, when Lyons could reflect on the tour from the comfort of his Washington drawing room, that he realized its "wonderful success." "I have now had time to talk quietly about it with men whose opinion is worth having," he wrote, "and also to compare newspapers of various shades of politics."[56] He had seen nothing to make him wince, or even complain. During this period of political uncertainty, the American press had found in the ever-obliging Prince of Wales the one subject that did not stir controversy. Even the Anglophobic *New York Herald* announced "that henceforth the giant leaders of Liberty in the Old World and in the New are united in impulse and in aim for the perpetuation of Freedom and the elevation of man."[57]

But six weeks after the prince had sailed away to the strains of "God Save the Queen," Lyons confided to the Duke of Newcastle that all their exertions might have been for naught. "It is difficult to believe that I am in the same country which appeared so prosperous, so contented, and one may say, so calm when we travelled through it," he wrote. "The change is very great even since I wrote to you on the 29th October. Our friends are apparently going ahead on the road to ruin with their characteristic speed and energy."[58]

THREE

"The Cards
Are in Our Hands!"

Seven states secede—"Slaveownia"—Seward rises to the occasion—
Bluster—Adams is offended—William Howard Russell at the White
House—The April Fool's Day memorandum—The Confederate cabinet—
The fall of Fort Sumter—Lincoln declares a blockade—Southern confidence

"It seems impossible that the South can be mad enough to dissolve the Union," Lyons wrote to the foreign secretary, Lord John Russell, after Lincoln was elected president on November 6, 1860. Yet South Carolina had already announced it would hold a special convention to decide whether to secede, and the news sent the price of shares tumbling on the New York Stock Exchange. The financial markets suffered another blow when a merchant vessel departed from Charleston, South Carolina, on November 17 with only the state flag flying from its mast. President Buchanan pleaded in vain with his proslavery cabinet to agree on a united response.

Lord Lyons cursed the little pig from San Juan Island and its penchant for Farmer Cutlar's potatoes. He wished he had been able to settle San Juan's boundary dispute during the Prince of Wales's visit. With the secession crisis gathering momentum and Buchanan growing increasingly feeble in the face of his colleagues, he doubted that the issue could be resolved before Lincoln's inauguration. Lyons suspected that the Republicans would be far less inclined than the Democrats to agree on a compromise. He had noticed that the Republican Party as a whole—not just Seward—tended to pander to anti-British sentiment as a way of showing that its abolition platform was independent of foreign opinion.

It was important not to give the Republicans a reason to complain, Lyons wrote to Lord John Russell, and he suggested that the government refrain from making any public statements about the current political turmoil in America.

Lord John Russell received Lyons's letter on December 18, the same day the South Carolina convention began its debate on the question of secession. The British cabinet had become increasingly concerned by the South's reaction to Lincoln's victory. Palmerston assumed it meant a second American Revolution was at hand. "There is no saying what attitude we may have to assume," he wrote with concern to the Duke of Somerset, "not for the purpose of interfering in their quarrels, but to hold our own and to protect our Fellow subjects and their interests."[1] Lyons's insistence that Britain stand aloof seemed eminently sensible. "I quite agree with Lord John Russell and Lord Lyons," Palmerston stated in a memorandum for the cabinet. "Nothing would be more inadvisable than for us to interfere in the Dispute."[2] The law officers of the Crown assured Russell that the South Carolina ship flying its state flag could dock at Liverpool without any fuss. Customs officials there would treat the questionable flag as though it were a bit of holiday bunting, beneath anyone's notice and certainly not a matter for official comment.[3]

The imperative to stay out of America's troubles was one of the few issues that united Palmerston's fractious cabinet. The other was Giuseppe Garibaldi's campaign to unite Italy. Here, too, the cabinet had agreed in July that the best course was to remain neutral and allow Garibaldi to fail or succeed on his own. Since setting out in the spring of 1860 to lead the Sicilian revolution against the Bourbon monarchy, Garibaldi had inspired hundreds of British volunteers to join his brigade. Dozens of officers had taken a leave of absence from the army in order to don the famous red shirt. Two ships from the navy's Mediterranean squadron were almost emptied as sailors left en masse to form their own battery. Even the Duke of Somerset, Palmerston's First Lord of the Admiralty, could not dissuade one of his own sons from running away to join the English battalion. The willingness of so many volunteers to help the Italians left the army and navy chiefs with little doubt that they would have a problem on their hands if war erupted in America, where both sides spoke English and the ties of friends and family were even stronger.

"We have the worst possible news from home," the assistant secretary of the American legation, Benjamin Moran, wrote in his diary. A few days later he stood with the American minister, George Dallas, in front of a wall map of the United States, speculating with him as to which of the Southern states would go.[4] "The American Union is defunct," pronounced Moran after the next diplomatic bag revealed that South Carolina had voted to secede on December 20, 1860.

Moran was relieved by the reaction of the British press to what it called the "cotton states."[5] *The Times* scoffed at the idea of secession: "South Carolina has as much right to secede from . . . the United States as Lancashire from England."[6] But *The Economist* was less sympathetic, calling South Carolina's secession poetic justice since Americans were always bragging about their perfect democracy. The *Illustrated London News* was the worst, in Moran's opinion, since it asked "our American

MONKEY UNCOMMON UP, MASSA!

Punch tells the Southern planters that the days of slavery are numbered, December 1860.

Cousins" to let the cotton states go in order to avoid making the same mistake as Austria, which had almost bankrupted itself resisting the Italians' desire for independence.[7] Yet most newspapers followed the line of *The Times*. Words such as "sharp," "ignoble," and "unprincipled" were frequently used to describe South Carolina. *Punch* suggested that the seceding states could name their new country "Slaveownia."[8]

The boastful rhetoric of Southern politicians was also attacked in the press. Senator Louis Wigfall of Texas came in for particular censure for his arrogant speech to the Senate on December 6, 1860. The South would be able to dictate her own terms to the world, he declared, because "Cotton is King. . . . He waves his sceptre not only over these thirty-three states, but over the island of Great Britain." Queen Victoria herself, Wigfall roared, must "bend the knee in fealty and acknowledge allegiance to that monarch." The South could turn off the supply of cotton and cripple England in a single week. The cabinet feared Wigfall could be right and agreed with Palmerston "that no time should be lost in securing a supply of cotton from other quarters than America."[9]

———

The South owed more than $200 million to the North, with most of the debt concentrated in New York, a city whose commercial ties with the cotton states were so close that some banks accepted slaves as collateral. The financial community was sent into a panic by the readiness of Southern businesses to use South Carolina's self-declared independence as an excuse to repudiate their debts. The *New York Post* denounced the practice as treachery, declaring, "The city of New York belongs almost as much to the South as to the North." The victims of the financial crisis were not only New Yorkers. In Britain, investors had almost $400 million in U.S. stocks, bonds, and securities; Benjamin Moran lost most of his savings in a matter of weeks. But the impact went deeper and wider in New York, and included victims such as Dr. Elizabeth Blackwell, whose hard-won funds for her women's medical college simply evaporated. Mayor Fernando Wood was so anxious about the state of the financial markets that he briefly entertained a proposal for New York to secede from the Union and become a "free city."

In late December, with Lincoln still in Illinois going through appointment lists and President Buchanan having retreated to his bedroom in the White House, Seward took the lead role in guiding the North's response to the seceding states. Thurlow Weed's prediction that Lincoln would "share" power—and the escalating crisis—had convinced Seward to put aside his hurt pride and agree to become secretary of state.[10] His self-belief and ambition returned in full force once the decision was made: "I have advised Mr. L that I will not decline [the post]," Seward wrote to his wife on December 28. "It is inevitable. I will try to save freedom and my country."[11]

The Senate had appointed the "Committee of Thirteen," and the House of Representatives the "Committee of Thirty-three," to address Southern grievances. Seward not only dominated the Senate committee but also made sure that his supporters—particularly Charles Francis Adams—were among the thirty-three. Their work became all the more urgent after news reached Washington that the Southern states were seizing federal arsenals and forts. Seward's strategy was to conciliate and delay for as long as possible. The South had been threatening to secede for years; he was convinced that if the hotheads could be contained, the moderates would gradually reassert control. He talked with such assurance that young Henry Adams felt he was in the presence of greatness.[12] But to Charles Sumner, Seward's willingness to guarantee the institution of slavery in order to save the Union was an insupportable betrayal of abolition principles. Sumner cornered Henry's brother, Charles Francis Adams, Jr., when he visited the Senate and ranted at him like a "crazy man," blaming "the compromisers, meaning Seward and my father."[13] As far as Sumner was concerned, his friendship with Adams was irreparably broken.

Seward ignored Sumner's ravings, confident that his conciliation plan would work given sufficient time. But in early January, two delegations from the New York business community were told by Southern leaders in Washington that a movement had started that could not be stopped. Mississippi voted to secede on January 9, Florida on the tenth. Alabama, Georgia, and Louisiana followed in quick succession; their senators left Washington and went to Montgomery, Alabama, where a special convention was due to begin on February 4. Texas followed on February 1, 1861, the seventh state to secede from the Union. On the morning of the third, Seward paid a surprise call on Lord Lyons, to reassure him that the South would be back in the fold in less than three months. Lyons had been wondering for several weeks when either the old or the new administration would remember the existence of the diplomatic community. He did not discount the value of being able to talk privately with the incoming secretary of state, but everything else about the interview made Lyons dread his future relationship with Seward. He sent two reports of the meeting to Lord John Russell. In the official dispatch, which would be printed for public consumption in the parliamentary "Blue Book," he gave a bland description that only hinted at the threats and preposterous claims Seward had leveled at him. Seward had, wrote Lyons with classic understatement, "unbounded confidence in his own skill in managing the American people."

In the separate dispatch marked "private and confidential," however, Lyons admitted that he had been horrified by Seward's mix of cynicism and naïveté. The secretary of state had tried to persuade him that there was enough federal patronage at his disposal to bribe the South back into the Union. As far as Seward was concerned, there was no need to discuss the international ramifications of the conflict because none existed. As long as there was no bloodshed, he told Lyons, the seceding states would eventually change their minds. Seward also repeated to him a recent conversation with the minister for Bremen (one of the smaller states of the German Confederation), "no doubt for my instruction." The hapless diplomat had complained about the Republican Party's election promise to place tariffs on foreign imports, saying that such a move would turn Europe against America at the moment when she most needed friends. Seward claimed to have replied that nothing would give him more pleasure, since he would then have the perfect excuse for an international quarrel, "and South Carolina and the seceding states would soon join in." "I am afraid," concluded Lyons, "that he takes no other view of Foreign Relations, than as safe levers to work with upon public opinion here."[14]

A few days later, Lyons heard that Seward was trying to pass a message to him and the French minister that they should ignore anything he might say about either Britain or France, since underneath he had "the kindest motives towards the two countries." Lyons thought that Seward's visit to Britain the previous summer had given him not only a handful of fond memories but also the dangerous misconception "that England will never go to war with the United States" and therefore "could be safely played with without any risk."[15] Lord John Russell advised Lyons to be blunt with Seward: he should understand that England's "forbearance sprung from a consciousness of strength, and not from the timidity of weakness."[16]

On February 8, 1861, Henry Adams wrote to his brother that Seward was in high spirits "and chuckles himself hoarse with his stories. He says it's all right. We shall keep the border states . . . the storm is weathered." The next day in Montgomery, Alabama, the Provisional Congress of the Confederate States of America elected Senator Jefferson Davis—one of Seward's closest Washington friends before the crisis—as provisional president. William Lowndes Yancey, the voice of secession, proclaimed memorably "that the man and the hour have met." Davis was inaugurated on February 18. A future general in the Confederate army informed his wife that "the firm conviction here is that Great Britain, France and Russia will acknowledge us at once in the family of nations."[17] Davis placed so much confidence in the power of cotton that he appointed Yancey, who had never been abroad, to lead the Confederate diplomatic mission to Europe.

Seward was still offering deals to Southern negotiators, even though Confederate troops were threatening the tiny federal garrison at Fort Sumter in Charleston, when Lincoln arrived in Washington on February 23. Everything about the new president proclaimed his rusticity. The two years he had spent in Congress during the late 1840s appeared to have left him in the same unpolished state as when he first entered it. During Seward's first private conversation with him, Lincoln admitted with startling candor that he had no idea about international relations, saying, "I shall have to depend upon you for taking care of these matters of foreign affairs, of which I know so little, and with which I reckon you are familiar." More extraordinarily still, Lincoln showed Seward his inaugural address and invited him to give his comments.[18] Less than a week before Lincoln's arrival, Seward had insisted to the Bremen minister that the presidency was a matter of luck—rather like the monarchy—and no one took the officeholder seriously. "The actual direction of public affairs belongs to the leader of the ruling party here."[19] Seward was obviously referring to himself, as though he was expecting Lincoln to settle meekly into his role as the ceremonial leader of the country, leaving him in charge.

No matter how hard Seward argued and cajoled, however, Lincoln would not be swayed from his notion that he alone had the right to select the members of his cabinet. Nor did he accept Seward's contention that the United States should abandon Fort Sumter rather than take a stand against Southern threats. Seward dared not reveal his promises to the Southern negotiators that Fort Sumter would not be reinforced.

While Seward struggled to assert his will over Lincoln, the Northern Republicans in the Senate took advantage of the missing Southern politicians, who were free-traders to a man, to pass the Morrill Tariff on February 27. The protectionist bill placed high import duties on most imported manufacturing goods; since 40 percent of Britain's export trade went to the United States, the effect of the tariff on Britain would be devastating. Its impact on international relations ought to have been of the highest priority to the State Department.*

Seward was bitterly disappointed by Lincoln's refusal to alter his appointments to the cabinet. His dismay was not palliated by the fact that the six other members were either neutral toward the president or former rivals, and equally suspicious of one another. Three—Caleb Smith (Interior), Edward Bates (attorney general), and Simon Cameron (War)—were cool toward him. But the others—Salmon Chase (Treasury), Gideon Welles (Navy), and Montgomery Blair (postmaster general)—were outright enemies.† Seward tendered his resignation on March 2. Lincoln calmly offered him the American legation in Britain as an alternative. He already had a second choice for secretary of state: William L. Dayton, the attorney general of New Jersey. "I cannot afford to let Seward take the first trick," Lincoln explained to his private secretary. Furious at being outsmarted by the novice leader, Seward conceded defeat before Dayton could be alerted of his good fortune. He withdrew his resignation on March 4, and the unsuspecting Dayton was put down for London. But having lost the battle to keep some of his greatest enemies out of the cabinet, Seward became even more determined that no one should interfere with his conciliation strategy, and all through March he feverishly schemed and maneuvered behind Lincoln's back.

———

Among the diplomatic community in Washington, the main topic of conversation was whether the North would employ any commercial

---

* The taxation on foreign goods depended on the economic interests of various Northern states; sugar, raw wool, iron, flaxseed, hides, beef, pork, grain, hemp, coal, lead, copper, and zinc all received protection from outside competition—as did dried, pickled, and salted fish.

† "He is obtrusive," complained Welles, "assuming and presuming, meddlesome, and uncertain, ready to exercise authority always, never doubting his right until challenged; then he becomes timid, uncertain, distrustful, and inventive of schemes to extricate himself. . . . I think he has no very profound or sincere convictions."[20]

sanctions against countries doing business with the South. Lyons agreed with Lord John Russell that Britain's commercial interests were paramount, but he also thought that it would be a calamity if the North forced the "maritime Powers of Europe to interfere" to protect their cotton supply since, in his view, the "stain of slavery" made the South "loathsome to the civilized world."[21]

On March 20, Seward made another of his unscheduled visits to Lyons, this time to sound out the minister's opinion on how the British would react if the North "interrupted" the South's commerce. Realizing this meant a blockade of Southern ports, Lyons attempted a little bluster of his own and threatened point-blank that if the North recklessly deprived Britain of cotton, she would fight back, and "the most simple, if not the only way, would be to recognize the Southern Confederacy." Recognition, in legal terms, meant granting the South the status of a sovereign country. The North would not only then suffer a psychological blow but might also find itself facing a united Europe that was prepared to protect the supply of cotton at the point of a gun.

Lyons was unaware that he had committed a grave error. He had given the impression to Seward, who thought that Lyons was too unimaginative to be bluffing, that Britain was looking for an excuse to recognize the South. Seward pretended that he agreed with Lyons's position, a tactic he often employed when he wanted to buy time. According to Seward's political philosophy, a frightened enemy was better than an untrustworthy friend. When he left the legation, it was to think about how to keep Britain at bay rather than how to help her avoid a disruption to her cotton industry.

The following day, Lyons gave a formal dinner that included Seward and the senior members of the diplomatic corps. Though Washington had not taken to the minister, it welcomed his copious champagne and French chef. The dinner itself passed without incident, but by the time the guests had moved to the drawing room, Seward was lubricated and loquacious. His gravelly voice suddenly rose above the gentle hum, causing Lyons to stop his conversation and turn around. He saw that Seward was having a heated discussion with the French and Russian ministers. Seward impatiently motioned him to join them.

"When I came up," Lyons reported, "I found him asking M. Mercier [the French minister] to give him a copy of his instructions to the French Consuls in the Southern States." Unsure whether Seward was mad or just grossly ignorant, the Frenchman retreated behind a veil of diplomatic coyness, assuring him that the instructions contained nothing more than an exhortation to protect French commerce while observing strict neutrality. Seward then repeated the demand to Lyons, who employed the same device. This was tantamount to poking a rhinoceros. Seward lost control of himself. According to witnesses, he accused Lyons of threatening him with Britain's acknowledgment of the South. "Such recognition will mean war!" he is said to have shouted. "The whole world will be engulfed and revolution will be the harvest."[22] Lyons avoided being specific in his own report, merely saying that Seward had become "more and more violent and noisy," so he had turned away, taking "a natural opportunity, as host, to speak to some of the ladies in the room."[23]

The French minister, Henri Mercier, was a large, hearty figure who did not cave easily. He was sufficiently irritated by Seward's badgering to suggest to Lyons that they obtain discretionary power from their governments to recognize the South whenever they saw fit. Lyons was appalled by the idea and persuaded Mercier that it would put them in considerable personal danger from Northern and Southern extremists. He proposed a different plan—that they keep to a unified policy at all times. Seward would be less ready to pick a quarrel if it meant engaging America in a battle of two against one, and he would never be able to use one country as his tool against the other. Mercier agreed. A few days later, Lyons heard that there had been a "stormy sitting of the Cabinet" on the day of his dinner and assumed this was the reason for Seward's outburst.

———

In only three weeks, Seward had changed from being the self-appointed "ruler" to the odd man out in Lincoln's cabinet. He tried to maintain his old mastery while struggling to find a place in the new order. His ability to dictate to Lincoln had come down to thwarting Charles Sumner's bid to become the minister to Great Britain. Seward managed to persuade Lincoln that Charles Francis Adams should have the post. William Dayton was once again moved around the checkerboard of patronage and given the Paris legation, despite being unable to speak French. It was a pyrrhic victory for Seward, however, since by staying in Washington, Sumner became the new chairman of the Senate Committee on Foreign Relations. The post would give him great power and leverage against Seward, if he could change Lincoln's impression of him as a pompous know-it-all. "Sumner," Lincoln allegedly said after their initial meeting in late February, "is my idea of a Bishop."[24]

Adams was no longer sure he wanted to be a minister when the telegram announcing his appointment arrived in Massachusetts. "The president had seemed so intent on the nomination of Dayton, that the news finally came on us like a thunderbolt," recalled Charles Francis Jr. "My mother at once fell into tears and deep agitation; foreseeing all sorts of evil consequences, and absolutely refusing to be comforted; while my father looked dismayed. The younger members of the household were astonished and confounded." Mrs. Adams was surprised, continued Charles Francis Jr.,

> when presently every one she met, instead of avoiding a painful subject or commiserating her, offered her congratulations or expressions of envy. So she cheered up amazingly. As to my father, he had then lived so long in the atmosphere of Boston, that I really think the great opportunity of his life when suddenly thrust upon him caused a sincere feeling of consternation. He really felt that he was being called on to make a great personal and political sacrifice.[25]

Adams's poor opinion of Lincoln had increased after the inauguration ball, when the president did not even pretend to recognize him. He traveled to Washington to accept his appointment in a state of deep pessimism. Breakfast with Seward on March 28 made him feel worse; "he spoke of my appointment as his victory," complained Adams indignantly, "whilst he made a species of apology for the selection of Mr. Wilson which seemed to me a little lame." Charles Wilson was to have the important post of legation secretary as compensation for missing out on the plum job of heading the Chicago Post Office, a position with a high salary and little responsibility.[26] Seward admitted that the Illinois newspaper editor could hardly be less qualified or suited to work under Adams, but Lincoln had insisted on the move as a quid pro quo for replacing Dayton.

Seward accompanied Adams to the White House for his interview with Lincoln. Adams was shocked by the "ravenous crowd" of office seekers who milled around the building, blocking stairs and corridors.[27] Inside Lincoln's office they found the president in deep conversation with a congressman over other potential candidates to fill the much-discussed Chicago Post Office job. When Adams began to express his gratitude for the appointment to London, Lincoln hurriedly cut him short, saying it was all Seward's doing. He then turned his back on Adams in order to engage Seward and the congressman in further discussion on "the Chicago case." Adams waited, uncertain whether the conversation was over, until a gesture from Seward indicated he had been dismissed.[28]

Adams was insulted. "Such was his fashion of receiving and dismissing the incumbent of one of the two highest posts in the foreign service of the country!" he complained in his diary. Nor had he been invited to attend the first state dinner of the White House, taking place that night, a gross slight considering that Seward was bringing as his guest William Howard Russell of *The Times,* who had arrived in Washington shortly after Lincoln's inauguration.

––––

The forty-year-old war correspondent William Howard Russell, known to his friends as Billy, was the most famous journalist in the world. His honest and searing reports during the Crimean War had made a heroine of Florence Nightingale as they had rocked the Aberdeen administration.

Russell was the ideal choice to represent *The Times* in the United States. Overeating and excessive drinking were his chief vices—especially drinking, which had grown worse as his wife, Mary, became increasingly frail and dependent on him. Their four older children were in boarding school, but Russell had left her nursing their four-month-old son, Colin, who seemed as weak and poorly as his mother. After saying goodbye, "I went to the station in a storm of pain," Russell wrote in his diary, feeling guilty that the night before he had been enjoying himself at the Garrick Club, where the novelist William Makepeace Thackeray proposed a toast in his honor.[29]

The qualities that made Russell an unsatisfactory husband to Mary were precisely those that John Thadeus Delane, the editor of *The Times,* hoped would endear him to the Americans. Russell was at his happiest in company; over dinner his round face and bright blue eyes would come alive as he amused his listeners with witty observations and stories. He could converse easily with anyone, which Delane knew was a vital prerequisite for success in democratic America.

Although the circulation of *The Times* was small by U.S. standards, hardly more than 65,000, the paper's influence was felt around the globe. Unlike its newer rivals, such as the *Daily Telegraph* and the *Daily News,* *The Times,* which was founded in 1785, had the financial resources to provide the latest news from distant countries. There were many who resented its power: "What an absurd position we are in, so completely dictated to and domineered by one newspaper," complained the MP Richard Cobden, who was nevertheless grateful when, in April 1859, a fellow passenger on a Mississippi steamboat, Senator Jefferson Davis, had offered to share his copy with him.

William Howard Russell soon discovered that celebrity in America had its drawbacks. A drunken night at the Astor Hotel with the Friendly Society of St. Patrick made the front pages. Apparently—since he could not remember the evening's events—Russell had made a rousing speech in favor of the Union. He confessed in his diary: "O Lord, why did I do it?" When Delane learned of the episode, he asked him the same question. English writers had a poor reputation in the South for coming "with their three *p*'s: pen—paper—prejudices."[30] Russell had jeopardized the paper's credibility and his own, which was not as high in America as he had assumed.[31] "I should imagine that you must be very perplexed in England," a British immigrant in New York remarked to his relatives. "The idea is somewhat amusing to us here that Mr. Russell should be sent over specially to report on American politics, as we are perfectly confident no novice could possibly be acquainted with the ins and outs, schemes, shifts and knaveries of this glorious disunion."[32]

During his journey to Washington in March, Russell had shared a railway carriage with Henry Sanford, the new American minister to Belgium. They talked at great length; Russell had no idea that he was conversing with the future head of the U.S. secret service in Europe. Sanford, on the other hand, grasped Russell's usefulness to the North and invited him to dine with Seward and his friends that evening. Seward dominated the dinner with his jokes and confidential anecdotes, giving Russell the opportunity to study him at length. He liked the way Seward's eyes twinkled when he talked, although he suspected it was from self-importance rather than kindliness. Seward strutted as though he was "bursting with the importance of state mysteries, and with the dignity of directing the foreign policy of the greatest country—as all Americans think—in the world."[33]

The following day Seward showed him around his kingdom, a plain
brick building that housed the State Department. There were usually a
hundred people scattered throughout its offices, but a recent purging of
Southern sympathizers made the place seem almost devoid of activity.
Seward's own office was surprisingly modest in Russell's view, merely a
"comfortable apartment surrounded with book shelves and ornamented
with a few engravings." Also in evidence was his liking for cigars.[34] In the
afternoon, Seward introduced him to Lincoln. The president may have
been new to the role of national leader, but he was an old hand at flattering men's vanities. "Mr. Russell," he said. "I am very glad to make your
acquaintance, and to see you in this country. The London *Times* is one of
the greatest powers in the world—in fact, I don't know anything which
has more power—except perhaps the Mississippi. I am glad to know you
as its minister."

Russell was "agreeably impressed with his shrewdness, humor, and
natural sagacity." But it was impossible for him to overlook the sheer un-
gainliness of the president. Lincoln was a "tall, lank, lean man," he wrote,
"considerably over six feet in height, with stooping shoulders, long pendulous arms, terminating in hands of extraordinary dimensions" that
were exceeded only by his enormous feet. "He was dressed in an ill-
fitting wrinkled suit of black, which put one in mind of an undertaker's
uniform at a funeral." His ears were wide and flapping, his mouth un-
naturally wide, his eyebrows preternaturally shaggy. Yet all was mitigated
for Russell by the look of kindness in his eyes.[35]

The state dinner from which Charles Francis Adams had been excluded was fascinating to Russell for the view it provided of Lincoln's relationship with his new cabinet. The formality of the occasion did not
deter some of them from continuing their arguments with the president
over the dispensing of patronage. Russell observed that the difference
between Lincoln and politicians "bred in courts, accustomed to the
world" was that they used sophisticated subterfuge to escape awkward
situations whereas the president told shaggy dog stories. But the effect
was the same: Lincoln disarmed his enemies without causing offense. As
for the secretaries, they all seemed like men of ordinary or average ability, with the exception of Salmon Chase, the secretary of the treasury,
who "struck me as one of the most intelligent and distinguished persons
in the whole assemblage." Mrs. Lincoln caught Russell's attention for
other reasons. She was not as ludicrous as the Washington gossips had

led him to believe, but her energetic fanning and overuse of the word "sir" were a decided distraction.

Russell returned to his rooms at Willard's after the dinner, unaware that Lincoln had asked the cabinet to remain behind for an emergency meeting. Fort Sumter had become the flash point in the tense relations between the North and South; the decision whether to abandon it or fight to preserve federal control could no longer wait. The cabinet deliberations continued the next day. Seward tried every expedient to prevent Lincoln from forcing a decision: he had practically promised Southern negotiators that the president would sacrifice the fort in return for peace and loyalty to the Union. Seward saw dishonor facing him if his double-dealing became known, and his efforts to prevent troops from being sent became ever more serpentine.

Seward was conspicuously absent when William Howard Russell visited the White House again, on March 31, for a near-deserted reception given by Mrs. Lincoln. Nor did he attend Lord Lyons's dinner that evening, which gave Charles Sumner the field to himself. The other missing person was Charles Francis Adams, who ought to have paid his respects at the British legation after accepting his post but had hurried home to Massachusetts instead. "My visit has changed my feelings much," he wrote. "For my part I see nothing but incompetency in the head. The man is not equal to the hour." Like William Howard Russell, he dismissed the rest of the cabinet as "a motley mixture, consisting of one statesman, one politician, two jobbers, one intriguer, and two respectable old gentlemen."[36] Adams was determined to avoid inconveniencing himself or his family any more than was necessary. Although the last of the Southern diplomatic envoys had already left for London, Adams could not see why he should chase after them. He was going to arrange his affairs, pack in an orderly fashion, and, most important of all, attend his oldest son's wedding in Massachusetts. Decades later, his son Charles Francis Jr. severely criticized his father for being so petulant:

Every stage of our action was thus marked by extreme deliberation; and the Confederate Commissioners took full advantage of the fact. There can, I think, be no question that my brother John's marriage on the 29th of April 1861, led to grave international complications. It is creditable to neither Seward nor my father that the latter was allowed to dawdle away weeks of precious time because

of such a trifle. It was much as if a general had permitted some social engagement to keep him away from his headquarters on the
eve of a great battle.[37]

Adams's casual neglect of Lord Lyons was another serious mistake.
Lyons would have been able to give him valuable insights and directions
in his dealings with the British government, among them that the British
genuinely desired to keep aloof. He might even have discovered, as Russell did, that Lyons was "strong for the Union." The information might
have been helpful to Seward as well, whose paranoia was increasing by
the day. A few days in Seward's company had allowed Russell to see
through the bonhomie to the ambiguities of his character. Initially he
had found him to be slightly absurd, but the more Seward insisted that
there was no imminent civil war, and that neither England nor France
was allowed to refer to it as such, the more Russell inclined to Lyons's
opinion that Seward was either a deluded narcissist or a desperate bully,
and possibly both.

Seward was tormented by his declining political influence, telling his
wife that he felt like "a chief reduced to a subordinate position, and surrounded with a guard to see that I do not do too much for my country,
lest some advantage may revert to my own fame."[38] He made one last effort to reassert his authority and composed a memorandum entitled
"Thoughts for the President's Consideration," which was delivered to
Lincoln's office on April 1. It is often called the "April Fool's Day Memorandum," and in it Seward argued that a foreign war was the only salvation for the Union. What possessed him to make such a bizarre proposal
has puzzled historians ever since.[39] Seward criticized the administration,
meaning Lincoln, for being "without a policy, either domestic or foreign." As a remedy, Seward proposed to reunite the country by creating a
foreign threat—in his words, to "change the question before the Public
from one upon Slavery . . . to one of Patriotism or Union."[40]

Seward concluded his letter with the statement, "Whatever policy we
adopt, there must be an energetic prosecution of it. Either the president
must do it himself . . . or devolve it on some member of his Cabinet. . . .
It is not in my especial province, but I neither seek to evade nor assume
responsibility." This was sheer flummery. Seward was making a last grab
for power. He had forewarned Henry Raymond, the editor of *The New
York Times,* and shown him the memorandum so that a positive story

would accompany the sudden change in policy.[41] As it happened, Raymond had nothing to report. Lincoln shrugged off Seward's attempt to coerce him with magnificent indifference. The proud secretary of state was gradually being corralled. Once the cabinet decided upon a relief expedition to Fort Sumter, the only concession Seward was able to wrest from Lincoln was that the South Carolina authorities be forewarned. It was not much, but it would save him from appearing to have deliberately and recklessly misled the Southern negotiators about the president's intentions.

By April 6, the time for deals and machinations had drawn to a close. A relief fleet bearing provisions for the hungry guards of Fort Sumter was making its way toward Charleston. The expectation in Washington was that its appearance would almost certainly provoke violence. William Howard Russell sent a note to Seward asking him for a definite answer regarding the truth about a relief expedition. He was rewarded with an invitation to dine on April 8. The evening began with a foursome of whist beside the fire. As the game progressed, Seward became more vehement in his pronouncements about the government's intentions. Suddenly, he put down his cards and ordered his son to fetch his portfolio from the office. His daughter-in-law understood the hint and left the room. When they were alone, Seward handed Russell a cigar and removed a paper from the portfolio. It was, he told Russell, the dispatch he was about to send to Charles Francis Adams.

Seward proceeded to read the dispatch aloud, "slowly and with marked emphasis," almost as though he were declaiming a speech in front of a large audience. "It struck me," wrote Russell in wonderment,

> that the tone of the paper was hostile, that there was an undercurrent of menace through it, and that it contained insinuations that Great Britain would interfere to split up the Republic, if she could, and was pleased at the prospect of the dangers which threatened it. At all the stronger passages Mr. Seward raised his voice, and made a pause at their conclusion as if to challenge remark or approval.[42]

Russell did not know what to make of such a performance. Ignorant of Seward's conversations with Lyons, he was baffled why Seward should want to turn a potential ally into an enemy.

The following day, April 9, Davis's Confederate cabinet agreed to attack Fort Sumter before the Federal relief fleet could arrive. In Washington, Russell scouted in vain for information, sloshing through the rain from one department to the next. He wanted to investigate conditions in the South before one or both sides imposed travel restrictions across the lines, but at the same time he was loath to leave the capital in case he missed something of importance. Finally, on the twelfth, he bought a train ticket for Charleston. As he paid a final round of calls to his new acquaintances, he received strong hints that something was about to happen. In fact, the first Confederate gun had fired on Fort Sumter at 4:30 that morning.

Lord Lyons was keen to hear from Russell during his travels, and invited him to rely on the consulates for his postal needs. The offer soon proved to be indispensable to Russell. He had noticed a certain ugliness creeping into the public mood as he progressed farther south. Virginia was relatively calm, but in North Carolina, he wrote, "the wave of the secession tide struck us in full career."[43] A "vigilance committee" in Wilmington demanded to know his sympathies and refused to let him telegraph his copy to New York. At subsequent train stops, Russell observed drunken posses brandishing their guns.

He reached Charleston on April 16, 1861, two days after the federal garrison had surrendered to the elaborately named Confederate general Pierre Gustave Toutant Beauregard. The boisterous celebrations on the city's streets reminded him of Paris during the last revolution there. Russell did not pretend to understand the South, but "one thing is for certain," he asserted to Lyons, "nothing on earth will induce the people to return to the Union."[44] Russell was surprised when the British consul in Charleston, Robert Bunch, revealed that less than a quarter of the Southern population owned all 3.5 million slaves. Even if slavery were abolished tomorrow, calculated Russell, fewer than 300,000 whites would be affected out of a population of 5.5 million. Yet every conversation demonstrated a support for slavery and independence that was inextricably entwined with a hatred of the North.

Robert Bunch had been the consul in Charleston since 1853 and was regarded by many as a permanent fixture in Southern society. He gave a dinner for Russell on April 18 that was singular in the brutal frankness with which the guests predicted Britain's swift humiliation by the South if she did not immediately recognize the Confederate government. Only the day before, Virginia had provisionally voted to join the Confederacy, raising the number of seceded states from seven to eight. Arkansas, North Carolina, and Tennessee looked certain to follow. Mr. Bunch's Southern guests were exultant. "It was scarcely agreeable to my host or myself," wrote Russell, to be told that England owed allegiance to the "cotton kingdom." "Why, sir," sneered one of the guests, "we have only to shut off your supply of cotton for a few weeks, and we can create a revolution in Great Britain. There are four millions of your people depending on us for their bread. . . . No, sir, we know that England must recognize us." Russell and Bunch maintained a polite silence as all the Southern guests present voiced their agreement.[45]

Two days later, the Charleston papers reported that a local shipping company was starting its own direct line to Europe. Almost as an aside, the papers noted that Jefferson Davis had invited civilian ships to apply for "letters of marque" and that Abraham Lincoln had declared a blockade of Southern ports.* When Russell questioned a businessman about the wisdom of launching a shipping line in the midst of a blockade, he was told, " 'If those miserable Yankees try to blockade us and keep you from your cotton, you'll just send their ships to the bottom and acknowledge us. That will be before autumn, I think.' It was in vain I assured him he would be disappointed."[46]

Lincoln's cabinet in Washington had argued furiously over whether to blockade the South. The president's decision in April to call for 75,000 volunteers had been universally approved, but the blockade issue thrust Seward squarely into a challenge against his foe Gideon Welles, the secretary of the navy. Welles and his supporters in the cabinet wanted Southern ports closed by federal mandate rather than blockaded by the U.S. Navy. He pointed out that a blockade was bound by a set of legal definitions and practices. First and foremost, a country could not blockade itself. A blockade was a weapon of war between two sovereign countries, or "belligerents" in technical terms. By formally blockading the South, the North would in effect be granting it belligerent status, which would

---

* A letter of marque was a government license allowing a civilian ship to attack the merchant shipping of an enemy in time of war. Ships that carried such letters were called privateers, to distinguish them from pirates. Davis had resorted to this old-fashioned method of sea warfare because it would be many months before the Confederacy had its own navy.

be extremely useful to the Confederacy. This quasi-recognition of its existence conferred on the South the power to raise foreign loans and purchase supplies from neutral nations. Its navy would have the right of search and seizure on the high seas. It would also be able to enlist foreign volunteers in countries that had not declared neutrality. These would be no mere trifles.

Welles argued that Europe would almost certainly go the next step and recognize the existence of the Confederacy. Nevertheless, it was Seward who prevailed, although whether he truly understood the difference between a blockade and a port closure, or why it mattered in international law, remains open to conjecture.[47] In addition to declaring a blockade, Lincoln announced that captured privateers would be treated as pirates and executed.[48]

Lord Lyons sided with Seward, not about the execution of Southern privateers, but about the blockade, since it would force the North to abide by the Declaration of Paris of 1856.* He soon realized, however, that the secretary of state had no interest in knowing the Paris rules, let alone following them. Seward ignored or failed to carry out even the most basic responsibilities demanded by the declaration.[49] Neither the U.S. ministers abroad nor the diplomatic community in Washington were given advance warning. When Seward finally sent an official notice to the foreign ministers on April 27, Lyons was dismayed by the vagueness of the document. It appeared to have been written on the fly, without addressing a single question as to how and when the blockade would be enforced.

Lyons had never quite given up hope that Britain might support the North, either actively or surreptitiously; it was part of the reason he was working so hard to keep the French in check. Henri Mercier had revealed that France was prepared to ignore the blockade if Britain agreed to the same policy. Having known Mercier since their Dresden days, when they used to partner each other in whist, Lyons thought it was typical of him to devise a plan so fraught with danger. He also disagreed

---

* The treaty had been drawn up and signed by the seven Great Powers of Europe—Austria, France, Great Britain, the Ottoman Empire, Prussia, Russia, and Sardinia—after the Crimean War in order to establish a set of international laws governing both blockades and privateering. Ironically, America had not signed the treaty because President Franklin Pierce refused to relinquish the right to use licensed privateers.

with Mercier's alternative, which was for Britain and France to respect the blockade until the beginning of the cotton season in September. This would be giving the South "a moral encouragement scarcely consistent with neutrality," he reprimanded Mercier. Furthermore, it might "entail utter ruin upon the [Northern] Administration and their supporters."[50]

Lyons could not go any further than this with Mercier; Seward's behavior had made it impossible. "I confess I can see no better policy for us than a strict impartiality for the present," he wrote sadly to Lord John Russell on May 6.

> The sympathies of an Englishman are naturally inclined towards the North—but I am afraid we should find that anything like a quasi alliance with the men in office here, would place us in a position which would soon become untenable. . . . My feeling against Slavery might lead me to desire to co-operate with them. But I conceive all chance of this to be gone for ever.[51]

Seward's earlier messages to ignore his public statements made Lyons fairly certain that the current display of aggression was for the benefit of the Northern public. It perplexed him that a man of Seward's intelligence could not see the danger he was courting.[52] With an army of 16,000 men and a navy of 9,000, the United States was a military midget compared to any of the Great Powers. "If Seward does not pick a quarrel with us," wrote Lyons to Lord John Russell, it would not be because "of the insanity which doing so at this crisis . . . would seem to indicate." Seward clearly had no intention of "conciliating the European Powers or at all events of not forcing them into hostility."[53] Charles Francis Adams, Jr., later admitted that his family had worshipped a false god. Seward was not the grand strategist or great statesman they had believed him to be. Seward had

> found himself fairly beyond his depth; and he plunged! The foreign-war panacea took possession of him; and he yielded to it. The fact is, as I now see him, Seward was an able, a specious and adroit, and a very versatile man; but he escaped being really great. He made a parade of philosophy, and by it I was very effectually deceived.[54]

President Jefferson Davis declared an official state of war on May 6, the same day that Lyons decided Britain could not risk making common cause with the North. William Howard Russell saw the bill lying on Davis's desk when he arrived to interview him for *The Times*. Davis proudly informed Russell that more than 400,000 volunteers had answered his call to arms, far more than they needed or could equip. "He asked me if I thought it was supposed in England there would be war between the two states," wrote Russell. "I answered, that I was under the impression the public thought there would be no actual hostilities." "And yet you see we are driven to take up arms for the defence of our rights and liberties," Davis had replied.[55]

Russell had witnessed for himself the Southern version of liberty. During a break in his journey to Montgomery, a slave girl, hardly more than ten years old, had begged him to take her away from "the missus." She promised to serve him faithfully in return, since "she could wash and sew very well."[56] The incident helped Russell to clarify his feelings about the South. At first glance, its ruling class was just like the English aristocracy. "They travel and read, love field sports, racing, shooting, hunting, and fishing, are bold horsemen, and good shots," he admitted. But behind the façade was not an enlightened society founded on the ideals of ancient Rome but "a modern Sparta—an aristocracy resting on helotry, and with nothing else to rest upon. . . . Their whole system rests on slavery, and as such they defend it."[57]

Montgomery, Alabama, was dreary and hot. "I have rarely seen a more dull, lifeless place," he wrote. "It looks like a small Russian town in the interior."[58] The ubiquitous slave auctions filled him with disgust. He was also unnerved by the discovery that he was the only white man in the city who was not carrying a loaded revolver. His interview with Davis had been a strange anticlimax. Both men were aware that the meeting could have far-reaching consequences. This was Davis's first, and perhaps only, opportunity to speak directly to Great Britain. Thousands of miles away, there was an audience waiting to meet the man who could hold Britain's textile industry for ransom should he so choose. Yet Davis was too proud to make a grand statement or appeal. "He proceeded to speak on general matters," wrote Russell, "adverting to the Crimean War and the Indian Mutiny." But apart from asking the journalist whether

"England [thought] there would be war between the two states," Davis hardly mentioned the crisis at all. Their conversation was so ordinary that Russell padded out his report for *The Times* with a description of Davis's appearance. The former secretary of war under President Pierce was "about fifty-five years of age," wrote Russell, "his features are regular and well-defined, but the face is thin and marked on cheek and brow with many wrinkles, and is rather careworn and haggard. One eye is apparently blind, the other is dark, piercing and intelligent."[59] Russell avoided mention of Davis's tic or his demeanor, which, though gentlemanly, was cold.[60]

Russell was equally disappointed with the Southern secretary of war, Leroy Walker, and the secretary of state, Robert Toombs. The former spat and chewed while talking mostly nonsense, not being a military man; the latter seemed earnest though dim. "Seward had told me," Russell wrote, "that but for Jefferson Davis the secession plot could never have been carried out. No other man of the part had the brain, or the courage and dexterity." Consul Bunch had said something similar to him during his stay in Charleston. In a frank appraisal protected by diplomatic seal, Bunch had commended Davis for his statesmanlike qualities but dismissed the rest of the Confederate cabinet as "the dead level of mediocrity."[61] Having now made their acquaintance, Russell agreed.

———

The one Southern cabinet member who did make a forcible impression on Russell was Judah P. Benjamin. Russell disliked Jews in general, but he could not help warming to Benjamin, describing him as "the most open, frank, and cordial of the Confederates whom I have yet met."[62] Benjamin, he learned, was not a native Southerner. He had been born in the Caribbean on the island of St. Croix, which technically made him a British subject. His family moved to the South when Benjamin was a baby, eventually settling in Charleston when he was eleven years old. Benjamin's undeniable brilliance propelled him to Yale Law School when he was only fourteen. Something else—the cause has never been revealed—led to his expulsion. Russell noted in his diary that Benjamin was "clever keen & well yes! What keen and clever men sometimes are"—referring, perhaps, to a certain ambiguity about Benjamin's sexuality.[63] Women enjoyed his company (although not his wife, Natalie, who had moved to Paris with their daughter in 1847); he could banter with them for an entire evening in English or French on any subject they pleased. But behind his perpetual smile there was a mysterious veil that none could penetrate.

Though he was only attorney general, Benjamin had already made himself indispensable to Davis. There was so little for him to do at the newly formed Department of Justice that Benjamin could devote most of his energies to whatever appealed to him. For the time being, he was acting as the president's grand vizier. He shielded Davis from the office seekers and took on the burden of sorting through many of the tedious but necessary details of government. "When in doubt," recorded a visitor, all strangers were referred to "Mr. Judah P. Benjamin, the 'Poo Bah' of the Confederate Government."[64]

In contrast to his inarticulate colleagues, Benjamin immediately engaged Russell in an intelligent debate. Referring to the blockade and the legality of letters of marque, Russell asked, "Suppose, Mr. Attorney-General, England, or any of the great powers which decreed the abolition of privateering, refuse to recognise your flags?" What if, he added, "England, for example, declared your privateers were pirates?" In that case, replied Benjamin, "it would be nothing more or less than a declaration of war against us, and we must meet it as best we can." He did not seem too downcast by the possibility. It was obvious to Russell that Benjamin was thinking about next season's cotton crop. Benjamin confirmed his suspicion by saying with a smile, "All this coyness about acknowledging a slave power will come right at last . . . we are quite easy in our minds on this point at present."[65]

Many years later, when Benjamin was an exile in London, Russell bumped into him at a dinner party. They walked home together, reminiscing about the war. Russell reminded him of their meeting in Montgomery, and how Benjamin had been so certain that the British and French would intervene as soon as their cotton stocks were low. "Ah, yes," Benjamin replied, "I admit I was mistaken! I did not believe that your government would allow such misery to your operatives, such loss to your manufacturers, or that the people themselves would have borne it."[66]

Benjamin was too discreet to say that when the Confederate cabinet held their first meeting, his had been the lone voice in favor of making preparations for a protracted war. The secretary of war, Leroy Walker, remembered the meeting with shame: "At that time, I, like everybody else,

believed there would be no war. In fact, I had gone about the state . . .
promising to wipe up with my pocket-handkerchief all the blood that
would be shed," he recalled despairingly.

There was only one man there who had any sense, and that man
was Benjamin. Mr. Benjamin proposed that the government purchase as much cotton as it could hold, at least 100,000 bales, and
ship it at once to England. . . . For, said Benjamin, we are entering
on a contest that must be long and costly. All the rest of us fairly
ridiculed the idea of a serious war. Well, you know what happened.[67]

Benjamin allowed himself to be swayed by his colleagues' optimism.
Europe would end the blockade by the following October, he explained
genially to Russell, "when the Mississippi is floating cotton by the thousands of bales, and all our wharfs are full."[68] Shortly after Russell left
Montgomery for Mobile, Alabama, the Provisional Confederate Congress voted to prohibit all trade with the North in order to prevent cotton from being shipped via Northern ports. "The cards are in our
hands!" proclaimed the editors of the *Charleston Mercury,* obviously unfazed by the doubts expressed by Russell when he visited their offices,
"and we intend to play them out to the bankruptcy of every cotton factory in Great Britain and France or the acknowledgement of our independence."[69]

FOUR

Expectations Are Dashed

Where is Adams?—Debate in the Commons—The neutrality proclamation—First interview with Lord John Russell—Seward's horseplay—The power of Uncle Tom

A poem in *Punch*, on March 30, 1861, neatly expressed Britain's cotton dilemma:

> *Though with the North we sympathize,*
> *It must not be forgotten,*
> *That with the South we've stronger ties,*
> *Which are composed of cotton.*

The journalist William Howard Russell's revelation that the South hoped to exploit these ties, along with his poignant descriptions of slave life, provoked outrage in England when his reports started to appear in April. But the North gained less support than Southerners had feared, since, in his inaugural address on March 4, Lincoln had promised not to interfere with slavery. The Morrill Tariff, with its rampant protectionism and whiff of anti-British bias, was an even greater gift to the Confederacy.[1]

At the U.S. legation, Benjamin Moran read the angry protests against the new tariff and took it to mean that the country as a whole had turned against the North. But George Dallas, the outgoing American minister whose existence was barely acknowledged by Seward, was much more sanguine about the hostile opinion expressed in newspapers. Britain "cannot be expected to appreciate the weakness, discredit, complications, and dangers which we instinctively and justly ascribe to disunion," he told Seward on April 9. "English opinion tends rather, I apprehend, to the theory that a peaceful separation may work beneficially for both groups of states and not injuriously affect the rest of the world."[2] He had obviously heard this said by many different people: even Thackeray had written to an American friend, asking, "In what way will it benefit the North to be recoupled to the South?" After all, at this time, England had not wanted "the Colonies" to go their own way, "and aren't both better for the Separation?"[3]

Nor did Dallas believe there was anything to be feared from the British government. Lord John Russell had rebuffed Seward's demand for a promise never to have any dealings with the South or its representatives, but "his lordship assured me with great earnestness that there was not the slightest disposition in the British government to grasp at any advantage," Dallas reported to Seward.[4] Far from looking for an advantage, the cabinet was approaching a state of panic over American affairs. Russell was shocked that six weeks after Lincoln's inauguration there was still no replacement for the now irrelevant Dallas, and he was mystified as to what could be delaying the arrival of Charles Francis Adams at such a perilous moment in his country's history.

Benjamin Moran thought Dallas's benign view of the British made him either an idiot or a crypto–Southern sympathizer. Dallas was certainly neither, but the knowledge that he was soon to go home may have made him apathetic when he should have been wooing potential Northern allies in Parliament. Moran also knew of at least one MP who was collaborating with the nascent Southern lobby in England. William Gregory, the MP for Galway, had given notice in the House of Commons that he was going to propose recognition of the South on May 1. Moran thought the move had been prompted by Gregory's friend Robert Campbell, the American consul in London.*

Campbell was a genial though strident secessionist from North Carolina who had supplied Gregory with letters of introduction for his tour of the United States in 1859. In Washington, he had stayed in a boarding-

---

* The U.S. consulate in London was a separate entity from the legation in the nineteenth century, and dealt primarily with matters arising from shipping and trade.

house popular with Southern senators; their "fire-eating talk" of independence, interspersed with liberal amounts of whiskey, had swept the
MP into their ranks. Privately, he thought their humanity had been
dulled by slavery, but Gregory accepted his new friends' claim that
emancipation was morally and economically impossible.[5]

Moran was furious with Dallas for failing to curb the pro-Southern
activities of consuls who had not yet been replaced by Republican appointees, but he dared not speak when his own future seemed so uncertain. He remained in suspense until confirmation of his reappointment
arrived on the fifteenth. Moran's other fear—that he was the only loyal
American official left in Britain—seemed a raging certainty after he
caught one of the new Southern envoys, Ambrose Dudley Mann, sneaking into the legation to see Dallas.

The arrival of the Confederate envoys was not unexpected; their
identities had been public knowledge for several weeks. Consul Robert
Bunch wrote from Charleston to warn the foreign office that they were
three of the rankest amateurs ever to have been sent on so sensitive a
diplomatic mission. He attributed President Davis's selection of such
men to Southern arrogance and the belief that the Confederacy did not
need proper advocates when cotton could do the talking. Mann had
served as a U.S. minister to Switzerland but Bunch dismissed him as "a
mere trading politician, possessing no originality of mind and no special
merit of any description." The second envoy, William Lowndes Yancey,
had never been anything but a rabble-rouser. His campaign to reopen the
slave trade, not to mention his support for expeditions against British
territories in Central America, made him a peculiar choice to send to England. Bunch was particularly disdainful of Yancey: "He is impulsive, erratic and hot-headed; a rabid secessionist." Bunch could not see a single
reason for the appointment of the third envoy, Pierre Rost, apart from his
friendship with Jefferson Davis's family and his proficiency in Creole
French.[6]

Moran despised Dallas's excuse that Mann was an old and valued
friend until he, too, was forced to choose between loyalty and patriotism. A few days after Dudley Mann visited the legation, Moran received
a letter from a friend in London who asked him for the Confederate
envoy's address. The friend, Edwin De Leon, until recently the U.S.
consul in Egypt, had invited him to his wedding two years earlier, but
Moran was appalled at his request and wrote sorrowfully that "I would

do anything in reason for him, but could not find it in my conscience to assist treason."[7]

————

Forcing a debate in the House of Commons had become William Gregory's mission, and he would not be thwarted. Palmerston pulled the pro-Confederate MP aside in the Commons on April 26 and demanded to know why he saw fit to place the government in such an awkward position. He reminded Gregory that the speeches would be reprinted in Southern and Northern newspapers and that both sides would end up being "offended by what is said against them, and will care but little for what is said for them; and that all Americans will say that the British Parliament has no business to meddle with American affairs." He reported to Lord John Russell that Gregory "admitted the truth of much I said, but said he had pledged himself to Mr. Mann, the Southern envoy. . . . Perhaps your talking to Gregory, either privately or in the House, might induce him to put his motion off."[8] Russell was anxious about being pushed to make a public statement ahead of events. George Dallas had shown that he was as ignorant of the situation as the Foreign Office. During his last interview with Russell on May 1, he had insisted that a blockade was not under consideration, since there was no mention of the fact in the latest State Department instructions; it had to be a fabrication of the New York press. But Russell discovered the next day from Lord Lyons's dispatches that the idea was very much under consideration.

The day after Palmerston's confrontation with Gregory, the British government learned that the Confederates had captured Fort Sumter. The initial newspaper reports were brief, but it appeared as though the South had won an easy victory. (The Thompson family in Belfast became the envy of the neighborhood after they received a long account of the battle from their son, a Union private in the Sumter garrison.)[9] "We cut a sorry enough figure indeed," complained Moran as he read through the dailies. "Everybody is laughing at us." Many papers described the news as "a calamity" and "a subject of regret, and indeed of grief," but Moran's attention was held by the *Illustrated London News,* which printed a pious editorial in favor of peace and "no coercive measures," next to an announcement that Frank Vizetelly, the paper's star artist, war reporter, and brother of the editor, was taking the next steamer to New York.[10] The tutting and clucking in the British press about the demise of the democratic experiment and the sorry state of "our American cousins"

A FAMILY QUARREL.

Punch depicts the North and South as a mismatched couple.

also grated on Moran's nerves. *The Economist* recalled Britain's futile re-action to the American Declaration of Independence and advised the North to settle the dispute with grace; to continue fighting now, its edi-tor, Walter Bagehot, scolded, would be "vindictive, bloody and fruit-less."[11] The conservative *Saturday Review* could not resist making a dig at Seward, who, "though he cannot keep the Federal fort at Charleston, has several times announced his intention of annexing Canada."[12]

Lord John Russell had still not spoken to William Gregory when the Southern commissioners Yancey and Rost finally reached London on April 29, a week after Mann. Unaccustomed to foreign travel, they had passed two miserable days in Southampton and had arrived in the capital feeling bewildered and frightened. Rather than pausing for a moment to consider the best way of contacting the Confederate community, they sent a telegram to the American legation addressed to Ambrose Dudley Mann. "The unblushing impudence of these scoundrels," ranted Moran, "to send their message to the US Legation for one of their fellow traitors."[13] The timing and announcement of their arrival was fortunate for Lord John Russell, since it gave him a bargaining chip with Gregory, who agreed to postpone his motion to June 7 in return for a Foreign Office meeting with the Southerners on May 3.

Russell was not making a great concession, since it was standard Foreign Office practice to receive representatives from breakaway countries. These meetings never carried official weight, nor were the emissaries accorded diplomatic rank. Russell assumed that Dallas had lived in England long enough to know this, and that Charles Francis Adams could have it explained to him when he eventually arrived. Russell was disturbed by the thought of Confederate privateers roaming the seas, and, at his request, the Admiralty was already taking precautionary measures to reinforce the North Atlantic squadron. The prospect of encountering lawless privateers so frightened Dallas that he booked passage for his wife and three daughters for May 1, hoping they would be home before transatlantic travel became impossible.

Russell's satisfaction over his dealings with Gregory lasted only twenty-four hours. On May 2 he received a run of telegrams: the first announced that Lincoln had decided on a blockade rather than port closures; the next, that Virginia, that mainstay of the American Revolution, had seceded, depriving the North of the large weapons arsenal at Harpers Ferry; and finally, that Maryland had erupted in violence, leaving eleven people dead in Baltimore during street fighting between Federal troops and Southern protesters.* "This is the first bloodshed and God knows where it will end," Moran wrote in his diary. It surprised and comforted him when several Englishmen called at the legation vainly asking to join the Federal army. But the reaction of Russell's predecessor at the Foreign Office, Lord Clarendon, showed that old resentments had a habit of reviving: "For my own part if we could be sure of getting raw cotton from them, I should not care how many Northerners were clawed at by the Southerners & vice versa!"[14]

When Russell went to the House of Commons that evening, he was bombarded with questions from MPs, not a few of whom shared Clarendon's view. He could give little enlightenment, but to those who expressed a desire for British intervention he warned against such a reck-

---

* It took ten days for a newspaper report in New York to be reprinted in *The Times*. There was a slightly quicker diplomatic route: if Lord Lyons needed to send an urgent message, he could send a telegram to Halifax, Nova Scotia, where it would be taken by steamer to Liverpool and telegraphed to London; this could cut the delay to eight or, in good weather, seven days.

less move. "Nothing but the imperative duty of protecting British interests, in case they should be attacked, justified the government in at all interfering," he told the House. "We have not been involved in any way in
that contest. For God's sake, let us if possible keep out of it."[15] He delivered a similar message to the Southern envoys when they arrived for
their interview on Friday, May 3. Gregory had warned them about Russell's notorious shyness, but they had not expected the frigid politeness
with which they were received. Russell caught them off guard by declaring he had "little to say." William Yancey stumbled through a speech
about the Constitution, liberty, and states' rights. He insisted the slave
trade would not be revived, which Russell disbelieved, threw in a warning about cotton, which Russell ignored, and finally asked for immediate
recognition, which Russell refused. The envoys returned to their lodgings at 40 Albemarle Street thoroughly disheartened.

Lord John Russell spent the weekend of the fourth and fifth of May
carefully analyzing the choices open to the British government. He
hoped that antislavery would become the overriding cause of the war,
but feared that the North would throw it over without hesitation if the
Union could thus be saved. He was also torn between despising the
South for its dependence on slavery and admiring its spirited bid for independence. Above all, he agreed with Lord Lyons that to give preferen-
tial treatment to the North would be unwise and possibly dangerous
with Seward at the helm. Accepting the legality of the blockade, which
would require a declaration of official neutrality, struck him as the wisest
course, he told his colleagues, especially in light of Seward's evident
keenness to manufacture a reason for declaring war.

The cabinet was not enthusiastic about adopting a policy that was so
dangerous to the country's cotton industry. Palmerston agreed with the
proposal, though he felt it was a heavy price for staying out of the conflict. "The South fight for independence; what do the North fight for,"
asked the home secretary, Sir George Cornewall Lewis, "except to gratify
passion or pride?"[16] William Gladstone was privately even more outspoken for the South and compared Jefferson Davis to General Garibaldi.
When his friend Harriet, Duchess of Sutherland, heard about his views,
she was outraged and demanded to know how he could "think the
Southern states most in the right—I did not hear you say; I don't believe
it."[17] Nor did she accept his explanation that the wishes of minorities
ought to be respected.[18] Only the Duke of Argyll, her favorite son-in-

law, wholeheartedly supported Russell. He abhorred revolutionary movements on principle; moreover, his friendship with Charles Sumner had given him an insight into American politics. He rightly understood that the Union had to be safeguarded since the South would never abolish slavery on its own.

In declaring neutrality, Russell was convinced he had chosen the best alternative; he had consulted the law officers of the Crown, as he always did when in doubt, and in their opinion the crisis in America was not a minor insurgency but a genuine state of war. The blockade could and should be recognized, they told him, and so should the right of the South to employ privateers. Russell endured some aggressive questioning in Parliament when he announced the government's decision on May 6. He was also pressured by Gregory into seeing the Confederate envoys for a second time, on the grounds that the Northern blockade had not been confirmed at the first meeting. Russell suspected they would try to make more of the neutrality announcement than the government intended. Their exultant demeanor on May 9 showed that his instincts had been correct.[19] The envoys were unaware, however, that even as they pressed their arguments on him, the law officers were composing an additional proviso to Britain's declaration of neutrality that would make it illegal for a British subject to volunteer for either side in the war. Russell had meant it when he said "for God's sake, let us if possible keep out of it."

Yancey, Rost, and Mann were dumbfounded when they read the "Queen's Proclamation of Neutrality" in *The Times* on May 14. A close examination of the wording showed that Russell had taken away many of the advantages that belligerent status had initially seemed to give to the Confederacy. He had invoked the rarely used 1819 Foreign Enlistment Act, under which British subjects were forbidden to volunteer for a foreign cause or encourage others to do so.[20] The act also prohibited the selling or arming of warships to either belligerent; those who disobeyed the proclamation would be prosecuted, and the offending items confiscated.[21] The more populous, industrial North would be able to overcome these obstacles on its own, but not the smaller, agrarian South.

The Southern envoys realized that their two interviews with Russell had failed to make the slightest impression on him. Yancey ascribed their failure to Russell's prejudice against the "peculiar institution," as Southerners euphemistically called slavery: "We are satisfied that the public mind here is entirely opposed to the Government of the Confederate States of America on the question of slavery," he reported to Robert Toombs, the Southern secretary of state. "All we can do at present is to affect public opinion in as unobtrusive a manner, as well as we can."[22]

———

Charles Francis Adams also read the neutrality proclamation in *The Times* on May 14. He had arrived in London the night before, having endured the worst sea crossing of his life. The three children, Henry, Mary, and Brooks, had, like him, been prostrate with seasickness. Abigail, his wife, had stayed below deck for a different reason: Cassius Clay, Lincoln's appointment to the legation in Russia, had embarrassed them by sauntering around the boat like a *Punch* caricature of the boorish American, with three pistols at his belt and a toothpick between his teeth.

Adams knew nothing of what had passed between Seward and Lyons. But even if he had, his outrage at the British government's decision to act without waiting for his arrival and consulting him first would have been the same. "Charles Francis Adams naturally looked on all British Ministers as enemies," acknowledged Henry Adams in his autobiography. "The only public occupation of all Adamses for a hundred and fifty years at least, in their brief intervals of quarrelling with State Street, had been to quarrel with Downing Street, and the British Government."[23]

That first morning, Adams was ready to confront Lord John Russell, so he asked George Dallas, who arrived at the hotel after breakfast, to escort him to Russell's house. To his dismay, the foreign secretary was not at home; a footman informed them that the family had been called suddenly to Woburn Abbey. Russell's brother, the Duke of Bedford, had collapsed and was not expected to recover. Forced to delay his confrontation for a few days, Adams turned his attention to the family's living situation. London had changed so much that he barely recognized it from the memories of his childhood. The city seemed ostentatious and gaudy; "shops fail in taste in everything here," he wrote.[24] His disapproval of English exhibitionism did not blind him to the fact that Dallas's residence was far too modest for its purpose; the family would have to remain at the hotel until something grander was found. He was also irritated with Dallas for having neglected to renew the legation's lease, which was ending in five days' time.[25] Adams responded to these twin challenges with stoicism, but Abigail's fragile courage deserted her. Benjamin Moran was called to the hotel to reassure her that the

Adamses would not be made social pariahs. Unconvinced, she insisted that he give the family a course in social etiquette. "Altogether I feel pretty sick and tired of the whole thing," Henry Adams complained to Charles Francis Jr.[26]

Adams's first invitation was from an MP named William Forster. Dallas's inquiries about him revealed that Forster belonged to the Liberal Party and had been an MP for all of three months. Like John Bright, Forster was a Quaker from a northern mill town, in his case Bradford, whose wealth came from manufacturing. But there the similarities ended. Bright was not interested in small acts or minor details; in Anthony Trollope's damning judgment, "It was his business to inveigh against evils, and perhaps there is no easier business."[27] Forster was a modest and sincere man who sought neither power nor popularity. These attributes inclined the House to be gentle toward the newcomer. His maiden speech on the slave trade had been listened to without interruption (although afterward he was informed by a fellow MP that in London one said *la-MENT-able,* not *LA-ment-able*).

Forster's father had twice visited the United States to preach against slavery, in some places risking his life to be heard. Forster Sr.'s experiences had provided his son with an unsentimental attitude toward the South's desire for secession. "A Mr. Gregory, MP, for Galway, who lately travelled in the South," Forster wrote to a friend in America, "has returned well humbugged by the Southerners." Gregory was talking all sorts of nonsense without anyone's daring to challenge him: "I wish it had fallen into the hands of a member of more experience to stand up for the North and the Union; but I must do what I can."[28] Forster decided his first step should be to organize a meeting of pro-Northern MPs.

Adams accepted Forster's invitation even though the date was set for May 16, the day of his presentation at court. When he arrived at Forster's house, he was disconcerted to discover that there were only seven people at the meeting, three of whom were Americans. Neither John Bright nor Richard Cobden had bothered to come. Cassius Clay and the historian John Lothrop Motley were the other Americans. Forster introduced the first two MPs so quickly that Adams missed their names. But the third, Richard Monckton Milnes, impressed Adams at once. "One might discuss long whether, at that moment, Milnes or Forster were the more valuable ally, since they were influences of different kinds," recalled Henry Adams.

Monckton Milnes was a social power in London . . . who knew himself to be the first wit in London, and a maker of men—of a great many men. A word from him went far. An invitation to his breakfast-table went farther. . . . William E. Forster stood in a different class. Forster had nothing whatever to do with May Fair [the fashionable center of London]. Except in being a Yorkshireman he was quite the opposite of Milnes. He had at that time no social or political position; he never had a vestige of Milnes's wit or variety; he was a tall, rough, ungainly figure. . . . Pure gold, without a trace of base metal; honest, unselfish, practical.[29]

"I found them all very tolerably informed and strongly inclined to the anti-Slavery side," Adams wrote in his diary. However, Milnes declared he had come "mainly for the abominable selfishness of the South in breaking up a great country"; Adams could not decide whether that was English irony or a genuine statement.[30] John Motley informed the meeting that he had received a letter from the Duke of Argyll, who insisted that the British government had no alternative but to declare neutrality. "When the American colonies revolted from England we attempted to treat their privateers as pirates, but we very soon found this would be out of the question," he wrote. "The rules affecting and defining the rights and duties of belligerents are the only rules which prevent war from becoming massacre and murder."[31]

Cassius Clay refused to be persuaded of England's good intentions. He was already tired of the country, with its rude servants and hotels that claimed not to have his reservation. Adams was also dubious, though he might have felt less wretched about the small number of MPs around the table had he known that the Southern envoys were in no better position. Gregory had managed to introduce Yancey to only two MPs, John Laird, owner of one of the largest shipbuilding firms in the country, and William Schaw Lindsay, a self-made shipping magnate. Both professed interest in helping the South achieve independence, but only on the understanding that slavery would eventually be abolished.

Adams went home after the meeting to change for his presentation at court. This was not the time, he told Moran, "for indulging oddities of any kind," nor for wearing clothes that made them look like servants caught on the wrong side of the green baize door.[32] The plain black uniform mandated by the State Department was to be put away; under his tenure, the legation would attend royal functions in the usual brocade and breeches of the diplomatic corps. Dallas and Adams arrived at Buckingham Palace twenty-five minutes early, giving Adams the chance to study the paintings in the Great Saloon while he steadied his nerves. "I reasoned with myself with severity," he wrote in his diary.[33] Queen Victoria received him with a few gracious words and then asked with polite disinterest whether he had ever been to England before. Keeping his composure, Adams replied that he had, when young.

George Dallas and his son left for Southampton immediately after Charles Francis Adams's presentation. Adams wrote in his diary, "From this time I take the burden on my shoulders."[34] He was justifiably uneasy about his staff; the legation secretary, Charles Wilson, displayed a lingering disappointment at being denied the Chicago Post Office. Benjamin Moran's open hostility toward Dallas was also an ill omen. "I part with the whole lot with joy," Moran crowed when the two Dallases set sail. He felt they had taken him for granted, never asking about his late wife during her illness, nor bothering to include him at legation dinners. His job was all he had, and he clung to it with ferocious desperation. Moran did not know that retaining him at the legation had been Henry Adams's idea or that he was the one who arranged it with the State Department.[35] From the moment Moran set eyes on Henry he regarded him as a rival, even though the young Adams was only his father's private secretary with no official standing at the legation.

———

Minister Adams received his first dispatch from Seward on May 17. Its tone and the peremptory demands of the British government worried him, but he obeyed Seward's orders and requested an interview with Lord John Russell, who had returned to London following the death of the Duke of Bedford. Russell replied with an offer of lunch that day if Adams was prepared to come to his house, Pembroke Lodge, in Richmond Park. In his haste, Adams arrived at the house before his message of acceptance, which caused Russell to greet him with more reserve than he had intended. Both men were struck for a moment by the physical similarities between them. Their small stature, coupled with their bald crowns, meant that from the back they could be taken for twins. Since neither had the least facility for small talk, the meeting quickly escalated into an acrimonious debate about the neutrality proclamation. Each thought the other rude and arrogant, and each set out to prove his superior knowledge of diplomatic history. They continued arguing after the bell rang for lunch. However, by the end of the meal their animosity had given way to a grudging respect. Russell showed his goodwill by inviting Adams for a stroll around the grounds. "I like Adams very much," he wrote a few weeks later, "though we did not understand one another at first."[36]

When he reflected on the interview, Adams thought he had acquitted himself reasonably well, but he was less positive about the state of relations between the two countries.[37] He never imagined the sense of emergency he had created in Lord John Russell. During the closing days of May, the British cabinet spent many hours trying to divine Seward's real purpose. The Duke of Newcastle's conversation with him the previous October was again analyzed. It was recalled how Napoleon had always reacted to failure with aggression; was Seward of the same mold, they wondered? If the South became independent, would he try to deflect public anger by attacking Canada? The question became not whether but how many regiments they should send to reinforce the Canadian border. The Duke of Argyll agreed to warn Charles Sumner about the effect of Seward's threatening behavior. "Mr. Seward knows Europe less well than you do," Argyll explained in his letter of June 4; "he may be disposed to do high-handed and offensive things which would necessarily lead to bad blood, and perhaps finally to rupture."[38]

"The great question of all is the American," Lord John Russell wrote to Lord Cowley, the British ambassador in Paris, "and that grows darker and darker every day. I do not expect that Lyons will be sent away, but it is possible. Seward and Co. may attempt to revive their waning popularity by a quarrel with Great Britain, but if we avoid all offence, I do not see how they can do it."[39] Since Russell was blind to his remarkable ability to make speeches that offended all parties, his confidence was perhaps misplaced. The cabinet had made a decision on privateering that it hoped would soothe Northern irritation with the belligerency issue: they had stretched the meaning of neutrality as far as it could go by closing British ports in every part of the globe to privateers and their captures. Since the North had no need of privateers, the new prohibition affected only the South and its ability to wage war at sea.

However, the South was picking up backhanded support from politicians who were keen to rub John Bright's nose in the apparent failure of democracy. "We are now witnessing the bursting of the great republican bubble which had so often been held up to us as a model on which to re-cast our own English Constitution," Sir John Ramsden, MP, proclaimed in the Commons on May 27 to a scattering of sarcastic cheers. Gladstone and Russell hurriedly disowned Ramsden's speech. "I do not think it just or seemly that there should be among us anything like exultation of their discord," Russell chided. Unfortunately, he diminished the good effects of his speech with some unnecessary observations on the failings of American democracy.[40]

Reports of the Commons debate reached an American audience al-ready infuriated by excerpts of William Howard Russell's candid travel-ogues that had found their way back across the Atlantic. Northerners objected to his description of racism, and especially his honest appraisal of pro-Southern feeling in New York. Southerners were offended by his depiction of them as heartless and arrogant. ("Charleston people are thin skinned," commented the Southern diarist Mary Chesnut; "I expected so much worse.")[41] Seward was incensed for a different reason. All along he had insisted there was a silent majority of pro-Union voters in the South, but Russell's letters from Georgia and South Carolina revealed the very opposite. Seward was sure they had influenced Britain's deci-sion to award belligerent rights to the South and was determined to make Russell pay for his reporting when he returned to the North.

Seward had also learned from Dallas that Lord John Russell had met the Southern envoys. Whether his reaction was driven by fear or embar-rassment, it was nevertheless a gross miscalculation with regard to his own standing with Lincoln as well as his future relations with Britain. On May 21, 1861, he composed an insolent and threatening dispatch for Adams to read to Lord Russell, which stated there would be war if En-gland had any dealings with the Confederacy or its envoys. This infa-mous letter came to be known by its number in the sequence of dispatches: Dispatch No. 10. Lincoln was no more inclined to declare war on England in May than he had been in April. According to Charles Sumner, the president showed him Seward's dispatch and asked for his opinion. Seward's blunder was Sumner's opportunity to ingratiate him-self with the White House. Sumner encouraged Lincoln to make drastic changes to the document. The more offensive phrases were removed, the threats toned down. Adams was no longer ordered to present the dis-patch to Russell; it was simply for his own guidance.

Washington gossip related that Sumner paid an unscheduled visit to

98 Portland Place
home of Charles Francis Adams

24 Upper Seymour Street
home of James Murray Mason

17 Savile Road
home of Henry Hotze

34 Sackville Street
home of Rose Greenhow

94 Piccadilly, Cambridge House
home of Lord Palmerston

87 Chesham Place
home of Lord John Russell

Seward and lectured him on the danger of misusing his powers.[42] Already furious at having his dispatch amended, Seward allegedly lost control and kicked his desk, shouting, "God damn them, I'll give them hell," referring to Britain and France. "I'm no more afraid of them than I am of Robert Toombs [the Confederate secretary of state]." It was a delicious victory, made sweeter for Sumner when he recounted the interview to Lincoln. "You must watch him and overrule him," he urged the president.

Seward asserted his independence by reversing some of Lincoln's changes before the dispatch was sent. He also preserved the original document in the State Department's files so that when the annual compilation was published, it was his letter rather than the amended dispatch that appeared.[43] But he could not erase the perception among the diplomatic community in Washington that Charles Sumner was the more reasonable and better statesman of the two.[44] All the foreign ministers heard the gossip about Dispatch No. 10, including Lyons, who was able to give Lord Russell a fair indication of its contents before the letter reached London. Seward accused Britain of deliberately ruining his plan to quarantine the South by encouraging the Confederates to believe that full recognition was imminent. Britain had acted precipitously and maliciously in declaring neutrality, he argued, since the president had only announced his *intention* to declare a blockade.

Seward was ignoring such inconvenient facts as the four British merchant ships that were seized by U.S. Navy blockaders when they tried to sail from Southern ports.[45] He was also discounting the desire of neutral countries to have their legal rights as neutrals acknowledged. Earlier in the month, the State Department had been misinformed about a Canadian steamer named the *Peerless* that was alleged to have been purchased by the Confederacy. In fact, it was Federal agents who had purchased the ship, but this had not been communicated to Seward. Seward threatened to send the U.S. Navy into Canadian waters to seize the *Peerless* unless Britain voluntarily handed over the vessel. "I said," Lyons informed Lord Russell, "that even if the *Peerless* should in fact be sold to the Seceded States, she could never cause the United States anything like the inconvenience which would follow a deliberate violation of neutral rights."[46]

The longer Seward reflected on the belligerency issue, the more he portrayed himself—and by extension the North—as the victim of British machinations. His language toward Lord Lyons was so coarse that the minister sought to avoid social occasions where they might meet. Seward was using his relationship with the New York press to whip up public excitement against Britain; he even went so far as to write an anonymous attack on Lyons for the *Daily Herald*.[47] "I shall do my best not to be a discredit to you," Lyons promised Russell after a group of senators demanded his expulsion, "but I am on very dangerous ground."[48]

The French had yet to announce neutrality officially, although Seward was aware that France and Britain had agreed to work in tandem on American issues. It suited him to claim that England had acted alone and precipitately. He refused to receive Lyons and Mercier together or to acknowledge that there was an official understanding between the two countries. Mercier did not mind, since he was rushing ahead with schemes to end the blockade, which required extreme tact and patience on Lyons's part to discourage.

"Every imaginable accusation of hostility to the United States is brought against Her Majesty's Government," Lyons reported to the Foreign Office. Seward's propaganda campaign had succeeded in convincing the entire country that Britain had wronged the North. "Disappointment and exasperation are universal and deep," wrote a New York lawyer in his diary. "The feeling of cordiality toward England—of brotherhood, almost of loyalty, which grew out of the Prince's visit last fall (how long ago that seems!)—is utterly extinguished."[49] Lyons's advice to London was to be firm but conciliatory, stay abreast with France, and "manifest a readiness on our part for war [though] the possibility of our being forced into hostilities is so painful a subject that I shrink from contemplating it." Nevertheless, on June 10, Lyons telegraphed in cipher to Rear Admiral Sir Alexander Milne, the commander of the North Atlantic squadron, to be ready for the following signal: "Could you forward a letter for me to Antigua?" Milne sent a notice to his officers: "Be on your guard and prepared. States may declare war suddenly."[50]

Charles Francis Adams first heard of the British government's anxiety about Seward on June 1, during a dinner party at Lord Palmerston's house. Lady Palmerston had chosen the guest list with care, inviting people who were known friends of the North, such as Richard Monckton Milnes. Hoping this would have put Adams at his ease, after dinner Lord Palmerston spoke to him about Seward's behavior. "He intimated," recorded Adams, "that his ways of doing things towards Lord Lyons had been ungracious and unpleasant." This was the first time Adams had heard of the tensions in Washington. It seemed unbelievable, and he almost told Palmerston that it had to be a misunderstanding. After reflecting on the conversation the following morning, Adams decided that Seward's brusque manner was probably the cause, and he resolved to warn his friend to be more circumspect.[51]

On June 7, Ambrose Dudley Mann went to the Commons to observe William Gregory make his motion for recognition. Moran was also sitting in the Strangers Gallery and noticed with glee that the Southern envoy Mann "scowled awfully" as speakers from both sides of the House criticized Gregory for his unseemly haste. At length the scolding became unbearable, and Gregory withdrew his motion. Adams was writing his report of the debate when Dispatch No. 10 arrived at the legation. "I scarcely know how to understand Mr. Seward," he wrote in disbelief. "The rest of the government may be demented for all that I know, but he surely is calm and wise." Henry Adams was less forgiving. "A dispatch arrived yesterday from Seward," he informed his brother on June 11, "so arrogant in tone and so extraordinary and unparalleled in its demands that it leaves no doubt in my mind that our Government wishes to face a war with all Europe. . . . I urged papa this morning, as the only man who could by any chance stop the thing, to make an energetic effort."[52]

Adams was still angry and embarrassed that the neutrality proclamation had been issued on the day of his arrival. He considered Lord John Russell's explanation to be spurious and self-serving. Nor did he accept Mr. Forster's contention that "GB had done all they could to aid us." Cunard had offered to lease twenty steamships to the Federal navy, which would have doubled its force of working steamers, until the Foreign Enlistment Act made such transactions illegal. But it was difficult for Adams to take the moral high ground when Seward seemed so intent on giving it away.

During an interview with Russell on June 12, Adams rephrased much of Seward's dispatch and "softened as well as I could the sharp edges." He also threw in a question about the *Great Eastern*, which had departed for Canada the week before with more than two thousand troops on board.[53] Russell answered bluntly that it was due to Seward's threats to seize a British vessel in Canadian waters; more regiments were on their way, he added. This was "another curse of Seward's horseplay," Adams recorded in irritation.[54] He could easily imagine how news of the reinforcements would be received in Washington, and he consoled himself with the fact that he had not yet signed the lease for his house: Henry Adams thought they would all be home in two months.

The expectation of his recall lent an unreal cast to the London season; Charles Francis Adams attended the first drawing room of the season feeling more like an observer than a participant. In his diary he admitted that as far as aristocracies went, the English managed theirs tolerably well but the system remained deficient. "My feelings, as you know, have never been partial to the English," he wrote to a friend.[55] He resented the relatively low status accorded to him by the rules of English society. The American legation in London had none of the social and political importance enjoyed by its British counterpart in Washington, and the fact that he was the third Adams to represent America counted but little among families whose record of diplomatic service went back two or three hundred years. The feeling that "he was there to be put aside" was magnified by the English reluctance to speak to strangers. "No effort is made here to extend acquaintances," Adams complained after the family went to a ball only to spend the entire evening in a lonely cluster.[56] Yet he knew this had not been the experience of Charles Sumner, or of John Motley, and he wondered whether Sumner was poisoning his English friends against him and Seward.[57]

But those who did try to be friendly to Adams were often put off by his stiff manner. Five cabinet members gave dinners in his honor in June; only one, the Duke of Argyll, was prepared to repeat the experiment. "I have not yet been to a single entertainment where there was any conversation that I should care to remember," Adams complained to Charles Francis Jr.[58] The Argylls were able to look past Adams's reserve since they regarded him more as a cause than a person. Adams unbent a little once he experienced the difference between a normal London dinner and the informal, lively gatherings at Stafford House. "The Duke and Duchess," he recorded in his diary, "have the simplest and most engaging manners of any of the nobility I have yet seen."[59]

Even Americans could find Adams difficult to approach. "He said he was very glad to see me," recorded a visiting diplomat, "in a tone which no doubt was intended for kindness. It was certainly courteous. But there was a lack of warmth and stiffness about it which . . . made me feel as though the temperature of the room had dropped several degrees."[60] Adams was incapable of producing charm on demand, a serious handicap for a diplomat. "My own wish," he wrote in his diary, "is to be silent when I have nothing to say, and not to be compelled to make conversation on topics which do not interest me."[61] Lord and Lady Macclesfield went out of their way to welcome the new minister, only to be met with suspicion. "I am at a loss to know the cause of their civility to us," he wrote, adding, "It is always irksome to me, who have the same cold manners [as the English] to attempt to make acquaintances, so that I hardly know how I shall get on."[62] Yancey sneered in his report to the Confederate secretary of state that "in his diplomatic and social relations, Mr. Adams is considered a blunderer," though the same could be said of him.

Adams would have welcomed any excuse to stay at home. "We are invited everywhere, and dine out almost every day, but this brings us no nearer [to belonging]," he admitted to Charles Francis Jr.[63] Henry Adams yearned to cut a dash among the fashionable young men, like any twenty-three-year-old, but, as an "American who neither hunted nor raced, neither shot nor fished nor gambled, and was not marriageable," there was no obvious circle for him to join. Nor did he have school or university ties to ease his entry. Tagging along to events with his father made him feel like a burden. "Every young diplomat," he wrote, "and most of the old ones, felt awkward in an English house from a certainty that they were not precisely wanted there, and a possibility that they might be told so."[64] Henry's introduction to the season began with a dance given by the Duchess of Somerset, where he was forced into a Scottish reel with the daughter of the new Turkish ambassador. He could not remember a more excruciating twenty minutes.

Adams was too busy to notice his son's unhappiness. Seward showed more restraint in his subsequent dispatches, but he continued to insist on a retraction of the neutrality proclamation.[65] The Queen's Advocate, Sir John Harding, claimed that his sympathies lay with the North, but, recorded Adams, when "I tried to explain to him the nature of my objection, which is much misunderstood here, he defended it with the usual argument."[66] The British attitude in general dismayed him. "People do not quite understand Americans or their politics," he wrote to Charles Francis Jr. He had heard that Richard Cobden thought separating from the South would be good for the North,[67] and John Bright had come out strongly for "strict neutrality."[68] "They think this a hasty quarrel," complained Adams. "They do not comprehend the connection which slavery has with it, because we do not at once preach emancipation. Hence they go to the other extreme and argue that it is not an element of the struggle."[69]

Adams was himself guilty of mischaracterization. The English reaction was far more complicated than he allowed. The celebrated novelist Mrs. Gaskell, an ardent admirer of the United States, confessed to being "thoroughly puzzled by what is now going on in America." "I don't mind your thinking me dense or ignorant," she wrote candidly to the future president of Harvard, Charles Eliot Norton. "But I should have thought (I feel as if I were dancing among eggs) that separating yourselves from the South was like getting rid of a diseased member." She added: "You know I live in S. Lancashire where all personal and commercial intimacies are with the South. Everyone looks and feels sad (—oh so sad) about this war. It would do Americans good to see how warm the English heart is towards them."[70]

Charles Darwin, whose *Origin of Species* had been published in 1859, highlighted another aspect that troubled the English. "Some few, and I am one of them, even wish to God," he wrote to the botanist Asa Gray, "that the North would proclaim a crusade against slavery."[71] A leading abolitionist, Richard Webb, voiced a similar complaint from Ireland: "Neither Lincoln nor Seward has yet spoken an antislavery syllable since they took office."[72] Seward had specifically instructed all U.S. ministers and consuls to avoid mentioning the word in connection with the Union. The deliberate omission was a grievous miscalculation. Seward had sacrificed the North's trump card in Britain in the hope that it would appease the South. Instead, he had provided ammunition to his critics who accused the North of hypocrisy. *The Economist* had already stated, "The great majority of the people in the Northern States detest the coloured population even more than do the Southern whites."[73] At the beginning of June, Moran's nemesis, Sarah Parker Remond, gave credence to the charge in an article about her family's persecution as free blacks in New England. Though she included a plea for England to support the North, it sounded absurd against the backdrop of her heart-rending experiences.[74]

Yet for all the finger-pointing and public criticism of the North, the Southern envoys failed to make the slightest change in Britain's policy. "We are satisfied that the Government is sincere in its desire to be strictly neutral in the contest," Yancey repeated in his next letter to Secretary Toombs, "and will not countenance any violation of its neutrality."[75]

Writing to a close friend in the South, Yancey admitted that the mission was not turning out the way he had envisioned: "In the first place, important as cotton is, it is not King in Europe." Furthermore, he added, "The anti-Slavery sentiment is universal. *Uncle Tom's Cabin* has been read and believed."[76]

FIVE

The Rebel Yell

*William Howard Russell in New Orleans—Sam and Mary Sophia Hill
volunteer—Elizabeth Blackwell inspires the U.S. Sanitary Commission—
"On to Richmond"—The Battle of Bull Run—Not a fight but a stampede*

"There is on the part of the South an enormously exaggerated idea of its own strength," William Howard Russell wrote to Lord Lyons from New Orleans on May 21, 1861.[1] The city was celebrating succession with parades and fireworks as though the war was already won. All the public buildings and many private houses were flying the new Confederate flag.* There were no doubts here about the power of cotton. It was "not alone king but czar," remarked the *Times* journalist after he was told for the dozenth time that the shipping season just past had been the most profitable in the city's history.[2]

Russell was not enamored with the Deep South. The unceasing battle against mosquitoes, the crude sanitation, and the greasy food that typified Southern cuisine made him consume more alcohol than his liver could tolerate. "Too much talk, smoke & brandy & water" was becoming a frequent complaint in his diary.[3] The South's erratic postal service was also a source of torment. It had taken a month for a plaintive letter from his wife, Mary, to reach him. He knew she would assume he had not

---

* The Confederate flag changed several times; for the moment it sported nine stars in a circle inside a blue square next to three bars of red and white.

bothered to reply. "God comfort her," he wrote sadly in his diary on May 25, "and make me worthy of her."[4]

William Mure, the British consul in New Orleans, rescued Russell from many hours of lonely reflection by inviting him to stay at his house. The extensive commercial ties between New Orleans and Liverpool were reflected in the social prominence of the British consulate; Mure's generosity gave Russell the best possible introduction to the South's biggest and wealthiest city. New Orleans was the fourth-largest port in the world and a commercial juggernaut compared to Richmond, Virginia, which had been chosen as the Confederacy's new capital. Known as the Crescent City because of the way it curved around a deep bend of the Mississippi River, New Orleans was the epicenter of the slave trade and the gateway not only for the majority of the South's cotton crop, but also for its tobacco and sugar. As business opportunities came and went, so, too, did many of New Orleans's foreign immigrants. The 1860 census had revealed that little more than half the population of 168,000 had been born in the South.[5] Russell grasped at once how an outsider like Judah Benjamin could find opportunities here that were denied him elsewhere in the Confederacy.[6]

New Orleans had belonged first to Spain and then France until the Louisiana Purchase of 1803 made it part of the United States. The original French and Spanish settlers called themselves Creoles, and their descendants still lived in the sixty-six blocks downtown known as the Vieux Carré, or the French Quarter. Here they built their houses in the Caribbean style with inner courtyards, pastel façades, and ornate balconies that allowed the occupants to see and be seen from the street. The English-speaking newcomers had congregated uptown, on the other side of the canal that ran through the city, in the so-called Garden District. They pointedly built their houses in the Greek Revival style, using red brick instead of plaster, and planted lush gardens that screened the buildings from the street.

New Orleans's French culture was reflected in the number of volunteer regiments for the Confederate army with names such as Chasseur, Lafayette, and Beauregard in the title. Russell noticed that the foreign immigrants tended to cluster together; hence there was the Irish Brigade, the Garibaldi Legion, and the European Brigade.[*] Russell was especially

---

[*] At the beginning of the war, a Confederate regiment generally consisted of 1,100 officers and men divided into ten companies.

taken with the Dickens-inspired "Pickwick Rifles," though the name it-self suggested Mure had not been entirely successful in persuading Britons to adhere to the Foreign Enlistment Act.[7]

It was not the willing recruits that concerned Mure, however, but rather those who were forced to volunteer whether they wanted to or not.[8] King Cotton ruled with a brutal hand in New Orleans. British sub-jects were being marched to recruiting posts by self-appointed vigilantes, "not in twos or threes, but in tens and twenties," the consul told Russell. One woman had complained to him that her husband was held hostage and beaten for three days until he agreed to enlist; his face was so badly disfigured when they brought him home that she failed to recognize him. Dissent was treated in the same harsh manner. "Every stranger is watched, every word is noted," Russell wrote in one of his dispatches to *The Times.* People who stated "their belief that the Northerners will be successful are sent to prison for six months."[9]

Throughout the Confederacy intense pressure was being exerted on the 233,000 foreign residents to prove their loyalty to the South. For William Watson, a Scotsman working as a mechanic in Baton Rouge, failure to follow his friends into the Pelican Rifles of the 3rd Louisiana Infantry would have been unthinkable. "I would never take up arms to maintain or enforce slavery," he wrote in his memoirs. But Watson's friends told him he would be fighting for independence, a cause so wor-thy that he could not remain aloof "without injury" to his honor.[10] A Welsh immigrant in Texas joined for similar reasons: "Every man and child that can carry a gun is a soldier in the South," he explained to his family.[11]

In Arkansas, another Welsh immigrant, twenty-year-old Henry Mor-ton Stanley (who would later achieve fame by "finding" Dr. Livingstone in Africa), was shamed into enlisting in the Dixie Grays of the 6th Arkansas Infantry by a neighbor who sent him the Southern equivalent of a white feather. He received a parcel "which I half-suspected, as the address was written in a feminine hand, to be a token of some lady's re-gard," he wrote. "But, on opening it, I discovered it to be a chemise and petticoat, such as a Negro lady's-maid might wear. I hastily hid it from view, and retired to the back room, that my burning cheeks might not betray me."[12]

Even without the threat of ostracism or harassment, there were other, more prosaic forces bearing down on the British community. The blockade was not only hurting the city financially, it was also an impediment to those who wished to leave the South. Many unemployed Britons were trapped in New Orleans; "nothing remains for them but to enlist," admitted Russell.[13] Two Anglo-Irish siblings from England, Mary Sophia Hill and her twin brother, Sam, were among the early victims of the blockade. The merchant families who sent their daughters to Mary's seminary in the Garden District were suddenly unable to pay the fees. Six weeks after the blockade began there was not a single pupil left in the school.

Mary and Sam were an eccentric pair. She was tight-lipped, fussy, and prone to shrillness; he was quiet, absent-minded, and passive. Despite having trained as a civil engineer under Isambard Kingdom Brunel, Sam had never been able to withstand the rigors of an occupation, and over the years his dependence on her had become absolute. The siblings had arrived in New Orleans in 1850 so Sam could take up yet another new position. His inevitable failure gave Mary the idea that they should start a school together. She would teach English, French, and music; Sam, if he were able, could teach mathematics.

"In my eyes," wrote Mary, "the only blot I ever saw in the sunny South was slavery; but as a stranger, an alien, I had no right to meddle."[14] But her sympathy for the South did not extend to Sam volunteering: "I was, and still am, and ever will be, a British subject," she wrote in her diary.[15] Nevertheless, her brother had joined the Irish Brigade after a furious argument over the failure of the seminary. Mary woke up one morning in early June to discover he had packed his bags and disappeared. She had seen the placards calling for Irishmen to join the 6th Louisiana Volunteers, as the Irish Brigade was officially designated, but never once did she think that her introverted and clumsy brother might heed the call. Nor dared she imagine how the Irish Catholic volunteers would treat a Protestant whose loyalty was not to Ireland but to the Crown:

> I tried all I could to get him free [Mary recalled]; went to Mr. Muir [sic], who was then Consul, to see what he could do, but with no good result. It nearly broke my heart to see my only brother and only near male relative leave me and leave the flag we were born under for a stranger, and perhaps get killed for his folly; so I concluded I would follow him to Virginia to care for him

where I knew he would sadly want a woman's care, and that I would, whenever needed, care for the wounded, the sick and the distressed. Miss Nightingale God bless her taught us, women of the British flag, this lesson of humanity.[16]

Sam's regiment was in need of a nurse, and Colonel Isaac Seymour was willing to overlook the fact that Mary was unmarried, since he doubted that the forty-two-year-old spinster would interest the men. "So," she recorded, "having no particular ties; being as the law has it, a *femme sole,* I made up my mind to this humane calling." Two weeks later Mary jotted in her diary: "My brother quite miserable at the step he has taken. I am so glad I made up my mind to look after him."[17]

———

Mary Sophia Hill would have found it much more difficult to become a nurse in the North. There was no shortage of women wanting to help. British-born Elizabeth Blackwell, the first woman to qualify as a doctor in the United States, was deluged with nursing applicants after the Federal surrender of Fort Sumter.* She was cross that the same society ladies who had previously claimed to be scandalized by the infirmary were now begging to be admitted for training.[18] But she soon realized there would never be a better opportunity to attract support for her medical college. With the aid of Henry Bellows, the charismatic pastor of All Souls Unitarian Church, she invited "the women of New York" to attend a mass meeting at the Cooper Institute. They expected large numbers, but not the four thousand who crammed into the hall.

The result of this historic event was the creation of the Women's Central Association of Relief. Elizabeth envisioned it as a kind of civilian

---

* Elizabeth Blackwell (1821–1910) was not only the first woman to earn a medical degree in the United States, but also the first female doctor to be placed on the British General Medical Council's register. Born in England and having lived and studied in both countries, she was the quintessential British American, having lived and studied in both countries, though "I look upon England as my home, and must always do so," she wrote to her best friend, the feminist writer Barbara Bodichon in 1860. Dr. Blackwell had been unable to raise sufficient funds to start a medical school for women in London, but since 1853 had been running the New York Infirmary for Indigent Women and Children, where her aim was to train women to become doctors in the course of serving the poor. The novelist George Eliot met Elizabeth Blackwell in 1859, recording in her diary: "Esteemable for the courage and perseverance she has shown . . . but very repulsive and schoolmistress-like in manner."

central command that would direct the various relief efforts on the home front, from the training of nurses to the distribution of woolen socks. The WCAR would work side by side with the army, ensuring that the needs of soldiers were met as quickly as possible. The Reverend Henry Bellows and a delegation of male doctors went to Washington to seek government approval for the plan. But during the thirteen-hour train journey they conceived a different idea: a national organization modeled on the British Sanitary Commission, which had been formed in response to Florence Nightingale's exposure of army hospital conditions during the Crimean War. Bellows suggested they call it the United States Sanitary Aid Commission.[19]

The Army Medical Bureau resented any interference or infringement on its domain and tried to block the commission from receiving official sanction. President Lincoln shared the bureau's doubts over the wisdom of allowing philanthropists and women to interfere with the work of professionals.[20] Yet on June 18 he reluctantly signed the United States Sanitary Commission into existence, remarking as he did so that it would probably be a "fifth wheel to the coach." The commission was awarded an office in the treasury building along with a table and some chairs. Still fighting a rearguard action, the army medical chiefs succeeded in limiting its operations to the new volunteer regiments. The sixteen thousand regulars that made up the standing army would be kept safe from the civilians.

Elizabeth Blackwell's name did not appear in any literature put out by the Sanitary Commission. Although she had been the initial force behind the volunteer movement, neither she nor the infirmary were invited to participate. "We shall do much good but you will probably not see our names," Elizabeth wrote to her best friend, Barbara Bodichon, on June 6:

> We would have accepted a place on the health commission which our association is endeavoring to establish in Washington and which the government will probably appoint—but the Doctors would not permit us to come forward. In the hospital committee, which you will see referred to in the report, they declined to allow OUR little hospital to be represented—and they refused to have anything to do with the nurse education plan if the "Miss Black-wells were going to engineer the matter." Of course as it is essen-

tial to open these hospitals to nurses, we kept in the background, had there been any power to support us, we would have found our true place, but there was none.[21]

Elizabeth and her sister Emily accepted their exclusion gracefully. Elizabeth became chair of the WCAR's nurse registration committee, and together the two sisters began to interview and select those who showed the most promise. Each candidate received a month's training at the infirmary, followed by a further month's practical experience at Bellevue or New York Hospital.

Dr. Blackwell had no doubt that her nurses would prove themselves in the field, as long as the well-meaning but catastrophically inept Dorothea Dix was prevented from ruining the enterprise. The fifty-nine-year-old veteran campaigner for the mentally ill had arrived at Washington in early May to offer herself as superintendent of army nurses. A lack of candidates had given her the position by default. Miss Dix was a "meddler general" without peer, complained Elizabeth. "For it really amounts to that, she being without system, or any practical knowledge of the business."[22] She soon confirmed Elizabeth's fears: erratic, disorganized, and quarrelsome, she was a positive hindrance to the scheme. Most applicants were turned away on ludicrous grounds, such as being too pretty or too recently widowed, but Elizabeth's trained nurses she dared not refuse.[23]

"If the Doctors would only do the part they have chosen and educate that material, we should have a capital band of nurses," Elizabeth wrote to Barbara Bodichon in June.[24] She also hoped they would accept the field hospital designs sent over by Florence Nightingale, but feared that the same chauvinism and anti-British prejudice that had led to her exclusion from the Sanitary Commission might also extend to anything originating with Miss Nightingale.[25] There was nothing to be gained from being associated with England since the neutrality proclamation. "To be scolded now whenever I enter a friend's house with 'well what do you say to England's behaviour . . . ' is a great irritation to me," complained Elizabeth. "I have been deeply chagrined by the tone our papers have been taking towards England."[26]

The Anglophobia encouraged by Seward was growing in strength. The *New York Herald* was the worst offender. Its Scottish editor, James Gordon Bennett, had no qualms about printing incendiary articles if they whetted public appetite for more. The *Herald* had toned down its antiwar rhetoric after a mob tried to burn down the paper's headquarters, but attacking England remained a popular alternative. New York had transformed from the ambivalent, even apathetic, city described by William Howard Russell in *The Times* into a noisy carnival of war. The shops along Broadway had become recruiting offices; posters and handbills advertising new regiments covered the city.

"The outbreak of the Civil War has given me a great addition of new and extraordinary duties, in the incessant applications for protection, and advice, etc.," wrote the British consul in New York, Edward Archibald.[28] He was rising to the challenge with valiant enthusiasm. A career diplomat for almost thirty years, Archibald was a devoted family man who spent his Sunday afternoons visiting sick and needy Britons. Since taking up his post in 1857, he had diligently collected statistics, written reports, resolved commercial disputes, found lost relatives, sent home destitute Britons, and performed all the myriad duties, both practical and pastoral, that were a consul's lot in a busy city like New York. Until Archibald shocked his superiors by denouncing the rebellion in an official dispatch, the Foreign Office had considered him their most reliable consul in the United States.[29]

Forced volunteering was not solely a Southern phenomenon, and the greatest call on Archibald's time was the plight of Britons who had been imprisoned or punished for their refusal to join a regiment.[30] His task was made more difficult by those who had joined willingly but had changed their minds and were looking for an excuse to escape.[31] Despite Archibald's efforts to publicize the Foreign Enlistment Act, Britons were volunteering in droves.* The slightest hint of a conflict between the North and Britain had also encouraged thousands of Irish immigrants to join the war effort.

The language employed by Irish recruiters was so explicit that

---

* Nineteen-year-old Thomas Beach, for example, was working for a British bank in Paris when the war began. "Friends and associations, many of them American, were leaving on every hand for the seat of war," he wrote. As a lark, Beach decided to go along with a group of friends who were sailing for New York. They all joined the same regiment: "Regarding the whole proceeding more in the light of a good joke than anything else, [I called] myself Henri Le Caron." (Under this name, during the 1870s he became one of the most notorious and successful spies in the British Secret Service.)[27]

Archibald warned the Foreign Office to prepare for a new threat. Posters urged their fellow Irishmen to train in America in order to fight the British oppressors back home. At least three regiments in New York were filled with Irish recruits, the majority of whom were avowed Fenians. Michael Corcoran, the colonel of the infamous 69th Infantry Regiment—the unit that had refused to parade in honor of the Prince of Wales—was also the commander of the Fenian movement's military wing.[32] Another well-known Irish revolutionary in the 69th was Thomas Meagher, whose stature among the New York Irish community was almost godlike since his escape from a penal colony in Tasmania, where he had been banished for sedition.[33] (Meagher's friend and fellow escapee, John Mitchell, had thrown his lot with the South.)

A large number of British immigrants volunteered out of idealism, but there were just as many, like twenty-five-year-old George Henry Herbert, who joined to stave off destitution after the company that had recruited him from England went bankrupt. He had been unemployed since Christmas and was down to his last pair of socks. They were holding up well—"There is only one hole in the heel of one of them," he had written cheerfully to his mother—but he could no longer continue without work. Such was the clamor for new recruits that even a man as short and overweight as Herbert could join a popular regiment like the 9th New York Volunteers, better known as Hawkins's Zouaves.* Unlike the majority of the new volunteers, who enlisted for ninety days, Herbert signed up for two years and in return was awarded the rank of first sergeant. He was grateful for any sort of position but harbored secret hopes of becoming an officer: "I study as much as I can," he wrote to his mother, "and do not despair of getting a commission sometime or other."[34] Herbert's hope of promotion would depend on his popularity with the men, since the volunteer regiments were allowed to elect their own officers.

---

* The original Zouaves were an elite North African corps in the French army whose uniform of white leggings, baggy blue trousers, magenta jacket, and bright red fez made them unmistakable on the battlefield. A Chicago lawyer named Elmer Ellsworth had started the American craze for Zouave regiments in 1859. He formed his own outfit, trained the men in the complicated drills and swordplay of a Zouave regiment, and took them on a nineteen-city tour of America. Colonel Hawkins had seen a demonstration by Ellsworth's Zouaves the previous summer, which was all the encouragement he needed to organize a New York version. His small company of Zouaves was among the first to be granted permission to recruit a full regiment, hence its designation as the 9th New York Volunteer Infantry.

"There is a British Regiment gotten up here," one English immigrant, Edward Best, told his aunt Sophie in Somerset. "It seems to be very popular and I trust will carry its flag through this affair with credit to our dear old country."[35] Consul Archibald, however, was embarrassed when the recruiters for the British Volunteers opened their office in the same building as the consulate.[36] He sent a letter to the main newspapers denying any involvement, though this provoked the press to label him a Southern sympathizer.

The British Volunteers started off well and could be seen training each morning in the drill room at the Astor Riding School.[37] But the regiment soon became a magnet for anti-British hostility, as did a regiment in Massachusetts that called itself the British Rifle Club.[38] "It is not right that British residents should be taunted and twitted without cause," complained the *Albion,* a weekly journal for the British community in New York.[39] The British Volunteers lost its appeal to recruits after one of the captains was accused of being a Confederate agent, a charge that was repeated in the press even after the unfortunate captain was exonerated.

By mid-June the British Volunteers' difficulties became insurmountable and they merged with an Irish regiment to become the 36th New York Volunteers. There were frequent fights and stabbings in the new outfit between the English and Irish factions, and mealtimes could be explosive. The violence encouraged many of the former British volunteers to join the 79th New York Highlanders, which in contrast to the Irish 69th had provided the Prince of Wales's honor guard during his visit in 1860. It was safe to be called Scots, Irish, or Welsh, but not British or English, noted Mr. Archibald.

A young Englishman named Ebenezer Wells had joined the 79th Highlanders when he arrived in New York in 1860 in order to have something to do on the weekends. "When the Civil War broke out, the regiment volunteered for the war," he wrote in his memoirs. "I was buglar [*sic*] and being away from parental restraint thought it would be a splendid excursion."[40] The men were thrilled when they received their orders in early June. "It was a beautiful Sunday when we marched down Broadway amidst deafening applause," wrote Wells. The crowds adored their tartan uniform, especially the officers' kilts. Nothing about the occasion hinted at the hardships ahead. Their knapsacks were packed with every conceivable delicacy as though they were on a Sunday outing. But,

Wells added ruefully, if they had known what lay in store for them, "how depressed instead of elated would our spirits have been."[41]

Ebenezer Wells experienced his first brush with violence as the regiment passed through Baltimore. He was ambushed by a stone-throwing mob and lost his cap and blanket before being rescued by members of his company. The 79th Highlanders were tired and hungry when they finally reached Washington on June 4. The sweltering city had become a vast military camp. Rows of white tents and parked artillery occupied the green fields around the half-finished Capitol building. Long trains of covered wagons filled the dusty thoroughfares.[42] At night, the city resonated with wild shouts and hoots, and thunderous fireworks were answered with rounds of gunfire.

The Highlanders were allocated temporary quarters at Georgetown University. The 69th had only recently vacated the premises, and their detritus still littered the grounds. The campus was eerily silent, all but fifty of the student body having volunteered to fight for the South. The men were nervous. The Confederate army, under the command of the hero of Fort Sumter, General Beauregard, was only seventeen miles to the west. "We lay every night with our muskets by our sides, ready cocked, and one finger on the trigger," wrote one of the recruits from the old British Volunteers. "It is a tough life, I can tell you."[43] His sentiment was widely shared in camps around the city. No regiment was so experienced or so confident that its men did not live in fear of an ambush or a surprise raid. The roar of the bullfrog, the screech of the night owl, "every rustle of the wind among the trees," wrote the newly arrived war reporter and artist Frank Vizetelly, "every sound that breaks the stillness of the night, is taken for the advance of the Secessionists."[44]

Vizetelly had accompanied the 2nd New York Regiment to their camp on the border between Washington and Virginia. The sounds of the forest did not frighten him; the thirty-year-old Vizetelly had spent the past ten years in the midst of battles and revolutions all over Europe. He had never known any other life than journalism. His father and grandfather were both well-known printers and engravers on Fleet Street. His three brothers were also in the trade; Henry, the second oldest, was one of the founders of the *Illustrated London News,* which was the first weekly newspaper to illustrate its articles with eyewitness drawings.

Vizetelly's fame in England rested on his pictures of Garibaldi's Sicily campaign. Dispatched by Henry to provide sketches of the fighting for

Attack on the pickets of the Garibaldi Guard on the banks of the Potomac, by Frank Vizetelly.

the *Illustrated London News,* Frank soon abandoned any pretense of objectivity and allied himself with Garibaldi. It was not in his nature to be impartial: his drawings were not only skillful depictions of a moment or tableau but moving narratives that engaged the emotions of the viewer. His images demanded a reaction, not unlike Vizetelly himself, whose craving to be the center of attention was insatiable. "He was a big, florid, red-bearded Bohemian," recalled an admirer, "who could and would do anything to entertain a circle."[45] Whether sitting around a campfire or dining in an officers' mess, Vizetelly would transfix his listeners with vivid stories, replete with voices and accents, or lead them in boisterous sing-alongs that lasted until the small hours.

William Howard Russell envied Vizetelly in just one respect: he was unmarried and could travel wherever he pleased without upsetting his family. Otherwise he pitied him. Vizetelly constantly teetered between depression and mania, and when not distracted by the thrill of danger, he became self-destructive and reckless. Vizetelly partially understood his limitations and chose to live rough with the 2nd New York Volunteers, even though the camp was infested with rattlesnakes and "myriads of bloodthirsty mosquitoes," rather than lounge in the saloon at Willard's.[46]

Sometimes he visited the camp of the Garibaldi Guard to swap stories with the handful of genuine veterans in the regiment. (The colonel there was a Hungarian con man, and most of the volunteers were not Italian but adventurers from the four corners of the globe.) On one of the few occasions Vizetelly did go to the capital, he received an invitation to dinner from Seward. He arrived expecting to regale his host with stories about the American volunteers he had encountered among Garibaldi's Red Shirts, but Seward was interested only in the tenor of his sympathies and whether he was planning to visit the South like that villain William Howard Russell. "I disclaimed any idea of so doing," reported Vizetelly.[47]

Once Seward took against a person, it was rare for him to change his mind. Russell had sensed at their first meeting that he could be a dangerous enemy. During his return journey from the South, Russell had read enough of the Northern press to warn him of the reception awaiting him in Washington. But "I can't help it," he wrote on June 22 to his fellow *Times* correspondent in New York, J. C. Bancroft Davis; "I must write as I feel and see. . . . I would not retract a line or a word of my first letters." He hoped that Northern newspapers would reprint his *Times* reports from the South, which would show that he was not a rebel sympathizer.[48]

Russell arrived in Washington on July 3, 1861. This time he stayed away from Willard's and found lodgings in a private house on Pennsylvania Avenue. He regretted the decision as soon as he unlocked the door to his room and caught the stench of the privy beneath the window. Once he had changed his clothes, Russell called on Lord Lyons to give him a report on the South, glad for the excuse to escape his lodgings, if only for a few hours. The legation was almost as dark as his bedroom, since Lyons had ordered the gas lamps to be kept unlit in order to avoid adding unnecessary heat. "I was sorry to observe he looked rather careworn and pale," Russell wrote afterward.[49] One of the attachés whispered to Russell as he was leaving that "the condition of things with Lord Lyons and Seward had been very bad, so much so Lord L would not go near State Dept. for fear of being insulted by the tone and manner of little S."[50] Ever since the neutrality proclamation had become known, Seward had been threatening and plotting to force a reversal of the South's belligerent status. Lyons was constantly on the watch against Seward's stratagems to weaken Britain's leadership and Mercier's attempts to sabotage the blockade. Try as he might, Lyons could not make Seward understand that Europe was only respecting the blockade out of deference to Britain. Russell returned to his lodgings feeling depressed by Seward's misguided behavior toward Lord Lyons. There was no other foreign minister in Washington, Russell wrote in his diary, "who watches with so much interest the march of events as Lord Lyons, or who feels as much sympathy, perhaps, in the Federal Government."[51]

"Sumner makes it appear he saved the whole concern from going smash," Russell wrote after he bumped into him on the street and had to stand for an hour in the blistering heat while Sumner gleefully enlarged on "the dirty little mountebankism of my weeny friend in office."[52] Russell was not sure whether to believe him until he called on Seward the following day and was subjected to another of his tirades. The secretary of state informed Russell that if he wished to go anywhere near the army, his passport would have to be countersigned by Lord Lyons, himself, and General-in-Chief Winfield Scott. He ended the interview with a lecture on the impropriety of Britain's granting belligerent status to the Confederates: "If any European Power provokes a war, we shall not shrink from it. A contest between Great Britain and the United States would wrap the world in fire, and at the end it would not be the United States which would have to lament the results of the conflict." Russell tried to appear serene during this outburst, but as he listened to Seward's monologue he could not help seeing the funny side. There they were "in his modest little room within the sound of the evening's guns, in a capital menaced by [Confederate] forces," and yet Seward was threatening "war with a Power which could have blotted out the paper blockade of the Southern forts and coast in a few hours."[53]

"Seward is losing ground in Washington and New York very fast," Charles Francis Adams, Jr., reported to his father on July 2. "Sumner has been here fiercely denouncing him for designing, as he asserts, to force the country into a foreign war."[54] It was true that Seward had not calculated on Sumner's relentless plotting against him, or that Sumner would try to set himself up as a rival secretary of state from the Senate; but both William Howard Russell and Charles Francis Jr. had been misled by Sumner. Far from being humiliated, Seward was reemerging in triumphant form, as the crush at his parties attested. June had been a month of consolidation and reconciliation between the president and his wayward secretary; Lincoln had won Seward's support through a combi-

nation of firmness and magnanimity in victory. Displaying more states-
manship than his detractors would admit, Seward recognized that Lincoln possessed the skills required in a president, "but he needs constant
and assiduous cooperation."[55]

The alteration in Seward's attitude toward Lincoln was accompanied
by a realization that neither bribery nor the lure of fighting Britain would
make the Southern states return to the Union. The change in Seward
could be discerned in early July after Gideon Welles engineered a bill
through Congress that gave Lincoln the authority to close Southern
ports by decree. The foreign ministers in Washington warned Seward
that Europe would ignore any attempt by the North to impose legal restrictions on ports it did not physically control. If he genuinely sought a
foreign war, all Seward had to do was demand compliance with these fic-
titious port closures, and the Great Powers would revolt. Seward believed them and persuaded Lincoln to say nothing publicly about the bill.

A few days later, on July 19, Seward paid a private visit to the legation.
He "proceeded, with some hesitation," reported Lord Lyons, "and with
an injunction to me to be secret," swearing "that he had used strong language in his earlier communications to Foreign Powers . . . from the necessity of making them clearly understand the state of Public Feeling
here." He added that his only motive had been to prevent disunion, not
begin a foreign war. "I was not altogether unprepared for the change in
Mr. Seward's tone," Lyons admitted; he had heard from the French legation that Seward had made a similar speech to Mercier a few hours earlier. He thought the real question was whether the change was
temporary or permanent—and that would depend on the Federal army's
progress in Virginia.[56]

———

The decision to send the army into battle rather than wait until the civilian recruits had been trained into soldiers had been made by the president's cabinet on June 29. The military advisers at the meeting had
argued against the idea: General Scott had already presented Lincoln
with a strategy, derisively called the "Anaconda Plan" by critics, which
aimed to minimize the bloodshed on American soil by trapping the
South behind its own borders and slowly applying pressure. But Northern newspapers were demanding a battle. Horace Greeley's *New York
Tribune* had started running the same banner headline every day: FOR-
WARD TO RICHMOND! FORWARD TO RICHMOND! THE REBEL CONGRESS CANNOT

BE ALLOWED TO MEET THERE ON 20 OF JULY!, which incited newspapers in other states to follow suit.[57] Lincoln explained to General Scott that it would be politically impossible to delay a fight, and even if it were not, there was the problem of the 75,000 volunteers whose ninety days were about to expire.

General Winfield Scott had fought in every American war since 1812 and was a revered national figure, although some of the younger officers in the army referred to him as "Old Fuss and Feathers." He was too old and infirm to lead the troops himself, so the command of the new Federal army at Washington went to Irvin McDowell, a young officer on his staff, whose drive and intelligence had already marked him out as a future general. McDowell had not been Scott's first choice; he had originally offered the position to Colonel Robert E. Lee, who lived in Arlington, just across the Potomac River from Washington. But Lee declined, deciding that his loyalty belonged to Virginia and therefore the South.

McDowell was energetic, but he had never actually commanded an army, nor was Scott convinced that he would remain calm under pressure. He had sufficient experience, however, to know that the 35,000 would-be soldiers currently camping in the woods around Washington were more of a danger to themselves than to the Confederacy. His objections were dismissed by Lincoln, who told him: "You are green, it is true, but they are green, also, you are all green alike." McDowell diligently executed Lincoln's order to engage the enemy and devised a plan that he thought would answer the country's wish for a quick and dramatic victory. He would march his men into Virginia to Manassas, where a Confederate army of 22,000 soldiers was stationed under the command of General Beauregard. Manassas was a small town some twenty-five miles west of Washington; though it was hardly more than a hamlet, its railroad junction linked two important rail lines going west and south into Virginia. If McDowell could smash the Confederate army blocking the way, the North would have an open route into northern Virginia, and from there it would indeed be "forward to Richmond."

William Howard Russell liked General McDowell, whose manner, despite some personal peculiarities (Russell had never met a teetotal glutton before), he found to be engagingly frank and honest. When Russell bumped into him on July 16 at Washington Station, McDowell admitted that he was there looking for two missing batteries of artillery.

The army had started its march toward Manassas that morning and already there was utter chaos at his headquarters. Even "the worst-served English general has always a young fellow or two about him," thought Russell pityingly as the forlorn figure walked up and down the platform, poking his head into each train carriage. He was almost tempted to accept McDowell's offer to travel with him on the train but decided it was impractical without his bags or a servant.

Over the next four days, the Federal army picnicked and pillaged its way from Washington to Manassas, leaving a trail of burning houses, discarded army kit, and stragglers that stretched for many miles. Although small by European standards, McDowell's army was the largest ever assembled in America's short history. He had organized it as best he could into five divisions with a total of thirteen brigades.* Almost all the commanders were officers from the regular army, which gave McDowell confidence that at least he would have men who knew how to give and receive orders. The commander of the 3rd Brigade was Colonel William T. Sherman, who would become the greatest Union general after Ulysses S. Grant. Sherman had asked for the 79th New York Highlanders and the 69th New York Irish because of the large number of European veterans in their ranks, but his hope that they would display more professional behavior than some of the other regiments was dashed from the outset. The Highlanders had refused to leave their camp because they had been given Model 1816 smoothbores instead of the modern rifled Springfields.† Colonel James Cameron restored order by promising that every man would receive his own rifle as soon as possible, and since the colonel's brother was the secretary of war, the men decided they could believe him.[58] The situation was worse at the camp of the 69th, where Captain Thomas Meagher, the Irish "Prince of New York," almost started a mutiny by arguing that their ninety days were up and that they should all be allowed to go home. Colonel Corcoran eventually managed to persuade the men to stay until after the anticipated battle.

The army's destination was Centreville, a pretty town whose tree-

---

* A regiment was composed of around a thousand officers and men divided into ten companies; a brigade generally consisted of four to six regiments; and a division normally had three or four brigades. In theory, a division contained twelve thousand men.

† The effective range of a smoothbore was about 100 yards, compared to the more deadly and accurate 1861 Springfield, which had a range of 300 yards.

lined streets promised the relief of shade to the dusty and parched soldiers. The Federal troops arrived in such a state of disarray and exhaustion that McDowell spent an entire day trying to reshuffle the various
disorganized parts into some semblance of order. More regiments announced they were leaving since their ninety days had expired.[59] The
Confederate army was massed along an eight-mile line a little farther to
the south behind a narrow, winding stream called Bull Run. Over the
previous two days, General Beauregard had been receiving reinforcements from General Joseph E. Johnston's army in the Shenandoah Valley. According to McDowell's plan, this second army was supposed to be
engaged by General Patterson in a diversionary battle so that the Confederates at Manassas would remain outnumbered. But Johnston had
eluded his attackers and was, at that moment, piling his men onto trains
bound for Manassas.

Generals Beauregard and McDowell had been classmates at West
Point. They had studied the same military classics, learned the same tactics, and admired the same generals. Beauregard's recent success at Fort
Sumter had unleashed his Napoleonic tendencies to an unfortunate degree and given him visions of a great victory. Now, not only was his numerical disadvantage being rectified, but he had been prepared in
advance for McDowell's attack with the help of spies in Washington.
Rose Greenhow, the alluring pro-Southern society hostess, had stayed
behind in Washington with the express purpose of sending information
to the Confederacy. She had been supplied with a cipher key for writing
in code and had organized her own spy ring of pretty young women who
charmed their way past Union guards to deliver messages, sewn inside
their petticoats, to a Confederate contact in Virginia. The most important of Rose's sources was Senator Henry Wilson of Massachusetts,
chairman of the Military Affairs Committee, who swore, "You well
know that I do love you—and will sacrifice anything," which may explain how a copy of McDowell's route ended up in her possession.[60]
Rose also knew the date of McDowell's departure and when he proposed
to attack.[61]

Although Jefferson Davis was not tied down by the Federal law that
limited the service of state militias to a mere ninety days, Beauregard was
hampered by other problems, including a severe shortage of arms and
equipment. The 6th Louisiana Volunteers, Sam Hill's regiment, had arrived at Manassas Junction with only their personal rifles and homemade

uniforms. "The men badly off for clothes," wrote Mary Sophia Hill in her diary. When Sam ripped his uniform she had to repair it with red flannel. "Just imagine a patch of this behind and on your knees!" she complained.[62] Sam had been unable to master the most basic skills of soldiering, but his commanding officer turned down Mary's plea to assign him to a nonmilitary function. The hard truth was that Sam fulfilled a function already, if only by being there to stop a bullet destined for someone else.

In Washington, Russell realized he had made a costly mistake by turning down McDowell's offer at the station. He had failed to engage a servant, and there was not a horse or any kind of transport left in the city; what the army had not requisitioned had been hired by civilians who wanted to watch the spectacle. On Saturday, July 20, Russell heard from Federal officers in the city that McDowell's attack would take place the next morning. His search for transport became frantic; Russell revisited one of the larger livery stables and begged the owner to rent him his last remaining carriage. He paid the exorbitant price demanded and rushed to General Scott's headquarters to have his pass countersigned. "But the aide-de-camp shook his head, and I began to suspect from his manner and from that of his comrades that my visit to the army was not regarded with much favour."[63] Russell would not be able to leave until the morning.

> I returned to my lodgings [he wrote], laid out an old pair of Indian boots, cords, a Himalayan suit, an old felt hat, a flask, revolver and belt. My mind had been so much occupied with the coming event that I slept uneasily, and once or twice I started up, fancying I was called. The moon shone in through the mosquito curtains of my bed, and just ere day-break I was aroused by some noise in the adjoining room, and looking out, in a half dreamy state, imagined I saw General McDowell standing at the table . . . so distinctly that I woke up with the words, "General, is that you?"[64]

By the time Russell was fully awake on the twenty-first, McDowell's army had already marched into position and was awaiting orders. The two opposing generals had formed precisely the same plan: to trick the enemy with a feint against one side while mounting the real attack on the other. McDowell moved first, and his initiative appeared to bring rewards. Vizetelly placed himself rather precariously in a field and made sketches of the Federal regiments charging into their Confederate opponents. Both sides displayed unexpected courage and determination in their first introduction to warfare. It was the Confederates who wavered and were gradually pushed back; they ran toward the crest of a rise known as Henry House Hill, after the little white farmhouse that overlooked the ridge.

Confident that McDowell was on the verge of driving the Confederates off the field, Vizetelly galloped back to Centreville to give his first sketches to a waiting courier. A journalist for *The New York Times* also left and returned to Washington to write a report on McDowell's victory. On the way back to the fighting, Vizetelly bumped into a hot and perspiring Russell accompanied by Frederick Warre, one of the more adventurous attachés from the legation. The driver of the gig had left them at Centreville and they were wandering around in search of something to eat. Vizetelly offered to share his lunch with them, and they found a shady spot on a hill overlooking Manassas.

A large crowd of sightseers, including several senators and their wives, was also on the hill to observe the battle. The smoke and haze made it impossible to see what was actually happening, although whenever there was a loud explosion a woman beside them would shout, "That is splendid. Oh my! Is not that first-rate? I guess we will be in Richmond this time tomorrow." Russell knew better: "I was well convinced," he wrote, "no advance of any importance or any great success had been achieved, because the ammunition and baggage wagons had never moved." On the other hand, an Englishman whom Russell did not recognize "came up flushed and heated from the plain," saying that the Federals were behaving "most gallantly."[65] His announcement that the Confederates were retreating provoked "gutteral 'hochs' from the Deutschland folk and loud 'hurroos' from the Irish."[66]

Russell's instincts were correct. McDowell was no longer leading but reacting; when urgently asked for orders by his subordinates, he told them to wait. "For some three hours previous, we had seen long lines of dense dust rising from the roads leaving from Manassas," wrote Vizetelly. The dust clouds were in fact the last of the Confederate brigades arriving off the trains from the Shenandoah Valley.[67] One of these fresh regiments, led by a former professor named Thomas J. Jackson, ran to Henry House Hill, where the Confederate stand was starting

**First Bull Run
or Manassas**
July 21, 1861

Main Federal advance, McDowell's army – morning

William Howard Russell
and
Frank Vizetelly

Sudley Springs Ford

Sudley
Ford

Sudley
Springs

Sudley
Church

Ebenezer
Wells

Bull Run

Red House Ford

Cub Run

Rocky Run

Federal advance

To
Centreville

morning movement

Evans Bartow

Bee

Sherman's
advance

Farm Ford

Warrenton Turnpike

Site of Federal
confusion during
retreat in late
afternoon

Stone House

Young's Branch

Tyler
Stone Bridge

Groveton

Robinson
House

Lewis Ford

Henry House

Bull Run River

Ricketts' and Griffin's
Fed. batteries

Ball's Ford

Blackburn's Ford

Jackson's morning approach

Johnston's and
Beauregard's
Confederate HQ

Confederate
reinforcements
in afternoon

Scene of
fighting
July 18

New Market

Mitchell's
Ford

To
Manassas Gap

Manassas Gap R.R.

N

Manassas – Sudley Road

W   E

S

Federal forces

Orange &
Alexandria R.R.

To
Alexandria

Confederate forces

Manassas
Station

Miles

0   1   2

to crumble. There, according to legend, Jackson's firmness and bravery under fire inspired a Confederate general to rally his troops with the cry: "Look at Jackson standing like a stone wall! Rally behind the Virginians!"[68] So began the legend of Stonewall Jackson.

The sudden increase of firepower caught the Federal soldiers at the bottom of Henry House Hill by surprise. While Sherman was preparing his regiments to make a charge, some of the men threw themselves flat on the ground as others sought refuge behind trees. Sherman urged them to stay in formation. It was useless, he shouted, to duck after the explosions. Just then there was a loud bang above his head, causing him to duck involuntarily. "Well, boys," said Sherman with a grin, "you may dodge the big ones."[69] The 79th was the second regiment to make the attempt. "We were met by a terrible raking fire," recalled one of the survivors, "against which we could only stagger."[70] A second assault with the same result convinced the survivors that it was time to retreat. By the time the Highlanders had reached the safety of the river, they had suffered 198 casualties, including their colonel and half the regiment's officers.

The field was littered with bodies when Sherman ordered the 69th to make their charge. By now it was late afternoon and many Union soldiers had reached the end of their strength. Sensing his enemies' exhaustion, in one of his few sensible decisions that day, General Beauregard ordered the Confederates to make a countercharge. The rebels surged forward, letting out wild, whooping screams as they ran. The "rebel yell," as it became known, froze the Union soldiers in their tracks. Just as Colonel Corcoran shouted to his men to rally to the flag, two other Federal regiments on the hill smashed into them, pursued by Confederate cavalry.

The urge to flee spread to other parts of McDowell's army. Russell had ridden down to the turnpike bridge and was about to cross it when he saw a mob running toward him. The Union retreat had turned into a mass rout. "The crowd from the front continually increased," he wrote; "the heat, the uproar, and the dust were beyond description. I got up out of the road and into a cornfield, through which men were hastily walking or running, their faces streaming with perspiration, and generally without arms."[71] Vizetelly was riding to Centreville to hand over another set of drawings to a waiting courier when he was forced off the road by a roaring cavalcade of horses and wagons. He turned around and saw a dense cloud, thick and impenetrable like an explosion, hurtling toward him. He quickly joined the churning sea of humanity to avoid being trampled. Soldiers and spectators became tangled in a bloody struggle to escape.

Ebenezer Wells was not far behind. "I had been detached into the transportation department, having volunteered for such, and was on my way to the front," he wrote.

> When an officer met me and ordered me to turn back saying the troops were retreating, I answered I dare not accept any orders but from Headquarters, as I had ammunition. He drew his revolver threatening to shoot me if I disobeyed. . . . I went on but soon found it was too true. The Army was on the retreat, and after having had a view of some of the renowned Southern Black Horse Cavalry I turned and joined in the run. And it was indeed a run, some never stopped until they reached New York. We lost more men then by desertion than all the rest of the war put together.[72]

Russell also became part of the flight. "What occurred at the hill I cannot say," he wrote, "but all the road from Centreville for miles pre-

The stampede from Bull Run, by Frank Vizetelly.

sented such a sight as can only be witnessed in the track of the runaways of an utterly demoralised army." He asked one soldier why he was running. " 'I am not afraid of you,' replied the ruffian, levelling his piece at me and pulling the trigger. It was not loaded or the cap was not on, for the gun did not go off."[73] Shaken, Russell concentrated on surviving the ride home. It was almost midnight when he reached his lodgings. Lightning played about the sky. Russell shut the door and sat down at his desk, intending to write his report before daybreak. A messenger arrived from Lord Lyons, who had become alarmed after Warre returned to Washington without him. Russell scribbled a quick note in reply, then returned to his report. But after a few minutes of writing, his pen slipped and he slumped in his chair. "I awoke from a deep sleep this morning, about six o'clock," he wrote.

> The rain was falling in torrents and beat with a dull, thudding sound on the leads outside my window; but louder than all, came a strange sound, as if of the thread of men, a confused tramp and splashing, and a murmuring of voices. I got up and ran to the front room. . . . I saw a steady stream of men covered with mud, soaked through with rain, who were pouring irregularly, without any semblance of order up Pennsylvania Avenue towards the Capitol.[74]

Russell stayed at his desk all day, occasionally pausing to watch McDowell's dejected army stumble past his window. Hundreds of prisoners, including Colonel Corcoran of the 69th, remained at Manassas. Mary Sophia Hill caught a glimpse of them whenever she ran between hospital tents. She had been working without a rest since the morning of the battle. "They have not half the supplies," she wrote. "I tore down all the window blinds, and rolled them into bandages." She cleaned, bandaged, fed, and comforted scores of wounded soldiers, all of whom reminded her of Sam. Some of the men begged for water, others pleaded with her to remove bullets from their shattered limbs. "I heard and saw it all," she recorded, "war in its grandeur and war in its meanness."[75] Only later did she learn that Sam's regiment never actually fired a shot.

SIX

War by Other Means

McClellan takes charge—Prince Napoleon at the White House—Sanford's spies—Desperate for arms—The British join up—The raging storm

Frank Vizetelly diplomatically skimmed over the Federal rout in his dispatch for the *Illustrated London News;* William Howard Russell could describe little else, since it was the only part of the battle he had actually witnessed. Knowing how dreadful it would sound, he was careful not to condemn the soldiers for the mistakes of their leaders. "The men were overworked," Russell explained in his report, "kept out for 12 or 14 hours in the sun exposed to long-range fire, badly officered, and of deficient regimental organization." The army's lack of experience, he added, made an orderly retreat all but impossible.[1]

Russell also blamed the generals for the subsequent mayhem in the capital; Washington was held hostage for two days while drunken soldiers roamed the city. "The Secretary of War knows not what to do, Mr. Lincoln is equally helpless," Russell recorded. "There is no provost guard, no patrol, no authority visible in the streets."[2] He wondered why the Confederates did not simply march in and take the city while it lay helpless and disorganized. The French minister agreed with him. "Ever since I first met M. Mercier," wrote Russell, "he has expressed his conviction that the North never can succeed in conquering the South, or even restoring the Union." Mercier felt the South might have lost more men in the Battle of Bull Run than it was publicly admitting. Nothing else, he thought, could explain the Confederacy's failure to exploit the chaos of the Federal army.

Rose Greenhow sent messages to General Beauregard urging him to strike while the city was undefended: "Come on! Why do you not come?" she pleaded.[3] Beauregard did not come because his forces were almost as disorganized as the defeated Federals. The problem of supplies was as acute as ever, his men were exhausted, and he knew that McDowell's army had not been destroyed at Manassas (as the Confederates called the battle)—it had simply run away.[*] But Southern public opinion agreed with Rose Greenhow. Newspapers voiced anger toward Beauregard for not finishing the task, but also expressed overweening confidence, even exultation, in the superiority of the Confederate army. The light number of casualties at Manassas contributed to the belief that the war would soon be over with little cost to the South.[4]

In the North, the expressions of shame and horror were also accompanied by calls for better leadership. Lincoln responded decisively. Less than twenty-four hours after the Battle of Bull Run he dismissed Irvin McDowell and ordered his replacement, General George McClellan, to come at once to Washington. He also asked Congress for a million additional soldiers. Lincoln used the intervening time until McClellan's arrival to write a private memorandum setting out his thoughts for the next phase of the war. The defeated army would be renamed the Army of the Potomac, the other Northern armies in the field would also be reorganized, and the army chiefs would be assigned a clear set of objectives. He even added a list of what the objectives should be, starting with the capture of Manassas, followed by Virginia and Tennessee.[5]

General McClellan arrived in Washington on July 26; by then most of the army had staggered back to camp, although it was still an unruly rabble. Two regiments were in outright rebellion and more could follow unless McClellan imposed his authority quickly. The 79th Highlanders was one of the regiments in mutiny; it was not the lack of rifles that upset the men but the appointment of a new colonel without their consent. McClellan sent in trustworthy regiments to put down both rebellions, and the 79th was marched in shame through Washington under armed

---

[*] The Union and Confederacy often gave different names to their battles. The Confederates generally preferred the name of the nearest town, the Federals, the nearest river or landmark.

guard.[6] He hung the regiment's colors in his office as a warning to others.

The thirty-five-year-old McClellan possessed a flair for organization, and within a few weeks the changes to the Army of the Potomac were so noticeable that the press was hailing him as America's answer to Napoleon Bonaparte. He was treated with almost reverential deference by the president's cabinet and greeted with lusty cheers whenever he rode into the camps. McClellan reacted to the adulation with the calm acceptance of a man whose life had hitherto been blessed by an unbroken train of good fortune. He came from a wealthy Philadelphia family; in addition to good looks, intelligence, and physical prowess, he could boast an adoring wife and a wide circle of friends.

William Howard Russell was not altogether surprised by the general's meteoric rise. Russell had met McClellan in the Crimea, where the latter was there as a military observer for the U.S. Army, and thought him a rather overconfident young man. He did not know if McClellan had outgrown his youthful arrogance, but he noticed that his riding style had not changed; the general "is stumpy and with an ungraceful seat on horseback," he noted in his diary.[7]

McClellan's lack of horsemanship did not prevent him from becoming the star attraction when a real Prince Napoleon and his entourage arrived in Washington on August 2. Prince Joseph Charles Bonaparte—"Plon-Plon" in certain circles—was a cousin of Napoleon III (who himself was Napoleon Bonaparte's nephew). He had fled from France to avoid a duel, although this was not known in the North. No one had informed the administration that Plon-Plon was coming, which led to an unintended snub when Baron Mercier accompanied the prince to the White House. The doorbell was rung, the knocker pulled, and yet the front door remained closed. The royal party waited impatiently to be let in until "an employee, who happened to be passing by, took care of this duty," recalled an aide.

The prince had his revenge on Lincoln by not uttering a word after the initial introduction. The president and Seward, who was also present, were both overcome with confusion. Lincoln bought some time by inviting the prince to sit down, which required the fetching and repositioning of several chairs. "But once these new positions were acquired," wrote the aide, "the two parties sat opposite each other . . . the Prince, impatient because he had had to wait, took a cruel pleasure in remaining silent. Finally, the President took the risk of speaking." He tried to ask the prince about his father, but mistakenly referred to a childless uncle. "This incident made him lose his confidence still further." Mercier stepped in with a comment about the weather in general, and then about the rain of a few days past. Lincoln resorted to another round of hand-shaking that used up just enough time to allow the party to be shown to the door without undue haste.[8]

Lord Lyons took advantage of the temporary *froideur* between France and America to give a dinner in the prince's honor. Seward, Charles Sumner, and General McClellan were all invited, but not William Howard Russell, to the latter's disgust.[9] Lyons had intended the event to be a grand demonstration of the Anglo-French alliance, and though he admired Russell, he considered the dinner far too important to include a mere journalist. The next morning Lyons wrote proudly to his sister, "It went off very well," despite the appalling heat, "as it was not hotter in my dining room than everywhere else."[10] The French had unwittingly scored a blow for England in the battle of wits between Lyons and Sew-ard. McClellan had glowed with pleasure under the flattery lavished on him by the prince's military aides. Sumner, too, had been the recipient of extravagant compliments. But to Seward they displayed a Gallic aloof-ness that was noticeable and embarrassing. The French considered him uncultured, unpolished, and profoundly nonintellectual. Seward "does not speak any language but English," wrote one of the aides contemptu-ously, "and knows Europe very little, though he customarily declares in a comically emphatic way that he has travelled throughout Europe for several years."[11]

Seward was not amused when Prince Napoleon requested a pass to visit the Confederate headquarters. He pretended at first not to under-stand his hints and forced him to make a direct application. The French party, once again accompanied by Baron Mercier, traveled to General Beauregard's headquarters, where they listened with great respect to the Confederate version of Bull Run.[12] As word spread through the camps of the prince's arrival, French volunteers, including some who had fought in Garibaldi's army, stopped by to pay their respects. "Such strange and romantic personalities!" recorded the aide, surprised that even members of the French aristocracy were coming across the Atlantic to fight for the Confederacy. Beauregard had appointed as his assistant inspector general

Lieutenant Colonel Prince Camille de Polignac, whose father, Jules de Polignac, had served as prime minister under Charles X and whose grandmother Yolande had made the family rich and powerful through her notorious friendship with Marie Antoinette.[13]

The prince returned to Washington unconvinced by the South's arguments or its military confidence, although his aides, he confessed with a laugh to Lord Lyons, "seemed to think that they would rather command the Southern soldiers." Baron Mercier escorted the prince and his party to New York on August 11 before anyone in Washington could discover their views. As they were leaving, a report reached the French legation that Seward had ordered the arrest of Charles James Faulkner, the former American minister to France and a citizen of Virginia, on suspicion of treason. Faulkner had been popular in France, and his detention sealed the party's dislike of the secretary of state.

Faulkner's arrest was not the only diplomatic upset of that week. On August 16, Lyons was called to the State Department by Seward, who informed him, with a gleam in his eye, that one Robert Mure, a naturalized American of Scottish birth, had been arrested in New York as he was about to sail for Liverpool. Mure had been caught with treasonable correspondence hidden inside a diplomatic bag he was carrying from the British consulate in Charleston. So began a long-drawn-out affair that caused Lyons many sleepless nights. Seward pestered him with alleged crimes committed by British subjects who were said to be in cahoots with the rebels. Lyons suspected that much of Seward's professed outrage was bluster, but he could not deny there was an element of truth about some of the British consuls. One or two were highly partisan— especially Consul Bernal in Maryland.[14]

An investigation by Lyons revealed that Consul Bunch in Charleston, however, was not one of the alleged Southern sympathizers. Bunch had entrusted his diplomatic pouch to Robert Mure, who was heading to England via New York, because the Northern blockade prevented its going directly by sea from South Carolina and the Southern ban on "commercial intercourse" meant there was no post between the states. It was Mure who made the egregious error of allowing the bag to be contaminated with private letters and documents. Seward had been waiting for one of the British consuls to make a slip and was amply rewarded by the contents of this bag. He graciously allowed the sealed dispatches to be sent to London unopened, but the rest he passed on to the press. Not surprisingly, many of the letters contained vitriolic comments about the North.[15]

There was a fresh outcry for Lyons's expulsion that almost made him wish for his own removal. "I am getting a longing for home which it will be difficult to gratify," he confided to his sister on August 23, "for I don't see how can I well get out of the scrape of happening to be the Minister here just now. . . . I don't believe the Americans mean to quarrel with us and I would rather not be removed in consequence of making some blunder—and I see no other means of getting away."[16] William Howard Russell dined at the legation that evening and was shocked by the sadness emanating from Lyons.

Russell felt guilty because he suspected that his own actions had contributed to Lyons's difficulties. The first copy of his Bull Run report in *The Times* arrived in New York on August 18. Within forty-eight hours nearly every newspaper in the North carried front-page denunciations of Russell. He was branded a liar and Confederate sympathizer. One newspaper claimed he was never at Bull Run; another, that he had incited the panic himself.[17] *The New York Times* derisively called him "Bull Run Russell." He received hate mail and death threats; shop owners would not serve him; the Lincolns ignored his greeting when their carriage passed by. Seward received a mass petition from Philadelphia, demanding Russell's expulsion. Sherman and other senior officers assured him that his description of the rout was perfectly fair, but the feeling among the lower ranks was implacably hostile. A German soldier leveled his gun at Russell, shouting, "[B]ull Run Russell! You shall never write [B]ull's Runs again!" Somewhat recklessly, Russell rode up to the man and challenged him. Although the soldier later claimed it was a "choake," "as his rifle was capped and loaded and on full cock, with his finger on the trigger, I did not quite see the fun of it." General Irwin McDowell commiserated with him, saying he was "very much rejoiced to find that I was as much abused as he had been."[18]

From Beauregard's headquarters in Virginia, Samuel Phillips Day, the English correspondent for the *Morning Chronicle,* brought more ire on Russell by sending an inflammatory letter to *The New York Times* about Northern cowardice at Bull Run.[19] The day after the letter was printed, a young English officer named Henry Ronald Hislop MacIver called at Russell's lodgings asking if he knew how to find Mr. Day.

MacIver bored Russell with stories of his military adventures in India and Italy until he realized the journalist had no intention of helping him, at which point he left rather crossly. A few days later Russell heard that MacIver had been caught trying to sneak across the lines into Virginia; he assured Lord Lyons that this was one arrest the legation could ignore.

"I feel it is my doom to be the best abused man in America on both sides," Russell lamented to *The Times'* New York correspondent, J. C. Bancroft Davis. Southern newspapers were being almost as vicious about him as those in the North. "He prefers to attribute Bull's Run to Yankee cowardice rather than to Southern courage," complained the diarist Mary Chesnut.[20] In Richmond, Samuel Phillips Day was forced to deny that he had anything to do with *The Times.* Russell was furious with London editor John Thaddeus Delane for ignoring his request to preface the Bull Run report with others from American papers.[21] But the opportunity to embarrass John Bright, who had finally announced his support for the North, was too great for Delane to resist; he not only printed Russell's report without any additional commentary, but mischievously also placed the account next to a bombastic editorial from the *New York Herald* about the retribution coming to Europe once the war was won.[22]

———

Since Frank Vizetelly's last dispatch in the *Illustrated London News* had been so laudatory about Northern recruits, the contrast between his suggestion of an easy victory and Russell's description of the Union army collapse was stunning. The effect on public opinion was just as Delane hoped. Prince Albert's private secretary, General Charles Grey, whose views were typical of a certain kind of crusty conservative, celebrated Bull Run as a victory for England. "I confess I cannot help being pleased with the course things are taking in America," he wrote to his brother, Earl Grey, "because I think it will before long put an end to the fighting and leave the world in a much safer state."[23] General Grey thought a divided America would be too busy quarreling with itself to bother with Britain. The Federal army's collapse on the battlefield also appeared to vindicate those who claimed that the North was fighting the war out of vanity whereas the South was fighting for independence.[24]

The image of the rout was so powerful that no British bank was now prepared to invest in Union bonds. August Belmont, the American agent for Rothschild's, the largest bank in the world at the time, was unable to convince his own employers, let alone any of its rivals. Bull Run also overshadowed the North's subsequent successes in the following months. In late August, when the Union gained control of Cape Hatteras, North Carolina's main route to the Atlantic, the victory was largely ignored by the English press. George Henry Herbert's family was among the few who followed the campaign. Herbert's regiment, the 9th New York Volunteers, was part of an amphibious attack on the two Confederate forts guarding the inlet. The rebels were shelled out of their position, leaving Herbert and the invaders to the poisonous snakes, toads, ticks, and mosquitoes that inhabited the forty-mile-long sandbank.[25] Until recently, he had been the target of much mockery from his comrades, but the horrors of war had brought the men together.[26] "I have now quite a love for my profession," he wrote in a letter home after the battle.[27]

In London, the occupants of the American legation had their suspicions confirmed by the North's vilification in some British newspapers. "I cannot conceal from myself the fact that as a whole the English are pleased with our misfortunes," Charles Francis Adams confided miserably to a friend. "There never was any real good will towards us. Of course, you will keep these views to yourself. It is not advisable in these days for ministers abroad to be quoted."[28] It was just as well he was unaware of Palmerston's quip that Bull Run should be renamed "Yankees Run." Adams had finally settled in his new life when William Howard Russell's report of the battle appeared in *The Times*. The legation had moved into new premises in Portland Place, the archives had been unpacked and a new cataloguing system put in place. Defeat robbed these improvements of their luster. Benjamin Moran sulked in the basement, and Adams's doubts about his mission returned; recalling Seward's threatening dispatches with embarrassment, Adams wrote in his diary "we deserve it all."[29] Harriet Martineau continued to write supportive articles in the *Daily News* and *Morning Star,* but she, too, had decided that Seward was the most dangerous politician she had ever encountered: "Seward in the Cabinet is enough to ruin everything," she complained to a friend.[30] She blamed him for having allowed the passage of the Morrill Tariff, since the bill was practically "inviting the world to support the Confederate cause."[31] The Rothschild's agent, August Belmont, agreed; during the American banker's unsuccessful visit to England to drum up interest in Union bonds, he was repeatedly asked to justify the attack on British trade. Palmerston told him at a private meeting shortly after Bull Run: "We do not like slavery, but we want cotton, and we dislike very much your Morrill tariff."[32] Even the pro-Northern *Spectator* appeared to have lost patience, complaining on June 15, "The Americans are, for the moment, transported beyond the influence of common sense. With all of England sympathizing, more or less heartily, with the North, they persist in regarding her as an enemy, and seem positively anxious to change an ally . . . into an open and dangerous foe."

The eighteenth of August was Adams's fifty-fourth birthday. That evening he was despondent. "My career in life is drawing on to its close," he wrote in his diary, seeing no future for himself or his country. Yet the situation in Britain was not as desperate as he believed. Immediately after the Battle of Bull Run, Vizetelly's *Illustrated London News* had sternly reminded readers "that the victory of the South places its cause in no better position in English eyes."[33] In Liverpool, the authorities ordered Southern ships to haul down the Confederate flags that had suddenly appeared after the battle. But the most significant development by far was the rejection of the Southern envoys' request on August 7 for a formal interview with Lord Russell.* Undeterred, the Confederates sent him a thirty-nine-page letter outlining the reasons why the South had attained the right to recognition. Russell's reply was short and pointed. "Her Majesty," he replied on August 24, "has, by her royal proclamation, declared her intention to preserve a strict neutrality between the contending parties in that war."[34]

Russell's rebuff brought the relations between the Confederate diplomats to a new low. They had been arguing among themselves for some time, and after this latest blow their disagreements became increasingly personal. Not only were they isolated in England, but weeks went by while they waited for instructions from Richmond. "Our sources of information are the New York and Baltimore papers," the envoys complained to the Confederate secretary of state.[35] Left to their own devices, Yancey became the odd man out as Rost and Mann turned to Edwin De Leon, the former U.S. consul in Egypt, whose arrival in London had caused Benjamin Moran so much heartache. De Leon, a journalist by training, had originally intended to plant a few articles in the press before going home. But he soon realized that Mann needed his help; Yancey had to be controlled. "He was not a winning or persuasive man," wrote De Leon, "but a bold, antagonistic and somewhat dogmati-

---

* Lord John Russell became Earl Russell in July and moved to the House of Lords.

cal one; abrupt in manner, regardless of the elegancies and small courtesies of life, a refined man in feeling, but not deportment."[36]

Mann and De Leon tried to distract Yancey with busywork while they negotiated a secret deal with Paul Julius de Reuter's telegraph agency. Shortly before Bull Run, Reuter had personally approached both the U.S. legation and the Southerners for the exclusive right to distribute their official reports from America. Benjamin Moran had indignantly rebuffed him, but the Southerners knew there was great potential in the deal, since many English and European newspapers relied on Reuter's telegrams for their American news.[37] Moran soon rued his mistake; Reuter "is against us," he grumbled in his diary. "He systematically prostitutes the monopoly he holds to depreciate the Union . . . there is no way to remedy the business but by buying the fellow up. This I would not do."[38] The sudden alteration from a pro-Northern to a pro-Southern tone made the U.S. consul in Leith wonder if the Scottish editors had been bribed. They "exaggerate as might be expected all the little mistakes of our Northern Army into a mountain," he protested. "No sheet in South Carolina could serve them better."[39]

William Yancey was also resentful of the patronizing way he was treated by the four purchasing agents who were buying arms for the South.[40] It was his friendship with John Laird, MP, Yancey liked to point out, that had opened the door to the largest shipbuilding firm in Liverpool. In many ways, the Confederate cabinet regarded weaponry as of greater importance than diplomacy.[41] Before the war, the North had manufactured 97 percent of the country's weapons.[42] The Confederacy had declared its independence with a mere 160,000 firearms and limited means of manufacturing any more. Only one factory in the entire South, the Tredegar Ironworks in Richmond, was capable of producing artillery. There was not enough time for the chief of the Ordnance Bureau, Major Josiah Gorgas, to develop the iron mines, erect the foundries, and build the factories required to equip a modern army. The soft-spoken Confederate secretary of the navy, Stephen Mallory, found his department in an equally deprived state. The Confederate navy had no warships and only two naval dockyards, in Pensacola, Florida, and Norfolk, Virginia. Its three hundred officers were on shore leave until Mallory could provide them with vessels. From the outset, Mallory accepted that he could not construct an entire navy; the best he could hope for, and perhaps all he really needed, was a few raiders to attack

Northern merchant ships, and a small fleet of ironclad warships to attack the Federal blockade.[43]

The two Confederate agents selected by Gorgas and Mallory to run the international war effort were a far cry from the amateurs in charge of Southern diplomacy. Caleb Huse, the purchasing agent for the army, and James Dunwoody Bulloch, whom Mallory assigned to acquire ships for the navy, were men of the highest integrity and resourcefulness. Both had family and business connections in the North, but it was to the Confederacy's immeasurable good fortune that their hearts belonged to the South. Major Huse was an artillery officer who had spent six months in Europe, courtesy of the U.S. Army, studying the armaments industry.[44] The forty-year-old Bulloch was a former naval officer who had been working for a Northern mail company at the start of the war. He had not seen his native Georgia for ten years, but, he wrote, "my heart and my head were with the South."[45] He was about to sail his mail ship out of New Orleans when the guns at Fort Sumter began firing. In the face of bitter Southern opposition, Bulloch scrupulously insisted on returning the vessel to its rightful owners in New York. Only then did he offer his services to the Confederacy.

When Huse arrived in England in April, he had discovered that Northern agents had almost stripped the country of surplus arms. They were paying cash in advance, as though part of their mission was to prevent guns from reaching the Confederacy. Huse had come with limited funds; Edwin De Leon lent him $10,000 of his own money, but it was not nearly enough to outbid the Federal agents.[46] Huse was rescued by Charles Prioleau, the director of the merchant shipping firm Fraser, Trenholm and Co. in Liverpool, who agreed to advance him the payments for his weapons. Prioleau was from Charleston, a fact he proudly advertised by fixing the "bonnie blue" star of South Carolina above his front door. Moreover, his firm was the British arm of a large Charleston firm called John Fraser and Co. There was already an agreement in place between the Confederacy and Fraser, Trenholm for the company to act as the South's financial agents in Europe. But Prioleau was going much further by giving credit to Huse without a guarantee in place.

He did the same for James Bulloch when the naval agent arrived the following month in a similar condition. Bulloch had no difficulty finding Fraser, Trenholm's Liverpool headquarters, which took up an entire three-story building near the docks.[47] Although he took the precaution of using the back door, Bulloch was spotted by Federal spies who had been waiting for him. The Union report compiled on him had provided an extremely detailed description of his features; he was a "very dark, sallow man with black hair and eyes, whiskers down each cheek but shaved clean off his chin and . . . about 5'8" high."[48] For the first few days, Bulloch continued to creep about the city, until he read in the local newspapers the precise details of his mission. The information was all there, from the number of ships he was seeking to his means of paying for them. It was, Bulloch wrote in astonishment, "as if the particulars had been furnished direct from the Treasury Department or from the pages of my instructions."[49]

The man behind the exposure was the flamboyant American diplomat Henry Sanford, who had introduced William Howard Russell to Seward in March. Shortly thereafter, he had left Washington to take up the post of minister to Belgium. Sanford inspired contradictory reactions in people. Charles Sumner was one of his most loyal supporters; Charles Francis Adams had loathed him from the moment they met. Sanford was not awed by the Adams name; he himself was wealthy and well connected, had studied abroad, could speak several languages, and, although he was only thirty-eight, had served in numerous legations including those at St. Petersburg and Paris. In his own mind he was an ingenious sophisticate, a ladies' man, and a puppeteer. To others, such as Lincoln's secretary of the navy, Gideon Welles, Sanford might have been tolerable were it not for his insatiable desire "to be busy and fussy, to show pomp and power."[50]

Seward had diverted Sanford to Paris to serve as the interim minister until William L. Dayton could settle his affairs at home. But he expected Sanford to perform many roles and to travel widely. At one time, Seward entertained serious hopes that Garibaldi would agree to lead the Union war effort, since he had briefly lived in the United States during his exile in the 1850s, and one of Sanford's tasks was to persuade Garibaldi to accept Seward's offer. (Garibaldi told Sanford he was not interested unless abolition became the main objective of the war and he was made supreme commander of all U.S. forces.) Sanford's most important mission was to counteract Confederate activity in Europe "by all proper means."[51] Sanford took these words literally, and from the moment he arrived in Europe focused his formidable energy on creating a surveillance network that stretched from London to Belgium. He wanted every rebel to have at least one Federal operative dogging his footsteps.[52]

Sanford knew even before Huse and Bulloch that two more Confederate agents were on their way. One of them, navy lieutenant James North, had orders to buy or commission two armored warships for the Confederacy. The other, Major Edward Anderson, would be working with Caleb Huse.[53] They landed at Liverpool on June 25, by which time Sanford had hired a private detective of murky reputation named Ignatius Pollaky. Sanford told Seward that Pollaky operated his own agency and "knows his business." Together they were going to destroy the Confederate network from the inside. "How it will be done," wrote Sanford on July 4, "whether through a pretty mistress or a spying landlord is nobody's business; . . . but I lay . . . stress on getting . . . full accounts of their operations here. . . . I go on the doctrine that in war as in love everything is fair that will lead to success."[54] Letters and telegrams could be copied, messages intercepted, informants bribed, or perhaps the odd accident might befall an unlucky Confederate agent. One of Sanford's ideas involved paying postmen a pound a week to reveal the frequency and origin of every letter received by the Confederates.[55]

An English arms manufacturer tipped off the Confederates to the fact that they were under surveillance. "My attention was brought to these people by Mr. Isaacs who came over to my quarters one morning and asked me if I knew I was being watched," wrote Edward Anderson. "Come with me to your window then, said he, and I will point out to you a shadow that never loses sight of you—at the same time directing my notice to a rough looking fellow standing across the street on the corner." Anderson immediately went down and tried to embarrass the detective by asking for street directions, which he gave rather awkwardly.

> He was a plain, countrified looking man, roughly clad and by no means bearing about him the appearance of a detective officer. Subsequently, when I came to know him better I was impressed with the effect produced by dress, for when I met my man on the following day, he was accoutred in a neat suit of black clothing like a gentleman, and on subsequent occasions in different costumes . . . sometimes with moustache and whiskers and again clean shaved. I never failed however to recognize my shadow. Assisting him were one or two others.[56]

On another occasion, while returning on the night train from Paris, Anderson shared a carriage with one of his shadows. "We had some little talk together," he recorded in his diary, "but neither of us learned much of the other."[57] He was not alone in having such face-to-face encounters. Suspicious figures seemed to loiter in every doorway. "They have agents employed for no other purpose," commented Caleb Huse.[58] Sanford intended to keep all the Confederates under surveillance, but he realized that James Bulloch had to be the chief target. "He is the most dangerous man the South have here and fully up to his business," he told Seward. "I am disbursing at the rate of £150 a month on this one man which will give you an idea of the importance I attach to his movements." He hoped that Bulloch might try to slip off to the Continent, where it would be relatively easy to have him arrested for failing to carry the proper documentation. "Of course, no one official would appear in the matter," he assured Seward.[59] Sanford was less concerned about Lieutenant North, whose contribution to the Southern war effort puzzled the detectives. North appeared to be working on his own, but what he was doing, apart from costing Sanford money in espionage expenses, remained a mystery. He seemed to spend a great deal of time moping and, from the look of his intercepted mail, complaining.

Sanford's fears about Bulloch had been prescient. The Confederate agent knew that the real threat to his operations was not from the spies (who were irritating), but from the legal obstacles created by the Foreign Enlistment Act. Before he set about any naval business, Bulloch obtained expert legal opinion on what the act allowed and disallowed, hoping to uncover any loopholes. To his surprise, he discovered it would be relatively easy to circumvent the rules: the act forbade a belligerent nation from outfitting or equipping warlike vessels in British waters, but there was nothing to prevent the construction of a ship with an unusual design. A vessel could be built in Britain with gun ports, for example, but it could not leave with any guns on board; it could have a magazine to store gunpowder, but would not be allowed to set sail with the powder present.

Bulloch went to work as soon as he received his legal advice. Within a few weeks he had made two contracts, one for a gunboat and the other for a top-of-the-line warship with copper-plated bunkers and enough storage space to hold a year's worth of spare parts. For the first, Bulloch used an intermediary to hide the involvement of the Confederacy and invented some Italian owners who were expecting delivery in eight months' time.[60] To give authenticity to the Italian claim, the vessel was called the *Oreto* for the time being. But the other ship did not require the same subterfuge, since it was being built by Laird and Sons, the Liverpool company owned by Yancey's friend John Laird. With a nod and a wink, Lairds accepted the explanation that the modifications were innocent. This vessel, Project No. 290 on Lairds' books, was going to cost a staggering £47,500, to be paid in five installments.[61]

With the first part of his mission now fulfilled, Bulloch turned his attention to helping Caleb Huse buy munitions. The victory at Bull Run lent urgency to their mission. "We want arms," implored LeRoy Walker, the Confederate secretary of war, "and must have them if they are to be had . . . the enemy is daily augmenting his supplies."[62] By the end of August, the agents had amassed so considerable a quantity of supplies that their most pressing problem was the threat of discovery by the authorities.[63] Now the Confederates found themselves stymied by the neutrality proclamation. Bulloch was unable to persuade any shipping owner to break the blockade. Finally, after much negotiation, Bulloch and Anderson made a deal with Fraser, Trenholm to rent space on the *Bermuda,* one of the company's fastest steamers, which was docked at Hartlepool on the east coast and already slated for use during the cotton season, when the blockade would be tested in earnest.

Henry Sanford knew about the *Bermuda* and had a plan that involved the U.S. Navy pouncing on her as soon as she reached the open sea "no matter what her papers." "We can discuss the matter with the English afterwards," he asserted confidently.[64] Seward ignored his suggestion, and Lord Russell turned down Charles Francis Adams's request to detain the *Bermuda,* since the minister was unable to show that she was anything other than a private ship on a private commercial venture. The officials in Hartlepool had observed her loading, and even noted that arms and ammunition were being "packed to resemble earthenware."[65] But there was no legal reason for her detention and the vessel sailed away on August 22, despite the fact that everyone concerned knew her real purpose and destination.

Fraser, Trenholm and Co. had great hopes for the *Bermuda.* Every Southerner, not to mention every British merchant with a half-decent cargo ship, believed that the blockade was a fiction. Latest estimates put the entire U.S. Navy blockading fleet at forty-two steamships. The Southern coastline extended over 3,500 miles, from the tip of Virginia to the banks of the Rio Grande in Texas, and included hundreds of ports, bays, and inlets. Almost two hundred navigable rivers fed into the sea;

many harbors had several entrances and numerous channels for hiding ships. Much of the South lay behind enormous sandbars that acted like a double coastline, allowing ships to sail from port to port without ever having to go out onto the open sea. When these considerations were added to the poor condition of the U.S. Navy, it seemed incomprehensible to Southerners that any country, let alone Britain, would accept that the blockade met the main legal requirement for its international recognition, namely, that it was real and being enforced on a daily basis. They were hoping that the Royal Navy would sweep away the miserable little wooden ships stifling the South's commerce and declare the ports once again open to the world.

Ordered by the Foreign Office to keep a record of blockade activity, the various British consuls responded by saying there really wasn't any. Phrases such as "totally inefficient" and "totally ineffective" appeared with regularity.[66] Yet the picture conveyed by the statistics was misleading. The South was not one vast open harbor, ready to receive and distribute all the goods that Europe cared to ship. If that had been the case, New York would never have been so vital a trade partner. Only ten Southern ports were deep enough for transatlantic shipping; and just five of those (Charleston, Mobile, New Orleans, Savannah, and Wilmington) were adequately provided with road and rail links.[67] The U.S. ships merely needed to be well placed rather than omnipresent. The Union Blockade Board, instituted by the secretary of the navy in June, was already at work analyzing the Confederacy's strategic weaknesses.

Two days after the departure of the *Bermuda,* Anthony Trollope and his wife, Rose, set sail for Boston. They arrived on September 5, after a brief stop in Halifax, beating the *Bermuda* to America by two weeks. Trollope had long wanted to visit the United States in order to write a travel book. It would be a break from writing fiction and perhaps, he hoped, might even put an end to the notoriety attached to the Trollope name. His mother had intended to be amusing rather than offensive in her *Domestic Manners of the Americans,* but the book had caused such damage to Anglo-American relations that Trollope had often thought, "If I could do anything to mitigate the soreness, if I could in any small degree add to the good feeling which should exist between two nations which ought to love each other so well . . . I should."[68]

Boston literary circles welcomed the Trollopes with warmth that belied the harsh statements against Britain in the press. The only sharpness they encountered was directed at Rose; people often asked her if she regretted writing *Domestic Manners,* to which she patiently replied that she was not her mother-in-law. Trollope had the occasional argument over Britain's neutrality. Bostonians, in common with the rest of the North, believed that England's greed for cotton was the real reason it had granted belligerency to the South.

But no one abused Trollope with the freedom or viciousness with which Washingtonians insulted William Howard Russell. Every obstruction was now thrown in Russell's way. Although General McClellan was unfailingly polite to him and never turned down his request for a pass, Russell found that the guards and sentries took a mean delight in turning him away. He did not know when his punishment would end, and while it continued, he was useless as a war correspondent.

Frank Vizetelly had no such impediments and was able to witness the rehabilitation of the 79th Highlanders when he visited them on September 11. Among them, Ebenezer Wells had been promoted to wagon master, a change that increased the young man's chances of survival but kept him on the move all day long. During one grueling marathon, his raw and bloody feet swelled out of their boots. "After cutting my boots here and there," he wrote, "I was obliged to throw them away and marched the last six miles on a stony road, nearly barefoot."[69] The 79th Highlanders were now deemed trustworthy enough to participate in a reconnaissance mission on a Confederate outpost near Lewinsville, a small town less than thirteen miles from Washington.

Vizetelly sketched the aftermath as McClellan greeted the returning soldiers with a dip of his hat. The artist was delighted to have something to occupy himself for a couple of days; the endless training was driving him mad.[70] Russell was also bored. "Time passes away in expectation of some onward movement, or desperate attack, or important strategical movements; and night comes to reassemble a few friends, Americans and English, at my rooms or elsewhere, to talk over the disappointed hopes of the day, to speculate on the future, to chide each dull delay, and to part with a hope that tomorrow would be more lively than to-day," he wrote in his diary on September 11. General McClellan would probably spend all winter pummeling his volunteer army into shape, a prospect Russell found extremely disheartening. "I like the man," he wrote in his diary. "But I do not think he is equal to his occasion or his place."[71] "In truth," he added, "life is becoming exceedingly monotonous and uninteresting. . . . But for the hospitality of Lord Lyons to the English residents, the place would be nearly insufferable."[72]

"The only thing that makes me stick out here," Russell wrote to Delane on September 13, "is the determination not to show a white feather for these fellows." He refused to follow the suggestion of Mowbray Morris, the managing editor of *The Times,* to seek safety in the British legation. The quickest way to stop the death threats and petitions against him, Russell told Delane, would be to tone down the anti-Northern bias in the newspaper: "I don't want to ask you to sacrifice the policy of *The Times* to me, but I would like you if possible not to sacrifice me."[73] He warned Delane that his penchant for quoting the rabble-rousing *New York Herald* as though it were the chief mouthpiece of the Union would eventually rebound on *The Times,* but the editor denied he was baiting the Americans. It was, Delane wrote back, "simply that we don't mean to be bullied by a so-called Power that can scarcely defend its capital against its fellow-citizens."[74]

Delane's sarcastic reply to Russell showed how little attention he was paying to the journalist's reports. By the beginning of October, McClellan had equipped and trained more than 100,000 soldiers who, even if he felt they were not yet ready to be deployed, would never drop their arms and stampede off the battlefield as they had done at Bull Run.[75] The humiliation suffered in July had made the North determined to crush not only the South but also her perceived allies. The treatment of blockade runners became harsher. When Edward Archibald, the British consul in New York, went to Fort Lafayette to check on the welfare of an imprisoned crew from a captured blockade runner, he found thirty men squeezed into a small, airless cell with barely enough headroom to stand. A bucket in the corner was the only lavatory, a small basin on a table their only access to water. Archibald took down their statements by the light from the doorway "using my hat for a desk. The men had lost everything except for the clothes on their backs and these were filthy and infested." The prisoners were so dejected that he arranged for new clothing to be sent to them at his own expense.[76] The international treaty governing the application of blockades forbade the sentencing or imprisonment of foreign blockade runners; they could be held for questioning only. But the timing of their release was at the discretion of the authorities. It could take just three days or, if Archibald lodged a complaint, as long as five months.[77]

Bull Run also made Northern politicians more realistic about the challenges ahead. Seward quietly reserved his nationalism for his dispatches and began to encourage foreign officers to volunteer for the Union, knowing that the army would benefit from their experience.[78] His open-door policy caused problems for the American legation in London, where would-be volunteers were constantly calling on Adams, expecting to be given a commission and free passage to America.[79] But Seward was unrepentant; he would rather keep them "on the Northern side," he told William Howard Russell, "lest some really good man should get among the rebels."[80]

The New York Times began to carry frequent reports of a major or colonel, late of the British Army, "who has tendered his services [to] the President."[81] Major General Charles Havelock—the brother of the more famous Major General Henry Havelock of India—discovered that this was not always the best way, however. When Lincoln appointed him to McClellan's staff, the general retaliated for the encroachment on his authority by refusing to acknowledge Havelock's presence. Leonard Douglas Hay Currie, captain of the 19th Regiment of Foot and a distinguished veteran of the Indian and Crimean wars, had more success by applying to the governor of New York. "Thinking I might be of use," he explained, "I was glad when an opportunity was offered me to place my services at the disposal of the government."[82] He was sent to Brigadier General W. F. "Baldy" Smith, who immediately took him on as his assistant adjutant general.

Seward was responsible for recruiting one of the least likely British volunteers to appear in Washington: Major John Fitzroy De Courcy, the British magistrate on San Juan Island during the "Pig War." De Courcy lived for soldiering, and rather than molder on the island during the ongoing stalemate, he wrote to Seward to ask if he could lead a regiment. Amazed and delighted by the irony, Seward invited him to Washington. Frances and Fanny Seward were disappointed to have the brusque soldier thrust upon them during their brief visit to the capital. Fanny, Seward's eighteen-year-old daughter, complained that De Courcy's presence spoiled her last evening with her father. She might have forgiven him had he been handsome, but De Courcy's face reminded her of a rocky beach and he suffered from "an imperfection in one of his eyes." It was

Reconnaissance made by General Stoneman, accompanied by the Comte de Paris and the Duc de Chartres, by Frank Vizetelly.

typical of Seward to sacrifice the needs of his family for a moment of transient importance; but he did follow through on his promise to De Courcy, who was made a colonel of the 16th Ohio Volunteers.

The hostility with which Britain was regarded in the North meant that none of the British volunteers received as much attention as the Comte de Paris, the Bourbon pretender to the French throne, and his brother the Duc de Chartres. The arrival of another set of French royalty (albeit the exiled kind whose only hope of gaining military experience was to go to America) was hailed as proof of the excellent relations between the two countries. Seward waived the rules so that they would not have to take the U.S. oath of allegiance. The count entered the army as plain "Captain Paris" and his brother as "Captain Charters." Their uncle, the Prince de Joinville, who had accompanied his nephews on the journey in order to place his son in the U.S. Naval Academy, politely turned down the offer of a command in the navy.

Lord Lyons ignored the spectacle of Seward paying assiduous attention to the former British magistrate of San Juan Island. Of all the provocations he had endured since August, the welcome given to De Courcy was among the least troubling. Seward "is at present very wild with Lord

Lyons," William Howard Russell remarked to Delane in September, after the secretary of state had embarrassed Lyons by leaking to the press a portion of their correspondence—selectively edited to make the minister appear arrogant and Seward patriotic.

The letters in question concerned the arrests of British subjects on charges of sedition. Seward's power over Lyons had increased dramatically during the summer. Every case of forcible enlistment and underage volunteering went through his office, and now, since Lincoln had suspended the writ of habeas corpus for a large section of the North, Seward had gained the additional power to detain indefinitely all persons suspected of treason. "I am afraid that he takes a personal pleasure in spying and arresting," Lyons wrote to Lord Russell in a rare outburst after Seward harangued him for an hour before casually taking out his pen and signing the release of a British prisoner.[*83]

Lyons was relieved that the arrests for sedition were not solely confined to British subjects, though they made up almost 15 percent of the suspects in prison.[84] No one was exempt, he informed the Foreign Office. Lyons had heard from his friend the English actress Fanny Kemble, who remained tied to the United States because of her two daughters, that her former husband had been arrested in Philadelphia and incarcerated without trial at Fort Lafayette in New York. The family was discovering, as had Lyons, that "it is vain to resort to the Courts of law for redress."[85] Rose Greenhow was also arrested during one of Seward's sweeps of rebel sympathizers in Washington; in deference to her status in Washington she was placed under house arrest rather than carted off to prison in a blaze of publicity.

Russell watched as the military authorities hounded Samuel Phillips Day out of Washington when the English journalist came through the lines on October 1. Edmund Monson, Lord Lyons's private secretary, told Day that the offensive letters he had been sending to *The New York Times* put him beyond the help of the legation. Day sailed for home on October 12 on the *Young America,* already planning his revenge on the

---

* Seward's bullying of Lyons on the subject of political arrests played into the hands of his critics. A story spread through Washington and into the history books that he boasted to Lyons, "My Lord, I can touch a bell on my right hand, and order the arrest of a citizen of Ohio. I can touch the bell again, and order the arrest of a citizen of New York. Can the Queen of England, in her dominions, do as much?" Seward's "little bell" became famous throughout both North and South.

North. Russell envied him. "Could it not be possible to arrange for me to go home for a month?" he begged Delane two days later. He missed his family, but even if he wanted to stay, "It is impossible to express one's opinion freely. The press and the politicians would desire nothing better than to hunt me out of this country."[86]

Seward "will probably play out the play and send me my passports," Lyons wrote to Lord Russell two weeks later. "If he is in his present mood, he will be glad to find a pretext for performing other half-violent acts of the same kind." But, he added despondently, "this cannot go on forever." Some incident would push the war of words into a war of arms; Lyons felt the crackling animosity in the air. William Howard Russell could sense it, too. A fury and desire to punish England was evident in the press, in politics, in the army, and among ordinary citizens. "The storm may blow over," he wrote to Delane; "now it rages furiously."[87]

SEVEN

"It Takes Two
to Make a Quarrel"

An unlikely friendship—The Fingal *escapes—The success of Confederate propaganda—Seward rues his mistake—Appointment of Mason and Slidell—Capture of the* Trent

The departure of Samuel Phillips Day on the *Young America* from New York in the middle of October coincided with the escape of the *Theodora* out of Charleston. The cargo on board the swift blockade runner was not cotton, but the successors to Pierre Rost and William Yancey. Frustrated by their failure to secure diplomatic recognition after the victory at Manassas, Confederate president Jefferson Davis had selected two of the South's most prominent and experienced politicians, Senators James Mason and John Slidell, to be the new Confederate commissioners in Europe. Slidell was to go to Paris, Mason was to remain in London, and Ambrose Dudley Mann would be transferred to Brussels.

In place of the broad suggestions given to the original commissioners, Mason carried with him a long and detailed set of instructions on how to approach the British government. In particular, the Confederate cabinet ordered him to ram home the illegality of the blockade under the Declaration of Paris, in the hope that this would encourage Britain to force the reopening of Southern ports. Without its own fleet, the Confederacy remained incapable of lifting the blockade. So far, just one cruiser had been launched: a converted passenger ship renamed CSS *Sumter,* whose limited capabilities made it effective only as a raider against merchant ships.

The chronic shortages caused by the blockade were forcing whole regiments to sit idle for want of arms and munitions. Even before the departure of Mason and Slidell, Davis had sent an agent to England, his instructions hidden for safekeeping inside the sole of his boot, imploring Caleb Huse to "send forward supplies as rapidly and as securely as possible. . . . You will not allow yourself to be governed by the political agents of the Government, but act upon your own responsibility."[1] Davis's exhortation had been anticipated; frustrated by the slow pace of shipments, Edward Anderson and James Bulloch had pooled their funds and bought their own steamship, the *Fingal*.

The challenge for the Confederates lay in keeping the identity of the *Fingal* from Henry Sanford's spies; otherwise the U.S. Navy would have no difficulty in tracking and capturing the cargo before it reached Savannah. They were helped by one of Anderson's most important suppliers, who had a relative in the Foreign Office. "Money will accomplish anything in England," wrote Anderson. "The bait took, and every night before I retired to bed I was thoroughly advised of all [Charles Francis Adams's] operations for the day."[2] He was counting on the mole to give sufficient warning if the *Fingal* was discovered.

Anderson frequently passed Federal agents in the street, but he had learned to tell the difference between those who were genuine arms purchasers like himself and those whose real business was to keep a watch on his own movements. "My friend McGuire is indefatigable in his attentions towards me," he observed. "His instructions must be very stringent for he posts himself opposite the very door of the Hotel." Ignatius Pollaky, Sanford's detective, insisted that he had a "fix on upon every agent of the rebellion," but still the name and location of the *Fingal* remained a mystery.[3] Sanford had been successfully intercepting the Confederates' telegrams until clerks at the Liverpool telegraph office became suspicious and uncovered the operation. This blunder enabled the Confederates to lodge an official complaint with the authorities. Reports appeared in the press, accusing the U.S. legation of setting up an illegal "system of political espionage and terrorism" in Britain.[4] Charles Francis Adams was mortified to be blamed for Sanford's handiwork. The spying "has been productive of great evil," raged Moran in his diary. "Not one farthing of good has it done us."[5]

Adams had never imagined that his post would be so troublesome and difficult. "Indeed the position of a minister at this Court is far more important and responsible than I had supposed," he admitted in his diary.[6] It disturbed him that Seward would stoop to playing dirty tricks against his opponents. "Early training in the school of New York State politics" had blunted some of his finer qualities, Adams thought. "[This] shows itself in a somewhat brusque and ungracious manner towards the representatives of foreign nations . . . [and], in a rather indiscriminate appliance of means to an end." Adams had no desire to be a part of Seward's schemes, but equally he resented learning about them in the press.

A suspicion that Seward's behavior was the real reason behind Lord Russell's invitation to stay at Abergeldie Castle in Scotland made Adams extremely reluctant to accept. He had no wish to travel a thousand miles in order to be grilled about his wayward chief, especially since his confidence in Seward had declined over the summer. Benjamin Moran was delighted to have the opportunity to act as the minister's conscience. "I have advised him to go, and he probably will," he wrote complacently in his diary on September 21. Two days later, Adams reluctantly boarded the train for the overnight journey to Aberdeen.

Although Seward's threats of war had died down since Bull Run, the substitution of high rhetoric for low-level harassment had made the British cabinet nervous about the U.S. secretary of state's intentions. Knowing that Adams shared his dislike of ceremony, Lord Russell had asked him to his private retreat in Scotland in the hope that the informal setting would enable them to be frank toward each other; it had worked with John Lothrop Motley, who had visited earlier in the month before taking up his new post at the U.S. legation in Vienna. During Adams's visit, Russell deliberately avoided any searching interviews or prolonged conversations of the type the minister dreaded. Their "desultory" talks ebbed and flowed around family meals and bracing country walks along the wooded banks of the river Dee.

Russell's campaign to charm Adams was a complete success. "He was for the first time," recorded Adams, "easy, friendly, I might almost call it genial . . . I liked him better the nearer I saw him." Some of the misunderstandings and fears from the summer, which had seemed so intractable, simply melted away. "The result of this protracted interview was decidedly advantageous," wrote Adams. "In the first place we tacitly grew into more confidence in one another."[7]

Refreshed by his initiation into the pleasures of alfresco tea with Scotch eggs and boiled peat water, Adams's good mood lasted until his return to the legation on September 27, where he found a scene of per-

fect chaos. Benjamin Moran was losing his temper at an unruly crowd of
would-be volunteers and passport seekers while the secretary, Charles
Wilson, who, if not drunk, was only recently sober, sat hunched behind
his desk reading the newspapers. Only after the legation had been
cleared and the latest surveillance reports retrieved from the piles of rubbish in Wilson's corner did Adams learn that no progress at all had been
made in finding Bulloch's secret cargo ship. He was about to give up on
the project when a stranger came to the legation on October 1 offering to
sell information about the rebels. Much as it offended Adams's sensibilities to pay him, he realized it was their best chance to thwart the Confederates: "The truth is," he wrote in his diary, "of late they have been too
cunning for us."[8]

Ten days later, the Confederates' mole in the Foreign Office sent
word that Adams knew the name and the location of the *Fingal*. Anderson and Bulloch went down to Holyhead in Wales on October 15 but
were too late to prevent a customs officer from boarding the *Fingal,* his
pen and notebook in hand. Bulloch was aghast: "I thought of the rifles
and sabres in the hold, and the ill-armed pickets on the Potomac waiting
and longing for them."[9] The two men took a desperate risk. Anderson
tricked the customs officer into leaving the steamer. Then, instead of
sailing into dock as promised, Bulloch ordered the *Fingal* to weigh anchor and "we cracked on all the steam her boilers would bear." They expected to be fired upon or chased by a customs ship, but nothing
happened. "It was half past eight o'clock before we got fairly out to sea
beyond the reach of batteries and pursuit," wrote Anderson. "How my
heart lightened as I looked at the blue water again and found myself on
board a good staunch ship once more."[10]

Shortly after the *Fingal*'s escape, the U.S. legation heard that the
Bermuda had arrived at Savannah. "Wilson pretends to disbelieve it,"
complained Moran on October 17. "But I fear it is fact." Otherwise, he
thought, there would not be so many advertisements in *The Times* for investors to buy shares in blockade-running ships. "John Bull would violate every law of honor and every principle of justice if he can secure his
own ends thereby," Moran declared.[11] The same criticism was being leveled, with equal rancor, by the British government against Seward.

"Mr. Seward appears to have deemed it advisable to get up a little excitement about the European Powers again" was how Lord Lyons

wryly characterized the situation to Lord Russell on October 22.[12] William Howard Russell was not constrained like Lyons by the language of diplomacy. Seward was up to "his usual tricks," he noted in a letter to J. C. Bancroft Davis. "He is determined to resort to his favorite panacea of making the severed States reunited by a war with England."[13] Neither Lyons nor William Howard Russell thought it was a coincidence that Seward's latest salvos against England had started when public confidence in the Lincoln administration was wavering. "A victory would do much to set things straight," Lyons had written privately to Lord Russell in September, "but some of the illusions with which the war was begun are gone forever. The appearance of unanimity in the North has completely vanished."[14] Lyons was referring to the political controversy started by Union general John C. Frémont in the border state of Missouri, who in August had announced the emancipation of all slaves in the state belonging to Confederate sympathizers. Frémont's impetuous act not only threatened to tear the army apart, with some regiments appearing ready to resign en masse rather than fight for the Negro, but also gave the strongest possible incentive to Missouri and the other slave-owning border states to join forces with the Confederacy.

Lincoln was already considering the removal of Frémont from his post when General McClellan suffered his first significant defeat. It was only a small engagement between two brigades at a place called Ball's Bluff, forty miles upriver from Washington, but the high number of Federal soldiers killed and wounded shook Lincoln's confidence in his new military commander. The possibility that the South might grow from eleven to thirteen or fourteen states could tip the scales against the North. The next day, October 22, Lincoln announced to his cabinet that he was repudiating both Frémont and his emancipation declaration. He was prepared to lose the support of the radical abolitionists in his own party, but not that of Kentucky, Missouri, and Maryland, which would make "the job on our hands," Lincoln confessed, "too large for us."[15]

Lord Lyons had at first paid little attention to Seward's rather obvious attempts to distract attention from the U.S. government's woes.[16] He was too busy trying to prevent the secretary of state from undermining the Anglo-French alliance. Seward had begun to woo Emperor Napoleon III in the delusion that France was the friendlier of the two nations.*[17] When Henri Mercier, the French minister, warned him that his government was losing patience with the blockade, Seward hinted that if the emperor withdrew his recognition of Southern belligerency, the North would do everything in its power to ensure a steady supply of cotton. Rather than being grateful for this show of favoritism, the French saw it as further proof that the North was heading for defeat. Mercier regarded Southern independence as a fait accompli and was trying to persuade Lyons that it was in everybody's interest for the Great Powers to recognize the Confederacy. Logic must prevail over sentiment, Mercier patiently but persistently argued. Lyons refused to be drawn in: "I take, perhaps, a more hopeful view than M. Mercier does of the Military prospects of the North," he explained to Lord Russell.[19]

However, Lyons could not ignore Seward's declaration on October 26 that the North was "expelling" Consul Bunch from Charleston (where it had no effective jurisdiction) for holding talks with the Confederacy about privateering. The staff at the British legation was furious that Seward had made no reference to the French consul, who had also taken part in the negotiations. Lyons maintained a stony silence during his interview with Seward, knowing that it would annoy the secretary of state to be denied a reaction. "Mr. Bunch has merely been selected as a safer object of attack than the British or French Government," he reported angrily to Lord Russell after the meeting.[20] It was not the transparency of Seward's motives that worried Lyons but the American's failure to realize the impact of his words and deeds on the international stage. "He always tries violence in language first," observed Lyons, "and then runs the risk of pledging himself and the nation to violent courses, if he be taken at once at his word."[21]

When Lord Russell heard the news about Consul Bunch, he understood that his efforts with Adams were unlikely to have the slightest effect on Seward's behavior. "It is the business of Seward to feed the mob with sacrifices every day," he wrote to Lord Palmerston, "and we happen to be the most grateful food he can offer." As long as there were no actions ac-

---

* Lyons suspected that Seward and Mercier had only a vague idea of what the other was saying, and although he faithfully reported all that Mercier told him, Lyons warned Lord Russell not to take his words too literally. "Your Lordship will not fail to recollect that the conversation, which was carried on in English, was repeated to me by M. Mercier in French, and that it took place between a Frenchman not very familiar with English, and an American having little or no knowledge of French."[18]

companying the secretary of state's words, Russell thought the safest course was to ignore him, since Seward was a "singular mixture of the bully and coward."[22] Palmerston agreed, although he wished that more regiments had been sent to Canada as a warning to Seward against becoming too cocky. But the British cabinet's anxieties were dismissed by the new secretary for war, Sir George Cornewall Lewis, who advised them not to be fooled by Seward's charade of aggression: "The Washington government is violent and unscrupulous," he wrote, "but it is not insane."[23]

Throughout Britain, however, the effect of Seward's threats, which he ensured were known to the press, was to swing public opinion dramatically away from the North. The mills had already moved to short time in order to preserve their dwindling cotton stocks. *Reynolds's Newspaper,* a popular weekly aimed at the working classes, blamed the North-

KING COTTON BOUND;
Or, The Modern Prometheus.

Punch acknowledges the threat posed by the Union blockade to "King Cotton."

ern blockade rather than the Southern cotton embargo for the looming crisis. "England must break the Blockade," cried an editorial in early autumn, "or Her Millions must starve."[24] Henry Adams was trying without success to plant favorable articles in the press. "I hope that you will see in some of the London newspapers if not my writing, at least my hand," he wrote in confidence to his brother Charles Francis Jr. "They need it, confound 'em."[25] Benjamin Moran was convinced that the Confederates were either feeding Reuter with false information or encouraging him to slant his news. "That he is under the influence of the rebels is too clear to be the subject of doubt," he fulminated in his diary. Only after the news service turned a recent Federal victory into a defeat was Moran able to persuade Charles Francis Adams to deliver a friendly warning to Reuter.[26]

Henry Adams complained to Charles Francis Jr. that their father would not engage in any form of journalism or public speaking. Although the senior Adams received many more invitations than his Confederate rivals, he invariably turned them down. While he agreed to attend the Lord Mayor's dinner on November 9 on the assurance that he would not be called upon to speak, William Yancey eagerly accepted an invitation to the less coveted Fishmongers' Company because there was a chance that he might.[27]

The departing Confederate commissioners had been working hard, they informed Richmond, to cultivate anyone "likely to bring to bear a favorable influence on the British cabinet."[28] But the greatest Southern propaganda coup had nothing to do with the envoys' efforts. In September a book entitled *The American Union,* which defended the South's claim to independence, became a surprise bestseller. The author was a Liverpool businessman named James Spence whose travels in America had persuaded him that while slavery was doomed, the cultural and economic differences between the North and South would never be overcome. In his opinion, it was politically and morally unfeasible for two such distinct entities to remain united.

The great strength of *The American Union* was its sober style and earnest attempt to discuss the merits of secession. Although Northern sympathizers disagreed with Spence's arguments, they had to admit that the book was too well written to dismiss. "It is studiously suited to the English taste," explained the abolitionist Richard Webb, "being moderate in tone, lucid in style, and free from personalities."[29] Moreover, the subject matter—independence—appealed to English sensibilities. "I believe Englishmen instinctively sympathize with rebels," the American vice consul, Henry Wilding, commented to his former superior, Nathaniel Hawthorne, so long as "the rebellion be not against England."[30] "Why do the Southern agents have it all their own way?" grumbled Charles Francis Jr. when he heard about the success of *The American Union* and other polemics. "Our agents abroad apparently confine their efforts to cabinets and officials and leave public opinion and the press to take care of themselves."[31]

Henry Adams assured his brother that the situation in England was worse than he could imagine; even "our own friends fail to support us." Lincoln's rejection of General Frémont and his emancipation proclamation had played into the Confederates' hands; without the slavery issue, the North was simply a large country fighting a rebellion in its nether regions. "Look at the Southerners here," Henry wrote indignantly on October 25; "every man is inspired by the idea of independence and liberty while we are in a false position."[32] *The Times* seemed to take a malicious pleasure in repeating as often as it could the hoary claim that the war was a contest between one side fighting for "empire" and the other "for independence."[33] The only politician who was prepared to attack Delane's crafty misrepresentation of the conflict was the Duke of Argyll, who delivered a ringing defense of the Union at his annual estate dinner on November 2. "I do not care whether we look at it from the Northern or from the Southern point of view," the *Illustrated London News* reported him as saying. "Gentlemen, I think we ought to admit, in fairness to the Americans, that there are some things worth fighting for, and that national existence is one of these."[34]

The public in both countries would have been shocked had they known Seward's real thoughts about the state of Anglo-American relations. Although the secretary of state was always talking as though he were locked in a life-and-death struggle with Britain, he knew that there was no desire in London for conflict with the North. Even if he discounted Lyons's protestations and Adams's dispatches, John Motley, whose opinion Seward trusted, had been giving him verbatim reports of his conversations with persons of note in England, including Lord Russell, Prince Albert, and the Queen. Motley's letters contained "a most cheering account of the real sentiment of honest sympathy existing in the best Class of English Society towards us," exclaimed the president's private secretary John Hay, who was present when Seward read out sections to Lincoln.[35]

The truth was that Seward cared little for what foreign governments thought about the war so long as they obeyed his directive to regard it as a minor insurrection and not a fully fledged rebellion. He worried even less about foreign sentiment and persistently ignored the warnings from his consuls and Henry Sanford that the North was squandering its goodwill abroad.[36] "Foreign sympathy . . . never did and never can create or maintain any state," Seward wrote flippantly to John Bigelow, the new American consul in Paris.[37] But once he learned that the new Confederate commissioners were to be Senators Mason and Slidell, Seward started to feel anxious about the North's representation in Europe. John Bright's complaint about the Morrill Tariff having "done immense harm to the friendly feeling which ought to exist here towards you," and Motley's observation of the "very great change in English public sympathy since the passing of the Morrill Tariff," suddenly became the talk of the State Department.[38]

William Howard Russell had disregarded rumors that Seward was looking for emissaries to send to Europe until he bumped into him on November 4 and learned that the stories were true. "He begged of me to come and dine with him tomorrow," Russell recorded in his diary, "to meet Mr. Everett who is here as one of a secret commission."[39] But having embraced the need for special agents abroad, Seward discovered that it was no easy task to find the right men. The august Edward Everett, a former secretary of state, minister to Britain, governor of and senator for Massachusetts, and the greatest orator of his generation, changed his mind two days later, and several other candidates showed a similar reluctance. Finally Seward was able to enlist four suitable representatives: General Winfield Scott, who had been forced to retire from the army; John Hughes, the Roman Catholic archbishop of New York, who would battle with Slidell for the sympathy of the French; the Episcopal bishop of Ohio, Charles McIlvaine, who was to woo the Anglican clergy; and his own old political partner Thurlow Weed, who Seward knew would be more than a match for James Mason. William Howard Russell could see why Seward admired Weed as a political lobbyist, although he doubted that the skill would serve him as well in a foreign environment. "Thurlow is a crafty old fellow," he wrote to the *Times* correspondent in

New York, "but he will be of small weight among the polished politicians of France or England."[40] Weed, Archbishop Hughes, and General Scott sailed together on November 8 from New York. Weed was angered by a newspaper report that exposed the nature of their mission. He was sure that Charles Sumner had either written it or told the writer what to say in order to embarrass Seward. Weed had seen him the day before and noticed that he had a "hang-dog look." But they had only Seward to blame for the pandemonium on the docks.

All persons wishing to depart from New York, including foreigners, were suddenly required to have their passport countersigned by the secretary of state. Among those most severely affected were British travelers passing through New York on ship connections to other ports. British consul Archibald's Manhattan office was filled with stranded families seeking his help. Some of them would have to wait another month for the next boat to their destination. Even a British Army officer who was en route from Canada to his regiment in Nassau was forcibly detained at the quayside. Archibald begged Lyons to make Seward appoint a civil servant with signatory powers, so at least the process might be done in New York.[41] Archibald assumed that the purpose of all this was to annoy England.[42] He was not alone in thinking so; Anthony Trollope accused Seward of having "resolved to make every Englishman in America feel himself in some way punished because England had not assisted the North."[43]

The real reason lay with Mason and Slidell. Initial reports claimed that they had managed to sail out of Charleston on board CSS *Nashville,* another converted steamship like the *Sumter.* The secretary of the navy, Gideon Welles, had immediately dispatched several warships to run her down before she reached Europe, but the only ship that spotted the *Nashville*—USS *Connecticut*—lost sight of her in the pursuit. Then Seward received a different report: the Confederates had traveled by way of Cuba and were going to dock in New York in early November.[44] No longer sure what to believe, Seward imposed the passport regulation to save the administration from the embarrassment of the Confederates' escaping in full view.

The *Nashville* was not carrying the envoys, although her mission was no less dangerous to the North. The Confederate secretary of the navy, Stephen Mallory, had ordered her to England to be fitted as a war steamer. The *Nashville* had reached St. George's harbor in Bermuda when the *Fingal* arrived on November 2, carrying Edward Anderson and James Bulloch. The two ships anchored only a few hundred yards from each other. "The *Nashville* ran up the Confederate flag as we stood in," recorded Anderson, "& I supposed had been sent out by Mr. Mallory for the express purpose of communicating with us, but how to learn this was the question." Their disguise was working a little too well. "To all intents and purposes we were an English merchant steamer," he recorded. "We were sporting the British flag, had an English captain and crew, and desired above all things to keep our movements secret. To send a boat to the *Nashville* direct would be to betray ourselves." It was a ridiculous situation. The ships rocked gently side by side, neither daring to make the first move. Anderson grew impatient. "Taking a spyglass from one of the quarter masters I affected to be admiring the surrounding objects until by degrees my vision turned upon the *Nashville*. Her officers were on deck scrutinizing us." He ordered coded signals to be raised, but it soon became clear that they meant nothing to the *Nashville*. Finally, one of the *Fingal's* officers rowed over on the pretext of asking for a casket of fresh water and was recognized by a former crewmate.

The captain of the *Nashville* turned out to be a former naval colleague of Anderson's named Robert Pegram. That night, as they swapped news and experiences, Pegram warned Anderson and Bulloch to banish any thoughts of an easy entry into Savannah: if his encounter with the *Connecticut* was anything to go by, they would be chased all the way from the Outer Banks.

Five days later, on November 7, the *Fingal* set sail for the South during a tropical storm. After five nights of hurricane-force wind, the weather calmed, and the Confederates were glad to realize they were only 140 miles from Savannah. "The night closed in upon us bright and clear, with the moon shining sweetly down upon us," wrote Anderson. "Everyone was on the alert." The moment of reckoning had come. It was not long before they caught sight of a Federal ship bobbing on the water. "The silence of the dead was preserved on board our vessel," Anderson continued. "In my anxiety as I stood beside the helmsman, I could hear the throbbing of my heart." As dawn approached, the heavy night dew condensed into a thick, wet fog. Suddenly, one of the caged cockerels began its morning crow. A dozen hands reached frantically into the coop. The creature was strangled and thrown overboard. A second cockerel awoke, and then a third, forcing the crew to pitch the whole cage into the sea. It was too late for secrecy now. The *Fingal* raced toward the harbor, somehow managing to elude the steam frigate that guarded the entrance. At last, wrote Anderson on November 12, "everything had come about just as I had dreamed of."[45] Thousands lined the quayside to cheer the *Fingal*'s entry into Savannah.[46]

Anderson and Bulloch's arrival in Richmond, however, was overshadowed by the Federal capture of Port Royal in South Carolina on November 7. The South had lost the only good harbor between Charleston and Savannah, while the North gained a second base on the Confederate coast that could provide fuel and supplies to the blockading fleets. The battle had brought together the largest U.S. battle fleet ever assembled up to that time. Seventy-seven vessels carrying 12,000 troops had set sail on November 1 from the recently captured Cape Hatteras. Ebenezer Wells and the reinstated 79th were among the three regiments on board USS *Vanderbilt*.

The expedition began smoothly enough, but by nightfall the wind had picked up and the flotilla began to lose its cohesion. The next day a fierce gale assaulted the Union convoy. A supply ship went down with all hands; another jettisoned its guns in a frantic attempt to stay afloat. On the *Vanderbilt,* the terrified soldiers and animals howled in unison. As the storm continued to rage, the horses were driven into such a frenzy that a dozen were able to struggle free and went careering about the ship. Unable to capture or subdue them, Wells was forced to kill the animals by slitting their throats. Their blood spilled out across the deck and down through every crack and crevice, traumatizing the already shattered soldiers. When the battered fleet reassembled outside the sandbank off Port Royal on November 7, the 79th Highlanders were too sick and exhausted by their journey, recorded Wells, to care whether they were in the South or in Hell.

The uplifting sight of artillery shells smashing through the Confederate defenses at Port Royal brought the soldiers back to life. "We took them on completely by surprise," recorded Wells. In less than a day, the two forts guarding the entrance to the port were bombarded into submission. The Federals followed up their victory by sweeping inland and seizing the town of Beaufort. "The soldiers and inhabitants all left in a hurry so much so that when we landed some of us had the satisfaction of sitting down to unfinished breakfasts and finishing them," Wells wrote. Afterward he and his friends made a thorough inspection of the empty plantations, riding around in the owners' carriages and generally helping themselves to anything of interest.[47]

Southerners, observed Anderson, "were frightened to death by the capture of Port Royal" and looking for someone to blame.[48] At the Confederate War Department, he learned that President Davis was considered in some quarters to be the main culprit because of his constant meddling and countermanding of orders. Leroy Walker had resigned as secretary of war in September, and the new secretary, Judah P. Benjamin, had no qualification for the post other than his loyalty to Davis.

In Benjamin's defense, he had inherited a badly organized and unhappy department. Boredom and disease were sapping the strength of the Confederate armies. Sam Hill's regiment, the 6th Louisiana Volunteers, was losing half a dozen men a month.[49] "Our hospital tents are full of sick; I am always busy," wrote Mary Sophia Hill from their camp in northern Virginia after yet another healthy young man died from typhus. One of her dying charges asked for a letter to be written to his mother in England, giving "an account of his death, and his reason for joining the Southern army." It was done as he requested, although she thought the letter contained little to comfort the young man's mother. Some of Mary Sophia's friends urged her to leave the camp for her own safety. "But I will risk it," she wrote on November 13. "I am determined to keep my brother in view, and I have no other means of protection."[50] Sam was always losing something, his blanket one day, his belt and cartridge box the next. He had no idea how to forage for himself and remained dependent on the food parcels sent to Mary by their friends in New Orleans.

The Southern press demanded to know why their troops were so poorly supplied. "We are credibly informed," expostulated the Richmond *Examiner,* "that there has not been a day within the past two months when full rations were served to the army. There has been great and almost constant want of candles and soap; sometimes and for the past ten days allegedly no sugar or rice."[51] Judah Benjamin was valiantly trying to reorganize the sclerotic relationship between the army and the commissary, but neither department was willing to compromise or take responsibility for mistakes. Yet he was also guilty of shortsightedness, as Edward Anderson discovered when he tried to interest him and Mallory in running a joint operation to improve the flow of supplies from England. Believing that Mason and Slidell would soon be in Europe, Benjamin thought there was no need to take action against a blockade that would not be around for much longer. Mallory also regarded the blockade as merely a stumbling block rather than a threat to the South's existence. "Mallory met my suggestions with evident discourtesy," Anderson recorded, "and yet he knew nothing whatever of the details of my arrangements."[52] Benjamin failed to understand the importance of Anderson and his ideas, and although the agent begged to be sent back to London, he allowed Anderson to be reassigned to General Robert E. Lee's staff. Anderson spent the rest of the war commanding the forts and batteries around Savannah, his expertise and brilliance wasted.

James Bulloch fared somewhat better than Anderson, suggesting to Mallory that they use the *Fingal* to ship cotton to England and take the profits to pay for supplies brought back on the return journey. But once the *Fingal* was loaded with cotton and made ready to go, Bulloch realized that she was too slow to outrun the blockading fleet. Rather than allowing him to transfer the cargo to a faster vessel, Mallory lost confidence in the idea and ordered Bulloch to return to London on a civilian blockade runner. Like Benjamin, Mallory decided that the shipping business was a distraction from far more pressing matters; the privateering scheme had failed to attract many volunteers, and for the moment all he had was the *Sumter* and the *Nashville,* neither of which would stand up against an actual naval vessel. On reflection, Mallory thought it was just as well that the new Confederate commissioners had traveled on a private vessel rather than the easily identifiable *Nashville.*

The three U.S. warships dispatched by Secretary Welles had searched in vain for the arriving Confederate commissioners Mason and Slidell. One of the vessels, the *James Adger,* limped into Southampton on November 2 after being damaged in a storm off the coast of Ireland. The *Adger's* unexpected arrival led Henry Sanford to consider using it against a Confederate cargo ship called the *Gladiator,* which was about to set sail from a London dockyard. Sanford's plan was complicated and probably illegal: he thought that if he could bribe the *Gladiator's* pilot to steer the ship into a mud bank on the Thames, the *Adger* could seize the cargo and the crew and steam away before the authorities had time to react.

Sanford hurried to the U.S. legation to share his idea, expecting some resistance from Adams but not the furious tirade that greeted him.

Adams interrupted Sanford in midflow to reveal that his spy system was being shut down. "Whilst he was quietly sitting on the other side of the channel without any responsibility for the acts of the worthless people whom he was employing," Adams told him, "the odium of their dirty conduct was inevitably fastened upon me." But no more: he had obtained Seward's agreement that from now on Sanford would have to confine his activities to Belgium, where he belonged. Shocked and bewildered, Sanford first protested, then pleaded, and finally tried bargaining with Adams, but the minister cut him off by rising from his chair. Mortified, Sanford followed suit, saying goodbye with as much dignity as he could muster; "but," wrote Adams, "I imagine he will never forgive me."[53] Benjamin Moran had always envied Sanford, and his humiliation felt like justice served: "One million of dollars were placed at this man's disposal for Gov't purposes and it has been greatly squandered to our injury," Moran wrote in his diary. "With one half of what he threw away in odious espionage I could have bought the British Press . . . every newspaper writer in London can be purchased, from those of *The Times* down. . . . I do not mean to say that each would openly take cash; but each will take a consideration suitable to his taste."[54] .

Adams was still uncertain whether Sanford had left for good when a polite summons arrived from Lord Palmerston on November 12. Regardless of its tone, the request for an immediate meeting suggested trouble. Adams was filled with trepidation as he made his way to Cambridge House at 94 Piccadilly through another London fog. He had never been there during the day, but the yellow gloom that shrouded the city made the difference seem slight. Flaming pyres only partially illuminated the forecourt. Inside, gaslights threw off as much smoke as light.* Palmerston was waiting for him in a library that was untenably dark by American standards. He was alone, and "at once opened on the subject then evidently weighing on his mind": the government knew the true purpose of the *James Adger.*[55] For a moment Adams thought that Sanford had carried out his plan, but as Palmerston talked it became clear that his concern had nothing to do with the *Gladiator.*

The British government, he said, had learned that the North was

---

* Cambridge House, wrote Sir George Trevelyan memorably, was "Past the wall which screens the mansion, hallowed by a mighty shade, / Where the cards were cut and shuffled when the game of State was played."

hunting for the Confederate commissioners Mason and Slidell, though its latest information on the duo was sketchy and contradictory. The Foreign Office could not be certain, but their reports suggested that the Confederates were traveling on a British mail ship, and that the *Adger* had been sent to intercept her. Palmerston was less concerned about the *Adger*'s right to seize the rebels—although he did consult the law officers on the question—than the obvious threat such an act posed to national honor, since an attack on a British ship could not pass unchallenged. The Confederates could send an entire fleet of commissioners to England, he informed Adams gravely, without its having the slightest effect on the British government's actions. The North would do better to leave all British ships alone. Offended by Palmerston's assumption that the United States would stoop to waylaying British mail packets, Adams explained rather huffily that the *Adger* had been chasing a rebel cruiser called the *Nashville.* Having failed to find her, the captain was waiting for the departure of the *Gladiator,* which—he labored the point—was laden with arms and munitions for the South. Palmerston refused to be drawn in and responded with the candid assertion that the North might eventually crush Southern resistance, "but that would not be restoring the Union."

After the meeting, Adams's relief that it had nothing to do with Sanford was tempered by his indignation at Palmerston's accusations. A week later, on the twenty-first, the *Adger*'s prey, the *Nashville,* sailed into Southampton with a Confederate flag brazenly flying from its mast. Although the Confederate commissioners were not on board, there were thirty prisoners from a Northern clipper called the *Harvey Birch,* which the *Nashville* had captured and burned in the English Channel. Lord Russell promptly sent orders that she was not to receive any military supplies or fittings. Her arrival was embarrassing and obviously provocative to the North. Charles Francis Adams demanded the arrest of Captain Pegram on the charge of piracy. Pegram responded with a letter to *The Times* pointing out that he was a regularly commissioned officer of the Confederate navy and therefore not a pirate. The locals in Southampton preferred Adams's version and treated Pegram like a swashbuckling hero.

Russell naturally refused Adams's request, since the *Nashville* was a bona fide ship of war belonging to a recognized belligerent, but he did agree to keep her under surveillance in case the Confederates attempted to smuggle guns on board.[56] The torrent of correspondence between the legation and Whitehall was now so great that Henry Adams and the two secretaries were overwhelmed by the drudgery of copying and archiving each and every letter. Benjamin Moran's tirades and twitterings made life in the office almost intolerable for Henry, who struggled "to resist complete nervous depression" resulting from the prolonged exposure.[57] On the morning of the twenty-seventh, the subject of Moran's ire was Lord Russell's latest response, which he characterized as unforgivably "hostile." The embittered secretary cursed Russell and Palmerston "for playing into the hands of the rebels." The prime minister had hated America since the War of 1812, contended Moran, and "has deliberately determined to force us into war."[58] He believed it was only a matter of time before Palmerston found some pretext to unleash his designs.

The moment came sooner than Moran expected. At precisely half past twelve, a messenger called with another telegram from the U.S. consul in Southampton. This time it was not about the *Nashville*. A ship from St. Thomas had arrived, bearing the astonishing news that Mason and Slidell had been captured off the coast of Cuba. They had been traveling on the *Trent*, a British mail packet bound for St. Thomas, when USS *San Jacinto* under Captain Charles Wilkes forcibly stopped the vessel and took the commissioners prisoner. The jaded occupants of the U.S. legation began cheering, even though, Henry Adams admitted, they knew it meant "not merely diplomatic rupture—but a declaration of war." His opinion was echoed around the country: "Have these Yankees then gone completely crazy to carry out this mad coup with the Confederate Commissioners?" Friedrich Engels asked Karl Marx, whose prodigious journalistic output from his home in Manchester included weekly articles about the Civil War. "To take political prisoners by force, on a foreign ship, is the clearest *casus belli* there can be. The fellows must be sheer fools to land themselves in war with England."[59]

Charles Francis Adams was not at the legation to hear the news. He had accepted an invitation from Richard Monckton Milnes to join a large house party at Fryston Hall in Yorkshire. Neither Charles Francis nor Abigail had experienced life in a grand country house before; Fryston's "somewhat ancient" decoration and total lack of modern conveniences confirmed their prejudices about the superiority of New England to Olde England. The wet weather forced the guests to huddle together in Milnes's library, whose relatively efficient fireplace made it also double as the breakfast room. By the twenty-seventh, the guests had become restless. Unable to stand the confinement any longer, the group—which included the MP William Forster, the novelist Elizabeth Gaskell, and Austen Henry Layard, the excavator of the ancient city of Nineveh (who had recently put away his tools to become Lord Russell's undersecretary for foreign affairs)—accepted Milnes's invitation to brave the rain for a visit to the ruins of Pomfret Castle.

A messenger bearing Moran's telegram from London tracked Adams down at the ruins. The minister would always remember standing in the persistent drizzle making polite conversation with his fellow guests while in his hand he clutched the news about the *Trent*. "We had a very dark and muddy walk home," he recorded. William Forster accompanied him, but Adams did not reveal the contents of the telegram, Forster told his wife, until "as we got in, Adams said, in his cool, quiet way 'I have got stirring news.'" Forster continued: "I think he is as much grieved as I am, and does not think a hundred Masons and Slidells would be worth the effect on us." The news had spread by dinner, making it a torturous affair. No one knew what to say, and Forster's attempts to make conversation were so ham-fisted that Adams could not help commenting in his diary: "He is no courtier." In the end, it was left to a local manufacturer who had been invited to make up the numbers to fill the void, which he did at great length in a diatribe addressed solely to Adams on the iniquities of the Morrill Tariff.[60]

The next morning, Layard and Forster went to London immediately after breakfast. Adams thought it best to travel by a different train and left at noon. Milnes and his wife were so warm and earnest at the parting that Adams felt rather emotional; it seemed at that moment as though no one in England had ever been so kind to him. He arrived at the legation in the evening to find Henry, Moran, and Wilson overexcited and once again making inappropriate comments to a crowd of visitors. A note from Lord Russell was waiting on Adams's desk. The hour was late, he realized with a tinge of relief. The meeting would have to wait until tomorrow, giving him a little more time to prepare.

"There was a shade more of gravity visible in his manner, but no ill will," Adams wrote after the interview on the twenty-ninth. He had decided to be frank with the foreign secretary. "Not a word had been whispered to me about such a project," he confessed. This seemed to reassure Russell, who then asked whether the *Adger* had received orders respecting British vessels. Adams replied no, not as far as he knew. There was nothing more to be said by either man. "The conference lasted perhaps ten minutes," Adams recorded. He could not imagine Seward being as civil in similar circumstances. But he was under no illusions that Lord Russell's politeness signified an unwillingness to retaliate. During the carriage journey home, Adams wondered if this had been his final visit to the Foreign Office: "On the whole, I scarcely remember a day of greater strain in my life."[61] The press, he saw, was urging the government to stand up for British rights. Even liberal papers like the *Manchester Guardian* accused the American government of testing "the truth of the adage that it takes two to make a quarrel."[62]

Lord Russell described his conversation with Adams at a hastily called cabinet meeting on Friday, November 29. Every member was present, except for the Duke of Argyll, who was on holiday in France. Palmerston was bristling with pugnacious indignation. He had spent the past few days calculating ship distances and totting up troop numbers. Whether Captain Wilkes's act had been premeditated or not, Palmerston had decided it was time "to read a lesson to the United States which will not soon be forgotten."[63]

EIGHT

The Lion Roars Back

Captain Wilkes seizes the Trent—*Northern glee—Britain prepares for war—Prince Albert's intervention—Waiting for an answer—Seward's dilemma—Lord Lyons takes a risk—Peace and goodwill on Christmas Day*

"A cold, raw day," William Howard Russell noted in his diary on November 16, 1861. "As I was writing," he continued, "a small friend of mine, who appears like a stormy petrel in moments of great storm, fluttered into my room, and having chirped out something about a 'jolly row,'—'Seizure of Mason and Slidell,'—'British flag insulted,' and the like, vanished." Russell hastily grabbed his coat and followed him outside, where he bumped into the French minister, Henri Mercier, coming from the direction of the British legation. "And then, indeed, I learned there was no doubt about the fact that [on November 8] Captain Charles Wilkes, of the U.S. steamer *San Jacinto*, had forcibly boarded the *Trent*, a British mail steamer, off the Bahamas, and had taken Messrs. Mason, Slidell, [and their secretaries] Eustis, and Macfarland from on board by armed force, in defiance of the protests of the captain and naval officer in charge of the mails."[1]

The American press was jubilant over the capture. "Rightly or wrongly, the American people at large look upon it as a direct insult to the British flag," wrote Lord Lyons.[2] But the opportunity to humiliate England was not the only reason behind the public's excitement. Mason and Slidell had been needling the North from the Senate floor for many years, and their banishment to Fort Warren in Boston Harbor was

LOOK OUT FOR SQUALLS.

Jack Bull. "YOU DO WHAT'S RIGHT, MY SON, OR I'LL BLOW YOU OUT OF THE WATER."

Punch sends a British warning to the United States, December 1861.

deemed a fitting punishment.* *The New York Times'* first editorial on the affair called for Wilkes to be honored with a medal or a public holiday. The Philadelphia *Sunday Transcript* went further and committed the country to war, reminding its readers that American soldiers had routed "the best of British troops" in 1812 and would do so again. "In a word, while the British government has been playing the villain, we have been playing the fool," the paper declared. "Let her now do something beyond driveling—let her fight. If she has a particle of pluck . . . if she is not as cowardly as she is treacherous—she will meet the American people on land and on the sea, as they long to meet her, once again, not only to

---

* It may have disappointed Northerners to know that the prisoners ate far better and had larger rooms than the regulars at Willard's.

lower the red banner of St. George . . . but to consolidate Canada with the union."[3]

What was not clear to Russell, however, was whether Captain Wilkes had acted on his own or in accordance with secret U.S. government instructions. His visits to the State and Navy departments on November 18 were inconclusive, since the former was not prepared to comment, but the latter had obviously been taken by surprise.[4] No one at the Navy Department had a good word to say in Wilkes's defense. Although a renowned cartographer, he had the reputation of being a bully and a braggart.[5] The command of the *San Jacinto* had been given to him with great reluctance; "he has a super-abundance of self-esteem and a deficiency of judgment," warned an official in August. "He will give us trouble."[6] Since his appointment, Wilkes had been trawling the oceans in defiance of his actual orders on a personal hunting expedition for Confederate ships. It was sheer luck that he stumbled onto the Confederate commissioners, and it was pure Wilkes—his colleagues told William Howard Russell—to decide that a search and seizure of the four men on a neutral ship would be legal under international law.

At the British legation, Russell encountered Lord Lyons politely fending off questions from a group of foreign ministers who had come ostensibly to offer their support, but really to ascertain England's probable response. This, Lyons made clear, would have to come from London. He explained to Russell that his overriding concern was to prevent anything coming from himself or the legation that might help the warmongers. The staff had been given orders not to discuss the *Trent* with anyone, although Russell could see from the look on their faces that they thought war was inevitable.

The following day, Russell prepared his letter to *The Times*. "I rarely sat down to write under a sense of greater responsibility," he admitted in his diary.[7] Russell assumed that his report would be "the first account of the seizure of the Southern Commissioners which will reach England," and the thought of how the public would react to the news filled him with foreboding. He was no longer just describing the attack on the *Trent*, but also the North's exultation and the U.S. government's silence, which he feared would be as provocative to the English as Wilkes's original act. Without excusing the Lincoln administration, Russell tried to explain the pressures placed upon it by democracy: "There is a popular passion and vengeance to be gratified by the capturing and punishment of Mr. Mason and Mr. Slidell," he wrote, "and I believe the Government will retain them at all risk because it dare not give them up."[8]

Russell was only partially correct about the administration. Public opinion naturally played a role in its deliberations, but from the start virtually all the members of the president's cabinet were adamantly opposed to releasing the commissioners. Lincoln allegedly complained to a journalist on November 16 about the embarrassment Wilkes had caused the country. "I fear the traitors will prove to be white elephants," he reportedly said. "We must stick to American principles concerning the rights of neutrals. We fought Great Britain for insisting, by theory and practice, on the right to do precisely what Captain Wilkes has done."[9] If that is true, Lincoln would have been the only member of his administration, apart from Montgomery Blair, the postmaster general, to accept that Wilkes had violated international law and the only member to realize the grave threat to America's moral reputation if the government supported him. The United States had fought the War of 1812 in part to defend its broad interpretation of "neutral rights." It had protected the slave trade, allowing it to flourish, and had expelled the British minister, John Crampton, in 1856, risking a third Anglo-American war, for his perceived violation of these rights. The United States would be inviting the censure and mockery of the entire world if the government suddenly repudiated a fundamental principle of American foreign policy because it was no longer expedient to maintain.

Regardless of how Lincoln originally understood the issue, within twenty-four hours of hearing the news he had joined the celebrations. He wrote about the seizure with exclamation marks to Edward Everett, the former American minister in London. To General McClellan, who came to deliver a warning from the Prince de Joinville that England would demand an apology, Lincoln replied categorically that the commissioners were not going to be released. The cabinet, excepting Montgomery Blair, behaved shamefully. The worst offender was the attorney general, Edward Bates, who gave ill-judged and incorrect legal advice to his colleagues. "Some timid persons are alarmed, lest Great Britain should take offense at the violation of her Flag," he wrote in his diary. "There is no danger on that score. The law of Nations is clear upon the point, and I have no doubt that, with a little time for examination, I could find it so settled by English authorities."[10]

General McClellan also called on Seward to give him Joinville's

1. Richard Bickerton Pemell Lyons, 2nd Lord Lyons (1817–87). Lyons arrived at the British legation in the spring of 1859 and stayed until December 1864, when he returned to England, having worked himself to exhaustion.

2. The British legation at Rush House, 1710 H Street, Washington.

3. The U.S. Capitol, Washington. Charles Dickens visited the capital in 1842 and thought the city had "Magnificent Intentions," with "streets [a] mile long, that only want houses, roads, and inhabitants." Fifteen years later, these intentions remained unfulfilled. A disagreement between the U.S. Federal government and a local landowner had stranded the unfinished Capitol building on top of a steep hill at the edge of town, facing the wrong way. The dome was finally completed on December 2, 1863.

4. President Lincoln's inauguration in front of the incomplete Capitol on March 4, 1861. In his inauguration speech, Lincoln tried to reassure the Southern states about his intentions toward slavery, but by then it was too late to stem the tide of secession: the war began six weeks later.

5. The U.S. Senate. Here, on May 22, 1856, Congressman Preston Brooks of South Carolina ambushed Senator Charles Sumner, who was sitting at his desk reading, and beat him with his cane. By Brooks's own account, he struck Sumner thirty times before the cane splintered.

6. President Abraham Lincoln (1809–65). Lincoln's physical appearance astonished people. The British journalist William Howard Russell was introduced to him at around the time this photograph was taken in 1861: "There entered, with a shambling, loose, irregular, almost unsteady gait, a tall, lank, lean man, considerably over six feet in height, with stooping shoulders, long pendulous arms, terminating in hands of extraordinary dimensions which, however, were far exceeded in proportion by his feet. He was dressed in an ill-fitting wrinkled suit of black, which put one in mind of an undertaker's uniform at a funeral." By the end of the war, the world saw past Lincoln's appearance to his humanity and magnanimity toward his foes.

7. William Seward (1801–72), U.S. secretary of state, Lincoln's rival for power before the war but who became his greatest ally during it. Seward's frequent statements that Canada would one day belong to the United States, coupled with his unscrupulous playing to American Anglophobia, made him the most detested U.S. politician in Britain.

8. London, view of the Royal Exchange. In 1861, Britain was the richest nation on earth. A trading country par excellence, its exports in the 1860s counted for a quarter of the world's manufactured goods.

9. Cambridge House, Piccadilly, where Prime Minister Lord Palmerston lived from 1855 to 1865. Sir George Trevelyan wrote of it: "Past the wall which screens the mansion / Hallowed by a mighty shade / Where the cards were cut and shuffled / When the game of state was played."

10. The chamber of the House of Commons. The pro-Northern faction of MPs led by William Forster and John Bright successfully prevented all attempts by pro-Southern MPs to persuade the house to vote in favor of recognizing Southern independence.

11. Lord John Russell, 1st Earl Russell (1792–1878), foreign secretary. A cultured and intellectual man, but an abrasive politician, Russell held thirteen political offices during his long career in politics and was twice prime minister. He and Palmerston were referred to by Queen Victoria as "those two dreadful old men."

12. Henry John Temple, 3rd Viscount Palmerston (1784–1865), prime minister, popularly known as "Lord Cupid" when young and "Pam" when an elder statesman. His dislike of the United States went back to the War of 1812, when he was secretary at war, and was exacerbated by America's protection of the slave trade. Palmerston's brinkmanship was successful during the *Trent* crisis of 1861, but his bluff was called three years later by the Germans.

13. Charles Sumner (1811–74), senator for Massachusetts. Until the Civil War, he was the most revered U.S. politician in Britain on account of his unflinching campaigns to abolish slavery and win equal rights for blacks.

14. Frederick Douglass (1818–95), writer, orator, and leading abolitionist in America. Douglass campaigned in Britain several times, and in 1859 briefly fled to London to avoid persecution after the radical abolitionist John Brown tried to start a slave uprising by raiding the armory at Harpers Ferry, Virginia.

15. Gideon Welles (1802–78), U.S. secretary of the Navy. Nicknamed "Father Neptune" by Lincoln because of his flowing beard, Welles was a lawyer and journalist with no maritime experience before his appointment. His loathing for William Seward, the secretary of state, interfered with their ability to work together.

16. Salmon P. Chase (1803–73), U.S. secretary of the treasury. An effective treasurer who established a national banking system and paper currency—the greenback—he was also a schemer who tried to engineer the dismissal of William Seward in 1862 and the removal of President Lincoln from the Republican ticket in 1864.

17. General George McClellan (1825–65), commander of the U.S. Army of the Potomac, 1861–62. He was removed by President Lincoln after the Battle of Antietam for being overly passive and cautious.

18. The 69th New York Irish Regiment, the "Fighting 69th," one of the five Irish-dominated regiments that made up the Irish Brigade of the Union Army of the Potomac. The regiment suffered disproportionate losses at the Battle of Fredericksburg.

19. U.S. General William Sherman (1820–91). Sherman began the war in command of a single brigade (which included the "Fighting 69th"), but he so distinguished himself that General Grant gave him control over all the Union armies west of Virginia. Sherman implemented a policy of total war against the South during his march from Atlanta to Savannah, Georgia, in 1864.

20. William Howard Russell (1820–1907). "Russell of the Crimea" was the most famous journalist in the world when he arrived in the North to cover the Civil War. His unbiased reports for *The Times* were considered insufficiently favorable to the North and in 1862 he was harassed into leaving the country.

21. Edward Dicey (1832–1911), pro-Northern English journalist for the *Spectator*. He published an account of his travels after his return home.

22. The Hon. Francis Lawley (1825–1901), pro-Southern British journalist for *The Times*. The war gave Lawley a second chance to redeem himself after his gambling debts forced him into exile. He became so enamored with the South that he willingly misrepresented events to show the Confederacy in a better light.

23. Frank Vizetelly (1830–83), British war artist and pro-Southern correspondent for the *Illustrated London News*. "He was a big, florid, red-bearded Bohemian," recalled an admirer, "who could and would do anything to entertain a circle."

24. Confederate President Jefferson Davis (1808–89). Davis seemed an ideal choice for the Confederate presidency, having served as a senator for Mississippi and as secretary of war under President Franklin Pierce, but he was notoriously thin-skinned and incapable of delegating. Davis was shocked and disappointed when Britain failed to recognize Southern independence.

25. The inauguration of Confederate President Jefferson Davis in Montgomery, Alabama, on February 18, 1861. Davis used his speech to prepare Southerners for war: "We have entered upon the career of independence and it must be inflexibly pursued."

26. The Confederate White House, Richmond, Virginia. The Davis family lived here from 1861 to 1865. Tragedy struck in 1864 when five-year-old Joe Davis was killed by a fall from a first-floor balcony.

27. Richmond, Virginia, during the war. Known as the "City of Seven Hills," it was named after Richmond in London because the view of the James River from its highest hill reminded the city's founder, William Byrd, of the Thames from Richmond Hill.

28. General Robert E. Lee (1807–70), Confederate commander of the Army of Northern Virginia. The South's most famous general was admired by both sides during the war, and British travelers were invariably starstruck when introduced to him. Lieutenant-Colonel Garnet Wolseley of the British Army wrote that Lee was "a splendid specimen of an English gentleman, with one of the most rarely handsome faces I ever saw. . . . You only have to be in his society for a very brief period to be convinced that whatever he says may be implicitly relied upon."

29. General Thomas J. "Stonewall" Jackson (1824–1863), Confederate commander of the famous Stonewall Brigade, who earned his nickname during the First Battle of Bull Run. He went on to form a successful partnership with Lee until his death from friendly fire at Chancellorsville in 1863. On hearing that Jackson's arm had been amputated, Lee replied: "He has lost his left arm; but I have lost my right arm."

30. Arlington, Virginia, plantation home of General Robert E. Lee before the war, seized by the Union in 1861.

31. General Josiah Gorgas (1818–83), Confederate chief of ordnance. He kept Southern armies supplied with arms throughout the war despite the blockade and an immense shortage of raw materials.

32. Judah P. Benjamin (1811–84), Confederate secretary of state. Known as "Jefferson's Pet Jew," Benjamin served Davis unquestioningly and even took the blame for mistakes that were not his own. The blockade prevented him from directing an effective or timely foreign policy.

33. Stephen Mallory (1817–73), Confederate secretary of the navy, one of the longest-serving members of President Davis's Cabinet. Mallory's strategy of building the Confederate navy in Great Britain almost brought the Northern and British governments to war.

34. James Dunwoody Bulloch (1823–1901) (*left*), with his half-brother Irvine. Bulloch was the Confederacy's chief secret agent in England and architect of the program to build Confederate commerce raiders in Britain and France. "He is the most dangerous man the South have here and fully up to his business," claimed the head of the U.S. secret service in Europe.

35. Henry Hotze (1833–97). Hotze was sent to England to be the chief Confederate propagandist in Europe and founded the pro-Southern journal *Index*. He was an expert at influencing public opinion: an editor "should see with the eyes of the public, and hear with the ears of the public, and yet have eyes and ears of his own."

36. James Murray Mason (1798–1871), Confederate commissioner in England. Mason and his fellow commissioner John Slidell were sailing to Europe to take up their posts when their ship, the British mail packet *Trent*, was stopped by Captain Wilkes of the U.S. Navy. Britain demanded an apology for the "attack" on her mail ship and the release of the two men. The *Trent* affair very nearly took the United States and Britain to war.

37. John Slidell (1793–1871), Confederate commissioner in France. "He is an excellent judge of mankind, adroit, persevering, and subtle, full of device and fond of intrigue," wrote William Howard Russell. If Slidell were shut up in a dungeon, he "would conspire with the mice against the cat rather than not conspire at all."

38. The shipyard of the Laird brothers, Liverpool, builders of the CSS *Alabama*. The cotton trade had helped to make Liverpool rich and had given it deep ties with the South. The majority of blockade runners sailed from Liverpool, and Fraser, Trenholm, the Confederacy's bankers, had their offices at 10 Rumford Place. Lord Russell complained that the city was "addicted to Southern proclivities, foreign slave trade, and domestic bribery."

39. Federal troops marching through New Orleans. Before the war, New Orleans was the fourth largest city in the country and the South's premiere port. It also had the largest immigrant population of the South.

40. Charles Francis Adams, Jr. (1835–1915) (*second from the right*), the only son of Charles Francis Adams to volunteer during the war, who rose from 1st lieutenant of the 1st Massachusetts Cavalry in 1861 to colonel of the 5th Massachusetts (Colored) Cavalry in 1865 and led one of the first colored regiments through Richmond after its fall on April 3, 1865.

41. Henry Adams (1838–1918). Henry accompanied his father, Charles Francis Adams, to London as his private secretary and later recorded his isolation and loneliness in *The Education of Henry Adams*. "Every young diplomat," he wrote, "and most of the old ones, felt awkward in an English house from a certainty that they were not precisely wanted there, and a possibility that they might be told so."

42. Charles Francis Adams (1807–86), U.S. minister to Great Britain. Adams was the son and grandson of U.S. ministers and presidents. Though he was dutiful, honest, and hardworking, his family legacy cast a shadow over his entire life. "Charles Francis Adams naturally looked on all British [statesmen] as enemies," wrote Henry Adams.

43. Henry Feilden (1838–1921), British volunteer in the Confederate army. He was surprised to discover that he was not the only Englishman to offer his services to the South: "A good number have, prior to this, come out to this country," he wrote in 1863, "and I believe have been obliged to serve as volunteers in the Army or on some General's staff until they have proved themselves fit for something."

44. Francis Dawson (1840–89), British volunteer in the Confederate navy and subsequently the Confederate army. "My idea simply was to go to the South, do my duty there as well as I might, and return home to England." In fact, Dawson stayed in the South after the war and became editor of the *Charleston News and Courier.*

warning, but the secretary of state did not want to hear bad news—especially from McClellan, whom he disliked. He resented having his expertise questioned and told the general that his information about England was based on ignorance. "I said I thought I was right," recorded McClellan; "he again contradicted me & I told him that the future would prove the correctness of my story." McClellan left, inwardly cursing that "so weak and cowardly a thing should now control our foreign relations."[11] Seward's unfounded optimism that Britain would not dare make a protest thoroughly depressed Lord Lyons. "I am so worn out with the never ending labour of keeping things smooth," Lyons wrote to Lord Russell on November 22. He had heard about Seward's reaction and was beginning to wonder whether the policy of keeping quiet was "leading these people to believe that they may go all lengths with us with impunity. . . . I am sometimes half tempted to wish that the worst may have come already," he confessed. "However I do not allow this feeling to influence my conduct and I have done nothing which can in the least interfere with any course which you may take concerning the affair of the 'Trent.' "[12]

There was apparently limited discussion of the *Trent* affair at the cabinet meeting on November 24. Lincoln agreed that they would wait to hear Britain's response before the government publicly committed itself on the legality of the seizure. No one remarked on the South's euphoric reaction to the capture or questioned why its press was so quick to agree that the British had been given a studied blow. President Jefferson Davis had laid particular stress on the insult in a speech to the Confederate Congress on November 18. "These gentlemen were as much under the jurisdiction of the British Government upon that ship and beneath its flag as if they had been on its soil," he said. Wilkes's act was no different from a kidnapping on Piccadilly.[13]

After the cabinet meeting, Seward realized that it would be impossible to keep Charles Francis Adams in limbo for two or three more weeks. He composed a dispatch on November 27 saying as little as possible about the affair except to admit that Wilkes had acted without orders. The administration was waiting for Britain's reaction, he informed Adams. That night, the apotheosis of Wilkes continued. The governor of Massachusetts spoke at a public banquet in his honor, praising him for giving "illustrious service" to the war and for humbling the "British lion" to boot. Gideon Welles ignored Lincoln's injunction to wait and published a letter of congratulation to Wilkes, which, fortunately, mentioned that the captain had acted on his own initiative.

When Congress reconvened on December 2, Lincoln did not specifically refer to Wilkes in his speech, but the House of Representatives passed a vote of thanks and awarded him a gold medal. In Boston, Anthony Trollope was forced to pronounce on the subject, though he felt there was more farce than force to the affair. "Who ever before heard of giving a man glory for achievements so little glorious?" he asked. Trollope was amused when people quoted obscure legal authorities at him in order to justify the *Trent* affair. " 'Wheaton is quite clear about it,' one young girl said to me. It was the first I had ever heard of Wheaton, and so far was obliged to knock under," he wrote. "All the world, ladies and lawyers, expressed the utmost confidence in the justice of the seizure." Yet, Trollope added, "it was clear that all the world was in a state of the profoundest nervous anxiety on the subject."[14] As the countdown began for the arrival of newspapers from London, the press began to change its tone as editorials asked: What if the British lion roared back?

———

The "lion" had been roaring since November 27. On Palmerston's orders, the secretary of state for the colonies, the Duke of Newcastle, advised the governor-general of Canada to prepare for war: "Such an insult to our flag can only be atoned by the restoration of the men who were seized," he wrote, "and with Mr. Seward at the helm of the United States, and the mob and the Press manning the vessel, it is too probable that this atonement may be refused." His opinion was shared in both Houses; peace, argued Lord Clarendon (who had been foreign secretary in the 1850s), was not "worth the price of national honour."[15]

Although the law officers were unanimous that the seizure was unlawful, at a meeting on November 29 the British cabinet was unable to agree on the proper measure of response to the Americans. If it were too strong, argued Gladstone, the Lincoln administration would be denied a graceful exit. Too weak, countered Palmerston, and it would send a false impression of Britain's intentions. They resolved to leave the drafting of the letter to Lord Russell. He was to state the facts of the case and demand the restoration of the commissioners along with an apology for the outrage. Failure to do so within seven days of receiving the letter would mean the immediate departure of Lord Lyons to Canada and war between the two nations.

When the cabinet reconvened the following day, nobody had a positive comment about Russell's resulting draft, which was clumsy and
overly obsessed with national honor. The three main principles at stake
(the rights of neutral countries in time of war, the right to free movement on neutral ships, and the protection of diplomatic correspondence)
were not made clear at all.[16] But the more the cabinet tried to amend the
letter, the more defensive Russell became, until finally they agreed that
Lord Lyons should receive two letters. The first would outline the case;
the second would contain the threat that the United States had seven
days to comply with Britain's demand. The temporary truce collapsed
immediately, as they now had not just one but two letters over which to
fight. Gladstone incensed Palmerston with his musings on whether the
law was entirely on their side.*[17] Finally there came a point when further
discussion was useless, and even though no one was satisfied, the drafts
were sent to the Queen and Prince Albert for their approval.

The prince lay ill with typhoid fever when the letters arrived at Windsor Castle on November 30. He had been kept informed of the cabinet's
discussions and had rightly feared that the official response would be
pompous and aggressive. In the last of the prince's many services to his
adopted country, he roused himself from his bed and composed a memorandum (though he could hardly hold a pen in his hand) on what the
letter ought to say. There should be "the expression of a hope," he wrote,

> that the American captain did not act under instructions, or, if he
> did, that he misapprehended them—that the United States Gov-
> ernment must be fully aware that the British Government could
> not allow its flag to be insulted, and the security of her mail com-
> munications to be placed in jeopardy; and Her Majesty's Govern-

---

* Gladstone was posturing for effect; Wilkes had clearly violated international law
  both by taking the Confederates off the ship and by acting as his own court of law
  in determining that they could be taken instead of going to a prize court, which
  alone had the authority to make such a ruling. The prize court would have set the
  Trent and the Confederates free, since people can't be kidnapped willy-nilly off the
  high seas. Wilkes's argument, that the Confederates were a living, breathing dispatch, which made them in legal terms "contraband of war," would have been
  laughed out of court. But the likelihood is that Wilkes would have precipitated a
  crisis even if he had sailed to a prize court, because England would have demanded
  an apology from the United States for stopping a British mail ship without cause,
  and the apology would have become the sticking point.

ment are unwilling to believe that the United States Government intended wantonly to put an insult upon this country.

Gone were the peremptory demands and in their place were merely polite statements of expectation.[*18]

Russell conceded that the changes were necessary, but even so he doubted that they would temper Seward's reaction or produce an apology.[19] He therefore composed a third letter to Lyons, describing how the demands should be presented. Russell wanted him to be tactful but unequivocal; the release of the prisoners would negate the need for atonement, but no words or species of apology would appease Britain's anger if the prisoners were retained.[20] With any luck, Seward would realize that retreat was preferable to war, but it would be up to Lyons to make the secretary of state understand that there could be no amateur dramatics, no clever little feints or attempts at bargaining. Only a straightforward answer would do.

The postmaster general, Lord Stanley, was keeping his wife informed of the cabinet's deliberations. "The accounts from America," he wrote on December 2, had confirmed their fears; Northern public opinion could be summed up as "great exaltation at the insult to England, great satisfaction at the capture of Mason and Slidell and the deification of Capt. Wilkes."[21] The next day Captain Conway Seymour boarded the Boston-bound *Europa* with the cabinet's letters.[22] Lord Stanley chafed when he realized how long it would be until they received a reply: "It cannot get to [Lord Lyons] in less than 12 days & another 12 days to return will be the earliest we can get any intelligence of its reception." As soon as the messenger left, however, Russell began to suffer misgivings about the plan. "I cannot imagine their giving a plain yes or no to our demands," he wrote. "I think they will try to hook in France, and if that is, as I hope, impossible, to get Russia to support them."[23] At the bottom of Russell's anxiety was the sense that the Americans had misunderstood his actions and that he was being wrongly blamed for reasons he still could not understand. "Not a word had been spoken, not a deed done by him but what showed the friendliest feeling," Lady Russell wrote loyally about her husband's dealings with the North.[24]

---

[*]Years later, Queen Victoria wrote of the memorandum: "This draft was the last the Beloved Prince ever wrote."

Palmerston thought that the United States would not even bother with negotiation. The "masses," he categorically stated, will "make it impossible for Lincoln and Seward to grant our demands; and we must therefore look forward to war as the probable result." George Cornewall Lewis, the secretary for war, complained that they were doing France's dirty work, which was rather ungrateful of him considering that Napoleon III had promised his support. "It is quite certain that the French Govt wish for war between England and America," wrote Lewis. "The blockade of the South would be raised, and they would get the cotton which they want."[25]

Late on December 3, Russell and Palmerston called another cabinet meeting. The Treasury had received an alarming report that a Federal agent had bought up the country's entire saltpeter reserves—about 4.5 million pounds. Most of it was due to be shipped the following day. The cabinet agreed to an immediate export ban; lacking sufficient mines of their own, the Federals would be hard-pressed to manufacture gunpowder without this precious commodity.[26] The Admiralty issued a worldwide alert to every station. Admiral Milne's instructions to ready his squadron reached him in Bermuda, where he replied: "The ships' companies are in a high state of excitement for war, they are certainly all for the South. I hear the Lower Decks to-day are decorated with the Confederate colours."[27]

The next day, the fourth, Stanley scribbled to his wife, "I write from the Cabinet where it has been decided to issue another Order in Council, prohibiting the exportation of arms & munitions of war, in addition to the former order prohibiting the exportation of saltpetre. I fear that the prospects of a satisfactory & amicable settlement are small."[28] One or two of his colleagues had protested against the ban, fearing that it would ruin Britain's arms trade, but Stanley was entirely with Palmerston and Russell. "If we are to be at war it is as well not to let them have improved rifles to shoot us with."[29] "If this goes on," added Stanley, "a Brigade of Guards will go out, one Battalion out of each Regiment." His younger son, Jonny, would be among the first to go.

The cabinet agreed to form a six-member war committee. Military experts were called in, and at the War Office, strategic plans drawn up during previous periods of tension were taken out for revision. Maine was to be the first target, with simultaneous actions by the Royal Navy to blockade Boston, New Bedford, Newport, Long Island, New York, and the Delaware River. If necessary, some of these ports would be bombarded into submission. "War has no doubt its honours and its evils," Admiral Milne reminded the secretary of state for the navy, who deprecated such wanton destruction, "but to make war felt it must be carried out against the Enemy with energy, and every place made to feel what war really is."[30]

The strategic difficulties were indeed formidable. The Canadian border was more than 1,500 miles long, thinly fortified and connected by only the most basic roads and waterways. It would require a minimum of 10,000 regular troops and 100,000 militia volunteers to repel an invasion.[31] Moreover, as *The Times* had pointed out, "We can sweep the Federal fleet from the seas, we can blockade the Atlantic cities; but we cannot garrison and hold 350,000 square miles of country." If the Americans chose to attack Montreal or Quebec, they would face a paltry British force of less than 5,000. Canada's only real defenses were snow and bad weather.[32] Their best option was to launch the first strike and capture Maine. "Do not be surprised if you hear of us all being made prisoners of war before the end of February," one of the departing officers wrote pessimistically.

> If the Yankees are worth their salt, they will at once make peace with the South and pour 100,000 men into Canada where they can easily compensate themselves for their losses of the Confederate states, and England be perfectly unable to prevent it. Unless the British Government at once make up their minds to fitting out an expedition which can start (as soon as war is declared) to seize Portland, and open up the railway communication from there to Quebec, I cannot see how we are to maintain our position in Canada this winter.[33]

Lord Stanley went down to Southampton to see his son off. Lady Stanley was too distraught and remained in London. The navy did not have the eighteen troopships on hand to transport the 11,000 soldiers who were going to Canada in the first wave. Jonny's vessel, the *Adriatic,* had been purchased from an American shipping firm and refitted in such haste that the U.S. flag could still be seen on the paddle box. As the *Adriatic* passed the *Nashville* on Southampton Water, the Guards band started to play "I'm Off to Charleston." This cheeky act of bravado elicited a few halfhearted cheers from relatives who had gathered on the banks to wave farewell.[34] "It will be very cold in Canada and I am afraid Jonny will feel it," Stanley wrote to his wife.[35] Their son was sailing at a dangerous time. Ice was beginning to close Canada's navigable rivers, and monster storms would soon lash her seas.[36]

"The all engrossing question is will America be foolish enough to go to War with us," wrote James Garnett, the owner of a large mill in Clitheroe in Lancashire. "Many people think it will."[37] Yancey and Dudley Mann fervently hoped so. They had not wasted any time in presenting Lord Russell with a letter of protest, and they had followed up two days later, on November 29, with a list of ships that had slipped through the blockade since April. Here was proof, they had argued, that the Northern blockade was ineffective and therefore not binding on neutral countries. Russell's cold response on December 7 left them temporarily crushed, until they reflected on the thousands of British soldiers who were leaving for North America. This was a case, they decided, of actions speaking louder than words.

———

Charles Francis Adams was both furious and humiliated that his knowledge of the *Trent* affair was no better than what a reader could glean from *The Times*. "Mr. Seward's ways are not those of diplomacy," he wrote bitterly on December 9. "Here have I been nearly three weeks without positively knowing whether the act of the officer was directed by the govt or not."[38] Henry Adams was equally indignant. "What Seward means is more than I can guess," he told his brother Charles Francis Jr. "But if he means war also, or to run as close as he can without touching, then I say that Mr. Seward is the greatest Criminal we've had yet." The seizure had undone all his father's hard work. "We have friends here still, but very few. Bright dined with us last night, and is with us, but is evidently hopeless of seeing anything good. . . . My friends of the *Spectator* sent up to me in a dreadful state and asked me to come down to see them, which I did, and they complained bitterly of the position we are now in."[39]

Henry was not exaggerating the difficulties confronting Northern supporters. William Forster lamented to his wife that his efforts for peace resembled "the struggles of a drowning man."[40] John Bright was at first too nervous to speak about the *Trent* affair, explaining apologetically to Adams that since his opposition to the Crimean War he had lost his appetite for being a national hate figure. Given Bright's violent rhetoric,

Adams rather hoped that this was true. Unfortunately, Bright overcame his fears and made a speech in Rochdale on December 4 that blasted the country for not being sufficiently pro-Union. This was too much even for the *Spectator,* which accused Bright of being prepared to sacrifice any principle if it did not sit well with America.[41] Harriet Martineau was one of the few English writers who could write with authority, since she was personally acquainted with Captain Wilkes, and even she was careful in her choice of words. Wilkes was not, she stressed in her articles for the *Daily News,* an Anglophobe or a warmonger, "but he lacks judgement and knowledge."[42]

Benjamin Moran realized the extent of the feeling against the North when he chanced to look out the window of his taxi and see that the American owners of the Adelphi Theatre had added the Confederate flag next to the usual Stars and Stripes. "The sight of this base emblem of slavery, treason and piracy made me ill with rage," he wrote in his diary.[43] The Confederates and their supporters were also putting up posters in railway stations and distributing rebel banners to street hawkers. Hackney cabs were given miniature Union Jacks crossed with the Confederate flag.[44] Moran heard that such overt displays of Confederate sympathy were even more prevalent in Liverpool. The new consul, Thomas Haines Dudley, reported that Southern exiles living in the city were gleefully capitalizing on the *Trent* incident.

Although Moran longed to have an American representative in the country who would not be afraid to engage with the press, he regarded Thurlow Weed's arrival on December 2 as a mixed blessing. "This morning's *Times* contains a letter from Thurlow Weed defending Mr. Seward," wrote Moran in mid-December. "The letter is strong in some things, but weak in others and *The Times* assails its vulnerable points with its usual malignity."[45] Until the *Trent* affair, Weed had been in France working with Henry Sanford on schemes to influence European opinion.

Seward's idea to send the three emissaries—Archbishop John Hughes, Bishop Charles McIlvaine, and Thurlow Tweed—"seems to me of no value," Charles Francis Adams had written frankly to Edward Everett. But Weed disagreed; when he arrived at the U.S. legation on December 6, his first thought was that he should have come earlier. There was a general air of disarray about the place. The misfits in the basement made him wonder how business was done, while upstairs, Charles Francis Adams was in an alarming state: bewildered and angered by Seward's silence, paranoid about England's intentions, and mentally more than halfway home.[46]

Weed immediately sent out letters and left his cards in all the great houses of London. The relative ease with which he connected with "intelligent and influential English friends of the North" led him to suspect that Adams had not tried very hard to penetrate society. Weed was able to arrange an interview with Lord Russell and had a perfectly sensible, albeit noncommittal, conversation with him. Although he did not say it in so many words, Weed was appalled that Adams had allowed Seward to become so thoroughly feared and hated.[47] "You have been infernally abused, and are wholly misunderstood here," Weed told Seward. Everyone he met believed that the secretary of state was determined to have a war. This was true even of Seward's friends. Lady Napier unhappily related to Weed a remark Seward had made just before their departure from Washington. "On some occasion," wrote Weed, "you talked about the incoming Administration going to war with England; that subsequently when alone with you, she asked, 'Why do you talk about war with England?' and that you replied seriously, 'that it was the best thing that could happen for America.'"[48] More damning still, *The Times* printed the story of his "joke" to the Duke of Newcastle, during the Prince of Wales's tour of America in 1860, that when in power he would manufacture a quarrel with England.[49]

It was already midnight on December 10 when Thurlow Weed sat at his desk to compose one of the most serious letters he had ever written to his friend. "I have finally got Lord [*sic*] Newcastle's own version of what was said to him," he wrote; "whatever you did say—was said. This, with the allusions to Canada . . . is regarded as evidence of your determined enmity to England, and even the Friends you made here—many of whom I have met—are carried away by this idea. And consequently War, unless you avert it, is inevitable. I pray that I am not mistaken in the hope that you comprehend the disastrous effects of such a war."[50]

The days passed and still there was no word from Washington. Nothing, however, worried Weed so much as his friend's silence. He sent a letter to Lincoln, imploring him to "turn the other cheek"; Adams sent yet another letter to Seward.[51] On December 14, *Punch* published a cartoon entitled "Waiting for an Answer," which showed Britannia ready to fire a cannon. At the Foreign Office, Lord Russell continued to fret over whether they had made the right decision. Their dispatch to Lyons left

WAITING FOR AN ANSWER.

Britannia ready to fire, *Punch,* 1861.

no room to maneuver if Seward prevaricated or refused point-blank. But "I do not think," wrote Russell, "the country would approve an immediate declaration of war." A "peace meeting" at Exeter Hall in the Strand had attracted four thousand people. Russell asked Palmerston if they should give the United States a second chance, should the worst happen, so long as Seward's letter was a "reasoning, and not a blunt answer."[52]

On Monday, December 16, London was plastered with black-bordered announcements of Prince Albert's death. He had died at eleven o'clock on Saturday night. Moran knew about the prince's alteration of the cabinet dispatch to Lord Lyons, and though he feared his action could be misinterpreted, he went defiantly to Buckingham Palace and signed his name in the condolence book. For good measure he added the names "Mr. and Mrs. Adams" next to his own. Late that same night, a messenger arrived with a dispatch from the State Department. The letter was short, too short considering the nature of the crisis, but it did contain Seward's admission that Wilkes had acted "without any instructions" as well as the remark that the American government hoped that London would "consider the subject in a friendly temper." Adams thought this "was not discouraging" but hardly a clear endorsement for peace. He wondered whether it was even worth showing to Lord Russell. Alarmed by this untimely display of diffidence, Moran and Wilson pleaded with Adams to go to the Foreign Office. Troopships were still departing for Canada and time was running out.

———

The British lion had turned tail, or so Washington thought during the first week of December. Mercier's execrable English created such confusion that Lincoln came away from their conversation believing that the British minister had given Mercier good news about England, and that Britain's law officers saw nothing wrong in the commissioners' seizure. "There would probably be no trouble about it," Lincoln cheerfully asserted to his friend Senator Orville Browning after the meeting.[53] Lincoln was also being misled by Charles Sumner, whose straightforward and sensible position on the *Trent* had become infected by his craving for popularity. At the beginning of the crisis, Sumner had assured the Duchess of Argyll that he would do everything in his power to resolve "any ill-feeling between our two countries."[54] But after he saw Lincoln on December 1 and realized that the president had no desire to release the prisoners, he abandoned his original position and suggested that they turn the case over to international arbitration. The plan protected the United States' pride and salvaged Sumner's; he had not been consulted or included in any of the cabinet discussions about Captain Wilkes. Sumner had no hesitation about blaming Seward: "The special cause of the English feeling is aggravated by the idea on their part that Seward wishes war, they say—'very well—then we will not wait,'" he told a friend in New York. "If the [British] Govt & the people could be thoroughly satisfied of the *real good will* of this Administration, a great impediment to Peace would be removed." That impediment, of course, was Seward.[55]

The arrival of the British newspapers on Friday, December 13, brought an abrupt end to all the speculation and celebrations that had been allowed to proliferate unchecked since November 16. The angry leaders and articles demanding reparation left no doubt as to how the British regarded Wilkes's act. On Monday morning in New York there were rowdy scenes at the stock exchange as investors dumped their bonds and rushed to buy commodities such as gold, saltpeter, and gun-powder. A run on the banks suspended all business, including the pay-ment of a loan to the Treasury that Secretary Chase had been expecting in mid-December. The New York offices of Barings and Rothschild's closed their doors, and Rothschild's transferred their American holdings to France to safeguard them from confiscation by the U.S. government.[56]

Dr. Elizabeth Blackwell took a brief rest from her teaching duties at the New York Infirmary to explain to her friends in London that it was all a terrible mistake. "Indeed, I have never before had cause for so much gloom," she wrote. "The *Trent* affair was no intentional insult to the En-glish flag—on the contrary . . . the whole thing is marked more by the *ill-breeding* of Americans and a reckless ignoring of consequences than by . . . deliberate insults which England attributes to her." Her friends and relatives were keenly divided on the issue. "With part of our own family furiously American and part as furiously English—disapproving as we do of the conduct of both countries—it is a terrible trial of feeling," she admitted.[57]

In Washington, Seward was aghast, having received over the weekend the first of Adams's dispatches regarding the British response to the *Trent* affair. A plaintive letter had also come from the Duchess of Sutherland begging him to stay true to his ideals: "I do not know if you will recollect me; but I think so. I liked much having known you. Your feeling toward England seemed so friendly. Your aspirations, your earnestness against slavery were so great, I rejoiced in hearing you speak," she wrote.[58] The letters so shook him that he ran across the street to the White House. He burst in on Lincoln, who was entertaining a few friends, to announce that Britain was preparing for war. "I don't believe England has done so foolish a thing," declared Orville Browning, one of the senators present. After Seward had read out Adams's dispatch, their incredulity turned to outrage. Browning jumped up and urged Lincoln to "fight to the death."[59]

More newspapers arrived on the sixteenth, with reports that Britain was backing up her demands with thousands of "crack troops." Perhaps almost as disturbing for Seward was the discovery that Sumner and Lin-coln had been discussing the *Trent* affair behind his back. Seward realized he had three choices: to press for war, to follow Sumner's lead and sup-port arbitration, or to argue for the correct but unpopular course de-manded by England. Seward hated all three options. That night he went to the Portuguese minister's ball looking bloodshot and disheveled. He ruined his attempt to appear relaxed by swearing and speaking too loudly. Toward the end of the evening Seward unsteadily approached a group of guests, which included William Howard Russell and the Prince de Joinville, and began boasting of what would happen to Britain if she forced the United States into war. "We will wrap the whole world in flames!" he exclaimed. "No power so remote that she will not feel the fire of our battle and be burned by our conflagration."[60]

William Howard Russell assumed that Seward had made up his mind to fight, even though a guest at the ball had scoffed that the secretary of state "always talks that way when he means to break down." Russell's letters from home showed that war was a foregone conclusion over there; *The Times* was already making arrangements for him to report from Canada. The following night, however, Russell went to Seward's house for dinner and was greeted by the secretary of state as if the events of the previous day had never happened. Seward smoothly assured him "that everything consistent with US honour would be done" to assuage Britain's feelings.[61] Russell silently disagreed with Seward's prediction; he thought the public would never stand for it and neither would Congress.[62] From his military contacts, Russell heard that the army's commanders were confident they would whip the British, which he found rather amusing, having recently spent an evening with Captain Leonard Currie, the English assistant adjutant general to General Smith, who told him "amusing stories of utter want of subordination, mutiny in refusing to go on guard or on duty, etc."[63]

Seward's dinner was in full swing when the *Europa* sailed into Boston Harbor. Quietly and unobtrusively, Captain Conway Seymour boarded the Washington train for the last stage of his journey. He had been traveling for only a few hours when the train came to a shuddering halt in the dark countryside. Hearing that repairs would not take place until the morning, Seymour commandeered a horse and rode all night to Baltimore, where he succeeded in chartering a special train to Washington. Finally, a little before midnight on Wednesday, December 18, the white-faced and exhausted Queen's messenger climbed the steps of Lord Lyons's house.

The following day, at three o'clock in the afternoon, Lyons presented himself at Seward's office. (In one of those strange quirks of timing, on the other side of the Atlantic, Charles Francis Adams had his meeting with Lord Russell on the same day, at the same hour.) Everything, it seemed to him, depended upon his delivery. He had to persuade the secretary of state to bring his games to an end without provoking him into making some last desperate attempt at bravado. Lord Russell was confident in his minister, but his namesake, William Howard Russell, shuddered to think that peace depended on the shyest man in North America. "Lord Lyons is a very odd sort of man," he wrote to the editor of *The Times* on December 20, "and not quite the person to deal with this crisis tho' he is most diligent, clear headed and straight viewed. He is nervous and afraid of responsibility—and he has no personal influence in Washington because he never goes into American society tho' he gives dinners very frequently."[64]

Lyons was nervous, but he carried himself with surprising aplomb. Seward let him speak without interruption and then asked to know the truth: What would happen if the government refused or requested further discussion? "I told him that my instructions were positive and left me no discretion," reported Lyons. Seward looked straight at him and begged for more time; he would never be able to bring around Lincoln's cabinet, let alone the country, in only seven days. Lyons believed him and agreed to return in two days, at which point the clock would be started. He went home feeling that his mission was already lost; he sincerely doubted that two, ten, or twenty days would make a difference. Rear Admiral Milne was sent a coded telegram instructing him to be ready to transport the legation staff to Canada.

When Lyons returned to Seward on Saturday, December 21, he was met with a plea for a couple more days. Ordinarily Lyons never disobeyed orders, but he knew that Seward was in a corner. Lyons had received an assurance from Baron Mercier that France's letter in support of Britain would be arriving any day. If Seward did not succeed in convincing the president's cabinet, the United States would be fighting an Anglo-French alliance in the North and the Confederacy in the South. A new appointment was set for Monday the twenty-third at 10:00 A.M., but this had to be the final meeting, he told Seward. The official protest would be presented on Monday, and the United States would have seven days to respond. That afternoon, Lincoln told Senator Browning that Seward had asked Lyons to read the demands to him in two days' time. The president had "an inkling of what they were," reported Browning, unaware that Lincoln knew exactly what they were since Seward had been keeping him informed from the beginning. After Seward's first meeting with Lyons, Lincoln had approached the editor of the *Philadelphia Press* for his help in "preparing the American people for the release of Mason and Slidell."[65] But Lincoln was being pulled in different directions; Sumner had also come by the White House to show him letters from John Bright and others that supported arbitration. Frustrated by his three-way conversation with Lyons, Lincoln asked Sumner why he could not speak to the minister himself. "If I could see Lord Lyons, I could show him in five minutes that I am heartily for peace," he said.[66] But Sumner would not allow it, saying without justification that a meeting between the president and a minister would be a breach of protocol. Sumner went further and not only extracted a promise from Lincoln to show him any correspondence before it was sent to Lord Lyons, but also set him up to defy Seward.

On the twenty-third, Lord Lyons went to the State Department for the third time, wondering if the meeting with Seward would be their last together. There was little for them to say to each other after he presented Lord Russell's letter; but Lyons could not help feeling sorry for Seward. He knew that the secretary of state was carrying an immense burden. Lyons had tried to make the situation easier for him by granting the extra time; if the transatlantic cable had still been working, he would not have had the discretion, but as it was, Lyons boldly made the decision in his belief that Seward would do his utmost to prevent a war. "You will perhaps be surprised to find Mr. Seward on the side of peace," Lyons explained to Lord Russell. But "ten months of office have dispelled many of his illusions . . . he no longer believes . . . in the ease with which the United States could crush rebellion with one hand, and chastise Europe with the other." Lyons was optimistic that Seward had learned his lesson and would never again regard relations with England as "safe playthings to be used for the amusement of the American People."[67]

Seward persuaded Lincoln to call a cabinet meeting for ten o'clock on Christmas morning. The secretary of state began by passing around copies of Lord Russell's "seven-days" letter. As he talked, however, it became clear that the cabinet remained opposed to releasing the Confederate commissioners.[68] Sumner, who was also present, spoke after Seward; he had come armed with letters from England. John Bright's was particularly eloquent about the aristocratic mob screaming for war. Sumner outlined to the cabinet what he had previously told Lincoln: since capitulation was politically impossible, an offer to go to arbitration was the government's only option. Otherwise Britain and probably France would break the blockade. The ironclad ships of the Royal Navy would smash the wooden U.S. fleet, the North would in turn be blockaded and its ports destroyed. The Confederacy, in the meantime, would sign a free trade agreement with England, "making the whole North American continent a manufacturing dependency of England."[69]

Sumner was still speaking when the door opened and a messenger brought in the official French response to the crisis. The dispatch unambiguously denounced Wilkes's act as a violation of international law. For a second, Seward was crestfallen, until he realized that his case had just been made for him. Edward Bates, the attorney general, was the first to see that Sumner's proposal for arbitration was hardly less dangerous than retaining the commissioners. Bates recorded in his diary: "I . . . urged that to go to war with England is to abandon all hope of suppressing the rebellion. . . . The maritime superiority of Britain would sweep us from the Southern waters. Our trade would be utterly ruined and our treasury bankrupt. In short . . . we *must not* have war with England. There was great reluctance on the part of some of the members of the cabinet—and even the President himself—to acknowledge these obvious truths."[70] The situation was too galling, objected Salmon P. Chase, despite, or possibly because, the country was facing bankruptcy unless he could raise another loan. The markets had reacted almost as badly to the notion of arbitration as they had to that of the prisoners arriving in Fort Warren. Banks were nearly at the bottom of their reserves, government bonds were plummeting again, and gold was running high.[71]

The meeting adjourned at 2:00 P.M. with an agreement to reconvene the following day. Before he left, Lincoln turned to Seward and asked him to summarize his arguments on paper. The president would do the same for Sumner's arbitration idea, and they would debate the two positions in the morning. Seward wrote all night; Lincoln made a half-hearted attempt before accepting that it was useless to delay the inevitable. When Senator Browning anxiously questioned him after dinner, Lincoln reassured him that there was not going to be a war with England.

By morning Seward had drafted a twenty-six-page response to Lord Lyons, which in effect dismissed the entire imbroglio as a consequence of Wilkes's forgetting to take the *San Jacinto* to a prize court for adjudication. He hoped it answered all the cabinet's objections, but he was too tired to judge. He left his house on Lafayette Square early and paid a surprise visit to Chase. If the secretary of the treasury could be persuaded, he thought, the others would follow his line. In fact, Chase, like Lincoln, had already begun to come around to Seward's way of thinking. Seward showed him the letter and explained why his idea was so much better than Sumner's. Rather than risk war by insisting on arbitration, they should pack the commissioners off to London and claim it as a victory for American neutral rights.[72] Chase consoled himself with the thought that if that happened, revenge on England would only be postponed.

Emotions were running high in the Senate. A last-ditch attempt by Senator Hale to force a resolution against releasing the rebel commissioners prevented Sumner from attending the meeting on the twenty-sixth. His absence allowed Seward to explain his letter to a far less critical audience. Seward kept expecting Lincoln to offer his alternative, but the president said nothing, and after comparatively little discussion, the cabinet approved Seward's proposal. He could hardly believe the sudden change of opinion. When the others had filed out, Seward turned to Lincoln and asked him why he had not made the case for arbitration. Because "I could not make an argument that would satisfy my own mind," the president replied.[73]

The cabinet had agreed to say nothing of the matter until Lyons received Seward's letter on the following morning, the twenty-seventh. That night, Sumner was in an ebullient mood when he attended a dinner given by William Howard Russell. After some diversionary talk about Prince Albert's death, the discussion turned exclusively to the *Trent*. Even at this late stage, Russell told the group, he had not heard a single voice in favor of giving up the Southerners; the government would never be able to pull off something so unpopular. But Sumner corrected him. There was no need for the administration to do anything so drastic, he insisted. "At the very utmost," he declared, "the *Trent* affair can only be a matter for mediation." Russell assumed that he was hearing the official line, since Sumner was in "intimate rapport with the President."[74]

The next day Russell was reading the Washington newspapers, which were still insisting that the rebels would never be given up, when he received a note from one of the secretaries at the British legation. "What a collapse!" he wrote, a trifle disappointed that it was back to business as usual. Sumner's surprise was even greater. Not twenty-four hours ago, the president had been adamantly opposed to any such settlement. Sumner had already accepted Seward's invitation to dinner that night. Begging off now would only call attention to his defeat.

Among the guests at Seward's was Anthony Trollope, who was oblivious to the drama unfolding in front of him.[75] Charles Sumner was unusually quiet and left the talking to Senator Crittenden, who made disparaging comments about Florence Nightingale to Trollope, no doubt unaware that the woman whose reputation he was trashing had recently donated her sanitation reports and hospital plans to the U.S. War Department.[76] Seward played the genial host to the hilt; after dinner, he invited the four senators at the table to accompany him to his study. He bade them all sit down while he took out the dispatches from London and Paris. To these he added his twenty-six-page reply to Lord Russell, his dispatch to Charles Francis Adams, and his response to the French foreign minister. Sumner and the others then had to sit in silence while Seward read out every line.[77]

A week later, on January 1, 1862, the two Confederate commissioners and their secretaries sailed for England on board the warship HMS *Rinaldo*. "[The Americans] are horribly out of humour," Lyons wrote to Lord Russell on December 31. He did not think this was the end of the story, but for now they could put their faith in Seward. "For he must do his best to maintain peace, or he will have made the sacrifice . . . in vain."[78] Seward had triumphed, but only just, and only for the moment. His reply to Russell, which Seward had composed with his domestic audience firmly in mind, failed as a legal document or as a new elaboration of U.S. foreign policy, but it successfully appealed to Northern readers, especially the part where he claimed that because of the *Trent* case, Britain would never again attempt to impress American sailors (a practice last used in 1812).

Sumner tried to diminish Seward's victory by claiming that the president had preferred arbitration but the need for a quick decision had forced him into a hasty act.[79] There was perhaps some consolation to him in the vitriolic and bitter speeches that enlivened Congress during the first week of January. On the ninth, Sumner gave a long speech in the Senate that was meant to explain and justify the government's decision. All the press, most of the president's cabinet, nearly every senator, and all the foreign ministers—except Lord Lyons—went to hear the performance. Senator Sumner had dressed for the occasion. Afterward, he was remembered as much for his olive-green gloves and tailored suit as for what he said. It was notoriously hard to follow Sumner. "He works his adjectives so hard," a journalist once commented, "that if they ever catch him alone, they will murder him."[80] He spoke for three and a half hours, flatly contradicting many of the arguments Seward had employed in his dispatch to Lord Russell.

The public's response exceeded all Sumner's expectations. There were tributes and editorials in the press. People who usually avoided him because of his abolition politics were eager to shake his hand.[81] Sumner's previous criticisms of Seward's reckless diplomacy were repeated and turned into the reason for Britain's "overreaction." The remarkable

"UP A TREE."
Colonel Bull and the Yankee 'Coon.
'Coon. "AIR YOU IN ARNEST, COLONEL?"
Colonel Bull. "I AM."
'Coon. "DON'T FIRE—I'LL COME DOWN."

Punch crows after the Union backs down, January 1862.

courage and patriotism Seward had displayed in forcing the cabinet to make an unpopular decision were brushed aside.

Lord Lyons knew what it was like to have one's intentions maligned and efforts discounted, and he was among the few people in Washington who secretly applauded Seward for his bravery. The shy minister did not know it, but he, too, had gained an admirer on account of his behavior during the crisis. As "one who witnessed the difficulties of Lord Lyons's position here, and how his pathway was strewn with broken glass," wrote Adam Gurowski, the State Department's chief translator, "[I] must feel for him the highest and most sincere consideration. . . . During the whole *Trent* affair, Lord Lyons's conduct was discreet, delicate, and generous . . . a mind soured by human meanness is soothingly impressioned by such true nobleness in a diplomat and an Englishman."[82]

NINE

The War Moves to England

Hard times in Lancashire—Burnside captures Roanoke—The sorrows of Lincoln—A victory at last—Mason and Slidell arrive in Europe—Dawson joins the Nashville—*Southern propaganda—The debate in Parliament*

"We are beginning the New Year under very poor prospects," recorded a cotton spinner named John Ward from Clitheroe on January 1, 1862. Twenty-seven thousand workers in Lancashire had been fired and another 160,000 were, like him, surviving on short time. Families on his street were selling their furniture to buy food. "A war with America" would be the final straw, wrote Ward, "as we will get no cotton. . . . Every one is anxious for the arrival of the next mail, which is expected every day."[1]

In Liverpool, crowds gathered each morning on the quayside waiting for America's response. The arrival of the *Africa* on January 2 caused brief excitement, but she carried only newspapers in her hold. The telegrapher Paul Julius de Reuter came to see Charles Francis Adams on Monday the sixth to ask if the minister would be so kind as to alert him the minute there was news. "He little imagines how entirely my government keeps me without information," Adams wrote angrily.[2] Two days later, it was Reuter who did Adams the kindness; his office had received an early telegram announcing the commissioners' release. Weed came an hour later to confirm that it was all over London. Adams's relief was tempered by his vexation at being the last to know.

Benjamin Moran rushed to St. James's, the club of the diplomatic

NAUGHTY JONATHAN.

Mrs Britannia. "THERE, JOHN! HE SAYS HE IS VERY SORRY, AND THAT HE DIDN'T MEAN TO DO IT—SO YOU CAN PUT THIS BACK INTO THE PICKLE-TUB."

Punch depicts the United States as a recalcitrant child in need of a whipping.

corps on Charles Street and probably the only club in London that would have him. For once he was the center of attention as two dozen minor diplomats and secretaries "sprang to their feet as if electrified," he wrote. Several even shook his hand before running off to the telegraph office. "In a few minutes messages were flashing over the wires to all the Courts of Europe." In the West End theaters, evening performances were already under way, but as soon as the curtains fell on the first act the news was announced, causing audiences to rise spontaneously and cheer.[3] Within the British cabinet, however, reactions were rather more mixed: "The Admiralty is flat and dull, now there is to be no war," the Duke of Somerset wrote sarcastically to his son, Lord Edward St. Maur.[4]

More than £2 million had been spent in the scramble to get ships and troops to America. It would be some time before soldiers came home. Jonny Stanley wrote to his parents from Montreal to say that he was safe although lonely. The infinite forests and frozen lakes of Canada were "very dull, and the people, however socially inclined, thoroughly different in manners and ways of thinking."[5] The troops had so little to do that a sizable number would slip away over the winter months, only to reappear on the other side of the American border as Northern volunteers.[6]

The press assumed that relations between the two countries would quickly return to normal. The *Illustrated London News* congratulated England for having dealt with the crisis so adroitly. "We are therefore clear of all blame in the whole transaction," it opined on January 11, "and legally, morally, and even sentimentally, we have shown ourselves friends to the Americans."[7] This was not the view of 20 million Americans. Huddled in his frozen headquarters in northern Virginia, Union general George Meade wrote to his wife that "if ever this domestic war of ours is settled, it will require but the slightest pretext to bring about a war with England."[8] A congressman from Illinois swore on the floor of the House that he had "never shared in the traditional hostility of many of my countrymen against England. But I now here publicly avow and record my inextinguishable hatred of that Government. I mean to cherish it while I live and to bequeath it as a legacy to my children when I die." From Paris, Seward's unofficial emissary Archbishop Hughes exhorted him to remember that the "awful war between England and America must come sooner or later,—and in preparing for it, even now, there is not a moment to be lost."[9]

Charles Francis Adams had neither the clarity of anger nor the cushion of complacency to comfort him. The news about the *Trent* had been followed by a letter from Charles Francis Jr. informing his family that he had joined the 1st Massachusetts Cavalry. The unexpected blow made ordinary business seem "utterly without interest," wrote Adams.[10] The upset to the family was not enough, however, to divert attention from an embarrassing gaffe by Henry Adams. On January 10 *The Times* revealed that "Mr. H. Adams," the younger son and private secretary of the American minister, had published a mildly insulting article about English society for the American press. Henry had never intended to acknowledge "A Visit to Manchester" as his own, and so he had vented some of his frustrations about his social isolation in London society, pointedly remarking, "in Manchester, I am told, it is still the fashion for the hosts to see that the guests enjoy themselves. In London the guests shift for themselves . . . one is regaled with thimbles full of ice-cream and hard seed cakes." Charles Francis Jr. had accidentally left Henry's name on the manuscript when he sent it to the editor of the *Boston Courier*.[11] Until then, Henry had been enjoying great success as the *New York Times'* anonymous London correspondent. "The Chief," as Henry called his father, gave his son a sharp dressing-down, so sharp that Henry briefly considered self-exile on the Continent.[12] He was teased without mercy by Benjamin Moran, who repeated ad nauseam "it is not every boy of 25 who can in 6 mos. residence here extort a leader from *The Times*."[13]

When he visited the Foreign Office on January 11 for his first meeting since the *Trent* crisis, Adams hoped that Lord Russell had not seen the *Times* article about his son. There was no cause for concern: Russell could be curiously obtuse about what he read in the papers. (Lady Russell had a far better understanding of the power of the press than her husband; she thought the American public had been goaded beyond endurance by the "sneering, exulting tone" in English newspapers after Bull Run.)[14] The two men passed the first half of the interview congratulating each other on preserving the peace, after which it was down to business again. Russell's current concern was the risk to peace posed by Union and Confederate cruisers. The *Sumter* had recently arrived at Cadiz, having destroyed a number of U.S. merchant ships along the way. The government expected a confrontation with a U.S. Navy ship but would not tolerate a free-for-all in British waters, which in Palmerston's words would be a "scandal and inconvenience." In Southampton, the disruption to ordinary business had risen to unsupportable levels; the crews of the CSS *Nashville* and USS *Tuscarora*—which had been pursuing the *Nashville* since December—were fighting each other in the streets.[15] Adams was caught by surprise, not having given a thought to either vessel during the past few weeks. It was back to the old state of affairs, he realized.

Life for all the occupants of the American legation was slowly returning to normal. People had stopped inviting them, Henry told Charles Francis Jr., "on the just supposition that we wouldn't care to go into society." The drought ended with a dinner at the Argylls' on January 17. The evening passed far more enjoyably than the U.S. minister expected; Gladstone sat next to him and showed genuine interest in his views, and the guest on his other side praised him for "my conduct during the difficulties." But Adams's enjoyment was curtailed when the conversation turned to Seward and his now infamous quip to the Duke of Newcastle. "I feel my solitude in London much more than I do at home," Adams wrote in his diary a short time later. "The people are singularly repulsive.

With a very considerable number of acquaintances, I know not a single one whose society I should miss one moment."[16]

———

Adams did not know the true state of affairs in Washington, and Seward did not wish to enlighten him. The *Trent* was only one of many crises that threatened the administration during the winter of 1862. Criticism of the Federal government's lack of progress was growing ever louder, with Lincoln receiving the largest share of the blame. The border states had not been secured, and the vast Army of the Potomac encamped around Washington had yet to do anything other than drill. Its leader, General McClellan, remained bedridden with typhoid. The War Department was riddled with incompetence and corruption and the Treasury had run out of gold, leaving Secretary Chase with no alternative but to print more money. On the night of January 10, Seward received a summons to the White House. There he found Chase, Assistant Secretary of War Peter Watson, and two generals gathered in a solemn huddle around the president. They had to act now, Lincoln told them, and find a way to produce victories or face the possibility "of our being two nations."[17] Frustrated by the generals' objections, Lincoln decided he would issue a presidential order for all naval and military forces to begin an advance on February 22, regardless of obstacles or delays.

The president's frustration presented an opportunity for Seward to strengthen their relationship at a time when his own allies were deserting him in droves. "There is a formidable clique organized against Mr. Seward," the attorney general noted in his diary on February 2. "I do not think I heard a good word spoken of Mr. Seward as a Minister even by one of his own party," observed Trollope of his time in Washington. "He seemed to have no friend, no one who trusted him."[18] Frank Blair, the powerful congressman from Missouri, complained to colleagues that Seward was "selfish, ambitious and incompetent" and apparently more concerned with fighting England than the South.[19] A senator attacked Seward for being "a low, vulgar, vain demagogue."[20]

Seward gave loyal service to Lincoln; while Mary Lincoln seemed incapable of fulfilling the role of confidante, the former contender for the White House found that he could adapt to the role with ease. Seward could not solve the president's military problems, but he was able to smooth the way for the secretary of war's departure on January 14, 1862, and the appointment of Edwin Stanton. The new secretary was arrogant and devious but, in contrast to Cameron, was efficient and would attack the department's problems with energy. The amiable but useless Cameron chose to spend his forced retirement in Russia, where he replaced the equally useless Cassius Clay as minister.

Simultaneously with Cameron's removal, some flicker of life appeared in the North's military machine. On January 14, the English volunteer George Henry Herbert learned that the "Zou-Zous"—as members of the 9th New York Infantry (Hawkins's Zouaves) were affectionately called—were going to evacuate from Hatteras Inlet. Despite the monotony of drilling and digging at Camp Wool, Herbert had never felt so content with his life. "Since I wrote to you I have received my promotion. I am now 2nd Lieutenant," he informed his mother. He promised to send a photograph of himself in his new officer's uniform in his next letter in case it was his last. "Our boys here are in high glee, we are going to leave Hatteras in a day or two," he explained. "We are part of an expedition under the command of General Burnside. It consists of somewhere about an hundred vessels of all sorts, containing a land force of as near as I can learn, about 10,000 men of all arms. Its destination is unknown. The rumour is New Orleans. I fervently hope so."[21]

The rumors were unfounded. Thirteen thousand men were leaving Cape Hatteras, heading up the North Carolina sounds to the mysterious Roanoke Island, a forlorn stretch of grass and swamp between the mainland and the Outer Banks. Its first inhabitants, Sir Walter Raleigh's ill-fated colonists, had survived in the New World for less than four years before they mysteriously disappeared. Three hundred years later the island seemed as untamed as ever. Its chief importance was strategic: whoever owned Roanoke held the key to Richmond's back door.[22]

General Ambrose Burnside (whose name and prodigious whiskers inspired the word "sideburns") had convinced General McClellan that he could lead a combined amphibious force in light-draft and flat-bottomed boats that would have no trouble navigating the shallow waters of Roanoke Sound. The Confederate garrison guarding Roanoke was small and unlikely to withstand a sustained assault. Burnside was so confident that he gave permission for journalists to accompany the expedition. William Howard Russell heard the news from his sickbed in a hotel in New York. The journalist had been worn down by the unrelenting campaign of abuse against him: "There is a sort of weakness and lan-

USS *Picket* leading the ships of the Burnside expedition over the Hatteras Bar in North Carolina, by Frank Vizetelly.

guor over me that I never experienced before," he told Delane. Frank Vizetelly would go and report for both of them.[23]

Vizetelly, so deep in debt that even Russell would no longer lend him money, was overjoyed at the prospect of escaping Washington. He joined Burnside's flotilla on January 10 with nothing else except a small bag containing a change of clothes and his pencils. "Woe is me!" he wrote after several days of crashing seas and hurricane winds. One night, a thunderous wave hit the boat with such force that he was catapulted from his bed against the cabin door, which burst open, depositing him with a thud in eight inches of briny water. He decided this would be his first and last amphibious expedition.[24]

The first phase of the attack was easily accomplished and the southern half of Roanoke Island was captured on February 7 without Herbert or his friends firing a shot. "Day broke cold, damp, and miserable," Vizetelly wrote on the eighth. "After a drink of water and a biscuit for each man, the Federal force prepared to advance into the interior."[25] Cannon fire alerted Herbert that it would soon be his regiment's turn to leave the makeshift camp. "Near the centre of the island it is very narrow and at the narrowest point a battery was erected," he explained to his mother. "The road is in fact nothing but a cow path through fine woods and a thick growth of underbrush."[26] The men had to march along the track two by two in order to allow room for the stretcher bearers carrying the wounded back to the ships. "I remember after that," commented a private in the regiment, "a sort of sickening sensation as if I was going to a slaughter-house to be butchered."[27]

"At last we came in front of the battery," wrote Herbert. The order came to charge and they plunged into the knee-deep swamp that surrounded the Confederate position. Vizetelly watched as they hurled themselves up the slope of the battery. The men behaved, he continued, "in the most brilliant manner, dashing through the swamp and over the stumps of the pine-clearing, and into the battery, which the Confederates were hastily leaving." When they reached the top, they discovered that the rebels had fled. The 9th took up the chase for four miles and finally cornered the defenders at the northern tip of the island, in their own camp.

Herbert was delighted to hear that a journalist from the *Illustrated London News* was with them, and he asked his mother to look out for his reports. A total of 264 Union solders and 143 Confederates had been killed in the attack; later, he would consider such casualty numbers remarkably small, but for now he thought he had survived a great battle. Vizetelly admitted to being impressed. "I will not attempt to prophesy a triumph for the Federalists," he told readers at home, "but, seeing the improved condition in the morale of the Union forces, and feeling somewhat competent to give an opinion, I am inclined to believe that these first successes are not to be their last. I have watched the Northern army almost from its first appearance in the field. I have seen it a stripling . . . I now see it arrived at man's estate."[28]

News of Burnside's success on Roanoke Island reached Washington while the city was still under the rosy glow of Mary Lincoln's triumphant White House ball held on February 5. The capital celebrated even harder when it learned that a great victory had been won in Tennessee. General Ulysses S. Grant had captured Fort Henry on the sixth and Fort Donelson on the fifteenth, giving him control of Tennessee's two main rivers, the Cumberland and the Tennessee. An important water highway had been opened for the North, which ran from the north of Kentucky all the way down to Mississippi and Alabama.

Lord Lyons wished in his heart he could escape while there was rela-

The 9th New York Volunteers (Hawkins's Zouaves) and the 21st Massachusetts in a bayonet charge on the Confederate fieldworks on Roanoke Island, by Frank Vizetelly.

tive calm. "I don't expect to be ever free here from troubles," he wrote.[29] There would always be another incident. "I have no doubt that for me personally this would be the moment to give up this place. I can never keep things in as good a state as they are," he confided to his sister two days after the ball. "However, I cannot propose this to the Government, especially after the GCB—and of course feel bound to stay as long as they wish to keep me."[30] Lyons was referring to the Order of the Bath, which Lord Russell had arranged to have bestowed upon him for his handling of the *Trent* crisis. When he had learned of the honor, Lyons had written to Russell with his characteristic humility that he had done nothing "brilliant or striking;" "the only merit which I can attribute to myself is that of having laboured sedulously, though quietly and unobtrusively . . . to carry out honestly your orders and wishes."[31] He also commended his staff for their exemplary behavior during the crisis— although he would not have been able to say the same for them now. Since the resolution of the affair, the attachés and secretaries had been living up to their nickname of "the Bold Buccaneers." Two of the more literary members of the group had decided to put on a play, and persuaded Lyons to allow them to perform it at the British legation.

The attachés' youth and high spirits insulated them from the subdued atmosphere that pervaded Washington after the sudden death of
Lincoln's middle son, Willie, on February 20. The precocious eleven-
year-old, who had reigned as the undisputed favorite of the family, was
suspected to have died of typhoid fever. Mary Lincoln withdrew into her
own private agony of grief, leaving her devastated husband with the burden of caring for their other boy still at home, seven-year-old Tad, who
was battling the same illness that had killed his brother. The *Spectator*'s
correspondent Edward Dicey was introduced to Lincoln not long after
Willie's funeral and noted the "depression about his face, which, I am
told by those who see him daily, was habitual to him, even before the recent death of his child." During their short interview Lincoln earnestly
interrogated him about English public opinion. "Like all Americans,"
commented Dicey, he "was unable to comprehend the causes which
have alienated the sympathies of the mother country."*32

The same question about England's sympathies was being asked in
the South. "Seward has cowered beneath the roar of the British Lion,"
bemoaned John Jones, a clerk in the Confederate War Department.
"Now we must depend upon our own strong arms and stout hearts for
defense."33 Even the shrewd and unflappable diarist Mary Chesnut had
given in to her optimism during the *Trent* affair. For a brief moment she
had shared the belief so prevalent in the South that the Royal Navy
would appear off the coast and blow the blockade to smithereens. Now
she wondered if the British were laughing at them, "scornful and scoff-
ing . . . on our miseries."34 Despite the brouhaha over their release, she
feared that Commissioners Slidell and Mason were chasing a chimera.
"Lord Lyons has gone against us. Lord Derby and Louis Napoleon are
silent in our hour of need," she wrote. The loss of Roanoke and the forts
in Tennessee caused an uproar in Richmond. Someone had to bear the
blame for these dreadful and unexpected defeats, and who better than

---

* Dicey never realized how much his references to the "mother country" alienated
Americans. His innocent, if tongue-in-cheek, comparison of New York with London caused great irritation. "Everything around and about me looked so like the
Old Country," he wrote. Landing on the docks, "Irish porters seized upon my luggage as they would have done at the Tower steps in London. Street newsboys
pestered me with second editions of English-printed newspapers. An Old-
fashioned English hackney coach carried me to my destination, through dull, En-
glish-looking streets, with English names; and the driver cheated me at the end of
my fare, with genuine London exorbitance."

the Confederate secretary of war, Judah Benjamin? "Mr. Davis's pet Jew," as his critics called him, was accused of having sacrificed Roanoke Island by refusing to send reinforcements. Benjamin's stint at the War Department had been hampered from the start by his lack of rapport with the military, and this latest crisis would make his position untenable. However, the truth in the case of Roanoke, which out of loyalty he never revealed to Davis, was that there were neither arms nor men to spare.[35] Two or three arms shipments a month from England were not enough to maintain one army, let alone several across hundreds of miles.

The freedom experienced by the four ex-prisoners on board HMS *Rinaldo* as she crossed the Atlantic in early January was far worse than the dull confinement the Confederate commissioners had endured at Fort Warren. To walk on the icy deck was to risk a thousand deaths. Huge icicles dangled above their heads. Any person not wearing a safety rope was liable to slip or be blown out to sea. Before the journey's end, many of the sailors had suffered frostbite. "If you have no news of 'Rinaldo,' I fear she is lost— horrible to think of," William Howard Russell wrote to Delane on January 16. Horrible but somehow not unexpected, considering the appalling misfortunes that had already blighted the Southerners' mission.[36]

"Mr. Slidell," declared a Northern journal, "is the ideal of a man who would think it a privilege to get into a scrape himself, if he could only involve his host and patron too." Mr. Mason, on the other hand, was "more of a bull-dog, ready to fasten on friends and foes alike."[37] Yet, until the *Trent* affair, there had been nothing in their previous histories to suggest that either James Murray Mason or John Slidell was the type of man whose fate would move armies. They so neatly fitted into Southern stereotypes as to be walking caricatures of a Virginia aristocrat and a Louisiana politician. Mason, who had been brought up amid elegant surroundings and liveried servants, could trace his family back to the English Civil War, in which one of his Cavalier ancestors commanded a regiment at the Battle of Worcester. Slidell, on the other hand, was the son of a moderately successful New York candle maker who had fled the city after a scandal involving a pistol fight and reinvented himself as a successful lawyer in New Orleans.[38] Slidell had few hatreds, but one of them was for New Yorkers who refused to forget his humble beginnings.[39] He was happier in New Orleans, where he could lift his finger and see his puppets raise their hands.

William Howard Russell had met both men and found them tolerable. Mason was tall, heavyset, and crowned with a bouffant hairdo that was once leonine but had started to recede into a mohawk. His bright blue eyes and ruddy cheeks made him appear kindly, but out of his small, thin mouth came the most unashamedly racist and proslavery statements Russell had ever heard. His proudest achievement up to this point had been the drafting of the 1850 Fugitive Slave Act, which denied escaped slaves any place of sanctuary in the United States. Mr. Mason, Russell informed readers of *The Times* on December 10, "is a man of considerable belief in himself; he is a proud, well-bred, not unambitious gentleman, whose position gave him the right to expect high office," though, as would become apparent, not necessarily the talent. His ten years as chairman of the Senate Foreign Relations Committee had left no discernible trace of experience on him. Mary Chesnut considered him to be one of the bigger imbeciles among her acquaintances: "My wildest imagination will not picture Mr. Mason as a diplomat," she had written after hearing of his appointment. "He will say 'chaw' for 'chew,' and he will call himself 'Jeems,' and he will wear a dress coat to breakfast. Over here, whatever a Mason does is right in his own eyes. He is above law." Mary knew the English horror of tobacco chewing, too. "I don't care how he pronounces the nasty thing but he will do it," she wrote. "In England a man must expectorate like a gentleman if he expectorates at all."[40] This last observation was certainly true, and it would count against Mason almost as much as his passionate belief in slavery.[41]

By contrast, "Mr. Slidell," Russell wrote in his diary, "is to the South something greater than Mr. Thurlow Weed has been to his party in the North." Like Mason, he was tall and well built, but feline rather than bluff with "fine thin features, [and] a cold keen grey eye."[42] His French was excellent, thanks to his Creole wife, as was his taste in wine. His suave manner was the antithesis of Mason's chomping heartiness. "He is not a speaker of note, nor a ready stump orator, nor an able writer, but he is an excellent judge of mankind, adroit, persevering, and subtle, full of device, and fond of intrigue . . . what is called here a 'wire-puller.' "[43] He could destroy a man or make him, as he did Judah Benjamin, who owed his entire political career to Slidell's connections. If the attainment of power was a belief, then Slidell was a practicing zealot. On all other questions he was agnostic. Slidell's urge to politick was so great, wrote Russell, that if he were shut up in a dungeon he "would conspire with the mice against the cat rather than not conspire at all."[44]

The Confederates arrived in England on January 29 to little fanfare. The press, including *The Times,* had warned the country against turning them into heroes; the Confederate commissioners were representatives of a government that was waging an undeclared war against Britain's cotton industry. Mason asked his friend William Gregory, MP, whom he had not seen since Gregory's visit to Washington in 1859, whether British resentment of the cotton embargo was the reason for the "harsh" treatment meted out to the *Nashville* and Captain Pegram, who had been forbidden to make any military alterations to his ship or stay longer once his repairs were completed. Gregory told him that, on the contrary, this was in accordance with the neutrality proclamation.

The *Nashville* set sail from Southampton on February 3, cheered on by thousands of well-wishers. (William Yancey's departure, on the same day but in a different ship, went unremarked.) With her Confederate flags and black-painted hull, the ship managed to look warlike and dashing at the same time. HMS *Shannon*—with gun ports open and engines running—stood guard between the *Nashville* and *Tuscarora*. There could be no engagement between the warring vessels in British waters. Much to Captain Craven's chagrin, the *Tuscarora* would have to wait twenty-four hours before she could begin her pursuit of the *Nashville.*[*]

Unbeknown to Captain Robert B. Pegram, a young man who called himself Francis Dawson had joined the crew under false pretenses as its fifty-first member. Pegram had thought he was dealing with a boy of sixteen or seventeen when Dawson first asked to come on board. He offered him a position "as a sailor before the mast," meaning the lowest rank of seaman, and assumed that this would be the last he saw of him. Dawson boarded the ship with the help of one of the master's mates. But he was no teenage runaway; he was in fact a twenty-one-year-old who had failed to break into the theater as a playwright and was looking for a new occupation. His real name was Austin Reeks; his father had ruined the family through one idiotic financial speculation after another, leaving

---

[*] Under the Declaration of Paris, when two belligerent ships arrived at a neutral port, their departure had to be separated by twenty-four hours to forestall the risk of a battle in the neutral country's waters.

his mother dependent on the charity of relatives. A widowed aunt who paid for Austin's education was the inspiration for his new name: Francis Warrington Dawson. Mrs. Dawson's late husband, William Dawson, had been an officer in the Indian Army. The change of identity and the leap into an adventure was not untypical behavior for Austin. He had never wanted to be himself, living in poverty with a father who made him ashamed and a mother he pitied. "My idea simply was to go to the South, do my duty there as well as I might, and return home to England," Dawson wrote in his reminiscences. One of his great strengths was that he believed his own stories. Once he had claimed that he was motivated to fight for the South by idealism, it became true.

He needed every shred of his sense of duty to survive his difficult initiation into life at sea. On his second day, Dawson's trunk was broken open and his belongings stolen. The old sea hands disliked the interloper who spoke fine English and said his rosary at night. They resented even more his obvious rapport with the ship's officers, and they punished him with the worst jobs. After nearly three weeks of hazing from the crew, Dawson decided that his life was "truly a hard one. I could not have borne it but that I know how judicious is the step I have taken. . . . Time does not in the least reconcile me to the men in the forecastle! More and more do I detest and loathe them." Fortunately, once Captain Pegram discovered Dawson's presence, he took pity on him and gave orders for his bunk to be moved to the upper deck. He soon felt an avuncular concern for the impetuous youth and was overheard saying that he would do something for Dawson once they reached home. Dawson hoped so. "I am told that I may make a fortune in the South if I chose," he wrote his mother. "God grant that I may for your sakes."[45]

Dawson was part of a small but growing number of potential recruits who were trying to reach the South in spite of the blockade. "There may be some whose experience in the field or for drill may be useful," Mason wrote to Richmond after several ex-officers called at the new headquarters of the Confederate commission at 109 Piccadilly. "Will you please advise me what I am to say to such applicants."[46] While he waited, Mason was careful to be encouraging without committing himself or the commission to anything illegal under the Foreign Enlistment Act. The British authorities' punctiliousness over the *Nashville* had shown him that there would be no leniency as far as the law was concerned. Slidell could afford to be less fastidious. Soon after his arrival in Paris, he received a visit from a tall, leather-faced Englishman in his mid-fifties who declared his intention of joining the Confederate army. Impressed by the man's soldierly past and bearing, Slidell agreed to supply him with letters of introduction. In late spring the Knoxville *Register* announced that an English volunteer, Colonel George St. Leger Grenfell, had arrived in Charleston, South Carolina, on board the blockade runner *Nelly*.[47]

In Parliament, William Gregory was pleased to learn that Richmond had instructed Mason to challenge Britain's observance of the blockade; safeguarding the country's economy would be taken much more seriously by MPs than independence for slave owners. The commissioner had come armed with statistics that proved it was a blockade on paper only. True, the records stopped at the end of October, but they nevertheless showed that more than six hundred vessels had succeeded in getting through since April. The first step was to bring Mason together with Lord Russell. Gregory helped Mason draft a note, asking for an *unofficial* interview. He reminded Mason to use the correct form: "The Right Hon. Earl Russell, Foreign Office. I should not address your letter to his private house."[48] While they were waiting for Russell's reply, James Spence, the pro-Southern author of *The American Union,* introduced himself to the group. The Liverpudlian businessman had realized that there were social and financial opportunities to be gained from befriending the nascent Confederacy; in a bid to prove his usefulness, Spence offered to help Mason prepare for his meeting with Lord Russell.

Russell had no wish to see Mason. "What a fuss we have had about these two men," he exclaimed.[49] He had heard that William Gregory and William Lindsay had decided to force a debate on the blockade after the opening of Parliament on February 6. Russell already had a fair idea of the number of ships getting through from the diligent reports of the local consuls, but he balked at challenging its legality. There was no telling when Great Britain might find herself in the similar position of mounting a feeble blockade.[50] At the meeting on February 10, Russell resorted to his usual method with the Confederates and forced Mason to do most of the talking. Mason noticed that the foreign secretary "took very little part in the conversation," and he felt that he had been played throughout the interview. "On the whole," wrote Mason, "it was mani-

fest enough that his personal sympathies were not with us, and his policy inaction."[51] This was true. "At all events, I am heart and soul a neutral," Russell wrote to Lord Lyons just before the meeting.[52]

The Confederate lobby's obstinacy exasperated Palmerston and Russell. Both were highly sensitive as to how it would appear to the North if
Parliament debated whether to disregard its blockade. Coming so soon
after the *Trent* affair, it would add credence to the charge that Britain was
simply looking for an excuse to turn on the United States. No one in the
cabinet believed that the war could last much longer. Why irritate either
side, was the general consensus, when all they had to do was wait for perhaps only three more months? The Lord Chancellor, Lord Westbury, expressed himself in his customary splenetic way: "I am greatly opposed to
any violent interference. . . . Let them tear one another to pieces."[53] To
try to forestall a debate, Russell invited James Spence to attend a meeting
at the Foreign Office, since it was known that he was held in high esteem
by the Confederates. Spence was delighted with his newfound importance. He listened gravely as Russell explained why he should use his influence to stop the Confederates from forcing a vote. As soon as the
interview was over, Spence hurried to the commission's headquarters on
Piccadilly to urge the group to redouble its efforts.

Charles Francis Adams had heard that the Confederates' political
friends were pushing the blockade question. He wrote to Seward on
February 7 urgently requesting any facts and statistics he could pass on to
the North's supporters in Parliament. It was embarrassing personally
and diplomatically, he hinted, for the State Department to leave him so
ill informed. Adams had become reconciled to Thurlow Weed's presence, "but my patience is gradually oozing out of me at this extraordinary
practice of running me down with my own colleagues," he wrote in his
diary. "Mr. Seward was not brought up in the school of refined delicacy
of feeling or he would not have continued these inflictions."

What they needed, Weed told Seward, was a host of unofficial representatives whose sole purpose was to shape public opinion. Adams was a
good man but useless for anything other than strict diplomacy. "We may
want the good-will of England before our troubles are over, and it can be
had on easy terms," he wrote. "I believe now that nine tenths of the English People would rejoice to see us successful."[54] But this was hinged on
precarious foundations. It did no good for Seward to argue that slavery
was de facto abolished in the small areas of the South held by the Federal

army. He would have to say publicly that this was a war for abolition.[55] Could not Seward help them a little, Weed asked, by at least granting passports to free blacks? It would help counter the claim that the North was just as racist as the South and hypocritical as well.[56]

For the upcoming debate in Parliament, Weed and Adams looked to William Forster rather than John Bright to outmaneuver William Gregory and the small but growing Confederate lobby. "On the whole Mr. Forster has been our firmest and most judicious friend," Adams admitted privately. "We owe to his tact and talent even more than we do to the more showy interference of Messrs. Cobden and Bright."[57] The latter seemed to relish his powers of alienation. On February 17, Bright made a blistering speech in the Commons against aristocratic supporters of slavery, which struck his listeners as ludicrous considering that Lord Shaftesbury was leading a national campaign to reunite a fugitive slave named Anderson with his wife and children. One MP commented afterward, "I don't think the people of England like [Bright] and his policy better than they do his friends the Yankees."[58]

"We are miserably prepared to meet and answer objections," Weed grumbled to Seward on February 20. "Members of Parliament beset me for materials, and I cannot get anything official. I have picked what could be found of the Newspapers."[59] Although still chastened by his recent exposure in the press, Henry Adams discreetly tried to aid his father by pushing Frederick Seward, Seward's son, to send over any reports that could be of use. "The truth is, we want light here," Henry told him. "Our friends have got to be stuffed with statistics and crammed with facts. . . . The Southerners will parade a great number of vessels which have run it. Our side must show an equal or greater number either captured, or chased, and must have at hand any evidence." Otherwise, he warned, the Confederates would argue that the fourth provision of the Declaration of Paris was not being met—that the blockade actually exist and be effective—and therefore the blockade was illegal.[60]

As the day of the debate approached, Adams noticed a rise in the number of newspaper articles sympathetic to the South. He blamed the "unscrupulous and desperate emissaries" who were prepared to spread any number of lies—even that slavery in the South would be abolished after independence—on a credulous British public.[61] The "emissaries" were actually one agent, Henry Hotze, a journalist from Mobile, Alabama, who had been appointed by the Confederate State Department to liaise between the commission and the press. Hotze had arrived in England on the same day as Mason and Slidell, but he had not traveled with them. Although he was only twenty-seven years old, Hotze exuded the confidence of someone twice his age. He was fluent in French and German, having spent his childhood in Switzerland. His charm and powers of conversation were still legendary in Brussels, where he had served as the secretary of the American legation during the late 1850s.[62]

The mission to England had been Hotze's own idea. During the autumn he had spent a few weeks in London on behalf of the War Department checking on the progress of arms shipments. This was long enough to convince him that the South needed to "educate" the English press, and that he was the person to do it. Although Hotze despised Mason and abhorred his tobacco habit, he accepted that he was dependent on Mason's contacts until he could make his own.[63] Fortunately, Mason had no idea of Hotze's feelings toward him, and during their first weeks in London he invited the journalist to accompany him everywhere he went. In this way Hotze forged many useful acquaintances and learned a great deal in a short amount of time.

On February 23, Hotze gleefully informed the Confederate State Department that his attempts to cultivate the press had succeeded far beyond his initial expectations. After only three weeks in London he had placed his first editorial in an English newspaper—a feat Henry Adams had failed to achieve in nearly a year. Furthermore, the newspaper was the Morning Post, Lord Palmerston's own mouthpiece. "With this I have acquired the secret of the 'open sesame' of the others I may need," he wrote from his new lodgings in Savile Row. He had expected weeks, if not months, of disappointment. "Although this success is due to an accidental combination of fortunate circumstances which I could not have concerted . . . it has nevertheless greatly encouraged me."[64]

In the days running up to the debate, Hotze and James Spence helped several of the Southern supporters with their speeches. Meanwhile, the American legation was still frantically putting together a rebuttal of the Confederates' statistics. Benjamin Moran spent every waking hour with William Forster coaching him on his answers, hoping that Forster's debating skills were more polished than his manners. Moran was flabbergasted to discover that the MP was married, and his wife "a nice and ladylike person."[65]

On Friday, March 7, the combatants assembled in the Commons to watch their proxies fight. The Confederates appeared confident despite the news in the previous day's papers of the Federals' double victories at Roanoke and Forts Henry and Donelson. The House was more crowded than normal for a Friday evening and from his vantage point in the Diplomatic Gallery, Moran noticed there were a large number of ministers present. William Gregory's pro-Southern speech was in his usual ebullient style. Every cheer from the House brought a smile to the Confederates and a grimace to their opponents. His claim that Britain was supporting an illegal blockade to the detriment of her own workers appeared to strike home with many members. After he sat down, a large number left for dinner, evidently having decided there was no need to listen to any more speeches in support of the motion. Forster was well into his speech when the House refilled. "We watched closely," recorded Mason, "as Forster went on with his exposé, and reduced the tables down almost to nil." To his surprise, Forster's speech received an even more favorable reception than Gregory's. Palmerston appeared to be listening intently, and Gladstone had actually turned around to watch Forster.

After Forster sat down, however, the Federal and Confederate observers realized that the ministry had merely been biding its time while it waited for the supporters of both sides to declare themselves. Sir Roundell Palmer now rose to speak on behalf of the government. A thin, pale man with an unfortunate lisp and squeaky voice, Palmer was no one's choice as a debater, but as the solicitor general he was more qualified than anyone else present to speak on the legality of the blockade. Palmer's shyness had always made him seem devoid of emotion—"bloodless," his critics called him. Tonight, though, unmistakable moral outrage against the South and all that it represented ran through his speech. The government would remain neutral, he declared, because "honour, generosity and justice" demanded it "and because it was the only course consistent with the Divine law, that we should do to others as we would wish others to do to ourselves." Years later, at the end of a long and illustrious career, he remembered the debate with pride. "The speech . . . gained me more applause than, perhaps, any other which I ever made."[66]

There were more speakers—Thurlow Weed had primed at least twenty to speak on the North's behalf—but it was obvious to all except Mason that the Confederates had lost the debate. When Gregory rose for

OVER THE WAY.

Mr. Bull. "OH! IF YOU TWO LIKE FIGHTING BETTER THAN BUSINESS, I SHALL DEAL AT THE OTHER SHOP."

Punch's John Bull knows there is an alternative supply of cotton.

the second time, it was to withdraw his motion. Weed was immediately surrounded by a dozen MPs who came over to shake his hand, while only a couple sauntered over to commiserate with Mason.[67]

The following morning, Adams tucked into a celebratory breakfast at the legation with Weed, Bright, Forster, and several other supporters. Adams admitted to the group that he had ceased to worry about the debate once he learned of the Federal victories. "Mr. Gregory," he announced, "could not have selected a more difficult moment for himself as the current of opinion is setting much the other way. Nothing shines so dazzling to the military eye of Europe as success."[68] Adams was allowing his cynicism too much rein. Moreover, if such success could sway political opinion, so could a cotton famine. Though it had not happened yet, Mason informed the Confederate State Department on March 11 that supplies "were now very low," and the cotton workers were dependent on charity "to keep them from actual starvation."[69] The cause of the South in England, he assured them, was by no means lost.

TEN

The First Blow Against Slavery

Ambiguous attitudes—Consul Dudley vs. James Bulloch in Liverpool—
Henry Adams is embarrassed—Rise of the ironclads—Farewell to Russell—
A brilliant maneuver

Not once during the blockade debate had any of the speakers referred to slavery. The issue was an embarrassment to both sides. Northern supporters were not allowed to claim that the war was to end slavery, and Southern supporters naturally could not say, as John Stuart Mill had so trenchantly put it in an essay published shortly before the debate, that the South was fighting for the right "of burning human creatures alive."*[1] Nor would they, since every Confederate sympathizer in Britain assumed that the South would abolish the "peculiar institution" as soon as its economy could sustain free labor.

A speech by Gladstone to an audience in Manchester in April 1862—many of whom were being financially drained by the war—revealed the extent to which ambiguity over the slavery question benefited the South and damaged the North. Gladstone asked the question that was deeply troubling his listeners: Were they suffering for nothing? There was "no

---

* William Yancey arrived back in New Orleans thoroughly disheartened by his mission. Cotton was a false god, he announced to the crowd that had gathered to greet him. The Queen favored the North, and Lord Palmerston was not interested in aiding the South. "Gladstone we can manage, but the feeling against slavery in England is so strong that no public man there dares extend a hand to help us. We have got to fight the Washington Government alone."[2]

DIVORCE À VINCULO.

Mrs. Carolina Asserts her Right to "Larrup" her Nigger.

Punch reminds the British that the South was fighting to keep its slaves.

doubt," he declared, "if we could say that this was a contest of slavery and freedom, there is not a man within the length and breadth of this room, there is, perhaps, hardly a man in all England, who would for a moment hesitate upon the side he should take."[3]

The Duke of Argyll berated Gladstone for allowing himself to be blinded by fashionable opinion. "That this war is having a powerful, a daily increasing effect on the hold of slavery over opinion in America is, in my judgment, a fact so evident . . . that I cannot understand its being in question," he wrote impatiently.[4] But Gladstone felt vindicated for expressing his doubts after he received a letter from a Liberian diplomat named Edward Wilmot Blyden, who declared that he was "very glad of the position which England maintains with reference to the war. . . . Both sections of the country are negro-hating and negro-crushing."[5]

Seward's interdiction against calling the conflict a war for abolition was so strict that Adams was placed in the invidious position of having to turn away Northern supporters who wanted to help. When a deputation from the British and Foreign Anti-Slavery Society visited the American legation in April, "expressing interest and sympathy with our cause," he could only say a few platitudes about voluntary emancipation after the war.[6] This "was not much to their liking," according to Benjamin Moran.[7] It was not enough for Adams to echo John Stuart Mill, that one set of people were fighting for independence in order to keep another in bondage; his listeners wanted him to promise abolition.

Although the slavery question was a persistent stumbling block for both sides in their bid to win public support in Britain, there was nothing to prevent them from waging unrestrained and barely concealed war on every other front. "Both the Northern and Southern parties have chosen to make this country a kind of supplemental fighting ground," railed the *Liverpool Mercury* on April 10, 1862. "Their respective agents here have been extremely active in their efforts to promote their own cause, as well as to discover and thwart the plans of their opponents. Each party has a place here which may be styled its headquarters; each party has in its service a number of agents, scouts and spies."

James Bulloch, the Confederate navy's purchasing agent and architect of its overseas fleet, had returned to England on March 10 aboard one of Fraser, Trenholm's commercial vessels. He had been expecting to hear that the *Oreto*—one of the two raiders commissioned the previous year—was already launched. Instead, he found the vessel bobbing uselessly in Liverpool harbor, in plain view of the world. He quickly went looking for a captain and crew who could sail it out of port before the authorities became suspicious of the empty but martial-looking ship in their midst.

Bulloch was too late. Federal agents had known about the *Oreto* for several weeks and were already trying to have her seized for contravening the Foreign Enlistment Act. Now that Henry Sanford had been forced to confine his operations to continental Europe, Bulloch's new adversary was Thomas Haines Dudley, a dour but intrepid Quaker from New Jersey. As a young lawyer, Dudley had actively fought against slavery, taking extraordinary risks such as disguising himself as a slave trader, complete with whip and pistols, and traveling to the South to rescue a free black family who had been kidnapped and forced into slavery. But at the age of thirty-six, Dudley narrowly survived a ferryboat fire that killed more than thirty people, leaving him with permanent physical and mental scars. After his recovery he concentrated on politics; Lincoln, who owed him a sinecure for his help in securing the Republican nomination, had offered him either the legation in Japan or the lower position of consul in Liverpool. Dudley had chosen Liverpool because he thought the doctors would be better in England. Yet he did not intend to ride out his appointment like the timeserving secretary Charles Wilson at the legation in London.[8] Dudley's experience on the ferryboat had left him determined to live the rest of his life with force and conviction.

His personal appearance pleased no less a critic than Benjamin Moran, who thought him "as intelligent as he looks."[9] Tall and wavy-haired, with a sad-looking face that was framed by a neatly trimmed beard, he seemed unthreatening to Moran; but then Moran was not on the receiving end of Dudley's surveillance operations. Within six months of his arrival at the Liverpool consulate, Dudley had created a new intelligence network that far outstripped Sanford's effort. The team consisted of himself, his vice consul, Henry Wilding, the London consul, Freeman H. Morse, and a large number of operatives under the direction of Matthew Maguire, Ignatius Pollaky's more reliable replacement. It was expensive to find spies who were both effective and trustworthy, but this was one area where Seward was prepared to be generous.[10]

Dudley was able to insert his men only around the fringes of Confederate society, but it was enough to penetrate their defenses. One operative gained hold of the list of Confederate agents in Britain; another obtained proof that the suspicious ship with the capacity to carry sixteen guns in Liverpool was definitely one of Bulloch's raiders.[11] Charles Francis Adams forwarded Dudley's report to Lord Russell, and the British government began quietly conducting its own investigation.[12] By the middle of March, Dudley believed that he had all the information he needed to lodge a protest with the city's customs officials. He could also prove that the Oreto was not destined for the Italian navy, as claimed by its builders, William C. Miller & Sons.

Bulloch was aware of Thomas Dudley's scrutiny, however, and already had a strategy, based on the legal advice given to him the previous year, to thwart his attempts to have the vessel seized. An English captain and crew would sail the ship out of Liverpool without a single military component on board; once in neutral waters, the Oreto would rendezvous with the *Bahama* to receive her guns and supplies. Caleb Huse was put in charge of procuring the arms shipment for the *Bahama*. The timing could hardly have been worse for him. His funds had run out and he was forced to borrow small sums from friends in Liverpool—£200 here, £1,000 there—to cobble together the cargo, all the while being "watched by the agents of the United States wherever I may go," as he complained to Major Josiah Gorgas of the Confederate Ordnance Bureau.[13]

When the Liverpool authorities inspected the *Oreto* at Dudley's request, they found nothing that actually contravened the Foreign Enlistment Act, even though it was unusual for a merchant ship to have gun ports. They refused to impound her until Dudley could produce more concrete evidence. Bulloch was lucky, but it would only be a matter of time before something or someone incriminated them and the ship's clearance would be revoked. On the chill, misty morning of March 22, the *Oreto* was slowly guided out of the harbor, ostensibly to test her engines. On board was a small party with female guests to give credence that the vessel was simply going on a Saturday outing. But as soon as she left the harbor, the passengers clambered down into the pilot boat and the *Oreto* steamed out to sea. From now on she would be known under her new name, CSS *Florida*.

Bulloch had taken a gamble by sending the *Florida* off without arms or a proper crew. Although the captain, James Duguid, knew the truth, since he was William Miller's son-in-law, the rest of the English crew had been told they were bound for Palermo. Bulloch was relying on John Low, a Scotsman who had emigrated to the South in his early twenties, to protect his investment. Low was traveling on the *Florida* as a passenger, though in reality he had command of the vessel. His orders were to have the *Florida* delivered to Nassau in the Bahamas, where he was to hand the ship over to Lieutenant John N. Maffitt (whom Bulloch knew well and believed was resourceful enough to know what to do with her) or, in his absence, to any Confederate officer.

Thomas Dudley was convinced that the Liverpool customs officers had dragged their feet during the investigation into the *Florida*. A report in late March that the U.S. Navy had captured Captain Pegram and the *Nashville* off the coast of North Carolina cheered the Federals a little but did not lessen their sense of grievance against the British authorities, whom they suspected of ill-concealed bias toward the South. Adams went to see Lord Russell on March 25 to protest against England's laxity over Confederate violations of the Foreign Enlistment Act. Russell listened sympathetically until Adams's indignation took on such a strident tone that he undermined his case. "Adams has made one of his periodical blistering communications about our countenancing the South," reported an internal Foreign Office communiqué after the meeting.[14]

Russell found the American minister's charge of bias especially unfair after the British government's myriad concessions to the North, not least its propping up the shaky legal foundations of the blockade.[15] Their relations deteriorated further after Adams complied with Seward's instruction to remonstrate once more against Britain's declaration of belligerency. This was not some "local riot" of twelve months' duration, expostulated Russell. Furthermore, he complained, when it came to blockade violations, why was Britain always being made out to be the villain when other nations were following the same practice?[16]

Ironically, while Adams was accusing Lord Russell of being insincere, the French emperor was playing a multiple hand between his own ministers and the rival American camps. Much to the annoyance of everyone except the Confederates, Napoleon held several private interviews in April with William Schaw Lindsay, MP (who was also a shipping magnate). Lindsay had played a significant role during Anglo-French negotiations of the 1860 trade treaty and was easily able to gain an audience with the emperor without exciting the suspicion of the British embassy. Napoleon said everything Lindsay wished to hear.[17] John Slidell's spirits soared when Lindsay reported back to him. "This is entirely confidential," he wrote to James Mason in London, "but you can say to Lord Campbell, Mr. Gregory etc. that I now have positive and authentic evidence that France only waits the assent of England for recognition [of the South] and other more cogent measures."[18] Russell was so annoyed by Lindsay's interference that he refused to meet him when the MP returned to England. The Confederates were elated, however, by the news from France; Consul Morse reported to Seward that the "Rebels here confidently predict two or three great Southern victories and the recognition of the Confederate States before the adjournment of Parliament."[19]

The commencement of Parliament had brought with it the resumption of Lady Palmerston's "at homes." Neither James Mason nor Henry

Hotze was on the guest list, but Benjamin Moran was able to finagle an invitation for himself, Charles Wilson, and Henry Adams. He was one of the first guests to arrive at Cambridge House on March 22 and spent the early part of the evening gawking at his surroundings. The "drawing rooms are not so large as one might expect," he pronounced, but they were brilliantly lit for the occasion, and as more people entered they "began to assume an animated and even gorgeous appearance."[20] Too shy to speak to strangers, he hovered in corners and by tables. Henry Adams, on the other hand, arrived determined to make this his entrée into society. He longed to be friends with "Counts and Barons and numberless untitled but high-placed characters."[21] Henry just hoped that the "unfortunate notoriety" caused by his caustic comments on English high society in "A Visit to Manchester" had been forgotten in the intervening three months. At the foot of the lofty staircase he gave his name to the footman, only to hear it called up as "Mr. Handrew Adams." He corrected him and the footman shouted loudly, "Mr. Hantony Hadams." "With some temper," Henry corrected him again, and this time the footman called out, "Mr. Halexander Hadams." Henry accepted defeat and "under this name made [my] bow for the last time to Lord Palmerston who certainly knew no better."[22] After this painful event, Henry decided it was not worth trying to storm the social ramparts of 94 Piccadilly.

"I have no doubt that if I were to stay here another year, I should become extremely fond of the place and the life," Henry mused to his brother Charles Francis Jr. on April 11. But for now he had a "greediness for revenge." He approved of the chief's "putting on the diplomatic screws." England should not be allowed to wriggle out of her responsibility for aiding the Confederates. At least the *Nashville* "has been taken or destroyed," he added. Moreover, it turned out that the *Harvey Birch,* which Confederate captain Pegram had triumphantly claimed as his first capture, belonged to Confederate sympathizers. Writing on the same day, Bulloch warned the Confederate secretary of the navy, Stephen Mallory, that Pegram's mistake had caused them considerable embarrassment. Indiscriminate attacks on Northern ships were perhaps not the best method of waging war.[23]

Despite Charles Francis Adams's complaints to Russell, Bulloch knew better than anyone else the truth about the British government's intentions. It "seems to be more determined than ever to preserve its neutrality," he wrote in disappointment; "the chances of getting a vessel to sea in anything like fighting condition are next to impossible." The fate of his prize cruiser under construction, Lairds' Project No. 290, now preoccupied him. He had her moved to a private graving dock, where she would be masted and coppered out of sight of prying eyes. But with the *Nashville* captured and the *Florida* sailing off on a blind adventure, defenseless and without a real crew, Bulloch was beginning to wonder whether they were pursuing the right course of action. His anxiety was, for the moment, misplaced. Three days later, on April 14, Benjamin Moran recorded in shock: "It seems as though the *Nashville* was not captured at Beaufort, N.C., but escaped. This is one of the most mortifying events of the war to us. Our naval officers on the sea-board have covered themselves with disgrace."[24]

"I cannot say that my value as a sailor had increased materially during the voyage," wrote Francis Dawson after the *Nashville* arrived at Morehead City, North Carolina, on February 28. He was so relieved to be on dry land that it hardly mattered to him that he was homeless and friendless. Captain Pegram departed for Richmond as soon as they docked, bearing boxes of much-needed supplies, including stamps and banknote paper. Dawson was left to find his own lodgings. "I had determined to take my discharge from the *Nashville,* and decide, by tossing-up, which one of the various companies named in the newspaper I should join." Pegram, however, made good on his promise. "I also wish to call specially your attention to the sacrifices made by Mr. Frank Dawson," he wrote to Stephen Mallory in early March. The "young Englishman" had "left family, friends, and every tie to espouse our cause," and, "not to be put off by any difficulties thrown in his way, insisted upon serving under our flag, performing . . . the most menial duties of an ordinary seaman."[25] On the strength of this recommendation, Dawson was appointed master's mate, the lowest officer rank in the navy. Pegram personally gave him the news, "one furious cold morning," while Dawson was "scraping the fore-yard, wet through with the falling sleet and intensely uncomfortable."[26]

Dawson's orders were to report for duty at the Norfolk shipyard in Virginia. This was the same destination as Pegram, who was going to take command of a ship that was still in dry dock. "To crown my satisfaction," Dawson recorded, "Captain Pegram told me that he intended to make a visit to his family, in Sussex County, Virginia, and would be glad if I

The Confederate steamer *Nashville,* having run the blockade, arrives at Beaufort, North Carolina.

should accompany him, and remain with him until it was necessary to go to Norfolk." They left Morehead on March 10 and took the train up to Virginia. The young man was fascinated by the alien landscape that rolled past his window; there were no neat hedgerows and green pastures filled with sheep, only mile after mile of scrub and woodland. Dawson's short stay at the Pegrams' plantation exceeded his wildest expectations. The family adored him, and local worthies hailed him as a foreign knight come to their rescue. Dawson was already a convert to the Southern cause; all the attention he received gave him personal as well as fanciful reasons to embrace the Confederacy. "You may rest assured," he wrote earnestly to his mother, "that while one of her children has power to wield a sword or pull a trigger, the South will never desist from her struggle against the Northern oppressor."[27]

On the day of Dawson's departure, news reached the plantation of

CSS *Merrimac*'s encounter with USS *Monitor*. The ships were the result of a frantic race between the North and South to construct the first American ironclads. The Confederates won (by twenty-four hours) when they launched the *Merrimac* (renamed CSS *Virginia*) on March 8, 1862. The vessel was an old U.S. warship that had been burned by Union sailors when they abandoned the Norfolk Navy Yard in Virginia the previous summer. Since then, the *Merrimac* had been completely remodeled except for her engines, which the Confederates had not had time to repair. Engineers literally "clad" the *Merrimac* in iron plates and added a ram to the stem of the ship. Long and squat, she looked more like an iron champagne bottle than a ship. Her speed was terrible, but the armor plating made her invincible. When the *Merrimac* slowly steamed into Hampton Roads to confront the Federal blockading fleet, nothing like her had ever been seen before. Hampton Roads is a wide body of water where three large rivers converge before flowing into Chesapeake Bay and out into the Atlantic. The Union navy had been in control of the bay and Hampton Roads for almost a year. Stephen Mallory knew that it was vital for the Confederacy that he take them back, and as the wooden Union gunboats fired ineffectively at the *Merrimac*'s hull, it seemed as though he would.

There was cheering in Richmond and hysteria in Washington after the battle. Lincoln called a special cabinet meeting at which the new secretary of war, Edwin Stanton, made a spectacle of himself, ranting that every city on the Eastern Seaboard would now be laid waste. The secretary of the navy, Gideon Welles, however, was unfazed. The newly clad and outfitted *Monitor* was already on its way to Hampton Roads, and he expected a more favorable outcome than the previous day's rout. The secretary's hopes were justified. The equally strange-looking Federal vessel, described by some as a "tin can on a shingle" (the tin can being a revolving turret that could fire in any direction), could not sink the *Merrimac*, but was powerful enough to pin her down. After four hours of point-blank firing, both ships withdrew, damaged but not inoperable. The possibility that the *Merrimac* might yet force its way to Washington had almost as powerful an effect on Edwin Stanton as the first Hampton Roads bombardment. To stop the Confederate monster, he wanted the main water channels to Washington blocked with sunken ships.

Lord Lyons was fascinated by reports of the encounter between the two ironclads. "This is, I suppose," he wrote to Lord Russell, "the severest test to which the system of coating vessels in iron armour has yet been exposed." The officers of Admiral Milne's North Atlantic squadron were equally agog. The ironclad warships in the British and French navies had, for obvious reasons, never been tested in the same way. Milne's entire fleet would gladly have assembled to watch another encounter, but the coveted task was awarded to Commander William N. W. Hewett of HMS *Rinaldo,* who was told to loiter near Fortress Monroe (at the entrance of Chesapeake Bay) "in order to obtain as much information as possible."[28] Newspapers in the North and South were hailing the battle as a revolution in naval warfare, not to mention proof that America would one day rule the oceans.[29] Francis Dawson saw the *Merrimac* when he reported to Norfolk Navy Yard. He noticed something that Commander Hewett had been too far away to see: that the vessel's armor plating was actually railroad ties rolled flat.

———

Lyons was frustrated that he had no eyewitness reports of the battle to pass on to the Admiralty. None of the British journalists he relied upon for news had been present; increasingly of late, their applications for military passes were being turned down by the U.S. War Department. The worst affected was William Howard Russell. He had returned from a two-month sojourn in Canada on March 1, having failed to persuade *The Times* to release him from his contract. "I am writing to you, my dear Morris, as a friend," he pleaded with the managing editor of the paper, Mowbray Morris. Russell listed all the reasons—family, finances, even life and death. "I have not met a man in Canada who has not declared to me he never thought I should have left the United States alive. . . . If you could see what I have had to bear in railway trains and in the street you would at least give me the credit of no common devotion."[30]

Russell's fears were soon confirmed. It was useless to remain in Washington, he told Morris, because no one would speak to him. "They are determined, I hear, to throw every impediment in my way," he wrote:

> McClellan is never to be seen by me, his staff are all surly . . . the officers I know are fearful of being attacked in the press if they are pointed out for any civility to me. Therefore I never get any intelligence of what is going to be done and secrecy on all points is so well kept I don't hear of any event coming off, and so cannot get a chance of describing it.[31]

His friends were sympathetic, but there was nothing they could do to reduce the prejudice against him.

The small band of British journalists in Washington had increased by two with the arrival of Edward Dicey of the *Spectator* and, recently, a freelance writer named Francis Lawley. They were liable to suffer the same penalty as Russell if they traveled together, but neither was as keen to see action as Russell: a little excursion to General Louis Blenker's camp and back was sufficient war reporting for them. Blenker, a German exile from the Revolution of 1848, headed a division "filled with black sheep of every nation under the sun," wrote Dicey. "The word of command had to be given in four languages, and the officers were foreigners almost without exception."[32] Francis Lawley was rather grateful for the opportunity to take things easy for a time. He had joined Anthony Trollope for part of his tour of the Midwest after Rose Trollope went home to England. Lawley and Trollope were friends and distant cousins, a tie that played an increasingly important role as the journey became more challenging. Neither was accustomed to traveling rough, and each thought the other was a ninny over the hardships they endured. After 120 miles on a provincial railroad, Lawley declared that an Englishman did not know discomfort until he had experienced a crowded American railway carriage going fifteen miles an hour across flat nothingness for an entire day.

At thirty-six, Lawley was still young enough to retain the air of a man of promise. But by this stage in his life he had already taken that promise and squandered it several times over until it seemed to his friends and family that it would never be fulfilled. He was the youngest son of the first Baron Wenlock. Success had come to him easily. He was a fellow of All Souls College (the academic citadel of Oxford) at twenty-three, and an MP at twenty-seven. Six months later, in 1852, he achieved an even greater coup when the then chancellor of the exchequer, William Gladstone, made him his private secretary. In 1853 his name was put forward for governor-general of South Australia. To those who did not know him, it seemed as though he was leading a charmed existence. Only those closest to him knew his terrible secret: Lawley was a gambling addict.[33] Ironically, the governorship, which he only accepted to escape his racing debts, proved to be his undoing. The colonial secretary objected to sending an unreformed gambler to govern the South Australians. This unexpected rejection led to some unsavory revelations. Since Lawley had already resigned his seat in Parliament, believing the post was his, he was suddenly faced with the loss of his reputation, his career, and his only source of income. He fled England to escape his creditors.

Lawley made a new life for himself, of sorts, as a freelance writer in New York. He admired the energy and optimism of Americans, telling his close friend and fellow gambler William Gregory, "this nation is destined to be greater than the greatest."[34] When the war started, Lawley was able to increase his income slightly by writing articles for English newspapers. He was not sure it was gentlemen's work. "It is hard," he confessed to his family, "to write and enter into very minute details without trenching upon information gained in the familiarity of private conversation, and to this I have an intolerable aversion." He was fortunate in that the *Daily Telegraph* took a relaxed attitude to the objectivity of its foreign reports. Lawley was resolutely pro-Northern and had no intention of touring the South: "I can do better as a correspondent in the North," he wrote, "seeing it only and writing from a one-sided view, than if I saw both sides and was embarrassed thereby."[35]

Washington suited Lawley very well. His travels with Trollope had trained him to be less delicate about the presence of mud, and his chronic shortage of funds merely put him in a large enough company for it to go unremarked. The "Buccaneers" at the British legation welcomed him at once, and he was given a role in their production of a burlesque opera called *Bombastes Furioso*. A large part of the English community in Washington was in the play. William Howard Russell reported to Mowbray Morris that it "was a complete success at the legation and Shiny William, as I call Seward, complimented me immensely."[36] This was an impolitic admission for one who was seeking his recall on compassionate grounds. "It is your business to report the military proceedings of the Federal Army," complained Morris, "and so I repeat: Go to the Front or come home."[37]

Russell felt that neither Delane nor Morris understood his position or else they would not keep insisting that he go where he was barred from entering. Russell could not help worrying that he had made a mistake in returning to Washington. Vizetelly had decided to go west, and the idea no longer seemed so harebrained; a significant battle had taken place on March 7 at Pea Ridge, near the Arkansas-Missouri border. President Jefferson Davis had sent a new general, Earl Van Dorn, to take over the disorganized forces in the region. This much Van Dorn achieved. The little general with a large ego boasted to his wife that he would take his army all the way north to St. Louis in Missouri. His plan was simple: a Union army of only 11,000 men, under General Samuel R. Curtis, controlled the passage from northwest Arkansas into Missouri; Van Dorn would divide his own army into two forces, surround the Federals front and back, and then pounce in a surprise attack.

William Watson, the Scotsman who had joined the 3rd Louisiana Infantry in New Orleans the previous summer, was at first relieved by Van Dorn's arrival, but he soon developed misgivings over whether the new general understood the limitations posed by territory or was aware of the real condition of the Confederate army. Their supplies were already low when Van Dorn gave the order for every man to be ready to march with ten days' rations in his haversack. But Union sympathizers had sent word to General Curtis of the Confederates' approach: Curtis was waiting for them when they attacked.

The Battle of Pea Ridge, Arkansas, began on March 7 as the fog lifted from the trees to reveal a gray winter morning. Watson and his fellow soldiers had been marching through frost and snow with little sleep and no food for almost seventy-two hours. "Cold, hungry, and fatigued we moved sullenly along," he wrote, "some of the lads almost sleeping on their feet." They thought they had marched to the rear of the Federal forces only to discover "that they were also in our rear, and they had the advantage of being in a strong position." Watson's regiment had stumbled into the center of the waiting Federals; when the firing died down, the 3rd's officers were all either dead or missing, except for one lieutenant. Fortunately, the sun was beginning to set, and the soldiers who had survived were able to creep away under the cover of darkness. The following morning, a Federal counterattack smashed the Confederates' line and the rebels fled the battlefield, Van Dorn first. Watson and his fellow soldiers were left to fend for themselves. It was a ninety-mile march to the nearest Confederate stronghold, a trek through rattlesnake-infested country, without food or maps. Seven days later, Watson staggered into the border town of Van Buren, four hundred miles from Van Dorn's stated destination of St. Louis. In retrospect, Watson admitted, "I never got what the Americans would call the 'hang' of this battle. . . . It was a mass of mixed up confusion from beginning to end."[38] Nevertheless the outcome was clear; the Confederates had suffered 2,000 casualties, the Federals 1,384, and General Curtis's victory ensured that the key border state of Missouri would stay in Northern hands.

This Federal victory in the west made General McClellan's failure to commit the Army of the Potomac in a major battle look all the more inexplicable. Lincoln had tolerated the general's arrogance (though he did not know that McClellan referred to him as "the gorilla") and shown leniency when the army did not advance into Virginia on February 22 as directed. But his patience was now at an end. Lincoln ordered McClellan to have the Army of the Potomac in motion no later than March 18. Russell could hardly believe that something was finally going to happen after almost eight months of anticipation. He visited McClellan's headquarters and asked permission to accompany the march. McClellan agreed, with the usual proviso that Russell first obtain the necessary pass from the War Department. As Russell busily wrote letters of request, reports began to filter through of a general retreat by the Confederate army. Confederate general Joseph E. Johnston had also heard of McClellan's order to move south and had concluded that his own army of 40,000 men would be wiped out in its present position near Manassas. On March 8, Private Sam Hill and the 6th Louisiana were ordered to dismantle the camp that had been their home since July of the previous year and prepare to march twenty-five miles south of Manassas to the Rappahannock River. Leaving behind nearly everything of value, including precious batteries, food supplies, and arms, Johnston's army trudged along single-track roads through incessant rain. Many fell sick with chills and diarrhea. "I remained doing what I could," wrote Sam's sister, Mary Sophia Hill, about her own activities during the dreadful trek through knee-deep mud. She had left the regiment in December in order to visit New Orleans "to see my sister, and get money from Ireland." The blockade prevented her remittance from coming in, but Mary still raised $150 in donations for the regiment and obtained several boxes of clothes and medicines. Her efforts were for naught, however; by the time she eventually reached Virginia, all but one of her trunks had been stolen. The old civilities of the South were gradually giving way to a harsher reality. Richmond itself was under martial law.

Sam Hill's brigade finally reached its new camp on the south bank of the Rappahannock on March 17, acting as the rear guard while the rest of Johnston's army continued on to Orange Court House, an Italianate building in a town of that name, with sweeping steps and a rectangular bell tower not unlike some of the grand residences in New Orleans. Mary managed to find rooms in a little cottage nearby. Here was a pleasant place to rest, even under the leaden skies of a wintry spring. Although the Louisianans were waiting for orders, Mary was kept busy with wounds and injuries, often the result of fighting among members of Major Chatham Roberdeau Wheat's 1st Louisiana Special Battalion. The Louisiana "Tigers" were such a lawless lot that the commander of the Louisiana Brigade had two of them executed by firing squad. Major Wheat was a veteran of Garibaldi's Sicily campaign, and in March he received a visit from a friend he had not seen since leaving Italy. The visitor was Henry MacIver, the young man who had annoyed William Howard Russell by asking for directions on how to sneak across Federal lines after Bull Run. MacIver had managed to escape his prison cell in Alexandria, steal the clothes and weapon of a Union soldier, and slip into Confederate territory. After being briefly detained as a Yankee spy, MacIver was finally able to achieve his wish and join the Confederate army. He was made a cavalry instructor with the rank of lieutenant and attached to General Thomas "Stonewall" Jackson's staff.

General McClellan was embarrassed that Joe Johnston, whose timely arrival at Bull Run had caused the Federals to flee, had now succeeded in moving to a new, unknown position. The Confederate's actions led McClellan to alter his plans and adopt a far more radical strategy involving the transportation by sea of a hundred thousand soldiers, plus supplies, horses, and equipment, to Fortress Monroe on the tip of the Virginia peninsula. From there, the army would march seventy miles east to capture Richmond. The first troops began to be shipped out from Alexandria on March 17. Edward Dicey was able to join a group of observers that included Nathaniel Hawthorne, who had become a great friend, but Russell was once again forced to stay behind. On March 24, he wrote in his diary, "One of the saddest days I have had in all my life, and Heaven knows I have had some sad ones, too."[39] Russell was referring to an article in the *New York Herald* that accused him of having speculated on the stock exchange using information obtained from the British legation during the *Trent* affair. The paper printed a copy of a telegram sent by Russell to his friend the lobbyist Sam Ward that appeared to support the allegation. But it was false. All Russell had done was telegraph Ward in New York ahead of the official announcement that the commissioners were being released. This was perhaps unwise, yet Russell claimed that the news was all over Washington by the time he sent the notice. Ward had a copy of the real, undoctored telegram, which proved Russell's innocence of any financial dealings, but no newspaper would print his explanation.

Russell was mortified by the slur on his character, especially after Lord Lyons let it be known that he regarded the telegram as a gross breach of trust. Not surprisingly, Francis Lawley sympathized with Russell's predicament and tried to smooth his relations with the legation. Russell found Lawley's earnest attempts to help almost as humiliating as the original slander. It was not comfortable to be told to stay "as far as you can, from the British legation, during the next five or six weeks" and to refrain "from any step which, however remotely, has the appearance of a desire to push yourself into the old relations." Although the attachés claimed they believed Russell's protestation of innocence, he feared they would never fully trust him again. He was lonely and fed up. His friend William W. Glenn, a Southern journalist, offered to provide him with safe passage to the Confederacy. Russell was tempted, but decided he could not, "with honour or propriety go South immediately after so long a residence among the Northern armies."

Lord Lyons forgave Russell and, at the end of March, invited him back to the legation for dinner. Russell was doubly grateful, not only for the rehabilitation of his character, but also because it gave him the opportunity to corner Edwin Stanton and embarrass him into writing out a pass then and there. Stanton was, however, determined to confine Russell to Washington even if it meant revoking the pass of every war correspondent in the country. On April 2, 1862, the War Department announced that it would no longer recognize press passes, and all reporters currently following the army in Virginia were to return to Washington or be arrested.[40] After two days of uproar, the department clarified its stand so that only foreign journalists were affected. Russell wrote to Stanton on the second, pleading with him to reconsider: "I can not conceive Sir, the object of such conduct." What, he asked, was the "cause for the change on your part towards me."[41] Stanton never replied. By now Russell had written to Lincoln, four generals, Seward, Sumner, and "innumerable Senators," all without success.

"In the South," Russell wrote ruefully, "the press threatened me with

tar and feathers . . . the Northern papers recommended expulsion, duck-
ing, riding rails, and other cognate modes of insuring a moral conviction
of error." He would not have allowed himself to be cowed by these
threats, but he accepted defeat "when to the press and populace of the
United States, the President and the Government of Washington added
their power." Sam Ward tried hard to dissuade Russell from leaving, and
he complained to Seward that Stanton had "tomahawked" the North's
most valuable foreign asset.[42] The secretary of state paid scant attention
to Russell's departure. Stanton's appalling blunder of driving away the
world's most famous war correspondent would only become clear later
on when the North had no foreign journalists reporting from its side.

Russell set sail for England on April 9 on board the *China*. "I saw the
shores receding into a dim gray fog," he wrote; "our good ship pointing
thank Heaven, towards Europe."[43] His wife and children had not seen
him in more than a year, his financial affairs were in a deplorable state,
and his career, so it seemed to him, was crumbling. Russell used his final
dispatch from New York, on April 3, to explain to readers why he was
abandoning his assignment. They were probably more forgiving than his
employers, John Delane and Mowbray Morris, who both sent frantic letters begging him to continue at his post. "It is lamentable that at such a
time we should be practically unrepresented," grumbled Delane, since
J. C. Bancroft Davis had also resigned, on grounds of ill health. *The Times*
did agree to reimburse the £1,340 that Russell had paid out of his own
pocket while in America, but took nearly two years to verify every receipt
and expense.[44]

———

Years later, Lord Lyons told William Howard Russell that his presence in
Washington during the first year of the war had greatly enlivened the
British legation and that the capital was a duller place after he left.
Lyons's irritation with Russell over the telegram scandal had had less to
do with the offense than with its timing. Lyons was in the middle of secret negotiations with Seward on a joint slave-trade treaty when the *New
York Herald* published its accusation against Russell. Lyons could not afford to have the legation dragged into a disreputable row when so much
depended on discretion and staying out of the public eye.

Lyons had always believed that an antislavery treaty between the two
countries was impossible. Only three years before, the mere possibility
that the Royal Navy might try to stop an American vessel to search for

slaves was sufficient to provoke threats of war. Britain had backed down, and the slave trade had flourished. There was scant hope in London that the Lincoln administration would have congressional support to revisit so contentious an issue. In May 1861, Seward had tried to skirt Congress by offering to sign a secret memorandum allowing the Royal Navy to stop and search suspected American slavers. But since the offer had coincided with his menacing dispatches to Adams, Lyons and Lord Russell had agreed that Seward's word was "worth little or nothing" when it came to Anglo-American relations.[45] They had misjudged the sincerity of Seward's intentions, however. The secret memorandum idea was no trick on his part, even if he had not thought through the impact on the public if a Royal Navy vessel sailed into New York Harbor with a captured slaver in tow.

The slave trade issue was revived when Captain Nathaniel Gordon was sentenced to death on February 7 by a New York court for the crime of participating in the Atlantic slave trade. It was the first successful prosecution of a slave trader in forty-four years, and the outcry for Lincoln to pardon Gordon was considerable, though not deafening. Lord Lyons wondered whether this was a sign that he should speak to Seward about a treaty. Slave trading was on the increase again, since blockade duty had taken away U.S. Navy ships that had been patrolling the west coast of Africa.[46] The only practical way to stop it was to give Royal Navy ships the right to challenge slavers flying the American flag.

With relations between the British legation and the U.S. State Department still in a honeymoon period after the *Trent* affair, Lyons suggested to Lord Russell that they revive the slave trade question while Seward was still "in the mood."[*47] As it turned out, Seward had also been toying with the idea of resurrecting negotiations, but neither Lyons nor Seward had given the issue as much attention as Lord Russell had. On February 28, 1862, he surprised Lyons with a printed draft of a slave trade treaty, with all the provisions and exclusions that the Americans might demand already included. Russell also gave Lyons discretionary power

---

[*] One of the biggest areas of contention between Lyons and Seward had recently been removed when the U.S. War Department assumed responsibility for political arrests. "I think it is well that the arrests should be withdrawn from Seward," Lord Lyons had written on February 18; "he certainly took delight in making them, and, I may say, playing with the whole matter. He is not at all a cruel or vindictive man, but he likes all things which make him feel that he has power."

on any changes, so that momentum would not be lost. Seward's reaction to the document would show him in his best light, as a gifted politician whose creative manipulation of people and issues could bring about results that were otherwise unobtainable.

Seward liked the proposed treaty and was determined to have it ratified. His abhorrence of the Atlantic slave trade became evident to the journalist Edward Dicey, who went to dinner at his house on March 22, when the secret negotiations were under way. It was another of Seward's foreign military dinners: Colonel De Courcy, General Blenker and his aide de camp, Prince Felix Salm-Salm of Prussia, were also present. Poor Fanny Seward had taken a violent dislike to De Courcy: "He appeared very well as long as he kept still and did not say much at the dinner table," she wrote. "But after dinner his brilliant capability of making himself disagreeable showed forth with undimmed luster. Added to being ill bred, awkward, and a terrible stare-er, he has the distinction of one of the most ugly and repulsive of faces." Dicey was also falling in Fanny's estimation until she scrambled her knitting and he sat on the floor to help her untangle the mess.[48] After dinner, Dicey stayed behind after the others had left and discussed the slave trade with Seward. The journalist did not pick up that the secretary of state was speaking in the past tense: "The Republican Administration would have merited the condemnation of every honest man if whatever else it had left undone, it had not put a stop to the Slave Trade."[49]

The "whatever else" referred to Lincoln's failed attempt to win support from the border states for a gradual emancipation bill.[50] In January, Carl Schurz, the U.S. minister in Spain, had visited the White House to discuss the reasons for the North's unpopularity in Europe. After being told by Schurz that it was a mistake to hide the antislavery aims of the war, Lincoln replied to him:

> "You may be right. Probably you are. I have been thinking so myself. I cannot imagine that any European power would dare to recognize and aid the Southern Confederacy if it becomes clear that the Confederacy stands for slavery and the Union for freedom." Then he explained to me that, while a distinct anti-slavery policy would remove the foreign danger . . . he was in doubt as to whether public opinion at home was yet sufficiently prepared for it. He was anxious to unite, and keep united, all the forces of

Northern society and of the Union element in the South, especially the Border States, in the war for the Union. Would not the cry of "abolition war" such as might be occasioned by a distinct anti-slavery policy, tend to disunite those forces and thus weaken the Union cause? This was the doubt that troubled him, and it troubled him very much.[51]

The objections of the border states to any form of emancipation within their own state lines forced Lincoln to go far more slowly than he wished. To avoid the same difficulties as Lincoln, Seward asked Lyons to play an elaborate game of subterfuge with him. In a brilliant political maneuver, he used the border states' traditional antipathy toward England to trick them into supporting the slave trade proposal. He altered the wording of the draft so that the proposal came from the United States to Great Britain, rather than the reverse. Then he added a ten-year limit to the treaty and asked Lyons to make objections to it at first, only to allow himself to be publicly beaten down by the force of Seward's arguments. "Mr. Seward's long experience of the Senate, and his well-known tact in dealing with that Body, gives his opinion on such a point so much weight," explained Lyons to the Foreign Office on March 31, "that I naturally thought it prudent to be guided by it." Lord Russell responded drily that credit for the treaty was "immaterial" to Her Majesty's government so long as the slave trade was suppressed.[52] Lyons dutifully performed his role as directed by Seward, and grudgingly "changed" his mind after a testy exchange of notes.

Lincoln's cabinet was unanimous in its congratulation of Seward—with the exception of Gideon Welles, who would not be dissuaded that Britain had an ulterior motive in agreeing to the treaty. "Yesterday was the anniversary of my arrival three years ago at Washington," Lord Lyons wrote to Lord Russell on April 8. "I celebrated it by signing the Treaty for the Suppression of the Slave Trade."[53] Nothing, except permission to go home, could have given him greater satisfaction. "Weary years they have been in many respects," he wrote, but the treaty made them seem worth the sacrifice. April was a good month for the abolitionists; a week later, on the sixteenth, President Lincoln signed into law a bill abolishing slavery in Washington. (Sumner had accused him of being the largest slave owner in America for his delay in freeing the three thousand slaves in and around the capital.) At the beginning of the war "it was the fashion amongst English critics," wrote Edward Dicey, "to state that the whole Secession question had no direct bearing on nor immediate connection with the issue of slavery. As to the letter, there was some truth in this assertion; as to the spirit, there was none." Finally, one year after the Federal evacuation of Fort Sumter, the "letter" and the "spirit" of the "Secession question" were converging.

ELEVEN

Five Miles from Richmond

Shiloh—Fall of the Crescent City—The "Woman Order"—Vizetelly's change of heart—The Seven Days' Battles—"Percy, old boy!"—Lord Edward is duped—General Lee takes the field—McClellan retreats—"This is Butler's doing"

Lyons and Seward were quietly congratulating each other over the success of the slave trade treaty when the North won its first major military victory of the war on April 7, 1862, at the Battle of Shiloh. The battle, which took place on Tennessee's southern border, was a first on several counts. It was the first time Americans witnessed the mass slaughter that comes with large-scale combat. It was also the first intimation that no single battle, no matter how terrible, would end the war; and for young Henry Morton Stanley of the Dixie Grays, it was "the first time that Glory sickened me with its repulsive aspect, and made me suspect it was a glittering lie."[1]

More than a hundred thousand soldiers fought in the two-day battle. Stanley's side was led by General Albert Sidney Johnston—who was regarded by his Northern opponents as the ablest general in the Confederacy—and by Confederate general P.G.T. Beauregard, the hero of Fort Sumter and Bull Run. They had hoped to launch a surprise attack against General Grant while he rested his army of forty thousand men along the wooded ravines of the Tennessee River at Pittsburg Landing. "Shiloh," which means "place of peace" in Hebrew, was a small Methodist church where Brigadier General William T. Sherman's division had set up camp.

Shiloh or Pittsburg Landing
April 6–7, 1862

N
W · E
S

Snake Cr.

L. Wallace

Grant

Buell

Tennessee River

To Savannah

Federal forces a.m. April 6
Federal forces p.m. April 6
Federal forces night April 6
Federal front April 7
Confederate forces a.m. April 6
Confederate forces p.m. April 6
Confederate forces night April 6

Sherman
McClernand Hurlbut

Pittsburg Landing

Artillery

Henry Morton Stanley

Owl Creek

Sherman

Hardee

McClernand

Polk

Dill's Branch

Tyler
Lexington

Robert Neve

Grant

(a.m., p.m.)
W. H. L. Wallace

Sherman

McClernand

Bragg

Horner's Nest

Prentiss
Hurlbut

Hurlbut

Breckinridge

Nelson

Shiloh Church

Prentiss

Bragg

Buell

Breckinridge

W. H. L. Wallace
Johnston killed

Sherman

Hardee

Polk

A. S. Johnston
Beauregard

Hardee
Bragg
Polk
Breckinridge

To Corinth

Miles
0   1   2

Johnston had chosen to attack Grant at Pittsburg Landing because he knew that an additional 25,000 reinforcements under General Don Carlos Buell were coming from Nashville. Once the two armies combined, Grant's numerical superiority would be overwhelming, and Johnston had no doubt that capturing the strategic railroad junctions at Corinth, which was only twenty-two miles from Pittsburg Landing, would be their next object. Johnston's own army was 44,000 strong, but he hoped that General Van Dorn and the survivors of Pea Ridge would arrive in time to give him additional support.

The plan, drawn up by Beauregard, was modeled on Napoleon's strategy during the Waterloo campaign, where he had divided his forces to pick off the allies one by one. Historic plans rarely translate well, and those of the defeated even less so; yet the first day of the battle, April 6, began promisingly for the Confederates. Grant was taken by surprise. Sherman's troops were sitting by their tents eating their breakfast in the warm morning sun when the rebels came yelling and whooping out of the woods. "Stand by, Gentlemen," Stanley's captain had ordered while they gathered in formation. The boy standing next to Stanley stopped down to pick a small posy of violets. "They are a sign of peace," he told Stanley. "Perhaps they won't shoot me if they see me wearing such flowers." Impulsively, Stanley also stuck a sprig in his cap. Once they charged, "We had no individuality at this moment. . . . My nerves tingled, my pulses beat double quick, my heart throbbed loudly, and almost painfully," Stanley recalled. The rebel yell jerked him out of his fear. "The wave after wave of human voices, louder than all other battle-sounds together, penetrated to every sense." He remembered he was not alone but surrounded by four hundred other companies. "I rejoiced in the shouting like the rest."[2]

The Union soldiers had fled Shiloh by the time Stanley's regiment arrived. The Confederates were stopped in their tracks by the sight of such abundance. Here was a neat little village of tents, many with a smoking stove in front, and all surrounded by mounds of new equipment. Everything was superior to their own camp, even the bedding. The sudden resumption of cannon fire recalled them to their senses, and the soldiers moved off. A short while later—whether it was five minutes or five hours Stanley did not know—he heard a piteous cry behind him. "Oh stop, *please* stop a bit." He glanced back. It was the boy with the violets. He was standing awkwardly on one leg, staring at the remains of his foot.[3] Henry

Stanley continued to run until something hit his belt buckle with such force that he flipped over and landed on the ground headfirst. When he came to, his regiment had disappeared and all was silent.

As he stumbled through the forest, he almost fell again, tripping over a body lying faceup. The eyes of the dead soldier seemed to stare back at him. With a shock, Stanley recognized him as the "stout English Sergeant of a neighbouring company. . . . This plump, ruddy-faced man had been conspicuous for his complexion, jovial features and good humour." The more he ran, the more bodies he encountered. The dead, he recalled, "lay thick as the sleepers in a London park on a Bank Holiday." The rest of the day became a series of wordless images. By the time he found his company again only fifty men remained.

Johnston and Beauregard's Waterloo strategy fell apart in an area known as the Hornet's Nest, where a sunken road acted like a defensive trench for the Federal troops, enabling them to hold steady for six hours against dozens of Confederate assaults. General Johnston was killed leading the final charge. A bullet tore through an artery in his leg, causing him to bleed to death in minutes. The Union soldiers holding the nest surrendered at 5:30 P.M., but by then Grant had formed a new defensive line along the river. He had been driven back two miles, but his army was still intact. "We've had the devil's own day, haven't we?" remarked Sherman to Grant after the fighting stopped. "Yes," he said, with a short, sharp puff of the cigar; "Lick 'em tomorrow, though."[4]

Grant always used simple language when he spoke. The forty-year-old general was a quiet, plain figure whose forcefulness and intelligence were cloaked behind an unassuming manner. Associates struggled to describe him: "He is rather under middle height, of a spare, strong build; light-brown hair, and short, light brown beard," wrote an aide to General Meade. "His face has three expressions: deep thought, extreme determination; and great simplicity and calmness." Unlike McClellan, Grant had never aspired to become an American Napoleon; he had not even intended to become a professional soldier. "A military life had no charms for me," Grant wrote of his time at West Point, "and I had not the faintest idea of staying in the army even if I should be graduated, which I did not expect." But Grant remained in the army for eleven years, fighting in the Mexican War of 1846–48 and spending the next six years on mindless garrison duty, developing and failing to conquer a drink habit. Although happily married to his wife, Julia, and a devoted father to their four children, Grant floundered in civilian life. One year he was reduced to pawning his watch to buy Christmas presents for the family. When the war broke out, Grant was working as a clerk in his father's tannery in Galena, Illinois—a humble climb down for the former captain. Within six months of volunteering, however, Grant had risen from colonel to brigadier general and, in addition to his old nickname in the army of "Sam"—for his initials U. S. (Uncle Sam)—had acquired the new national nickname of "Unconditional Surrender Grant" because of the terms he had offered to the defeated Confederates at Fort Donelson.[5]

Sherman's short conversation with Grant on the night of the sixth was actually one of the first between them. Sherman had suffered a nervous breakdown during the autumn of 1861 and had only recently returned to duty. Sherman was the opposite of Grant in mannerisms: his tall, wiry frame was always moving, he gesticulated as he spoke, and he often worked himself up into an excitement during conversation. But in many ways the pattern of his life was similar to Grant's: Sherman had also struggled in civilian life; he, too, loved his wife and adored his children; and he had also fought his own private battles of the mind. The latter forged an unbreakable bond between them. Sherman later remarked: "Grant stood by me when I was crazy and I stood by him when he was drunk. And now we stand by each other always." In turn, Grant said of him: "Sherman is impetuous, faulty but he sees his faults as well as any man." Both were realists, neither was an abolitionist, and each approached the task of warfare in the same relentless and dogged spirit. Sherman had briefly wondered if they should retreat on the sixth, until speaking to Grant reaffirmed his resolve.

During the night, General Buell and his reinforcements sailed down the river to Pittsburg Landing. By contrast, flooded roads and a damaged rail system meant that Van Dorn's battle-ravaged army was still sitting 250 miles away in Little Rock, Arkansas. This was good news for William Watson and the 3rd Louisiana Regiment, who were spared the fight, but it was a disaster for Beauregard. The weather turned, and a harsh downpour pelted the living and the dead. Flashes of lightning revealed the presence of wild pigs, attracted by the smell of fresh meat. Neither side had expected such a high number of casualties, and many of the ten thousand wounded were left out on the field all night, their screams so terrible that a Confederate soldier wrote, "This night of horrors will haunt me to my grave."[6]

For many of the reinforcements, including an Englishman named Robert Neve of the 5th Kentucky Volunteers, this was their baptism of war. "Boys," said Neve's commander in the morning, just before sending the Union regiment off into the woods, "we shall beat them today, for their general is killed. He was shot yesterday in leading a charge." The news had no real meaning for Neve except that his side was apparently doing better than the rebels. Yesterday the Confederates had attacked; today it was their job to return the favor. Neve's regiment surged through the woods like hunters flushing out their prey. Occasionally, a stray shell interrupted their momentum. With every foothold gained, Neve's confidence rose; fighting was not so bad after all.

The exhausted Confederates made a game effort to repel the invaders. Henry Morton Stanley's company marched forward in skirmishing order. The young soldier stood in a daze until his captain barked, "Now, Mr. Stanley, if you please," which mortified him. He rushed blindly forward, straight into a pocket of Federal soldiers from Ohio. Two of them wanted to shoot him immediately, but an officer saved his life. As he was marched off to the Union camp, they chatted about "our respective causes, and, though I could not admit it," he wrote later, "there was much reason in what they said." The slavery question "could have been settled in another and quieter way, but they cared all their lives were worth for their country."[7]

General Beauregard ordered his army to retreat to Corinth, more than twenty miles away. In the confusion after the battle, along with the abandoned wagons and artillery guns that had become stuck in the mud, hundreds of wounded men were also left behind. Beauregard's reputation for tactical genius was also a casualty, although Grant's received a knock, too, for the way he was taken unawares on the first day. The total number of casualties was staggering: more than 23,000 men, or 25 percent of the forces engaged.

Shiloh was not the only blow to the Confederacy. That same day, the famously abrasive and arrogant Union commander General John Pope captured another strategic point: Island No. 10 on the Kentucky-Tennessee border. Journalist Edward Dicey had traveled west to Cairo, a commercial depot on the Mississippi River just above the Mason-Dixon Line. He watched as great hospital steamboats disgorged their wounded from Shiloh and Island No. 10. "All day and all night long you heard the ringing of their bells and the whistling of the steam." Piles of coffins waited on the jetty "with the dead men's names inscribed upon them, left standing in front of the railway offices."[8]

———

In Virginia, General McClellan had already landed two-thirds of his army at Fortress Monroe, which guarded the entrance to Hampton Roads, and was marching up the peninsula toward Richmond when the Confederate secretary of the navy, Stephen Mallory, sent a small fleet to attack the remainder of the ship transports. On April 11, the *Merrimac,* accompanied by six vessels, steamed toward the Federal fleet and its *Monitor.* Francis Dawson had been assigned to the *Beaufort,* which, despite its grand-sounding name, was only a small tugboat with one gun. "The general idea was that the *Monitor* would be overwhelmed by the combined attack," wrote Dawson. But the *Monitor* refused to leave the cover of Fortress Monroe, disappointing HMS *Rinaldo* and the two French warships that had moved in to observe the fight. One of the Confederate gunboats did manage to capture three transports, which elicited an indiscreet cheer from the *Rinaldo,* but otherwise little was achieved in the expedition. When Dawson returned to the base, he was relieved to learn that he was being transferred. Captain Pegram had been given command of an ironclad in New Orleans, and Dawson was to join him.[9]

The French minister, M. Mercier, visited Richmond a few days later, on April 16, expecting to hear talk of surrender.[10] Instead, that afternoon, the Confederate Congress—which had only 26 senators and 135 representatives—passed a draft law conscripting all able-bodied men between eighteen and thirty-five. When Mercier met with his old friend Judah Benjamin, who had been transferred by Davis from the War Department to the State Department in March, he was told that the South would fight to her last breath. Northerners were "a people for whom we feel unmitigated contempt as well as abhorrence," Benjamin declared with uncharacteristic heat.[11] Sitting in the new Confederate secretary of state's spacious but austere office in the former U.S. Customs House, Mercier realized that Benjamin was hoping that the French could be enticed into breaking the blockade in return for cotton and the promise of a free trade agreement. But Mercier knew it was not France that needed persuading.

When Mercier returned to Washington on April 24, Lyons went to see him immediately, worried that his impetuous colleague had made promises to the Confederates that would undo their joint policy of neutrality. Mercier was more excited than usual. He spoke eloquently of the Southern spirit and the reasons why France and Britain should cease dallying and recognize the Confederacy's independence. The South was preparing to recoup its losses, he insisted. Even now, the Confederates were on the verge of completing a second ironclad that would render New Orleans invincible to naval attack. Moreover, they were prepared to lose Richmond, Tennessee, "New Orleans and all their seaports, and indeed the whole of the coast."[12] But even as Mercier was talking, a fleet of U.S. gunboats was bearing down on New Orleans, having subdued the supposedly impregnable forts that defended her.

The city officially surrendered on April 26. The train on which Francis Dawson and his friend Captain Pegram were traveling was within twenty miles of New Orleans when it pulled onto a side track. To their astonishment, train after train came rumbling past in the other direction, each one packed with evacuating Confederate soldiers. "There was no choice for us but to go back to Virginia," Dawson wrote. The much-vaunted ironclad that should have been Pegram's next command was out of their reach. "The journey back was worse than the journey down, as the delays were multiplied," Dawson remembered. Despite Mercier's optimism, this last defeat was sending waves of panic through the South. "New Orleans gone—and with it the Confederacy," came the anguished cry of the diarist Mary Chesnut.[13] Rumors that General McClellan was almost at Richmond sent people rushing out of the city. Clerks packed up the government archives and prepared them for removal; President Davis put his wife and children on the train for Raleigh, North Carolina.[14]

———

For six days, until the arrival of Union general Benjamin Butler and his 15,000 troops, New Orleans was a city on the verge of anarchy. Fires burned unchecked; looters roamed at will; all commerce, including the delivery of foodstuffs, abruptly stopped. Rioters stormed the mint, and one, William Mumford, succeeded in tearing down the U.S. flag that had been installed on Union admiral David Glasgow Farragut's orders. It was then dragged through the streets of the city. In retaliation, Farragut warned that he was sending his men ashore and would bombard the city unless the U.S. flag was flown from City Hall. The desperate mayor turned to the foreign consuls to save New Orleans from immolation. He begged them to send the 4,500-strong European Brigade, which was made up of foreign neutrals who were not liable for the draft, but who had volunteered for civil defense duty.[15] The arrival of the French war-ship *Milan* allayed the consuls' trepidation about sending a group of middle-aged "merchants, bankers, underwriters, judges, real-estate owners and capitalists" into riot duty. The Brigade proved to be a poor substitute; as darkness descended each night, recalled an observer, the city glowed by the light of the arsonist's torch, and the faint but urgent ringing of fire bells wafted out across the water.[16]

On May 1, twenty-five hundred Northern soldiers marched through rubble and trash-strewn streets to take up positions in the chief public buildings. The residents of the magnificent St. Charles Hotel in the French Quarter were turned out to make way for General Butler and his retinue, while the customs house became his headquarters. Butler let it be known that henceforth every citizen would live and abide by his rules alone. "The hand that cuts your bread can cut your throat," he an-nounced.[17] Butler was one of the first politicians to be made a general in the volunteer army. It was his success in raising regiments—and his sup-port for the war as a Democrat—rather than any previous military expe-rience that won him the rank. He had joined the Massachusetts militia as a twenty-one-year-old, and had risen to become a brigadier general with-out ever hearing a shot in battle. A successful lawyer by profession, Ben Butler could fight hard and dirty when circumstances demanded. Force of will and astute backroom tactics had won him the military command of the New Orleans operation—a remarkable feat considering that his two previous commands had been marred by breathtaking incompe-tence.

Among Butler's first acts was the capture and execution of William Mumford, who was strung up from the same flagpole that had flown the desecrated U.S. flag. He also issued a raft of edicts: Any house used by sharpshooters would be destroyed.[18] Shopkeepers who refused to sell to Union officers would have their goods confiscated. Overt displays of partisanship would be judged without mercy—a woman who laughed loudly at a passing Union funeral cortege was sentenced to two years' imprisonment.[19] Almost anyone who wished to do business in the city was first required to take an oath of allegiance.

Nor was Butler troubled in the least by diplomatic niceties. When the foreign consuls protested against their citizens' having to take loyalty oaths, he invited them to leave the city. He declared all foreign funds in their safekeeping to be Confederate contraband and therefore liable to seizure. Union soldiers forced their way into the Dutch consulate and bullied the hapless consul into opening his vault. When Butler attempted the same with the French consulate, however, Count Mejan reminded him that a French warship was moored on the river. Butler also punished members of the British Guard (a company in the European Brigade) who had sent their uniforms and weapons to friends in the Confederate army. Two were imprisoned and another thirty-seven were forced to leave the city.[20]

Lord Lyons thought it was "very imprudent" for the British Guard to engage in such partisan behavior, but he was sufficiently alarmed by Consul Mure's reports to order the *Rinaldo* to proceed to the city. New Orleans had always been a byword for lawlessness and truculence, and the absence of menfolk did little to cow its abandoned wives and daughters. These female Southerners wore Confederate colors, sang songs, hissed, spat, turned their backs, and on one famous occasion dumped the contents of a chamber pot on Union soldiers. In retaliation, on May 15, Butler issued General Order No. 28, which held that "hereafter, when any female shall by word, gesture, or movement, insult or show contempt for any officer or soldier of the United States, she shall be regarded and held liable to be treated as a woman of the town plying her avocation." Washington dismissed the document as a crude piece of Southern propaganda, until newspapers from New Orleans confirmed it.[21]

Butler's "Woman Order" galvanized the South more effectively than any speech or partial victory might have achieved.[22] The Confederate armies in the west had become demoralized after the recent spate of defeats. The loss of Island No. 10 had increased federal control of the Mississippi River to within attacking distance of Memphis, the Confederacy's fifth-largest city and the river gateway into Mississippi. Many of the regiments in General Beauregard's army had come to the end of their twelve-month terms and wanted to return home. One of his corps commanders, Braxton Bragg, who was promoted to general after Shiloh, refused to let them go, and to make his point, deserters were shot without trial. William Watson's 3rd Louisiana were among the twelve-month regiments. The men were furious with Bragg until the "Woman Order" became known. "The feeling of indignation which was roused by Butler's acts overcame in a great measure the disaffection that had been fast spreading through the army," wrote Watson. "Many were roused to a spirit of revenge . . . not that they hated Davis and his Bragg the less, but that they hated Lincoln and his Butler the more."[23]

———

By mid-May, Beauregard's Army of the Mississippi had swelled to around 70,000 Confederates. But he was facing a massive new entity called the Army of the West, which had 120,000 soldiers. The Union general leading this army was Henry Halleck, the second most senior general after McClellan. Known as "Old Brains" for his treatise on military theory, Halleck had taken charge after Shiloh as the senior general, and had combined the three Federal forces under Buell, Grant, and Pope. Although Halleck was moving slowly toward Corinth, Mississippi, Beauregard did not think that the time available would allow him to prepare any better for the Federals' arrival. But he understood the city's importance to the South. "If defeated here," he wrote to Jefferson Davis after the army had retreated to Corinth from Shiloh, "we lose the whole Mississippi Valley and probably our cause."[24] But given the choice between railroads and men, Beauregard chose the latter. His chief concern now was to save his army.

Halleck arrived at the outskirts of Corinth on May 26. The pickets in Watson's regiments traded jokes and insults with their Northern counterparts. "We were glad to hear they had an abundance of coffee," wrote Watson, "as we trusted that it would fall into our hands." In just a few more days, Corinth would be completely surrounded, and no more supplies would reach Beauregard's wilting army. On the twenty-ninth, Watson was on a picket duty when his squad was late returning and became lost in the darkness. "We therefore concluded to seek out a quiet, snug place in the woods and lie down till daylight." The next morning they awoke to an unnatural silence. Walking back to camp, they discovered it was empty. During the night Beauregard had succeeded in evacuating his entire army. It was one of the greatest military maneuvers of the war. Like most of the rank and file, Watson had been utterly ignorant of Beauregard's elaborate plans to deceive Halleck.

Watson and his men headed off in the direction of Corinth. There they found the railroad and walked along its broken track. Every now and then they came across large groups of Confederate deserters. These were mostly volunteers from Bragg's division—Tennessee men whose main concern now was to protect their farms and families from looting soldiers. Watson did not blame them. He, too, wished to return home to

New Orleans. The Queen's proclamation of neutrality meant that the new conscription law did not apply to him. "I now considered that I had faithfully fulfilled my engagement to the Confederate States, and trusted they would do the same by me."[25]

General Halleck's soldiers marched into Corinth on May 30 only to find a filthy ghost town. The general was furious at being denied his great battle, but "most of the men and officers were glad of it," wrote Robert Neve of the 5th Kentucky Volunteers. The Englishman wrangled a pass into town and went scavenging around the defensive works, kicking over discarded treasures and occasionally finding something interesting, like a bowie knife. "I also found a note directed to General Halleck. It said: 'If you think there is no HELL or here-after, follow us. Yours, Blythe's Regiment, Mississippi Volunteers.' "[26]

———

The peaceful capture of Corinth did not result in the praise Henry Halleck had expected. Indeed, quite the reverse. The Chicago *Tribune* sneered at his "barren triumph" and called it "tantamount to a defeat."[27] Newspapers across several states followed suit. The acrimony over the Confederates' retreat revealed Halleck's poor relationship with the press. Reporters wishing to follow his army were firmly discouraged from making the attempt, as Frank Vizetelly discovered.[28] It had felt like a deep personal sacrifice to say goodbye to his friends in the Army of the Potomac; "I was proud of the position I had achieved among them," he wrote. During the past twelve months, "I have sought my fortune with the soldiers of the Potomac . . . so thoroughly had I become identified with them that numbers of the officers and—I am not ashamed to say it—men, looked upon me as an old friend."[29]

On May 14, Vizetelly informed readers of the *Illustrated London News* that he had transferred from the U.S. Army to the U.S. Navy. "The last you heard of me, [I] was waiting in St. Louis for a reply from General Halleck," he wrote. The response to his request had been disappointing; Halleck had not officially barred him from the Army of the West, but he had forbidden him to use government transport. It amounted to the same thing, Vizetelly pointed out, since he could not paddle a canoe, "charter a steamer specially to carry me, or swim up the Ohio and Tennessee Rivers," just to follow the army. Happily, he discovered that the naval authorities were indifferent to his presence. Vizetelly was granted permission to observe the river operations on the Mississippi.

Confederate sharpshooters firing from the banks of the Mississippi at the Federal fleet, by Frank Vizetelly.

"Leaving St. Louis late in the afternoon," wrote Vizetelly, "I found myself steaming down its rapid current in one of those floating palaces." There seemed to be no shore along the river; "nothing but submerged forests for miles and miles back, with here and there a clearing showing the locality of a plantation." His destination was Fort Pillow, the last Confederate obstacle before Memphis. Vizetelly remained on board for six weeks as the Union fleet wound its way down the Mississippi River. Despite the growing heat, he was often confined to his tiny cabin, as sharpshooters hidden in the tangled thickets along the river proved to be far too accurate for safety. Vizetelly was convinced that the South was wasting her men on a losing cause. "We find that each day the North is developing her gigantic resources," he wrote. The South had no shortage of brave men, "but her army is growing weary." "I have spoken with numerous deserters, prisoners, and others, and they have, with few exception, expressed themselves heartily sick of the war."[30]*

---

* Northerners had pointed out to Vizetelly the staggering disparities between the two sides. The last economic figures before the war showed that the Southern states had 18,026 "industrial establishments," the North, 110,274.[31]

At daybreak on June 6, the Union and Confederate flotillas steamed toward each other in their final confrontation. As the city of Memphis came into view, Vizetelly saw that a line of eight Confederate vessels waited to block them. High above, stretched out along the bluff in front of the Tennessee city, were thousands of spectators. Their cheers turned to wails as the Confederate fleet was smashed to pieces. "Never was a success so complete and so cheaply purchased by the victors; never an enemy so humiliated," Vizetelly wrote in jubilation. "The stars and bars have been trailed in the dust . . . verily the Memphians have eaten dirt."[32]

However, when the readers of the *Illustrated London News* next heard from their war correspondent, Vizetelly was suffering from a crisis of conscience. "Your readers must understand that I never saw anything of Southern people until I landed at Memphis," he wrote. "A 'peculiar institution' of theirs had prejudiced me somewhat against them, and I believed from all I heard that the Secession movement was but skin deep after all." But "in Memphis and its immediate neighbourhood I made it my business to mix with all classes and test their loyalty or disloyalty . . . all were clamouring for separation. If then, such are the sentiments of the entire South, and defeat does not bring them nearer to the Union, what is to be the result of all this bloodshed?"[33] For the first time he questioned whether he had been supporting the right side.

Vizetelly was not the only Englishman to undergo a change of heart in June. Henry Morton Stanley, formerly of the Confederate Dixie Grays, joined the Union army on June 7. Stanley had been sent to Camp

Destruction of the Confederate "cottonclads" off Memphis, by Frank Vizetelly.

Douglas, outside Chicago, along with hundreds of other Confederate prisoners.[34] About twenty-six thousand men were sent there during the war; at least six thousand never came out. The inmates called it "80 acres of hell." "The appearance of the prisoners startled me," Stanley recalled. Every man was filthy, emaciated, and crawling with vermin.[35] To reach the latrines Stanley was forced to step over half-naked men lying in great puddles of feces, either too weak or too delirious to move. "Exhumed corpses could not have presented anything more hideous than dozens of these dead-and-alive men," he wrote. "Every morning, the wagons came to the hospital and dead-house, to take away the bodies; and I saw the corpses rolled in their blankets, taken to the vehicles, and piled one upon another."[36]

More than three hundred of the eight thousand prisoners in the camp claimed to be British subjects, and a group of them demanded to see the British consul, John Wilkins. He turned to Lord Lyons for advice. Surely, Wilkins asked, they should try to secure the release of those who had been forcibly conscripted into Confederate service. Lyons encouraged him to "exert all his influence unofficially in their favour," but he deemed it hopeless to use official channels, since it would be impossible to prove whether a man had enlisted willingly.[37] Consul Wilkins argued and pleaded to see the British prisoners, but the authorities would not allow him inside the camp.[38]

Stanley solved his predicament by switching sides and enlisting for three years in Battery L of the 1st Illinois Light Artillery. The "increase in sickness, the horrors of the prison, the oily atmosphere, the ignominious cartage of the dead, the useless flight of time, the fear of being incarcerated for years . . . so affected my spirits that I felt a few more days of these scenes would drive me mad." He had never cared about politics anyway: "There were no blackies in Wales."[39] In mid-June the battery was shipped to Harpers Ferry in western Virginia, where Stanley was hospitalized for dysentery on the twenty-second. Soon afterward, he went for a stroll around the hospital grounds and did not return. He went home to Wales, eager to get as far away from the war as possible.

Stanley was lucky not to have been assigned to Battery K, which was sent to Tennessee to help Union general George W. Morgan seize the Cumberland Gap from Confederate control. The Gap was a mountain pass through the Appalachians, where Virginia rubbed borders with neighboring Kentucky and Tennessee. The rugged Cumberland Mountains suddenly parted there, as though a spade had dug a thousand-foot-deep slice through the rock, allowing the aptly named Wilderness Road to wind its way down to the rich basin known as the Bluegrass region. General Morgan realized that the Confederate stronghold could not be taken by a direct attack. The only option was to split up his brigades and have them clamber up and over the Cumberland Mountains along mule tracks so they could launch a surprise assault on the Confederates from the other side.

Colonel Fitzroy De Courcy was ordered to lead his brigade through a steep gorge flanked by sheer rock on one side and the Cumberland River on the other. It had been eight months since he had been given command of the 16th Ohio Volunteers. His men were pleased to have one of the best drillmasters in the Union as their colonel. But the ways of the British Army were not those of a volunteer regiment, and the Ohioans considered him unduly harsh and exacting. He was no more popular with them than he had been with Fanny Seward. De Courcy was at his best when commanding larger forces in which individuals were less likely to be the victims of his scathing comments. But General Morgan had realized that a soldier of De Courcy's experience was invaluable and had promoted him to brigade commander.

The trek took more than two weeks and cost De Courcy many of his horses and all his supply wagons, which either broke or became lodged in the rocks. The brigades were weary and hungry when they reunited on the other side of the Gap on June 18. The next day, they discovered that the terrible odyssey had been for nothing. The Confederates, believing that General Morgan possessed a force of more than fifty thousand, had abandoned the Gap.[40] Nevertheless, Morgan became emotional when he reflected on the hardships endured by De Courcy's troops. "Pardon me for speaking of the heroic bearing and fortitude of the Seventh Division," he wrote to General Buell and Secretary Stanton. "A nobler band never marched beneath a conquering flag." He singled out De Courcy in particular and asked that he be promoted to brigadier general. "He is an accomplished officer and is every inch a soldier." His request was ignored.

———

McClellan's peninsula campaign to capture Richmond was already under way by June 20, although not in the manner expected by the War Department. McClellan was laying elaborate sieges to Yorktown (where a British army had surrendered in 1781) and Williamsburg, towns that the three British military observers with him believed could have been taken with a bit of dash and very little fuss. They held their tongues, though, and whenever anyone asked them for their opinion they confined themselves to praising the general's wonderful job in transforming civilians into soldiers. This was exactly what Lord Palmerston wanted. He later reminded Lord Russell that all officers observing "federal forces in the field . . . should be Strictly cautioned not to make any Criticisms which might be useful to the Federals in pointing out to them Faults or Imperfections. . . . The Federals are luckily too vain to attach much value to the opinions of Englishmen, but our officers might be told to open their Eyes and Ears and to keep their mouths Shut."[*41]

A combination of poor intelligence gathering and McClellan's own paranoia had led him to believe that he was heavily outnumbered by the Confederates defending Richmond. His demands for reinforcements brought about the deployment of the 1st New Jersey Cavalry, known as the Cavaliers, which had been left behind to guard Washington. The morale of the regiment had improved since the arrival of Sir Percy Wyndham, a twenty-nine-year-old English soldier of fortune, on February 19, who had been assigned as its colonel by the War Department in an attempt to resolve the regiment's officer problems. Few men would willingly have accepted such an unhappy outfit, but Sir Percy was not the reflective kind. In the words of one officer, "he strode along with the nonchalant air of one who had wooed Dame Fortune too long to be cast down by her frowns."[42]

The regiment found Sir Percy's eccentricities rather endearing. Dark hair crowned his head in a Byronic wave, and a mustache and beard extended from his lips like bushy Christmas trees. He seemed to love dressing up and would change his uniform on the flimsiest of excuses. He looked younger than his years even though he had been a soldier since the age of fifteen and had served in the French, Austrian, and British armies. Wyndham's parentage was dubious and his knighthood Italian (bestowed upon him by King Victor Emmanuel for his services during Garibaldi's campaign), but his skills and bravery were authentic.[43] Although he dressed like a dandy, he possessed a temper that terrified the

---

* The Prince de Joinville excused McClellan's performance, claiming that the general had been constantly hamstrung and interfered with by Washington.

men. When enraged—which was apparent by the way he twiddled his mustache—Sir Percy was capable of anything, so much so that officers from other regiments insisted on wearing sidearms when around him. The men learned how to drill because if one person made a mistake, he would force the entire regiment to keep repeating the maneuver until they dropped from fatigue. But instead of hating him, the soldiers felt an extraordinary sense of pride. "Under our new Colonel our affairs have improved so much that we consider ourselves equal to almost any Cavalry Regiment in the field," wrote its surgeon.[44]

The regiment was en route to the Army of the Potomac when a special messenger arrived with instructions to turn around and head for the Shenandoah Valley as quickly as possible, where it was to join a force under General McDowell, of Bull Run fame. Jefferson Davis's military chief of staff, Robert E. Lee, had ordered Stonewall Jackson to create a diversion in the Shenandoah Valley so that Lincoln would not dare to send all the soldiers at his disposal to McClellan. The valley was like a gently undulating corridor with high, wooded mountain ranges on either side. The Shenandoah Valley Turnpike stretched 125 miles from the Potomac River all the way down to the bottom of the valley, making it an ideal conduit for an invading force.

Stonewall Jackson, a dour Presbyterian who rarely spoke, even to explain his orders, had originally been sent to defend the valley's abundant orchards and lush pastures. His performance in Virginia during the winter had been lackluster, but since the beginning of McClellan's peninsula campaign, he had beaten every force sent to stop him. He disabled one Federal army, under Frémont, on May 8. Next he turned on Union general Nathaniel P. Banks on the twenty-third at Front Royal. This was Sam Hill's, and the 6th Louisiana's, first experience of fighting. Their commander, Dick Taylor, recorded in his memoirs that at midday on May 23, they were marching along a road heading north, when

there rushed out of the wood to meet us a young, rather well-looking woman, afterward widely known as Belle Boyd. Breathless with speed and agitation, some time elapsed before she found her voice. Then, with much volubility, she said we were near Front Royal, beyond the wood; that the town was filled with federals, whose camp was on the west side of the river, where they had guns in position to cover the wagon bridge, but none bearing

on the railway bridge below the former. . . . All this she told with
the precision of a staff officer making a report.[45]

It has been disputed whether Belle Boyd's courageous dash through
active battle lines did indeed provide Jackson with new intelligence, but
it was certainly news to Taylor, who ordered his troops to storm the
town. The Federals surrendered after five hours of fighting. Colonel
Henry Kyd Douglas, a childhood friend of Belle Boyd's, bumped into
her "standing on the pavement in front of a hotel, talking with some few
federal officers (prisoners) and some of her acquaintances in our
army. . . . As I stooped from my saddle she pinned a rose to my uniform,
bidding me remember that it was blood-red and that it was her 'colors.' "[46]

Two days after the Confederates' success at Front Royal, Sam Hill's
brigade tore through Winchester, liberating it from Federal occupation.
Mary Sophia Hill heard that Sam had been killed, "so off I started for
Staunton," she wrote, "nearly crazy." She eventually found Sam in a
makeshift hospital. He was dirty and in shock, but his wounds were not
life-threatening. She became determined to have him transferred out of
his regiment.[47]

On June 1, Sir Percy and his rerouted Cavaliers arrived at Strasburg,
to the west of Front Royal, just as Stonewall Jackson's troops were evacuating the area. Turner Ashby, a recently promoted Confederate
brigadier general, was picking off Union soldiers who had had the ill
luck to advance too far forward. Sir Percy was fed up with hearing about
the "Black Knight of the Confederacy," as Ashby was called, and had declared to a journalist covering Federal movements that he was going to
"bag" the rebel. Shortly after breakfast on June 6, Sir Percy learned that
one of Stonewall Jackson's wagon trains was stuck in the mud on the
road to Port Republic, guarded by just a handful of Ashby's men. His orders did not include mounting offensives, but he could not resist the
prize. Just before two o'clock, he ordered his cavalry into formation and
started off at a gallop in the direction of the stranded wagons. But Ashby
and his entire cavalry were actually grazing their horses not far away. As
Sir Percy galloped toward the woods straddling the road, he was stopped
by a fierce countercharge from Ashby. The regiment's colors, sixty-four
Cavaliers, and Sir Percy himself were captured. Sir Percy was furious
with the behavior of his troops, whom he felt had barely put up a fight.[48]

"He would have stopped right there in the road and engaged in fisticuffs if he could have found a partner," wrote a Confederate soldier.[49]

Sir Percy was still seething with rage when he arrived as a prisoner at the Confederate base, where an old comrade from the Garibaldi campaign, Roberdeau Wheat, immediately recognized his voice. According to Dick Taylor, Wheat shouted, "Percy, old boy!" "Why, Bob!" the other rejoined. Wheat good-naturedly chided him for fighting on the "wrong" side, and then stepped aside so that the colonel could be brought before Stonewall Jackson.[50] That evening, while the two men were chatting in Jackson's office, news came that Turner Ashby had been shot through the heart during a later skirmish. A member of Jackson's staff quickly led Sir Percy away so that the general could be alone.[51]

By sunset on June 9, the bulk of the Union forces in the Shenandoah Valley were in full retreat. A newspaper in Richmond declared: "Strange as it may appear, news from the armies within five miles of [this city] is of secondary importance. Invariably the crowds which daily flock around the bulletin boards ask first 'What news of Jackson?' "[52] With only 17,000 troops at his disposal, Jackson had succeeded against a combined Union force three times his strength, attacking it piecemeal, making full use of the valley's terrain. Yet the events taking place around Richmond were just as significant; on May 31, Confederate general Joseph E. Johnston had launched an attack against McClellan's army. Known as the Battle of Fair Oaks, or Seven Pines, the campaign failed in all its objectives, but it did produce one stroke of luck for the Confederacy: the obstinate and ineffectual General Joe Johnston was struck by a bullet. President Davis replaced him with General Robert E. Lee, who had never before commanded troops in battle. He will "be timid and irresolute in action," sneered General McClellan when informed of Lee's appointment.[53]

Spring flooding postponed further movement by either army; and the lull had all Washington on tenterhooks. The five miles between McClellan and the city of Richmond seemed a mere hop and a skip to victory. Seward boasted to Charles Sumner that the war would be over in ninety days or less. Lord Lyons could not help wondering whether he was about to miss its most exciting moment. He had at last received permission to take a holiday and was leaving on June 18. Life in Washington was no "bed of roses," he had often told his sister. But it was not until May that he had finally summoned up the nerve to ask Lord Russell for a leave of absence.[54] Lyons had grown despondent waiting for an answer; "my chance of getting home seems less and less as I reflect upon it," he wrote to his sister.[55] By the beginning of June, he had persuaded himself that his case was hopeless. Then, on the sixth, came Lord Russell's letter granting him three months' leave.[56]

Lord Lyons's final week in Washington started out well with only the usual routine work.[57] This satisfactory state of affairs was ruined, however, by the arrival of Lord Edward St. Maur, a younger son of the Duke of Somerset, First Lord of the Admiralty. It was Lord Edward's older brother, Lord St. Maur, who had briefly fought as a Red Shirt under Garibaldi. Lord Lyons thought that Lord Edward was risking his career in the Foreign Service for a cheap thrill and warned him that the presence of a British cabinet minister's son could lead to all kinds of unexpected trouble. But even he had not anticipated Lord Edward's falling into the hands of Consul Bernal in Baltimore and his secessionist cronies. The Southern journalist W. W. Glenn remembered his first meeting with Lord Edward St. Maur very well. "He was quite young," he wrote, "and had a great dread of having his name in the newspapers . . . on account of his father's position in the English Cabinet. . . . He was quite Northern [supporting] too." Glenn had plans for the youth, however.

> I determined to devote myself to giving intelligent Englishmen every facility for acquainting themselves thoroughly with the true condition of Southern affairs and the spirit of the Southern people . . . it might prove useful to make so intelligent a convert: Lord Lyons of course attempted to dissuade him from carrying out his project, and went as far as to tell Lord Edward that if he was caught and thrown into prison, he need expect no aid from him as Minister. Lord Lyons from the beginning did everything he could to prevent the slightest offense being given to the Federal Government. . . . He made later several remonstrances to me through his attachés.[58]

Dread at what might happen to Lord Edward overshadowed Lyons's otherwise joyful departure on June 18. In Washington, President Lincoln shook his hand and asked him to convey "his good intentions towards the people of Great Britain." When Lyons reached New York, Seward stopped by his hotel to say goodbye. He promised that if anything did arise between the two countries while Lyons was away, he would place the matter on hold until his return.[59] Lyons was touched by these displays, although he had no illusion that the goodwill toward him was anything other than temporary and capricious. If he, rather than Mercier, had visited Richmond to explore the views of the Confederate government, the result would have been expulsion from the country and an apology demanded from Britain. The contrast between the public's attitude toward Britain and France also disturbed him. The French attempt to topple the Mexican government in the spring, Lyons noticed, had been accepted with an angry shrug, even though it mocked American claims to be the sole power in the region.* They "are more civil to France than to England," he asserted to Lord Russell, "partly because they never will have, do what she will, the same bitterness against her as they have against England."[60]

———

Lord Edward knew that crossing the lines into Southern territory might be risky, but "there is no imprudence in what I am doing—I have asked good advice," he assured his parents on June 19. "I do not intend to get into any chance of difficulties."[61] Nor did he; Glenn's contacts proved their worth, and Lord Edward was safely deposited in Richmond on June 26. He did not think it odd that with the Confederacy fighting for its life, President Davis would make time to see him. Lord Edward was perhaps too young and naïve to realize what the presence of an English cabinet minister's son would mean to Southerners. All Lord Edward had to do was say his name and government officials, staff officers, and influential citizens opened their doors to him. "There is a remarkably friendly feeling towards England . . . the only sign of ill-feeling that exists is on the subject of recognition," he not surprisingly concluded. "I saw and talked to everybody, I was very kindly treated indeed."[62]

He was so well treated that other British subjects—many of whom were desperately trying to find any means of leaving the South—became quite jealous. The Confederates deliberately shielded him from the hardships and persecution often suffered by ordinary Britons. A young Scottish journalist named Gabriel Cueto, for example, had been held

———

* France's invasion of Mexico made the presence of Joinville and the Orleans exiles politically embarrassing, and they departed from America at the end of June. But Joinville continued to defend McClellan from abroad, publishing a long pamphlet, entitled "The Army of the Potomac," which appeared the following October.

without charge since May.[63] Lord Edward never heard about him, and Cueto's case did not receive a mention in England either, although he would spend nine months in a Confederate prison essentially for speaking his mind.[64] An English governess named Catherine Hopley, who was stranded in Richmond, thought it was outrageous that "Lord Seymour [*sic*] should be able to obtain a passport from the Confederate government without any trouble," while the rest of them were left to rot in the city. "I went the first thing in the morning, to see Mr. Cridland," she wrote, "at what the 'blockaded British subjects' used to call 'anything but the Consolation Office.' " She also visited the Confederate secretary of war, George Randolph, and Stephen Mallory of the Confederate navy, and offered herself as a courier to Europe. But both men scarcely looked up from their papers. Their curt dismissal was especially wounding since "I was sympathising so deeply with them all, and wishing I could take messages and letters to England for them, and feeling worthy of being trusted even with the gravest secrets."[65]

The Confederates did not require Miss Hopley's services when their own native-born women were perfectly willing to carry out dangerous operations. Rose Greenhow, the Washington hostess who had exposed herself to Northern wrath by passing military secrets to the South, had arrived in Richmond after months of house arrest and then incarceration in a Federal prison. President Davis made a point of calling at her hotel and was shocked to see the ravages wrought by her ordeal. She had the air of someone "shaken by mental torture," he wrote sadly to his wife.[66] Moreover, she was homeless and penniless. Judah Benjamin promptly sent her $2,500 as a mark of the Confederacy's gratitude.

Lord Edward's arrival had coincided with the beginning of General Lee's counteroffensive against McClellan. Bored with his leaky tugboat, Francis Dawson resigned from the Confederate navy to join an artillery battery commanded by Willie Pegram, a nephew of Captain Pegram's. On June 26, Pegram's battery was ordered to cross the Chickahominy River, northeast of Richmond. According to Lee's plan, the troops under General A. P. Hill (to which the battery belonged) were to form one element of a four-part attack against McClellan's somewhat incoherently placed divisions. If all went well for Lee, the Federal invaders would be attacked on every side and could disintegrate.

But one vital piece was missing: Stonewall Jackson and his men had not yet arrived from the Shenandoah Valley. After anxiously waiting until three in the afternoon, General Hill ordered his men to begin their assault without him. "The guns were instantly loaded, and the firing began," Dawson recalled. "A solid shot bowled past me, killed one of our men, tore a leg and arm from another, and threw three horses into a bloody, struggling heap. This was my chance, and I stepped to the gun and worked away as though existence depended on my labours."[67] He worked feverishly until a blow knocked him off his feet. "That Britisher has gone up at last," he heard. Dawson examined his leg and saw that a shell fragment had ripped away six inches of flesh. But strangely, he felt nothing. "I went back to my post, and there remained until the battery was withdrawn after sunset." Of the seventy-five men in Pegram's battery, only twenty-eight were still standing.

Dawson managed to hobble for several miles to a field hospital. While trying to obtain some morphine for a friend, he saw surgeons, their bare arms smeared with blood, cutting and sawing into rows of limbs. Below one table lay "arms, feet, and legs, thrown promiscuously in a heap, like the refuse of a slaughter house." Dawson decided not to stay and obtained a ride on an ambulance going to Richmond. His adventures with Willie Pegram had been brief, but he was gratified to read about himself in the Richmond *Dispatch* a few days later as the "young Englishman" who had "received a wound while acting most gallantly."[68] He was a hero, as tens of pretty young lady nurses told him every day.

Dawson soon began to regret his fame. When one of his friends in the Confederate navy, James Morgan, came to visit him, Dawson begged for his help. "The day was hot," Morgan recalled,

and I found my friend lying on a cot near the open front door, so weak that he could not speak above a whisper, and after greeting him and speaking some words of cheer I saw that he was anxious to tell me something. I leaned over him to hear what he had to say, and the poor fellow whispered in my ear "Jimmie, for God's sake, make them move my cot to the back of the building." I assured him that he had been placed in the choicest spot in the hospital, where he could get any little air that might be stirring; but he still insisted that he wanted to be moved, giving as a reason that every lady who entered the place washed his face and fed him with jelly. The result was that his face felt sore and he was stuffed so full of jelly that he was most uncomfortable. . . . Shaking with laughter, I

The Seven Days
June 25 – July 1

Federal Forces
Confederate Forces

N
W E
S

Miles
0   5   10

Hanover Junction

Hanover Court House

Richmond, Fredericksburg and Potomac R.R.

Virginia Central R.R.

Stuart's raid

Stuart's raid 12–15 June

Jackson

Pamunkey R.

Old church

Ebenezer Wells

BATTLE OF
MECHANICSVILLE
JUNE 26

Lord Edward
St. Maur

Meadow
Bridge

D. H. Hill

Francis
Dawson

Beaver Dam Cr.

Jackson

Ellerson's
Mill

A. P. Hill

Gaines's Mill

BATTLE OF
GAINES'S MILL
JUNE 27

Mechanicsville

Porter

Longstreet

Porter

Tunstall's Sta.

D. H. Hill

Longstreet

New Bridge

Golding's Farm

Boatswain's Swamp

Grapevine Bridge

Trent Farm

White
House

McClellan

Lee

Magruder

Richmond

Huger

Old
Tavern

Fair Oaks

Oak Grove June 25

BATTLE OF FAIR OAKS
OR SEVEN PINES MAY 31–JUNE 1

Seven Pines

Franklin

Sumner

Heintzelman

Keyes

Savage Sta.
June 29

White Oak Swamp

Richmond and York River R.R.

Bottom's Bridge

Jackson

Chickahominy R.

Chaffin's
Bluff

Stuart's raid

New
Market

Drewry's
Bluff

James R.

June 30

Glendale

Frayser's Farm

Forge Bridge

Richmond & Petersburg R.R.

BATTLE OF
MALVERN HILL
JULY 1

Malvern Hill

Charles City
Court House

Federal Army July 2
Harrison's Landing

James R.

Appomattox R.

delivered his request to the head surgeon, who pinned a notice on Dawson's sheet to the effect that "This man must only be washed and fed by the regular nurses."[69]

The Battle of Mechanicsville, as Dawson's engagement was called, was a costly disappointment for Lee. Jackson's failure to arrive on time resulted in Confederate troops having to attack without adequate support. Lee was still feeling his way into his new command, but the one quality he did not lack was determination. The following day, General Hill's troops once again led the assault. But by now Jackson and his men, including the Louisiana Brigade, had arrived and they too rushed into battle. Seeing his men stagger beneath a barrage of fire, Major Wheat galloped in front of the Louisiana Tigers, urging them to follow. Both he and his horse were immediately riddled with bullets. The fighting continued so hotly that Wheat's body lay where it fell for twenty-four hours.

For the next seven days, beginning on June 25, Lee and McClellan clashed along the Chickahominy River, around the perimeter of Richmond, in one bloody encounter after another. Although McClellan lost none of these battles, he was unnerved by Lee's attacks and began retreating southward, away from Richmond. Lee wanted to demolish "those people," as he referred to the Federals, with another all-out attack on July 1. By now, the Union army was entrenched around Malvern Hill, fifteen miles southeast of Richmond. The terrain favored the Federal soldiers sitting atop the 150-foot-high plateau. McClellan still had 115,000 men with 100 pieces of artillery and, unlike their general, their nerves were holding steady.

The Confederate attack was so disjointed that isolated brigades ran forward only to be chewed up by artillery fire. This "was not war—it was murder," a Confederate general later said of Lee's failed assault. The Louisianans (minus Sam Hill, who was happily drawing up maps, thanks to some clever wrangling by his sister) were mauled by Irishmen in blue, including the 69th New York. The total Confederate loss on this terrible day was five and a half thousand, nearly twice the number of casualties sustained by the Federals.*

---

* Among the Union wounded was a cousin of William Gladstone's, twenty-one-year-old Herbert Gladstone, who had joined the 36th New York British Volunteers the previous year. He survived an agonizing journey back to the capital with a bullet lodged in his left leg, after which his family in England lost track of him.

About a quarter of Lee's eighty-thousand-strong army was either dead or wounded. McClellan could have ordered a counterattack, and many of his generals urged him to do so, but he had lost the will to fight. The next morning, July 2, the mist lifted from the battlefield to reveal so many bodies that the terrain appeared to be masked by a bloody quilt. Some were dead, but many still crawled feebly like stricken insects. Despite having inflicted a stunning blow against Lee's army, McClellan continued his retreat, and the Seven Days' Battles were a strategic victory for Lee, despite his heavy losses. On June 3, McClellan had been five miles from Richmond; on July 3, he was thirty. The casualties for the two sides amounted to more than 35,000 men.

McClellan left behind a treasure trove for the undersupplied Confederates. "All along the road," wrote an English observer, "cartridge boxes, knapsacks, blankets and coats may be picked up. The rebels, as they pass, generally cast away their own worse equipments and refit. . . . Here were cartridge boxes, unopened and perfectly new."[70] Five days later, on the eighth, Lincoln sailed down to Harrison's Landing on the James River in order to see the situation for himself. His impatience with McClellan was echoed all over the North. Only the general seemed to think that his withdrawal was nothing other than a "change of base." The rest of the country called it a reckless squandering of a brilliant opportunity to capture Richmond and win the war.

Lord Edward St. Maur set off for Washington after the Seven Days' Battles and arrived under a flag of truce at McClellan's camp on July 15. He had planned to stay for some time, but his admission to having observed the campaign from the "other side" provoked a reaction from the Union officers "which was really childish," he protested to his father. Unwisely, he fell into arguments with them about the reasons for the war and other sensitive subjects. Lord Edward's opinions had undergone a complete transformation, just as the Southern propagandist W. W. Glenn had hoped. "I did not start with any feeling one way or the other," he insisted, "but I defy any candid man to go south, without being convinced that this war must end in separation." If the split did not happen soon, he expected it to become a long and "very cruel war." He had heard from Southern officers that there had been instances of Louisiana regiments killing their Northern prisoners. "This," decided Lord Edward, "is Butler's doing."

TWELVE

The South Is Rising

Beast Butler—Palmerston is offended—Hotze and Spence join forces—
Lindsay goes too far—The Alabama escapes—Déjà vu at Bull Run

"Beast Butler," as the South dubbed General Ben Butler, was enjoying what the Scotsman William Watson called a "perfect reign of terror" over New Orleans. Watson received his discharge at Camp Tupelo and set off by train and steamboat to New Orleans. During his journey south, he witnessed unsettling scenes: Federal soldiers marching onto a plantation and putting down a slave revolt at gunpoint; Confederate "guerrillas" using women and children as human shields. When he reached New Orleans, Watson went straight to the consul, George Coppell, to ask for a certificate of British nationality. "He informed me that the certificate would be of no use or protection, if I violated neutrality. I then looked about for a day or two to see the state of things under Butler's rule."[1]

Watson found a city ruled by whim—the whim of a Union soldier, a Butler-appointed bureaucrat or judge, or an anonymous informer. "Butler continued to hunt for treason, and all material that could contribute to it he confiscated. He found it existed extensively in the vaults of banks," wrote Watson, "in merchants' safes, in rich men's houses, among their stores of plate and other valuables."[2] A judicial ransom system was in effect. Men of means would be arrested on some unknown charge and their wives prevailed upon to secure their release by handing over thousands of dollars to a "fixer" who happened to know the right judge.

Watson had been in the city for only a few days when he experienced Butler's justice for himself. It began with a thoughtless comment he made in a café. A short while later, Watson was accosted on the street by three men and forcibly marched to the customs house. He was questioned by detectives who "seized my pocket-book, as they had seen in it treasonable documents in the shape of bank-notes." He asked to see a lawyer and to have his arrest made known to the British consul, which made his interrogators laugh. After a night behind bars, Watson was taken to see General Butler on the charge of having used "treasonable language." Years later, the memory of his interview still made Watson bitter. Butler's head "was large and flabby," he wrote, "and nearly destitute of hair—except a little at the sides, which was just the color of his epaulets." The general jeered at him and asked if he knew why he was there. "I said I was a British subject, and would have counsel to attend to my case. 'Oh, a British subject of course,' roared he. 'I know that they are all British subjects now in New Orleans.' "

Butler's manner throughout the interview led Watson to expect a lengthy prison term. Instead, he was sent before a judge, who examined his certificate of nationality and then offered him some words of advice about incautious jokes in a city under martial law. "I was quite astonished at having got off so easily." His pocketbook was also returned, with some of the money still there, "which was considered a most extraordinary and unaccountable circumstance."[3] Watson wondered if the presence of HMS *Rinaldo*, lately arrived on Lyons's orders, had anything to do with his swift release. Butler, he thought, made a great deal of noise about foreigners and the interference of foreign powers, particularly "John Bull." But it was all calculated to frighten, rather than eradicate, the foreign population. Nevertheless, Watson was determined to leave New Orleans. All he had to do was find a weakness at one of the checkpoints and sneak past the guards. One sultry summer's day, Watson and two friends set off for a picnic and simply carried on walking.

On May 13, 1862, almost three weeks after Butler's arrival in Louisiana, Henry Adams was surprised by the spectacle of his father performing a victory dance in the hall at London's American legation. "We've got New

Orleans!" his father shouted. Henry ran out of the house to look for Thurlow Weed. Finding him "near his hotel, I leaped out of the cab, and each of us simultaneously drew out a telegram which we exchanged. . . . I went round to the Diplomatic Club and had the pleasure of enunciating my sentiments."[4] That evening, Weed's celebrations at the Reform Club were underscored by the shrill cry of newspaper boys who passed beneath the windows, shouting "Rumored Capture of New Orleans." Even more gratifyingly, the next day *The Times* admitted that it had been "mistaken" in accepting Southern assurances that the city would never fall. William Howard Russell added spice to the mix by reminding readers of McClellan's "magnificent army" that "hated them like the devil and would want to have something to do" once the war was over. Russell's warning appeared to strike a chord. At a reception on May 15, John Bright wagged his pudgy finger at Henry, saying, "If you Americans succeed in getting over this affair, you mustn't go and get stuffy to England. Because if you do, I don't know what's to become of us who stood up for you here." Henry laughed and replied that Bright would be welcome as a member of Congress.[5]

News of the victory had reached London on the anniversary of Charles Francis Adams's arrival in England. The coincidence seemed fitting; life in England had grown quite bearable of late. "There is just now," Adams wrote to Charles Francis Jr., "nobody who professes to think well of the South."[6] It helped that they had moved to a new residence in Upper Portland Place. Situated between Regent's Park and Regent Street, the house at No. 5 enjoyed unobstructed light that streamed through the full-length windows all day long. An invigorated Adams told his mortified secretaries that from now on they were going to behave like gentlemen and cease turning their offices into "slut holes." Confident in her improved surroundings, and armed with a new cook, Mrs. Adams held her first "at home." To the family's relief, recorded Benjamin Moran, "it was quite largely attended."[7]

With the social season in full swing and despite a house suitable for entertaining, Henry was disappointed by his lack of friends. "I can't succeed in finding any one to introduce me among people of my own age," he complained to his brother Charles.[8] He sensed he had made a fool of himself when an acquaintance introduced him to William Howard Russell. Rather idiotically, Henry began blathering away about the pity of his returning to England. Russell looked "embarrassed" at this, and then laughed, remarking "that personally he was glad [to be home], but he regretted having lost the chance of showing his goodwill to us by describing our successes."[9] Russell ended the conversation by pointedly saying he would like to call on Henry's father.

William Howard Russell was anxious to clear his name with Minister Adams. It was only once he arrived home that Russell realized the extent to which *The Times* had slanted his reports. The diarist Henry Greville, whose friendship with Fanny Kemble made him take an interest in American affairs, was shocked to learn of Russell's belief "that the North will in the end carry all before them." "If this be his opinion," wrote Greville on May 10, "his correspondence must have been carefully cooked before insertion, for nothing that has appeared in it can bear this construction."[10] Delane had no use for Russell now that he was in England and stopped taking his articles on the war. The rebuke was not unduly troubling for Russell, however, since he was able to return to his job as editor of the *Army and Navy Gazette.* Nor did he regret his decision to leave America; less than a month after his arrival, he suffered the loss of his one-year-old son, Colin, and the total collapse of Mary, his wife. The children were now utterly dependent on him. Fortunately, Delane soon forgave Russell; "here you are and we must make the best of it," he wrote, and *The Times* awarded Russell a pension of £300 a year for life.[11] Delane resumed commissioning him for special assignments, but the ban on American subjects remained in place.

Charles Francis Adams now almost looked forward to his interviews with the other Russell, the foreign secretary. They were more like jousts than conversations; "about once a week," joked Henry, "the wary Chieftain sharpens a stick down to a very sharp point, and then digs it into the excellent Russell's ribs."[12] The foreign secretary enjoyed returning the compliment, and it was not uncommon for the meeting to conclude with an invitation to continue the argument over dinner. On May 19, all five members of the Adams family went to Pembroke Lodge for an outing with the Russells. "One year ago, yesterday," the minister wrote in his diary, "I went over this same ground on a very chilly day." Then, he had been nervous about meeting Lord Russell; but now, he decided, "Lord and Lady Russell are pleasanter as seen in their domestic life than elsewhere. No family is more thoroughly a home circle."[13] The harmonious relations between the legation and the Foreign Office were sufficiently encouraging for Henry to write to his brother on June 6 that the

Confederate commissioner was no longer a threat to them: "I hear very little about our friend Mason. . . . He has little or no attention paid him except as a matter of curiosity."

A week later, however, General Butler's "Woman Order" became known. The British were shocked by the implication behind Butler's promise to treat "any female" who insulted a Northern soldier as a "woman of the town plying her avocation." The press was not appeased when Lord Russell explained, during a heated debate in the House of Lords, that Butler was probably extending a law already used to curb prostitution to include Southern women who breached the peace in other ways. Even papers that normally supported the North condemned the order. For Confederate sympathizers in Parliament, it was a gift that they shamelessly exploited. William Gregory conjured up for his fellow MPs images of women, not unlike their own wives and daughters, being thrown to the mercy of the very dregs of society. Lord Palmerston was unable to restrain himself. "Sir," he declared, "an Englishman must blush to think that such an act has been committed by one belonging to the Anglo-Saxon race." His sincere outrage struck a chord in the House of Commons; previously neutral MPs began to wonder whether Britain had a moral duty to intervene in the conflict.[14]

This latest innovation in modern warfare was, Palmerston told Russell, "without example in the history of nations."[15] The more he thought about it, the more he wished to make an official remonstrance to the North. When Russell would not agree, he went ahead anyway. "Even when a Town is taken by assault," Palmerston protested in a letter to Charles Francis Adams on June 11, "it is the Practice of the Commander of the conquering army to protect to the utmost the Inhabitants and especially the Female Part of Them." By contrast, Butler was handing over the women of New Orleans "to the unbridled license of an unrestrained soldiery."[16]

The U.S. minister did not know what to make of the protest. The letter was marked "confidential," and yet it did not seem like a private matter. A professional diplomat might have been more cautious in his response, but Adams had only his instincts and twelve months' experience to guide him. Rather than try to avoid a row, as Lyons would have done, Adams bristled with self-righteous indignation. "My relations with the Prime Minister can never again be friendly," he wrote in his diary.[17] Over the next few days he badgered Palmerston with demands for a clarification of his comments. After Adams twice called at his office to complain, Lord Russell realized that the minister had been pushed to some sort of breaking point. At the second visit, Russell tried to calm him down by agreeing that "the thing was altogether irregular." Adams went home elated. "I now saw that I had all the advantage," he wrote on June 19. Meanwhile, Russell suggested to Palmerston that he withdraw his letter. But once the prime minister sensed that Adams was turning the incident into a battle of wills, he refused. The most he could stomach was an ambiguous reply that admitted nothing. Unfortunately, Adams could not resist having the last word. In his final letter, he declared that henceforth he would only accept letters from Palmerston that came through official channels.

Henry was proud that his father had forced Palmerston into a retreat. But in truth, it was a small victory. The next time the two men encountered each other, Adams noticed that Palmerston deliberately ignored him.[18] Invitations to Lady Palmerston's parties also ceased.

———

Whatever the provocation, now was not the time for Adams to quarrel with the prime minister; the cabinet was assessing the economic damage caused by the cotton famine. A report by the Poor Law Board read to the Commons in May revealed a bleak picture of inadequate public help and growing private misery. In twelve months, the number of charitable cases in Britain had risen from 40,000 to 150,000. More than 400,000 workers were either unemployed or working part-time, causing great hardship for a further 1.5 million people whose care or livelihood was dependent on them.[19] Journalists were beginning to write accounts of their tours to the hardest-hit towns, pricking consciences with their descriptions of once proud, industrious families who were forced by "the iron teeth of poverty" to accept weekly handouts of food and coal.[20]

The U.S. consuls' descriptions of the suffering in Lancashire convinced Seward that the British would not hesitate to interfere in the war if the alternative meant starvation across wide swaths of England. Thurlow Weed had been urging him since the spring to show that the North was prepared to help Britain overcome the Southern cotton embargo. "Let the enemy refuse [to send] the cotton," he advised him.[21] In May, Seward declared the four Southern ports under U.S. control open for cotton export. But his scheme failed when the Treasury throttled the plan with too many regulations. The initiative therefore lay with the South, and Judah P. Ben-

jamin was determined to use it. A year ago, the Confederate cabinet had attempted to wield cotton like a blunt instrument. No one had listened to
Benjamin's objections then. But now he was secretary of state and could
introduce a more sophisticated cotton policy without hindrance or argument, since Southern coffers certainly needed the revenue.[22]

Benjamin was still hoping that he could bribe France with cotton, but
he could not be sure. The emperor Napoleon's invasion of Mexico also
raised the interesting possibility that France might need Southern help in
securing its conquest. The problem for Benjamin was his inability to
communicate with his commissioners in a timely fashion. James Mason
had yet to receive a single dispatch (although one sent in April eventually
arrived in late June), and Slidell was in a similar position.[23] Benjamin was
obtaining most of his news from journals and old newspapers. He was
pleased to see, however, that even without his supervision, the commissioners and propaganda agents were making great strides in their efforts
to influence public opinion. James Spence and Henry Hotze had become a formidable team. Spence had offered his services to Mason back
in April. All he asked for in return was the promise that after independence the South would appoint him as its financial agent, which would
help him to recoup some of his losses caused by the 1857 panic. "I assume," he had written boldly,

> that it will be of value to your Government to have on this side a
> man of intellect, zealous in their cause, fertile in expedients, vig-
> orous in action, of wide mercantile experience; one accustomed to
> deal with large and difficult things, able to influence public opin-
> ion through the press, and not afraid of any encounter as a
> speaker. In what measure I may claim to possess some of these, it
> is not for me to say. I simply state facts, easily verified, from which
> to draw your conclusions.*[24]

---

* In the same letter, Spence also suggested that the Southerners consider changing
their name from Confederate States to "Southern Union," which sounded better to
English ears. When Mason forwarded his request to Benjamin, he asked the secretary
of state not to take offense. Spence's objection to the word "Confederacy" sounded
lunatic, Mason admitted, but he was speaking "from an English business point of
view." He assured Benjamin that on all other matters Spence was a "man of large research, liberal and expanded views." Moreover, he had close ties to *The Times,* and his
book, *The American Union,* continued to outsell every other work on the subject.[25]

Liverpool was the perfect arena for Spence's genius as a propagandist and social organizer. "We are southern almost to a man," a Liverpudlian friend confirmed to the MP Richard Monckton Milnes. "There is even a secret club here—they call it the 'Wig-Wam' . . . in this club all the Southern news is discussed, southern newspapers find their way and arrangements are made for sending arms and ammunitions. . . . No club was ever more practical or more secret: large contributions are constantly coming in."[26] The manufacturing areas around the city were also fertile territory; Spence engaged two veteran strike leaders, William Aitken and Mortimer Grimshaw, to organize mass demonstrations in the worst-hit cotton districts. Their motives may have been tinged by a desire to revive their glory days, but they were also passionately against the sacrifice of English cotton workers for the benefit of Northern capitalists.

Hotze naturally gave the protest meetings great prominence in his new weekly, the *Index*. He had started the journal at the end of April with the help of donations from friends in order to have his own vehicle for reporting Anglo-American matters. It was designed to be cosmopolitan and worldly, as though its Southern sympathies were an inconsequential and harmless feature rather than the sole raison d'être of the paper. Hotze explained to a potential writer that for the *Index* to be respectable it had "to be tolerant and yet not indifferent; to be moderate and yet have strong convictions, to be instructive and yet not dull." Above all, the information had to be dressed "in the most attractive manner" and displayed "in the most accessible way."[27]

The *Index* did not require a large circulation so long as it was read in all the clubs and by MPs. Hotze sought out contributors with deliberate calculation. He wanted writers with connections to other newspapers rather than ardent partisans. The more they wrote for him, he reasoned, the more they would absorb Confederate views that would in turn carry over into their articles for other newspapers. British journalism was a small enclave within the already small world of educated society.[28] Once inside the charmed circle, Hotze discovered it was easy to influence content without being obvious. Newspaper editors were so eager for American news that they would take his manufactured "letters from a traveler" and rework them to appear as editorials or reportage.[29] One of Hotze's favorite methods was to supply an acquaintance with fresh information in the shape of a pro-South editorial that required little editing. If the article was printed, Hotze would always insist that the submitter keep the ten-guinea fee. For the moment, Hotze was concentrating on two themes that he thought would resonate with English readers: the needless suffering of cotton workers, and the "blood" relationship between the Southern gentry and their British cousins.[30]

Henry Adams thought the tone of the *Index* was "so excruciatingly never conquer" that "one is forced to the belief that they think themselves very near that last ditch."[31] He discounted the Confederates' methods at his peril, however. Thurlow Weed, Seward's emissary, was not a "clubbable" man in the English sense, and Grub Street hacks prided their independence too much to accept his money.[32] He was an expert at pulling the more vulgar levers of corruption, but the subtle game of co-opting English journalists had eluded him. When Weed departed from England at the beginning of June, it was with a sense of regret that he had only partially fulfilled his mission. On a personal level, he was confident that his conversations with various editors and politicians had disabused them of the more pernicious myths about Seward. On the other hand, Weed knew that his efforts to establish a Northern lobby similar to Henry Hotze's stable of propagandists and opinion formers had failed.

There was more disappointment for Weed once he arrived home and discovered that his control over the New York press had slipped during his absence. His views on Britain had mellowed during his time abroad, yet he found editors resistant to the idea of adopting a more benign view of Anglo-American relations. Bravely, Weed took on the burden himself and published an open letter to New York City's Common Council in which he urged his countrymen to reconsider their hostility to England. Regarding the *Trent* affair, "I am bound," he asserted, "in truth and fairness, to say, that that Government and people sincerely believed that *we* desired a rupture with *them,* that we sought occasion to taunt and snub them." Moreover, America's recent behavior toward Britain included supporting Russia in the Crimean War, the expulsion of the British minister on a technicality, and Seward's oft-repeated claim that one day Canada would belong to the United States: "Some of these grounds of complaint were, as we know, well taken." He begged his fellow New Yorkers to remember that "the Union has many ardent, well-wishing friends in England, and can have many more if we act justly ourselves."[33]

Though wise and admirably sane, Weed's letter failed to address the intense bitterness caused by *The Times* and other newspapers. Edward

Dicey was disconcerted when he visited the house of a Northern acquaintance who forced him to gaze at the portrait of a young man.
" 'How,' he said to me, 'would you like, yourself, to read constantly that
that lad died in a miserable cause, and, as an American officer, should be
called a coward?' " Dicey admitted that "I could make no adequate
reply."[34] The fact that many American newspapers were just as rude
about Britain was a rather hollow argument in the face of such grief.[35]
The U.S. consul in Paris, John Bigelow, warned Lord Russell that it
made Americans deeply resentful to learn from the British press "that we
are barbarians, that our system of government is a nuisance, that our
statesmen are knaves or imbeciles."[36] The British consulate in New York
noticed that ordinary Britons suffered every time there was a controversy
in the press, and Lord Edward St. Maur wrote home about a new term
being bandied about the city: "Anglo-Rebels."[37]

―――

Despite Butler's offensive "Woman Order," the MP William Schaw
Lindsay was discovering just how difficult it could be to turn goodwill in
Parliament into action. Nine-tenths of the House of Commons, he in-
sisted to James Spence, "was in favor of immediate recognition" of the
Confederacy. Spence thought he should wait for a Southern victory before forcing a vote, but Lindsay disagreed; his interviews with Emperor
Napoleon in April had made it clear that the only impediment to Southern independence was the British cabinet. As proof, he could point to the
leading article in *Le Constitutionnel* on June 1 that appeared to argue that
France should offer to mediate in the conflict without bothering to wait
for Britain.* On June 17, Lindsay sent an arrogant letter to Russell warning him that the government would look weak and foolish if its foreign
policy ended up in the hands of backbenchers like himself. "Within the
next fortnight," he boasted, support for the Confederacy would be unstoppable. James Mason fervently hoped that his friend was right. He
was feeling rather downcast by their lack of progress. "We must wait for
'King Cotton,' " he wrote to Slidell on June 19, "to turn the screw still
further."[39]

---

* *Le Constitutionnel* was generally considered to be the mouthpiece of the French government. This "seems like a preparation of the public mind for a mediation on the
part of France in the American conflict," noted the diarist Henry Greville on June
2, "and to-day *The Times* has put forth a leader strongly advocating it."[38]

Two weeks later, Mason's wish seemed close to being granted. The supply of cotton bales went down while the number of workers on poor relief jumped by another 11,000.[40] There were more mass meetings in Lancashire. Even though the results of these meetings were often ambiguous, they were sufficiently heated to alarm the Union's supporters.* Lord Lyons had been back in Britain for only a few days, but he immediately grasped the seriousness of the situation. He reported to William Stuart, secretary of the legation in Washington, that cotton was "the real question of the day." Obviously, Lyons was powerless to do anything from England, but, he told Stuart, "if you can manage in any way to get a supply of cotton for England before the winter, you will have done a greater service than has been effected by Diplomacy for a century."[42] The Duke of Argyll, John Bright, and Richard Cobden all wrote to Charles Sumner begging him to use his influence in facilitating the flow of cotton from the South.[43]

The U.S. legation was in a high state of anxiety. They had hoped to derail Lindsay by exposing the MP as an arms supplier or blockade runner for the South, but discreet inquiries into his business dealings revealed that the shipping magnate was scrupulously honest.[44] Their best hope lay in a military success. "[We are] waiting the event of the struggle at Richmond," Henry told his brother on July 4, 1862.[45] London was swirling with rumors that Lee had defeated McClellan. "No one but me is sorry for it," wrote Lord Lyons; until now he had not understood how sharply public opinion had turned against the United States.[46] Despite the wild ups and downs of the past twelve months, he had never ceased to hope that the two countries might form some sort of an alliance, but "public opinion will not allow the Government to do more for the North than maintain a strict neutrality," he wrote pessimistically on July 5, "and it may not be easy to do that if there comes any strong provocation from the US."[47] Adams tried dropping heavy hints to Seward that the North could not afford to alienate Europe while her armies looked so

---

* Although the strike leaders Aitken and Grimshaw were able to call out large meetings all over Lancashire, achieving an unambiguous vote in favor of Southern independence was proving to be a considerable struggle. A meeting in Ashton, which was one of the most deprived towns in the area, ended with a resolution in favor of recognition for the Confederacy, but someone from the floor successfully tacked on an amendment that urged Britain and France to "crush the abettors of slavery and oppression."[41]

vulnerable. The "insurgent emissaries" here, he warned on the eleventh, were eager to seize on "every act" that might "cast odium on the [U.S.] Government."[48]

After the latest news put McClellan in full retreat, Lindsay decided that the time for his motion had come. But over the next few days, the "nine-tenths" he had boasted of began to doubt the wisdom of forcing the British government's hand. After initially encouraging him, the Tory leadership came to its senses and realized that the American war brought out too many conflicting passions to unify the opposition. "In fact, it seems that there is nothing good to be got out of this American question," wrote a senior Tory on July 14.[49] Lord Lyons was also quietly lobbying senior politicians against making any change to the current policy.[50]

Lindsay began to feel uncomfortable. Perhaps, he admitted, Spence was right after all; they needed something exceptional to sweep members off their collective feet. Two days later the longed-for moment arrived when Parliament received the official figures on employment in Lancashire. The report was sufficiently dire to revive Lindsay's courage. He announced that he would be introducing a debate on the Civil War on July 18. While Lindsay was composing his speech, the news reached London that Lee had crushed the Federal army in the Seven Days' Battles. Henry Adams stared in amazement at the bold headline of his evening paper. " 'Capitulation of McClellan's Army. Flight of McClellan on a steamer. Later from America.' This astounding news for a moment made me almost give way," he wrote.

William Forster, MP, came rushing to the legation to find out if it was true. "Such odd things have occurred of late, that we can't be sure now that our generals won't run away from their own soldiers," wrote Moran bitterly.[51] Charles Francis Adams received Forster in his study, looking ashen. "This has gone too far," he wrote in his diary, "that I think I should be glad to be relieved of the mission. Nothing but a sense of duty to the public reconciles me to the trial a moment longer."[52] "Things look well for Lindsay's motion tonight," gloated James Mason.[53] *The Times* helped maintain the appearance by suppressing information that contradicted the surrender report.[54] The legation, however, had the latest newspapers from New York. "A single glance at dates showed us that it was an utter swindle," wrote Henry; "we had bulletins from McClellan two days later than the day of the reported surrender."[55]

Adams was aghast at how quickly the falsehood was spreading, and he asked William Forster to take the American newspaper to the House of Commons so that MPs could see for themselves that the Federal army had retreated but was still intact. Benjamin Moran went along to watch and was surprised by the enormous crowd that had turned up for the debate. There was much jostling between Northern and Southern supporters over seats in the gallery. James Mason had a shouting match with the doorkeeper and had to be rescued by William Gregory, who led him to the floor. Moran was pleased to see that the Southern commissioner was wearing the wrong type of coat for the occasion. The only people not present were Adams and Lord Lyons, who both stayed away deliberately.

Adams might have felt calmer if he had known that the McClellan rumor would not affect the British government's policy. Three weeks earlier, Lord Palmerston had candidly informed the Confederate agent Edwin De Leon that the Federals could be pushed back and Washington besieged and it would still not be enough to guarantee recognition.[56] Knowledge of this would have saved Lindsay from making a fool of himself. He was such a poor speaker anyway that several members went off for a drink until he had finished. Moran seethed as he listened to the debate, forgetting that politicians generally consider foreign countries to be fair game. No speaker challenged Lindsay's assertion that slavery was not the cause of the war or that the North was fighting out of greed and a desire for power. At half past one in the morning, Lord Palmerston rose slowly from his seat and the boisterous House of Commons fell silent. The seventy-eight-year-old politician surveyed his listeners with a grandfatherly air. He reminded the House that a report of the debate would be read in America and would probably offend both sides. But, more important, there had never been "a contest of such magnitude between two different sections of the same people." Recognition or mediation was not something to be considered lightly. It was for the government alone to decide "what can be done, when it can be done, and how it can be done." The House burst into applause. "As I came away," recorded Moran with satisfaction, "I met Mason alone, looking sullen and dejected."[57]

With remarkable persistence, James Mason presented the Foreign Office a week later with a formal demand for recognition of the Confederacy. The document was accepted without comment. Yet the debate had helped to shape public opinion in a way that was advantageous to the

South. First, as Adams complained to Seward, the Confederates had succeeded in positioning themselves as the underdogs and victims in the
war.[58] Second, and more dangerous still, they had made the idea of
British mediation seem like a humanitarian duty to end the bloodshed.
Make the war about slavery, Adams urged Seward, otherwise the British
government could end up caving in to pressure.[59] After the debate, Lord
Russell admitted to Lyons that he was astonished by the passions it had
stirred. "The great majority are in favour of the South," he concluded.
Furthermore, "nearly our whole people are of [the] opinion that separation wd be [of] benefit both to North and South."[60]

Russell's concern about national sentiment may have blinded him to
more practical and immediate issues such as the Confederates' violations
of the Foreign Enlistment Act. Charles Francis Adams had repeatedly
asked him to investigate reports of a formidable cruiser that was under
construction at Lairds shipyard. His consul in Liverpool, Thomas
Haines Dudley, had amassed such damning evidence that only an outright partisan—as the customs collector of Liverpool happened to be—
could claim with a straight face that the mysterious No. 290 at Lairds was
simply a merchant ship of unusual design.[61] The vessel was ready to depart before Russell finally realized the danger, and he ordered all the rel-
evant documents to be delivered immediately to the law officers. This
was on July 23. Over the next six days a tragicomedy unfurled without
anyone realizing its true importance until it was too late. The papers arrived at the house of the Queen's Advocate, Sir John Harding, on the day
he suffered an irreversible nervous breakdown. Meanwhile, an anonymous Confederate sympathizer in the Foreign Office alerted James Bulloch that his ship was about to be seized. Harding's illness created a
bureaucratic vacuum; in the ensuing muddle of confused responsibilities and departmental paper shuffling, the Confederates bribed a local
customs official and quietly sneaked No. 290 out of Liverpool. By the
time the telegram ordering her arrest reached Liverpool on July 31, the
steamer was on her way to the Azores. There she would receive her guns,
a new captain, and a new name: CSS *Alabama*. Northern shipping was
about to face its greatest threat since the War of 1812.

––––

Lord Russell still thought the best hope for ending slavery was for the
North and South to separate.[62] Like many Englishmen, he assumed that
the effect of international moral pressure and enlightened domestic

opinion would eventually force Southern leaders to abolish slavery, just as Czar Alexander II had abolished serfdom in 1861. Gladstone shared his view; he was one of the few members of the British cabinet who had actually read James Spence's *The American Union,* and the debate on July 18 sent him spinning further into the Confederates' arms. Gladstone had fallen in love with the humanitarian argument. "It is indeed much to be desired," he wrote to a friend on July 26, "that this bloody and purposeless conflict should cease." Four days later, a mutual acquaintance succeeded in placing Henry Hotze next to him at dinner. The evening passed like a dream for Hotze; Gladstone hung on his every word. By the end of the night they were discussing where the boundary ought to lie between the two Americas, and whether it would be better to divide the border states in half.[63]

Gladstone would not be the first English politician or the last to fall under the spell of a foreign agent, but the way Henry Hotze played him was especially masterful. In his report after their "chance" meeting, Hotze described to Judah Benjamin how he carefully drove the conversation to make it seem as though Gladstone was in control. "I purposely abstained from introducing any topic," he wrote on August 6; he allowed Gladstone to waffle on about "supposed difficulties" over the Confederacy's border. Then, when he thought the moment was right, Hotze casually referred to the South's (nonexistent) intention to revalue its currency to make it more favorable for the pound, "a prospect which I knew would be peculiarly agreeable to him." Over the next few days he commissioned sympathizers to write articles that discussed the South's economic policies, hoping that they would keep Gladstone's interest alive. This was Hotze's usual tactic. "Thanks to friends," he continued, he knew which arguments appealed to individual cabinet members, "and to these from week to week I devoted myself." The results appeared to be promising. "Just as I close this," finished Hotze, "a reliable friend steps in to inform me that there have been three successive cabinet meetings . . . and that each time the cabinet was evenly divided, Mr. Gladstone leading the party in favor of recognition."[64]

Hotze's "reliable friend" had given him an accurate report of the state of opinion in the cabinet. Leading the faction against immediate recognition was the pugnacious Duke of Argyll, who resented Gladstone's attempt to browbeat them with fallacious moral arguments. "I retain my opinion unchanged," wrote the duke after a bruising correspondence with Gladstone; no war "has been more just or more necessary. . . . It is not inconsistent to sympathize with revolts which are just, and to fight against other revolts which are unjust." In his usual blunt way, Argyll informed Gladstone that he was deceiving himself if he believed that separation was good for the "anti-slavery cause."[65]

Argyll's reproach stung Gladstone, but the latter was mollified by his success with Palmerston, who "has come exactly to my mind," he told his wife after the final cabinet meeting of the session.[66] Palmerston did not in fact share Gladstone's moral qualms, and he certainly did not wish to fight a war on behalf of the South. But if the Confederates continued their run of victories, and the North proved obdurate, he could see no reason why the question should not be considered. The French had been advocating October—when the cotton season was normally in full swing—as the time for Europe to decide, which seemed reasonable to Palmerston.[67] Gladstone had also succeeded in pricking Russell's conscience. Though he saw the complications and subtleties of the question that the crusading chancellor of the exchequer conveniently ignored, Russell was also becoming bewitched by the siren call of the humanitarian argument. On August 6, Russell suggested to Palmerston that they try to bring the opposing sides to an armistice. But, he asked on reflection, "On what basis are we to negotiate?" It seemed to him there was little hope that Lincoln "and his Democracy will listen to reason."[68]

The deliberations in the cabinet soon leaked out; *The New York Times* reported that the Great Powers were contemplating mediation. France and Russia were said to be keen; England was apparently undecided.[69] Without Lord Lyons to reassure him, Seward assumed the worst. Senator Orville Browning bumped into him at Lincoln's office and asked him point-blank "if there was any danger of intervention in our affairs by England and France. He said there was," recorded Browning, "unless volunteering went on rapidly, and our army was greatly increased."[70] Seward sent one of his wrap-the-world-in-flames dispatches to Adams, hoping that it would scare the British into inaction. He also rather cleverly sent out a circular on August 8 to all consuls in Europe offering inducements to immigrants seeking work opportunities in America.

The circular, No. 19, seemed innocent enough, but it was actually a back-door route for army recruitment. Consulates were encouraged to display information on the cash bounties awarded to volunteers. Seward knew the game he was playing. "Nobody is authorized to do anything or pay anything, for once entering into this kind of business there would be no end of trouble," he warned his consul in Paris, since official recruitment was illegal; but "to some extent this civil war must be a trial between the two parties to exhaust each other. The immigration of a large mass from Europe would of itself decide it."[71]

Throughout August, every utterance and report from England was picked over and analyzed for clues. It was at this precise moment that the irascible John Roebuck decided to try his hand at Anglo-American relations. The Liberal MP was growing old, and change frightened him. Anything that retarded the modernizing, democratizing tendencies of the United States seemed like a cause worth supporting. Forgetting that the South was also a democracy, he championed its independence because separation would hurt the North. On August 14, Roebuck and Palmerston attended the same banquet in Sheffield. Knowing that the prime minister's presence would ensure that the speeches were reported in the press, Roebuck theatrically turned to Palmerston and exhorted him to admit that the South's time had come. "The North will never be our friends," he bellowed, to a few "hear, hears." "Of the South you can make friends. They are Englishmen; they are not the scum and refuse of Europe." The mayor of Manchester leaped to his feet and shouted over the boos and cheers, "Don't say that; don't say that." Roebuck responded: "I know what I am saying. [The South] are Englishmen, and we must make them our friends."[72]

Reports of the Manchester banquet confirmed Northern fears and revived Southern hopes. Palmerston was no longer "considered [by Southerners] as the personal enemy of the confederacy—a most rabid abolitionist—who is suppressing the sympathies, which England would otherwise show for the south."[73] All over the South, people waited anxiously for foreign news, believing that their fate hung on his change of view.

———

McClellan's failure to capture Richmond had convinced Lincoln that there was no real substance or drive to the general. McClellan looked and talked the part, he realized, but lacked the will to act. Without even bothering to consult him, Lincoln announced McClellan's demotion on July 11. He lost his position as general-in-chief of the U.S. armies, which was given to Henry "Old Brains" Halleck, whose commanders out west had produced the victories at Shiloh and Island No. 10; and he was ordered to merge his army with General John Pope's army, which was fighting in northern Virginia. Pope, not McClellan, would command this new mammoth army.

Lincoln had to have a military victory; volunteering practically ceased after the Seven Days' Battles, and the 600,000 extra soldiers he requested were not stepping forward without the lure of large bounties. Furthermore, he knew that if he played the emancipation card while the North appeared to be losing the war, it would be interpreted at home and abroad as the desperate move of a floundering government—in Seward's words, "our last shriek on the retreat."[74] Lincoln had accomplished as much as he could for the moment: Washington was now in line with the rest of the North, free of the taint of slavery; among the recent bills passed by Congress was a law prohibiting the return of fugitive slaves to their masters, and another allowing "persons of African descent" to join the army. But Lincoln had not been able to persuade the border states to accept emancipation in return for compensation for their slaves; slavery remained legal in the United States.

Notwithstanding the installation of Henry Halleck as the new general-in-chief, August turned out worse for the North than July. Despite the capture of three important Southern ports, the "Anaconda" strategy of a total blockade of the South's coastline was far from being achieved.* Nor had the North (with the exception of New Orleans) been able to extend its control of the Mississippi River beyond the border states. Worse, even gains had slipped into losses. Kentucky and Tennessee looked vulnerable once more.

Jefferson Davis had replaced the popular General Beauregard following his retreat from Corinth with the widely disliked Braxton Bragg. At the end of July Bragg had taken his army on a seven-hundred-mile maneuver into Kentucky, where he intended to install a pro-Southern governor. If the Confederacy could secure this border state, he reasoned, the others might follow. Halleck had sidelined Grant after Shiloh and put his faith in General Buell, whose timely arrival on April 6 had saved the Federal army from defeat. But Buell was fretting uselessly, sending his troops hither and thither without actually trying to intercept Bragg. Robert Neve of the 5th Kentucky Volunteers had vivid memories of the

---

* Although General Winfield Scott's "Anaconda Plan" to isolate and squeeze the South was never formally adopted, this effectively became the strategy of the war.

relentless marching: of the thirst, the hunger, and the ever-present dust. He recalled with sadness a man they "found dead on the road who had died through excessive fatigue. As the army passed along there, he laid like a dog as if no one cared who he was. It was," he wrote, "a bad sight to see a poor soldier die in such a way."[75] While Neve and thousands like him labored to keep moving under the broiling sun, Confederate raiders preyed on Buell's weaker outposts.

On the far eastern side of Kentucky, the small Federal force that had wrested the Cumberland Gap from the Confederates was itself surrounded. Colonel De Courcy's commander sent a desperate telegram to the War Department on August 10 warning that their supplies would last three weeks at best. That was his last communication with the outside world. A few hours later, Confederate guerrillas organized by John Hunt Morgan and his English staff officer, Colonel George St. Leger Grenfell, cut their telegraph line. The beleaguered Federals had no way of knowing whether help would come; still, when the Confederates ordered their surrender, they replied defiantly: "If you want this fortress, come and take it."[76] Morgan and his raiders ignored the challenge, confident that starvation would do the work for them.

Lincoln's cabinet was grim when it learned that a Confederate army was marching unopposed toward Kentucky. As Lincoln's frustration with Buell increased, he turned to General Pope to stop the run of bad news. Pope, at least, claimed to be thirsting for battle. The self-promoting victor of Island No. 10 had recently boasted to the press that his soldiers only ever saw the backs of the enemy. Pope liked to make "hard war." Unlike McClellan, he was less concerned about keeping casualty figures to a minimum, nor did he believe in protecting civilians from the ravages of war. He wanted Southerners to suffer, because he thought it would make them more willing to surrender. But in one important sense, Pope was just the same as McClellan: he underestimated his opponent.

The Seven Days' Battles had brought out the fighter in Lee. The once cautious officer had undergone a metamorphosis into a resolute and audacious general. He had private reasons, too, for wanting to throw the Federals out of Virginia. At the start of the war he had lost the family home of Arlington, across the river from Washington. Shortly after the Seven Days' Battles, his other home, the White House plantation in central Virginia, was burned to the ground by Federal soldiers, forcing his wheelchair-bound wife, Mary, to seek refuge in Richmond.[77]

Lee divided his army of fifty thousand into two "wings" so that he could attack Pope from several directions, a risky tactic given his inferior numbers. Stonewall Jackson was given command of one, and General James "Old Pete" Longstreet, who had performed well during the Seven Days' Battles, the other. Jackson's division struck first, tearing into Pope on August 9. He launched another surprise attack against Pope two weeks later, and followed it up on the twenty-seventh with a raid on Pope's supply depot at Manassas Junction. "Huzza," crowed John Jones, the usually cynical clerk at the Confederate War Department. "The braggart is near his end."[78]

Jackson's raid gave away his position; Pope ordered his commanders to prepare the men for battle. The name Manassas conjured up dreadful memories for the North. "Everything is ripe for a terrible panic," Charles Francis Adams, Jr., wrote to his father from Washington. "I have not since the war began felt such a tug on my nerves."[79] Pope had superior numbers to Jackson but not by an overwhelming margin. McClellan had played into Lee's hands; mortified by his demotion, he had resisted for as long as possible Halleck's orders to reinforce Pope. He knew that a battle was fast approaching and wanted to watch his rival "get out of his scrape by himself." Among the reinforcements who did reach Pope, however, was Sir Percy Wyndham, who had been exchanged and was able to rejoin his regiment just in time to participate in the "scrape."[*]

The Second Battle of Bull Run began piecemeal on August 28 and roared into life on the twenty-ninth. In the thirteen months since the first battle, the armies had grown in size and the men had become hardened and more experienced. Once again, Henry House Hill became the focus of bitter fighting, although this time it was the Federals who held the hill and the Confederates who were cut down trying to dislodge them. Pope had no idea that Lee and Longstreet had arrived with the other half of the Army of Northern Virginia. After the firing drew to a halt on the evening of the twenty-ninth, Pope was so confident he had won that he sent a dispatch to Washington announcing his victory. He

---

[*] The North and South copied the European system of parole and exchange of prisoners. Prisoners gave their word—their parole—not to take up arms until they were formally exchanged for an enemy prisoner of equal rank. If the wait for exchange was going to take more than a few days, parolees could go home or to a parole camp and wait until they received notice that the paperwork had been completed.

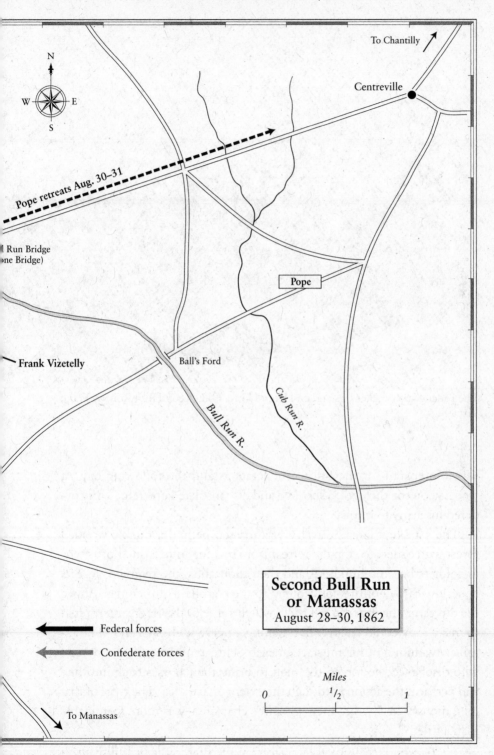

To Chantilly

Centreville

Pope retreats Aug. 30–31

Run Bridge
one Bridge)

Pope

Frank Vizetelly

Ball's Ford

Cub Run R.

Bull Run R.

**Second Bull Run
or Manassas**
August 28–30, 1862

Federal forces

Confederate forces

Miles

0   ¹/₂   1

To Manassas

The Federal army makes its stand on Henry House Hill, Second Bull Run, by Frank Vizetelly.

was unprepared for the full Confederate assault the following day. At 7:00 P.M. on the thirtieth, a shocked and disconsolate Pope reluctantly ordered his army to retreat.

The 1st New Jersey Cavalry was massed behind a thickly wooded forest with orders to stop the retreat from turning into a rout, but as tens of soldiers became hundreds and then thousands, the regiment lost its cohesion. Stray gunfire contributed to the Cavaliers' difficulties. Above the din came the order to fall back, which some of the riders interpreted to mean they could gallop off, touching a nerve with Sir Percy. The familiar twiddling of his mustache began. Threatening to shoot any man who disobeyed, he forced the men to bring their horses back into line and perform the action as though they were on parade. "The twirl of that long moustache," wrote the regiment's chaplain, "was more formidable than a rifle."[80]

There were five thousand casualties at the first Battle of Bull Run; at the second, twenty-five thousand. Lee had lost proportionately more men, however, and his army was in no shape to pursue the Federals.*

Lincoln had eaten dinner at Secretary Stanton's house on the thirtieth, thinking that Pope was his man. But by the time he retired to bed, the news had come through of the army's defeat. Once again, the residents of Washington woke up to the sight of leaderless soldiers pouring through the streets, filthy, hungry, and clearly in search of a drink. Only this time, behind them came wagon after wagon of the wounded and dying. "So," lamented the treasurer of the U.S. Sanitary Commission, George Templeton Strong, "after all this waste of life and money and material, we are at best where we were a year ago."[82]

---

* Among the Confederate prisoners was the accident-prone Garibaldi veteran Lieutenant Henry Ronald MacIver, who had received a bullet in the wrist. An Irish Federal surgeon bandaged his arm with more skill than he could have hoped for, and afterward MacIver was transferred to Alexandria. He was, wrote his biographer, "somewhat dismayed to find himself face to face with his old jailer . . . he saw that the man recognised him as his former prisoner the instant they met."[81]

THIRTEEN

Is Blood Thicker Than Water?

*The possibility of intervention—Lee invades the North—Antietam, the
bloodiest day—Dawson experiences Northern hospitality—The splendors
and shortages of Richmond—Meeting the Confederate generals*

"The suspense was hideous and unendurable," Henry Adams recalled, as he waited for news from America.[1] On September 9, 1862,
came a telegram from Reuter's agency announcing a victory for Union
general John Pope at Bull Run. "This has been a Red Letter Day," Moran
wrote euphorically. "If this be true it is the beginning of the end."[2]

Four days later, Moran learned they had been misled; Pope had been
defeated, and the Confederate army was just twenty miles from Washington. "My heart sunk within me," he wrote. "The rebels here are elated beyond measure. The Northern people are looked upon as cravens, and the
Union is regarded as hopelessly gone." He was alone at the legation; the
Adamses were away and Charles Wilson had taken a leave of absence "for
his health." With no one to act as a moderating influence on his behavior,
Moran happily insulted a British Army officer who called at the legation
to volunteer for the Federal army; "they think we are unable to attend to
our affairs, and that they can settle them," he remarked testily.[3]

The Adams family said goodbye to their hosts and returned to London
as soon as they heard the news. Mrs. Adams told Moran that it would have
been "torture" to remain, since there were Confederate sympathizers
among the house party. Henry suffered pangs of guilt that so many were
risking their lives while he was fighting the battle of the drawing rooms.

"After a sleepless night," Henry subsequently wrote of his younger self, "walking up and down his room without reflecting that his father was beneath him, he announced at breakfast his intention to go home into the army."[4]

Lord Russell had been wavering over whether Britain should intercede, until he received the reports about the Second Battle of Bull Run.[5] Charles Francis Adams had come away from their meeting on September 4 thinking it was business as usual, since Russell had assured him "I [could be] quite at ease in regard to any idea of joint action of the European powers in our affairs. I laughed and said I was in hopes that they all had quite too much to occupy their minds . . . to think of troubling themselves with matters on the other side of the Atlantic."[6] But a day later, the Confederate commissioner in Brussels, Ambrose Dudley Mann, reported that he had just received a letter from his informant in London, "an influential Englishman," who wrote that there was "a steady progress of opinion in one direction" regarding Palmerston and Russell. As to the latter, "I am informed upon the most credible authority, [Russell is] perfectly satisfied that there is not so much a shadow of a chance for the Yankees to overpower the united and resolute South, and that he would not be opposed to intervention if a reasonable hope could be entertained of its acceptance by the administration at Washington."[7]

Whether or not Russell was "perfectly satisfied" before Second Bull Run, afterward he became a thorough convert to the idea that the war must be stopped. "I agree with you that the time is come for offering mediation to the United States Government, with a view to the recognition of the independence of the Confederates," he wrote to Palmerston on September 17. "I agree further, that in case of failure, we ought ourselves to recognize the South States as an independent state." Russell ordered their ambassador in Paris, Lord Cowley, to have a quiet word with the French foreign minister, Édouard Thouvenel, about cooperation from the emperor.[8]

For the Confederates, Lee's victory at Second Bull Run was the signal to begin creating a groundswell of public sympathy in favor of Southern recognition. In France, Confederate commissioner John Slidell had heard through intermediaries that the emperor would not state publicly that the Powers should intervene until he had received unambiguous reassurances from Britain that it would follow suit. Henry Hotze put his stable of writers to work. "Since one journalist usually writes for several publications," he explained to the Confederate secretary of state, Judah P. Benjamin, "I have thus the opportunity of multiplying myself, so to speak, to an almost unlimited extent." He was not worried about "the sympathies of the intelligent classes [which] are now intensified into a feeling of sincere admiration." But James Spence's failure to stir up unrest in the manufacturing districts made Hotze fear that the working classes were implacable enemies of the South. "I am convinced," he admitted, "that the astonishing fortitude and patience with which they endure [the cotton famine] is mainly due to a consciousness that by any other course they would promote our interests."[9]

Hotze was overestimating his success with the "intelligent" classes and underestimating the unpopularity of the North among the workers. But what united all the classes in England, regardless of his efforts, was an ingrained hatred of slavery; the institution was an insurmountable stumbling block. Slidell and Mason could and did mislead potential Southern sympathizers when the occasion demanded. Camouflaging the South's total dependence on slavery was the only way, for example, that Slidell was able to persuade the veteran abolition campaigner Lord Shaftesbury to give them his support. Slidell had targeted Shaftesbury because "his peculiar position as the leader of an extensive and influential class in England, and the son-in-law of Lady Palmerston gives a value and significance to his opinions beyond that of a simple member of the House of Lords," he explained to Benjamin. But the relationship almost foundered in September when Shaftesbury asked him, in all innocence, "if the [Confederate] President could not in some way present the prospect of gradual emancipation. Such a declaration coming from him unsolicited would have the happiest effect in Europe." Slidell circumvented the question by replying that abolition was an issue for the individual states to decide and he could not speak for all of them.[10] Slidell was grateful that Lincoln was still publicly maintaining an ambivalent stance on slavery.[11] On August 19, Lincoln declared in a letter published by the *New York Tribune,* "If I could save the Union without freeing any slave I would do it, and if I could save it by freeing all the slaves I would do it."* It enabled him to suggest to Lord Shaftesbury

---

* Lincoln continued to be hamstrung by the opposition to emancipation from influential leaders such as John Hughes, the archbishop of New York, who had already issued this warning: "We Catholics . . . have not the slightest idea of carrying on a war that costs so much blood and treasure just to gratify a clique of Abolitionists in the North." With elections coming up and the military tide against him, Lincoln felt that he could not afford to alienate anyone.

that the chances of emancipation "were much better if we were left to ourselves than if we had remained in the Union."[12]

Slidell heard from Shaftesbury that a decision regarding Southern
recognition was "close at hand, a very few weeks at the furthest." Ironically, of all the concerns that might delay or precipitate the decision,
Palmerston and Russell never mentioned slavery or public opinion as
being among them. They were far more worried that the North would
simply reject Britain's offer to mediate. The Duke of Argyll had warned
Palmerston at the beginning of September that the Americans would
never accept any interference from Europe. "I think it right to tell you of
a letter we have had from Sumner," wrote the duke on September 2. "He
says that there is *no thought* of giving up the Contest. He speaks, indeed,
as if doing so were simply impossible." It would therefore "be folly, I
think, to attempt any intervention."[13]

But there had been more momentous news from America since Russell and Palmerston had agreed to hold a cabinet meeting on the subject.
General Lee had apparently marched with his Confederate army north
into Maryland. "The two armies are approaching each other to the
North of Washington and another great conflict is about to take place,"
Palmerston wrote to Russell on September 22. "Any proposal for mediation or armistice would no doubt just now be refused by the Federals.
[But] if they are thoroughly beaten . . . they may be brought to a more
reasonable state of mind."[14] Two days later, on the twenty-fourth,
Palmerston informed a delighted Gladstone about the mediation plan.
"The proposal would naturally be made to both North and South," he
wrote. "If both accepted we should recommend an Armistice and Cessation of Blockades with a View to Negotiation on the Basis of Separation." If only the South accepted, "we should then, I conceive,
acknowledge the Independence of the South." Russell had suggested
that the cabinet meeting should be held at the end of October, but
Palmerston was now thinking it should be sooner. "A great battle appeared by the last accounts to be coming on . . . a few Days will bring us
important accounts."[15]

———

Britain was waiting for news even as thousands of American families
were already grieving after the single bloodiest day of the war. Forty-
eight hours after his victory at Second Bull Run, Robert E. Lee had indeed ordered his Army of Northern Virginia to move north. On

September 4, his exhausted and underfed troops traversed the Potomac River into the border state of Maryland. Lee's plan was to reach Pennsylvania, cut the rail links there, and isolate Washington from the rest of the country. He understood as well as the Confederate government that Europe was waiting for a clear-cut victory, but this was not the reason behind his decision to invade the North. He hoped that the very presence of Confederate soldiers on Northern soil would give President Davis the authority to demand "of the United States the recognition of our independence."[16] If that failed, Lee thought it would be a sufficient shock to the North to make the upcoming elections, which included several state governorships, turn in favor of the antiwar Democrats.

On September 12, Lincoln overruled his cabinet and reinstated General McClellan to lead the Army of the Potomac. The soldiers trusted Little Mac, as they called him, and Lincoln felt strongly that this was no time for Washington to play favorites. Among the 80,000 troops who chased after Lee were Ebenezer Wells of the 79th New York Highlanders and George Herbert of the 9th New York Zouaves. Five major battles and twelve engagements in eighteen months had drained the regiments of their lifeblood. In the words of one chronicler, the Highlanders had withered to a "body of cripples."[17]

Ebenezer Wells had been wounded during the Second Battle of Bull Run. "My Sargent said to me, Wells, leave the field," he recalled. "I said what for, he pointed to my leg. I looked and saw blood, I soon felt where it came from: I had been shot in the side. . . . [In] the intense excitement of that minute I only remember of having felt a slight stitch." He was well enough to join the exodus from Washington a week later. The knowledge that McClellan was again their leader "revived the spirits of the men and without any rest we marched into Maryland." It was probably fortunate that McClellan preferred to move his army at a crawl rather than a jog. Once again, the general's remarkably inefficient intelligence had magnified Lee's forces to twice their actual size, causing McClellan to become hypercautious.

Ill fortune was, however, dogging Lee at every turn. His army should have had at least 15,000 more men, but many had straggled to the point of desertion or refused on principle to invade the North. Lee himself began the incursion with a nasty fall that left both his hands in splints. Generals Jackson and Longstreet also suffered minor but incapacitating injuries. All three had to be conveyed through Maryland in ambulances rather than gallantly leading their men on horseback. As the shoeless army tramped its way through the quiet countryside, it became clear that the Marylanders would not rise up or even offer breakfast to the Confederates. The men had to feed themselves with unripe apples and green corn snatched from the fields.[18] Lee naturally worried about his supply line. Aware that there were Federal forces behind him that could cut off his army, he decided that he would have to neutralize the threat they posed before he proceeded farther north. He would have to detach his small army into even smaller, autonomous divisions—a risky maneuver, but it had worked against Pope, and Lee believed that he had the initiative.

On September 13, the 27th Indiana Volunteers trailed into an abandoned Confederate camp outside Frederick. Four of them lay down on the grass to talk and rest in the late summer haze. One soldier, the future president of Oregon State University, noticed a yellow envelope lying in the field.[19] Inside, the group found three cigars and Lee's detailed plans for the next four days. The document, entitled Special Orders 191, was speedily relayed up the chain of command to McClellan. Almost as quickly, a Confederate sympathizer galloped off to report the dreadful news. At first, McClellan believed the orders were a trick, but a captain from Indiana recognized the handwriting and could vouch that the copyist on Lee's staff had been a friend before the war.[20] "I have all the plans of the rebels, and will catch them in their own trap," McClellan telegraphed Lincoln. "Will send you trophies."[21]

McClellan delayed his move for two days, even though his 95,000-strong Army of the Potomac was facing a Confederate force of only 18,000. By September 16, Lee had managed to reunite two-thirds of his divided army and take up a position around a quiet Maryland village named Sharpsburg. About a mile away, on the other side of Antietam Creek, McClellan's soldiers gathered in readiness. "Our Brigade stole into position about half-past 10 o'clock on the night of the 16th," recalled a private in Company G of the 9th New York Volunteers. "No lights were permitted, and all conversation was carried on in whispers." Their place in the line was inside a thin cornfield that sloped down toward a creek. They sat down on the plowed earth and watched dark moving masses in the distance. "There was something weirdly impressive yet unreal," the private continued, "in the gradual drawing together of those whispering armies under cover of the night—something of awe and

North Woods

Hooker

Cornfield

Stuart

N
W   E
S

Mansfield

Franklin

East Woods

Morning Fighting

West Woods

Dunker Church

Hood (Longstreet)

Hagerstown Turnpike

Sumner

Pry House McClellan's HQ

McClellan

Bloody Lane or Sunken Road

Federal artillery
Confederate artillery

R. H. Anderson

D. H. Hill

Lee

Jackson and

Boonsboro Road

Antietam Creek

Porter

Sharpsburg

Lee's HQ

(Longstreet) D. R. Jones

George Henry Herbert

To Shepherdstown

Longstreet

Toombs

Toombs

Burnside

Rohrbach Bridge taken 1 p.m.

To Boteler's Ford

A. P. Hill arrived late afternoon

Harpers Ferry Rd.

From Harpers Ferry

Ebenezer Wells

Antietam or Sharpsburg
September 17, 1862

dread, as always in the secret preparation for momentous deeds."[22] The fighting began as the first rays of dawn revealed the countryside. At first there was sporadic firing, which grew louder and heavier as pockets of engagement blossomed into fields of thunder and flying debris.

As in previous battles, the landscape imposed itself on the fighting. "At Antietam it was a low, rocky ledge, prefaced by a corn-field," wrote a Union soldier. "There were woods, too, and knolls, and there other corn-fields; but the student of that battle knows one cornfield only—*the* corn-field . . . about it and across it, to and fro, the waves of battle swung almost from the first." By 10:00 A.M. the Confederates were in possession of the field that, instead of corn, contained the bodies of more than a thousand dead and wounded men.[23] When the fighting shifted to the woods, Federal troops discovered to their horror that a battery of Confederate artillery had been swiftly moved to block the retreat. John Pelham, the twenty-four-year-old captain in charge of the artillery, was already something of a hero in the South. During Antietam, his unflinching precision under fire made him a legend. After the battle, Stonewall Jackson said of him, "Every army should have a Pelham on each flank." Henry MacIver happened to be delivering a message to Pelham when Federal cavalry attacked the position. The charge was so swift that Pelham and his men had only enough time to draw their revolvers. But the Scotsman never had a chance to use his: a bullet smashed through MacIver's mouth, taking four teeth and part of his tongue with it before exiting through the back of his neck.[24]

After the cornfield and the woods came a sunken road, which, over the course a terrible morning, was christened the Bloody Lane. For several hours along an eight-hundred-yard-long dirt track, a small but well-entrenched Confederate force was able to beat back each Federal charge. (The Irish Brigade lost half its men in less than twenty minutes; Brigade General Thomas Meagher, "the Prince of New York," survived by being too drunk to ride.) But eventually they were overwhelmed and surrounded. "We were shooting them like sheep in a pen," recalled a private from New York.[25] The break in the Confederate line offered McClellan a clear way through; he could have destroyed Lee's center and then turned to crush each wing. Yet McClellan never called forward his reserves.

In the afternoon, the hardest part of the fighting was at Rohrbach Bridge, which spanned Antietam Creek and led directly toward the Con-

federate brigades under General "Old Pete" Longstreet. Ambrose Burnside, who had led the Union capture of Roanoke in February, now commanded McClellan's IX Corps, which included both the 9th New York
and the 79th Highlanders. The bridge in question was only 12 feet wide
but 125 feet long. Burnside divided his corps, sending some, including
the 9th, to ford the river farther down; the rest, including the 79th, he ordered to charge across the bridge. The Confederates easily repulsed each
assault until the 79th ended up having to trample over the bodies of their
comrades in order to reach the other side.

For three hours, various regiments made disjointed attempts to fight
their way across Burnside's Bridge, as it became known. "We had a heavy
struggle crossing Antietam Creek," George Herbert told his brother
Jack. He had been in charge of the battery that was covering the ford and
had watched as his friends waded through waist-deep water while bullets
and shells picked them off one by one. The 9th was the first to reach the
far bank. As soon as they were reunited, they were ordered to storm the
Confederate position on the other side of a plowed field. It was three in
the afternoon. "When the order to get up was given, I turned over
quickly to look at Col. Kimball, who had given the order, thinking he
had suddenly become insane," wrote the regiment's historian. "I was
lying on my back . . . watching the shells explode and speculating as to
how long I could hold up my finger before it would be shot off, for the
very air seemed full of bullets."[26] The men around him were similarly
battle-crazed. One wrote how "the whole landscape for an instant turned
slightly red."[27]

The regiment managed to stagger on until they were within fifty
yards of the Confederates. The two sides stared at each other and then
roared into hand-to-hand combat. It was the Confederates who turned
and fled toward Sharpsburg. The officers leading the 9th struggled to restrain their troops from chasing after them and finally resorted to taking
out their revolvers and threatening to shoot.[28] But at 4:30 P.M., the Union
victors were blindsided by a fresh attack from Confederate reinforcements. The last of Lee's divided forces had arrived at the battlefield, and
the 9th had no choice but to retreat. Some of the men cried as they stumbled back down the hill. McClellan had failed to send reinforcements.
When a courier from Burnside arrived with a plea for men and guns,
McClellan replied: "Tell General Burnside this is the battle of the
war. . . . Tell him if he cannot hold his ground, then the bridge, to the last

man!—always the bridge! If the Bridge is lost, all is lost!" Burnside held the bridge but little else.[29]

"Antietam was a fearful struggle," wrote Ebenezer Wells. During the night of the seventeenth he had led his team of wagons to a hill; "the thickest of the fight had been just there. The road ran parallel with a stone wall which formed a good breastwork for the Southerners, and it was a heavy slaughter for our men. . . . It was a moonlit night, and I went to speak to a man sitting across the wall. I wondered what he stayed for." Wells addressed a few words to him, only to realize that he was dead. "He must have been killed instantly, as he was in a nearly upright position as though in the act of climbing over. The bodies were piled up in heaps all about us."[30] Nearly six thousand men lay dying or dead in ditches and creeks, around fences and knolls, under trees, and across blackened fields. Another seventeen thousand were either waiting for medical attention or receiving what passed for care under hideous conditions.[31] Remarkably, Henry MacIver was alive. He had been dragged from the field and carried to a nearby house. By the time he was seen to, he had almost drowned in his own blood. To prevent him from choking to death, the doctor put a silver tube down his throat.

McClellan was so dazed by the scale of the battle that he did nothing to impede Lee's retreat across the Potomac into Virginia. The shocking number of casualties on September 17 would make Antietam the single costliest day of the war. Twenty-five thousand men were killed, wounded, or missing. McClellan had lost nearly 15 percent of his men; Lee, almost a quarter. The Confederate general might have been defeated once and for all, with his army destroyed, if McClellan's attacks had been better coordinated. McClellan had shown that he could take a strong hand and throw it away. Yet Antietam was still a victory of sorts for the North because Lee's invasion had been halted. Although McClellan made the fatal mistake of allowing Lee to escape, he had pricked the aura of invincibility that had grown around the Confederates since the Seven Days' Battles. He had proved that the Army of Northern Virginia could be stopped.

A few days later, when both armies had deserted the battlefield, the Marquess of Hartington went to inspect the site in order to give a report to his younger brother, Lord Edward Cavendish, who was serving in one of the regiments sent out to defend Canada during the height of the *Trent* affair. Hartington had been in the United States for nearly a month, avoiding his expensive mistress, Catherine Walters (whom he affectionately called Skittles). Now, he walked over the silent terrain in appalled wonder. "In about seven or eight acres of wood," he reported to his father, the Duke of Devonshire, "there is not a tree which is not full of bullets and bits of shell. It is impossible to understand how anyone could live in such a fire as there must have been there."[32]

Lord Hartington's impression of Washington after the Battle of Antietam was that it resembled a vast camp. "You see hardly anything but soldiers and baggage-wagons, and stores moving up to the troops. . . . Washington is now completely surrounded by [forts], I think there are between forty and fifty," he wrote on September 29, 1862. "No drink is allowed to be sold, and, though the place is full of soldiers, it is very quiet." He admired the bearing of the volunteers and thought it "a great pity that such fine material should be thrown away, as they very likely may be, by having utterly incompetent officers."[33] Naturally, he was entertained by Seward, Lincoln, and a host of Washington dignitaries who had become friends with his other brother, Frederick, during the latter's visit in 1859. By now the Americans were used to titled foreigners in their midst. Seward reminisced at length about his stay in England and the titled personages he had met. Lincoln was civil "and also told us stories. I said I supposed we had come at a bad time to see the country, and he said, 'Well!' He guessed we couldn't do them much harm." Secretary of War Stanton revolted Hartington for being a "most atrocious snob," worse even than Seward. General McClellan, he thought, was quiet and modest in comparison, but Hartington was surprised by the general's hatred of abolitionists.[34]

Lincoln regarded Antietam as the victory he had been waiting for in order to issue his preliminary Emancipation Proclamation. "I think the time has come now," he told the cabinet after the announcement on September 22. "I wish it were a better time. I wish that we were in a better condition." But, he continued, "I must do the best I can and bear the responsibility of taking the course which I feel I ought to take." The proclamation declared that on January 1, 1863, all slaves in the rebellious parts of the country would be "forever free."[35] Lincoln also included the prospect of compensated emancipation for slave owners—and emigration for freed blacks—in order to soften the objections of both Democratic voters and the border states. Seward had his reservations but supported the president. On September 26, he told his daughter that he hoped the proclamation had not been issued prematurely.[36]

———

Francis Dawson learned about the Emancipation Proclamation from his prison guard. His bravery had earned him a commission as a first lieutenant of artillery. "The cup of my happiness was full," he wrote in his memoir. "My new uniform was a gray tunic with scarlet cuffs and scarlet collar; an Austrian knot of gold braid on each arm . . . gray trousers with broad red stripes."[37] The Englishman had acquired legions of admirers. "I am very highly thought of here; pardon the apparent egotism of the remark," he wrote candidly to his mother. "I have a troop of wealthy and influential friends here who will do anything for me. Mr. Raines of whom I have spoken to you before has even expressed a wish to adopt me as a son."[38] His popularity was fortunate, since he had not actually received any pay and inflation was already turning ordinary articles into priceless objects. He was dismayed to discover that a plain calico shirt cost twenty Confederate dollars.

Dawson went to Richmond to receive his orders and, while there, had his portrait taken; "if I am killed it shall be sent to you," he promised his mother. From anyone else such words might have been mere bravado, but Dawson was serious. He astonished the chief of ordnance, Colonel Gorgas, by informing him that he did not wish to be relegated to the rear. The colonel complied. "He gave me a letter to General Longstreet, requesting that, if any particularly hazardous service should fall within the line of my duty, it might be given to me."[39] Gorgas had assigned him as brigade ordnance officer under Colonel Manning, in Longstreet's division.[40] But during his first assignment in early September, Dawson was captured along with the wagons he was taking to Longstreet's camp. By morning the prisoners were in Pennsylvania on their way to Harrisburg. Dawson's fresh-looking uniform and general foreignness once again attracted attention. The Union officers escorting the train took such a liking to him that he was able to borrow one of their blankets and a spare toothbrush. But by the journey's end, Dawson had discovered that it was possible to be too popular. When they reached Harrisburg, one of the officers insisted on showing him around the town. The commandant thought this was a doubtful idea, but the captain was adamant. Supper in the town's principal hotel

passed without incident. Unfortunately, this only emboldened the U.S.
officer:

> After supper [Dawson recalled], we walked out to the front of the
> hotel, where my companion slapped me on the shoulder and said
> in a loud voice: "Here is a real live Rebel officer! The first man
> that says a word to him I will knock his damned head off!" This
> was not a very pacific speech to make to a crowd of fanatical Penn-
> sylvanians, who had just heard that the battle of Sharpsburg [Anti-
> etam] had begun.[41]

From the hotel they went to a music hall. They entered as the performers were leading the audience in a rendition of "The Union and
McClellan forever." Undaunted, the captain escorted Dawson down the
aisle to the front row, calmly ignoring the growls and murmurs from the
crowd. "By this time," he noticed, "my companion was decidedly exhilarated." Dawson had no choice but to wait and see what suicidal es-
capade the captain would think up next. About half an hour later, the
officer jumped from his seat and shouted at the top of his voice that he
would beat any man who laid on a finger on his friend. His action unleashed the crowd. Just before Dawson lost consciousness, he heard
shots being fired. When he recovered, he learned that the commandant
had come looking for them. The captain had emerged barely alive. It
transpired that he had a notorious drinking problem.

Dawson was almost relieved when he reached the relative safety of
Fort Delaware. The grim fort turned prison was situated in the middle of
the Delaware River on a swamp-infested island known locally as Pea
Patch. The only other inhabitants beside the inmates and guards were
malaria-carrying mosquitoes and rats. As an officer, Dawson was housed
inside the fort rather than in one of the wooden barracks outside. "The
Time dragged heavily," he wrote. Ninety unwashed men were crammed
into a thirty-foot room and never allowed out except for meals, which
were short and sparse. After three weeks he was paroled and shipped
back to Richmond.

He arrived in the city on October 6. "I can hardly realize now," he
wrote, "that the time, counted by days and weeks, was really so short.
And yet, it must have been so." There was an air of anxiety in Richmond
that he had not felt before. All leave had been canceled, and uniformed

men were thronging the streets. The hotels were full and there was nowhere for him to stay. The wounded from Antietam filled every spare bed and couch in the city. More than ten thousand soldiers were being treated in Richmond's hospitals. Having heard that there was a shortage of nurses, Mary Sophia Hill temporarily left Sam and went to help at Chimborazo, which had grown so quickly since its establishment in 1861 that in a few more months it would be the largest military hospital in the world.

Dawson could not rejoin Longstreet's army until his exchange was official, which would not be until the end of November, but he was able to wangle a military pass from Colonel Gorgas, who recognized that the foreign volunteer could simply resign if he became fed up. Dawson left the city to visit the Pegrams. Though he did not like to admit it, he was in love—in love with the South, with its people, its culture, and at this particular moment, with Miss Pegram. "You will think me partial, but it is not so," Dawson insisted in a letter to his mother. Yet he could not help dwelling on certain attributes of Captain Pegram's niece: "Loving brown eyes, perfect hands and a rich mass of glorious auburn hair."[42] The delightful Miss Pegram had nursed him during his convalescence in the summer, and was pleased to do so again.

Dawson's departure from Richmond at the beginning of October coincided with the arrival of Francis Lawley and Lieutenant Colonel Garnet Wolseley. They had met in Baltimore shortly before the Battle of Antietam when they were trying to slip into the Confederacy, the former to report for *The Times,* the latter, who was stationed in Canada, to satisfy his curiosity about volunteer armies. The twenty-nine-year-old Wolseley had been among the first wave of soldiers sent out by the British government during the *Trent* affair. After the possibility of war had subsided, Wolseley continued to be fascinated by the events south of the border. "It is not easy to describe the breathless interest and excitement with which from month to month, almost from day to day, we English soldiers read and studied every report that could be obtained of the war as it proceeded," he wrote later. Wolseley badgered his superiors until he and a friend secured a two-month leave of absence.[43] They then flipped a coin to decide who would go to the North and who would have the harder task of going to the South. Wolseley "won" the South.[44]

During the summer, *The Times* had offered Lawley the now vacant post of special correspondent. The middling poet and bon vivant Charles

Richmond

sheds

New Fair Ground

Fush
Hill

Capitol Street

Baptist
College

Richmond, Fredericksburg & Potomac R.R.

Alley St.

18th

Confederate camps

Richmond Hill

Main Street

23rd

21st

20th

19th

hospitals

Oline St.

Old Fair Ground

Confederate
hospitals

Pearl St.

Front St.

N
W E
S

forts

Hollywood

Cemetery

mills

Richmond and Kanawha Canal

Tredegar Iron Works

Belle Island

battery

prisoners
of war

Arsenal

Fort Winder

Richmond & Danville R.R.

Manchester

Shockoe Creek

earthworks and batteries

15th

14th

13th

12th

11th

10th

9th

8th

7th

6th

5th

swamp

fort

fort

Virginia Central R.R.

Confederate
camps

Jefferson Davis's
house

The Capitol

Capitol Square

Government
House

Alms House

Church Hill

Old
St. John's
Church

Main Street

depot

Libby Hill

James

falls

Railroad Bridge

rapids

Mayo's Bridge

River

canal

foundry

depot

Haxall Mills

earthworks

Mackay had replaced J. C. Bancroft Davis in New York and was supplying the paper with business and political analysis.* But Delane needed
the eyewitness reports previously supplied by Russell. Lawley knew
nothing about military matters, but in two other important respects he
had changed a great deal since February. He was a hardier traveler, and he
had decided that the South had a right to independence. No single event
was responsible for Lawley's apostasy, but the Anglophobia displayed before and during the *Trent* affair, not to mention the untrammeled hound-
ing of his friend William Howard Russell, had helped to convince him
that a strong Confederacy was essential if the North's aggressive tendencies were to be restrained.[45]

Just surviving the tortuous journey past Federal pickets and scouting
parties into Confederate territory was an education for Lawley. W. W.
Glenn's contacts were finding it harder to slip back and forth. Lawley
had never before shared a room, let alone a bed, with several dirty
strangers. In his autobiography, Field Marshal Viscount Wolseley, as he
was to become, recalled with amusement being woken up in the middle
of the night by Lawley, who was standing in the corner of the farmer's
shed where they were sleeping, frantically waving his stick at the rats
scurrying over his feet. Less comical was their train ride from Fredericksburg to Richmond. The travelers had to squeeze in beside hundreds
of amputees who were being conveyed to hospitals in the city. The men
lay stretched across the seats and were bumped and jolted continuously.
"That train," wrote Wolseley, "opened Frank Lawley's eyes to the horrible side of war, made all the more in this instance because no chloroform
or medical supplies of any sort were available."[46]

When Lawley and Wolseley reached Richmond, they were lucky to
secure an attic room in the Exchange Hotel. Frank Vizetelly, they
learned, had snagged the last remaining bed at the Spotswood, the
Willard's of Richmond. He was glad of their company and went with
them to the war secretary's office to obtain a travel pass. The sight of the
captured flags of the enemy lying in heaps on the floor shocked Wolseley,

---

* Mackay had been a foot soldier in the army of underpaid hacks until 1843, when, at
the age of twenty-nine, he made his reputation with a book called *Extraordinary
Popular Delusions and the Madness of Crowds*. But in his heart he always considered
himself a poet rather than a journalist. He did not intend to do any traveling for *The
Times*. Mackay had toured the United States in 1858 and felt that he had experienced enough trains and American hotels to last him a lifetime.

but he held his tongue while they received their papers and letters of introduction. The following day, October 9, the little party set off to find General Lee's headquarters.

Wolseley came away with fragmentary but vivid impressions of the city. Richmond had hardly changed since Charles Dickens had described it in 1842 as "delightfully situated on eight hills, overhanging the James River." It was still a city of churches rather than saloons, and despite the arrival of five railway lines over the past thirty years, the pace of life remained slow and decorous. The residents prized the city's reputation as the premier cultural center of the South. Richmond boasted five daily newspapers, a literary journal, several theaters, and an academy of fine arts. The city did share one characteristic with Washington: its hotels were similarly uncomfortable and dirty. But otherwise the capitals were a study in contrasts. Washington was a city built to order, lacking in history or tradition; Richmond was formed shortly after the first settlers arrived in Jamestown, and its history was indistinguishable from many of the most famous events of the Revolutionary era. Patrick Henry's "Give Me Liberty or Give Me Death" speech in 1775 was made in St. John's church on Broad Street.

Unlike the domeless Capitol building in Washington, Richmond's neoclassical capitol was not only finished but also widely admired and imitated. Designed by Thomas Jefferson, it stood proudly on the highest hill of the city, within a twelve-acre park called Capitol Square, dominating the skyline like the Parthenon on the Acropolis. Here, in a cluster of classical buildings, lay the seat of the Confederate government. The Confederate presidential residence was situated four blocks away, in an Italianate mansion that had been donated to the government by the owner.

Richmond was built on a rising slope, and its streets were regular and easy to navigate. The industrial district—the flour mills, tobacco and wheat processing plants, and ironworks—was down by the river. Shops and businesses of the better class were below Capitol Square, along Main Street, and the residential neighborhoods were on the crests of the hills. The city's busiest slave auction house, owned by Robert Lumpkin, was only three blocks from the capitol. Wolseley avoided it when he went exploring, though it was almost the only establishment in town with goods to sell. The bookshops were empty of books, and the general stores were denuded of everyday items like shoe polish and pins.

View of Richmond from the west, by Frank Vizetelly, who sketched his own image on the left, under the tree.

Before they left, Lawley gave his *Times* dispatch to the French consul, who was less of a stickler than Consul Moore when it came to preserving the sanctity of the diplomatic bag. Like Wolseley, Lawley had noticed the effects of the blockade, but he airily dismissed them in his article as merely depriving Southerners of a few unnecessary luxuries. Nor did it matter, he declared, that Confederate soldiers often had to march without shoes, hats, or coats: "These men, many of them bearing some of England's most honoured names, and descended from England's best families, are in the field, and have been so for 19 months, fighting against [Northern] mercenaries!" (The article prompted the paper's managing editor, Mowbray Morris, to remind Lawley that they required his news-gathering skills, rather than his opinions, since they had plenty of the latter at home.)[47] Had he read the dispatch, Consul Moore would have been infuriated by Lawley's insouciance. The beleaguered diplomat was, at this moment, writing pathetic letters to the Foreign Office saying he was wretchedly understaffed, overwhelmed, and unable to buy even such commodities as coal for the office: "I leave it to your Lordship to judge if we are not entitled to extra aid."[48]

Lawley had never had to suffer a moment's hardship that was not the direct result of his own profligacy. Perhaps this was why he came to idolize the Confederate army. The young plantation aristocrats who so readily sacrificed everything for the sake of an ideal put his own idle existence to shame. Many of them, like the ambulance driver who conveyed Lawley and his friends away from Richmond, were utterly unsuited for soldiering. The driver, the son of a wealthy farmer, had accepted the relatively menial occupation because his battle wounds were too severe to allow him to continue to fight. Yet he had no idea how to look after himself, even to the extent of becoming drenched because he had never had to fetch his own blanket before.[49]

Observing the Southerner's inability to shift for himself, Wolseley decided that the difference between a professional army and a collection of armed volunteers was, for want of a better term, the existence of esprit de corps. Without it, as he and other English observers noticed, nothing worked as it should.[50] There appeared to be little internal cooperation or forward thinking. Regiments would march along muddy roads, making them worse, without stopping to lay new tracks so that the next regiment would not become bogged down. Wolseley admitted to feeling "sorely puzzled" about the South. Slaves were referred to as "servants," and white servants as "the help," but the euphemisms were simply window-dressing the obvious. Its people combined genteel manners with ancient barbarism; they were brave in the face of appalling deprivation, and personally charming even when proclaiming their bitterness at being betrayed by their British cousins.[51]

As the three Englishmen traveled to General Lee's headquarters near Winchester, they were treated to the full glory of Virginia in the autumn, the gentle golden light reminding Wolseley of a country scene from a Claude painting.[52] When they arrived at Lee's camp in the Shenandoah Valley in mid-October, Wolseley and Lawley were surprised by its spartan appearance. The headquarters was nothing more than eight pole tents placed in a row on hard, rocky ground. Horses roamed loose, wagons were pitched willy-nilly and were clearly serving as makeshift beds for some of the officers.

Lee himself inspired a strong reaction in the travelers; Wolseley developed an immediate case of hero worship. Though still recovering the use of his hands, the Confederate general was a "splendid specimen of an English gentleman, with one of the most rarely handsome faces I ever saw. . . . You only have to be in his society for a very brief period to be convinced that whatever he says may be implicitly relied upon." Wolseley recognized in Lee a military genius: "I never felt my own individual insignificance more keenly than I did in his presence."[53] Lawley was equally enthusiastic. Lee was "impressive and imposing," he wrote, "his dark brown eyes remarkably direct and honest as they meet you fully and firmly. . . . It is certain that General Lee has no superior in the Confederacy and it may be doubted whether he has any equal."[54] Vizetelly quickly set about sketching a portrait of him for English readers while Lee conversed with the visitors. Not once, Lawley and Wolseley observed, did the general express any bitterness toward the North, even though his homes had been pillaged without restraint. Nor did Lee discuss the recent battle at Antietam.

Unable to spare even a single tent for the travelers, Lee gave them a two-horse wagon so that they would be able to visit the camps of the other generals. "Upon leaving him," wrote Wolseley, "we drove to Bunker's Hill . . . at which place Stonewall Jackson, now of world-wide celebrity, had his headquarters." The normally taciturn Jackson made a particular effort with his guests, and even reminisced about his time in England, leading them to think that his reputation for moroseness was rather overblown. Indeed, the general talked so much that the three visitors never had the chance to ask him anything. "As we rode away," wrote the Confederate officer escorting the group, "I said: 'Gentlemen, you have disclosed Jackson in a new character to me, and I've been carefully observing him for a year and a half. You have made him exhibit *finesse,* for he did all the talking to keep you from asking too curious or embarrassing questions. I never saw anything like it in him before.' "[55]

Jackson's ruse did not prevent the visitors from making their own judgments. Lawley noticed that the general had achieved a kind of mythical stature. Civilians flocked to his camp just for a glimpse of the great man; even his staff regarded him with reverence. The journalist thought it was dangerous that the hopes of so many should rest on just one commander. Yet he could understand why. Jackson lived the part. "Dressed in his grey uniform," wrote Wolseley, "he looks the hero that he is."[56]

General Longstreet, their final stop on the tour, could only suffer by comparison to Lee and Jackson. Lawley, however, saw much to praise. "His frame is stout and heavy, his countenance florid and cheery, and eminently English in appearance."[57] They watched a review of ten thousand of his soldiers. "Among this body there were no shoeless or barefooted sufferers," wrote Lawley; "a finer or more spirited body of men has never been assembled together on the North American continent." According to Wolseley, the boots and shoes had only recently arrived in a large shipment from England.

Wolseley's leave was coming to an end and he had to begin his journey home. He was able to achieve only a brief glimpse of Lee's cavalry commander, J.E.B. ("Jeb") Stuart. The travelers arrived at his headquarters, an elegant plantation house called "The Bower," to discover that the famed general was off on a raid in Pennsylvania. The Bower's owners were still there, however, as were numerous pretty female relatives whose chief raison d'être appeared to be making the officers comfortable. Stuart returned on October 10 with twelve hundred captured horses and not a single man lost. Wolseley observed the riders galloping home and was impressed by their superiority to Northern cavalry, "who can scarcely sit on their horses, even when trotting."[58]

Francis Lawley and Frank Vizetelly were a great hit among Stuart's staff. Lieutenant Colonel William Blackford recalled the officers' delight

General Jeb Stuart scouting in the neighborhood of Culpeper Court House, Virginia, by Frank Vizetelly.

when they returned to camp on October 16 and found the journalists·
waiting to meet them. "These gentlemen were often after this our guests,
and we all became very fond of them," he wrote. They already had a
Prussian officer serving as a volunteer aide, Major Heros von Borcke,
and were used to eccentric foreigners.[59] A partially recovered Henry
MacIver was also pottering in and out of Stuart's camp, trying to be useful but more often simply passing the time with friends from his
Garibaldi days. He was delighted to see Vizetelly again. The hard-
drinking journalist "was the most interesting narrator I have ever listened to around a campfire," wrote Blackford.

> There was not a disreputable or reputable place of prominence in
> the civilized world that he did not know all about. . . . We had a
> shrewd suspicion that he drew a little on his imagination for his
> facts, but what difference did that make to us. Late into the night
> we all sat around the embers of our fire out under the grand oaks
> listening to the fascinating tales he told, his expressive counte-
> nance and gestures giving full effect to his words by their play. Mr.
> Lawley was an exceedingly intelligent and refined Englishman

Night amusements in the Confederate camp, by Frank Vizetelly.

and in another style we enjoyed his instructive conversation very much, but Vizetelly was fascinating.[60]

Blackford and Borcke invited them to pitch their tents on the vacant plot next to their own. "Regularly after dinner," Borcke recalled, "our whole family of officers, from the commander down to the youngest lieutenant, used to assemble in [Vizetelly's] tent, squeezing ourselves into narrow quarters to hear his entertaining narratives."[61]

During the journey home, Wolseley mused on the scenes he had witnessed down south. He had seen many armies, "but I never saw one composed of finer men, or that looked more like *work,*" he wrote. "Any one who goes amongst those men in their bivouacs, and talks to them as I did, will soon learn why it is that their Generals laugh at the idea of Mr. Lincoln's mercenaries subjugating the South."[62] By the time he reached Montreal, he had made up his mind to campaign for Southern recognition. Wolseley was aware that the question remained open in Britain. Like so many Englishmen, he assumed that slavery would quickly die out after independence. The real moral issue, in his eyes, was how long the suffering should be allowed to continue. In a bid to reach the widest possible audience, he decided to write an essay for the literary *Black-*

wood's Magazine entitled "A Month's Visit to the Confederate Headquarters." "The first question always asked me by both men and women was," he declared in the article, "why England had not recognised their independence. . . . Had we no feelings of sympathy for the descendants of our banished cavaliers? Was not blood thicker than water?"[63]

FOURTEEN

A Fateful Decision

British reaction to Antietam—Gladstone's Newcastle speech—Battle in the
cabinet—The emperor proposes joint intervention—Russell turns tail

Britain did not receive word of Antietam until the very end of September. "I hope more than I dare express," wrote Adams in his diary on the twenty-ninth. "For a fortnight my mind has been running so strongly on all this night and day, that it seems to almost threaten my life." His son Charles Francis Jr., now Lieutenant Adams in the 1st Massachusetts Cavalry, had last written to the family to say that his regiment was joining the Army of the Potomac in Maryland. The following day, on the thirtieth, the legation heard that Lee's advance had been stopped. "But [McClellan] failed to follow it up and let them escape," raged Benjamin Moran.[1] Adams was also disappointed. Nor were his fears allayed about his son. It was several more days before they received a letter from Charles Francis Jr. His regiment had sat on their horses in readiness while shells exploded on the surrounding hills, but McClellan never sent them into battle.

Reports of the terrific slaughter at Antietam shocked the nation; the 25,000 casualties on a single day seemed almost inconceivable, especially when compared to the 25,000 Britain suffered during the entire Crimean War.[2] "The Federals in their turn have had a victory; and so it goes on; when will it end? Fanny Kemble says not until the South is coerced back into the Union," wrote Henry Greville, reflecting the horror felt by many people at the thought that the war might continue for many months more.[3] Five days later, on October 5, 1862, there was a second uproar in the press, this time over Lincoln's Emancipation Proclamation. As Seward had feared from the outset, the Proclamation was widely denounced as a cynical and desperate ploy. Charles Francis Adams understood its symbolic importance, but even pro-Northern supporters could not understand why Lincoln had allowed the border states to keep their slaves, unless the emancipation order was directed against the South rather than slavery itself. "Our people are very imperfectly acquainted with the powers of your Federal Government," explained the antislavery crusader George Thompson to his American counterpart William Lloyd Garrison. "They know little or nothing of your constitution—its compromises, guarantees, limitations, obligations, etc. They are consequently unable to appreciate the difficulties of your president."[4]

The *Spectator* declared itself to be disappointed with the Proclamation: "The principle is not that a human being cannot justly own an-

"NOT UP TO TIME;"
Or, Interference would be very Welcome.

As the French and British governments ponder intervention, *Punch* argues the time is now.

other," it insisted, "but that he cannot own him unless he is loyal to the United States."[5] For the radical Richard Cobden, the moral contradiction proved that "the leaders in the Federal government are not equal to the occasion."[6] *The Times* went further and accused Lincoln of inciting the slaves in the South to kill their owners, imagining in graphic terms how the president "will appeal to the black blood of the African; he will whisper of the pleasures of spoil and of the gratification of yet fiercer instincts; and when blood begins to flow and shrieks come piercing through the darkness, Mr. Lincoln will wait till the rising flames tell that all is consummated, and he will rub his hands and think that revenge is sweet."[7]

Lord Palmerston reacted to the two announcements with a far cooler head than either Russell or Gladstone. All along he had been a proponent of mediation while the outcome of the war seemed obvious. But Lee's check at Antietam, regardless of his miraculous escape across the Potomac, had revealed a serious weakness in the Confederate army. The prime minister's confidence in the mediation plan was further shaken by

ABE LINCOLN'S LAST CARD; OR, ROUGE-ET-NOIR.

Punch portrays Lincoln's Emancipation Proclamation as a last desperate move.

a strong remonstrance from Lord Granville, the Liberal leader in the House of Lords, who argued in a letter to Russell on September 27 that any sort of interference in the war—no matter how good or charitable the intention—would only result in Britain becoming dragged into the conflict. "I return you Granville's letter which contains much deserving of serious consideration," Palmerston wrote to Russell on October 2. "The whole matter is full of difficulty, and can only be cleared up by some more decided events between the contending armies."[8]

Russell had come to the opposite conclusion. He wanted the cabinet meeting to discuss mediation brought forward by a week, from October 23 to the sixteenth. The news of Antietam and the Emancipation Proclamation had convinced him that only Britain had the power to stop the humanitarian crisis unfolding in America. The answer to Granville's objections, he thought, was to build an international alliance involving France and Russia to force the warring sides to agree to an armistice. "My only doubt is whether we and France should stir if Russia holds back," he told Palmerston.[9]

Gladstone was also moved by his belief that a humanitarian crisis was at hand, though he saw two—the one in Lancashire as well as the one in Virginia. Unlike Russell and Palmerston, he did not think that the Confederates had suffered a significant setback at Antietam. "It has long been clear enough," he wrote, "that secession is virtually an established fact." When Gladstone talked about the undecided questions in America, he meant whether "Virginia must be divided, and probably Tennessee likewise."[10] He patiently brushed aside the Duchess of Sutherland's objections, telling her that "Lincoln's lawless proclamation" would be far more destructive to America than a separation between the states. When the duchess informed her son-in-law, the Duke of Argyll, about this latest twist to Gladstone's view of the war, the duke sent him a blistering rebuke. "I would not interfere to stop [the war] on any account," he wrote. "It is not our business to do so; and even short-sightedly, it is not our interest. Do you wish, if you could secure this result tomorrow, to see the great cotton system of the Southern States restored? Do you wish to see us almost entirely dependent on that system for the support of our Lancashire population? I do not."[11] The combination of his worries about Lancashire and his disgust with the Emancipation Proclamation pushed Gladstone over the edge. On October 7, the day after the Proclamation appeared in *The Times,* he went to Newcastle to attend a banquet in his honor. He had been thinking all day about "what I should say about Lancashire and America: for both these subjects are critical."[12] Gladstone later told his wife that the acoustics were terrible and he had struggled to make himself heard. It would have been better for him, perhaps, if he had not been heard at all. The words that caught everyone's attention were these: "We may have our own opinions about slavery; we may be for or against the South, but there is no doubt that Jefferson Davis and other leaders of the South have made an army; they are making, it appears, a navy; and they have made what is more difficult than either; they have made a nation."

Gladstone's startling announcement was telegraphed all over Europe almost before he had sat down. Ambrose Dudley Mann in Brussels wrote to Richmond that same night: "This clearly foreshadows our early recognition."[13] Thirty-four years later, Gladstone admitted that his speech was a mistake of "incredible grossness." "I really, though most strangely, believed that it was an act of friendliness to all America to recognize that the struggle was virtually at an end." He hated to think of the damage he had caused, "because I have for the last five and twenty years received from the . . . people of America tokens of goodwill which could not fail to arouse my undying gratitude."*[14] But at the time he was unrepentant, until Russell pointed out to him that he had created a controversy where none had existed.

Benjamin Moran worked himself up into one of his customary rages after he read the morning news on October 8. Adams was not sure what to think. He knew enough about British politics now to realize that it would be highly unusual for a change in cabinet policy to be announced in this way. The press seemed hesitant as well. When Adams saw William Forster four days later, he revealed that Seward had given him secret instructions that he was to withdraw from his post if recognition or intervention became government policy. Forster thought this was something

---

* Two years after the conclusion of the war, in 1867, Gladstone admitted in a letter to the American author and abolitionist Charles Edwards Lester: "I had imbibed, conscientiously if erroneously, an opinion that 20 or 24 millions of the North would be happier, and would be stronger . . . without the South than with it, and also that the negroes would be much nearer to emancipation under a Southern Government than under the old system of the Union, that had not at that date [August 1862] been abandoned. . . . As far as regards the special or separate interest of England in the matter, I . . . had always contended that it was best for our interest that the Union should be kept entire."[15]

the Foreign Office ought to know before it made any irretrievable decisions. But, Adams wondered, was this the Foreign Office at work, or just
Gladstone? Feeling depressed, he cheered himself up with a trip to the
theater to see *Our American Cousin.* "The piece has no literary merit
whatever," he wrote. "I laughed heartily and felt better for it."[16]

It seemed to Adams that his question about the British cabinet's intentions was answered a week later when Sir George Cornewall Lewis
gave a speech in Hereford contradicting Gladstone's claim that the South
was an established nation. His speech received favorable comment in the
North and caused uproar in the South. Gladstone's "made a nation" remark was forgotten. Britain was the clear leader in Europe, complained
the influential *Richmond Enquirer:* Lewis had extinguished the light and
closed "the last prospect of European intervention."[17] At home, a relieved
Adams decided that Gladstone had spoken only for himself in Newcastle and "had overshot the mark."

After these two conflicting statements, there were no more public
comments by any of the cabinet. But furious arguments were taking
place behind the scenes. Gladstone and Lewis had long been rivals. Only
one of them could become Palmerston's heir, and each was conscious of
the other's near presence. Allowing his emotions to cloud his judgment
was exactly what the aloof and scholarly Lewis expected of Gladstone.
Russell, whenever he thought that the liberal Whig traditions of the
house of Bedford were at stake, did the same, and this, Lewis knew, was
their weak point.

Russell issued a memorandum to the cabinet on October 13 that laid
out why they should intervene and settle the war. Lewis pounced on it
and wrote a scathing countermemorandum on the seventeenth, pointing
out that it was not a debating club that would be receiving the mediation
proposal but "heated and violent partisans," who would reject it in an instant. The South would not be grateful for the help, thought Lewis, and
the North would swear vengeance on Britain.[18]

Many years later, Henry Adams decided that the real reason why the
cabinet fell into such a muddle over the American question was because
the English were, by habit, eccentric:

> The English mind took naturally to rebellion—when foreign—
> and it felt particular confidence in the Southern Confederacy be-
> cause of its combined attributes—foreign rebellion of English

blood—which came nearer ideal eccentricity than could be reached by Poles, Hungarians, Italians or Frenchmen. All the English eccentrics rushed into the ranks of the rebel sympathizers, leaving few but well-balanced minds to attach themselves to the cause of the Union. . . . The "cranks" were all rebels. . . . The Church was rebel, but the dissenters were mostly with the Union. The universities were rebel, but the university men who enjoyed most public confidence—like Lord Granville, Sir George Cornewall Lewis, Lord Stanley, Sir George Grey—took infinite pains to be neutral for fear of being thought eccentric. To most observers, as well as to *The Times,* the *Morning Post,* and the *Standard,* a vast majority of the English people seemed to follow the professional eccentrics; even the emotional philanthropists took that direction . . . and did so for no reason except their eccentricity; but the "canny" Scots and Yorkshiremen were cautious.[19]

Senior Tories also voiced their concerns after they discovered that Russell was on the verge of approaching the French with his intervention plan; the opposition still maintained its stance that Britain should avoid becoming entangled with either side. Lord Derby had no doubt, wrote Lord Clarendon, "we should only meet with an insolent rejection of our offer."[20] But Russell was no longer listening to his critics. He had already made overtures to the emperor via the British ambassador in Paris, Lord Cowley. However, the French cabinet was undergoing one of its periodic crises, and the foreign minister was clearing his desk for his successor. The Confederate commissioner in Paris, John Slidell, was in a state of nervous excitement. By now, he wrote to the Confederate secretary of state, Judah P. Benjamin, on October 20, "I had hoped to have had it in my power to communicate something definite as to the Emperor's intentions respecting our affairs." Instead, everything seemed to be in confusion. Slidell's informants were giving him conflicting accounts of the two countries' intentions. All he knew for certain was that the emperor was their friend and that Lord Lyons most decidedly was not. Slidell ended his letter with the rueful admission: "I have no dispatches from you later than 15 April."[21]

It was mortifying to James Mason to hear that John Slidell was having another interview with the emperor. The Confederates in England envied Slidell for his easy access to senior French politicians. "I have seen none but Lord Russell," Mason admitted to his wife, and that was "now nearly a year ago."[22] Henry Hotze had to scavenge for news, seizing on scraps and tidbits from friends with "connections to high places" without ever quite knowing whether he was receiving supposition or fact. He was mesmerized by the unprecedented cabinet brawl over the recognition question. "This species of ex-parliamentary warfare was opened with the sparring between Mr. Roebuck and Lord Palmerston," he wrote. "Since then it has grown more serious, and in the case of Mr. Gladstone and Sir George C. Lewis into almost open animosity." In trying to divine the tea leaves, Hotze put great weight on the fact that Lord Lyons was still in London. He hoped it meant that the cabinet was teetering on the side of the South. He tried giving a gentle shove toward Southern recognition by encouraging his "allies in the London press" to increase their output. Some writers, including one at the Tory-leaning *Herald,* were even willing to let Hotze dictate their articles. There was, however, one person whom Hotze wished he could silence. "I almost dread the direction his friendship and devotion seem about to take," he confessed. James Spence had been inspired by the Emancipation Proclamation and was now convinced that the South should issue one of her own. Hotze was furious with Spence for bringing the subject into public view again, but he was at a loss how to divert him.[23] Mason was encountering a similar problem from his friends in the Tory Party, who were trying to extract a pledge from him that the South would renounce slavery.

Hotze's fears that the slavery question might prevent recognition were allayed after he learned that the cabinet meeting and Lyons's departure had again been delayed. This, he thought, was proof that intervention was imminent. In fact, the meeting of October 23 had not been so much delayed as sabotaged. Palmerston had become alarmed by Russell's apparently blind enthusiasm for the mediation plan. "I am very much come back to our original view of the matter, that we must continue merely to be lookers-on till the war shall have taken a more decided turn," he told Russell on October 22. Rather than argue with Russell face-to-face, Palmerston stayed away from the cabinet meeting, which meant that nothing official could be decided. The members who did turn up argued heatedly with Russell and Gladstone, both of whom were so shaken by the experience that each afterward wrote detailed defenses of his position. Russell was especially upset with Lewis, whose memorandum had made him look foolish. The document accused him of propositions "which I never thought of making," Russell wrote grumpily to Palmerston.[24] He was beginning to feel cornered. A visit from Charles Francis Adams on the same day as the aborted cabinet meeting only served to increase his discomfort.

Adams had finally given in to his anxiety over all this talk of Confederate recognition and possible intervention and had sought an official interview with Lord Russell. He waited restlessly on the day of the twenty-third, watching the hours tick by until it was time for him to leave for his three o'clock appointment. He was disappointed when he arrived at the Foreign Office to find several ambassadors lolling about the antechamber still waiting for their meetings. Seeing his pained look, one of them tried to cheer him up but soon relinquished the attempt. Adams did not see Russell until half past four. By then he had rehearsed his position so many times that he was able to put his question to Russell as effortlessly as an afterthought. They were speaking about Lord Lyons, who had called on Adams that morning, and Adams casually "expressed the hope that he might be going out for a long stay. I had indeed, been made of late quite fearful that it would be otherwise. If I had entirely trusted to the construction given by the public to a late speech, I should have begun to think of packing my carpet bag." Just as casually, Russell replied that Gladstone had been misunderstood and that the cabinet's position remained unchanged. They talked on, but Adams was so relieved he no longer felt the need to press the issue, except to remark that the North would not take kindly to Gladstone's speech.[25] Russell did not detain him, equally relieved that he had been able to lie while sticking to the letter of the truth.

Lord Lyons left for New York on October 25. "I have sent off Lyons without instructions," Russell informed Palmerston, "at which he is much pleased."[26] Lyons had never ceased waging his discreet but determined campaign, speaking quietly to both senior Tories and Liberals about the folly of interfering in the war. He felt a profound sense of loyalty and gratitude to Russell, but he refused to acquiesce in a policy that he believed to be morally and practically wrong. The cancellation of the latest cabinet meeting signaled to him that the proposal had died. "I am quite satisfied with the course the government means to take at present with regard to American politics—which diminishes the annoyance of going back," Lyons told his sister on the twenty-fourth. During their four months together they had talked frequently about his coming home, and he promised, "My object now will be to bring my mission to America to an end as soon as I can with credit and propriety." They probably both knew that this was a vain hope.[27]

Lyons was also mistaken about Russell's proposal. It was napping rather than dead or dying. John Slidell's informant wrote on October 28, "I have just returned from Broadlands ... and have also seen several leading political men in town. My impression is that little or no progress has been made as regards your question."[28] During the last week of October the memorandum war continued as more cabinet members felt compelled to state their positions. When Russell received George Grey's letter on the twenty-eighth, he thanked him "for writing me a letter instead of printing a Memorandum," and compared it to Lewis, "who sprang a mine on me." But why, he asked, did people think inaction was morally superior to intervention? "If a friend were to cut his throat," he wrote, "you would hardly like to confess, 'he told me he was going to do it, but I said nothing as I thought he would not take my advice.' "[29] Clarendon observed, "Johnny always loves to do something when to do nothing is prudent."[30] When Lord Lyons realized that Russell had not abandoned his plan, he sent him repeated warnings "that at this moment Foreign Intervention, short of force, could only make matters worse."[31]

Russell was still feeling put upon when Lord Cowley sent him the news that the emperor had ordered his new foreign minister to approach Britain with a proposal of Anglo-French intervention. Russell was delighted. Once again he could be an angel of peace and prevent any further bloodshed in America. "Was there ever any war so horrible?" he asked Cowley rhetorically.[32] Now he could call a new cabinet meeting and his plan would have to be discussed. Palmerston had the opposite reaction. If the North wished to waste the lives of thousands of emigrant Germans and Irishmen, it was not, he decided, England's business to interfere. Moreover, his suspicion of anything French made him skeptical of the proposal. The French have no morals, he told Russell, and would probably agree to all kinds of egregious provisions for slavery. "The French Government are more free from the shackles of principle and of right and wrong on these matters, as on all others than we are," he insisted.[33]

By November 7, rumors about the emperor's proposal had leaked to the press. Adams's spirits sank in proportion to the rise among Confederates. Russell was like a child anticipating a birthday. After reading that a mass meeting of cotton workers in Oldham had passed a resolution in favor of intervention, Russell could not help asking the mayor what had changed in the district. Nothing, the mayor replied; the gathering was small compared to previous American war meetings in Oldham, and it had been intentionally packed with Confederate supporters. (James Spence's agents provocateurs, Aitken and Grimshaw, were so disheartened by their inability to form a genuine social movement that they ceased their activities shortly afterward.) But in London, James Mason was growing more optimistic. "The cotton famine," he was pleased to report, "is looming up in fearful proportions." He added that 700,000 workers were currently living off charity and that typhoid appeared to be on the rise. "The public mind is very much agitated and disturbed at the

ONE HEAD BETTER THAN TWO.

Louis Napoleon. "I SAY, HADN'T WE BETTER TELL OUR FRIEND THERE TO LEAVE OFF MAKING A FOOL OF HIMSELF?"

Lord Pam. "H'M, WELL, SUPPOSE YOU TALK TO HIM YOURSELF. HE'S A GREAT ADMIRER OF YOURS, YOU KNOW."

Punch's characterization of Louis-Napoleon advocating a joint approach—Palmerston holding back, November 1862.

fearful prospect for the winter, and I am not without hope that it will produce its effects on the counsels of the Government," he wrote.[34]

The effects were not as great as he believed: every economic indicator showed that the country was absorbing the cotton shock, and civic and church leaders were confident that mass unemployment in Lancashire could be alleviated if private individuals throughout the country donated sufficient funds to help the workers. Lord Derby set the example with a donation of £12,000, the largest ever given by one person to a particular cause at that time. He was the chairman of the Central Relief Fund that was overseeing the efforts of 143 committees to collect money and clothing. The workers were unemployed, but many were not sitting idle; Harriet Martineau and others were organizing schemes to help them learn new trades and skills. The sewing and cooking schools, she noted, were proving to be especially popular with the women.[35]

Charles Francis Adams had been so satisfied with Lord Russell's explanation that he saw no reason to alter his holiday plans. He was in Tunbridge Wells with his family when the cabinet met on November 11 to debate the French proposal. Benjamin Moran was equally sanguine. "Lord Russell gave Mr. Adams assurances at their last interview that nothing would be done without notifying him," Moran wrote in his diary on the eleventh. "I rest undisturbed . . . I infer the French proposal will be rejected."[36] But while he was pottering about the empty legation, there was open war in the British cabinet. George Cornewall Lewis and the Duke of Argyll were the leaders of the opposition to Russell and Gladstone. The week before, Lewis had sent around a second memorandum—this one over fifteen thousand words—that answered every single one of Russell's and Gladstone's arguments. He had also enlisted his son-in-law, the gifted lawyer William Vernon Harcourt, to write a companion piece for *The Times* under the pseudonym "Historicus."

Russell's ship was sinking, though he steadfastly remained at the helm. He opened the cabinet meeting by explaining his position once again. When he had finished, he turned expectantly to Palmerston. Russell's desperate glare told him that retreat was impossible. The cornered prime minister made a few halfhearted comments about not letting Lancashire down. "I do not think his support was very sincere," wrote Lewis; "it certainly was not hearty: The proposal was now thrown before the Cabinet, who proceeded to pick it to pieces. Everybody present threw a stone at it of great or less size, except Gladstone, who supported it, and the Chancellor and Cardwell, who expressed no opinion."[37] As they debated throughout the morning and into the following day, it became obvious to Lewis that Russell had been rather too forward with the French and feared the consequences of declining their offer. But he remained unmoved by Russell's embarrassment or his dread of annoying France. Lewis scolded Russell for his unrealistic faith in the ability of outsiders to impose peace on America: "What would an eminent diplomatist from Vienna, or Berlin, or St. Petersburg know of the Chicago platform or the Crittenden compromise?" The idea of the Great Powers dictating the terms of agreement between the North and South was ludicrous.[38] He continued to harry the foreign secretary until, in Gladstone's words, "Lord Russell rather turned tail. He gave way without resolutely fighting out his battle." Not surprisingly, Gladstone was disgusted with his colleagues. "But I hope," he wrote to his wife, "[the French] may not take it as a positive refusal, or at any rate that they may themselves act in the matter. It will be clear that we concur with them, that the war should cease."[39]

Russell hoped that his reply to the emperor on November 13 was open-ended and flattering enough to soften the awkward fact that his offer was being turned down. Napoleon was indeed annoyed with the foreign secretary, especially since the Russians had also been lukewarm about his proposal. But the emperor's anger paled beside that of the Confederates, who still perceived Russell as their archnemesis. Henry Hotze's self-confidence suffered a precipitate fall. He wondered whether his attempts to manipulate opinion had backfired. Worse still was the shock of discovering that the government had far greater control over the press than he had ever imagined. Once it was announced that the French proposal had been declined, Hotze could not find a newspaper willing to print his attack on Lord Russell, not even *The Times*.[40]

There is no single reason why the British cabinet voted against intervening in the war. Economically, it did not make sense to interfere; militarily, it would have meant committing Britain to war with the North and once again risking Canada and possibly the Caribbean for uncertain gains; politically, there was no support from either party or sufficient encouragement from the other Great Powers apart from France; and practically, the decision to intervene would have required a majority consensus from a cabinet that had never agreed on the meaning or significance of the war. But there is also an individual whose name is rarely mentioned and yet who deserves his place among the reasons, and that is Seward. From the beginning of the war, eighteen months earlier, Seward had threatened Britain to stay out of the conflict or face the consequences. His bluster and posturing had driven away a potential ally, but the message was heard. A few months after the cabinet discussion, William Harcourt joked to Lewis that it was "a little amusing that the whole wrath of the South and the imputation of being the real obstacle to Intervention should fall on Lord John. It only shows how little is known of the real history of affairs. . . . It reminds me of what Sir R. Walpole said: 'don't tell me of history; I know that *can't* be true.' "[41]

When Charles Francis Adams returned from Tunbridge Wells in mid-November, he straightaway paid a visit to Russell's house in Chesham Place. Naturally, they discussed Britain's reply to the French emperor. Adams told him, "I hoped it would open the eyes of the [American] people to their mistake as to the disposition of the Emperor and make them more liberal to England." Russell's hearty assent to this was no doubt driven by a combination of guilt and embarrassment. Adams mistakenly thought it was due to the foreign secretary's having scored a diplomatic coup. "His Lordship seemed a little elated by his paper and was more cordial than usual," he wrote in his diary on November 15. "He alluded to the alleged audience granted to Mr. Slidell . . . and said that if the Queen had granted any such to Mr. Mason there would have been no end to the indignation in America. I said, yes."

As November drew to a close, the public's interest in the intervention question waned. In spite of himself, Russell was being credited with having behaved with propriety. Even some British Confederate sympathizers agreed with the government's decision to remain neutral.[42] Only the ever optimistic James Mason still believed that "events are maturing which must lead to some change in the attitude of England."[43]

PART II

FIRE ALL AROUND THEM

FIFTEEN

Bloodbath at Fredericksburg

*Lincoln suffers at the polls—the Battle of Fredericksburg—The Senators
attempt a coup—The Marquis of Hartington's conversion—Victory or
annihilation*

Lord Lyons returned to Washington on November 12, 1862, having
spent a few days in New York speaking to Democratic and Republican
leaders. He was relieved to find that they were far more willing to share
their personal views than the politicians in the capital, who were wary of
appearing too familiar with him. The "Peace Democrats" had performed
well in the November elections, picking up the governorships of New
York and New Jersey as well as taking control of several state legislatures.
Their declared aim of peace and compromise over slavery chimed perfectly with the large number of Northern voters who had felt blindsided
by Lincoln's Emancipation Proclamation. McClellan's failure to chase
after Lee following the Battle of Antietam in September had also contributed to a growing doubt in the North over whether the war was
worth the enormous sacrifice in human lives. There had been nine
major battles during the past eleven months, resulting in more than
150,000 casualties between the two sides, and yet there was no indication
of any end in sight.

Across the Atlantic, the results of the midterm elections seemed
much worse to Charles Francis Adams than they really were—the Republicans still controlled Congress by a large majority—and his bitterness toward Lincoln threatened to overwhelm his peace of mind.

Benjamin Moran was shocked by Adams's indiscreet tirades against the administration (though he secretly enjoyed them, too) and recorded each outburst with relish. "Mr. Adams had a long talk with me about Lincoln," he wrote in his diary on November 19.

> He thinks the recent political defeats a natural result of his man-agement. . . . Mr. Adams regards Lincoln as a vulgar man, unfitted both by education and nature for the post of President, and one whose administration will not be much praised in the future.[1]

Ordinarily, Adams would never have confided in a gossipy malcontent like Moran. But despite having made a large circle of acquaintances during the past eighteen months, he felt as friendless as the day he arrived in London. The U.S. minister in Spain, Carl Schurz, pitied his social isolation. Adams "performed his social duties with punctilious care," Schurz wrote after a brief visit to England, but was not "a shining figure on festive occasions [and] lacked the gifts of personal magnetism or sympathetic charm that would draw men to him."[2] His wife, Abigail, felt upstaged by the social success of the American expatriate Mrs. Russell Sturgis, whose soirées were a feature of the season.

The frustration and sense of alienation at the American legation were not all that dissimilar to the loneliness experienced by Lord Lyons and his staff in Washington. Lyons's new first attaché, twenty-five-year-old Edward Malet, had been warned by his friend William Kennedy, who had been seconded to the legation in September, to prepare himself for ghastly weather and few distractions.* "However," Kennedy added, "there is lots of work to do and so one has no time to walk about or grumble, especially as we dine every night with [the minister]."[3] Since Malet had been serving as an unpaid attaché at the British legation in Petropolis, Brazil, where Emperor Pedro II kept his summer residence, he could hardly wait to experience the so-called discomforts of Washington. A salary of £300, and his promotion to "the most important mission next to the Embassies," were, Malet wrote happily to his parents, more than enough compensation.

Lord Lyons's dislike of change, particularly with regard to his own staff, made him prickly toward Malet at first, even though the young at-

---

* The previous incumbent, William Brodie, had pleaded with the Foreign Office to send him anywhere so long as he could escape Washington.

taché's background echoed his own. Malet's father, Sir Alexander, was currently serving his tenth year as minister to the German Federation, placing upon his son the same burdens of expectation and family tradition that had overshadowed Lyons's early career.[4] This unacknowledged connection between them may have been another reason why Lyons was so much harder on Malet than on the others. Malet often had his draft letters returned for rewriting, accompanied by such acerbic comments as "Brevity is the soul of wit, but I object to absolute nonsense—L."[5]

Malet found that Kennedy had not been exaggerating about the long hours. "I have only visited one American house," he wrote to his mother after a month in the capital. The glorious days of the "Buccaneers" were already over. Rarely stopping for lunch, the attachés' first break from their desks came at 7:00 P.M., when they dashed to Willard's to gulp down as many cocktails as they could before returning to the legation at eight for dinner with Lyons. In addition to the daily bundles of diplomatic correspondence that required copying and filing, the attachés were also handling hundreds of cases on behalf of British subjects who were seeking redress or protection from various authorities; and in the past year a large number of cases had arisen that concerned missing, conscripted, injured, or dead British volunteers. Most weeknights Malet was obliged to return to the chancery after dinner and continue working until past midnight. But his situation was different from Henry Adams's in one important respect: the presence of ten bachelors gave the legation in Washington a rather hearty feel, not unlike an undergraduate college or an officers' mess. There was none of the poisonous claustrophobia that infected the legation in London. Nor did Malet have to live with his parents; he was able to rent a spacious house with Kennedy just down the street from the legation, at 227 H Street North. It came with a garden and entertaining rooms large enough to inspire him to try his hand at decorating. He was quite pleased with the results: one room was pink with gold buds, the other white "with lots of small gold stars."[6] All that was lacking were the people to fill them. Malet passed his precious spare time wandering up and down Pennsylvania Avenue, watching "the queerest figures I ever saw in my life—and nearly always troops of prisoners being taken from one place of confinement to another."[7]

The latest prisoners to arrive in Washington were Confederates captured during a skirmish on November 2, 1862, at Snickers Gap, one of the three main passes in the Blue Ridge Mountains that linked the eastern part of Virginia with the Shenandoah Valley. General McClellan's new plan involved advancing along the base of the Blue Ridge, methodically taking each gap, until he reached the Manassas Gap railroad. Once there he intended to decide whether to attack a portion of Lee's army that was known to be only twenty-five miles away, or to avoid a fight and march east to the town of Fredericksburg, which lay along the bank of the Rappahannock River, sixty miles due north of Richmond. In his telegram to Lincoln that afternoon, McClellan made his usual plea for more men and cavalry, though "I will do the best I can with what I have got," he added.[8]

Lincoln was no longer interested in McClellan's best. He had already made up his mind to dismiss the general after the midterm elections and appoint a successor who was less preoccupied with maneuvering and more interested in attacking. On the night of November 7, McClellan was writing a letter to his wife when two visitors knocked at his door. Snow covered their clothes and their faces were raw from the cold; McClellan realized that this was not a courtesy call. The older of the two, General Catharinus P. Buckingham, had come by special train from Washington to deliver the order from Lincoln removing McClellan as commander of the Army of the Potomac and replacing him with General Ambrose Burnside. "I read the papers with a smile," wrote McClellan, and "turned to Burnside [who was standing next to Buckingham] and said, 'Well Burnside, I turn the command over to you.' "[9] McClellan told his wife, "They have made a great mistake," and in his heart Burnside suspected it, too. Although his victory at Roanoke the previous spring had raised his reputation with Lincoln, Burnside's limitations as a military leader had been revealed by his muddled thinking during the Battle of Antietam. Many soldiers broke ranks and tried to touch McClellan's boots as he rode out of the camp and into retirement on November 9. He had failed to lead them to victory, but his commitment to their welfare had touched their lives in ways that only the soldiers themselves could appreciate.

Sir Percy Wyndham was disgusted by what he considered to be incompetent army management by the War Department. He had been assigned against his wishes to General Franz Sigel's XI Army Corps in early September and was given temporary command of the cavalry brigade, which was on guard duty in northern Virginia.[10] Bored by his new command, Sir Percy asked General Samuel P. Heintzelman of the III Army Corps for his help in obtaining a transfer. He was especially annoyed that connections seemed to count far more than merit: "The names of a great many Colonels in the service have been recommended to the President for Promotion," he wrote, but "I, not being acquainted with any political parties of person of influence, naturally have no chance of being recommended in like manner. I would consider it a lasting favour if you would use your influence in obtaining me a position, and if possible in your own command." Heintzelman was experiencing his own difficulties with the high command and had no influence to spare; so bitter were the rivalries in Sigel's corps that a jealous officer sabotaged Sir Percy Wyndham's request by accusing him of disloyalty. "I hear it from a field officer of cavalry that Wyndham said to him in the presence of a private of his Regiment that he would soon as leave to fight for the Confederates as for the Union, and that he would if our Government did not give him what he wanted," claimed the embittered informer.[11]

Even the jovial English lieutenant of the 9th New York Volunteers, George Henry Herbert, was becoming disillusioned, despite his recent promotion to ordnance officer for the division. "The system is radically wrong," he complained. "With the exception of a few regiments, officers and men treat one another as equals, no punishments are inflicted. The private under you today may, if a friend of his gets into office, be a Colonel in another regiment tomorrow."[12] Herbert's experience was confirmed by an English military observer who was fascinated by the different styles of leadership of the two armies. In the South, though many officers were just as unqualified as their Northern counterparts, the plantation system fostered a strong sense of social hierarchy. "The Regimental Officers are mostly men of Known families in the districts from whence the regiment is raised," he wrote, "and the 'mean whites' look up to and obey the sons of the Great Planters." In the North, it was not uncommon for the soldiers to disregard "their Captains and their Lieutenants, whom they regard as equals."[13]

Herbert had just returned from Washington after requisitioning stores for the regiment when he heard the news about General McClellan. Apart from General George Getty, the commander of his division, who was a professional soldier, Herbert had little faith in his superiors, and certainly none in General Burnside after Antietam. "Everything is rotten to the core," he repeated to his brother Jack. "Generals are appointed, I guess, on account of incapacity. Most or at least many are such as no gentleman can serve under and retain self-respect."[14]

Burnside decided to head straight for Fredericksburg and use pontoon bridges to cross the Rappahannock River. With luck he would be on the other side before Lee even knew where the Federal army had gone. From there it would be a straight movement along the Richmond–Fredericksburg railroad. Each regiment was to have twelve days' rations, which Burnside considered more than sufficient for the enterprise. Lincoln had some misgivings about a plan that placed so much emphasis on timing, but he acquiesced, only urging Burnside to move as quickly as possible.

First nature and then Washington, however, began to thwart Burnside at every turn. As soon as the soldiers began their march, the clouds gathered and dumped a steady, hard rain on their heads. "Talk about roads," Herbert commented to his brother; "it would do your heart good to see this specimen of a Virginia dirt road. I suppose you have often heard of mud knee deep. You will find it literally deeper than that. It took me 2½ hours to ride seven miles. This is a singular soil. It is a crust of clay over quicksand. As soon as it is thoroughly wet the sand settles, and the first thing you know you break through the crust and down you go four or five feet."[15] Nevertheless the Army of the Potomac managed to arrive at Fredericksburg in good time on November 20, only to find that the pontoons were notably absent. Burnside refused to consider an alternative plan, and so the entire army waited for the missing pontoons for the next two weeks. Herbert was furious: "All this time was spent by the rebels in fortifying the hills in rear of the town, mounting heavy guns, etc. And a splendid job they made of it."[16] Meanwhile, the soldiers used up their rations and discovered that administrative bungling meant no more were coming. Herbert's New York Zouaves celebrated Thanksgiving on November 27 with a feast of water: even the hardtack and coffee had run out. The misery of the army's situation led to pilfering and fights between regiments. Ebenezer Wells's Highlanders had a vicious struggle with the 2nd Michigan for the last remaining wooden fence in the vicinity, each desperate to chop it up for firewood.[17] There was so much sickness in the camps that Herbert wondered if more than half the army was actually present for duty.

Behind the Confederate lines, Francis Dawson reported to General James "Old Pete" Longstreet's headquarters on December 6, and realized after his brief and unceremonious meeting with the general that his history as an English volunteer held no interest for him. Longstreet maintained a professional relationship with his staff members, which, for a junior officer such as Dawson, meant almost no personal contact at all. Adding insult to his lowly status was the discovery that he was expected to do the work of three men: "Colonel Manning had no taste for anything but marching and fighting, and Lieutenant Duxberry was too fond of pleasure and show to be of much practical use," wrote Dawson. "The whole responsibility in the Ordnance Department of Longstreet's Corps devolved upon me."[18]

Lee was incredulous that Burnside was still seriously contemplating Fredericksburg as a crossing place. He ordered Longstreet's First Corps into position along a seven-mile range of wooded hills that overlooked Fredericksburg and the Rappahannock River. The batteries were clustered thickly, ready to fire on the plain below. When Longstreet asked his artillery commander whether any more guns were needed, the officer replied, "A chicken could not live on that field when we open on it."[19] The Confederate army was so well entrenched above the town that a Federal advance seemed completely implausible. Yet "the Yankees were in plain view on the other side" of the area and "evidently very active," wrote Heros von Borcke, Jeb Stuart's Prussian volunteer aide, after his reconnaissance. Union general Edwin Sumner sent orders to the mayor to evacuate all civilians. The majority of the inhabitants of the eighteenth-century town were women and children. "I never saw a more pitiful procession than they made trudging through the deep snow," wrote a Southern artilleryman.

> There were women carrying a baby in one arm, and its bottle, its clothes, and its covering in the other. . . . Most of them had to cross a creek swollen with winter rains, and deadly cold with winter ice and snow. We took the battery horses down and ferried them over, taking one child in front and two behind, and sometimes a woman or a girl on either side with her feet in the stirrups, holding on by our shoulders. Where they were going we could not tell, and I doubt if they could.[20]

Sheet ice coated the roads, making the horses fearful and skittish. Reconnaissance "was anything but pleasant," wrote von Borcke.[21] But the

atmosphere at General Stuart's camp remained almost festive. The
Maryland journalist William W. Glenn had sent across two more English
visitors to the Confederacy. Captains Lewis Phillips and Edward Wynne
had succumbed to the temptation that was affecting so many British officers in Canada, to slip through Northern lines for a peek at the Confederate army.[22] Wynne fell ill when they reached Richmond, leaving
Phillips to continue by himself. Phillips found the Confederate officers
touchingly keen to demonstrate to him the quality of their men. Borcke
recalled the Englishman watching a shabbily dressed South Carolina
brigade parade before him in a marching style that would have earned
swift punishment if performed on British soil, and pronouncing with
perfect sincerity that he was impressed.[23]

The picket lines of the two armies had come so close to each other
that rebel and Federal soldiers could jokingly trade insults across the
river. Sam Hill's regiment, the 6th Louisiana, enjoyed a brief bartering
system with unknown Union pickets, exchanging letters and tobacco for
coffee and old editions of *Harper's Magazine*. One letter actually reached
its destination in New Orleans.[24]

On the night of December 10, word spread through the Confederate
camp that ammunition was being doled out among the Yankees, indicat-
ing that a battle was imminent.[25] The officers at Stuart's headquarters
nonetheless decided that there was time to take Captain Phillips to a
country ball that was being held nearby. The ten-mile wagon ride to the
plantation was a rash and dangerous journey to attempt—several of the
Confederates were flung with their musical instruments into a snow-
bank when the wagon veered off the frozen road, but, laughing and
bleeding, they righted the vehicle and continued. After another hour of
bumps and near misses, they arrived at the house. Borcke recalled that
"the mansion was brilliantly lighted up, many fair ones had already assembled and the whole company awaited, with impatience and anxiety,
the arrival of their distinguished guests and promised music." They
danced quadrilles and Virginia reels until the small hours. "Our English
captain," wrote von Borcke, "entered into the fun quite as heartily as any
of us."[26] By the time they had returned to camp it was almost daybreak,
and muffled sounds were coming from the Federal lines.

General Burnside had ordered his engineers to begin throwing pontoons across the Rappahannock. Fog emanating from the river gave them
some cover, but the soldiers remained at the mercy of Confederate

sharpshooters. Burnside's response was to shell the town, giving those who had refused to leave their homes a taste of what was to come. Having fiddled and fretted for more than two weeks, he was now impatient to move. His intelligence reports wrongly implied that Lee's army was in poor condition, lacking in artillery and at only half its normal 72,000 strength. The Army of the Potomac was, on paper at least, almost twice its size and equipped with 350 heavy guns. Burnside's natural optimism increased as his army began crossing the river. Lee could hamper the Federals' progress but he lacked the firepower to mount an effective counteroffensive.

Burnside thought he could surprise Lee with a brilliant, sweeping attack.[27] Lee, on the other hand, was confident that the Federal advantages in troops and artillery were more than offset by his own high defensive position above the town; all he had to do was wait for the Army of the Potomac to expose itself on the plain. By nine o'clock on the evening of December 12, George Herbert and the 9th New York Volunteers were among the fifty thousand Union troops in control of the town. Herbert was shocked to learn that a family friend was among the five hundred Confederate prisoners, but he was unable to speak to him before they were transported to the rear.[28]

The following morning, December 13, Captain Phillips solemnly shook hands with Jeb Stuart's officers and set off in search of Robert E. Lee. In the meantime, the two journalists Lawley and Vizetelly were having breakfast with the general and his staff. Lee appeared calm while they waited for the dawn mist to clear from the plains below. His hat and coat were spotless and, as always, the only sign of his rank was the three stars on his collar. After breakfast, the party rode the length of the Confederate line, looking down at the Federals below as they prepared to march out of Fredericksburg. Longstreet's First Corps remained spread out, but his artillery was massed in tight formation along a low ridge called Marye's Heights, which faced the center of the town. The gently sloping plain would provide little cover for the Federal advance. Lawley told his readers, "It is no wonder that every Southerner from the Commander-in-Chief down to the youngest drummer-boy, understood the strength of the ground, and contemplated the coming shock of battle with serene confidence and composure."[29]

As soon as the shelling began, the skyline of Fredericksburg was transformed from quaint rooftops and spires into a broken, flaming ruin.

Fredericksburg
December 13, 1862

Falmouth

To
Aquia Creek

George
Henry
Herbert

Rappahannock River

Stafford

Canal

Marye's Heights

Sunken
road
and wall

Fredericksburg

Burnside

Plank Road

Longstreet

Hooker

Heights

Francis
Dawson

Hazel
Run R.

Old Richmond Road

Pickett

Richmond, Fredericksburg & Potomac R.R.

Hood

F r a n k l i n

W.F. Smith

Lee

R e y n o l d s

Doubleday

Gibbon

Meade

A. P. Hill

Knoll

J a c k s o n

Mine Road

D. H. Hill

Early

Hamilton's
Crossing

Stuart

Pelham
(held various
positions in area)

┼┼┼┼	Pontoon bridges
▬▬	Federal forces
⊡⊡	Federal artillery
▬▬	Confederate forces
⊡⊡	Confederate artillery

Yards
0   1,000   2,000

In a letter to his brother, Herbert tried to describe what happened next: "Two miles back of the town, the ground rises gradually and forms a semi-circular range of hills somewhat in this form." He drew a rough sketch. "This semi-circle was a mass of guns. The fire of which crossed in every direction and completely swept the plain." The range was Marye's Heights, and at its base lay a sunken road behind a four-foot-high stone wall. Impregnable to rifle fire, the wall provided almost total cover to the Confederates crouching behind. Regiment after regiment was sent up the plain without adequate protection as generals tried to interpret Burnside's confused battle plan. One body of soldiers crammed into the relative safety of an isolated house. When it became full, those forced outside tried to create a protective barrier with human corpses, or took refuge behind dead horses.[30]

"General George W. Getty, my division commander, and myself," wrote Herbert's brigade commander, Colonel Rush Hawkins, "were on the roof of the Slaughter house, a high residence at the lower end of the city. . . . From this prominent position our repeated repulses and the terrible destruction of the Union troops had been witnessed." At three o'clock, the two officers were ordered to send in Getty's division. "The order was obeyed but not until I had tried to induce General Getty against its obedience and general waste of life."[31] The instructions became muddled, however, as couriers failed to return and anyone with a horse was commandeered to deliver messages. Ebenezer Wells happened to be at headquarters and was beckoned over by a general. Someone handed him field glasses, and a distant spot was pointed out on the plain. He was so shocked by what he saw that he almost stumbled. "I was ordered to go and deliver my verbal despatch . . . and if shot it was to be my dying words for it to be carried on," he recalled.[32] Wells was one of the few who returned unscathed, but the fate of his message is unknown. George Herbert's regiment misinterpreted their orders to mean they were to advance to a nearby battery rather than toward Marye's Heights. As it turned out, this saved their lives—the only instance of Burnside's inability to communicate with his officers proving to be fortuitous. The moral, declared a young British Army officer who studied the battle twenty years later, was "Let your instructions be explicit, plainly-worded and capable of no double construction."[33]

Lawley and Vizetelly watched, awestruck, as six Federal advances were mowed down by a combination of Longstreet's artillery and the

rebel troops behind the stone wall. "From the point where I stood, with
General Lee and Longstreet," wrote Vizetelly, "I could see the grape,
shell, and canister from the guns of the Washington artillery mow great
avenues in the masses of Federal troops rushing to the assault, while the
infantry, posted behind a breastwork just under the battery, decimated
the nearest columns of the enemy."[34] Looking through his field glasses at
the carnage below, Lee commented, "It is well that war is so terrible—we
should grow too fond of it."[35] Francis Dawson was stationed just out of
range to hear Lee's remark. In any case, he was almost spellbound by the
battle: "Never in my life do I expect to see such a magnificent sight
again," he wrote to his mother; "the whole scene of conflict was before
our eyes, and at our feet, the glorious sun shining as tho' bloodshed and
slaughter were unknown on the beautiful earth; the screaming of shells
and the singing of the rifle bullets adding a fearful accompaniment to the
continued booming of the heavy guns." He saw the Federal army hurl itself at the Confederate guns. "It was thrilling to watch the long line advance, note the gaps in the array, as the wounded fell or else staggered to
the rear, and see the gallant remnant melt away like snow before our
withering fire," he wrote. The Irish Brigade's distinctive green and gold

The bombardment of Fredericksburg, Virginia, by the Federals, December 1862, by
Frank Vizetelly.

flag made its charge one of the easiest to follow from start to terrible finish. George Hart, an English volunteer in the 69th, wrote bitterly, "It was not a fight, it was a massacre."[36]

The guns began to silence as night drew in. At 9:00 P.M. Colonel Hawkins interrupted the generals as they were planning the following day's attack. "I listened until I was thoroughly irritated," he wrote. None of them seemed to have grasped the day's defeat. Exasperated, the commander took out his pencil and drew a diagram of what the Confederates would likely do to a second attack. This brought them to their senses. But although they were now unanimous about a withdrawal, no one wanted to go to Burnside's headquarters with the request. Hawkins took it upon himself, riding in pitch-blackness through mud and debris to Burnside's camp. He arrived before the general himself and waited. "As [Burnside] came through the door he said: 'Well, it's all arranged; we attack at early dawn, the Ninth Corps in the centre, which I shall lead in person'; and then seeing me he said: 'Hawkins, your brigade shall lead with the 9th New York on the right of the line, and we'll make up for the bad work of to-day.' " Undaunted, Hawkins launched into a calm but emphatic explanation as to why there could be no second attack. The unanimous agreement of the generals forced Burnside to concur. Strangely, there were still regiments who had yet to fire a shot; Charles Francis Adams, Jr., had spent all day in the woods reading the poems of Robert Browning while he waited for orders.

"A ride along the whole length of the lines told a sad tale of slaughter," wrote Lawley. "It is doubtful whether any living pen could do justice to the horrors." But "when the eye had once rested upon the fatal slope of Marye's Heights the memory became fixed upon the spot." Fourteen Federal brigades had been thrown at the wretched stone wall. "There, in every attitude of death, lying so close to each other that you might step from body to body, lay acres of the Federal dead."[37] Vizetelly stopped counting the bodies when he neared seven hundred. Intermingled with the dead were the wounded and dying. With no truce agreed, they could not be rescued from the field. Their screams and moans filled the cold night air. The survivors huddled together in ravines, behind walls, and at the bases of trees for warmth, forbidden to light fires lest they provide a target for the enemy. As the dead stiffened in the freezing temperatures, they were propped up to look like sentries.[38]

All day on the fourteenth, Lee waited for Burnside to resume the offensive. But instead of fighting, Union soldiers turned what had been casual looting of Fredericksburg into a full-scale rampage. The historian of Ebenezer Wells's regiment claims that the three terrified women discovered by the 79th in a filthy coal cellar were treated with kind respect. If so, they were among the few who were not taunted or molested. Soldiers went from house to house stripping the valuables and methodically smashing the rest. The streets became blocked with broken detritus; everything from pianos to petticoats lay in mangled heaps across the roads. The anarchy horrified and disgusted many Federal soldiers, but the destruction continued throughout the day. Even Martha Washington's tomb was ransacked and used for target practice. At night, the madness below seemed to be reflected in the sky—the Northern Lights had never been seen so far south, and bright-red tongues of light flickered and crackled over the soldiers' heads. When dawn came, the rising sun revealed a remarkable change on the battle plain. Hardly a shred of blue remained. The dead had been stripped naked by Confederates seeking to exchange their tattered uniforms for good Northern cloth.

Lee was still waiting on the fifteenth when Burnside requested a flag of truce for burial and retrieval. Lee acquiesced, which, according to Wolseley, was a tactical mistake of the gravest kind. In his history of the battle, written in 1889, he would describe the general's actions as "inexplicable." "Burnside's army was at Lee's mercy," wedged tight between the Confederates and an unfordable river. Lee should have launched an all-out attack and obliterated the mighty Army of the Potomac while it remained vulnerable. Such a decisive victory, Wolseley believed, would have convinced the European Powers that neutrality was no longer an option. The Lincoln administration might well have fallen, and with it the national will to prosecute the war.[39] But Lee always contended that he had no means of knowing the true extent of Burnside's losses on December 13. The Confederates had suffered nearly five thousand casualties—a total that seemed high until they learned that the Federals had experienced another Antietam-style bloodbath, with casualties approaching thirteen thousand. While Lee hesitated, Burnside was able to carry out a rapid and silent retreat during the night. The Confederates awoke on the sixteenth to discover that they were alone.

Mary Sophia Hill went to Fredericksburg to offer her help and found it a ghost town: "If ever you saw a city of desolation it was this."[40] Every house was perforated by cannonballs; whole streets lay in rubble. But when Captain Phillips, who had been reunited with his friend Captain Wynne, went down into the town to investigate, they discovered it was far from empty. Major von Borcke accompanied them, recalling in his memoirs, "A number of the houses which we entered presented a horrid spectacle—dead and wounded intermingled in thick masses."

As they trod carefully over human debris, Phillips suddenly grabbed von Borcke's arm and pointed to the body of a soldier who was missing a part of his skull: "Great God, that man is still alive!" His cry caused the soldier to open his eyes and stare "at us with so pitiable an expression that I could not for long after recall it without shuddering." Helpless, the men knelt down and stayed with him for a moment.*[41] Francis Lawley was gripped by similar scenes in other parts of the town. "Death, nothing but death everywhere," he wrote afterward; "great masses of bodies tossed out of the churches as the sufferers expire; layers of corpses stretched in the balconies of houses as though taking a siesta . . . horrified and aghast at what I saw, I could not look."[42] Sickened by the unrelieved suffering around him, he returned to Richmond without waiting for his friends.

The first of the wounded began to arrive in Washington on December 14. These were the men who could drag themselves off the battlefield and board steamers without assistance. It was another two days before the seriously injured were brought from the field hospitals. An English military observer at one of these hospitals thought he had never witnessed anything so barbarous:

> There were about 60 surgeons without coats (chiefly French, German and Irish), covered in blood and dirt, chatting, arguing, and laughing and swearing, and cutting and sawing more like the devils and machines than human beings. Large heaps of legs, and arms were piled here and there, all sizes, and stages of decomposition . . . I thought I could stand a good deal but . . . I felt myself grow pale and dared not speak for a few minutes.[43]

It seemed incredible that any patient could leave such a place alive.

---

*Jeb Stuart took a grim satisfaction from Wynne and Phillips's reports: The "Englishmen here," he wrote to General Lee's eldest son, George Washington Custis Lee, "who surveyed Solferino [the battle that inspired Henry Dunant to found the Red Cross] and all the battlefields of Italy say that the pile of dead on the plains of Fredericksburg exceeds anything of the sort ever seen by them."

The hospital ships disgorged thousands of stretchers along the crowded waterfront. The wounded lay on the ground for hours until ambulance drivers heaved them onto wagons and ferried them to various hospitals around the city. The new pavilion-style hospitals advocated by Florence Nightingale were being built as quickly as possible. The haste produced careless mistakes: one hospital was left without a mortuary, forcing administrators to stack the dead in an adjacent lot until burial; another was placed next to an open sewer. The newest hospital, Lincoln General, opened the week of the Battle of Fredericksburg, but even though it had a capacity of 2,575 patients, the number of casualties far exceeded the available beds: hotels, churches, warehouses, even a floor of the Patent Office were converted into makeshift wards. The novelist Louisa May Alcott had been a nurse for all of three days when a line of carts drew up outside the old Union Hotel in Georgetown. The ballroom became Ward Number One with forty beds. The filthy, blood-smeared arrivals were undressed and washed before they were allowed to lie on the sheets. Miss Alcott amazed herself by performing the task without shuddering. Then a British surgeon dressed their wounds. "He had served in the Crimea," she wrote, "and seemed to regard a dilapidated body very much as I should have regarded a damaged garment; and, turning up his cuffs, whipped out a very unpleasant looking housewife [sewing kit], cutting, sawing, patching and piecing, with the enthusiasm of an accomplished surgical seamstress."[44]

The vast need for surgeons and medical personnel had opened the doors to any foreign doctor with a degree and a proficiency in the English language. Though not in the same numbers as foreign soldiers, they came by their tens and hundreds to Washington. Until two months before, twenty-five-year-old Charles Mayo had been the house surgeon at the Radcliffe Infirmary in Oxford. There were loud protests from the staff and patients when the popular and well-respected doctor announced his intention to go to America to gain more medical experience.[45] After seeing Mayo's qualifications, the new surgeon general, Dr. William Hammond, who was valiantly trying to overhaul the entire system, offered him charge of 125 beds at the Armory Square Hospital in Washington. This was not what Mayo had in mind, and he politely declined the offer, preferring to take the assistant surgeon examination instead. But to his chagrin, his marks were so high that the president of the examining board put in a special request for Mayo to be stationed in the capital.

In the aftermath of Fredericksburg, Mayo worked all day and long into the night, hurrying

> from place to place to the assistance of maimed and exhausted men, pursued all the while by messengers with notice of fresh arrivals . . . scarcely a hotel or boarding-house in the city but contained someone that required the doctor's help. It became impossible to keep a detailed visiting list, or to remember the names of one's patients. "Lieutenant A and five others, Colonel B and six others; Captain C and four others," are specimens of the kind of record that had to suffice for the contents of a particular house or hotel.[46]

Occasionally, he remembered men by their stories; for example, a wounded officer in the Irish Brigade who was saved by the butt of his revolver, which took the full force of a minié ball. But for the most part, he was too busy to become friendly with his patients. Mayo noticed that many of them arrived dying from tetanus—the result of incompetent butchery at the field hospitals, he concluded. There was nothing he could do for these wretched men except try to ease their pain. One particular case stayed in his memory: a healthy young major with a botched amputation who lingered for several days, eventually dying in the arms of a kind and decent hotel keeper who could not bear the thought of her guest dying alone.

Washington was in an uproar over Fredericksburg, and General Burnside was accused of criminal stupidity. "What astonishes me is that such a battle should ever have been fought," the new attaché Edward Malet wrote to his father. "I do really think that all those men who fell were murdered."[47] Lincoln's reputation as a war leader suffered a serious blow. The president wrung his hands as he listened to accounts of the battle, repeatedly asking, "What has God put me in this place for?"[48] To many people, not just in the capital but also throughout the country, the answer was obvious: it was time for Lincoln to make way for a successor. The treasurer of the Sanitary Commission, George Templeton Strong, wrote in his diary on December 18 that "Old Abe's grotesque genial Western" jokes simply nauseated him now; "if these things go on we shall have pressure on him to resign."[49] Three days later, Strong recorded with surprise that it was Seward and not Lincoln who had resigned. "Edward Everett and Charles Sumner are named as candidates for the succession. I do not think Seward a loss to government," he wrote. "He is an adroit, shifty, clever politician, he believes in majorities, and it would seem, in nothing else."[50]

A campaign to oust Seward had been gaining momentum for several months. The previous September, Lincoln had fended off an anti-Seward delegation from New York that claimed to represent the wishes of five New England governors by declaring that the administration would collapse without the secretary of state. The statement was debatable, since Seward's power had shrunk considerably since the heady days in December 1860 when he boasted to his wife that the future of the government rested on his shoulders.[51] Seward had successfully forged a close relationship with Lincoln as his second in command and confidant, but his relations with the rest of the cabinet had actually worsened during the past two years. The other members resented the way Seward had managed to insinuate himself into Lincoln's inner circle. They disliked arriving at cabinet meetings and finding him already there, or, when they left, watching him stay behind for a private "chat." Gideon Welles's diary was peppered with fulminations against Seward and his wish "to direct, to be the Premier, the real Executive."[52] The treasury secretary, Salmon Chase, whose views on emancipation were far more radical than Seward's, loathed him so heartily that he seized every opportunity to undermine the secretary of state. He repeatedly used the phrase "back-stairs influence" when referring to Seward, until it took on a life of its own and became a universal cry.

Charles Sumner had been hoping for some time that Seward would make a mistake that would finish him permanently. He believed that such a moment had come after the publication in early December of the State Department's diplomatic correspondence for the first half of 1862. By now the State Department was overseeing 480 consulates, commercial agencies, and consular agencies abroad, and the literature Seward offered to the public was extensive. The British section contained letters from Charles Francis Adams that the minister had never imagined would become public. Benjamin Moran arrived at the legation on December 22 to find Adams mortified to the point of tears after the London press gleefully published some of the juicier anti-British dispatches, which included his complaints about *The Times* "and the sympathies of the higher classes," whom Adams accused of "longing to see the political power of the United States permanently impaired."[53]

Seward's decision to publish every letter was "almost amounting to insanity," Moran declared savagely. "Mr. Adams thinks his usefulness at this post is destroyed. . . . At one time during the day I thought he seriously contemplated resigning, and I told him he could not be spared—that it was his duty to remain. . . . This he agreed to . . . but that he would be more guarded in his future Dispatches to Mr. Seward." Where, Adams wondered, was Seward's sense of tact or diplomacy? "I scarcely imagine it wise in diplomatic life to show your hand in the midst of the game."[54] Now that the whole country knew that he accused the aristocracy of wishing "to see the Union shattered," Adams doubted if polite society would ever receive him again.[*]

Sumner was interested in only one letter—a dispatch sent to Adams on July 5, 1862, in which Seward betrayed his contempt for the hard-line abolitionists and their universal emancipation agenda.[†] This, Sumner believed, would be sufficient to ruin Seward in the eyes of the radical wing of the Republican Party. All he needed was an event or catalyst to mobilize his fellow senators—which had been provided by the disaster at Fredericksburg.

On the evening of December 16, the thirty-two Republican senators gathered for a meeting in the Senate reception room to discuss their response to the defeat. Lincoln did not escape censure, but the general feeling in the chamber was that the president's mistakes were—as Chase

---

[*] Seward's printed correspondence provided some of the most interesting reading the Foreign Office clerks had seen in years. But Lord Lyons adopted a judicious view of the letters. "[Seward's] tone towards the Foreign Powers has, however, become much more civil than it appeared in the correspondence printed last year," he pointed out to Lord Russell. As for Adams and his indiscreet comments, Lyons thought he showed "more calmness and good sense than any of the American Ministers abroad. He is not altogether free from a tendency to small suspicions—but this, I think, proceeds from his position, not from his natural character—it is, too, a very common mistake of inexperienced diplomats."[55]

[†] The line that really upset Sumner was this: "The extreme advocates of African slavery and its most vehement opponents were acting in concert together to precipitate a servile war—the former by making the most desperate attempt to overthrow the federal Union, the latter by demanding an edict of universal emancipation."[56]

repeatedly charged—the direct result of Seward's baleful influence. Ironically, Seward's deliberate attempt to foster an aura of power and mystique about himself, which William Howard Russell had noticed in 1861, now told against him. By the end of the meeting, all but four of the senators had agreed that Lincoln should be confronted about Seward. In Sumner's view, the secretary of state's own words had damned him by revealing his lack of commitment to the war. But there was a deeper intent among some of the senators: Seward would be only the first casualty. The other moderates in the cabinet would follow, and then Lincoln himself, leaving the way clear for Chase to become president with a cabinet of fellow radicals.[57]

One of Seward's few remaining friends on Capitol Hill had sneaked out of the Republican meeting to warn him of the impending coup. His immediate reaction was to resign first in order to deny his enemies the satisfaction of seeing him humiliated.[58] By the time Lord Lyons heard about the senators' attack, their delegation had already met with a clearly distressed Lincoln on December 18 and presented their demands for Seward's removal and a reorganization of the cabinet.[59] Lincoln had been able to parry their claim that the cabinet was divided, but he had no answer to Sumner's accusation that Seward was sending "offensive dispatches which the President could not have seen, or assented to."[60] To buy time, he invited them to resume the discussion the following day.

Lyons still regarded Sumner as a reliable ally in Anglo-American controversies, but he thought the Republican Party as a whole combined an unhealthy mix of zealotry and ignorance that made them unpredictable. "We may have to be ready for squalls," he wrote to Lord Russell on the nineteenth. That evening, Lincoln received the Republican delegation for the second time. But he had a surprise for the plotters. He had invited the cabinet—with the exception of Seward—to hear their allegation that the secretary of state had usurped its powers. It was an awkward moment for Chase, who, even more than Sumner, had been the prime mover behind the attempted coup. He panicked over whether to portray himself as loyal to Lincoln, which would mean denying the senators' allegations that the cabinet was disgruntled, or to throw in his lot with the delegation and support its claims. He lost his nerve and pretended to be surprised that there were rumors against Seward. His cowardice abashed several of the senators, but not Charles Sumner, who angrily repeated his previous complaints about Seward's record. Still, when confronted with testimonials that the cabinet was united behind Lincoln, the majority of delegation felt too embarrassed to insist on Seward's removal. The meeting adjourned at one in the morning with nothing actually decided.

Lyons thought that the outcome would depend on whom Lincoln could least afford to lose; "a quarrel with the Republican Members of the Senate is a very serious thing for him." As two more days slipped by without any definite news, Lyons pondered a future without his erstwhile nemesis: "I shall be sorry if it ends in the removal of Mr. Seward," he wrote a little ruefully on Monday, December 22. "We are much more likely to have a man less disposed to keep the peace. . . . I should hardly have said this two years ago."[61] But that afternoon he paid a visit to the State Department, and to his relief he found Seward back at his desk, behaving as if nothing had happened. Over the weekend, just as Seward had started to accept the coup against him, and Lincoln had begun to rationalize to himself why his chief ally in the cabinet had to be sacrificed to placate the radicals, Chase had become frightened that Seward's friends and supporters would take their revenge on him. To save himself, he offered his resignation in the hope that this would clear him of any imputation of harboring ambitions for the presidency. Lincoln realized that Chase had lost his nerve. In a deliberate show of authority, the president rejected his resignation, replied that both secretaries were indispensable, and declared all discussion about a cabinet reorganization at an end. The senators' protest had achieved precisely the opposite effect of what they had intended. But it was obvious, Lyons wrote to Lord Russell on December 26, that "Mr. Seward was plainly not in a position to make any concessions at all to neutrals."[62] He would not dare risk his remaining political capital on helping Britain to obtain cotton, or indeed on helping Britain at all.

That same day, the twenty-sixth, President Jefferson Davis told Southerners to relinquish their hope for British intervention. He was speaking to the legislature in his home state of Mississippi at the end of a morale-boosting tour through the western parts of the Confederacy. Davis did not need to rouse his listeners' indignation—many already had firsthand or secondhand knowledge of the devastation wrought by Union armies. Nor did he need to warn them against complacency: beyond Virginia, the South was shrinking as more and more territory came under Federal control. What the lean and shabbily dressed listeners required from their president was reassurance that the North might smash their homes but not their moral purpose. Davis damned Northerners as the blighted offspring of Cromwell's fanatical Roundheads. It was in their blood to oppress others, he declared. Their ancestors "persecuted Catholics in England, and they hung Quakers and witches in America." The liberty-loving South could never live in harmony with such monsters of intolerance. But having given his audience its dose of tonic, Davis proceeded to administer a series of bitter pills. The last, and most shocking to the once-mighty kings of cotton, was the fact of the South's utter isolation. "In the course of this war our eyes have often been turned abroad," admitted Davis:

> We have expected sometimes recognition, and sometimes intervention, at the hands of foreign nations; and we had a right to expect it . . . but this I say: "Put not your trust in princes," and rest not your hopes on foreign nations. This war is ours; we must fight it out ourselves. And I feel some pride in knowing that, so far, we have done it without the good will of anybody.[63]

The Marquis of Hartington was moved by Davis's speech. He and his traveling companion, Colonel Leslie, had arrived in Richmond on December 23, five days after leaving Baltimore in the dead of night. Hartington had wanted to ask the U.S. government's permission to cross into the South, but the legation had warned him against the idea. "They said they thought it was very doubtful," he explained to his father, the Duke of Devonshire, "and if we were refused there would be more difficulty in going out on our own hook." He promised they would not resist if they were captured during the attempt.[64] Fortunately, with the assistance of the ubiquitous Maryland journalist W. W. Glenn, they had been able to travel from one safe house to the next without encountering any Federal patrols.

The difference between the countryside of Maryland and that of Virginia was striking. "The country looks terribly desolated," wrote Hartington. "The fences are all pulled down for firewood, a good many houses burnt, and everything looking very bare." The contrast between Baltimore and Richmond was even greater. The Southern capital had doubled in size in less than two years, but it was worse off in every aspect. Hartington was surprised by the shoddy appearance of all classes. "They have had no new clothes since the war began," he wrote, "and are not likely to get any till it is over." Yet "these people say they are ready to go on for any length of time, and I believe many of them think the longer the better, because it will widen the breach between them and the Yankees, against whom their hatred is more intense than you can possibly conceive."[65]

Hartington had arrived in America in August with no strong feelings about the war. After a couple of weeks in New York, he felt "inclined to be more a Unionist than I was." The moderation of New Yorkers impressed him, since "I believe, if they could lick them, and the South would come back to-morrow, they would be willing to forget everything that had happened, and go on as usual." But as he saw more of the North he became less certain about the point of the war: "I understand nothing about it, and I can't find anybody except Seward who even pretends that he does. . . . They mix up in the most perplexing manner the slavery question, which they say makes theirs the just cause, with the Union question, which is really what they are fighting for."[66] He found the Peace Democrats he spoke to in the North a rather unattractive lot, which made him waver: "I think their arguments are weak and their objects not by any means desirable," he wrote from Chicago in mid-October.[67]

But once Hartington reached Virginia, it took less than a week for him to be won over. Like Frank Vizetelly and Francis Lawley before him, he was smitten. "I hope Freddy [his younger brother, Lord Frederick Cavendish] won't groan much over my rebel sympathies, but I can't help them," he wrote to his father on December 28, 1862. "The people here are so much more earnest about the thing than the North seems to be, that it is impossible not to go a good way with them, though one may think they were wrong at first."[68] The Southerners were certainly putting on a good show for him. He was introduced to Jefferson Davis and his cabinet, who seemed like moderate and sensible men to him, fighting the laudable cause of self-determination; he had spoken with Lee and Jackson, who were modest in victory; and he had been shown a couple of carefully selected plantations. "The negroes hardly look as well off as I expected to see them," he wrote afterward, "but they are not dirtier or more uncomfortable-looking than Irish labourers." Southern fears of a "servile insurrection" inspired by Lincoln's Emancipation Proclamation had proved to be unfounded.*[69] On the twenty-ninth, Lawley accompa-

---

* In New Orleans, Acting Consul George Coppell had tried to obtain permission for British subjects to arm themselves in case of a race riot against whites.

nied Hartington and Colonel Leslie to General Jeb Stuart's headquarters. Forewarned by a telegram from Lawley, the officers ransacked their own belongings to provide the party with comfortable accommodation. Scarce luxuries like blankets and stoves were sacrificed for the visitors. The fattest turkey in the camp was killed and plucked for dinner. Hartington appreciated their efforts, and he endeared himself to his hosts by insisting "we should not make any change for them in our ordinary routine, but let them fare exactly as the rest." To demonstrate his sincerity he helped to beat the eggs for "a monster egg-nog."[70] But as Hartington joined in the revelries, he suddenly realized the scale of suffering it would require to crush the spirit of rebellion. The South "can never be brought back into the Union except as conquered provinces," he wrote, "and I think they will take a great deal of conquering before that is done."[71]

SIXTEEN

The Missing Key to Victory

New Year's Day—Heartbreak at Vicksburg—General Banks assumes command at New Orleans—The Alabama *embarrasses the U.S. Navy—Seward returns to his old ways*

The English volunteer Dr. Charles Mayo finally took a break from work on New Year's Day to attend a public reception at the White House. By the time he reached the front of the queue outside the Blue Room, Lincoln had been shaking hands for more than two hours without a break. "His presence is by no means majestic," wrote Mayo, "and I could not but pity the poor man, he looked so miserable."[1] A journalist observing the occasion wrote that Lincoln's gait had become "more stooping, his countenance sallow, and there is a sunken, deathly look about the large, cavernous eyes."[2] The president had also hosted the official reception for dignitaries, foreign diplomats, and politicians earlier in the day. It was the only occasion when the ministers were expected to wear their dress uniforms to the White House. Notwithstanding the finery on display, the atmosphere had been subdued. Seward hardly left Lincoln's side, Lyons noticed, and made no attempt to engage his colleagues in conversation.

Once the White House had emptied, Lincoln could concentrate on the immediate problem at hand: General Burnside had called in the morning to offer his resignation. Though the president had lost confidence in Burnside's capabilities, he was not sure that it would be right to give the Army of the Potomac its third leader in three months. Over the past few days, telegrams had been arriving from out west that filled him

New Year's Day reception at the White House, by Frank Vizetelly.

with anxiety. The Federal armies in Mississippi and Tennessee both appeared to be on the brink of defeat.

———

Only five months earlier, Lincoln had complained that Europe concentrated far too much on the North's failures in the East and entirely ignored the great successes it enjoyed in the West, where Federal armies were "clearing more than a hundred thousand square miles of country."[3] But since then, the U.S. Navy had been unable to take control of the Mississippi River, and General Grant had failed to capture the river port of Vicksburg, his next objective. For as long as Vicksburg stayed in Confederate hands, the mighty Mississippi remained the South's most precious supply route and means of communication between its eastern and western parts. The significance of the river as the economic backbone of America was no mere story to Lincoln; during his youth he had worked on it, traveling on flatboats from Illinois down to New Orleans. "Vicksburg is the key," he had told his generals in 1861. "The war can never be brought to a close until that key is in our pocket. . . . We can take all the northern ports of the Confederacy, and they can defy us from Vicksburg."[*4]

———

* Confederate president Jefferson Davis also had emotional ties to Vicksburg. His family home, Brierfield plantation, was only twenty miles south of the town along

Since that discussion, the Federal army had grown to just under a million men, twice the Confederate total of 464,000. Lincoln wanted this numerical superiority exploited; a week of Fredericksburgs would wipe out Lee's Army of Northern Virginia but cause only a dent in the North's fighting capacity.

Vicksburg was roughly equidistant between Memphis, Tennessee, and New Orleans; the next fort was Port Hudson, 150 miles farther south, which guarded the approach to Baton Rouge, Louisiana. Nick-named the "Hill City" before the war, but now referred to as the Gibral-tar of the Mississippi,* Vicksburg owed its defensive strength to the spectacular geography of the Mississippi Delta. Situated along a sprawl-ing chain of hills overlooking a sharp bend in the river, surrounded by alligator-infested swamps and densely wooded bayous whose emerald-colored waters obscured a netherworld of poisonous snakes and snap-ping turtles, Vicksburg afforded few approaches that could not be defended from the town. Before the war, Vicksburg had been a thriving commercial center of four thousand inhabitants, with six newspapers, several churches of different denominations, and even its own syna-gogue. But now its purpose was simply strategic, to be defended or cap-tured at all costs.

The lack of progress in opening up the Mississippi River had political and military implications that Lincoln could not afford to ignore. The Democratic politician turned general John McClernand warned that if control of the river were not soon achieved, the Midwestern states of Ohio, Illinois, and Indiana might lead a second mass exodus from the Union, creating a separate Confederacy of the Northwest, which would make its own peace with the South.

There was also the problem of General Ben Butler down in New Or-leans. His eight-month rule had resulted in a profoundly alienated pop-ulation as well as a raft of missed opportunities to gain more of the Mississippi. Lincoln decided to replace Butler with another political gen-eral, Nathaniel P. Banks. Though his military record was not inspiring—

---

a part of the river known as Davis Bend. He described Vicksburg as the "nail-head that held the South's two halves together."

* The phrase referred to the Great Siege of Gibraltar during the American War of In-dependence. Though vastly outnumbered and outgunned, the besieged British forces on the Rock had defied a combined Spanish and French invasion fleet for three years and seven months, one of the longest sieges in history.

Stonewall Jackson had thrashed his first army in the summer of 1862—
Banks was a popular and respected Massachusetts politician. From humble beginnings as a bobbin boy in a cotton factory, he had risen through
his own talents to become the Speaker of the House of Representatives.
Banks's leadership qualities were not in question, nor was his honesty—
an important consideration after the accusations of corruption leveled
against Butler.

The immaculately dressed and well-spoken Banks (he had carefully
erased all traces of his working-class roots) appeared to be the perfect
choice. His political connections meant that he had no trouble working
with the governors of New York and New England to recruit an entirely
new army of volunteers; he had already displayed his tact and administrative skills after he was sent to quell unrest in Maryland in 1861; and he
was ambitious for military glory. Lincoln gave Banks two objectives
when he asked him to go to New Orleans in November 1862. Militarily,
the general was to lead his army up the Mississippi, sweeping away Confederate resistance as he proceeded, until he joined forces with General
Grant at Vicksburg, some 225 miles to the north. Politically, he was to ensure the election of a new, pro-Northern legislature in Louisiana that
would enable the state to be readmitted to the Union.

Lincoln adopted the same pragmatic approach when General
McClernand asked permission to raise an army of volunteers from the
Midwest with the sole aim of attacking Vicksburg. The president believed that the political gains to the administration from McClernand's
project outweighed any potential annoyance that might be felt by the
army chiefs.

However, Lincoln underestimated how much Halleck and Grant—
neither of whom had any liking for enthusiastic amateurs, regardless of
their political usefulness—would resent the encroachment on their authority. Grant immediately made plans to reach Vicksburg before
McClernand. He ordered his trusted lieutenant William T. Sherman to
take 33,000 men and sail down the Mississippi to about fifteen miles
north of Vicksburg, where he was to leave the river and enter its tribu-
tary, the Yazoo. There was a bluff along a bend in the Yazoo that was easy
to scale and would allow Sherman to follow an overland route to the
town. Grant intended to march toward Vicksburg with the rest of the
army, luring the Confederates into a battle and thus leaving the way open
for Sherman. The operation began on December 20, 1862, as a fleet of

troopships, floating hospitals, and gunboats set sail from Memphis. But while Sherman was traveling downriver, Confederate raiders destroyed Grant's supply base, forcing him to turn back toward Tennessee. Sherman continued on his mission unaware that he would be facing the enemy alone.

The floating attack force came to a halt on Christmas Day, a few miles short of the proposed bluff. The sinking of a gunboat, USS *Cairo,* revealed the existence of underwater mines around an area of the Yazoo known as Chickasaw Bayou. Still ignorant of Grant's return to base, Sherman decided to alter his plan slightly and disembark at Chickasaw. There was more swamp than dry land here, but above the bluffs were the Walnut Hills and a road that led straight to Vicksburg. Sherman was not fazed by his first solo mission under Grant; he knew that the Walnut Hills were largely devoid of Confederate troops, and assumed that the taking of the bluffs would be achieved in a matter of hours.

But he waited four days before launching the attack, giving ample time for the Confederates to prepare a defense. Sherman's plan would now require the troops to cross a wide, open plain while being shot at from above, echoing Burnside's folly at Fredericksburg. In his memoirs, Sherman described his division commander Brigadier General George Morgan cheerfully receiving the order of battle with the words "General, in ten minutes after you give the signal I'll be on those hills."[5] Morgan's memory of the meeting on December 28 was rather different: he had tried to dissuade Sherman from the idea, warning him that a direct frontal attack would turn the gloomy swamps of the bayou into a mass grave. But Sherman was suffering from an excess of bravado, not uncommon among generals when given their first independent command. "Tell Morgan to give the signal for the assault," he ordered an aide. "We will lose five thousand men before we take Vicksburg, and may as well lose them here as anywhere."[6]

The battle commenced the following day, December 29. Morgan was furious with Sherman. The men to be lost were *his* men, the survivors of Cumberland Gap and the harrowing retreat through barren wilderness. Colonel John F. De Courcy was commanding Morgan's 3rd Brigade. His sense of duty prevented him from questioning his orders, but, knowing what was about to happen, he insisted on hearing the orders from Morgan himself: " 'General, do I understand that you are about to order an assault?' To which I replied, 'Yes; form your brigade,' " Morgan recalled many years later. "With an air of respectful protest he said: 'My poor brigade! Your order will be obeyed, General.' " De Courcy had also been changed by his experiences at Cumberland Gap; gone was the martinet, and in his place a commander whose loyalty to his regiment was reciprocated by the men.

General Morgan watched as the brigade charged through the marshes into the freezing water. "All the formations were broken," he wrote. "The assaulting forces were jammed together, and, with a yell of desperate determination, they rushed to the assault and were mowed down by a storm of shells, grape and canister, and minié-balls which swept our front like a hurricane of fire."[7] De Courcy raced back and forth as he tried to keep cohesion to the regiments. Some managed to cross the small river in front of the bluffs only to become trapped, others fell back, while a few remained on the near side. After the battle, Morgan and De Courcy were accused of failing to put more muscle into the attack, and Sherman was especially critical.[8] Yet a survivor from De Courcy's regiment, the 16th Ohio, wrote afterward that they were so close to the enemy that they could not retreat without being shot in the back, "so there was nothing left for us to do except to surrender."[9]

Sherman was pacing up and down at his headquarters when Morgan went to see him about collecting the wounded from the field. Unable to accept the extent of his failure, Sherman at first refused a flag of truce, condemning many of the wounded to death and the rest to capture. His initiation into independent command had cost the lives of 1,800 men, half of them from De Courcy's 3rd Brigade.[10]

Five days later, on January 3, De Courcy and his shattered regiments slunk into camp at Milliken's Bend. The army was divided between those who believed Morgan and De Courcy, who hotly asserted that they did move forward (and had the casualties to prove it), and those who accepted the account of Brigadier General John Thayer, who claimed that he had passed them with his soldiers while they cowered in the first rifle pits. The dispute would never be resolved; years later, Private Owen Hopkins of the 42nd Ohio Infantry wrote that De Courcy's brigade had followed behind his own, "but the boys pressed forward so vigorously in the daring onset that it was difficult to tell who was in the advance."[11]

The growing dissension in the camp was halted by the arrival of General McClernand; in his pocket was an order inveigled out of President Lincoln assigning all of Sherman's troops to his command. Ever mindful of his future political career, McClernand had a grand vision to implement. He informed a stunned but helpless Sherman—who had known nothing about McClernand's visit to Washington—that the force was going to be renamed the Army of the Mississippi, with Sherman and Morgan as the two corps leaders under him.

McClernand was not as inept as his contemporaries claimed.[12] He did at least recognize a superior soldier when he saw one and was willing to listen to Sherman. At the start of the Chickasaw expedition, a Confederate raid had captured one of the Federal steamers, which was taken to Fort Hindman, some forty miles up the Arkansas River, which fed into the Mississippi. Sherman now suggested to McClernand that they capture the fortification. It held no more than five thousand troops, but its strategic location enabled the Confederates to sneak onto the Mississippi at will, wreaking havoc against Federal ships before escaping back up the Arkansas. This was the time, urged Sherman, when they had 32,000 men at their disposal, to erase this Confederate menace and claim the Mississippi north of Vicksburg.

The Federals landed three miles below Fort Hindman on January 10, 1863. Morgan ordered De Courcy to hold his brigade at the rear, guarding the boats against an ambush, while the rest of the army began its assault. Admiral David Dixon Porter's gunboats hammered their target—which was not much more than a bastioned dugout—with continuous fire for twenty-four hours. When Sherman gave the order for an all-out attack on the following day, there was only halfhearted firing from the fort. The first advance brought the soldiers to within "handshaking distance of the enemy," according to Brigadier General Morgan, but "the fight continued with sullen stubbornness." Several times a white flag appeared only to be hastily hauled down. Realizing that a little more effort would tip the scales, Morgan sent orders for De Courcy to march his brigade into action. The troops emerged from the woods along the riverbank and charged, double file, toward the fort. Within minutes, another white flag appeared on the parapet, and this time it remained.[13]

The attack resulted in a thousand Federal casualties, almost ten times the number inflicted on the Confederates. But McClernand and Sherman had netted nearly five thousand prisoners, depriving Arkansas of a quarter of its troops. Although Grant initially blasted the operation as a monument to McClernand's vanity, after a few days' reflection he accepted that it had given a much-needed victory, both tactically and psychologically, to the army.

On January 17 a snowstorm turned the blackened terrain a dazzling white as the troopships steamed back down the Arkansas River to the Mississippi. The commanders took advantage of the quiet hours during the journey to compose their reports. In his letter to the secretary of the navy, Gideon Welles, Admiral Porter laid the entire blame for Sherman's failure at Chickasaw on De Courcy: "But for the want of nerve in the leader of a brigade, the army should have succeeded." Farther down the fleet, Brigadier General Morgan sat in his cabin writing precisely the opposite report: De Courcy's "gallant brigade lost 580 men at Chickasaw Bluffs," he observed, "and, with Blair's brigade, bore the brunt of that hard-fought but unsuccessful day. Col. John F. De Courcy deserves promotion."[14]

De Courcy tried to resign, but the request was denied. His longing to escape his present location was exacerbated by the wretchedness of camp conditions. Rain followed the snow in a gray downpour that continued day after day. The ground beneath the tents flooded, causing the camp's rudimentary latrines to overflow and poison the water wells.[15] The only dry land was occupied by hospitals and graves, which presented the men with the choice of sleeping among the dead or alongside the barely living. Yet Grant could not afford to have his army lie idle while they waited for the weather to cooperate. He had slapped down McClernand's ambitions, taking control of the Army of the Mississippi himself so he could merge it with the other Federal forces in the area. His best course of military action was politically impossible, since it would mean starting the campaign afresh and leaving the vicinity of Vicksburg. This the Northern public would have interpreted as another defeat. So Grant had the men begin several canal projects in the somewhat forlorn hope of engineering an alternative route to the town. The men were sent out with shovels and ordered to dig. Sherman thought the whole enterprise was "a pure waste of human effort."[16]

Every officer in De Courcy's regiment fell ill with swamp fever, and De Courcy himself lasted just two weeks before suffering a total collapse. The army doctor took pity on him and recommended his removal from the camp. The patient had suffered much "both in body and mind," he wrote on February 14, 1863, making him prey to "typho-malarial fever." A few days later, De Courcy joined a wagon train heading east. He would not see his old regiment for many months. His destination was Cincinnati, Ohio, seven hundred miles from Vicksburg, and the long journey was almost as harrowing as the life he left behind. By the time De Courcy was examined by another doctor on March 14, his body had become almost skeletal in appearance. He was immediately placed on sick leave and declared unfit for duty for sixty days.

At the War Department in Washington, reports of Grant's futile engineering works caused alarm, especially since there were rumors that the general was drinking again. Lincoln had already been forced to step in and countermand an order by Grant that threatened to have serious political repercussions: General Order No. 11, which Grant issued in late December, had called for the arrest and expulsion of all Jews in the parts of Mississippi and Tennessee under Union control.* Lincoln revoked the order two weeks later, leaving it to General Halleck to explain to Grant about the wisdom of proscribing "an entire religious class, some of whom are fighting in our ranks." But the reversal was too late for local Jewish communities, including thirty families in Paducah, Kentucky, who were driven from their homes and dumped into riverboats bound for Ohio.[17]

Lincoln and his secretary of war, Edwin Stanton, decided to send Charles A. Dana, a former journalist and troubleshooter for the War Department, to Grant's headquarters. The reason given was the department's concern about inefficiencies in the paymaster service, but in reality Dana's mission was to be the eyes and ears of the administration. There were too many calls in Washington for Grant's removal for Lincoln to do nothing.

The Vicksburg campaign had assumed even greater importance since the Battle of Murfreesboro in central Tennessee on New Year's Day. U.S. general William Rosecrans and Confederate general Braxton Bragg had fought each other to a stalemate. Each had lost a third of his army, putting both out of action for many months; crucially, neither general would be able to send reinforcements to Vicksburg. When Dana reached the main army camp at Milliken's Bend, just above Vicksburg, Grant and his staff chose the wise course of bringing him into the military family. Dana was allowed full access to everything that was happening in the

---

* Grant apparently believed that "Jewish peddlers" were to blame for the army's supply problems.

Army of the Tennessee, and soon came to admire Grant as a resourceful and determined leader.

Francis Lawley also visited the Vicksburg area during the great digging operations. Naturally, he did not go near Grant's headquarters, and so he had no opportunity to take the measure of the man who was staking his reputation and career on Vicksburg's capture. In Lawley's opinion, the town was impregnable. "The swollen state of the river, the dreary wastes of oozy swamp and fen," he wrote for *The Times*, were more powerful weapons "than sword or bullet." Through his telescope he could see the parlous state of the soldiers in the Federal camps.[18] Lawley departed for Atlanta confident that Grant would never succeed.

———

General Banks's army in New Orleans—which he called the XIX Corps—consisted of fifty-six regiments, many of them less than four months old and totally ignorant of military life. One of the newest regiments was the 133rd New York Infantry Volunteers, also known as the 2nd Metropolitan Guard because the recruits were mostly New York policemen—tough working-class men whose fighting skills had been honed against the feral gangs that terrorized lower Manhattan. The 133rd were bemused and dismayed to have a British Army officer as their commander.

Colonel L.D.H. Currie, as he liked to style himself, was the young officer whom William Howard Russell had referred to in his diary as laughing ruefully at the total lack of military discipline in McClellan's army. The thirty-one-year-old career soldier and veteran of the Crimea* had been sent to Brigadier General W. F. "Baldy" Smith's division, where he quickly showed himself to be far too useful to be relegated to administrative work. By the beginning of 1862, Currie was taking part, if not the lead, in cavalry expeditions against Confederate pickets in northern

---

* During the Crimean War, the 19th Regiment of Foot was sent to the evocatively named Calamity Bay, where it took part in the bungled fight against the Russians for the Alma Heights. Currie was brought down by a bullet that tore a large hole through his left foot. He was rescued from the field, conscious, and therefore able to prevent the regimental surgeon from amputating his foot. For several months Currie lay festering in the notorious Scutari hospital until he was rescued by his brother, who brought him home on a stretcher. Currie made it his mission to walk again. Through sheer force of will he dragged himself on crutches to his medal ceremony at Buckingham Palace on May 19, 1855. His ashen countenance so alarmed Queen Victoria that she asked to be kept informed of his recovery.

Virginia.[19] When McClellan was threatening Richmond in June, Currie's unflappability stood him in good stead after his horse was killed under him. By July there was a groundswell of support for giving Currie a regiment of his own. Four generals, including McClellan, sent letters on his behalf. "I believe him capable of filling any military position which may be assigned to him," wrote Major General William B. Franklin.[20]

Whether Currie was capable of commanding the unruly 133rd remained to be seen. Already furious at having been assigned to a foreigner, the regiment saw nothing positive about being in New Orleans. The women still turned their backs and scowled at the slightest provocation. The male inhabitants seemed to divide into two distinct species: those who wished to fleece them and those who were waiting for an opportunity to kill them. The city was like a poisonous flower: beautiful to behold but dangerous to touch. General Butler had cut down the murder rate, but every other vice had been allowed to flourish. General Banks was appalled to discover that many of the stories that had reached him were true. Federal officers treated private property in the Crescent City as theirs for the taking. A family might receive an eviction notice with orders to move out the same day, taking nothing except clothes and necessities. The occupier would move in the following day, and the plundering would begin.

The Scotsman William Watson observed Banks's attempt to impose civic order on the city and almost felt sorry for him. The Northerner was, wrote Watson, "altogether too mild a man to grapple with the state of things then existing in New Orleans."[21] "Everybody connected with the government has been employed in stealing," a horrified Banks wrote to his wife in mid-January. "Sugar, silver plate, horses, carriages, everything they could lay their hands on." He also discovered that nothing happened without a bribe. Among his first directives was an order for all officers to leave civilian accommodation and return to army quarters.[22] Mary Sophia Hill had recently returned to New Orleans carrying hundreds of messages and letters for the marooned families of Confederate soldiers, and was similarly appalled by the moral degradation that had spread through the city.

The 133rd was sent north to Baton Rouge, where Currie did his best to continue training the men, teaching them the rudiments of drill. By the end of January he was just beginning to make some headway when he learned that the War Department had received serious allegations against him. A former member of the regiment had been trying to persuade his old colleagues to make a joint protest against Currie. When he failed to whip up enough support, he went ahead on his own, concocting an absurd list of crimes allegedly committed by the colonel. Currie knew he would be exonerated if the authorities questioned his fellow officers, but he recoiled at the thought of an investigation. It would, he was sure, undermine his hard-won authority. Moreover, he found the whole affair deeply offensive. "I have been engaged in a humble way, but to the best of my ability in suppressing rebellion, and maintaining constitutional government, which is scarcely compatible with such charges," he wrote to his superiors; "if, after a life of fourteen years of active employment in a profession of honour, my character requires defence, it is not worthy of it." They agreed. On February 4, 1863, Currie's commander declared that no attention should be paid to the allegations.[23]

Currie's exoneration was followed by an order to lead a scouting expedition through the bayous west of Baton Rouge. After Vicksburg, the Mississippi River meandered for about 150 miles until it reached another deep bend carved into eighty-foot-high bluffs. Here the little town of Port Hudson was perched on top of the eastern bank, the perfect site for heavy artillery to bombard enemy ships as they slowed down to navigate the sharp turn. The bastion not only kept the Federal army bottled up between New Orleans and Baton Rouge, it also protected the Confederates' chief supply route west of the Mississippi. The romantically named Red River, so called for the rust-colored clay along its northern banks, flowed from the corner of northern Texas all the way down and across Louisiana, finally emptying into the Mississippi just above Port Hudson. It passed through some of the most fertile regions of the Confederacy. If Banks could take Port Hudson, he would also have the Red River, its grains and cattle, and, most important of all, its rich cotton plantations.

Since Banks could not approach Port Hudson from the Mississippi, he wondered if he could bypass the area altogether by finding a way through the mazelike bayous and lesser tributaries that fed the river. Currie's regiment was sent on a two-week trek through densely wooded swamps and across alligator-infested rivers. They were prey not only to the wildlife but also to local Confederates who lay in wait for them. One private was killed and two others were snatched during an ambush. The men returned at the end of February, nervous and physical wrecks. They were "used up," in Currie's words: "In my opinion the country is impracticable for all arms of the service."[24]

There was no alternative but to face Port Hudson's batteries. General Banks invited his naval counterpart, Admiral Farragut, to his headquarters at the palatial St. Charles Hotel to discuss a joint assault. The general knew that his troops were no match for a seasoned Confederate army, but they could provide cover for Farragut's warships. Banks would attack Port Hudson from the land, hopefully causing enough confusion to allow the navy to steam up the river. The great question hung on Banks's ability to deliver a solid enough diversion.[25]

Just how green some of his troops were had been demonstrated on February 20 when a small detachment sent to the levee to oversee the departure of Confederate prisoners bound for Baton Rouge was responsible for a disgraceful incident. As word spread through the city that rebel officers were being escorted onto steamboats, thousands of well-wishers, most of them women and children, ran down to see them off. Mary Sophia Hill was among them. Weeping and cheering, they waved red handkerchiefs in mass defiance of the order against displays of Confederate sympathy. The Union troops soon lost control of the crowd, which heaved and swayed with emotion. Panicking, the Federal officer in charge sent an urgent request for more troops, who arrived with bayonets fixed. They came "at a canter," recalled Mary. "The guns were rammed and pointed at this helpless mass of weakness." The women were literally beaten back from the levee. "As I never yet ran from an enemy," she continued, "but always faced them, I walked backwards, with others, to some warehouses, where we were again chased by Federal officials in uniform."[26]

No one was killed, but there were cuts and broken bones; and with every retelling the officers became more brutal and the danger more desperate. Once again the Northern occupiers had succeeded in presenting themselves in the worst light. Southern newspapers sarcastically labeled the affair *"la bataille des mouchoirs"* (the battle of the handkerchiefs). Banks's reputation plunged: "Some say Banks never saw a battle, as he was always running; but he did, he won this, which is well remembered," wrote Mary scornfully.[27]

The navy was also contributing its share of frustration and disappointment to Lincoln. On January 11, 1863, CSS *Alabama* attacked the U.S.

"Scene on the Levee at New Orleans on the Departure of the Paroled Rebel Prisoners," February 1863.

blockade at Galveston, Texas. Once a forsaken collection of wooden buildings along a dreary sandbar that stretched for twenty-seven miles, Galveston had become a boomtown in recent years, sporting large modern warehouses and New Orleans–style mansions. Profits from shipping cotton—three-quarters of Texas's produce passed through the seaport—had paid for colonnades of palm trees and lush oleanders to line streets that had formerly been mud tracks in the grass. The U.S. Navy had begun blockading Galveston in July 1861, and a Federal force had briefly held the port until Confederate general John Magruder (nicknamed "Prince John" by his enemies on account of his flashy behavior in front of ladies) recaptured the town on New Year's Day 1863. Reinforcements to the naval blockade had just arrived when Captain Raphael Semmes and the *Alabama* cautiously approached the Union fleet.

In only six months the *Alabama* had become the most famous ship afloat. The entire English-speaking world knew her history, beginning with her audacious escape from under the noses of the British authorities. In addition to her aura of daring, she was beautiful to behold. The fifty-four-year-old Semmes had loved the *Alabama* from the moment he first saw her. During his thirty-seven years in the navy, he had never sailed on such a well-crafted vessel. "Her model was of the most perfect symmetry," he wrote, "and she sat upon the water with the lightness and grace of a swan."[28] The Confederate navy agent James Bulloch had asked Lairds to build him a ship that could survive the harshest of conditions for months on end. He knew that the *Alabama* would never have a home port or a regular source of supply.[29] The result was a 230-foot vessel with three masts, built for roving and raiding, capable of sail and steam power, equipped with two engines, a liftable screw propeller, and eight powerful guns. Her cabins could comfortably accommodate 24 officers and a crew of 120.

Semmes had been in command of CSS *Sumter* until the vessel required such extensive repairs that in the summer of 1862 he was forced to sell her in Gibraltar. When he and his second in command, Lieutenant John Kell, arrived in England, Bulloch realized that they were the obvious choice to take command of the *Alabama*. The new crew soon nicknamed their captain "Old Beeswax" on account of his highly waxed mustache. The sharpened tips—which looked both debonair and dangerous—were symbolic of the divergent nature of his character: Semmes was always perfectly correct and mild-mannered in his demeanor, but behind the mask was a stern and relentless fighter. He had strong literary and intellectual tastes, and, in contrast to many of his peers in the navy, he had no trouble adapting to home life when on furlough. During the long gaps between his deployments at sea, Semmes had established his own law practice. He was also a gifted writer, having published two well-received memoirs of his experiences during the Mexican War.

Despite frequent buffetings from rough weather and unruly sailors, Semmes soon imposed his will on the ship. The seamen were almost all British, "picked up, promiscuously," wrote Semmes, "about the streets of Liverpool . . . they looked as little like the crew of a man-of-war, as one can well conceive. Still, there was some *physique* among these fellows, and soap, and water, and clean shirts would make a wonderful difference in appearance."[30] The officers, on the other hand, were mostly Southerners, the notable exceptions being the master's mate, twenty-one-year-old George Townley Fullam from Hull, and the assistant surgeon, David Herbert Llewellyn, a vicar's son who had recently completed his residency at Charing Cross hospital.[31] Semmes considered the *Alabama* to be a ship of war rather than a privateer, and he demanded navy-style obedience from the men. "My code was like that of the Medes and Persians—it was never relaxed," he wrote. "I had around me a staff of excellent officers, who always wore their side arms, and pistols, when on duty, and from this time onward we never had any trouble about keeping the most desperate and turbulent characters in subjection."[32] The highest wages of any fleet and the promise of fantastic amounts of prize money also helped to maintain discipline.

The *Alabama* scored its first capture on September 5, an unarmed whaler, which was raided for supplies and then set afire. The merchant crew was allowed to go ashore in its whaleboats. Those men were lucky; other crews were held prisoner belowdecks until Semmes could unload them at a neutral port. By Christmas, the *Alabama* had successfully pounced on ten U.S. ships.[33] One capture often led to another, since Semmes would use the information gleaned from logbooks and timetables to chase after sister ships. But at Galveston, Semmes was offered a different opportunity—to prove to the world that the *Alabama* was capable of much more than merely preying on civilian ships. For the first time, she was meeting adversaries of her own class.[34]

As soon as Semmes caught sight of the five blockading ships in front of Galveston, he ordered the *Alabama* to retreat slowly, hoping to entice one of the vessels into a chase. The Federal captain of the *Hatteras* took the bait, believing that he had caught a blockade runner in the act, and hardly noticed that Galveston was becoming smaller and smaller in the distance. "At length," recounted Semmes, "when I judged that I had drawn the stranger out about 20 miles from his fleet, I furled my sails, beat to quarters, prepared my ship for action, and wheeled to meet him."[35] The ships faced each other nose to nose, a mere hundred yards apart and yet only partially visible in the clear, moonless night. Using a bullhorn, the warship challenged first, ordering the unknown vessel to identify herself. Semmes cheekily shouted back, "This is her Britannic Majesty's steamer *Petrel*." There followed an awkward pause while the captain of the *Hatteras* pondered his next move. He had no wish to provoke the Royal Navy, but there was something suspicious about the ship floating before him. After some rapid calculation of consequences, he announced he was sending over a boarding party. Semmes called back that he was delighted, thus buying the *Alabama* a few precious minutes to load her guns. They heard orders being shouted and the creaking sound of a boat being lowered into the water. This was the signal for First Lieutenant Kell to cry out, "This is the Confederate States Steamer *Alabama*!" followed by a broadside from the cannons. The captain of the *Hatteras* quickly returned fire. Each time the *Alabama* landed a shell on her adversary, one of the sailors was heard to shout, "That's from the 'scum of England'!"[36] In less than fifteen minutes the *Hatteras* was completely disabled and starting to sink. The survivors from the warship were picked up and held in the brig until the *Alabama* docked at Port Royal in Jamaica on January 20.

If that were not enough to shake the U.S. Navy's morale, a week later the blockading fleet at Mobile Bay in Alabama failed to stop the midnight escape of the infamous CSS *Florida,* the ship originally known as the *Oreto.* After her hurried exit from Liverpool in March 1862, the vessel had suffered one setback after another. The British authorities in Nassau detained her for nearly four months, although the courts there finally determined that she was not in defiance of the Foreign Enlistment Act. But once free, Captain Maffitt lost half his crew to yellow fever, including his own stepson. Even when the *Florida* eventually sailed into Mobile in September, she continued to be dogged by misfortune. It took three months to complete the repairs to her damaged hull. Finally, on January 17, 1863, nine months after leaving Liverpool, the *Florida* began its long-delayed career as a Confederate commerce raider. Two days later, Captain Maffitt captured his first prize, a cargo ship bound for New York.

The Confederate gains at sea were taking place at a sensitive time for Anglo-U.S. relations. For the past two months, a group of twelve New York businessmen calling themselves the New York International Relief Committee had been soliciting donations for Lancashire's suffering cotton workers.[37] On January 9, the *George Griswold* set sail carrying a large cargo of provisions that included 13,000 barrels of flour and 500 bushels of corn, all paid for by the committee. The ship was bedecked with symbols of Anglo-American friendship, including the flags and pennants of the two nations. As the *Griswold* was towed out of New York Harbor, she received salutes from the British vessels that had gathered to see her off. Four more ships soon followed the *Griswold;* the irony that they could be captured and destroyed by the *Alabama* was not lost on the Northern press, nor on Seward.*[38]

The secretary of state used the public's resentment over the *Alabama* and the *Florida* to his advantage. Over the New Year, he had met with Senator James Grimes, chairman of the Naval Affairs Committee, and persuaded him to propose an armed response against Britain. There was nothing anti-British in Seward's motives. His only concern was how to shore up his weak position among Republicans; with any luck, Sumner would oppose Grimes's measures and look like an apologist for England, costing him popularity in the press. After the Galveston attack by CSS *Alabama*, Grimes announced that he was reviving the bill to allow President Lincoln to issue letters of marque. Arming civilian privateers was necessary, he argued, because the Confederates were building their own fleet in England. Lincoln should have the power "to let slip the dogs of war" against them.[39]

As Seward had hoped, Charles Sumner could not resist attacking such a poorly conceived idea. "This revival of Letters of Marque is [Seward's] work. I have protested to the President against their issue, but I fear that I shall not entirely succeed," he complained to John Bright. "There is not a Senator—not one—who is [Seward's] friend politically,

---

* Lord Lyons naturally took heart from the *Griswold*, perhaps far too much. The ship was proof, he told Russell, that Americans liked to complain about Britain, but behind the posturing "there lies a deeper and more enduring feeling of good will and kindly affection, which will be a lasting bond of feeling between the two kindred nations."

the larger part are positively, and some even bitterly against him. . . . In the House of Reps., he has no friends; nor among his colleagues of the cabinet." Lord Lyons was crestfallen once he realized that Seward had resorted to the same anti-British line that had made the first year of the war so acrimonious and difficult. "It looks like a return to the old bluster," he wrote sadly. "Whether he does it to recover his position with the Radical party and with the people at large . . . or . . . he really thinks he can frighten England and France with his privateers, I can not say. He is more cordial than ever with me personally, and I do my best to prevent his getting into hot water either with France or with me."[40]

Sumner was speaking the truth, however, when he warned Bright that the Confederate navy program had to be stopped. "The feeling towards England runs high and I hear it constantly said that war is inevitable unless those ships now building are kept from preying on our commerce."[41] Northern newspapers were blaming the *Alabama* and the *Florida* for the precipitous decline of U.S. shipping (rather than the lack of Northern investment in the merchant marine).[42] "England will be hated for it, till the last American now on the stage goes to his grave," threatened the *New York Times*.[43]

SEVENTEEN

"The Tinsel Has Worn Off"

*Democrats versus Republicans—Burnside in the Virginia mud—Arrival of
General Hooker—Mosby's Raid—A crisis of conscience—Volunteering for
the South—An encounter with Stonewall Jackson*

Lincoln's troubles made the Democrats bolder in their denunciation
of Republican "fanaticism" for persisting with the war. "You have not
conquered the South," thundered Clement Vallandigham in the House
on January 14, 1863. "You never will."[1] The Ohio congressman and
leader of the Peace Democrats had been unseated by the Republicans in
the congressional elections, and this was his farewell speech. Though far
from being an Anglophile, Vallandigham was deliberately echoing the
Earl of Chatham's warning to the House of Commons during the American War of Independence: "My Lords, you cannot conquer America!"
Although Vallandigham had been defeated in the violent and expensive
contest, he was confident that his opposition to the war—and to Lincoln's Emancipation Proclamation—would win him the governorship of
Ohio in ten months' time. "Sir," he concluded, "there is fifty-fold less of
anti-slavery sentiment to-day in the West than there was two years ago;
and if this war be continued, there will be still less a year hence."[*]

---

[*] Vallandigham reveled in being called a "Copperhead," a term used by the Republicans to imply that the Peace Democrats were like snakes, ready to strike on behalf
of the South without warning—and by the Democrats themselves to symbolize
their commitment to freedom and states' rights, since copper pennies bore the
word "liberty."

Vallandigham's "make peace now" speech was received by a public still trying to comprehend the staggering death toll from Fredericksburg, Chickasaw Bluffs, and Murfreesboro. Discontent with the war, wrote Lyons on February 10, "is undoubtedly increasing, and if we have no success before the Spring . . . it will be impossible to keep up the numbers of the Army."* One hundred and thirty regiments were about to reach the end of their term of enlistment, George Herbert's among them. "I am waiting as impatiently as you can for 4th of May," he wrote to his mother. Like most of his comrades, he had no intention of reenlisting: "The tinsel has worn off the thing," he admitted.[2] Congress, aware that it faced a potentially crippling manpower shortage, was preparing a bill for a national draft.

The recent spate of defeats was not the only reason for the lack of enthusiasm for volunteering. The War Department's mishandling of wounded soldiers had become a national scandal. Dr. Mayo never saw the gross abuses of the system, since he was caring for officers who were well enough to recuperate in private establishments, but another English doctor, twenty-five-year-old Charles Culverwell, was a reluctant witness to the neglect suffered by soldiers who were sent to the convalescent hospitals.[3] Ironically, Culverwell had never wanted to be a doctor. He was addicted to the theater, but his father had pleaded and "reasoned with me, until at last he suggested a compromise. 'Get your diplomas; get a means of livelihood at your fingers' ends, and then you may do whatever you like.' "[4] Culverwell dutifully qualified, married in 1860, became a father himself, and set out to support his family as a doctor by day while acting at night under the stage name Charles Wyndham. The public was unconvinced by either role. "No patient darkened my door," he wrote, and the theater company went bankrupt in August 1862. There are conflicting accounts as to why he enlisted as a surgeon in the Federal army.[5] But regardless of whether he went freely or was pushed by his

---

* Dr. Mayo was shocked when he visited Congress. "In both houses," he wrote, "the occupation of members seemed to consist of calling each other traitors." He was a witness to some of the least edifying scenes in Senate history. On January 27, 1863, Senator Willard Saulsbury of Delaware made his infamous harangue from the Senate floor. He was, recorded the doctor, "in a state of hopeless drunkenness, and insisted on making a speech, and when rebuked by the chairman and threatened with removal by the sergeant-at-arms, drew and cocked his revolver, and threatened to shoot any body who interfered with him." The standoff continued for some time, until Saulsbury was persuaded to leave.

family, Culverwell later claimed that he relished the prospect of adventure: "I was bound for America, the land of freedom where equality was adored, favoritism abhorred. . . . I was convinced that on my arrival there I had only to hold up my little finger and every State in the Union would rush at me with a commission." He arrived in America in October 1862 with just $45. The rest of the family's savings was left with his wife, Emma, who remained in London, pregnant with their second child. They had agreed she would come out as soon as he was financially secure.

The plan went awry from the beginning. Culverwell had arrived without letters of introduction; they were offered to him, including one to General Nathaniel Banks, but he had turned them down, believing they would not be needed in the egalitarian New World. Not knowing what else to do, Culverwell parked himself in the public sitting room at Willard's Hotel and placed his illustrated book on surgery on his knees. He sat there reading for two days, hoping that someone would ask him if he was a doctor. At the end of the second day he noticed an elderly gentleman being approached by autograph seekers. He recognized the face but could not recall the name; however, this was enough to give him courage. His heart beating with excitement, Culverwell went up to him and asked for help. The stranger politely declined. Not knowing what else to do, Culverwell returned to the public room the following day. This time, the elderly gentleman sought his eye and asked him:

> "How was it you were so foolish to come to America without letters? They are absolutely indispensable here." I explained to him that I was stupid enough to believe America different from other countries, and the mere fact of introductions being used in Europe stamped them as superfluous here. I told him that a letter to General Banks which had been offered to me, I had even refused to wait for, as it had come from Paris. "I know General Banks," he replied; "I'll give you a letter to him if you like, but I shall be bound to say I know nothing about you." "So long as I am able to get to him," I said, "I should ask for nothing more."[6]

Culverwell discovered that the kind stranger was none other than the impresario P. T. Barnum. His letter opened the way to an appointment as acting assistant surgeon, a position that allowed the holder to resign and

rejoin at will. But Barnum's influence evidently had its limits: Dr. Culverwell was sent to one of the "contraband camps" near Alexandria, the
most unpopular posting in the medical corps. He lasted two weeks in the
pestilential and stinking shantytown that contained the South's runaway
slaves.* His request for a transfer resulted in the army's second most unpopular assignment: duty at Camp Convalescent, Fort Ellsworth, known
locally as "Camp Misery," where wounded soldiers too sick to be discharged instead died of neglect. "We don't get any vegetables at all," wrote
an inmate of Camp Convalescent. "We are in tents, five in each tent, no
beds.... We don't get our cooking done ... it is one of the meanest
places I have come across.... They need not talk of the misery of the
rebels, let them come down here and it will open their eyes."[7] Culverwell
lasted for two months there before he could stand it no longer and again
asked to be transferred. This time the authorities were merciful, and on
January 20, 1863, he was sent to Jefferson Barracks in St. Louis, Missouri,
one of the largest military hospitals outside Washington.

———

It was not only the sick who suffered deprivations. Theft and bureaucratic incompetence were so widespread throughout the army that the
soldiers were often short of basic supplies such as fuel, blankets, and
fresh food. Lorenzo D. Sargent, the new colonel of Charles Francis
Adams, Jr.'s regiment, the 1st Massachusetts Cavalry, exemplified one of
the criticisms made by British military observers of the Northern system
of command: he fraternized with the lower ranks as a way of showing
solidarity with the men, but failed to concern himself with their physical
or moral welfare. "He considers himself a tactician and yet he could not
drill a corporal's guard without making ludicrous blunders," Charles
Francis Jr. wrote to his family. "His mistakes on the drill ground, his the-
ories of war and his absurdities in camp are ... the laughing stock of the
regiment.... He has already cost us the best officers in our regiment,
and we all fear that he will ultimately ruin it."[8]

Charles Francis Jr.'s frustration with the lack of accountability in the
army was a common complaint among the soldiers; recruits were desert-

* It was General Butler who invented the term "contraband." He was the commandant of Fortress Monroe in 1861 when three runaway slaves arrived asking for sanctuary. When their former Southern masters requested their return, Butler refused,
arguing that slaves were "contraband of war," since the South was using them as
"tools" to sustain the war effort. The term stuck.

ing in Virginia at the rate of a hundred a day. There were frequent fights and disturbances in the camps. Percy Wyndham's cavalry brigade was in a state of uproar after he gave the colonel of one of his regiments a ferocious beating and threatening to shoot him if he continued to disobey orders. The officers in the brigade retaliated by petitioning the War Department for the right to wear sidearms in his presence. Disgusted with his men and with the failure of leadership from above, Sir Percy resigned his command on January 18, 1863.[9] But General Heintzelman considered his skills and experience too precious to lose. "Colonel Wyndham is such an excellent Cavalry officer when under the orders of a suitable commander and has behaved so gallantly on frequent occasions," he wrote, "that I would most reluctantly see his resignation accepted. His service with the main army in the front would I am satisfied be eminently valuable."[10] The army accepted his suggestion of returning Wyndham to the 1st New Jersey Cavalry, where he was still liked and admired.

General Burnside knew that his generals were conspiring against him and he had to act swiftly before his army disintegrated. To save his command and the army's morale, he decided to challenge the Confederates again, but from a different vantage point several miles north of Fredericksburg. George Herbert predicted disaster. Yet the weather seemed to favor the general, remaining cold and dry while the troops packed their belongings and tore down the camps. In the predawn hours of January 20, the men stood in smart rows with three days' rations in their packs, ready to march across the Rappahannock. However, by midafternoon they felt the first spots of rain on their heads; by late evening they were struggling against a steady downpour. "In two hours the roads were impassable," wrote Herbert.[11]

George Herbert watched as mules sank up to their necks in mud. Every few yards, the New York Zouaves had to dig themselves out and then attempt to free the artillery, which was mired in three or more feet of icy sludge. Ebenezer Wells of the 79th Highlanders watched helplessly as a loaded wagon slid off a cliff, pulling six horses to their death. "We let it go for it was bitter cold," he recalled. The men concentrated on survival: "I was nearly frozen to death, if I had have given way to sleep which seemed to almost overpower me I never should have felt any more pain. I cut my thumb thinking it would cause circulation," he wrote. "I felt as though I could cry aloud in despair." To survive, Wells lay down next to his horse, Bill, who had been trained to perform circus tricks, "putting my feet between his hind legs, my body against his and my face in his breast."[12]

Burnside admitted defeat after forty-eight hours and ordered his men to return to their original campsites. Dubbed the "Mud March" by the army and the press, this was Burnside's final debacle as commander of the Army of the Potomac. By January 27, the general and a few loyal staff members were on a train bound for New York. General "Fighting Joe" Hooker (a nickname that would return to haunt him) took Burnside's place. Hooker's intrigues against Burnside had been notorious throughout the army. When George Herbert learned the news, he put the promotion down to "right smart bobbery" and thought his "appointment will create a great disturbance."[13] Charles Francis Adams, Jr., told his brother Henry that Lincoln had created more problems for himself by selecting a man "who has not the confidence of the army."[14]

Hooker was a heavy drinker, and although his name did not inspire the slang term for prostitute, as is popularly believed, his headquarters often resembled a saloon bar in the worst part of town. The qualities that had caught Lincoln's attention were his energy and ambition, on display as soon as he took control of the Army of the Potomac. On February 5, the soldiers learned that they were being divided into eight numbered corps, each with its own badge and insignia. Hooker also created a separate cavalry corps under General George Stoneman, just as Lee had done with Jeb Stuart. In one stroke Hooker eliminated the muddles and regimental rivalries that had driven Percy Wyndham into an armed standoff against his fellow officers. Charles Francis Adams, Jr., revised his earlier opinion, writing happily, "At last we are coming up and winning that place in public estimation which we have always felt belonged to us of right."[15]

Dr. Mayo visited the Army of the Potomac during Hooker's reorganization. He had been promoted from assistant to staff surgeon, and now served on the three-member board that certified volunteer surgeons. Mayo was interested to see how Hooker was managing the health of the soldiers. "I was here able to see how the wheels of the medical department of an army of more than a hundred thousand men are kept in motion by their chief director, Dr. Letterman—an able manager, if ever an army had one." With Hooker's support, Dr. Jonathan Letterman instigated a new, healthier regime. The railway line was repaired and supplies were being brought quickly and efficiently to the front. "The army was now therefore pretty comfortable," wrote Mayo.

> All had tents, or shelter of some kind, and plenty of rations. . . . Almost all had built themselves fireplaces and chimneys . . . and had plenty of fuel to keep themselves warm. In fact, as camp life goes, there was little to complain of but the mud, which was certainly some of the dirtiest (always excepting that of Washington), brownest, deepest, stickiest, and most ubiquitous that can be conceived.[16]

He could not say the same for the inhabitants of Fredericksburg, who were surviving on twice-weekly handouts of food. Mayo watched as huddled figures, including children, sat for hours in the snow on the banks of the river, a fishing rod in one hand and a bucket in the other. Before Mayo returned to Washington, he paid a visit to the Irish Brigade. So many of its officers had passed through his care after Fredericksburg that he felt a special affection for the men. It was melancholy for him to walk through the half-empty camp. Fewer than 600 of the 1,100 remained; yet they were, he wrote in astonishment, "as jovial and hospitable as ever." The marked lack of bitterness among the brigade even extended to its wounded.*

————

Aside from the downpours and sticky sludge, the chief impediments to Hooker's massive reorganization were the Confederate raids on outlying camps. They occurred without warning, and though little was taken except for a few wagons or an unlucky soldier on picket duty, the effect on Federal morale was severe. Hooker had been in command for less than a week when, on January 29, 1863, a small force led by one of the most effective Confederate outfits—John Singleton Mosby and his Partisan Rangers—pounced on the Federal pickets guarding Percy Wyndham's

---

* These included former employees from the Irish estate of William Gregory, the leading Confederate sympathizer in Parliament. Gregory's gamekeeper, Michael Conolly, had followed his family to America and volunteered for the North. His action cost him his arm at Fredericksburg. Several of Conolly's cousins were also wounded, but his two brothers had come out of the battle unscathed. "As for my part," Conolly wrote to Gregory from his hospital bed, "I will not be able to join the company again."

base around Fairfax Court House. Nine horses and their riders were captured. Wyndham ran to his horse and marshaled two hundred cavalrymen to chase after Mosby, but the raiders had vanished into the darkness. The raids against the Federals had made Mosby a hero among Virginians, which surprised everyone who had known him before the war. A lawyer by profession, he was small and thin, slightly hunched, and very plain with strawlike hair and a narrow hatchet face. He looked more like nineteen than his real age of thirty, but his unprepossessing exterior belied a superior ability to infiltrate enemy lines and cause mayhem. His surprise attacks were forcing Federal authorities to divert large numbers of troops into wasteful defensive operations.

On the evening of March 8, Mosby and twenty-nine volunteers set off toward Fairfax Court House. He had devised a plan to sneak into Wyndham's headquarters and kidnap him from his bed. Mosby had not told the men what he aimed to do, since he reasoned that they would undoubtedly have refused so suicidal a mission. It was a frosty, pitch-black night, which helped the marauders slip past Federal pickets. Mosby knew exactly where to find the gaps in the line. "We passed along close by the camp-fires, but the sentinels took us for a scouting party of their cavalry," he wrote. "I had felt very cold in the early part of the night, but my blood grew warmer as I got farther in the lines, and the chill passed away. I had no reputation to lose by failure but much to gain by success." It was midnight when they reached the village of Fairfax. Mosby's men were shocked when they realized where they were, but not more so than the Federal guards, who at first refused to believe what was happening.[17]

Mosby quickly organized his men into raiding parties; one to gather the prisoners, the other to collect the horses. The telegraph lines were cut and the operator subdued. The Confederates moved stealthily from house to house, rousing officers from their beds with the warning that they would be shot if they made a noise. Mosby waited impatiently for Wyndham to appear. "But for once fortune had been propitious to him," recalled Mosby. Wyndham had taken the train to Washington that afternoon. The raid on his house produced only two sleepy staff officers and Wyndham's uniform, which Mosby decided to keep as a trophy. As he prepared to leave with his dumbfounded prisoners, who outnumbered the Confederates four to one, Mosby was told that Brigadier General Edwin Stoughton was billeted in the town.[18]

The twenty-five-year-old Stoughton was as famous for his unlikely promotion as he was for his high living. He should not have been in Fairfax at all, since his brigade was five miles away, but the general liked his independence. The two-story brick house that served as his headquarters was never empty or silent. Unable to resist the challenge, Mosby tricked his way inside by claiming to have a dispatch from the 5th New York Cavalry. He then grabbed the surprised Union officer, "whispered my name in his ear, and told him to take me to General Stoughton's room. Resistance was useless and he obeyed." Stoughton was sleeping off a rowdy night. Mosby woke him by spanking his bottom. "He asked in an indignant tone what all this meant. I told him that he was a prisoner, and that he must get up quickly and dress. I then asked him if he had ever heard of 'Mosby,' and he said he had. 'I am Mosby,' I said." Stoughton intrigued his captor by taking such inordinate care in getting dressed that one of the Confederates standing guard politely handed him his watch after he left it on the bureau.[19]

Sir Percy Wyndham was humiliated. It hardly mattered that he was in Washington at the time. He felt unable to face his men again. For three weeks he hid himself away, ignoring orders to return to his regiment, the 1st New Jersey Cavalry. A final order, underlined "commendatory," roused him from his funk. Still preoccupied with thoughts of revenge, Wyndham sought permission to form his own regiment of ranger scouts. When his request was denied, he asked for and obtained a leave of absence.

Abraham Lincoln apparently laughed when he heard about Stoughton's capture, joking, "I can make a better general in five minutes, but the horses cost one hundred and twenty-five dollars apiece."[20] Yet behind the ludicrous picture of a general being taken from his own bed was the worrying possibility that anyone could be Mosby's next victim. The military authorities ordered a thorough review of Washington's defenses. New men were put in command; the outposts were strengthened and pulled closer together; a new system of passwords was introduced. Just in case Mosby had designs on the capital, troops guarding the Chain Bridge, the chief bridge linking Washington with Virginia, were ordered to remove the planks every night.

The authorities suspected that Mosby was receiving local assistance. Fearing that it could be anyone and everyone in Virginia, they issued a blanket warning to commanders to have their men on high alert at all times. Sentries had strict injunctions to reject "It's me" or "We're with

The Chain Bridge across the Potomac above Georgetown, looking toward Virginia, by Frank Vizetelly.

the Fourth" and other such casual identifications. Any information that might be helpful to the enemy, such as duration of stays and destinations, was deliberately withheld from the troops. The tightening net closed on the two British captains Lewis Phillips and Edward Wynne during their return journey to the North. Phillips's luck had always been better than his companion's, and he made it through to Maryland; Wynne was caught while crossing the Potomac River. The legation learned of his arrest a few days later. "He seems to have behaved very foolishly," wrote the new attaché, Edward Malet. "He gave himself up to the federal pickets . . . being brought before the commanding officer seems to have chaffed him and [he] tried to carry matters with a high hand."[21] Wynne maintained that he had said nothing objectionable beyond admitting he had been "very well treated whilst in the South" and was therefore grateful to its people. It is unlikely he stopped there, however, since he was soon brought under guard to the Old Capitol prison in Washington.

Lord Lyons forbade the attachés to write to Wynne or make it seem as though the legation had any interest in his release. He had "had some trouble," explained Malet to his family, "as the government are very much put out at our soldiers going South and then returning rampant secessionists and now that they have caught one they wish to make an example of him." The Old Capitol prison was a decaying, makeshift jail in the middle of Washington. Once the temporary meeting place of the U.S. Congress, then a school, and later a boardinghouse, it had become an unsavory haven for snakes and vermin when the authorities began using it to house political prisoners. Nothing was done to delouse or repair the inside; the windows were simply boarded up and a fence erected at the back. Smugglers, blockade runners, suspected rebel sympathizers, spies, and the odd Federal military offender soon joined the political prisoners. They smoked and played cards all day long, waiting to be charged, or released, or sometimes executed. Captain Wynne was "prisoner no. 6." Malet visited him several times, bringing him cigars and newspapers. He tried to cheer him up, pointing out that the officials had allocated Wynne a private room. His efforts had little effect; Wynne shunned the other prisoners, preferring to sit in his cell plotting his escape.

The Marquis of Hartington and his friend Colonel Leslie were exploring Charleston when they learned of Wynne's imprisonment. The Charlestonians "are much better off here than at Richmond for most things," Hartington observed to his father. "Though most people have removed their property and slaves . . . in case of an attack by the enemy." But being "better off" was not the same as being comfortable. Hartington was more candid about the situation to his mistress, Skittles: "I have lost all my luggage, & I can't get any things here; at least very few things; & I have had to get along on one suit of clothes for a fortnight & shall for some time longer. . . . We have had some hunting as they call it, but it is not much like Leicestershire."[22] Apart from the ruined areas from the fire in 1861, the city was clean and orderly. The hotels were not crammed with shabby refugees like those in Richmond. But there was no escaping the fact that Charleston was under siege. The cost of living had risen eightfold since April 1861. Consul Bunch reported that salt was seventy times more expensive, there was no coal at any price, and the only cloth available for purchase was sailors' blue serge.

Hartington had been inclined to sail out of Charleston in a blockade runner since "there is scarcely any risk at all of being taken in one of them, especially in running out, and it would not do us much harm if we should be caught as they could only take us to some other port and then let us go."[23] Now he feared the ignominy of his position if he were to be thrown into the Old Capitol like Wynne. With the help of their new friends, Hartington and Leslie devised an overland route that relied on safe houses all the way to Washington. On February 9, Edward Malet was woken by sinister noises coming from his garden. He went outside to investigate and found Hartington and Colonel Leslie prowling in the back. They were terrified of being caught by the police; Captain Wynne had escaped from the Old Capitol prison earlier that day, causing a hue and cry in the capital.[*]

Malet took Hartington and Leslie in for the night. "The best advice we could give them," he wrote, "was to be off as fast as possible and stop nowhere till they were in New York." Hartington and Leslie arrived in New York a week after their rescue by Malet, having traversed almost three hundred miles without a single incident. Hartington made up for it now by creating a wonderfully embarrassing one: he attended a ball given by the Rothschilds' banker August Belmont, and either accidentally or purposefully sported a Confederate badge on his lapel. However, when a Union lieutenant on sick leave angrily confronted him, Hartington apologized and removed it, not wishing to be thought of as anti-Northern even though his sympathies now lay with the South.[†]

The more the blockading squadron tried to tighten its grip, the more Charlestonians enjoyed watching the blockade runners evade them and triumphantly steam into the harbor. The ships brought not only precious supplies but also news and, from time to time, British volunteers for the army. One of the first to arrive in January was Captain Stephen Winthrop, from Warwickshire and formerly of the 22nd Regiment of Foot, who braved the winter mud to seek out Robert E. Lee in Camp Fredericksburg. The general welcomed Winthrop with great courtesy, though he neither needed nor wanted another volunteer on his staff.

----

[*] Wynne had escaped by "breaking out a panel in his door." He was one of only four escapees in the prison's history. Wynne always insisted that he acted on his own, and the legation's records are silent on the matter.

[†] Hartington's faux pas took on a life of its own. The lapel badge story was repeated ad nauseam as incontrovertible proof of the English aristocracy's hatred of the United States. The American poet and literary critic James Russell Lowell included the incident in his diatribe against European arrogance in his essay "On a Certain Condescension in Foreigners" (1869), changing the story slightly in order to have Lincoln meet Hartington after the ball and deliberately insult him for having shown disrespect toward the North.

After a short deliberation over what to do with the Englishman, Lee sent him to General Longstreet with his regards.

Winthrop was shortly followed by two more volunteers: Henry We-myss Feilden of the Black Watch and Bradford Smith Hoskins, formerly of the 44th Regiment of Foot and the Garibaldi Guard. The latter ended up with Jeb Stuart, who sent him to replenish John Mosby's staff; Feilden was assigned to the defense of Charleston. Feilden's background was similar to Colonel Currie's; both men were public-school-educated career officers with a strong sense of personal honor and public duty. After leaving Cheltenham College in 1857, Feilden had joined the Black Watch, properly known as the 42nd Royal Highlanders. He spent his nineteenth birthday in India preparing to recapture Cawnpore, the scene of one of the worst massacres of British civilians during the Indian Mutiny. His twenty-first was celebrated in China while floundering in the deep swamp that surrounded the Taku forts; it was here that U.S. commodore Josiah Tatnall disobeyed the order to be a mere observer and sent aid to the British forces.

Feilden's grandfather Sir William was a mill owner from Blackburn, Lancashire, who had made a fortune in the cotton business. But Henry was the second of seven children, and one of four sons; there was never any doubt that he would have to earn his living. He sold his army commission in 1860 and returned to England in the hope of going into business. Four years of hard fighting had matured Feilden in unexpected ways; in addition to possessing considerable courage and self-confidence, he felt a strong sense of compassion for the weak and vulnerable. Many years later, Rud-yard Kipling, one of Feilden's closest friends, said of him, "I don't believe the Colonel ever gave a man a shove downwards in all his life."[24]

The family connection with Southern cotton made Feilden all the more susceptible to Confederate propaganda. He believed the canard that the South would abolish slavery once independence had been achieved. Shorn of its moral perils, the South looked immensely attrac-tive, especially through the sympathetic reports of Vizetelly and Lawley.[25] Feilden resolved to run the blockade with a cargo of supplies, sell them at a profit, and then join the Confederate army. But once he arrived at Bermuda, Feilden discovered that Francis Lawley's claim that Charleston was an open port was a gross exaggeration. It took three at-tempts and two different captains before he reached the Confederacy at the end of January.

Feilden eventually arrived at Richmond on February 15, 1863. "The city is one great camp," he wrote to his aunt.

Indeed the whole country is, everyone is a soldier, and everyone is trying for military distinction. The demand for appointment as officers is enormous, so many thousand have extraordinary claims on the Executive that it is impossible to do one half of them justice. I saw at once that my chance of getting a military appointment was very small, and indeed I could not expect it otherwise. I paid a visit to the Secretary of War, presented my letter to him and other influential men, was told that if possible something would be given to me, and I received from all of them that kindness and courtesy so distinctive in the Southern gentlemen. A good number of Englishmen have, prior to this, come out to this country, and I believe with very rare exceptions they have been obliged to serve as volunteers in the Army or on some General's staff until they have proved themselves fit for something.

A Confederate sympathizer in Nassau had asked Feilden to deliver a box of goods to Stonewall Jackson in camp at Hamilton's Crossing near Fredericksburg. Eager to meet the general, Feilden set off on the fifty-mile journey as soon as there was a lull in the rain and snow. But "the day I went to camp the rain came down with redoubled fury, as if it was proud of showing the earth's dirty face, and dissipating the white mantle of snow," he wrote.

I stumbled through mud, I waded through creeks, I passed through pinewoods. Wet through I got into camp about 2 o'clock and made my way to a small house—the General's Head Quarters. I wrote my name, gave it to an orderly and was immediately told to walk in. The General rose and greeted me warmly—he is so simple and unaffected in his ways and habits. I cannot illustrate this better than by telling exactly what he did—he took off my wet overcoat with his own hands, made up the fire, brought wood for me to put my feet on to keep them warm whilst my boots were drying, and then began asking me a great many questions on many subjects. We had a very pleasant conversation till dinnertime when we went out and joined the members of his staff. At dinner the General said Grace in a fervent, quiet manner that struck me much; there is a something about his face that you cannot help reverencing. He is a tall man, well and powerfully built but thin, with a brown beard and hair; his mouth is very determined-looking, the lips thin and compressed firmly together; his eyes are blue dark, with a keen and searching expression in them; his age is 38 and he looks about 40. I expected to see an old, untidy-looking man, and was surprised and pleased with his looks.

Henry returned to his room after dinner. The general sought him out again and offered his bed to share:

I thanked him very much for the courtesy, but said goodnight, and slept in a tent, sharing the blankets of one of his aides-de-camp. In the morning at breakfast I noticed the General said Grace before the meal with the same fervour as I had remarked before. An hour or two afterwards it was time for me to return to the Station. This time I had a horse, and I turned up the General's Head-quarters to bid adieu to him. His little room was vacant so I stepped in and stood before the fire: I noticed my great coat stretched before the fire on a chair. Shortly after the General entered the room. I was saying goodbye, and as I finished he said, "Captain, I have been trying to dry your great coat, but am afraid I have not succeeded very well." That little act shows the man, does it not! To think that in the midst of his duties, with the cares and responsibilities of a vast army on his shoulders, with the pickets of a hostile army almost within sight of his quarters, he found time to think of and to carry out these little acts of thoughtfulness!

Feilden had never encountered such personal courtesy from a British general. He returned to Richmond desperately hoping that the War Department had accepted his application. He would have accepted anything, and was thrilled to receive the offer of a captaincy and the position of assistant adjutant general in Charleston. In only a few weeks he had become as ardent a Confederate as any native-born Southerner. For the first time in years, Feilden felt at home: "I am tired of going to sea myself, I am sick of seeing new places," he wrote, "never did I feel happier than at the present moment." He was an efficient adjutant and quickly

made friends among his fellow officers; General Beauregard pronounced himself satisfied with the latest addition to his staff.

Charleston society was delighted with the handsome and personable
English captain. "The people are the kindest I ever met," Feilden wrote
in wonder, unaware that he was making up for the loss of Consul Bunch,
whose recent departure from the city had left a void that he filled perfectly. (Though the "cotton is king" attitude of the South had never
ceased to irritate the consul, he had been heartbroken to receive the Foreign Office's order to return to England.)[26] Feilden's lodgings were in
one of the boardinghouses used by English blockade runners. This gave
him unfettered access to breakfast, lunch, and dinner. Until then, he told
his aunt, he had been eating the diet of ordinary Southerners: "coffee
made out of rye, or else water, crackers and old bacon or tough meat. The
people of the South are suffering very much for want of good food."[27]

Neither the threat of attack nor the scarcity of luxuries had diminished Charleston's social calendar. Francis Lawley attended a ball before
setting off on his travels through the western part of the Confederacy,
and he was impressed by the Southerners' determination to keep up appearances; the shimmering silks and starched collars defied the truth of
the two-year-old blockade. It was as though the closer the city came to
danger, the more its inhabitants clung to their old habits. "I am finishing
off this scrawl as the gentleman who is taking this to England leaves tomorrow," Feilden wrote on March 4, 1863. "We are living here very comfortably and enjoying ourselves, although every day we expect to be
attacked by the Yankee Armada."[28]

EIGHTEEN

Faltering Steps
of a Counterrevolution

Attack on Charleston—British public opinion begins to change—The illustrious Maury, Pathfinder of the Seas—Espionage—Lord Russell is thwarted by John Bright—Wilkes again

The "Yankee Armada" set sail for Charleston at the beginning of April 1863. Frank Vizetelly was still in the city and could hardly wait for the clash to take place. His reports for the *Illustrated London News* became increasingly one-sided as he watched the city prepare for the attack. "I have every faith in the result of the coming encounter," he wrote, "for never at any time have the Confederates been more determined to do or die than they express themselves now."[1] More important than the Confederates' determination, however, was the lack of preparedness of the U.S. invasion force. Dr. Mayo inspected the fleet of seven monitors* and two ironclads before it left the Washington Navy Yard "and sincerely pitied those who had to go to sea in it." The decks of the monitors were barely a foot above water. He thought the slightest turbulence would probably swamp the vessels and send them to the bottom of the sea.[2] Admiral Samuel F. Du Pont was similarly pessimistic about his fleet, but the public clamor to capture and punish Charleston for starting the war was gathering force. Lincoln interpreted Du Pont's reluctance as McClellan-

---

* Monitor ships were different from ordinary ironclads on account of their heavy guns, revolving turrets, and flat bottoms, which enabled them to lie low in the water.

Confederates deploying torpedoes by moonlight in the harbor channel, Charleston, May 1863, by Frank Vizetelly.

like timidity. "Doom hangs over wicked Charleston," boomed the *New York Herald Tribune* on the eve of the fleet's departure. "If there is any city deserving of holocaustic infamy, it is Charleston."[3]

Du Pont's fleet sailed into the harbor on April 7. At 3:00 P.M. urgent peals rang across the city, alerting the inhabitants to take cover. Confident in Beauregard's defenses, many chose to watch from rooftops and balconies rather than hide in their houses. Frank Vizetelly ran from the Charles Hotel down to the Battery Promenade, where he jostled with the spectators for an unobstructed view of Fort Sumter. "I sketched the scene," he wrote for the *Illustrated London News,* "and finished the drawing in the evening, while the garrison of Fort Sumter were repairing the damages." Admiral Du Pont's gloomy prediction that his fleet would be overwhelmed was soon fulfilled. The fight lasted a mere two and a half hours. But in that time his fleet was crippled and his best ironclad steamer, the *Keokuk,* was sunk.

"I don't think the Yankees can capture Charleston, do what they will," Henry Feilden wrote after the battle. "In six weeks more the unhealthy season will come on, and the scoundrels will die on this coast like rotten sheep." It was his firm belief that the South would win its independence by Christmas. In the meantime, he planned to convert his entire savings into Confederate currency while it was still cheap to buy. Vizetelly was similarly ebullient about the South's prospects of victory. "The fight may be renewed at any moment if the Federals have the stomach for the attempt," he informed his readers back home, "but I think they have suffered too much."[4]

The U.S. secretary of the navy, Gideon Welles, was furious with Du Pont for failing to put on a better show. Embarrassed by yet another naval defeat, he wondered whether it was even worth making a further attempt: "Nothing has been done, and it is the recommendation of all, from the Admiral down, that no effort be made to do anything," Welles wrote gloomily in his diary. "I am by no means confident that we are acting wisely in expending so much strength and effort on Charleston, a place of no strategic importance. But it is lamentable to witness the . . . want of zeal among so many of the best officers of the service."[5]

Vizetelly's triumphant reporting of the Union's repulse contributed to the sour mood in Washington. The secretary of war, Edwin Stanton, was an avid reader of the English press, particularly those journals that were sympathetic to the South. Stanton would shut his office door, settle down on the sofa, and spend the afternoon discovering from Britain's finest journalists why the North deserved no pity and why he, especially, was the worst sort of bungler. According to one of his clerks, it was almost a form of relaxation for him.[6]

———

Contrary to Stanton's belief that all of England sympathized with the South, support for the North was growing. The London consul, Freeman H. Morse, whose duties had expanded to include propaganda and public agitation, told Seward that there had been a "revolution" since Lincoln's Emancipation Proclamation.[7] Despite the initial skepticism toward the Proclamation and the best efforts of *The Times* to portray it as a cynical ploy to encourage race riots—or at the very least force Southern soldiers to return to their homes to protect their families—the message that the war had a moral purpose seemed to be reaching the British public.

Among the initial signs was a rise in pamphlets and books putting forward the case for the North. James Spence's seemingly unassailable arguments in *The American Union* for recognition of the South were picked apart to devastating effect by the economist John Elliot Cairnes in his book *The Slave Power,* which appeared in the autumn of 1862 and went through several editions after the Emancipation Proclamation. Cairnes was followed by the actress Fanny Kemble, who published her diary,

Journal of a Residence on a Georgian Plantation in 1838–1839, written during her exile on her former husband's slave plantation in Georgia, and William Howard Russell, whose account of his stay in America, entitled *My Diary North and South,* verified many of her observations.[8] The *Spectator* journalist Edward Dicey also wrote a travelogue—*Six Months in the Federal States*—that tried to correct many of the distortions and caricatures of Northern culture that pro-Southern journalists had propagated. An increase in the number of volunteers calling at the legation reflected the changing perception of the war. "Applications for service in our army strangely fluctuate," wrote Benjamin Moran in his diary on January 14, 1863. "For some time past they have been but few. Since the announcement of the President's determination to adhere to his emancipation policy they have again become numerous and today we have had a French and British officer seeking employment."[9] Moran was surprised by the wide range of motives and financial circumstances of these would-be volunteers; as far as he could tell, some were genuine idealists, but others were simply looking for an escape from their daily existence. Another surprise was waiting for him when he went to church. The vicar had never mentioned the war before, but on this Sunday he announced during prayers, "Our hearts in this great contest are with the North," which was answered with a deep "Amen" from the congregation.[10]

"Emancipation Meetings continue to be held in London every week, sometimes four or five a week at some of which two and three thousand people have been present and in a majority of cases unanimously with the North. Other portions of the country are following the example of this city and holding meetings with about the same result," Consul Morse reported to Seward.[11] James Spence spoke passionately at an antislavery meeting in Liverpool, but to his surprise he failed to convince a mixed audience of merchants and tradespeople that the South would also abolish slavery as soon as it won independence.[12] The public was far more interested in hearing from President Lincoln than from Spence. Encouraged by Charles Sumner, Lincoln had written an eloquent letter to the "Workingmen of Manchester" thanking the cotton workers for their patience and sacrifice. "Whatever misfortune may befall your country or my own," declared the president, "the peace and friendship which now exist between the two nations will be . . . perpetual."[13]

Morse was being helped by Peter Sinclair, a formidable and energetic Scotsman who had spent the past six years building a Canadian-

American temperance organization called Bands of Hope. Sinclair had lately returned to England with the specific intention of giving his aid to the North. "Mr. Sinclair has been laying facts, figures and arguments before a committee of the old Emancipation Society, one of the most influential organizations in England," Morse informed Seward in January. Even though some veteran campaigners like Bishop Samuel Wilberforce and Lord Shaftesbury remained unconvinced (much to Henry Hotze's glee), Sinclair had been remarkably successful in convincing a wide range of individuals—including "merchants, bankers, lawyers, literary men, etc."—that abolition was possible only in a united America. The hitherto pacifist British and Foreign Anti-Slavery Society changed its stance and became actively involved in the counterpropaganda war, secretly supplying Moran with information about Confederate activities in the financial markets.[14] Sinclair was also the leading organizer of the Emancipation Society's massive demonstration at Exeter Hall on January 29. Henry Adams managed to secure a seat at the meeting and was thoroughly uplifted by the experience. The politicians, Henry told his brother afterward, were going to have to listen to their constituents or risk being "thrown over."*

—

Henry Adams had cheered up considerably since September, when the powerfully connected Richard Monckton Milnes made the improvement of the twenty-five-year-old's social life his pet project.[15] But his father continued to be tormented by doubts and anxieties; Charles Francis Adams felt especially angry toward Seward. It was not only the dispatches publication fiasco. On January 28, the legation received a telegram from the vacationing secretary of the legation, Charles Wilson, announcing his imminent arrival in London. Benjamin Moran was in despair. Adams was horrified. Both had assumed that Wilson would never return from his government-funded vacation in Chicago. Neither could stand working with the uncouth and obnoxious secretary, whose

* Henry Adams was like his father in his tendency to exaggerate the division of opinion between the social classes. Friends, neighbors, and even families disagreed with one another, such as the Devonshires at the top of the scale—where Hartington leaned toward the South, and his brother Lord Frederick Cavendish toward the North—and the Collings family at the lower end, where Jesse Collings, a hardware merchant, bombarded the local press with letters in support of the North, and his brother Henry, a commercial sailor, joined the Confederate navy and fought on board CSS *Merrimac*.

only reason for being at the legation arose from a serpentine bargain between Seward and Lincoln over patronage. Without consulting or explaining his thoughts to Moran, Adams decided that the best way to keep Wilson at a distance—without its looking like a direct snub—was to exclude both legation secretaries from all social functions. Moran was crushed when he discovered that the Adamses were entertaining behind his back. "This is a deliberate slight," he raged in his diary. "All other Ministers invite their secretaries to their state dinners; but it seems to be a pleasure to ours to degrade his by acts of omission."[16] Charles Francis Adams was far too preoccupied to notice Moran's wounded dignity. A thick yellow fog had descended on London, quite different from the usual kind at that time of year. It made the day seem like endless night, and the world outside even more claustrophobic than the world within. The sense of being trapped exacerbated Adams's fears; he was dreading the opening of Parliament on February 5 and could think of little else.

As it happened, although several speakers referred at length to the American war, there were no clarion calls for immediate recognition of the South, no hints from the government about a change in policy. The issue was certainly alive: in the Lords, the Earl of Carnarvon asked Lord Russell to explain Britain's position on the fate of Her Majesty's subjects currently held without trial in Northern prisons.[17] But America did not seem to resonate in Parliament as it had before Christmas. Adams mentally thanked the Poles for their revolution on January 22, 1863, which was keeping the House distracted.

Adams was also nervous about his meeting with Lord Russell on February 7, the first since the publication of his uncomplimentary dispatches, and he expected some sort of rebuke or coldness. "I was a little prepared to find him rather more reserved than heretofore," Adams wrote in his diary. "In his place I think I should have been so. But so far as I could see there was no difference." (Adams might have felt differently toward Russell had he known of the foreign secretary's strenuous efforts to unite the cabinet behind his mediation plan.) The fog dissipated, "yet I felt rather sad," Adams confessed in his diary. "The unsettled condition of our public affairs and the doubt that overhangs the future both financially and morally cast a shadow upon everything."[18] When he did venture out, Adams was not particularly sociable. Even dinner at the Argylls' was a chore for him, though he liked them as a rule. "The Duchess is an interesting woman, but she is not very easy in con versation. She labors at starting subjects without knowing how to keep them going. He is much in the same way," he complained on February 11, forgetting that a conversation requires two willing partners.[19]

Nearly three weeks later, Adams came face to face with Lord Palmerston at a royal levee. The two had not spoken to each other since the "Butler letters" the previous June. "Of course I was called to decide something, so I made a formal bow and put out my hand." To Adams's relief, "He bowed in return and took my hand so that no perceptible difficulty took place. Most of the other Cabinet members treated me with great cordiality."[20] Adams was still trying to make sense of the encounter when he received an invitation from Lady Palmerston, the first in over a year. "This was certainly a change," he wrote in puzzlement, unaware that Benjamin Moran had left his card at Cambridge House. The dictates of diplomatic protocol obliged Lady Palmerston to respond to the gesture by inviting the assistant secretary to her next party, which she could not do without also including the senior members of the legation. But it cannot be said that Adams made the most of the opportunity. Afterward he wrote, "The same old crowd and the same people whom I did not know."[21] Although Adams often spoke as though he cared nothing for social advancement, Benjamin Moran was not fooled: "One of the leading characteristics, if not the leading one of English society," he wrote in his diary, "is its perfect exclusiveness. To get through this barrier is almost impossible. Americans who try it once and fail, generally stop; but not the Adamses. Their desire to get thro' the charmed wall and into the circle is a disease . . . altho' they are constantly pretending they are indifferent to it."[22]

———

The Confederate commissioner James Mason had never seen the inside of Cambridge House and was thus denied the luxury of being bored by the Palmerstons' parties. During the past twelve months, Mason's most intimate encounter with the higher echelons of government had been the thirty minutes he had spent in Lord Russell's office shortly after his arrival. On the other hand, Mason could boast that he had seen the Egyptian Hall of Mansion House, the official residence of the Lord Mayor in the City of London, many more times than Adams, since the South enjoyed strong support from financial institutions with historic ties to the cotton industry.

The Lord Mayor's banquet on February 11, 1863, came just at the

Great emancipation meeting held at Exeter Hall, March 1863.

right time for Mason. Russell had become more elusive than ever. Mason did not know what to make of this "strange contumacy from such a quarter." To make sure his correspondence was not falling victim to Federal skulduggery, he had had his secretary personally deliver the last Confederate letter to the Foreign Office. That had been more than a month ago. The banquet at Mansion House appeared to confirm Mason's belief that the foreign secretary was out of step with the rest of the country. "When my name was announced by the Mayor, it was received with a storm of applause," Mason wrote in his diary. When he was unexpectedly invited to address the hall, almost every sentence he spoke elicited loud cheers, especially when he referred to the commercial ties between the City and the South, and he thought he had acquitted himself rather well. One of James Spence's friends had been among the guests and was convinced that he had witnessed a momentous event. "My dear Spence," he wrote the next day,

> I was at the Mansion House last night and heard the Lord Mayor virtually recognize the South in the quietest and most inoffensive way that could be imagined. . . . As I came out I rubbed shoulders with Captain Tinker, Grinnell's partner and I said, jocularly, "Well, you see the Lord Mayor has been and gone and done it." He laughingly replied, "Oh yes, it's all over now." Depend on it, this expression of opinion from the heart of England's middle classes must tell. It will reverberate thro' the land and find an echo.[23]

The only Southerner in England who did not rejoice after the Lord Mayor's banquet was Commodore Matthew Fontaine Maury, who thought Mason was wasting his time. "Many of our friends here have mistaken British admiration of Southern 'pluck,' and newspaper spite at Yankee insolence as Southern sympathy. No such thing," Maury had written to a friend in late January. He was adamant: "There is no love for the South here. In its American policy the British Government fairly represents the people. . . . There is no hope for recognition here, therefore *I* say withdraw *Mason*." After the banquet Maury wrote: "We are gaining ground here, it is true, but before we can expect any aid or comfort we must show our ability to get along without it—then it will be offered right and left."[24]

Matthew Maury would have been a much better Southern commissioner than William Yancey or James Mason. He was one of the Confederacy's few international heroes, having received six honorary knighthoods, a clutch of medals and seals, and membership in several royal societies for his contribution to the study of oceanography. Maury's research of sea charts and weather patterns had led him to uncover the hidden pathways of the sea, taking the guesswork out of trade routes and opening the oceans to further exploration. It was Maury's discovery of the North Atlantic shelf that had emboldened Cyrus Field to lay his ill-fated telegraph cable in 1858.

But in America, Maury's blunt and often captious behavior had made him as many enemies as admirers. The navy pushed him into retirement, although it relented and made him a commander after he fought to be readmitted. When the war began, Maury was fifty-five years old, happily married, and the father of nine children, having run the Naval Observatory in Washington for nearly seventeen years. But on April 20, 1861, though he neither owned slaves nor approved of slavery, Maury chose his native state of Virginia over his loyalty to the federal government. He walked out of the observatory for the last time with tears streaming down his face, leaving on the desk his sword, his naval uniform, and a letter of resignation to Abraham Lincoln.

Maury soon discovered that old quarrels had not died with the new Confederacy. It was unfortunate that his future ended up in the hands of three of his greatest rivals: Jefferson Davis, Judah P. Benjamin, and Stephen Mallory. Maury's pioneering work on torpedoes and mines received scant official support. When he received his orders in August 1862 to go on a purchasing mission to London, Maury assumed it was an attempt to consign him to oblivion.[25] He knew there was already a clutch of agents in England competing with one another for scarce resources. After long, anguished discussions with his wife, Ann, the Maurys agreed that their youngest child, thirteen-year-old Matthew Jr., known as Brave, would accompany him to England. The rest of the family would try to live quietly in northern Virginia.

Maury and young Brave traveled to Charleston to wait for room to become available on a steamer running the blockade. As the weeks passed, Maury became a frequent guest at Ashley Hall, home of George A. Trenholm. Built in the Regency style according to Southern taste, the house was a skillful combination of intimidation and opulence. Few families could maintain such an establishment at those times, but the blockade had transformed Trenholm from the chairman of a middle-sized shipping firm into the wealthiest man in the South. Life at Ashley Hall was not only untouched by the war, it was better than ever. Dinner guests were treated to delicacies that had not been seen elsewhere in Charleston since 1861. Maury hardly noticed seventeen-year-old James Morgan at other end of Trenholm's dinner table, looking uncomfortably hot in his woolen naval uniform. A random series of events had brought Morgan to Trenholm's door. Since helping his English friend Francis Dawson, escape the overenthusiastic nursing of some female volunteers, Morgan had been transferred from one ship to another. His current posting was on a little ironclad still in dry dock. With nothing to do and nowhere to go, Morgan had taken to roaming aimlessly around Charleston until Trenholm took him under his wing. On the sultry night that brought Maury and Morgan together for the first time, Trenholm turned to the youth and "asked me if I would like to go abroad and join a cruiser," recalled Morgan. "On being assured that I would give any-thing to have the chance, he returned to Commodore Maury and re-sumed his conversation about the peculiarities of the 'Gulf Stream.' " The next morning, Morgan received orders from the secretary of the navy to accompany Maury to London. There, he was to report to James Bulloch for further instructions.[26]

Maury's worst fears about his mission were confirmed when he ar-rived in England in late November 1862. The Confederates were low on funds and had been surviving on credit since the previous summer. Caleb Huse had warehouses full of precious guns, medicines, blankets, and shoes for Lee's army that he could not afford to ship. James Bulloch himself had two half-completed ironclad rams at the Lairds shipyard in Liverpool, costing £94,000 each, that would never leave dry dock if he did not pay up in time. In Scotland, two agents for the Confederate navy, one of them the hapless James North, were in an equally perilous rela-tionship with the shipwrights on the Clyde. If these ships could be let loose upon the Federal navy, they would, in Bulloch's words, "sweep away the entire blockading fleet of the enemy."[27] The modifications he had suggested would enable his cruisers to fight in any waters. Mobile, heavily gunned, and armed with menacing iron rams, they were a new breed of fighting machine. But in the meantime, Bulloch had until March to come up with the final installment.

Bulloch was polite to Maury, but clearly regarded him as an added burden. Apart from the financial headache of yet another agent seeking pay and expenses, he feared that every new Confederate operation threatened the security of his own. Just before Maury's arrival, Bulloch had informed Richmond via a secure channel that sneaking the ships past the British authorities would be difficult, and "will require to be conducted with such caution and secrecy that I fear to mention the plan even in this way." The chief British ports had received orders to prevent the departure of any other *Alabama*s. Hampered by one of the worst winters in many years, the builders had put up temporary sheds and were using expensive gaslight in order to work around the clock. Even so, construction was coming along slowly.[28] "Have tried very hard to hasten the completion, but insurmountable difficulties have occurred," Bulloch wrote in code, trusting that the cipher had not been broken by Federal agents. "No armoured ships for Admiralty have ever been completed in time specified; whole character of work new, and builders cannot make close calculations; great labour and unexpected time required to bend armour-plates; and the most important part of the work, the riveting, is far more tedious than anticipated."[29]

The first attempt to solve the Confederates' debt crisis was made by James Spence and William Schaw Lindsay, MP. Spence had at last achieved his wish and been appointed the South's financial agent for Europe. Eager to untangle the Confederates' wayward affairs, he and Lindsay came up with the ingenious idea of floating cotton bonds on the London market, sidestepping the fact that two-thirds of the Confederacy's wealth was tied up in slaves and land. As long as the Southern government could guarantee the flow of cotton to England, it would be a cheap way of raising money. Mason enthusiastically endorsed the idea. But Spence was outmaneuvered by John Slidell and Caleb Huse, who championed an alternative loan proposal by the French banker Frédéric Emile, Baron d'Erlanger. There were several reasons why Slidell preferred to work with the Frenchman. Erlanger et Cie was one of the great European banking houses, similar to Rothschilds and Barings, and had lent money to the French government. Moreover, the baron was desperately in love with Slidell's daughter, the beautiful Mathilda. He had been introduced to her during a business trip to New Orleans and had never recovered from the meeting. (The two were married in October 1864).[30]

Spence and Slidell fought over the Erlanger proposal throughout January 1863. The baron was amazed to have his dealings questioned by a provincial businessman and flicked Spence's questions aside. Such treatment only incensed Spence all the more: he refused "to be treated with something like polite contempt," he told Mason. "I am not the man to take it easily." He had no choice. The Confederate secretary of state, Judah P. Benjamin, did not like the terms of the Erlanger loan, particularly the 5 percent commission, but he was anxious to drag the emperor into closer ties with the Confederacy. On January 29, the Confederate Congress voted to approve the Erlanger loan.[31]

The real threat to Bulloch's ironclad rams, however, was not the lack of funds but Federal infiltration of his inner circle. The U.S. consuls, Thomas Haines Dudley and Freeman Morse, had finally succeeded in placing an agent close to the Confederates' center of operations.[32] Soon Morse and Dudley were able to relay precise descriptions of the blockade runners leaving England, making it easier for the ships to be intercepted.[*][33] One capture resulted in the loss of the sorely needed provisions Maury had bought for his family.[34] Another netted the North a large cache of documents, which on inspection turned out to be two months' worth of official correspondence between Richmond and the Confederates in England. Among the revelations was James Spence's employment by the South, which ruined his cover as a disinterested advocate.

The consuls also exposed the Cunard shipping line as the secret carrier of Confederate dispatches between Nassau and England; they even uncovered how the *Alabama* was able to send and receive messages. "It has all the time been a mystery to me how Capt. Semmes could get his letters and papers," wrote the agent known only as WFGA. The system turned out to be quite simple. The lighthouse keeper on the Hole in the Wall, at the south end of the Abacos Islands in the Bahamas, was being paid to act as a go-between: every two weeks, the *Alabama* would sail by and exchanges would be made.[35] The Confederate operations might have been completely compromised were it not for the parsimonious attitude of the U.S. State Department. Espionage was an expensive game, and the two consuls were always running out of money. Seward had not

---

[*] The consuls reported on January 9, 1863, for example, "an armed steamer is to leave Liverpool to-morrow with important dispatches from Commodore Maury (who is still in England), Mason, and Slidell. A man by the name of Hope is the bearer of these dispatches and will go out on the steamer."

increased their budget for some time, his estimation of their work having been colored by one or two blunders that had undermined their credibility.

"Think British Government will prevent iron ships leaving," Bulloch informed Richmond on February 3, "and am much perplexed; object of armoured ships too evident for disguise."[36] The only Confederate project that had not been compromised was Matthew Maury's. Using privately financed cotton bonds, he had bought a Scottish steamer called the *Japan,* which could be easily converted into a fighting ship. A colleague in the Royal Danish Navy was generously helping to oversee the construction on the Clyde. But Northern agents heard rumors about the ship once Maury began to assemble a crew and arrange for the delivery of guns and supplies. He needed fifty seamen and twenty-one officers. There were nine Confederate naval officers scattered around London, living in boardinghouses under assumed names. Maury used his rank to commandeer them for the *Japan.* That still left eleven vacancies that had to be filled with British officers. It was hardly ideal for the Confederates to be in the minority on their own cruiser, but the imminent threat of exposure left him with no other choice.

Maury was finalizing the last details for the *Japan*'s departure when permission to sell cotton bonds through the Erlanger banking house finally arrived from Richmond. Erlanger issued the prospectus on March 18. The public's response was little short of frenzied, which made Spence's objections look self-serving. By the third day more than $16 million worth of bonds had been sold.[37] In his report, James Mason admitted that there had been "a strong opinion in moneyed circles of the City that the enterprise was a hazardous one, and likely to fail in the market." But the Confederates had managed to overcome the City's skepticism by touting the loan as a risk-free investment. Mason assured subscribers that no matter which side won the war, the bonds would always have to be honored.[38]

"Cotton is King at last," crowed Mason.[39] "It is financial recognition of our independence," John Slidell declared to Richmond.[40] His sentiments were echoed in London. Confederate sympathizers raised the issue of recognition in the House of Lords on March 23, but Russell made a forceful speech that put an end to the debate before it had even properly started. Charles Francis Adams was surprised and thought it the best Russell had given on the war.[41] He did not know, of course, that

Sumner was sending hysterical letters to the Duchess of Argyll and other English friends warning them to be prepared for Northern privateers preying on English ships, or that Lord Lyons had advised Russell to treat the Confederate activities in England as a real threat to peace.[42] "The outcry in America about the *Oreto* and the *Alabama* is much exaggerated," Russell replied to Lyons, "but I must feel that her roaming the ocean with English guns and English sailors to burn, sink and destroy the ships of a friendly nation, is a scandal and a reproach. I don't know very well what we can do."[43] After Richard Cobden bluntly spelled out the danger of being a passive observer, Russell decided that the House of Commons should debate whether the current Foreign Enlistment Act needed to be strengthened.

Russell asked Charles Francis Adams what he wanted the government to say in the debate, to which Adams replied they "should declare their disapproval of the fitting out of such ships of war to prey on American commerce." Russell thought this was eminently sensible and relayed the message to Palmerston just before the Commons discussion on March 27, 1863. The House knew that Lairds had built the *Alabama* and was in the process of building more like her. "I think you can have no difficulty in declaring this evening," Russell wrote to Lord Palmerston, "that the Government disapprove of all such attempts to elude our law."[44]

"The government itself is getting alarmed," Freeman Morse wrote excitedly to Seward on the morning of the debate. "This country is now thoroughly agitated on what they call the American question."[45] The debate began with William Forster asking the government whether new laws were required to prevent the Confederates from building their warships in Britain. There should have been no difficulty, except that no one had counted on John Bright's appearing in the Commons. Adams had tried to dissuade him from speaking, knowing how Bright's "help" often had the opposite effect. The night before, Bright had enjoyed a standing ovation at a trade union meeting when he roundly denounced the "privileged class" for being foes of freedom. Still intoxicated by the cheers of his audience, he gave a similar-sounding speech to the House, forgetting that his listeners were members of this afflicted class. They should have "looked in the faces of three thousand of the most intelligent of the artisan classes in London, as I did," he told an indignant House, "and heard their cheers, and seen their sympathy for [America]."[46] Bright was answered by John Laird, who had spent the evening hearing himself denounced as a cheat and warmonger. After pointing out that his firm had been approached by both the North and the South at the beginning of the war, "I have only to say that I would rather be handed down to posterity as the builder of a dozen *Alabama*s, than as the man who applies himself deliberately to set class against class," he bellowed, to the accompaniment of cheers from both sides of the House.[47]

In addition to dragging the shipbuilding question into the trenches of class war, Bright also challenged Palmerston to apologize to the Americans. That promptly killed any hope that the House would vote to strengthen the Foreign Enlistment Act. Rather than voicing his disapproval of Confederate evasions of the law, Palmerston declared he would never amend Britain's laws simply to satisfy international pressure.[48] Seizing this as their cue, Confederate sympathizers introduced a new subject in the debate: the U.S. Navy's harassment of British merchant ships. Adams believed that Bright had provided Palmerston with an excuse to avoid strengthening the act. "Had he been really well disposed he never could have written me the private note which caused our differences last year," he wrote bitterly.[49]

Furious that John Bright's blundering speech had thwarted the government's attempt to strengthen the Foreign Enlistment Act, Russell ordered his staff to treat seriously all allegations against suspect ships. It was not long before the government had details of several Confederate vessels. Matthew Maury's *Japan* on the Clyde was one of the first to be unmasked. Maury learned from a report in the newspapers that that project was out in the open. He immediately sent orders for the cruiser to leave England whatever her condition. The crew and stores were to sail on a separate ship and rendezvous in neutral waters. A messenger delivered a cryptic note to the lodgings where James Morgan had been hiding since his arrival in England. He was ordered to proceed with the utmost care to a house on Little St. James's Street, where a "Mr. Grigson" would give him further instructions. Morgan hurried through the streets, hoping that he was not being followed. At the house he found half a dozen nervous Confederate officers. They jumped every time there was a knock at the door, fearing it was Consul Morse with the police. Nobody dared leave the house until well after sunset.

> At half-past nine that evening [wrote Morgan] we all proceeded to a railway station where we took a train for White Haven, a little

seaport about an hour's ride from London. There we went to a
small inn, where we met Commander Maury, Dr. Wheeden, and
Paymaster Curtis, and were soon joined by others—all strangers
to me. We waited at the inn for about a couple of hours; there was
little, if any, conversation, as we were all too anxious and were all
thinking about the same thing. In those two hours it was to be decided whether our expedition was to be a success or a failure. If
Mr. Adams, the American Minister, was going to get in his fine
work and balk us, now was his last opportunity.[50]

The Foreign Office had already issued instructions to detain Morgan's
vessel. But by some mysterious chance, the telegram remained in an out-
box until after the port's telegraph station closed for the day. The delay
enabled the *Japan* to escape in the early hours of April 1, 1863.[51] Eight
days after leaving England, off the coast of Brittany, Matthew Maury's
cousin Commander William Lewis Maury hoisted aloft the Confederate
flag, and the *Japan* began its service as CSS *Georgia*.

The appearance on the high seas of a third Confederate commerce raider
ratcheted up the already high tension between the United States and
Royal navies. The U.S. blockading squadron at Mobile, for example—
which was still smarting from the embarrassment of having allowed CSS
Florida to escape—started firing live rounds at passing Royal Navy vessels, each time claiming to have mistaken the unambiguous appearance
of a British warship for a civilian blockade runner.* Conversely, British
frigates patrolling the Caribbean were as unhelpful as possible toward
the U.S. vessels trying to chase down blockade runners.

   Admiral Milne, commander-in-chief of the Royal Navy's operations
in North America and the West Indies, was annoyed by his officers' failure to maintain a strictly neutral stance. He despised the blockade runners and had ordered the fleet to refrain from giving them any assistance.
Sometimes the so-called offense against the United States was simply
tactless behavior, such as the fraternization between British crews and
CSS *Alabama* when she sailed through Jamaican waters in January. But at

---

* In New Orleans, a young sublieutenant on shore leave from HMS *Galatea* was
beaten up and thrown into the stocks. An investigation revealed that he had been
strolling down Canal Street singing rebel songs. The dim-witted officer defended
his conduct, saying "I did call them stinking cowards but that was nearly all."[52]

other times, Milne detected more than a hint of partisanship. In February he removed HMS *Petrel* from Charleston after Captain George W. Watson and his officers became far too friendly with the blockaded townspeople.[53] The last straw was a clearly biased report by Watson about the weakness of the blockading fleet. Milne upbraided him for "mixing himself so conspicuously and unnecessarily with the Confederate authorities," and ordered Watson to a remote part of the Caribbean. "I cannot trust him either at Nassau or on the American coast," Milne complained on March 20 to Sir Frederick Grey of the Admiralty.[54] Milne also punished the captain of HMS *Vesuvius,* who had agreed to transport $155,000 in specie past the blockade at Mobile because, allegedly, it was interest owed to bondholders in Britain. (Fearful of the reaction in Washington, Lyons promptly dismissed the British consul who had arranged it.)

Milne made it his general rule to adopt a lenient approach regarding complaints about American harassment of "innocent" cargo ships. He also held firm even when the U.S. Navy widened its net to include merchant ships sailing between the West Indies and the Gulf of Mexico. The chief destination of these ships was Matamoros, a miserable, drought-ridden town on the Mexican border about thirty miles from the mouth of the Rio Grande. Powdery white dust covered every surface in Matamoros, including the hair and clothes of the inhabitants, making them look like the walking dead. The town would have dissolved back into the scrubland were it not directly across the river from Brownsville, Texas, another miserable little town whose existence was saved by the Civil War.

These two places, more than fifteen hundred miles from Richmond, were the only open gates into the Confederacy. The narrow, winding Rio Grande was a neutral river, and so, according to international law, it could not be blockaded. At first the North paid little attention to Matamoros. It was situated in a barren waste that spread for hundreds of miles; there were no port facilities or roads, and its only connection to Brownsville was a rickety ferryboat. But even with these obstacles, cotton sellers were prepared to risk their lives hauling long wagon trains across the Texas plains and over the river. By early 1863, nearly two hundred ships a month were calling at Matamoros, bringing supplies to the Confederacy and leaving with cotton.

Although he could not admit it publicly, Russell was anxious for the sake of the British cotton industry that this tiny chink in the blockade should stay open. He ordered Lyons to protest the U.S. Navy's habit of seizing any British ship heading toward Mexico. There was no way of proving whether the guns and matériel were destined for the South or for the beleaguered Mexican government, whose twelve-month resistance against a French invasion force was showing signs of fatigue. But Milne was loath to interfere with the practices of the U.S. Navy; HMS *Phaeton* was already cruising the gulf as a friendly reminder of British neutrality. The only help that Milne was prepared to give to British merchantmen was the advice to anchor on the Mexican side of the Gulf, where the U.S. Navy was powerless to molest them.

The fate of several British merchant ships was already worrying the Foreign Office—and the readers of *The Times*—when U.S. admiral Charles Wilkes once again exercised his uncanny ability to create an international crisis. Learning that a British-owned merchant ship called the *Peterhoff* was leaving the Danish island of St. Thomas to sail to Matamoros, Wilkes ordered USS *Vanderbilt* to stop her as soon as she left the

"BEWARE!"

Keeper. "HE AIN'T ASLEEP, YOUNG JONATHAN; SO YOU'D BEST NOT IRRITATE HIM."

Punch warns the United States not to irritate the British lion, May 1863.

harbor. As the *Vanderbilt* approached, one of the *Peterhoff*'s passengers was observed throwing a large packet into the water. Her captain was nowhere to be seen, since he was busy burning papers in his cabin. The captured ship was brought to Key West in Florida on March 10, 1863, where the British vice consul said that the vessel could not possibly have been involved in anything so low as blockade running since Captain Stephen Jarman was a lieutenant in the Royal Naval Reserve. Moreover, she had been transporting the Lloyd's insurance agent for Matamoros and a bag of mail from the Post Office. The return of the mail became an instant cause célèbre in England. The poisonous combination of Charles Wilkes and British property provoked *Trent*-like hysteria, with the press insisting that national honor was at stake.[55]

Lyons warned Russell that the mood of the Northerners was just as violent.[56] Whatever their disagreements over the war and the merits of abolition, they were united by their resentment toward Britain. "Everybody is furious with England and with everybody and everything English," Lyons wrote sadly.[57] The Northern press was claiming that the British were building a navy for the Confederates, supplying their armies, lending them money, and providing moral if not actual support to the *Alabama,* the *Florida,* and the *Georgia.* Lyons telegraphed Admiral Milne to make his fleet battle-ready—once again, the signal for war would be "Could you forward a letter for me to Antigua?"[58] Milne complied, though he was fearful that putting his ships on alert would provoke the very collision he was laboring so hard to prevent.

NINETEEN

Prophecies of Blood and Suffering

Blockade running becomes a serious business—Two cautionary tales—
Seward is courageous—General Longstreet feeds an army—A murder—
Hooker's "perfect plan"

In London, Benjamin Moran laughed sourly when he read the naïve response of the British vice consul in Florida. There was no doubt that Captain Jarman had been blockade running; Moran had in his possession a copy of the subscription letter offered by the *Peterhoff*'s owners, which stated that the purpose of the voyage to the West Indies was to supply arms to the Confederacy in exchange for cotton. Nor could the uproar over Admiral Wilkes's action disguise the fact that Bermuda and the Bahamas had become the chief supply depots for the South.

The Bahamas was the preferred route for commercial blockade runners because of their proximity to the Southern coast. It took only three days to sail from Nassau to the main Southern ports. The same trip from Bermuda—which was almost nine hundred miles due east of Charleston—took at least five days and sometimes more in poor weather. But by late 1862, Josiah Gorgas, the Confederate chief of ordnance, had realized that Bermuda's relative inaccessibility was an advantage for his government since the competition for docking facilities and warehouses was less fierce. The Ordnance Department's small fleet of blockade runners used the tiny island of St. George, which lay at the top end of the archipelago. Its port was closer to the open sea than the main island's, and the approach from the South was an easy passage through crystalline waters. On the return jour-

Unloading cotton from blockade runners at the port of Nassau, by Frank Vizetelly.

ney, the ordnance fleet unloaded its cargoes at Wilmington in North Carolina rather than sailing to Charleston, which was expensive and crowded. Though not as convenient as Charleston—Wilmington was twenty-five miles from the sea, on the east bank of the Cape Fear River—the port could be reached via two different approaches and enjoyed the advantage of being guarded by Fort Fisher, whose large guns could hit any blockader attempting to enter the river.

The supply system between Bermuda and Wilmington was growing so rapidly that in early 1863 the Confederate Ordnance Department appointed Major Norman Walker to oversee its operations on the island. From his headquarters at the Globe Hotel on St. George, the industrious Walker arranged for 80,000 Enfield rifles, 27,000 Austrian rifles, and 21,000 muskets to be shipped in February alone. He also filled orders for steel, copper, and saltpeter and sent hundreds of cases packed with screwdrivers, cartridges, buckles, stirrups, percussion caps, buttons, and all other daily necessities required by the Confederate armies. Soon the U.S. consul in Bermuda reported that Confederate steamers were coming and going with the regularity of mail ships.[1] As he was naturally resented by the locals for his attempts to interfere with this lucrative trade, the consul's life became a daily round of harassments both petty and great. One morning in March a group of "colored blockade running seamen" took their revenge by loudly singing Confederate songs beneath his window.[2]

The Globe Hotel was a three-story stone building, painted a pretty shade of pink with black shutters. Built in 1699 as a residence for the governor, it was one of the oldest houses on the island. With each change of ownership the place had become a little more run-down and frayed about the edges, and it was currently a boardinghouse run by a widow and her three spinster sisters. But "it was a Palace to me," wrote Major Walker's pregnant wife, Georgiana, who arrived on March 24, 1863, with three young children in tow and what remained of their belongings. (One bag contained the Confederate flag and a pouch filled with Virginia soil. Georgiana intended to give birth with the flag draped symbolically above the bed and the soil placed underneath to ensure that the baby was a true Virginian.) Desperate to join her husband in Bermuda, Georgiana had approached every blockade runner in Wilmington pleading to be taken on as a passenger, until finally the captain of the *Cornubia,* the leading steamer in the Ordnance Department's squadron, had taken pity on her. Georgiana became the first woman to run the blockade.

At times, Georgiana could count as many as a dozen Confederate flags in the harbor. Some of the vessels' captains were Southern, but many were British, usually Royal Naval Reserve officers. One, the Hon. Augustus Charles Hobart-Hampden, a younger son of the sixth Earl of Buckinghamshire, even resigned his commission to dedicate himself to blockade running, and there seemed to be no shortage of thrill seekers from either branch of Her Majesty's forces. On the steamship from Halifax to Liverpool in November, Matthew Maury and James Morgan had been surprised to learn that among the passengers was a group of English army officers who had used their leave to try blockade running. The Earl of Dunmore, who became friendly with Maury and Morgan, boasted of his capture and confinement in a Northern prison. The earl had "passed through the Federal lines and gone to Richmond and thence to Charleston," wrote a clearly impressed Morgan.

He had travelled incognito, under his family name of Murray. The boat he took passage on successfully eluded the Federal fleet off Charleston, but an outside cruiser captured her the very next day. The prisoners were of course searched, and around the body of "Mr. Murray," under his shirt, was found wrapped a Confederate flag—the flag of the C.S.S. *Nashville,* which had been presented to him by Captain Pegram. Despite his protestations that he was a Britisher traveling for pleasure, he was confined, as "Mr. Murray," in Fort Lafayette. The British Minister, Lord Lyons, soon heard of his predicament and requested the authorities in Washington to order his release, representing him as being the Earl of Dunmore, a lieutenant in Her Majesty's Life Guards. But the commandant of Fort Lafayette denied that he had any such prisoner and it required quite a correspondence to persuade him that a man by the name of Murray could at the same time be Lord Dunmore.[3]

Lord Lyons implored his staff to discourage their friends and acquaintances from visiting the Confederacy. Two months after Edward Malet's midnight encounter with Lord Hartington, the legation attaché was again called to the aid of an English civilian. The Federal security measures implemented after Mosby's raid had snared another victim. George Alfred Lawrence was famous throughout England as the author of *Guy Livingstone.* Published in 1857, the novel eulogized a handsome daredevil Guards officer who defies social convention to the point of blackguardism but ultimately knows right from wrong. Five years later, Lawrence's dashing alter ego still haunted its sedentary creator. In December 1862, Lawrence shocked his wife and friends by announcing his intention to serve as a volunteer staff officer to General Lee. In contrast to the devil-may-care Guy, Lawrence had carefully planned his adventure. He obtained highly laudatory letters of introduction, including one from James Mason, made financial provisions for his family, and secured an appointment from the *Morning Post* as its Southern correspondent.

Lawrence was greeted with adulation by the young attachés at the legation. Lord Lyons invited him to dinner, although he was not as taken with the author as his impressionable staff, one of whom supplied Lawrence with the address of the ever-obliging pro-Southern journalist W. W. Glenn. This time, however, Glenn regretted his involvement; Lawrence was captured on April 10 a few miles from the last Federal outpost in Greenland County, West Virginia. He was high-handed with his Federal interrogator and melodramatically refused to answer questions except to say "I am the author of *Guy Livingstone* and other works of fiction, I took no letters from Baltimore to carry and none were found on me."

According to the army report, hidden among Lawrence's personal belongings was a letter from Mr. Glenn giving directions on where to find his guide, "and the route to take, the persons to trust and to avoid . . . it reflects a disloyal and traitorous light." There was also a scurrilous verse in his handwriting: "Jeff Davis rides a white horse, Abe rides a mule, Davis is a gentleman, Abe a fool." William Seward was robustly unsympathetic when Lord Lyons wrote to him about releasing Lawrence from the Old Capitol prison.

The publicity attending Lawrence's arrest was deeply embarrassing for Lord Lyons. He also feared what the English papers would say once it became known that the "author of *Guy Livingstone*" was being held in prison without charge. Despite persistent prodding by Lyons to bring Lawrence to trial or else release him, Seward did nothing for two months. The secretary of war, Edwin Stanton, insisted that Seward make an example of Lawrence and showed his anger by refusing to grant any more passes to British military observers, including Lieutenant Colonel James Eli Crowther, who had been sent by the British Army as an official observer.*

George Lawrence whiled away his time in prison writing irritable letters to Lyons swearing that there was not "a shadow of foundation" to the charge he had sought to join the Confederacy. The attachés visited him weekly bearing little care packages, which the guards kept for themselves. Lawrence loathed his loquacious cellmate, whose "narrative riches about matched those of the knife-grinder."[5] His sole consolation, he wrote, was the occasional sight of a beautiful female prisoner who once threw him a white rose from her window. Apart from this innocent little romance, Lawrence kept to himself. When Seward finally ordered his release in June, Lawrence returned to New York a chastened man. Henceforth he would continue his campaign against the North from the safety of his study.

Lord Lyons might have been more persuasive with Seward if

---

* Stanton was like Seward in his inability to resist an aristocratic title. He granted a visitor's permit to Lord Abinger, who was stationed in Canada with the Scots Guards. Abinger went down to the Army of the Potomac, was treated to a grand review, and had his photograph taken with Hooker's staff. Owing to his discreet and affable nature, no one among his hosts had the faintest idea of his true feelings. In contrast to the neutral Crowther, Abinger was thoroughly sympathetic to the South. The previous April, he had invited Commissioner James Mason to dine at the regimental mess in Eastbourne. Mason was most gratified to have the notice of a Scottish peer and recorded every detail of the outing in his diary.[4]

Lawrence's arrest had not coincided with that of another adventure-hungry Briton. Twenty-year-old Alfred Rubery was one of life's nincompoops. The death of his father, John, the largest umbrella manufacturer in Birmingham, had given him a modest independence. Leaving his older brother to manage the family business, Alfred went to San Francisco in the summer of 1862 with dreams of making his fortune in mining. He had not been in the city for long when he fell into a barroom argument with a Federal officer. Young Rubery had visited the South before the war. Naturally, as one who owed his wealth and social position to factory smoke, he idealized Southern society and thought it the most perfect on earth. He said all this and more to the incensed Lieutenant Tompkins, who happened to be the descendant of a New York State governor. "High words followed," according to witnesses, "and Tompkins made a remark that touched Rubery's honor. The latter simply said, 'You will hear from me, sir,' and left the room."[6]

The virtually friendless Rubery needed a second for his duel with Tompkins. An acquaintance put him in touch with Asbury Harpending, a Confederate veteran who had fought at Shiloh. Only a year older than Rubery, Harpending seemed to be living proof that fantasies can come true. Brought up in Kentucky, he had run away from home as a teenager and made his way to Mexico, where he discovered a gold mine, becoming rich overnight. But the chronic anarchy and violence that bedeviled Mexico soon separated Harpending from his new source of wealth. Undaunted, when the war began, he went to San Francisco with fresh schemes in mind. His first idea was to organize a chapter of the Knights of the Golden Circle, a secret pro-Southern society, and have each member recruit a hundred volunteers. This, he reckoned, would give him a big enough force to seize California's government buildings and declare the state's allegiance to the South. When that failed, he somehow got himself to Richmond, where he wrangled an officer's commission in the Confederate navy.

Harpending returned to San Francisco with a new plan. He and a friend named Ridgley Greathouse were going to charter a ship, sail it into Mexican waters, and lie in wait for the Pacific Mail steamer and its cargo of California gold. After offloading the passengers, they would equip the steamer as a privateer and send the gold to Richmond. Thus armed, they would prey on Californian cargo ships and, with luck, disrupt the supply of gold to the North. The only hitch to the plan was the $25,000 required to see it through to execution. Harpending was therefore delighted to meet the pro-Southern and apparently well-heeled Rubery.

But first, Harpending had to rescue his friend from the duel with Tompkins. Alfred Rubery's physical prowess lagged far behind his enthusiasm. "I tried him at pistol practice," recalled Harpending, "and found that, with extra good luck, at ten paces he could hit a barn." The American could fast-talk his way out of anything; he used his gift now to make the duel disappear. With Tompkins safely dispatched, the three conspirators began looking for a suitable ship. They soon happened upon the *J. M. Chapman,* a ninety-ton schooner that had just made a record-breaking voyage from New York. As soon as ownership was transferred to them, they proceeded to hire a crew and purchase enough firepower to make a formidable warship. "It only remained to secure a navigator who could be implicitly trusted," wrote Harpending. When none materialized, they were forced to engage William Law, a sea captain and ex–slave trader who had been dismissed by the Pacific Mail Company. Law had only eight fingers and "was the most repulsive reptile in appearance that I ever set eyes on," wrote Harpending. His antipathy proved well founded.

The day of departure was set for March 15, 1863. The night before, Harpending and Rubery hid in a dark alley behind the American Exchange Hotel and waited for the crew to arrive. They then divided into three squads to avoid suspicion and "slipped through the dimly lighted streets, past roaring saloons and sailor boarding houses" and reached an unfrequented part of the waterfront unnoticed, where the privateer was moored. Rubery and Harpending "were exultant." But,

> when we scrambled aboard the *Chapman,* Greathouse was pacing the deck in agitation. Law was not there. I experienced a shock such as a man receives when a bucket of ice water is emptied on him in his sleep. The suggestion of treachery could not be avoided. We cast loose from the wharf and anchored in the stream. But we were helpless. We could not sail without our navigator. We had nothing to do but wait.[7]

Shortly after dawn the three conspirators awoke to find the *Chapman* surrounded by U.S. gunboats. The authorities had been keeping careful surveillance for several days. Rubery and Harpending had neglected to supply the local revenue officers with a cargo manifest, thereby piquing official interest in the mysterious boxes that were being loaded in such a hurry. The luckless three were taken to Alcatraz, where Rubery was soon visited by Consul William Lane Booker, who thought him to be a rather unsympathetic, cocky youth who fully deserved his punishment. "He has nothing to complain as to his treatment," Booker reported to Lord Russell, "beyond being deprived of his liberty."[8] The evidence against Rubery was so overwhelming that Lyons made no attempt to intervene on his behalf. While searching through Rubery's baggage, the Federals had found a plan for capturing San Francisco's military forts, a proclamation to the people of California urging them to join the Confederacy, and a declaration of allegiance for those who did.

Rubery's family could not accept that their little Alfred had played a central role in the conspiracy. For the past three months he had been spinning a tale to them about a mining venture in Mexico. Determined to prove his innocence, they showed the letters to Birmingham's two MPs, John Bright and William Scholefield. Neither shared the Ruberys' delusion: "They seem to be wholly unaware that he can have committed himself so as to justify his arrest," wrote Scholefield pityingly.[9] "[Alfred] must be wonderfully stupid to have engaged in any conspiracy," decided John Bright, "and yet I hear that he is sharp and clever, and was educated at the London University." The Rubery name and fortune carried sufficient weight in Birmingham to make it impossible for the MPs to ignore the family's request for help. John Bright reluctantly wrote to Charles Sumner, "Is it too much for me to ask you to procure his liberation on condition that he shall at once return to England?"[10] It was. Rubery remained at Alcatraz.

———

Lord Lyons refused to let either George Lawrence or Alfred Rubery disrupt his enjoyment of the first days of spring. It was not only possible but also delightful to walk down streets abloom with flowering trees. The great drying-out attracted crowds of tourists and distinguished visitors to the city. Seward's house became lively again, and nineteen-year-old Fanny Seward briefly relinquished her reserve to enjoy a brief flirtation with an English naval surgeon on leave from USS *Commodore Morris*.

Washington society turned out en masse, including President Lincoln, to watch the self-styled "youngest star in the world," John Wilkes Booth, play Hamlet at Grover's Theatre. Dr. Charles Culverwell observed Booth's debut in the capital. Having heard that the lesser parts were open to audition, Culverwell took a leave of absence and auditioned under the name Charles Wyndham. To his great surprise, he won the part of Osric. On the handbills for the play, Culverwell was described as "Charles Wyndham: first appearance of a gifted young actor." After the opening night on April 14, 1863, no one mentioned Osric, but Booth received praise from every quarter. Many years later, Culverwell still retained vivid memories of his brief encounter with Booth:

> During my introductory rehearsal I wandered about the stage and finally chose an advantageous position at a little table where I could command a good view of all the proceedings. John Wilkes noticed me there and smiled. . . . The courtesy and kindness shown to me by John Wilkes made way for friendship between us, and we frequently were together after the play. He was a most charming fellow, off the stage as well as on, a man of flashing wit and magnetic manner. He was one of the best raconteurs to whom I have ever listened. As he talked he threw himself into his words, brilliant, ready, enthusiastic. He could hold a group spellbound by the hour at the force and fire and beauty of him . . . as an actor, the natural endowment of John Wilkes Booth was of the highest. His original gift was greater than that of his wonderful brother, Edwin. . . . He was the idol of women. They would rave of him, his voice, his hair, and his eyes. Small wonder, for he was fascinating. . . . Poor, sad, mad, bad, John Wilkes Booth.[11]

Lord Lyons was never given the opportunity to watch Booth play Hamlet; a careless clerk in the Foreign Office had forwarded the legation's correspondence to the printers of the parliamentary "Blue Book" without first removing the censored passages. Its arrival in mid-April caused such controversy that Lyons suffered the same hideous embarrassment that had ruined Charles Francis Adams's Christmas. "The goodwill to me personally, which miraculously survived so long, seems at last to have sunk altogether," wrote Lyons. The political damage was also considerable. The Blue Book had offended or alienated both supporters and enemies alike: "Unluckily the book contains just the passages in my dispatches which are most irritating to each of the parties, and which it is most inconvenient to them to have published."[12] Lyons was especially worried about how the Blue Book would affect his relationship with Seward. He had heard that the secretary was annoyed and feared that it made him appear weak in his dealings with the diplomatic corps.

Lyons also braced himself for a difficult time over the *Peterhoff* affair, with Seward making public threats and statements about what the United States would and would not stand for, similar to his recent grandstanding about letters of marque. But Seward surprised him; rather than allowing the controversy to take on a life of its own, he courageously defied the objections of the abinet and returned the *Peterhoff*'s captured mailbag to Lyons. He even prevailed upon his rival Gideon Welles to transfer Admiral Wilkes to the Pacific Ocean, where there were fewer opportunities to cause trouble. The U.S. navy secretary grudgingly gave the order, but in secret Welles fantasized about the dire retribution awaiting Britain—"years of desolation, of dissolution, of suffering and blood."[13] Welles's supporters started a whispering campaign against Lyons. "Among other devices," wrote Lyons, "is that of representing me as having made the most violent and arrogant demands about the *Peterhoff*." This led to an unpleasant encounter with Charles Sumner at a dinner party. The senator dragged Lyons into a corner and proceeded to rail at him for overstepping his prerogative. Lyons was dumbfounded at first, then swore he had never made anything resembling a demand. He finally offered to show Sumner copies of his correspondence with Seward.[14]

Lyons wondered whether he was wasting his efforts to bolster good relations between the two countries. "One hardly knows whether to wish the North success or failure in the field," he had written to Russell during the *Peterhoff* affair.[15] Yet the Confederacy was equally bitter against England, Lyons learned from the diplomatic bags that occasionally made it out of the South.* "It ought to have been known here from the first, but was not, that England could be no friend to the Confederacy or its

---

* It was no longer the exception but the rule for British subjects to be conscripted into the army or jailed if they refused. By some miracle, Lord Lyons received a letter from a Yorkshire lad in a Southern jail in Mississippi. The writer was desperate for help: "I was, like a very dog, ordered to 'fall in,'" he wrote, "and were sent to this place and placed in artillary [*sic*] companies. I again told my captain of my immunity from the service but it availed nothing. . . . I was sick from exposure and sent to hospital where I have been ever since, except the last two weeks when I was arrested and sent to Jail, where I now write this, charged with cursing the Confederacy and trying to escape the place, which they term desertion."[16]

cause," declared the *Richmond Enquirer*, for example. "We have been long in finding out the truth and, before we would admit it, have endured some humiliations and insolent airs on the part of that Power, which surprised us very much, but ought not to have done so. At last the thing has become too clear."[17]

Southern rage against Britain placed Francis Lawley in a difficult position. He had completed his tour of the Confederacy and returned to Richmond at the end of March, but his report for *The Times* was taking longer than usual to compose. Anything less than unqualified praise, Lawley had discovered, was not tolerated by his hosts. He confided his exasperation to William Gregory. "I cannot impress upon you the difficulty which I find in the discharge of my present office, in avoiding topics which will be calculated to ruffle the amour propre . . . of the most susceptible people and government on earth."[18]

Lawley still believed in the purity of the Southern planter class as the epitome of all that was noble and intelligent in the human race. But in his opinion, the rest of the Southern population was going to the dogs: "Richmond and in a less degree, Charleston and Mobile, strike me as immense gambling booths." He would know—many of his friends and acquaintances, including Judah Benjamin, made up the chief clientele of Richmond's illicit "hells." Profiteering, corruption, and hoarding were rampant. Lawley felt a visceral disappointment whenever he observed Southerners behaving like ordinary human beings in time of war, and he tried as much as possible to shut his eyes to the messy aspects of the South. He required moral clarity from the Confederates, especially now that the North was growing stronger and more aggressive. Part of him was confident that "Fighting Joe" Hooker stood no chance against Lee. But he had seen enough of the Federal army to have doubts, even if he preferred not to express them out loud. "My sole and only hope is in the demoralization of the Yankees but I have little faith in it," he wrote to Gregory. "The truth is that the Yankee fights much better than he has been represented as fighting."[19]

On April 2, 1863, a few days after Lawley had unburdened himself to Gregory, there were bread riots in Richmond. The Confederate capital was a microcosm of the many hardships being endured across the South; hunger and disease were spreading. Smallpox had invaded the poorer neighborhoods as more refugees arrived, begging for space even if it meant sleeping outside on a porch or in a garden shed. Everything was scarce. Women who before the war bought only the finest scented soaps from France were using soap made from kitchen grease mixed with lye. Ordinary articles such as pins and buttons were so hard to come by that John Jones, the diarist in the Confederate War Department, walked to work every day with his eyes fixed on the ground hoping to find some carelessly dropped treasure in the gutter.

Lee's Army of Northern Virginia was also suffering; the men had been on half rations for so long that many were showing the first signs of scurvy. There were still plenty of foodstuffs in southern Virginia and North Carolina, particularly in the fertile tidewater regions near the coast, but over the past year, transportation had become almost impossible. The Federal occupation of Norfolk, Suffolk, Plymouth, Washington, and New Bern—all of them strategically important towns along the south-eastern seaboard—was choking the Confederate supply line. On the morning of the bread riots in Richmond, General Longstreet—Francis Dawson's new commander—received permission to attack Suffolk. The Union garrison there was weakly held, and Longstreet believed he could take it with twenty thousand men. The Confederate general had hoped to launch a surprise attack, but an intercepted message alerted the Federals to his plan.

Washington promptly dispatched thousands of troops to strengthen the garrison, forcing Longstreet to alter his battle plan from an attack to a siege. The no longer plump Englishman George Herbert of the 9th New York Volunteers ("Hawkins's Zouaves") was among the Union re-inforcements. The regiment was thunderstruck by its mobilization. The men had only six weeks left before the terms of their enlistment expired. They had expected to remain in camp at Newport News, Virginia, where the most strenuous activity of the day was a game of baseball against the 51st New York. The men "are all anxiously looking forward to our final march up Broadway," Herbert told his mother. Few of them intended to reenlist: Herbert was already planning his future in England. "I guess I shall have somewhere about $400 when I am mustered out and the more gold falls the richer I shall be," he mused on March 31.[20]

Eleven days later, on April 11, Herbert and his comrades disembarked at Portsmouth Naval Yard. The regiment stood listlessly under pelting rain as inquiries revealed that Suffolk was already under siege by Longstreet's forces. The trains had been canceled and there were no available wagons. The soldiers were forced to march twenty-seven miles over railroad ties, loaded down with all their equipment. It was dark by the time they reached the Suffolk camp. No one had bothered to prepare for the regiment's arrival, so the men went from tent to tent seeking a place to sleep. The lieutenant colonel, Edgar Kimball, found an old friend from the Mexican War and spent a few hours warming himself with his tent companion's whiskey.

A little after 2:00 A.M., Kimball remembered his orders to report to General George Getty's headquarters. On the way, however, he came across General Michael Corcoran, the boisterous commander of the Irish Brigade. In one version of what happened next, Kimball went to the aid of a sentry who was shouting at several men on horseback. Corcoran, on the other hand, claimed that Kimball suddenly emerged from the darkness and grabbed his bridle, demanding that the countersign be given. But according to all versions of the incident, Corcoran refused to give it, saying, "I am General Corcoran and staff." This was not enough for Kimball, who began brandishing his sword, whereupon Corcoran shot him at point-blank range. Journalists at the camp rushed to telegraph the news of his death.

Kimball's insistence on the proper countersign was initially commended as a wise precaution when the guerrilla John Mosby was about: "Under the circumstances, with a Rebel force in close proximity, an enemy might have said the same thing," wrote a New York correspondent. When the Zouaves learned of their colonel's death, many of them picked up their weapons and started for Corcoran's camp. Fearing a riot, General Getty had the bugle sounded for assembly, which the men instinctively obeyed. He sat on his horse in front of the regiment and made a conciliatory speech, promising that there would be an investigation into Kimball's shooting. The soldiers calmed down as they listened. At first they were rather pleased to hear that the general was sending them away from the camp at once. A few hours later, when they had reached Fort Nansemond, the men realized that the general had ordered them to the "extreme front." The Zouaves spent the next twenty-two days under continuous fire from Confederate rifle pits, "so fully occupied with the enemy in front," wrote the regiment's historian, "that if his satanic majesty had wished to brew mischief he could have found no heart or hands in the regiment to do it for him." None of the regiment was allowed to attend Kimball's funeral in New York on April 20.[21]

As more Union troops were sent to reinforce Suffolk, Longstreet realized that his small army would soon be radically outnumbered. He saw no reason to continue the siege, since enough bacon and grain to feed Lee's army for two months had been collected during the so-called Tidewater Campaign. Longstreet was preparing to withdraw his men when a telegram arrived on May 3, 1863, ordering his immediate return to the Army of Northern Virginia: "Fighting Joe" Hooker was on the move. Longstreet tried to move as quickly as he could without jeopardizing the safety of the long wagon trains filled with supplies.

George Henry Herbert's term of enlistment ended on the same day as Longstreet's retreat. The Zoaves threatened to mutiny if they were kept at Suffolk a minute longer, sufficiently alarming the authorities into providing troop transports to take the Zouaves straight to New York.

Longstreet doubted that he would reach Lee in time to help him stop General Hooker's advance. Suffolk was more than 150 miles from Fredericksburg and "Fighting Joe" had been counting on this when he devised his battle plan. The two armies had passed the winter facing each other across the banks of the Rappahannock River. Hooker tried to give the impression that he was contemplating another frontal assault on Fredericksburg in order to hide the fact that he was looking for places to ford the river upstream. Richmond was still his objective, and the Confederate army was still blocking the way; but Hooker's strategy—one of the boldest on the Union side for the entire war—involved a sophisticated deception. He intended to force the Confederates out of their entrenched position at Fredericksburg by attacking them simultaneously from several different directions. To achieve this, he needed to disguise the whereabouts of his army until it was too late for Lee to do anything other than react defensively.

Hooker knew that the Army of the Potomac had a two-to-one advantage over Lee, whose Army of Northern Virginia numbered fewer than 65,000 men. The Union general thought he could increase the odds even more by sending his 12,000-strong cavalry corps on raids around Richmond, with instructions to "Let your watchword be fight, fight, fight." He wanted the cavalry to isolate Richmond from the rest of the state, causing panic in the capital and, with luck, forcing Lee to detach a part of his army for its defense. Sir Percy Wyndham's regiment had a merry time ripping up railroads and cutting communications north of Richmond, rarely encountering opposition. Predictably, Wyndham went too far and began thinking up his own assignments, which led to his arrest for insubordination; after vigorous protests by his supporters, he was released with a censure for disobeying orders.

Hooker was in a jubilant mood once the Army of the Potomac started moving on April 29. Leaving 40,000 troops at Fredericksburg, under the capable command of General "Uncle John" Sedgwick, he ordered the rest, numbering almost 80,000 men and officers, to cross the Rappahannock River at two different places and rendezvous at Chancellorsville, nine miles west of Fredericksburg. The name applied not to a village but to a clearing in a wood that spread over seventy square miles in such dense thickets that locals simply labeled it "the Wilderness." A crossroads cut through the middle of the clearing, passing close to the veranda of an old brick mansion named Chancellor House. Here Hooker and his staff set up their temporary headquarters, flushing the indignant female inhabitants out of the parlor to their bedrooms on the floor above. He was ready to launch his surprise attack. "My plans are perfect," he declared on the eve of the battle; "may God have mercy on General Lee, for I will have none."[22]

TWENTY

The Key Is in the Lock

A great gamble—Death of Stonewall Jackson—Grant reaches Vicksburg—
Arthur Fremantle meets the famous Colonel Grenfell—Feilden in love

The discovery that Hooker had divided his army and was planning to crush him like a nut between two hammers came as a tremendous shock for Lee, who was unused to being tricked by his Federal opponents. Having weighed the various risks and options for his army, Lee decided that the greatest danger came from Hooker's advancing forces rather than the 47,000 Federals still remaining at Fredericksburg. Fortunately, Lee had avoided the trap of dispatching part of his army to defend Richmond, having correctly guessed that the Federal cavalry raids around the capital were nothing more than a feint. Even so, Lee could afford to leave only 10,000 men to hold Fredericksburg. The remaining 52,000 he ordered to turn around and take up defensive positions just beyond Chancellorsville. Lee planned to attack Hooker's troops as they emerged from the Wilderness, using the advantage of surprise.

The fighting began on May 1, 1863. At Fredericksburg, General Sedgwick fired some artillery at the Confederates and engaged in a few skirmishes. It was hardly the aggressive movement envisaged by "Fighting Joe" Hooker, but to the raw and untested second lieutenant Henry George Hore, it seemed as though he had participated in a marvelous triumph. Hore had joined Sedgwick's staff only a few weeks earlier, having sailed from England to do his part in freeing the slaves. "We are victorious and captured [the Confederates'] batteries, men and all," Hore wrote in the afternoon to his cousin Olivia; it had been "the Battle of Fredericksburg the Second."[1]

Francis Lawley had rushed from Richmond as soon as he heard that Hooker was on the march but was disappointed that the Wilderness's impenetrable scrub made it impossible for him to see what was happening. What blinded him also hindered Hooker's generals as they tried to lead their men through the woods. At 2:00 P.M., after meeting relatively light pockets of resistance from the Confederates, Hooker suddenly called off the advance and ordered his army to retreat back to Chancellorsville. His commanders begged him to continue fighting. Hooker was obstinate: "I have got Lee just where I want him," he told General Darius Couch, who walked away from the meeting convinced that "Fighting Joe" "was a whipped man." Hooker was never able to explain his decision afterward except to say that all of a sudden he lost faith in himself.[2]

That night, Lee and Stonewall Jackson discussed how to take advantage of their adversary's hesitation. They agreed to divide their already outnumbered army into even smaller segments. Jackson would take thirty thousand men and march around Hooker's army, relying on local guides to find a way through the Wilderness, and surprise him from the rear, while Lee remained in front with just fifteen thousand troops. In any other battle, the enemy cavalry would have spotted such a maneuver, but Hooker's was miles away, destroying barns and canals.

When Hooker was informed that large troop movements were taking place, he decided that it meant the Confederates were retreating back to Fredericksburg. It never occurred to him that Lee would attempt an attack from two different directions, using the same divide-and-surprise tactic that he himself had intended to employ. The next day, May 2, at five o'clock, just as the Federals were sitting down to cook their dinners, Stonewall Jackson ordered his men to charge. "Swift and sudden as the falcon sweeping her prey, Jackson had burst on his enemy's rear and crushed him before resistance could be attempted," wrote Francis Lawley in a sudden fit of poetry.[3] The rout was so complete that an entire wing of the Union force collapsed and ran back toward headquarters, some two miles away. The first Hooker learned of the battle was when one of his staff officers happened to walk out onto the veranda and look through his field glasses. "My God, here they come!" he shouted.[4] The lines between the two armies became blurred as the twilight turned to darkness.

Hooker was not beaten yet, however. Though strangely passive with regard to his immediate danger, he had no trouble directing the operations at Fredericksburg. Furious that Sedgwick had been poking rather than smashing the Confederates' positions, Hooker sent him a terse message demanding the capture of the town, and instructed the message bearer to stay until Sedgwick had moved into action.[5] The direct order had its effect.

Henry Hore was up early on May 3, riding hard between Sedgwick's headquarters and the batteries. Now he saw real fighting instead of the tepid firing of the day before. It was a shock for him to discover that the rebel soldiers handled their rifles with far greater accuracy than his own side. Sedgwick's troops were flailing until the Federal artillery unleashed its guns. There was such a long delay before the first explosions, wrote Hore, "that I thought [the rebels] would take the guns before we fired. At last came the word: 'Depress pieces' and I quite felt sick, they were just about fifty yards or so from my horse who was as much excited as myself."

The next hour was Hore's initiation into the sordid truth of war. "Good God, my dear girl, it was awful," he admitted to his cousin Olivia. "Their dead seemed piled heaps upon heaps, the shot went right clear through them, completely smashing the front of the columns." Sedgwick ordered ten regiments to charge across the plain toward Marye's Heights, the same attack formation that had decimated the Irish 69th and so many other regiments in December. But this time there was only a thin line of Confederates behind the famous stone wall, and in half an hour the attackers were up and over, lunging forward with their bayonets. Sedgwick was so excited that he tore a page from a letter meant for his wife and scribbled an order for more artillery. He gave it to Hore with the command to ride as fast as he could and return with every gun he could find. A fellow officer named Hansard, who had abjured his home state of South Carolina to support the North, offered to accompany him.

The two officers were almost at the rear when a Confederate raiding party came crashing through the trees with terrifying whoops and yells.[6] Hore wheeled his horse around, hoping that Hansard was with him. But when he looked behind him he saw one of the raiders spur his horse on and reach out to grab Hansard's bridle. Hore made a split-second decision to turn around. As he did so, the two riders struggled and fell to the ground. Hansard landed on his back. While he lay helpless, a Confeder-

Chancellorsville
May 2–6, 1863

▰▰▰▰ Federal forces, May 2   ▰▰▰▰ Confederate forces, May 2

▬▬▬▬ Federal forces, May 3–4   ▬▬▬▬ Confederate forces, May 3–4

◀▬▪▬ Federal withdrawal, May 5–6

Hooker

Rappahannock River

Falmouth

Richmond, Fredericksburg & Potomac R.R.

Henry
Hore

Banks'
Ford

Sedgwick
May 4

Fredericksburg

Sedgwick
May 3 attack

Sedgwick

Lee holds off Sedgwick
at Salem Church May 3
and attacks May 4

McLaws

Plank Road

Early

Anderson

Early

Early's withdrawal
May 3 and Lee's attack
May 4

Sedgwick
May 3
attack

Old Richmond Road

Mine Road

Miles

0   1   2   3

ate cavalryman whipped out his sword and plunged it into his chest. Hore watched, aghast, as the raider leaned forward and tore off Hansard's shoulder straps. The rebel locked eyes with Hore and shook the straps at him. "I now felt as if he or I must be killed," wrote Hore. Time slowed and each movement became exaggeratedly clear in his memory. He pulled out his revolver and galloped toward the cavalry-man: "I had made up my mind I would kill him if I could." The rebel either had no gun or forgot he had one. When Hore was sure he would not miss, he fired straight at him: "This did not take 30 seconds," he wrote, "not near so long as it takes me to write. I sighted him along the barrel of my revolver and if I had not killed him the first time would have shot again, for H[ansard] was a good friend to me."[7]

Hore remembered little else of that day. Once the Federal army had breached Marye's Heights, the Confederates pulled back toward Chancellorsville, making a new stand in the woods around Salem Church. Though still outnumbered, the Confederates managed to hold down Sedgwick's troops. Hore was confused and thought that the Confederate retreat meant another victory. "They have not gained (the Rebels I mean) a single yard," he wrote, "and we don't mean they shall," not realizing that in Hooker's plan, Sedgwick should have been at Chancellorsville by now, helping to smash Lee's little army. By this time, Hooker was sorely in need of Sedgwick. Shortly after nine o'clock on the morning of the third, a Confederate cannonball had smashed into the veranda of Chancellor House, knocking Hooker unconscious. Though still groggy after coming to, he insisted on resuming command, much to the dismay of his staff. Contrary to his commanders' wishes, Hooker ordered a general retreat.

Shortly after Hooker's departure, Chancellor House went up in flames.* Lee trotted up to the burning house as Confederates came running toward him, cheering and shouting wildly. Behind them the Wilderness had been transformed into a roaring furnace, trapping the lost and wounded. Men closest to the conflagration could see figures waving in the inferno. Union and Confederate soldiers braved the sear-

---

* Mrs. Chancellor and her six daughters were rescued by one of Hooker's aides, Lieutenant Colonel Joseph Dickinson. He disobeyed orders and remained with the women until they were safely across the Rappahannock, earning their eternal friendship and gratitude.

ing heat to pull out anyone they could. Two enemies fought together to rescue a trapped youth: "The fire was all around him," recalled the Federal soldier. They could see his face: "His eyes were big and blue, and his hair like raw silk surrounded by a wreath of fire." In vain, they burned their hands trying to reach him. "I heard him scream, 'Oh Mother, O God.' It left me trembling all over, like a leaf." The defeated rescuers fled the forest. Although it was agony to open their fingers, "me and them rebs tried to shake hands."[8]

There was no cathartic pain for Henry Hore. On the night of the fourth, taking advantage of the full moon, he led a burial party to look for Hansard's body. They found him lying next to the dead rebel. Hore dug a grave and buried Hansard, but he deliberately left the Confederate raider to rot out in the open. "My dear Cousin you must think me quite savage," he wrote afterward in the bleak surroundings of a dark, filthy barn, "but the carnage of this frightful war and the horrid sights I see every day made me indifferent to human life. At one time I should have never thought of killing anyone, but now can shoot a man without a shake of my hand. I think I am writing to you more as if you were a hard hearted man than a very pretty girl."

On May 5 the balmy weather was replaced by lashing wind and rain. The Confederate commanders informed Lee that another attack was beyond their men's strength. The storm provided the Union army with perfect cover as it slowly crawled back over the Rappahannock River. Charles Francis Adams, Jr.'s cavalry regiment was on the other side, part of the skeleton force of mounted troops Hooker had kept behind. He initially discounted the tales from the abject stragglers who stopped to ask for food or shelter, but "in the afternoon came the crusher," he told his father. They received the order to saddle up and return to their old camp. They found it "deserted, burned up, filthy, and surrounded with dead horses. We tied up our horses and stood dismally round in the pouring rain."[9]

Henry Hore arrived at Fortress Monroe on Hampton Roads a few days later, on May 9, a young man no longer.[10] The magnitude of Hooker's defeat was numbing: 17,000 casualties to Lee's 13,000, without gaining the slightest moral or tactical advantage. Lincoln was horror-struck when he read the telegram, exclaiming, "My God, my God, what will the country say?" The press was predictably harsh: "Everybody feels," wrote Joseph Medill, the editor of the *Chicago Tribune,* and a close friend of the president's, "that the war is drawing to a disastrous and disgraceful termination."[11] The *New York World* railed that the "gallant Army of the Potomac" had been "marched to fruitless slaughter" by "an imbecile department and led by an incompetent general."[12]

The country's frustration with its leaders made the gratitude felt toward the volunteers all the deeper and more profound. A flotilla of boats swarmed the troopship carrying the 9th New York Volunteers as it approached the Battery, at the southern tip of Manhattan. Thousands of well-wishers lined the pier, throwing flowers and waving flags, and a military band escorted the soldiers along Broadway to Union Square. The men were still wearing their filthy uniforms from the siege at Suffolk, but their disheveled appearance seemed to delight the crowds. This was the enthusiastic reception that the seven hundred survivors of the regiment had been imagining for weeks. On May 20, 1863, George Henry Herbert handed over his weapon at the armory, shook hands with his comrades one last time, and walked away. After a disastrous beginning that had made him the butt of the regiment's jokes, Herbert had grown to love his life in the army. He sailed for England richer by $400, ready to start life afresh.

Lee had maintained a sanguine demeanor throughout the battle—until the moment he learned that Stonewall Jackson had been shot. Jackson had been reconnoitering positions when he accidentally galloped into his own picket line. The nervous Confederate guards shot blindly at the group, killing several riders and striking Jackson. Two bullets tore through his left arm; another hit his right wrist. He was also dragged along by his horse and dropped by his stretcher bearers. The damage to his left arm was irreparable; the limb had to be amputated the next morning. Lee sent Jackson a message via the chaplain begging him to recover quickly, adding, "He has lost his left arm, but I have lost my right arm." As soon as doctors deemed he could be moved, Jackson was loaded onto an ambulance and taken on a twenty-seven-mile journey to a plantation at Guinea Station.

Francis Lawley followed behind, arriving at the plantation on May 7. Jackson had been moved to the estate office, where he could recuperate in private. "With a beating heart I rode up to ask after him," wrote Lawley. The doctor stepped outside so that he could speak plainly; the general's wife and infant daughter were inside. Jackson had appeared to be recovering, but late the previous night the classic signs of pneumonia had set in. Lawley knew what this meant: "I gave up all hope of his recovery."[13]

Lawley could not bear to wait for the end, so he boarded one of the trains taking the wounded back to Richmond. On May 8 he sent a letter to the Confederate secretary of war, James Seddon, warning him of Jackson's desperate condition. Two days later, on the tenth, Jackson died. Lee cried when he learned the news; there was not a man or woman, North or South, who failed to understand the meaning of Jackson's death or his vital importance to the Confederacy.*

The loss of Jackson posed a dilemma for Lawley. If he made too much of it in his reports, readers might think that the South had suffered a mortal blow. Yet here was an opportunity to create a mythic figure whose heroic end would elevate the entire Southern cause. Lawley did his best, eulogizing Jackson as both an earthly saint and a military genius whose death would only inspire the South to "deeds of more than mortal valor." (Unfortunately, the blockade was playing havoc with Lawley's dispatches; his obituary of Jackson reached London before the news of his shooting.)[15]

Lawley was so concerned about presenting Jackson's death in the best possible light that he deliberately obscured the gravity of the situation out west. On May 19, 1863, he finally revealed to the English public that Vicksburg might not be impregnable after all. The news was "contrary to my own and the general anticipation," Lawley admitted at the end of yet another article on Stonewall Jackson. General Grant had won a series of tactical victories, beginning with a successful night raid by the Union navy on April 16 that enabled the fleet to steam up the Mississippi River past Vicksburg's thirty-one guns. Grant stopped all the useless digging and canal building and set his army loose against the Confederates. On May 1 his troops crushed the small force holding the town of Port Gibson, thirty miles south of Vicksburg. Suddenly it was as though the wind was at their backs. The Federal army raced toward Vicksburg, fighting four battles in seventeen days, swatting aside the Confederates' resistance. General Sherman razed most of Jackson, the capital of Mississippi, on May 14, in a fiery portent of what was to come in 1864.

---

* In his history of the Civil War, Winston Churchill wrote: "Chancellorsville was the finest battle which Lee and Jackson fought together. Their combination had become perfect."[14]

Grant's success frightened Richmond, but there was no agreement on how he should be stopped. Longstreet thought they should provoke a battle against the Union Army of the Cumberland, which was stationed in Tennessee. This, he argued, would force Grant to divide his forces between the two theaters. Jefferson Davis wanted to send reinforcements to the two Confederate generals defending Mississippi, John Pemberton and Joseph E. Johnston (now fully recovered from his bullet wound). But Lee had his own plan, one so bold and risky that its very audaciousness made any other suggestion appear timid and lackluster. He proposed to lead his army north again—for an invasion of Pennsylvania. The state was unprotected. Hooker would have to withdraw from Virginia to defend Washington. At the very worst, the North would look vulnerable to its own citizens, and possibly, in the eyes of the international community, incapable of winning the war. The Confederate cabinet debated Lee's proposal for two days and at last agreed, with only the postmaster general, John Reagan, dissenting. Davis decided that Vicksburg would have to be reinforced with regiments from all parts of the South except Virginia.

In May 1863, Frank Vizetelly was on board one of the relief trains carrying troops to Vicksburg. He was going out west, Vizetelly informed his readers, because "the campaign in the valley of the Mississippi will, I believe, decide the duration of the war."[16] He offered no explanation as to why he had missed the Battle of Chancellorsville. Given the state of his debts and his propensity to fall off the wagon, Vizetelly's absence and his sudden decision to go to Vicksburg were probably connected. The train juddered slowly across Georgia and Mississippi, the track so worn and buckled in places that it was derailed three times. On the last, Vizetelly was thrown hard against the carriage and suffered a concussion. For an hour or two he thought his arm was broken and was relieved to find it only badly bruised. The engineers managed to keep the train going until they reached Jackson, Mississippi, forty-five miles east of Vicksburg. Sherman's departure was so recent that the city was still burning. Nothing of any value was intact, certainly nothing that might repair the damaged train. "The Yankees were guilty of every kind of vandalism," Vizetelly wrote with indignation. "They sacked houses, stole clothing from the negroes, burst open their trunks, and took what little money they had."

Train with reinforcements for General Johnston running off the tracks in the forests of Mississippi, by Frank Vizetelly.

Now he was not sure where to go. The news from Vicksburg was ominous. The Federal army had surrounded the hilltop town; Confederate general John Pemberton's army of thirty thousand men was holed up inside, along with three thousand luckless civilians. The Confederate army had enough rations to last sixty days. The fatherless families who cowered in its midst, on the other hand, had only their gardens, their fast-emptying cupboards, and, in the final resort, their pets. Vizetelly decided he had no choice but to stay in and around Jackson. His exploration of the surrounding countryside revealed dozens of dismal encampments, where women and children had clustered together for protection. It was an unexpected sight, he wrote. "Ladies who have been reared in luxury" were living rough like country peasants, "with nothing but a few yards of canvas to protect them from the frequent thunderstorms which burst in terrific magnificence at this season of the year over Mississippi."[17]

Only two months before, Northern newspapers had branded Grant a failure and a drunk. But since then, he had marched 130 miles and won every battle. Charles A. Dana, the observer sent by Lincoln and Stanton to Grant's headquarters, had seen much that troubled him: the callous, even brutal, attitude toward the sick appalled him, but he never saw

Grant incapacitated. In fact, closer acquaintance made Dana appreciate the general's particular genius for waging war without ever faltering or second-guessing himself. This determined quality stood Grant well once he reached Vicksburg: his first assault on May 19 was a dismal failure. A thousand Federal soldiers fell in the attack, but not a foot was gained. On the second attempt, three days later, he lost another three thousand men. Grant insisted that the army remain where it was. But he also refused to request a flag of truce to allow the wounded to be collected. The injured lay strewn among the dead for two days. The only witness to their suffering was the harsh sun, which putrefied the dead and flayed the living. Finally driven mad by the screams and stench from the ditches, the Confederates sent a message to Grant, begging him "in the name of humanity" to rescue his men.[18]

It then dawned on Grant that all he had to do was be patient and starve out the inhabitants. Inside the town, no one believed such a calamity would come to pass. General Pemberton and his men were waiting for General Johnston to lead his army to their rescue. But the cantankerous Johnston had warned Pemberton not to retreat to Vicksburg, and now that it had happened he wrote off the town and the army as lost. Nothing, not even the urgent telegrams from President Davis and Secretary of War Seddon, could make Johnston change his mind and risk his small force of 24,000 men against a Federal army three times the size. His one concession was to send out a request for volunteers to sneak supplies through the Federal lines into Vicksburg. Vizetelly accompanied some of the missions. These forays were exceedingly dangerous. The scouts had to crawl on their hands and knees in the dark for miles, "avoiding every gleam of moonlight, and prepared at any moment to use the revolver or the knife." Many previous attempts, Vizetelly informed his readers, had ended with the volunteers being either captured or shot. During one particular mission, the intrepid band scrambled along gorges and through pathless woods until they were twelve miles from Vicksburg. There they left Vizetelly and disappeared into a ravine. "As I lay on the ground in the calm, quiet night I could distinctly hear sounds of musketry between the loud booming of mortars," he wrote. Whether that meant success or failure he could not tell and would not know until the next day.[19]

Shells continually rained down on Vicksburg, shaking nerves and buildings alike. Parishioners of St. Paul's Catholic church attended mass even though the church was dangerously situated on one of the highest points of the town. On one occasion a shell crashed through a window and exploded above the altar. Stunned but unhurt, Father John Bannon calmed his screaming congregation and continued with the service.[20] The townspeople retreated to their cellars and to caves dug deep into the hillside, but there was no respite from the thunderous noise. Afterward, witnesses wrote in wonder at the little touches of comfort people added to their caves. As the siege went on, rugs, chairs, even beds were dragged underground. But bravado, enterprise, and fortitude ultimately gave way to hunger, fear, and despair.

The barrage was not all one way. As long as they had shells, the gunners in Vicksburg had their choice of sitting targets outside. Each time he led his wagon trains out to forage, Ebenezer Wells, the English wagon master of the 79th New York, bade farewell to his friends. On several occasions he returned to camp with bullets lodged in his saddle and blanket. "Our over-tasked mule-teams," wrote an officer, "were obliged to drag all the supplies under a broiling sun from the reeking banks of the Yazoo, or over the long road that wound through the hilly and desolate region."[21] Sometimes Wells's teams made it back to the camp but not the sorely needed supplies, which had to be left behind along with the wounded or dying mules.

Among the Federal soldiers who held their breath as cannonballs whizzed over their heads was the British doctor Charles Mayo. He was furious to be at Vicksburg. One of his former patients, Major General George Hartsuff, had invited him to join his headquarters at Louisville, Kentucky. Mayo received permission for the transfer and was set to leave when he discovered that a clerk had written down the wrong department on his orders, sending him to General Grant instead of General Burnside. Hartsuff advised Mayo to go to Vicksburg anyway and wait for him to sort out the clerical error with the surgeon general.

Mayo caught typhus as soon as he arrived on June 1. He put on a brave face for his family's sake, telling them that he had a nice tent "pitched with that of the Medical Director of the Corps, under a pair of fine beech-trees on a hill," neglecting to mention that there were nine others in the tent. He had been placed as staff surgeon-major and medical inspector of the XIII Army Corps, with 25,000 men under his care. Mayo found the survivors of the May 22 assault in a miserable state, many having been left to the care of unwilling and unsympathetic civil-

Confederate scouts with percussion caps for the garrison of Vicksburg, running the Federal pickets, by Frank Vizetelly.

ians. Ever practical, he immediately set about imposing some order on the shambolic situation. He had all the wounded collected and placed together under an open shed made of rough poles and boards. For beds, he copied an innovation found in a deserted Confederate camp and used cane poles and strips of bark braided together to make a mat. The contraption was strong enough to support a man's weight and flexible enough to conform to his body.

The army medical department was more of a hindrance than a help to him. But "we had one excellent and trustworthy friend," he wrote, "namely, the Sanitary Commission." The volunteer organization had depots and agents for every army in the field. "The principal agent with Grant's army was a thoroughly good fellow, and consequently was of very great use to us, indeed without the aid of his supplies the sick must have suffered far more than they did," Mayo wrote. The medical department always had an excuse, and whatever it did send was never enough. By contrast, the Sanitary Commission agent was so determined to secure the very best for the injured that he even managed to haul ice from

Cincinnati to the camp, an unimaginable luxury in the searing heat. "But no man alive could have counteracted the effects of that climate," wrote Mayo. "Malaria, salt pork, no vegetables, a blazing sun, and almost poisonous water, are agencies against which medicine is helpless. They soon began to tell on myself, as they did on others much more nearly accustomed to the climate. The hope of being recalled also vanished."[22]

Mayo's sense of duty kept him at his post, but by the middle of June he realized that if he did not do something about his situation he would be dead by the autumn. He had become used to the constant shelling, but the malarial conditions were sapping his strength. "Vicksburg still holds out," he wrote miserably to his sister on June 19. A week later, Mayo had become so desperate that he sent a plea for help to Lord Lyons. It embarrassed him to write to the minister, particularly as Lyons had urged him not to accept an officer's commission since it would put him beyond the help of the legation: "I was led to believe that I should have no difficulty in getting an order of transfer to a climate in which I could be of some use; if I had thought that they had intended to leave me here I would have left the service rather than come. Now, however, I cannot pass the lines of the army." Mayo begged Lyons to give his letter of immediate resignation to the secretary of war.[23]

While Mayo looked to Washington for deliverance, the wilting Federal army turned its eyes to the South. Grant had been expecting General Banks to steam up the Mississippi River; he was meant to have taken Port Hudson by now and opened the way for joint river operations against Vicksburg. Where was he? Washington had been asking the same question. General Henry Halleck sent two angry letters to Banks, expressing his disappointment "that you and General Grant are not acting in conjunction."[24] Banks had captured Alexandria, the state capital of Louisiana, but Halleck dismissed this as a selfish quest for glory. The judgment was unduly harsh; Banks was trying to devise a way of capturing Port Hudson that did not require a river attack. His first attempt on May 27 had resulted in almost 2,000 casualties compared to a Confederate loss of only 235. The total repulse mirrored Grant's disaster at Vicksburg a few days earlier, but Banks, at least, was prompt in retrieving the wounded.

Staff at Banks's headquarters noticed a precipitous drop in morale after the failed attack. The men had lost faith not only in their general but also in themselves. Banks, on the other hand, saw no reason why he should not be more successful the second time around. He brought in additional artillery so that by June 11 he had more than 130 guns. Ever punctilious, he sent a letter to Confederate general Franklin Gardner inside the fort at Port Hudson suggesting that he surrender to "avoid unnecessary sacrifice of life." Gardner declined even though his men were already exhausted and starving.

On the fourteenth, Banks attacked Port Hudson for the second time. Colonel Currie's luck ran out at a place called Priest Cap. His division commander, General William Emory, was hit first; the Englishman took his place, shouting "Get on, lads" as he ran toward the fort. Within minutes Currie was struck by bullets in both arms. Almost a hundred members of the 133rd went down behind him. Some four thousand Federals were either killed or wounded that day.

Currie was rescued by his own men and dragged back to safety. His wounding came as a terrible blow to the regiment. He was no longer considered alien but eccentric; his English manner of speaking was regarded as quaint rather than foreign. A hospital ship transported Currie down to New Orleans, where he remained for a few weeks until he was well enough to be sent to Philadelphia to recuperate. It would be several months before he rejoined his regiment.

The survivors of the 133rd went about their duties without enthusiasm. "I think the hope of taking the port without force is a forlorn one," wrote the regiment's assistant surgeon. "General Banks has offered a promotion and medals to one thousand who will volunteer to storm their works. . . . We can see their camps and their soldiers and also the Secesh flag very plainly. We have the Fort completely surrounded but I suppose they have enough provisions inside to last them probably a year." When the regiment left Baton Rouge there were 800 men and officers; "now we scarcely number 400."[25] But Banks had no intention of withdrawing until Port Hudson surrendered.

The Northern and Southern forces remained in their respective fortifications, slowly shrinking through disease and malnutrition. The only general with the ability to move was the Confederate Joseph Johnston, and he was in a state of passive dejection. He had repeatedly urged Pemberton to evacuate Vicksburg, arguing that the town could always be retaken but his army was irreplaceable. Grant's siege made escape impossible now; an English army officer traveling through Mississippi asked Johnston about his plans. The general "was too weak to do any good, and he was unable to give me any definite idea as to when he might be strong enough to attack Grant."[26] The officer, Lieutenant Colonel Arthur James Lyon Fremantle, had arrived in the South on April 8. This was the first time he had encountered anything less than total confidence and determination from a Confederate general. Fremantle's initial response to the war had been one of casual interest. "In common with many of my countrymen, I felt very indifferent as to which side might win," he wrote, "but if I had any bias my sympathies were rather in favour of the North, on account of the dislike which an Englishman naturally feels at the idea of slavery." His support for the North did not, however, survive Seward's early misfires in international diplomacy: "Soon a sentiment of great admiration for the gallantry and determination of the Southerners, together with the unhappy contrast afforded by the foolish bullying conduct of the Northerners, caused a complete revulsion in my feelings, and I was unable to repress a strong wish to go to America and see something of this wonderful struggle."[27]

The twenty-six-year-old officer applied for a leave of absence from his regiment, the Coldstream Guards, which had been stationed in Canada since the *Trent* affair. In contrast to many of his fellow officers, Fremantle was prepared to enter the South only in a manner that did not violate the rules of neutrality. This ruled out running the blockade or slipping through Federal lines from the North. Such circumspect behavior was typical of the young man. A keen sense of military honor was engrained in the Fremantle family; his grandfather and father had both served in the army, and all his brothers were officers, too.

Fremantle had been posted to Gibraltar as the assistant military secretary to the governor when the U.S. Navy chased Commander Raphael Semmes in his first commerce raider, CSS *Sumter,* into port in January 1862. Semmes vividly remembered their meeting. The governor had sent Fremantle to present a memorandum to Semmes that outlined the strict rules of neutrality the authorities intended to observe toward both navies while the Federals and Confederates remained at Gibraltar. Having warned Semmes that no breach would be tolerated, Fremantle then confessed to him "that he was an ardent Confederate, expressing himself without any reserve, and lauding in the highest terms our people and cause. He had many questions to ask me, which I took great pleasure in answering."[28] Semmes probably gave Fremantle the idea of reaching the

Col. John F. De Courcy

Haynes Bluff

Yazoo R.

Snyder's Bluff

Sherman
April 30

Chickasaw Bayou
attack

Sherman fails
Dec. 1862

Milliken's Bend

Sherman

McPherson

Pemberton

Duckport Canal

Young's
Point

Sherman

Williams'
Canal

McClernand
(ORD)

Vicksburg

Vicksburg
surrenders
July 4

Mississippi River

Warrenton

Pemberton

New
Carthage

McClernand
McPherson

Big Black River

Hard Times

Grand
Gulf

Evacuated
May 2

Bowen

Bruinsburg

Port Gibson
May 1

Miles

0   10

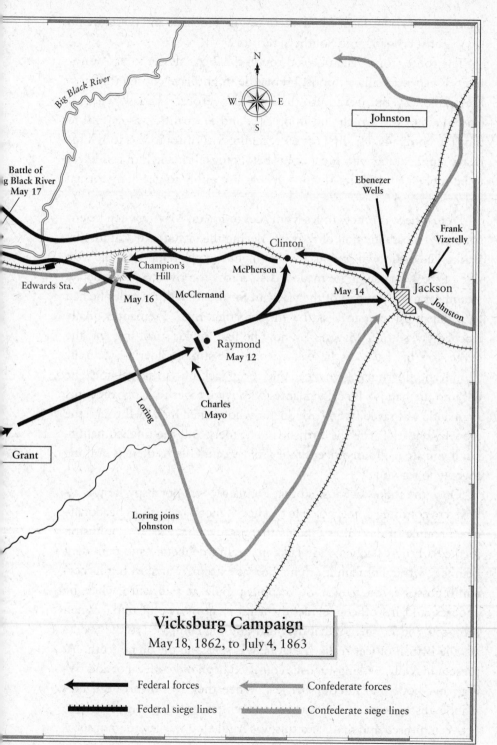

Big Black River

Battle of
g Black River
May 17

N
W E
S

Johnston

Ebenezer
Wells

Frank
Vizetelly

Clinton

Champion's
Hill

McPherson

Edwards Sta.

May 16

McClernand

May 14

Jackson

Johnston

Raymond
May 12

Loring

Charles
Mayo

Grant

Loring joins
Johnston

Vicksburg Campaign
May 18, 1862, to July 4, 1863

Federal forces   Confederate forces

Federal siege lines   Confederate siege lines

Confederacy via Mexico, where there was no blockade and therefore no laws against crossing into Southern territory.

The route from Matamoros through the Texas desert to San Antonio was exceptionally arduous. Fremantle might have chosen the most honorable way, but it was also the most dangerous. The law, where it existed at all, was rough and imprecise, and Fremantle was careful to travel in company. His first act on reaching San Antonio was to sell his heavy trunk, along with most of his belongings. It made him less likely to be robbed, and it was obvious he was not going to need any formal attire.

Fremantle was ninety miles from Alexandria on May 10 when he encountered a pathetic trail of refugees fleeing the city after its capture by Banks. Having grown anxious that he might become trapped on the west side of the Mississippi, he made a dash across the river. A Confederate steamboat took him part of the way, but for the final thirty miles he had to paddle upstream in a skiff with six other men. Fremantle finally reached Jackson on May 18. By now he had only a small bag and the clothes on his back. As he walked past the still smoldering Catholic church and the ruins of what had once been Jackson's principal hotel, he fell into the hands of local vigilantes who were eager to hang someone. Fremantle was saved by an Irish doctor who pushed his way through the crowd, saying, "I hate the British Government and the English nation, but if you are really an officer in the Coldstream Guards there is nothing I won't do for you."[29]

Once the mob was satisfied that Fremantle was not a spy, he was allowed to continue on his way. He reached General Johnston's headquarters a couple of days after Grant's first assault on Vicksburg. Johnston seemed a little detached: "He talks in a calm, deliberate and confident manner," wrote Fremantle; "to me he was extremely affable, but he certainly possesses the power of keeping people at a distance when he chooses, and his officers evidently stand in great awe of him." When Johnston told Fremantle that they had nothing compared to the Federals, the British officer realized that he was speaking the literal truth. "At present his only cooking-utensils consisted of an old coffee-pot and frying pan—both very inferior articles." When they sat down to eat, Fremantle discovered "there was only one fork (one prong deficient) between himself and Staff, and this was handed to me ceremoniously as the 'guest.' "[30]

Fremantle encountered the same polite behavior wherever he went. The Confederates were curious about him, and he was constantly peppered with questions, such as whether the Coldstream Guards really wore scarlet into battle. Inevitably someone would ask him whether he thought British soldiers could fight as well or better. During one train journey there was a lively debate in the carriage as to whether the British could have defeated Lee at Fredericksburg.

It was May 28 when Fremantle arrived in Chattanooga, Tennessee, where General Bragg and his long-suffering army were encamped. He was not the only visitor at Bragg's headquarters. The staff introduced Fremantle to an unexpected guest: three days earlier, Clement Vallandigham, the dissident Democrat and leader of the so-called Copperheads, had been unceremoniously dumped in front of Confederate pickets and ordered by his Federal guards not to turn back.

The exiled politician was outraged at his treatment by the U.S. government. On May 1 he had attended a rally in Ohio where he gave one of his usual antiwar speeches. It was a deliberate provocation, and General Burnside—who had been transferred to run the Department of Ohio, which oversaw all military matters across seven states from Wisconsin to West Virginia—fell into the trap. On May 4 Burnside sent soldiers to Vallandigham's house in Dayton. They smashed down his back door and dragged the politician off to a waiting train. Vallandigham's arrest had the effect that he was hoping for: newspapers throughout the Midwest declared him a martyr to free speech and freedom of conscience. Burnside hastily assembled a military tribunal of eight army officers to "try" the case. It was a farce, Vallandigham indignantly told Fremantle; one of the officers was not even American. (The unknown officer was Colonel John Fitzroy De Courcy, who had returned to duty and was anxious to be of use to Burnside in the hope it would lead to his reinstatement with the 16th Ohio.)

The tribunal listened to the evidence for two days and came to a unanimous agreement on the defendant's guilt. They had more difficulty deciding what to do with him. One thought he ought to be shot; another suggested exile; eventually they agreed he should be imprisoned in a fort somewhere.[31] But the ensuing national uproar over Vallandigham's trial severely embarrassed the administration, and Lincoln swiftly commuted the sentence to banishment. But Vallandigham had no more wish to be in the South than the rebels had to receive him. He had been made, in Fremantle's words, "a destitute stranger" in his own country. General Bragg was puzzled as to how to treat his reluctant visitor; Vallandigham's platform of compromise and reunion was no more popular in the South than Lincoln's policy of forced reunion. He was relieved to learn that Vallandigham wished to travel to Bermuda, where it would be possible for him to take a ship to Canada. Vallandigham preferred not to mix with his hosts while they waited for permission from Richmond to allow him to travel to Wilmington. He did not consider himself a Confederate sympathizer and was not interested in meeting foreign supporters of the South; he politely declined an introduction to the sole English volunteer on Bragg's staff.

Colonel Fremantle, on the other hand, was delighted to meet his compatriot. "Ever since I landed in America, I had heard of the exploits of an Englishman called Colonel St. Leger Grenfell," he wrote on May 30, two days after his arrival at Bragg's headquarters. "This afternoon I made his acquaintance, and I consider him one of the most extraordinary characters I ever met. Although he is a member of a well-known English family, he seems to have devoted his whole life to the exciting career of a soldier of fortune." Grenfell was Bragg's inspector general of cavalry, having left the raiding outfit led by the Confederate guerrilla John Hunt Morgan the previous Christmas. Fremantle was surprised to learn that Grenfell was fifty-five years old and that he had a wife (who had thrown up her hands some years before and was running a successful girls' school in Paris) and two grown-up daughters.[32] Grenfell told Fremantle that he had fought the Barbary pirates in Morocco, followed Garibaldi in South America, and joined the Turks against the Russians in the Crimea. The last was undoubtedly true, as he had been Colonel De Courcy's brigade major in the Turkish contingent.[33] Neither Grenfell nor De Courcy ever knew that their paths had again crossed during the Federal occupation of the Cumberland Gap.

"Even in this army," wrote Fremantle,

which abounds with foolhardy and desperate characters: [Grenfell] has acquired the admiration of all ranks by his reckless daring and gallantry in the field. Both Generals Polk and Bragg spoke to me of him as a most excellent and useful officer, besides being a man who never lost an opportunity of trying to throw his life away. He is just the sort of a man to succeed in this army, and among the soldiers his fame for bravery has outweighed his unpopularity as a rigid disciplinarian. He is the terror of all absentees, stragglers and deserters, and of all commanding officers who are unable to produce for his inspection the number of horses they have been drawing forage for.[34]

Grenfell always wore a red cap, which made him conspicuous in battle and therefore more esteemed among the officers.

Grenfell took Fremantle on a tour of the outposts. During the ride he was frank about the army's deficiencies, as well as his own troubles: "He told me he was in desperate hot water with the civil authorities of the State, who had accused him of illegally impressing and appropriating horses, and also of conniving at the escape of a negro from his lawful owner, and he said that the military authorities were afraid or unable to give him proper protection." Three days later, on June 3, "Grenfell came to see me in a towering rage," wrote Fremantle. He had been arrested. "General Bragg himself had stood bail for him, but Grenfell was naturally furious at the indignity. But, even according to his own account, he seems to have acted indiscreetly in the affair of the Negro, and he will have to appear before the civil court next October. General Polk and his officers were all much vexed at the occurrence.[35] Bragg's surety was misspent. A week later, Grenfell packed his bags and disappeared. No one heard anything of him for three months.

By then, Fremantle had already left for the east. After another tortuous train ride, which had the single distinguishing feature of a female soldier in their midst, he arrived at Charleston.* One of the first people to greet him was Captain Henry Feilden. Fremantle was amazed to come

---

* While Fremantle was in Charleston, the local newspapers reported: "The Western army correspondent of the 'Mobile Register' writes as follows:—'The famous Colonel St. Leger Grenfell, who served with Morgan last summer, and since that time has been Assistant Inspector-general of General Bragg, was arrested a few days since by the civil authorities. . . . If the charges against him are proven true, then there is no doubt that the course of General Bragg will be to dismiss him from his Staff; but if, on the contrary, malicious slanders are defaming this ally, he is Hercules enough and brave enough to punish them. His bravery and gallantry were conspicuous throughout the Kentucky campaign, and it is hoped that this late tarnish on his fame will be removed; or if it be not, that he will.' "

across another English volunteer. "A Captain Feilden came to call upon me at 9 A.M.," he wrote in his diary. "I remember his brother quite well at Sandhurst."[36] The younger Feilden seemed entranced with the South. Naturally, Fremantle could not know of the momentous event that had taken place in Feilden's life that week: Miss Julia McCord of Greenville, South Carolina, had visited the office, seeking a military pass to visit her brother.

TWENTY-ONE

The Eve of Battle

A message to the shipbuilders—British reaction to Jackson's death—Henry Hotze resurgent—All eyes on Lee—Sir Percy Wyndham finds glory at Brandy Station—A lost boy

"My father heard about your going out to America to see me," the Marquis of Hartington wrote to Skittles after his return to London in early spring. "He has been told all about the whole thing, which he had no notion of before [and] is in a terrible state about it." He added disingenuously: "I told him you had given me up and he knows that I am very unhappy." The truth, as they both knew, was that he was gently putting his mistress aside, or at least was trying to, with so far limited success.[1] Yet Hartington would not have the luxury of dithering for much longer; he had received an invitation from Lord Palmerston to join the government, which would mean assuming greater responsibilities while enjoying fewer of life's pleasures. "I think it would be a most horrible nuisance," he wrote.[2] On April 13, 1863, however, the decision was made for Hartington by the unexpected death of George Cornewall Lewis, the secretary for war.* Earl

---

* It was the second tragedy to strike the Lewis family. Lewis's daughter had died in childbirth some weeks before, leaving the infant son to be brought up by her grieving husband, William Vernon Harcourt. The double loss (Lewis had been like a father to Harcourt) led to Harcourt's temporary withdrawal from public life. He stopped writing his pro-Northern essays, which had appeared in *The Times* under the pen name "Historicus," and remained a widower until 1876, when he married Elizabeth Motley, the daughter of the American historian John Lothrop Motley.

A certificate for the 7 Per Cent Cotton Loan, signed by Emile Erlanger and J. Henry Schroeder, and by Colin McRace and John Slidell for the Confederacy.

de Grey was promoted from undersecretary to secretary, and Hartington was offered de Grey's former position, an honor not even he
could refuse.[3]

The Confederates in England had reviled Lewis ever since his speech
against recognition the previous November. They were not sure what de
Grey or Hartington might achieve for their cause, but the simple fact of
there being two more known supporters in positions of power was
enough to rescue the Confederates from their gloom. Nothing had gone
right for them since the launch of the Erlanger-sponsored cotton bonds
in March, and even these had ultimately proven to be a disappointment.
Rumors spread by Federal agents that Jefferson Davis intended to default
on the bonds had caused the price to plummet. Only secret buying on a
massive scale by the Confederates was keeping them at a reasonable
level.

The secret ship-construction program had also suffered a spate of
reversals. A week after the *Georgia*'s escape on April 1, Matthew
Fontaine Maury learned that John, his eldest son, was missing at Vicksburg and presumed dead. "Oh my dear, dear wife," he wrote, "my heart
is gone from me."* Maury's only mementoes of his lost son John were
a short letter and his old winter coat, which had been shortened to fit
his twelve-year-old-son Brave; this at least "has its memories," he
wrote.[4] Heartbroken, Maury abandoned London and went with Brave
to live in Bowdon, on the outskirts of Manchester, refusing to see anyone except his closest friends. Almost simultaneously, the government
impounded the *Alexandra* in Liverpool, which Fraser, Trenholm had intended to donate to the Confederate navy; and James Bulloch heard
that the former paymaster of the *Alabama,* a man named Clarence
Yonge, was exacting revenge for his dismissal by telling both the Federals and the British government everything he knew about the Confederates' operations.

Bulloch tried to guess what his enemies would learn from Yonge.
The Lairds rams currently under construction would be safe, he

---

*John had disappeared while leading a reconnaissance mission at Vicksburg. A
friend on the Federal side made inquiries but could find no record of his capture.
An investigation after the war found evidence that he had run into a Federal scouting party, which shot him and dumped his body.

thought, since Yonge had left England the previous July: "I do not think he was ever in the Birkenhead works, or that he has any personal knowledge of what is going on there. He surely can have no knowledge of the *Alexandra*."[5] But the government's evident willingness to use Yonge to build its case against the *Alexandra* made Bulloch fearful that the era of legal loopholes and fly-by-night escapes had passed. He became convinced of this toward the end of April, after Charles Francis Adams was allowed to commit a serious diplomatic blunder without incurring any official sanction.

Shortly after the seizure of the *Alexandra,* Adams had written in his diary, "The course of the government has raised the whole hive of sympathizers, as it was never stirred before. What with the case of the *Alexandra,* and that of the *Peterhoff* . . . the effect is to stimulate ill temper. The greater the necessity of keeping as quiet and calm as possible."[6] But instead of heeding his own advice, Adams became entangled in a blockade-running scandal involving two American gunrunners who were shipping arms to Mexico. Admiral Wilkes's capture of the *Peterhoff* had made insurance for sailing in Mexican waters prohibitive for small firms. The gunrunners, General Juan Napoleon Zerman and Colonel Bertram B. Howell, asked Adams to provide them with an affidavit stating they were aiding the Mexicans and not the South. This, they hoped, would lower their insurance premium, since their ship would no longer be at risk of capture by the U.S. Navy. In spite of Moran's warnings, Adams not only provided Howell and Zerman with a letter of indemnity, but also embellished it with pointed jabs at Lloyds for underwriting "dishonest enterprises" such as blockade running.[7] As is so often the case with compromising letters, one copy became several. The letter went from Lloyds to the owners of the *Peterhoff,* thence to the Foreign Office, and finally to *The Times.*

The press called Adams a hypocrite for protesting against British arms sales to the South while secretly helping Americans to supply Mexico. One newspaper wondered if he was selling protection; another accused him of plotting to drive British shipping from the Americas. *The Times* returned to its favorite theme of Northern hypocrisy. The paper often reminded its readers of the example set during the Crimean War, when President Franklin Pierce had rebuffed Britain's protests over the shipments of American-made weapons to the Russians with the retort: "Americans sold munitions of war to all buyers without troubling themselves about the ports to which the goods would be consigned, or the purposes to which they would be put."

The French also issued a strong protest to the U.S. minister in Paris. The Foreign Office was incensed with Adams and thought "his explanation of it . . . very lame." The embarrassed ministry desperately tried to stave off a debate on the subject but finally yielded on April 23. Aided by the Tories, pro-Southern MPs excoriated the government for allowing the North's envoy to become "the Minister for Commerce in England." One sarcastically remarked that Adams's notion "of honesty and neutrality is remarkable. Every thing is honest to suit his own purposes." Some of the speeches that followed were so insulting toward the North that the speaker of the House later apologized to Adams. Calm was restored only after Palmerston and Russell assured their respective listeners in the Commons and the Lords that Seward would disavow Adams's "extraordinary" and "unwarrantable" act.

The government had to work hard to stifle the controversy, muzzling its party members and planting stories in the press that the Foreign Office was satisfied with Adams's protestations of innocence. Palmerston twisted Delane's arm into having *The Times* imply that Howell and Zerman had tricked Adams. But none of these efforts to protect Adams diminished his sense of grievance. He remained convinced that his behavior had been above reproof, and for weeks afterward he badgered Lord Russell to retract his speech in the Lords. Henry Adams loyally supported his father, telling his brother Charles Francis Jr., "When the whole *Peterhoff* story is told, we shall reverse everything and overwhelm these liars."[8] Nevertheless, he could see that his father was floundering and was relieved when the prominent New York lawyer William M. Evarts arrived on May 1. Evarts, one of Seward's closest political confidants, had been sent by him to liaise with the Crown prosecution lawyers in the *Alexandra* trial. But instead of bolstering Charles Francis Adams's confidence, Evarts's arrival had sent him into further decline. Evarts was the fourth U.S. agent to arrive that spring. Henry could joke about having a "complete Cabinet of Ministerial advisers and assistants," but he was not the one whose competence appeared to be in doubt.

Hartington's maiden speech as the new undersecretary for war took place on May 14, 1863. He managed to arrive late for the debate—regarding a bill to regulate the country's volunteer militias—and without his papers, but the House appeared to accept his apology once he demonstrated a sound grasp of the subject. The Confederate sympathizers in the Commons held their breath, waiting to see whether he might use the opportunity to praise the South; finally, after keeping them in suspense until the end of his speech, Hartington fulfilled their hopes by making a long and favorable comparison between English volunteer soldiers and the brave fighting men he had recently seen in the Confederacy. By itself, Hartington's speech was a minor event, but its timing turned out to be extremely fortunate for the South, coming as it did four days before the news of Lee's victory at Chancellorsville. James Mason's supporters in Parliament were so elated that they immediately laid plans to rattle the government again about Admiral Wilkes and Northern interference with British ships in the West Indies. In France, a friendly meeting with the Spanish ambassador lifted Commissioner Slidell's spirits.

It was the news of Stonewall Jackson's death, however, that made the Confederates spring into action. They were amazed and delighted by the spontaneous outpouring of public grief in England. Newspapers carried long eulogies to the fallen hero; *The Times* even compared Jackson's death to Admiral Nelson's at Trafalgar. Flags flew at half-mast at many cotton mills. Public expressions of sympathy were hastily drawn up for Jackson's widow. The unexpected intensity of the reaction delivered the Confederates from their despair even as it threw the U.S. legation and its supporters into deeper vexation. The querulous Liberal MP John Roebuck, whose youthful affection for America had changed in his old age to a blazing dislike, held a mass meeting in Sheffield that voted to recognize the Confederacy. A few days later, on June 1, the pro-Confederate owner of the *Saturday Review*, Alexander Beresford Hope, formed a committee calling itself the "British Jackson Monumental Fund." Beresford Hope, whose vociferous support for the Confederacy stemmed from a misguided belief that its political system was more aristocratic than the North's, announced that the fund was going to commission the Irish sculptor John Foley, designer of the Albert Memorial in Hyde Park, to make a statue of Stonewall

Jackson that would be presented to the people of Virginia upon completion.* Not to be outdone, publishing houses hastily called for biographies about the general. The race was won by the English governess stranded in Richmond during Lord Edward St. Maur's visit, Catherine Hopley, who pipped the competition with her *Stonewall Jackson,* published in August.[10]

The Confederates also regarded it as a good sign that the newest of their three cruisers, the *Georgia,* had made contact with the *Alabama* in Brazil. The vessels had met in the harbor of Bahia quite by chance. "Day broke and we found ourselves very near two men-of-war," wrote James Morgan.

> What was their nationality? It seemed an age before the hour for colors arrived, but when it did, to our great delight, the most rakish-looking of the two warships broke out the Stars and Bars! "It is the *Alabama!*" we gasped, and commenced to dance with delight. The officers hugged one another, each embracing a man of his own rank, except the captain and myself. Like the commander, I was the only one of my rank aboard, so I hugged myself.[11]

The shipping magnate William Schaw Lindsay had succeeded William Gregory as the Confederacy's chief political lobbyist in the Commons. He was a safer choice than Roebuck, less volatile and more popular among his fellow MPs. Lindsay was elated by the commotion over Jackson's death, believing it meant the country was ready to recognize Southern independence. He invited Mason and Roebuck down to

---

* The wealthy Beresford Hope and his brother-in-law Lord Robert Cecil, the future Marquis of Salisbury and prime minister, were both haunted by the fear that American-style democracy might one day infect British politics. But whenever Beresford Hope adopted a cause, he embraced it with fanatical intensity. He romanticized the South to an absurd degree, publishing three pamphlets in support of its independence. "I honestly and entirely believe," he wrote, "that the cause which will tend to the confirmation of all the evils of slavery, is that of the North, and that the cause which is most likely to prove a benefit to the slave, and in the end relieve him of his shackles, is that of the South." A. Beresford Hope, *The Remnants of the American Disruption,* p. 44 (London, 1862). The statue of Stonewall Jackson was not finished until 1874, but Beresford Hope had remained committed to the project and paid the shipping costs. The unveiling ceremony took place in Richmond, Virginia, the following year in front of fifty thousand people, including many survivors of Jackson's cavalry.[9]

his estate in Surrey for a concentrated weekend of plotting. After the
meeting, Roebuck wasted little time. In the first week of June he met
with Benjamin Disraeli, who said all the things that an opposition leader
would when offered the chance of attacking the government without actually committing himself or his party to a change in their policy of non-
interference in the American war. But this was encouragement enough
for Roebuck, who gave notice in the House of his intention to revisit the
question of Southern recognition. The debate was slated for the end of
June. The Confederates took the news with a degree of caution. Roebuck was an asset to the extent that the MP represented himself as a man
of the people, but (in the words of one observer) vanity was "written all
over his face when you came near it." They trembled at the idea of letting Roebuck loose in the Commons without an explicit move by the
French beforehand. John Slidell drew up a memorandum for Emperor
Napoleon's attention, which outlined all the reasons why an independent South suited French interests, and requested an interview.

When Mason returned to England, he found Waterloo Station placarded with posters depicting the British Union Jack crossed with the
Confederate flag. Hackney cab drivers were displaying the emblems in
miniature. Hotze was working at a feverish pace, distributing posters,
placards, and circulars up and down the country. The *Morning Herald* and
the *Standard* agreed to print editorials demanding recognition every other
day until the debate. Spence was also in his element. During the past two
years he had changed from being a businessman of no great talent or success into a canny political operator respected by the Southerners in England and feared by the Northern lobby. For the new push in Parliament,
Spence formed two separate organizations. One was a respectable club,
called the Manchester Southern Club, whose purpose was to distribute
Confederate material in the north of England; the other was his own private army of agitators. The group successfully broke up an abolitionist
meeting at the Manchester Free Trade Hall. "These parties are not the
rich spinners but young men of energy with a taste for agitation but little money," Spence wrote to Mason.

> It appears to my judgment that it would be wise not to stint
> money in aiding this effort to expose cant and diffuse the truth.
> Manchester is naturally the centre of such a move and you will see
> there are here the germs of important work—but they need to be

tended and fostered. I have supplied a good deal of money individually but I see room for the use of 30 or 40 pounds a month or more.[12]

Almost no one outside the legation had the least suspicion that public opinion was being cleverly manipulated. "The intelligence of the country is now unanimous in our favor," Henry Hotze wrote proudly. He was exaggerating his success, but there had been an undeniable shift back toward the South since the initial excitement aroused by Lincoln's Emancipation Proclamation at the beginning of the year. Hotze's genius lay in his understanding of who and what constituted fashionable opinion. He knew how to portray the South in ways that appealed to particular constituencies, such as the clergy, university students, journalists, actors, and artists, whom he considered to be natural proselytizers as well as role models.

The Ladies' London Emancipation Society tried to beat Hotze at his own game by distributing more than a hundred thousand excerpts from Fanny Kemble's plantation diary, but neither they nor the indefatigable Harriet Martineau could match Hotze's tentacle-like connection with the press. By early May, Martineau had given up trying to change the North's poor image in England and was concentrating on the message "that it is not necessary to admire the Yankees very much to be on their side in the quarrel."[13]

Hotze was being helped, of course, by the absence of pro-Northern English journalists covering the war in America. Since Charles Mackay's arrival in America to replace the *Times*' ailing New York correspondent, J. C. Bancroft Davis, Mackay had been obediently sending back articles that showed the North in a poor light. The managing editor, Mowbray Morris, was pleased with the reports and told Mackay, "Your views are entirely in accordance with those of the paper and I believe of the majority in this country."[14] (The Morris fortune had disappeared almost overnight after emancipation released the slaves on the family's sugar plantation in the West Indies.) Francis Lawley was treading a far more precarious line. He was writing his reports to make it seem as though a Confederate victory was inevitable, but was also trying to force the government's hand by provoking public outrage over Southern suffering.

The combination of Lawley's eyewitness reports and Frank Vizetelly's emotive drawings certainly acted powerfully on the public

Southern refugees camping in the woods near Vicksburg, by Frank Vizetelly.

conscience. "I assure you the sympathy of all England is with the South and I think justly so," a housekeeper from Manchester informed her relatives in Michigan. "[The Northerners] are jealous of us as a mightier nation and hate us because we do not take their part, but it is a family quarrel and they must make it up themselves."[15] At the other end of the social spectrum, the Hon. Lucy Lyttleton, at the time an impressionable twenty-two-year-old debutante, was shocked to discover that not everyone supported the South. "During dinner America was the topic," she wrote in her diary on June 13, 1863, while staying with the Duchess of Sutherland at Cliveden. "The Duke and Duchess [of Argyll] are Northern! in their sympathies." Lucy did not feel confident enough to argue with them or with the widowed William Vernon Harcourt, the other guest present. "It does make one's heart ache to think of such grief," she wrote; "he joins in conversation, and puts on no affectations of sorrow; but his face tells it all. The little baby lives."[16]

Henry Hotze could not have hoped for a more positive reception to his propaganda. He was delighted by the lamentations of the pro-Northern *Bradford Observer* on June 19 that the Northerners were losing the argument: "We have men really wishing for the universal abolition of slavery expressing earnest wishes for the success of the section of a nation who are the most deeply tainted with the crime of slavery."

Yet the Confederate lobby was still not satisfied. There was a rumor going around the Tory Party that the French emperor would not openly support the South. Roebuck and Lindsay agreed they had to receive a personal assurance from Louis-Napoleon himself before they exposed themselves to the massed ranks of the House. John Slidell prepared the ground for their meeting during his own interview with the emperor on June 18. Once again Louis-Napoleon said he hoped the South would win, not least because he considered the Confederates more supportive of his own venture in Mexico. He also agreed to allay the fears of the two English MPs. Slidell could almost hear the trumpets of independence in his ears. Two days later, on June 20, Roebuck and Lindsay went to the Tuileries. James Spence had run through all the possible arguments with Roebuck in advance. The emperor reassured them that he had not changed his mind. However, he added, his cabinet was opposed to any sort of formal communication with London, fearing that Lord Russell might use the offer as leverage to gain favor with Seward. The French ambassador had been instructed to make only an informal approach about a joint move between the two countries.

In London, James Spence attended a campaign dinner for nearly sixty guests given by Beresford Hope. He sat between the publisher John Murray and the Whig politician Lord Elcho, both of whom made flattering remarks about his *Times* articles. But Spence could not enjoy himself while the Tories' participation remained an open question. The Confederate lobby discussed whether they should go ahead without the Conservative Party and simply rely on the emperor's promised support. Mason, Hotze, and Spence were more worried about the *Alexandra* trial, which they feared might throw out something embarrassing or prejudicial at precisely the wrong moment.

The trial began on June 22, with the Crown prosecution laying out the facts against the ship. Lord Russell had moved the proceedings to London, certain that Liverpool would never allow a conviction against one of its own. That city, he wrote in exasperation, was "addicted to Southern proclivities, foreign slave trade, and domestic bribery."[17] The *Alexandra* was, said the solicitor general, Sir Roundell Palmer, obviously a vessel built for war. To bolster his argument, he produced Clarence Yonge, the ex-paymaster of the *Alabama,* who admitted that James Bulloch and Fraser, Trenholm were in cahoots and confirmed that Confederate naval and military officers had the run of the company's headquarters. But Sir Hugh Cairns, Bulloch's defense lawyer, tore apart poor Roundell Palmer. Despite the best efforts of Consul Dudley, the American lawyer William Evarts, the Home Office's Secret Service, the chief law officers, and a Confederate turncoat, all the evidence produced was circumstantial. After three days of testimony, the case went to the jury on June 25. Guided by the presiding judge, Justice Pollock (who happened to be a great friend of Lindsay's as well as a stickler for legal precedent), the jury found against the Crown; the seizure of the *Alexandra* was ruled to have been illegal. The Confederates and their supporters were jubilant. Pollock had interpreted the Foreign Enlistment Act to mean that only fully armed ships were covered under the law; "war-like" ships could be built without interference. But James Bulloch knew in his heart that the case was only a temporary victory. Lord Russell demonstrated his determination to win by ordering Palmer to appeal the ruling.

———

The day after the acquittal, London heard stunning news from America. General Lee was marching toward Maryland, or possibly Washington. "The English hope it will be our destruction," wrote Benjamin Moran in his diary.[18] Lee's invasion thrilled the Confederate lobby. The timing could not have been more auspicious for them. They had already decided to prepare the way for Roebuck's motion by having one of Gregory's friends in the Lords, the Marquis of Clanricarde, ask Russell whether the French had made any sort of important proposal that ought to be made known to the country. This, they thought, would force Russell's hand.[19]

On June 26, 1863, Clanricarde fired the first salvo and asked Russell whether he had received a communication from the French. Russell replied that he had not. This rather flustered Clanricarde, who tried to retrieve the situation by asking whether the noble lord thought it was time to recognize the South. Russell replied that he did not, and so ended the exchange. This was not how the Confederates had expected the day to end. Either Russell or the emperor was lying to them. In Paris, Slidell paid a hasty visit to the foreign minister, who assured him that a note had indeed been sent to Baron Gros, the French ambassador. In London, Roebuck went to see the ambassador, who could only say that he had not made a formal approach to Russell, which the Englishman already knew.

Louis-Napoleon had actually instructed his ambassador to speak to Palmerston about jointly recognizing the South, but the prime minister was ill with gout. Baron Gros, unsure whether he was required to convey the same message to the foreign secretary, merely met with Lord Russell instead but dropped a hint about the emperor's intentions and left it at that. All this nodding and winking was creating a scenario for a perfect tragicomedy of errors, unless decisive reports arrived from America.[20]

With some trepidation, given John Bright's previous performance in the Commons, the pro-Northern lobby asked him to lead the counterattack against Roebuck and Lindsay. Bright agreed, though he was worried that another military victory by Lee would make any further debate about recognition a pointless exercise. He was having dreams about the war in which he was surrounded by telegrams that he could see but not read.[21]

Charles Francis Adams asked Bright to attend a working dinner a few nights before Roebuck's planned motion for recognition of the South. Several of Seward's recent emissaries were present, including William Evarts, John Murray Forbes, and William H. Aspinwall.* A sense of grievance against the Lincoln administration weighed down the conversation. "The impression here is that your Government is incapable, that it lacks two essential qualities, foresight and force," Bright explained to Sumner. "Among the Americans here, friends of the North, there is great want of confidence in your Cabinet at Washington, and I cannot but feel that great losses of men, and means, and long delays, and apparent mismanagement, must have the effect of creating a disgust with the war."[22]

Having witnessed the government's difficulties, Evarts thought Washington was not giving Lord Russell the credit he deserved for his attempts to secure a conviction against the *Alexandra*'s owners. Forbes and Aspinwall concurred; they were returning to America in a few days and intended to speak to Seward about his role in the British public's negative perception of the North.

Forbes and Aspinwall left for New York on June 30, the day of Roebuck's motion in the Commons, a few hours too early to know the re-

---

* Forbes and Aspinwall were two wealthy businessmen and philanthropists who had arrived in the spring bearing $10 million in government bonds. Seward had sent them to England on a secret mission to purchase any ships that could be used by the Confederates for their navy. Only a handful of people were meant to know the details, but Forbes and Aspinwall had been in England for less than a week when *The Times* received a tip-off. Thwarted by their exposure, they gave a considerable portion of their money to Consuls Dudley and Morse for their espionage operations— with more immediate and probably far more effective results.

sults of the debate. In America, the last newspaper reports placed the Confederate army near the border of Pennsylvania; Harrisburg, the state's capital, was standing by to evacuate the legislature. The Confederates in London were feeling confident; Roebuck did not know that Bright was to be his opponent in the House. When asked by a Southerner whether he would fear such an encounter, "No, sir!" Roebuck replied sententiously. "Bright and I have met before. It was the old story—the story of the sword-fish and the whale! No sir! Bright will not cross swords with me again!"[23]

————

The death of Stonewall Jackson had not dented the Confederate army's confidence, even though Lee had been forced into a drastic reorganization to make up for the loss of his best general. He created three infantry corps, one under "Old Pete" Longstreet and the others under Richard Ewell and Ambrose P. Hill. Jackson's cavalry was assigned to Jeb Stuart. Longstreet had already demonstrated his abilities; the rest would have to prove themselves on the field. But at least Lee had sufficient stores and enough men, eighty thousand in all, to justify leading the army into enemy territory.

Thirty days of hot, cloudless skies had left Virginia parched and dry. As the Army of Northern Virginia pulled away from Fredericksburg during the first week of June, rising columns of dust betrayed its movements to General Hooker's scouts. Hooker realized that Lee was heading north and wrongly assumed that the Confederates were going to attack Washington. He was prevented from discovering his mistake for several days by the newly appointed Ambrose Hill, who had been ordered to block the Federals at Fredericksburg for as long as possible. The strategy worked insofar as it occupied the attentions of Union general "Uncle John" Sedgwick, but Lee had underestimated the strength and size of Hooker's cavalry corps, who were also on the hunt.

The debonair Jeb Stuart had passed the time since Chancellorsville organizing grand reviews of his troops. His headquarters was in Culpeper County, thirty miles east of Fredericksburg on the other side of the Rappahannock River, where the Orange–Alexandria railroad passed through a small village at Brandy Station.[24] The grandest of the reviews was on June 5, involving all ten thousand soldiers and the horse artillery, followed by a ball in the evening. Thousands of spectators watched as Stuart put on a performance of knightly dash worthy of *Ivanhoe*. There

45. A colored regiment poses for the camera. By the end of the war, there were more than 180,000 colored troops serving in the Union army. Their entry into the U.S. Army was slow and difficult and did not begin until Congress passed an act in July of 1862 that allowed them to enlist.

46. Group of "contrabands," Cumberland Landing, Virginia. Escaped slaves were not sent back to the South because they were classed as "contraband of war," meaning they were part of the Southern war effort and were therefore liable for "confiscation." Thousands of slaves from Virginia fled to shanty towns around the outskirts of Washington.

47. A slave auction house in Atlanta, Georgia.

48. The Rohrbach Bridge. During the Battle of Antietam on September 17, 1862, the bridge became known as Burnside's Bridge after U.S. General Burnside ordered his men to cross it while being fired upon by the Confederates from the bluffs above the river.

49. The dead after the slaughter at Antietam. The battle ended in a draw and was the single bloodiest day of the war. The two sides combined suffered more than 25,000 casualties.

50. President Lincoln and U.S. General McClellan meeting after the Battle of Antietam. Lincoln was furious with McClellan for not pursuing General Lee and crushing the Confederate army while it was in retreat.

51. General Ambrose Burnside (1824–81), commander of the U.S. Army of the Potomac for less than three months. His exuberant facial hair allegedly gave rise to the term "sideburns."

52. Fredericksburg. Confederate General Robert E. Lee won a stunning victory over Burnside at the Battle of Fredericksburg on December 13, 1862. Burnside ordered the Federal soldiers to charge across a plain overlooked by a seven-mile range of wooded hills filled with Confederate artillery. When asked if any more guns were needed, the artillery officer in charge replied, "A chicken could not live on that field when we open on it."

53. Marye's Heights. The famous stone wall along the heights of Fredericksburg gave the Confederates perfect protection while they fired upon the Federals below. Burnside sustained 12,600 casualties to Lee's 5,000.

54. Admiral Raphael Semmes (1809–77), who commanded two commerce raiders of the Confederate navy. His exploits on CSS *Alabama* inspired the Junior United Service Club of Great Britain to present him with a "magnificent sword, which had been manufactured to their order in the city of London, with suitable naval and Southern devices."

55. Commander Matthew Fontaine Maury (1806–73), Confederate navy, nicknamed "pathfinder of the seas" for his study of the ocean currents, which made travel easier and faster. Maury was sent to England during the war to purchase commerce raiders for the Confederate navy.

56. Lieutenant James Morgan (1845–1928), Confederate navy, friend and future brother-in-law of the English Confederate volunteer Francis Dawson. Morgan served on Commander Maury's commerce raider CSS *Georgia,* whose cruise ended in madness and savagery after only six months at sea.

57. Colonel John Fitzroy De Courcy (1821–90), 31st Baron Kingsale (*left*), British volunteer in the Union army and colonel of the 16th Ohio Volunteer Infantry. In 1863 De Courcy captured the Cumberland Gap from the Confederates with a force less than half the size of his opponents by tricking them into believing they were surrounded by a huge army.

58. Colonel Sir Percy Wyndham (1833–79), British volunteer in the Union army, knighted by King Victor Emmanuel for his services during the Garibaldi campaign to liberate southern Italy, and colonel of the 1st New Jersey Cavaliers. Sir Percy only ever twiddled his moustache when angry.

59. Dr. Charles Culverwell (1837–1919), British volunteer surgeon in the Union army, who yearned to become an actor and between campaigns appeared several times on the stage, including with John Wilkes Booth in *Hamlet* at Grover's Theater. "They would rave of him, his voice, his hair, and his eyes. Small wonder for he was fascinating . . . Poor sad, mad, bad John Wilkes Booth." After the war, Culverwell became Sir Charles Wyndham, one of the most successful actors of his generation.

60. Battle of Gettysburg, July 1–3, 1863. The bloodiest battle of the Civil War resulted in more than 43,000 casualties. Confederate General Robert E. Lee withdrew first, giving the psychological edge to U.S. General George Meade.

61. Little Round Top, Gettysburg. U.S. Colonel Joshua Chamberlain and his 20th Maine held Little Round Top for Meade, depriving Lee of the high ground that the Confederate General needed in order to seize control of the battle. Chamberlain later received the surrender of Lee's army in 1865.

62. U.S. Secretary of State William Seward taking a party of diplomats to see Trenton Falls in New York on August 18, 1863. (*left to right*) William Seward, Russian Minister Baron Stoeckl, Nicaraguan Minister Luis Molina, British Minister Lord Lyons, French Minister M. Mercier, German Minister Rudolph Schleiden, Bertinatti (Italian legation), Swedish Minister Count Piper, M. Bodisco (Russian legation), George Sheffield (British legation), and Mr. Donaldson (U.S. State Department).

63. Rose Greenhow (1817–64), Confederate spy and envoy, with her daughter Little Rose, in a photograph taken in Federal prison. Jefferson Davis sent her to England in 1863 in the hope that she would persuade either Lord Palmerston or Emperor Napoleon III to recognize Confederate independence.

64. Belle Boyd (1844–1900), Confederate heroine, spy, prisoner, and dispatch carrier for the Confederate government. Belle's attempt to run the blockade out of Wilmington in 1864 was foiled by the Federal blockade. She fell in love with her captor and they were married in St. James's Church, Piccadilly.

65. General Braxton Bragg (1817–76), Confederate commander of the Army of Tennessee and the most unpopular general in the South. His subordinates wrote to Richmond in October 1863, after the Battle of Chickamauga, asking for a different leader, but Davis insisted that Bragg stay.

66. Civilians hunting for souvenirs the day after the Battle of Chattanooga on November 25, 1864. General Bragg had to retreat, throwing away the victory of Chickamauga in September and opening the way for a Federal invasion of the Deep South.

67. Jacob Thompson (1810–85), Confederate commissioner in Canada. Jefferson Davis gave him $1 million in gold to fund secret operations against Northern targets, both civilian and military. Thompson's plots became increasingly destructive and terror-driven as the war progressed.

68. Clement C. Clay (1816–82), Confederate commissioner in Canada. Clay was sent out at the same time as Jacob Thompson, but they were temperamentally unsuited to working together and operated out of different cities.

69. Confederate plotters meeting on the Canadian side of Niagara Falls, July 1864. (*left to right*) George N. Sanders, Captain John B. Castleman, Colonel George St. Leger Grenfell, British volunteer in the Confederate army, and Captain Thomas H. Hines. Together they hatched a plot to take Chicago and liberate Confederate prisoners in the surrounding camps. Castleman and Grenfell were captured, but only Grenfell was sentenced to death. He drowned while trying to escape the harshest Federal prison in the U.S., Fort Jefferson, on the Dry Tortugas in the Gulf of Mexico.

Among the innovations of the American Civil War was the use of observation balloons, heavier and more accurate artillery, and the reliance on railways to mass-transport troops and arms.

70. Mounted cannon—the "Dictator," most powerful mortar in the war, so heavy it had to be fitted to a specially reinforced railway car.

71. Massed field artillery.

72 . A Federal observation balloon.

73. U.S. Lieutenant General Ulysses S. Grant (1822–85), center, whose victories in the Western theater of the Civil War led to President Lincoln appointing him general-in-chief in March 1864. Grant was relentless in war and magnanimous in victory.

74. Battle of Cold Harbor, May 31–June 3, 1864. The fourth phase of U.S. General Grant's campaign against Confederate General Lee ended in defeat for the Union. Grant was labeled "Butcher Grant" because of the high number of Federal casualties. The fighting took place over the same area as the Battle of Chancellorsville in 1863, and soldiers could not help treading on human remains.

75. CSS *Alabama*. In twenty-two months the Confederate commerce raider covered more than 75,000 miles, captured or sank sixty-five Northern merchant ships, destroyed $5 million worth of Northern goods, and caused a massive sell-off of U.S. merchant marine.

76. CSS *Stonewall*. A Confederate ironclad ram, she was commissioned by James Bulloch in England and built in France, though delays prevented her from reaching the South before the end of the war.

77. The crew of USS *Kearsarge*. The sloop-of-war, commanded by Captain John Winslow, defeated CSS *Alabama* in an extraordinary duel in the English Channel on June 19, 1864.

78. Fort Sedgwick, the bomb-proof Union quarters at Petersburg, called "Fort Hell" by its occupants. Opposite was Fort Mahone, known as "Fort Damnation." The siege of Petersburg cost the lives of 70,000 in nineteen separate battles.

79. The trenches of Petersburg. Between June 1864 and April 1865 the two armies were spread out in a maze of trenches stretching more than thirty miles. "All day long," wrote a British observer, "the men sat in their fetid dugouts, sweltering in the heat, until the night shift relieved them. . . . Soldiers talked about fearful slaughtering they had witnessed in vague tones, as if they wished to forget it."

80. Charleston at the end of the war. Charleston was regarded with special hatred by Union forces because it was here that the war began on April 12, 1861, when Confederate General Beauregard fired on the Federal-held Fort Sumter, forcing its surrender. "If there is any city deserving of holocaustic infamy, it is Charleston," declared the *New York Herald Tribune*.

81. Richmond after its fall on April 3, 1865. Fire threatened to engulf the entire city and the Federal invaders became firefighters, saving what they could. Fifty-five blocks, the entire business district, went up in flames.

82. and 83. Victory parade of the U.S. Army down Pennsylvania Avenue and the front of the Capitol on May 24, 1865. More than 620,000 soldiers and 50,000 civilians died in the war. At least a further 470,000 soldiers were wounded or maimed, including 50,000 amputees. The North lost 10 percent of its white males ages 20 to 45; the South lost 30 percent.

84. Lincoln Memorial, old Calton Cemetery, Edinburgh. On the west side, the inscription reads: "Unveiled 21st August 1893. This plot of ground given by the Lord Provost, Town Council of Edinburgh to Wallace Bruce, US. Consul as a burial place for Scottish soldiers of the American Civil War 1861–5." On the east: "To preserve the jewel of liberty in the framework of peace. Abraham Lincoln." Around the base: "Suffrage—Union—Education—Emancipation."

85. The British Stonewall Jackson Memorial, Richmond, Virginia. The inscription on the plaque reads: "Presented by English gentlemen, as a tribute of admiration for the soldier and patriot, Thomas J. Jackson, and gratefully accepted by Virginia in the name of the Southern people. Done A.D. 1875, in the hundredth year of the commonwealth. 'Look! There is Jackson, Standing like a Stone-Wall.'"

were even buglers and flower girls who scattered petals before Stuart's arrival.

When Lee and his army reached Culpeper Court House on June 9, Stuart put on another review, this time without the flower girls. But the feeling among the observers was that the cavalry general had become far too interested in showmanship. Lee commented acidly to Stuart about a Northern commander who had also bedecked himself with flowers— just before a defeat. Francis Lawley wrote damningly that Stuart was "much too fond of frolics and dancing and being flattered."[25] As soon as the performance ended, the men dispersed in readiness for the long march in the morning. Lee planned to take the army across the Blue Ridge Mountains into the Shenandoah Valley and head due north; Stuart was meant to be diverting attention rather than attracting it, so that Lee would have time to put sufficient distance between himself and his pursuers.

At 4:30 in the morning on June 9, the first divisions of Union general Alfred Pleasonton's 11,000-strong cavalry corps splashed across the Rappahannock on a mission to "to disperse and destroy the rebel force" at Culpeper. Stuart's antics had led the Federal cavalry straight to him; fortunately for the Confederates, Hooker's information was several days old and he was unaware that the entire Army of Northern Virginia was nearby or that it was about to begin the journey northward. Woken by the sound of firing, Stuart scrambled out of his tent on Fleetwood Hill, which overlooked Brandy Station, and shouted to his officers to block the river fords. He was too late; half the Federal cavalry was already across the river.

Sir Percy Wyndham, restored to brigade command and in high spirits, led the second half of the corps, which forded the Rappahannock in midmorning. He was trotting toward Brandy Station when an artillery gun on top of Fleetwood Hill began firing shells at their feet. There was only the one gun at Stuart's headquarters, but Wyndham could not know that. He shouted for the brigade to halt and take up a defensive position. A Federal artillery gun was pointed in the offending direction and fired back. Half an hour later, the 1st New Jersey Cavaliers made the first of six charges against Stuart's position on Fleetwood Hill. Wyndham had trained his men to use their sabers, which at the time they had scoffed at as fancy Old Worldism, but now that they were fighting up close with the horses wheeling and rearing, the saber proved by far the most effective weapon. Their Confederate opponents were outraged and bewildered; one of them shouted, "Draw your pistols and fight like gentlemen!"[26]

The thunderous galloping of thousands of horses caused a swirling brown cloud to envelop the hill as cavalry units charged and counter-charged one another for almost seven hours. At various times during the day, each side briefly gained control of the crest. The Confederates captured Wyndham's artillery and two of his best officers were killed, yet the 1st New Jersey Cavaliers fought on until they were surrounded and their only path of retreat was through the enemy. Wyndham remained in command, despite a bullet having sliced through his calf, until all his men were off the hill and safely back across the Rappahannock.

Wyndham exhorted the regiment to take pride in its performance. Though they had not ended with possession of the hill, his troops had behaved nobly, he wrote the following day, "standing unmoved under the enemy's artillery fire, and when ordered to charge, dashing forward with a spirit and determination."[27] The Battle of Brandy Station fulfilled Wyndham's dream of leading his own cavalry charge. The disappointments and frustrations of the past year were eclipsed by the brilliant performance of his troops under fire. The exhausted soldiers relished his delight. Wyndham "paid the regiment the highest compliments for its steady and dashing charges," wrote one of his officers to the governor of New Jersey on June 10. "He goes to Washington today [to the hospital]. We hope he will soon return, as he cannot be spared from his command."[28]

The Battle of Brandy Station was a turning point for the Federal cavalry. Though its 866 casualties were nearly twice as many as the Confederates', the Union cavalry had come of age. Even Charles Francis Adams, Jr., whose squadron played only a small part in the fighting, gained confidence from the fight. But for Pleasonton's mistiming of the two river crossings, he told Henry, they would have "whipped Stuart out of his boots."[29] Charles Francis Jr. was right. If Pleasonton had coordinated the corps better so that the two divisions had attacked simultaneously rather than six hours apart, Stuart would have been smashed to pieces. Reflecting on the battle many years later, one of Stuart's officers commented that Brandy Station "made the Federal cavalry."[30] Similarly, the battle ruined Jeb Stuart's aura of invincibility; the fact that he had ultimately held his ground did not excuse his carelessness in allowing the surprise attack or lessen the shame of his having to call on infantry reinforcements for help.

————

Lee could not afford to let the near debacle at Brandy Station slow the momentum of his army. The departure for Maryland proceeded as planned. The Second Corps under Ewell headed toward the lower Shenandoah Valley, with Longstreet following close behind. On June 13 the Third Corps quietly slipped away from Fredericksburg, leaving their Federal opponents to discover that the weeklong sparring had simply been a feint rather than the preparation for a large battle. General Hooker realized he had been tricked, but his latest intelligence told him only that the Confederate army was somewhere in the Shenandoah Valley. The best he could do was to keep the Army of the Potomac moving north while protecting Washington against surprise attacks.

The skirmishing at Fredericksburg had been a gentle introduction to warfare for Company F of the 7th Maine Infantry, a unit of new recruits that arrived in Virginia on May 23, 1863. Walking fresh into a battle-hardened regiment was not usually a pleasant experience for recruits. But the newest and youngest member of Company F had no difficulty in endearing himself to his comrades. Nineteen-year-old Frederick Farr was a runaway from England who had enlisted under the alias Frederick Clark. His father was the celebrated epidemiologist William Farr, who pinpointed the cause of the great cholera epidemic of 1848. The last that Farr Sr. had heard from his son was in January, when Frederick wrote to say he was studying hard for his civil service exams. Three weeks later, on February 26, Frederick had secretly boarded the *Anglo-Saxon* for Portland, Maine.

Back at home, Dr. Farr called at the American legation to swear an affidavit that Frederick was underage and had enlisted without his parents' permission. He also fired off letters to his Northern friends in the U.S. Sanitary Commission and the Statistics Office begging for their help. Joseph Kennedy of the Census Bureau petitioned Seward, Lyons, and even General Hooker on Farr's behalf. Kennedy tried to have Frederick transferred to General Pleasonton's staff, where his own son was an aide, and he engaged a local lawyer in Maine to visit the boy. The lawyer returned with unexpected news: the youth had only ever wanted to be a soldier and had refused his help. "He is very popular with his superior officers and is as disinclined to leave the service at present as they are indisposed to part with him." All the lawyer could do for now was ask the regiment's colonel and the governor of Maine (both of whom were personal friends) to take an interest in Frederick's welfare.[31]

On June 8, Joseph Kennedy cornered Lord Lyons at a ball given by the Brazilian minister. Kennedy continued pressing Farr's case until Lyons explained that even in the best circumstances—when the law had been clearly transgressed—his appeals to Seward often failed to win a release.[32] That day, Lyons had been shown one of the saddest letters yet received by the legation. A Miss Hodges in Baltimore had written about her fiancé, Bradford Smith Hoskins, who had been killed on May 30, during a skirmish between Federal cavalry and Mosby's Rangers. Hoskins had been in America for less than six months, and with Mosby for only six weeks. Federal troopers had carried the mortally wounded officer into a nearby farmhouse belonging to the Green family, who took pity on the Englishman dying so far from home and buried him in their family plot in the cemetery across the way. Unfortunately, the Federals' magnanimous gesture was undermined by the theft of his personal effects. Miss Hodges begged Lord Lyons to track down the missing articles and have them returned to Hoskins's father in England. The minister dutifully began the laborious task of finding the thief.[*34]

Lyons was longing for a respite from the daily grind of appeals and rejections. He half hoped that the rumors of an imminent attack by the Confederates were true. "There is some chance of communication between Washington and the North being interrupted, as it was at the beginning of the war," Lyons wrote to his sister on June 16. "The interruption of my correspondence for a few days would be a most enjoyable relief to me."[35] But he suspected there was no real danger, except to Lee. Lyons thought the general had made "a perilous move" by launching another invasion, even though the mere suggestion of his coming had created panic in Washington. Sir Percy Wyndham was ordered out of his bed and told to round up all available horsemen for the city's defense.

---

* Several months went by as the case moved slowly down the chain of command until it reached the colonel of the 5th New York Cavalry. He discovered that it was one of his troopers who had taken the bag. The article was proffered up, with Hoskins's belongings still inside, and passed back up the chain to Washington. It was a melancholy triumph for Lyons, but he was glad to inform the Reverend Hoskins in Kent that his son's belongings were on their way home.[33]

TWENTY-TWO

Crossroads at Gettysburg

The anguish of Charles Francis Adams, Jr.—Colonel Fremantle meets Robert E. Lee—The view from the oak tree—The Federals hold—Lawley's painful duty

The train carrying the English colonel Arthur Fremantle pulled into Richmond on the morning of June 17, 1863, while more than a hundred miles away the Army of Northern Virginia was crossing the Blue Ridge Mountains into the Shenandoah Valley. Francis Lawley had already left Richmond, hoping to reach Lee before the army disappeared entirely. Lawley was weighed down by a sense of foreboding, even though his reports maintained their jaunty tone. His boast that "Vicksburg will never fall" was simply propaganda, he had admitted to the Marquess of Hartington in a confidential letter of June 14. It looked increasingly doubtful that the besieged town could withstand Grant for much longer. "If it falls the Confederacy may hold out and will strive to hold out for years," he wrote. "But bisected & perforated everywhere by its enemies its fortunes will be at zero. No successes which Lee can gain in Virginia will be set off against the fall of Vicksburg." Mindful of Hartington's new position as undersecretary for war, Lawley appealed to his military instincts, urging him to lobby for Southern recognition so that Britain would have an ally if the North turned its million-strong army toward Canada.[1]

"I hear everyone complaining dreadfully of General Johnston's inactivity in Mississippi, and all now despair of saving Vicksburg," Fremantle wrote in his diary. He had spent his first day in Richmond visiting with

as many government officials as would receive him.*[2] He eventually
managed to gain access to the Confederate secretary of state, Judah P.
Benjamin—"a stout dapper little man" in Fremantle's opinion—whose
anteroom was crowded with supplicants waiting for an audience. Benjamin gravely pressed upon him England's moral responsibility in allowing the bloodshed to continue—one word about recognition and the war
would end, he claimed. When Fremantle brought up the specter of
Britain's losing Canada if she grappled with the North, Benjamin
laughed at the possibility: "They know perfectly well you could deprive
them of California . . . with much greater ease." This was a novel idea
that Fremantle was too polite to pursue.[3]

After their interview, Benjamin escorted Fremantle to Davis's house.
The president served him tea, the first that Fremantle had seen during
his travels, while they discussed the risks to England if she supported the
Confederacy. Although Davis avoided talking about the current fighting,
he alluded bitterly to the suffering wrought by Union armies. His own
family had been made homeless after Federal soldiers torched his
brother's plantation in Mississippi, having forced the tearful occupants
out onto the lawn to watch the destruction. He defended the behavior of
Confederate soldiers and denied that they shot men who surrendered.
(The fate of Negro regiments at Charleston and also Port Hudson in
1864 would put the lie to this claim.) This gave Fremantle the opportunity to question him about Colonel Grenfell's legal trouble with the state
authorities. "He was very sorry when I told him," wrote Fremantle, as
"he had heard much of his gallantry and good services."[4] But Davis was
not unduly troubled by Grenfell's departure; there seemed to be no
shortage of foreign volunteers.[†]

"When I took my leave about 9 o'clock, the President asked me to call
upon him again," wrote Fremantle. He felt sorry for him; Davis looked

---

* Despite not having met a single Southerner who was prepared to free his slaves
under any conditions, Fremantle wrote after his visit to Charleston: "I think that if
the Confederate States were *left alone,* the system would be much modified and
amended."

† Only the week before, on June 9, a letter from Lieutenant Sydney Herbert Davies
had appeared on his desk. Davies had resigned from his regiment in Canada in
order to carry secret dispatches to the South. "I have now the honour to apply for
a major's commission in the CSA," he wrote. "I am in possession of a first class certificate as an instructor of musketry and am not ignorant of warfare." He was rewarded with a commission of first lieutenant.[5]

much older than his fifty-five years. He face was lined and emaciated, his eyes were evidently hurting him, yet "nothing can exceed the charm of his manner, which is simple, easy, and most fascinating."[6] This was an uncharacteristic description of a man who was generally considered to be haughty and cold, and too enamored of his military record during the Mexican-American War to listen to the advice of his generals. On the night of June 19 there was an explosion of thunder and lightning over Richmond. The clattering of rain followed by a rush of cool air made a pleasant end to Fremantle's last hours in the city. He was packing in preparation for a dawn departure by train to Culpeper, where he hoped to obtain a horse and ride to Lee's headquarters at Berryville.

The drought also broke at Middleburg, near the northern Virginia border, finally ridding the countryside of its pervasive smell of rotting horses.[7] Water flowed through the camp of the 1st Massachusetts Cavalry, flooding the tents, many of which stood empty. Charles Francis Adams, Jr., was alone in his, struggling to make sense of the past forty-eight hours. Only four days ago he had been studying William Howard Russell's published diary for accuracy and bias, wondering if the authorities had forgotten the regiment's existence. After the Battle of Brandy Station, General Pleasonton had ordered the cavalry to pursue the Confederate army into the Blue Ridge Mountains and bring him definitive intelligence of its direction. Jeb Stuart had placed his troopers in front of the three mountain gaps to hold the Union cavalry off. Both he and his men were trying to blot out their recent near humiliation; Pleasonton's cavalry were no less determined to prove that they were the Confederates' equals or better. The 1st Massachusetts Cavalry had always previously ended up on the sidelines or been held in reserve, but this time they were assigned to Kilpatrick's brigade and sent to break the Confederate hold at Aldie, the northernmost gap in the Blue Ridge. They roared into the village on the morning of the seventeenth, easily driving off the rebel pickets, but when they turned back for another sweep, they were hit by a countercharge of Confederate reinforcements. Charles Francis Jr.'s squadron became trapped at the foot of a hill. "My poor men were just slaughtered and all we could do was to stand still and be shot down," he wrote in anguish to his brother Henry. "In twenty minutes and without fault on our part I lost thirty-two as good men and horses as can be found in the cavalry corps. They seemed to pick out my best and truest men, my pets and favourites. How and why I escaped I can't say, for my

General Longstreet's corps crossing the Blue Ridge from the Shenandoah to the Rappahannock, by Frank Vizetelly.

men fell all around me."[8] He was racked by guilt and grief over his losses. The army's leaders were butchers, he wrote bitterly to Henry; the "drunk-murdering-arson dynasty" of Hooker and the rest had to be expelled before they did Lee's work for him.

Jeb Stuart succeeded in driving the Federals away from the passes, but he could not prevent General Pleasonton from obtaining the information sought by Hooker. By June 22 the Federals knew for certain that Pennsylvania and not Washington was Lee's objective. Stuart was unsure what Lee wished him to do in the face of so many threats—should he guard the gaps, follow the Confederate army up the Shenandoah Valley, or create a diversion and try to maintain the deception that the capital was in danger? Lee sent him two notes, on June 22 and 23, which the cavalry commander interpreted to mean that he could use his own judgment, provided he rejoined the main body of the army in good time. Stuart decided to go riding and raiding in between the Federal army and Washington.[9]

Fremantle at last arrived at Lee's headquarters at 9:00 A.M. on June 22. He recognized the general immediately but refrained from going up to him; the expression on Lee's face discouraged frivolous interruption. Instead, Fremantle asked a member of the staff where he might find Francis Lawley. After introducing him to Lee's aides, Lawley invited Fremantle to join them for breakfast. There was another guest at the table, a Prussian captain named Justus Scheibert, who was an official observer from the Royal Prussian Engineers. The conversation centered mostly on Jeb Stuart and his successful repulse of Pleasonton's cavalry at the mountain passes. For the moment, at least, Stuart's reputation was on a reprieve. But he had lost one of his most popular volunteers—the Prussian soldier Heros von Borcke, who had been severely wounded at Aldie.

Lawley understood Fremantle's desire to meet Lee, but persuaded him to wait until the atmosphere was less frenetic. He suggested they leave the camp and deposit themselves ten miles farther north, at Winchester, where there would be decent lodgings and a blacksmith for Fremantle's suffering horse. They spent the next couple of days together, exploring the battle-scarred countryside and staying out of the Confederates' way. The houses looked bleak and dilapidated, with those still inhabited being used as hospitals for the wounded. The travelers visited the mud hole that had once been Commissioner Mason's elegant plantation. "Literally not one stone remains standing upon another," wrote Fremantle, surprised at the vitriol behind the Federal attack.

On June 24, leaving Lawley to write his *Times* dispatch, Fremantle went foraging for their horses without success. He eventually found virgin grass four miles outside town, but all the hay and corn had been seized long ago. He was experiencing on a small scale one of Lee's greatest anxieties: how to feed his army. As usual, Lawley hid the situation from his readers. He conceded that the Southern army was "still ragged and unkempt" but declared that all had good shoes and that the animals were "for the most part sleek and fat." Lawley was unable to finish his report that day or the next. He became so ill, probably with dysentery, that they had to stay behind in Winchester even though the Confederate army had resumed its northward progress. On June 25, Lawley forced himself to mount his horse and they rode all day in the rain, trying to catch up with Lee. They managed to pass some divisions of Longstreet's corps, but the generals had already crossed the Potomac.

"It was a dreary day! The rain was falling in torrents," recalled Francis Dawson. "General Lee, General Longstreet and General Pickett were riding together, followed by their staffs. When we reached the Maryland shore we found several patriotic ladies with small feet and big umbrellas waiting to receive the Confederates who were coming a second time to deliver downtrodden Maryland." One of the four women held an enormous wreath that had been intended to adorn the neck of Lee's horse, Traveler, but its size frightened the animal and it was handed to one of the general's aides to carry. More ladies greeted them at Hagerstown, just south of the Pennsylvania state line. This time one of them asked for a lock of Lee's hair, which he refused, offering one of General George Pickett's instead. "General Pickett did not enjoy the joke," wrote Dawson, "for he was known everywhere by his corkscrew ringlets, which were not particularly becoming when the rain made them lank in such weather as we then had."[10]

Lawley and Fremantle rode into Hagerstown late at night on Friday, June 26. They had almost caught up with the army, but Lawley was so weak that he slumped alarmingly on his horse. Fremantle's had gone lame; "by the assistance of his tail, I managed to struggle through the deep mud and wet," he wrote, until after seventeen very long miles they bribed a Dutchman with gold to let them stay the night. "I dared not take off my solitary pair of boots, because I knew I should never get them on again," recorded Fremantle. Twenty-four hours earlier, in England, the *Times*' managing editor, Mowbray Morris, was writing optimistically to Lawley to keep going just a little bit longer. The only real hardship was the blockade, he asserted; once that was raised, "your position will be comparatively easy and your work pleasant."[11]

The following day Lawley was too ill to be moved. Deciding that his friend required medical attention, Fremantle took Lawley's horse, which seemed marginally less likely to collapse, and set off in search of Longstreet. He found him after only an hour. Longstreet immediately sent an ambulance to fetch Lawley, and invited Fremantle to join his mess during the campaign. He informed the surprised Englishman that they had already crossed into Pennsylvania, Maryland being only ten miles wide at that point. They were heading toward Chambersburg, a small town twenty miles from Hagerstown.

After a couple of days' observation, Fremantle realized that he was witnessing a rare event in military history: an invasion unaccompanied by mass rape and murder. Northern blacks were being robbed, assaulted, and in some cases forced at gunpoint into slavery. But since these crimes happened along the fringes of the army, Fremantle saw only minor infractions such as fence breaking or Northern whites being forced to accept worthless Confederate dollars for their goods. Fremantle thought they were remarkably ungrateful for the army's restrained behavior "and really appear to be unaware that their own troops have been for two years treating Southern towns with ten times more harshness."[12] Francis Dawson felt proud to be riding in Longstreet's corps. "The army behaved superbly in Pennsylvania," he declared. "The orders against straggling and looting were strict." He saw Lee dismount in front of a field of broken rails and tidy them up himself: "It was the best rebuke that he could have given to the offenders." When the army entered Chambersburg, Dawson was surprised to see young men lolling on street corners. Suddenly Lee's invading army of sixty thousand seemed small and vulnerable; there were no such "spare" men in Virginia. Dawson visited the prison where he had been held after the Battle of Antietam. There were Yankee prisoners in the yard, and for a brief moment he wanted to pelt them with stones, as had been done to him.

To maintain order, Lee had decreed that only generals and their staff were allowed into Chambersburg without a special pass. But this official reassurance was not enough to calm the townspeople: all the shops and hotels were closed and shuttered. The commissary officers could not find anyone willing to sell provisions, though they threatened to seize them by force if necessary. Lawley was recuperating at the Franklin Hotel, which was kept locked to casual passersby. Fremantle had to hammer on the doors, shouting that he was an English traveler, until they were cautiously opened.

Fremantle went to Lawley's room to give him the latest news and discovered that the journalist was not alone. An Englishman dressed in the full uniform of the Hungarian hussars was sitting in the chair, recounting his journey through the lines. He had crossed into the South in late May, aided as usual by the Maryland journalist W. W. Glenn, in the hope of meeting the famous Robert E. Lee. Fremantle could not stop himself from smiling; the thirty-eight-year-old Captain Fitzgerald Ross had spent the past thirteen years in Austria and had succumbed to the country's fondness for military pomp. He was dressed as though on parade, and brushed aside Fremantle's warning that the Confederates would tease him mercilessly.

All day during the twenty-eighth and twenty-ninth, Fremantle walked quietly among the Confederates, observing their unhurried preparations to move farther north. The army corps was dispersed for miles around, employed in the unending search for food and water. The Confederate army had marched more than ninety miles from its base at Fredericksburg. Every bullet and shell had been brought with them in long wagon lines. Despite these difficulties, Longstreet's headquarters had a relaxed air about it. The normally taciturn general passed the early part of the evening with Fremantle, reminiscing about his time in Texas. But shortly after the Englishman departed, Longstreet received another visitor, a scout, who brought devastating news. The Union army had crossed into Maryland and was only days, if not hours, behind them.

Jeb Stuart was meant to be Lee's eyes and ears, but at this moment the cavalryman was fifty-five miles away, his progress slowed by 125 captured wagons. He was rather pleased with his expedition; on June 28 he had come within six miles of Washington, sending tremors down Pennsylvania Avenue. Lord Lyons ordered his staff to pack their bags in case they needed to make a hasty departure. Since being hustled back into duty, Sir Percy Wyndham had succeeded in rounding up three thousand riders. But he had found horses for only two-thirds of them. (In his search for more, some of his actions had bordered on outright theft, earning him powerful enemies in the capital.)

Lee had no means of sending a message to Stuart, but he dispatched hurried instructions to his generals, who were spread out in a forty-five-mile radius, to collect their scattered corps and meet outside the village of Cashtown, eight miles west of Gettysburg. On June 30, Lee heard that "Fighting Joe" Hooker had resigned after a petty quarrel with General-in-Chief Henry Halleck and been replaced by George Gordon Meade. Lee was not happy with the change: Hooker would have been a far weaker opponent. Meade was a Mexican War veteran, a no-nonsense professional soldier whose hair-trigger temper had earned him the nickname "the Old Snapping Turtle." Fremantle traveled with Longstreet to join Lee, who was in the midst of moving his headquarters closer to Gettysburg. Ten different roads went through the town, making it a useful launch site for a confrontation with the Federal army. The general betrayed no sign of anxiety to Fremantle, who thought him "the handsomest man of his age I ever saw." He was wearing his customary long gray jacket and Wellington boots, both of which were surprisingly clean.

One of the Confederate brigades had spotted Union cavalrymen lurking around Gettysburg. When Lee received the news, all knew that a

battle was imminent. Still elated by the recent victory at Chancellorsville, Lee's officers had no doubt about the outcome. Lawley was
equally optimistic. Though weak, he had managed to eat breakfast in the
hotel dining room in Chambersburg with Captain Ross on July 1. The
complaints and anti-Southern comments of the other diners, all locals,
so irritated Lawley that, to Ross's acute embarrassment, he held a
twenty-dollar Confederate bill aloft and declared "in a month it would
be worth more than all their greenbacks in the North put together."[13]

As Lawley and Ross were eating their breakfast, four Confederate infantry brigades set off in search of a warehouse reported to be full of
shoes. Three miles from Gettysburg they stumbled into the 1st Cavalry
Division of the Union army. Thus began the Battle of Gettysburg, without the orders or knowledge of the two commanders. It was eleven
o'clock when the faint echoes of artillery fire alerted Lee to the battle taking place. He was furious at this unexpected development, which added
to the difficulties forced upon him by not knowing where his enemy lay
or how many he faced. At this moment there were in fact more Confederates than Federals at Gettysburg—a massed attack by the Southerners
could have captured the town.

An hour later, at noon, Longstreet was marching at the head of his
corps toward Gettysburg. Fremantle followed on horseback while Lawley and Captain Ross traveled at the back of the wagon line. "At 2 P.M. firing became distinctly audible in our front," wrote Fremantle. Soon they
passed a ghastly parade of stretchers and the walking wounded coming
the other way. The soldiers were so accustomed to such scenes that they
barely glanced at them. Finally, at 4:30 P.M., the travelers found General
Lee on the top of Seminary Ridge, observing the battle below.

Fremantle climbed to the top of an oak tree in order to obtain a better
view of the Federal defense. The town lay within an undulating basin,
surrounded by ridges and boulder-strewn hills. Lee had realized that control of these ridges was paramount; as at Fredericksburg, whoever held
the high ground outside the town had the advantage. General Ewell's orders were to drive the Federals from Cemetery Ridge "if possible." Fatally
for Lee's plans, as the next two days would prove, Ewell decided it was not
possible, and remained where he was.[14] Nevertheless, when the firing
dwindled away at dusk, the Confederates appeared to have won the day.
They had lost six thousand men compared to the almost nine thousand
casualties suffered by the Federals, and Gettysburg was theirs.

Chambersburg Pike

E w e l l

Howard

A. P. Hill

Gettysburg

Reynolds
(Doubleday)

Hanover Road

Hagerstown Road

Seminary Ridge

Howard

Cemetery Hill

E w e l l

A. P. Hill

Lee

Pettigrew

Newton

Culp's Hill

Arthur
Fremantle

Trimble

Hancock

Cemetery Ridge

Slocum

Frank
Vizetelly

Pickett

Willoughby Run

Longstreet

Peach
Orchard

Wheat
Field

Sickles

Birney

Meade

Charles
Francis
Adams Jr.

Baltimore Pike

Devil's Den

Little Round Top

Francis
Dawson

Longstreet

Sykes
Big
Round Top

Sedgwick

Frederick
Farr

Emmitsburg Road

Taneytown Road

N
W   E
S

Rock Creek

Gettysburg
July 1–3, 1863

Federal forces, 1st day
Confederate forces, 1st day
Federal forces, 2nd day
Confederate forces, 2nd day
Federal forces, 3rd day
Confederate forces, 3rd day

Yards
0   1,000   2,000

The Union army, however, had seized the best defensive positions around the perimeter of hills and ridges south of town, near the local cemetery. That evening Fremantle and Lawley witnessed a tense debate between the Confederate generals. "The enemy's new position," reported Lawley later, made Longstreet fear that a direct assault would be too dangerous. He wanted Lee to move the army to a better location and force Meade to come after them. But Lee disagreed. "The enemy is here," he argued; "if we do not whip him, he will whip us." They would renew the attack the following day. Lawley thought Longstreet was right, ignorant as he was of the risk. The Confederates had no intelligence of Meade's numbers or position other than what they could see with their own eyes.

"The universal feeling in the army was one of profound contempt for an enemy whom they have beaten so constantly, and under so many disadvantages," wrote Fremantle. But never before had the disadvantage been one of terrain or information. When General Meade arrived at Cemetery Hill that night, he was relieved to find that his army held the high ground. The ridge occupied by the Federals was several miles long and in some parts more than 140 feet high. Lee's army was spread out in a thin semicircle below.

The four European observers nevertheless shared the Confederates' optimism. Lawley's malady had returned, but he insisted on breakfasting at 3:30 A.M. with the Prussian observer Scheibert, Fremantle, and Captain Ross, who had shaved his beard and waxed his mustache in anticipation of the day's battle. He made silly comments about Mars calling, which the others accepted in good humor.

They returned to Fremantle's oak tree on Seminary Ridge and there found Lee and his generals discussing the plan of attack. Longstreet was still trying to persuade Lee to retire from Gettysburg. Fremantle was amused to see Generals Longstreet and John B. Hood whittle at sticks while they talked. The habit struck him as peculiarly American. Ross soon lost interest in the Confederates' conversation and stared at the Federal positions through his field glasses. He experienced a jolt when he saw them looking straight back at him through their own.[15]

In the morning, despite being ordered to move his troops into attack formation, Longstreet procrastinated for several hours, giving Meade more time to prepare. Federal reinforcements had been arriving throughout the night, including the 7th Maine Infantry (and the English runaway Frederick Farr), which was sent to shore up the extreme end of the Union line. "Order from General Gibbon read to us," recorded a private in one of the Minnesota regiments occupying Cemetery Ridge. "He says this is to be the great battle of the war and that any soldier leaving the ranks without leave will be instantly put to death."[16]

The concentration of troops now numbered 60,000 Confederates and 85,000 Federals, yet all was quiet during July 2 until late afternoon. Bored with waiting, Ross and Fremantle left the other two by the tree and went exploring. They bumped into two members of Longstreet's staff. One of them, Colonel James B. Walton, was in charge of the reserve artillery. The Confederates shared their cherries with them, and afterward they all went for a dip in the stream. When the Englishmen returned to the oak tree, Jeb Stuart had at last reappeared with the missing cavalry. Lee was so angry he could barely acknowledge him.

"No one would have imagined that such masses of men and such a powerful artillery were about to commence the work of destruction," wrote Fremantle. "We began to doubt whether a fight was off to-day at all." The sudden explosion of Confederate artillery at 4:45 P.M. gave the answer. An hour later, Longstreet ordered his corps to storm the Federal defenses. Fremantle was amazed by Lee's behavior once the fighting began. The general sat by himself on a tree stump. No one spoke to him. He received only one report and sent just one message. He had become an observer in his own battle. "I know not whether I am mistaken," Lawley wrote later; "Lee struck me as more anxious and ruffled than I had ever seen him before, though it required close observation to detect it."[17] In previous battles, Lee had encouraged his subordinates to use their initiative, but at Gettysburg the practice allowed for increased confusion. Without a leader to coordinate its movements, the Confederate assault was like a random firecracker display. To add to the strangeness of the scene, a Confederate marching band "began to play polkas and waltzes, which sounded very curious, accompanied by the hissing and bursting of shells."[18]

The cannonade sounded "one deep prolonged bellowing roar," wrote Lawley. "A thick canopy of smoke, constantly rent by bright darting flashes of flame, cast its dense pall over the struggling, bleeding thousands who toiled and died in its centre."[19] Lee's plan called for a specific type of attack known as "en echelon," meaning that the divisions were to attack in sequence, parallel to one another—first hitting the south side of

Meade's line, which held Little Round Top hill, and then the north side, which overlooked the cemetery near the town. En echelon assaults were complicated, requiring precision timing and execution; it would have been a risky maneuver for Lee under the best of circumstances, and to attempt one now, when two of his three corps commanders were new and untried, was asking a great deal. The Federals had orders to hold Little Round Top "at all hazards"; Father William Corby, one of the chaplains of the Irish Brigade, climbed to the top of a boulder and called out that any soldier killed on the battlefield would be given a full Christian burial, but God help those who ran away.[*20] Almost half the brigade was killed or wounded that day, shot to pieces in the infamous Wheat Field, which lay near the bottom of Little Round Top. Meanwhile, General Ewell's attacks against Meade's northern lines along Cemetery Hill teetered on the brink of victory, but fierce Federal counterattacks drove the Confederates back to the town. When the sun went down, each army had suffered almost ten thousand casualties.

Lee was hemorrhaging men, yet he still believed that one more assault would dislodge the Federals and allow him to pick off the fleeing divisions one by one. He wanted all 65 batteries and 282 guns ready and primed for action for the next day, July 3. Longstreet had argued against fighting the Federals at Gettysburg, and he now vehemently protested against Lee's proposal to attack the Union center, which, as far as he could tell, would simply be a repeat of Fredericksburg, only this time with the Confederates on the plain and the Federals firing at them from above. Lee was confident that if he sent Jeb Stuart to attack Meade from behind at the same time as the assault in the front, the Federals would be too confused to repel both.

General Meade sensed that Lee was going to throw at him everything within his grasp. Conscious that he was the sixth general to lead the Army of the Potomac, he invited all the generals to a war council at the little white farmhouse that served as his headquarters. The dozen or so commanders discussed whether to retire or continue the battle and then took a vote: they would remain at Gettysburg for one more day and, since they held the higher ground, allow Lee to launch another attack.[21]

---

[*] Gettysburg, like Antietam, Fredericksburg, and Chancellorsville, had its own lexicon of horrors where thousands died contesting a patch of ground: the Wheat Field, Devil's Den, and the Peach Orchard.

The Confederate reserve artillery was ordered into position, facing the center of Meade's line. One of the English volunteers who had run the blockade in the spring, Captain Stephen Winthrop, was assigned a battery and told to take it to Captain Charles W. Squires of the Washington Artillery. Although he had been appointed to Longstreet's staff in late April, Winthrop had arrived at his headquarters only a day or so before the battle, and the order flummoxed him. He tried to memorize the directions, but it proved impossible to navigate the country roads without a map. He became lost and did not arrive until midnight. Squires was so angry that he had Winthrop placed under arrest. The unlucky Englishman was held under arms until the morning, when Colonel Walton came to his rescue.[22]

Early in the morning the four observers joined Lee's and Longstreet's staff as they reconnoitered the battleground, the first time the Confederates had done so since the battle erupted. It was unnerving for Fremantle to walk past the bodies of fallen soldiers, some of whom turned out to be still alive, opening their eyes as they heard him approach. The conspicuous party attracted the attention of a sharpshooter, which led to an encounter with a hidden battery. A few shells whizzed over their heads. One landed on a Federal field hospital, trapping the wounded inside when the building went up in flames.

Although Lee had wanted simultaneous artillery and infantry attacks, Longstreet was inordinately slow in placing his men. As a result, all the fighting that morning took place in one location around Cemetery Hill. By noon, there were 3,500 casualties. Hundred of horses were dead or dying, including sixteen killed by a shell in the yard next to Meade's farmhouse. Then the battlefield went silent for a while, which allowed the midday sun to clear the enveloping smoke, and the next stage of Lee's mangled plan went into motion. Francis Dawson was recovering from dysentery, but even in his weakened state he worked feverishly to transport ordnance to the 164 artillery crews facing the Federal center line: "Every arrangement was made to shell the enemy's position, on Cemetery Hill, and follow this up by an attack in force," he wrote. "Three or four hundred pieces of artillery were being fired as rapidly as the cannoneers could load them. Being in the centre of the front line, I had an excellent view of the fight."[23]

Leaving Lawley and Scheibert at their post by the oak tree, Fremantle and Ross went down into the town, thinking that the view from the cupola above Ewell's headquarters would offer a spectacular panorama. The idea became less attractive as shells began bursting from all directions. They had managed to reach the tollgate when flying shrapnel sliced into their guide. A little boy who had latched on to them began screaming and laughing hysterically each time another shell burst. Fremantle realized they had to get away as quickly as possible. But at the next explosion the child darted off before they could stop him. "I never saw this boy again, or found out who he was," wrote Fremantle sadly.[24]

The two observers were still dodging shells when Longstreet finally ordered his corps to prepare for the attack. The Federal guns had stopped firing, leading him to assume that his own barrage had successfully destroyed their defense. He did not know that his artillerists' aim had been slightly off, or that the Federals were simply conserving their ammunition for the expected assault. The Confederates, on the other hand, had used up all their long-range shells. Longstreet's artillery chief, Edward P. Alexander, begged him to call the charge before the Federal guns started up again.

Dawson watched as 14,000 Confederate soldiers assembled in the woods. One division, led by the ringleted George Pickett, was almost exclusively Virginian. Prayers were read to the brigades, almost as though the men were receiving the last rites. "This is a desperate thing to attempt," Dawson heard one of the brigadier generals remark. "Just then," Dawson continued, "a hare which had been lying in the bushes, sprang up and leaped rapidly to the rear. A gaunt Virginian, with an earnestness that struck a sympathetic chord in many a breast, yelled out: 'Run old heah; if I were an old heah I would run too.' "[25]

The Federals could not see the Confederates massing in the woods across from them. "From our position the eye ranged over a wide expanse of uneven country, fields broken by woods, showing nowhere any signs of an army movement, much less of conflict," Charles Francis Adams, Jr., wrote in his memoirs. Even at the height of the battle, Gettysburg seemed pleasingly pastoral: "a quiet, midsummer, and champagne country. Neither our lines nor those of the enemy were visible to us; and the sounds of battle were hushed." When the Confederate artillery fire began, Charles Francis Jr. and the survivors of the 1st Massachusetts Cavalry had been lying on the grass, near their horses, while they waited for orders. The thick heat and soft buzzing of insects acted as a kind of soporific. "Lulled by the incessant roar of the cannon," he recorded, "while the fate of the army and the nation trembled in the balance, at the very crisis of the great conflict, I dropped quietly asleep. It was not heroic; but it was . . . war."[26]

Forty-seven Confederate regiments spaced over the distance of a mile began advancing across the 1,400-yard field that lay in front of Cemetery Ridge. Francis Lawley—too ill to climb the tree himself—shouted up to Justus Scheibert to describe the charge to him. The Prussian started a running commentary full of technical descriptions, prompting Lawley to bellow at him in frustration to use layman's terms, but Scheibert was at a loss for further words, having never witnessed such butchery. The closer the Confederates stumbled toward the concave Federal line, the easier targets they presented. Fremantle entered the wood where Pickett's division had gathered only a few minutes before. Federal shells were bringing down huge tree limbs, and yet the wood was full of gray-clad soldiers, "in numbers as great as the crowd in Oxford Street in the middle of the day." Then he saw that every single one was wounded.[27]

The woodland scene confused Fremantle. When he found Longstreet, who was sitting on a rail at the edge of the wood, he made an exceptionally thoughtless comment. "Thinking I was just in time to see the attack," he wrote contritely, "I remarked to the General that 'I wouldn't have missed this for any thing.' " Longstreet gave a hollow laugh. "The Devil you wouldn't! I would like to have missed it very much; we've attacked and been repulsed; look there!"[28] Longstreet asked wearily for a drink, and Fremantle offered him a sip of rum from his flask. Scattered in heaps and fragments below were nearly seven thousand Confederate soldiers. George Pickett had lost two-thirds of his division, including all thirteen colonels. "I suppose that I was the first man to whom Pickett spoke when he reached the line," wrote Francis Dawson. "With tears in his eyes, he said to me: 'Why did you not halt my men here? Great God, where, oh! where is my division?' I told him that he saw around him what there was left of it."[29]

Fremantle was surprised by Longstreet's calm demeanor. A Federal charge at this moment would have smashed the Confederate army into pieces. When one general protested that he could not gather his men, Longstreet sarcastically told him not to worry, the enemy would do it for him. Lee came riding up the hill to help rally the soldiers. "His face, which is always placid and cheerful, did not show signs of the slightest disappointment," wrote Fremantle. His only concern was to ready a line of defense. Lee asked Colonel Edward Alexander whether they had enough ammunition to repel a Federal attack. The artillerist gave a bleak answer. Lee bravely acknowledged his part in the failed charge. "It was all my fault this time," Lee told the dazed fugitives from Pickett's charge; "form your ranks again when you get back to cover."[30] At 7:30 P.M., when he was certain that there would be no more fighting that day, Fremantle returned to camp to describe the recent events to Lawley.

On the following day, July 4, the battlefield was soaked by a long, steady downpour. "Many dear friends had yielded up their young lives during the hours which had elapsed," wrote Charles Francis Jr., "but, though twenty thousand fellow creatures were wounded or dead around us, though the flood-gates of heaven seemed open and the torrents fell upon the quick and the dead, yet the elements seemed electrified with a certain magnetic influence of victory, and, as the great army sank down over-wearied in its tracks, it felt that the crisis and danger was passed—that Gettysburg was immortal."[31]

Lee now had just one aim—to retreat with the remnants of his army before Meade attacked. In all, 70,000 Confederates had fought at Gettysburg; only 48,000 were leaving. The Federal army had one field hospital for every 12,000 soldiers; the Confederates simply gathered as many of the injured as they could and loaded them onto wagons. Thousands were left behind, and countless men died from their wounds or starved to death waiting for someone to rescue them. Two weeks after the battle, a civilian stumbled upon one of the abandoned camps. A party was sent to collect the survivors. A shocked witness wrote:

> One boy without beard was stretched out dead, quite naked, a piece of blanket thrown over his emaciated form, a rag over his face, and his small, thin hands laid over his breast. Of the dead none knew their names, and it breaks my heart to think of the mothers waiting and watching for the sons laid in the lonely grave on that fearful battlefield. All of those men in the woods were nearly naked, and when ladies approached they tried to cover themselves with the filthy rags they had cast aside. The wounds themselves, unwashed and untouched, were full of worms. God only knows what they suffered.[32]

Lincoln would never forgive Meade for not driving after Lee. But the Union commander had lost a quarter of his army; 23,000 men were dead, wounded, or captured. His generals supported his decision to wait until they were sure of Lee's movements. A temporary halt while the injured were removed and the supply trains arrived did not seem like an intolerable delay. The Federal cavalry caught up with the Confederates two days later. "As we approached Hagerstown, we heard some fighting ahead, between our cavalry and a cavalry force of the enemy. I rode ahead to see if any artillery was needed," wrote Colonel Alexander.

> During the day I had an accession to my staff. Capt. Stephen Winthrop . . . on the march from Gettysburg [had] negotiated with Gen. Sorrel, Longstreet's adjutant, to be transferred to me. Sorrel asked me if I would consent—which I did very willingly, and he joined me about noon on the 6th. He was well built, stout & very muscular, good grey-blue eyes, a full, oval face, with a British mouth and nose, good natured, jolly, & brave. He was an excellent and admirable representation of his country. . . . That very afternoon he got a chance to show the stuff he was made of.[33]

Winthrop was returning with a fresh horse from Alexander's reserve when he rode into one of Jeb Stuart's regiments as it prepared to attack a Federal battery. He introduced himself and asked to carry their colors. The Confederates were too surprised to decline his request. He positioned himself at the front of the charge and leaped forward. "Winthrop's horse was killed by a canister quite close to the guns, but the charge was repulsed. He got another horse, and went in a second charge," recalled Alexander. Though armed with only his saber, he rode into the body of the Federal cavalry and plunged his sword into one of them, "coming out with his sabre bent & bloody all over." Winthrop went off to look for Alexander, satisfied that his honor had been redeemed after his humiliating arrest at Gettysburg.

"The March back to the Potomac was dreary and miserable indeed," wrote Dawson. "The rain fell in torrents. The clothing of the men was worn and tattered, and too many of them were without shoes. It was a heart-breaking business, and gloom settled down upon the army." A trail eighteen miles long slowly ground through the mud toward Hagerstown in Maryland. During the journey, Longstreet talked to Fremantle and Lawley about the reasons for the Confederate defeat, placing the failure on numbers rather than tactics.[34] "He said the mistake they had made was in not concentrating the army more, and making the attack yesterday with 30,000 men instead of 15,000," reported Fremantle. "The advance had been in three lines, and the troops of Hill's corps who gave way were young soldiers, who had never been under fire before." Longstreet would retract this opinion after the war, however, writing in his own memoirs that forty thousand men "could not have carried the position at Gettysburg."[35]

Lawley, Fremantle, Ross, and Scheibert arrived at Hagerstown on the seventh and took rooms together at the Washington Hotel.[36] Lawley had a hard task ahead of him and was left alone by the others so he could write in peace. He could not disguise the grief in his heart: "For the first time during my residence in Secessia," he began, "it is my province to record, as having happened under my own eyes, a failure of the Confederate arms."[37]

TWENTY-THREE

Pressure Rising

Fiasco at the House of Commons—Vicksburg surrenders—An economy without cotton—Rioting in New York—A summer jaunt—Rose Green-how's diplomatic mission

The House of Commons was full on Tuesday evening, June 30, 1863, when Henry Adams entered the Strangers Gallery, pretending not to notice the Southerners seated around him. According to the latest news from America, Lee's army had marched without hindrance all the way to Pennsylvania. But the news appeared to be having a dampening effect on support for Roebuck's motion—several MPs had questioned the need for a debate on recognition when the Confederacy was on the verge of winning independence without English help. It was yet one more dilemma weighing on Roebuck's mind when he entered the Commons. Earlier that day, in the House of Lords, Russell had denied for a second time that the French emperor had written to him about recognizing the South.

James Spence had always felt uncomfortable with Roebuck as the South's main spokesman in the Commons, but even he never imagined the extent to which the MP would self-immolate that evening. Roebuck's speech began unpromisingly with an overflow of bile before descending into such balderdash that he alienated his listeners. There were cries of "No!" when Roebuck insisted that Negroes were worse off in the North than in the South, where "black children and white children are brought up together. I say it without fear of contradiction from any one whose contradiction is worthy of notice. . . . There is a kindly feeling in the minds of the Southern planters toward those whom England fixed there in a condition of servitude." But the real damage came toward the end when he referred to his interview with Louis-Napoleon. Roebuck explained afterward that Russell's denial had given him no choice but to bring up the matter because his own honor was at stake. But rather than simply saying in a few words that France was eager to cooperate on a policy of recognition, Roebuck gave a blow-by-blow description of their interview, including Louis-Napoleon's complaints about double-dealing by the Foreign Office.

At that moment he was doomed, the Confederate lobby discredited. Roebuck had broken a cardinal rule: he, a backbencher, had wedged himself into the middle of Anglo-French relations. The Tories abandoned Roebuck to his fate—even MPs known to sympathize with the South expressed their disapproval of the motion, and the undersecretaries from the Home and Foreign offices were scathing in their criticism of his interference. Gladstone's telling-off was merciful by comparison, though the cabinet was furious with Roebuck for dredging up the question of recognition. But there was more to come.

John Bright had watched his prey stagger and bleed from a thousand little cuts before he moved in for the kill. He recalled with biting sarcasm that "only about two years ago" Roebuck had stated categorically, "I have no faith in the Emperor of the French," and yet he was appearing before the House as the emissary of "the great French ruler." As to the confusion between Roebuck and the Foreign Office over what the emperor had actually communicated:

> I will say this in justice to the French Emperor, that there has never come from him, not from any one of his ministers, nor is there anything to be found in what they have written, that is tinctured in the smallest degree with that bitter hostility which the hon. and learned Gentleman [Roebuck] has constantly exhibited to the United States of America and their people.[1]

Observing Roebuck's humiliation, Henry Adams wrote that Bright "caught and shook and tossed Roebuck, as a big mastiff shakes a wiry, ill-conditioned, toothless, bad-tempered Yorkshire terrier." Bright's crushing of the MP was so complete that Henry "felt an artistic sympathy with

Roebuck, for, from time to time, by way of practice, Bright in a friendly way was apt to shake him too, and he knew how it was done." A Southerner described it as "the most deliberate and tremendous pounding I have ever witnessed."[2] The House adjourned for the night, leaving Roebuck's motion prostrate on the floor.

There was consternation in Whitehall and the Quai d'Orsay as to how Anglo-French policy could have degenerated so swiftly into public farce. The French foreign minister, Édouard Drouyn de Lhuys, dispatched a telegram to Ambassador Gros in London asking for an explanation of the British government's denial.[3] At the Foreign Office, Lord Russell asked Lord Cowley, Britain's ambassador to France, whether he had knowledge of a proposal from the emperor. Russell vaguely recalled Baron Gros's aside about the emperor's support for Southern recognition, but it had never occurred to him to treat it as an official communiqué to the government. Just as troubling to the cabinet was the claim in Roebuck's speech that Louis-Napoleon had complained of his peace overtures being ridiculed by the British. The Foreign Office clerks were ordered to comb through every diplomatic dispatch of the past twelve months to see if there was any truth to the allegation.

When Mason reported the debacle to Slidell, his chief concern was whether they would be able to procure written evidence to prove Roebuck's claim. James Spence and William Gregory, on the other hand, wanted only to be rid of the controversy; they pleaded with Roebuck to withdraw his motion. "The members are 10 to 1 in favour of the South," wrote Spence to Commissioner Mason, but the minute the emperor of France was dragged into the debate, the issue became a matter of national pride and "on this point the vote might be 5 to 1 against Southern interests."[4] Roebuck, as Spence had feared, would not be swayed, nor would he listen to Palmerston, who wrote to him on July 9 saying he was welcome to make his motions in support of the South, but he was treading on dangerous ground when he interfered in matters of state. Roebuck was defiant. That same day, *The Times* predicted the capture of Washington by Lee.[5]

On Friday, July 10, Roebuck tried to resume his motion, only to find himself blocked by his friends. William Schaw Lindsay urged him to wait until after the arrival of the *Scotia* in three days' time—bringing definitive news of Lee's victory—which would cast the debate in an entirely differ-

ent light. The Confederates added their own entreaties, terrified that
Roebuck was on course to destroy the South's political chances in the
Commons permanently. All Henry Hotze desired now was a "decent retreat" before the House had the opportunity to vote down Roebuck's
motion.[6]

The Times helped the Confederates by printing an editorial on Monday, July 13, urging Roebuck to withdraw his motion. Finally Roebuck
listened to the pleas from the chorus around him. That same evening
he announced to the House his decision to withdraw his motion. Benjamin Moran was in the gallery, watching as the Southern lobby
squirmed during Roebuck's speech. William Lindsay spoke immediately after, telling the members that whatever else they thought of his
friend, he was not a liar; the emperor truly had told them of his desire
to recognize the South. The speech was "a long rambling half mad
jumble," wrote Moran, "which the House alternately laughed and
jeered at. Then Palmerston rose, and while patting the two dupes on
the head, expressed the hope that the unusual proceedings . . . would
never be repeated."[7] The Confederates were never happier to see a motion die.

Charles Francis Adams attended a reception at Lord Derby's later
that night, his recent depression almost lifted by the Confederate fiasco
in the Commons. The Tories pressed him for news, forcing him to
admit that, like them, he was waiting for the Atlantic steamer to arrive.
But when the Scotia did come, on Thursday, July 17, the reports about
the battle at Gettysburg were unclear. Adams could not tell whether Lee
had suffered a defeat or merely been checked for a day or so. The Times
hedged but leaned toward a momentary delay. Two days later, however,
Henry Adams came down to breakfast and found his father reading the
victory telegram from the State Department. "I wanted to hug the army
of the Potomac," Henry wrote of his joy at that moment. "I wanted to
get the whole of the army of Vicksburg drunk at my own expense. I
wanted to fight some small man and lick him." The telegram announced not only Lee's retreat from Gettysburg but also the fall of
Vicksburg.

An uneven line of soiled white flags had signaled the surrender of Vicksburg on July 4. As the medical inspector of the XIII Army Corps, Dr.
Charles Mayo was among the first wave of Federal officers sent to in-

spect the situation inside the town.* Seven thousand mortar shells had been lobbed into Vicksburg during the forty-three-day siege. In some streets, every single house had been hit; shattered glass and wooden shards lay strewn everywhere. "The blackened ruins that had once been houses" made Mayo wonder how Londoners would fare in similar circumstances. "We knew quite well that the besieged would be unable to take charge of their own. As it was we found their sick in a most miserable plight," he wrote. "The state of their hospitals was such that a regard for our own safety compelled us to place them in the hands of our own medical officers for instant purification and speedy abolition. They had come to the end of their resources. About 15,000 men fit for duty was all that remained of Pemberton's army: his sick numbered 6,000 or 7,000."[8]

The fighting continued, however, and although Pemberton had finally given up Vicksburg, General Johnston had no intention of surrendering the regiments under his control. He decided to make a stand at Jackson, whose citizens were still struggling to resurrect the city after its occupation in May. Frank Vizetelly reluctantly decided that it was time for him to leave the Mississippi Delta before the Federals seized control of the last railroads going east. He made it out just in time: on July 7, 46,000 U.S. troops, led by General Sherman himself, crossed the Big Black River and were only twenty miles from Jackson. But the journey quickly became a nightmare once the parched and dusty soldiers discovered that the retreating Confederates had fouled all the wells. Sherman was forced to send his mule teams back to the Big Black River to collect drinking water for his thirsty army. At Jackson, he encountered another problem: the Confederates were too well entrenched to be dislodged by

---

* While Mayo was exploring Vicksburg, he was the subject of cheerful conversation at home. On July 11, 1863, the *Medical Times and Gazette* reported on the dinner held by the Southampton Medical Society: "Mr. Dayman spoke at length: 'A son of one of their old associates, Mr. Mayo, of Winchester (hear, hear), was at that moment with the army in America.' (A deeply-toned Voice: Yes, but on the wrong side—laughter.) "There were no wrongs on the side of Surgery." (Hear.) (A Voice: I should prefer his being in the south. Another Voice: The north is more bracing, and laughter.) 'Their young friend, Dr. Chas. Mayo, was with the army in North America.'—(A Voice: The right man in the right place, and laughter.) 'He was gone out as a volunteer Surgeon, taking with him no prejudiced views of the supremacy of Military Surgery, but content to carry into the field the principles which had made his father. . . . Might their young friend do justice, not only to Hampshire, but also to England.' (Applause.)"

Rebels marching out of Vicksburg and stacking arms.

anything except a sustained artillery barrage—the kind that required much more ammunition than the Federals had brought. It took less than an hour for the Union batteries to fire all their available shells. Sherman hastily sent his ordnance officers to round up all the army's reserves. In the meantime, the guns remained silent.

Helpless until the ammunition arrived, the Union soldiers fortified their positions with heavy bales of cotton brought in from the surrounding countryside by heavily guarded wagon trains. Undaunted by the capture of the previous wagon train, Ebenezer Wells set off with his, despite having an escort that was only half strength. "I was about six miles out, riding along in front of my teams," he wrote, when "I was startled by a shot passing close to me." It seemed to be coming from a nearby cornfield. One of the guards became frightened and jumped into a wagon. As he landed, his gun went off, firing a bullet into Wells's best friend. Torn between saving the wounded officer and protecting the supply train, Wells shouted for the wagons to keep moving without him and carried his friend to the edge of the road. "I knelt beside him while he told me his last message home," he recorded. The officer begged him to send his watch and Bible home to his family. "Then, asking me to take his hand but not to move it for the pain, he told me to go as I was in danger." Wells reluctantly galloped off after his wagons. Traveling down the same road on the return journey, he was horrified to see a large red stain where his friend had lain. "By great favour the general allowed me to have a funeral," wrote Wells. The ammunition had arrived and the guns were firing when the burial took place, the priest's words drowned out by the roar of the artillery.[9]

The next day, July 17, 1863, a lone black civilian was spotted walking away from the city carrying a white flag.[10] Johnston had led his army out during the night, leaving Jackson silent and empty but for a few hundred frightened citizens. The Federals marched in and captured some Confederate stragglers, among them an Englishman named Captain Frederick Hampson of the 13th Louisiana Regiment. Two years later, after he had escaped to England, Captain Hampson still shuddered at his treatment:

The surrender of Vicksburg—view of the city from the riverbank showing part of the river batteries.

When captured by the enemy I was stripped of my clothes, even my shoes then robbed of my money, watch and rings. [I] was then marched a distance of 45 miles to Vicksburg *barefoot,* and on the route was grossly insulted by the privates and some officers of the Federal Army: I experienced fearful suffering from hunger, exposure and thirst, not being allowed to leave the ranks, and when we bivouacked [we had] no tents or covering to protect us from the weather; it raining almost all the time. . . . I remained in their hands until about the middle of August, when I succeeded with two more brother officers in effecting my escape from Vicksburg, thence to New Orleans, and from there made the best of my way (via New York by water) to England.[11]

Ebenezer Wells had fallen victim to "Mississippi fever" and was too ill to celebrate the Federal capture of Jackson, becoming another of the delirious, groaning soldiers whom Dr. Mayo tried to keep alive long

enough to be transported to the North. Mayo had more than five hundred patients in his field hospital, ninety of them under his personal care.
He was no longer living in a tent, but on a steamboat next to the hospital ships. Lord Lyons's reply to his letter reached him there. Though disappointed by the minister's refusal to pass his resignation on, Mayo was
gracious in his response, apologizing for placing him in an uncomfortable position: "Of course I had no right to expect any other reply than
that which I have just received," he replied to Lyons in late July. "Two
months of sickness in a climate like this, incurred through a blunder
made by a Washington office-assistant do not tend to improve a man's
temper, nor to reconcile him to his position. I intend to leave this district
with or without orders, at the first opportunity."[12]

"The fall of Vicksburg has made me ill all the week," James Spence wrote
to Mason.[13] *The Times* downplayed the news at first, but on July 23,
Charles Francis Adams noted that the paper "condescends to admit this

morning that Vicksburg is taken." Three days later, *The Times* was also forced to concede the Federal capture of the Mississippi River—Port Hudson had surrendered to General Nathaniel Banks on July 9 after a forty-eight-day siege.

As soon as Henry Hotze recovered from the shock of the news—no one had expected Vicksburg to surrender, let alone General Lee to falter—he began rallying his supporters in the press. It was imperative that they halt the now precipitous slide of Confederate bonds. "You will not be surprised that I am giving to my operations an extension which only the urgencies of the crisis could warrant," he informed Judah Benjamin. Hotze had pulled off the extraordinary feat of persuading a religious publishing house to include in every publication, religious and nonreligious, for the next two months, a Southern pamphlet entitled "Address to the Christians Throughout the World." Signed by the ninety-six clergymen of Richmond, the "Address" urged fellow Christians to protest against Lincoln's Emancipation Proclamation.[14] Hotze estimated that it would be read by 2 million people.[15] This and the obvious shock felt by the British public were his only comfort.

There was outrage in the legation at the lack of enthusiasm in England over the Northern successes. *The Economist* described Lee's defeat as a tragedy because it meant a prolonging of the war.[16] "The salons of this great metropolis are in tears," Adams wrote cynically in his diary. "Tears of anger mixed with grief." He was still smarting over the ignominious end to Mrs. Adams's weekly parties; not even Benjamin Moran bothered to attend the final one.* The assistant secretary had ceased to attend out of protest, having been cast into a jealous agony ever since George Sheffield, one of Lord Lyons's unpaid attachés, visited the legation and innocently revealed that Lyons invited the junior diplomats to every dinner. Moran blamed Henry Adams for stealing his rightful place. Ironically, Henry had recently written to Seward's son, Frederick, pleading for an increase in salary in recognition of Moran's services: "He is an

---

*Adams had also canceled the legation's Fourth of July celebration. The previous year's dinner had been a desultory affair. He expected this year's to be no better, and he feared a visit from the popular orator Henry Ward Beecher, brother of the author Harriet Beecher Stowe, who was visiting England on a lecture tour. Beecher was arousing the British public, but for all the wrong reasons, telling a gathering of temperance campaigners, for example, that the North was losing because its army officers could not stay sober.

invaluable man," he wrote, "a tremendous worker, and worth any ten ordinary officers to Government, but here he has borne nine tenths of the
labour of the Legation for seven years, and gets for it a miserable pittance
of $1500 a year; about enough to support a respectable cab-driver in this
city."[17]

Unaware of Henry's intercession on his behalf, Moran behaved
toward him with appalling rudeness and spite. It pained him to watch
Henry slowly navigate his way into English society and start to enjoy a
real life outside the legation. The younger Adams had become a member
of the Cosmopolitan Club, which did not have permanent premises like
Brooks's or Boodles, but whose members were all notable figures on the
literary or political stage. Henry was mystified why Lord Frederick
Cavendish had championed his admission: "Whether he feels his conscience touched by the vagaries of his brother Hartington; or whether he
desires to show a general and delicate sympathy with our position," he
wrote to Charles Francis Jr., "I don't know and can't guess." But more
important even than joining a club or being proposed by a peer, Henry
had finally made a genuine friend, Charles Milnes Gaskell, known as
Carlo, the son of James Gaskell, a Yorkshire MP and supporter of the
North. They became lifelong friends.[18]

The season was drawing to a close. "The streets are full of Pickford's
vans carting furniture from the houses, and Belgravia and May Fair are
the scene of dirt and littered straw," Henry wrote to his brother. He
knew he would miss the excitement. Despite everything, he liked going
about in London society, "and some day in America," he wrote, "I may
astonish myself by defending these people for whom I entertain at present only a profound and lively contempt."[19]

Their father was looking forward to the summer recess: though the
year had begun disastrously, none of it now seemed to matter. "The great
causes of our apprehension have died away," he wrote. "The cotton
famine and Lancashire distress have not proved such serious troubles as
we had feared."[20] Newspapers no longer carried alarming reports of
protest meetings and "disturbances" in the mill towns. The Earl of
Derby's Central Committee was efficiently distributing almost £500,000
worth of charity, and the Poor Law Board was overseeing a £2 million
public works program in Lancashire, paying the unemployed cotton
workers to build sewers, pave roads, and create public parks and recre-

ation grounds.[21] Some mills were using cotton from India, even though it was of inferior quality to Southern cotton, which had almost doubled imports from 536,000 bales in 1861 to over a million in 1863. Moreover, there were plenty of opportunities for workers who were willing to move away from the cotton districts. The British linen and woolen industries were enjoying a renaissance, for example, the profits from blockade running were swilling around Liverpool, and the armaments industry was having its best year ever.[22] The latest figures showed that even with the dragging effects of the Morrill Tariff, the value of British trade was rising and would top £444 million for 1863. All of these developments were an encouraging counterbalance to the troubles of the cotton industry.

———

The legation was settling into its usual summer routine when Benjamin Moran noticed something strange. He wrote on July 27: "The steamer this week brought no Despatches whatever. This never occurred before in my time."[23]

The abrupt silence had been caused by the complete breakdown of civic order in New York. For five days, between July 13 and 17, the city lay at the mercy of fifty thousand rioters who exacted gruesome revenge on the two classes of persons they considered most responsible for the war: Negroes and those who defended them. There had been signs of working-class resentment ever since the Draft Act became law on March 3, 1863. In theory, it provided Washington with more than 3 million potential new soldiers; in practice, it netted about 100,000 reluctant conscripts and 70,000 substitutes. The draft applied to all able-bodied white males between the ages of twenty and forty-five, but the exemptions for particular family circumstances, such as only sons with widowed mothers to support, as well as the provision that allowed a man to purchase a substitute for $300, mostly benefited the middle class and native-born Americans.[24] For immigrant laborers earning an average of 85 cents a day, the sum of $300 was a cruel joke. Nowhere was the resentment greater than among the 200,000 Irish immigrants of New York, many of whom felt that they had been enticed into emigrating so that they could provide "food for [gun]powder." The editor of the *Freeman's Journal,* a popular Irish newspaper in New York, demanded to know why the Irish were expected "to go and carry on a war for the nigger."[25]

Although aliens were specifically excluded from the draft, the State

Department had recently tightened the rules and increased the burden of proof required from resident foreigners. Consul Archibald was struggling to keep pace with the demand for his help. There had been a sharp increase since the spring in the number of "crimpings"—kidnappings and illegal conscriptions of British subjects. The latest complaint to reach the consulate involved three Caribbean sailors who had disappeared from the *Mary Harris* only to reappear as unwilling seamen on board USS *Tulip*. Archibald wondered whether the recent strike by Irish dockworkers had something to do with the *Tulip* case; the shipyard owners had brought in contrabands—freed slaves—to replace the workers. The combination of the looming draft and black strikebreakers was an especially inflammable mix. The working-class Irish community was outraged that the draft applied only to whites and feared that cheaper— and better educated—black workers were out to steal their jobs.

On Saturday, July 11, 1863, the authorities chose a half-developed block of Manhattan—Forty-seventh Street and Third Avenue—to hold the first of two lotteries for the draft. Colonel Robert Nugent of the Irish 69th New York Volunteers had been asked to oversee the lottery in the hope that this would calm Irish objections. But no other preparations had been made in case the event turned violent; there were only eight hundred policemen on duty for the entire city, and almost every New York regiment was at Gettysburg with General Meade.[26] The drawing of names passed without incident, however. There were a few more fires than usual over the weekend, and the crowds watching them seemed to be on the large side, but the authorities had no hint of what was about to happen on Monday.

When the famous *Great Eastern*—the largest passenger ship in the world—docked at New York on Sunday night, the disembarking passengers felt an air of menace from the onlookers. The financial agents John Murray Forbes and William H. Aspinwall were among them; in Forbes's trunk were $6 million worth of bonds. He was standing on the quayside, fearful that he was about to be mugged, when an Irish cab driver recognized him from a goodwill visit Forbes had once paid to his regiment and offered to take him anywhere he wanted. "We rattled safely over the rough, dark streets, and I was soon glad to deposit my charge among the heaps in the old Brevoort House [Hotel]," wrote Forbes.[27] A few hours later, Lieutenant Colonel Fremantle's train pulled into New York from Pennsylvania. He had said farewell to his friends on July 9, when the

Confederate army was still resting at Hagerstown in Maryland, and turned back toward the North. Fremantle's steamship, the *China,* was scheduled to depart for England on Wednesday, July 15, and until then he had arranged to stay at the Fifth Avenue Hotel on Madison Square. Even though the city was searing hot, Fremantle walked the length of Broadway on Monday. "On returning to the Fifth Avenue," he wrote, "I found all the shopkeepers beginning to close their stores, and I perceived by degrees that there was great alarm about the resistance to the draft which was going on this morning." Inside the hotel he found a scene of pandemonium, with terrified guests begging the equally frightened concierges for protection. A mob had torched several blocks nearby and was holding back the fire brigade. Fremantle decided it would be better to wander around anonymously rather than be trapped in the hotel: "I walked about in the neighbourhood, and saw a company of soldiers [from the invalid corps] on the march, who were being jeered at and hooted by small boys, and I saw a negro pursued by the crowd take refuge with the military; he was followed by loud cries of 'Down with the bloody nigger! Kill all niggers!' "[28]

The British consul was able to rescue Ann Anderson, a Barbadian ship's cook, who was being chased down West Street by a mob. Fortunately, she had time to hammer on the doors of the consulate at No. 10 and be pulled to safety. Twenty blocks north of Fremantle's hotel, at Forty-third and Fifth, stood the Colored Orphan Asylum, home to 237 Negro children aged twelve and under. Three thousand rioters gathered at the front, forcing the asylum superintendent hurriedly to evacuate the small occupants through the back. One little girl was left behind. She was found cowering under her bed by the rioters and beaten to death.[29]

Farther downtown, another mob, heavily armed and ten thousand strong, appeared in front of the police headquarters on Mulberry Street and were confronted by two hundred club-wielding policemen. After twenty minutes of hand-to-hand fighting, the mob turned tail.[30] The violence was sporadic but clearly the result of direction. Small working parties cut down the telegraph poles along Third Avenue, isolating each of the twenty-six police precincts from central command. Others stopped railroad cars and pulled up the tracks. Rioters broke into the Armory at Twenty-first Street and Second Avenue, helping themselves to the rifles and carbines within. A separate mob headed over to Newspaper Row, across from City Hall Park, where the *Tribune* and *The New York*

Times had their offices. The *Times* editor, Henry Raymond, kept the crowd at bay with three borrowed Gatling guns, but the *Tribune* building had only a small band of policemen guarding its entrance.[31] Rioters burst through the doors to find that the staff had used bales of newspaper to barricade the stairs. Unable to push their way through, the mob set fire to the counters and went off in search of other prey.

By sunset, the orange sky was streaked with columns of black smoke. Hiding inside the St. Nicholas Hotel, the mayor of New York, George Opdyke, and the U.S. Army general in command of the Department of the East, John Ellis Wool, passed their responsibilities back and forth as a group of prominent citizens implored them to declare martial law. At 9:30 P.M. the New York head of the telegraph service, Edwin Sanford, sent a wire to Washington from Jersey City, whose station was still operating: "In brief the city of New York is tonight at the mercy of a mob whether organized or improvised, I am unable to say. . . . The situation is not improved since dark. The program is diversified by small mobs chasing isolated Negroes as hounds would chase a fox."

Fires burned uncontrollably all over the city. Establishments that employed blacks as well as whites, such as bars and brothels, were particularly targeted. Dr. Elizabeth Blackwell feared for her infirmary and ordered the servants to close the shutters and lock the doors. Every light was extinguished, leaving the occupants sitting in darkness as the muffled but unmistakable shouts of a lynch mob torturing its victim could be heard through the walls. Some of the white patients became hysterical, begging Dr. Blackwell to save the hospital by expelling the black occupants. She had almost succeeded in calming them down when one of the contraband patients went into labor. Terrified that the woman's cries might be heard from outside, Elizabeth and two nurses carried her to the back of the infirmary. There, in a dimly lit room, they worked all night to deliver the baby.

Meanwhile, mobs were prowling the waterfront, attacking British vessels known to have black crew members. One black sailor was lynched and another suffered life-threatening injuries. Archibald turned the consulate into a safe house, but with limited space at his disposal he had to ask the legation in Washington for help. Although there were no carriages or omnibuses running, an intrepid secretary managed to reach Jersey City to send a ciphered telegram to Lord Lyons: "I consider a man-of-war essential here immediately to receive and protect British

Black crews." Lyons replied that HMS *Challenger* was on its way, but the warship would not reach New York for at least another twenty-four hours. Archibald could not wait that long. In desperation, he contacted the French consulate, which arranged for Admiral Reynaud to offer the *Guerriere* to British blacks. The French frigate steamed into the harbor, opened the gun ports, and let down rope ladders. The captain shouted through his megaphone that all colored Britons were to board the vessel by order of Consul Archibald. Seventy-one black British sailors clambered aboard, and a further seven British vessels moored alongside her.

The violence on Tuesday included mass looting as well as more raids on the armories. Rioters sacked Brooks Brothers, burned the 26th Precinct house, destroyed the Harlem River Bridge, demolished the Washington Hotel, and attacked the mayor's house. Fifty to sixty thousand people were said to be out on the streets; barricades were being erected at various points in the city to hinder the movement of police. "Immediate action is necessary, or the Government and country will be disgraced," Edwin Sanford telegraphed the War Department. The governor of New York, Horatio Seymour, declared a state of insurrection and also asked Washington for troops. A politician to his fingertips, he assured the angry crowd outside City Hall that he was their friend and supporter against the draft, but his appeal failed to stop the violence. Finally, late on Tuesday night, Washington ordered five regiments to the city.

"Wednesday begins with heavy showers, and now, (ten A.M.) cloudy, hot, and steaming," wrote the treasurer of the Sanitary Commission, George Templeton Strong, in his diary; "there will be much trouble today."[32] When Fremantle went down for breakfast he found soldiers guarding the hotel (Robert Lincoln, the president's eldest son, was coming home from Harvard and happened to be one of the guests). But outside, the immediate streets were deserted; the entire city appeared to be in the middle of a mass exodus. There were no carriages, and he had to walk down to the waterfront. "I was not at all sorry to find myself on board the *China*," wrote Fremantle, his final memory of the city "a stone barricade in the distance, and [the sound of] firing going on."[33] The mob and the military had evidently found each other.[34]

At midmorning a small funeral cortège started out from West Fifty-third Street. Dr. Charles Culverwell's wife, Emma, could no longer wait for the rioting to subside. Their three-year-old daughter had died the previous Sunday of infant cholera. Emma did not know where Charles was, although he had promised to come to them. Terrified for herself and her surviving daughter, she attempted to slink unnoticed past the rioters. They barred her way, forcing Emma to plead for permission to bury her child.[35] All this time Culverwell had been begging his hospital superiors in St. Louis to grant him compassionate leave. In desperation he annulled his contract on July 16, donned civilian clothes, and headed for New York.

By Wednesday night, HMS *Challenger* had still not appeared; however, a U.S. warship had joined the *Guerriere,* training its guns on Wall Street to deter an attack on the financial district. On Thursday, rioters discovered they were fighting not just a few brave souls but ten thousand veterans of Gettysburg. During the night there was a final, bloody convulsion at Gramercy Square on Twentieth Street that left one soldier and fifteen rioters dead. But at noon on Friday, the roars and explosions ceased as suddenly as they had begun; Elizabeth Blackwell unlocked the doors of the infirmary for the first time in forty-eight hours. Edwin Sanford telegraphed Washington at 3:45 P.M. that the "city continues very quiet." George Templeton Strong blessed the change in weather: "Rain will keep the rabble quiet tonight."[36] Early estimates put the death toll at anywhere from a hundred to a thousand people, but the physical devastation was obvious. Whole blocks had been burned and more than three hundred buildings destroyed.[37] Among the homes that had been ransacked was Colonel Nugent's—a punishment for his role in enforcing the draft.

"It is a fact that the rioters have been almost entirely Irish," Archibald wrote to Lord Russell, and their fury toward "the poor Negro people" had not abated simply because of the presence of troops.[38] HMS *Challenger* arrived on Saturday and accepted transfer of the refugees from the *Guerriere.* The seventy-one colored seamen remained sequestered below for several days. "There are, however, many lawless characters still about the wharves," Archibald wrote on July 20, "and the masters assure me that it is not safe for the Negro sailors to return to their own vessels."[39] Although the consul was due to take his annual leave, he remained in the smoldering city until he was confident that the danger had passed.

———

Lyons had not heard from Seward during the crisis; violence had flared in other parts of New York, and the secretary's own house in Auburn was

attacked. The incident was relatively minor—a rock hurled through a
downstairs window—but for several nights Frances Seward had stayed
awake, waiting for the sound of breaking glass. Be prepared for the loss
of our home, Seward wrote stoically to his wife; if the war brings an end
to slavery, "the sacrifice will be a small one."[40]

Despite Archibald's brave conduct during the riots, British subjects
"are far from being pleased either with HM Government or with HM
Minister here," Lord Lyons told Lord Russell on July 24. No one
thought that the legation was doing enough to protect Britons from the
rampant cheating and illegal conscriptions that accompanied the latest
draft effort. The legation staff was working late into the night trying to
keep abreast of the rapidly increasing number of case files. Few cases, if
any, were straightforward.[41] Young Frederick Farr refused to be helped;
he ignored the attachés' inquiries and would not respond to letters from
his father's friends. "That is a queer boy of yours," one of them wrote to
Dr. Farr in exasperation. "I have not been able to draw a line from him."

"ROWDY" NOTIONS OF EMANCIPATION.

" THE mob on the corner, below my house, had hung up a negro to the lamp-post. In mockery, a cigar was placed in his mouth. * * * For hours these scared negroes poured up
Twenty-seventh Street, passing my house. * * * One old negro, 70 years old, blind as a bat, and such a cripple that he could hardly move, was led along by his equally aged wife with a
few rags they had saved, trembling with fright, and not knowing where to go."—MANHATTAN's *Letter in the Standard, July 30th.*

Punch accuses President Lincoln of doing nothing to save free blacks from the rioting Irish.

Farr's commanding officer reported that the boy was "in excellent health and spirits" after Gettysburg and only wanted to be left alone.[42]

Lyons knew there was nothing to be gained from telling British subjects that they should count themselves fortunate to be in the North and not in the South, where the situation was far worse. In addition to being tricked or beaten into joining regular regiments, Britons were being rounded up to man "home defence militias," and there was nothing the consuls could do about it; Judah P. Benjamin expelled Consul George Moore from Richmond in June for allegedly exceeding the limits of his purview. One of the very few British conscripts to escape to the North, a Mr. R. R. Belshaw, thanked Lyons "for the interest which you have taken in my case," but, he complained, "thousands of British subjects are daily suffering in the Confederate army as I have done and yet there is no relief; though England speaks she says nothing."[43]

Lyons did not have a satisfactory answer for Belshaw; the diplomatic situation in the South was beyond his control and yet somehow still perceived by Washington and London as his responsibility.* Lord Russell pondered whether they ought to send a military agent or commissioner to Richmond, taking the same route as Fremantle in order to avoid running the blockade, but Lyons persuaded him against the idea. The North would object, and the Confederate government would no doubt ignore the agent as it did the consuls. Seward was adamant that any British attempt to contact the Southern authorities would be regarded by the United States as an act of deliberate provocation, if not war.

Lyons did not understand what drove the secretary of state. Sometimes they seemed to be in the most perfect harmony. Tucked away in the Seward archives are private letters showing that Lyons often coached Seward on how to frame his official responses to British complaints.[45] But Seward was always playing more than one game at a time. In early August he asked Lyons if Britain would be prepared to join the North in

---

* The secretary of the navy, Gideon Welles, had a strangely inflated idea of Lyons's power. It was mortifying, he complained, "the extent Lord Lyons shapes and directs, through the Secretary of State, an erroneous policy to this government." CSS *Florida* had recently sailed within sixty miles of New York, leaving a trail of burning ships and bruised egos in her wake. Welles sent six cruisers to chase after the elusive Captain Maffitt and his crew, but a false lead had led them up the East Coast toward Nantucket. This, too, was somehow Lord Lyons's fault.[44]

fighting the French takeover of Mexico. "It would no doubt be a relief to Mr. Seward," Lyons reported after the interview, if Britain assumed the burden of defending the Mexicans—and the Monroe Doctrine—against the emperor's imperialist designs. But "England would run the greatest risk of being ultimately sacrificed without scruple by the United States."[46]

Four days later, on August 7, Lyons was distressed to see his suspicions confirmed. "An impending quarrel with England is allowed to be put forward as a lure to Volunteers for the Army," he informed Russell. Seward's latest dispatch to Charles Francis Adams predicted war if the British government failed to halt the Confederates' shipbuilding program. Seward knew that Adams would never show such a threatening letter to Lord Russell; and Lyons knew it too, telling Russell, "It will not, I suppose, be communicated to you, but will first see the light when Congress assembles in December."[47]

Lyons was about to leave for a short visit to Canada when Seward waylaid him with a proposition to spend the last two weeks of August exploring northern New York State: all the foreign ministers had been invited. Lyons could think of few things less appealing than being dragged through the wilds with the very people he wished to escape. But, he confessed in a private letter to Lord Russell, Seward "has made such a point of my going with him, that it has been impossible to get off without telling him plainly that I'd not choose to travel with him. This of course I could not do; and he deserves some consideration from us."[48]

Lyons would not have felt so guilty if he had known the reasons behind Seward's invitation. The secretary of state had been entertaining for some time the idea of a summer jaunt with the diplomatic corps, which would allow him to demonstrate his charming side and the North's booming economy all at the same time, but he only went forward with his plan when he needed a cover for visiting Judge Samuel Nelson of the Supreme Court. Opponents of the draft were mounting legal challenges and the administration wanted to be sure that the Court would make the right decision. Judge Nelson happened to live in Cooperstown, in upstate New York.

On August 15 the large party of diplomats and officials boarded a special train for New York; Lyons had brought along two attachés so he would not have to do all the talking. Contrary to his fears, Seward behaved with impeccable manners throughout the journey; ice cream was provided when it was hot, and carriages for those who preferred to explore sitting down. This rarely seen side of Seward touched Lyons. The secretary of state was incurably vain, he told Russell, but the more one knew of him, the more there was "to esteem and even to like." The trouble lay in Seward's tendency to overplay his hand, which required Lyons to exercise his "patience and good temper to be always cordial with him."[49]

The two-week excursion ended with a visit to Niagara Falls on August 25. Seward had a long conversation with Lyons before the minister departed for Canada. He began by referring to the problem of British antipathy toward the North. Lyons assured him that pro-Southern sentiments in Britain would dissipate as soon as the war ended, since there would be "nothing to keep it alive. I told him that the important point was public opinion in the United States." But Seward insisted that something had to be done to change British opinion: "The President could not travel, and the United States had no Princes." Lyons listened, wondering where this was leading. Then it dawned on him that Seward was floating the idea of paying a goodwill visit to England. The prospect seemed baffling, and Lyons suspected Seward was thinking more of his domestic audience, perhaps for a future presidential run. Guessing how the cabinet would react to such a tour, Lyons gently discouraged the plan. When he heard of it, Palmerston was indeed horrified: "I hope Seward will not come here," he wrote to Lord Russell. The visit would not change British policy—except for the worse if Seward said something silly. "He is . . . vulgar and ungentlemanlike and the more he is seen here the less he will be liked." He would drink brandy with "some editors of second rate newspapers," and be fêted by the manufacturing towns, but "I doubt whether Seward would be very well received in Society."[50] Seward soon dropped the idea—to a silent chorus of relief in England.

After the tour's conclusion, Lyons traveled to Canada in the hope of finally obtaining some rest from his labors. But there he found that the conflict was being enacted in miniature north of the border. Crimpers and recruiters were doing a brisk business along the border towns, turning Canadian public opinion dangerously pro-Southern. The authorities suspected that the Confederates were planning to use Canada as a base for operations, although so far there was little evidence to support these fears.

The idea of launching raids from Canada had indeed been suggested to Jefferson Davis, but he remained undecided, worrying that the international community would regard such a move as a last, desperate measure. For the moment, Davis had decided to pursue an alternative course. The North was constantly sending emissaries to meet with influential members of British society, and he was sure that the South had suffered as a result. To redress the balance, Davis had asked Rose Greenhow—whom he remembered as one of the most powerful hostesses in Washington before the war—to travel to England and, as important, to France, with the express purpose of explaining the case of Southern independence. Slidell would help her gain an audience with the emperor, but the rest would be up to her own efforts.

Rose had been living quietly since her arrival in Richmond in June the previous year. Between looking after her ten-year-old daughter, also named Rose, and writing a memoir of her imprisonment in Washington, she had managed to make a semblance of a life for herself. But she had not been happy. The Southern ladies had not welcomed her into their circle; Mary Chesnut waspishly described Rose as "spoiled by education—or the want of it."[51] President Davis's request was a welcome rescue not only from her grinding day-to-day existence, but also from the petty disapproval of Richmond society.

There were no other travelers at the Mills House Hotel when Rose arrived in Charleston during the second half of July; the other guests were all black marketeers of some description. Within hours of unpacking, she received a visit from General Beauregard. Knowing that she had a direct link to President Davis, he gave her a frank report of the situation and explained why he needed more artillery. The Federal bombardment was about to resume, and this time the Confederates expected it to continue until the city surrendered.

Rose's next guest was Frank Vizetelly. "He gives me all that he gathers, altho' under the seal of confidence as I told him I should tell you," she informed President Davis. Vizetelly believed that the shortage of drinking wells around Jackson would soon exact a crushing toll on Grant's army, having witnessed "eight men within a space of thirty feet fall down from want of water." This fact alone, he told her, guaranteed that General Johnston would not be driven out of the city. In reality, even as Vizetelly spoke, the Confederates were retreating from Jackson, and in a few hours the city would be in flames. Vizetelly's passionate advocacy of the Southern cause had temporarily robbed him of his critical faculties. Every judgment, every prediction he made to Rose would turn out to be wrong.

Rose soon came to the conclusion that Charleston Harbor was useless as a means of escape, and she boarded a train with little Rose for Wilmington. Her rooms at the Mills House Hotel did not remain empty for long. On August 7, Fitzgerald Ross and Captain Scheibert checked into the hotel, having left Francis Lawley behind in Richmond. The journalist had pushed himself to the brink of collapse at Gettysburg and was too weak to travel. The pressure of maintaining an optimistic tone in his *Times* reports had also been taking its toll on him.

Fitzgerald Ross recognized Vizetelly from Lawley's description when the journalist showed up at the Mills House Hotel for dinner. According to Scheibert, "this hotel had the best service of any tavern" in the South. It charged the highest prices, too: $100 per person for a three-course meal.[52] General Beauregard welcomed Vizetelly's new friends when they called at his headquarters, and introduced them to the English officer on his staff. Henry Feilden was growing used to his role as Beauregard's mouthpiece and cheerfully gave a tour of the preparations against the next phase of the Federal siege. The consuls observed with alarm that more gunships were sailing into the harbor. The city itself was obviously the next objective. The British consul, Henry Pinckney Walker, sent a message to the legation in Washington that somehow slipped through, beseeching Lord Lyons to send a British warship to rescue the "several thousand" British women and children who were in the direct line of fire.[*53]

At 10:45 P.M. on August 21, a note from Union general Quincy Adams Gillmore was delivered to Beauregard's headquarters announcing the imminent bombardment of the city. He had neglected to sign it, so no one took the threat seriously. Three hours later, the shelling began. "At first I thought a meteor had fallen; but another awful rush and whirr right over the hotel and another explosion beyond, settled

---

[*] The British consul was exaggerating; the number was less than a thousand. Lyons's chargé d'affaires, William Stuart, telegraphed Rear Admiral Milne for his advice. Milne replied in the negative. It would be unthinkable, he wrote, to send in a ship now and interfere with Federal naval plans.

any doubts I might have had," wrote Vizetelly. He threw on his clothes and ran down the stairs, fighting his way past hysterical businessmen. "One perspiring individual of portly dimensions was trotting to and fro with one boot on and the other in his hand, and this was nearly all the dress he could boast of. . . . Another, in a semi-state of nudity with a portion of his garments on his arm, barked the shins of everyone in his way in his efforts to drag an enormous trunk to the staircase."[54] Out in the street, women were running in all directions, their heads ducked, some carrying children in their arms. Many people were stampeding toward the station in the wild hope that a train would be waiting to convey them away. Vizetelly found Ross and Scheibert coolly standing around in the Mills House bar. He persuaded them to come with him down to the promenade, where they would have a better view of the bombardment. To their surprise, a large crowd had already gathered there. For an hour they stood out under the open canopy of stars, with Vizetelly and Ross taking bets as to whether the shells would fall short and land on their heads.[55]

The next morning, General Beauregard sent a furious note to Gillmore demanding a halt to the firing until all the civilians could be evacuated. The British consul called on General Gillmore under a flag of

Downtown Charleston under fire from Union forces, by Frank Vizetelly.

truce with a similar request. The Federal commander granted a cease-fire of twenty-four hours before resuming the bombardment. After three weeks of continuous shelling, the excitement wore thin, and the three friends began to discuss their departure from Charleston. On September 14, Ross and Vizetelly bade farewell to Scheibert, who was returning to Prussia. "I fear our troubles have only begun," Thomas Prioleau wrote to his cousin Charles Prioleau, the head of Fraser, Trenholm in Liverpool. "The fire brought against us is immense and incessant, yet we do not despair."*[56]

---

* Francis Lawley's optimistic reporting about the shelling of Charleston did not deceive William Howard Russell: "Such rubbish!" he wrote in his diary on September 28. "I really believe on the U.S. question the great John Bull has lost his head and is distracted by jealousy to such an extent that it has not only ceased to be just and generous but to be moderately reasonable."

TWENTY-FOUR

Devouring the Young

Rose Greenhow arrives in England—The British government vs. the rams—
Commissioner Mason leaves his post—A new breed of volunteer—General
Bragg's justice

With Rose Greenhow and her daughter on board, the blockade runner *Phantom* was the only ship to escape from Wilmington on the night of August 5, 1863. "We passed the *Elizabeth* and the *Hebe,* who had each got aground, but our anxiety was too great on our own account to bestow much thought upon our friends," she wrote in her diary; "the Yankees threw up rockets, which revealed to us the fact that we were in the midst of five of the 'blockaders.'" After rounding Cape Fear with the pursuers mercifully far behind, "Capt. Porter had a mattress spread upon deck, upon which I lay," Rose continued in her diary, "watching the moon which had risen and was shining gloriously high in the Heavens, and pitying myself as the victim of that most unfortunate infirmity of seasickness." Little Rose also felt wretched and "crouched by my side, amidst the cotton bales which crowded the deck."[1]

The *Phantom* sailed unmolested into St. George's harbor, Bermuda, on August 10, 1863. Rose's steamship to England was not leaving for three weeks, which gave her ample opportunity to study Major Walker's shipping operation. "The entire trade of the island is Confederate," she remarked. The willingness of the British authorities to ignore his activities was a reflection of Bermuda's desperate plight before the war. A devout believer in "the wise and beneficial system of servile labor," Rose hoped that the British now regretted their folly in abolishing slavery in 1833. Had it not been for the Confederate community on the island, all of whom shared her prejudices, she would have been miserable during her stay; living cheek by jowl with a free black population seemed unnatural and offensive to her. But in contrast to her treatment at Richmond, Rose was the center of attention in St. George. "She is one of the most beautiful women I ever saw," gushed Georgiana Walker. "She knows this and like a sensible woman, does not pretend to think the contrary."[2] The fact that Rose was traveling on a diplomatic mission made her seem even more glamorous.

Rose had expected to be in Liverpool by September 11 or 12 at the latest, and she was taken by surprise when the captain announced that he was changing their destination. The *Harriet Pinckney* was a new Confederate steamer, he explained, and too precious to risk becoming "Yankee prey" on the return journey. They were heading south instead, to Falmouth on the coast of Cornwall. "This was unexpected to us all," Rose wrote in her diary, "and everyone set to work to know where Falmouth was and what sort of a place."[3] The captain was being overly cautious; the closest threat to the *Pinckney* was USS *Kearsarge,* which was sailing around the Azores in the hope of finding one of the Confederate raiders.

———

Captain Maffitt would not have sailed the battle-scarred *Florida* into Brest, France, had he known that his arrival would attract the attention of Federal agents, putting in jeopardy the six Confederate raiders under construction at Nantes and Bordeaux.[*] James Bulloch had moved his operations across the Channel after the detention of the *Alexandra* in the spring. The emperor had given his permission for the switch to France with the proviso that if the United States uncovered the existence of the Confederate ships, the authorities would deny all knowledge of the program.[4] Lucien Arman, owner of the largest shipbuilding firm in the country, was building four *Alabama*-style raiders for Bulloch in Bordeaux and had also helped to arrange the contract for the two smaller ships at Nantes.

———

[*] Maffitt could not resist lingering in the Channel in the hope of snatching a last-minute prize, and he was rewarded for his daring with the *Anglo-Saxon,* a U.S. ship carrying coal to New York. He removed the passengers, appropriated the coal, and burned the ship. The Royal Navy was affronted by Maffitt's cheek at carrying out a raid so close to British waters and sent a frigate to patrol the area. But by then Maffitt had docked at Brest.

The obliging Arman—whose wealth and position had grown in step with the emperor's desire to modernize his navy—also introduced Bulloch to the brokerage firm of Bravay and Company. Monsieur Bravay agreed to buy the Confederate rams nearing completion at Lairds shipyard in Liverpool for a nominal sum (plus a large commission) and maintain that they were destined for his client, the pasha of Egypt. The intricate web of deception had been working well until the *Florida* sailed imprudently into Brest with its Confederate flag flying from the mast. The foreign minister, Drouyn de Lhuys, was furious, and proceeded to sit on Captain Maffitt's request to use the port's repair facilities for four days before reluctantly assenting on the condition that the visit be kept secret from the American legation.

In London, the *Florida*'s arrival went almost unremarked amid the furors over the imminent departure of the Lairds rams. Charles Francis Adams had warned Lord Russell that their very existence presented the greatest threat to Anglo-American relations since the *Trent* affair. Two ram raiders could not, of course, win the war for the Confederacy, but they could threaten the Federal stranglehold on Charleston or Wilmington. Moreover, argued Adams, if the rams were allowed to leave, there would be nothing to prevent the Confederacy from building twenty more in Britain. War between America and England would be unavoidable if the government failed to clamp down on all Confederate violations of British neutrality; and this, he was convinced, would never happen under Lord Palmerston.

———

U.S. consul Thomas Haines Dudley in Liverpool had uncovered every aspect of the Confederates' operations: how they recruited sailors, who paid them and when, how they procured supplies, and on which vessels the cargoes sailed. But he had failed to unearth a single piece of written evidence against the rams that could be presented in a court of law. The Lord Mayor of London warned the Home Office that it would be a waste of time sending government agents to investigate Lairds, since nothing would be found. But Lord Russell ignored the advice, which he believed to be tainted by the Lord Mayor's pro-Southern bias, and sent the agents anyway. The hostility experienced by pro-Northerners in Liverpool could be overwhelming at times: "I have . . . done myself a great deal of damage," complained one of Dudley's informants.[5]

The Duke of Argyll noticed Charles Francis Adams's agitation when the U.S. minister and his family went to stay in Scotland in the middle of August. One morning after breakfast, Adams had a frank conversation with the duke about the probability that the North would declare war if the government allowed the rams to depart. He was surprised to discover that he was not the first to say so. "He said that he had received a letter from Sumner," wrote Adams on August 28, 1863, "dwelling very strongly on the danger of war." Adams was too circumspect to discuss Seward's latest dispatch (the threatening and bombastic letter Lord Lyons had seen earlier in August), but he hinted that there were instructions he was deliberately holding back for the moment. Adams, however, had no way of knowing that Seward was actually quite sanguine about the rams. "The English Ministry are our friends," Seward had recently admitted to the navy secretary, Gideon Welles. The very day Adams poured out his fears to the duke, Seward told Welles to cease worrying because "the armored vessels building in England will not be allowed to leave."[6] Adams's continual fretting about the rams ruined the enjoyment of his visit to Inveraray Castle, and he left for London on August 31 thinking he would never see Scotland again. This, he decided, would not be a great loss: "Half of it is fit only for the habitation of the beasts and the birds. The other half has nothing especial to recommend it either."[7]

Benjamin Moran was hysterical when Adams arrived back at the legation on September 3. One of the Lairds rams had actually been taken out for a test run, yet Lord Russell had replied to Adams's latest protest with what seemed to him the usual empty assurances. The legation was reliving the escape of the *Alabama*. The effect on Adams was dramatic. He sent a warning to Russell that day, and a stronger one the next. On the fifth, having received nothing but a bland note in reply, he lost his temper. "This is war," he wrote to Russell, war by stealth and deceit. If the government allowed the two rams to depart, to destroy New York and Boston at will, the United States would retaliate. If the circumstances were reversed, Adams declared, Britain would do the same. He would communicate his government's response forthwith.[8]

Adams assumed that Lord Palmerston was interfering—or, worse, restraining Lord Russell from responding properly. It would have been far better for his peace of mind and the future of Anglo-American relations had he been kept informed of the strenuous efforts of the Home and Foreign office clerks to find a legal way of stopping the rams. Since June, the government had been secretly conducting an international investigation into their true ownership. The British consul in Egypt had been ordered to pry the truth out of the pasha as to how he had become mixed up with the Confederates. The information trickling in only heightened Russell's suspicions about Bravay and Company. Palmerston agreed that he, too, was worried about "this ship building business." Yet there was no obvious remedy: Seward's threats and Adams's letters made it politically impossible for them to amend the Foreign Enlistment Act without appearing to bow to U.S. pressure.

The British cabinet's concern had increased in August after Richard Cobden shared with them his most recent correspondence from Charles Sumner. The senator, reported Cobden, had made a volte-face about England, and instead of being her chief ally in the U.S. capital was now her loudest critic. Sumner appeared to be so bent on revenge for Britain's accumulated wrongdoings that Cobden had felt constrained to remind him, "We have been the only obstacle to what would have been almost a European recognition of the South."*[10] The more Russell heard about the state of opinion in the North, the less he agreed with the advice of the law officers to wait until there was positive proof against the rams. Finally, on August 31, the Foreign Office received a telegram from the British consul in Egypt confirming that the pasha story was a ruse. Yet still the legal advisers to the Customs and Treasury departments rejected his entreaties for action.

Although he was still on holiday in Scotland, Russell telegraphed his undersecretary for foreign affairs, Austen Henry Layard, on September 3 to say that he would return to London for a confrontation with the law officers if necessary. Palmerston concurred with Russell: the Confederates were dragging the government into "neutral hostility." He consid-

---

* The Duke of Argyll told Sumner that he would not show his letters to Lord Russell because the foreign minister would dismiss them as gibberish. The duchess also tried to reason with him. "I like you to be quite frank with me, but wish you did not hope for what is impossible," she wrote earnestly. "We must be neutral, as a Government. . . . I sent some of the newspaper extracts you sent me to Lord Russell. He replied: 'We must be neutral. . . . We do not "fit out ships by the dozen," and Mr. S. must know the allegation to be untrue. One—two—three ships may have evaded our laws, just as the Americans evaded the American laws during the Canadian Contest. . . . You will have seen that the Government did their best in the *Alexandra* case. As to the ironplated ships, there seems to be great difficulty in getting at the truth.' "[9]

ered the possibility of having to pay damages to Lairds to be worth the risk—it would certainly be cheaper than a war with the United States.[11] Layard obediently sent the detention order that day. Fearful that his telegram might lose itself—in the way that unpopular messages were wont to do in the Treasury Department—he wrote to them again two days later.[12] His persistence paid off, and a customs official informed Lairds of the order.

Lord Lyons's secretary of the legation, William Stuart, received instructions to explain to Seward that the vessels were being detained even though the government did not expect a favorable decision from the courts. Unfortunately, no one remembered to share this concern with Charles Francis Adams, or indeed to apprise him of the recent developments regarding the rams. Russell's sudden reticence may have been prompted by a fear of leaks, or a desire to wait until he had definite news, but most likely he had become annoyed with the aggressive tone of Adams's letters and decided that the minister could afford to wait a little while.

Over the next two weeks, there was frenetic correspondence among the members of the cabinet as they debated whether the detention order had been the right step. As if to remind the ministry how fraught the issue remained in Parliament, the *Liverpool Courier* declared on September 12 that a government that truckled to U.S. pressure was worthy of impeachment. The next day, Palmerston suggested to the First Lord of the Admiralty, the Duke of Somerset, that the navy should purchase the rams from M. Bravay, which would avoid the embarrassment of another legal battle. At the very least, he wrote in all seriousness, "we are short of iron clads and it takes time to build them." The rams would be a useful addition to British naval capacity just in case "[the Federals] should be disposed and able next year to execute their threatened vengeance, for all the forbearance we have shown them."[13]

In October, Captain Hoare, the Royal Navy attaché to the British embassy in Paris, visited M. Bravay with a line of credit and a list of questions. Their conversation left Hoare with no doubt of the rams' true ownership. The Frenchman's nods and winks were irritating but illuminating—had James Bulloch witnessed this display of self-important puffery, he would have been furious at Bravay's indiscretion. Nevertheless, the Frenchman refused to sell the rams at any price, and Hoare returned home with nothing except a poor opinion of the Confederates' dealings. By coincidence,

British crewmen from the *Florida* arrived in Liverpool during the week of Hoare's meeting with Bravay. Captain Maffitt had let them go to save money, but everyone, including Consul Dudley, assumed they were coming to take the rams out of Lairds shipyard while there was still time. This mistaken belief sent officials into a frenzy. Russell saw another *Alabama* incident in the making and wanted the marines to become involved; the Home Office ordered the Liverpool constabulary to keep a close watch on the sailors.[14]

If Lord Russell had expected gratitude from Charles Francis Adams, he was soon disabused. The U.S. minister was only just beginning to express his pent-up frustration with the British government. Ignorant of Russell's marathon negotiation with the law officers, Adams assumed that it was his "war letter" that had frightened the English into action, and he fired another cannonade of unfortunate remarks on September 16: "If Her Majesty's Government have not the power to prevent the harbours and towns of a friendly nation from being destroyed by vessels built by British subjects, and equipped, manned, and dispatched from her harbours," he raged, "then . . . all international obligations, whether implied or expressed, [are] not worth the paper on which they are written."[15] His letter was passed around the cabinet, accompanied by various noises of disgust and outrage. "It seems to me that we cannot allow to remain unnoticed his repeated and I must say somewhat insolent threats of war. We ought, I think, to say to him in civil Terms 'you be dammed,'" declared Palmerston. Russell thought the same. In his reply on September 25 he dispensed with the usual expressions of "regret and concern" and went straight to the point: "There are, however, passages in your letter," he wrote, that "plainly and repeatedly imply an intimation of hostile proceeding towards Great Britain on the part of the Government of the United States unless steps are taken." These threats would not be tolerated: Her Majesty's Government will never "overstep the limits of the law" for the sake of appeasing another government, and "they will not shrink from any consequences of such a decision."[16]

Adams came to his senses after he received Russell's indignant reply and hastily apologized for his letter. Henry Adams, on the other hand, was unrepentant. "They meant to play us, like a salmon," he told Charles Francis Jr., until their father's threat of war ended "the little game. . . . Undoubtedly to us this is a second Vicksburg. It is our diplomatic triumph, if we manage to carry it through."[17] It was Russell's fault that the legation wrongly assumed Adams had scored a victory over him. His pride had brought him the worst of all outcomes: his efforts unacknowledged, his reputation tarnished, and the government made to look weak. Adams's apparent diplomatic coup was naturally the talk of Washington. William Stuart was so alarmed that he spoke to Seward's son, Frederick, on September 18 to explain the real sequence of events. But the myth of the British lion cowering under the onslaught of the American eagle had already taken hold.

Seward could not resist making capital out of England's embarrassment. He had asked Thurlow Weed to plant newspaper stories about the dangerous rams in England, so that he could fight a "battle" and emerge the victor. Gideon Welles was infuriated by the ease with which his rival manipulated the news. "I am under restrictions which prevent me from making known facts which would dissipate this alarm," he wrote in his diary. "It does not surprise me that the *New York Times* . . . and all the papers influenced by Seward should be alarmed. [He] knows those vessels are to be detained, yet will not come out and state the fact, but is not unwilling to have apprehension excited. It will glorify him if it is said they are detained through protest from our minister."[18]

Charles Sumner unwittingly played into Seward's hands. The rage and paranoia that had recently alarmed his friends burst into public view on September 10. Several thousand people crowded into the Cooper Union in New York to listen to him deliver a four-hour tirade against Britain. "I am disappointed and disgusted with Sumner's own conduct," wrote Lord Lyons after he had read the speech in full.[19] Its real purpose, he believed, was to strengthen Sumner's position against Seward. If the rams were stopped, people would remember the Cooper Union speech as being instrumental in the diplomatic victory; but if the warships were allowed to set sail, Sumner would be able to point to his speech as proof that he, at least, had been willing to confront the British. The vehement denunciations of Britain were baffling to Sumner's friends. Some attributed his excess of feeling to his old head injury, others to grief over the recent death of his brother; all agreed on the calamitous damage to his reputation. Having positioned himself as the voice of moderation, his new bellicosity made him look like the worst kind of political opportunist. Lord Lyons would never trust him again; "I had hoped better things of him," he wrote.[20] One of the few letters of approval came from Seward, who, with exquisite irony, sent Sumner his hearty congratulations.[21]

The Economist announced there was no hope for Anglo-American relations if a "friend" like Sumner could make such a hostile speech. His accusation that the British government was conniving with the Confederates had to be answered, which Russell duly did in a widely praised speech. Sumner became agitated by the criticism coming from the other side of the Atlantic and obstinately stuck to his position, even after he learned that Russell had detained the rams *before* his Cooper Union speech. Protests from English acquaintances simply made his declarations more extreme. "If Russell wants cotton, let him withdraw all support . . . for the Rebellion," he ranted to John Bright who, for all his faults, pandered to no man and refused to play along with Sumner's characterization of Russell.[22]

Adams was disappointed that few people in England other than his own son gave him credit for stopping the rams. But a bruised ego was the least of his worries. On September 28, Moran recorded that the legation messenger had grievously swindled the family. Letters had been intercepted, Adams's wine cellar ransacked, money taken, even checks forged. Feeling that their sanctuary had been violated, Mrs. Adams was already pining to leave London when an anonymous letter arrived at the legation:

Dam the Federals
Dam the Confederates
Dam you both
Kill you damned selves for the next *10* years if you like; so much
    the better for the world and for England. Thus thinks every
    Englishman with any brains.
NB.PS. We'll cut your throats fast enough afterwards for you if
    you aint tired of blood, you devils.[23]

This decided the matter. Adams found a large seaside retreat for rent in St. Leonards-on-Sea, near Hastings. There, he led Henry and Brooks into the slate-blue water for bracing plunges before breakfast.[24] It was a relief to leave behind the chaos and discord of the legation. "My state of depression of spirits is becoming chronic," he wrote in his diary in a rare moment of self-reflection. "This way of living does not suit me, and the condition of public as well as of my private affairs at home is not satisfactory."[25]

Adams's chief solace was that his difficulties paled beside those of the Confederates in London. Mason had announced on September 21 that he was closing the commission. Benjamin Moran was almost sorry to see him go: "Mr. Mason was the unfittest man they could have sent here, and has proved an ignominious failure."[26] Mason's English friends had feared just such a reaction to his departure and had entreated him to stay; the press, including *The Times,* considered his resignation ill judged. But Mason was acting on Judah Benjamin's instructions. The Confederate secretary of state had ordered him to relocate to France under the new designation of "special commissioner to the Continent" and to give as his reason for the move Southern dissatisfaction with Britain.[27] Yet the state of affairs in France was no better for the Confederates. A disgruntled clerk at the offices of Bravay and Company had passed incriminating documents to the U.S. legation. The French authorities naturally professed to be shocked to learn that the Confederates were using their dockyards, and the foreign minister, Drouyn de Lhuys, glibly assured William L. Dayton, the U.S. minister in Paris, that there would be a thorough investigation into the matter. The deception granted Bulloch a reprieve, but it was no guarantee that his construction program would be allowed to continue.

There was a funereal atmosphere at James Mason's house in Sackville Street when Rose Greenhow arrived for dinner on September 17. She had seen him the day before. "He was very kind—and we had a long talk," she wrote in her diary.[28] Mason apologized for leaving her in such an awkward position. She had been expecting to make a life for herself in London as the Confederate commission's political and social hostess, recreating her role in Washington before the war, and his departure would deprive her of an essential platform for her mission. Mason had also performed a vital function for the Confederates and their sympathizers in England by containing the personal differences between them to a sustainable level. It had not mattered quite so much that Spence dismissed Henry Hotze's propaganda journal, the *Index,* as a waste of time and money, or that Hotze considered Spence to be a deluded abolitionist, when there was a third party to keep them apart. How they would work together once he was in France had not been resolved. Spence and Hotze vied with each other to help Rose. Spence took her to Richard Bentley and Sons, Charles Dickens's publishers, who eagerly acquired the memoir she had been writing in Richmond, *My Imprisonment and the First Year*

of Abolition Rule at Washington. Hotze trumpeted Rose to the readers of the
Index as one of the great martyrs of the Southern cause, a heroine whose
"spirit and talent [were] not common even among women of the
South."[29]

––––––

For all of Hotze's genius at shaping public opinion, he failed to understand the gravity of the situation in Liverpool. "The Rams in the Mersey
are more than ever the centers of attention. The efforts of the Government to insure their detention are really ludicrous," he sneered to Benjamin. Bulloch, on the other hand, saw nothing amusing about the
government's actions. On October 8, Russell decided that Lairds could
not be trusted, and he changed his detention order to outright seizure.
The Duke of Argyll congratulated Russell and urged him not to regret
defying the law officers: "They would never have advised you to do what
you have so rightly done," he wrote. "I say, three cheers for the House of
Russell."[30] Palmerston agreed with Argyll that there "was no moral
Doubt that [the rams] are intended for Confederate service." Even the
Queen became involved, telling Gladstone that the rams business should
not be allowed "to endanger the Government." Despite her concern,
Gladstone thought "she did not appear to lean towards over-conciliation
of the Federal Government."[31] James Bulloch insisted in his memoirs
that he never intended the rams to sneak out of England. If that was so,
Lairds had done him a disservice with their suspicious activity.

    The task of guarding the rams was one of the least rewarding experi-
ences of Captain Edward Inglefield's career in the Royal Navy. He and
his men were threatened wherever they went in Liverpool. An intelligent
and empathetic officer, he realized that the anger directed toward them
chiefly stemmed from a fear that the five hundred craftsmen working on
the rams would lose their jobs, and he advised the Home Office to allow
the work to continue until the ships were completed. Inglefield deliberately refrained from putting on a show of force: he moored his sloop at
some distance from the rams, carried nothing more threatening than an
umbrella, and ordered his men to remember that on this mission they
were peace preservers, not war makers. It was a sensible but risky move.
One ram looked primed to leave: "Her turrets are very nearly completed,
and excepting stores she can be ready for sea almost any day," he reported. "I have taken upon myself not to permit the boilers to be run up,
or the fires laid even for presumed experimental purposes."[32]

Bulloch was surprised that the government had seized the rams without first obtaining legal sanction or charges against Lairds. After a month went by without any sign of legal action, he began to wonder if the process was being deliberately drawn out in order to give the law officers more time to prepare their case. On October 28 "Historicus" attacked the rams in *The Times* (this was William Vernon Harcourt's return to print after the death of his wife in April), condemning the Confederates' illegal use of British shipyards and arguing for a determined response from the government. Bulloch realized that "Historicus" was preparing public opinion for the government's clampdown on Confederate operations in England; whether or not the rams case went to court, the ships would never be allowed to leave. The following day brought more disappointing news. CSS *Georgia* had dropped anchor at Cherbourg in so dilapidated a state as to be on the verge of sinking.

The raider had destroyed nine ships during her six-month adventure. But according to Lieutenant James Morgan, the final weeks had resembled a gothic horror story, full of madness and savagery. Captain Maury had suffered a nervous breakdown near the Cape of Good Hope, and the enforcement of discipline had fallen to the charming but weak Lieutenant Evans. There were constant fights and several attempted mutinies: "things had gone from bad to worse than bad until one day some of the stokers discovered that a coal bunker was [all that] separated [them] from the spirit-room," wrote Morgan;

The Royal Navy keeping watch over the Lairds' rams in the Mersey.

and inserting a piece of lead pipe into the hole they got all the liquor they (temporarily) wanted. This they distributed among the crew and soon there was a battle royal going on the berth deck which the master-at-arms was unable to stop. . . . Here was a pretty kettle of fish! . . . I suddenly leaped upon the man and bore him to the deck, where, in a jiffy, the master-at-arms placed the bracelets on his wrists. The other mutineers, quietly extending their arms in sign of submission, were placed in irons, and confined below. The discipline of the ship needed as much repairing as the vessel did herself. It was time the *Georgia* sought a civilized port for more reasons than one.[33]

Clerks at Fraser, Trenholm had carefully stored the crew's letters, to be distributed on their eventual return to port, and receiving news from home helped calm the febrile atmosphere on the ship. "There was great rejoicing for all save me," recorded Morgan after the letters were delivered at Cherbourg. He had received two: the first told of the death of his brother George, a captain serving in the 1st Louisiana Infantry in Virginia; the second, that Gibbes, his other brother and a captain in the 7th Louisiana, had died a prisoner of war on Johnson's Island in Lake Erie. Morgan's adventures at sea suddenly seemed trivial to him after the terrible news from home. From this moment, his one ambition was to return to the South and fight the Federals.

———

In the Southwest, the capture of Vicksburg and Port Hudson had brought a temporary quiet to the Mississippi region. General Banks's XIX Corps returned to camp, and the 133rd New York Volunteers, Colonel Currie's regiment, resumed its garrison duty in Baton Rouge. Currie had recovered from his wounds, and much as he retained a fondness for his men, he loathed inaction more and had applied for a transfer. "I have at least one strong arm left," he wrote to Thurlow Weed, "and I am only desirous that any merit I may possess . . . may meet with equal favor with my compeers."[34] Currie's eagerness to be in the thick of danger was rare: most of the injured and sick wanted to be as far away from the fighting as possible.

Ebenezer Wells and Dr. Charles Mayo were both sent north, Wells to a hospital in Kentucky and Mayo to Saratoga Springs in New York to recover from typhus. His last weeks in Vicksburg had been a blur to him, but the illness saved his life in an unexpected way. On August 18, Mayo had become so unwell that a friend insisted he spend the night in town with him rather than on his ship, the *City of Madison*. During the night there was an explosion on the *Madison* that claimed the lives of all those on board. After this near brush with death, the authorities finally took pity on Mayo and shipped him out of Vicksburg. The War Department accepted his resignation from the army on September 8, although it was another two weeks before he was well enough to sail for England on the twenty-second, never to return to America.*

Mayo's quiet departure contrasted with the noisy and sometimes violent integration of the thousands of new army recruits produced by the draft, many of whom were determined to desert at the first opportunity. Even the volunteers were often cynical about their situation. "As I fully intend to desert if I don't get good treatment, I enlisted under the name of Andrew Ross," James Horrocks wrote to his parents on September 5, 1863. The nineteen-year-old had run away from Lancashire to escape the financial burden and shame of having fathered an illegitimate child.[35] Volunteering in the Federal army seemed like an excellent prospect to the prodigal son: "I shall get when mustered in $200 from the state of New Jersey, 50 dollars from Hudson City (where I enlisted) and 25 dollars from the Government. This, together with a month's pay in advance, will make $288 cash down," he told his parents. "I shall be able to save more money as a soldier than as a clerk with 400 dollars a year (that is a pretty good salary in New York)."[36]

Horrocks was surprised by the large number of foreigners who had enlisted with him. "The Company I am in is a motley assembly—Irish, Germans, French, English, Yankees—Tall, Slim, Short, and Stout. Some are decently behaved and others uncouth as the very devil," he wrote home. One-fifth of the regiment was English, including all the sergeants. Nevertheless, he was pretending to be a Scot in order to avoid the anti-English prejudice among the Americans.[37] The desertions began as soon as the men received their bounty money; but far from deserting himself, Horrocks was sent out with several others to find the absconders and returned with more than a dozen. The ecstatic spirit of patrio-

---

* Nine years later, in 1872, while taking a break between wars, an old friend from the Vicksburg campaign went down to Oxford to pay Dr. Mayo a visit. The friend was General Sherman.

tism and duty that had animated the first wave of volunteering in 1861 had died out; Horrocks's desire "to keep myself pretty secure and safe" reflected the feelings of a large majority of the new soldiers, especially among the conscripts.

In the South, where there were neither untapped reserves of young men nor legions of foreigners arriving each week, part-time raiders and guerrilla outfits were playing an increasingly important role in the war effort. Northern Virginia, where Charles Francis Adams, Jr., was stationed, was Mosby country. The eastern shore of the Chesapeake Bay, two hundred miles to the south, had become John Yates Beall country.

As with Mosby, the war had enabled the twenty-eight-year-old Beall to redefine himself. His father's death when Beall was twenty had forced him to sacrifice a promising legal career in order to care for his widowed mother and five younger siblings. Service in the Confederate army had provided an honorable escape route from domestic responsibilities, until a bullet to his right lung seemed to cut short his military career.

Beall moved to Canada in 1862, where he tried to establish a business selling game, until a friend told him about the Confederate navy operations in England. It sounded so exciting that he wanted to "join them and take of their fortune for good and evil."[38] In the time it took Beall to reach Richmond in February 1863, he had changed his mind about going to England, however, and instead saw himself as a waterborne version of John Mosby. The Confederate navy secretary, Stephen Mallory, was skeptical of the idea. He appointed Beall acting master on March 5—the usual commission for gentleman volunteers—but gave him no other help or encouragement: Beall would have to supply his own boat, uniform, weapons, and volunteers, none of whom could be eligible for conscription. Furthermore, although they would be able to keep whatever booty they captured, they would not be paid.

Beall set about recruiting from the groups still open to him—the middle-aged, stranded foreigners, and wounded veterans like himself. By September 1863, his Confederate Volunteer Coast Guard, or "Beall's Party," as it was known, had grown to eighteen and included two newspaper editors and their apprentices, a couple of sailors, and two Scotsmen: Bennet Graham Burley and John Maxwell. Burley had recently been imprisoned in Castle Thunder, the converted warehouse in Richmond that housed spies and political prisoners. The twenty-three-year-old Glaswegian had arrived in the South the previous year, bearing designs for a powerful underwater limpet mine, which in theory could penetrate armor plating. (The explosive device had been invented by his father, Robert Burley, Jr., the owner of a toolmaking factory, who, unable to secure commercial interest in his invention at home, had given the plans to his son to take to America.)

Bennet Burley had chosen the South on the assumption he would have a better chance of being noticed. His hunch was correct, though for all the wrong reasons. Fortunately, the new chief of the Confederate navy's Bureau of Ordnance and Hydrography, John M. Brooke, was also an inventor. As soon as Brooke saw Burley's plans, he knew that the youth was no spy and arranged for his release. Having regained his freedom, Burley displayed the daring and initiative that later made him one of the most famous war correspondents of his generation and persuaded Brooke to let him test the mine on a Federal ship. John Maxwell was assigned to help Burley carry out his mission, but Burley's father had missed something in the design and at the final moment they were unable to ignite the fuse.

The mine's failure to explode merely whetted Burley's and Maxwell's appetite for danger, and they officially joined Beall's Party on August 13, 1863, the day their navy commissions as acting master came through. Having acquired two small boats, the black *Raven* and the white *Swan,* the raiders went on to harass Federal shipping around Cape Charles and Fortress Monroe so successfully that a joint U.S. military and naval expedition was ordered to find them.[39] Beall's dream of emulating Mosby had come true.

John Mosby himself had received a bullet wound in August and had only recently returned to active duty. He decided to prove his recovery by reprising his spectacular raid against Sir Percy Wyndham in March. This time the target was Francis Pierpont, the governor of pro-Union West Virginia, who was staying in temporary quarters in Alexandria. The raid was unsuccessful, but it reminded Wyndham, whose recovery from his leg wound had been reported with great excitement by local newspapers, that the contest between them was still alive.[40]

Wyndham's New Jersey Cavaliers were camped at Bristoe Station, right in the center of Mosby country, but Wyndham was unable to indulge his fantasies of revenge, having again been moved up to brigade command. Union general George Meade had ordered his cavalry corps to find out where Lee was moving with the Army of Northern Virginia.

Despite almost constant skirmishing with Jeb Stuart's troops, the caval-rymen were able to report that Lee had dispatched General Longstreet and the First Corps to an unknown destination. "I should be glad to have your views as to what had better be done, if anything," Meade asked General Halleck on September 14. Lincoln wondered what Meade was waiting for: "He should move upon Lee at once," the president wrote impatiently to Halleck.[41]

Meade did indeed move, but slowly and deliberately, to the relief of the Confederates. President Davis and General Lee had decided that there was no alternative to sending Longstreet to Tennessee, which was in danger of being captured by Union general William Rosecrans and his Army of the Cumberland. If Rosecrans succeeded, yet more vital rail-roads would be lost, railroads that were Virginia's only lifeline to the much reduced Confederacy. Tennessee lay across the top of the South like an elongated anvil, touching the borders of Arkansas, Mississippi, Alabama, Georgia, North Carolina, and Virginia; the Confederates feared that its conquest would allow the North to carve up the South like a joint of beef. The implications of such a disaster added to the Rich-mond cabinet's anguish after the summer of defeats. The chief of ord-nance, Josiah Gorgas, mourned in his diary: "Yesterday we rode on the pinnacle of success—today absolute ruin seems to be our portion. The Confederacy totters to its destruction."[42]

During July, Rosecrans had pushed his Confederate adversary, Brax-ton Bragg, into the eastern corner of Tennessee. Bragg still held Chat-tanooga, with its all-important rail depots, but the irascible general was leading a demoralized army that had already been defeated twice in bat-tle. Bragg's bullying manner made him despised by his officers and loathed by the men. "I had seen men shot, and whipped, and shaved, and branded," wrote Sam Watkins, a private in the 1st Tennessee Regiment. He thought he was used to Bragg's ways, but at Chattanooga worse was to come. He watched the hanging of two "Yankee spies." "I saw a guard approach," he wrote, "and saw two little boys in their midst. . . . I saw that they were handcuffed. 'Are they spies?' I was appalled; I was horri-fied; nay, more, I was sick at heart . . . the youngest one began to beg and cry and plead most piteously. . . . The props were knocked out and the two boys were dangling in the air. I turned off sick at heart."[43]

TWENTY-FIVE

River of Death

Colonel De Courcy wins and loses—Longstreet arrives at Chickamauga—
The Confederate generals' revolt—Two English travelers—Contrasting good-
will tours—"They are all down on us"

The timing of Longstreet's arrival in Chattanooga depended on eastern Tennessee's remaining under Southern control. If the railroads or the road through the Cumberland Gap stayed open, Longstreet would be able to reach General Bragg in a matter of days. If these were closed, the only other possible train route went south through the Carolinas, west through Georgia, and finally north to Chattanooga, taking at least a week, if not two. However, Federal forces led by General Burnside captured Knoxville, Tennessee, on September 2, 1863, cutting the Virginia–Tennessee rail link. This left the Cumberland Gap, which had been guarded by a garrison force of 2,500 Confederates since starvation drove out Colonel De Courcy in 1862. The new Confederate commander at the Gap, Brigadier General John Frazer, was struggling. Only two regiments were in a fit state for duty; the other two had been so depleted by illness and desertions that they were in a state of near mutiny. Frazer had been receiving conflicting orders about whether to evacuate or defend the fort. In the end, he decided to fight.[1]

Burnside did not want to be caught up in an arduous struggle for a single pass when he had an ideal candidate for the task in Colonel De Courcy, whose familiarity with the area was unmatched. Burnside assigned to him an independent brigade of 1,700 men, with orders to attack the Confederates from the northern side of the Gap. For De Courcy, the command signaled that his rehabilitation was complete, his reputation no longer tainted by the accusations of cowardice at Chickasaw Bluffs.

De Courcy's happiness was shortlived. He discovered after the expedition had begun that he was leading a brigade that consisted of the flotsam and rejects of Burnside's army; one regiment was just three months old, another a mere two weeks. Worse still, the ordnance supplies had failed to arrive on time. His artillery regiment had lost most of its guns; his two cavalry regiments had no revolvers; and the infantry regiments were down to thirty bullets per man. Their bread ration was enough to last them for four days, perhaps seven if cut in half. De Courcy ordered a slow march, hoping that the rations and munitions would catch up with them along the way. None came. By September 7, De Courcy had grown so outraged by the lackadaisical incompetence of Federal headquarters in Kentucky that he was bombarding them with hourly messages demanding to know, in the strongest language possible, when he could expect the arrival of his supplies. His brigade had now crossed the Cumberland Ford, and the Gap was less than half a day's march away.[2]

When he learned that no wagons had been dispatched because the commissary officer in Kentucky had been on a drunken spree for several days, the best and worst aspects of De Courcy's character came to the fore. "What is to be done?" he wrote to a member of Burnside's staff on September 7. "My men will begin to get sick before many hours for want of bread. Little corn here, and I have only ammunition enough to bluster with and persuade the enemy to evacuate or capitulate if he be so inclined but I cannot make a serious attack."[3]

De Courcy's first instinct was to telegraph his resignation. But as he thought about his predicament, he realized that the Confederates had no means of knowing the state of his forces. This gave him the idea of deceiving the Confederates into thinking his brigade was four times its actual size—by having his men march in a continuous loop within earshot of the fort. Thus heartened, he made the fatal mistake of falling in love with his cleverness, and when help arrived in the form of a cavalry brigade under General James M. Shackelford, De Courcy became fearful that he would interfere. He should have dispatched a messenger to explain his intentions. Instead, he sent a letter asking Shackelford to stay out of the Gap because "I fear you have not been made acquainted . . . that I am fully acquainted with all the roads and locations on both sides of the gap, and further that I have been in the military profession almost continuously since my sixteenth year." Shackelford ignored De Courcy and sent a message to General Frazer ordering him to surrender, which he refused to do.

Between his furious telegrams to Kentucky and his tactless behavior with Shackelford, De Courcy was leaving a trail of ill will.[4] On September 8, De Courcy sent a polite communication to General Frazer. The situation was hopeless, he said. The fort was surrounded, and any attempt to fight their way out would only result in "a cruel loss of life." All this time, the same Federal regiments had been marching around and around, making it seem as though the Confederates were facing several thousand men. De Courcy naturally hedged when Frazer replied asking to know the number of Federal troops opposing him. For twenty-four hours the Confederate general held firm, but after a day of absolute stillness—De Courcy would not even allow the men to load their rifles in case one of the new recruits accidentally pulled the trigger and started a firefight—Frazer's nerve started to buckle. De Courcy thoughtfully sent back the Confederate go-between with a gift of two gallons of good whiskey. He followed up with a note: "It is now 12:30 P.M., and I shall not open fire until 2 P.M., unless before that time you shall have struck all your flags and hoisted in their stead white flags in token of surrender."[5]

During these tense negotiations, General Burnside had marched up from Knoxville, Tennessee, with an additional infantry brigade. He, too, sent a demand for surrender to General Frazer. By now the Confederate had received three orders in three days from three separate forces. As far as he knew, tens of thousands of Federal troops were poised to blow his position to pieces. Frazer drank De Courcy's whiskey and considered his options. In the meantime, an irritated Burnside tried to assert his authority over the situation. He was incensed to learn that De Courcy had ignored Shackelford's command. Ignorant of the colonel's plan and the reasons behind it, Burnside regarded his action as veering close to insubordination.

At three o'clock on September 9, Frazer ordered his staff to run up the white flag. De Courcy's troops fell into line and marched into the fortified camp, singing "The Girl I Left Behind Me." The Confederates were unaware that their Federal captors were carrying unloaded rifles. The soldiers looked at the small force with astonishment; one shouted, "Where are the rest of the men?"[6] De Courcy went to find Frazer, who was sitting in his tent, the last of the whiskey in one hand, his snuffbox in the other. In the meantime, a quarter of the Confederates quietly slipped away from the gap, taking their guns and knapsacks with them. De Courcy was not interested in the loss of four hundred or so prisoners. He had captured the pass without firing a single bullet. He savored the moment. "The whiskey worked," he remarked, according to one of his aides.[7] When Richmond learned of the surrender, Josiah Gorgas recorded in his diary that the Cumberland Gap had been given away by "a drunken Brigadier, named Frazer."[8]

Burnside trotted up the road an hour later, expecting to see the Confederates in formation and Frazer standing at the front, ready to hand over his flag. The sight of De Courcy walking around as though he owned the place made Burnside snap. Enraged, he ordered two officers to escort the colonel back to his camp. The following day, De Courcy was taken to Kentucky under armed guard. The charge was insubordination, but the rumor swirling through the ranks was that he had colluded with General Frazer to let the prisoners escape. No charges were actually brought against him, but once again he was in limbo and his character under suspicion. On September 18, 1863, De Courcy wrote to the assistant adjutant general on Burnside's staff pleading for a court of inquiry so he could clear his name. An investigation "has now become absolutely necessary to save my character—as an officer and a gentleman."[9]

Down in Louisiana, the 16th Ohio Volunteers received a vague report that De Courcy was no longer on detached duty with Burnside. They still missed him. "Hear that Col. De Courcy is ordered back to his regiment," wrote the regiment's drummer in his diary on September 21, 1863. "Hope it is true."[10] In Kentucky, Burnside's harsh treatment of De Courcy won the colonel a large degree of sympathy. "It is stating the case very mildly to say that the officers of De Courcy's brigade were highly indignant at this summary way of dealing with the leader—a leader whose sterling qualities they had seen occasion to admire," wrote Lieutenant Colonel Robert McFarland of the 86th Ohio Infantry. The officers wrote a protest on De Courcy's behalf and sent it to President Lincoln. Even Burnside's own staff felt that the summary arrest without charge was an overreaction to the incident. One of the assistant adjutant generals, Lieutenant Colonel Charles Loring, added his voice to the clamor: "I feel for him that he would suffer under very grave imputations if the circumstances of the case be not made publicly known."[11] But the protests only annoyed Burnside all the more. He refused to grant De Courcy's request for a court of inquiry. Instead, on September 29, Burnside distributed a public letter that lambasted De Courcy for his arrogant behavior.[12]

———

The detour forced on Longstreet by the capture of the Cumberland Gap meant changing trains at least ten times to reach Chattanooga. "Never before were such crazy cars—passenger, mail, coal, box, platform, all and every sort, wobbling on the jumping scrap-iron—used for hauling soldiers," recalled one of his aides.[13] The men were not bothered by their unorthodox conveyances, however, and even enjoyed themselves. "When we reached South Carolina we received attentions which had long ceased to be common in Virginia," wrote Francis Dawson. "A number of ladies were waiting for us on the platform, armed with bouquets of flowers and with well filled baskets of cake, fruit, and more substantial fare. There was an abundance, too, of lemonade for the dusty soldiers."[14] But to Mary Chesnut, who caught a glimpse of the rumbling cavalcade, the sight was macabre. Miles of flatcars cars passed by, with "soldiers rolled in their blankets lying in rows with their heads all covered, fast asleep. In their grey blankets, packed in regular order, they looked like swathed mummies." The sight made her sad: "All these fine fellows were going to kill or be killed. Why?"[15]

The imminent arrival of more Confederate troops renewed Bragg's confidence. A battle was imminent, but he would no longer be fighting a numerically superior enemy. Rosecrans had divided his army into three isolated forces. If Bragg could lure each of them in turn into one of the deep valleys that marked the terrain around Chattanooga, he might be able to destroy the entire Federal army. His plan depended on General Burnside's remaining in Knoxville, and on his own generals' following his exact orders. Burnside obligingly fiddled and fussed, but Bragg's second requirement proved to be impossible. The Confederate commander had made himself so despised that his generals ignored him, allowing opportunities to attack to slip through their grasp. Bragg desperately needed Longstreet, if only to restore order and spirit to his army.

When news of Longstreet's departure for Tennessee reached Charleston, Frank Vizetelly and Fitzgerald Ross took the first available train to Georgia, accompanied by a British Army officer named Charles H. Byrne, who had run the blockade in order to join the staff of the renowned Irish Confederate general Patrick Cleburne. The travelers arrived in Augusta on September 15. The town owed its prosperity to the Savannah River; "most of the goods which run the blockade into Charleston and Wilmington are sold by auction here, whence they are dispersed all over the interior," reported Ross, whose appetite for running after the action remained strong despite the misery of Gettysburg. "We found several English friends in Augusta engaged in the blockade-running business." An invitation to stay proved too tempting to resist, and the three companions had such a merry time that they were caught by surprise when Longstreet's train passed through on September 19. Realizing that they were in danger of missing the battle, they begged a ride on the next train. On the twentieth they lurched to a halt outside Ringgold, several miles south of Bragg's army, unable to travel any farther because of broken track. It was obvious from the crowded pens of Federal prisoners in the middle of the town that the battle for east Tennessee had already begun.

Longstreet arrived at Bragg's headquarters near the Chickamauga River ("River of Death" in Cherokee) just before midnight on September 19; the bulk of his troops were with him, although the artillery train carrying Francis Dawson was still en route. Bragg had mismanaged the first day of fighting, making uncoordinated attacks that were readily crushed by the Federals. For the morrow, he told Longstreet, the army was to be divided into two, with Longstreet commanding one wing and General Bishop Leonidas Polk the other, in order to hit Rosecrans in synchronized blows, left and right.[16] The blows did take place, but, because of a combination of undelivered orders, misunderstood directions, and the difficulty of operating in a thickly wooded terrain that screened parts of the fighting, the synchronization did not. Even so, Longstreet was magnificent. While Bragg was panicking and calling the battle lost, "Old Pete" realized that the Federal line had split and sent in his wing to exploit the opportunity. The Confederates almost succeeded in breaking Rosecrans's entire army. But one U.S. general, George H. Thomas—who was henceforth known as "the Rock of Chickamauga"—held his position and prevented a total Federal disaster.

It was late afternoon when Vizetelly and Ross heard about Longstreet's assault. Vizetelly wanted to rush to the front, appalled that he was missing the battle. They did not arrive at Longstreet's camp until evening: "We had walked a dozen miles," wrote Ross, "and, not knowing

To Chattanooga

Rosecrans

Crossroads

N
W   E
S

Miles

0   1

To Chattanooga

Breckinridge

Federal Right
retreats after
defeat

Granger to Thomas's support

Thomas

Snodgrass
Hill

Polk

Bragg

Francis Dawson
Fitzgerald Ross
Frank Vizetelly

Wood
4 Sept.

Longstreet

Widow Glenn

West Chickamauga Creek

Lafayette–Rossville Road

Lee and Gordon's Mills

Chickamauga
Sept. 20, 1863

Federal forces, a.m.

Federal forces, p.m.

Confederate attack

where to find our friends, we concluded to stay where we were all night." They had missed one of the most dramatic and bloody days of the war. Longstreet's attack had spread mass panic among his opponents, reminiscent of the Federal flight during the First Battle of Bull Run in 1861. Rosecrans's army, and indeed Rosecrans himself, had fled to Chattanooga, leaving the Confederates in possession of his deserted headquarters. As soon as it was light, the companions resumed their search for Longstreet. "We had been very much disappointed at being too late for the battle," wrote Ross, "but I think what we saw today rather moderated our regret." In all, 36,000 men had been killed or wounded during the two-day fight, nearly a third of the total who had taken part. During the night, while Ross and Vizetelly slept, the battlefield had been a hive of activity as small details of soldiers and civilians searched for survivors, holding their lanterns aloft to avoid treading on hands and feet.

The Confederate private Sam Watkins had helped to carry the wounded to the field hospitals. "Men were lying where they fell, shot in every conceivable part of the body," he wrote afterward. "Some with their entrails torn out and still hanging to them and piled upon the ground beside them, and they were still alive." He passed a group of women who had been looking for relatives. One of them cradled a dead soldier's head on her lap, crying, "My poor, poor darling! Oh, they have killed him, they have killed him!" He turned away, but there was nowhere to look without being assaulted by gore and terror. A man whose jaw had been torn away, leaving his tongue lolling from his mouth, tried to talk to him. Another stumbled past with both his eyes shot out, though one was still hanging down his check. "All through that long September night we continued to carry off our wounded," he recorded.[17]

Bragg was transfixed by the bloodshed. Longstreet argued, even pleaded with him to be allowed to launch another attack on the Federals before they had time to fortify Chattanooga and briefly thought he had persuaded the general to follow up his victory. But Bragg saw the thousands of corpses, the dead horses and shattered wagons, and despaired. He ordered the entire army to take up a new position along the crest of Missionary Ridge, which overlooked Chattanooga. Rather than endure another battle, he planned to starve Rosecrans into surrender, just as Grant had done to the Confederates at Vicksburg. Vizetelly and Ross realized that they were in the midst of an uproar in the camps and that the troops were furious with their leader. "I do not know what our Generals thought," wrote Sam Watkins. "But I can tell you what the privates thought. . . . We stopped on Missionary Ridge, and gnashed our teeth at Chattanooga."[18] Watkins would have been gratified to know that Bragg's commanders shared his outrage. Several of them were discussing with Longstreet whether they should risk their careers by sending an official complaint to Richmond.

Vizetelly was circumspect in his report of the Battle of Chickamauga for the *Illustrated London News*. He made no mention of the generals' revolt against Bragg, or that Longstreet was leading the cabal.[19] His shame at having arrived late may have pushed him to exceed his usual exuberance in camp. Every night he sang songs and entertained the senior officers as though his life depended on their enjoyment. The Confederates were mystified by their riotous visitor who could drink them all under the table, but were deeply appreciative of his efforts. "It was no uncommon thing to see a half dozen officers, late at night, dancing the 'Perfect Cure' which was one of the favorite songs . . . in the London music halls, and was introduced to our notice by Vizetelly," wrote Francis Dawson, who was thrilled to share his tent with him.[20] Years later, Longstreet's artillery chief, Edward P. Alexander, could still remember Vizetelly teaching them the words to "Tiddle-i-wink."* "He was really a man of rare fascination and accomplishments," reminisced Alexander. "He made great friends everywhere, but especially in Longstreet's corps."[21]

The evening frolics could not mask the fact that the Confederate Army of Tennessee was in crisis. Bragg had suspended two popular generals, Bishop Leonidas Polk and Thomas Hindman, for their failure to carry out his orders during the battle. Longstreet had secretly sent an official complaint to Richmond against Bragg and was waiting for a reply. The fourteen other senior generals were on edge, as Francis Dawson discovered. He had been made acting chief of ordnance while his superior, Colonel Peyton T. Manning, recovered from a head wound, and his temporary promotion gave him a seat at the staff dinners. One night, Major Walton,

---

* The Confederates loved this song, which Vizetelly composed himself: "'Twas in the Atlantic Ocean in the equinoctial gales; / A sailor he fell overboard, amid the sharks and whales. / And in the midnight watch his ghost appeared unto me; / Saying I'm married to a mermaid in the bottom of the sea. CHORUS: Singing Rule Britannia! Britannia rule the waves. / Britons never, never, never will be slaves."

who I had always disliked heartily [wrote Dawson], said that
when the Confederate States enjoyed their own government, they
did not intend to have any damned foreigners in the country. I
asked him what he expected to become of men like myself, who
had given up their own country in order to render aid to the Confederacy. He made a flippant reply, which I answered rather
warmly, and he struck at me. I warded off the blow, and slapped
his face.

The next morning, Dawson asked Ross to deliver his challenge to Major
Walton. Ross had relished the prospect of a duel, but he was deprived of
the spectacle by Walton's offer of a written apology. Dawson waited for
two days. When none came, he sent Ross to see Walton again. The major
informed him that he had changed his mind. Delighted, Ross responded
that the major must choose his weapons, since the challenge still held.
"This brought Walton to terms," wrote Dawson, "and he made the apology I required."[22] Dawson felt vindicated, but he still had to dine with
Walton every day.

The tensions in Bragg's army increased until, on October 5, twelve
generals signed a petition asking for him to be removed from his command. Francis Lawley hoped that Longstreet would take over from General Bragg. "I have done my very utmost to get him to the helm," he
wrote to a friend. "The disappointment and indignation of his own
corps, if he is put under Bragg, will be great and dangerous."[23] Lawley
was still feeling weak as well as unappreciated by his employers; he had
recently received a reprimand from Mowbray Morris at *The Times,* who,
in a momentary pang of editorial responsibility, had asked him to tone
down his "extravagant partiality to the Southern Cause."[24]

Lawley arrived from Richmond just as Bragg learned of the attempted coup against him. He was unsurprised by the "heartburning
recrimination" that had infected all ranks of Bragg's army.[25] When
Jefferson Davis arrived at the camp on October 9, Lawley assumed that
the president had made the difficult journey expressly to remove the unpopular general. "The conclusion is irresistible," Lawley told *Times* readers in his new spirit of semi-impartiality, "that General Bragg failed to
convert the most headlong and disordered rout which the Federals have
ever seen . . . into a crowning victory like Waterloo." Cold, driving rain
accompanied Davis's visit. Francis Dawson had to dig a trench around

their tent to keep the water from flooding in during the night. The rain did not deter wild hogs from feeding on the dead, but most other activity ceased. The guns could not be moved, as the wagons became stuck. "Few constitutions can stand being wet through for a week together," wrote Ross. They were fortified, however, by the box of provisions Lawley had brought with him from Virginia. He had also arrived with a spare horse, which enabled the observers to follow President Davis as he visited the different headquarters. Davis stayed for five days, and every day the generals, the travelers, indeed the entire army, expected an announcement.

On September 22, 1863, the telegraph office in Washington had erupted into frenzied activity as the first reports came through from Chickamauga. The message from General Rosecrans was blunt: "We have met with a serious disaster."[26] The news was bewildering to the cabinet. Their most recent message from Rosecrans had announced his effortless capture of Chattanooga. Although Lincoln and General Halleck had been concerned that General Burnside was taking too long to march from Knoxville to join forces with Rosecrans, it had never occurred to them that the Army of the Cumberland was in any real danger from Bragg. Tennessee had appeared to be falling like a neat row of dominoes, especially now that the Gap was in Federal hands. Indeed, Lincoln was so confident that he had started to make plans to strengthen Tennessee's pro-Northern state government.[27]

The rest of the cabinet had shared Lincoln's optimism. William Seward had been feeling sufficiently cheerful to allow his work to be interrupted by a visit from Leslie Stephen. The Englishman had arrived in Washington with a letter of recommendation from John Bright. The future editor of the *Dictionary of National Biography* (and father of Virginia Woolf) was, at the age of thirty-one, entering the final months of his career as an Anglican clergyman. Recently, Stephen had suffered a crisis of faith and was on the verge of leaving the Church and his academic post at Trinity Hall, Cambridge. His wild red hair and unkempt beard made him an alarming figure, but his combination of being a friend of John Bright and the cousin of the pro-Northern journalist Edward Dicey overcame Seward's resistance. He invited Stephen to accompany him to the White House. A cabinet meeting was slated to begin in half an hour, but in the intervening time Seward introduced Stephen to Lincoln as a friend of the "great John Bright." "Bright's name is a tower of strength in these parts," Stephen wrote in surprise to his mother:

> They all talked of him with extraordinary admiration, and I was obliged to conceal the very distant nature of my relations to him by ingenious prevarication. I said that I had not seen him since the end of the Parliamentary session, as I had been absent from England since that time, and I did not let on that I had only seen him once, two years before that epoch, and then from the gallery of the House of Commons when he was on the floor.[28]

British descriptions of Lincoln had led Stephen to expect a clumsy, elephantine figure of bizarre proportions, not the "benevolent and hearty old gentleman" who laughed and smiled so readily. "I felt quite kindly to him," Stephen recorded. He thought Lincoln was far more impressive than Seward, whose initial good impression was undermined by his fatal propensity to swagger. "He is a little, rather insignificant-looking man, with a tendency to tell rather long-winded and rather pointless stories," wrote Stephen dismissively. "He rather amused me by the coolness with which he talked about government affairs to me as a total stranger. Within five minutes after he saw me he said that if England permitted the rebel rams to start, they would declare war."[29]

Taking advantage of the military pass Seward had written out for him, Stephen had visited General Meade's headquarters in Virginia, where no one, either during the journey or in Meade's camp, believed him when he said that England remained unconvinced that slavery was the real cause of the war. "They perfectly laugh at me," Stephen wrote to his mother after he had arrived in New York at the end of September. "I might as well tell them that in England we did not think the sun is the cause of daylight." Nor did Americans believe him when he tried to explain the confusion that had led many Englishmen to support the South. "Assuming that Englishmen had really understood the nature of the quarrel, I should feel ashamed of my country myself. Of course, I know they didn't," he added, "but it is no use trying to drive that into Americans, it only produces shrugs of their shoulders and civil grins."[30]

Exasperation with English attitudes to the war had also led an acquaintance of Stephen's, Henry Yates Thompson, to visit America in order to gain firsthand knowledge about the situation. His own family had fallen victim to the fashionable moralizing that dismissed the North as an empire-seeking nation of hypocrites and elevated the South as the last bastion of a preindustrial paradise. "I am quite staggered by your letter," he had written crossly to his mother from Philadelphia on September 19 in response to her comment that Northern racism was as bad as, if not worse than, Southern slavery. "If you really think slavery pleasanter, all I say is you don't know what slavery is," he raged. "I am so certain myself of the good to humanity of this War that, if the North were not winning, I should be inclined to volunteer myself, and have a shot at some of those accursed people you are all praising so loudly."[31]

Thompson arrived in Washington at the beginning of October, shortly after Stanton had ordered twenty thousand reinforcements to General Rosecrans at Chattanooga. He visited Seward on the second: "I was quite shocked by his appearance: he was so bowed," he wrote to his brother Sam. "I was told afterwards that he has a son very ill just now with one of the armies. If I had known that before, I should not have gone. . . . The photographs of Seward look quite different from how he really appears now."[32] Thompson did not feel comfortable bothering Seward for a pass to Meade's headquarters, nor did he try to impose himself on the president. His only sight of Lincoln was a glimpse of a cadaverous face through the window of a carriage, its wheels churning such a cloud of pale dust that the cavalry trotting behind looked like the four horsemen of the Apocalypse. Thompson was right to avoid the White House; the Lincolns were in silent mourning for the unmentionable side of Mary's family. Her brother-in-law, Confederate general Todd Helm, had been killed at the Battle of Chickamauga. Three of Mary's brothers had already died for the South.[33] Thompson stayed only a few days in the city and then headed out west.

Henry Yates Thompson's departure from Washington coincided with the return of Lord Lyons from his holiday in Canada. The minister had spent the previous week in New York, taking the temperature of the city. "It is a pity I cannot come here oftener," he told Lord Russell. "This is so much the best place for obtaining a knowledge of what is going on in the political world."[34] It was a strange time for Lyons to make a visit. Tiffany and Co. was flying the Russian flag on the front of its building, and American and Russian flags lined the whole of Broadway.

Two weeks earlier, four Russian warships had sailed into New York

Harbor. Their appearance took the country by surprise. The press speculated that Czar Alexander II had sent the fleet as a goodwill gesture to the North. Some people even wondered whether the czar was making a covert offer of military aid—"Thank God for the Russians," wrote Gideon Welles in his diary. But when Seward questioned the Russian minister, Baron Stoeckl, about the fleet's visit, the baron was vague. The real reason the czar had sent his fleet to North America was in order to keep it ready in case Russia resumed hostilities against England and France. The Russian admiral of the fleet had orders to give every impression of military support short of actually lying.[35]

The city organized a parade and an elaborate banquet in honor of the Russian visitors. In the midst of the excitement, the arrival of Admiral Milne on the flagship HMS *Nile* was hardly reported in the press. It was the first visit by a British admiral since the War of 1812, and a genuine gesture of goodwill that Milne and Lyons had been planning for several weeks. But the Russian presence crushed their hopes of making a strong impression on the American public. In contrast to the throngs who visited the Russian ships, not a single vessel approached the *Nile*. The closest Milne came to a public honor was a dinner party given for him and his wife at Cyrus Field's house in Gramercy Park. The admiral did not mind the indifference shown to his visit, though Lyons was disappointed, given the multiple occasions on which Milne had restrained his officers and punished those who displayed less than strict neutrality in the conflict. Milne instinctively warmed to the energy and spirit of the North.[36]

Before the end of Milne's visit, the commander of the Brooklyn Navy Yard came to his senses and invited the admiral for a tour. Milne was introduced to Major General Irvin McDowell of Bull Run fame and other official dignitaries. "Although on our arrival there was evidently much coolness," Milne reported to the Duke of Somerset, "yet before we left the tide in our favour had evidently turned." As Lyons had discovered for himself during their first meeting in Canada, it was impossible not to like and respect the admiral.

Washington was more welcoming toward Admiral Milne. Seward once again set aside his work for the mixed pleasure of escort duty, and Gideon Welles suspended his loathing of Britain for the hour he sat next to Milne at a dinner at Willard's. The navy secretary had a good memory for courtesies as well as slights: the previous July, HMS *Phaeton* had happened to sail past the U.S. Virgin Islands on Independence Day. Mindful of Milne's order to show respect when in American waters, the captain had surprised the Federal warship moored in the harbor by hoisting the U.S. flag and firing a twenty-one-gun salute.

Admiral and Lady Milne sailed back to Canada on October 12. "I believe my visit has done much good in many ways, and I would strongly recommend that such visits should be repeated," he wrote to the Duke of Somerset.[37] The British weekly newspaper in New York, the *Albion*, thought Milne deserved official praise for his courage in forcing the issue. "And now that the ice is broken, we trust that hereafter and in happier times, the British Admiral commanding . . . may make frequent visits to this port."[38] He could see that Americans cared about British opinion to an astonishing degree. Yet this vital part of diplomatic relations was left solely to the whim of the press. If nothing else came from Milne's visit, his sober assessment of Britain's unpopularity gave credibility to Lyons's repeated warnings to the Foreign Office. As if to underline the point, the treasury secretary, Salmon Chase, made a bizarre speech in Ohio shortly after Milne's visit about wanting to seize "Old Mother England by the hair" and give her a good shaking.

Lyons and, lately, the Foreign Office had come to believe that Seward was Britain's best hope for keeping relations level between the two countries, and both were rooting for him in his ongoing battles with Gideon Welles and Charles Sumner.[39] (No one outside the British government knew that Seward was giving Lyons off-the-record advice on how to forestall some of the congressional attacks on British interests.)[40] Contemplating the immediate future, Lyons saw only dangerous corners and looming obstacles now that he knew for certain "that Mr. Sumner and the ultras will make another onslaught on Mr. Seward when Congress opens."[41] Worse still was Baron Mercier's revelation that he had requested a leave of absence. His wife had put up with Washington for his sake, Mercier explained to Lyons, but she could stand it no longer. Lyons could not help himself, but he hoped that the French Foreign Ministry would share his anxiety and consider Mercier too important to be replaced.

When trouble for Lord Lyons did come, it was from the South rather than the North. On October 23, he read in the *National Intelligencer* that the four remaining British consuls had been ordered to leave the Confederacy in retaliation for Britain's alleged support for the North.[42] The consuls' unceasing efforts on behalf of conscripted Britons had been an irritant to the Confederate State Department for more than a year, and they made convenient scapegoats that Judah Benjamin had no scruple about using. Acting consul Allan Fullarton in Savannah had provided the excuse when on October 3 he sent to Richmond a belligerent protest on behalf of six drafted British subjects. Four days later, on October 7, Benjamin convened a special cabinet session to discuss the consuls. Jefferson Davis was conveniently in Tennessee with General Bragg and therefore protected from any international outcry that might follow. The decision to expel them was apparently unanimous.[43] If Benjamin did not gain any popularity by the move, at least he did not lose any, and he doubted that the Confederacy would suffer, either.

———

The troubles endured by the Scotsman William Watson showed the importance of the consuls to the British community. Tired of struggling to find work in the South after leaving the Confederate army, Watson had decided to try his hand at blockade running. During the summer he sailed from New Orleans to Belize. There, fear of the Confederate commerce raiders had led to a glut of cheap U.S.-owned ships for sale. He bought a flat-bottomed vessel, christened her *Rob Roy,* and headed for the Gulf of Mexico. When Watson eventually reached Galveston, he discovered that the city was barely functioning. "It was now virtually in ruins, and the grass was growing in the streets," he wrote. Anarchy and martial law ruled simultaneously.

Watson was powerless to prevent a local commander from impounding the *Rob Roy* for defense duty. But he had faith in Consul Arthur Lynn. "When I saw that gentleman and reported the matter he was a little surprised, but said he would scarcely be much astonished at anything these people—the Confederates—would do. They were now desperate, and would not let any regard for international law or individual rights interfere with any project they meant to carry out."[44] In the face of Consul Lynn's protests, Confederate general John B. Magruder promised that he would release the *Rob Roy* if an alternative vessel could be found.[45] Naturally disappointed by this response, Watson went to Magruder's headquarters himself. The officers were sarcastic toward him until he was recognized by a former member of the 2nd Texas Regiment. "I was quite astonished at the great effect which this little incident had upon the demeanor of the officials towards me," wrote Watson. The *Rob Roy* was returned, and Watson was again free to face the ordinary hazards of blockade running.[46]

Several weeks passed before Consul Lynn learned of Benjamin's order for the British consuls to leave, and when he read the order itself, he noticed that his name had been left off the list. He decided to remain at his post until circumstances changed. Consul Frederick Cridland in Mobile had also escaped Richmond's notice and was determined to stay. Every white male between the ages of sixteen and sixty was being conscripted. "Letters are received and applications are made to me daily by British subjects to interfere and prevent their being forced into military service, but I cannot assist them," he wrote on November 14. Yet he hoped that his presence still retained some moderating effect. Cridland's letter caused much indignation in the Foreign Office over the plight of Britons in the South; it sickened Lord Lyons each time a letter appeared from the Confederacy pleading for help that he was unable to give.[*47]

Most Southerners did not believe that British residents were suffering at all. Southern newspapers rarely, if ever, reported when Britons were chained to wagons and dragged through towns to encourage "volunteering," or hung upside down and repeatedly dunked in water, or threatened with being shot through the knees.[48]

---

[*] When HMS *Virago* eventually made it through to Mobile in January 1864, Consul Cridland told the captain that he had not heard from the Foreign Office for six months. Later, in April, a pathetic message from Consul Lynn miraculously arrived in Washington, begging for guidance: "If I am however, to remain at my post it would afford me sincere gratification if Your Lordship would direct me what course to pursue." The consuls in the South could not know of the extraordinary efforts made by the Foreign Office in trying to reach them. Lyons pleaded unsuccessfully with Seward to allow a special envoy through the blockade so that Britain could make a direct protest to the Confederate government.

TWENTY-SIX

Can the Nation Endure?

Jefferson Davis's choice—Saved by the "Cracker Line"—Lincoln addresses the country—Fighting in the clouds—The center breaks—The South holds

Francis Lawley had been so sure that Jefferson Davis would dismiss General Bragg that in his *Times* dispatch on October 8, 1863, he wrote as though an announcement was imminent. Yet Bragg's removal was not preordained. The Battle of Chickamauga had been a stunning victory for the South—the only one since Chancellorsville in May. Longstreet had complained to the secretary of war, James Seddon, "that nothing but the hand of God can help as long as we have our present commander," without reflecting how his doom-laden letter would appear to the world beyond Tennessee and Georgia. To Davis, the charge seemed self-serving and melodramatic; he agreed with Bragg that it would have been impossible for his shattered army to chase after Union general William Rosecrans even for the ten miles to Chattanooga. Furthermore, aside from the obvious dangers presented by the Confederates' internal disputes, the Army of Tennessee looked not only secure but on the verge of another success.

Chattanooga was not quite a one-horse town, but with few more than two thousand residents it certainly did not have the resources to feed and shelter an army of more than fifty thousand. The Tennessee River looped the town in a U-bend on three sides, with the fourth, which faced south, overlooked by an undulating chain of mountains. At the southwestern end rose Lookout Mountain, which towered two thousand feet above the town; toward the northeastern end, the six-mile-long Missionary Ridge gently curved around like a natural amphitheater. Since Bragg held both these high points and the railroads in the valley, the Federals' only safe supply route was a single road through the backcountry that eventually reached Chattanooga via the far side of the Tennessee River. During the rainy season, which was just beginning, the road was expected to become an impassable mud track, leading to inevitable starvation for the Federals.

President Davis had already demonstrated his willingness to be firm with generals who opposed him. Despite public criticism he had shunted aside both Joe Johnston and Pierre Beauregard. But with Braxton Bragg, a man he liked and trusted, Davis was strangely protective. Not even the shocking number of Confederate casualties at Chickamauga—higher than those suffered by Lee at Gettysburg and far higher than those suffered by Rosecrans—shook Davis's faith in him. After allowing the unhappy generals to air their objections for a couple of days, Davis climbed atop the appropriately named "Pulpit Rock" on Lookout Mountain and made a brief but spirited defense of Bragg to the Confederate troops assembled below, warning his listeners that "he who sows the seeds of discontent and distrust prepares for the harvest of slaughter and defeat." Davis may have felt that there was no other credible alternative to General Bragg, but the Army of Tennessee disagreed. When Davis boarded his return train on October 14, 1863, much of the army's will to fight went with him. Instead of giving him three cheers, soldiers shouted, "Send us something to eat, Massa Jeff! I'm hungry! I'm hungry!" (Bragg's ability to manage the supply operations for the army was no better than his skills as a leader of men.) The news of Davis's decision spread so quickly that two days later, Consul Cridland wrote to Lord Russell from Mobile, Alabama, that everyone was in despair because President Davis was "retaining General Bragg in command against all opposition."[1] Bragg's retribution was swift. The leading rebels found themselves sidelined or dismissed; Longstreet's command was reduced to the fifteen thousand soldiers who had accompanied him from Virginia, and he was sent to guard Lookout Mountain, as far away from Bragg as possible.

Lawley, Vizetelly, and Ross stayed with Longstreet for another week, loyally enduring the short rations and incessant rain until they could

Chattanooga and the Federal lines from the lower ridge of Lookout Mountain, by Frank Vizetelly.

stand it no longer. Vizetelly completed a couple more sketches and Lawley one more dispatch, this time not even trying to sugar over his contempt for Bragg. There was no compelling reason for them to remain, but leaving proved more difficult than they expected, as the few trains running from Chickamauga were reserved for the sick and wounded. Ross solved their problems by making friends with the stationmaster, who retained a proud memory of being inspected by Lord John Russell at the beginning of the war. At first "I tried to explain that he might be mistaken," wrote Ross, who realized that the man had confused Lord Russell with William Howard Russell. Since the stationmaster found them room in a covered wagon (which let in the rain only at the corners), he decided to drop the point.[2]

They arrived back in Augusta, Georgia, two days later, on October 24. To their relief, the Planters Hotel had rooms for all of them. "A clean bed with actual sheets," exclaimed Lawley, "plenty of water to wash in, decent food, a table to write on, candles"—these were luxuries to a man "who has long floundered in the mud of General Bragg's camp."[3] The weather was less harsh, too, and a gentle autumn wind replaced the cruel downpours of Tennessee. The men passed the afternoons on their hotel balcony in shirtsleeves, smoking and chatting. They tried out the local theater and discovered it to be quite passable. Vizetelly's only complaint was the tea served at the Planters, which was so weak he wondered how it managed to reach the spout.[4]

Little news filtered down to Augusta from Bragg's camp, and certainly none from the besieged Federals in Chattanooga. The three friends were unaware that Washington had sent 23,000 troops from the Army of the Potomac to reinforce Rosecrans. Lincoln had acted decisively; there was only one general he truly believed in, and he called upon him now. Ulysses S. Grant was summoned from his headquarters in Cairo, Illinois, and ordered to Chattanooga. Lincoln had written to

Grant after Vicksburg, "When you turned northward, east of the Big Black, I feared it was a mistake. I now wish to make the personal acknowledgement that you were right and I was wrong."[5] The president showed his newfound faith in Grant by placing him in overall command of the three main Federal armies in the west.

Lincoln was taking a risk by interfering with the Army of the Cumberland. "Old Rosy," as the soldiers called Rosecrans, remained beloved by the men; he had meticulously looked after their welfare, and many of them were sorry to see him dismissed. "Worst of all," wrote the English volunteer Robert Neve of the 5th Kentucky Volunteers, worse than the short rations, lack of blankets, and leaking tents, "was the order for General Rosecrans to be relieved. It was read to us on parade."[6] Rosecrans's popularity with the soldiers was the chief reason why Lincoln waited until after the election for state governor in Ohio on October 13 to dismiss him, fearing that to do otherwise could push the soldier vote toward Vallandigham (who lost by a wide margin). But once the election was out of the way, he agreed that General Rosecrans could be replaced by the "Rock of Chickamauga," General George Thomas, who had prevented a complete Federal rout at that battle.

The Confederate siege of Chattanooga was so tight that after a mere three weeks, sutlers in the town were charging six cents for a mouthful of bread—the usual price for two loaves. In the animal pens, the horses and mules were staggering in the last throes of starvation. Every building in the town had been transformed into makeshift hospitals, except for the Catholic church where Rosecrans worshipped. Grant arrived at Chattanooga on October 23, still using crutches after a fall from his horse in August. But the painful injury had not affected his vigor or determination. The 23,000 reinforcements from Virginia had arrived, led by a chastened "Fighting Joe" Hooker. General Sherman's corps was coming from Mississippi. Grant was confident he could best his opponent; the real enemy he feared was Tennessee's geography. Somehow he had to ferry food and grain to Chattanooga before the entire Army of the Cumberland collapsed or surrendered.

If Rosecrans had at least been able to hold on to Lookout Mountain, the situation facing the Federals would not have been so dire. With the Confederates now in possession of it, all the southern routes into the town, including the river, roads, and railway, were exposed to enemy fire. But the engineers of the Army of the Cumberland had come up with a plan. It required a furtive night expedition along the Tennessee River, beneath the Confederate guns on Lookout Mountain. If successful, they would be able to build a pontoon bridge two miles upriver, where a bend in the river would put the Federal forces beyond the reach of artillery fire.

At 3:00 A.M. on October 27, fifty pontoon boats, each carrying twenty-four soldiers and two rowers, silently paddled past the Confederates. Robert Neve was in the fourth boat. "It was a fine moonlit night and very still," he wrote. "We passed down very quiet and could even see the Rebel pickets standing before their fires. It did not create any alarm."[7] They seized the landing with relative ease, driving back a small Confederate counterattack with few losses. "The next job was to cut down all trees . . . all day long we had to work felling trees and making small breastworks. Here we were all but starving. Rations were very short." A Confederate attack was expected, and it came at midnight on the twenty-eighth. This should have been Longstreet's second triumph at Chattanooga, his opportunity to defeat Grant without having to engage in a major battle. But Longstreet had not been paying attention to the Federal inroads along the southern end of the valley, and he made a serious mistake now by sending only four brigades against the attack force. The Confederates were easily overwhelmed and had to retreat back up Lookout Mountain.

The next day, the first supply wagons carrying hardtack (called "crackers" by the army) and dried beef came rolling through along the "Cracker Line." The route stretched back for hundreds of miles. In northern Kentucky, a partially restored Ebenezer Wells led a wagon train of more than two thousand pack animals, fighting fever and exhaustion to keep the supplies moving. Robert Neve soon noticed the difference in his rations. Over the next two weeks more supplies arrived, including fresh vegetables and new uniforms. "Our rations were getting better, and we felt better as well." His regiment was so close to the Confederate pickets that they agreed to take turns on picket duty. "We would wave each other's caps and then exchange newspapers." The reversal of their fortunes was complete; it was now the Confederates who were outnumbered, starving, and miserable and the Federals who were growing in confidence and strength.

General Bragg grasped the magnitude of Longstreet's mistake in failing to prevent the Federal bridgehead into Chattanooga, but his reaction to the disaster was perverse. Instead of trying to plug the gap or reinforce his position, Bragg chose to send Longstreet away, along with twenty thousand men, on an expedition to take Knoxville, Tennessee, from General Burnside. There was some rationale to the decision: if Burnside could be forced back to central Tennessee, the Confederates would re-possess the three railways that passed through Knoxville and the all-important Cumberland Gap, which would restore the quick route to Virginia. But at best the mission was a dangerous sideshow when Federal supplies and troops were pouring into Chattanooga.

Bragg relished the thought of Longstreet's having to operate on his own, hoping that this would expose some of his rival's weaknesses. "One of General Longstreet's most serious faults as a military commander was shown at this time," admitted Francis Dawson. Longstreet made few preparations for the campaign and never bothered to speak to Dawson about ordnance. "Not one word was said to me by him on the subject. I had an inkling, however, of what was going on, and obtained ample sup-plies. Had I not done so, we should have been in an awkward predica-ment by the time that we reached Knoxville. Had anything been lacking, it is certain that the blame would have been placed on me."[8] The army reached its destination with less than half the number of wagons and an-imals required for a campaign. But Dawson's prescience protected him from Longstreet's growing fury as the general watched his army wilt under the twin assaults of hunger and cold.[9] The capture of a Federal wagon train on November 15 eased some of the pain.

Longstreet desperately wanted to avoid a siege, and hoped to make Burnside fight him outside the town. On November 16, he thought he had succeeded. Burnside's army was strung across a narrow valley out-side Knoxville—a "beautiful position" for taking, recalled a Confederate officer. But the situation began to go wrong almost at once. When the cannons opened fire, Dawson was horrified to discover that the ammu-nition he had worked so hard to acquire was defective. Instead of raining fire and shot upon the enemy, the shells exploded prematurely or not at all. Two days of fighting ended with severe losses to the Confederate corps.

Longstreet vacillated while his enemy built stronger defenses. "There was a good deal of delay, for one reason and another," wrote Dawson, "and we were so near the town that we could hear the tunes played by the band at Fort Sanders. The favourite air then was: 'When This Cruel

War Is Over.' "[10] Longstreet had assured Bragg that Knoxville would be captured long before Grant's reinforcements arrived at Chattanooga. This was impossible now that Burnside occupied the town. But since he had not heard from Bragg for several days, Longstreet wrongly assumed there was no imminent danger to the besiegers.

Francis Lawley, Frank Vizetelly, and Fitzgerald Ross left Georgia in early November, once they knew for certain that General Longstreet would not be returning to Chattanooga. Vizetelly and Ross set off for Charleston, while Lawley, who was mystified by his friends' enthusiasm for danger, headed for Richmond. Charleston was again being bombarded; if the Federals succeeded in taking the city, it would be one more disaster that Lawley would have to fudge for his readers. The strain of always putting the best face on Confederate fortunes was beginning to show in his most recent dispatches. When he arrived in Richmond on November 14, Lawley wrote a report for *The Times* that admitted far more than he perhaps realized. The enemy, he wrote, "hems in the edges of the 'rebellion' on every side." The North had surrounded the South "with a cordon of vessels so numerous as for the first time in 30 months to make access to the Confederate coast really dangerous and difficult."[11]

Lawley thought the city looked beautiful. A light dusting of snow covered most reminders of the war and imparted charm to even the most dilapidated buildings. President Davis had returned to Richmond a few days earlier, having toured Charleston's defenses and delivered an encouraging speech to its embattled citizens. During his absence the Confederate cabinet had learned that the precious Lairds rams were almost certainly lost to them. The secretary of the navy, Stephen Mallory, still hoped that James Bulloch would find a way to rescue the vessels; with the exception of the *Alexandra,* the agent had always come through. But the rest of the cabinet thought the news vindicated its decision to expel the British consuls. They were convinced that the Royal Navy could have broken the blockade at any time during the past three years if the British had been truly in favor of Southern independence. The existence of the British blockade runners made no difference to Southern resentment toward Britain—though without them Lee's army would be suffering even greater privations.

Lee had not fought a battle since Gettysburg and yearned to launch an attack against General Meade and the Army of the Potomac. It went against the grain with him to remain on the defensive, but, as he had explained to his wife in late October, "thousands were barefooted, thousands with fragments of shoes, and all without overcoats, blankets or warm clothing. I could not bear to expose them to certain suffering on an uncertain issue."[12]

General Meade was troubled by many worries, but the condition of his army was not among them. At the beginning of October, a scandal had threatened to tarnish the reputation of the cavalry corps, but it was quickly hushed up by the War Department. All the cavalrymen knew about it was that Sir Percy Wyndham had been escorted to Washington under armed guard. It was not clear why he had been removed. The War Department refused to say anything other than that he had been relieved "for the time being." Sixteen years later, in 1879, the *Decatur Daily News* of Illinois ran an article that claimed to clear "an old mystery." Apparently, two unnamed informants had accused Wyndham of plotting to surrender his regiment to the Confederates for $300,000. "Mr. Stanton could not, getting his information as he did, place Col. Wyndham under arrest . . . so the only road open was to remove him from command."[13] The informants had first brought the accusation to Secretary Chase, who took the matter to Stanton. They claimed to have a letter from the Confederate secretary of state, Judah P. Benjamin, that laid out a strategy to entice Wyndham into surrendering his cavalry.[14] The War Department does not seem to have investigated whether Wyndham actually considered the bribe, nor was he interrogated about the letter.

Speculation about Wyndham's removal from active duty was rife: Lord Lyons received protests from the public after stories appeared in the New York press that accused him of being the instigator. "I have to say that there is no foundation whatever for the assertion made respecting me," Lord Lyons wrote to a Mr. John Livingston in New York. He had not, as Livingston claimed, solicited or made "representations of a disparaging character against that brave officer."[15] On November 5, *The New York Times* intervened unexpectedly—probably at Seward's behest—with an article on the controversy that explicitly denied Lord Lyons's involvement and repeated the War Department's stance that Wyndham was on temporary relief from duties. It would turn out to be a very long relief.

The Union cavalry wondered about the unexplained removal of its most colorful brigade leader; Wyndham's habit of twiddling his mustache whenever he became angry was remembered with humor rather than the fear it once provoked. The corps would have been happy to have him back, especially after it suffered a humiliating defeat by Jeb Stuart's troopers at Buckland Mills on October 19, which was dubbed "Buckland Races" by the Confederates after the Federals were chased upcountry for several miles. Meade was summoned by Lincoln for an interview in Washington and given to understand that he was expected to destroy Lee, not play cat-and-mouse with him. The result of the meeting was a small engagement near Fredericksburg on November 7, which netted Meade more than 1,600 prisoners, eight battle flags, and four artillery guns.

The secretary of war, Edwin Stanton, remained unimpressed and wanted Meade to push harder. Nothing about the situation in Virginia pleased him. But on November 14, Stanton received one piece of news that did give him satisfaction: the combined land and sea force sent to capture John Yates Beall had at last succeeded in cornering its prey. Bored with lying low in Richmond, Beall had resumed his raids on November 10. He managed to seize just one vessel before his whereabouts were exposed and the full might of the North pounced on the little band. Bennet G. Burley was one of only two who managed to escape. Beall and his crew were taken to Fort McHenry in Baltimore, where they were kept in manacles for six weeks until the Confederate secretary of the navy, Stephen Mallory, ordered eighteen Federal prisoners of war—picked at random—to be similarly shackled in retribution, which led to a relaxation of their treatment.*

"I have seen your dispatches," Lincoln telegraphed Meade after the fight at Fredericksburg, "and I wish to say, 'Well done!' " He then wrote to Burnside at Knoxville, giving him the news about Meade's success and asking pointedly, "Let me hear from you."[16] Lincoln was also waiting anxiously for news from General Grant: the "Cracker Line" had saved the Army of the Cumberland from starvation, but far more was at stake than a battle over logistics. "If we can hold Chattanooga and eastern Tennessee," Lincoln had written to Rosecrans before the general's removal, "I think the rebellion must dwindle and die."[17]

---

* Unwilling to volunteer for the regular Confederate army, Burley briefly tried his hand at journalism before turning to the stage. He joined the New Richmond Theatre, run by the British theater manager Richard d'Orsay Ogden. Burley's first role was a small part in the aptly named *The Guerrillas,* a Confederate melodrama set during Stonewall Jackson's military campaign in 1862.

On November 19 the president was going to Gettysburg—whose 23,000 Union casualties in July remained the highest of any battle of the war— to speak at the dedication of the town's new war cemetery. The solemn and painful task was made worse by the uncertainty in the west; Lincoln would have to address the mourners with Rosecrans's disaster at Chickamauga still fresh in their minds. However, Lincoln did not wish to dwell on the dangers facing the country, or why duty had to be its own reward at such a time. He already had a theme for the speech, one advocated three months earlier by Seward's financial emissary to London, John Murray Forbes, whose perspective on the meaning of the war had sharpened during his travels abroad. "John Bright and his glorious band of English republicans can see that we are fighting for democracy," Forbes had written to Lincoln on September 8. "After we get military successes, the mass of the Southern people must be made to see this truth, and then reconstruction becomes easy and permanent."[18]

A large retinue accompanied Lincoln to Gettysburg, including Seward, several governors and senators, and the French minister, Henri Mercier, but not Lord Lyons, who did not receive an invitation. Although the reasons for the visit were somber, the crowds greeted Lincoln with enthusiasm and lined up in large numbers to shake his hand. The principal speaker at the ceremony was not the president but the great orator Edward Everett, whose age and infirmities were sadly evident in parts of his speech. Everett spoke for more than two hours during the unusually hot afternoon, tripping up occasionally and at one point confusing Meade with Lee.[19]

When he was finished, the audience steeled itself for another long speech, not knowing that Lincoln had been asked by the organizers to be short and concise. The two-minute address was over so quickly that the photographer did not have time to focus his lens, and many among the fifteen thousand listeners had not yet settled down. Lincoln himself believed that his words had fallen flat. Several newspapers criticized him for failing to live up to the occasion.[20] Antonio Gallenga, a temporary correspondent for *The Times*, thought that Lincoln's speech had been a total failure. English readers were told that the "imposing ceremony" was "rendered ludicrous by some of the luckless sallies of that poor President Lincoln."[21] But Lincoln's private secretary John Hay recorded in his diary that the president spoke "in a firm free way, with more grace than is his wont."[22] Edward Everett had no doubts about the momentous nature of Lincoln's speech. He congratulated Lincoln, confessing that he wished "I came as near to the central idea of the occasion, in two hours, as you did in two minutes."[23] Everett realized that Lincoln had captured the essential nature of the war. In a mere 272 words, the president had defined the moral purpose of the country's existence—democracy, freedom, equality—not only for the mourners at Gettysburg but for every subsequent generation of the American people. The Revolution of 1776 had brought forth:

> a new nation, conceived in liberty, and dedicated to the proposition that all men are created equal. Now we are engaged in a great civil war, testing whether that nation, or any nation so conceived and so dedicated, can long endure.
>
> We are met on a great battle-field of that war. We have come to dedicate a portion of that field as a final resting-place for those who here gave their lives that that nation might live. It is altogether fitting and proper that we should do this.
>
> But, in a larger sense, we cannot dedicate—we cannot consecrate—we cannot hallow—this ground. The brave men, living and dead, who struggled here, have consecrated it far above our poor power to add or detract. The world will little note nor long remember what we say here, but it can never forget what they did here. It is for us, the living, rather, to be dedicated here to the unfinished work which they who fought here have thus far so nobly advanced. It is rather for us to be here dedicated to the great task remaining before us—that from these honored dead we take increased devotion to that cause for which they gave the last full measure of devotion; that we here highly resolve that these dead shall not have died in vain; that this nation, under God, shall have a new birth of freedom; and that government of the people, by the people, for the people, shall not perish from the earth.[24]

———

Henry Yates Thompson arrived at Bridgeport, Alabama, forty-seven miles downstream from Chattanooga, on Friday, November 20, carrying a letter of introduction from Edward Everett to Dr. John Newberry, the head of the Western Department of the Sanitary Commission. It was late, so instead of continuing his journey to the commission's headquarters, Thompson bedded down in one of their tents at Bridgeport. "Before I went to sleep," he wrote, "I heard a solemn thudding sound outside. I asked my companion what was it and he said: 'Oh, the last of Sherman's men crossing the pontoons.' "[25]

Grant had been waiting for Sherman's troops to arrive before he made his attack against General Bragg. By November 21 he had accumulated more than sixty thousand men. Staring down at them from Lookout Mountain and Missionary Ridge was a diminishing army of 33,000 Confederates. The "Cracker Line" had answered the Federal hunger pains, but no such relief had come to Bragg's army. "Never in all my whole life do I remember of ever experiencing so much oppression and humiliation," wrote the Confederate private Sam Watkins. "The soldiers were starved and almost naked, and covered all over with lice and camp itch and filth and dirt. The men looked sick, hollow-eyed, and heart-broken, living principally upon parched corn, which had been picked out of the mud and dirt under the feet of officers' horses."[26]

Thompson and Dr. Newberry boarded a steamboat for the last leg of the journey. It was another two days of arduous travel before they reached Chattanooga on November 22. That day, Bragg stacked the cards against himself still higher by sending two more divisions to Knoxville. "I had a fine view of the whole Rebel position on Missionary Ridge about three miles distant across a wooded valley," wrote Thompson on the twenty-third:

> The pickets and the skirmishers of both sides were behind their respective rifle pits in the valley below us and the Rebel pickets were plainly visible from Fort Wood, about half a mile from where I stood. All those round me were expecting immediate fighting. Soon I saw a sight I shall never forget. The whole Union army in the town—about 25,000 men under General Thomas—left their tents and huts and marched out past Fort Wood in long winding columns creeping into the valley and into line of battle round the town. From Fort Wood it all looked like a great review. But it was in deadly earnest.

Thompson was observing Grant's test of Bragg's resolve, to see whether the Confederate general was prepared to fight over Chattanooga or was planning to withdraw. The Union line charged toward

Orchard Knob, a fortified hillock at the base of Missionary Ridge. The Confederates in the rifle pits, as mesmerized as Thompson by the bright spectacle rushing toward them, fled. Federal private Robert Neve was surprised to take the hill so easily: "We kept rushing on until we got in sight of their works, which we took with little opposition, and captured a number of prisoners. I took two myself," he added. Thompson watched as the prisoners were brought in and noticed that they were "rough and ragged men with no vestige of a uniform." During the night, while Neve lay shivering on the ground listening to every rustle and snap, Thompson rolled bandages for the Sisters of Mercy. He had not expected so much noise or, perhaps, so much blood. "This is war with a vengeance," he wrote.[27] The men had seemed universally brave and determined. Robert Neve could have enlightened him that nothing was ever uniform in battle: "I noticed in this fight that several officers and men got sheltered behind the trees, and kept waving their hats and cheering men up to a great degree, not even caring about firing a shot at the enemy."[28]

After breakfast on November 24, Thompson returned to Fort Wood to watch the second day of the Battle of Chattanooga. Bragg had managed to recall one of the two divisions sent to Knoxville—General Patrick Cleburne's—and had placed it at the far end of Missionary Ridge to shore up his right. Grant's overall plan for the day was simple: to capture the extreme ends of Bragg's position and then take the middle. "Fighting Joe" Hooker's day had come.

> I began to think nothing was doing [wrote Thompson] when at about midday, when I was dividing my lunch with one of the gunners on the fort, heavy reports of cannon and musketry from Lookout Valley made all of us hurry to that side of Fort Wood. I joined two officers looking through telescopes towards Lookout Mountain and we soon saw Hooker attacking, his men plainly visible to us sweeping round the steep face of Lookout.
>
> Close by me was General Grant in a black surtout with black braid on and quite loose, black trousers and a black wideawake hat and thin Wellington boots. He looked clean and gentlemanly but not military having a Stoop and a full reddish beard, the moustache much lighter than the ends which were trained to a peak.
>
> We saw Hooker's men fall back once—then they advanced

Tennessee River

Chickamauga Creek

Sherman advance
Nov. 24
and attacks Nov. 25

Tunnel
Hill

Cleburne

Mountain supply route

Brown's
Ferry

Cracker
Line

Hardee

Fort
Wood

Grant

Thomas

Robert
Neve

Breckinridge

Missionary Ridge

Chattanooga

Moccasin
Point

Hooker

Fort
Negley

Henry
Thompson

Bragg

Nov. 24

Lookout
Mountain

Hooker advance
Nov. 25

Chattanooga
Nov. 24–25, 1863

N

W   E

S

Federal Forces, Nov. 24

Confederate Forces, Nov. 24

Federal Forces, Nov. 25

Confederate Forces, Nov. 25

Miles

0   1   2

again. After some little suspense we saw the Rebels run round the face of Lookout near the top and Hooker's line advance after them, rifles popping all along the face of the mountain and guns shelling the retreating Rebels from Moccasin Point and Fort Negley. An officer beside me with a telescope cried out: "There they are and the Rebels are running." His glass was pointed to the steep face of Lookout more than half way up—and there sure enough, just three miles from us along the sparsely wooded face of the mountain, we saw a running fight with the Rebels retreating before Hooker's men.

When Hooker's men planted that large U.S. flag near the top of the mountain, the whole of the troops, and the people in and around Chattanooga, who must number some 60,000 at least, seemed to hurrah together.

The only man who seemed unmoved was General Grant himself, the prime author of all this hurly burly. There he stood in his plain citizen's clothes looking through his double field-glasses apparently totally unmoved. I stood within a few feet of him and I could hardly believe that here was this famous commander, the model, as it seemed to me, of a modest and homely but efficient Yankee general. I stood next to General Grant for quite some time. If the battle had been a pageant got up for my benefit I could not have had it better.[29]

Thompson had witnessed the "Battle Above the Clouds," so called because a light fog had formed on parts of the mountain during the fight, obscuring the valley below. Hooker's victory had been achieved with surprisingly little cost; his casualties, including those missing and captured, were fewer than two thousand. The following day, the twenty-fifth, was supposed to be Sherman's turn for glory. Grant expected his man, who had served him so well at Vicksburg, to complete the rout and drive the Confederates off Missionary Ridge. But Sherman's adversary was General Patrick Cleburne, a former corporal in the 41st (Welsh) Regiment of Foot, who was the best commander in the Army of Tennessee. Cleburne's new British volunteer aide-de-camp, Captain Charles H. Byrne, who had accompanied Ross and Vizetelly on their journey from Charleston in September, described the fight for his friends. "Three times did they charge our position, and three times were they repulsed," he wrote. "The third charge was the most determined of the lot. They managed to reach the crest of the hill, and there they fought us for about two hours at a distance varying from twenty to thirty paces;—so close were they that our officers threw stones."[30] Byrne's horse was shot in the neck. Rather than abandon his comrades, he chose to remain and fight on foot.

The bravery and sacrifice of Cleburne's soldiers became immaterial after Grant exploited the fact that Bragg had allowed the center of the Confederate line to thin dangerously during the fight to only fifteen thousand men. At Gettysburg, the Confederate charge at Meade's center had proved fatal because Lee had failed to dent the Federal strength; but here there was a genuine weakness and Grant prevailed. General Thomas's division of twenty-five thousand rose from the base of Orchard Knob and smashed through the Confederate defenses at the top of the Ridge. No one had ordered the men to go that far; rage and madness simply took hold of them. "We had all got mixed up," wrote Robert Neve. "Every man done as he liked, firing to the best advantage until we got twenty yards from the top. Someone cried out, 'Fix bayonets!' and 'Forward to the charge.'" The Confederates ran, "leaving cannon, wagons, horses, tools and everything. It was a perfect rout."[*31] Four thousand Confederates were captured on the Ridge, twice the number of casualties for the battle.

Bragg was powerless to halt the men as they came hurtling down the other side of the mountain toward Ringgold. Sam Watkins saw him ride. "Bragg looked scared. He had put spurs to his horse, and was running like a scared dog. . . . Poor fellow, he looked so hacked and whipped and mortified and chagrined at defeat, and all along the line, when Bragg would pass, the soldiers would raise the yell, . . . 'Bully for Bragg, he's hell on retreat.' "[32] The only division that did not panic was Cleburne's, which held off the Federals long enough to enable the bulk of Bragg's army to escape off the mountain. The Confederates managed to stay ahead of their pursuers, crossing through Ringgold Gap into Georgia toward the station town of Dalton. Grant did not have the wagons and

---

* This was also Robert Neve's final day of the war. Already sick with dysentery, he was sent to the hospital after the battle and was never again well enough to fight. He mustered out of the army in September 1864 and returned to England. His health permanently damaged by the war, he died in his mid-thirties in 1879, and his wife, Charlotte, successfully applied to Washington for a widow's pension.

supplies for an incursion into enemy country, and he forbade his generals to pursue the Confederates past Ringgold.

Henry Yates Thompson explored Bragg's deserted headquarters two days after the battle, on November 27. Since the twenty-fifth he had been helping Dr. Newberry by identifying the dead and pinning their names to their jackets. The first slain Federal he found turned out to be named John Bull. As Thompson wandered among the bullet-scarred trees, picking up souvenirs, he stumbled across a pile of bodies. He had not noticed them at first because their faded uniforms were the same color as the leaves. They had no hats or shoes.

> I went on to a knoll commanding the ridge in both directions [he wrote]. I found two Rebels—one dead and one just alive unattended since the battle. I gave the wounded man what brandy I had left in my flask and he spoke a little. His brains were protruding— the wound was in the back of his head. He seemed thankful for the brandy. I minced and mixed some meat, onions and biscuit and put water with them. He tried to eat but could not chew. A Federal came to help and washed his face.

While combing through the field, Thompson had a second shock. He saw two children, a little girl and boy, scavenging among the dead. They were collecting bullets. "The little girl said she lived 'over there,' pointing to Bragg's headquarters. She had been in the house all through the battle," he wrote. No one seemed to be responsible for them. The children seemed unaware of the danger that had passed over their heads, or of the perilous future that awaited them once the soldiers were no longer around to share their rations.[33] The pageantry Thompson had seen from afar had darkened to a scene of gore and horror. "The impression left on me by my walks the next day through those blood-stained woods," he wrote later, "fixed a conviction in my mind, a conviction of the absolute and essential wickedness of those who talk lightly of war and still more of those who lightly begin a war."[34] Thompson was ready to return home. "Now I am tired to death," he wrote. His ship was not leaving until December 23, but Thompson felt he had witnessed enough suffering and intended to spend the final weeks of his stay in America visiting friends and enjoying himself as a tourist. His opinion of the North had grown higher still now that he understood the great suffering endured by its people.

"God be praised for this victory, which looks like the heaviest blow the country has yet dealt at rebellion," George Templeton Strong wrote in New York after hearing the news from Chattanooga. "Meade's army again reported in motion and across the Rapidan," he added to his diary entry. "The nation needs one or two splendid victories by its Eastern armies to offset those gained in the West."[35]

Two days later, on November 29, General Longstreet received a wire from Jefferson Davis confirming the Confederate defeat at Chattanooga and ordering him to abandon his siege at Knoxville so that he could provide support to Bragg. The telegram had come an hour too late for eight hundred Confederate and thirteen Federal soldiers. One of the worst-planned assaults of the war had just taken place in front of Burnside's defenses. Francis Dawson was so sickened by the fiasco that he could not bear to write about it in his memoir. All he could say about the twenty minutes of slaughter was that Longstreet's attack "failed utterly."

The Confederates began to march away from Knoxville on December 4. Fearing that General Sherman was on his way to help Burnside, Longstreet decided it would be safer to retreat farther east rather than head south toward Georgia. "The men suffered frightfully," wrote Dawson. "It is no exaggeration to say that on such marches as they were obliged to make in that bitter weather they left the bloody tracks of their feet on the sharp stones of the roads." Longstreet, stricken with remorse and self-doubt, wished to be relieved of command. His request was denied, but President Davis did accept General Bragg's resignation. The general blamed the defeat on the cowardice of his troops and the personal animosity of his commanders without ever examining his own part in either cause. President Davis had no other alternative than to recall his stubborn opponent General Joe Johnston and order him to take command of Bragg's Army of Tennessee.

In the Federal army, General Burnside, too, asked to be relieved. He was satisfied that his reputation as a commander had been redeemed by the capture of the Cumberland Gap and the defense of Knoxville. No longer would he be known solely for the disaster at Fredericksburg and the humiliating "Mud March" of January 1863. The real victor of the Cumberland Gap, Colonel De Courcy, was also determined to leave the army. The War Department, not interested in deciding the contest between a departing general and his disgruntled colonel, had never responded to De Courcy's complaints. He was saved from becoming bitter by the loyal support and admiration of the soldiers who had been with him on the campaign. "It was the unanimous opinion of the officers in De Courcy's brigade that this trouble actually grew out of jealousy caused by the brilliant result of De Courcy's tactics," Lieutenant Colonel McFarland of the 86th Ohio Infantry later claimed. "It will be borne in mind that 2500 men, well protected by rifle-pits, forts, and cannon, had surrendered to 800, who were without effective support of any kind."[36] The injustice meted out to De Courcy so grieved his old regiment that on December 19 the officers and men of the 16th Ohio Volunteer Infantry presented him with a commemorative sword, sash, and belt. Captain Hamilton Richeson declared:

> Officers there are who command the confidence of those under them, but who cannot win their respect. Others have the respect of the men but not their confidence. You, sir, not only possess the confidence, but also the respect of the soldiers of your regiment. . . . Indeed, through all the vicissitudes, dangers, privations and vexations of a soldier's life, while you were with the regiment you made so perfect, your conduct was admirable.[37]

De Courcy had always hoped that he would win their respect, though devotion had seemed out of the question because of his famously disciplinarian style. The 16th's parting gift demonstrated that he had achieved far more than he had believed possible. "If I did well it was because they did better," he replied. "Under fire they were ever firm, cool and self-reliant." De Courcy's Civil War experiences had been harsh and frequently heartbreaking, but were by no means in vain. The soldiers he had tried so hard to mold into idealized versions of British troops remained proudly and defiantly true to their American roots; rather, it was De Courcy himself who was transformed into an officer and leader worthy of his men.*

---

* In early 1864, De Courcy submitted his resignation. He received an ordinary discharge on February 19, which, after protests, was amended to an honorable discharge on March 3. He was forty-four years old. More than half his life had been spent in the service of one army or another, and he could not imagine beginning a new life in business or farming. De Courcy chose to go home to England. His future prospects were slim. But there was still one career open to him: he could marry well. On May 10, 1864, De Courcy married Elia, Comtesse du Bosque de Beaumont, a French widow of independent means.[38]

———

General Meade had suffered the misfortune of embarking on his new campaign against Lee the day after eastern newspapers reported Grant's boast that his army was "driving a big nail in the coffin of the rebellion." Meade had learned that the Confederate Army of Northern Virginia, which was little more than half the size of the 80,000-strong Army of the Potomac, was encamped in two separate locations some thirty miles apart. His plan was to creep across the Rapidan River, strike at one Confederate corps with all his might, and then quickly go after the other. But gross incompetence by one of his generals, who became lost, and miserable weather, which slowed down the others, wrecked Meade's beautiful design. By the time all the Federals were across the river and in place, Lee had his full army ready and properly entrenched. The area, known as Mine Run, was only eight miles from Chancellorsville. It was a thickly wooded area divided by a stream that ran into the Rapidan River. When Meade surveyed his army's position on November 30, he knew in his heart that he had failed. Though Lee had fewer than fifty thousand men at his disposal, they were expertly placed behind impregnable defenses. A soldier from Massachusetts looked across at the Confederate works and "felt death in my very bones."[39]

Meade made the courageous decision to call off the attack, though he knew he would be dubbed a coward by the Northern public, and quietly pulled his army back over the Rapidan. During the retreat a sudden freeze almost paralyzed the Army of the Potomac. The 7th Maine Infantry, young Frederick Farr's regiment, suffered its worst night of the war as it crossed the Rapidan on December 1. "We halted after marching for a short time, and the night being intensely cold we made fires," wrote a friend of Frederick's. "This was the last that has been seen or heard of him. It is supposed that wearied out by the exceptional hardships he had undergone, he fell asleep by one of the fires and did not awake till the rebel cavalry came up to him and took him prisoner, as the Rebs followed close at our heels."[40] No one had received word from Frederick, but it was assumed that he was in one of the prisons near Richmond.

The Army of the Potomac retired to its winter camps, which were spread out between the two "Raps," the Rappahannock and Rapidan rivers. The Army of Northern Virginia followed suit on the other side of the Rapidan, and out west, the opposing armies under Grant and Johnston did the same. There would be no more fighting until the spring. Although the Federal offensive in Virginia had not materialized, it was Lee rather than Meade who was on the defensive, and the same pattern was being repeated all over the South. Charleston held, despite the continued bombardment of its forts, but the question was for how much longer. Wilmington was still open, but Mobile and Galveston, though nominally under Confederate control, were receiving only a trickle of blockade runners. John Jones, the War Department clerk in Richmond, had heard that the capture rate was one in four blockade runners; "we can afford that," he wrote.[41] But Jones had also heard in the War Department that soldiers were threatening to desert in order to feed their families and protect their farms. Grant's victory at Chattanooga had given the Union a base from which to attack not only the heart of the South, but also its munitions and gunpowder factories in Georgia.

Fredericksburg, Chancellorsville, and Chickamauga—the three Confederate victories in 1863—had not taken the South one step closer to independence, whereas Gettysburg had restored the morale of the Northern public, and Vicksburg had showed that victory was possible. "The signs look better," Lincoln wrote after the Mississippi River was reopened to travel and commerce. "The Father of Waters again goes unvexed to the sea." Much of Mississippi, Tennessee, West Virginia, and Virginia north of Fredericksburg were under Union control; the Gulf and Atlantic coasts were also closed off from the Confederacy; and Texas, Arkansas, and most of Louisiana were inaccessible to Richmond. But these advantages seemed less certain when the core of the Confederacy—Virginia, the Carolinas, Georgia, and Alabama—remained intact; two formidable Confederate armies and the great Robert E. Lee were at Davis's disposal; and the fighting spirit of the South remained unbroken.

PART III

If Only We
Are Spared

TWENTY–SEVEN

Buckling Under Pressure

Time for a vacation—The Alabama*—The Irish—Confederate woes in Europe—The Liberal government clings to power*

"They are wearing out, down there," Henry Adams wrote to his brother Charles Francis Jr. after *The Times* published Francis Lawley's reports from Tennessee. "He says it took him forty hours to go by rail the hundred and thirty miles from Atlanta to Chattanooga, in the filthiest, meanest cars he ever saw."[1] The effects of the Federal blockade were far worse than Henry knew. The Confederate government cupboards were practically bare: in recent months the purchasing orders for its agent James Bulloch in Liverpool had broadened from military supplies to include such ordinary items as "one dozen erasers," "two dozen memorandum books of different sizes, and 12 dozen best lead pencils."[2]

Francis Lawley was feeling worn out himself. After three years of reporting from the field, he had decided to take a leave of absence in the New Year. He stayed in the Confederate capital over Christmas while his friends Frank Vizetelly and Fitzgerald Ross went to the headquarters of Confederate general Jeb Stuart near Orange Court House in Virginia. The celebrations were not as jolly as those of the previous Christmas, though Stuart chivalrously lent them his own tent, and Ross was delighted to meet Stuart's new assistant inspector general of the cavalry corps, Colonel George St. Leger Grenfell. After their visit, Ross wrote that the English cavalry officer had "told us some capital stories of his various adventures. . . . The Colonel . . . has only lately been transferred to this army, and looks back with regret to the stirring and fighting time when he was with [General John Hunt] Morgan in the West . . . [they] adored their 'fighting old Colonel,' and would have followed him anywhere."[3]

Grenfell had failed to achieve the same popularity among Stuart's men. When the Englishman had resurfaced in Richmond after his mysterious disappearance from Bragg's army, his value as an expert cavalryman convinced the Confederate authorities not to prosecute him for his original crime of helping a slave to escape, or for having jumped bail ahead of his trial. But Grenfell's placement on Stuart's staff in September caused fierce resentment among the tight-knit group. By the time Ross met Grenfell, the colonel had become so fed up with his treatment that he was on the verge of joining forces again with General Morgan. The Kentucky raider's recent escape from a Federal prison in Ohio had raised his reputation in the South still higher, and hundreds of volunteers were answering his invitation to form a new guerrilla outfit.[4]

After Christmas, Ross and Vizetelly returned to Richmond to say goodbye to Lawley. Though his spirits were waning, those of Richmond society were not; amateur theatricals were the craze that winter. Vizetelly had been the mainstay of every production—painting scenery, rehearsing songs, adapting parts, and sometimes even acting. On January 12, 1864, he performed in a comedy before a select audience that included President Davis and General Stuart. Vizetelly's part "was to dandle and stifle the cries of a screaming baby," wrote the diarist Mary Chesnut, while three soldiers behind a curtain simulated the child's cries. "When Mr. Vizetelly had exhausted all known methods of quieting an infant (in vain), his despair was comic. He threw the baby on a chair and sat on it," prompting great roars of laughter.[5]

Two weeks after Lawley left for England, Vizetelly realized that he, too, was exhausted and should return home to rest before the fighting resumed in the spring. In his last dispatch from the South, Vizetelly admitted that his two years in the Confederacy had affected him more than any other assignment; "every soldier of the army of Northern Virginia was a comrade. We had marched many weary miles together, and I had shared in some of their dangers," he wrote. "This brought me nearer to them than years of ordinary contact could have done." As he rode away from Jeb Stuart's camp in late January, Vizetelly stopped to look back at

Winter quarters of Jeb Stuart's cavalry, by Frank Vizetelly, who sketches himself on the left.

the little gathering of tents, suddenly afraid for "the many friends who were lying there, some of whom would breathe their last in the first glad sunshine of [the] coming spring."[6]

As Lawley and Vizetelly made their separate journeys across the Atlantic, each having run the blockade at Wilmington, news of CSS *Alabama*'s latest raids on Northern ships was spreading. Captain Raphael Semmes daily expected to see a Federal fleet bearing down on the *Alabama,* but none came. "My ship had been constantly reported, and any one of his clerks could have plotted my track . . . so as to show [Gideon Welles] where I was bound." Instead, laughed Semmes, the U.S. navy secretary played an endless and unwinnable game of chase. All Semmes had to do was estimate how long it would take for intelligence of his whereabouts to reach Washington and make sure he left ahead of his pursuers.[7]

Since the Confederate commerce raider's launch in 1862, Semmes had burned or released on bond forty-two vessels, sunk the gunboat USS *Hatteras* at Galveston, and converted one captured vessel into a satellite raider (the *Tuscaloosa* would have a short career of six months and take only one prize). But by the summer of 1863 the *Alabama* and its crew were showing signs of battle fatigue. Still searching for prey, Semmes sailed down to Cape Town, South Africa, where to his surprise and relief he and his crew were fêted as heroes. Nothing so exciting or glamorous had visited Cape Town for a very long time, and the residents of this lonely outpost of the British Empire could hardly believe their good fortune. They were so welcoming—inviting the Southerners on big game and ostrich hunts—that twenty-one sailors deserted, leaving Semmes with a serious shortage of men. After much scraping around, his executive officer, 1st Lieutenant John McIntosh Kell, was able to find only eleven replacements. Fortunately, two Prussian naval officers who had been shipwrecked near Cape Town also joined as master's mates.[8] The appearance of the gunboat USS *Vanderbilt* off the Cape put an end to the *Alabama* crew's two-month respite from their harsh life at sea. At midnight on September 24, the ship set sail during a heavy gale for the fertile hunting grounds of the Far East, where Semmes knew he was not expected.[*]

An article entitled "Our Cruise" in the *Southern African Mail* by George Townley Fullam, one of the English officers on board the *Alabama,* eventually reached England in the autumn. Fullam described the ship's adventures, from her narrow escape from Liverpool harbor in July 1862 to her glorious entry into Cape Town twelve months later. Embarrassingly for the British government, Fullam claimed that someone in Her Majesty's Customs had alerted the Confederates to the *Alabama*'s pending seizure, allowing her to get away in time. Not surprisingly, the U.S. legation was incensed by this revelation. Charles Francis Adams ordered the article to be printed as a pamphlet and for a copy to be sent to Lord Russell with a strongly worded complaint attached.

Although Russell insisted to Adams that the British government could not be held responsible for the depredations of the *Alabama,* pri-

---

[*] That same night, in the Kell household, far away in McIntosh County, Georgia, six-year-old Jonny Kell cried as his mother buried his little sister, Dot, near the house. Jonny's younger brother, three-year-old Munroe, was too shocked to speak. Jonny frightened his mother by saying he wished to join "little Sissy" in heaven. Four days after her daughter's death, Mrs. Kell was relieved to hear that Munroe had regained his words. "Jonny, you may have my marbles," he said, "I don't want them any more." That evening he showed the classic signs of diphtheria. He was dead by the morning. "Oh God have mercy on my desolate broken heart," wrote Lieutenant Kell's despairing wife. "He has been gone so long, so long! Three long sad years."[9]

NEUTRALITY.

Mrs. North. "HOW ABOUT THE *ALABAMA*, YOU WICKED OLD MAN?"
Mrs. South. "WHERE'S MY RAMS? TAKE BACK YOUR PRECIOUS CONSULS—THERE!!!"

The Union and the Confederacy both rail at a determinedly calm John Bull, *Punch*, November 1863.

vately he was worried that the United States might carry out its threat—first made by Seward and Adams in 1862—to sue Britain for damages after the war.[10] Russell discussed with the law officers whether they should bar the raider from all British ports around the world, but in their opinion such a move could be interpreted as an admission of guilt regarding the *Alabama*'s escape. Russell was relieved when an alleged violation of British neutrality at Queenstown, Ireland—involving USS *Kearsarge* and sixteen Irish stowaways—for once reversed the direction of complaints, giving him the opportunity to play the injured party with the U.S. legation.*

---

* Captain John Ancrum Winslow had been searching for James Morgan's ship, the *Georgia,* when storm damage forced USS *Kearsarge* to put into Queenstown, Ireland, on November 3 for emergency repairs. While it was there, a local newspaper printed a story that the U.S. ship had come expressly to enlist volunteers. The following day the *Kearsarge* was surrounded by rowboats filled with men clamoring to be chosen. The *Kearsarge* set sail on November 5 with sixteen extra men. Winslow's explanation of the incident failed to say how the sixteen climbed aboard unnoticed and managed to find such perfect hiding places on an unfamiliar ship.

The British government was fully aware that large numbers of Irish-men were enlisting in the Federal army; Consul Archibald had observed the crowds at Castle Garden, the immigration depot on the southern-most tip of Manhattan, and estimated that every week, 150 Irish laborers were stepping off the boat and into the arms of recruiters.[11] A Home Of-fice clerk compiling passenger statistics first spotted the phenomenon in April 1863, when he noticed a sharp increase—it had almost tripled since 1862—in the number of single male travelers. After carefully reviewing all the statistics from the past three years, the Home Office discovered that the actual increase in the emigration of unmarried Irishmen was roughly ten thousand a year (a figure the government decided it could accept without too much heartache).[12]

The Confederate government was also concerned about the vast in-flux of Irish immigrants to the North, and in August 1863 sent its propa-gandist in France, Edwin De Leon, to Ireland, where he diligently spent several weeks publishing articles about the horrors of the war. James Mason followed in September, but his findings confirmed their worst fears. The Irish were so poor after two failed harvests, Mason wrote to the Confederate secretary of state, Judah P. Benjamin, on September 4, 1863, "that the temptation of a little ready money and promise of good wages would lead them to go anywhere."[13] But the draft riots in New York in mid-July had given Benjamin hope that it was not too late to stem the tide. The accusation that the U.S. government was throwing its Irish immigrants into the slaughtering pen was gaining credibility fol-lowing the near obliteration of the Irish Brigade at Fredericksburg and Gettysburg. Benjamin dispatched to Ireland two more agents, Lieu-tenant James Capston, a former Dubliner, and Father John Bannon of Vicksburg, with orders to discourage Irish immigration using all means at their disposal.

The exposure of the stowaways on the *Kearsarge* had been Lieutenant Capston's first success. But he could not uncover any proof for the Home Office that Captain Winslow had acted deliberately, nor did he find evidence of official Federal recruiting in Ireland. (The U.S. govern-ment had no need to send over agents when there were plenty of un-scrupulous entrepreneurs ready to assume the risk themselves in return for a large cut of the bounty paid for volunteers.) Capston and Bannon soon gave up that particular line of attack and concentrated instead on spreading anti-Northern propaganda. The two Confederate agents tried to tap into Irish nationalist sentiment by comparing the South's fight for independence with Ireland's. They distributed thousands of handbills warning potential emigrants that they would end up as cannon fodder if they went to the North. Father Bannon used his church connections to ensure that the injustices endured by the Irish community in the North were broadcast from the pulpit. Although emigration continued apace, the agents successfully rubbed off any glamour in volunteering for the North.

———

The danger of having their arms shipments seized by the U.S. Navy and their commerce raiders impounded by the government had driven the Confederates' activities in Britain underground. "The cheapest and most favorable market, that of England, was well nigh closed to the Confederacy, while the United States were permitted to buy and ship what they liked, without hindrance, and at the ordinary current prices," complained James Bulloch in his memoirs.[14] Matthew Fontaine Maury had hoped to launch a second Confederate cruiser, CSS *Rappahannock,* but he was forced to send the vessel from Sheerness, Kent, on November 24, 1863, with its hull and boilers still needing work simply to prevent its seizure by the authorities. The cruiser just managed to reach Calais, where it had remained since December, awaiting repairs.

The blockade was also drastically inhibiting the South's communications. Rose Greenhow had been in Paris since December, trying to arrange an interview with Emperor Napoleon III: "I would write you many interesting particulars," she wrote to a friend in Virginia, "but the publication of the late intercepted letters is a good warning to me to be careful. If you will get from Mr. Benjamin a cipher and use my name as the key, I can then tell you many things."[15] The "intercepted letters" were those from CSS *Robert E. Lee,* which had been caught on November 9, 1863, on its twenty-first trip between Wilmington and Nassau. The U.S. Navy also captured the Confederate Ordnance Department's two remaining supply ships the same night, but the real prize was the *Lee.* On board were two lieutenants from the Royal Artillery, the Belgian consul, and a mailbag containing dispatches from James Mason for the Richmond cabinet.[16] The mailbag also included the private correspondence of his colleague Edwin De Leon, which revealed every aspect of his propaganda campaign—from his attempts to bribe French journalists to his methods of spreading disinformation. But by the time De Leon's letters appeared in the New York and London press, the disgraced agent was already on his way back to the South, having been dismissed by Jefferson Davis not for the exposure, but for criticizing Judah Benjamin, who had taken the side of John Slidell in the acrimonious relations between the two agents.

Slidell had refused to work with De Leon after he learned that the propaganda agent had opened and read Confederate dispatches intended for him alone. Convinced that De Leon was after his position, Slidell tried to undermine him at every opportunity. He was equally hostile toward Rose Greenhow and discouraged his wife from helping her find a school for her daughter. (Eventually Rose accomplished the task on her own, placing little Rose in the Convent du Sacré Coeur, a Catholic boarding school with many foreigners among its two hundred girls.)[17] Slidell's suspicions about De Leon were groundless, but he was right to be fearful of interference from Rose: "I have come to the conclusion that we have nothing to hope from this side of the Channel," she wrote to President Davis on January 2, 1864.[18] The French mission was a waste of time and resources, she concluded: Slidell cared more about his social life than Confederate diplomacy, and Mason's grasp of French was too poor for him to be effective in Europe. She advised Davis to recall Slidell and send Mason back to London before the work of two years withered on the vine.

Rose thought Louis-Napoleon's sympathy was entirely mercenary: "They want tobacco now quite as much as the English want cotton . . . and I believe that if we were to stop the going out of either cotton or tobacco, it would have more effect than anything else."[19] Having failed to reach the emperor through friends or contacts, she audaciously wrote to him on January 11 requesting a meeting, and much to Slidell's annoyance, she was granted an interview at the Tuileries on the twenty-second. The little drama was observed by the Maryland journalist W. W. Glenn, who, having spirited Lawley, Vizetelly, and a host of other British visitors across Southern lines, was now in Paris visiting a friend. Glenn's own feelings about Rose were ambivalent—he had seen her once before in Mason's company and thought her "a handsome woman, rouged and elaborately gotten up"—but he was still amused by Slidell's consternation over her success with the emperor:

> Slidell, the moment he heard she was to have an audience, was so afraid of the apparent influence of the woman . . . that she might

injure him at Richmond by her letters, or on her return home, and thus perhaps effect his recall which he by no means desired, that he immediately went and left his card; and although he had declared she should not set . . . foot in his house or know his family, he sent Mrs. S. to call upon her too. When she went to have her interview, Mr. S. sent Eustis, his secretary of legation, with her to present her. She had them in fact all at her feet.[20]

Louis-Napoleon was not only charming and sympathetic—taking the Confederate heroine's hand and gently seating her on a cushion next to him—but he also surprised her with the depth of his knowledge about the war. "Tell the President," she recorded him as saying, "that I have thoughts on his military plans—he has not concentrated enough. The Yankees have also made true blunders. If instead of throwing all your strength upon Vicksburg you could have left that to its fate and strengthened Lee so as to have taken Washington, the war would have ended." He continued to be charming even when she asked him directly whether he would recognize the Confederate States. "I wish to God I could," Louis-Napoleon answered. "But I cannot do it without England."[21] At the end of their conversation, the emperor escorted Rose to the door and shook her hand. He seemed to be offering hope, and for a short while she was elated by the interview. She wrote in such glowing terms to Georgiana Walker in Bermuda that her friend recorded in her diary:

> Mrs. G. is much delighted with her visit to Paris, & considers her mission to have been a successful one. She had an audience of the Emperor, & was treated with marked attention. She says she advocated our cause warmly & earnestly, & left not one point uncovered; that the Emperor received her as one directly from the President; & bade her tell the President that his sympathy was all with him, & that he should do all in his power to aid him. The Empress says, "His Majesty is not averse to interviews with beautiful escaped prisoners." I have since heard that Mrs. Greenhow had attended a Ball at the Tuileries, & had supped in the room & perhaps at the table with their Majesties.[22]

But in reality the emperor had only uttered the same platitudes that Slidell had heard a dozen times before, and once Rose was able to reflect on the interview, she realized that she, too, had been fobbed off: "My belief is the stronger now that our only chance of recognition must now come from England and that, that is the place to which our efforts must be directed." She returned to London on February 6, 1864. "I left my little one behind and my heart was heavy," she wrote in her diary.[23] James Bulloch, who had arrived in France on January 27, escorted her to the station, helped her onto the train, and deposited her in the carriage reserved for women traveling alone. Aware of the heavy burdens upon him, Rose was touched by his courtesy.

Bulloch was too discreet to unburden himself, but he was that day suffering "a greater pain and regret than I ever thought it possible to feel."[24] He had crossed the Channel in a last-ditch effort to save the rams, which were still being held at Lairds in Liverpool. Since they belonged to a French subject, M. Bravay, the emperor could, in theory, request their return to France. But Louis-Napoleon refused to intervene. Slidell assumed that the emperor was simply paying lip service to Northern demands, but Bulloch knew better. "There was a good deal said about the personal sympathy of the Emperor for the South; and his earnest desire that by some means or other we might get our ships out," he wrote angrily after the war, but "the sympathy and hope were sheer mockery."[25]

The day after Rose's departure, on February 7, Bulloch sent a letter to Bravay authorizing him to sell the Lairds rams as quickly as possible. (It took several months, but after considerable haggling the Admiralty bought the ships for £180,000.) Bulloch's distress was not only for the loss of the rams; Slidell had decided that the ship construction operation was jeopardizing his relationship with the emperor and ordered Bulloch to sell the unfinished ironclads in Bordeaux. Determined not to be thwarted, Bulloch pretended to acquiesce while he sought a broker who would agree to buy the vessels on paper only.

Even legitimate Confederate enterprises were buckling under pressure. The price of the Confederate cotton bond had dropped precipitously, from £70 to £34, after Grant's victory at the Battle of Chattanooga and now fluctuated around the £50 mark. The cost of shipping supplies to the Confederacy and the increasing likelihood of capture were wiping out the profits of blockade running.[26] For the first time since the war, the survival of Fraser, Trenholm and Co.—the Southern shipping firm and financial clearinghouse for the Confederacy in Europe—appeared to be in doubt. "Every consignment to us is closely scrutinized and anything at all suspicious would be seized at once," Charles Prioleau in Liverpool explained to a would-be arms supplier. Nor could he extend further credit to the Confederate government, not even to purchase replacement blockade runners for the Ordnance Department. Prioleau calculated that if every available cotton bale arrived at Liverpool, the company would still be owed £70,000.

Six months earlier, the Confederate propaganda agent Henry Hotze had suggested to Benjamin that Richmond should assume control of all the Confederacy's international dealings, from arms supplying to blockade running. Now he begged the secretary of state to do it before the market damned the Confederacy for good. "Prohibit the exportation of cotton, except for Government account," he wrote. "Prohibit the importation of luxuries on any pretence, and import shoes and clothes as well for the citizens as the Army." Most important of all, he urged him to void all contracts that had not been negotiated by Colin McRae, the South's official purchasing agent.[27] With cotton selling for more than 23 shillings a pound (five years before, it had been worth only 7 pence), there were vast profits awaiting the Confederate government if it could put an effective export system in place.

Hotze also wanted to be rid of the South's official financial agent, Liverpool businessman James Spence, whose support for the abolition of slavery had become a burden and an embarrassment for the Confederates in England. The ardent supporter of Southern independence was roaring up and down the country in preparation for the opening of Parliament in February. Spence had studied the methods of the antislavery societies and was imitating them to good effect: publishing pamphlets before each meeting, preparing fact sheets for the local press, circulating petitions during the meeting, and creating local affiliates of his Southern Independence association.[28] The aim, he told Lord Wharncliffe, the head of the Manchester affiliate, was to make it seem as though pro-Southern feeling was increasing, since nothing should be allowed to dampen the already fragile spirits "of our people who of late have had much to dismay them." But all the good work had been ruined, in Hotze's opinion, by the Association's antislavery manifesto, which stated explicitly: "The Association will also devote itself . . . to a revision of the system of servile Labour, unhappily bequeathed to them by England, in accordance with the spirit of the age, so as to combine the gradual extinction of slavery with . . . the true civilisation of the negro race."[29] This, Hotze believed, was unacceptable and far outweighed Spence's success in attracting four peers and nine MPs to the committee.

James Mason hastily wrote to Benjamin from France that he had been unable to prevent the antislavery manifesto: the Southern Independence Association represented the "views of Englishmen addressed to English people . . . it was in vain to combat their 'sentiment.' The so-called 'antislavery' feeling seems to have become with them a 'sentiment' akin to patriotism."[30] Mason's defense was not enough to save Spence's position as financial agent, and his operations were transferred to Colin McRae. But Benjamin was so flattering and apologetic in his letter of dismissal on January 11 that the Confederacy was able to retain the Liverpudlian's goodwill. "As a man of the world," Benjamin wrote, "I would meet you on the most cordial terms without the slightest reference to your views on this subject; but . . . 'as a member of a government,' it would be impossible for me to engage you in its service after the publication of your opinions."[31] It helped that Benjamin agreed to reimburse Spence for the money he had expended on propping up the South's declining bonds.

"It is a singular feature of this struggle in America that its merits should be debated at popular meetings held all over this kingdom," Adams wrote to Seward shortly before the opening of Parliament. "The association of sympathizers with the Insurgents have of late been assiduously engaged in sending paid agents to deliver lectures in behalf of their cause at various places. This has given occasion to counter efforts. Frequently discussions are held by representatives of both sides. I very much doubt whether anything precisely similar ever took place before."[32]

Adams knew that the Confederacy's supporters were waiting for the new parliamentary session with great anticipation. The Liberal government appeared to be tottering toward collapse, and Palmerston had become mixed up in a bizarre divorce case.* Seward had also contributed to the British government's weakness. "That Solomon has . . . exercised his usual indiscretion," raged Benjamin Moran on February 11, 1864, after

---

* The eighty-year-old premier had been cited as the guilty party in the divorce proceedings of Timothy O'Kane against his wife, Margaret, prompting the society joke: "She was Kane, but was he Able?" Benjamin Disraeli grumpily predicted that the case—though spurious—would do wonders for Palmerston's popularity and no doubt give him a sweeping victory at the next election.

Seward included in the official publication of the State Department's correspondence for 1863 dispatches that were never sent to the Foreign Office, such as his provocative July letter on the Lairds rams.[33] By playing fast and loose with the State Department record of official dispatches, Seward had made any British concession seem like weakness in the face of Northern threats.

Fortunately for the government, the Tories did not mind castigating Russell for his handling of the Northerners, but they had no desire to be seen as the defenders of slavery, or of rebellion.[34] Nor were they by any means confident that their party had enough support in the House for a change of ministry.[35] Confronted by the possibility of a change in government, Charles Francis Adams decided that he preferred Palmerston to survive. Adams still attended Lady Palmerston's weekly parties with gritted teeth, but the sight of the eighty-year-old prime minister standing jauntily at the top of the grand staircase no longer oppressed him.

Adams's usual cynicism about British politics was in partial abeyance owing to a happy family event. Charles Francis Adams, Jr., had at last taken his furlough and come to England. The term of the 1st Massachusetts Cavalry had expired at the end of 1863, but Charles had encouraged his company to follow his example and reenlist. "They seem to think that I am a devil of a fellow," he wrote. "These men don't care for me personally. They think me cold, reserved and formal. They feel no affection for me, but they do believe in me, they have faith in my power of accomplishing results and in my integrity."[36]

Benjamin Moran envied Charles Francis Jr.'s assured deportment. "He is a sturdy weather tanned man of about 30 years—stout and strong with a bald head; and is a good deal taller than either his father or his brother Henry [and] is coming to Europe to dip into English society," he wrote in his diary. Moran's hope that it would only be a little dip was soon dashed. "Mr. Adams can't introduce his secretaries to their rights," he thundered, "but he and his wife go out of their way to *stuff* their son into every possible house in London, when he really has no business there."[37] At a party given by Lady de Grey, Moran sidled up to a crowd that included the poet Robert Browning and the artist John Everett Millais. "When, Lo! Mrs. Adams appeared forcing her way through followed by the Captain at her apron string. I was disgusted," he wrote. "She was in her element and talked as loud and vulgarly as ever. Holding her finger up and shaking it towards him, she said, 'here Charley, here, here,' and on his joining her presented him to Browning and Tom Hughes [the author of *Tom Brown's Schooldays*]. . . . I got out of the way and went down stairs."[38]

Moran was outraged when "the Captain" failed to pay a visit to the legation offices. "He is pure Adams," Moran wrote spitefully. But his opportunity for revenge on the family came sooner than he expected. Charles Francis Adams wished to take both his sons to the Queen's levee on March 2. "This morning," wrote Moran on March 1, "Mr. H. B. Adams came into the Legation and rather insolently insisted that he was entitled to outrank us at Court." Henry ought to have known that Moran would not allow a threat to his rank as assistant secretary to pass unchallenged. As a mere private secretary, Henry had no official rank.

"I even questioned the propriety of his going to Court at all—to say nothing about his right," recorded Moran. With extraordinary timing, Sir Edward Cust, the Queen's Master of Ceremonies, called at the legation at the height of the argument and confirmed that the right of attendance was extended only to daughters of ministers, not to sons or private secretaries. Naturally, exceptions were allowed, but unofficial private secretaries such as Henry Adams would certainly be ranked behind the last attaché or assistant secretary. Moran had been waiting to hear this ever since Henry's arrival. The look of triumph on the secretary's face was too much for Henry, and he swore never to go to court again. "I don't think anyone will regret that decision," wrote Moran smugly.[39]

Shortly after the altercation with Moran, Henry and Charles Francis Jr. left for Paris, "a city for pleasure," wrote Charles Francis Jr.[40] The brothers took every advantage of their freedom. Charles recorded that they spent their last night drinking a beautiful Burgundy "and started for London smiling and happy with wine." He was sober, though a little jaded, for his presentation at court on March 12. During the carriage ride, Charles further annoyed Moran by grumbling about the occasion. "This cant is abominable," wrote Moran afterward. "If he didn't know what he was going for, why in the name of decency did he go?"[41] Henry was still smarting from the argument and stayed at home.

———

Henry Hotze was pleased when he heard that the Reverend John Sella Martin and Andrew Jackson, both former slaves, had ended their lecture tours and were going home to America. Their presence had threatened to overshadow his successful infiltration of the down-market press. With sufficient funds, the South could be parlayed into a national cause, Hotze often told Benjamin:

> The North has two papers, one 3-penny and one penny paper, which it subsidizes lavishly. We also have two, a 3-penny one and a penny one, and in respectability, standing, and influence no one would venture to institute even a comparison between the respective champions. We have moreover the advantage over the subsidized writers of the North that our cause is pleaded with the force of personal conviction and with the zeal of personal friendship and political sympathy. . . . In the neutral press, both daily and weekly, we have also important connections, equally honorable, while the North, beyond its own organs, has nothing. All this, I unhesitatingly declare, is due to the *Index*.[42]

Hotze was also looking for ways to dilute the impact of Henry Yates Thompson's recent articles. Since his return from the battlefields of eastern Tennessee, Thompson had been writing for the *Daily News* and touring the country giving talks about his experiences in the North, somewhat to his family's embarrassment. Leslie Stephen was another irritant, since he was unafraid to take on the South's supporters at Cambridge and force them to defend their views on slavery. Neither man was an eccentric or a fanatic, and their opinions on the war could not easily be dismissed. Hotze hoped that Colonel Fremantle's *Three Months in the Southern States,* which had been published just before Christmas, would become so popular that dissenting voices would be ignored.[43] Still, even Fremantle's book contained passages that upset Hotze. At James Mason's request, Fremantle had removed passages that made the South seem foreign in English eyes, but he refused to take out his impressions of Southern slavery.[44]

Lawley's arrival in England in February briefly revived Hotze's hope of a propaganda coup. The journalist had been traveling for nearly three weeks, and the enforced rest had restored him to health. William Howard Russell saw him twice in the same week and noted that he was "in splendid fettle, grey but as clear and handsome as paint." His eloquent reports of the Confederacy's sufferings had won him a following of swooning females, but Russell was not deceived. Lawley, he wrote, was as "hard as nails."[45] However, Lawley could not afford to bring public attention to himself lest he alert his creditors. The best he could do for Hotze and the Confederates during the short time he dared spend in England was to speak privately to his former colleagues in Westminster. None of these meetings produced anything of substance, although his interview with Disraeli on February 19 had seemed promising at the time.[46]

At the beginning of March, Lawley passed through Paris on his way to Italy. Slidell reported to Benjamin that Lawley "had a long and very interesting interview with the Emperor. The Conversation turned entirely upon American affairs and was most satisfactory . . . the Emperor is prepared to take any action in our favor in concert with England, but adheres to his determination not to move without her cooperation."[47] *The Times* barely touched on American affairs while its special correspondent was away, and when it did, Hotze found the articles quite unsatisfactory. His impatience was shared by the managers of *The Times*. Mowbray Morris reluctantly granted Lawley an extra month's vacation in return for his promise to be in Virginia before the start of the spring campaigns.[48]

On March 25, Charles Francis Adams, Jr., set sail back to the United States. The brothers had been surprised by how much they enjoyed each other's company. Henry even accompanied him to Liverpool and waited on the tugboat as Charles Francis Jr.'s steamer pulled out of sight. "Henry nodded to me good-bye from the tug," wrote Charles Francis Jr., "and I, with a bitter taste . . . in my mouth, was off for home."[49] His departure for America was followed a few days later by that of Rose Greenhow for France. Little Rose sobbed when her mother appeared at the convent. Her distress made Rose dread the inevitable parting. "I know I ought not to be miserable," Rose wrote in her diary as she reflected on the decisions that had brought them to Europe, "and yet I am, and tears which I try to keep back flow down my cheek and blind me."[50] On April 2 she celebrated little Rose's eleventh birthday with the one gift that her daughter craved above all: her undivided attention.

TWENTY–EIGHT

A Great Slaughter

Grant takes command—A disastrous campaign—Lord Lyons labors on—
The new volunteers—Return to the Wilderness—An unstoppable force

General Ulysses S. Grant arrived in Washington on March 8, 1864, to accept his promotion to lieutenant general. In giving him command of all the Union armies in the field, Lincoln promised that he would not interfere as long as the strategy remained one of relentless attack. They both knew that the South could not possibly compete with the North for manpower or resources.[1] The Capitol's gleaming new dome—finished on December 2, 1863—was a powerful advertisement for the healthy state of the U.S. Treasury, especially compared to the hyperinflation and financial chaos that were crippling the South.*

Yet the year had not begun well for the North: the Confederate cavalry under General Nathan Bedford Forrest had hampered Sherman's attempts to wreck Mississippi's rail system; a Union incursion into Florida was beaten back in late February; and in Charleston, the Federal navy encountered a new and potentially devastating weapon of war: the submarine. The experimental CSS *H. L. Hunley*—named after its inventor—sank the gunboat USS *Housatonic* during an evening attack on Feb-

---

* At the start of the war in 1861, one dollar in gold had equaled $1.10 in Confederate dollars; three years later in 1864, it equaled $20. At the same time, in the North, one gold dollar equaled $1.55 in U.S. greenbacks in 1864.

ruary 17. (All but five of the Federal crew survived, but the *Hunley* mysteriously sank during its return journey to Fort Moultrie, drowning the
six sailors inside. The tragedy dissuaded the Confederates from building
any more submarines.)

Grant had prepared a strategic plan for the next phase of the war: to
subdue the western half of the Confederacy first before moving east to
crush Lee's Army of Northern Virginia. But he discovered on his arrival
in Washington that Lincoln's promise not to meddle in military actions
contained qualifications. Lincoln, along with General Henry Halleck
(who had been relegated to the newly created administrative post of chief
of staff), wanted a major push up the Red River into Texas.

The fertile cotton plantations along the Red River were too enticing
for the administration to ignore. Lincoln also liked the idea of keeping
troops in Texas just in case the Confederates attempted to join forces
with the French in Mexico. The fall of Mexico City in June 1863 had effectively ended the Franco-Mexican War, although the victorious French
army was still fighting the defeated Juarist regime in parts of the country.
Archduke Ferdinand Maximilian, the younger brother of the Austrian
emperor Franz Joseph I, had been cajoled by Louis-Napoleon into accepting the imperial crown of Mexico and was due to arrive in the country sometime in April.* Even though Grant did not think either reason
was sufficiently compelling to deprive him of the forces he needed for an
attack against Mobile, Alabama—which he considered a vital stepping-
off point for capturing the rest of the state—Lincoln and Halleck went
ahead with their plan anyway.

On March 12, General Nathaniel Banks's troops began slogging from
Franklin, Louisiana, toward Shreveport, the Confederate capital of Louisiana since the capture of Alexandria in 1863. The campaign was a joint
army-navy expedition, with Admiral David Dixon Porter leading a
flotilla up the Red River to converge with Banks at Shreveport. Some of
the infantry regiments were only two months old. The 17th Infantry

---

* The emperor of the French breezily assured Maximilian that the United States was
"well aware that since the new regime in Mexico is the work of France they cannot
attack it without immediately making enemies of us." But Seward had nonetheless
let it be known through the U.S. minister in Paris that the United States would
never recognize a French puppet regime in Mexico—which put Louis-Napoleon
in a bind and complicated his relations with the Confederates. He could only support the South if its victory was assured; otherwise the new emperor of Mexico
would have a powerful and vengeful United States as his neighbor.[2]

Corps d'Afrique, for example, was made up of freed slaves from Nashville, Tennessee. Its officers were white volunteers from across the North, among them Dr. Charles Culverwell from New York.* The generous signing bonus of $227 had persuaded him to apply for the post; part of it paid for his photograph in a new uniform purchased specially for the expedition. Many years later, he made light of his participation in the Red River campaign, joking that he had expected to show off his crisp new jacket to the inhabitants of captured Confederate towns, only to find that the opportunity never came.

Few excursions in the war encountered so many mishaps or ended so ignominiously as Banks's Louisiana campaign. The start had been exceptionally smooth; he reached Alexandria on March 26 and immediately began to organize elections for the new pro-Union state legislature. But after that, nothing went right. This plan to revive economic ties between Southern plantation owners and the North was undone by Admiral Porter's officers, who seized all the cotton for themselves before the official cotton brokers, who accompanied Banks, had a chance to transact any legitimate business. Even the Red River turned against him; instead of rising to its usual winter levels, it began to shrink at a rapid rate. Porter just managed to haul his vessels over the rapids above Alexandria before the fast-emerging rocks made the journey impossible. The U.S. fleet ground to a halt near Grand Ecore, a small trading town perched atop a ninety-foot bluff, more than seventy miles from Shreveport. Banks was able to push his army a little farther upriver, but the single-track route he had chosen turned the journey into a slow-moving haul through foul slurry.

The Confederate general Richard "Dick" Taylor ended Banks's advance at the Battle of Mansfield on April 7, some forty miles south of

---

* After the death of his child during the draft riots in July, Culverwell had accepted a post at MacDougall Hospital in the Bronx, New York, so he could be close to his family. Still determined to try his luck as an actor, he had resigned in the autumn to join Mrs. John Wood's company at the Olympic Theatre in Manhattan. He promised his long-suffering wife that it would be his final attempt to conquer the stage. Mrs. Wood had given him the role of the ardent young poet in the burlesque *Brothers and Sisters*. Culverwell had never performed such lengthy speeches before, and his nervousness grew in anticipation of the first night. His opening speech began with the line "Drunk with enthusiasm I . . ." On October 8, Culverwell leaped onstage and declared, "Drunk." With that he died a thousand deaths, unable to utter another word. The next morning "Ma Wood" dismissed him, and Culverwell returned to the Federal army.[3]

Shreveport. Taylor had only 8,000 men against 12,000 Federals, but he was one of the ablest generals in the South and had already demonstrated his aggressive fighting skills while serving under Stonewall Jackson in 1862. In this campaign, Taylor also benefited from having several excellent subordinates, including the French aristocrat Prince Camille de Polignac (affectionately dubbed "Prince Polecat" by his Texan troops), who had volunteered for the South in 1861. The Confederates cost the Federals 2,000 men at Mansfield; the loss shattered Banks's confidence in the mission, and he ordered a general retreat, much to the chagrin of his own troops. His men never forgave him for making them look like cowards, and whenever he passed by marching columns he was greeted with rude songs and catcalls. Prevented from fighting the real enemy, Federal soldiers instead punished the surrounding communities, leaving a swath of burning homesteads all the way back to Alexandria. Porter's fleet was now stranded above the rapids, forcing Banks to stay put with his glowering army until the Red River rose or someone found a way to carry the ships over the rocks.

Toward the end of April, with Porter's ships still floating in three feet of water rather than the usual nine, Colonel Joseph Bailey, the acting military engineer of the XIX Corps, devised a complex plan for damming the river to create a surge over the falls. "This proposition looked like madness, and the best engineers ridiculed it," wrote Admiral Porter in his report. But Bailey convinced his superiors that the plan would work. On April 30, three thousand Federal troops began hacking and sawing. "Trees were falling . . . quarries were opened; flat-boats were built to bring stone down from above, and every man seemed to be working with a vigor I have seldom seen equalled," wrote Porter. He singled out a few officers and regiments for praise, in particular the 133rd New York and its English colonel, L.D.H. Currie, adding that "the noble men who succeeded so admirably in this arduous task, should not lose one atom of credit so justly due them."[4] With his wounds healed, Currie had decided against transferring to another command and was back once more with his men, guiding them through the perils of Banks's final campaign.

On March 1, Confederate troops near Richmond stopped a bold attempt by a small Union cavalry outfit to liberate the Federal prisoners in Belle Isle camp on the James River. One of the leaders of the expedition, Colonel Ulric Dahlgren, was killed during the retreat. Southerners were appalled that Dahlgren, who had strong family ties to the Confederacy, would turn against his own. Even more shocking was the discovery of papers on his body that outlined a plan to massacre the entire Confederate cabinet.[5]

The days of "Rosewater chivalry" were at an end, declared the *Richmond Enquirer* on March 5; henceforth the Confederacy must fight "barbarity with barbarity."[6] A week after Dahlgren's raid, Davis summoned Captain Thomas Hines, who had masterminded the prison escape of the Kentucky raider General John Hunt Morgan, to a secret meeting in Richmond. He ordered Hines to travel to Canada via Chicago and other cities in the Northwest to recruit propagandists and fighters for the South. Once in Canada, his mission was to collect the scattered survivors of Morgan's command, plus any displaced Southerners or former prisoners of war, and encourage them to rejoin the Confederate army. Hines could, in the carefully chosen words of the Confederate secretary of war, James Seddon, by "any fair and appropriate enterprises of war" engage in "any hostile operation" against the North.[7]

Hines presented Colonel Grenfell with a dilemma after he invited his former comrade to join his operations in Canada. At first, Grenfell felt honor-bound to keep his promise to serve Morgan as his adjutant general.[8] But the offer of adventure proved too enticing, and two weeks after Captain Hines received his departure orders, Grenfell resigned his commission and announced he was leaving the Confederacy. The resignation was obviously a contrivance, both to extricate him from his commitment to Morgan and as part of a scheme to make it appear that he was disenchanted with the South. His official disengagement from the Confederacy would theoretically enable Grenfell to travel without hindrance through the North, picking up information for Hines all the while.[9]

The Confederate government's willingness to violate British neutrality in Canada had increased after the unexpected arrival on April 1 of a special messenger sent by Lord Lyons carrying a letter from Lord Russell to Jefferson Davis. Seward had permitted this first and only direct communication between London and Richmond, no doubt amused by its humiliating content for the South. Russell had written a remonstrance to Davis for using British ports to build Confederate warships, and in his inestimable way he had managed to prick every sensitive part of Southern pride. The worst insult for Davis was Russell's continual references to "the so-called Confederate States." It was a week before Davis could

bring himself to answer Russell's letter, and even then he was so offended that he had his private secretary write on his behalf. In future,
Davis dictated to the secretary, any communication containing the
phrase "so-called Confederate States" would be returned without a reply.
British neutrality, he raged, was nothing more than "a cover for treacherous, malignant hostility."[10]

That same day, April 7, Davis sent a wire to Colonel Jacob Thompson, a former cabinet secretary under President Buchanan and a veteran
of Vicksburg, who had returned to his plantation in Oxford, Mississippi,
after its surrender. It read: "If your engagements will permit you to·ac-
cept service abroad for six months, please come here immediately."[11]
Thompson arrived a few days later and accepted the appointment of
"Commissioner for Special Service in Canada." The post was quite unlike Mason and Slidell's in Europe. Davis was not interested in playing
diplomatic games. Instead, Thompson's mission was to foment anti-
Northern feeling in Canada until it created a crisis in Anglo-American
relations. Davis also wanted him to supervise Thomas Hines's propaganda operations in the Northwest. The existence of the secret pro-
Southern society the Knights of the Golden Circle and its recent
offshoot, the Sons of Liberty, had convinced Benjamin and Davis that
there were tens of thousands, if not hundreds of thousands, of disaffected Midwesterners who, with the right encouragement and sufficient
funds, would take up armed resistance against the Republican administration.[12]

Jacob Thompson was an intelligent man but a poor judge of character and given to impulsive behavior. With proper oversight and a sufficiently large organization behind him, he might have been a good choice
for the post. But the deputy selected by Davis was Clement C. Clay, a
popular Alabama senator before the war, whose poor health and obsession with appeasing his spoiled wife made him an unsuitable candidate
for any sort of clandestine operation. Thompson needed a stronger and
steadier hand than Clay's, someone with more caution and a more cynical attitude toward the self-described Confederate agents currently making a nuisance of themselves in Canada. Davis had also entrusted
Thompson with $1 million in gold, far too large a sum to be under the
control of one person.

Thompson and Clay ran the blockade at Wilmington on May 5 without encountering any particular difficulty, despite Judah P. Benjamin's indiscreet letter to Slidell in Paris. "We have sent Jacob Thompson of Mississippi and Clement C. Clay of Alabama to Canada on secret service," he had written on April 30, "in the hope of aiding the disruption between the Eastern and Western States in the approaching election at the North. It is supposed that much good can be done by the purchase of some of the principal presses, especially in the North-West."[13]

———

A second important decision Jefferson Davis made in April was to recall General Beauregard from Charleston. Although Davis still loathed the Creole general, he had bowed to his friends' urgings to make use of Beauregard's popularity as the victor of First Manassas (Bull Run). Davis's own popularity had suffered since Bragg's defeat at Chattanooga, emboldening his enemies in the Confederate Congress. Davis could not afford to allow politically connected generals like Beauregard to remain disaffected.[14]

The news that he was being transferred to the command of the military operations in North Carolina and southern Virginia below Richmond caught Beauregard by surprise. Although he had felt sidelined in Charleston, he was anxious about leaving when the Federals were building up their fleet for another assault. He had so little confidence in his replacement, General Sam Jones, that he decided not to take all his staff with him in the hope that some continuity would be maintained. The English volunteer Captain Henry Feilden, whose admiration for the departing commander bordered on hero worship, was crestfallen to learn that he was one of those staying behind. The general called him to his office on April 19 to explain the situation, promising to send for Feilden if his new appointment became permanent. "I don't think I have any chance of getting to Virginia with him for some time, though I flatter myself that he has too much regard for me to debar me from sharing the privations and dangers of the field with him," Feilden wrote after the meeting.[15]

This was not what the recipient of the letters wished to hear. Feilden had recently become engaged to twenty-six-year-old Julia McCord, the daughter of the late congressman David James McCord—known in his day as "Handsome Davy"—who had been a powerful figure in South Carolina politics during the 1830s. Julia should have been brought up amid great comfort and security, but the early death of her parents had robbed her of both. Before meeting Feilden she had lived quietly and obscurely with a spinster cousin in Greenville, South Carolina.

Julia had fallen in love with Feilden when she visited his office in June 1863 to obtain a military pass to visit her half-brother. (She preserved the little piece of paper for the rest of her life.) Her effect on Feilden was equally dramatic: "I have only one thing to say and that is you must have no doubts of my love for you, darling," he promised in one of his earliest letters to her.[16] His protectiveness toward her extended to playing down the dangers that faced Charleston. "Don't be alarmed about my overworking myself, the business of the office is already decreasing," he lied on April 30. As soon as various troop movements had been completed, "we shall have a very quiet summer."[17] But with Beauregard gone, a Federal fleet of almost fifty ships gathering outside the harbor, and General Jones so short of manpower that the city's fire brigade was being used in place of real soldiers, there was no chance of a quiet or peaceful summer.[18]

———

"I doubt whether people in Europe are aware of the extent of the progress of this country in military strength," Lord Lyons had written to Russell during Grant's Chattanooga campaign. In answering Russell's question as to whether Britain could still defeat the United States in a war, Lyons had replied that any British invading force would be outnumbered "by five to one" and would have no chance of winning. But he did not "think the government here at all desires to pick a quarrel with us or with any European power."*[19] Lyons's conviction that an Anglo-American war was now unlikely did not mean that he was any less dispirited by his failure to change U.S. attitudes toward Britain. "It is not my purpose here to explain the bitter feelings of the great majority of the American people against England," he wrote to Russell on April 25. "The feeling is the less to be combated, because it is utterly unreasonable and

---

* Lord Lyons accepted the extra burdens placed upon the legation because of the war, but he refused to spy for the Foreign Office. When Lord Russell asked him to obtain drawings of the American-made Parrott gun, a new invention that showed destructive promise, he answered: "I consider it to be of the utmost importance that not only this Legation should not be employed in such practices, but that both myself and every other member of it should be absolutely and bona fide without any knowledge of their existence."

utterly regardless of facts or arguments."[20] Recently, *The New York Times* had speculated with undisguised glee on the hope of a war between Britain and Germany. A new German navy would arise, the newspaper predicted, "manned, equipped, and armed" in American ports.[21]

———

Lyons was not sure that he could stand living in Washington for much longer. He particularly missed the company of Henri Mercier, who had returned to France on New Year's Eve. ("His wife was so miserable here that she could bear it no longer," Lyons told his sister.)[22] Without the Merciers, Lyons's intimate social circle had contracted to the Russian minister, Baron Stoeckl, and his American wife, Elisa. More seriously, Lyons had grown to dislike his work at the legation. In early spring Lyons wrote a frank letter to Lord Russell expressing concern that he was no longer fit for the post. "I am worn out, and utterly weary of the whole thing," he confessed. "The people here too are beginning to get very tired of me; and I feel that if I can by any means get through this summer without breaking down in health, and without getting in to any very serious scrape, it will be as much as I shall be able to do."[23] Russell replied sympathetically and emphatically that Lyons belonged in Washington.

The legation staff were also tired, and demoralized by their inability to help or make contact with British subjects in the South. The anguish of ignorance was a common lament among families in Britain with relatives in Confederate prisons. Dr. William Farr had tried every possible approach to obtain news of his son, Frederick, who had been captured the previous December. After being informed by the legation that there was no communication between Washington and Richmond, he had befriended the Confederate community in England in the hope that someone would be able to pass along information. In late February, an agent working with the purchasing agent Caleb Huse wrote to the assistant commissioner of exchange in Richmond, Captain William Hatch, saying that "a good friend of our cause" was seeking to know if his son was still alive.[24] There were more than twenty prisons in and around Richmond. It would take some time for Captain Hatch to discover the whereabouts of Private Frederick Farr and, even if he was found, to convey the news to England. While the Farrs waited for news, not even knowing if the search was indeed under way, young Frederick became ill with typhus— a disease endemic in the filthy and overcrowded Southern prisons—and died on March 23, 1864.

———

"Suppose I were ill for a week," Lyons's attaché Edward Malet wrote despairingly to his mother. "I think it is rather hard upon me, for a Legation ought not to be left in such a condition that it cannot get on without one man."[25] The Foreign Office had refused to increase the number of attachés and yet had denied them holiday leave on the grounds that the legation was dangerously overstretched.[26] Most of the new work was coming from a steep rise in forced enlistment cases and arrests of British subjects for desertion. "Every effort has been made by us to obtain redress for those which have appeared to be well founded," Lyons assured Lord Russell. "In few cases, however, have our efforts produced any satisfactory results." The form was always the same:

> The remonstrances addressed by me to the Sec of State are duly acknowledged and transmitted to the War or the Navy Department. The Department orders an investigation. . . . I do my best to elicit the truth, and to obtain evidence—a controversial correspondence between the US government and me ensues. The Department always claims that the men were willing volunteers; the Government accepts the statement, and the men are retained.[27]

Lyons cited as an example the case of sixteen-year-old Henry Usher, the grandson of Admiral Usher, who was kidnapped by crimpers while on his way to a job interview at the British consulate in New York. With the legation's help, Consul Archibald had eventually tracked Usher down in Beaufort, South Carolina, where the boy had been enlisted in the 5th New York Heavy Artillery as "John Russell."[28] This had been in January, and four months later the War Department was still dragging its feet.

If it required strenuous efforts for the overworked legation to rescue a British subject from the armed services, the circumstances had to be extraordinary for a Briton to be released from prison—such as the presidential pardon given to Alfred Rubery in December. Rubery's guilt in the attempted seizure of the *J. M. Chapman* in California was undeniable, but the request to Federal authorities for his release had come from John Bright, whose photograph was currently hanging above the mantelpiece in Lincoln's office. The official decree announcing the pardon declared that the president's decision should be regarded "as a public mark of the esteem held by the United States of America for the high character and steady friendship of the said John Bright." The unabashedly pro-Southern Rubery also had his $10,000 fine commuted so long as he left the country within thirty days and made no attempt to help or enter the Confederacy.*

Lyons would never have championed Rubery's release if it had been up to him; as a rule, he refused to bother Seward with cases involving self-described British Confederate volunteers. "To do so," Lyons told Lord Russell, after the Foreign Office forwarded a protest from Private Joseph Taylor, a Yorkshireman who had been incarcerated in Fort Delaware since Vicksburg, "could in fact hardly fail to cause annoyance. There are, I am sorry to say, a very large number of British Subjects who are Prisoners of War as Mr. Taylor is, and who, like him, entered the Confederate Service in disobedience to the Queen's commands, and in defiance of Her Majesty's warning that they would do so at their peril."[30] However, Seward was not entirely deaf or blasé about the myriad injustices created by the war. British prisoners of war in Federal hands were given the option of swearing an oath of allegiance to the United States in exchange for their release.†[31] Hundreds of British prisoners took advantage of the oath.

Lyons suspected that forced enlistments in the Federal army would continue until the War Department ceased to regard the practice as a necessary evil to make up for the shortfalls in the draft. But there were signs that the sheer volume of crimping was beginning to have an adverse impact on the army. After watching the execution of two such victims for

---

* Bright also used his influence to rescue seventeen-year-old Alfred Massey Richardson. Alfred had been working for the chairman of the Union and Emancipation Society of Manchester. The previous August, his head filled with ideas about freeing the slaves, Alfred and a friend, Stephen Smelt, had run off to New York. They both joined the 47th New York Volunteers, but not before being beaten up and robbed of their bounty money. "Can you undertake to obtain [Richardson's] discharge?" Bright wrote to Sumner on the same day that Lincoln signed Rubery's pardon. "I think Mr. Stanton will be able to spare so young a boy, if you apply to him." Sumner took Bright's request literally and secured the release of Richardson but neglected to mention young Smelt, to the grief of his parents.[29]

† The North had ceased conducting prisoner exchanges with the South, ostensibly in protest against Confederate mistreatment of colored soldiers. But with 611,000 men under arms, the North could afford to have several thousand penned up, whereas the South, whose total armed force did not exceed 277,000, could not. Many British prisoners were relieved by the halt to the exchanges. Presented with the choice between a Federal prison and return to the South, they often preferred to stay in prison.

attempting to desert, General Isaac Wistar sent a protest to General John Dix in New York about the dishonest recruiting practices in the city:

> Nearly all are foreigners, mostly sailors both ignorant of and in-
> different to the objects of the war in which they thus suddenly
> find themselves involved [he wrote]. Two men were shot here
> this morning for desertion; and over thirty more are now awaiting
> trial or execution. These examples are essential as we all under-
> stand but, it occurred to me, General, that you would pardon me
> for thus calling your attention to the great crime committed in
> New York of kidnapping these men into positions where, to their
> ignorance, desertion must seem like a vindication of their rights
> and liberty.*[32]

The lax discipline and poor attitude of the new recruits and draftees was also a problem for the Federal army. "If I was in England or in the English service I should consider that it was a shame and a sin to desert," wrote the English volunteer James Horrocks. But here, "in the land of Yankee doodle," desertion is "regarded universally as a *smart thing* and the person who does it a *dem'd smart fellow.*"[33] Yet Horrocks was a soldier of uncommon ability and rectitude compared to James Pendlebury, who enlisted as a private in the 69th New York Infantry on January 27. Pendlebury was an unemployed mill worker from Lancashire with a family, a drinking problem, and a gamey leg. At home he used to spend every night in the pub boring the regulars until "one day I was talking energetically about the Slaves and full of fire when my comrades said I ought to go to America," recalled Pendlebury. "One said he would give me twopence if I would go and others also offered pennies."[34]

Pendlebury collapsed upon arriving in New York and spent several weeks in the hospital. After his discharge he was arrested for drunken-ness in Jersey City. The judge agreed to waive the fine if Pendlebury en-listed: "A policeman came with me to see that I really did enlist.

---

* The passenger line Cunard, for example, was losing sailors faster than it could re-place them. The company's chairman, Sir Edward Cunard, ordered his lawyers to help rescue the drafted men although he despaired at finding many of them. "The truth is that the English are in a much worse position here than any other nation," he wrote to an MP. Cunard acknowledged that Consul Archibald was working hard, but Lord Lyons, he complained, was "entirely too easy going and diplomatic."

However, when I went under the standard, I was too short. They . . . ran me down to Williamsburg and there I was big enough to join the 69th New York Irish Brigade. . . . On joining I got 400 dollars down, so I thought I would send it home." Instead, he spent it on whiskey. When the money ran out, Pendlebury's ailments returned. The members of the Irish 69th were familiar with the problem:

> Now if there is a drinker here [wrote Pendlebury], he will know how dreadful he feels after a spree, when he is nearly dying and can't get any more drink—that was how I felt. When [the guard] answered I looked up into his face and said, "Can you save a life because I fear I shall be dead before morning." He asked me what I meant, so I told him. He then poured me a tea cup of whisky and I drank it and fell asleep.[35]

Pendlebury had found a home for himself, and despite his English nationality, his Irish comrades accepted him among their ranks, finding an alcoholic volunteer preferable to a reluctant conscript.[36]

Edward Lyulph Stanley, the headstrong younger son of the British postmaster general, Lord Stanley, arrived in Washington on April 14, 1864, having spent three weeks in New York listening to strangers make pointed comments about England's treachery.* He had not been the slightest bit fazed, being able to hold his own in any arena. According to family lore, when young Lyulph was five years old, "he was one day naughty and scolded by his mother; when she had finished, he said, 'Proceed, you interest me.' "[38] "Stanley is a clever young man," wrote Lord Wodehouse after being introduced to him in 1862, "& will be very pleasant when he has rubbed off a little juvenile conceit, which however is pardonable, as he has just taken a first class at Oxford. He is a staunch Northerner which is singular and a finer Radical. I like to see a young man begin with rather extreme opinions. They 'tone' down fast

---

* When Fitzgerald Ross arrived in New York at the end of April, he was warned by the *Times* correspondent Charles Mackay not to discuss the war or politics in New York because of the vicious differences in opinion. "It is considered very mauvais genre" to bring up either topic, he wrote. The safest way to begin a conversation was "to abuse England, which everyone is glad to do, and as everybody agrees on this point, there is no difference of opinion."[37]

enough."[39] But Stanley was showing no signs of toning down. He visited the Adamses before his departure and exhausted them all with his rapid, earnest talk about American politics.[40]

Seward was treated to a similar verbal onslaught when he invited Stanley to dinner on April 17. In contrast to Lord Edward St. Maur, Stanley saw no need to be circumspect simply because of his father's position in Palmerston's cabinet, and he grilled Seward on every subject that arose. "Mr. Seward struck me as sharp and on the whole a kindly amiable man," wrote Stanley after the encounter, "but rather shrewd than really able or wide in his views, and prone to be captious and technical instead of statesmanlike in his way of handling great questions." He was far more impressed by Lincoln, who, he wrote, "spoke very reasonably and without any vulgarity tho' with some quaintness and homeliness of expression."[41] The president obviously warmed to the Englishman, since he allowed his private secretary John Hay to take the next morning off to show Stanley around Washington. (They went to General Lee's former home, Arlington, which by Stanley's standards was "dirty and small.") Hay's opinion of England had been colored by Lawley's reports, Stanley noticed with regret. He discovered, like every visitor before him, that "Americans see hardly any English newspaper but *The Times,* which is considered here as the true exponent of English opinion."

Stanley had come to America to learn how British supporters might help the soon-to-be-emancipated slave population, but he was not averse to visiting the front lines, too. On Friday, April 22, he took the train to Brandy Station in Culpeper County, Virginia, to visit the Army of the Potomac. Waiting for him at the station was Charles Francis Adams, Jr. Captain Adams's contempt for his commanding officers had finally made him accept a transfer to General Meade's cavalry escort, which meant that he was in a position to introduce Stanley to both Meade and General Grant. The former, wrote Stanley, was "a thorough gentleman and very captivating," the latter "very modest and unassuming in manner" but clearly a man of "character and a will of his own." In conversations about the future of Negroes in the army, Grant was honest about his initial doubts and why he had changed his mind in their favor after observing how well they fought as soldiers at Vicksburg.

Stanley spent two days with Charles Francis Jr. The monotony of camp life surprised him: the soldiers' daily routine seemed cheerfully domestic, and wintertime relations between the Federal and Confederate armies were strangely cordial. "I am told there is a most friendly feeling between the [opposing] armies," wrote Stanley; "it is almost impossible to prevent their mixing, and exchanging coffee and tobacco and playing cards together, though there are very strict orders against it."*[42] Unlike every other visitor to the Army of the Potomac before him, he had no interest in staying to watch it fight. He was anxious instead to visit New Orleans to see how the city's emancipated blacks were faring under Northern rule. He left Meade's headquarters as hundreds of covered supply wagons were being assembled in long lines.

Charles Francis Jr. was not sure whether they were preparing to attack Lee or taking precautionary measures in case of a sudden move by the Confederates. "The feeling about Grant is peculiar," he noticed; "a little jealousy, a little dislike, a little envy, a little want of confidence." A "brilliant success will dissipate the elements," he thought, but until then Grant would be regarded as an interloper.[43] Grant was also taking over at a time when the term of enlistment for thousands of soldiers was about to expire. The 79th Highlanders had only two weeks more to serve, and their dress uniforms had already been bought for the parade up Broadway. They were furious at being sent to Virginia; during a parade review, the regiment marched past Grant in silence, refusing to answer the call for three cheers.

Banks was still struggling against the Red River when Grant decided that the spring campaign should be directed against the South's two largest armies, Lee's and Johnston's. There were to be no more uncoordinated battles in various parts of the South. On April 3, 1864, he ordered Sherman to leave Chattanooga and head with his 98,000 men for Atlanta, Georgia. "You, I propose to move against Johnston's army," Grant told Sherman, "to break it up and get into the interior of the enemy's country as far as you can, inflicting all the damage you can against their war resources."[44] Once Atlanta had been taken, Sherman was to march across

---

* Some authorities were content to turn a blind eye to even flagrant fraternization. "Our regiment had plenty of coffee but not tobacco," wrote James Pendlebury. "We made boats of paper and floated the boats containing the article we wished to exchange down to the other side. One day we ran short of paper and one of the Confederates offered to swim across the river if he would not be taken prisoner. This was cordially agreed upon, but the officer in charge on our side did not carry out his promise and the man was taken prisoner. He was taken to General Hancock's quarters and the general very kindly let him go back."

the state to Savannah and then up the coastline through the Carolinas to Virginia, where he was to join Grant at Richmond.

Theoretically, Grant had 185,000 soldiers with which to attack Lee, but political considerations had whittled down that number to a little over 100,000. The secretary of war, Edwin Stanton, insisted on keeping back 20,000 for the defense of Washington; and a further 65,000 were divided between the Army of the James, led by General Butler (of the New Orleans "Woman Order" fame), and the Army of West Virginia, under the command of the German general Franz Sigel. To his frustration, Grant discovered that these "political" generals not only owed their rank to Lincoln but were also protected by him and could not be shunted aside, despite their proven inability in the field.

Grant tried to limit their potential for disaster by giving Butler and Sigel mere supporting roles in his spring campaign. Their objective would be to deprive the Confederate Army of Northern Virginia of its supplies, while Grant went after Lee himself. "Beast" Butler started out first on May 3 with 30,000 soldiers, along with their horses and heavy guns, crammed into an assortment of steamboats and ferries for the two-day journey up the James River toward Richmond. As there was only a light smattering of Confederates forces south of Richmond, there was no reason why Butler could not disembark his army at one of the many landings along the river and march unmolested all the way to the capital. Grant wanted Butler to plant his forces just below Richmond, blocking every route from the south and west. If Butler had been acting solely at his own discretion, Grant might have worried. But two veteran commanders had been appointed as Butler's subordinates to prevent him from wrecking the venture.

The 5th Battery, New Jersey Artillery, containing the English private James Horrocks, was among the units placed under Butler's command. When Horrocks saw Butler in person he was startled by his notorious ugliness. "Imagine a bloated-looking bladder of lard," he wrote to his parents. "Call before your mental vision a sack full of muck . . . and then imagine four enormous German sausages fixed to the extremities of the sack in lieu of arms and legs."[45] Butler had been ordered to drive hard toward Richmond, smashing the rail link between Petersburg and Richmond as he went. But Horrocks did not notice any particular sense of urgency after his regiment arrived on May 5 at a deserted City Point, less than twenty-five miles from the Confederate capital.

The day was warm and sunny, far too pleasant to waste idling on the banks. "I took a walk with another fellow," wrote Horrocks. "We passed several little shanties, and at every one the soldiers . . . were ransacking and taking everything worth taking." Horrocks and his friend hurried on. "We walked on about a mile and a half and then came to a fine residence of a planter, in which about a dozen soldiers were making free with everything." As they approached the gate, a couple of soldiers came out laden with struggling livestock. A headless lamb was slung over the shoulder of one, its neck still dripping with blood. The gray-haired owner of the house sat hunched on the doorstep, moaning as Horrocks stepped around him. Once inside, he heard screams and the crashing of wood as soldiers forced open every door and cupboard. The black house servants were cowering in the corner of the parlor while the elderly wife of the owner shouted hoarsely at the men to leave. Horrocks walked down the hall to escape the noise. "In the next room, which was extremely well furnished, was a piano. I sat down and played Home, Sweet Home! with variations." The playing soothed him, and without another thought, he joined in the looting. "I took a flute and a package of beautiful wax candles and a piece of scented soap." He also found a wad of Confederate notes, which he was about to pocket when the old lady entered the room and shamed him into putting them back. Suddenly, Horrocks wished to slip away as quickly as possible.

The troops were starting to move out when Horrocks returned to the landing place. No one had missed him. They marched for several hours through thick piney woods. "Every now and then we passed some poor fellow who had given out and lay on the side of the road with his knapsack and musket alongside of him and then we passed portions of their kit . . . scores of blankets and overcoats, and boots and shoes." Like Frederick Farr, these men had been left behind, "thrown away," in Horrocks's words, "in order to lighten the load."[46] Horrocks promised his parents that he would take the greatest care with his life; he expected to be fired at soon and was curious how it would feel. "When I have felt it, I will tell you how it is."[47]

Horrocks's eagerness to encounter Confederate bullets was delayed by General Butler, who, instead of blocking the approaches to Richmond from the south and west, had become diverted by the nonexistent need to build fortifications and trenches, giving the Confederates enough time to insert General Beauregard's small force of 18,000 men between the Union Army of the James and the capital. Butler's failure to reach Richmond meant that Grant would be setting his spring campaign into motion with his plan damaged from the outset.

The Army of the Potomac began moving on May 4. If Grant's ultimate objective was to reach Richmond, Lee's was just as straightforward: to hold down the enemy long enough to convince the Northern public to vote for a pro-peace president in the November election. He was relieved when his scouts confirmed that the Federals had crossed the Rapidan River and were marching along the Germanna Plank Road. The route Grant had chosen passed through the Wilderness, whose dense wasteland had helped to give the Confederates their victory at the Battle of Chancellorsville in 1863.

Instead of marching quickly through the Wilderness, the Federal commanders took a leisurely pace, so that by midnight the advance of the army was still less than halfway through. In the darkness, there was many a startled yell as an accidental kick or stumble over a mound of leaves revealed human remains beneath. Many soldiers were too frightened to sleep that night, but not the new volunteer James Pendlebury, who lay down on the ground curled up like a dog. Pendlebury had made the beginner's mistake of throwing away his knapsack during the hot and tiring march. "In throwing away the knapsack I also threw away my cartridge box," he wrote. During the night, his captain "came and wakened me with his foot, and, handing me a cartridge box, said, 'Here take that, and don't ask any questions.' He had stolen it from one of the other men because he was so fond of me."[48]

Pendlebury's regiment was part of General Hancock's II Corps, one of the first to enter the Wilderness on May 4. There was no possibility he would be able to hide from the fighting once it began. "This was my first battle and I can't say that I was a brave man, for I wished I was at home," he wrote in his memoir. "But after I had fired a few times I began to get accustomed to the work and soon I had no fear about me." His baptism started at 4:00 P.M. on May 5. Lee had succeeded in placing two of his three corps inside the Wilderness even though General Longstreet was still a day's march away. Forty thousand Confederates pitched into seventy thousand Federals. Just as Lee had hoped, the Union regiments lost their sense of direction, firing wildly into the trees and charging hither and thither. At sunset many soldiers had no idea where they were and resorted to lying behind improvised breastworks. There was nothing to see except the outlines of tree trunks. But the noises coming from the woods were terrifying. As at Chancellorsville, stray sparks lit the dry underbrush, and fires spread along the forest floor, burning everything in their path.

Yet neither army flinched. At dawn on the sixth the fighting resumed with the same ferocity. Under General Hancock's direction, Pendlebury's corps suddenly found its cohesion and began to overpower the Confederates. Lee was near the Orange Plank Road when he saw hundreds of troops running toward him. Realizing that the line had broken, he spurred his horse forward in a desperate attempt to rally the men himself. At that moment, the first of Longstreet's regiments—a brigade of Texans—came storming up, having marched through the night from the Old Fredericksburg Road. The sight of Lee caused them to shout in dismay, "Lee to the rear! Lee to the rear!"[49] The Texans rushed ahead of him; but of the eight hundred who went forward, only three hundred returned unhurt.

Longstreet's corps had tramped through little-used tracks, taking every shortcut no matter how snarled and wild in order to reach Lee, the boom of gunfire spurring them on when exhaustion threatened. Captain Francis Dawson, who had passed his artillery examination in April, was exhilarated despite his arduous ride. "You know that until I left I had never been in the saddle in my life," he wrote to his parents, "but in sober truth the saddle is the headquarters of a staff officer and by dint of long practice you cannot fail, however stupid, to become moderately expert."[50] Dawson was riding with Longstreet and his staff when Lee met them. Displaying none of the hesitancy that had undermined his leadership at Knoxville, Longstreet saw immediately that the woods could aid them if he ignored conventional tactics and allowed the terrain to dictate the formation of his battle line.[51] His troops ran forward, with Longstreet and his staff, including Dawson, riding ahead of the surge.

The breastworks of the Irish Brigade caught fire under the barrage of artillery, scorching some of James Pendlebury's comrades, but the flames protected them from being overrun by the Confederate charge. But other Federal regiments turned and ran. The 79th Highlanders had been positioned at the rear of the line by General Hancock. "You have done your share," the general told Ebenezer Wells. Relieved to be spared a fight, the Highlanders were dumbfounded when they were ordered to beat the fleeing regiments back into line. "Our men bayoneted a few," re-

Wilderness

Germanna Ford

Rapidan River

Ebenezer Well

Gordon's
flank attack
late May 6

Sedgwick
May 5

Wilderness
Tavern

Burnside
May 6

Ewell
May 5

May 6

Orange Turnpike

Warren
May 5

Hancock

May 6 p.m.

A. P. Hill

May 5

May 5

Orange Plank Road

Longstreet, May 6

Confederate
withdrawal
May 7

Lee

Francis Dawson

The Wilderness and Spotsylvania
May 5–12, 1864

▬ ▬ ▬▬▬▬▬ Federal forces
▬ ▬ ▬▬▬▬▬ Confederate forces

James Pendlebury

Rappahannock River

Falmouth

Chancellorsville

Fredericksburg

Federal Advance
May 7–8

Salem Church

Grant

Meade

Richmond, Fredericksburg & Potomac R.R.

Hancock May 12

Bloody Angle

Wright

Warren

Burnside

Spotsylvania
Court House

N
W ✳ E
S

Miles

0   1   2   3   4   5

called Wells, "and others of us not liking to do so to our own men, knocked them down with the butt end of the rifles."[52] The 79th could not prevent a general rout, however, and by late morning the Orange Plank Road belonged to the Confederates. Longstreet had smashed the Federal line with a panache that recalled Stonewall Jackson's stunning victory the previous May at Chancellorsville. Dawson trotted up behind Longstreet as the general led a small group of staff and commanders along the road. The Confederates were congratulating one another on their signal success.

Though it was a date few liked to remember, it was exactly a year and a day since General Jackson had been accidentally shot while scouting three miles farther west, near the Orange Turnpike Road. The Orange Plank Road was similarly hemmed in by trees, which made it difficult for the isolated pockets of Confederate troops on either side to see one another. "There were but about eight of us together, all mounted," described Dawson. "*Without a moment's warning* one of our brigades about 2000 strong, only 50 or 60 yards distants [*sic*] poured a deliberate fire into us." "Friends," shouted one of Longstreet's officers, too late. Seconds later, four of the eight were on the ground. Three were dead or dying; Longstreet was slumped over his saddle, choking and coughing up blood. Dawson and two others lifted him from his horse and carried him over to a large tree. "My next thought was to obtain a surgeon," continued Dawson, "and, hurriedly mentioning my purpose, I mounted my horse and rode in desperate haste to the nearest field hospital. Giving the sad news to the first surgeon I could find, I made him jump on my horse, and bade him, for Heaven's sake, ride as rapidly as he could to the front where Longstreet was. I followed afoot."[53]

Dawson arrived as Longstreet was being carefully laid in an ambulance. The general had been hit by a single bullet, which passed through his neck and out his right shoulder. He was bleeding heavily but conscious. Dawson joined the silent group riding in the ambulance. They met Lee on the way to the hospital. "I shall not soon forget the sadness in his face," wrote Dawson, "and the almost despairing movement of his hands, when he was told that Longstreet had fallen." Longstreet's appearance convinced Lee that the Wilderness had claimed his other most reliable commander. Visibly shaken, he rode away to assume control of Longstreet's attack. But Lee could only guess what Longstreet had planned to do, and not all of it made sense to him. It was four o'clock when he gave the order to attack, several hours after Longstreet had intended his final assault to begin. During the delay, the Federals had regrouped and were prepared for the onslaught. The firing ceased at nightfall with neither side conceding their ground.

The following day, May 7, saw skirmishes but no real fighting. The two armies needed time to replenish their ammunition, fill places left by the dead and wounded, and eat and sleep after two days of continuous fighting. In the past forty-eight hours, 11,000 Confederate and 17,500 Federal soldiers had been killed or wounded in the Wilderness. Troops in the Army of the Potomac watched with a baleful eye as the supply wagons were hitched to horses and led toward the rear. They took it as a sign that Grant had ordered a retreat, just like Hooker after Chancellorsville and Burnside after Fredericksburg. The casualties from the battle were certainly enough to make most commanders unwilling to risk another clash with Lee; but Grant was different from his predecessors. The wagons were moving because Grant was continuing the advance to Richmond. He informed General Meade that the entire army must be on the march by midnight. Once the long lines began moving, Grant took his place at the front so that the men would know he was leading them toward, rather than away from, battle.

Lee was prepared for the news. He knew he was facing a far tougher opponent than his previous adversaries. He assumed Grant was heading for the crossroads at Spotsylvania Court House—the road south from there being the swiftest route to Richmond—and raced to get there ahead of him. Over the next couple of days, the two armies converged on Spotsylvania, skirmishing all the way.[54] Lee managed to stay in front, but barely: using bayonets and tin cups, his army hastily dug itself in along the intersection at the court house in a thin line that extended for about three miles. The Confederates braced for Grant's attack on the tenth. During the afternoon, Union regiments clambered through the woods and out into the open in an attempt to punch a hole in Lee's defenses. The Confederate line bulged in the middle, where the ground was higher than the rest of the undulating landscape. Here, at a point dubbed "the Mule Shoe" because of its U shape, a Federal attack succeeded in capturing twelve hundred prisoners, temporarily threatening the integrity of Lee's line. A simultaneous attack on the Confederate position around Spotsylvania Court House was led in part by the 79th New York Volunteers. Though Ebenezer Wells was furious at being in the front lines when his release was less than three days away, he feared being called a coward even more than he feared dying.[55] But here the Confederates held their position, and the attack ended at darkness with once again nothing achieved. The Highlanders were kept at the front lines until the final minute of their enlistment, when the regiment was ordered to march to Fredericksburg with two hundred prisoners in tow.

Grant tried to shake Lee from Spotsylvania by sending Major General Philip Sheridan and 10,000 cavalrymen to attack the Confederate defenses in front of Richmond. The raid forced Lee to dispatch Jeb Stuart and 4,500 troopers to pursue the Federals, and the two cavalry forces clashed on May 11 at Yellow Tavern, only six miles from Richmond. Stuart received a fatal shot in his stomach as he attempted to rally his outnumbered corps. Sheridan could have destroyed Stuart's cavalry, but Lee's nephew, Fitzhugh Lee, known as Fitz, immediately took charge and was able to effect a skillful retreat.

When first checked by Lee, Grant had sent a telegram to General Halleck in Washington, which read in part: "I propose to fight it out on this line [of attack] if it takes all summer." He showed his determination by launching a second attack against the Mule Shoe on May 12. The nature of the ground invited the attackers in, but getting out—especially once the earth had been churned to mud—was almost impossible. The Highlanders had escaped by a hair's breadth on a day that cost the two armies more than ten thousand men. The brutal hand-to-hand fighting between the Federals and Confederates led to the area's being christened "the Bloody Angle." "Rank after rank was riddled by shot and shell and bayonet-thrusts, and finally sank, a mass of torn and mutilated corpses," recalled a horror-struck member of Grant's staff who witnessed the assault. "Then fresh troops rushed madly forward to replace the dead, and so the murderous work went on."[56]

The Army of the Potomac had suffered twice as many casualties as the Army of Northern Virginia since May 5. A rough estimate showed that on May 13, 83,000 Federals remained of the 119,000 who had crossed the Rapidan River on the fourth. But Lee had not only lost a quarter of his army: a third of his commanders were also gone, and more responsibilities were devolving onto his shoulders. Grant, on the other hand, though he did not want for commanders, had far too many who were a positive help to the enemy. Nothing useful had come out of General Sigel's Shenandoah Valley campaign, and General Butler had become trapped behind his trenches eight miles south of Richmond. He had fought so feebly that even James Horrocks could see that the Army of the James was poorly led. "There is no confidence felt in the *beast* at all," he informed his father.[57]

Grant's reaction to the failure of Sigel and Butler was to push his own soldiers to march faster and fight harder. Only four days after the fighting at the Mule Shoe, the Army of the Potomac began another move southward. The effect on the army, wrote Charles Francis Adams, Jr., to his father, was almost the same as real victory, "when in fact it has done only barren fighting. For it has done the one thing needful before the enemy—it has advanced. The result is wonderful. . . . It is in better spirits and better fighting trim today than it was in the first day's fight in the Wilderness."[58]

TWENTY-NINE

"Defiance to Her Enemies"

Garibaldi's visit—James Mason falls for the trick—Battle in the English Channel—A tale of corruption in New Orleans—The beautiful Belle— A fatal arrogance

The English were shocked by the descriptions of the fighting in the Wilderness and at Spotsylvania. "There has been a great deal of news from America this week," wrote the Lancashire cotton worker John Ward on May 29, 1864, "giving an account of some of the most terrific battles with the most terrible carnage and slaughter for eight days that has ever been known in the world, and with little result."[1] Most newspapers described the duel between Grant and Lee as a festival of slaughter. In *The Times*, Charles Mackay compared Grant to Javert from Hugo's *Les Misérables*: "But still he holds his way undaunted, seeing nothing, caring nothing, but Richmond."[2] The "unprecedented death toll" in May was a popular subject with newspaper editors and cartoonists. "It is mortifying that we get no telegrams direct from officials at Washington," complained Benjamin Moran. "If we had reports of our own to give early to the press, we could greatly modify opinion here."

Yet the Confederate agent James Bulloch was also feeling stymied at every turn. He was desperate to make use of the propaganda skills of Henry Hotze or Francis Lawley; but Hotze was in France trying to revive the newspaper contacts abandoned by Edwin De Leon, and Lawley was in Italy, unable to return to London after his interview with the emperor for fear of alerting his creditors. Frank Vizetelly was in England, but since his arrival in mid-April he had divided his formidable energy between his favorite literary haunts, the Cheshire Cheese public house in Fleet Street and the Savage Club in Drury Lane. He had not thought about the Confederacy except to let Francis Dawson's family know that "he is very much liked, and is a very good officer, and, I have no doubt, will make his way."[3]

The court's decision against the Confederate warship *Alexandra* had been overturned on appeal, but Bulloch knew it was too late to resurrect his dream of a British-built Confederate navy.* In France, the Marine Department had ordered the two unfinished vessels in Nantes to be detained. "Every pledge has been violated, and we have encountered nothing but deception and duplicity and are now their victims," Bulloch wrote indignantly of the French.[5] He understood better than Slidell that the Confederacy was simply a pawn in the emperor's grand designs for Mexico. Only three raiders remained afloat: the *Georgia,* currently undergoing refurbishment in Cherbourg; the *Alabama,* whose last known whereabouts put her near Cape Town; and the *Florida,* which was thought to be near Bermuda. Bulloch hoped to keep them all at sea, if only to deter investors from using U.S. shipping firms. He would rather have sold Matthew Maury's unseaworthy *Rappahannock,* still at Calais, and used the money to repair the *Georgia,* but he was overruled by the senior Confederate naval commander in Europe, Commodore Samuel Barron, who decided to do the opposite, strip the *Georgia* of her fittings and use them on the *Rappahannock.*

The empty *Georgia* crept out of Cherbourg on a moonless night and arrived in Liverpool on May 2. "She was a poor miserable little tin kettle of a craft, but I loved her," wrote Lieutenant James Morgan. "My life, as the youngest of her officers, and the only one of my grade, had been very lonely, still she had been the only home I had known for thirteen

---

* The Confederates had used every possible trick, including jury tampering, to influence the outcome of the court cases. On May 17, 1864, for example, Charles Prioleau directed one of their agents to make sure there was a favorable decision in an upcoming court case: "The enclosed list contains the names of the Juries to try the case on the 6 June. It is important to know the sympathies of as many of them as possible . . . find out whether any of them or how many are, by opinion or interest, enemies to the cause of the defendants or the contrary. . . . Any expenses incurred we will of course discharge—you have carte blanche in this respect."[4]

The Confederate cruiser *Georgia*.

months."[6] On his first night ashore he went to the theater; "as soon as my gray uniform was noticed a whisper went through the audience that the *Alabama* had arrived in the port. Someone proposed three cheers for the *Alabama,* and they were given with a will."[7] An evening of applause— and then only because of mistaken identity—was Morgan's chief reward for the nine vessels captured by the *Georgia*. The ship was decommissioned on May 10. The crew assembled on the quarterdeck as the Confederate flag was lowered for the last time. "We bade good-bye to our shipmates," wrote Morgan, who was more determined than ever to return home, "many of us never to meet again."[8] James Bulloch sold the *Georgia* for £15,000.* It was not a bad sum, considering his options. He planned to purchase several more blockade runners with the money, hoping that the vessels would pay for themselves after a couple of runs or else be converted by Southern engineers into gunships.[9]

The faithful William Schaw Lindsay, MP, wrote to James Mason after the *Georgia*'s sale begging him to return to England. The movement was adrift without him, he confided. Lindsay tried to instill a sense of urgency in his friend: "Matters seems to be coming to a crisis on the other

---

* In current terms, about $1.6 million.

side of the Atlantic . . . the question is quite ripe for fresh agitation, and from experience I find that that agitation must be started by a debate in Parliament."[10] The British government's majorities in both houses were so slim that Palmerston was desperately casting about for allies. Two weeks later, Lindsay sent Mason stunning news. The prime minister had invited him to a private meeting on May 26 to discuss the wording of a resolution to offer mediation between the warring states. Lindsay never considered whether Palmerston might be trying to buy off the pro-Southern MPs in Parliament. "You should come here as soon after receipt of this letter as possible," Lindsay begged Mason. Palmerston had even indicated he was open to a meeting with the Confederate commissioner, but Mason refused to come to London unless summoned by the prime minister himself.

The Confederate commissioner's obduracy was shaken by a letter from the Reverend Francis Tremlett, the vicar of St. Peter's, Belsize Park. Tremlett reminded Mason that he had started the Society for Promoting the Cessation of Hostilities in America a few months before, and "as you were good enough to get us a good lift some little time since . . . I feel that you would naturally like to know what we have been doing with the money." Mason hardly remembered Tremlett, although the vicar kept open house for any Confederate in need. Tremlett's organization was not lobbying MPs and peers for Southern independence per se; the vicar knew that such activity would imply an acceptance of slavery. Instead, the Society presented itself as a religious body whose sole aims were peace and the revival of Lancashire's cotton trade. Mason was astonished to learn that the Society was organizing a deputation to meet Lord Palmerston.[11] He also discovered that Tremlett had been working with Commodore Matthew Maury for several months until illness had curtailed Maury's activities. The vicar was intending to lead deputations to Russell as well as Palmerston; "of course I shall have enough to do to look up influential people to form the Deputation, but if I can't find these, I will go even if I have to go alone," he told Maury.[12]

Mason left Paris within a day of receiving Tremlett's letter and arrived in London on June 5. As soon as Palmerston learned of Mason's presence, he knew that the Confederacy's supporters in Parliament would not dare risk their chances of a pro-Southern resolution by voting with the Tories to bring down the government. He now strung them along, continuously requesting delays to Lindsay's resolution for British mediation in the war. The Confederate lobby nervously discussed the import of this tactic and decided that the prime minister was waiting for news from Virginia. They were also reassured by Henry Hotze, who had heard from a source that the opposition was again considering its own motion for Southern recognition. "Indeed, I am satisfied that so general, almost universal, is popular sentiment in England with the South," Mason wrote to Judah P. Benjamin on June 9, "the ministry, even if disposed to resist, would have to yield to the popular sentiment."[13]

During the second week of June, the reports from America seemed to confirm Mason's optimism. He regularly called at Rose Greenhow's lodgings in Mayfair to discuss the latest telegrams. "He agrees perfectly with me in considering the news excellent," she recorded in her diary after they read in the press that Grant and Lee had clashed again on June 3, just south of Spotsylvania at a crossroads called Cold Harbor.[14] According to the reports, seven thousand Federals had been killed in less than an hour while trying to drive the Confederates from their fortified trenches.* Mason did not bother with Tremlett's group after he learned about Grant's setback even though Lord Russell had agreed to meet with the vicar's "deputation."

The Confederates noted every utterance and passing remark that indicated a politician's preference for one side or the other, while remaining blind to the obvious pressures squeezing the government. For the past six weeks a conference of nine European powers had been meeting in London to try to settle the dispute between Germany and Denmark over the sovereignty of Schleswig-Holstein, but Lord Russell's efforts to impose a resolution were going so badly that Britain was suddenly looking less like a Great Power that could dictate the destiny of other nations than an inconsequential island nation. "A few feeble barks [by the Confederates] have been raised against us, but without much effect as far as I can see," Henry Adams wrote airily to Charles Francis Jr. on June 10.[16]

---

* For several days after the battle, Grant refused to call a temporary truce to allow the wounded to be retrieved. By the time he changed his mind, it was too late for many of the trapped and helpless soldiers. After the war, Grant expressed his remorse for the unnecessary suffering he had caused at Cold Harbor. Among those affected by his actions was Seward, who—for the second time in the war—spent several sleepless nights waiting to learn the fate of his son, Captain William Seward, Jr. He had read in the newspapers that two captains from his son's corps had been wounded at Cold Harbor, but neither had been named.[15]

The *Alabama* was spotted outside Cherbourg harbor on June 10, 1864, having spent six months in the Far East followed by a return visit to Cape Town. The ship looked battered and dirty. "Our bottom is in such a state that everything passes us," Captain Semmes had written in his journal on May 21. "We are like a crippled hunter limping home from a long chase."[17] The last four months of her two-year voyage had pushed the vessel and her crew past endurance. The *Alabama*'s seams were opening; damp and mold had invaded every corner, including the magazine that housed Semmes's dwindling supply of gunpowder. The repairs would take at least a month, provided he had the cooperation of the French, and he was worried that they were going to turn him away. "The last batch of newspapers captured were full of disasters," Semmes wrote in his memoirs. "Might it not be, that, after all our trials and sacrifices, the cause for which we were struggling would be lost? . . . The thought was hard to bear."[18]

The French port admiral informed Semmes that he had made a mistake in choosing Cherbourg over Le Havre. Cherbourg was a naval station and subject to government oversight; Le Havre was a commercial port with many private docks where the *Alabama* could have settled without interference. The admiral could not allow Semmes to dry-dock his ship without permission from the emperor, who was enjoying a brief sojourn in the country. While they waited for the emperor's return to Paris, USS *Kearsarge* sailed into view. (The American legation in Paris had alerted Captain Winslow to the arrival of the *Alabama*.) Although Captain Winslow led his crew in a rousing cheer when he announced they were going to fight the *Alabama* at last, he was feeling as exhausted as Semmes. "I find I have not the health that I had," he wrote on June 13. "I am fast running down hill."[19]

"Here we are," wrote Semmes's English assistant surgeon, David Herbert Llewellyn, to one of his old colleagues at Charing Cross Hospital. "An enemy is outside. If she only stops long enough we go out and fight her. If I live, expect to see me in London shortly. If I die, give my best love to all who know me."[20] Semmes could have waited for the emperor's permission to dry-dock, but he deliberately chose to fight the *Kearsarge*. "The two ships are so equally matched that I do not feel at liberty to decline it," Semmes wrote in his journal, ignoring the difference between the *Kearsarge*'s spruce condition and the *Alabama*'s dilapidated state.

Accordingly, on Sunday morning, June 19th, between 9 and 10 o'clock [recalled Lieutenant John Kell], we weighed anchor and stood out of the western entrance of the harbor, the French iron-clad frigate *Couronne* following us. The day was bright and beautiful, with a light breeze blowing. Our men were neatly dressed, and our officers in full uniform. The report of our going out to fight the *Kearsarge* had been circulated and many persons from Paris and the surrounding countryside had come down to witness the engagement.[21]

Seven miles beyond French waters, the *Kearsarge* floated quietly while Captain Winslow carried out the Sunday inspection of the ship and crew. The routine seemed no different from the week before, except that today the guns were loaded and, perched high above the deck, special lookouts were scanning the horizon.[22] The *Alabama* sailed into view with a growing flotilla of spectator ships behind her. A band aboard one vessel played "Dixie"; on another the crew gave "three cheers for the *Alabama*." In the few moments left before battle stations, Semmes made his final speech to the crew, telling them:

> Remember that you are in the English Channel, the theatre of so much of the naval glory of our race, and that the eyes of all Europe are at this moment, upon you. The flag that floats over you is that of a young Republic, who bids defiance to her enemies, whenever, and wherever found. Show the world you know how to uphold it![23]

When the two ships were a mile apart, they turned broadside to broadside and began firing at each other in classic dueling fashion. On the *Alabama,* Dr. Llewellyn was operating on a wounded sailor when a shell burst open the wardroom, sweeping the table and patient from under him.[24] Two more shells struck the pivot gun, killing its crew. Just one of the *Alabama*'s guns scored a direct hit on the *Kearsarge*—a shell landed on the sternpost—but it failed to explode. The *Kearsarge* demolished the *Alabama* in less than an hour. Only when the vessel was clearly listing did Semmes give the order to abandon ship. Nine of the crew were dead; at least two dozen more lay wounded about the deck. Dr. Llewellyn came up to help load the worst injured onto a dinghy. The master's mate, George Fullam, was ordered to row to the *Kearsarge* and request assistance. According to eyewitnesses, an uninjured sailor tried to leap into the dinghy but was held back by Llewellyn: " 'See,' he said, 'I want to save my life as much as you do, but let the wounded men be saved first.' " He refused the occupants' offer to row him over with them to the *Kearsarge.* " 'We can make room for you,' " argued Fullam. " 'I will not peril the wounded men,' was his reply."[25]

Once Captain Winslow accepted that the white flag was not a trick, he dispatched two boats to rescue the survivors before they were dragged under by the vortex swirling around the stricken ship. Two French boats also arrived to help, as did the *Deerhound,* an English pleasure yacht. They were unable to save seventeen of the crew, including two of the black sailors serving on board, nor Dr. Llewellyn, who was last seen clinging to two cartridge boxes.[26] Captain Semmes was among the forty-two survivors rescued by the *Deerhound.* The *Kearsarge* picked up another seventy, three of whom died soon after being brought on deck. One of the French boats delivered its human cargo to the *Kearsarge;* the other headed to shore. But the owner of the *Deerhound* asked Semmes for directions, to which he managed to splutter "any part of Great Britain." Captain Winslow was outraged when he realized that she was sailing toward England, but there was nothing he could do to prevent the Confederates' escape.

The *Alabama*'s crew received a heroes' welcome on their arrival at Southampton. "One thing is very noticeable, that the destruction of the *Alabama* is much lamented by a majority of this people," Consul Zebina Eastman remarked crossly to Seward. "The London *Standard* says, 'Every TRUE Englishman will regret to learn that the gallant Alabama has gone to her last resting place.' "[27]

The cabinet's view regarding the *Alabama*'s demise was more practical. Lord Russell hoped that Adams would cease making claims for compensation, though he doubted the Northerners would be bought off that easily. Palmerston, as usual, asked what lessons could be learned for the navy: "The Fate of the *Alabama* certainly shews that the days of unprotected wooden ships are fast fading away, and it makes one rather uneasy about the fore and aft unprotected parts of the [iron-hulled, armor-plated warship HMS] *Warrior,*" he warned the Duke of Somerset.[28]

Henry Adams was disgusted with the way the papers were "trying to make a sea-lion of this arrant humbug."[29] On June 24 an advertisement appeared in the *Telegraph* asking for contributions from army and navy officers to a fund to replace the sword lost by Semmes when the *Alabama* went down. The press interest was so great on both sides of the Channel, and the reports so detailed and numerous, that Édouard Manet was able to paint a depiction of the battle that persuaded people he had witnessed it himself.*[30] Captain Semmes and Lieutenant Kell recuperated at the Reverend Francis Tremlett's vicarage while the papers debated the significance of the *Alabama*'s role in the war. In two years the cruiser had captured or destroyed a total of sixty-five U.S. ships, causing more than $5 million worth of losses to the Northern merchant marine trade. Had Britain behaved with propriety, was she blameless over the existence of the *Alabama*, asked several newspapers. The Duke of Argyll pressed the cabinet for an answer. "It will be found important to be able to say that we did our best to protest against the legitimacy of such proceedings," he had warned shortly before the duel. Otherwise, "in the first war in which we are engaged, 'Alabamas' will certainly be fitted out against us from neutral ports."[31]

When news of the *Kearsarge*'s victory reached Washington, Gideon Welles ordered the Navy Department to fly its largest Union flag. In Baltimore harbor, U.S. troopships sailing past HMS *Phaeton* hooted and chanted the *Alabama*'s name.[32] Glad to have something other than casualty lists and homecoming parades to report, *The New York Times* discussed the sinking of the *Alabama* for several weeks.†

* Yet many of the details in the press were wrong. Henry Adams read that Semmes hid under a tarpaulin during the battle. Across the Atlantic, the Confederate arms agent Edward C. Anderson mistakenly believed that his son had been killed. "My worst fears are realized and my noble boy is no more," he wrote. "According to the newspaper account which is all I have of the battle, my darling son was blown overboard by a shell, leaving his leg on deck. The news came like an earthquake upon me. . . . My darling boy is the only officer killed in the battle."

† The 79th New York Highlanders had their homecoming parade up Broadway and soon dispersed. "We were mustered out of the service June 9th, 1864," recalled Ebenezer Wells. "I stayed a few weeks in N.Y. then returned to England, being away 4 years and 5 months." The adjustment to civilian life proved to be hard. But eventually Wells found peace through prayer and a sense of pride that he had fought on the side of justice. "[I] have marched in triumph amid the plaudits of noble hearts, have felt the throb of nobility and patriotism as I fought for country dear," he wrote, "and have come back to my own home to receive the kiss of love."[33]

The best that could be said for Grant in June was that he remained undaunted despite having lost 55,000 men since May. But the sheer fact he was still marching forward was vitally important for Northern morale in light of the humiliating end to General Banks's Red River campaign. Lincoln's ability to shield his friend did not extend to outright disaster, and Banks's replacement to lead the XIX Corps, Major General Edward Canby, was appointed even before the defeated Federals arrived back in New Orleans.

Banks retained his title of commander of the Department of the Gulf, but his role was purely administrative. General Canby began a complete reorganization of his army. Among the changes was the formation of a "marine brigade" under Colonel L.D.H. Currie, whose task was to guard the Mississippi River from guerrilla attacks.[34] Dr. Charles Culverwell, however, chose to return to his family. May was the start of the sickly season, when swarms of mosquitoes rose like shimmering clouds out of the swamps. But the only assignment that would take him back to New York was escort duty for eleven soldiers who had become insane during the Red River campaign. Only seven survived the journey. Culverwell could cope no longer. Shortly afterward he resigned from the army and returned to England, never again to repeat the experiment of military life or indeed of being a doctor.[*]

The return of General Banks to New Orleans coincided with Edward Lyulph Stanley's arrival in the city. The Englishman was told that Banks had been laboring hard to improve the condition of freed slaves, having established nine military schools to teach literacy to the black recruits and ninety-five regular schools for black children.[36] But Stanley quickly realized that the white population were putting up a fierce resistance to Banks's reforms. "The whites here have been accustomed to maltreat the negroes without any notice being taken of it," he observed to his family on May 17.[37] He went to a supposedly well-run plantation—the same one visited by William Howard Russell in 1861 and the Marquis of Hart-

---

[*] Using his stage name of Wyndham, Culverwell toiled steadily in the world of provincial theater while he built up his skill and reputation. When he visited America again in 1870, it was as Charles Wyndham, one of the leading comic actors of his generation. Shortly before he was knighted in 1902, Wyndham gave a fund-raising speech on behalf of the British soldiers fighting in the Boer War: "I served with the Federal forces during the longest and most bitter conflict of modern days. Then I learned for the first time, and at first hand, what war really means, war—which if it does not make life worth the living, at least makes death worth the dying."[35]

ington in 1862—and thought it exposed the myth of "the contented slave." He was appalled by the dirty state of their hovels, by their despair, and by their fear of him as a white man. "I am quite satisfied that [the plantation] is being very badly managed in the interest of the negro," he declared.[38]

Stanley doubted how much more Banks could achieve without the wholehearted support of his staff. One New Orleans resident admitted to Stanley that she preferred the certainty of Butler's misrule to the arbitrary and capricious administration that now governed the lives of ordinary citizens. Banks had little control over his subordinates, she complained; rather than step in to curb abuses, "he was so undecided and would keep putting you off, and giving you no satisfactory answer."[39]

Mary Sophia Hill, the former British schoolteacher who had become a Confederate nurse after her twin brother, Sam, enlisted in the army, was one of the victims of General Banks's poor administration. She had left the South after the Battle of Gettysburg to visit relatives in Britain. But on her return to New Orleans in the spring of 1864, she had found herself under increasing scrutiny from Federal officials. "Imagine how my English blood boiled with indignation at being treated like a criminal," she complained to her brother on May 20. "I will never forget it [sic] to the Yankees—never; not that it would be possible for me to hold them in greater contempt than I do at present."[40]

Mary had attracted attention because she always seemed to have a letter or parcel to deliver to someone in the city. She received two visits from a stranger named Ellen Williams, who offered to convey any letters to the South since she was departing for Galveston. Ellen also tried to give her a note from Confederate general Dick Taylor addressed to a Mrs. Hill, which Mary refused to take: "I told her I was not Mrs. Hill and the letter was not for me." But Mary injudiciously gave her three letters, including one for Sam. A few days later, on May 26, Mary came home to find a Captain Frost from the provost office waiting in the parlor. He bundled her into a cab and drove her to the women's prison on Julia Street.

The jailer, Mr. Laurence, took a hearty dislike to the new prisoner and her repeated declarations of British nationality. He boarded up Mary's window, removed the sheets from her bed, and prevented her from having contact with her sister or brother. "I often wonder since

[how] I kept my senses," she wrote later, "for many have lost their reason for less cruelty." The main charge against her, she eventually learned, was passing information to the enemy. "I wrote to Mr. Coppell, acting Consul, who wrote me word he would attend to my case: it was not necessary to see me. I differed with him. It was his duty to see me and hear what I had to say, he knowing me to be a British subject."*[41] After three weeks of solitary confinement, Mary was allowed a visit from her sister and brother-in-law, who were so appalled by her condition that they forced the authorities to allow her to be seen by a doctor. "Had it not been for him, I would have died," she wrote.[42] She was held in prison without being officially charged or given a date for her trial, while she grew weaker and more desperate by the day.

———

Mary Sophia Hill was not the only nuisance to the Federal authorities. Belle Boyd, the Confederate spy and heroine of the Battle of Front Royal in 1862, was also in custody. Her ability to pry information out of impressionable Federal soldiers was legendary. It was only with the greatest reluctance that Stanton had sanctioned Belle's release from prison the previous December after she contracted typhoid.

Belle had recuperated in Mobile, Alabama, under the care of Mary Semmes, the wife of Captain Semmes, who "treated me with as much attention as though I had been her own daughter." Mary's tales of the *Alabama* inspired Belle to try a new kind of adventure, and she wrote to Judah P. Benjamin offering to carry Confederate dispatches to England. Benjamin was delighted and provided her with $500 in gold, a letter of introduction to Henry Hotze, and passage on a blockade runner out of Wilmington. As dawn broke on her twentieth birthday, May 9, 1864, the *Greyhound* carried Belle and two other passengers past the blockade out

---

* Coppell had received Mary's distress call when he was himself at a particularly low ebb. He had been working without pay since September 1861. "I should not have troubled your Lordship on this occasion but that my individual resources . . . are inadequate to the present large demands upon them," he had written to Russell on May 20. Knowing it would be some time before he received a reply, he labored at his duties with waning enthusiasm. When his letter eventually arrived in London the Foreign Office was amazed that he had never said anything before. No one had bothered to check whether the legation or London was meant to be paying his salary. Russell immediately granted him £350 per annum and a £200 war allowance.

into the open sea. She did not get far; USS *Connecticut* captured the *Greyhound* at 1:40 P.M. on the following day.

The U.S. naval officer in charge of taking the *Greyhound* to Boston, Lieutenant Samuel Hardinge, was a handsome young fellow without a girl back home. He did not know, at first, that the widowed "Mrs. Lewis" was the infamous Belle Boyd—and by the time he discovered her true identity he was so besotted that she was able to persuade him that the captain of the *Greyhound* ought to be released. Hardinge took Belle shopping for clothes when the *Greyhound* stopped briefly in New York, and finished by proposing marriage to her when the vessel docked at Boston. "So generous and noble was he in every thing," Belle wrote later, "that I could not but acknowledge that my heart was his. I firmly believe that God intended us to meet and love."[43]

This had not, however, been the intention of the Navy Department. Gideon Welles ordered Lieutenant Hardinge's arrest. "My dear Miss Belle, It is all up with me," Hardinge wrote dejectedly on June 8. "The Admiralty says that it looks bad for us; so I have adopted a very good motto, viz: 'Face the music!' "[44] Welles and the war secretary, Edwin Stanton, were incensed that Belle had managed to make both their departments look foolish and were determined it should never happen again. The provost marshal in Boston received a telegram ordering her immediate removal to Canada, and "if I was again caught in the United States, or by the United States authorities, I should be shot," she wrote. Two days later she was on the train to Montreal, missing Hardinge but excited at the "delightful prospect of breathing free Canadian air."[45]

Stanton had been in the midst of deciding what to do with Miss Boyd when one of his clerks informed him that an Englishman, a former volunteer in the Confederate army, was asking for an audience. The military governor of New York, General John Dix, had hesitated to accept Colonel Grenfell's tale about his disenchantment with the South and had sent him to Washington to apply directly to the War Department for permission to travel through the North as a tourist. Annoyed at the presumption on his time, Stanton nevertheless agreed to see Grenfell out of curiosity. Two days later, on June 13, Grenfell was shown into Stanton's office.[46]

Stanton received Grenfell with a stenographer present, which ought to have been a warning that this was not the time to play games. Heedless of the danger, Grenfell behaved like a second-string actor at his grand moment. He not only offered the incredulous secretary "inside" information about Lee's army, but he also professed himself ready to join the U.S. Army. Stanton declined the offer. But he did extract a promise from Grenfell to make no further contact with or provide any help to the Confederacy. The colonel left Stanton's office believing that his performance had been masterful. He had received permission to travel anywhere in the North without having to register his presence with the local provost marshals. It had not occurred to Grenfell that the authorities could keep watch on him by other means. Believing his mission accomplished, Grenfell returned to New York where his new friend, Fitzgerald Ross, was waiting to begin their tour of northern New York and Canada, unaware of the sinister reason for the journey.

THIRTY

"Can We Hold Out?"

A Welsh visitor to Washington—Tit for tat—Return of Lawley and Vizetelly—An intolerable stench—Battle of the Crater—The Negro regiments—Devastation in the valley

On June 22, 1864, Griffith Evans, a Welsh army veterinary surgeon stationed in Canada, called at the British legation in Washington seeking advice on how to reach the front. Lyons explained that it was doubtful Seward would give him an official pass. "Lord Lyons entertained me very hospitably," wrote Evans. "He took my hand in both his when I left, and gave it a good shaking." Evans felt sorry for him: "He looks a kind, good natured middle-aged man who was staggering under the burden of safeguarding the rights and liberties of nearly 3 million British subjects." Evans was shocked to learn that crimping was never punished, nor legal redress available for the victims:

> The usual mode is to drug the food or drink, whether it be alcohol or tea. The person loses consciousness and recovering some time after in a distant place finds himself dressed in the US uniform, he remonstrates but is assured he enlisted himself, finds some money in his pocket which he is told is part of his bounty, and that he has spent or lost the rest. Such are the complaints received daily. All the Embassy can do is to request the War Department to investigate the case, to give it a fair trial and report. Some

are then retrieved and some not, but none of those relieved get Army compensation.[1]

Lyons did not discuss his civil cases with Evans. That week, British subjects in Memphis had protested to him about a rule that banned their employment unless they joined the Federal militia; a black Canadian had been arrested for breaking the state of Delaware's ban on colored people; and Mary Sophia Hill had written to him from prison begging for his intercession. "Imagine, my Lord, a woman and a British subject so threatened," she cried. "My object in writing this letter is to ask Your Lordship to see justice done me and to protect me until I am proved as not belonging to the Glorious Flag of Old England."[2]

Consul Coppell admitted to Lyons that he had failed to visit the prisoner, but advised him, "From personal knowledge I do not think the case one for Your Lordship's interference."[3] Lyons had no reason to doubt him, experience having taught the minister that cases such as Mary's usually came with a long and tangled history of mutual antipathy between the prisoner and the authorities. He would not help her while there were others who were truly innocent and helpless. William Seward was amazed by Lord Lyons's tenacious advocacy for such pathetic cases. The old rules of warfare had been swept away, he told him during a contentious interview. Seward pointed to the latest news from Charleston, where the Confederates had moved fifty Northern officers to a converted prison in direct range of the U.S. gunboats.

General Sam Jones in Charleston had decided it was time for the Federals to feel what the city's civilian population had been enduring for the past eight months, and fifty Federal prisoners of war (all officers) had been moved to a converted prison in one of the most heavily shelled neighborhoods. He knew that an attempt to capture the city was still being prepared—his scouts had reported that thirteen warships and forty-six troop transports were anchored less than a hundred miles away in Port Royal Sound, which had been captured by the Federals early on in the war.[4] But the timing of the attack remained a mystery. Captain Henry Feilden was not taking any chances: he had drawn up a will in Julia's favor even though their wedding had not yet taken place. If he were to be killed now, he told her,

I should feel as if I was leaving a wife behind in you, and it is my duty to attend to your wants. I thought of you, darling, last night whilst I was sitting out on the ground, I thought of you and felt happy to be able to render my small mite in defence of your country. You will trust me dearest, wont you, to love you ever as I do now, whatever happens if I am alive you will be protected . . . someone who will think of nothing else for the rest of his life but making you happy.[5]

General Beauregard had recommended Feilden for promotion:

Though I do not think there is much chance of their refusing it, personally I do not care whether they do or do not [Feilden admitted]. I really look forward to the war ending this year, and if [only] we are spared to one another, we shall be able to settle so comfortably in Charleston. I will go into some business and work very hard, and then I shall have you to comfort me and inspire me. Then you will be able to amuse yourself with all your old friends and acquaintances. Dearest Julie, if I can only make you as perfectly happy as we mortals can expect to be, I shall have no other wish on this earth.[6]

Feilden's respect for General Jones plummeted after the Federal officers were used as human shields. He had urged Jones to reconsider the order, pointing out that retaliation would probably follow. "My argument then and now was the homely adage that 'two wrongs can never make a right,' " he related to Julia.[7] Feilden was so troubled that on June 30 he went down to check on the Federal prisoners. He wore his best uniform for the visit, "to show that we are not quite ragged yet in the Confederacy." There were five generals among the fifty officers. Feilden struck up a conversation with General Truman Seymour, who was so interesting and pleasant that he regretted the folly of General Jones all the more: "I hardly ever met a Yankee before, never a Yankee General and thought the contact would make one's flesh crawl, but strange to say, I could not blow Seymour from a gun or hang him without a good deal of repugnance. Indeed, I felt more inclined to ask him to dinner and show him around Charleston."[8]

Feilden's prophesy of retaliation was soon fulfilled. The commandant of Fort Delaware, on Pea Patch Island in the Delaware River, received an order to select fifty officers from among the 12,500 Confederate prisoners and dispatch them to one of the captured forts in Charleston Harbor so that they would be in the line of Confederate fire. The inmates assumed that there would be more random selections in the future, and the thought spurred many to look for a way of escape. There was only one route out, however, through sewage drains that led to the Delaware River. Among the six prisoners willing to try was the Scotsman Bennet G. Burley, who had been captured on May 12, 1864, while planting torpedoes on the Rappahannock River. When Burley was searched, they found an unusual pass that granted him the freedom to cross Southern lines at will. Regular soldiers did not carry such passes. Burley was labeled a spy and treated accordingly.

Burley weighed the risks and decided that his prison conditions could not significantly worsen if he tried to escape and was recaptured. One night, when the drains were full and water was seeping up through the floor, Burley and his five comrades pried open the grille in their barracks and, taking a big breath, lowered themselves into the pitch-dark pipe. Burley's powerful physique enabled him to thrust his body along for twenty-five yards until he reached the end and could heave himself into the rushing river. Only one other Confederate managed the same feat. Burley was rescued by a passing sailboat, telling the crew that he had capsized while night fishing, which the captain either believed or chose not to question. He was taken to Philadelphia and from there he headed north to Canada, where he would be safe.

———

In Virginia, the Army of the Potomac was edging toward Richmond. "We must destroy this army of Grant's before he gets to the James River," Lee had urged General Jubal Early on May 29. "If he gets there, it will become a siege, and then it will be a mere question of time."[9] Two weeks later, on June 12, the Federals had not only reached the James but also crossed it, using pontoon bridges. Now only the small town of Petersburg, population 18,266, lay between Grant and the Confederate capital.[10] The town straddled the five remaining railways and two main roads that connected Richmond to the rest of the state. From June 15 to 18, Grant ordered a continuous wave of attacks, losing more than ten thousand men over four days without breaking the Confederate defenses. "We have assaulted the enemy's works repeatedly and lost many lives, but I cannot understand it," Charles Francis Adams, Jr., wrote in anguish to his father on June 19. "Why have these lives been sacrificed? Why is the Army kept continually fighting until its heart has sickened within it? I cannot tell . . . Grant has pushed his Army to the extreme limit of human endurance."[11]

The U.S. generals complained that their troops had lost their courage for frontal assaults. The men would make a show of going forward before hunkering down under cover. Grant tried one last time before he accepted the necessity for a long siege. He dispatched Sheridan on another cavalry raid with orders to attack Lee at his vulnerable points—the bridges, water tanks, and supply lines. On June 22, Grant ordered an assault against one of the five railroads. The 69th New York Volunteers were among the attackers.

> Our Captain asked permission to lead us [wrote James Pendlebury]. He had been under arrest for some time and told me that he had a foreboding that in the next encounter he would be killed. . . . As we were entering into the charge he received a shot and fell at my side. I turned and said, "Captain, are you mortally wounded?" He said, "I am Jimmy, don't leave." There was one thing I had learnt always to have beside me, which I knew was most refreshing; I carried a supply of water because the first thing men who are wounded cry for is water. The captain thanked me for it and I stood beside him. I, myself, was so very thirsty that I lay down and literally slaked up every drop of water that I found in the imprint of a horse's shoe in the clay. I forgot it was muddy I was so thirsty. I gave to my Captain many a drink during the throes of death. I turned him over many times and did all I could for him. After a while I got him on my shoulder and carried him into the shelter of the trees out of the sound of the whizzing bullets. I really thought I would never get out alive. By and by the Captain died and I got him on my back and carried him back to our works. We buried him in the breast works in front of Petersburg, Virginia.

Grant ordered a second charge, but many of the troops were done with fighting. The 69th was drunk before the attack—Pendlebury wandered forward in a daze, thinking he would dodge Confederate bullets if they came—and the men were captured en masse.[12]

The Confederates were no less shaken by the six weeks of relentless fighting. Francis Dawson had suffered so many near misses that he was certain the next bullet would find him.[13] But his spirits had recovered since the return of Lawley and Vizetelly, who ran the blockade at Wilmington together on June 5. Vizetelly had brought with him a letter from Dawson's mother. "Little did I think, when years ago, I saw drawings and sketches in the [London] Illustrated by our 'special artist F. Vizetelli,' or even when we had many a frolic together in the mountains of Tennessee," Dawson wrote home on June 26, "that he, the same joyous, corpulent artist would have proved a source of such happiness to my dear parents and myself." Dawson's happiness was complete after Vizetelly drew a picture of his corps on a midnight march through burning woods.[14]

"I am satisfied General Grant will make no more onslaughts upon the Confederate breastworks," Lawley wrote from Lee's headquarters on June 27. "Weeks and weeks will probably pass without amending Grant's prospects before Petersburg." The Confederates' defenses stretched for over thirty miles in a protective semicircle of trenches and

A corps of the Confederate army marching by night through burning woods, by Frank Vizetelly.

View of Petersburg from General Lee's headquarters—watching the Federals through binoculars, by Frank Vizetelly.

bombproof shelters, connected by walkways that in some places were six feet deep and up to twelve feet wide. Lawley recognized that the real danger to the Confederacy came from Sherman in Georgia. Only Confederate general Joseph E. Johnston and the Army of Tennessee stood between Sherman and Atlanta, the last strategic target of the South. The great question on Lawley's, indeed everyone's, mind was whether the Northern electorate would decide to end the war before Sherman reached Virginia.

Three days later, on July 1, Lee's artillery commander, General Edward Porter Alexander, arrived at the Confederate headquarters with disturbing news. He had seen activity that convinced him the Federals were digging a tunnel under the trenches. Lawley asked him how long it would have to be to clear their works: "I answered about 500 feet," Alexander recalled. "[Lawley] stated that the longest military tunnel or gallery which had ever been run was at the siege of Delhi, and that it did not exceed 400 feet. That it was found impossible to ventilate far greater distance." Alexander reminded him that the average coal mine went much farther and it would not be too taxing for the Federals to ask any volunteer from the Pennsylvania mines about ventilation. Lee had no option but to wait and see who would turn out to be right.[15]

Lawley and Vizetelly suffered as the summer heat cast a pall over the trenches. To pass the time, Vizetelly drew portraits of Lee and his staff watching the Federals through field glasses. The biggest excitement was the arrival of a captain from the British Army, G. T. Peacocke, who reported to duty as a volunteer aide to General Pickett.[16] Lawley filled his reports with stories of "African savagery" and Federal brutality toward women and children, but he neglected to describe the hunger that now afflicted Lee's army. One of the more colorful English blockade runners, the Hon. Augustus Charles Hobart-Hampden, the third son of the Earl of Buckinghamshire, whose later exploits with the Turkish navy won him the title "Hobart Pasha," visited the front lines in July. He came armed with boxes of sausages and sardines, which were eagerly gobbled up by the grateful Confederates. "For months past [they] had tasted nothing but coarse rye-bread and pork washed down with water," wrote

Hobart-Hampden. "There were several Englishmen among the officers composing the staff," he added with surprise. "I often wonder what has become of them."[17]

Hobart-Hampden saw Petersburg and Richmond, where nearly every other female was dressed in deep mourning, and even snatched a half-hour conversation with Lee himself, yet still he believed Lawley's optimistic prediction of Southern victory. "Though a line of earthworks hurriedly thrown up in a few hours at Petersburg was nearly all that kept Grant's well-organized army from entering the capital; though the necessaries of war, and even of life, were growing alarmingly short," he wrote after the war, "still everyone seemed satisfied that the South would somehow or other gain the day." Lawley he could excuse, since the journalist was "so carried away by his admiration of the wonderful pluck shown by the Southerners . . . whereas all of us . . . should have seen the end coming months before we were obliged to open our eyes to the fact it was come."[18]

The Welsh army veterinarian Griffith Evans had obtained an observer's pass from the Medical Department and was visiting the Federal lines at the same time that Hobart-Hampden was with the Confederates. He, too, had little sense that the South was struggling when he arrived at Petersburg. His first visit was to General Butler's camp on July 3, where the flies were already a pestilence. (They were the biting kind and "are very troublesome indeed," James Horrocks complained to his brother.)[19] All day long, wrote Evans, the men sat in their fetid dugouts, sweltering in the heat, until the night shift relieved them. It was a dreadful existence, and he pitied them. Soldiers talked to him about the "fearful slaughtering" they had witnessed in vague tones, "as if they wished to forget it."

Driving around the countryside, Evans thought he had never beheld anything so hideous, so redolent of biblical destruction: "Fences pulled down for fuel, the crops in the fields trodden down, houses deserted or occupied by troops, or burnt down, thousands of recent graves of men killed or died lately, and those so shallow that the stench from them was in places intolerable. Dead cattle and horses, men's accoutrements, etc., strewn about, etc. etc. It was indescribable and the effect was sad and sickening."[20] He could not imagine how the soldiers would tolerate their conditions for much longer.

A rumor was spreading through the camps during Evans's visit. The army discouraged discussion of it, but the news eventually leaked out. Sir Percy Wyndham had ridden into the camp of the 1st New Jersey Cavaliers insisting that he was once more their colonel. Although the men knew that the New Jersey state legislature had petitioned Washington for Wyndham's reinstatement for the second time on June 4, there had been no indication that Stanton had changed his mind. After a tense standoff, the lieutenant colonel of the regiment ordered the arrest of Wyndham, who refused to leave quietly. Wyndham created such an uproar that General Meade had him escorted to Washington under guard on July 1. His discharge papers were waiting for him when he arrived. On July 5, 1864, Sir Percy Wyndham was officially mustered out of the army, and strongly encouraged to leave town.*

Griffith Evans's own return to Washington was impeded by a Confederate raid on the perimeter. The audacious attack led by Jubal Early was an attempt by Lee to force Grant into detaching part of his army to defend Washington. "There is a large Confederate force within three or four miles of Washington, and some perhaps think they will make an attempt to take the town today," Lord Lyons informed his sister on July 13. But though there was panic in the city, the legation was not even bothering to pack up the archives. "Even if the town was taken my physical comfort would not be likely to be disturbed," Lyons decided. "I don't really expect to have to move, and I daresay you will hear next week that things have lapsed into their odious condition."

Lyons was far more worried about the state of his staff. He repeatedly told the Foreign Office that it could no longer assign the same number of attachés to Washington as it did to Ulan Bator. The secretary, William Stuart, and one of the junior staff had left before the arrival of their replacements. "The heat is overpowering," Lyons wrote to Lord Russell. "I am anxiously looking out for [their] arrival . . . and I hope they will be immediately followed, if they are not accompanied, by one or more Third Secretaries or Attachés—otherwise the whole Legation will be knocked up."[21] A letter from Joseph Burnley, the new secretary, brought

---

* Sir Percy briefly attempted to run a riding academy for cavalry officers in New York. Its failure convinced him to return to Italy to serve on Garibaldi's staff for the next couple of years. Ever the roving adventurer, he moved to Asia and started a humorous journal in India, the *Indian Charivari,* and a logging business in Mandalay, Burma. He was killed in Mandalay at the age of forty-nine in 1879 while demonstrating a hot-air balloon of his own design, which exploded in midair.

terrible news: he was coming out with his wife and children. "A dreadful prospect for me—and still worse for him, poor man," wrote Lyons. No woman had disturbed the monastic peace of the legation for the past five years.[22] Lyons set about trying to dissuade Burnley from bringing his family. He could, with complete honesty, describe the lonely existence of a British diplomat in Washington. With Henri Mercier gone, and the Russian minister, Baron Stoeckl, on leave for the summer, Lyons had received not a single invitation to dinner for weeks.[23]

Griffith Evans was concerned for Lyons when he visited the legation on July 20, though the minister sheepishly declined his sympathy. Evans should reserve his pity for the country's leaders, Lyons told him: "Mr. Lincoln is not the man to look at that he was four years ago." The Welshman realized the truth of this statement when he visited the White House a few days later. He walked through the "Grand Reception Room," which he thought was "very seedy looking," into Lincoln's office without anyone's challenging his presence. Lincoln was so exhausted and put upon that he did not think to ask why a stranger was in his office. "He shows marks of mental overwork," decided Evans after a few minutes' conversation.[24]

The pressures on Lincoln were increasing. Grant's failure to capture Richmond and Jubal Early's raid near Washington had shaken the cabinet's confidence. The tense divisions between the members resurfaced in violent quarrels and a resumption of the old plots and counterplots against one another. Seward, whose son Will had been wounded while defending Washington against Early, turned some of his frustration on Lord Lyons. He rudely dismissed as exaggeration the minister's complaints that the Central Guard House in Washington was using water punishments against alleged deserters. Lyons had evidence from six separate cases, and he was outraged by the State Department's explanation that a cold shower was pleasant in the summer. Turning water cannons on prisoners was not "in conformity with any law or regulations," he bluntly wrote to Seward on July 25. It was used for one reason only: "for the purpose of extorting, by the infliction of bodily pain, confessions from persons suspected of being deserters."[25] Nor was this his only complaint against the army. That same week, Lyons received evidence from the New York consulate of British subjects being hung by their thumbs until they agreed to sign confessions of desertion.

The legation's only success in July was the rescue of Admiral Usher's grandson, Henry, who had walked into the New York consulate on the thirteenth, painfully thin and unsteady on his feet. "Usher has been for about a week in hospital in this place, too ill to report to me until today," recounted the deputy consul. Now that they had him, they were not allowing him out of their sight. One of the clerks went to the ticket office to purchase a berth for the boy, and another stayed by him until he boarded the steamer. The attachés celebrated the news that young Usher had departed from New York by having a drink at Willard's.

The president has "called for 500,000 more recruits," Lyons reported to London on July 22. "It will depend very much on the events of the present campaign whether he gets them."[26] Thurlow Weed believed this new draft to be an act of political suicide.[27] The army knew little of Grant's intentions, and its spirits sank as the soldiers broiled and sweated in their camps, waiting for orders. "Here we are just where we have been so long and no one knows anything," Charles Francis Adams, Jr., complained to his brother. "I am tired of the Carnival of Death."[28]

Charles Francis was unaware that the five-hundred-foot tunnel at Petersburg was almost complete. In a couple more days, Grant intended to blow up the center of the Confederate lines. In preparation for the daring assault, Grant ordered a diversionary attack north of the James River, close to Richmond. The troops selected for the mission included Colonel L.D.H. Currie and the 133rd New York Volunteers, lately arrived from Louisiana. Grant wanted Lee to be caught between defending Richmond and Petersburg and, with luck, ruffled into making mistakes. But it was the Federals who ended up committing the errors by their failure to plan adequately for the assault. Colonel Currie, who had been appointed acting commander of the 3rd Brigade, 1st Division, discovered that many of his troops were new recruits. He became increasingly worried the more he witnessed their lethargic response to his orders. The men had been assigned to hold one of the creeks that fed the James, but at the first sign of trouble they broke cover and ran for their lives. "Colonel Currie is as much annoyed at the conduct of his troops as myself," reported his commanding officer: "They had the most explicit instructions from Colonel Currie, who even went so far as to tell them if they broke, the troops in the rear had orders to fire on them."[29]

Currie's threats could not match the actual feel of gunfire for many of these men.* General Godfrey Weitzel, the acting chief of staff of the XIX Corps, vigorously defended Currie's conduct to his irate superiors. He "bears three honorable wounds," Weitzel wrote indignantly, "and is promoted for gallantry. He was Major-General Smith's adjutant-general all through the campaigns of the Army of the Potomac." But Currie was denied the opportunity to correct the poor impression made by his raw troops. The next day, on July 27, he was ordered to take his brigade to Washington in anticipation of another attack by Jubal Early. Two days later, on July 29, the diversionary expedition was abandoned and the Federals recrossed the James River. The mine tunnel was scheduled to explode in a few hours' time.

A hitch had been discovered, however. The troops especially trained for the mission happened to be from colored regiments, and all of a sudden it seemed politically hazardous to use them; white regiments were substituted. Notwithstanding Grant's declaration that "they will make good soldiers," there was still widespread resistance to the idea of blacks in uniform, as well as doubts about their abilities. "Can a Negro do our skirmishing and picket duty?" asked Sherman rhetorically. "Can they improvise bridges, sorties, flank movements, etc., like the white man? I say no."[31] The second-class status of the colored regiments was reflected in their pay for the first two years—which stayed at $7 a month, only just over half the $13 paid to whites—until Congress rectified the inequality. Yet the number of black volunteers was increasing, from none before 1862 to fifteen thousand in 1863 to more than a hundred thousand by the summer of 1864. Moreover, they were not only serving their country, they were dying for it, too, and at a higher rate than white soldiers. The Confederates rarely took black prisoners alive.†

---

* Some of them were victims of crimpers, like twenty-one-year-old Edward Sewell from Ipswich, who had arrived in 1862 to work as a mechanic for a New York firm. He had been kidnapped in May while riding on the train to work: "I sat by myself in the corner and believe I began to doze [wrote Sewell]. About three or four in the afternoon I woke up and found myself on board a steam-packet on its way to Hart's Island. . . . I found that I was then in uniform as a soldier, and had been robbed of my money, jewels, and clothes, except a ring on my finger."[30]

† A notorious example of Confederate rage against black soldiers had taken place only three months before, on April 12, at Fort Pillow in Tennessee. The Federal force of approximately 262 black and 295 whites surrendered to General Nathan Bedford Forrest, but fewer than 75 black soldiers walked out alive.

At 4:45 A.M. on July 30, the fuse was lit and four tons of gunpowder exploded underneath two unsuspecting South Carolina regiments. Two hundred and fifty men were buried instantly; several hundred others were blown to fragments. The hole formed by the explosion was more than 150 feet long, 97 feet wide, and 30 feet deep. "Into this crater," wrote Confederate general Edward Parker Alexander, "the leading [Federal] division literally swarmed, until it was packed about as full as it could hold."[32] The Federal soldiers were trapped as the Confederate regiments on either side of the crater formed a new defensive line and trained their guns into the crater. Alexander's English staff officer, Stephen Winthrop, and three others ran to one of the artillery pieces that was still working and started firing. The Federal soldiers were slaughtered like animals in a pen. Almost four thousand were lost in the debacle, including most of the black troops who were sent in after the white regiments. "The effort was a stupendous failure," wrote Grant.[33]

Francis Lawley was two miles away at Lee's headquarters when he heard the muffled boom and saw the "dark curls of smoke" billowing from the crater. He embellished the fiasco in his report to give a false picture to British readers of white bravery and black cowardice. "The panic-struck negroes," he lied, "crowded into the empty crater of the mine, and cowered down in abject terror." While he was crafting his *Times* dispatch, a messenger arrived with the news that Jubal Early had torched the Pennsylvania town of Chambersburg. Lawley added this to the end of his report, to show that Lee still retained the ability to attack Northern targets: "Richmond never laughed more scornfully at the puny onslaught of her foe."[34]

"We have met with a sad disappointment at Petersburg," Seward wrote to his wife on August 5. "And now we have to deal with a disappointed, despondent, and I fear discontented people, who expect the Administration to guarantee success."[35] Lincoln traveled down to Fort Monroe for a private conference with Grant. The general blamed the war secretary, Edwin Stanton, for insisting "that defending Washington was more important than chasing the enemy, even if it allowed Early to feint and pounce wherever he chose."[36] A few days after the meeting, Grant had his way and General Phil Sheridan was allowed to lead a force of forty thousand men into northern Virginia. Sheridan's instructions were clear: to make the fertile Shenandoah Valley unfit for human habitation and destroy Jubal Early's army. Grant's precise words were for

Sheridan "to follow him to the death."[37] The key was mobility, which could only be achieved if Sheridan's supply lines kept up with him. The "thankless and arduous" task of guarding the continuously moving wagon trains was given to Colonel Currie.[38]

Lee had hoped that Early's raids would force Grant to send reinforcements to northern Virginia; he was even prepared to sacrifice a whole division of his army if it diverted the Federals away from Petersburg and Richmond. Francis Dawson was among the cavalry force under General Fitz Lee, which arrived in the Shenandoah Valley on August 8. "I then realized, as never before," wrote Dawson, "the devastation of war. . . . The brutal Sheridan was carrying out his fell purpose . . . columns of smoke were rising in every direction from burning houses and burning barns."[39] Yet he prevaricated to his parents, telling them the Confederacy was "tattered but like our soldiers it stands well."[40]

The detachment of forty thousand Federal troops made little difference to Grant's strength in southern Virginia, whereas Lee needed every man in the trenches. Grant was relentless, probing and attacking any perceived weakness in the Confederate defenses. "[He] is a man of such infinite resource and ceaseless activity," wrote Charles Francis Adams, Jr., admiringly on August 13. "Scarcely does one scheme fail before he has another on foot; baffled in one direction he immediately gropes round for a vulnerable point elsewhere—that I cannot but hope for great results the whole time. He has deserved success so often that he will surely have it at last."[41]

General Butler's Army of the James finally had worse things to worry about than the biting flies. "We have had no fighting here since I last wrote," James Horrocks admitted to his parents just before the army was deployed on August 14. "We have been remarkably quiet. I believe we have not fired a shot nor had a shot fired at us for over a month." But Horrocks came down with typhus and did not take part in the march to Deep Bottom (so named after a deep bend in the James River about eleven miles southeast of Richmond), where Grant planned to mount a second attack—the first had ended badly on July 27—against Lee's defenses at Chaffin's Bluff.[42] Horrocks's illness saved him from participating in what turned out to be the second of three assaults at Chaffin's Bluff. On this occasion, a lack of proper planning meant that the ships carrying the troops along the river were too big to dock at the designated landing areas. The schedule for the operations was thrown into disarray, and the Confederates succeeded in driving the Federals back to the river.

Among the three thousand casualties on August 14 was Robert Moffat Livingstone, the eighteen-year-old son of Dr. David Livingstone, the celebrated missionary and explorer. The boy had been missing for more than a year. Livingstone had ordered Robert to sail from England and join him in Kilmane, Portuguese East Africa, in early 1863, but the wayward youth had changed his mind and journeyed only as far as Natal, South Africa, where he absconded with the ship's money box.[*43] Robert worked his passage to America and joined the 3rd New Hampshire Infantry in January 1864, enlisting under the name of Rupert Vincent. His regiment had suffered several losses at Deep Bottom, including their colonel, Josiah Plimpton; but it was actually heatstroke that felled Robert, a common problem that week. He was taken to a field hospital, where he became lost in the system for more than a month, leading his commanding officers to assume he had deserted. At least his family now knew where he was; Robert finally wrote to his favorite sister, confessing that army life was not at all how he had envisioned.[44] "Robert has gone all to the bad," lamented Dr. Livingstone when he heard the news. Despite his grief, Livingstone did not give up on him entirely, resolving that if Robert behaved himself, he would try to help him obtain an officer's commission.[45]

The heat that had put Robert in the hospital was reaching some of the highest temperatures in recent memory. Lawley wrote in *The Times* that the past twenty days had been the worst he had ever known. "Night and day the mercury of the Fahrenheit has touched 90, and has sometimes gone considerably above that figure." Visiting Richmond, he saw that people cleaved at all times to the shady side of the streets, flitting like "pale shadows" under the harsh sun.[46] "The drought still continues to

---

[*] Since the death of Livingstone's wife, Mary, in 1862, relations between father and son had become strained to the breaking point. Dr. Livingstone had not seen his son—or any of his other children—for several years, though he continued to send them long, disapproving letters from East Africa. Robert was a restless, lonely boy—"dour, determined, impulsive," was how one contemporary described him. Far from acceding to his father's wish for him to train as a doctor, Robert wanted to join the army or navy. At one point, he absconded from school and became lost for a short time in the underworld of Limehouse in London, where sailors' hostels operated side by side with opium dens and brothels.

the total destruction, I fear, of all crops, especially of our vegetables," the Confederate chief of ordnance, Josiah Gorgas, wrote despairingly.[47] Naturally, this was not something that Lawley cared to admit, and in his next dispatch he managed to turn every adversity into a seeming virtue. "Lee has, as usual, the odds against him," he allowed, "and yet at no moment has the confidence of Secessia in the security in Richmond and Petersburg been more serene."[48] The true feelings of "Secessia" were more accurately expressed by Gorgas, who wrote in his diary on August 29: "Can we hold out much longer?"[49]

THIRTY-ONE

The Crisis Comes

Not enough men—Lincoln upholds the message of Gettysburg—Lord Lyons insists—Colonel Grenfell's new mission—Failure of the Copperheads

The South was nearly bankrupt. In mid-July, President Davis persuaded George A. Trenholm to take over from Christopher Memminger as secretary of the treasury—even though the businessman told him frankly that it was too late to improve the Confederacy's finances. Its rampant inflation and crippling shortages were evidence of an economy that was no longer functioning. The South's military position also looked critical, especially in the West, and on July 17, 1864, Davis removed General Joe Johnston from command of the Army of Tennessee. The cabinet unanimously backed the decision. General William T. Sherman had invaded Georgia on May 7 with a force of a hundred thousand men, and for the past three months Richmond had been expecting to hear of a great battle between the two armies. But Johnston had insisted on pursuing a strategy of attrition, arguing that he could wear Sherman down through defensive maneuvering and then attack once the numerically superior Federals were too weak to resist.

The problem for Johnston was that whenever he settled his men into a seemingly impregnable position, Sherman simply marched around him and continued toward Atlanta. Johnston succeeded in having one battle of his choosing, at Kennesaw Mountain on June 27, less than thirty miles from Atlanta, but Sherman easily absorbed the three thousand casualties and moved forward. Johnston abandoned the mountain, but before he could establish a new defensive line the Federals had crossed the last natural barrier before Atlanta—the Chattahoochee River—on July 8. Now there were no more mountains or rivers to stand in the way of Sherman's advance. Losing Atlanta would not only be politically disastrous; Davis knew that its capture would "open the way for the Federal Army to the Gulf on the one hand, and to Charleston on the other." The South would be split in two: "It would give them control of our network of railways and thus paralyze our efforts."[1] Davis replaced Johnston with one of his subordinate commanders, thirty-three-year-old General John Bell Hood, who had been lobbying for weeks to be allowed to wage a more aggressive campaign.

Atlanta was not the only city under threat. Mobile's defenses were crumbling, and the survival of Charleston—where the Federal bombardment was under way—rested on Fort Sumter's continuing to keep the enemy out of the harbor. Captain Henry Feilden was fighting his own battles with the Ordnance Department for more guns. (There was still no word of his promotion, despite General Jones's having added his own letter of recommendation to General Beauregard's.) He did not wish to sound defeatist, but if Mobile were to fall, Feilden told General Gorgas, "Farragut's fleet would be set at liberty for operations to the eastern coast, and there can be little doubt that Charleston would be the first place assailed . . . in our present position, I feel deeply apprehensive as to the result of a grand naval attack."[2]

Feilden was unable to press his point further; in August he was sent on a special mission to Florida. "Throughout this State but especially on the Coast there are large numbers of deserters and desperadoes who have fled from our armies and hid themselves in these almost inaccessible wilds," he explained to Julia. "The General now wishes to apply the policy of reconciliation, and I shall go down amongst them as an ambassador. I think with good care we may have some success, but they will be a hard crowd to deal with."[3] Feilden kept Julia amused with wry descriptions of his journey along the country roads of the Deep South. He made a brief stop in Savannah, Georgia, where he stayed at a plantation remarkably untouched by the war. His bedroom, he told Julia, was decorated with French china: "You will think me very foolish perhaps noticing all these things, but I am so fond of pretty house arrangements." While he was there, he dined with an aging officer who remembered selling cotton to his grandfather, old Sir William Feilden.[4]

The South could not afford Feilden to return empty-handed. It had run through its reserves of able-bodied men, and there were now so few officers left that one of the Confederate brigadier generals killed at Deep Bottom was only twenty-four years old. The War Department clerk John Jones had heard that General Bragg was recommending "publication be made here, in the United States, and in Europe, encouraging enlistments of foreigners in our army."[5] Bragg had probably been inspired by the unexpected arrival in Richmond of four Polish army officers in early August who claimed that thousands of Polish exiles would fight for the South in return for grants of land after the war. The manpower shortage was so acute that Davis was willing to believe them; he authorized the South's financial agent in Britain, Colin McRae, to spend £50,000 to charter transport ships for the Poles allegedly waiting to enlist.[6] Benjamin also agreed to Henry MacIver's request for passage on a blockade runner so he could return to Scotland and raise volunteers for the Confederacy. (The arrangement brought to a close the Scottish officer's disappointing career in the Confederate army, which had ended with him sidelined to provost marshal duties and beset with health problems brought on by syphilis.)[7]

The Confederate Navy Department was lacking not men, but ships. At the beginning of August, the Confederate navy secretary, Stephen Mallory, detached the *Tallahassee* from the fleet defending Wilmington and sent it on a commerce raid up and down the East Coast. The vessel was a former blockade runner purchased by Mallory from an English blockade-running firm and converted into a raider. The *Tallahassee* destroyed twenty-six vessels during its nineteen-day voyage—Northern papers reacted as though the entire Eastern Seaboard was under attack—but the brief sensation was won at a terrible cost to Southern supplies. Lee had argued strongly against the plan, and his fears were proved right. The *Tallahassee* consumed the last of Wilmington's supply of smokeless coal, forcing blockade runners to burn the more conspicuous black variety, which led to the capture of seven ships. The Federal navy took advantage of the *Tallahassee*'s absence to double the size of the blockading fleet around Wilmington. Fresh sailors were sent to the U.S. Navy ships, including Henry Morton Stanley, whose previous history as both a Confederate and a Federal deserter was unknown to the authorities.[*]

The *Tallahassee* was an embarrassment to Lord Lyons as well as the U.S. Navy Department. The Northern press, Lyons informed Russell, constantly referred to the vessel as the "Anglo-Rebel pirate." He suspected that the stalemate in Virginia and Georgia had created more than the usual need to find scapegoats, and advised the foreign secretary to refrain from making any sort of public statement about American affairs. "I should say the quieter England and France were just at this moment the better." The subject was too volatile, especially since the "Peace Party" was becoming bolder in its demands for an armistice. Lincoln's popularity had fallen precipitously since the slaughter in Virginia and the fiasco of the crater explosion at Petersburg. The latest news from Atlanta was also disappointing: Sherman had defeated Hood in three separate engagements, and yet the city remained in Confederate hands. Newspapers throughout the North harped on the administration's failures: "Who shall revive the withered hopes that bloomed at the beginning of General Grant's campaign?" asked the Democratic *New York World*. "Who is responsible for the terrible and unavailing loss of life . . . after the opening of a campaign that promised to be triumphant?"[9] Lyons feared that "Mr. Lincoln's chance of the Presidency for a second term seems vanishing."[10]

———

Jefferson Davis had been praying for this moment: the Northern public and press were growing weary of the war. His original belief that Southern independence would be achieved through British recognition had been proved wrong, and his hopes that Lee would deliver independence through his victories had been dashed, but he still had faith that the South would prevail if it could break the Northern will to fight. He now realized that Britain's neutral stance was not a curse but a boon to the Confederacy, since Canada was the perfect staging post for waging psychological warfare against the North. The special commissioners in

---

[*] Stanley had returned to the North from Wales in January 1863, having failed to reconcile with his family or to find satisfactory employment. But he had fared no better in America, and after working at various jobs he joined the U.S. Navy on July 19, 1864. He was assigned to USS *Minnesota* as a ship's clerk, a light position that would expose him to danger only if the vessel received a direct hit. Otherwise, he anticipated a summer of little excitement other than the occasional chase of an unarmed blockade runner.[8]

AMERICA
ANOTHER FEDERAL
DEFEAT

VERY PROBABLE.

Lord Punch. "THAT WAS JEFF DAVIS, PAM! DON'T YOU RECOGNISE HIM?"
Lord Pam. "HM! WELL, NOT EXACTLY—MAY HAVE TO DO SO SOME OF THESE DAYS."

Punch's view that Britain (Palmerston) will soon have to recognize the Confederacy (Jefferson Davis).

Canada, Jacob Thompson and Clement C. Clay, could move about with relative ease, and even if they failed to inflict serious damage on Northern targets, their activities might provoke Washington into declaring war against Britain. Davis was sure that recognition of the South would be among the first steps, if not the very first, that Britain would take against the North.

Thompson and Clay had quickly realized that they would never work well together, but they had created enough separation between their projects to minimize potential friction. Clay preferred to work with James Holcombe, a former law professor at the University of Virginia who had been in Canada for the past five months on a separate mission for the Confederate State Department.*[11] Clay was hoping to romance disaffected Northern politicians into believing that an armistice was in the interest of both sides. It seemed to him that the peace advocates were willing to believe almost anything. "We have not dispelled the fond delusion of most of those with whom we have conversed, that some kind of common government might—at some time hereafter—be established," he wrote archly to Benjamin.[12] One of these intermediaries convinced the editor of the *New York Tribune,* Horace Greeley, that Clay and Holcombe had been given the authority to negotiate peace terms with the North.[13] Greeley used the power of his newspaper to confront Lincoln over his reluctance to consider the Confederates' terms: "I entreat you to submit overtures for pacification to the Southern insurgents," he urged melodramatically. "Our bleeding, bankrupt, almost dying country also longs for peace."[14] The public, Greeley insisted, would vote for a Democratic president in November if Lincoln seemed to care more about war than peace.

Lincoln knew enough about the Confederate commissioners in Canada to be certain that political embarrassment rather than peace was their goal, but he also knew that he could not afford to be portrayed as deaf to potential overtures from the South. Yet there were no terms that the South could offer—other than the abolition of slavery and restoration of the Union—that he would accept. In contrast to many Northerners, and even some conservative Republicans, Lincoln's belief in the principles articulated at Gettysburg—liberty and democracy—was unshakable, and he would not trade them for peace, or for his reelection in November.

---

*On December 7, 1863, seventeen Confederate sympathizers—many of them British—had boarded the steamer *Chesapeake* in New York and hijacked it once they were in international waters. The intention was to turn the vessel into a privateer, but the adventure quickly degenerated into farce. The *Chesapeake* ran out of coal and most of the crew deserted. The vessel was captured by a U.S. warship and towed into Halifax harbor on December 15. Once it became known that a Canadian was among the prisoners, a furious crowd took over Queen's Wharf, determined to free him. Five more U.S. Navy ships appeared in the harbor and a tense standoff ensued. Finally, on December 19, the U.S. naval officers bowed to pressure and all the prisoners were rowed to shore, whereupon the crowd "rescued" the Canadian. Holcombe had been ordered to find any legal argument, no matter how weak, to claim the *Chesapeake* as a Southern prize. But to his embarrassment he discovered that none of the Chesapeake privateers were actually from the South, and the Confederates had no claim to their services or the vessel.

Lincoln skillfully wrong-footed Greeley by inviting him to be the North's representative in these apparently genuine discussions for peace. Greeley had no choice but to accept, and on July 18, with Lincoln's private secretary John Hay accompanying him as a witness, he met with Clay and Holcombe on the Canadian side of Niagara Falls. Hay was carrying a letter from Lincoln to the commissioners, addressed "To Whom It May Concern." It offered them safe conduct to Washington to discuss the war under the following terms: "the integrity of the whole Union, and the abandonment of slavery"; no other condition would be acceptable. The discussion unfolded much as Lincoln had expected, with Clay admitting that he had no authority to negotiate a peace and Greeley and Hay returning empty-handed. But the Confederates had pried out of Lincoln a statement about slavery and its fundamental place in the war that could only make him more unpopular with the great mass of voters in the West, who still thought they were fighting for the Union rather than abolition.

The "To Whom It May Concern" letter was indeed the last straw for some Lincoln supporters. The treasurer of the U.S. Sanitary Commission, George Templeton Strong, thought "his letter . . . may cost him his election. By declaring that abandonment of slavery is a fundamental article in any negotiation for peace and settlement, he has given the disaffected and discontented a weapon."[15] Charles Francis Adams, Jr., was shocked by the palpable sense of defeat among the cabinet when he visited Washington at the end of August. (He was on furlough, recovering from an attack of jaundice caused by malaria.) He had transferred from Meade's staff to an all-black regiment, the 5th Massachusetts (Colored) Cavalry, and was waiting to take up his commission as lieutenant colonel in September. His own convictions about the aim of the war and the necessity of seeing it through remained strong despite his recent experiences in Virginia; but a meeting with Seward left him deeply concerned. "His tone was very different from that of last spring," Charles Francis Jr. wrote to his father on August 20, "when he seemed to me so buoyant and confident of the future. . . . I was pained to feel how discouraged he was. He too gave me the impression which all here do, of 'going it wild' and not seeing where this thing is going to come out."[16]

Contrary to Charles Francis Jr.'s fears, Seward was one of the few politicians not scheming to replace Lincoln or flirting with ideas for a negotiated peace. But "the Tide is setting strongly against us," warned the editor of *The New York Times*, Henry Raymond, on August 22. As chairman of the Republican National Committee, Raymond had substantial influence. He saw no hope for Lincoln, barring a sudden military success, unless the administration declared its willingness to consider reunion with slavery intact.[17] Even Edwin Stanton, whose longevity at the War Department owed much to his loyalty to Lincoln, decided that it might be worth finding out from the Confederate commissioners what sort of terms the South would be willing to discuss. On August 19, 1864, Judge Jeremiah Black, a moderate Democrat and old friend of Stanton's, visited Commissioner Thompson in Toronto. Three days after the meeting, Thompson wrote to Mason and Slidell in France that Stanton had sent Black to him because he had lost all confidence in the Republicans' reelection. "Judge Black has come to me to learn the state of feeling in the Confederate States, and to know whether I was able to say if negotiations for peace could be opened without the ultimatum of final separation."[18] Stanton never did learn the answer, because on August 22 the *New York Herald* exposed the meeting, which frightened him into repudiating any connection with the visit. Facing treachery in his cabinet, abandoned by the Republican National Committee, and excoriated in the press, Lincoln believed that his chances of reelection were slim. Yet "I honestly believe that I can better serve the nation in its need and peril than any new man could possibly do," he told Thaddeus Kane, the chairman of the House Ways and Means Committee.[19] The following day, the twenty-third, Lincoln put his cabinet to the test: he asked them to demonstrate their loyalty by signing their names at the bottom of a covered document. They did not know it, but each man was committing himself to the war until the last day of the Lincoln presidency, assuming the Democrats won the White House in November:

> This morning, as for some days past, it seems exceedingly probable that this Administration will not be re-elected [read the memorandum], then it will be my duty to so cooperate with the President elect, as to save the Union between the election and the inauguration; as he will have secured his election on such ground that he can not possibly save it afterwards.[20]

While these somber proceedings were taking place in Lincoln's office, across the parched park of Lafayette Square, Lord Lyons was writing his assessment of the president's future. The situation was indeed bleak, but "there is still a *possibility*," Lyons insisted to Lord Russell, "of some military successes before the winter, which might make a great change in public feeling."[21] Lyons had hoped for some sign of progress before he left for Canada to discuss with the governor-general, Viscount Monck, how to restrain Confederate operations in North America. The trip had been planned since July, but Lyons was loath to leave the legation before at least some of his cases were settled. "I heartily wish I could get away from Washington, and go at once to Canada," he had written to Russell on August 9, "but with two Members of the Legation away on account of their health, and two more ailing, I am afraid the work cannot be done at all without me."[22]

Those unresolved cases included that of Mary Sophia Hill, who had written again to the legation. She had been tried in a military court and a verdict apparently reached. "But no official statement has been made, or any public verdict given, nor can I get any satisfaction," she wrote in a shaky hand on August 20:

> I have been tried according to their own laws, and after four weeks, common justice, I should think, would demand a verdict . . . the shocks my nervous system has received from the confinement and from the rough treatment I received from my jailer and assistant, as well as the excitement of my trial, and now four weeks suspense as to result, will make me an invalid for life and has very nearly upset my reason. I am not, never ever have been, guilty of the charges brought against me. . . . But there seems a spirit of bitterness against HM's subjects here, and very little law or justice for them.[23]

Lyons agreed that the law and justice were becoming two quite separate entities for British subjects. Whether Mary was as innocent as she claimed would make no difference, he was quite certain, in her treatment by the military authorities. It was only a gross injustice—resulting in the death of a conscripted Briton—that had recently forced a change in the War Department's approach to disputed enlistments so that alleged British subjects were removed from the battlefield while their cases were under review.*

At the end of August, Lyons decided he could not take another day in the capital: "The thermometer in the House literally stands as high at midnight as at noon." He ordered his two favorite attachés, Edward Malet and George Sheffield, to be ready to leave for Canada with him on the thirtieth. The new secretary, Joseph Burnley, would just have to do his best.

———

The Canadian authorities had warned London that the Confederates in British North America were not only "hostile in spirit" to the North but also "prepared to give expression to that hostility in overt acts."[25] Fitzgerald Ross was astonished by the brash behavior of the Confederate community on the Canadian side of Niagara Falls. He and Colonel Grenfell had arrived at Clifton House in mid-July to find the hotel awash with conspiracies. "The 'season' had hardly yet commenced," wrote Ross, but the place was so busy that it seemed to be in midflow. Scores of survivors from John Morgan's failed raid into Kentucky were hanging around the colonnaded hotel and were "delighted to meet their old Colonel again." In his travel account, Ross tried to make the meeting sound coincidental and harmless. The Morgan raiders passed the time "talking Secesh politics and plotting mischief against the Yankees," he wrote, as though the conspirators were nothing more than nostalgic veterans who liked to reminisce about the glory days and plan the occasional nuisance.[26]

Ross's breezy memoir left out the real details of their stay at Niagara. It was the week of Commissioner Clement C. Clay and James Holcombe's peace conference with Horace Greeley; it was also the week that

---

* The victim was Andrew Cunningham, a British subject who had been kidnapped and forced into the 39th New York Volunteers on January 8, 1864. Lyons was alerted to his plight on February 11 and immediately petitioned for his release. The facts regarding Cunningham's kidnapping were never in dispute, but even so the usual delays followed. Finally, on June 7, 1864, after considerable nudging from Lyons, Seward gleaned from the War Department that Cunningham's release had been ordered. Six weeks went by without further communication on the subject. Seward had completely forgotten about Cunningham when, on July 23, 1864, he received a sheepish note from Charles Dana, assistant secretary of war. They had been unable to find Private Cunningham because he had been killed in battle on May 10, 1864, four weeks before his discharge.[24]

Grenfell was reunited with the Confederate agent Thomas Hines.[*27] Grenfell sent a mysterious letter from Niagara to his daughter, Mary. "There is still work to be done and I am awaiting events," he wrote, before warning her that he was planning to disappear "for a month or so I hope, before I again get into the saddle. . . . It is impossible to give a safe opinion upon what may take place in the South within the next three months, but they cannot subjugate it, never, never!"[28] Ross parted from Grenfell at the end of July and returned to England in the autumn, intending to write a book about his adventures in the South. He never imagined that the "mischief" had actually grown into a conspiracy involving the exiled Copperhead Clement Vallandigham and the underground group the Sons of Liberty.

Vallandigham had been living a lonely and frustrating existence in Windsor, Ontario, since his expulsion to the South in 1863 and subsequent escape on a blockade runner to Bermuda. Windsor's chief recommendation was its location on Canada's southern boundary, facing Detroit. Vallandigham's suite on the second floor of the Hirons House hotel afforded him a fine view of the forbidden fruit across the river. The hotel was also situated next to the ferry landing, which made it convenient for pilgrimages by Copperheads and loyal allies in the Democratic Party.[29] Desperation had driven Vallandigham to accept an offer from the Sons of Liberty to become its "Supreme Grand Commander." The original Sons of Liberty was a revolutionary organization formed before the War of Independence to demoralize and intimidate the loyalist supporters. In its new incarnation, the Sons of Liberty combined paramilitary aims with Masonic-like rituals, complete with secret signs, elaborate initiations, and large stockpiles of weapons in several states.

Far more popular in the Northwest than anywhere else in the country, the Sons of Liberty nevertheless attracted an eccentric constituency, and its numbers fluctuated wildly from a few thousand across the country to 18,000 in Indiana alone.[30] The grand commander of the organization, an Indiana printer named Harrison H. Dodd, needed Vallandigham

---

[*] The Confederate government believed there were four hundred escaped prisoners of war hiding out in Canada and Nova Scotia. James Holcombe had been ordered to advertise in local newspapers that he had the means to pay for their passage home. But his efforts to locate the missing four hundred yielded only six Confederates. Hines, on the other hand, had no trouble locating the survivors of Morgan's brigade, whom he trained for his operations against the North.

since the Sons of Liberty was in danger of collapsing unless it could find a national figure sufficiently credible to attract more members. Vallandigham needed the Sons of Liberty almost as much; his resounding defeat in the 1863 election for governor of Ohio had been a major setback. General McClellan looked certain to win the Democratic Party's nomination for president unless Vallandigham used the organizing capabilities of the Sons of Liberty to force his way into the selection process.

Thompson and Captain Hines's first meeting with Vallandigham took place at Windsor on June 11, 1864. "On my arrival here I heard that there was such an organization as the Order of the Sons of Liberty in the Northern States, and my first effort was to learn its strength, it principles, and its objects, and if possible to put myself in communication with its leading spirits," Thompson reported back to Judah Benjamin. "This was effected without much difficulty or delay. I was received among them with cordiality, and the greatest confidence at once extended to me." His investigations into the society revealed that the membership was not as large as Vallandigham had boasted to him, but

> its organization was essentially military. It had its commanders of divisions, of brigades, of regiments, of companies. The belief was entertained, and freely expressed that by a bold, vigorous, and concerted movement the three great Northwestern States of Illinois, Indiana, and Ohio could be seized and held. This being done, the States of Kentucky and Missouri could easily be lifted from their prostrate condition and placed on their feet, and this in sixty days would end the war.[31]

Vallandigham was hedging his bets. He was hoping to lead the Democrats to victory in the presidential election, but was prepared to reap the fruits of an armed uprising in the Northwest if his political ambitions failed. He was counting on Thompson to provide the arms and explosives for his members.

Thompson did not care whether Vallandigham wanted reunion or Southern independence so long as he was committed to fomenting a revolution in the North. He agreed to fund a joint venture between his Confederate raiders and Vallandigham's Sons of Liberty to make a coordinated attack on the three prisoner-of-war camps in Illinois and Indiana. The prisoners would provide a ready army to help the conspirators stage a coup d'état in the Northwest, and as soon as this was accomplished, they would return to the South to help finish the war. Thompson hoped that the prison break would bring an additional fifty thousand fighters to the Confederacy.

Captain Hines, Colonel Grenfell, and some sixty former members of Morgan's brigade were to attack the prisons; the Sons of Liberty would have the responsibility for rounding up the chiefs of the local legislatures and disposing of them. "All they need now is an 'occasion,' as they style it, to rise and assert their rights," Thompson had reported to Benjamin on July 7.[32] There was no attempt at any strategic planning, no discussion as to which camps would be liberated first or how the army of liberated prisoners would be fed, transported, and clothed; but this did not stop Thompson from writing hundreds of thousands of dollars' worth of checks. Confederate sympathizers and corrupt middlemen shipped cartloads of revolvers hidden in boxes marked "Sunday school books" to Ohio and Indiana. New York proved to be especially fertile ground for obtaining illicit guns and ammunition.

All the Confederates had assigned themselves aliases, which fooled no one and only served to give the conspirators a false sense of security. "Dear Hunter [the alias used by Thomas Hines]," wrote Grenfell on July 31 from Collingwood on the Canadian side of Lake Huron, "there is fair fishing round the place but better further North . . . if any news write immediately."[33] Grenfell was waiting for Hines to give him the signal to go south to Toronto, which was the agreed rendezvous point for the plotters. However, the date for the uprising was proving difficult to pin down with the Sons of Liberty, and the "occasion" had been pushed back several times. Vallandigham had returned to Ohio, hoping to be arrested by the authorities in the belief that this would provoke a public backlash violent enough to spark a revolt. But to his dismay, Lincoln gave orders for the troublemaker to be ignored, which deprived Vallandigham of the intoxicating power of indignation. Ironically, Grant's military failures in Virginia had also weakened the Sons of Liberty's resolve, since public weariness with the war made it seem likely that democracy rather than conspiracy would soon bring peace. Representatives for the Sons of Liberty tried to cancel the mission, telling Hines and Thompson on August 8: "The more we think of it the more thoroughly are we convinced that it will be unsuccessful."[34]

The organization had been successfully infiltrated and arrests were already beginning to take place, including those of fifty leading men from the Sons of Liberty in Kentucky on July 30. Two days later the state's grand commander, Judge Joshua Bullitt, was seized as he stepped off the ferryboat on his return from a conference with Thompson and Hines in Canada. A search of his belongings revealed a satchel full of gold, a check for $10,000 signed by Jacob Thompson, and many incriminating papers.[35] The leaders of the Indiana chapter, including Harrison Dodd, were arrested three weeks later. The Confederates were equally guilty of jeopardizing the mission. They knew U.S. detectives were tailing them but failed to alter their behavior. The same basic ciphers were used, the same routines followed, and there was much careless talk in public places. By now the Federal authorities had a clear idea that some sort of attack on Camp Douglas was being planned in a joint Copperhead-Confederate operation.

Thompson and Hines would not be put off, however, and managed to pry out of the Sons of Liberty a new date for the uprising. It would now take place on August 29 in Chicago during the Democratic National Convention. The obvious wavering of the Sons of Liberty made the Confederates anxious, but they reckoned that even if only half the promised five thousand members actually came, there would still be a reasonable chance of success. Hines sent out the long-awaited signal for his followers to convene in Toronto. On August 24 Thompson handed Hines his written orders and $24,000 to cover the expenses of the mission. Over the next few days, Grenfell and sixty others slipped into Toronto. Each man was provided with $100 in cash, a pistol, ammunition, and a return train ticket to Chicago. Hines outlined the plan: they were to travel inconspicuously, in groups not larger than three or four. Once in Chicago they would meet at the Richmond House hotel for the rendezvous with the Sons of Liberty. One force would make for Camp Douglas to liberate its 5,500 inmates. The other would travel two hundred miles west to Rock Island Barracks to release its 9,000 Confederate prisoners.

Grenfell left with Hines and a couple of others on August 26. He chose as his costume for the occasion a gray hunting suit, in the same hue as the Confederate uniform, two sporting guns, and a yellow-spotted hunting dog—a loud disguise entirely characteristic of him. When one of Grenfell's traveling companions pointed out that the suit would probably cause him to be arrested the minute he stepped off the train, he replied: "I have my English papers, and my gun and my dog, and if they ask me what I am doing, I will say I am going hunting."[36] The party reached Chicago on August 28 and proceeded straight to Richmond House. Grenfell signed the register under his own name. Hines, on the other hand, kept to his alias of Hunter. The Confederates had a suite of rooms—all labeled "Missouri Delegation"—which was deemed a sufficient disguise to allow them to blend in with the thousands of real delegates who were crowded four to a room in the city's overburdened hotels. (The plumbing, which had so irritated Anthony Trollope during his stay in the city, remained unimproved.)

That night, the Confederates and Sons of Liberty met for the first time since the secret conferences in Canada. They revealed "that something had gone wrong": no orders had been sent to the forty thousand members in Ohio or the fifty thousand in Indiana. By way of exculpation they pointed out that the mission had already been exposed in several newspapers and that Camp Douglas had received additional Federal troops.[37] The Confederates were incensed. It seemed impossible that the hundreds of thousands of dollars funneled to the Sons of Liberty would fail to produce a single fighter. Outside the hotel windows the city was heaving with antiwar protesters, many of them obviously wearing sidearms. At least some of them, Hines insisted, would be eager to see a little action.

The embarrassed conspirators agreed to supply the Confederates with five hundred men by the following evening. The Camp Douglas plan would be abandoned, and the less guarded prison at Rock Island would become the sole target. Under the new plan, one of Hines's deputies, John Castleman, and twenty Confederates would accompany the Sons of Liberty, while Hines and the remaining fifty would provide support by cutting the telegraph wires and stopping all trains in and out of Chicago. With the help of the prisoners from Rock Island Barracks, they would commandeer the trains and head two hundred miles south to Springfield, the state capital. In a few hours, Illinois would be theirs.

The Confederates waited uneasily for the sun to set. Outside, excited crowds tramped to and from the convention hall. Vallandigham avoided Richmond House: he was far too busy squeezing and working the delegate system. Prison breaks and political assassinations could not have been further from his mind. Only Charles Walsh, the leader of the Chicago chapter of the Sons of Liberty, and a couple of sidekicks bothered to return to Hines's rooms. He did not have five hundred men, or one hundred men, or even fifty men, although he thought he might be able to find twenty-five if given enough time. When the Confederates insisted this was not enough, Walsh suggested November 8—the day of the election—as the new date for the prison liberation. Hines agreed through gritted teeth, swearing he would hold them to that day no matter what the cost. Once the Sons of Liberty left, the Confederates passed the rest of the night pondering their options. The snippets of news that filtered along the corridors of the hotel indicated that Vallandigham had failed to derail McClellan's bid for the Democratic Party's nomination. Just about every expectation held by Hines, Grenfell, and the rest had turned out to be wrong. There was no seething undercurrent of revolution, no paramilitary organization of well-armed fighters, no willingness in any quarter to take risks.

It was too dangerous for the Confederates to remain in Chicago. Hines outlined their choices during a noisy meeting of the disappointed volunteers: they could use their tickets to return to Canada, attempt to sneak home, or stay with him and hide out in southern Illinois until November 8. Twenty chose Canada; another twenty-five said they would go south. The rest agreed to help Hines build a force from scratch among the Illinois members of the Sons of Liberty. Grenfell, as usual, made a fourth choice. He would maintain the hunting charade and shoot prairie chickens around Carlyle, Illinois, until called to duty.[38] "Tell the girls I am alive and well, although engaged in rather dangerous speculations, which you will know more of, probably, bye and bye," he wrote on August 31 to the Grenfell family business manager in London.

> The North West states are ripe for revolt. If interfered with in their election they will rise. All this is in favour of the South. . . .
> We are on the eve of great events. Abe Lincoln will either have made peace, or made himself a military dictator, within the next two months. In the latter case the N. W. Provinces secede, and there comes a row. Either course aids the South.[39]

Jacob Thompson shared Grenfell's delusion that the Northwest was smoldering with revolutionary aims. The Copperhead leaders were cowards, he claimed to Judah Benjamin, but "the feeling with the masses is as strong as ever. They are true, brave, and, I believe, willing and ready."[40] Indeed, Thompson was angry with Hines for giving up so quickly on the Chicago expedition. He refused to work with the Confederates who returned to Toronto, calling them "deserters." Thompson blamed everyone for the mission's failure, including Clay and Holcombe, whom he accused of weakening the Copperheads' resolve by having dangled the prospect of a negotiated peace at the Niagara Falls conference in July.

Thompson had become a bitter and vengeful man since his arrival in Canada; during his absence from home, Federal soldiers had burned his Mississippi plantation and assaulted his wife. Isolated from friends and family and surrounded by like-minded fugitives, Thompson turned his personal grievances into an excuse to inflict the greatest possible suffering on the North, and in particular on Northern civilians. Nothing, he complained to Clay, should distract the Confederates from delivering the message of violence.

THIRTY-TWO

The Tyranny of Hope

Clinging to power—How to orchestrate a public protest—Rose Greenhow
makes her decision—Petitioning for peace—Atlanta

Lord Palmerston was facing the prospect of defeat in the twilight of his parliamentary career. "They [the opposition] have had their Meeting and have agreed upon a vote of Censure," Palmerston wrote to Gladstone on June 28, 1864, after Lord Russell's peace conference in London ended embarrassingly for the British government, without an armistice agreement between Germany and Denmark. Palmerston could not escape the truth that it was his own pugnacious declaration the previous July—that Denmark could always rely on Britain's support—that had started the government's woes. The Danes had believed him; the French resented him; and the Germans had known he was bluffing—even if it was some months before Palmerston realized it himself.

There was a national uproar after Palmerston and Russell announced that Britain would not fight alongside the Danes after all. Whether the government's course was right or wrong mattered less than the obvious fact that it was a complete reversal from the one originally proposed. On July 4, Disraeli introduced in the House of Commons the motion against the government. "Yet I am more than doubtful about the result," the Southern propagandist Henry Hotze reported to Judah Benjamin. He considered the Tory Party to be destitute of policies; "the chief end of its tactics is to get into office without committing itself on either of the two great questions . . . the American and the Danish." This, feared Hotze, could be their undoing.[1]

Henry Adams was tickled to be so close to and yet untouched by the Liberals' political crisis. "Everyone who has an office, or whose family has an office, is in a state of funk at the idea of losing it," he chuckled to Charles Francis Jr. Recently he had been feeling flat and "more and more doubtful every day as to what life is made for," he had confided to his brother. "I am getting old, and must be at work. The *chef* can do without me, if he only tries."[2]

The parliamentary debates on the censure continued for four days. Gladstone's speech in the Commons sealed his position as the undisputed leader-in-waiting of the Liberal Party, although it was not strong enough to silence the government's critics. "I wish either that one could put one's nerves into one's pocket . . . or that one could run away from the future," Henry wrote to his brother on July 8. "The division takes place tonight, and the excitement in society is tremendous." Their father had heard that the government was down to a majority of two or four votes in the Commons. He was surprised to find himself hoping the Liberals would prevail.

The Confederate commissioner James Mason was still waiting for the interview with Palmerston that William Schaw Lindsay had promised in June. The prime minister had played his part with finesse, making no commitments to the pro-Southern faction in Parliament while ensuring that the Tories could not offer them anything that was not already under discussion. Rose Greenhow, who had become close to the opposition through a fortuitous friendship with the Tory hostess Lady Chesterfield, was convinced that the Confederates were wasting their time with the Liberals.[3] Despite telling Mason everything she heard in Lady Chesterfield's drawing room, she could not shake his faith in Palmerston. "Saw Mr. Mason who was very busy," Rose wrote on July 8. "He does not think we have anything to gain by a change in ministry. [For] Queens sake!"

Adams finished his work early that night so he could go to the House of Commons and watch the government fight for its life. He squeezed into the Strangers' Gallery at 5:00 P.M. and sat through seven speakers while waiting for Palmerston to make his stand. It was past midnight when the prime minister finally rose to address the House. "He is not a good speaker, his manner is hesitating," Adams wrote in his diary, which was true of Palmerston at the best of times. "And yet I cannot doubt," he added reluctantly, "that he makes the only real leader now to be found in English politics."[4] The division took place at half past two in the morning, with the Tories confident that they had the votes. Mrs. Greenhow waited impatiently at her lodgings: "I am anxious for news from Parliament," she wrote in her diary. "I am afraid the Government will have a majority."[5] Both Houses divided at the same moment. The peers went against the government by a majority of 9 votes; but in the Commons, the Tories discovered that a handful of MPs had switched sides during the debate, uneasy that the price of government would mean effectively declaring that Britain was no longer a Great Power but a feeble, blustering bully. The Liberals survived by a majority of 18 votes.

"Had the scale turned the other way, the scene would have been worth staying to see," wrote Adams, who left before the result was called. His early departure meant that he missed a first in the history of the Commons.[6] As soon as the numbers were called, Palmerston clambered up the stairs on his gouty foot to the Ladies' Gallery to embrace his wife in plain view of the House. She cared as much as Palmerston himself that when he did go out of politics, it would be on his own terms.

———

With the parliamentary crisis safely behind them, the Confederate lobby at Westminster stepped forward to claim its reward from Palmerston. Lindsay's resolution for mediation was to be the climax of a week of carefully orchestrated events. The Confederate lobby had reasoned— justifiably—that the previous failures in the Commons had been exacerbated by the problem of individuals acting on their own. In order to succeed, they had to appear united, representative of the entire country, and popular among MPs of all persuasions.

For several weeks, Spence's Southern Independence Association had been distributing petitions throughout England calling for British intervention in the war. These were intended to represent the voice of the ordinary public—some of them, like the Manchester petition, contained more than five thousand signatures.[7] Next, Mason was to have his interview with Palmerston, followed by the deputation from the Reverend Francis Tremlett's peace society. Separately, representatives from the cotton factories were to deliver a 90,000-signature-strong petition to Russell. Only then, after the government had heard from the rich and the poor, from manufacturers and merchants, all demonstrating that the country desired action on behalf of the South, would Lindsay put forward his resolution.

The plan began well. At Henry Hotze's instigation, *The Times* reported that the Northern armies had been checked on every front. Lindsay took Mason to see Palmerston at Cambridge House on July 14: "I was received with great civility, and after the ordinary topics of salutation Lord P. commenced the conversation," Mason wrote afterward to Judah Benjamin. Palmerston seemed interested in the South's military options, but he became evasive when Mason asked him for a definite answer as to whether Britain would join with Napoleon in offering to broker an armistice. (If Mason had paid any attention to recent debates in Parliament, he would have realized that the idea of an Anglo-French alliance on practically any issue was preposterous.) He tried not to be disappointed by the interview, but it hardly seemed worth the seven-week wait.

Palmerston was no less opaque when Francis Tremlett and James Spence arrived the following day with the delegation from the Society for Promoting the Cessation of Hostilities in America. Tremlett had collected an impressive group that included six MPs and the president of the Royal College of Surgeons. Palmerston listened politely but quipped, "Those who in quarrels interpose / Will often wipe a bloody nose" and sent them on their way. Lord Russell presented a more sympathetic demeanor to the factory workers who visited the Foreign Office on July 18. Their petition described the poverty and hunger endured by those in the once profitable cotton trade and begged Russell to "enter into concert with other European powers, with a view to restore peace on the American continent." But he was just as vague as Palmerston over when international mediation might be appropriate.

It would have been sensible for Lindsay to retreat at this moment, but the dogged MP would not give up, knowing that if he withdrew his resolution now, there would not be another opportunity to debate intervention for several months. While Lindsay pondered how best to use the limited means at his disposal, Rose Greenhow continued to plead with every member of the government who happened to come her way. She cornered Gladstone at a dinner given by Lord Granville on July 21 and reminded him that less than two years ago he had declared the Confederacy a nation. "Your sympathies have been with us of the South, but your Government have aided the Yankees," she scolded. "Your neutrality is a farce." Gladstone parried her accusations with a mixture of humor and obfuscation. Recognition, he told her, would not help the South and would only make the North angry. Rose tried again on July 24 when Lady Chesterfield brought her to Lady Palmerston's final party of the season and introduced her to the prime minister. Rose was annoyed that he used the same arguments as Gladstone. "Talked a good deal with him," she wrote in her diary. "He asked me how I got over. I said, 'Run the blockade.' "[8]

The next afternoon, Lindsay finally raised the subject in the House of Commons, though he was now certain of the answer. He did not bother trying for a resolution, but simply asked Palmerston the same question put by Mason during his private interview eleven days earlier: whether the government had any intention of ending the war in America. The curt response he received was the same: there was "no advantage to be gained" by doing so, even though "Her Majesty's Government deeply lament the great sacrifice of life and property in America and the distress which that war has produced in this country."[9]

"Thus has terminated an operation which has cost much labor and money to somebody or other" was Charles Francis Adams's sarcastic epitaph.[10] He had paid little attention to the Confederates after Palmerston's successful repulse of the Tory attack, being more concerned with the worsening asthma of his daughter Mary. He blamed the London fogs for undermining her health, adding the crime of bad weather to the long list of malicious and treacherous acts that Britain would one day be called upon to answer.[11] Adams also seemed to draw comfort from his belief that the British upper classes were united in favor of slavery and injustice. He wasted considerable time and effort in July arguing with Lord Russell, despite all evidence to the contrary, that the rescue of the *Alabama*'s officers had been prearranged with the owner of the *Deerhound*. Adams was so intent on proving a conspiracy that he neglected to make capital out of the genuine scandal surrounding the *Alabama:* that Southern officers had saved one another and left the English seamen to drown. Adams also squandered an opportunity to undermine accusations of Northern arrogance and hypocrisy when on July 28 the Commons debated the problem of British workers being kidnapped or tricked into the Federal army. Instead of supplying Northern supporters with information on the latest efforts to stop the abuse, Adams took umbrage against the tone of the complaints and insisted it proved the intent of "the higher classes" to destroy the Union.[12]

Rose Greenhow suffered from the same willful blindness as Adams, though she confused sympathy for Southern suffering (her own in particular) with acceptance of Southern slavery. Few people had the nerve or desire to challenge her fantasy, though the Duchess of Sutherland snubbed Rose in the most pointed manner possible when Lady Chesterfield introduced them at the Kensington horticultural show. Rose was able to comfort herself with the observation that the duchess's girth and "gaudy apparel" compared badly with her own remarkably youthful appearance. She had greater trouble putting aside her embarrassment at an incident during a dinner given by Lord Granville's sister, Lady Georgiana Fullarton. An unnamed earl had pressed her relentlessly on the subject of slave families until she lost her temper and shrilly revealed the ugly prejudices of her native country. Rose sensed the alienation of her audience and was furious. It was at moments like this that she hated the English almost as much as she hated the North.[13]

"My heart yearns to stay and also to go," she wrote in her diary after the prorogation of Parliament. Her diplomatic mission appeared to have fizzled into something resembling a goodwill tour. She had not extracted any new promise from the emperor, nor had she helped Mason and Lindsay achieve any material change in government policy. "I thirst for news from home. The desperate struggle in which my people are engaged is ever present," she wrote unhappily.[14] Rose's book sales had brought her more than £2,000, money she preferred to distribute in the South rather than waste on yet another jolly though meaningless outing with her Tory friends. She assured Mason and Spence that her absence would not be for long. After all, her elder daughter, Florence, had recently joined her in England, and she could not leave little Rose (who was still uncertain about boarding school life) for too long.*

Rose would be joining an exodus of Southerners. Captain Semmes was also making arrangements to go home, though he knew that prison and possibly execution were likely if the Federals caught him. He was

---

* Rose was not alone in feeling guilty about her comfortable life in Britain. When Matthew Fontaine Maury read that the birthday present of his youngest child was to be allowed to eat until full, he confessed to Francis Tremlett that he "felt as if I must choke with the sumptuous viands set before me on the Duke [of Buckingham]'s table."[15]

more than a little in love with Louisa Tremlett, the Reverend Francis Tremlett's sister, and, unwilling to leave just at the moment, had accepted the Tremletts' invitation to accompany them on a walking tour of Europe. Other survivors of the *Alabama* had already left, as had Lieutenant James Morgan of the ill-fated *Georgia*. Rose braved the Channel crossing to France one more time in order to say farewell to her daughter. They went shopping and Rose bought her a watch, "which made her very happy." It was one of the few times the child smiled. "My little darling very miserable that I am going away," wrote Rose on July 28. Two days later, she took little Rose back to the convent "and left her sobbing bitterly. It was a heavy trial . . . my heart is very sad."

Rose was, as usual, desperately seasick during the Channel crossing: "I got a bench on deck, and seated my maid and lay with my head on her lap." She arrived back at 34 Sackville Street on August 1 to find London almost empty. "The season [is] over. . . . Houses shut up. Streets blocked with baggage," she wrote with a tinge of regret. Georgiana Walker, the Confederate exile in Bermuda, had recently arrived with her children and was staying in lodgings on the floor below (she had come to England to consult an ophthalmologist about her younger daughter's failing eyesight). The glamour surrounding Rose as she made her final farewells put Georgiana in awe of her: "The Lords and Ladies and Duchesses are her constant visitors," she wrote in her diary, "and her invitations to dinner parties and balls innumerable."[16] James Mason was also leaving town: "I propose for the next two or three months to visit different points in England and in Ireland, not to return to London unless specially called," he informed Benjamin on August 4.[17]

Charles Francis Adams was about to go on holiday as well, albeit with reluctance. He liked London when it was empty; "to me it is usually a period of the most pleasant relief and satisfaction," he wrote in his diary. "Were my family contented I would cheerfully remain, at least during the warm weather."[18] But the family was most definitely not contented: "Mary and I are plotting to make sure that this be our last season," Henry wrote to Charles Francis Jr. "All this however is as yet unknown to the family, and much depends on Loo." Loo was Henry's married sister, Louise Kuhn, who had come with her husband, Charles, in July for an extended visit.[19] Ironically, Henry did not need his sister's help to persuade their father. Adams was longing for a "release from a continuance at this post before another season."[20]

Now that the era of perpetual crisis had passed, both Charles Francis Adams and Henry were restless. Neither felt that English society had learned to treat the Adams family with the proper respect. Rose Greenhow, at least, knew how to feed the Adams amour propre. Fearlessly, she visited the legation on July 11, shortly before her departure for the South, to procure a parole for Lieutenant Wilson, one of the *Alabama*'s officers who needed medical attention. Adams was unable to resist her flattery and handed her one of the few victories during her time in England.

Rose spent her final evening in London with her daughter Florence. "Until the last minute she had hoped that I would not go," she wrote in her diary. "But alas, inexorable destiny seems to impel me on."[21] Mason accompanied Rose to Glasgow where the blockade runner the *Condor*— the newest addition to the blockade-running fleet of Alexander Collie, an English shipbuilder—was preparing to leave on August 10. The commander was Captain William N. W. Hewett, the captain who had taken Mason and Slidell to England after the conclusion of the *Trent* affair. He was using the alias Samuel S. Ridge. "I like his looks and am quite sure he will not lose his vessel if courage and coolness will save it," decided Rose. Only when she was completely alone on board did the enormity of the decision to leave begin to weigh upon her. "A sad, sick feeling crept over me of parting, perhaps forever, from many very dear to me," she wrote. "A few months before I had landed as a stranger; I will not say in a foreign land, for it was the land of my ancestors. . . . But I was literally a stranger in the land of my fathers and a feeling of cold isolation was upon me."[22]

———

Henry Hotze had decided to leave England for a short while in order to expand his operations into Europe. He had pulled off a great triumph in France by cultivating Auguste Havas, the proprietor of the Havas Agency, the sole telegraphic and foreign news service in the country. "All translations from papers in other languages . . . are made for the whole French press [by] Havas," Hotze explained to Benjamin. Its monopoly on foreign news was complete and unassailable.[23]

Hotze's journal, the *Index,* was paying for itself. Circulation was increasing, as were revenues, and Hotze no longer had to write the majority of articles himself. The Southern poet John R. Thompson had agreed to come over from Richmond to help him, and Hotze had prevailed on John Witt, a nephew of the scientific racialist George Witt, to become the magazine's new editor. "My work being thus, both in England and France, reduced within manageable dimensions," Hotze told Benjamin, "I feel able . . . to devote some efforts to a field hitherto entirely neglected." Hotze's aim was to spread uncertainty in the European financial markets regarding the North's ability to pay its bonds. He had also heard that Poles were being recruited in Germany to fight for the Federal army. This, he thought, he could deal with quite easily by sending across John Witt to entrap a recruiter. Hotze had already dispatched the amenable Witt to Ireland on a mission to expose the activities of Federal recruiters there. "One conviction for violation of the Foreign Enlistment Act would make considerable noise," he explained to Witt. "Engage the services of a first rate detective . . . find some intelligent, non-commissioned officer . . . who could play the part of a decoy duck at the proper time."[24]

Although British subjects were more likely to be forced into the Confederate than the Federal army, the South's isolation from Europe meant that such reports rarely reached the outside world. As far as the British public was aware, the kidnappings, beatings, and torture of immigrants were all a Northern phenomenon.[25] The perception that crimping was rampant in the North lent veracity to Robert Livingstone's explanation to his father of how he became a Federal soldier. "I went to Cape Town where your agent Mr. Rutherford advised me to find employment on board a brig which brought me to Boston," Robert wrote from his hospital bed. "Here I was kidnapped and one morning . . . I found myself enlisted in the US army." He passed over his alias of "Rupert Vincent" by claiming, "I have changed my name, for I am convinced that to bear your name here would lead to further dishonour to it." Robert swore to his father that he was an unwilling combatant and a penitent son.[26] Dr. Livingstone tried to suppress his doubts and accept the letter at face value. "Our Robert is in the Federal Army . . . he was kidnapped he says," he told a friend.[27]

Livingstone joined the queue of anxious relatives making inquiries at the legation. "We get daily applications as to the fate of persons in our army, and I have a great deal to do to answer them," Benjamin Moran recorded in his diary. "At one time the letters all run on employment in the army—at another on free emigration—and now on the fate of relatives in our service."[28] He had noticed another change: for no apparent reason that he could discern, the public had gone wild over a petition ad-

SOMETHING FOR PADDY.

O'CONNELL'S STATUE (LOQ.). "IT'S A *REPALER* YE CALL YOURSELF, YE SPALPEEN, AND YOU'RE GOIN' TO DIE FOR THE *UNION*."

Punch's caricature Irishman is lured to fight for the Union (*left*),
while the Church (*right*) urges him to stay.

dressed to the U.S. government asking for the bloodshed to end. London had been placarded with advertisements for the so-called Peace Address: Not only are the walls covered with big posters inviting people to sign," he wrote, "but men are sent around from house to house in lanes and allies [*sic*] for signatures. The address is a most insulting one to the loyal American people, and is being extensively subscribed by children and fools. Shop girls and servants are inveigled into placing their names to it."[29] The U.S. consuls reported similar scenes in their districts. In Ireland, priests were reading the petition during the Sunday sermon and urging parishioners to sign. The Peace Address was in the form of a letter claiming brotherhood with the American people. The alleged author was Thomas Bentley Kershaw, a Manchester cotton factory foreman.

Consul Eastman in Bristol thought Kershaw was the front man for an international conspiracy directed at wavering voters in the North. He commented to Seward on August 24, "You will observe that under all these rumours of peace, there lies coiled the insidious project of Southern independence."[30]

Charles Francis Adams told Seward that the real instigators of the Peace Address had to be "the rebel emissaries themselves," never imagining that the Confederate lobby was furious with Kershaw for diverting the public's energy into a scheme that had no chance of achieving its goal.[31] Spence had tried everything short of sabotage to discourage him. William Lindsay would never have allowed the peace petition to continue, but a stroke in August had disabled him and his recovery was uncertain. Hotze had initially refused to give Kershaw any assistance in collecting signatures. The master propagandist knew that a peace petition from England would incite Northern Anglophobia without adding a single vote to the Democrats in the upcoming national elections.[32] Hotze was running his own peace campaign, writing letters and articles under various aliases for newspapers throughout the North. Kershaw's only usefulness to the Southern cause was in his keeping the issue alive among the "shop girls and servants." But even then, there were cheaper ways of attracting public sympathy than the £150 it cost to distribute the petition.[33] (When Kershaw eventually arrived in Washington with his petition in October, he was told that the U.S. government did not accept foreign petitions from nonaccredited individuals. After waiting for a few days, he gave up and returned home.)

———

Hotze was one of the first people to see Belle Boyd when she arrived from Quebec in early August. Though she had destroyed her dispatches when the Federals captured the *Greyhound,* Belle still possessed Benjamin's letter commending her to Hotze's protection. It was only natural that she would seek him out now that she was friendless and penniless. In a surprising twist, Hotze was himself holding a letter for Belle. "Upon opening it, I found that it was from Mr. Hardinge, informing me that he had come to England," wrote Belle in her memoirs, "but not being able to learn my whereabouts, had proceeded to Paris, in the faint hope of finding me there. I was deeply touched at this new proof of his honest attachment, and immediately telegraphed a message to him, stating where he would find me in London."[34]

Belle and Acting Ensign Samuel Hardinge had spent a total of three weeks in each other's company. They might well have married even without Hotze's encouragement, but the propagandist worked so swiftly that neither was allowed the opportunity for second thoughts. Hotze arranged the entire wedding. He booked the church, invited the guests, and, most important of all, tweaked the interest of the press by portraying the young lovers as a modern-day Romeo and Juliet. The nuptials took place at St. James's, Piccadilly, on August 24, 1864. The main newspapers, including several in France, carried gushing accounts of the day, complete with a lengthy history of the brave and beautiful bride and her stalwart groom. Belle was inundated with wedding presents, which was fortunate, since the couple was beginning married life with nothing but the public's goodwill.

Benjamin Moran noted the Confederate wedding in his diary: "It seems the rebel strumpet Belle Boyd was married at St James' Church, Piccadilly, to-day to some poor idiot. He is said to be a deserter from our Navy by the name of Hardinge."[35] Moran was alone at the legation; the secretary, Charles Wilson, had left for Chicago on August 17, having decided that an honest day's work could not be half as trying as another hour spent in Moran's company. Naturally, Moran was frightened that Henry Adams was angling for the vacant post, unaware that Henry had not only refused it but also insisted to Seward that Moran was the only suitable candidate.

The Adams family returned to London on September 3, still anxious about Mary's health.[*] London would not begin to revive until the autumn and until then offered few distractions for the family. The most exciting part of the day was the arrival of the post, though the news from America made them despair. The North was suffering from war malaise, Charles Francis Adams wrote in his diary. "All accounts agree in saying that the President is deserted and his re-election in great danger."[36]

On September 11, rumors reached London that Sherman had captured Atlanta. The effect on the legation was electric, even though they

---

[*] The holiday had been a trial: Henry did not mind his brother-in-law, Charles Kuhn, but his sister Loo had turned into a peevish invalid. Rather like Alice James, the intelligent, thwarted sister of Henry and William James, Loo was too wealthy to have an occupation and too clever to be happy without a purpose other than herself. "She is evidently much bored by our life," Henry commented drily to Charles Francis Jr.

had to wait a full week before receiving confirmation of the news. The reports were "doubted by *The Times* and disbelieved in the City," Henry told his brother Charles. For the past month the press had been castigating Lincoln for his refusal to concede defeat. Even William Howard Russell had written in the *Army and Navy Gazette:* "The Northerners have, indeed, lost the day solely owing to the want of average ability in their leaders in the field."[37] The Confederates and their supporters tried to play down the strategic importance of Atlanta. Slidell assured the French emperor during a chance conversation at the races that Sherman's latest advance would be a pyrrhic victory for his overstretched and undersupplied forces. The emperor "expressed his admiration and astonishment at what we had achieved," the commissioner reported to Benjamin. But, he added bitterly: "A year ago I should have attached some important political signification to this incident."[38]

Knowing that Atlanta's fall would boost the chances of Lincoln's winning a second term, Hotze hastened his departure for Germany: "It is from Germany that the enemy must next spring recruit another army," he wrote. "It is upon Germany that he relies for the gold to carry on the war."[39] Georgiana Walker and her family also left England. Her husband, Norman, had joined them at the end of August, driven from Bermuda by an outbreak of yellow fever. The Confederates agreed that he should make Halifax, Nova Scotia, his new base for supplying the South until it was safe to return to the Caribbean. On September 30 the family set sail for Canada on the *Europa.* The chief drawback to the voyage, wrote Georgiana, was the number of "Yankee" passengers. "But I must admit that they behaved themselves as well as Yankees can behave and exhibited that respect for us, which all Yankees feel for Southerners."[40] She was expecting to be miserable in Halifax until she remembered that Rose Greenhow might still be there, waiting for a blockade runner to take her to Wilmington. The thought of being with her friend gave Georgiana hope that everything would turn out well.

THIRTY-THREE

"Come Retribution"

Burley and Beall are reunited—Lord Lyons meets Feo—Shipwreck—
Charleston under siege—Northern ambivalence—The enemy in ashes

Lord Lyons arrived in Montreal on September 15, 1864, with his two favorite attachés, George Sheffield and Edward Malet. Simply being away from the unhealthy climate of Washington was enough to restore Malet's health: "A change of air is all I wanted," he informed his mother, "and I now feel as if I had never been ill."[1] But Lyons, he noticed, remained weighed down by his fear that many tedious discussions awaited him in Quebec about Federal crimping and Confederate plots.

The governor-general of Canada, Viscount Monck, was in many ways as isolated as Lord Lyons. Though blessed with a genial manner and patrician ease at social gatherings, Monck's determination to avoid showing favoritism toward any party forced him to maintain a degree of aloofness from the Canadians, who could sense that he looked askance at their internal quarrels. Monck thought his ministers were among the most small-minded men he had ever encountered. None of them, he wrote in a confidential letter to London, "is capable of rising above the level of a parish politician."[2] It had been clear to him since his arrival three years earlier that the endemic suspicion and jealousy between Canada's provinces had been disastrous for the country's development. To survive and flourish, Monck believed, these separate provinces had to be persuaded that their future prosperity depended upon confederation;

and he had thrown himself into the project with energetic zeal.* He hoped that at the very least, political unity would strengthen Canada's relations with the United States, and that it might possibly even make the colonists more willing to pay for their own defense—an object dear to London.

Lord Monck had been concerned about Southern violations of British neutrality ever since the Confederate agents had appeared in the spring, petitioning—without success—to have five additional ships sent to patrol the Great Lakes. Personally, he was pro-Northern rather than neutral (or even pro-Southern like many Canadians), and was doing his best to discourage the Confederacy from sending its agents to Canada. In November 1863 he had foiled a Southern plot to attack the Federal prison camp on Johnson's Island in Lake Erie off Sandusky, Ohio— successfully, though only temporarily, dampening the Confederates' interest in launching raids from Canada against the North.[3]

During the summer, Commissioner Jacob Thompson had revived the plan to liberate the prisoners on Johnson's Island. The days when almost any force could have taken the island were long past, but the prison was still an enticing prospect for the Confederates because its position in Sandusky Bay was close to the Canadian border. Sandusky itself was a minor town; Charles Dickens had paid a fleeting visit in 1842 and thought the place bleak and the population "morose, sullen, clownish and repulsive."[4] But to the fugitive slaves who escaped captivity via the "underground railroad" to Canada, Sandusky represented their last stop before freedom. The U.S. authorities had chosen Johnson's Island for the opposite reason; without a boat, it was the last stop to nowhere.

The island's prison was badly built and poorly maintained: its latrines lacked drainage and the barracks had no running water. But the suffering of the 2,500 Confederate prisoners had only really begun in the spring, when the War Department decreed that conditions should mirror those of Southern prisons; food parcels were confiscated, and prisoners were

---

* The fourth Viscount Monck exceeded all expectations when he took up the governorship. He had only accepted the post because his Irish estates were so encumbered with debt that it was either Canada or bankruptcy. He had never displayed the least talent for politics or administration before; yet Palmerston had seen something in Monck that he liked, and his perspicacity was rewarded. Monck was a diligent, discreet, and scrupulously honest public servant who led the way to the British North American provinces' becoming the Canadian Confederation in 1867.

forbidden to supplement their rations except by capturing rats (which were, however, plentiful). These weak and diseased inmates were the men Jacob Thompson intended to use to bring terror to the United States' northern border.

The iron-hulled gunboat USS *Michigan* had been patrolling Sandusky Bay since Monck's exposure of the first Confederate plot against Johnson's Island. Before then, it had been employed to make draft protesters in Detroit think twice before they rioted.[5] The warship had never fired its guns and was too unseaworthy for deployment in battle, but since she was the only naval vessel on Lake Erie, whoever sailed her controlled the lake. In mid-July, Thompson believed he had found the right man to capture the vessel.

Twenty-seven-year-old Charles H. Cole was a mystery to everyone who knew him. He lied about his war record, hiding the fact he had been cashiered from the Confederate army in 1863 for dishonesty.[6] He had never held a leadership role, and yet in July he managed to dupe Thompson into giving him $4,000 to investigate the various possibilities for seizing the *Michigan*.[7] Cole used the money to treat his girlfriend to a luxurious holiday tour around the Great Lakes before finally settling down to business on August 11 and booking a room for "Mr. and Mrs. Cole" in one of Sandusky's better hotels. The West House overlooked Sandusky Bay, offering its clientele an unobstructed view of Johnson's Island and USS *Michigan,* which was usually anchored nearby. Cole's reports to Thompson were sufficiently optimistic to elicit the order that he should spend whatever it took to bribe the officers or purchase the *Michigan* outright. "He thinks everything looks favourable and is sanguine of success," Thompson told Clement Clay on August 13, 1864. Cole opened an account in one of the local banks, letting it be known that he represented an oil company from Pennsylvania, and began distributing his largesse among the *Michigan*'s officers. None responded to his cautious overtures. Even the captain, John C. Carter, who resented sailing around an empty lake while his peers were off chasing Confederate raiders, was beyond reach.

Cole wrote to Thompson in August telling him that he was ready to lead a team of Confederates to capture the vessel. The claim may have been nothing more than a maneuver to gain more time and funds. If so, he was caught out when Thompson not only ordered him to proceed but also sent him one of his best volunteers, John Yates Beall, late of Chesa-

British North America and the United States

QUEBEC
Montreal
Ottawa
St.-Jean-sur-Richelieu
St. Albans
Lake Champlain
ONTARIO
VERMONT
Lake Huron
Lake Simcoe
BRITISH NORTH AMERICA
NEW YORK
Toronto
Lake Ontario
Guelph
St. Lawrence R.
MICHIGAN
Welland Canal
Port Colborne
Niagara Falls
Rochester
Trenton Falls
Port Stanley
Buffalo
Syracuse
Auburn
Albany
Lake St. Clair
MASS.
Detroit
UNITED STATES
Windsor
Lake Erie
Binghamton
Toledo
Sandusky Bay
Cleveland
CONN.
Sandusky
Johnson's Island
N
OHIO
PENNSYLVANIA
W   E
New York
Pittsburgh
S
Miles
0   25   50   75   100
Gettysburg

peake Bay.[8] Once he met Beall, Cole realized that his comfortable little setup was at an end. Beall had crossed into Canada hoping to start his own privateering operations on the Great Lakes, but he dropped the idea after hearing about the Johnson's Island plan from Thompson. "I immediately volunteered," wrote Beall, "and went to Sandusky, Ohio, to meet Captain Cole, the leader. We arranged our plans, and separated. Cole stayed at Sandusky. I came to Windsor to collect men, and carry them to the given point."[9]

Beall remained in Windsor until the beginning of September, carefully working out the details of the plan with Thompson. He was overjoyed when Bennet G. Burley arrived after a difficult journey through the North. Burley's British nationality meant he could purchase the equipment and weapons required without inviting suspicion, and Cole's role was gradually reduced until his sole contribution was to arrange an evening of diversions for the *Michigan*'s crew.[10] Some were to be entertained on shore, the rest plied with drink on the vessel. While Cole was intoxicating the crew, Beall and his team were to capture the local Sandusky ferryboat called the *Philo Parsons* and, on Cole's signal, to sail alongside the *Michigan* and climb aboard. Then, with the element of surprise on their side, they would fire on the garrison guarding Johnson's Island, blow open the walls, and release the prisoners.

On September 17, two days before the date appointed for the raid, one of Beall's volunteers betrayed the group to the provost marshal of Detroit. Captain Carter of the *Michigan* was initially skeptical of the report, until he remembered that Cole had arranged a party for the *Michigan*'s crew at an inn on the outskirts of Sandusky. On the morning of the nineteenth, Carter sent a trusted officer to the West House hotel, who lured Cole onto the *Michigan* on the pretext of asking permission for the entire crew to attend the party. As soon as he was on the vessel, Cole was arrested and searched for papers. The documents Cole was carrying were not particularly revealing, but that did not stop him from confessing everything to Captain Carter. He also admitted that he had intended to abscond with Thompson's money before carrying out the final part of the plan: to rescue the prisoners.[11]

In the meantime, Beall and Burley had boarded the *Philo Parsons,* fully confident that Johnson's Island would be theirs by midnight. Burley persuaded the ferry captain to make an unscheduled stop at Sandwich, on the Canadian side of the river, to pick up three friends, one of whom he said was disabled; the ship's clerk noticed that the disabled man was miraculously cured as soon as the vessel started moving again. At the next stop, another sixteen men climbed aboard, bringing a large wooden trunk with them. The *Philo Parsons* continued chugging quietly along its scheduled route until 4:00 P.M., when the trunk was opened and Burley handed out two dozen revolvers and hatchets. Within half an hour, all the passengers and crew were locked in the cabin. No one was hurt, although a few shots had been fired.

Beall and Burley congratulated themselves on a superbly run operation. All they had to do was drop off the prisoners on one of the deserted islands in the lake and wait for Cole's signal to attack the *Michigan.* By 6:00 P.M. however, the plan was falling apart. Beall discovered from the engineer that there was no more wood, since it was company policy to take on only enough fuel for the scheduled trip. The raiders had no choice but to sail to the nearest fueling station, on Middle Bass Island. While they were there loading the wood, another ferry, the *Island Queen,* docked beside the *Philo Parsons.* Seeing the puzzled look on the captain's face, Beall ordered his men to seize the steamer. The fight proved more difficult than expected; among the passengers were twenty-six Federal soldiers on an illicit jaunt. Vicious hand-to-hand fighting ensued between the soldiers and Confederates, and the *Island Queen*'s engineer was shot in the face. It was thirty minutes before the last man surrendered.

With his strong sense of chivalry, Beall refused to allow the passengers to be molested. One turned out to be carrying $80,000 in his baggage, which he offered to share with Beall in exchange for his life. The Confederate haughtily explained that he was conducting a rescue mission, not a robbery, and all property was safe except for the ships themselves and their day's takings, which were legitimate prizes. As soon as there was sufficient wood on board to restart the engines, Beall ordered the passengers off the boat, first exacting a promise from each one to keep silent for the next twenty-four hours.

It was 9:00 P.M. when the Confederates finally sailed within sight of the *Michigan*. She had changed position since the morning and was facing the prison; ominously, her gun ports were open and steam was rising from her funnel. The raiders waited for Cole's signal. Burley's anecdotes of previous raids failed to impress the worried men, and after an hour they began to argue that they should turn back. None of them knew Beall or Burley well enough to risk their lives in what increasingly appeared to be a compromised mission. Beall pleaded and threatened without success. The ringleader of the mutineers explained they had nothing against him—they even admired him—but they were not prepared to die for him. When Beall asked if they were willing to put their opposition down in writing, they not only agreed, but all seventeen signed their names. The statement declared the mission to be hopeless: "We . . . take pleasure in expressing our admiration of the gentlemanly bearing, and courage of Captain Y. Bell [*sic*] . . . but . . . we cannot by any possibility make it a success, and having already captured two boats, we respectfully decline to prosecute it any further."[12]

Beall and Burley had little choice but to abort the mission. When the sun rose on Tuesday, September 20, 1864, the *Philo Parsons* lay partially submerged a few miles from Windsor. The Confederates had stripped her of everything valuable, including three mirrors and the piano from the saloon. Beall was already on his way to the northern wilds of Ontario; Burley went east to hide out with friends in Guelph, near Toronto.

The legation in Washington informed Lord Monck of Beall's raid by coded telegram. Anxious to forestall Northern accusations of connivance or indifference, he ordered the Canadian Rifles stationed at Windsor to provide all possible assistance to the U.S. authorities. Lord Lyons had been at Spencer Wood, the governor-general's official residence in Quebec, for only two days, and the news from Lake Erie so depressed him that he retired to bed with a crushing headache. The unwelcome discovery that there was a large number of houseguests also staying had already put him in a delicate state. He did not reappear for twenty-four hours.

Lyons roused himself for an excursion to Chaudière Falls, but he remained apart from the group and left them wondering when he failed to appear at the picnic lunch. Their suspicion that he was avoiding them was close to the mark. He would have stayed away from dinner, too, if he could have done so without offense. Just before the gong, there was a savage encounter between a house cat and a lapdog belonging to one of the guests. "With difficulty the animals were quieted, and we went in to dinner," recorded Lord Monck's sister-in-law, Frances Monck, whose husband, Colonel the Hon. Richard Monck, was the governor-general's brother and military secretary. "Lord L.'s amusement was great; he went on all the evening alluding to the battle."[13]

Feo Monck, as she was always known, was a force of nature, though a gentle one, who was perpetually missing trains, losing hats, and spilling anything hot and full to the brim. She was intelligent, too, though it could be difficult to tell behind the endless little dramas that punctuated her day. Feo and Lyons soon discovered that they shared the same dislike of hot weather, cold weather, exercise, and boats, and thereafter, as his attachés observed, he was a changed man. Sheffield and Malet had always assumed that Lord Lyons disliked women, but around Feo he revealed a hitherto unknown repertoire of after-dinner songs and became a tireless raconteur of hilarious anecdotes from the annals of diplomatic history. The more Feo laughed at his puckish comments, the wittier he became. "If you could hear Lord L.'s odd, grave, inquiring way of saying these things you would laugh as much as I am now laughing," she wrote in her letter journal after they had spent a week exploring the majestic rivers of Quebec.

By the time the house party visited Shawinigan Falls, the second-highest waterfall in Canada after Niagara, Lyons had thrown off the last traces of reserve, removing his boots and stockings and splashing about the shallow rocks like a child. "Lord L. has travelled much, but he says he never saw a more exquisite view than that day," recorded Feo. "When we had feasted our eyes on the Falls, and picked leaves, we went to our grand lunch laid on a table made with boards by the servants and boatmen. The sun was burning hot and the day perfection." During the long journey home "we talked and sang, and Lord L. repeated poetry."[14]

Lyons could not be so free when they visited Montreal and Niagara Falls. "We are to go to Cataract House at Niagara on the American side," wrote Feo, "as the Confederate people are met at the Clifton House [on the Canadian side], and Lord L. does not wish to seem to watch them."[15] For once, Lyons's caution made things worse; it would have been better if he had made a great show of watching them, thus sending a clear message to Jacob Thompson and his cohorts that their illegal operations in Canada would not be tolerated. But he was struggling both physically and mentally; only Feo Monck and the attachés knew how much he had dreaded his return to Washington. During one of their final excursions, he persuaded her to hide with him instead of meeting a deputation of local worthies who had gathered to greet their boat. "He gave me his arm," wrote Feo, "and we ran off out of the ship, and got into a cab without waiting for any of them," leaving the mayor standing disconsolately on the wharf. As the date of his departure on October 12 drew near, Lord Lyons became increasingly reckless and led Feo into all sorts of scrapes. On an outing to Lake Ontario they climbed up a steep ledge overlooking the lake, ignoring the prominent danger sign, and "we stood there," recalled Feo, "clinging to the railing till we saw a policeman coming, and were so afraid of being scolded that we jumped down and ran away!"[16]

Rose Greenhow had arrived at Halifax on September 6, 1864, and had been forced to wait for nearly three weeks while the Condor recoaled and took on supplies before she could begin the final part of her journey to Wilmington, North Carolina. Two more passengers were joining her: Lieutenant Wilson, whose parole she had obtained from Charles Francis Adams, and the Confederate commissioner James Holcombe, who had decided that he did not wish to participate in Thompson's or Clay's operations. The long delay until the Condor's departure on September 24 was enough time for the U.S. consul in Halifax to learn the names of the passengers and the ship's destination. As soon as the vessel steamed out of the harbor, he sent a telegram to Washington warning the Navy Department to ready the fleet at Wilmington. When the *Condor* reached Cape Fear in the small hours of October 1, every available blockader was waiting.

A storm was brewing as the vessel approached the Carolina coast. The roiling sea favored the *Condor,* and Captain Hewett was able to slip past the first line of blockaders. But as they approached New Inlet—the closer of the two entrances to Cape Fear River—Hewett saw that the sheer number of blockaders crowding around the entrance would make it impossible for him to escape detection. USS *Niphon* was the first to spot the *Condor,* and at 3:30 A.M. the chase began. The *Niphon* plowed through the waves, firing her guns in a steady roll. The *Condor's* passengers cowered beneath the deck listening to the explosions above their heads. Suddenly, the ship lurched hard to starboard and crashed to a stop. The pilot had mistaken the wreck of the *Night Hawk,* which had been chased down the previous night, for a Federal ship and turned hard to avoid it, hitting a sandbank in the process.

The *Condor* was close enough to Fort Fisher for its guns to afford her some protection against the *Niphon.* Captain Hewett thought he might still be able to make the final dash in a few hours, once the tide had lifted his ship off the bar, but he could not guarantee that it would hold against the pounding of the waves, or that the rest of the fleet would not join the *Niphon.* Rose Greenhow and James Holcombe both became hysterical. She was carrying dispatches from Mason and Hotze for Richmond, as well as £2,000 in gold, the entire profit from her book, and was rapidly becoming panic-stricken at the thought of being a Federal prisoner again.[17] Since the shore was only a few hundred yards away, she begged Captain Hewett to let down a rowboat. Holcombe added his pleas. At first Hewett refused, but when two sailors volunteered to row, he relented.

Rose, Holcombe, Wilson, and the *Condor's* pilot clambered with great difficulty into the rolling boat with the oarsmen. Rose had left everything behind on the ship except a copy of her book, the dispatches, and the money, which was in a pouch secured by a heavy chain. As they neared the surf, a wave flipped the boat over, spilling the passengers into the water. The men were able to swim to the surface and cling to the side of the boat, but Rose never reappeared. An hour later, the tide brought the rowboat in, allowing the battered and exhausted survivors to hobble onto the beach. Captain Hewett and his crew were rescued at dawn, although the *Condor* was left stuck in the sand.

Rose's body was found in the morning by Thomas Taylor, an English blockade runner who had gone down to the beach to supervise the salvage operation of his own vessel.* He had her remains carried to Fort Fisher, where the commandant's wife, Mrs. Lamb, prepared it for transportation to Delaware. The following day, October 2, Wilmington gave Rose a state funeral: church bells tolled as her flag-draped coffin led an immense cortege headed by representatives from the Confederate War Department, the army, and the navy. Mindful that she was being buried without her family present, the president of the Soldiers' Aid Society preserved Rose's hair for her daughters, "in case we ever hear from them."[19]

———

Rose Greenhow's death was a brutal reminder to Wilmington's inhabitants that the Federals were tightening their grip. Francis Lawley had become worried for the city's safety after his visit in mid-September. "There is abundant cause for thinking that Wilmington is the great thorn in the flesh of the Federals at this moment," he wrote on September 24. "We shall witness a desperate attack upon this place within the next seven weeks."[20] This was also the view of General Beauregard, who was growing exasperated by the lack of defensive preparations in both Wilmington and Charleston and had written to Captain Henry Feilden urging him to try his utmost to shake "the authorities of Charleston" out of their complacency.[21]

Beauregard's letter had been waiting for Feilden when he returned to Charleston from his secondment to General John K. Jackson. Though it was arduous and uncomfortable, the worst that had happened to him

---

* The vessel was the *Night Hawk,* which had confused the pilot on board the *Condor.* Thomas Taylor was the "supercargo," the officer in charge of a ship's cargo. Though only twenty-four, Taylor had the highest success rate of any English blockade runner. But his luck had run out the night before the *Condor*'s arrival. The *Night Hawk* was chased onto a sandbar and boarded by Federal sailors, who "acted more like maniacs than sane men, firing their revolvers and cutting right and left with their cutlasses," recalled Taylor. After beating up the crew, they set fire to the ship and left, not caring whether the blockade runners burned or drowned. Taylor had wanted to fight the flames, but his men dragged him onto a rowboat, "though the boiling surf seemed more dangerous to my mind than remaining on the burning ship."[18]

during his mission to bring back Confederate deserters from Florida was the loss of a ring given to him by Julia.[*] She had been talking about a grand wedding after the war, but Sherman's capture of Atlanta had convinced Feilden that it would be foolish to delay any longer. Charleston's defenses were holding for the moment, but seventy days of continuous shelling had left parts of the city in utter ruin—Feilden was not sure where they would live after the wedding. Lieutenant James Morgan of the defunct *Georgia* was dismayed when he visited Charleston during Feilden's absence and found many of the streets covered over with grasses and vines. "I felt ashamed of my new uniform," he wrote, after seeing the ragged state of the troops guarding Wilmington and Charleston.[22] Morgan had never imagined that conditions aboard his ship would compare favorably with those in the local barracks.

Feilden was so accustomed to keeping up a positive front for Julia that a general vagueness was creeping into all his letters. He gave his family every pertinent detail about his fiancée except her surname, and Lady Feilden was obliged to send an engagement present of gloves and a parasol addressed simply to Miss Julia. Feilden laughingly reassured Julia that the omission had not been for want of love. His feelings for her would never alter, he promised, nor would he ever give her a moment's distress by flirting or looking at another woman: "My wife will never be afraid of my misbehaving in that manner," he wrote firmly.[23]

Feilden's steadfast nature was one of the qualities that endeared him to his superiors. He had never complained about the state of headquarters even though his commanding officer, General Roswell S. Ripley, was a drunk and his staff not much better. It was nevertheless a great relief to him when Ripley was replaced at the beginning of October. "General Beauregard has recommended that Col. Harris be promoted to the rank of Major General, and that the defence of Charleston be handed over to him," Feilden wrote excitedly to Julia. The change in command almost certainly guaranteed his promotion:

> Col. [D. B.] Harris told me that he had told General Beauregard
> that he would only accept the command under certain conditions,

---

[*] Feilden promised the family he had stayed with in Florida that he would send them a reward if they ever found the ring. Two years after the end of the war, he received a small package with the ring inside. He kept his promise and sent all the money he could afford.

and one of them was that he should select his own staff, and not have Ripley's crowd palmed off on him. In that case he will apply for me as his AA General. It will be a capital thing for me if all this happens; it will give me my promotion to a Majority and put me in a position where I shall not be ranked by every ignoramus who has got influence enough to be placed on the staff of the Department of SC., Ga., & Fla. Colonel Harris is a splendid officer and just the man I should like to serve under. Charleston, with him in command, would make a splendid fight.[24]

Feilden's belief in the South was unshaken by the recent downturn in her fortunes. "I was intended to live in the midst of all these troubles," he wrote, "for I can keep up my spirits under all circumstances." True to form, his subsequent letters were all about their wedding.[25] But the flow of letters between Charleston and Greenville ceased in early October. Yellow fever had spread to the staff headquarters, and Colonel Harris was among the first to be struck with the disease. Feilden nursed him day and night for a week, but Harris was beyond help and died on October 10. Feilden stayed up for two nights, guarding the body from the depredations of rats and dogs until Harris's family could claim the body. He had lost not only a friend but also his best chance of promotion.

General Beauregard's choice to replace Harris was Lieutenant General William J. Hardee, a veteran of the Mexican War and the author of a drill manual used by both armies. Hardee had been looking for a new post since falling out with General Hood in Georgia, and he came with his own staff of trusted and experienced officers. Feilden's friends were determined to ensure that Hardee realized he was gaining an officer of exceptional quality. Colonel Thomas Jordan, Beauregard's chief of staff, wrote to General Hardee about Feilden on October 12: "He is of English birth and education and has seen service in the British Army. At first he was on inspection duty, but I had him transferred to my office, where he became my right-hand man—and I can recommend him as a judicious, well-informed, well trained staff officer."[26] The letter languished in Hardee's "to consider" pile. The general was appalled by the bedraggled state of his new troops and immediately launched a campaign for supplies. The soldiers lacked blankets and coats; "very many of my men are absolutely barefooted," he complained to Richmond on October 19.

Francis Lawley had seen for himself the weakened state of the South-

Rendezvous of General Mosby's men above the Shenandoah Valley, by Frank Vizetelly.

ern armies. It went against the grain with him to dwell on the Confederacy's deprivations, but he could no longer ignore the truth. "I cannot be blind to the fact, as I meet officers and privates from General Lee's army," he wrote to Lord Wharncliffe from Richmond on October 12, "that they are half worn out, and that, though the spirit is the same as ever, they urgently need rest." Their diet for the past 160 days had consisted of bread and salted meat, while the enemy had at its command "all that lavish profusion of expenditure and the scientific experience that the whole civilized world can contribute."[27] However, when Lawley praised "the patience and self-denying endurance of the troops," he was stretching an ideal already abandoned by his friends. Earlier in the week, the chief of ordnance, General Josiah Gorgas, had privately conceded that the soldiers' spirits were almost beyond saving: "Our poor harrowed and overworked soldiers are getting worn out with the campaign. They see nothing before them but certain death, and have, I fear, fallen into a sort of hopelessness, and are dispirited. Certain it is that they do not fight as they fought at the Wilderness and Spotsylvania."[28]

Frank Vizetelly witnessed the battles between Jubal Early's similarly exhausted Confederates and Sheridan's hard-driving cavalry in the

Shenandoah Valley. Early was relying on the help of John Singleton Mosby and his Partisan Rangers to harass the Federals, and at first Vizetelly was dazzled by Mosby, whose guerrilla raids reminded him of the daredevil spirit of Jeb Stuart. "His achievements are perfectly marvellous," wrote Vizetelly after hearing how the Rangers swooped down on a six-hundred-foot-long Federal wagon train in mid-August and captured the entire contents, suffering only two casualties in the raid.[29] Mosby had been able to outlast his former rival Sir Percy Wyndham, but his new opponent, the English colonel L.D.H. Currie, could not be tricked into making the sort of mistakes that had been Wyndham's undoing. Although Currie could not prevent Mosby's raids, he kept the wagon trains moving and intact. Nor were the raiders much help to Jubal Early in a real cavalry battle. Early had lost an entire brigade in a combined Union cavalry and artillery attack on September 24.* Since then, he had been able to mount only insignificant skirmishes against Sheridan, who was carrying out Grant's order to lay waste to the region. Vizetelly had covered many campaigns, but none that so explicitly targeted the enemy's will to fight. The sight of emaciated women pleading with soldiers for bread to feed their children led him to accuse Union troops of deliberately causing mass starvation among the civilians. Sheridan's declaration that "the people must be left nothing but their eyes to weep with over the war" was repeated many times in the British press. This sort of "wanton destructiveness," asserted the editor of the *Illustrated London News,* is "unknown to modern warfare."[†30]

There was nowhere safe for refugees anymore: families who thought they would find sanctuary in Richmond risked losing their adolescent sons to the Confederate army. Despite President Davis's dictum against "grinding the seed corn of the Republic," boys as young as fifteen were now being rounded up and marched to the trenches. "No wonder there are many deserters—no wonder men become indifferent as to which

---

* During a battle on September 24, 1864, at Front Royal, an English volunteer substitute, Private Philip Baybutt (1844–1907), seized the regimental flag of the 6th Virginia Cavalry. The prize enabled him to receive the only Medal of Honor awarded to a British subject during the Civil War.

† Sheridan ordered his troops to hang prisoners of Mosby's Rangers rather than treat them as prisoners of war, and six were executed on September 22, 1864. Mosby retaliated and executed five Union prisoners, chosen at random, on November 6. A week later he wrote to Sheridan suggesting that they call a truce on the executions.

side shall prevail," wrote the War Department clerk John Jones bitterly.[31] Nevertheless, those who risked the journey to Richmond sometimes met with surprising generosity. "Virginians of the real old stock," in Mary Sophia Hill's words, gave her a corner to sleep in when she arrived ill and penniless in early October. The military tribunal in New Orleans had returned a guilty verdict with the recommendation of imprisonment for the duration of the war. But her defense lawyer, a "Union man" named Christian Roselius, had protested against the sentence and won a commutation to banishment from New Orleans. Consul Coppell also interceded on her behalf, offering to buy passage for Mary on the *Sir William Peel,* which was about to depart for England, but General Banks refused, saying, "She will have to run the blockade. She will have plenty of trouble; perhaps it will teach her to behave herself the rest of her days."[32]

"He had his desire," recalled Mary. "I did have plenty of trouble." Despite the insistence of the new legation secretary, Joseph Burnley, that "everything that could be done in this matter has been done," Mary was carried across the picket lines into Confederate territory and left by the road to fend for herself.[33] Mary never revealed how she made the one-thousand-mile journey from New Orleans to Richmond without a horse or money, but the memory would forever haunt her, driving her to seek justice years after the war.

———

Mary had arrived in Richmond shortly after the Federals captured another of the forts guarding the approach to the capital on September 29. The enemy, wrote John Jones on October 4, "is now within five miles of the city, and if his progress is not checked, he will soon be throwing shells at us. . . . Flour rose yesterday to $425 a barrel, meal to $72 a bushel."[34] Mary risked her life to look for her twin brother, Sam, who had been sent to the trenches with the other engineers in his office. While crossing a pontoon bridge she stood aside to allow General Lee to ride past. "I consider it an honor," she wrote, "and a great one too, to have seen the General of the age, Robert E. Lee, the soldier's friend, the Christian warrior."[35]

Lee had grown used to such hero worship; his determination to endure the same hardships as his men was widely known, though it had not deterred Southerners, particularly women, from delivering food and gifts to his tent. But another side to Lee had become apparent of late. No

Punch's terrifying depiction of the human cost of the Civil War, September 1864.

man, not even the great "Christian warrior," could withstand the relentless attrition of troops, supplies, and options without showing the strain.
Francis Dawson was taken to Lee's mess and subjected to a tirade of sarcastic remarks:

> It was the most uncomfortable meal that I ever had in my life
> [he wrote]. My frame of mind can be imagined when General
> Lee spoke to me in this way: "Mr. Dawson will you take some
> of this bacon? I fear that it is not very good, but I trust that you
> will excuse that. John! Give Mr. Dawson some water; I pray
> pardon me for giving you this cup. Our table service is not as
> complete as it should be. May I give you some bread? I fear it is
> not well baked, but I hope you will not mind that." Etc., etc.,
> etc.; while my cheeks were red and my ears were tingling, and I
> wished myself anywhere else than at General Lee's headquar-
> ters.[36]

Only a month of fighting weather remained. On October 7, 1864, Lee
ordered his final large-scale assault of the year, sending two divisions
along Darbytown Road with orders to flush the Federals out of their new
position. They started off well and overran the first line of trenches, capturing more than three hundred soldiers in the process, among them the
English fugitive Robert Livingstone, who had been released from the
hospital on September 30 and had only rejoined the 3rd New Hampshire
Volunteer Infantry the day before. As Livingstone was marched away, he
could hear his side responding with a massive barrage of fire. The Confederates were faltering. Lee galloped toward the retreaters, waving his
hat and shouting for them to make another stand. On previous occasions
the very sight of him had been enough to stem a flight, but this time the
men continued to run.

Grant was sufficiently encouraged by his troops' handling of the
Confederate attack to order a follow-up assault on October 13, but this
time the Federals were driven back by the defenders. "We have had a
pretty brisk little fight today," Dawson wrote to his mother that evening.
"Grant has been feeling our lines on this [North] side of the River; he
made but two attacks on our ranks and each time was easily repulsed."
The setback to the Federals had an immediate effect on the Confederates' spirits. Dawson was almost giddy: "There are croakers [pessimists]

everywhere . . . but you must not allow any of them to persuade you that we are, as the Yankees say, 'in our last ditch.' " Moreover, his commander had returned: "I am happy to say that General Longstreet reported for duty today, his right arm and hand is still paralyzed from his wound but he could not be kept back any longer . . . he is a tower of strength to our cause, and he returns at a good time."[37]

Dawson's optimism was a testament to his ignorance of the true state of the Confederate defenses. He had laughed at the sight of black regiments during the recent fighting in and around Darbytown Road, considering their deployment proof of the North's weakness. But more experienced Confederate officers acknowledged their heroism and were asking why the South did not employ their slaves to solve the manpower shortage.* General Lee was considering the idea, although he did not say so in public.

Edward Stanley was fascinated by the North's ambivalence to Negro regiments. Even some members of the Adams family were shocked by Charles Francis Jr.'s transfer to a black regiment. "His uncle, Mr. Sidney Brooks, was I hear very disgusted that his favourite nephew would do this," wrote Stanley. "I am glad he has done this as the more people of position take these commands, the more it tends to raise the Negro." Stanley thought the experience would be good for Adams himself, who "was not quite free from the American prejudice against and repugnance to Negroes." Charles Francis Adams, Jr., had not regretted his decision the previous September to transfer to the 5th Massachusetts Cavalry (Colored), but he shared General Sherman's doubts that black troops would ever be the equal of white. The "Nigs" were angelic, he told Henry Adams after the regiment had sustained nineteen casualties and three dead in fighting at Petersburg on June 15. But "the rugged discipline which improves whites is too much for them. It is easy to crush them into slaves, but very difficult by kindness and patience to approach them to our own standard."[38]

Stanley had finished his tour of the North more pessimistic about the future of the freedman than when he started. Day-to-day relations between blacks and whites had the feel of an awkward jig to him. He had visited a school in Boston where a "quadroon" pupil was made to sit by

---

* The colored troops in the Darbytown Road engagements received fourteen of the sixteen Medals of Honor awarded to black soldiers during the Civil War.

herself, as though separated from the other girls by a cordon sanitaire.* The sight convinced him that the racial integration of the U.S. Army was vital to reforming American society. He knew this would not happen overnight, but he had been encouraged by the number of white soldiers willing to join colored regiments, especially among the foreign volunteers who wanted to become officers.

Private James Horrocks was among the whites applying to transfer to a colored regiment. "What do you think about it?" he asked his parents, as he weighed the army's unequal treatment of colored regiments against the possible improvement of his prospects:

> Chances of being shot greater; accommodations and comforts generally smaller, but pay much larger than what I have now. No horse to ride but a uniform to wear. And above all—an *Officer*'s real shoulder straps and the right of being addressed and treated as a gentleman, with the advantage of better society, and if I like it, this is a position I can hold for life, being United States troops, while Volunteers will undoubtedly be disbanded when the war is over.†[40]

Horrocks's confidence that peace could not be far away received a boost on October 19 at the Battle of Cedar Creek in the Shenandoah Valley. The Confederates under Jubal Early surprised the Federals in a dawn attack, routing two of Sheridan's corps and destroying their camps. But in the afternoon, Sheridan led a crushing counterattack, capturing hundreds of prisoners and most of Early's artillery. It was the Confederate general's third and final battle against Sheridan in the Shenandoah Valley. Every battle had been a Federal victory, and Early could not afford to risk

---

*Ernest Duvergier de Hauranne, a French journalist and liberal politician, was in New York on a similar cultural voyage as Stanley. He observed: "Between Broadway and the Hudson River there exists a filthy, rundown neighborhood inhabited by Irish immigrants and colored people exclusively. It is impossible to imagine anything more depressingly poor. . . . From time to time one sees with amazement a trolley car ride by which carries a sign: 'Colored People Admitted.' What in the world can be the meaning of this? Are there separate laws here for Negroes? No, but public prejudice persecutes them more powerfully, more tyrannically even than law."[39]

† For example, the English volunteer Thomas Beach, who had adopted a new identity as a Frenchman named Henri Le Caron, was able to leap from being a private in the 15th Pennsylvania Cavalry to a lieutenant in the 15th U.S. Colored Infantry.

another encounter. "We have only pistols, sabers and old fashioned rifles," wrote a Confederate cavalryman. "Above all, we have not enough food to keep the horses up."[41] Sheridan had achieved his purpose; the verdant Shenandoah Valley was now a wasteland of burned fields and ruined homesteads.

Sheridan's success in Virginia made some newspapers uneasy. "The laying waste of the Shenandoah Valley will undoubtedly call out acts in retaliation equally terrible," predicted the *Detroit Free Press* as reports began to filter through to the North of a Southern movement to exact revenge.[42] On October 15 the *Richmond Whig* urged Davis

> to burn one of the chief cities of the enemy, say Boston, Philadelphia, or Cincinnati. If we are asked how such a thing can be done, we answer, nothing would be easier. A million of dollars would lay the proudest city of the enemy in ashes. The men to execute the work are already there. There would be no difficulty in finding there, here, or in Canada, suitable persons to take charge of the enterprise and arrange its details. . . . New York is worth twenty Richmonds. They have a dozen towns to our one; and in their towns is centered nearly all their wealth. It would not be immoral and barbarous. It is not immoral nor barbarous to defend yourself by any means or with any weapon the enemy may employ for your destruction.[43]

The Confederacy's mood of despair and outrage would soon be reflected in its new cipher key, which would be altered from "Complete Victory" to the more ominous-sounding "Come Retribution."

THIRTY-FOUR

"War Is Cruelty"

The Confederates invade Vermont—Colonel Grenfell's mistake—War at sea resumes—The impact of Lincoln's reelection—March to the sea—Death in a prison camp

Instead of feeling restored by his holiday in Canada, Lord Lyons felt incapacitated by intense bleakness. Nothing inappropriate had taken place between him and Feo Monck; nor did he expect ever to see her again. But she had awakened something in him, a half-realized sense of liberty that would not be stifled and yet could not be indulged, and the prospect of Washington now seemed intolerable. Lyons could no longer avoid the truth: he did not belong in America, where his quiet eccentricities were out of step with the harsher rhythms of the young republic. The legation had been a haven for the past four years, but even this was about to be taken away from him, as it was time for his staff, including Edward Malet, to be transferred to new posts. In a couple of months Lyons would have to start all over again with a new set of faces.

Lyons's visit to New York in mid-October was uneventful until the night of the twentieth, when he attended a dinner party at which the guests included General John Dix, the military governor of New York State. Suddenly a messenger burst into the room and handed a telegram to the general, who read it and rushed out. He returned half an hour later to berate the astonished Lyons: twenty or so Confederate raiders had crossed the border from Canada and had attacked the Vermont town of St. Albans, looting more than $200,000 from its three main banks, setting fire to the square, and killing one citizen. He told Lyons that he had sent a force back across the border with orders to capture the raiders dead or alive. The news immediately conjured up in Lyons's mind the specter of another international crisis: if the North crossed the Canadian border and invaded British soil to seize the Confederates, the British government would have to protest and demand an apology along with restitution of the prisoners. The United States would refuse, forcing the government into an ultimatum—probably followed by a declaration of war.

Lord Monck, foreseeing the same catastrophic chain of events, had ordered the Montreal police to find the Confederates before they fell into the Northerners' hands. Thirteen raiders were caught within forty-eight hours, but the U.S. posse found their leader, Bennett Young, hiding in a farmhouse. Young—who had participated in the Chicago convention plot—might have swung from a tree were it not for the intervention of a British Army officer who happened upon the scene and persuaded the furious Northerners to escort the prisoner to the local garrison. Monck telegraphed the news to Seward, assuring him that the Confederates would remain in custody while the courts examined the case for their extradition. He hoped this swift action would forestall any thoughts of Northern retaliation.

The St. Albans raid had been organized by the Confederate commissioner Clement C. Clay without the knowledge of Jacob Thompson, who was furious that it had been kept from him. Thompson's own plots were nearing fruition and promised to be far more destructive and violent than mere banditry against a U.S. border town. He feared that this further violation of British neutrality would lead to increased cooperation between the Canadian and Northern authorities and create more obstacles for his operatives. As far as Thompson could tell, Canadians remained broadly supportive of the South, and he wanted nothing to jeopardize their goodwill. Halifax was still "intensely Southern," according to Georgiana Walker, who had arrived with her family on October 11. (For her, Rose Greenhow's death overshadowed the actions of a few hotheads. "My thought flew at once to the poor little orphan at the Sacré Coeur, now bereft of Father, Mother, Friends," she wrote, "truly [reliant] on the cold charities of the world.")[1]

General Sheridan was expanding the definition of "total war" to include deliberate starvation and the destruction of civilian property. Jacob

Thompson was taking it in another direction: that of terror and mass murder. He was far more systematic than any of the other Confederate agents working in Canada, and he had the men and resources to mount large-scale campaigns.[*2] Thompson had several schemes under way in late October, including a second attempt against USS *Michigan* by John Yates Beall and Bennet G. Burley, which involved the purchase and arming of a civilian steamer; but Thompson's chief plot was an undertaking in conjunction with the Northern Sons of Liberty to start a revolution on November 8, Election Day.

Two more members from General John Hunt Morgan's defunct brigade had been sent by Jefferson Davis to help Thompson: Lieutenant Colonel Robert Maxwell Martin and Captain John William Headley. They had originally hoped to lead the supposed uprising talked up so persuasively in June by Vallandigham, but Copperhead enthusiasm for conspiracies had subsided once Sherman and Sheridan's victories exposed the weakness of the Confederacy. By the beginning of November, the number of cities involved in the Confederate Sons of Liberty plot had shrunk to just two: Chicago and New York. "We were told that about 20,000 men were enlisted in New York under a complete organization," recalled Captain John Headley. "It was proposed by the New York managers to take possession of the city on the afternoon of Election Day and, in order to deter opposition, a number of fires were to be started in the city." As in the Chicago plot, the prisoners at Fort Lafayette would be freed, and the city's authorities, both military and civilian, would be either murdered or thrown in prison.[3] The Confederates expected the rest of New York State to follow or be taken as easily as the city.

Lord Monck was throwing the meager resources at his disposal into surveillance operations against the Confederates, but his system was

---

[*] A completely separate operation led by a Kentucky doctor, Luke P. Blackburn, had been inspired by the yellow fever epidemics in Bermuda. Dr. Blackburn was an expert on the disease and twice in 1864 offered his services to the Bermudan authorities, once in the spring and once in the autumn. Believing, mistakenly, that yellow fever could be transmitted via the clothes of deceased victims, Blackburn nursed the dying patients and then stored their belongings in large trunks. He had these transported to Halifax, where another agent shipped them to Washington to be auctioned off to unsuspecting civilians. Blackburn's ignorance that yellow fever is spread via mosquito bites rather than human contact spared the lives of hundreds, if not thousands. Blackburn's plot was exposed after the war, but he escaped punishment and became governor of Kentucky in 1879.

grossly inferior to the Federals'. Alerted by the U.S. consul in Halifax, Seward was able to telegraph General Dix on November 2: "This department has received information from the British Provinces to the effect that there is a conspiracy on foot to set fire to the principal cities in the Northern States on the day of the Presidential election." The warning was followed by the dispatch of General Butler and five thousand troops, who marched into New York on November 7. The New York Copperheads met Thompson's guerrillas that day and told them to go back to Canada, as no subversive would dare show his face while Butler was in town. But Martin and Headley would not be put off that easily, and they extracted from the Copperheads a new date for the uprising: Evacuation Day, November 25, so called because it was the day the British Army had been evacuated from Manhattan during the Revolutionary War.

Although the New York plotters had postponed their plan, the Chicago conspiracy was still in play, despite the arrest of John Castleman, Captain Thomas Hines's deputy, on October 2. Castleman's place was taken by the English volunteer Colonel Grenfell. "We have all got to live a certain time," Grenfell wrote to his daughter on October 11, "and when the end comes what difference will it make whether I lived in London or Illinois?"[4] The new plan relied on the help of twelve hundred Copperheads—a much smaller number than before—to launch a four-pronged attack on Camp Douglas. Once armed and liberated, the Confederate prisoners were supposed to break open the other prison camps in the state while the Copperheads, led by Grenfell, created a diversion throughout Chicago with fires and incendiary bombs. Hines expected to raise an army of 25,000 Confederate prisoners of war to capture Illinois.

The commandant of Camp Douglas, Colonel Benjamin Sweet, had informants inside the prison who were keeping him abreast of the conspiracy, but he did not know the full details of the plot until a Confederate turncoat named Maurice Langhorne called at his office on November 5 and offered to go undercover for him. Langhorne had briefly served under Confederate general Morgan and knew he would have no difficulty reconnecting with his former comrades. Grenfell was particularly incautious, freely discussing the plot not only with Langhorne but also with a second informant who was sent by Colonel Sweet to verify the information.

Shortly after midnight on November 7, Union troops arrested the leader of the Copperheads; another detachment went after Thomas Hines, although he managed to hide. A third went to the Richmond House hotel in search of Grenfell. A fellow conspirator had managed to get a note to him first, which read: "Colonel—you must leave tonight. Go to Briggs House," but Grenfell ignored the warning. The arresting officers found the note when they entered his room. He was sitting by the fire, fully dressed, though he could have run from the hotel at any time during the previous three hours.[5] Whether he was feeling ill (he was still recovering from influenza) or was simply overconfident, his inaction led to his becoming an inmate of Camp Douglas rather than its liberator. He was put in a special cell reserved for spies and irregular combatants—next to the latrines.

The legation read about the arrests on the morning of the election, but Lord Lyons himself was unaware of the failed plot. He had collapsed on November 6. "Two days after you left," George Sheffield wrote to Edward Malet, "Lord Lyons gave up the work of the legation to Burnley, and I am sorry to say, has been seriously ill."[6]

—————

Lord Lyons's last act of business before his collapse had been to speak to Seward about the problem of Confederate operations out of Canada. Seward believed his assurances that Lord Monck was trying his best to discourage them, and as a show of good faith he gave Lord Lyons a copy of the government's vehement protest before it was sent to Charles Francis Adams in London. Lyons was grateful, since foreknowledge would allow Lord Russell sufficient time to compose his response before it was officially delivered. "He said that it would be impossible to resist the pressure which would be put upon the government . . . if these incursions from Canada continued," Lyons reported confidentially to Lord Russell on October 28.[7] A way had to be found to stop Thompson and his agents.

Seward's protest to Lord Russell arrived at the legation while Adams was out of London. The family had moved to Hanger Hill House, a handsome Georgian mansion in the village of Ealing.* The apparent cer-

—————

* Formerly the home of Lady Byron, Hanger Hill was advertised by its current owners as a healthy retreat from London with the convenience of being only six miles from the city's center. Henry Adams liked Hanger Hill's aristocratic pretensions, but the unrelieved proximity to his family was a trial. Mary was weak and querulous, and "Loo will bore herself to death," he told his brother Charles Francis Jr.

tainty of a Democratic victory had made Charles Francis Adams lack-adaisical about coming in to London, conduct that exasperated Benjamin Moran.

"Mr. Adams got a letter this morning from Mr. Dudley reporting a suspicious vessel," Moran recorded on October 8. "I thought we should send the *Niagara* after her, but he said no." Moran reveled in injured silence when it was discovered that the vessel had been carrying the crew for the *Shenandoah*, James Bulloch's replacement for the *Alabama*.

The forced sale of the French ships had provided Bulloch with a large reserve of cash that he used to purchase a ready-built steamer.[8] The greatest challenge for Bulloch was how to assemble the Confederate officers in one place without someone talking or being discovered. In order to forestall potential leaks, Bulloch had furnished each crew member with explicit instructions. "You will proceed to London by the 5 o'clock train this afternoon," Bulloch informed 1st Lieutenant William Whittle on October 6, 1864,

and go to Wood's Hotel, Furnival's Inn, High Holborn. Take a room there and give your name as Mr. W. C. Brown if asked. It has been arranged for you to be in the coffee room of the hotel at 11 o'clock a.m. precisely to-morrow, and that you will sit in a prominent position, with a white pocket handkerchief rove through a buttonhole of your coat, and a newspaper in your hand. In this attitude you will be recognized by Mr. Richard Wright, who will call at the appointed hour and ask you if your name is Brown. You may say yes, and ask his name; he will give it, and you will then retire with him to your room, hand him the enclosed letter of introduction, and then, throwing off all further disguise, discuss freely the business in hand.[9]

Whittle and his fellow Confederates obeyed their orders, and the *Shenandoah* sailed secretly from London on October 8. But after the transfer of arms and crew had been made in neutral waters on the nineteenth, the new commander of the cruiser, James Waddell, discovered that the stabilizers for the gun carriages were missing. Without them, the guns would go crashing backward every time they were fired. But this was the least of Captain Waddell's problems. He had only 43 officers and men for a ship designed to carry a crew of 150.[10] The equipment had been salvaged from other Confederate ships, and in the rush to acquire guns and ammunition, ordinary necessities such as tables and chairs had been forgotten. Waddell was so concerned about the shortages that he contemplated abandoning the cruise, but his small crew persuaded him that they would be able to manage. Most were used to far worse deprivations, especially the transfers from the *Alabama.* "Every officer and man 'pulled off his jacket and rolled up his sleeves,'" recalled Lieutenant Whittle, "and with the motto, 'do or die,' went to work at anything and everything." They captured their first prize, the *Alina,* from Maine, on October 30. With a little encouragement, seven sailors from the *Alina* agreed to serve on the *Shenandoah,* giving hope to the overworked crew that more would follow.

James Bulloch argued that his little navy's record was spotless and that his raiders had attacked the Northern shipping trade without ever harming passengers or crew.[11] But there was nothing heroic about commercial warfare, and in real engagements the Confederate cruisers fared badly. On October 7, USS *Wachusett* had captured CSS *Florida*—the last of the original three commerce raiders—in the Bay of San Salvador, Brazil, without firing a shot.[12] Bulloch's real contribution to the South was his supply operation, which, under the steady direction of the Confederate agent Colin McRae, was working twenty-four hours a day. Since the beginning of autumn, McRae and Bulloch had sent the Confederacy more than five miles of wire, eight pairs of engines, six torpedo boats, four steamers for the navy, three British engineers, and a large quantity of miscellaneous goods including three unmarked boxes sent by Matthew Maury that contained the parts for a new kind of electromagnetic mine.[13]

Maury had "locked myself down" in his "experimental establishment of my own," as he told Louisa, the sister of the Reverend Francis Tremlett.* But he did take one day off to visit the Confederate bazaar in aid of

---

* Maury was working on improvements to his mines and what he termed "torpedoes," which were immobile electrical mines intended to detonate upon contact. Unfortunately, he failed to take into account the impracticality of using new technology that could not be easily replicated or repaired. Stephen Mallory could not afford to waste his dwindling resources on such rarified warfare. But the British Army had plenty of resources, and General Sir John Burgoyne of the Royal Engineers supplied Maury with acid, batteries, insulated wire, and all other necessary ingredients for mine manufacturing without asking too many questions about how much was actually required for experimental use.

the Southern Prisoners' Relief Fund.[14] Despite James Spence's fear that the bazaar would have too many contributors and not enough buyers, more than two thousand visitors crammed into Liverpool's St. George's Hall on October 18. Inside the neoclassical building were twelve stalls, representing the twelve Confederate states (though the twelfth, Kentucky, had actually remained in the Union). Confederate flags and portraits of Southern generals lined the walls. "This is purely an enterprise gotten up by English gentlemen and ladies, sympathizers with the South and of their own prompting," James Mason told his wife with great pride.[15] Spence had accumulated an extraordinary array of donations, from Robert E. Lee's pipe to wooden crosses made from the wreckage of Fort Sumter. In addition to persuading local businesses to donate all the food and drink, he arranged for a number of concerts to take place throughout the four days.[16] (Raphael Semmes had departed for the South on October 3, or Spence would have tried to make use of him as another attraction.) Encouraged by the large crowds, the organizers extended the fair from four to five days. Even after deducting expenses, their final profits were more than £17,000.

Although many newspapers accepted the organizers' claim that the bazaar was an exercise in charity rather than political propaganda, Northern supporters were not deceived. Benjamin Moran prayed to heaven that retribution would fall upon the English. "When the day of reckoning comes," he wrote to Dudley on November 1, "I hope I shall be oblivious of mercy towards this government."[17] Moran's desire to be merciless was granted a week later when Samuel Hardinge, Belle Boyd's new husband, paid an unexpected visit to the legation. He came "begging for a loan today," Moran recorded in his diary on November 7, 1864. "He looks like a traitor—is tall and about 21 years of age. He professes to be loyal." Moran triumphantly turned him away, but Hardinge returned the next morning, offering to spy for the Federals. Moran was supercilious: "I gave him no encouragement. He is evidently in very straightened [*sic*] circumstances, and wants money. After associating with rebels and marrying a spy, it is rather cool impudence in him to come here to beg. His coming here is proof to me that the rebels are in very great pecuniary troubles in London."[18] Hardinge returned to America shortly afterward—without Belle. He was arrested on his arrival in the North and taken to the Old Capitol prison, where he was told he would remain at the discretion of Edwin Stanton, the secretary of war.

The irony for the Confederates was that the bazaar had been too successful. The outpouring of support for the South by the British public would make it impossible for the U.S. government—had Seward been so inclined—to allow the distribution of the fund to Confederate prisoners without suffering a loss of face. "It would be a great relief to us if we could get permission to act openly," Spence wrote to Lord Wharncliffe on November 2, after he realized that the fund was in danger of turning into a thankless burden.*[19] He suggested that they write a letter to Charles Francis Adams asking leave to send "an accredited agent" on a tour of Northern prisons. At the very least it would demonstrate the organizers' good faith to the British public. The bazaar committee had already purchased two thousand blankets, ten thousand socks, and five thousand shirts, which were boxed and ready to be shipped. Wharncliffe duly wrote to Adams on November 9 begging him to show pity on "the suffering of American citizens, whatever their State or opinions."[20] Adams tersely replied that the matter was for the State Department to decide, not the legation, and he refused to answer any further correspondence on the subject. (Adams did not feel the least guilty about turning away the pro-Southern supporters; he had his hands full with cases he considered to be far more deserving.)

Henry Hotze was too absorbed by his own troubles to help Spence. His plan to step back from the day-to-day running of the *Index* had backfired in spectacular fashion.[†] The staff had revolted against John Witt, the new editor, imperiling Hotze's plan to expand his operations.[22] Nor had

---

* Spence had already assumed the task of unraveling Rose Greenhow's estate on behalf of her daughters and balked at taking on any more work. "She had faults, but who has not," Spence had written to Wharncliffe after learning of her death. His reference to her "faults" was a delicate allusion to the distrust she inspired in Francis Lawley and others as a shameless manipulator of men. Varina Davis, President Davis's wife, could only feel so much pity for Rose, "her poor wasted beautiful face all divested of its meretricious ornaments and her scheming head hanging helplessly upon those who but an hour before she felt so able and willing to deceive."

† Percy Gregg, a writer whom Hotze had always suspected of being slightly unhinged, had started the trouble by refusing to allow Witt to edit his copy. Witt had retaliated by dropping his stories altogether—with good reason: they were the ravings of a violent racist. "Of the passages altered or omitted there is scarcely one that I would have let stand," Hotze admonished Gregg on his return from Germany. "There are some I could mention to you which I should consider almost fatal to the paper." Hotze had never intended for the *Index* to be a pulpit for slavery. He was trying to massage, not bludgeon, public opinion. "It is a matter of real disappointment to me that one of my chief calculations, resting upon you, threatens to fail."[21]

anything come of his attempt to create a recruiting scandal in Ireland. Hotze had in fact discovered a genuine fraud in England involving three con artists from New York who enticed several hundred workers over to America on a false glass-manufacturing contract. But the press had shown only perfunctory interest in the case. The Tories were content to let it alone as well; Lord Derby ordered the party "to sit still" and allow the government to tear itself apart.[23]

Palmerston was not in the least interested in petty recruiting scandals, except as a counterargument to Northern complaints about the *Alabama;* he was only concerned with the Civil War insofar as it revealed a new military threat to Britain. "If the Americans go to war with us," Palmerston wrote to the First Lord of the Admiralty, the Duke of Somerset, "they will send out a swarm of fast steamers . . . sturdy enough to escape from our cruisers, and strong enough to capture any merchantman."[24] When Russell received Seward's protest about the Confederates' use of Canada on November 10, Palmerston reacted as though it was only a matter of time before the U.S. Navy's new Monitor-class gunboats seized control of the Great Lakes. Worried that the Americans could close off access to the St. Lawrence River, which connected the Great Lakes to the Atlantic, he suggested to the war secretary, Lord de Grey, that the river be protected by "floating batteries and heavy guns" powerful enough to "smash and sink monitors."[25] "Any Reduction of our real Naval Force," Palmerston warned Somerset, "in the face of all the warnings we have of contingent hostility on the part of the Federal States of North America would be taking upon ourselves a very dangerous responsibility."[26]

Adams, too, was worried by the aggressive language in Seward's protest to Lord Lyons. He knew the foreign secretary well enough now to be certain that the dispatch would be counterproductive. Unaware that Russell had already received an unofficial copy of the protest via Lord Lyons, Adams decided to rephrase Seward's letter before delivering it to the Foreign Office.

Adams was still struggling to find the right tone for the "improved" dispatch when the *Canada* arrived on November 21, bringing the results of the presidential election. Lincoln had carried all but two states, though a few went Republican by the slimmest of margins, including New York State by less than 1 percent of the popular vote. "Thus has the country passed safely through the most grave of its trials since the first outbreak of the war," wrote Adams with relief in his diary.[27] The British press concentrated on Lincoln's victory and ignored the Confederate government's latest message to Europe, which came in the form of a manifesto demanding immediate recognition. The South's request for "justice" from Great Britain, while it was deploying guerrillas and agents provocateurs in Canada, received a cold response from Lord Russell.[28] Under the circumstances, James Mason was fortunate to have any response at all. France, Sweden, and the Papal States were the only other countries to acknowledge receipt of the manifesto.[29]

Adams felt liberated. For the past three years, his life had been blighted by fear and anxiety. Lincoln's reelection—which would not have happened if the war were still going badly—seemed to herald the end of perpetual crisis. "The responsibility attending this post declines steadily with the progress of the war," Adams wrote in his diary. He felt that the change justified his asking Seward "about the possibility of my being relieved in the spring." When Henry Adams heard the news of the election, he feared his father would be too reticent in his request, and asked Charles Francis Jr., "Should you go to Washington, try and have a talk with Seward about our affairs."[30]

Adams delivered his amended version of Seward's protest on Confederate Canadian operations to Lord Russell on November 25. His lingering misgivings about deserting the legation fell away once he learned that Russell had not only received Seward's protest via Lord Lyons but also had already replied. "Mr. Adams is very angry with Mr. Seward about his conduct," reported Benjamin Moran. "His labor was all thrown away and he is made to look like a fool. It was a trick that no man but Seward could have played with Mr. Adams."[31]

"This election has relieved us of the fire in the rear," Charles Francis Jr. wrote to Henry Adams on November 14, "and now we can devote an undivided attention to the remnants of the Confederacy."[32] The Democrats' hopes of winning the White House had been upended by the twin victories of Sherman at Atlanta and Sheridan in the Shenandoah Valley. Grant's tenacity had made the Copperheads appear defeatist, if not unpatriotic, and the same message of "peace now" that had been so popular during the summer had alienated all but the Democrats' core supporters in the autumn. Ordinary Federal soldiers shared Charles Francis Jr.'s determination to finish the war; 78 percent had voted for Lincoln. The

Democratic candidate, General McClellan, had counted on the army without considering the psychological cost to men who were fighting for victory rather than for peace. Even many Federal prisoners of war "voted" for Lincoln. James Pendlebury had been a prisoner at Andersonville, considered to be the worst of the Confederacy's prisons, since his capture in June. Unable to cope with the sheer number of prisoners, the commandant of Andersonville, Henry Wirz, had allowed a small delegation to travel to Washington with a petition to resume the exchange system.[33] The failure to gain a response led to a second prison being built nearby to take some of the overflow. "We moved to Millen and while there I voted for Abraham Lincoln," Pendlebury wrote in his memoirs. "Our Captains allowed us to as they were anxious to carry McLennon [*sic*] because Abe Lincoln was a Republican and McLennon a Democrat.

THE FEDERAL PHŒNIX.

The Federal Phoenix rises again, according to *Punch*, from the flames of states' rights, free press, and the Constitution.

Now 19 out of every 20 voted for Lincoln so we were all 'docked' rations."* The defiance shown by Pendlebury was all the more remarkable given that the Federal soldiers knew Lincoln had refused to resume prisoner exchanges until the Confederates treated white and black prisoners on an equal basis. On some days, there were more than 150 burials at the prison: "We would fight like wild beasts that we might carry out the body of a fellow prisoner, because on those occasions we would get into the woods and come back with a supply of firewood with which to do our cooking."[35] After the prisoners were forbidden to go into the woods, they fought for the "privilege" of taking the bodies to the carts, since it was their only opportunity to scavenge for clothing.

The needless suffering of prisoners was a frequent accusation hurled at both administrations. But Lincoln and Grant were also blamed for deliberately sacrificing thousands of Northern soldiers in order to prevent the South from replenishing its empty ranks. The Regius Professor of History at Oxford University, Goldwin Smith, was on a lecture tour of the United States and took the opportunity to visit a Union-run prison camp in Chicago and a prison hospital in Baltimore. He thought neither unduly harsh, whereas the sight of returning Federal prisoners from Andersonville made him shudder: "I put my finger and thumb round the upper part of a large man's arm," he wrote. "It must be said that Grant was partly responsible, if, as was understood, he refused to exchange prisoners. No laws of war surely can warrant the retention of prisoners whom a captor cannot feed."[†36]

Goldwin Smith's popularity in the United States was second only to John Bright's on account of his vigorous pamphleteering in support of

---

* Hundreds of Federal prisoners took part in the sham vote. According to an early chronicler of Kansas state history, "When Sherman started on his march to Savannah the rebel authorities believed that a detachment of the Federal army would be sent to release the prisoners at Andersonville. Accordingly, in October 1864, [several Kansan prisoners] were taken to Milledgeville, Georgia, and from there to Savannah. While at Milledgeville, the Union prisoners went through the form of casting their votes at the general election. The soldiers in the field were given the privilege of voting for President. . . . The rebels were very much interested in the outcome, and advised those who wanted the war to come to a speedy close to vote for McClellan. However, the result of this balloting was about two to one in favor of Lincoln."[34]

† By the middle of 1864 the South had become so desperate for men that Davis agreed to a simple exchange—soldier for soldier—without regard to race. Prison exchanges resumed in November, albeit slowly.

the North, and he was entertained during his tour by a plethora of senators and generals.[37] Before the election, he stayed with Charles Sumner, who ranted so obsessively about Seward's blunders as secretary of state that Smith was glad to escape. Afterward, when Smith was in Washington, he stayed with Seward and realized that not all of Sumner's criticisms were unfair. Seward had fallen into the old habit of drinking and talking too much; he is "the least cautious of diplomatists," recorded Smith. With regard to Lincoln, Smith noted that the English perception of the president as an "ungainly and grotesque" figure was largely correct, "but on the face instead of levity, sat melancholy and care."[38]

The escalating tension along the Canadian border was a significant factor in Seward's return to bad habits. He needed to talk to Lord Lyons and was frustrated by his mysterious illness. In the beginning he had heard that it was typhoid; then the diagnosis changed to neuralgia or dyspepsia or a combination of both. Whatever it was, the minister was unable to leave his room or receive visitors. Seward had taken Lyons for granted for so long that he was shocked to discover how quickly matters could deteriorate when the British minister was absent. Seward broke protocol by writing directly to Lord Monck, rather than via the British legation in Washington, urging him to act swiftly and publicly before John Yates Beall's latest Lake Erie venture—known to be centered on an armed and reinforced steamship—created a mini-war on the Great Lakes.[39] Monck did not appreciate being accused of dilatoriness when he was devoting the greater part of his day to thwarting the Confederates (he even sent a chronology to Lyons showing how and when he had responded to each event), but he was not as attuned to Northern public opinion as Seward. The secretary of state knew there was trouble brewing long before *The New York Times* came out in favor of a retaliatory war: "Let it come," declared the newspaper. "We were never in better condition for a war with England."[40] Seward could only hope that his letters were being put into Lord Lyons's hands.[41]

Seward could at least take satisfaction from the growing dissension within the Confederate Congress over the war; calls for peace were appearing in the Southern press with increasing frequency. He was heartened, he wrote to his wife, "in the discovery that division is at last breaking out among the rebels."[42] Davis had been traveling through the remnants of the Confederacy giving speeches to the public and meeting with state governors in private, several of whom were on the verge of withdrawing their cooperation. Desertion was endemic, yet 85 percent of Mississippi's white adult male population was in the army, which made a mockery of Davis's exhortation to Confederate women in his speech to the congress on November 7 to "use your influence to send all to the front."[43] Varina Davis discerned a greater willingness in Richmond to cabal against her husband. "The temper of Congress is less vicious," she wrote, "but more concerted in its hostile action."[44] The Confederate Congress had reacted angrily as a body to Davis's proposal to appropriate forty thousand slaves as a supplement to the army. They would be diggers, cooks, and porters rather than soldiers, but their contribution would be significant enough to earn them their freedom after the war. The War Department clerk John Jones took Davis's proposal as a sign that normal life in the Confederacy was disintegrating.[45] Wood was $100 a cord and coal cost $90 a load, both beyond the means of a civil servant. When Confederate soldiers received their pay, which was not often, they encountered the same frustrating experiences as Jones. Captain Francis Dawson's monthly salary of $150 allowed him to purchase new trousers for $100, but not a new pair of boots, which cost $350. Dawson prayed that his current boots would see him through the final weeks of the autumn campaign. "After the 15th November, Richmond is safe," he informed his mother, for then the weather would be the Confederacy's best defense.

The Army of Northern Virginia was stretched like an elastic band along mile after mile of trenches and fortifications. Lee had already moved his headquarters to be closer to Petersburg, where Grant had made the greatest gains in territory. Dawson's prophecy was accurate almost to the day. The Federals settled into their winter dugouts during the second week of November. Private James Horrocks and the 5th Battery, New Jersey actually built little wooden cabins, complete with windows and brick chimneys.

Thank goodness I have a nice, warm log shanty to live in [he wrote to his parents]. Already the winter of Virginia begins to commence. This season is characterized chiefly by perpetual rain, and penetrating cold that pierces through one's clothing and makes one shiver. Mud of a sticky character takes one up to the knees and it is no rare occurrence to get up to the middle in it. . . .

The state of the ground renders the movement of Artillery almost impossible.[46]

General Longstreet occasionally ordered a round of artillery fire to keep the Federals on their toes, but his batteries were no less mudbound than those of his opponents. The relative quiet enabled him to reorganize his staff. There were several promotions and requests for transfers, including one by Francis Dawson. Longstreet had never shown the least interest in the Englishman, but he was suddenly indignant when Dawson was appointed chief ordnance officer on General Fitzhugh Lee's staff. "General Fitz Lee heard of me through some of our mutual English friends and made application for me," Dawson explained to his mother. Dawson was delighted to be able to say goodbye to his uncongenial messmates. "Although I have suffered but little," he wrote to his mother on November 24, "it is useless to deny that there is considerable jealousy displayed towards an Englishman."[47]

Dawson felt welcomed by his new mess officers from the beginning. "A better set of fellows on Fitz Lee's staff it would have been difficult to find," he wrote. "There was no bickering, no jealousy, no antagonism." The camaraderie he had craved—"we lived together as though we were near relatives"—made up for the hardship of his new post. Dawson had to work twice as hard with a smaller staff and no logistical support: "I found that it was no joke to organize the Ordnance Department of a couple of Divisions of Confederate Cavalry, but I adapted myself to circumstances."[48]

Lee had sent his nephew to reinforce Jubal Early's shattered army in the Shenandoah Valley, where there was clearly going to be no winter lull. General Sheridan's reputation so terrified civilians that the women of Harrisonburg had petitioned the government for the right to organize themselves into a regiment for local defense.[49] Their bravery inspired Dawson to chide his mother for complaining about his father's debts: "Tell him for me to keep a stout breast," he wrote. "Only think of the misery and desolation of this fair land and all will seem light by comparison."[50]

In Georgia, General Sherman had initiated his own version of scorched-earth tactics. The Federal Army of the Tennessee had occupied Atlanta since September 2; finally, on November 15, Sherman gave the order to evacuate. His next destination was the city of Savannah, 285 miles to the east. He did not expect much resistance from Lee, who could not afford to detach a single regiment from the siege around Petersburg; nor was he frightened of General Hood and his little Army of Tennessee, which was lurking somewhere in the countryside. Before he left Atlanta he set the city on fire and expelled its remaining residents, telling the mayor, "War is cruelty, and you cannot refine it."[51] Five thousand houses were burned to the ground in a single night. "Behind us lay Atlanta," Sherman recalled in his memoirs as the army began to march, "smouldering and in ruins, the black smoke rising high in air, and hanging like a pall over the ruined city."

Sherman's plan for Georgia was effective and simple. He divided his army into two wings and cut a devastating trough more than fifty miles wide through the state. Foragers, known as "bummers," had broad orders to do as they pleased short of mass rape and murder. Fearful that the Federals might first head south toward Andersonville, which was only 120 miles from Atlanta, Confederate prison commandant Wirz sent hundreds of Union prisoners on forced marches to various locations around the state. He could not feed them all anyway; James Pendlebury received a pint of corn for a four-day march. "A poor fellow asked if he could lie beside me and in the morning he was dead," he wrote. "During that march I don't think beasts could have been more savage."

The economic catastrophe caused by Sherman's march sent immediate ripples across the South. At Salisbury prison, North Carolina, where Robert Livingstone had been sent in October, ten thousand prisoners were living outdoors in a large pen. "Some dug holes in the ground to shelter themselves from the cold winds at night," wrote Archibald McCowan, a Scotsman who arrived at the same time as Livingstone. As the rations grew smaller and smaller, the prisoners feared that the Confederates would starve them to death before the war ended. Walking past the prison well on November 24, McCowan noticed a small group of prisoners lounging around, each carrying a club made from a tree branch. "One of these men was very conspicuous on account of his uniform; the red breeches and Turkish cap of a Zouave regiment." Suddenly, the group attacked the prison sentries. "Each of the other conspirators knocked down his man and with the arms thus obtained they rushed to the large gate which generally stood open to allow teams to pass in and out," wrote McCowan.[52] The other prisoners joined in. Two of the guards were killed before the sentries on the other side of the pen realized what was happening. In a few minutes, every prisoner was running toward the gates. McCowan had intended to join the mêlée, but a friend grabbed him by the arm and pulled him down. "Stay where you are you damn fool," he said. The commandant climbed to the roof and turned the prison's howitzer onto the crowd below. McCowan waited until all was silent before raising his head. He saw a number of bodies sprawled on the ground. "I learned later that 15 prisoners were killed and about 60 wounded, not one of whom knew anything about the matter." Robert Livingstone had tried to run away with the others and been shot down. He lived for ten days before dying of his wounds on December 4, when his body was dumped in a trough alongside the other casualties of the failed rebellion.

THIRTY-FIVE

"The British Mark on Every Battle-field"

The plot against New York—A parting of friends—Congress retaliates—
A Christmas gift—Wilmington falls—One last attempt

Despite the failure of his agents on Lake Erie and in Chicago, the Confederate leader of clandestine operations in Canada, Jacob Thompson, remained confident in his designs for a campaign of terror. He had particular faith in John Yates Beall and Bennet Burley, and believed that their new scheme—to purchase a steamer and convert it into a warship—had a far greater chance of succeeding than the ill-fated attempt to seize the *Philo Parsons*. Burley had been working at a foundry in Guelph, Ontario, overseeing the construction of the cannon and torpedoes that were to be fitted onto the converted steamship. "Everything is going on finely and I anticipate having the things finished early, perhaps this week," he had reported in October.[1] Beall was waiting to captain the vessel as soon as it was delivered to Canada's Port Colborne, at the southern end of the Welland Canal on Lake Erie, some thirty miles west of Buffalo.

Beall's plan called for the steamer, renamed CSS *Georgian*, to receive its battering ram and cannon at Colborne. The ram was designed to sink USS *Michigan*, and the cannon was to be used against the undefended cities along Lake Erie from Buffalo to Detroit. But when the *Georgian* sailed onto Lake Erie on November 1, it seemed as though every household within a two-hundred-mile radius of Colborne knew of her arrival.

"The whole lake shore was a scene of wild excitement," Thompson wrote to Judah P. Benjamin. "At Buffalo two tugs had cannon placed on board. . . . Bells were rung at Detroit. . . . The bane and curse of carrying out anything in this country is the surveillance under which we act."[2] To make matters worse, the *Georgian*'s propeller broke and a replacement had to be brought from Toronto. But the conspirators believed they were safe after the authorities searched the vessel and, since the weaponry had not yet been delivered, found nothing suspicious.

By November 16, 1864, the *Georgian* had been repaired and was sailing west toward Sarnia on Lake Huron to pick up the rest of her weaponry when Monck's agents finally achieved their first success against the Confederates. They intercepted the shipment before it reached Sarnia and found a large quantity of arms in three boxes marked "potatoes." The trail led straight back to Burley, who was arrested in Guelph the following day and taken to Toronto to face a trial for extradition to the United States. At first, the detectives thought they had captured Beall, and their confusion enabled him to go into hiding before they realized their mistake. The rest of the *Georgian*'s crew also scattered, leaving only Burley to take the blame for the plot. Thompson was prepared to kill civilians for the cause of Southern independence, but he was less insouciant about risking the lives of his own men. He hastily wrote to the Confederate navy secretary, Stephen Mallory, asking him to forward documents proving Burley's naval commission so that the charge of piracy—which carried a death sentence—could not be made against the Scotsman.[*3]

Disappointed by the sudden unraveling of the Lake Erie plan, Thompson waited anxiously for the outcome of the plot to set New York afire on November 25. There had been no word from Lieutenant Colonel Robert Martin or Captain John Headley since their aborted at-

---

* With great difficulty and expense, Jacob Thompson managed to send a message to Richmond using the latest techniques in photography. The message—a request for written evidence of Burley's naval commission—was written in extralarge letters and photographed, and the negatives were reduced to the size of five thumbnails, which were then placed under the cloth covering of the messenger's jacket buttons. "I (afterwards) met J. Davis at a dinner," recalled the photographer. "I asked him if he remembered the button message, and he seemed much pleased to meet the author of it." Stephen Mallory and Jefferson Davis both supplied the affidavits requested by Thompson. Davis claimed to have ordered the *Philo Parsons* expedition, and Mallory provided proof of Burley's naval commission.

tempt on the seventh. But the departure of General Butler and his Federal troops on November 15 gave Thompson hope that they would still carry out the mission. The small Confederate cell was more determined than ever "to let the Government at Washington understand that the burning homes in the South might find a counterpart in the North," as Headley recalled.[4] They were planning to use a new kind of incendiary bomb based on Greek fire—a mixture of phosphorus and carbon bisulfate—which could be transported easily in small bottles and produced a powerful explosion when exposed to air. The targets were New York City's hotels. The conspirators were to travel around with large satchels, and one by one leave the bottles in prebooked bedrooms.

On November 24, the day before the attack, Headley picked up the chemical concoction from a Southern sympathizer and carried it in his suitcase on a streetcar up the Bowery:

> I soon began to smell a peculiar odour—a little like rotten eggs—
> and I noticed the passengers were conscious of the same presence.
> But I sat unconcerned until my getting off place was reached,
> when I took up the valise and went out. I heard a passenger say as
> I alighted, "there must be something dead in that valise."[5]

Only six of the original eight took part in the plot on the twenty-fifth, two having lost their nerve. Each man put ten bottles of the Greek fire in a satchel and spread out through the city. They visited nineteen hotels in all, as well as two theaters and Barnum's Museum. But the Confederates had ignored the basic rule of arson—that fire requires oxygen to burn—and had planted the Greek fire in locked bedrooms and closed cupboards, causing the flames to peter out of their own accord.

One of the hotels set on fire, the Lafarge, was adjacent to the Winter Garden Theatre at Broadway and Thirty-first, where the three Booth brothers, Edwin, Junius Brutus, and John Wilkes, were playing together for the first and last time in their careers, giving a charity performance of *Julius Caesar* to raise money for the Shakespeare statue fund for Central Park; John Wilkes Booth was playing Mark Antony, and his more famous brother Edwin was Brutus. John Wilkes, a member of the Sons of Liberty, was already deep into his own plot, although at this time the scheme was limited to kidnapping Lincoln and forcing the release of all Confederate prisoners in exchange for his freedom. Booth had been meeting

Confederate agents in Canada, but the fragmented structure of their operations meant that he knew nothing about the New York conspiracy, and the arsonists were unaware of whose life they were risking when they set fire to the Lafarge. As news rippled across the auditorium that the hotel next door was burning, there were screams from the audience and people began to rise from their seats. "The panic was such for a few moments that it seemed as if all the audience believed the entire building in flames," reported *The New York Times*. But in that split second between calm and a stampede, Edwin Booth stepped forward and reassured the audience that the theater was not itself on fire: "In addition . . . Judge McCunn rose in the dress circle, and in a few timely remarks admonished them all to remain quietly in their places, and at the same time tried to show them the danger which would attend a pell-mell rush for the doors, and especially the uselessness of it."[6]

The fires caused mass panic throughout the city, but no recorded deaths. By the following evening, newspapers were carrying full descriptions of the six suspects, who all decided to leave for Toronto on the eleven o'clock train. They slipped into their berths and waited, fully dressed and armed, in case detectives boarded in pursuit. Much to their surprise, they reached Canada without being recognized. U.S. detectives came looking for them but returned to New York empty-handed.[*] General Dix announced that "such persons engaged in secret acts of hostility" would be caught, tried, and executed "without the delay of a single day."[8] The treasurer of the U.S. Sanitary Commission, George Templeton Strong, thought the arson attempt proved "that the South is thoroughly rotten, and the Confederacy a mere shell."[9] Such was the fear in the city that several newspapers called for Southern citizens to be rounded up and expelled, and Dix ordered all Southern refugees to register their names with the police department.

In the midst of the public outpouring of anger against the South (and at the British for harboring the conspirators in Canada), Mary Sophia Hill turned up without warning at the New York consulate to request

---

[*] Only one of the arsonists was caught and tried for the crime: Robert Cobb Kennedy, an Irishman, who was picked up by detectives in Detroit on December 29, 1864. He was tried in New York and sentenced to hang on March 25, 1865. Kennedy went to the gallows insisting that the plot was a legitimate act of war in retaliation for Northern atrocities, and that he had intended to destroy buildings rather than kill civilians.[7]

Archibald's assistance. She had come to complain about her trial and banishment from New Orleans, but Consul Archibald was less interested in the dangers she had overcome to reach New York than in the threat to her safety now that she had arrived. He purchased a ticket for her on the next steamship to England and made sure that she was on it.

Lord Lyons had not left his bedroom for more than a month, during which time Seward had continually assumed that in one more week or so the minister would reappear, looking tired, perhaps, but otherwise well. He was shocked when Lyons informed him on December 4 that he was leaving for England in two days' time. "I agree with you that it is best that you go away for a time," Seward answered Lyons's note by return messenger. "And yet I feel that my cares and difficulties will be seriously increased by your withdrawal."[10]

Lord Russell had hoped to keep Lyons in Washington for the duration of the war, and he was still counting on him making a full recovery after a month or two in England. He made it clear to Lyons that this was a respite rather than a transfer from his post. But the minister cared only that he was going home; he wrote to his sister, telling her to prepare an extra place for Christmas dinner.[11] The doctors had diagnosed his headaches as neuralgia, and he had been warned that the pain could become worse before it went away. Fortunately, his worries about the transatlantic crossing were soothed by George Sheffield, the last of the old guard at the legation, who offered to escort the invalid home. The suddenness of the decision—there were no farewell banquets and no time to engrave a watch or some such memento—imparted a sense of crisis to the news. On December 5, the morning after he received Lyons's note, Seward wrote to Charles Francis Adams urging him to impress on Lord Russell "how deeply this incident is regretted by this government, and how desirous we are for Lord Lyons's recovery and return to our country."[12]

A week later, on December 12, Lyons was helped up the gangplank of the *China* in New York by Sheffield. Within only a few hours of the minister's departure, Seward's fears about his burdens increasing came true. The extradition trial in Montreal of the St. Albans raiders ended suddenly after the magistrate in charge of the case, Judge Charles Coursol, ordered their discharge on grounds so technical that the explanation introduced a new and arcane area of debate for the Canadian judiciary. The pro-Southern audience in the courtroom swarmed the prisoners, cheering and shouting as they were led down the steps. By the time the news reached Lord Monck in Quebec City, the raiders had fled the area. General Dix had no qualms about sending his troops into Canada to find them. "All military commanders on the frontier" were ordered to chase and, if necessary, shoot the Confederate guerrillas "wherever they may take refuge." But even before Dix issued his proclamation, Monck had ordered new arrest warrants. "The police are making every effort to prevent their escape," he informed the legation.[13]

Monck's attempt to demonstrate his seriousness to Seward was undermined by an incident three days later that once again involved John Yates Beall. On December 16, a small team led by Beall tried to intercept a train taking seven Confederate generals from Johnson's Island prison to Fort Lafayette in New York. They failed to stop the train or find the generals, and two Union detectives captured Beall and another guerrilla on the American side of Niagara. "All the efforts of Confederates . . . had failed," lamented Captain Headley. "Now many of our best men were in prison. Burley at Toronto. Cole at Sandusky. Young and his comrades at Montreal. Beall and Anderson in New York City. Grenfell, Shenks, Marmaduke, Cantrill and Travers at Chicago."[14]

John Yates Beall suffered the same fate as Robert Cobb Kennedy, one of the New York arsonists. He was taken to New York, where he was found guilty by a military court of spying and piracy and was executed on February 24, 1865. Right up until the last moment he refused to accept the charges against him, claiming he was a Confederate naval officer and neither a spy nor a pirate. "It is murder," he is alleged to have said before mounting the gallows. "I die in the service and defense of my country."

Beall's conviction not only appeared to validate the desperate measures called for by General Dix, but also lent credence to those who argued that Britain deserved to be punished for allowing these plots to be nurtured in her territories.* Yet Seward, who might have been expected to inflate his rhetoric for maximum effect, surprised observers by mov-

---

* Anti-British feeling reached new heights. In Washington, for example, two policemen ambushed Arthur Seymour, one of the junior assistant secretaries at the legation, beating him almost senseless. The two policemen—and the magistrate who acquitted them—were caught in a lie when they claimed that Seymour admitted in court he was drunk that evening. Seymour had actually just finished work and was on his way to dinner.

ing swiftly to maintain calm along the Canadian border. He counter-manded General Dix's order, though he begged the legation secretary, Joseph Burnley, to keep quiet about this action until the fuss had died down. Seward also labored hard to manage the increasingly belligerent stance against Britain adopted by Congress. Charles Sumner's transfor-mation into Britain's harshest critic was now complete, and he was lead-ing the Senate movement for retaliatory steps to be taken against the mother country. His first target was the ten-year-old Reciprocity Treaty— a free trade agreement with Canada—which was scheduled to end in June 1865. Using his position as chairman of the Foreign Relations Commit-tee, Sumner pushed through a resolution for the treaty's suspension after June; he also attacked the Rush-Bagot Treaty of 1817, which limited the militarization of the Great Lakes, and prepared a list of grievances, begin-ning with the Queen's proclamation of neutrality in 1861, which he in-tended to be the basis of a campaign for massive financial restitution from Britain.

Charles Francis Adams, Jr., had breakfast with Sumner in Washing-ton in December and thought that he was half sane at best "and now out-Sumners himself."[15] The senator's brave and often lonely fight to achieve equal rights for Negroes had become lonelier of late because of his ten-dency to alienate potential allies.[16] Rather than being an asset in the White House's campaign to pass the Thirteenth Amendment, which ex-panded the Emancipation Proclamation to all U.S. states and not just those in rebellion, he was regarded as an obstacle to the deal making that had to be done to achieve its passage. The Senate had passed the amend-ment in April 1864, but it had been stalled in the House since.

Sumner's power in the Senate was waning. Lincoln no longer listened to him or trusted him. (Sumner owed his frequent appearances at the White House to Mary Lincoln, whom he assiduously courted.) Seward no longer feared him, but, according to Charles Francis Jr., he would exile Sumner as Minister to Anywhere if he could. Lyons had come to Wash-ington believing that Sumner was the greatest man in American politics. Five years later, he considered him a self-aggrandizing, sneaky Savonarola who tainted the very causes he affected to espouse. "If that man ever gets into power he will, under some highly moral pretence, sacrifice the high-est public interests to his position," Lyons complained to Professor Gold-win Smith, who happened to be a fellow passenger on the *China*. Of all public men in Washington, "he is the one for whom I have brought away the least respect."[17] Lyons's regard for Seward, on the other hand, had matured from barely concealed contempt to admiration. After an acrimonious beginning, each had learned and benefited from their forced collaboration. The politician had become a true statesman, the diplomat a true ambassador.

––––

The chief defect of Jacob Thompson's plots, in the opinion of the Confederate government, was that they were not working. Thompson defended his record to Confederate secretary of state Judah P. Benjamin: "I have relaxed no effort to carry out the objects the Government had in view in sending me here. I had hoped at different times to have accomplished more, but still I do not think my mission has been altogether fruitless."[18] Benjamin disagreed and appointed his replacement, telling Thompson in December:

> From reports which reach us from trustworthy sources, we are satisfied that so close espionage is kept upon you that your services have been deprived of the value which is attached to your further residence in Canada. The President thinks, therefore that as soon as the gentleman arrives who bears this letter . . . that you transfer to him as *quietly* as possible all of the information that you have obtained and the release of funds in your hands and then return to the Confederacy.[19]

The "gentleman" was Brigadier General Edwin Gray Lee, a cousin of Robert E. Lee's. Edwin Lee suffered from chronic lung disease and was no longer fit for active service, but he had experience in clandestine operations. He found on his arrival to Canada, however, that Thompson was not prepared to leave quietly or hand over control.

Jefferson Davis and Judah Benjamin knew that the Canadian operations were their only means of striking directly into the North. The South's last remaining army in the west, the Army of Tennessee under Joe Johnston's successor, John Bell Hood, was smashed to pieces over the course of seven battles between September and November—in the last, the Battle of Franklin on November 30, the attack of the Southern army was so ill-planned and uncoordinated that General John M. Schofield was able to inflict one of the bloodiest defeats of the war. Six Confederate generals were killed, including Patrick Cleburne, the highest-ranking Irish general in the South.* From then on, Sherman was determined to reach the Atlantic coast as quickly as possible. "I can make this march, and make Georgia howl!" he assured Grant. "I propose to . . . make its inhabitants feel that war and individual ruin are synonymous terms."[21] Leaving General Thomas behind to destroy the remnants of Hood's army, Sherman was able to move forward between ten and fifteen miles a day and cause at least $1 million worth of damage to Georgia. He entered Savannah on December 21, 1864, having completed his three-hundred-mile "march to the sea" in thirty-six days. He telegraphed Lincoln: "I beg to present you as a Christmas gift the City of Savannah, with one hundred and fifty guns and plenty of ammunition, also about twenty-five thousand bales of cotton."

Richmond did not learn of Savannah's capture for several days. But the Confederate government was transfixed by the threat to its last open port. "[Federal] Troops are moving toward Wilmington from here," wrote the chief of ordnance, Josiah Gorgas, "and a heavy armament has departed from Hampton Roads, supposed to be destined to the attack of that place. The great trouble to be met now is to feed the army here while the railroads southward are being repaired."[22] The situation was now desperate: the supply of food for the army would not even last the month without additional deliveries from Bermuda. The commissary general, Lucius Northrop, turned to Thomas Taylor, the English blockade runner, for help. "I said I would do my best," wrote Taylor, "and after some negotiations he undertook to pay me a profit of 350 per cent upon any provisions and meat I could bring in within the next three weeks!"[23] Taylor set out on the *Wild Rover* and returned from Bermuda on December 24, just as the

---

* Cleburne was the first Southern general to argue that the slaves should be promised their freedom if they fought in the army. On January 2, 1864, he wrote to General Joe Johnston: "Our country has already some friends in England and France, and there are strong motives to induce these nations to recognize and assist us, but they cannot assist us without helping slavery, and to do this would be in conflict with their policy for the last quarter of a century. England has paid hundreds of millions to emancipate her West India slaves and break up the slave trade. Could she now consistently spend her treasure to reinstate slavery in this country? But this barrier once removed, the sympathy and the interests of these and other nations will accord with our own, and we may expect from them both moral support and material aid. One thing is certain, as soon as the great sacrifice to independence is made and known in foreign countries there will be a complete change of front in our favor of the sympathies of the world."[20]

long-expected assault on Fort Fisher at Wilmington by General Butler and Admiral Porter was about to begin.

Francis Lawley and Frank Vizetelly had both rushed to Wilmington from Petersburg fearing they would be too late to witness the attack. The largest fleet ever assembled in the war—sixty-four Federal ships in total—were arranged in a three-mile-wide crescent, blocking the entrance to Cape Fear. Opposing them were fewer than a thousand Confederates manning the fort, some of them boys who had never fired a gun before. (The Confederate navy consisted of only fifty vessels now, and Mallory had not even bothered to send a defense.) "For five weary hours upon the 24th," wrote Lawley, "the iron hailstorm, without one instant's cessation, descended upon or around the fort, tore great rents . . . set fire to the wooden quarters of the garrison, swept away every vestige of flag or flagstaff . . . without injuring a hair of the head of its defenders."[24] The Federals' plan to explode a ship next to the ramparts merely resulted in a loud noise and a great deal of sea spray, but the Confederates' secret weapon—Matthew Fontaine Maury's electromagnetic mines—also failed, being too complicated and delicate to work properly under fire.

The first wave of Union troops fought all Christmas Day, coming within seventy-five yards of the walls. Rather than being buoyed by their proximity to success, however, General Butler was blinded by the possibility of defeat, and when darkness fell he called off the attack. Admiral Porter was furious. Five hundred properly led men could have taken the fort, he claimed to the navy secretary, Gideon Welles. To compound Porter's anger, the *Banshee II* and its vital supplies for Lee's army managed to slip past the Federal fleet in the early hours of December 26. Taylor was fired upon by several gunboats as he dashed toward the fort: "It was an exciting moment as we crossed the bar in safety, cheered by the garrison," he wrote, "who knew we had provisions on board for the relief of their comrades in Virginia."[25]

The South knew that the Federal attackers would return. "If Wilmington falls, 'Richmond next,' is the prevalent supposition," wrote the War Department clerk John Jones. "It is unquestionably the darkest period we have yet experienced. Intervention on the part of European powers is the only hope of many. Failing that, no doubt a negro army will be organized—and it might be too late!"[26] President Davis decided to make one last appeal to Britain. With nothing left to offer, and with no threat of blackmail or an Anglo-American war to dangle, Davis resorted to the previously unthinkable: he proposed to abolish slavery in return for recognition of Southern independence. On December 27, 1864, he asked Duncan F. Kenner, one of his few remaining allies in the Confederate Congress, to go to London to speak to Lord Palmerston.* Benjamin promised Kenner that he would prevent Mason and Slidell from interfering, and wrote to the commissioners that same day.[27] He dared not describe the mission in explicit terms in case the letter fell into the wrong hands, but he stated that Kenner's mandate came directly from the president and could not be questioned.[28] Meanwhile, Davis arranged a secret meeting between Kenner and the Confederate congressional leaders, who reluctantly accepted that there was no alternative. Partly to explain his departure, and partly because his position as chairman of the Confederate House's Ways and Means Committee made him the obvious candidate, Kenner was given additional powers to negotiate a government loan from European banks. Kenner would have authority to sell every last cotton bale in the South, if necessary, so long as he procured new funds for the bankrupt treasury.

But before Kenner could do any of these things, he first had to find a way of breaking the Federal stranglehold on the South.

———

Francis Lawley paid a brief visit to Charleston after the Battle of Wilmington and was sorry that he did: the empty streets reminded him of Boccaccio's description of Florence after the Black Death. Some blocks were nothing more than charred ruins, while others remained eerily pristine with "vacant verandahs and deserted sun balconies." There was grace and grandeur amid the ruins—the tall spire of St. Michael's Church remained intact, though no one would now dare, as Rose Greenhow once had, to climb the steps for a view over the harbor. "Nor can any one who visits Charleston to day be blind to the possibility," he wrote in his *Times* report, "that before the 13th of April 1865, arrives—the

---

* Kenner was the largest slave owner in the Confederate Congress, but this had not prevented him from trying to persuade Davis in early 1863 to ask Britain for recognition in return for gradual emancipation. Like General Patrick Cleburne, Kenner had realized that no British government would sully its antislavery record by recognizing the South while she remained a slave-owning nation. In 1863, when her fortunes were at the high-water mark, he believed the South could have made the offer from a position of strength and probably dictated her own terms.

fourth anniversary . . . a Federal watchman may from this same spire gaze down upon the sun-lit harbour and city beneath him."[29]

The city was not entirely devoid of troops or civilians; there were still twelve thousand soldiers garrisoned in the surrounding area, and Henry Feilden was as busy as ever. His wedding to Julia had taken place in Greenville, South Carolina, on October 27, 1864, but he could not allow her to live with him in Charleston. "How I miss you, dearest, and all your kindnesses and attentions," he wrote to his wife, who remained in Greenville. "But it was the right thing to do under the circumstances, for we shall soon have to undertake active operations." No one was sure whether Sherman would head to Charleston after Savannah or march to Richmond via Columbia, South Carolina's state capital. Either way, the state and its port were doomed. "One thing you may be sure of," promised Henry, "you will have to be looked after, and I will resign my commission sooner than not be able to do so." He had persuaded one of the last blockade runners in Charleston to take out £100 worth of cotton for them. This was all the non-Confederate money they possessed, "and will give us some little exchange in the hour of need."[30] Feilden had again been recommended for promotion, this time by General Beauregard and General Hardee. As it was, not only was there no response to the generals' requests, but Feilden also fell victim to the growing confusion in the War Department. He received contradictory orders, sending him hither and thither, much to the annoyance of Hardee and Beauregard, who both wanted him on their staff. He managed to have the orders rescinded, but his promotion remained in abeyance.[31]

On January 4, 1865, General Lee detached the veteran South Carolina regiments from his shrinking army and sent them home to defend their state. Feilden was already thinking about evacuation plans. "If we can't hold Charleston," he wrote to Julia on the fifth, "I am very sure we shall not burn it up, because there are now in the city and would be left behind, some 15,000 poor men, women and children and negroes, who cannot possibly leave the city in any case, for they would have no place to go, and would die of starvation." Julia had fantasies about burning their house rather than letting it fall into Federal hands. "It would be a good deal like cutting off one's nose to spite the face," he chided. "If Charleston is to be burnt, let the Yankees have the disgrace of doing it. Sherman's army will commence active operations in South Carolina in a few days."[32] Feilden tried to reassure Julia that a Federal occupation

would not be as terrible as she feared. He could not comprehend the
pent-up rage many Northerners felt toward South Carolina, and
Charleston in particular, for being the cradle of rebellion.[33] Nor did he
understand the Southern horror of "Negro troops." "I know it would
make no difference to me for I lived in places where there was nothing
but Negro troops, Nassau for instance," he wrote to her, "and I noticed
that people; Southerners, English and others seemed to enjoy life just as
much as if all the troops in the island were white."[34]

The South was undergoing a late but hard lesson in the fighting ability of black soldiers as five Negro regiments joined the Federal assault
force for the next attack on Wilmington. At four in the morning on January 13, Admiral Porter's fleet once again appeared on the horizon, and by
eight o'clock the first landing transports were disgorging troops onto the
beach. Frank Vizetelly had remained at Fort Fisher, hoping to draw a picture of the fighting. His patience was rewarded with a perfect view of the
attack. He was able to capture the entire scene for the *Illustrated London
News,* from the Federal soldiers landing in the distance to the Confederates desperately trying to shore up the fort's walls in the foreground.

The fort fell two days later, on January 15, although Wilmington itself
remained in Confederate hands for the moment. Feilden urged Julia to

The fall of Fort Fisher, by Frank Vizetelly.

remain in Greenville. "The people are now dreadfully scared here," he wrote on January 19. "Many I am sure are sorry that they did not clear out before this. It cannot be long before this city is attacked. I suppose we shall have to yield in the end unless strong reinforcements reach us, of which I see very little hope at present." Sherman had already set out from Savannah, and stories of Federal atrocities were preceding his advance.[35]

Julia may have been safe in Greenville, but she was living in the most primitive conditions, without winter shoes or proper undergarments. It was nevertheless easier for her to obtain flour and wood than it was for the inhabitants of Richmond. "We have famine, owing to the incapacity of the government, and the rapacity of speculators," complained John Jones on January 19. The city was swirling with rumors. He had heard that Secretary of War James A. Seddon had resigned—which was true—and that Jefferson Davis was going to be replaced by General Lee—which was not, although the Confederate Congress voted to make Lee "Commander-in-Chief" of all Southern forces. Four days later, on the twenty-third, Jones wrote, "It is rumored that a commissioner (a Louisianan) sailed to-day for England, to make overtures to that government."[36]

Kenner was not sailing for Europe; he had decided to make the three-hundred-mile journey to New York, and from there attempt to sneak onto one of the fast steamships. He set off on January 18 with two guides, who had been told that "Mr. Kinglake" was going to Canada to assist with the defenses of the Confederate prisoners. Their orders were to make haste but also to take extra care to avoid capture. Neither knew that their charge's identity was as fake as his brown wig, nor were they aware that the last messenger to attempt to reach Canada from the South had been captured in Ohio, tried by court-martial, and sentenced to death.[37]

In Canada, Lord Monck was fighting a rearguard action against pro-Southern prejudice and bureaucratic incompetence in order to preserve British neutrality in the region. Five of the St. Albans raiders, including Bennett Young, had been rearrested;* the Montreal chief of police had been forced to resign; the original judge in the St. Albans case, Charles Coursol, suspended; the St. Albans banks indemnified for the money

---

* Jacob Thompson tried to obtain copies of their commissions, just as he had done Burley's, but none of his messengers had succeeded in reaching Richmond.

stolen; the law changed to allow for the expulsion of aliens; and hundreds of troops deployed along the border. On January 11, the judge in Montreal had granted the St. Albans raiders a thirty-day recess on the grounds that they needed more time to prepare their defense. But Monck hoped this setback would be viewed against the success of the Bennet Burley trial in Upper Canada, where Burley's extradition had been ordered on January 20. Lord Monck signed the extradition papers, and on February 2, Burley was taken by special night train to Suspension Bridge station at Niagara Falls. Twenty armed guards rode the train, maintaining a vigil until the Union agents came on board to collect the prisoner.[38]

The secretary of the legation, Joseph Burnley, dismissed Burley as an undeserving case, just as he had done with the Chicago conspirator Colonel Grenfell. "If my cousin Charles would use his influence with Lord Lyons it might be of use to me," Grenfell had written in December to the chief clerk of the family firm, Pascoe Grenfell and Co., in London, unaware that Lyons was about to return to England. "I cannot say more at present. I know not a soul here nor have I a friend." He ended the note pathetically: "I leave it to you to inform my girls of my situation or not, just as you like."[39] Grenfell's cousin, Charles Grenfell, MP, did ask for help from the Foreign Office, which in turn ordered Burnley to raise the case with Seward. The legation secretary doubted they could do anything for Grenfell, whose guilt was so obvious that "everything seems to militate against him," but he asked the British consul in St. Louis, Mr. Wilkins, to make discreet inquiries.[40] "You seem to be on such good terms with the Authorities," he explained, "that I dare say you may be able to effect something privately when I should most likely fail officially."[41]

Grenfell's former commanding officer, General Joseph Wheeler, later claimed that the Englishman was innocent of the charges. Of the more than one hundred Confederate conspirators who had been arrested in November, only eight were put on trial in January, and Grenfell was one of them. "The trial of your grandfather, you must recall," Wheeler wrote to Grenfell's family, "was a time when there was most extreme and bitter partisan feeling, and the officials had around them a number of spies who were dishonorable men in the extreme, and who would commit any perjury to secure convictions."[42] Grenfell was in the most trouble because of the way he had tried to deceive the war secretary, Edwin Stanton, and his treatment in prison was undoubtedly the harshest, but he made his predicament far worse by his arrogant behavior. One of Grenfell's greatest weaknesses—the reason his life had been a catalogue of disappointments and bitter feelings—was his delusion that he was a prince among pygmies. He believed he was more intelligent than everyone else, braver, more principled, and certainly more deserving of special treatment. Occasionally, he impressed people with his bravado, but more often he turned them into inveterate foes. If the judge advocate had any animus against Grenfell before the trial, it was increased tenfold after Grenfell mocked him with a silly salute when stating his "not guilty" plea.

But Grenfell's British nationality would have worked against him even if he had been a model prisoner. Edwin Stanton wanted Britons in the Confederacy to suffer the same retribution as Southerners. Gideon Welles agreed and was disgusted with Seward's reluctance to sanction the seizure of British property in Savannah. Stanton told Welles not to worry: Sherman was taking a robust approach toward British cotton merchants who were trying to protect their cotton by "asserting it had the British mark upon it." Sherman told them in reply he had "found the British mark on every battle-field. The muskets, cartridges, caps, projectiles were all British and had the British mark upon them."[*43]

There were only eight objections to the resolution when the U.S. Senate voted to rescind its trade treaty with Canada on January 12, 1865. Charles Sumner's anti-British rhetoric was incomprehensible to his friends in England, particularly his slurs against Lord Russell, which were so outrageous that John Bright was forced into the unfamiliar posture of defending the foreign secretary's integrity.[44] But Sumner's position did not seem unreasonable, or unjust, to a Northern public still terrified that there were arsonists and insurgents ready to strike without warning.

When Davis's envoy, Duncan Kenner, reached New York on February 6 after a hazardous trek through the back roads of Virginia and Maryland, he discovered that the slavery issue had been taken out of his hands. On January 21, the U.S. House of Representatives had finally voted—by

---

* General Grant made a similar complaint to Seward, forwarding to him "specimens of fuses captured at Fort Fisher . . . and the statement of Col. Tal P. Shaffner that the same were manufactured at the Woolwich Arsenal, England, an arsenal owned and run by the British Government."

119 to 56—to ratify the Thirteenth Amendment, thus abolishing slavery on American soil. The Confederate Congress, on the other hand, had voted against Davis's proposal to arm the slaves. Kenner also learned that the two governments had engaged in halfhearted peace negotiations on February 3—known as the Hampton Roads Conference—which collapsed on the first day. These were all good reasons for him to give up, but he was determined to see the mission through to completion. He boarded the Southampton-bound *America* on February 11, posing as a Frenchman in order to confuse the detectives standing guard at the pier. Kenner believed the fate of the Confederacy lay in his hands: Wilmington was gone, Charleston was tottering, and Richmond was surrounded. But if Lord Palmerston could be persuaded that there was no longer any moral impediment to Southern recognition, Kenner still had faith that the combination of Britain's navy and Confederate courage would win independence for the South.[45]

THIRTY-SIX

"Richmond Tomorrow"

The truth cannot be hidden—A late success for Bulloch—Hysteria over Canada—Arrival of Davis's envoy—A hard line—Lord Lyons retires (temporarily)

Lord Lyons had been miserable for much of the journey home. Almost worse than the headaches was the persistent feeling that he had failed. He feared that he had ruined his prospects by leaving Washington and doubted that the relationship of mutual respect he had built laboriously between the legation and the State Department would survive his absence. Lyons's former attachés were also anxious about their chief's legacy undone. The "Buccaneers," as they had once styled themselves, had complained constantly of overwork while they were there, but their new assignments made them miss the camaraderie of the legation. "When we were very jolly in the evening we always used to sing, 'yonder lies the whiskey bottle empty on the shelf,' " sighed Malet.[1]

Lyons looked so ravaged when he arrived at the Foreign Office on Christmas Eve 1864 that Lord Russell was startled. He promised Lyons that his post in Washington would remain open until either his health was restored or he chose to give it up of his own volition. This reassurance lifted a great weight off Lyons; for the first time in many weeks he did not feel as though he had thrown away his career in a moment of weakness. A few days after the interview, Lyons composed his final report on American affairs, and wrote letters of recommendation for his long-suffering staff. There was much he regretted about the war, but it had served a purpose, he told Russell. Amid all the horrors and iniquities "there appears to be one gleam of consolation," he thought, for "slavery seems to be doomed."[2]

The Southern Independence Association was delighted that the South was finally coming around to Britain's way of thinking, and they composed a congratulatory address to President Davis on his boldness. To many people, however, the idea seemed far-fetched: nothing but sheer desperation would make them relinquish "the services" of their slaves, Lord Palmerston told John Delane, the editor of *The Times,* "but one can hardly believe that the South [*sic*] men have been so pressed and exhausted." Delane was inclined to agree, until he learned that General Sherman had reached the outskirts of Savannah. "The American news is a heavy blow to us as well as to the South. It has changed at once the whole face of things," Delane wrote to his deputy editor on December 25. "I have told Chenery to write upon it." The next day, he sent another note: "I am still sore vexed about Sherman, but Chenery did his best to attenuate the mischief."[3] James Spence also tried to play down the news, telling Lord Wharncliffe on January 5, 1865, to look out for his article in *The Times:* "You will find I do not attempt to deny the Federal success in Tennessee or the danger of Savannah, which I assume to be likely to fall [the news of Christmas Eve had not yet reached Britain], but I hope to show that public opinion overestimates the importance of the events and that upon the whole the year's campaign is a failure on the part of the Federals." Spence disliked writing such obvious propaganda for the South, "but then," he reasoned, "it is at such a time—the hour of need— that a friend is of value. When the South is victorious they can do without one's aid."[4]

The fall of Savannah was not the only disaster that James Spence was trying to present in a more favorable light. His Confederate prisoners' bazaar had inspired the London office of the U.S. Sanitary Commission to publish a pamphlet on Southern prison conditions.[5] Neither Spence nor Wharncliffe had stopped to consider whether highlighting the plight of Confederate prisoners might backfire if anyone queried the South's own record, though their campaign had worked so well at first that Mrs. Adams asked Charles Francis Jr. whether it was official policy to mistreat Confederate prisoners.[6] Lord Wharncliffe tried to calm the public outcry by forwarding letters to the press from English volunteers who had suffered in Federal prisons, but it was too late to reverse the damage.*[7] Families with relatives in Southern prisons, including Dr. Livingstone, began to insist that as British subjects they should be released at once under the prisoner exchange system.[8] Another father with a missing son in the Union army, Thomas Smelt, wrote directly to Abraham Lincoln, begging him "as a parent from a parent, that my son may be sent back to me, he has surely fought well and suffered much for your cause and deserves so much."[9]

James Spence did not realize how badly the Southern cause had suffered until *The Times* began to turn down his propaganda articles without explanation. After being met with silence for more than a week Spence conceded that his influence with the paper was at an end. "I doubt if they will insert anything more on the subject," he wrote to Lord Wharncliffe on January 16. "I see but one thing now that can save the South and that is arming the negroes. Tho, I have always expected they would do it, I am growing fearful lest they invited those fatal words—'too late.' "[10]

James Bulloch did not accept that time had run out on the Confederacy, especially since—after the disappointments of the previous year—he was experiencing a late surge of success.[11] The *Ajax,* one of two river steamers he had commissioned to defend the entrance to Wilmington, sailed from Glasgow undetected in the second week of January. "It is quite impossible to predict what may have transpired when you reach Nassau," Bulloch told the captain of the vessel, Lieutenant John Low. "Should [Wilmington] have been taken by the enemy . . . you will then proceed with the ship to Charleston, SC. . . . You may find Charleston itself closed to you, in which case there will remain no port on the Atlantic coast of the Confederate States into which you can take the Ajax." But

---

*One letter came from police constable Joseph Taylor, late of Company F, 5th Louisiana, who wrote to Lord Wharncliffe on January 5: "As one who has opposed the Northern Armies from Cedar Mountain fight which took place in August 1862 up to the Battle of Gettysburg, Pennsylvania, July 1863, and taken prisoner the day after that great Battle had terminated, I think it my duty to make this humble protest against the assertion of Mr. Seward that the prisoners taken by the Federals are so well treated that they are suffering no privations." Another English recipient of Lord Lyons's aid, Captain Hampson of the 13th Louisiana Regiment, wrote: "Looking in today's *Standard,* I wish so far as lies in my power to corroborate [Taylor's] statement in regard to the treatment of Confederate prisoners by the Federals. I have had personal experience of their kindness (!) to their fellow being whilst in their hands and prisoner."

even then Bulloch wanted Low to find a way to use the ship against the North: at the very least she could bring cotton out from Texas or Florida.[12]

He was already thinking of weapons other than cruisers to send across the Atlantic. His two remaining blockade runners, for example, were useless for fighting but could easily be deployed as rocket launchers against fishing towns in New England.[13] Bulloch had also managed to buy back one of the French ironclads that had been sold after the emperor ordered the secret construction program to end.* The cruiser, which he had decided to christen the *Stonewall,* was coming from Copenhagen, and Bulloch had arranged for a ship with a crew and arms to meet her in neutral waters. After waiting two weeks for news that the transfer had taken place, Henry Hotze suggested to Bulloch on January 25 that they should go ahead and announce the existence of CSS *Stonewall.* It would, he argued, cause panic on the East Coast and force the U.S. Navy to send ironclads to New York, opening the way for the *Stonewall* when she reached Wilmington.[14] Hotze's *Index* had been heavily advertising the *Shenandoah*'s last known captures for that very reason, unaware that the raider was now anchored at Port Phillip Bay, four miles from Melbourne, bereft of coal and in serious need of refurbishment. The Australians were delighted to be front-row spectators for a change, and thousands were visiting the Bay in the hope that the notorious Captain Semmes of the *Alabama* was the new commander of the *Shenandoah.*[15]

The diehards had no trouble accepting Hotze's propaganda. His own staff believed him. John Thompson wrote in his diary: "Am told we shall soon hear something of importance. I think it refers to an ironclad from

---

* In late December, Bulloch triumphantly informed Mallory that he was on the verge of a significant breakthrough. He had always assumed that the French-made cruisers were lost to them. After the emperor had ordered their sale, one had been bought by the Prussians, the other by the Danes, to be deployed at sea against each other, but the contest never took place, because the Danes were defeated before they received the ship and it became clear to Lucien Arman, the ship's builder, that the Danes had no use for his expensive vessel when it finally arrived in Copenhagen. Rather than insisting on the sale, Arman devised an outrageous plan to sabotage the ship during her trials, thereby providing the unsuspecting Danes with a legal excuse to break the contract. He already knew, of course, of a buyer who would pay twice the amount he had agreed with the Danes for such a powerful ship. Bulloch agreed to pay an exorbitant 455,000 francs for the return of the vessel.

Europe to attack Boston and New York."[16] The shipping owner Alexander Collie ridiculed James Spence for being "blue." "We might be prepared to hear of Wilmington and Charleston being captured, and of Richmond being evacuated," Collie wrote to Wharncliffe on January 23, "but, in spite of it all, the South will wear the North out and gain its independence." In the meantime, he was expecting his steamers to begin taking "three or four cargoes monthly for the next four months."[17]

The *Stonewall* was in greater danger than either Bulloch or Hotze knew. Her arrival at Quiberon Bay, on the south coast of Brittany, on January 24 was telegraphed to the U.S. minister in Paris. William Dayton was no longer in charge of the U.S. legation in France, having died under mysterious circumstances in December; John Bigelow, the consul in Paris, had been promoted to his place. A man of far greater intelligence and vigor than Dayton, Bigelow almost succeeded in scuttling the mission by his protests to the French authorities. But one of the worst storms in recent memory ultimately achieved his work for him; on January 29, only a day after the *Stonewall* sailed from Quiberon, the ship's bridge was smashed to pieces by giant waves. Unable to sail on to Wilmington, Captain Page took the damaged vessel to Ferrol, on the Spanish coast, and waited for repairs. Twenty-four hours later, Europe learned that the Federals had captured Wilmington's only defense, Fort Fisher.

"Glorious news reached us today," Benjamin Moran wrote in his diary on January 30, 1865. "The rebels are tired and will come back [into the Union] soon." Bulloch pressed on, however, and sent an engineer to Ferrol to oversee the *Stonewall*'s repairs. "The fall of Fort Fisher seriously deranges our plans for sending supplies, but all of us who are charged with such duties will speedily consult and make new and suitable arrangements," he promised Mallory.[18] Mason was also defiant, telling Benjamin that the Southerners in England approved of the Confederate Congress's declaration on December 13, 1864, to fight on "at whatever cost or hazard."[19]

The Economist criticized the public's overreaction to the news of Fort Fisher, since the South "still [has] large armies in the field, they have still the ablest generals of the Republic in their ranks," but most other papers now declared the Confederacy to be without hope.[20] It was common knowledge that the South would not be able to survive without its imports. During the past four years, 60 percent of the Confederacy's rifles had come through the blockade, 75 percent of her saltpeter, and 30 per-

cent of her lead, and, particularly after 1862, the blockade runners had
become the South's lifeline.[21] Consul Thomas Dudley in Liverpool had
recently completed his statistics for 1864 and amassed evidence against
113 steamships and 304 sailing vessels. Despite the U.S. Navy's efforts,
the South had managed to export 124,700 bales of cotton in return for
meat, shoes, arms, medicines, and all the other necessities of war. A total
of 303 steamships had successfully run into Wilmington during the war,
more than twice the number that reached Charleston.[22] The port had become indispensible to the Confederacy. On February 15, Consul Dudley
reported that the blockade-running business had died almost overnight.

It had taken four years and seven hundred U.S. ships at a cost of
$567 million to close every Southern port. During that time, there had
been 6,316 attempts and 5,389 runs past the blockade. The average capture rate for the whole war was only 30 percent, but this figure hides
the increasing success of the Federal navy over time. In 1861, roughly
nine out of ten blockade runners reached their destinations, but by
1865 the number was only one in two. Although criticized as inept at
the time, it is now clear that the blockade played a vital role in the
Northern war effort. Guns, meat, and shoes could be shipped in on the
blockade runners, but not the heavy cargoes such as iron rails, telegraph poles, and train carriages that the South needed in order to move
its armies, feed its people, communicate over long distances, and transport supplies. These hammer blows to the South cost only 10 percent
of the total expenditure of the war; except for Rose Greenhow and a
few others, almost no one was killed; and a mere 132,000 sailors were
employed by the Federal navy compared to 2.8 million soldiers in the
army.[23]

———

Mrs. Adams, Henry, Mary, and Brooks left London on February 1 to
begin a tour of the Continent. The family had given up the house in Ealing in the expectation that Charles Francis Adams would follow them
soon, assuming that Seward would grant his request and appoint a successor. They also were hoping for a visit from Charles Francis Jr., who
had surprised them by becoming the colonel of his regiment and proposing marriage to Mary Hone Ogden in the same month.

"Neither *Henry* nor Brooks Adams had the decency to bid me goodbye," Moran raged in his diary. "I didn't expect so much civility from the
boy, but I did from Henry." He was equally incensed with his new assis-

tant secretary, Dennis Alward, for ingratiating himself so easily into Adams's favor. "Mr. Adams is very civil, but it is the smile of the ogre," he wrote. The minister had wounded Moran to the quick by inviting Alward to ride in his carriage, and, at a reception given by the Countess of Waldegrave, he had taken "special pains to introduce Mr. Alward to everybody and equal pains not to introduce me at all."[24]

Parliament resumed business on February 7. "I have no reason to anticipate any modification in the policy of the ministry toward us," wrote Mason to Judah Benjamin. "Still, as we have a large body of earnest friends and sympathizers in both houses, it may be that something will arise during the session of which advantage can be taken."[25]

THE THREATENING NOTICE.

ATTORNEY LINCOLN. "NOW, UNCLE SAM, YOU'RE IN A DARNED HURRY TO SERVE THIS HERE NOTICE ON JOHN BULL. NOW, IT'S MY DUTY, AS YOUR ATTORNEY, TO TELL YOU THAT YOU *MAY* DRIVE HIM TO GO OVER TO THAT CUSS, DAVIS——" (*Uncle Sam Considers.*)

Punch depicts Lincoln advising restraint on the move to punish Canada by ending the free trade treaty, February 1865.

The "something" was the universal consternation over Congress's repeal of the two treaties with Canada, particularly the Rush-Bagot Treaty, which limited the naval power on the Great Lakes. The hysteria over the issue in Parliament alarmed Adams, who warned Seward on February 9: "The insurgent emissaries and their friends are busy fanning the notion that this is a prelude to war the moment our domestic difficulties are over." With uncharacteristic force, he charged the secretary of state to remember that the future of Anglo-American relations lay in his hands.[26]

All of Adams's meetings with Lord Russell since December had been very satisfying. The foreign secretary had taken care to explain the government's position regarding the Confederate operations in Canada and what steps had been taken to prevent them. They had both agreed that the two countries had survived far worse aggravations. "We had heretofore passed through so many troubles during this war," Russell told Adams, "so we might safely get over this one."[27] But in late January, Russell's tone had become anxious; he requested clarification on twelve U.S. steam launches under construction in British dockyards, and whether they were for military or civilian use. Adams realized that the government's concern was whether they would be used not against the South, but on the Great Lakes against the British. Palmerston was genuinely alarmed. "There is something mysterious about these launches," he wrote to Russell. "Could they have not got them sooner, more cheaply and as good in their own dockyards? What they are really meant for one cannot say. Their size is quite enough for carrying guns, and it is probable they are destined to cover the landing of troops on our shores in the Lakes."[28]

The British cabinet agreed that Quebec should be fortified as quickly as possible; the navy's budget was increased, and the Queen was warned on February 12 that the country was preparing for war. Her private secretary, Lieutenant General Charles Grey, argued unsuccessfully for a preemptive strike.[*29] Although the Queen deprecated the idea, she shared Grey's anxiety, acknowledging in her diary "the impossibility of our

---

* A short time later, the Duke of Somerset received a parcel containing the plans of the U.S. Navy's latest ships and their torpedoes. They had been secretly obtained by the master shipbuilder Donald McKay, who resided in New York but whose heart and family remained in Nova Scotia.

being able to hold Canada, but we must struggle for it."[30] Lord Lyons was summoned to the palace to give his assessment of the United States' intentions. Still in the grip of mental exhaustion and in great pain from his neuralgia, he could not help sounding bleak. Lyons "seemed bitterly disgusted with his post at Washington and with the dreadful people he has had to deal with—so insincere and ungentlemanlike," the Queen recorded after the interview. "He thinks the position a dangerous one, but does not believe in a war [between the United States and] us, at least he hopes it may not come to it."[31]

Lord Russell had been sincere when he told Adams in December that responsibility for preventing an Anglo-American war rested on the two of them finding "a safe issue from this, as we had from so many other troubles that had sprung up during this war."[32] In mid-February, he decided to send a protest to the Confederate government over its blatant abuse of British neutrality. Unlike the previous remonstrance sent in 1864, this one would be sent to Washington with a request that the U.S. government pass the letter on to Richmond. Russell showed the document to Charles Francis Adams. Addressed to Mason, Slidell, and Mann, it complained that Confederate acts in Britain and Canada had showed "a gross disregard of her Majesty's character as a neutral power, and a desire to involve her Majesty in hostilities."[33]

Adams was astonished by the passion in Russell's voice; "he read it over slowly and deliberately," the minister recorded in his diary. During the subsequent conversation, Russell agreed with Adams "that it looked ill" when Canadian and English juries repeatedly acquitted Confederate offenders. "People here now took sides, almost as vehemently on our questions as we did ourselves. It was to be regretted, but there was no help for it," Russell had argued, which received the blunt riposte from Adams that if Britain had become embroiled in the Prussian-Danish war, "in two months, Prussia would have been fitting out fast steamers in the port of New York, and we should not have been able to stop them. His Lordship candidly enough admitted that the idea had occurred to him."[34] "This conference was one of a most friendly character," Adams wrote to Seward, "and convinced me that whatever might be the desires of the French emperor, nothing but the grossest mismanagement on our part would effect any change in the established policy of this ministry towards us." Over the next few days, Adams repeated his warnings with greater vehemence.[35]

Adams wondered whether Seward was even bothering to read his reports, since the secretary of state rarely responded to specific points and had ignored Adams's request to leave London.[36]

The news that the U.S. Congress had ratified the Thirteenth Amendment, abolishing slavery, had an even greater effect on British public opinion than the North's recent military victories. No amount of sneering by Henry Hotze in the *Index* could diminish the moral grandeur of emancipation. He had been counting on the memoirs of Fitzgerald Ross and of Belle Boyd to create a sensation—and a diversion—but neither book was ready for publication. "I can do no better though I have tried very hard," Ross explained to his publishers. "Is it the general experience of authors that the preface is the most difficult part of the book to write?"[37] Belle Boyd was being helped with her book by the writer George Augustus Sala, who may also have become her lover; if he did, the affair was suddenly complicated by the return of Belle's husband, Sam Hardinge, who had been released without explanation from Fort Delaware on February 8 and had arrived in London with his health completely broken down.* Belle included Hardinge's prison diary in her memoirs, but there is no record of what happened to him once he reached England; he simply disappeared and was never mentioned again. She was similarly tight-lipped about the birth date of her daughter, Grace.[39]

James Mason was in Paris with Mann and Slidell composing a joint response to Lord Russell's protest when Duncan Kenner arrived on February 24.[40] The commissioners could not believe that the South they remembered would genuinely consider emancipation; to them, slavery was the core of Southern identity.[41] Yet Mason had recently received a letter from his eldest son, Lieutenant James M. Mason, Jr., who fully embraced the idea of offering freedom to the slaves in return for their

---

* Sala had reported on the war for the *Daily Telegraph* and was, like Lawley, completely pro-Southern. In the introduction he provided for Belle's memoir, *Belle Boyd in Camp and Prison,* he claimed that she possessed scandalous information about members of Lincoln's administration. Whether or not this was really the case, he helped her to draft a threatening letter to Lincoln on January 24 in which she offered to suppress her memoir if Hardinge was released by the beginning of March. "I think it well for you and me to come to some definite understanding," Belle had written boldly.[38]

fighting for the Confederacy: "With proper discipline they will fight as well as any mercenaries," he insisted. His regiment, the 42nd Virginia Infantry, had almost starved while fighting General Sheridan in the Shenandoah Valley, and it was hardly better off in Petersburg. He doubted any of them could survive another winter of such suffering: "If the North continues her present energy, the long night of ruin, misery and agony will surely come unless indeed, you in Europe, do something for our aid."[42]

Kenner had risked his life to deliver Davis's proposal of emancipation in return for recognition, and it did not matter to him whether the commissioners were relieved or outraged.[43] Slidell realized that they had no choice, and on March 4 he had an interview with the emperor, who repeated his condolences and sent the commissioner on his way. But Mason still could not bring himself to accept the truth; he accompanied Kenner to London and tried to keep him distracted with business arrangements for the Confederate cotton loan. Kenner could not be deflected from his real purpose for long, however, and he insisted that Mason arrange the meeting with Lord Palmerston.

The Confederate commissioner reluctantly complied, but had one more trick up his sleeve. At the last minute he succeeded in persuading Kenner to step aside and allow him to make the representation, on the grounds that the mission required the skills of an experienced diplomat. Mason met with Lord Palmerston on March 14, 1865. By his own account, he prevaricated for almost twenty minutes before finally asking whether "there was some latent, undisclosed obstacle on the part of Great Britain to recognition." Palmerston had already divined the real purpose of the conversation and replied without hesitating that slavery had never been the obstacle. Mason was elated until he recounted the conversation to a friend, Lord Donoughmore, who told him that Palmerston had said this precisely to forestall a last-minute appeal from the South: slavery had *always* been the chief impediment to recognition. The South had squandered her only chance of achieving it by not emancipating the slaves in 1863, when Lee was the undisputed victor on the battlefield. For a brief moment, Mason feared that he had been responsible for ruining the South's last hope of survival, and wanted to see Palmerston again so he could be much clearer this time, but Donoughmore assured him that "the [opportunity] had gone by now, especially that our fortunes seemed more adverse than ever."*[44]

Hotze informed his editorial staff that "the Confederate funds in Europe were in a state of bankruptcy . . . and the Index would probably be discontinued in two or three months." "This greatly disconcerted me," wrote his deputy John Thompson, "as I am at a loss to know how to live when my salary is cut off."[45] The Confederates in London were further demoralized by the debate in the Commons on the night of the fourteenth about the proposed cost of Canada's defenses. Benjamin Moran observed the proceedings from the Strangers' Gallery, expecting to hear the North denounced or the South eulogized. To his surprise, Southern recognition was not even mentioned, and "the marked feature was the tone of respect towards the US, Mr. Lincoln and Mr. Seward. This was in wonderful contrast to the jeers, the sneers and the disrespect common in that House on all occasions when these names were mentioned two and three years ago. . . . Forster made a speech that amounted to eloquence. I didn't think he had it in him."[46]

The revolution in British attitudes toward the North and South was also apparent in the Foreign Office's approach to persons who had run afoul of the U.S. authorities, as Mary Sophia Hill found to her disappointment. "I should like my trial denounced," she had written to Lord Wharncliffe in February.[47] Mary had written in a similar vein to Lord Russell: "I have come to this country for the purpose of carrying my case personally to your Lordship, and to ask for justice to be done me, and though but a humble individual, I feel assured not all is in vain. England's flag protects her subjects, wherever they may be scattered."[48] But he did not feel inclined "to ask for justice," and after reviewing all the documents in Mary's case, neither did Russell's legal advisers. "Her whole story is, moreover, extremely improbable," insisted the attorney general on March 18:

---

* The former Confederate secretary of state, Robert M. T. Hunter, stated the conundrum in stark terms on March 7, 1865, during the Confederate Senate debate on whether to use slave soldiers. "To arm the negroes is to give them freedom," he told the chamber. "If we are right in passing this measure, then we were wrong in denying to the old Government the right to interfere with the institution of slavery." He, for one, was not prepared to be a hypocrite. But the majority of the Senate chose survival over principle. They all knew that General Lee was desperate to have the negro recruits for his army. A week later, on March 13, the Confederate House of Representatives followed suit after a raucous and bitter debate.

It is not true, as she says, that she was acquitted; she was found guilty, and banished. It is certainly not improbable that she may have been rudely treated by the United States authorities; but the British Consul and Lord Lyons appear to have done all that was in their power to save her from the consequences of her own (to say the least) very imprudent acts. We are clearly of opinion, that there is no ground for your Lordship's interference in this matter.[49]

Robert Burley encountered a similar response to his requests regarding his son Bennet, the Confederate guerrilla in Canada. Frightened by the execution of John Yates Beall, Bennet's friend and coconspirator, Burley Sr. had enlisted the help of his local MP, Robert Dalglish, as well as MP William Forster, to take up the case with the Foreign Office and the American legation.[50] (Fitzgerald Ross became concerned for Colonel Grenfell and asked his publisher to remove all references to his friend from his memoir.) He also made a heartfelt appeal to Lord Russell to save his son. The foreign secretary scribbled on the back of Burley's letter: "Inform him a copy of his letter will be sent to Washington with instructions to do the best for his son."[51] Translated, it meant the government would not contest the charges.

Russell was so anxious about the apparent rise in Northern hostility toward England that he asked Lord Lyons to cut short his recuperation and return immediately to Washington. But to his surprise, instead of dutifully agreeing, Lyons resigned from the diplomatic service. "Lord Russell has been extremely kind to me, and so indeed has every one," Lyons wrote to his former secretary of the legation, William Stuart. Seward's subsequent letter especially moved him: "I accept your farewell with sincere sorrow," the secretary of state wrote on March 20. "But I reconcile myself to it because it is a condition of restoration of your health." Seward promised that Anglo-American relations would prosper after the war, although it saddened him that Lyons would not be around to enjoy the moment when the two countries "are reconciled and become better friends than ever. . . . But God disposes." It was bittersweet for Lyons to read these words. "I confess that I do not feel so much relief or even pleasure as might have been expected," he told Stuart. "I seriously thought of offering to go back immediately when I heard the decision of the Cabinet." That decision was the appointment of Sir Frederick Bruce, the former minister to China, as the new head of the Washington legation. It was not Bruce that troubled Lyons but the reality of being re-placed. He even missed "my Washington Mission." In Lyons's reply to Seward, he reflected on "the friendly and unconstrained terms on which we were" and how much good they had produced. "I am most anxious that my successor's intercourse with you should be placed at once on the same footing."[52]

"You are about to proceed to Washington at a very critical period," Russell informed Sir Frederick Bruce on March 24, 1865.[53] He warned Bruce on no account to mention the *Alabama* or allow Seward to speak to him about reparations for the Confederate cruisers built in Britain. If Seward brought up the Confederate cruisers, Bruce was to declare the subject beyond his remit.[54] That night, Benjamin Moran encountered Lyons and Bruce together at the French embassy ball. Lyons smiled wryly when Moran asked how he had enjoyed Washington, and he replied with monumental understatement that "he had had a very satis-factory time in the US, although rather hard worked."[55]

Charles Francis Adams was amused by the government's "singular panic in regard to what will be done by us, after restoration [of the Union]. A week or two since you could not drive the notion out of their heads that we were not about to pounce at once upon Canada."[56] But Adams took the greater satisfaction from seeing the humiliation of his former adversaries:

> One thing seems for the present to be settled. That is, that no hope is left for any aid to the rebel cause. England will initiate nothing to help them in their critical moment. . . . The volumi-nous intrigues of the rebel emissaries have been completely baf-fled, their sanguine anticipations utterly disappointed. They have spent floods of money in directing the press, in securing aid from adventurers of all sorts, and in enlisting the services of ship and cannon builders with all their immense and powerful following, and it has been all in vain. So far as any efforts of theirs are con-cerned, we might enter Richmond tomorrow. This act of the drama is over.[57]

THIRTY-SEVEN

Fire, Fire

Tom Conolly, MP, crosses the bar—Welly!—The last train out—Richmond burns—Grant breaks Lee's line

Henry Feilden reluctantly accompanied General Hardee as the Confederate army abandoned Charleston on February 17, 1865. "I cannot bear to think of leaving this dear old city which has been defended so long and gloriously," he wrote sadly to Julia. "I have given our house to an English family who will endeavour to save it for me." But he warned her, "We are going to see hard times."[1] His last view of the city before its fall was of golden flames flickering against the night sky as great fires consumed the wharves: the retreating Confederates had deliberately torched the remaining cotton and set fire to ships in the harbor. He was unaware that this "magnificent sight" had led to a horrific tragedy: a large crowd of civilians, mostly women and children, had been foraging in a warehouse that contained a lethal combination of food and gunpowder when it exploded, killing 150 and leaving many more to die in agony.[2]

Federal troops entered Charleston on February 18 and almost immediately went on the rampage. The contents of the houses, including pianos and four-poster beds, were either plundered or destroyed, depending on the humor and taste of the invaders. Consul Henry Pinckney Walker reappeared and invited any British subjects in the city to register at the consulate, although he did not offer the building as a refuge.[3]

Some women were not only afraid to leave their houses, but were unable to do so, since looters had stolen their dresses.

It was ten days before Feilden had another opportunity to write. During that time he had not changed his clothes or slept in a real bed. "I do not know how much more we have to endure," he wrote on the twenty-eighth, "but as far as I am concerned I am a stronger Southern Man at this moment than ever I was before, and I shall not give up till the very last moment."[4] His devotion was not a universal feeling among the retreating Confederates. General Hardee had come down with typhus shortly before the order to evacuate and was barely able to walk, let alone inspire courage or fortitude among his demoralized troops. Months of defensive duties had made the soldiers unfit for forced marches, and the struggle through frozen swamps in unceasing downpours caused many to faint with exhaustion. Whole companies disappeared in the darkness.[5] The officers' ability to prevent desertion during daylight was hardly more successful, and the small army was losing almost two hundred men a day. Hardee's destination was a small town north of Wilmington called Fayetteville, in North Carolina, an important supply base for the Confederates. General Johnston—whom Lee had recently reinstated—had ordered all available troops to meet there to make a last stand against Sherman's advancing forces.

Confederate regiments were already gathering at Fayetteville when Thomas Conolly, an Anglo-Irish MP from County Kildare, Ireland, arrived on March 2. Conolly had invested in the blockade runner *Emily II* and sailed to Bermuda with her, intending to run the blockade at Wilmington. A less eccentric character might have chosen to return home after the fall of Fort Fisher, but Conolly saw no reason to let a Northern victory get in the way of his visiting "Dixie." Leaving the *Emily II* at Nassau, he persuaded Captain Maffitt, who was taking his ship, the *Owl*, to Havana, to make a slight detour by way of the North Carolina coast and drop him off somewhere near Cape Fear. On February 26, Conolly and two friends climbed into a skiff and rowed through the pouring rain over the sandbar and into the neck of the Shallotte River, some thirty-seven miles north of Wilmington. Soaked to the skin and hungry, they called at several houses until they found someone willing to give them shelter for the night.[6]

It was only after he landed that Conolly learned of General Sherman's arrival in South Carolina. The news made him drop his plans to tour Charleston in favor of reaching Richmond as quickly as possible. He arrived at Fayetteville on March 2 to find it mobbed with wagons and soldiers. "The bar-room of the large Hotel is crowded with men in uniform, and a fine young fellow, very handsome, is hobbling about on a new wooden leg," Conolly jotted in his diary. The three travelers passed two days in the town while Conolly tried to negotiate the purchase of a horse. "So we make the best of it," he wrote, "and order a banjo band and whiskey to our room and ask all the wounded officers about and have a capital evening's amusement up to 1 o'clock dancing and singing."[7] Two days later, they ran into Frank Vizetelly, who obligingly offered to take them to Richmond.

The small party arrived at the capital on March 8. Conolly's penchant for bright red breeches looked incongruous amid the browns, grays, and deep mourning. "The aspect of Richmond at this time is wretched," he wrote. "Shops with nothing in them except enough to show how miserably they are run out. Stores with open doors and empty bales and broken up packing cases and dirty straw." Government clerks were quietly packing their archives in anticipation of having to leave the city. Vizetelly deposited Conolly at the Ballard Hotel and went in search of Francis Lawley. The Ballard was "now miserably furnished, scarcely anything in the bedrooms except the beds and a few broken chairs," Conolly recorded. The carpets had been torn up and sent to the army for coats. "Almost all the crockery in the Hotel is cracked and broken, and we had to buy 3 tumblers for our room at 25 dollars each." He was annoyed to discover that a bottle of brandy set him back $60.[8]

The first resident to receive a visit from Conolly was the wife of James Mason, the Confederate commissioner in London. "Plucky dear old Lady," he wrote. She was nursing her son, James M. Mason, Jr., who was one of the few survivors of a recent skirmish against General Sheridan.[9] The day had been proclaimed by Davis as one of fasting and prayer, and Conolly confined himself to muffins for tea, followed by oysters and cocktails. During the next few days he attached himself to various generals, his open and liberal purse helping to soften any objections to his presence. His persistence paid off, and on March 13, he received an invitation to supper at the Confederate White House at 9:00 P.M.

Conolly was impressed by President Davis's calm demeanor. "I never saw quiet determination more strikingly manifest in any person than in Jeff Davis," he wrote. "His conversation is easy, copious in illustration from foreign countries, and rich and animated!" Varina Davis, on the other hand, was less adept at hiding her true thoughts; though obtuse at times, Conolly knew when he was being put down. "Mrs. Davis is a very different character," he decided, "a great talker and very bitter. She is calculated to damage any cause however good."[10]

Had Conolly appeared a day later, it is unlikely that the Davises would have invited him to dinner. Lord Russell's protest to the Confederate commissioners was delivered to Richmond on March 14, the morning after. "Britain gives us a kick while the Federal generals are pounding us," the War Department clerk John Jones wrote bitterly.[11] But by then, Conolly had already left the capital and was being entertained by General Lee at Petersburg. Conolly's reaction to meeting Lee was similar to Colonel Wolseley's in 1863. Even in the hour of his greatest trial, Lee still retained an aura of magnificence. "The Hope of His Country is also the handsomest man in all that constitutes the real dignity of man that I ever saw," wrote Conolly. The general drew the line at allowing Conolly to stay the night, and General Pryor's wife was prevailed upon to take him in. However, she was quickly won over by Conolly's charm: "The MP proved a most agreeable guest," she wrote, "a fine-looking Irish gentleman with an irresistibly humorous, cheery round of talk."[12] During Conolly's final dinner at Petersburg, Lee opened a bottle of "very old Madeira." "Excellent! Just 2 glasses," wrote Conolly mournfully, not realizing that he had consumed all the vegetables and the only turkey in the mess. After saying goodbye to Lee, who gave him his photograph and a Confederate flag, Conolly braved a storm to attend a party at Petersburg with "some nice young fellows" and a bevy of pretty ladies.

The Confederate Congress was holding what would turn out to be its last session when Conolly returned to Richmond on March 18. Four days earlier, the politicians had agreed to allow owners to volunteer their slaves as soldiers, having voted unanimously "to prosecute the war with the United States until . . . the independence of the Confederate States shall have been established." But today the members adjourned with no thought of when they would meet again.[13] The city was tense and quiet as the residents waited to learn whether General Johnston would stop Sherman's advance now that Fayetteville had fallen to the Federals. "If Sherman cuts the communication with North Carolina," wrote John Jones, "no one doubts that this city must be abandoned by Lee's army."[14]

"We are falling back slowly before Sherman," Feilden had scribbled in a penciled note to Julia on March 13. "I hope that we may have a victory over this man Sherman. I should like to pursue him from here to South Carolina."[15] None of the Confederate generals, including Hardee, had expected Sherman to make it through the Carolina swamps so quickly, if at all. The right wing of Sherman's army was within marching distance of Raleigh, North Carolina's capital. In desperation, Hardee deployed his outnumbered and weakened forces in a surprise attack against Sherman's left flank on March 16.

The ambush slowed Sherman just enough for Johnston to organize his army into battle formation at Bentonville, North Carolina. There, for three days, beginning at dawn on March 19, 1865, a force of twenty thousand Confederates struggled against an army three times its size. The disparity between the two armies was exacerbated by the Confederates' muddled organization, but Johnston suddenly showed his critics that he could fight—and fight hard—when pressed. By March 21 Johnston's army had suffered more than twenty-five hundred casualties, to the Federals' fifteen hundred. Feilden was talking to General Hardee when a stray shot struck the tree beside them. The next bullet passed through Feilden's sleeve "near enough to jar my funny bone" and hit his horse, Billy, in the leg. The wound was just bad enough to prevent him from riding the horse in the next cavalry charge. Hardee's sixteen-year-old son, Willie, begged to take part, and in the heat of the moment, Hardee nodded his assent and kissed the boy farewell. A short while later, a Texas Ranger brought Willie back, shot through the chest. "He was a mere schoolboy," wrote Feilden in anguish. "He was as gallant a little fellow as ever fired a musket." The tragedy made him long to be with Julia: "Oh! My precious one, if we are only spared to meet again, and live together, what happiness it will be," he wrote. "I don't care how poor we may be. It will be the greatest blessing this earth can afford us."[16]

After the Battle of Bentonville, Sherman continued his march toward Richmond while the Confederates retreated to Raleigh, North Carolina— Johnston apparently too stunned to consider pursuit. He telegraphed Lee: "Sherman's course cannot be hindered by the small force I have. I can do no more than annoy him." Lee realized that in a few days he would be facing the combined forces of Grant, Sheridan, and Sherman, and he began planning the Army of Northern Virginia's evacuation from Petersburg. He knew that Richmond would then fall to the Federals, but if his army remained intact, the South would still have its fighting capability. On March 25, he launched a surprise attack against the Union Fort Steadman, on the east side of Petersburg, hoping to distract Grant long enough to enable the rest of the Confederate army to retreat southward, toward North Carolina. The assault was an outright disaster, costing Lee four thousand casualties against the Federals' fifteen hundred, without any weakening of Grant's line.

Thomas Conolly was in Richmond during the attack, but the news of its failure made no difference to his confidence in the ultimate outcome of the war: "Richmond thy sun is not setting, rather the Day is just about to break over your hero-crested virgin hills!" he wrote in his diary, adding for good measure: "Always darkest before the dawn! What a dawn, Independence!" Late on the twenty-fifth he received a note inviting him to visit Mrs. Mason's house. " 'Welly' is to be there!" wrote Conolly in surprise, learning for the first time that his friend Lieutenant Llewellyn Traherne Bassett Saunderson, of the British Army's 11th Hussars, had arrived in the South at the same time as he had, hoping to volunteer on General Lee's staff.[17]

The following day, March 26, Conolly went to church, where the vicar's sermon put him to sleep; "I hate argument, I like faith much better!" Conolly was oblivious to the fact that the city was emptying around him. Jefferson Davis had overridden his wife's protests and instructed her to take the family to Charlotte, North Carolina, three hundred miles to the southwest, and to go farther if necessary. Their furniture was sent to auction, and Varina distributed various mementos to friends and servants. Davis also asked his private secretary to accompany the family to safety. He gave Varina all his gold save for one five-dollar piece and a small Colt pistol, which she was to use in the "last extremity."

CSS *Georgia*'s former lieutenant James Morgan met the Davis family at the station. In his wildest dreams he had never imagined himself as personal guard to a mother and her small children. When summoned by the Confederate navy secretary, Stephen Mallory, to the Navy Department, he thought it was for some infraction: "I at once began to think of all my sins of commission and omission. To my surprise, he told me that I was to accompany Mrs. Jefferson Davis south, and added, with a merry twinkle in his eyes, that the daughters of the Secretary of the Treasury [George Trenholm] were to be of the party." (Morgan had become engaged to Trenholm's younger daughter, Helen, whom he met in Charleston the night of his introduction to Matthew Fontaine Maury.)

As Morgan observed the parting between Jefferson and Varina, he realized that the Davises were behaving as though it was their final moment together as a family. The two eldest children clung to their father, crying to stay with him. Davis kissed them all again, stroked the baby that lay asleep on a bench, embraced his wife, wished Morgan and the Trenholm girls a safe journey, and walked heavily down the carriage steps. What should have been a six-hour train journey took more than four days. When the creaking train pulled into Charlotte, a furious mob surrounded the carriage:

> I closed the open windows of the car so that the ladies could not hear what was being said [recalled Morgan]. We two men were helpless to protect them from the epithets of a crowd of some seventy-five or a hundred blackguards, but we stationed ourselves at the only door which was not locked, determined that they should not enter the car. Colonel Harrison was unarmed, and I had only my sword, and a regulation revolver in the holster hanging from my belt. Several of the most daring of the brutes climbed up the steps, but when Colonel Harrison firmly told them that he would not permit them to enter that car the cowards slunk away. When the disturbance had quieted down Mrs. Davis, her sister, and her children left the train.

The city's residents were frightened of showing courtesy to Varina and furious with her husband for mismanaging the war. "Mrs. Davis would have been in a sad plight if it had not been for the courage and chivalric courtesy of a Jewish gentleman, a Mr. Weil," wrote Morgan, "who hospitably invited her to stay at his home until she could make other arrangements. May the God of Abraham, Isaac, and Jacob bless him wherever he is!"[18]

Jefferson Davis waited anxiously in the Confederate capital while Lee sought to delay Grant's encirclement of Petersburg. The Army of Northern Virginia had dwindled to no more than 35,000 men, while Grant's Army of the Potomac had grown to over 125,000. President Lincoln was less than twenty miles from Richmond, having traveled from Washington on the *River Queen* to visit Grant's headquarters at City Point on the James River. (Mary and Tad accompanied him for the first days, but Mary behaved so strangely—raving at the slightest provocation—

that she was encouraged to stay in her cabin.) Lincoln's greatest concern was that peace, which seemed so close now, should not be a pyrrhic victory for the North. "I want no one punished," he told Sherman and Grant. Their armies were to be restrained from violence or vengeance. When asked about President Davis, Lincoln expressed a wish that the Confederate leader would emigrate, unnoticed and unmolested.

———

Lee and Grant had fought each other over seven hundred square miles of territory since June 9, 1864; more than seventy thousand soldiers had died in nineteen separate battles. Now, the struggle had narrowed to the possession of the Five Forks crossroads, fifteen miles from Petersburg. Lee needed to hold it just long enough for his forces to escape from Petersburg using the Southside Railroad. Tom Conolly was again at Lee's headquarters, where he watched the general outline the battle plan to his staff, using a stick and a "mud map." Conolly remained with Lee rather than following Generals Fitz Lee and George Pickett to Five Forks, and he was rewarded with the spectacle of a skirmish between two picket lines:

> This pleased [Conolly] so much, [wrote General Wilcox] that he offered his service to me for the coming campaign, and said if I would permit him he would remain with me until its close. I accepted his tender of service, and told him I would make him one of my volunteer aides. He thanked me, and asked if I would let him go under fire. I replied that it would hardly be possible for him to escape being under fire. He said he would return to Richmond, get his baggage and report to me early Monday morning [April 3].[19]

At Five Forks, Fitz Lee and Pickett had orders to hold the crossroads "at all hazard." Welly had been placed on Fitz Lee's staff, where he was delighted to discover another British volunteer, Francis Dawson. They rose at 3:30 A.M. on March 31, and "after a rough breakfast we all went down to General Pickett's headquarters where a Council of War took place. We remained here for 3 hours or so, smoking and telling stories in a downfall of rain the whole time."[20] Years afterward, Dawson also remembered the terrible rain that had chilled him to the bone. He had tried to keep warm by gulping coffee out of an old tin cup before the fighting commenced, scalding his lips in the process. Later in the morning another moment seared itself in his memory. "It was very difficult to rally the men," he wrote:

> One fellow whom I halted as he was running to the rear, and whom I threatened to shoot if he did not stop, looked up in my face in the most astonished manner, and, raising his carbine at an angle of forty-five degrees, fired it in the air, or at the tops of the pines, and resumed his flight. It made me laugh, angry as I was.[21]

Toward sundown, General Fitz Lee's men made a final, desperate charge against Sheridan's line. One bullet struck an overhanging branch just as Dawson lowered his head to ride under the tree; the next tore into his shoulder.

"Bad news from Pickett," recorded Welly on April 1. "He has lost 5,000 men out of 8,000, and the remainder are cut off from us." The two generals, Fitz Lee and Pickett, had ridden off to a picnic, having assumed that Sheridan would spend the day entrenching his men. Far from it: Sheridan launched a surprise attack. "We had no idea that the enemy were so close to us," wrote Welly, "when all of a sudden about 250 Yankees let drive at us, it was so sudden that nobody could help being startled. I looked round and the whole regiment had disappeared." Sheridan captured more than four thousand prisoners at Five Forks. As the scattered Confederates found one another, Welly was relieved to learn that "Dawson, one of my brother ADCs," had not been killed, but sent to Richmond at Fitz Lee's insistence.[22]

Dawson arrived in the city so befuddled with morphine that he was oblivious to the turmoil in the streets. At dawn on Sunday, April 2, Grant ordered an all-out attack on Lee's defenses, smashing through at almost every point. Lee realized he had to retreat immediately or risk being surrounded and captured. He ordered the troops to evacuate and sent a telegram to Davis advising him to leave Richmond. The message was delivered to Davis while he was at church. Conolly was sitting in a pew nearby and observed the sexton whisper in his ear. "He rises and leaves the Church. Then the same operation to one and a second member of the government, both follow suit; people begin to whisper . . . they rose in tens and 20s and left the Church, outside the secret was soon abroad." Only the most faithful remained for communion. Conolly fought his

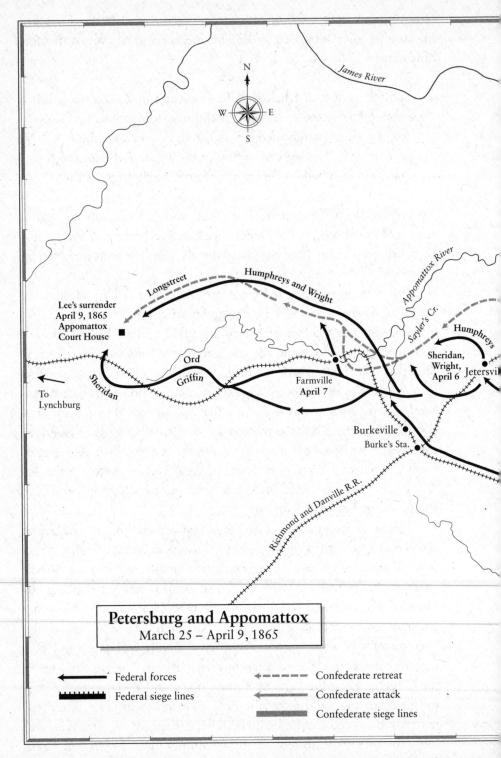

Petersburg and Appomattox
March 25 – April 9, 1865

Francis Dawson
Llewellyn Saunderson

Richmond, Fredericksburg & Potomac R.R.

Virginia Central R.R.

Charles Francis
Adams, Jr.

Cold Harbor •

Weitzel, April 3

Richmond & York River R.R.

Richmond

Manchester

James
Horrocks

Richmond & Danville R.R.

Ewell

Lee, April 4–5

Lee

Amelia
Court
House

Longstreet

Gordon

Anderson

Appomattox River

City Point

James River

Petersburg

Sheridan, April 5

Ft. Stedman,
March 25

Five Forks

Southside R.R.

Warren

Wright, April 2

Pickett,
March 31

Sheridan,
April 1

Dinwiddie
Court House

Hatcher's Run

Grant

Meade

Sheridan

Nottoway River

Richmond, Fredericksburg & Potomac R.R.

Miles

0   5   10   15   20

way through the streets—"a regular stampede has begun"—to the home of his friends Mrs. Enders and "her nice pretty daughters." He promised the distraught women he would spend the night, guarding the house for them. Having satisfied himself that they were safe for the moment, Conolly set off in search of Francis Lawley and found him packing his bags at the hotel: "We take a parting cup to our next merry meeting."

Jefferson Davis was also packing. Trains were being laid on to take the government and the treasury to Danville, forty miles southwest of Richmond. There was pandemonium in the city. People were fighting and clawing at each other to escape the city, "on horseback, in every description of cart, carriage and vehicle," wrote Lawley, "on canal barges, skiffs, and boats." Stephen Mallory and Judah P. Benjamin were already at the station waiting for the rest of the cabinet. Mallory had sent an order to Raphael Semmes, who had been placed in charge of Richmond's water defenses after his return to the South in November 1864, to destroy the fleet of nine ships on the James River and take his force to wherever Lee established his new headquarters. The Confederate navy secretary had not heard from James Bulloch in weeks. Each day he had waited for a telegram announcing the arrival of CSS *Stonewall,* but despite Bulloch's efforts, the cruiser had only set sail from Spain on March 28. Mallory had no idea of the whereabouts of CSS *Shenandoah* (the raider was in the Pacific, near the Eastern Caroline Islands, south of Guam), nor did it matter now. Judah Benjamin was inscrutable, but he, too, had to accept that his final gamble had failed. Even if Duncan Kenner had succeeded in obtaining Southern recognition from Palmerston in exchange for emancipation—which Benjamin seriously doubted after receiving Lord Russell's protest—it was too late for the Confederacy.

The trains began rumbling out of Richmond at eleven o'clock. First went the government train, followed by the treasury's, and finally the government archives. Every car was crowded with refugees; more were riding on the roofs and clinging to the sides. Some of the guards on the trains were boys, barely in their teens. "Up to the hour of their departure from Richmond," insisted Francis Lawley, "I can testify that Mr. Davis and the three most prominent members of his Cabinet went undauntedly forth to meet the future, not without hope that General Lee would be able to hold together a substantial remnant of his army."[23]

Tom Conolly stood by the front window of the Enders family home, keeping watch while the women lay on the sofas behind him, "weep[ing] and sob[bing] till their hearts seem breaking." Francis Lawley also remained awake. "During that memorable night there was no sleep in Richmond," he wrote. "In front of every Government bureau, of every auditor's office, around the Capitol, and upon each side of Capitol-Square, the glare of vast piles of burning papers turned night into day." The last regiments to leave Richmond had orders to destroy the ordnance depots to keep them from enemy hands, and to dispose of the city's liquor supply. In a well-intentioned but disastrous move, the Confederates emptied hundreds of whiskey kegs onto the streets. "Women and boys, black and white, were seen filling pitchers and buckets from the gutters," wrote John B. Jones in his diary.[24]

Both Conolly and Lawley heard the explosions, which seemed to shake every building in Richmond to its foundations:

> As I walked up between 5 and 6 in the morning of Monday, the 3rd, to catch the early train [wrote Francis Lawley], a vast column of dense black smoke shot into the air . . . as the eye ranged backwards along the James River, several bright jets of flame in the region of Pearl and Cary streets augured the breaking forth of that terrible conflagration which subsequently swept across the heart of the city. As the train moved off from the Fredericksburg depot about 6 o'clock, I parted with Mr. Conolly, the Member for Donegal, who had passed a month in Richmond, and was upon this eventful morning still undecided whether to follow General Lee's army or to strike northwards like myself.[25]

In the commercial district, hardly a single pane of glass remained unbroken, and from Main Street to the canal nearly a thousand buildings were on fire. The bridges were also destroyed. This, together with the "roaring and crackling of burning houses . . . made up a scene that beggars description and which I hope never to see again," wrote a departing Confederate officer; "a city undergoing pillage at the hands of its own mob, while the tramp of a victorious enemy could be heard at its gates!"[26] Lawley was overwhelmed at the sight. For the past four years he had venerated the South; he had perjured himself on its behalf and had perpetuated a dream, only to watch helplessly now as it transmogrified into a nightmare. "Hell is empty, and all the devils are here," he quoted from *The Tempest.*

Conolly returned to his hotel at sunrise, shoving aside anyone who attempted to get in his way. Hundreds of fires were still burning. He had almost reached the building when he heard a cry: "the Yankees, the Yankees." The city's bleary-eyed residents were astonished to see a combination of white and Negro regiments from the Union Army of the James—Butler's old army—riding through the streets. Many were singing "John Brown's Body" as they marched. The scene helped to make up Conolly's mind to quit the Misses Enders, and by midmorning he was riding for Fredericksburg. Already a Federal flag was hanging from the rooftop of the Capitol. "The ensign of our subjugation," lamented a female resident, but its appearance represented salvation just as much as disaster.[27] The general leading the Federal entrance, Godfrey Weitzel, hurriedly ordered his officers to organize teams of firefighters. The hotels, the banks, the better class of shops, the warehouses, depots, and hundreds of private houses were either charred heaps of brick or empty edifices. Fifty-five blocks in the center of Richmond had disappeared, but Weitzel's men saved many more.

Hundreds of families collected in Capitol Square, sitting in huddled groups with the detritus of destruction around them, waiting miserably for the Federals to take charge of their future. Hour by hour, order was gradually restored to the streets. By ten o'clock that night, when Charles Francis Adams, Jr., led the 5th Massachusetts Colored Cavalry into the city, an unofficial curfew made the place seem deserted. "To have led my regiment into Richmond at the moment of its capture is the one event which I should most have desired as the culmination of my life in the Army," he admitted to his father. "For the first time I see the spirit of the Virginians, the whole people are cowed—whipped out."[28]

Abraham Lincoln arrived at the city a few hours after Charles Francis Jr., on the morning of the fourth.[29] The black population was anything but "whipped out." They clustered about him, shouting ecstatically, touching his clothes, shaking his hand; he protested when some knelt down as he passed. Lincoln entered the Confederate White House and looked around Davis's office, even sitting in his chair. He seemed tired and worn to those around him. Victory was at hand, but not yet in his hands—not until the surrender of Lee's army, he reminded a Confederate delegation who called on him to discuss Virginia's political future. During the afternoon, Lincoln toured hospitals and prisons, showing a gentle courtesy to Federals and rebels alike. He displayed a magnanimity toward the defeated Confederates that was conspicuously absent among his colleagues in the cabinet.

Lee would be able to keep fighting if he could reach North Carolina and consolidate his army with the survivors of General Joe Johnston's. He ordered his commanders to head forty miles west, toward the court-house at Amelia Springs, where the scattered fragments of the Army of Northern Virginia could regroup and distribute supplies for the long journey ahead. But Grant was in pursuit, his forces moving so swiftly that Quartermaster Sergeant James Horrocks (since his promotion in March) returned from his furlough in New York to find his camp deserted. Not knowing where the 5th Battery, New Jersey Artillery had gone, he walked into Richmond and spent the night on the floor in one of the bedrooms in the Confederate White House. "So I had the honor of sleeping in the house of Jeff Davis," he wrote to his brother, "if there is any honor in that."[30]

THIRTY-EIGHT

"A True-Born King of Men"

*Lincoln in Richmond—Appomattox Court House—A final salute—From actor to assassin—*Punch *apologizes—The American example—Flight to the interior—Vizetelly's £50 note*

On April 5, 1865, Abraham Lincoln spent his second day in Richmond riding about in an open carriage. His bravery terrified the presidential retinue, but it no doubt contributed as much to the city's return to order as any overt display of arms. The aftermath of Richmond's burning was also observed by Thomas Kennard, an English railway engineer, who was so eager to be a part of the momentous events in Virginia that he had chartered a private yacht to take him and a small group of British and American tourists along the James River to the Confederate capital. They wandered through the streets, shocked to find "that nearly half the city has been reduced to ashes," though they thought the Federal soldiers' behavior was exemplary:

No pillage or destruction of property had taken place [wrote Kennard], and, to the great honour of the Federal arms be it fairly said, never before did cities like Petersburg and Richmond, entered by excited troops after years of siege, suffer to so trifling an extent. Tobacco was the only temptation that could not be resisted. There was not a whisper amongst the inhabitants conversed with, other than that they had been treated in the most humane and proper manner. We can all certify to the fact that out of the thousands upon thousands of troops we have seen only one man has been detected the worse for drink. This is accounted for by the fact that spirits are forbidden both in the army and navy on service. One could not fail to remark the deep mourning worn by the ladies moving about the streets, or the careworn expression of their countenances. The "darkie" element, on the contrary, was decidedly jubilant.[1]

Lincoln stopped at Capitol Square on his way to General Weitzel's headquarters in the former Confederate White House and addressed a crowd of newly freed slaves: "My poor friends, you are free," he said, "free as the air. You can cast off the name of slave and trample upon it. . . . Liberty is your birthright." But later, at the close of his meeting with Weitzel, Lincoln urged the general to treat the defeated white population with tact: "If I were in your place," the president told him, "I'd let 'em up easy, let 'em up easy."[2]

Lincoln was impatient for peace, and he urged General Grant, in a telegram on April 6, to finish off Lee's army before it escaped to Georgia: "Nothing . . . is to delay, hinder, or interfere with your work."[3] Grant had heard from Sheridan that the Confederates had massed at Amelia Court House, forty miles west-northwest of Petersburg, and were desperately foraging for food in the surrounding countryside, as their supplies had failed to arrive. Grant realized immediately that his adversary had only one course of action: "It now became a life and death struggle with Lee to get south to his provisions."[4] More than a million and a half rations of bread and meat were waiting for the famished Confederates at Danville, a hundred miles away on the Virginia–North Carolina border. "The soldiers are in a dreadful state from hunger," Welly wrote in his diary on the sixth. Lee had heard that the road to Danville was blocked, but there were 80,000 rations at Farmville, only eighteen miles from his present position; this had to be the next destination, or else his men would either collapse from starvation or desert.

Francis Lawley had changed his mind about fleeing immediately to New York, returning instead to observe the final scene of the drama that had absorbed his life since he became the *Times'* special correspondent. "All day long upon the 6th, hundreds of men dropped from exhaustion,"

Richmond, Virginia, after capture by the Federals, by Thomas Kennard.

he wrote, "and thousands let fall their muskets from inability to carry them any further."[5] Lee pleaded with his son Rooney, who was commanding a division of the cavalry corps, to keep up its spirits, exhorting him, "don't let it think of surrender. I will get you out of this."[6] But Sheridan pounced on the Confederate army as it retreated across Sayler's Creek. Two divisions, amounting to almost a quarter of Lee's forces, were cut off from their comrades; here, beside a naked line of trees, occurred the final battle between the Army of the Potomac and the Army of Northern Virginia.

> Shells screaming, passed us, some bursting a few feet off us, volley of bullets coming in every direction [wrote Welly]. Every now and then, I heard bullets go with a *thud* into some unfortunate soldier, who would give a scream and all was over. I had a very narrow escape by a Parrot [*sic*] shell passing within 2 inches of my head and bursting within a foot of me, by coming in contact with a tree, a piece of it killing a man about a hundred yards off. It certainly was very exciting. People may talk about hunting, but a good battle is a 100 times more exciting.[7]

The surrounded Confederates tried to fight their way through, many resorting to fists and teeth if they had no weapons.* But after five hours the two divisions surrendered, making prisoners of nine Confederate generals (including Custis, Lee's eldest son) and almost eight thousand soldiers. The gray countryside turned black with the smoke rising from burning wagons. Lawley looked about him and saw "exhausted men, worn-out mules and horses, lying down side by side—gaunt famine glaring hopelessly from sunken lack-lustre eyes—dead mules, dead horses, dead men everywhere—death, many times welcomed as God's blessing in disguise."[9]

Lee dragged the remains of his army across the Appomattox River and reached Farmville on April 7. The precious rations were waiting for him, but also the news that the way ahead to Appomattox Station, twenty-five miles west of Farmville—where the rest of his supplies had

---

* A former British Army officer in the Confederate army, Henry O'Brien, lay among the wounded, left for dead by his comrades. He had not expected the war to come to this: "I came to this country last winter," he explained a few weeks later from prison, his life having been saved by a Federal surgeon. "[I ran] the blockade at Wilmington, NC through a love of adventure and a desire of seeing something of active service on this continent."[8]

been sent—was blocked by Sheridan. Straggling had diminished Lee's army to fewer than 13,000 men, yet when he received a note from Grant on the evening of the seventh asking for surrender to avoid "any further effusion of blood," he tried to use the correspondence to buy time while his officers looked for an escape route to Danville. That night, General Fitz Lee sent Welly to deliver a note to his uncle, Robert E. Lee, who was, wrote the British officer, "quite calm, although the Army is in such a state."[10] The next day was even worse for the Confederates. "No food, and marching all day. It is a fearful sight to see the state of our Army, hundreds upon hundreds lying in the road, not able to move from hunger and fatigue," wrote Welly. "The enemy surround us on all sides." Lee's army was so depleted that one brigade had only eight men.[11]

During the night of April 8, Lee's senior commanders, Longstreet, Gordon, and Fitz Lee, gathered in a copse near Appomattox Court House to discuss the possible courses left open to them. Fitz Lee did not wish to be a part of any surrender, and informed his uncle that he would take the remainder of his corps and flee southward. But the others were prepared to surrender with Lee if their final attempt to escape failed. Though there were only 10,000 soldiers present for duty against a pursuing force of 116,000, the generals agreed there should be one last attempt to break through Grant's encirclement: "At 6 A.M., our line of battle is formed," wrote Welly. "The whole line move forward under heavy shelling from the enemy, our men seem mad with rage, they charge the enemy who are ten times their number, and drive them before them, killing all that come in their way, taking no prisoners, but for all that it is no good, the enemy's reserve come up and our men have to retreat, but they do it only inch by inch."[12]

At 8:30 A.M. Lee was informed that Gordon's attack had failed and the troops were falling back toward Longstreet's position, which was itself under fire from Federal forces. "Then," said Lee, "there is nothing left for me to do but to go to General Grant, and I would rather die a thousand deaths."[13] He had prepared for this moment, having dressed before the battle in his best uniform, with red sash, ceremonial sword, and gold scabbard (the last given to him by a group of English female admirers).[14] Welly was still exchanging fire with Federal soldiers when Fitz Lee received Lee's dispatch that he was surrendering the army that day.

When the Union and Confederate generals gathered at 1:00 P.M. in the parlor of Wilmer McLean's brick house a short distance from Appomattox Court House, Grant was struck by the extreme contrast between Lee's immaculate clothes and his own "rough travelling suit" (which was only a private's uniform adorned with the stars and epaulets of a lieutenant general). Lee had just two officers with him; Grant was accompanied by Generals Sheridan, Ord, and Porter and most of his staff, but the witnesses stood back respectfully as the two men chatted for a while, as though the occasion was no more than two veterans meeting for the first time since the Mexican-American War. "What General Lee's feelings were I do not know. As he was a man of so much dignity, with an impassible face, it was impossible to say," wrote Grant in his memoirs, "but my own feelings, which had been quite jubilant on the receipt of his letter, were sad and depressed."[15] Finally Lee could take the suspense no longer and brought the subject around to the surrender.

At four in the afternoon, Lee and his aides stepped out onto the sunlit porch of the McLean house, the document of surrender signed. Grant had offered generous terms: the Confederates were to lay down their weapons in perpetuity, but in return the officers could keep their horses and sidearms, and all could return to their homes unmolested. Grant had also offered to send rations to the famished Confederates. Lee mounted his horse, Traveller, and rode toward his own lines. "As the great Confederate captain rode back from his interview with General Grant," wrote Francis Lawley,

> the news of the surrender acquired shape and consistency, and could no longer be denied. The effect on the worn and battered troops—some of whom had fought since April 1861 . . . passes mortal description. Whole lines of battle rushed up to their beloved old chief, and, choking with emotion, broke ranks and struggled with each other to wring him once more by the hand. Men who had fought throughout the war, and knew what the agony and humiliation of the moment must be to him, strove with a refinement of unselfishness and tenderness which he alone could fully appreciate, to lighten his burden and mitigate his pain. With tears pouring down both cheeks, General Lee at length commanded voice enough to say: "Men, we have fought through the war together. I have done the best that I could for you."[16]

Lawley did not stay to watch the defeated Confederates stack arms and surrender their regimental flags on April 12. He was in New York, finishing his report on Richmond's evacuation, when the ceremony took place. His refusal to witness the final moments of the Army of Northern Virginia meant that he deprived himself of an experience that would surely have helped to heal rather than increase his sorrows. There was none of the crowing or ritual humiliation that he had feared; indeed, as the first line of Confederates stepped forward to deliver their weapons— members of Stonewall Jackson's old brigade—the Federal guard stood at attention and presented arms, inspiring the Confederates to do the same—"honor answering honor," in the words of the attending Union general Joshua Chamberlain.[17]

Word of Lee's surrender spread quickly throughout the South. "We were brought into the 4 mile camp at Vicksburg and I was lying there when news came of General Grant's great victory," wrote James Pendlebury of the 69th New York Irish Regiment. He had survived three months of relentless marching from one makeshift prison to another until his rescue by Federal troops. Sick and weak as he was, Pendlebury dragged his emaciated frame to the Vicksburg courthouse and rang the bell, which was answered by a volley of cannon fire off the surrounding hills. But in Richmond, the one-hundred-gun salute was ignored by the long shuffling lines of residents queuing at U.S. Sanitary Commission depots for their rations. Francis Dawson had regained consciousness, although he was incapacitated by the bullet wound to his shoulder. "What would you think of me were I to return to England, poorer than when I left her shores?" he wrote to his mother. He felt not just the defeat of the Confederacy but a sense of personal failure: "My life has been a useless one, productive only of grief to others whom I love the best and remorse to myself." He had always promised his mother that his absence from London would not leave her in want; however, his "worldly possessions" now consisted of "a postage stamp and what was left of a five dollar greenback that a friend in Baltimore had sent me."[18]

Farther south, at Danville, Jefferson Davis, his cabinet, and an escort of sixty midshipmen from the Confederate naval academy boarded their trains again, this time for Greensboro, North Carolina, where the armies of Beauregard and Johnston were said to remain intact. "People in the army wonder at my good spirits," Feilden wrote to Julia from his makeshift camp at Hillsborough, North Carolina, "for all that I cannot shut my eyes to our condition, though perhaps after all it is more philosophic to try and not think, but to float down with the current."[19] But, like Dawson, Feilden was prepared for a prolonged resistance to Federal rule. "To tell the truth," he wrote, "I would sooner be killed in this war than leave the country in its present distress of my own accord." Davis shared his sentiments, and when he reached Greensboro, the Confederate president became indignant with Beauregard and Johnston for telling him there was no alternative to asking Sherman for his terms of surrender. Davis insisted that the war was by no means over, not when there remained two undefeated Confederate armies—Johnston's in North Carolina and General Edmund Kirby-Smith's west of the Mississippi.[20] Driven by Davis's determination to fight on—and a fear that they would all be hanged for treason if caught by the Federals—the remaining members of the Confederate cabinet began making preparations to leave Greensboro on April 14. They were being hunted by Federal forces, but one determined seeker had already found them, though he was a friend: Frank Vizetelly, who had been trying to catch up with Davis since the fall of Richmond, was the only journalist to reach him.

———

Abraham Lincoln had been in Washington for five days on April 14 when he convened the cabinet to discuss the terms for readmitting the Southern states to the Union. The only member not at the meeting was William Seward, who was bedridden after suffering a carriage accident on April 5 that had left him with a dislocated shoulder and a broken jaw. His wife and daughter, Frances and Fanny, were nursing him. "His face is so marred and swollen and discolored that one can hardly persuade themselves of his identity," Frances wrote to her sister, nor was he able to communicate except by grunting.[21] Bereft of his closest ally, Lincoln found it much more difficult to persuade the cabinet of the wisdom of showing clemency toward the South. He even advised the war secretary, Edwin Stanton, to allow the Confederate plotters in Canada to escape to Europe. Stanton wanted Jacob Thompson arrested and tried in the United States. "Best to let him run," countered Lincoln.[22]

The president felt there was something momentous about this day—Good Friday. He was not sure what to expect, he told the cabinet, perhaps news of Johnston's surrender or the capture of Jefferson Davis, but the night before he had dreamed his recurring dream—the one that always seemed to precede good news—in which he was sailing "with great rapidity towards an indefinite shore."[23] When he joined Mary Lincoln for a carriage ride a couple of hours later, Lincoln was even more emphatic about his feelings: "I consider *this day,* the war has come to a close," he told her. "We must *both* be more cheerful in the future— between the war and the loss of our darling Willie—we have both, been very miserable."[24]

That evening the Lincolns went to Ford's Theatre to watch Laura Keane in her one-thousandth performance of Tom Taylor's *Our American Cousin.*[*] All of Washington knew that Lincoln was going to be there, and many people had bought tickets just so they could catch a glimpse of him. The information helped John Wilkes Booth to make up his mind; his previous attempts to kidnap the president had all been thwarted by faulty intelligence or human failure. Months of frustration had exacerbated his already volatile nature, and tonight he was determined "to live in history."[25] He expected three deaths to occur simultaneously: Lincoln's by his hand, Vice President Andrew Johnson's by the hand of George Atzerodt, and Seward's by the hand of Lewis Powell; and he had prepared a statement in advance for the *National Intelligencer* justifying the murders. The three men started out together, but George Atzerodt could not bring himself to perform the task and retreated to a hotel bar. At 10:00 P.M. Powell called at Seward's house, claiming to have brought medicine from the doctor. A servant took him to the third floor, where Fanny and a male nurse were tending to Seward. But Frederick, Seward's younger son, became suspicious and refused to let Powell enter the patient's room. Throwing off his pretense, Powell attempted to shoot Frederick, and when the gun failed to go off, he used it to beat him unconscious. Easily dispensing with the nurse who opened the door to investigate the noise, Powell ignored Fanny and went straight for Seward, who struggled to defend himself as Powell hacked at his head and neck with his bowie knife. Fanny's screams alerted Seward's older son, Augustus, who rushed into the room and

---

[*] Her first performance, on October 15, 1858, had coincided with Lincoln's final U.S. Senate campaign debate against Stephen A. Douglas. Although Douglas went on to represent Illinois in the Senate, Lincoln's extraordinary eloquence and clarity regarding the future of slavery had catapulted him to national prominence.

tried to grab the knife. Powell slashed at him wildly; breaking free of Augustus's grip, he hurled himself down the stairs and out of the house, stabbing a State Department messenger who happened to call at the wrong time.

A few minutes later, just after the curtain had risen for the third act of *Our American Cousin,* Booth talked his way into the presidential box and fired a single shot into the back of Lincoln's head. Before anyone could stop him, Booth leaped over the balustrade and onto the stage, the petrified actors watching helplessly as he hobbled out the back. Lincoln was carried to a house across the street where he lingered, unconscious, for nine hours, his decline observed by the cabinet and several doctors. Mary Lincoln became so hysterical that she was removed from the room several times, and she was absent when Lincoln took his final breath at twenty-two minutes past seven in the morning.

Seward lived, though his throat had been slashed several times and his right cheek nearly sliced off as he tried to fight his attacker. Frederick was in a coma, his skull broken in two places, and Augustus had suffered two stab wounds to the head and one to his hand. The secretary of state drifted in and out of consciousness for several days, unaware that Lincoln was dead or that Andrew Johnson had been sworn in as the seventeenth president of the United States. Although propped up on pillows so he could watch Lincoln's funeral procession on April 19, Seward admitted later that the black funeral plumes passing beneath his window had caught his eye but failed to register with him as anything significant or untoward.[26]

On April 21, Lincoln's funeral train pulled away from Washington station at 7:00 A.M. and began its seventeen-hundred-mile journey to Springfield, Illinois.* That day, in Virginia, the raider John Singleton Mosby disbanded his Partisan Rangers, although Mosby himself refused to give his parole. His two British volunteers confounded the Federals by asking for safe passage to Canada. The following day, General Fitz Lee wrote his final dispatch to Robert E. Lee, commending each of his staff officers "and Captain Llewellyn Saunderson, who,

---

* Consul Archibald broke Foreign Office protocol for the first time in his life to attend a memorial service organized by the British community in New York. He defended his action to Sir Frederick Bruce, arguing that to stay away would have offended not only his own sensibilities but also the entire city's.

having just arrived from his native country, Ireland, joined me previously to the fall of Petersburg, and remained with me to the last."*[27] Lincoln's train had reached Albany, the state capital of New York, when Joe Johnston surrendered his army to Sherman on April 26. The one important difference to the terms that Grant had offered Lee was Sherman's agreement to provide transport for the Southern troops from distant states. Henry Feilden had only a hundred miles to travel in order to reach Julia in Greenville, South Carolina, so he set off on his own horse.

> I have not heard anything about you for so long that I have been quite miserable. You are aware I suppose that the war has ended in this part of the country, and that we have given in on this side of the Mississippi. Considering the position we were in, General Johnston made excellent terms with Sherman for the army—that is to say—that we are not to be molested by the Yankee Government, and our personal property is respected. No one else in the country has any guarantee for either life or property, except from the magnanimity of our enemies, which does not amount to much. The feeling of indignation in the North against our late leaders is described by the Yankee officers as intense. General Schofield (a very old friend of General Hardee's) who now commands North Carolina advised him to leave the country at once. My own opinion is that our prominent men will be treated with great severity, if not executed. . . . The death of Lincoln was looked upon by our army as a great misfortune for the South. If he were alive we should have had no difficulty in getting terms.[28]

The flight of John Wilkes Booth, the man behind the South's "great misfortune," also came to an end on April 26. (Lewis Powell, the attempted murderer of Seward, had been caught ten days earlier.) Booth and another accomplice were found in a barn a few miles south of Port

---

*A paroled Confederate general, Cadmus Wilcox, who bumped into Thomas Conolly in New York on April 22, wrote: "[I] met Conley [sic] the first night. He gave an amusing account of his leaving Richmond in the night and his difficulties in reaching the Baltimore-Ohio railroad. He urged me to go to Ireland with him and, supposing I wanted money, offered me his purse freely."

Royal, Virginia, by a detachment of twenty-six Federal soldiers. When Booth refused to surrender, they set fire to the barn in the hope of flushing him out, but one of the soldiers, Boston Corbett, shot him in the neck while he remained inside. Corbett's desire for glory deprived the mourning nation of the chance to obtain justice for its slain president.

Lincoln's funeral train finally reached its destination at Springfield, Illinois, on May 3, 1865. After a twelve-day journey through more than 440 cities and towns, the bodies of Lincoln and his son Willie, who had died in 1862, would now be laid to rest in Oak Ridge Cemetery.

———

England was already "staggering," according to Benjamin Moran, over the news of Lee's surrender when the telegram announcing the assassination of President Lincoln arrived on April 26. John Bright felt "stunned and ill" when he heard the news. He was in mourning for his best friend, Richard Cobden, who had died on April 2, three weeks too soon to celebrate "this great triumph of the Republic," and his brother-in-law Samuel Lucas, the owner and editor of the Morning Star, who had died on the sixteenth. "I feel at times as if I could suffer no more and grieve no more," wrote Bright in his diary. "The slave interest has not been able to destroy the nation, but it succeeded in killing the President."[29] "I was horror struck," recorded Moran, "and at once went up with Mr. Alward [the new assistant secretary] to announce the intelligence to Mr. Adams. He turned as pale as death." Within a few hours the legation was overrun with visitors. Adams had expected to see Bright and Forster, and possibly Lord Houghton (formerly Richard Monckton Milnes), but certainly not the Duke of Argyll or Lord Russell, who showed "as much sympathy as he was capable of."[30] Lord Lyons also made a special trip to London to pay his respects and obtain news about Seward.

The British press was united over the tragedy of Lincoln's violent death. Newspapers that had routinely criticized the president during his lifetime rushed to praise him. On April 28 and again on May 1, The Times printed long eulogies to the late president. "The feeling which the death of Mr. Lincoln has excited in England is in no degree confined to the advocates of the Northern cause, it has shown itself just as strongly among the friends of the South," the paper declared. "We feel confident that a sorrow in which both nations may without exaggeration be said to share cannot pass without leaving them better acquainted with each other, and more inclined to friendship . . . than they were before."* This was a wild hope, and the editors knew it; William Howard Russell could not help writing smugly in his diary: "Had *The Times* followed my advice how different our position would be—not only that of the leading journal but of England!"[31]

Despite being the primary instigator and cause of *The Times'* wildly biased reporting of the war, Francis Lawley escaped vilification because he was not a journalist by profession. The paper's New York correspondent, Charles Mackay, on the other hand, was castigated for betraying his trade. The *Spectator* accused him of doing "probably more than any other single man to diffuse error concerning the great issue involved, and to imperil the cause of human freedom."[32] *The Times'* managing editor, Mowbray Morris, belatedly realized the damage caused to the paper's reputation by its pro-Southern reporting and dismissed Mackay from his post in a scathing letter that laid the entire blame for *The Times'* position on his shoulders alone. *The Economist* also felt obliged to explain away its previous condemnations of Lincoln, claiming that over the past four years "Power and responsibility visibly widened [Lincoln's] mind and elevated his character."[33] But it was *Punch* that performed the greatest volte-face. Three weeks earlier, on April 8, the magazine had placed Lincoln in a gallery of April Fools that included Napoleon III and the MPs Roebuck, Bright, and Disraeli. The combination of embarrassment, shame, and shock that Lincoln was killed while watching his play moved Tom Taylor, the magazine's senior contributor, to browbeat his colleagues into giving him a free hand to compose an abject apology and homage to the late president. The editor, Mark Lemon, supported him, telling the staff, "The avowal that we have been a bit mistaken [over Lincoln and the war] is manly and just." Taylor did not hold back: "Between the mourners at his head and feet, Say, scurril-jester, is there room for you?" he asked contritely. Lincoln "had lived to shame me from my sneer, / To lame my pencil, and confute my pen, / To make me own this kind of prince's peer, / This rail-splitter a true-born king of men. / My shallow judgment I had learned to rue."[34]

---

* Leslie Stephen prepared a devastating critique of *The Times'* reporting on the war, which he published later that year under the title "The Times and the American Civil War." The thirty-three-page pamphlet carefully dissected each report and essay for its bias and misrepresentation of facts.

BRITANNIA SYMPATHISES WITH COLUMBIA.

Britannia sympathizes with Columbia, *Punch*, May 1865.

Moran's usual cynicism was temporarily overcome when he attended a mass meeting at St. James's Hall, Piccadilly, on April 30:

The room was draped in black and three United States flags were gracefully entwined in crape at the east end of the room. The floor, the balcony, the galleries, and the platform of the great hall were literally packed with ladies and gentlemen. . . . The warmth of the applause, the earnest detestation of the murder, and the condemnation of slavery made me inwardly vow that hereafter I would think better of the feelings entertained towards us by Englishmen than ever before. And that if ever any chance of quarrel should occur between the two Countries, and I should hear an uniformed countryman of mine denouncing honestly and mistakenly, the spirit of England towards us, the recollection of what I saw then would nerve me to declare that we had friends in England in our day of sorrow, whose noble sympathy should make us pause.[35]

He wrote even more fulsomely the following day after observing the speeches in the House of Commons and the House of Lords.

The U.S. consuls described extraordinary scenes at public meetings. A resident of Liverpool, arguably the most pro-Southern city in Britain, recorded with surprise that the news "has turned all sympathy towards the North. Immense meetings on the subject have been held almost everywhere in England and the Queen herself has addressed a letter of condolence to Mrs. Lincoln."[36] Adams began to think that Lincoln had done more for Anglo-American relations by his death than by any other act during his life.

The great change in attitudes toward the North did not mean that the Confederates in England were being cast aside by their friends, however. James Spence disbanded the pro-Southern associations, because, he explained to a former member, it would be wrong to continue public action on behalf of the South: "I feel, too, that Englishmen cannot now take further part in this direction with propriety." But his personal loyalty to Mason was undiminished, and he was among those who offered to establish a subscription fund on the Confederate agent's behalf. (The Southern commissioner was too proud to accept such charity.) "The British believe that resistance is hopeless," Mason wrote to Judah P. Benjamin on May 1, "and that the war is at an end—to be followed, on our part, by passive submission to our fate. I need not say that I entertain no such impression, and endeavor as far as I can to disabuse the public mind."[37] The South's other chief agents in England—James Bulloch, Henry Hotze, Colin McRae, and Matthew Maury—were far more realistic. Hotze trimmed his staff on the *Index* and began looking for financial backers, announcing that journal's new cause would be the protection of "white man's government" against the "Africanization" of America.[38] Maury sent a formal letter of surrender to the U.S. Navy, promising to desist from all acts of aggression against the United States. Bulloch and McRae girded themselves for prolonged litigation from creditors both real and predatory on account of the Confederacy's unpaid bills. (Some firms, such as the London Armoury Company, which had turned away business in order to fulfill its lucrative orders from the Confederacy, would quickly go bankrupt.) The certainty that an investigation into their books would absolve them of wrongdoing counted for little against the knowledge that their personal sacrifices for the South had been to no avail.

John Slidell wrote to Mason from Paris urging him to open his eyes to the South's defeat: "We have seen the beginning of the end. We are crushed and must submit to the yoke. Our children must bide their time for vengeance, but you and I will never revisit our homes under our glorious flag."[39]

Jefferson Davis finally accepted defeat on May 3. He had been constantly on the move since leaving Greensboro on April 14, and he had reached Washington, in northeast Georgia. Right up until the day before, Davis had insisted to the cluster of cabinet members and generals surrounding him that resistance was not just possible but also a duty. He had carried on the normal functions of government, issuing orders and signing papers—albeit by the roadside instead of at his desk—as if it would only be a matter of time before the Confederacy was made whole again. Frank Vizetelly was present to sketch him doing so. "This was probably the last official business transacted by the Confederate Cabinet and may well be termed 'Government by the roadside,' " the war artist wrote next to his drawing.

"Three thousand brave men are enough for a nucleus around which the whole people will rally when the panic which now afflicts them has

Jefferson Davis signing acts of government by the roadside, by Frank Vizetelly.

passed away," Davis had told a member of his cavalry escort. The officer was speechless for a brief moment before replying that the three thousand troops guarding the Confederate president would risk their lives to save his, "but would not fire another shot in an effort to continue hostilities. . . . Then Mr. Davis rose and ejaculated bitterly that all was indeed lost. He had become very pallid, and he walked so feebly as he proceeded to leave the room that General Breckinridge [the new Confederate secretary of war] stepped hastily up and offered his arm."[40] Even then, Davis did not relinquish all hope. A few hours later he was approached by Lieutenant James Morgan of CSS *Georgia,* who had come in search of him after Varina Davis had relieved him of his escort duty.

> I begged him to allow me to accompany him, but he told me that it would be impossible, as I had no horse. He spoke to me in the most fatherly way, saying that as soon as things quieted down somewhat I must make my way to the trans-Mississippi, where we still had an army and two or three small gun-boats on the Red River, and in the mean time he would give me a letter to General Fry, commanding at Augusta, asking him to attach me temporarily to his staff.[41]

The Confederate cabinet began to break up as soon as the fugitives crossed into Georgia on the third. They were worn down by fatigue and fear. "I am as one walking in a dream, and expecting to wake," wrote General Josiah Gorgas.[42] Vizetelly drew one last picture of the complete party as it rode through the woods, and then Gorgas, Benjamin, and Mallory all set out on their own. A novice rider, Benjamin was physically incapable of keeping up with Davis and had struggled for the past few days. He assumed the disguise of a French businessman, bought a horse and buggy, and went off in the direction of Florida, where he hoped to take passage on a boat to the Caribbean.

"I saw an organized government . . . fall to pieces little by little," wrote Captain Micajah Clark, Davis's former private clerk, who had been placed in charge of the Confederacy's traveling treasury three days earlier. Vizetelly's final sketch showed Davis in Washington, Georgia, on May 4, shaking hands with the officers of his guard. "It was here that President Davis determined to continue his flight almost alone," wrote Vizetelly. "With tears in his eyes he begged them to seek their own safety

Flight of Jefferson Davis and his cabinet over the Georgia Ridge, five days before his capture, by Frank Vizetelly.

and leave him to meet his fate." The journalist thought that Davis had been "ill-advised" to travel with so large a retinue when there was a $100,000 bounty on his head.

With the postmaster general, John H. Reagan, his three aides, and a small cavalry detachment, Davis headed southward, expecting to catch up with Varina and the children in a day or two. He hoped that the wagons carrying the last of his government's funds—$288,022.90 in gold and silver coins—would reach a port and from there be transported to England, where it could be used to fund Southern resistance against Washington.* Davis, now realizing the extreme folly of attracting attention, made up a new identity as a Texas politician on his way home. Vizetelly's continued presence only endangered the party, and the journalist accepted that it was time for him to leave. Just before he rode away, sometime on or shortly after May 5, Vizetelly pressed a £50 note into Davis's hand, which would be enough to pay for the entire family to sail to England, third class.[43]

The next time Vizetelly had a report of the president's progress was

---

* The bulk of the money disappeared and has never been found.

from the news wires, announcing Davis's capture on May 10. The Federal commander at Hilton Head, South Carolina, signaled:

> Jeff Davis, wife, and three children; C C Clay and wife, Reagan, General Wheeler, several colonels and captains, Stephens (late Vice-President) are now at Hilton Head, having been brought here from Savannah this afternoon. They were captured by 130 men, 5th Michigan Cavalry, 120 miles south of Macon, Ga, near Irwinville. They had no escort, and made no resistance. Jeff. looks much worn and troubled; so does Stephens.[44]

The new British minister, Sir Frederick Bruce, informed London of the development. "There is no doubt that the Confederacy as a political body is at an end," he wrote to Lord Russell. He strongly advised that Britain refuse port entry to the two Confederate cruisers still at large unless she desired to irritate the U.S. government. "The moment is a critical one," Bruce warned on May 16.[45] CSS *Stonewall* had tried to obtain

Jefferson Davis bidding farewell to his escort two days before his capture, by Frank Vizetelly.

coal at Nassau and been sent on her way. The ship managed to make it to Havana, where its presence embarrassed the authorities for a few days until definitive news arrived of the Confederacy's collapse.*

Bruce had been in Washington since April 8, although he had not yet been presented to Lincoln when the president was assassinated on April 14. Since then, Bruce had waited anxiously to learn what the new administration's attitude would be toward Britain. A large banner had been draped across the State Department building proclaiming PEACE AND GOOD WILL TO ALL NATIONS, BUT NO ENTANGLING ALLIANCES AND NO FOREIGN INTERVENTIONS, which did not inspire him with confidence.[47] He was relieved when President Johnson went out of his way to reassure him of his cordial feelings toward Britain.[48] "I have not been accustomed to etiquette," Johnson admitted when Bruce was presented to him, "but I shall be at all times happy to see you and prepared to approach questions in a just and friendly spirit."† Charles Sumner had offered to be an intermediary between the British legation and the president, but Bruce was loath to call upon him despite his admiration for the senator's historic battle against slavery. There was something about Sumner's insistence that no one else in Washington was capable of discussing foreign affairs that made Bruce doubt his motives. "It struck me," wrote Bruce, "that the drift of his conversation was to lead me to the conclusion that I should enter into confidential communication with himself. This I am reluctant to do, as long as there is hope of Mr. Seward being able shortly to resume his duties." He disliked "the want of frankness in him" and

---

* The Scotsman William Watson was in Havana trying to salvage some of his profits from his blockade runner the *Rob Roy* when the *Stonewall* sputtered into the harbor. "As for the large fleet of blockade-running steamers thrown idle at Havana, it would be difficult to say what became of them all," wrote Watson. He was disappointed to discover that exorbitant taxes and charges had reduced his share to a sum comparable to the average yearly wage of a ship's master.[46]

† In contrast to "plain and quiet Lord Lyons," Bruce was "white-haired, white-whiskered, round-cheeked, with rich dark eyes, hearty, [and] convivial," wrote Oliver Wendell Holmes, the future Supreme Court justice. Bruce was a clever choice as minister; his successful partnership with Anson Burlingame, the U.S. minister in China, had already made him popular with the administration. Moreover, Bruce liked Americans, having served on a previous diplomatic mission to Washington in 1842; he felt comfortable among them, preferring the raw energy of the New World to the stuffy hauteur of the Old. Holmes was amazed to discover that Bruce was "pretty freely outspoken for our side as if he were one of us."[49]

suspected that Sumner was trying to discover his weaknesses in order to exploit them later.[50]

Bruce could see that the overwhelming desire in the country was for peace, and he no longer feared for the safety of Canada, although there were still serious frictions between Britain and America that remained unresolved. "The feeling against blockade runners, and foreigners who have served in a civil or military character in the South, is so strong as to make a fair trial almost hopeless," he wrote to Russell. "These cases require great delicacy in handling—for to insinuate unfairness on the part of the officers composing their Military Commissions, would render the execution of a sentence only more certain." Reflecting on Colonel Grenfell, who had been the only defendant in the Chicago conspiracy trial to receive the death sentence, Bruce thought that people were "against leniency where a foreigner is concerned and the Government will not openly thwart the popular sentiment in that respect."[51] Bennet Burley's trial would take place soon, and Bruce expected a similar outcome.

Bruce felt pity for the defeated South, but his overriding fears were for the colored population of the United States, whose future seemed so uncertain. "The antagonism [against] the Negro breaks out constantly," he wrote to Lord Russell. In Manhattan, a delegation of black New Yorkers was denied the right to walk behind Lincoln's funeral cortege. When the White House intervened, a police escort had to protect the black marchers from the violence of the mob. "At Philadelphia," continued Bruce, "though the Abolition element is strong, the pretension of the coloured people to ride in the railway cars [is] strenuously resisted, and threaten[s] to end in serious riots." He had also heard that Tennessee had barred the testimony of black witnesses except in trials involving black defendants.[52]

Many Southerners assumed that Northern fury would result in the execution of all the leading Confederates. Henry Feilden had heard that President Johnson was "burning with hatred against the South" (which was untrue, though Johnson did exclude owners of plantations worth more than $20,000 before the war from pardon), yet his own experiences showed him there was hope of eventual reconciliation between the two sides. He encountered mostly kindness from Federal troops as he slowly made his way to Charleston. Two Northern officers "acted as well as they could and were as kind and accommodating as possible," he told Julia. "For instance they insisted on paying all the expenses. We helped them to drink three bottles of whiskey en route. At Branchville they got the US officer to put our horses on the car and saved us 65 miles ride. By the way," he added, "the 102nd US Colored troops gave us lunch there."[53]

President Andrew Johnson proclaimed a general amnesty on May 29, 1865, three days after the surrender of the last Southern army in the field, General Edmond Kirby-Smith's Army of the Trans-Mississippi. The war was officially at an end, but for many people it was not over. During the past four years, Dr. Elizabeth Blackwell had rarely been absent from her work, training nurses at the New York Infirmary for Women; she tried to explain her state of mind to Barbara Bodichon, her friend in England:

> You cannot hardly understand and I cannot explain how our private lives have all become interwoven with the life of the nation's. No one who has not lived through it can understand the bond between those who have. . . . Neither is it possible without this intense and prolonged experience to estimate the keen personal suffering that has entered into every household and saddened every life. . . . The great secret of our dead leader's popularity was the wonderful instinct with which he felt and acted . . . he did not lead, he expressed the American heartbreak . . . it has been to me a revelation to feel such influence and to see *such* leadership. I never was thoroughly republican before . . . but I am so, thoroughly, now.[54]

Epilogue

Going home, staying on—A transatlantic cable—The Alabama *claims—*
Sumner's demands—Impasse—Last chance at Geneva—Conclusion

On May 23, 1865, more than 150,000 soldiers began marching down Pennsylvania Avenue to the White House in a grand review of the Union armies. The parade lasted for two days, and even then the spectators lining the route saw but a fraction of the victorious Northern forces. General Ulysses S. Grant—who would succeed Andrew Johnson as president in 1868—was now the commander in chief of the largest army in the world, with 1,034,064 soldiers at his disposal.[1]

Yet a mere eighteen months later, Grant's forces would consist of just 54,302 men in the regular U.S. Army, and 11,000 (most of whom were U.S. Colored troops) in the volunteer army.[2] The navy was also shrinking, selling its warships as quickly as the market allowed, until by 1870 only 52 of the original 641 vessels remained.[3] The rapid pace of demobilization reflected the country's desperate yearning for peace. In the aftermath of the war, a different kind of volunteer stepped forward, one motivated by a sense of debt to the nation's fallen, whose mission was not to kill but to collect statistics, identify remains, and reinter in military cemeteries thousands of rotting and neglected corpses.[4] The renowned Civil War nurse Clara Barton founded the Office of Correspondence to help families in their search for soldiers who were missing and presumed dead.[5] A total of 360,222 Federal soldiers were known to have died during the four years of the war, and another 271,175 had been injured or maimed. To Colonel L.D.H. Currie, the British commander of the 133rd New York Metropolitan Guard, this terrible human toll meant the loss of all but one of the regiment's founding officers. To the former British prisoner Private James Pendlebury of the 69th New York Irish Regiment, it meant returning to his regiment after ten months in captivity to find that he recognized less than half the faces.

The demobilized forces benefited from a steady economy and abundant land. The continuous influx of immigrants during the war—more than 800,000 by most accounts—had not crowded out the labor pool, and many of the British volunteers, including Colonel Currie, saw America as offering greater opportunities than the old country.[6] The errant father Private James Horrocks would not have returned to England even if he could have. He stayed in the U.S. Army until November 1865, by which time he had earned both the officer's commission he coveted and a considerable sum of money. "I have paid all my debts," he wrote to his family on the twenty-seventh, "bought . . . an excellent suit of citizen's clothes and everything I stood in need of and have still above $400 left." Horrocks joined the million-plus veterans who sought to make new lives for themselves after their wartime experiences. But his hopes of making a fortune were never quite realized: he married a woman from California, settled in St. Louis, Missouri, and passed into middle age as an accountant in a credit agency. Despite having no legitimate children of his own, Horrocks refused to acknowledge the illegitimate son in England whose birth had driven him from his home and into the ranks of the Federal army.[7]

Other British volunteers became true Anglo-Americans in the manner of Dr. Elizabeth Blackwell, who moved easily between the two countries until she fell out with her sister Emily over the management of the New York infirmary and went to live permanently in England in 1869. The most colorful example of this new breed was Henry Morton Stanley, the serial deserter. He jumped ship from USS *Minnesota* in February 1865 and spent the next two years pursuing various ventures in America, including gold prospecting in Colorado, while simultaneously trying to launch a career in journalism. His ability to spin a tale eventually brought him to the notice of James Gordon Bennett, the editor of the *New York Herald,* who hired him as a foreign correspondent. In 1871, Stanley set off on his famous expedition through present-day Tanzania to find the missing missionary Dr. David Livingstone, father of Robert, the British volunteer who had died in a Confederate prison camp shortly before the war's end. After spending almost two decades in Africa, Stanley returned to England in 1890, where he subsequently became an MP and was knighted in 1897.

The Britons who chose to go home took with them not just memories (and in some cases wounds) but also new attitudes based on American ideals. James Pendlebury received $875 from the army, which he spent in just two weeks and had to work his passage across the Atlantic. But his experiences had changed him for the better. "What did I learn from all this?" he asked in his memoirs. "I have learned that I never need want for bread as long as I have health and strength. . . . Nothing that is honest demeans a man and if he does not like his work; well, let him mend himself as soon as he can. This is what I learned in America. . . . Today, through going to America I am an independent gentleman." Pendlebury became a successful businessman and tried hard to stay off drink. In 1877 he took his family to the Isle of Man, where, according to his obituary, he purchased a mansion and became "a prominent figure at many public meetings . . . [unafraid] to express his opinions in the most vigorous language."[8]

The America that Pendlebury was describing did not extend to the South. Eighty-eight percent of America's wealth now resided in the North; in the Cotton States there was neither the industrial base nor the manpower to fuel economic growth. One in four white Southern males between the ages of seventeen and forty-five—some 258,000—had been killed in the war, and at least 260,000 had suffered debilitating injuries.[9] Nine thousand miles of railroad track had been destroyed, three-quarters of the South's merchant shipping was gone, and almost all the banks had been emptied of specie. Without slavery, the entire commercial infrastructure of the South collapsed. For the first year after the war, bartering was commonplace in many villages and communities. The labor-intensive cotton plantations were worth only a third of their prewar value, and even the parts of the South that had been untouched by actual fighting were soon brought to poverty and ruin. Frances Butler, Fanny Kemble's youngest daughter, had never shared her mother's pro-Northern sympathies, and in 1865 she returned with her father to the family's rice plantation in Georgia. For the first couple of years she lived in utter squalor:

So I cook, and my maid does the housework, and as it has rained hard for three days and the kitchen roof is half off, I cook in the dining-room or parlour. Fortunately, my provisions are so limited that I have not much to cook; for five days my food has consisted of hard pilot biscuits, grits cooked in different ways, oysters, and twice, as a great treat, ham and eggs. I brought a box of preserves from the North with me, but half of them upset, and the rest were spoilt. One window is entirely without a sash, so I have to keep the shutters closed all the time, and over the other I have pasted three pieces of paper where panes should be. . . . I think if it rains much more there will not be a dry spot left in the house.[10]

The exploitative aspects of Reconstruction—the punitive taxes, questionable expropriations, and legal chicanery that often ran unchecked—also hindered the South's recovery. Captain Henry Feilden, the English volunteer on General Beauregard's staff in Charleston, lost the title to his house, forcing him to live apart from his new wife, Julia. He went to Orangeburg, some seventy miles from Charleston, where he tried to set up a wagon hauling business, while Julia remained in Greenville with her aunt.[11] They endured the arrangement for a year before accepting defeat and moving to England. Feilden was reinstated in the British Army and served as paymaster in the 18th Royal Hussars. In later life, he combined his military service with a second career as a naturalist and eminent polar explorer. The marriage was a happy one, though childless, and a timely bequest in 1901 brought them a beautiful seventeenth-century house in the village of Burwash, Sussex. There, Rudyard Kipling and Feilden became neighbors and close friends. After Feilden's death in 1921, Kipling wrote, "He was the gentlest, gallantest English gentleman who ever walked."*[12]

Francis Dawson, General Fitz Lee's English ordnance officer, was also driven to manual labor. As soon as he had recovered from his shoulder wound he worked as a field hand on a plantation near Richmond.

---

* The poet Algernon Swinburne also became friends with Feilden. "I defy you not to like him if you knew him," Swinburne wrote to a friend in 1867. "[He is] one of the nicest fellows alive, and open as such men should be, to admiration of all fallen causes and exiled leaders. I am not saying they are equal in worth—heaven forbid—only I must say that failure is irresistibly attractive, admitting as I do the heroism of the North."

The job sustained him until businesses began to reopen and his education made him a desirable employee. In 1866 he joined the staff of the
Richmond *Examiner* for a short time before becoming the assistant editor of the *Charleston Mercury*. Unlike Feilden, however, Dawson not only
made the South his home, but he played a significant part in its revival as
the editor of the *Charleston News and Courier*. His second wife (the first
having died young) was the writer Sarah Morgan, an older sister of his
longtime friend Lieutenant James Morgan—who rounded out his own
picaresque career by becoming the U.S. consul general to Australia.
Dawson was playing an increasingly prominent role in Democratic politics when he was killed on March 12, 1889, during an argument with his
neighbor. Southern culture had always been more aggressive than
Northern, but the weakening of social and official authority after the
Civil War led to even greater levels of violence. Dawson's contribution to
the pacification of the South had been a long campaign against dueling,
an effort that a courtroom jury repaid by acquitting his murderer.

Neither of the two British participants in Jacob Thompson's guerrilla
war against the North—Colonel George St. Leger Grenfell or Bennet G.
Burley—ever returned to the South. Grenfell's death sentence was commuted to life imprisonment at Fort Jefferson in the Dry Tortugas Islands,
seventy miles west of the Florida Keys in the Gulf of Mexico. His other
cellmates were the four conspirators in Abraham Lincoln's assassination
who did not receive capital sentences. One, Dr. Samuel Mudd, who
treated the injured John Wilkes Booth during the actor's flight from justice, became good friends with Grenfell, and in 1867 he sent a description of Grenfell's treatment to his brother-in-law:

> Colonel St. Ledger Grenfel [*sic*] is kept in close confinement
> under guard. A few days ago, being sick, he applied to the doctor
> of the Post for medical attention, which he was refused, and he
> was ordered to work. Feeling himself unable to move about, he
> refused. He was then ordered to carry a ball until further orders,
> which he likewise refused. He was then tied up for half a day, and
> still refusing, he was taken to one of the wharves, thrown over-
> board with a rope attached, and ducked; being able to keep him-
> self above water, a fifty pound weight was attached to his feet.
> Grenfel is an old man, about sixty. He has never refused to do
> work which he was able to perform, but they demanded more

than he felt able, and he wisely refused. They could not conquer him, and he is doing now that which he never objected doing.[13]

On March 6, 1868, Grenfell tried to escape from the Dry Tortugas along with three other prisoners. They were caught in a storm and the little boat disappeared. Afterward there was the occasional "sighting" of Grenfell, but there is little doubt that he drowned somewhere in the Gulf.

Bennet Burley had better luck. He had been incarcerated in Port Clinton, the capital of Ottawa County, Ohio, and was awaiting his second trial (the first having resulted in a hung jury) when, in September 1865, a well-wisher brought him an apple pie to celebrate the start of apple-picking season. Hidden beneath the crust was a sharpened iron file. Burley escaped to Detroit, where he was able to cross the river to Canada and to freedom. He became a journalist and in 1881 settled down to a long career as the foreign correspondent for the London *Daily Telegraph*. Burleigh (he changed the spelling) was joined at the *Telegraph* by George Augustus Sala (Belle Boyd's sometime protector) and Francis Lawley, who had returned to England shortly after Appomattox. Dropped by Sala, Belle took advantage of the general amnesty declared by President Johnson in 1866 to go back to the United States, where she earned a living as an actress until her marriage in 1869 to Lieutenant John Swainston Hammond, a former British volunteer in the Federal army.[14] Lawley's return to England had a less happy outcome: his creditors continued to pursue him, and the salary he earned from writing about the turf (a subject he knew well) was not enough to stave off bankruptcy. There were still outstanding debts against his estate when he died in 1901. His fellow pro-Southern journalist Frank Vizetelly continued as a war artist and reporter until he was killed in 1883 while covering the fighting in the Sudan between the Anglo-Egyptian army under William Hicks (known as Hicks Pasha) and the Mahdi rebels.

Canada was a popular hiding place for many Southern fugitives. Jefferson Davis resided there for a time after his release from prison in 1867. At first it had seemed likely that the former Confederate president would be tried and executed for masterminding Lincoln's assassination. But when no evidence could be produced against him, the grounds for prosecution became more complicated. The question was still unresolved when Davis was given bail on May 13, 1867. It was a further two years before the threat of legal action against him and thirty-seven other Confederate leaders, including Robert E. Lee, was dropped by the U.S. government. Davis lived on for another twenty years, beset by financial misfortune and family tragedies, but a defiant relic of the Confederate States to the last. Lee, in contrast, was a firm advocate of reconciliation with the North. He became president of Washington College in Lexington, Virginia (later Washington and Lee University), a post he held until his death in 1870.

The last Confederate war secretary, John Breckinridge, and the commissioners James Mason, Clement C. Clay, and Jacob Thompson also returned to the United States from Canada once they were confident of receiving amnesty. Despite his leading role in the Confederates' terror operations in Canada, Thompson was never prosecuted for his crimes. He chose Memphis, Tennessee, as his new home, his wealth mysteriously untouched despite the war—there was always speculation that some of his fortune came from the $1 million entrusted to him by the Confederacy in 1864.

Thompson was extremely fortunate, especially in light of the terror and destruction he had tried to inflict upon the North. His colleagues in Europe never dared return to the United States, since they were not included in any of the official pardons. Ambrose Dudley Mann, the commissioner in Brussels, and John Slidell, the commissioner in Paris, stayed in France; the Confederate financial agent Colin McRae emigrated to Belize, and the chief of Confederate operations abroad, James Bulloch, remained in Liverpool. His brother, Irvine, was one of the last Confederates to surrender when his ship CSS *Shenandoah* sailed into Liverpool on November 6, 1865.* Both Bullochs are buried at Toxteth Park Cemetery in Liverpool.

The former Confederate secretary of state Judah Benjamin also died abroad. He arrived in England in July 1865 after a harrowing escape from Florida and retrained as a barrister. He became an expert in commercial

---

* The *Shenandoah* had been at sea for a year when Captain Waddell finally brought her back to England, six months after the war's end. During that time the cruiser had captured thirty-eight ships, the majority of them Northern whalers, and taken more than a thousand prisoners. Waddell had believed that the South would continue to fight after Lee's surrender. It was the capture of President Davis—which he learned from the British bark *Barracouta* on August 2, 1865—that persuaded him to surrender, too.

law and in 1868 he published a treatise on that topic, popularly known as "Benjamin on Sales"; the book's immediate success assured his financial stability for the rest of his life. Striving to put the past behind him (and burdened by many secrets), Benjamin generally avoided the other Confederate exiles. He made no effort to see Henry Hotze despite their close relationship during the war. Hotze, for his part, had no interest in refashioning himself to suit the times; he remained an unapologetic supporter of slavery and the creed of white supremacy. But his hope of publishing a magazine dedicated to crushing the aspirations of freed blacks was soon quashed, and he became a propagandist for hire, working for any government or ruler who required his arts. He died in Zug, Switzerland, in 1887.[15]

Lord Lyons died a few months after Hotze, having served in the Foreign Office for forty-eight years—the last twenty of them as the British ambassador to France, the highest-ranking post in the diplomatic service. Once Lyons had recovered from the neuralgia that had forced him to leave Washington, he found that retirement was far worse than being overworked, and he eagerly accepted Lord Russell's offer in October 1865 of the embassy in Constantinople. Lyons himself was too modest to recognize his altered standing in the Foreign Office, but instead of the lonely midlevel diplomat who had incited derision at Washington, he was now a highly respected representative of Her Majesty's government whose dignified though conciliatory approach in delicate situations made him invaluable. After only a year in Constantinople, he was rewarded with the Paris embassy, and there he spent the remainder of his life, in great comfort and satisfaction, served faithfully by several of his former attachés from the Washington legation.

In his own way, Benjamin Moran also reached the summit of his capabilities—if not his ambitions—when in 1876, after twenty-three years at the U.S. legation in London, he was sent to run the legation in Lisbon in 1876, where he showed that he was not without talentz as a diplomat. That year, The New York Times described him as "one of the most capable and experienced diplomats in the service of the United States."[16] He ruled over his little kingdom for six years, gleefully bullying his staff, until his retirement in 1882, when he returned to England and passed the last four years of his life in Braintree, Essex. At his death, the humble printer's son from Chester, Pennsylvania, was praised by The Times as the "ablest and most honest" representative the United States had ever sent to Great Britain.[17]

On July 27, 1866, Cyrus Field stood on the deck of the *Great Eastern* watching through his binoculars as engineers hauled the transatlantic cable ashore at Heart's Content, Newfoundland. Finally, after five attempts in nine years, a cable sturdy enough to withstand the rigors of the Atlantic was laid along the 1,800-mile undersea shelf between Ireland and Canada. The cable's first message, sent through on the twenty-eighth, announced the signing of the armistice between Prussia and Austria. The Americans had been as surprised as the rest of Europe by the speed and efficiency with which Prussia had defeated Austria in the Seven Weeks' War. The Battle of Sadowa on July 3 had involved nearly half a million soldiers, the largest concentration of troops to date in either Europe or America. The Prussian military observers in the United States during the Civil War had been impressed by how rapidly armies and artillery could be transported by railroad, and during the past year the Prussian war minister had created a Field Railway Section modeled on the Union Construction Corps. The Prussians had also benefited from the close attention they had paid to Civil War developments in artillery and communications.[18]

The second message to reach Newfoundland was from Queen Victoria to President Andrew Johnson, congratulating him "on the successful completion of an undertaking which she hopes may serve as an additional bond of Union between the United States and England." At the moment it was just a hope: Austria's recent defeat had added another layer of complexity to a relationship that was already tense as a result of the unresolved issues left by the Civil War. Prussia's emergence as the dominant military nation among her neighbors was redrawing of the balance of power in Europe. France was now menaced by a credible threat, and the German Confederation no longer answered to Vienna but to Berlin. It was too soon to tell how these changes would affect Britain and America, but British politicians were worried that it would be the same old story of England facing two threats at once. "It is the unfriendly state of our relations with America that to a great extent paralyses our action in Europe," Russell's replacement as foreign secretary, Lord Clarendon, would shortly admit. "There is not the smallest doubt that if we were engaged in a Continental quarrel we should immediately find ourselves at war with the United States."[19]

During a Commons debate on March 13, 1865, Prime Minister Lord

Palmerston had tried to brush away the many crises of the past four years by putting them down to a family quarrel: "The North wished us to declare on their side and the South on theirs, and we wished to maintain a perfect neutrality." But this simplification of the arguments between the two countries carried no weight outside the Commons, and little even there. According to *The Times* and a majority of the British public, both sides had behaved badly. The United States had never supported Britain in any war, including the Crimean, and yet neither the North nor the South had seen the contradiction in demanding British aid once the situation was reversed. Both had unscrupulously stooped to threats and blackmail in their attempts to gain support, the South using cotton, the North using Canada. Both were guilty in their mistreatment of Negroes, both had shipped arms from England, and both had benefited from British volunteers. In America, the perception that Lord Russell had behaved like a villain and that the British ruling classes had schemed with the Confederacy to overthrow the Union in the hope of destroying democracy was so pervasive that the historian George Bancroft digressed upon it during his eulogy on Lincoln before Congress on February 12, 1866.[20] Like most Americans, he shared the belief that the declaration of neutrality had been nothing more than an underhanded attempt at recognizing the independence of the South; that the British government had connived with the Confederates to send out the commerce raiders; and that the blockade runners had been allowed to operate with impunity because they enabled the South to keep fighting long after its own supplies were exhausted.

Senator Charles Sumner played a discreditable part in promulgating the myth that Britain had acted maliciously and illegally by awarding belligerent status to the South. His friends in England, especially the Duke and Duchess of Argyll, felt betrayed by his attacks. "You know how heartily my Duke has been with you all through," the duchess objected on July 4, 1865. "I protest again against your supposing it a proof of Lord Russell's ill-will. . . . As to the haste, I suppose there would have been less of it, if the consequence attached to it by you had been foreseen."[21] Lord Russell was so incensed by Sumner's slurs on his motives and intentions toward the North that he rejected Charles Francis Adams's proposal in the summer of 1865 for an international arbitrator to consider American claims against Britain, complaining that his successes against the Confederates seemed to count for nothing, whereas his failures—

none of which he believed were his fault—counted for everything. Palmerston's death on October 18, which elevated Russell to the prime ministership once again, removed the only person who would have had weight and influence to show Russell that there could be another approach to the claims.

William Henry Seward never accused Britain of having collaborated with the South. But he steadfastly maintained that relations could not be cordial until reparations had been paid for the *Alabama*'s depredations and an apology given for Britain having bestowed belligerent status on the South. For most of 1865, the secretary of state was content to allow Charles Francis Adams a free rein in his dealings with Lord Russell—as long as these points were not conceded. Seward did not have the strength to mount the kind of blustering campaign that had marked his first year in office. Physically, he would never return to his old self. His right arm was useless and speaking was difficult; "few of his old friends could meet him without a shock," wrote his son. However, it was the family tragedy following Powell's attack that inflicted the greatest damage on Seward. His sons Fred and Augustus slowly recovered from their wounds, but Frances, Seward's wife, went into a rapid decline and died on June 21, less than three months after the assassination attempt. Their relationship, although complicated, had not been unloving, and her loss severed Seward from what he had always considered to be the better part of himself. Almost immediately after Frances's death, it became clear that his daughter Fanny's health had also been affected, and she began to succumb to the tuberculosis that would kill her the following year.

Seward's troubles increased in 1866 as he struggled to find his footing in President Johnson's administration.[22] Having been partly responsible for the Tennessee pro-war Democrat's appointment as Lincoln's vice president, Seward wrongly assumed that Johnson would follow his lead, or at least listen to his advice. Instead, Johnson stubbornly pursued his own line, which leaned decidedly toward maintaining the wretched status of the black population in the South. Johnson's attempts to obstruct Southern Reconstruction lost him the support of the Republicans. The relationship between the White House and Congress deteriorated so quickly that in March 1866, Johnson vetoed the new Civil Rights Bill, which, among other guarantees, awarded full U.S. citizenship to American blacks. Congress responded by overturning his veto. Seward tried to serve Johnson as faithfully as he had served Lincoln, but even the British minister, Sir Frederick Bruce, noticed the lack of rapport between them and wondered whether the president regarded Seward as more of an obstruction than a help.

Bruce had no doubt that Seward was determined to keep the peace between England and America, but what other plans the secretary of state was harboring remained a mystery to him. Charles Francis Adams, however, soon divined exactly what game Seward was playing: the protests over belligerency and the *Alabama* claims were leverage to force Britain to make territorial concessions to the United States. Seward had heard that there was support in British Columbia for annexation by America, and this had given him the idea that perhaps all of Canada and possibly even parts of the Caribbean might be obtained for the Union. There was "no prospect of coming to an agreement," he told Adams on May 2, 1866, even though the American minister had been saying for some time that "the line of difference between the two countries was becoming thinner and thinner . . . assuming any tolerable share of good will [there was] no reason why earnest efforts might not eliminate it altogether."[23]

Seward's machinations were upset by a series of raids between May 31 and June 7 across the U.S.-Canada border. This time the guerrillas were not a handful of Confederates but Fenians—Irish Americans committed to Irish independence—who intended to conquer or hold Canada hostage until Britain proclaimed Ireland a free state. The existence and aims of the fifty-thousand-strong Fenian Brotherhood (many of whom were U.S. Army veterans) had never been a secret. The previous autumn, its leaders had approached Seward and Johnson asking to know how the United States would react to the establishment of an Irish republic on Canadian soil, and they had received the ambiguous answer that the government would "acknowledge accomplished facts." The Fenians had read into this the notion that the United States would send troops north in support once the initial invasion had taken place. The United States did end up sending troops, but it was to arrest rather than to help the Fenians.

Seward knew that the government's suppression of the Fenian raids would not play well in Washington or across many parts of the country. But a steep rise in Anglophobia aided his plan to force Britain to give up Canada. On July 26, 1866, two days before the completion of the transatlantic cable, the House of Representatives voted unanimously to remove restrictions on the building or selling of warships to foreign nations. It was a deliberate warning to the British government to be prepared in any future conflict for hundreds of *Alabama*-style raiders, built in U.S. dock-yards and manned by U.S. crewmen.

Early in 1867, Seward's long-held desire to acquire Canada appeared to be on the verge of fulfillment after the Russians offered to sell "Russian America" (Alaska) to the United States. With remarkably little haggling, he brought down the asking price to $7.2 million and signed the treaty of sale with the Russian minister on March 30. "I know that Nature designs that this whole continent, not merely the thirty-six States, shall be, sooner or later, within the magic circle of the American Union," Seward declared to an audience in Massachusetts. But to his surprise, the public disagreed and he was harshly criticized in the press for wasting millions on a distant "icebox." Nor did the prospect of having a U.S. border to the north and south of them encourage the Canadians to seek their absorption within "the magic circle." On July 1, 1867, British North America became the Dominion of Canada, initially a confedera-tion of four provinces—Ontario, Quebec, New Brunswick, and Nova Scotia—under a single Canadian parliament.[24] It looked probable that the other provinces, including British Columbia, would soon seek to join Canada rather than the Union.

The existence of a united, largely self-governing Canada allowed the new British government led by the Tory prime minister Lord Derby (Lord Russell having lost the general election in 1866) to breathe a little easier. Derby's foreign secretary, Lord Stanley, futilely hoped that Seward would realize that his plan to extract territory in exchange for dropping the *Alabama* claims had been compromised and would finally agree to begin negotiations. Stanley, Charles Francis Adams had noted in his diary in the spring of 1867, had little reason to be defensive about Britain's actions during the war and was more willing than Russell to discuss the two countries' differences. But no British politician was pre-pared to "confess a wrong and sell Canada as the release from punish-ment," nor was the Derby government any more prepared than its predecessor to revisit the question of belligerent rights.[25] Seward's re-sponse was uncompromising: "I feel quite certain that the balance of faults has been on the side of Great Britain," he told Adams on May 2, 1867, in a dispatch for communication to Lord Stanley. "Thus the whole controversy between the two states must remain open indefinitely."[26]

The British hoped that Seward was bluffing or blustering, as so often in the past, but his recent dealings with France suggested that he was not. Louis-Napoleon had secretly asked Seward at the end of 1865 whether the United States would recognize the validity of Emperor Maximilian's rule in Mexico in exchange for a complete withdrawal of the French army. Seward had not only turned down the offer, but allowed General Grant to send thirty thousand U.S. troops under General Philip Sheridan to the Rio Grande, where they provided arms and training to the Juárez rebels. Prussia's victory over Austria in 1866 convinced Emperor Napoleon that Mexico was a distraction compared to the threat on his doorstep posed by German militarization. He informed Maximilian that the French army would remain in Mexico only until March 1867, when he would have to choose between maintaining his throne unaided and abdicating. Napoleon urged him not to be proud and to abdicate, but Maximilian would not hear of leaving and paid for his misplaced idealism with his life. His rule collapsed within weeks of the French leaving Mexico, and despite a heroic rescue attempt by Prince Felix Salm-Salm, a former Prussian volunteer in the Federal army and colonel of the 68th New York Infantry, Maximilian was captured and executed by the victorious Benito Juárez on June 19, 1867.*

Canada was not Mexico, and the Fenians in the United States were never thought to be as dangerous as the Juaristas. The British desire to resolve the *Alabama* claims controversy came more from a growing sense that bygones should be bygones. "Surely it is time to forget ancient differences," declared the Duke of Argyll at a public breakfast in honor of the American abolitionist William Lloyd Garrison on June 29, 1867, just

---

* As a veteran of the Federal army, Prince Salm-Salm was almost unique among the 2,500 Americans who immigrated to Mexico after the Civil War. The exodus of ex-Confederates was orchestrated by Matthew Fontaine Maury, who offered his services to Emperor Maximilian in June 1865 and was appointed imperial commissioner of immigration. Most settled near Cordoba in a specially designated area known as the Carlotta Colony, where they eked out a miserable existence for a couple of years before returning to the South. Another nine thousand Southerners moved to Brazil, where slavery remained legal, and about a thousand went to British Honduras, now Belize. The community at Forest Home in Punta Gorda died out, and its cemetery is now a tourist attraction.

ten days after Maximilian's death. "This country desires to maintain with the American people not merely relations of amity and peace; it desires to have their friendship and affection. . . . I think we ought to feel, every one of us, that in going to America we are going only to a second home."[27] The breakfast was a final gathering of the old guard of pro-Northern supporters and included not just MPs and journalists but also many veteran black abolition campaigners such as Sarah Parker Remond and the Reverend John Sella Martin. Lord Russell was initially not invited, an omission that hurt him deeply. Too embarrassed to explain that Garrison subscribed to the American view that Russell had supported the South during the war, the organizers "found" his invitation. Russell then took advantage of the occasion to offer a public apology for his failure to understand why Lincoln did not simply abolish slavery in 1861:

> Distance and want of knowledge of the circumstances of America made me fall into error in that respect. I was afterwards convinced by . . . Mr. Adams . . . that I had not rendered due justice to President Lincoln, who was the friend of freedom, and not only the friend, but ultimately the martyr of freedom. (Cheers.) I now, therefore, acknowledge that . . . I did not do justice to the efforts made by the United States, but I am now persuaded that President Lincoln did all that it was possible to do, and that we are bound to give our tribute of admiration to the excellent policy which the President and his Government pursued.[28]

Lord Russell's attempts to make amends impressed Charles Francis Adams and John Bright but not Seward, whose continued intransigence puzzled British friends of the North.[29] Shortly before Christmas, however, Seward fatally undermined Adams's confidence in his judgment by proposing that instead of Canada, Britain could relinquish the Bahamas in exchange for settling the *Alabama* claims. Now convinced that personal ambition rather than principle was the main force driving Seward's foreign policy, Adams informed him that he was resigning effective April 1, 1868.

Once it became known that Charles Francis Adams was retiring after seven years in London, the American minister's stiffness and unsociability was no longer deplored but admired as proof of his integrity and demonstrable fairness toward England.[30] By April 1868 there had been four prime ministers in three years: Palmerston, Russell, Derby, and Benjamin Disraeli; Adams's longevity at the legation during a period of such rapid political transition changed his public persona from that of a Yankee crank to a pillar of the diplomatic community. Ever nervous about making speeches, he turned down the numerous offers to hold a banquet in his honor, but that did not mean he was insensible to the plaudits that came his way. Lord Russell's speech in the House of Lords on March 27, 1868, gave Adams the most satisfaction of all. "Here I may say I cannot mention that gentleman's name without expressing my high esteem and respect for him," declared Russell. "He did everything which honour and good faith and moderation could prescribe."[31]

————

Seward was becoming conscious of his legacy; he had served as secretary of state for almost a decade, but the past three years under Johnson had been a crushing disappointment. Seward's political reputation had been tarnished by his ill-judged attempts to play the conciliator between Johnson and his critics. In May 1868, Johnson survived an attempt by the Senate to remove him by impeachment for "high crimes and misdemeanors," but only by one vote. "I have always felt that Providence dealt hardly with me in not letting me die with Mr. Lincoln," Seward remarked bitterly. "My work was done, and I think I deserved some of the reward of dying there."[32] Seward was frequently accused of being drunk in public during the latter half of Johnson's presidency: "He no longer seemed to care," wrote Henry Adams, who visited Washington in 1868; "he asked for nothing, gave nothing, and invited no support; he talked little of himself or of others, and waited only for his discharge."[33] This was an exaggeration—Seward cared a great deal—but he had lost the facility of keeping his friends loyal and his enemies afraid. "His trouble," sneered a critic, "is not that the party to which he once belonged is without a leader, but that he wanders about, like a ghost—a leader without a party."[34]

General Grant's election to the presidency in November 1868 opened a fresh path of negotiations for both countries; for Seward it meant that he had only four months left in office to engineer one final diplomatic triumph. But his attempt to repair Anglo-American relations ended in failure. The increasingly anti-British tone in the capital arising from the prolongation of the *Alabama* claims dispute required the kind of political skills that the outgoing secretary of state had long ceased to possess. The

Senate rejected his proposed "Johnson-Clarendon Treaty," which would have resolved the majority of America's disputes with Britain, by 44 votes to 1. The triumphant architect of Seward's humiliation in the Senate was his old rival Charles Sumner.

On April 13, 1869, Sumner gave an address to the Senate in which he laid the entire cost of the war after Gettysburg in 1863 at Britain's feet. He estimated the financial damages caused by the Confederate commerce raiders to be $15 million, adding a further $2 billion for the indirect damages caused by Britain's "un-neutral neutrality." As a proportion of Britain's GDP, the same figures today would be $155 million for the commerce raiders and $265 billion for the indirect costs.[35] Sumner also demanded an unreserved admission of guilt and an apology from Britain, followed by a new treaty to arrange for the reparations. The speech rescued Sumner's flagging political career. It was one of the only instances in his life in which he correctly judged the prevailing public opinion and successfully capitalized on it to increase his power in Washington. A few weeks later, Sumner gave another speech in which he spoke of Britain's complete withdrawal from the Americas. Until that moment, Sumner's influence with the new Grant administration had looked tenuous, but now he had national popularity as well as his chairmanship of the Senate Foreign Relations Committee to reinforce his bargaining power with the president.

Sumner was aided by the fact that Grant's attitude toward England was cool, bordering on hostile, and that both the new president and his secretary of state, Hamilton Fish, were fascinated by the possibility of absorbing Canada into the United States.* But Sumner's resurgence in Washington did not last long. He overplayed his hand as chairman of the Foreign Relations Committee by making it abundantly clear that the administration could not make the smallest decision on foreign policy without his assent.

It was Sumner's active opposition to Grant's plan to purchase Santo

---

* In late March 1865, President Lincoln had discussed the *Trent* affair with General Grant, making it clear that Britain deserved to be punished: "We gave due consideration to the case, but at that critical period of the war it was soon decided to deliver up the prisoners. It was a pretty bitter pill to swallow, but I contented myself with believing that England's triumph in the matter would be short-lived, and that after ending our war successfully we would be so powerful that we could call her to account for all the embarrassments she had inflicted upon us."[36]

Domingo during the first half of 1870 that sealed his downfall. It was too great a challenge to the administration's authority to be allowed to go unpunished. Hamilton Fish's determination to break free of Sumner's control removed the impasse between Britain and America over the *Alabama* claims. The timing could not have been better: Gladstone's foreign secretary in 1870, Lord Granville, was as anxious to find common ground with the U.S. secretary of state as Fish was with him.

The sudden political will in Britain and America to end the differences between them produced one of the most remarkable and successful international conventions of the nineteenth century. "We are taking several bites out of that big cherry," Granville wrote triumphantly to John Bright in October 1870, "reconciliation with the States."[37] Two teams, each consisting of five commissioners, met in Washington on February 24, 1871. By all accounts, the commissioners got on remarkably well; the British were surprised to discover that their American counterparts were "a very gentlemanly good set of fellows socially" and that Hamilton Fish was "quite English in manner and appearance."[38] In only nine weeks, the two teams negotiated the Treaty of Washington, which settled most disputes, potential and historical, for the next twenty years. Fish was satisfied by the British apology over the *Alabama*'s escape, and in return he agreed to close any legal loopholes that would allow U.S.-made *Alabama*s to prey on British merchant ships in time of war. He also used Sumner's inevitable objections to the negotiations, since America's right to Canada was not part of the discussion, to engineer the latter's removal as chairman of the Foreign Relations Committee.

The Treaty of Washington established two tribunals, one to arbitrate the claims of private individuals against the United States for actions committed during the Civil War, the other to rule on the *Alabama* claims. At the first, Mary Sophia Hill finally had her say in court. In fact, she said far too much, and her claim was dismissed for indecorous language. Undaunted, she appealed the decision: "I leave my case in your honorable hands, feeling that justice, even at this late hour, will be done me, and the insult to our flag; through me, be canceled, as England always has and always will protect the most humble of her subjects. As I said before, my health is ruined, so I do not consider the damage of two thousand pounds excessive."[39] This time, the court decided that £2,000 was excessive but otherwise found in her favor, and on January 5, 1872, awarded her $1,560 in damages.

At long last, the *Alabama* claims tribunal met in Geneva in December 1871. Charles Francis Adams was called out of retirement to represent the United States on the panel of five international judges who were to decide on the case. Adams had not wanted the appointment, and when he met his fellow judges he thought his worst fears confirmed. The British representative, Lord Chief Justice Sir Alexander Cockburn, had so short a temper that he seemed unbalanced, while the three other judges—a Swiss, a Brazilian, and an Italian—had varying degrees of familiarity with the English language. America and Britain each sent two legal teams to argue their respective sides. The proceedings started calmly enough, until the British team discovered in early January 1872 that Sumner's "indirect claims" for $2 billion—at 7 percent interest—had been included by the Americans for arbitration. The British demanded that the claims be excluded, and the Americans responded with equal vehemence that they stay and be decided upon by the judges. There was outrage in Britain when the news became known. Prime Minister William Gladstone declared in the House of Commons on February 7 that the government would be "insane to accede to demands which no nation with a spark of honour or spirit left could submit to even at the point of death."

President Grant could not have dropped the indirect claims, even if he wanted to, without jeopardizing his reelection hopes in November. Yet the idea that the *Alabama* and her sister ships, the *Florida, Georgia,* and *Shenandoah,* were responsible for prolonging the war by two years, as Sumner claimed, was patently ludicrous. The proceeding stalled until Charles Francis Adams took it upon himself to prevent the tribunal from collapsing. He knew that neither government could be seen to back down, and therefore he persuaded the other judges on the panel to exclude the $2 billion claim from consideration.

Three months later, on September 14, 1872, the tribunal ruled that Britain owed $15.5 million, including interest, for the damage caused by the Confederate cruisers. Ironically, the sum was $500,000 more than the amount first proposed by Charles Sumner in 1869.* The American press

---

* Britain actually paid out $8,070,181, since the United States agreed to give Canada $5.5 million for the right to fish in its waters and also paid $1,929,812 in compensation as a result of rulings at the mixed commission on British and American claims.

complained that it was too little, the British press that it was too much, but there was a shared sense of pride in both countries that a high moral precedent had been set in allowing disputes to be resolved in an international court rather than on the battlefield.[40] Adams is usually praised on the unfounded assertion that he prevented Britain from supporting the South, whereas his real triumph—when he transcended his own limitations and acted with visionary patriotism—was his brave decision to intervene at the *Alabama* tribunal in June 1872.

Before Adams returned home, he briefly visited England in order to say one last farewell to Lord Russell, and to reassure him that his reputation had not been sullied by Britain's expression of regret for the escape of the *Alabama* or by the payment of the claims. This act of generosity toward Russell caused Adams to arrive back in the United States too late to say goodbye to Seward, who died on October 10. The former secretary of state's death received respectful attention, but not the national mourning that he deserved considering his service to the country. Seward was too complex and contradictory a person to be easily categorized; he was not, as is now sometimes claimed, one of the greatest secretaries of state in U.S. history; his chronic and sometimes dangerous manipulation of foreign relations to boost his domestic agenda precludes him from that title. But after a disastrous beginning at the State Department, Seward became essential to the preservation of peace between America and Britain. His restraint of the forces that could have destroyed the fragile neutrality of the British government remains one of his outstanding achievements.

Two months after the ruling in Geneva, Sergeant Gilbert H. Bates, formerly of the 1st Wisconsin Heavy Artillery Regiment, traveled to Britain on a personal goodwill mission. Starting in Scotland on November 6, 1872, Bates walked the length of the country, bearing aloft the Stars and Stripes, to prove to Americans that the British bore no ill will toward the United States. He had performed a similar feat in 1868, marching through the South from Vicksburg to Washington. At Bolton, northwest of Manchester, Bates was accosted by a man who declared that he, too, was a Federal veteran and wished to carry the flag through the town; it was James Pendlebury. Surprised, Bates handed him the flag and Pendlebury was allowed to have his moment of glory. Bates received a hero's welcome when he reached London on November 30. Addressing an appreciative crowd in front of the Guildhall in the City, he declared:

It has been asserted by the press that this is a Yankee test of English feeling towards the States, but as far as I am concerned, it is no test. It is only a proof that I was right . . . when I said the English people respected America. . . . I have met with nothing but the kindest treatment. I have not had even a cross look from any one. My own countrymen on the other side of the Atlantic have been watching the progress of the tour of my flag with the greatest interest, and therefore I am gratified that the English people have proved that I was right.[41]

The resolution of the *Alabama* claims brought the Civil War chapter of British-American history to a close. The prewar resentment between the two countries had finally played itself out and a new, less hysterical and suspicious relationship was forming. Thirteen years later, in 1885, Ulysses S. Grant could write about the two countries in his memoirs with hope instead of rancor. "England's course towards the United States during the rebellion exasperated the people of this country very much against the mother country," he wrote.

I regretted it. England and the United States are natural allies, and should be the best of friends. They speak one language, and are related by blood and other ties. We together, or even either separately, are better qualified than any other people to establish commerce between all the nationalities of the world.[42]

Almost immediately after the war, the British writer William Michael Rossetti (the brother of the artist Dante Gabriel) tried to explain its impact on English public opinion in an essay for the American *Atlantic Monthly.* Rossetti claimed never to have seen his compatriots so animated "in connection with any other non-English occurrences": the entire country had divided over the merits of the Civil War, and whether abolition, democracy, the Union, or the right to self-determination had been the real principle at stake. Expressions such as " 'I am a Northerner,' and 'I am a Southerner' " were "as common on Englishmen's lips as 'I am a Liberal' or 'a Conservative.' "[43] It has been the purpose of this book to restore to view the Anglo-American world that Rossetti described.

In 1925, the U.S. consulate in London collected information on British Civil War veterans for the Federal Pensions Bureau for the last time. By then, the largest survivors' organization in the country, the American Civil War Veterans (London Branch), had dwindled from 140 members to a mere 24 ex-soldiers and 21 widows. But already in histories of the war it was as though the British volunteers in the Union and Confederate armies had never existed.[44]

This is not to say that Britain was rubbed out of the Civil War, far from it: 1925 was also the year that the first major study of Anglo-American relations during the war was published, E. D. Adams's *Great Britain and the American Civil War*. After Adams came a trickle and then a flood of books on the subject as the role of international diplomacy gained ever greater prominence in the historiography of the Civil War. "No battle," observed Allan Nevins, author of the eight-volume series *Ordeal of the Union*, in 1959, "not Gettysburg, not the Wilderness, was more important than the contest waged in the diplomatic arena and the forum of public opinion." The seemingly inexhaustible scholarly interest in these two areas continues to endorse the truth of Nevins's insight. But studies of movements, forces, factors, and political calculations ultimately have to be anchored by individual experience. *A World on Fire* has been an attempt to balance the vast body of work on Anglo-American history in the 1860s with the equally vast material left behind by witnesses and participants in the war—to depict the world as it was seen by Britons in America, and Americans in Britain, during a defining moment not just in U.S. history but in the relations between the two countries.[45]

The histories of the British participants in what is and always will be an American story bring the sharper focus that often comes with distance. Though united by language and a shared heritage, the Britons in America were nevertheless strangers who happened to find themselves, for a variety of reasons, in the midst of great events. Their simultaneous involvement and detachment (even when their observations turned out to be misleading or mistaken) provide a special perspective on the war, one that by definition was not possible for native-born Americans.[46] There were also many instances when the intimate access granted to British observers meant they were the only independent witnesses to record a particular event—such as William Howard Russell on President Lincoln's first White House dinner, or Frank Vizetelly on the flight of Jefferson Davis after the fall of Richmond. For this reason their accounts remain not only fascinating but invaluable relics of the Civil War.

Rossetti concluded his essay about Britain and the American Civil

War with an apology that speaks for all those authors who venture into this complex history: "For anything I have said which may possibly sound egotistic or intrusive—still more for anything erroneous or unfair in my statements or point of view—I must commit myself to the candid construction of my reader, be he [or she] American or English."[47]

Acknowledgments

I would like to thank the following people for sending me their ancestors' papers: John Knight, Derrick Mayhew, and Iris Diggle; as well as John Hailey, Bill Torrens, and Beata Duncan for their help.

I have been greatly aided over the years by my assistants, who have done everything from photocopying archives to picking up the children from school: Heather Nedwell, Jay Knowlton, Lorena Crackett, Christina Galbraith, Elizabeth Uzelac, and Olivia Taylor. I also thank all those at Penguin and Random House who have worked on the book.

The following people and libraries provided invaluable material: Library of Congress; U.S. National Archives; U.K. National Archives; Massachusetts Historical Society; South Carolina Historical Society; Museum of the Confederacy; British Library; British Newspaper Library; Royal Museum of Central Africa; Ms. Sam Collenette—Bolton Archives and Local Studies; Roger Bettridge, Linda Haynes, and Bill Torrens—Buckinghamshire Record Office; Kate Fellows and Rachel MacGregor—Birmingham City Archives; John Hopkins and Esther Williams—Cheshire Record Office; Sam Johnston and David Thomas—Cornwall Record Office; Susan Worrall—Coventry Archives; Rachel M. Rowe—Smuts Librarian in South Asian and Commonwealth Studies, University of Cambridge; Diana Chardin—Trinity College Library, Cambridge University; Martin Beckett—State Library of New South Wales; David M. Bowcock—Cumbria Record Office; John Brunton, Susan Laithwaite, Janice Wood, and Tim Wormleighton—Devon Record Office; Jennifer Gill—Durham Record Office; Jane Hogan and Elizabeth Rainey—Archives and Special Collections, Durham University Library; Hugh Jaques and Deborah Stevenson—Dorset Record Office; Sarah Chubb—Dundee University Archives; Ian Flett—Dundee City Archives; Michael Read—Welsh College of Music and Drama; Marion M. Stewart—Dumfries and Galloway Archives; Robert Craigie; Philip Bye—East Sussex Records Office; Dr. Annette Hagan and Hazel Robertson—Special Collections, Edinburgh University Library; Elizabeth Pettitt—Flintshire Records Office; Karan Robson—Southampton University Library; Mr. P. R. Evans—Gloucestershire County Record Office; Pauline Kane—Glasgow Public Library; Lynne Dent, Niki Pollock, and Moira Rankin—Special Collections, Glasgow University Library; Elizabeth Ball—Glasgow University Archive; Steffan ab Owain and J. Dilwyn Williams—Caernarfon Record Office; Martin Taylor—Hull City Archives; Elizabeth Kirwan—Department of Manuscripts, National Library of Ireland; Helen Burton—Special Collections and Archives, Keele University; Bruce Jackson and Neil Sayer—Lancashire Record Office; Dr. Margaret Bonney—Leicestershire Record Office; Adrian Wilkinson—Lincolnshire Archives; Ruth Hobbins, Roger Hull, and Liz Williams—Liverpool Record Office; Stephen Freeth and James R. Sewell—Guildhall Library, Corporation of London; Susan Stead—Special Collections, University College London; Malcolm C. Davis, Paul Howell, and Gillian Moran—Special Collections, Leeds University Library; Gwen McGinty and Dr. Maureen M. Watry—Sydney Jones Library, University of Liverpool; Dr. John Nicholls—London City Mission; Robert Gerrelli; Stephen M. Dixon—Medway Archives and Local Studies Center; Dawn Littler—Merseyside Maritime Museum; John Hodgson and Peter McNiven—John Rylands University Library; Edith Philip—National War Museum of Scotland; Alastair Carroll, Anne Craig, and Michelle Kelly—Public Record Office of Northern Ireland; Helen Sellars—Florence Nightingale Museum Trust; Richard Aspin, Douglas Knock, Nyree Morrison, and Helen Wakely—Wellcome Library for the History and Understanding of Medicine; Helen Arkwright and Lesley Gordon—Special Collections, Robinson Library, University of Newcastle; Caroline Kelly and Elizabeth Tebbutt—Department of Manuscripts and Special Collections, Hallward Library, University of Nottingham; Jill Davies, Duncan Hartwig, and Kiri Ross-Jones—Manuscripts Department, National Maritime Museum; Tim Hughes; Mrs. S. Wood—Northumberland Record Office; Adrian Henstock—Nottinghamshire Archives; Caroline Dalton—New College Library, Oxford; Clare Brown and Melissa Dalziel—Special Collections and

Western Manuscripts, Bodleian Library, Oxford; Marie Lewis—Pembrokeshire Record Office; Steve Connelly—Perth and Kinross Council Archive; Josef Keith—Library, Friends House, London; Susan McGann—Royal College of Nursing Archives and U.K. Centre for the History of Nursing; Barbara Mortimer—Queen Margaret University College; Alan Readman—West Sussex Record Office; Angus Johnson and Brian Smith—Shetland Archives; Margaret Myerscough—Stockport Central Library; Di Tapley—Surrey History Centre; Len Reilly—Local Studies Library, Southwark; Robert Fotheringham, John McLintock, and Dr. Alison Rosie—National Archives of Scotland; Daniella Shippey; Dr. Iain G. Brown—National Library of Scotland; Alison Healey—Shropshire Records and Research Center; Christopher Lloyd—Tower Hamlets Local History, Bancroft Library; Rhys M. Jones and Meriel Ralphs—National Library of Wales; Steve Hobbs—Wiltshire and Swindon Record Office; Jeanette Grisold—Warwickshire Record Office; Dr. David Wykes—Dr. Williams's Library; Elen Wyn Hughes—University of Wales, Bangor; Lyons Papers, courtesy of His Grace the Duke of Norfolk, Arundel Castle; Bob Hale and Lyn Morgan—Sheffield Archives and Conservation Unit; Mrs. C. Boddington—East Riding of Yorkshire Archive; Judith A. Smeaton—North Yorkshire County Record Office; Andrew George, Paul Harris, Ruth Harris, Barbara Hick, and Jayne Rhodes-Gifford—West Yorkshire Police; Elizabeth Briggs—West Yorkshire Archive; Marvel Manning—Hoole Special Collections, University of Alabama; Jim Pate—Birmingham Public Library; Charlotte Chamberlain—Mobile Public Library; Barry Crompton—Archer Memorial Civil War Library; Laura Madokoro—National Archives of Canada; John Rhodehamel—Huntington Library; Richard A. Hanks—A.K. Smiley Public Library; Kathleen Burns—San Diego Public Library; Bonnie Linck—Connecticut State Library; Martha L. Bennett—Fort Delaware Society; Marjorie G. McNinch—Hagley Museum and Library, Wilmington; Lynn Conway—Georgetown University Library; Patrick Kerwin and Albert E. Smith—Library of Congress; Tony Gonzalez—National Union Catalog of Manuscript Collections; Faye Haskins—Washingtoniana Division, D.C. Public Library; Amy Elizabeth Burton—United States Senate Office; Glovenia E. Snead; Sydney Herbert Davis; C.F. Henningsen; Jim Taylor; Susan Watson—Hazel Braugh Records Center and Archives for the American Red Cross; Trevor Plante—National Archives; Alicia Clarke—Sanford Museum

Archive; Anne Thompson—Robert W. Woodruff Library, Emory University; John Phillip Albert—Georgia Historical Society; Melissa Bush—Hagrett Rare Book and Manuscript Library, University of Georgia; E. Cheryl Schnirring—Illinois State Historical Library; Olivia Chen—Chicago Historical Society; Andrea Telli—Chicago Public Library, Special Collections and Preservation Division; Kathy J. Koch—Archive, American Association of Nurse Anesthetists; Lori O'Connor—Kentucky Historical Society; Elizabeth Tunis—National Library of Medicine; Anne Sauer—Tisch Library, Tufts University; Pat Boulos—Boston Athenaeum; Diane Gallagher—History of Nursing Archives, Boston University; Alex Rankin—Boston University; Nicholas Graham—Massachusetts Historical Society; Barbara DeWolfe—William L. Clements Library, University of Michigan–Ann Arbor; Michael Hennen—Mississippi Department of Archives and History; Steve Zerbe; Megan Hahn Fraser—New-York Historical Society; Sha Fagan—Sarah Lawrence College; Jim Moske—New York Public Library; Nancy Martin—Rush Rhees Library, University of Rochester; Sarah DeSanctis; Fred Bassett—New York State Library; Mitch Frass—Duke University Library; North Carolina State Archives; Anne Skilton—Wilson Library, University of North Carolina at Chapel Hill; Connie Cedoz—Port Clinton Public Library; Jim Duffey; Nan Card—Rutherford B. Hayes Presidential Center; Albert Hallenberg—Public Library of Cincinnati; John E. Hass—Ohio Historical Society; Karen Drickamer—Musselman Library, Gettysburg College; John Heiser—historian, Gettysburg National Military Park; Molly Dohrmann—Jean and Alexander Heard Library, Vanderbilt University; Mary Jo Fairchild, Jackie McCall, Carey Lucas Nikonchuk, and Peter L. Wilkerson—South Carolina Historical Society; Ann Drury Wellford—Museum of the Confederacy; and Gregory Stoner—Virginia Historical Society.

Notes

To read the comprehensive bibliography for *A World on Fire,* please visit
www.amanda-foreman.com.

ABBREVIATIONS

BL British Library

BDOFA *British Documents on Foreign Affairs: Reports and Papers from the Foreign Office Confidential Print,* ed. Kenneth Bourne and D. Cameron Watt (Frederick, Md., 1986–)

MHS Massachusetts Historical Society

MPUS *Message of the President of the United States,* 37th Congress (Washington, D.C., 1862)

NARA National Archives and Records Administration, Washington, D.C.

ORN Official Navy Records

OR Official Records

PRFA *Papers Relating to Foreign Affairs Accompanying the Annual Message of the President of the United States*

PRO Public Record Office

Prologue

1. Virginia Clay-Copton and Ada Sterling, *A Belle of the Fifties: The Memoirs of Mrs. Clay of Alabama* (New York, 1904), pp. 116, 118.
2. *New York Times,* February 19, 1859.
3. Mrs. Roger A. Pryor, *Reminiscences of Peace and War* (New York, 1905), p. 57.
4. C. Vann Woodward (ed.), *Mary Chesnut's Civil War* (New Haven, 1981), p. 367.
5. Lyons nevertheless understood the importance of providing excellent food and wine at the legation dinners. Hence the chef was from Paris and the wine from his own family cellars. Source: Brian Jenkins.
6. James J. Barnes and Patience P. Barnes (eds.), *Private and Confidential: Letters from British Ministers in Washington to the Foreign Secretaries* (Selinsgrove, Pa., 1993), p. 213, Lyons to Lord Malmesbury, April 12, 1859.
7. Raymond A. Jones, *The British Diplomatic Service* (London, 1983), p. 99.
8. Calvin D. Davis, "A British Diplomat and the American Civil War: Edward Malet in the United States," *South Atlantic Quarterly,* 77/2 (1978), p.166.
9. 863,409 British and 1,611,304 Irish, PRO FO 115/394, f. 216. Two-thirds of

these "British" expatriates were actually Irish immigrants, who harbored a visceral hatred toward the mother country. Nevertheless, they enjoyed the same protection by the British minister as the 98 Scots in Dakota, and the 23,848 Englishmen in Massachusetts. The Foreign Office had recognized that the legation's staff of five was too small and the sixth attaché was on his way. Although the British government promulgated the official line of "once a Briton, always a Briton," in practice, Lyons was not expected to take up the cases of naturalized British subjects.

10. H. C. Allen, *Great Britain and the United States* (New York, 1955), p. 361. In 1819, the foreign secretary, Lord Castlereagh, warned his new British minister, "The jealousies as yet imperfectly allayed inclines the Government of the United States to maintain . . . [to us] a tone of greater harshness than towards any other Government whatever. The American people are more easily excited against us and more disposed to strengthen the hands of their Ministers against us than against any other State."

11. George Washburn Smalley, *Anglo-American Memories* (New York, 1912), p. 174.

12. Lord Newton (ed.), *Lord Lyons: A Record of British Diplomacy*, 2 vols. (London, 1914), vol. 2, p. 214.

13. John Evan (pseudonym of Evan John Simpson), *Atlantic Impact* (London, 1952), p. 210. This oft-repeated description of Lyons may possibly be apocryphal but the spirit of the story remains true.

14. The admiral became his son's champion: "Had it not been for your visit to England at the critical moment," he wrote to his father from his new post in Florence, "I should now have been no more than simple Secretary of Legation." Newton (ed.), *Lord Lyons*, vol. 1, p. 7.

15. Scott Thomas Cairns, "Lord Lyons and Anglo-American Diplomacy During the American Civil War," Ph.D. thesis, London School of Economics, 2004, p. 58.

16. As quoted in Brian Jenkins, *Britain and the War for the Union*, 2 vols. (Montreal, 1974, 1980), vol. 1, p. 44.

17. Sarah Agnes Wallace and Frances Elma Gillespie (eds.), *The Journal of Benjamin Moran, 1857–1865*, 2 vols. (Chicago, 1948, 1949), vol. 1, pp. 504–5, February 8, 1859.

18. Newton (ed.), *Lord Lyons*, vol. 1, p. 14, Lord Lyons to Lord Malmesbury, May 29, 1859.

19. Charles Dickens, *American Notes for General Circulation* (London, 1842; Penguin Classics, 2000), p. 129.

20. Edward Dicey, *Spectator of America*, ed. Herbert Mitgang (Athens, Ga., 1971), p. 62.

21. Ibid., p. 65.

22. Michael Burlingame (ed.), *Lincoln's Journalist: John Hay's Anonymous Writings for the Press, 1860–1864* (Carbondale, Ill., 1998), p. 50.

23. William Howard Russell, *My Diary North and South*, ed. Eugene H. Berwanger (New York, 1988), p. 41, March 26, 1861.

24. Clay-Copton and Sterling, *A Belle of the Fifties*, p. 139.

25. Mrs. Clay recalled that Lyons said, "Ah, Madam! do you remember what Uncle Toby said to his nephew when he informed him of his intended mar-

riage?" She, presumably not having read *Tristram Shandy,* had no idea what was coming next. "Then, without waiting for my assent, he added, 'Alas! alas! quoth my Uncle Toby, you will never sleep slantindicularly in your bed [any] more!' " Ibid.

26. Hudson Strode (ed.), *Private Letters of Jefferson Davis* (New York, 1966), p. 105, Varina Davis to Jefferson Davis, April 10, 1859.

27. Wilbur Devereux Jones, *The American Problem in British Diplomacy, 1841–1861* (London, 1974), p. 172.

28. Barnes and Barnes (eds.), *Private and Confidential*, p. 214, Lyons to Lord Malmesbury, June 21, 1859.

29. Newton (ed.), *Lord Lyons*, vol. 1, p. 14, Lord Lyons to Lord Malmesbury, May 30, 1859.

30. James O'Donald Mays, *Mr. Hawthorne Goes to England* (Ringwood, 1983), pp. 156–58.

PART I: COTTON IS KING

Chapter 1: The Uneasy Cousins

1. Wilbur Devereux Jones, *The American Problem in British Diplomacy, 1841–1861* (London, 1974), p. 169, Lord Derby to Lord Malmesbury, October 11, 1858.

2. Kenneth Bourne, *The Foreign Policy of Victorian England, 1830–1902* (Oxford, 1970), p. 334, Lord Palmerston to Lord Clarendon, December 31, 1857.

3. In 1807, HMS *Leopard* was prowling off the coast of Virginia when it came across USS *Chesapeake*. The *Leopard* fired on the *Chesapeake* after the vessel refused to heave to, killing three American sailors and wounding a further eighteen. Only one deserter was found.

4. Paul Ford Leicester (ed.), *The Writings of Thomas Jefferson, 1807–1815*, vol. 9 (London, 1898), p. 366, Jefferson to William Duane, August 4, 1812.

5. Thomas Low Nichols, *Forty Years of American Life*, 2 vols. (London, 1864), vol. 1, p. 409.

6. Jasper Ridley, *Palmerston* (New York, 1971), pp. 270–74, Palmerston to Russell, January 19, 1841.

7. Evelyn Ashley, *The Life and Correspondence of Henry John Temple, Viscount Palmerston*, 2 vols. (London, 1879), vol. 1, p. 408, Palmerston to H. S. Fox, February 9, 1841.

8. The raid had taken place in 1837. The USS *Caroline* was carrying supplies to pro-American Canadian insurgents. Tired of troublemakers fostering rebellion south of the border, a group of armed men seized the *Caroline,* killing an American sailor in the process, and sent it over Niagara Falls. While hogging his barstool, McLeod boasted that he was the killer. In truth, he was a pathetic fantasist.

9. James Chambers, *Palmerston, the People's Darling* (London, 2004), p. 199.

10. Ridley, *Palmerston*, p. 273.

11. The border dispute over New Brunswick and Maine was settled by British minister Lord Ashburton and U.S. secretary of state Daniel Webster.

12. H. C. Allen, *Great Britain and the United States* (New York, 1955), p. 136.

13. Ibid., p. 123.

14. Betty Fladeland, *Men and Brothers* (Champaign, Ill., 1972), p. 351.

15. Annie Heloise Abel and Frank J. Klingberg (eds.), *A Sidelight on Anglo-American Relations, 1839–1858* (Lancaster, Pa., 1927), p. 40.

16. Elizabeth Cady Stanton, *Eighty Years and More: Reminiscences, 1815–1897* (New York, 1898), pp. 71–92.

17. Jean Fagan Yellin, "Harriet Jacobs and the Transatlantic Movement," in *Sisterhood and Slavery: Transatlantic Antislavery and Women's Rights: Proceedings of the Third Annual Gilder Lehrman Center International Conference at Yale University* (Yale, 2001), p. 7.

18. Allen, *Great Britain and the United States*, p. 198.

19. William Brock, "The Image of England and American Nationalism," *Journal of American Studies*, 5 (Dec. 1971). Edward Everett, speech at Bristol, 1842, p. 227.

20. Nichols, *Forty Years of American Life*, vol. 1, p. 398.

21. Allen, *Great Britain and the United States*, p.147, quoting the *Edinburgh Review*, 1820.

22. It was often pointed out that Louisiana would still belong to the French if Barings Bank in London had not financed the purchase, selling more than $9 million worth of the $11 million total of bonds sold.

23. Charles Dickens to Macready, March 22, 1842, quoted in Walter Allen, *Transatlantic Crossing: American Visitors to Britain and British Visitors to America in the Nineteenth Century* (New York, 1971), p. 236.

24. What Seward actually believed in has been the subject of intense historical debate. In a speech in 1853 he declared it was his aim that the republic "shall greet the sun when he touches the tropics, and when he sends his gleaming rays towards the polar circle, and shall include even distant islands in either ocean." But Ernest Paolino argues that by 1857 Seward had abandoned the idea of annexing Canada by force. For one thing, a trip to Labrador convinced him that the Canadians would never accept it. Nevertheless, he liked to talk as though he believed it was just a matter of time, if only to annoy the British. In 1860 he made a speech congratulating the Canadians for "building states to be hereafter admitted into the American union." Ernest N. Paolino, *The Foundations of the American Empire* (New York, 1973), p. 8.

25. G. H. Warren, *Fountain of Discontent: The Trent Affair and Freedom of the Seas* (Boston, 1981), p. 56.

26. Henry Adams, *The Education of Henry Adams*, ed. Ernest Samuels (repr., Boston, 1973), p. 102.

27. David Herbert Donald, *Charles Sumner and the Coming of the Civil War* (New York, 1961), pp. 295–96.

28. *Letters of Sir George Cornewall Lewis*, ed. Sir G. F. Lewis (London, 1870), pp. 390–92, Lewis to the Hon. Edward Twisleton, January 21, 1861.

29. *Illustrated London News*, August 29, no. 814 (Aug. 1856), pp. 121–22. The Duchess of Sutherland made it a point of duty to support black performers who came to England. In 1853, for example, she invited Elizabeth Taylor Greenfield, known as "the Black Swan," to perform a concert at Stafford House in the presence of Queen Victoria. The event was so celebrated that it was turned into a song: "The Other Side of Jordan" (1853).

30. *George Douglas, Eighth Duke of Argyll (1823–1900): Autobiography and Memoirs*, ed. the Dowager Duchess of Argyll, 2 vols. (London, 1906), vol. 1, p. 412.

Chapter 2: On the Best of Terms

1. Kathleen Burk, *Morgan Grenfell, 1838–1988* (Oxford, 2002), p. 20.
2. John M. Taylor, *William Henry Seward: Lincoln's Right Hand* (New York, 1991), p. 107.
3. Jay Sexton, *Debtor Diplomacy* (Oxford, 2005), p. 138.
4. Playing to the gallery, Seward had urged President Buchanan to give Britain one year to withdraw entirely from Central America. If she refused, he argued, the United States would have the right to annex Canada. Cuba had become the largest importer of slaves after Brazil, prompting Lord Palmerston to order the Royal Navy to surround the island, if necessary, and board any suspicious-looking ship, whatever the color of its flag. By May 1858, the navy had boarded 116 suspected slave ships, of which 61 were American-owned. The New York press, in particular, raised an outcry, and Secretary of State Lewis Cass demanded that Britain stop such activities immediately. Senator James Murray Mason had steered a bill through the Senate to send a U.S. naval squadron to the Caribbean. The British government backed away from a confrontation and ordered the Royal Navy to desist from the practice. Palmerston was outraged by Derby's pusillanimity, but he placed the greater blame on the United States. Hugh Thomas, *The Slave Trade* (New York, 1997), p. 764.
5. Edwin G. Burrows and Mike Wallace, *Gotham* (New York, 1999), p. 676.
6. H. C. Allen, *Great Britain and the United States* (New York, 1955), p. 158.
7. Frederick W. Seward (ed.), *Seward at Washington* (New York, 1891), p. 372.
8. Taylor, *William Henry Seward*, p. 113.
9. H. F. Bell, *Lord Palmerston*, 2 vols. (London, 1936), vol. 2, p. 253. Her mother had been the great Lady Melbourne, a political hostess whose influence in the 1780s was second only to the Duchess of Devonshire's.
10. John Prest, *Lord John Russell* (London, 1972), p. 134. "You give great offence to your followers," his exasperated brother, the Duke of Bedford, once complained, "by not being courteous to them, by treating them superciliously or de haut en bas, by not listening . . . to their solicitations, remonstrances, or whatever it may be. . . . "
11. Ibid., p. 349.
12. Beverly Wilson Palmer (ed.), *The Selected Letters of Charles Sumner*, 2 vols. (Boston, 1990), vol. 1, p. 24, Sumner to Duchess of Argyll, May 22, 1860.
13. Seward (ed.), *Seward at Washington*, p. 390.
14. Sarah Agnes Wallace and Frances Elma Gillespie (eds.), *The Journal of Benjamin Moran, 1857–1865*, 2 vols. (Chicago, 1948, 1949), vol. 1, p. 545, May 21, 1859.
15. Ibid., p. 558, June 23, 1859.
16. Ibid., p. 504, February 8, 1859.
17. K. Theodore Hoppen, *The Mid-Victorian Generation* (Oxford, 1998), p. 202.
18. James Matlack Scovel, "The Great Free Trader by His Own Fire Side," *Overland Monthly and Out West Magazine* (1893), p. 129.

19. Seward (ed.), *Seward at Washington*, p. 380. Deborah Logan (ed.), *The Collected Letters of Harriet Martineau*, 5 vols. (London, 2007), vol. 4, p. 180, Martineau to Henry Reeve, July 6, 1859. Seward also told Harriet Martineau that he believed Sumner's ailments were mostly psychological.

20. Wilbur Devereux Jones, *The American Problem in British Diplomacy, 1841–1861* (London, 1974), p. 200.

21. Massachusetts Foundation for the Humanties: http://www.mfh.org/special-projects/shwlp/site/honorees/remond.html, Sarah Parker Remond to Abby Kelly Foster, September 1858. Sibyl Ventress Brownlee, "Out of the Abundance of the Heart: Sarah Ann Parker Remond's Quest for Freedom," Ph.D. thesis, University of Massachusetts, 1997, p. 119.

22. Wallace and Gillespie (eds.), *The Journal of Benjamin Moran, 1857–1865*, vol. 1, p. 608, November 22, 1859.

23. Ibid., p. 614, December 10, 1859.

24. Ibid., p. 616, December 16, 1859.

25. Brownlee, "Out of the Abundance of the Heart," p. 136.

26. David Herbert Donald, *Charles Sumner and the Coming of the Civil War* (New York, 1961), p. 348.

27. Taylor, *William Henry Seward*, p. 114.

28. James J. Barnes and Patience P. Barnes (eds.), *Private and Confidential: Letters from British Ministers in Washington to the Foreign Secretaries* (Selinsgrove, Pa., 1993), p. 223, Lord Lyons to Lord Russell, December 6, 1859.

29. Mason's report was published in June 1860.

30. Mrs. Roger A. Pryor, *Reminiscences of Peace and War* (New York, 1905), p. 98.

31. Rose Greenhow, *My Imprisonment and the First Year of Abolition Rule at Washington* (London, 1863), p. 192.

32. Martin Duberman, *Charles Francis Adams* (New York, 1961), p. 213.

33. Greenhow, *My Imprisonment*, p. 192.

34. Ernest Samuels (ed.), *Henry Adams: Selected Letters* (Cambridge, Mass., 1988), p. 21, Henry Adams to Abigail Adams, February 13, 1860.

35. Duberman, *Charles Francis Adams*, p. 21.

36. Charles Francis Adams would have argued back that he had not been a slouch during his adulthood: he served in the Massachusetts state legislature for five years, and was twice an unsuccessful candidate for vice president in 1848 and 1872.

37. San Juan Island remained under joint military occupation for the next twelve years. Then, after Britain and the United States signed the Treaty of Washington, the San Juan question was referred to Kaiser Wilhelm I. He established a three-man arbitration commission, which studied the issue for almost a year. On October 21, 1872, the commission ruled in favor of the United States. A month later, the Royal Marines packed their bags, said goodbye to their American friends, and marched out of the English camp for the last time. Two years later, the American camp was abandoned.

38. PRO 30/22/34, ff. 130–33, Lyons to Russell, April 10, 1860.

39. PRO 30/22/34, ff. 149–50, Lyons to Russell, May 22, 1860.

40. As recently as March 2, Sumner had told her, "I incline now more than ever

to think that Seward will be [our candidate]." Palmer (ed.), *The Selected Letters of Charles Sumner*, vol. 1, p. 19.

41. No one had actually counted the prince's entourages so it came as a terrible shock when there were too many bodies for too few beds. Buchanan gallantly offered up his room and slept on a sofa in the corridor.

42. Stanley Weintraub, *Edward the Caresser* (New York, 2003), p. 68.

43. Ibid., p. 71. The issue of slavery would force itself upon the prince one more time, in the North. On October 18, 1860, a delegation of African-Americans presented him with "An Address of Colored Citizens of Boston to the Prince of Wales," which offered "their profound and grateful attachment and respect for the Throne which you represent here, under whose shelter so many thousands of their race, fugitives from American slavery, find safety and rest . . . and where the road to wealth, education, and social position, and civil office and honors is as free to the black man as to the white." *Anti-Slavery Advocate*, 2/403/50, February 1, 1861.

44. Weintraub, *Edward the Caresser*, p. 73.

45. Edward Dicey, *Spectator of America*, ed. Herbert Mitgang (Athens, Ga., 1971), p. 11.

46. Lloyd Morris, *Incredible New York* (New York, 1951; repr. Syracuse, N.Y., 1996), p. 24.

47. Weintraub, *Edward the Caresser*, p. 76.

48. The 69th Regiment, New York State Militia, was the nucleus for the 69th New York State Volunteers, which was itself one of the three founding Irish regiments of the famous New York Irish Brigade.

49. Seward (ed.), *Seward at Washington*, p. 455.

50. Palmer (ed.), *Selected Letters of Charles Sumner*, vol. 1, p. 23, Sumner to Seward, May 20, 1860.

51. Glyndon Van Deusen, *William Henry Seward* (Oxford, 1967), p. 231.

52. Hallward Library, University of Nottingham; Newcastle, NEC/10885/134, Duke of Newcastle to Sir Edmund Head, June 5, 1861.

53. Sir Theodore Martin, *The Life of His Royal Highness the Prince Consort*, vol. 5 (New York, 1880), p. 204.

54. Ibid.

55. Martin Crawford, *The Anglo-American Crisis of the Mid-Nineteenth Century: The Times and America, 1850–1862* (Athens, Ga., 1987), p. 76, Morris to Bancroft Davis, October 30, 1860.

56. Lord Newton (ed.), *Lord Lyons: A Record of British Diplomacy*, 2 vols. (London, 1914), vol. 1, pp. 27–28, Lord Lyons to Duke of Newcastle, October 29, 1860.

57. Crawford, *The Anglo-American Crisis of the Mid-Nineteenth Century*, p. 10, October 12, 1860.

58. Newton (ed.), *Lord Lyons*, vol. 1, p. 29, Lord Lyons to Duke of Newcastle, December 10, 1860.

Chapter 3: "The Cards Are in Our Hands!"

1. Wilbur Devereux Jones, *The American Problem in British Diplomacy, 1841–1861* (London, 1974), p. 198.

2. Ibid.

3. *BDOFA*, part I, ser. C, vol. 5, p. 162, law officers of the Crown to Lord John Russell, December 7, 1860.

4. Sarah Agnes Wallace and Frances Elma Gillespie (eds.), *The Journal of Benjamin Moran, 1857–1865*, 2 vols. (Chicago, 1948, 1949), vol. 1, pp. 751, 753, December 7 and December 11, 1860.

5. Ibid., p. 765, January 9, 1861.

6. *The Times*, January 9, 1861.

7. *Illustrated London News*, January 19, 1861.

8. William S. Walsh, *Abraham Lincoln and the London Punch* (New York, 1909), p. 20.

9. Brian Jenkins, *Britain and the War for the Union*, 2 vols. (Montreal, 1974, 1980), p. 86. And *BDOFA*, part I, ser. C, vol. 5, pp. 169–70, Lord Lyons to Lord John Russell, December 18, 1860.

10. Glyndon Van Deusen, *William Henry Seward* (Oxford, 1967), p. 240.

11. Frederick W. Seward (ed.), *Seward at Washington* (New York, 1891), p. 487.

12. Ernest Samuels (ed.), *Henry Adams: Selected Letters* (Cambridge, Mass., 1988), p. 32, Henry Adams to Charles Francis Adams, Jr., December 9, 1860.

13. Charles Francis Adams, Jr., *Charles Francis Adams, 1835–1915: An Autobiography with a Memorial Address* (Boston, 1916), p. 82.

14. Charles Francis Adams, Jr., "The British Proclamation of May, 1861," *Massachusetts Historical Society Proceedings*, 48 (1915), pp. 190–241, at p. 216, Lord Lyons to Lord John Russell, February 4, 1861.

15. PRO Kew, 30/22/35, ff. 16–19, Lyons to Lord John Russell, February 12, 1861. Lord Newton (ed.), *Lord Lyons: A Record of British Diplomacy*, ed. Lord Newton, 2 vols. (London, 1914), vol. 1, p. 30, Lord Lyons to Lord John Russell, January 7, 1861.

16. *BDOFA*, part I, ser. C, vol., 5, p. 181, Russell to Lord Lyons, February 20, 1861.

17. Charles M. Hubbard, *The Burden of Confederate Diplomacy* (Knoxville, Tenn., 1998), p. 27.

18. Doris Kearns Goodwin, *Team of Rivals* (New York, 2005), p. 316.

19. Michael Burlingame, *Abraham Lincoln*, 2 vols. (Baltimore, 2008), vol. 2, p. 98.

20. *Diary of Gideon Welles*, 3 vols. (Boston, 1911), vol. 1, pp. 134–40.

21. *BDOFA*, part I, ser. C, vol. 5, Lyons to Russell, March 18, 1861.

22. Lynn M. Case and Warren F. Spence, *The United States and France: Civil War Diplomacy* (Philadelphia, Pa., 1970), p. 130. Norman Ferris maintained that the various accounts of the dinner by the foreign ministers were too dissimilar to be trustworthy. I believe that the sense in all of them is the same: Seward did not like their answers and became aggressive. Norman B. Ferris, "Lincoln and Seward in Civil War Diplomacy: Their Relationship at the Outset Reexamined," *Journal of the Abraham Lincoln Association*, 12 (1991), p. 21.

23. Newton (ed.), *Lord Lyons*, vol. 1, pp. 31–34, Lyons to Russell, March 26, 1861. Norman Ferris disputes Lyons's account but his argument is not persuasive.

24. David Donald, *Charles Sumner and the Coming of the Civil War* (New York, 1961), p. 383.

25. Adams, *Charles Francis Adams, 1835–1915*, p. 108.

26. MHS, Adams MSS, Diary of Charles Francis Adams, March 28, 1861.

27. David H. Donald, *Lincoln* (New York, 1995), p. 285.

28. Interestingly, Jack Shepherd, *The Adams Chronicles* (New York, 1975), p. 358, Martin Duberman, *Charles Francis Adams* (New York, 1961), p. 257, Philip Van Doren Stern, *When the Guns Roared: World Aspects of the American Civil War* (New York, 1965), p. 35, and Donald, *Lincoln*, p. 321, take the account from Charles Francis Adams, Jr.'s biography of his father, but it differs in minor but significant aspects from Adams's diary.

29. Alan Hankinson, *Man of Wars: William Howard Russell of "The Times," 1820–1907* (London, 1982), p. 152.

30. C. Vann Woodward (ed.), *Mary Chesnut's Civil War* (New Haven, 1981), p. 67, June 4–10, 1861.

31. Hankinson, *Man of Wars*, p. 157, Mowbray Morris to Russell, April 4, 1861.

32. Wiltshire and Swindon RO, 2536/10, Edward Best to Aunt Sophia, May 10, 1861.

33. William Howard Russell, *My Diary North and South*, ed. Eugene H. Berwanger (New York, 1988), p. 42, March 26, 1861; dashes added for clarity.

34. Ibid., p. 47, March 28, 1861.

35. Ibid.

36. MHS, Adams MSS, Diary of Charles Francis Adams, March 31, 1861.

37. Charles Francis Adams, Jr., *Charles Francis Adams, 1835–1915: An Autobiography* (Boston, 1916), pp. 112–13.

38. Van Deusen, *William Henry Seward*, p. 270.

39. Edward L. Pierce (ed.), *Memoir and Letters of Charles Sumner*, 4 vols. (Boston, 1894), vol. 4: *1860–1870*, p. 29.

40. The crux of his proposal was America's engagement with Europe. Seward stated that he "would demand explanation from Spain and France, categorically, at once. I would seek explanations from Great Britain and Russia, and send agents into Canada, Mexico and Central America, to rouse a vigorous continental spirit of independence on this continent against European intervention. And if satisfactory explanations are not received from Spain and France, would convene Congress and declare war against them." This was a scatter-gun approach, indicative of Seward's state of mind. At least regarding Spain, he did have a valid issue. With extraordinary timing, Spain had just annexed Santo Domingo—a direct snub to the Monroe Doctrine. But the others were mere wishful thinking.

41. Patrick Sowle, "A Reappraisal of Seward's Memorandum of April 1, 1861, to Lincoln," *Journal of Southern History*, 33/2 (May 1967), pp. 234–39.

42. Russell, *My Diary North and South*, p. 66, April 9, 1861.

43. Ibid., p. 77, April 15, 1861.

44. Martin Crawford (ed.), *William Howard Russell's Civil War: Private Diary and Letters, 1861–1862* (Athens, Ga., 1992), p. 43, William Howard Russell to Lord Lyons, April 19, 1861.

45. Russell, *My Diary North and South*, p. 92, April 18, 1861.

46. Ibid., p. 95, April 20, 1861.

47. There is still a lively debate as to whether the United States was right to have chosen a blockade over port closures. As Howard Jones has noted, the U.S. Constitution deemed that all ports must be treated on an equal basis. Lincoln

did not have the legal power to close only the Southern ports and leave the Northern ones open. He would either have to shut every port in the country, or declare that Northern ports were exempt from closure since they were not part of the United States, which would have been absurd. Jones, *Blue and Gray Diplomacy* (Chapel Hill, N.C., 2009), p. 56.

48. A letter of marque (marque meaning "frontier") was a cheap way for countries without a navy to wage war against an enemy's shipping. By international law, any captain with a vessel could become a privateer if issued with one. Thus shielded by the law, he could roam the sea, seizing enemy ships and taking them before an admiralty court. There it would be decided whether or not the ship was a legal prize and not, for example, the property of a neutral state. If judged a legal prize, the ship would be condemned and captain and crew entitled to the profits. Roland R. Foulke, *A Treatise on International Law*, 2 vols. (Philadelphia, 1920), vol. 2, p. 244. The last country to offer letters of marque was Mexico in 1847.

49. The declaration had four salient points: 1. Privateering is, and remains, abolished; 2. The neutral flag covers enemy's goods, with the exception of contraband of war; 3. Neutral goods, with the exception of contraband of war, are not liable to capture under enemy's flag; 4. Blockades, in order to be binding, must be effective. Also, the declaration was only binding upon countries that had signed the treaty.

50. Adams, "The British Proclamation of May, 1861," p. 218.

51. Ibid., p. 220, Lord Lyons to Lord John Russell, May 6, 1861.

52. In Lyons's words, "It may be impossible to deter this Government from offering provocations to Great Britain, which neither our honour nor our interest will allow us to brook." Ibid., Lord Lyons to Lord John Russell, May 20, 1861.

53. Ibid., Lord Lyons to Lord John Russell, May 6, 1861.

54. Adams, *Charles Francis Adams, 1835–1915*, p. 89.

55. Russell, *My Diary North and South*, p. 126, May 7, 1861.

56. Ibid., p. 104, April 27, 1861.

57. *The Times*, April 30, 1861.

58. Russell, *My Diary North and South*, p. 119, May 5, 1861.

59. *The Times*, May 7, 1861.

60. Russell, *My Diary North and South*, p. 124, May 7, 1861.

61. Adams, "The British Proclamation of May, 1861," p. 207, Consul Bunch to Lord John Russell, February 28, 1861.

62. Russell, *My Diary North and South*, p. 128, May 7, 1861.

63. Crawford (ed.), *William Howard Russell's Civil War*, p. 52, May 7, 1861.

64. Robert Douthat Meade, *Judah P. Benjamin: Confederate Statesman* (Baton Rouge, La., 2001), pp. 172, 175.

65. Russell, *My Diary North and South*, p. 128, May 7, 1861.

66. Meade, *Judah P. Benjamin*, p. 172.

67. Ibid., p. 166. During his long imprisonment after the war, Jefferson Davis allegedly told his doctor that he had wanted to send 3 million bales of cotton to Europe before the blockade took effect. It never happened because he "had not time to study and take the responsibility of directing until too late." *Prison*

Life of Jefferson Davis by Dr. Cravens, quoted in *Confederate Veteran*, 24 (1916), p. 207. Douglas B. Ball also exonerates Davis and instead blames the secretary of the treasury, Christopher Memminger, for being shortsighted and vacillating on the subject until it was too late: *Financial Failure and Confederate Defeat* (Champaign, Ill., 1991), pp. 88–96. Where the ships would have come from to ship 3 million bales, however, is not clear.

68. Russell, *My Diary North and South*, p. 130, May 7, 1861.
69. F. L. Owsley, *King Cotton Diplomacy* (2nd ed., Chicago, 1959), p. 24, June 4, 1861.

Chapter 4: Expectations Are Dashed

1. William S. Walsh, *Abraham Lincoln and the London Punch* (New York, 1909), p. 24.
2. *MPUS*, no. 330, Dallas to Seward, April 9, 1861.
3. Donald Bellows, "A Study of British Conservative Reaction to the American Civil War," *Journal of Southern History*, 51/4 (Nov. 1985), pp. 505–26, at p. 511.
4. *MPUS*, no. 330, Dallas to Seward, April 9, 1861.
5. Brian Jenkins, "Sir William Gregory: Champion of the Confederacy," *History Today*, 28 (1978), p. 323.
6. Charles Francis Adams, Jr., "The British Proclamation of May, 1861," *Massachusetts Historical Society Proceedings*, 48 (1915), pp. 190–241, at p. 209, Bunch to Russell, March 21, 1861.
7. Sarah Agnes Wallace and Frances Elma Gillespie (eds.), *Journal of Benjamin Moran, 1857–1865*, 2 vols. (Chicago, 1948, 1949), vol. 1, p. 809, May 13, 1861.
8. PRO 30/22/21, ff. 469–71, Palmerston to Russell, April 27, 1861. They were flummoxed by having no American to speak to on the issue. On May 5 (f. 472), Palmerston wrote to Russell that he had received a visit from an agent of Rothschilds, who read a letter from August Belmont urging mediation: "I stated to him also the obvious objections to any step on our part at the present moment but I admitted the great importance of the matter and it desires to be fully weighed and considered." Palmerston suggested they could try communicating "confidentially with the South by the men who have come over here from there; and with the North by Dallas who is about to return in a few days. Dallas, it is true, is not a political friend of Lincoln and on the contrary rather leans to the South, but still he might be an organ, if it should be deemed prudent to take any step."
9. PRO NI T/1585A, Private John Thompson to father, April 28, 1861.
10. *Illustrated London News*, May 4, 1861.
11. *Economist*, May 4, 1861.
12. *Saturday Review*, March 30, 1861.
13. Wallace and Gillespie (eds.), *The Journal of Benjamin Moran*, vol. 1, p. 796, April 5, 1861, p. 799, April 18, 1861, p. 802, April 27, 1861.
14. A. L. Kennedy (ed.), *My Dear Duchess: Social and Political Letters to the Duchess of Manchester, 1858–1869* (London, 1956), p. 154, Lord Clarendon to Duchess of Manchester, May 8, 1861.
15. British Sessional Papers, 1861, vol. 63, Command Paper No. 2910, pp. 210–11, May 3, 1861.

16. *Letters of Sir George Cornewall Lewis,* ed. G. F. Lewis (London, 1870), pp. 395–96, G. C. Lewis to Sir Edmund Head, May 13, 1861.

17. K. D. Reynolds, *Aristocratic Women and Political Society in Victorian Britain* (Oxford, 1998), p. 124, Duchess of Sutherland to Gladstone, May 25, 1861, BL Add. MS 44325, ff. 137–79, and Duchess of Sutherland to Gladstone, May 28, 1861, f. 144.

18. BL Add. MSS 44531, Gladstone to Duchess of Sutherland, May 29, 1861.

19. *BDOFA,* part I, ser. C, vol. 5, p. 199, Lord John Russell to Lord Lyons, May 11, 1861.

20. Even before the proclamation, the U.S. secretary of war, Simon Cameron, had to gently but firmly reject offers from Canadians who were eager to raise regiments for the North. OR, ser. 3, vol. 1, ser. 122, no. 6.

21. After the war, the United States claimed that Britain had acted without provocation and with malign intent. However, as D. P. Crook, C. F. Adams, Jr., and others argue, the cabinet had more than enough information and reason to take this route. Lord Russell knew by May 11, thanks to the consul in New York, that Lincoln had proclaimed the blockade and called for 75,000 soldiers—and that the Confederacy had a president, functioning legislature, a constitution, judges, customs officers, armies, and a flag. See, for example, D. P. Crook, *The North, the South, and the Powers, 1861–1865* (New York, 1974), passim.

22. ORN, ser. 2, vol. 3, p. 215, Yancey and Mann to Toombs, May 21, 1861.

23. Henry Adams, *The Education of Henry Adams,* ed. Ernest Samuels (New York, 1973), p. 116.

24. MHS, Adams MSS, Diary of Charles Francis Adams, July 11, 1861.

25. The legation shuttled first to 7 Duke Street on May 20, and then to 17 St. George's Place on June 1. The building was adequate but on the small side. The house he found for his family, 52 Grosvenor Square, had also been his grandfather's residence during his posting in London.

26. W. C. Ford (ed.), *Letters of Henry Adams, 1858–1891,* 2 vols. (Boston, 1930–38), vol. 1, p. 90, Henry Adams to Charles Francis Adams, Jr., May 16, 1861.

27. Quoted in Asa Briggs, *Victorian People* (London, 1954), p. 206.

28. T. Wemyss Reid, *Life of the Right Honourable William Edward Forster* (London, 1888), p. 333, Forster to Ellis Yarnall, May 10, 1861.

29. Adams, *The Education of Henry Adams,* p. 124.

30. Trinity College Library, Cambridge, Houghton MS CA9/66, Milnes to Sir Charles J. MacCarthy, June 25, 1861.

31. *George Douglas, Eighth Duke of Argyll (1823–1900): Autobiography and Memoirs,* ed. the Dowager Duchess of Argyll, 2 vols. (London, 1906), vol. 2, p. 170, Argyll to John Motley, May 14, 1861.

32. MHS, Adams MSS, Diary of Charles Francis Adams, May 15, 1861.

33. Ibid., May 16, 1861.

34. Ibid.

35. Charles Vandersee, "Henry Adams Behind the Scenes: Civil War Letters to Frederick W. Seward," *Bulletin of the New York Public Library,* 71/4 (1967), p. 248. Otherwise, Henry had written to Frederick Seward, every staff member would be new and "you will see at once what a position the Embassy would be in."

36. G. P. Gooch (ed.), *The Later Correspondence of Lord John Russell, 1840–1878*, 2 vols. (London, 1925), vol. 2, p. 320, Lord John Russell to Lord Cowley, June 13, 1861.

37. MHS, Adams MSS, Diary of Charles Francis Adams, May 18, 1861.

38. Edward L. Pierce (ed.), *Memoir and Letters of Charles Sumner*, 4 vols. (Boston, 1894), vol. 4: *1860–1870*, p. 31, Argyll to Sumner, June 4, 1861.

39. Gooch (ed.), *The Later Correspondence of Lord John Russell*, vol. 2, p. 320, Russell to Lord Cowley, June 13, 1861.

40. Hansard, 3rd ser., vol. 163, col. 277, May 30, 1861.

41. C. Vann Woodward (ed.), *Mary Chesnut's Civil War* (repr., New Haven, 1981), p. 67.

42. Seward's new accommodation was called the "Old Club House." Two years before he moved in, it was the scene of Daniel Sickles's notorious murder of Phillip Barton Key, his wife's alleged lover. Sickles shot Key in cold blood on the street in front of the house, and his victim was carried inside, where he bled to death in the room that became Seward's parlor.

43. David Herbert Donald, *Charles Sumner and the Rights of Man* (New York, 1970), p. 21.

44. Ibid., p. 25.

45. *Tropic Wind*, *Hiawatha*, *Octavia*, and *Haxall*.

46. BDOFA, part I, ser. C, vol. 5, p. 209, doc. 172, Lyons to Russell, May 2, 1861.

47. Adam Gurowski, *Diary from March 4, 1861 to November 12, 1862* (Boston, 1862), pp. 37–50.

48. PRO 30/22/35, ff. 96–98, Lyons to Russell, June 4, 1861; PRO 30/23/35, ff. 99–100, Lyons to Russell, June 10, 1861.

49. George Templeton Strong, *Diary of the Civil War, 1860–1865*, ed. Allan Nevins (New York, 1962), p. 145, May 22, 1861.

50. G. H. Warren, *Fountain of Discontent: The Trent Affair and Freedom of the Seas* (Boston, 1981), p. 84.

51. MHS, Adams MSS, Diary of Charles Francis Adams, June 1, 1861.

52. Ford (ed.), *Letters of Henry Adams*, vol. 1, p. 93, Henry Adams to Charles Francis Adams, Jr., June 10–11, 1861.

53. Designed by Isambard Kingdom Brunel, the ship was five times the size of its nearest rival. In addition to the 2,000 troops on board, there were more than 470 women and children, 122 horses, and 400 crew, making a total of around 3,000. During the voyage, two women gave birth, and five stowaways were discovered. G. H. Warren, *Fountain of Discontent*, p. 87.

54. MHS, Adams MSS, Diary of Charles Francis Adams, June 12, 1861.

55. Allan Nevins, *The War for the Union*, 4 vols.; vol. 2: *War Becomes Revolution, 1862–1863* (New York, 1960), p. 245.

56. MHS, Adams MSS, Diary of Charles Francis Adams, June 5, 1861.

57. W. C. Ford (ed.), *A Cycle of Adams Letters, 1861–1865*, 2 vols. (Boston, 1920), vol. 1, pp. 13–15, Charles Francis Adams to Charles Francis Adams, Jr., June 21, 1861.

58. Ibid., pp. 19–22, Charles Francis Adams to Charles Francis Adams, Jr., July 18, 1861.

59. MHS, Adams MSS, Diary of Charles Francis Adams, June 17, 1861.

60. Carl Schurz, "Reminiscences of a Long Life," *McClure's*, 26/1 (Nov. 1905), p. 642. Schurz went on to say: "I left Mr. Adams with the highest impression of his patriotism, of the clearness and exactness of his mind, of the breadth of his knowledge, and his efficiency as a diplomat. . . . He was, in the best sense of the term, a serious and sober man. Indeed, he lacked some of the social qualities which it may be desirable that a diplomat should possess. While he kept up in London an establishment fitting the dignity of his position as the representative of a great republic and performed his social duties with punctilious care, he was not a pleasing after-dinner speaker, nor a shining figure on festive occasions. He lacked the gifts of personal magnetism or sympathetic charm that would draw men to him."

61. MHS, Adams MSS, Diary of Charles Francis Adams, August 18, 1861.

62. Ibid., June 5, 1861.

63. Ford (ed.), *A Cycle of Adams Letters*, vol. 1, p. 7, Charles Francis Adams to Charles Francis Adams, Jr., June 7, 1861.

64. Adams, *The Education of Henry Adams*, pp. 197, 196, 134.

65. Wallace and Gillespie (eds.), *The Journal of Benjamin Moran*, vol. 2, June 25, 1861, p. 834.

66. MHS, Adams MSS, Diary of Charles Francis Adams, June 18, 1861.

67. Wendy Hinde, *Richard Cobden* (New Haven, 1987), p. 305. "As for the separation of the States," he wrote, "if I were a citizen of a free state, I should vote with both hands for a dissolution of partnership with the slave states."

68. Hansard, 3rd ser., vol. 163, col. 192, May 28, 1861.

69. Ford (ed.), *A Cycle of Adams Letters*, vol. 1, pp. 13–15, Charles Francis Adams to Charles Francis Adams, Jr., June 21, 1861.

70. J.A.V. Chapple and Arthur Pollard (eds.), *The Letters of Mrs. Gaskell* (New York, 1997), pp. 654–58, Gaskell to Charles Elliot Norton, June 10, 1861.

71. Belle Becker Sideman and Lillian Friedman (eds.), *Europe Looks at the Civil War* (New York, 1960), p. 62, Darwin to Asa Gray, June 5, 1861.

72. Clare Taylor, *Britain and American Abolitionists: An Episode in Transatlantic Understanding* (Edinburgh, 1974), p. 407, R. D. Webb, July 16, 1861.

73. February 2, 1861. But far more inflammatory had been Seward's recent note, sent to all foreign governments, asking them to refuse asylum to escaped slaves.

74. *Englishwoman's Journal*, June 1861.

75. ORN, ser. 2, vol. 3, p. 202, Yancey, Rost, and Mann to Toombs, July 15, 1861.

76. William L. Yancey Papers, Alabama Department of Archives and History, Yancey to R. Chapman, July 3, 1861.

Chapter 5: The Rebel Yell

1. Martin Crawford (ed.), *William Howard Russell's Civil War: Private Diary and Letters, 1861–1862* (Athens, Ga., 1992), p. 58, May 21, 1861.

2. William Howard Russell, *My Diary North and South* (Philadelphia, 1988), ed. Eugene H. Berwanger, p. 172, June 1, 1861.

3. Crawford (ed.), *William Howard Russell's Civil War*, p. 59, May 24, 1861.

4. Ibid., p. 58, May 25, 1861.

5. Out of a total population of 168,675, 66,268 were immigrants.

6. Crawford (ed.), *William Howard Russell's Civil War*, p. 62, May 29, 1861.

7. *The Times*, May 22, 1861. For a fascinating discussion on the ethnic components of Louisiana's regiments, see Ella Lonn, *Foreigners in the Confederacy* (Chapel Hill, N.C., repr. 2001), pp. 100–113.

8. PRO FO5/788, f. 171, Mure to Lord John Russell, July 9, 1861.

9. Russell, *My Diary North and South*, p. 166, May 27, 1861.

10. William Watson, *Life in the Confederate Army: Being the Observations and Experiences of an Alien in the South During the Civil War* (London, 1887; repr. Baton Rouge, La., 1995), pp. 122, 397.

11. Pembrokeshire RO, HDX/559/52, William Benyon to brother Thomas in Wales, May 15, 1861.

12. Nathaniel Cheairs Hughes, Jr. (ed.), *Sir Henry Morton Stanley, Confederate* (Baton Rouge, La., 2000), p. 95.

13. The other problem for Mure was the harassment of black British subjects. He arranged for a black Crimean War veteran to be spirited out of the city, and paid $17.40 from consulate funds to secure the release of Alexander White, another black British subject languishing in jail. PRO FO5/788, f. 171, Mure to Lord John Russell, July 9, 1861. Russell, *My Diary North and South*, p. 171, June 1, 1861.

14. Mary Sophia Hill, *A British Subject's Recollections of the Confederacy* (Baltimore, 1875), p. 7, June 8, 1861.

15. Ibid.

16. Ibid., p. 60.

17. Ibid., p. 8, June 20, 1861.

18. Columbia University, Blackwell MSS, Elizabeth Blackwell to Barbara Bodichon, April 23, 1861.

19. William Quentin Maxwell, *Lincoln's Fifth Wheel* (New York, 1956), p. 6.

20. Ibid., p. 8.

21. Columbia University, Blackwell MSS, Elizabeth Blackwell to Barbara Bodichon, June 6, 1861.

22. Ibid.

23. Dorothy Clarke Wilson, *Lone Woman* (Boston, 1970), p. 388.

24. Columbia University, Blackwell MSS, Elizabeth Blackwell to Barbara Bodichon, June 6, 1861.

25. Wellcome Institute, Verney MS 8999/24, Florence Nightingale to Sir Henry Verney, June 11, 1861.

26. Columbia University, Blackwell MSS, Elizabeth Blackwell to Barbara Bodichon, June 6, 1861.

27. Henri Le Caron, *Twenty-Five Years in the Secret Service: The Recollections of a Spy* (16th edn., London, 1893), p. 10.

28. PRO FO282/6, ff. 350–51, d. 20, Archibald to Lord Lyons, April 29, 1861.

29. PRO 33/22/39, f. 71, Archibald to Lord John Russell, April 24, 1861.

30. PRO FO282/6, ff. 335–46, Archibald to Lord John Russell, April 24, 1861.

31. Some, like Mr. Murphy from Petersfield, England, were running away from debts, wives, and other burdens. His wife tried everything to locate him, even writing to President Lincoln to ask "Your Majesty" for help since "myself and dear baby are starving. . . . Should he be with any of your magistys [*sic*] regiments will you send the word." NARA, RG94, entry 416, box 47, 1861 E–K, S. 396, Mrs. E Murphy to President Lincoln, August 29, 1861.

32. Corcoran's insubordination led to his arrest and appearance before a court martial. He was in limbo, still under arrest but with no trial in sight, until the Battle of Fort Sumter. Corcoran immediately offered the services of the 69th. This posed an uncomfortable dilemma for the authorities until Governor Morgan issued a pardon and the charges against Corcoran could be dismissed.

33. Richard Demeter, *The Fighting 69th: A History* (Pasadena, Calif., 2002), p. 59. The 69th's flag boldly proclaimed the allegiance of its members. Made of green cloth, at the top was the Fenian symbol of the sunburst, in the middle a golden harp, and along the bottom a wreath of shamrocks.

34. BL Add. MS 415670, f. 214, Herbert to mother, July 18, 1861.

35. Wiltshire and Swindon RO, 2536/10, Edward Best to Aunt Sophie, May 10, 1861.

36. PRO FO282/8, ff. 22–24, Edward Archibald to Lord John Russell, April 26, 1861.

37. The best history of the British origins of the 36th New York Volunteers can be found at http://www.conversantcomm.pl/36thNY/History2.htm.

38. *Boston Herald*, April 20, 1861, p. 4, col. 1.

39. *Albion*, May 25, 1861.

40. New-York Historical Society, *Narrative of Ebenezer Wells* (*c.* 1881), n.pp., *c.* June 2, 1861.

41. Ibid.

42. Russell, *My Diary North and South*, p. 376.

43. *Roxbury City Gazette,* June 27, 1861, p. 2.

44. *Illustrated London News*, July 6, 1861, p. 22.

45. James M. Perry, *A Bohemian Brigade: The Civil War Correspondents* (Hoboken, N.J., 2000), p. 190.

46. *Illustrated London News*, August 3, 1861, p. 121.

47. Ibid., July 6, 1861, p. 22.

48. Crawford (ed.), *William Howard Russell's Civil War*, p. 74, Russell to J. C. Bancroft Davis, June 22, 1861.

49. Russell, *My Diary North and South* (London, 1863), p. 377. Berwanger's 1988 abridged edition does not include this observation.

50. Crawford (ed.), *William Howard Russell's Civil War,* p. 80, Diary, July 4, 1861.

51. Russell, *My Diary North and South*, ed. Berwanger, p. 429.

52. Crawford (ed.), *William Howard Russell's Civil War*, p. 79, Diary, July 3, 1861.

53. Russell, *My Diary North and South*, ed. Berwanger, p. 227.

54. W. C. Ford (ed.), *A Cycle of Adams Letters, 1861–1865,* 2 vols. (Boston, 1920), vol. 1, Charles Francis Adams, Jr., to Charles Francis Adams, July 2, 1861.

55. Doris Kearns Goodwin, *Team of Rivals* (New York, 2005), p. 364.

56. PRO 30/22/35, Lord Lyons to Lord John Russell, July 20, 1861.

57. Allan Nevins, *The War for the Union*, 4 vols.; vol. 1: *The Improvised War, 1861–1862* (New York, 1959), p. 214.

58. William Mark McKnight, *Blue Bonnets o'er the Border: The 79th New York Cameron Highlanders* (Shippensburg, Pa., 1998), p. 23.

59. Russell, *My Diary North and South*, ed. Berwanger, p. 240, July 13, 1861. He

also doubted that any army could reconquer so vast a territory as the South. "It is one thing," he opined in *The Times,* "to drive the rebels from the south bank of the Potomac, or even to occupy Richmond, but another to reduce and hold in permanent subjection a tract of country nearly as large as Russia." *The Times,* July 18, 1861.

60. John Bakeless, *Spies of the Confederacy* (New York, 1970), p. 10.
61. The value of her work has since been questioned, but there is no doubt that she was able to send advance warning to General Beauregard to prepare for the imminent arrival of the Federal army in Virginia. Edwin Fishel, *The Secret War for the Union* (New York, 1996), p. 59.
62. Hill, *A British Subject's Recollections of the Confederacy,* p. 8, July 4, 1861.
63. Russell, *My Diary North and South* (London, 1863), p. 438. Berwanger's 1988 abridged edition does not include this exchange.
64. Russell, *My Diary North and South,* ed. Berwanger, p. 266.
65. Ibid.
66. *The Times,* August 6, 1861.
67. *Illustrated London News,* August 10, 1861, pp. 143–45.
68. James M. McPherson, *Battle Cry of Freedom* (London, 1990), p. 342.
69. McKnight, *Blue Bonnets o'er the Border,* p. 27.
70. Ibid., p. 28.
71. Russell, *My Diary North and South,* ed. Berwanger, p. 268.
72. New-York Historical Society, *Narrative of Ebenezer Wells.*
73. *The Times,* August 6, 1861.
74. Russell, *My Diary North and South,* ed. Berwanger, p. 277.
75. Hill, *A British Subject's Recollections of the Confederacy,* p. 10.

Chapter 6: War by Other Means

1. *The Times,* August 6, 1861.
2. William Howard Russell, *My Diary North and South,* ed. Eugene H. Berwanger (New York, 1988), p. 278.
3. Allan Nevins, *The War for the Union,* 4 vols; vol. 1: *The Improvised War, 1861–1862* (New York, 1959), p. 221.
4. The Confederates suffered 400 killed and 1,600 wounded, and the Federals 625 killed, 950 wounded, and 1,200 captured. James M. McPherson, *Battle Cry of Freedom* (London, 1988), p. 347.
5. James McPherson, *Tried by War* (New York, 2008), p. 41.
6. New-York Historical Society, *Narrative of Ebenezer Wells* (c. 1881), n.pp., August 15, 1861.
7. Martin Crawford (ed.), *William Howard Russell's Civil War: Private Diary and Letters, 1861–1862* (Athens, Ga., 1992), p. 110, August 26, 1861.
8. Camille Ferri Pisani, *Prince Napoleon in America,* trans. Georges Joyaux, (Bloomington, Ind., 1959), p. 100.
9. Crawford (ed.), *William Howard Russell's Civil War,* p. 100, August 7, 1861.
10. West Sussex RO, Lyons MSS, Box 299, August 5, 1861.
11. Pisani, *Prince Napoleon in America,* p. 113.
12. Ibid., p. 130.

13. Jeff Kinard, *Lafayette of the South* (College Station, Tex., 2001), p. 19.

14. PRO 30/22/35, Lord Lyons to Lord Russell, September 6, 1861. Bunch had been entrusted with secret negotiations between the South and Britain and France to end privateering. This too was exposed in the diplomatic bag.

15. Another piece of bad luck was Robert Mure's surname—the same as the consul's in New Orleans. U.S. newspapers erroneously claimed that the two men were related, which made it look as though the British consuls in the South were in cahoots with one another against the North.

16. West Sussex RO, Lyons MSS, Box 299, Lord Lyons to sister, August 23, 1861.

17. Alan Hankinson, *Man of Wars: William Howard Russell of "The Times," 1820–1907* (London, 1982), p. 170.

18. Russell, *My Diary North and South*, pp. 301, 305.

19. The letter was purportedly from an English soldier, R. Young Atkins, "late of the Garibaldi Brigade," who fought at Bull Run. The real Atkins was from Cork, his name was Richard Goring, and whether he wrote any of the rubbish in the letter remains doubtful.

20. C. Vann Woodward (ed.), *Mary Chesnut's Civil War* (New Haven, 1981), p. 159, August 23, 1861.

21. Brian Jenkins, *Britain and the War for the Union*, 2 vols. (Montreal, 1974, 1980), vol. 1, p. 154. It was a coincidence that John Bright broke his public silence about the Civil War just three days before the news of Bull Run. Neither the timing nor his views found favor with the voters of Rochdale and the Radical candidate lost the election.

22. Stanley Morison, *The Times: The History of The Times; The Tradition Established, 1841–84* (London, 1939), p. 367.

23. Durham University, General Charles Grey MSS, GRE/D/VI/6, General Grey to 3rd Earl Grey, August 31, 1861.

24. Susan St. John Mildmay and Herbert St. John Mildmay (eds.), *John Lothrop Motley and His Family: Further Letters and Records* (London, 1910), p. 112.

25. BL Add. MS 415670, f. 216, George Henry Herbert to Jack, October 12, 1861.

26. He had allowed his mind to wander during drill practice. Unfortunately, wrote the regimental historian, when the order to march was given he "failed to move, and as a consequence the regiment 'stood fast' while all the other regiments moved off. For an instant the General seemed paralyzed with astonishment." He then bellowed at the top of his voice, " 'Move! Move! For God's sake, you little bandy-legged man, move!' Herbert moved." When the practice was over, five hundred men turned in Herbert's direction and shouted in unison, "Move! Move, you little bandy-legged man!" Matthew J. Graham, *The Ninth Regiment New York Volunteers* (Lancaster, Ohio, repr. 1997), p. 66.

27. BL Add. MS 415670, f. 216, Herbert to Jack, July 18, 1861.

28. Sarah Forbes Hughes (ed.), *Letters and Recollections of John Murray Forbes*, 2 vols. (Boston, 1900), vol. 1, pp. 234–35, Charles Francis Adams to J. M. Forbes, August 30, 1861.

29. MHS, Adams MSS, Diary of Charles Francis Adams, vol. 76, August 6, 1861.

30. Deborah Logan (ed.), *The Collected Letters of Harriet Martineau*, 5 vols. (London, 2007), vol. 4, p. 283, Martineau to Henry Reeve, July 28, 1861.

31. *Morning Star*, July 15, 1861.

32. *Letters, Speeches, and Addresses of August Belmont* (n.p., 1890), p. 77, Belmont to Seward, July 30, 1861.

33. *Illustrated London News*, August 10, 1861.

34. ORN, ser. 2, vol. 3, p. 247, Lord Russell to Yancey, Rost, and Mann, August 24, 1861.

35. James D. Richardson (ed.), *A Compilation of Messages and Papers of the Confederacy Including the Diplomatic Correspondence, 1861–1865*, 2 vols. (Nashville, Tenn., 1905), vol. 2, p. 53, Yancey and Mann to Robert Toombs, August 1, 1861.

36. Charles McCaskill, "An Estimate of Edwin DeLeon's Report of His Service to the Confederacy," MA thesis, University of South Carolina, 1950, p. 24.

37. ORN, ser. 2, vol. 3, p. 233, Mann to Toombs, August 3, 1861. Mann continued: "The modus operandi would be this: That you should employ a strictly trustworthy individual to prepare a short statement of the most important occurrences, and transmit it per Cunard steamer to us, under cover to 'M'Iver, agent Cunard Packets, Queenstown, Ireland.' Reuter will give him directions to telegraph the contents to us the moment the steamer touches at that place. If it were deemed important to communicate twice a week, then a dispatch might be sent to 'Joseph Sharpe,' Southampton, England."

38. Sarah Agnes Wallace and Frances Elma Gillespie (eds.), *The Journal of Benjamin Moran, 1857–1865*, 2 vols. (Chicago, 1948, 1949), vol. 2, pp. 868–69, August 26, 1861.

39. NARA, M.T-396, roll 4, vol. 4, U.S. consul in Leith to Seward, August 29, 1861.

40. For example, Edward Anderson complained, "I called last night on Mr. Yancey to protest against his recommendation of English adventurers for appointment in the Confederate Army. The case in point was that of a young man who for some days had been hanging around my quarters seeking to get a recommendation to the authorities in Richmond, and who from all I could gather was an unprincipled trifling fellow. I had refused to endorse him and he went from me to Yancey who, without any knowledge whatever of the man, gave him letters to the Secy of War which procured him employment as an officer. I subsequently learned that this fellow turned out a Yankee spy." W. S. Hoole, *Confederate Foreign Agent: The European Diary of Major Edward C. Anderson* (Tuscaloosa, Ala., 1976), pp. 43–44, August 7, 1861.

41. Joseph A. Fry, *Henry S. Sanford: Diplomacy and Business in Nineteenth-Century America* (Reno, Nev., 1982), p. 50.

42. McPherson, *Battle Cry of Freedom*, p. 318.

43. Frank J. Merli, *Great Britain and the Confederate Navy* (Bloomington, Ind., 1965), p. 17.

44. R. I. Lester, *Confederate Financing and Purchasing in Great Britain* (Charlottesville, Va., 1975), p. 148.

45. James D. Bulloch, *The Secret Service of the Confederate States in Europe*, 2 vols. (New York, 1884), vol. 1, p. 32.

46. McCaskill, "An Estimate of Edwin DeLeon's Report of His Service to the Confederacy," p. 22.

47. At 10 Rumford Place.

48. David Hepburn Milton, *Lincoln's Spymaster: Thomas Haines Dudley and the Liverpool Network* (Mechanicsburg, Pa., 2003), p. 29.

49. ORN, ser. 2, vol. 2, pp. 83–87, James Bulloch to Mallory, August 18, 1861.

50. Fry, *Henry S. Sanford*, p. 37.

51. Harriet Chappell Owsley, "Henry Shelton Sanford and Federal Surveillance Abroad, 1861–1865," *Mississippi Valley Historical Review*, 48 (Sept. 1961), p. 212.

52. Ibid., pp. 212–13.

53. Anderson never told Huse that his original mission had been to report on the latter's operations and, if necessary, send him home. Huse's determination to beat out Federal competition looked like reckless spending to the Confederate authorities, who had no idea of the obstacles impeding their agent. Some even suspected him of harboring Union sympathies because he did not hate all Northerners. But after three weeks' acquaintance Anderson was able to report that Huse's only defect was that he sometimes lacked discretion.

54. Neill F. Sanders, "Consul, Commander and Minister: A New Perspective on the Queenstown Incident," *Lincoln Herald*, 81/2 (1979), pp. 102–15, at p. 103, Sanford to Seward, July 4, 1861.

55. Owsley, "Henry Shelton Sanford and Federal Surveillance Abroad," p. 214.

56. Hoole, *Confederate Foreign Agent*, p. 64, September 26, 1861.

57. Ibid., p. 36, July 25, 1861.

58. Samuel Bernard Thompson, *Confederate Purchasing Operations Abroad* (Gloucester, Mass., 1973), p. 16.

59. Owsley, "Henry Shelton Sanford and Federal Surveillance Abroad," p. 214.

60. Warren F. Spencer, *The Confederate Navy in Europe* (Tuscaloosa, Ala., 1983), p. 18.

61. David Hollett, *The Alabama Affair: The British Shipyards Conspiracy in the American Civil War* (Wilmslow, 1993), p. 16.

62. OR, ser. I, vol. 4, no. 127, p. 577, L. P. Walker to Caleb Huse and Edward Anderson, August 17, 1861.

63. ORN, ser. 2, vol. 2, pp. 83–87, James Bulloch to Stephen Mallory, August 18, 1861.

64. Neill F. Sanders, "Lincoln's Consuls in the British Isles, 1861–1865," Ph.D. thesis, University of Missouri, 1971, p. 34.

65. Peter Barton, "The First Blockade Runner and the 'Another Alabama': Some Tees and Hartlepool Ships That Worried the Union," *Mariner's Mirror*, 81 (1995), pp. 45–64.

66. F. L. Owsley, *King Cotton Diplomacy* (2nd ed., Chicago, 1959), p. 233.

67. Stephen R. Wise, *Lifeline of the Confederacy: Blockade Running During the Civil War* (Columbia, S.C., 1988), p. 24.

68. Anthony Trollope, *North America* (repr. London, 1968), p. 20.

69. New-York Historical Society, *Narrative of Ebenezer Wells*, October 13, 1861. Despite the relative disappointment of Lewinsville, McClellan decided that the 79th merited the return of its colors. They were handed over during a solemn ceremony.

70. Vizetelly provided the *Illustrated London News* with a sketch of the wounded being greeted by General McClellan. The accompanying description was completely over the top: "He raised his hat as each poor fellow was borne from the ambulance to the hospital; and many whose eyes were fast glazing in death raised themselves . . . and smiled a last smile at their young and beloved General."

71. Russell, *My Diary North and South*, p. 318, October 10, 1861.

72. Ibid., p. 313, September 11, 1861.

73. Crawford (ed.), *William Howard Russell's Civil War*, p. 125, W. H. Russell to Delane, September 13, 1861.

74. John Black Atkins, *The Life of Sir William Howard Russell*, 2 vols. (London, 1911), vol. 2, p. 72.

75. Nevins, *The War for the Union*, vol. 1, p. 300. McClellan actually had 152,000, but one-third were absent, under arrest, or otherwise unfit for duty.

76. PRO FO5/779, desp. 131, Consul Archibald to Lord Russell, September 25, 1861. By late summer, Archibald was making the five-hour journey to Lafayette on a weekly basis. He discovered extreme malnutrition among the men. Their food allotment should have been worth 43 cents a day, but theft by the guards reduced this to 10. Eugene H. Berwanger, *The British Foreign Service and the American Civil War* (Lexington, Ky., 1994), pp. 53–54.

77. Ibid., p. 55.

78. On September 25, Benjamin Moran wrote: "We have some very fine young fellows to see us for service in our army." Two days later, he wrote again: "There were several fine gentlemanly Englishmen here today." Wallace and Gillespie (eds.), *The Journal of Benjamin Moran*, vol. 2, pp. 883, 884, September 27, 1861.

79. Adams wrote that he was plagued with visitors because of "the notice current in the papers that I have authority to engage officers for the American service. The wish for adventure and pay is great in all the countries of Europe. I see something of it from almost every nation." MHS, Adams MSS, Diary of Charles Francis Adams, vol. 76, September 30, 1861. Adams had to be extremely careful lest he attract the same charge of recruiting that led to the English minister, John Crampton, being expelled from Washington during the Crimean War. As far as he was concerned, the would-be Federals could do whatever they wished so long as the legation was not made a party to their plans.

80. Russell, *My Diary, North and South*, p. 291.

81. One issue of *Frank Leslie's Illustrated Newspaper* listed the Count de Sayre, the Baron de Schonen, and Major General Charles F. Havelock of the Imperial Ottoman Army all arriving simultaneously in Washington. Ella Lonn has identified dozens of British officers and soldiers of fortune who held positions of responsibility in the Union army. Two of the most distinguished were Robert Johnstone and John Lambert. Ella Lonn, *Foreigners in the Union Army and Navy* (New York, repr. 1969), p. 283. Robert Johnstone was lieutenant colonel of the 5th New York Cavalry until August 1863. When questioned about his reasons for joining, he explained that all his life he had delighted in anything big, and that he could not remain idle while so big a nation was being split asunder. And John Lambert was a captain in the 33rd New Jersey Volunteers who later became acting inspector general on General David Hunter's staff.

82. New York State Library, Edwin Morgan MSS, box 19, f. 11, L.D.H. Currie to Governor Morgan, March 2, 1863.

83. PRO 30/22/35, f. 229–24, Lord Lyons to Lord Russell, September 9, 1861. (The origin of the anecdote remains a mystery. Lord Lyons merely wrote:

"Seward exercises upon the reports of spies and informers, the power of depriving British subjects of their liberty, or retaining them in prison, or liberating them, by his sole will and pleasure.")

84. Berwanger, *The British Foreign Service and the American Civil War*, p. 53.
85. *BDOFA*, part I, ser. C, vol. 5, p. 307, Lord Lyons to Lord Russell, September 6, 1861.
86. Crawford (ed.), *William Howard Russell's Civil War*, p. 150, Russell to Delane, October 14, 1861.
87. Ibid., p. 125, Russell to Delane, September 13, 1861.

Chapter 7: "It Takes Two to Make a Quarrel"
1. Hudson Strode, *Jefferson Davis: Confederate President*, 3 vols. (New York, 1959), vol. 1, p. 141.
2. W. S. Hoole, *Confederate Foreign Agent: The European Diary of Major Edward C. Anderson* (Tuscaloosa, Ala., 1976), p. 66, September 26, 1861.
3. Harriet Owsley, "Henry Shelton Sanford and Federal Surveillance Abroad, 1861–1865," *Mississippi Valley Historical Review*, 48 (Sept. 1961), p. 215.
4. Joseph A. Fry, *Henry S. Sanford: Diplomacy and Business in Nineteenth-Century America* (Reno, Nev., 1982), p. 45.
5. Sarah Agnes Wallace and Frances Elma Gillespie (eds.), *The Journal of Benjamin Moran, 1857–1865*, 2 vols. (Chicago, 1948, 1949), vol. 2, p. 899, October 31, 1861.
6. MHS, Adams MSS, Diary of Charles Francis Adams, September 21, 1861.
7. MHS, Charles Francis Adams, Notebook Reminiscences, September 18 1867. Russell was able to reassure Adams that Britain had no intention of going to war with Mexico.
8. MHS, Adams MSS, Diary of Charles Francis Adams, vol. 76, October 1, 1861.
9. James D. Bulloch, *The Secret Service of the Confederate States in Europe*, 2 vols. (New York, 1884), vol. 1, p. 115.
10. Hoole, *Confederate Foreign Agent*, p. 82, October 15, 1861.
11. Wallace and Gillespie (eds.), *The Journal of Benjamin Moran*, vol. 2, p. 892, October 17, 1861.
12. PRO 30/22/35 ff. 295–300, Lyons to Russell, October 22, 1861.
13. Martin Crawford (ed.), *William Howard Russell's Civil War: Private Diary and Letters, 1861–1862* (Athens, Ga., 1992), p. 159, Russell to J. C. Bancroft Davis, October 19, 1861.
14. PRO 30/22/35 ff. 229–40, Lyons to Russell, September 6, 1861.
15. James M. McPherson, *Battle Cry of Freedom* (London, 1988), p. 357.
16. These included a letter sent to all the governors of states that possessed a port or coastal city, telling them to be prepared for a foreign invasion.
17. Sumner certainly knew the truth about France. Harriet Martineau wrote to him, "I know that our Cabinet has had, and still has, the utmost difficulty in preventing the French and Spanish governments from breaking the blockade." Deborah Logan (ed.), *The Collected Letters of Harriet Martineau*, 5 vols. (London, 2007), vol. 4, p. 307, Martineau to Sumner, c. November 1861.
18. *BDOFA*, Part 1, ser. C, vol. 5, doc. 336, pp. 331–32, Lyons to Russell, October 28, 1861.

19. PRO 30/22/35 ff. 263–78, private, Lyons to Russell, October 4, 1861.

20. E. D. Adams, *Great Britain and the American Civil War*, 2 vols. in 1 (New York, 1958), vol. 1, p. 194.

21. PRO 30/22/35 ff. 340–44, Lyons to Russell, December 6, 1861.

22. Adams, *Great Britain and the American Civil War*, vol. 1, p. 194.

23. University of Southampton, Palmerston MSS, PP/GC/LE/144, Lewis to Palmerston, September 3, 1861.

24. *Reynolds's Newspaper*, September 29, 1861.

25. W. C. Ford (ed.), *A Cycle of Adams Letters, 1861–1865*, 2 vols. (Boston, 1920), vol. 1, pp. 48–50, Henry Adams to Charles Francis Adams, Jr., September 28, 1861.

26. Wallace and Gillespie (eds.), *The Journal of Benjamin Moran*, vol. 2, p. 911, November 25, 1861.

27. He gave one of his typical barnstorming speeches, eliciting cheers from the audience. However, Yancey overplayed his hand and referred to the South as "the land of the free and the home of the oppressed," which prompted *Punch* to remind him that the whites were the free and the blacks were the oppressed. Winthrop Donaldson Jordan and Edwin J. Pratt, *Europe and the American Civil War* (New York, 1931), p. 23.

28. ORN, ser. 2, vol. 3, pp. 222–23, Yancey and Mann to Robert Toombs, July 15, 1861.

29. R.J.M. Blackett, *Divided Hearts: Britain and the American Civil War* (Baton Rouge, La., 2001), p. 138.

30. "I often think of you, and wonder what your feelings are with regard to the fearful events now happening," Wilding told Hawthorne. In a long letter, he analyzed the current situation thus: "The anti-slavery people profess to believe that slavery has nothing to do with the struggle; that the Federal Government are no more contending for the abolition of slavery than are the Confederates. They won't see that the contest is for the abolition of slavery in the only way that reasonable men in America have ever supposed it possible, by confining it to its present limits; and that the South, rather than submit to that, will, if they can, destroy the Union. There are many reasons for this feeling in England. In the first place, I believe Englishmen instinctively sympathize with rebels—if the rebellion be not against England. A great many also desire to see the American Union divided, supposing that it will be less powerful, and less threatening to England. All the enemies of popular government—and there are plenty even in England—rejoice to see what they suppose to be the failure of Republican institutions." Julian Hawthorne (ed.), *Nathaniel Hawthorne and His Wife*, vol. 2 (Boston, 1884), pp. 165–66, Wilding to Hawthorne, November 14, 1861.

31. Ford (ed.), *A Cycle of Adams Letters*, vol. 1, pp. 52–53, Charles Francis Adams, Jr., to Henry Adams, October 6, 1861.

32. Ibid., pp. 61–63, Henry Adams to Charles Francis Adams, Jr., October 25, 1861.

33. Lord Russell told an audience in Newcastle on October 14, "I cannot help asking myself as affairs progress in the conflict, to what good can it lead?" According to *The Times*, Russell then warned his listeners that a moment might come when intervention in the American war would be inevitable. After all,

the paper reported him as saying, the war was not about slavery but about one side fighting for "empire, and the other for independence." (In fact, Russell had said "power" rather than "independence," which was less inflammatory. But someone at the paper had decided the phrase was too anodyne.) Norman Ferris, *Desperate Diplomacy: William H. Seward's Foreign Policy, 1861* (Knoxville, Tenn., 1976), p. 238, fn.

34. *Illustrated London News*, November 2, 1861.

35. Michael Burlingame and John R. Turner Ettlinger (eds.), *Inside Lincoln's White House: The Complete Civil War Diary of John Hay* (Carbondale, Ill., 1997), p. 26, October 12, 1861. Seward claimed absurdly to his wife on October 29 that the wicked machinations of Britain "made it doubtful whether we can escape the yet deeper and darker abyss of foreign war."

36. The consuls in Belfast, Glasgow, and Dublin all wrote strong letters on the subject.

37. John M. Taylor, *William Henry Seward: Lincoln's Right Hand* (New York, 1991), p. 192.

38. MHS, "Bright-Sumner Letters, 1861–1872," October 1912, pp. 93–165, Bright to Sumner, November 20, 1861. But if the *Leicester Guardian* was anything to go by, there was still an opportunity to influence public opinion toward the North: "By the domestic fireside, on the exchange, and in the counting house . . . every tide of events has been anxiously watched," it commented. The emotional response to the war was not "on account of the great commercial interests involved but the feeling that those taking part in the contest are bone of our bone, and flesh of our flesh." Blackett, *Divided Hearts*, p. 6.

39. Crawford (ed.), *William Howard Russell's Civil War*, p. 165, Russell to J. C. Bancroft Davis, November 6, 1861.

40. Ibid.

41. PRO FO5/779, desp. 164, Archibald to Lyons, November 2, 1861. PRO FO282/9, f. 79, d. 163, Archibald to Lyons, November 1, 1861.

42. Seward has "the power," Lyons added angrily, "of depriving British Subjects of their liberty, or retaining them in prison or liberating them by his own will and pleasure." PRO FO282/9, f. 79, d. 163, Archibald to Lyons, November 1, 1861.

43. Anthony Trollope, *North America* (repr. London, 1968), p. 139.

44. Edward Chalfant, "A War So Near," *Journal of Confederate History*, 6 (1990), p. 146.

45. Hoole, *Confederate Foreign Agent*, p. 88.

46. Stephen R. Wise, *Lifeline of the Confederacy: Blockade Running During the Civil War* (Columbia, S.C., 1988), p. 54.

47. New-York Historical Society, *Narrative of Ebeneezer Wells* (c. 1881), n.pp., c. November 9, 1861.

48. Hoole, *Confederate Foreign Agent*, p. 101.

49. James P. Gannon, *Irish Rebels, Confederate Tigers* (Mason City, Iowa, 1998), p. 10.

50. Mary Sophia Hill, *A British Subject's Recollections of the Confederacy* (Baltimore, 1875), p. 60.

51. Quoted in Robert Douthat Meade, *Judah P. Benjamin: Confederate Statesman* (Baton Rouge, La., 2001), p. 182.

52. Hoole, *Confederate Foreign Agent*, p. 102.

53. MHS, Adams MSS, Diary of Charles Francis Adams, vol. 76, November 2, 1861.

54. Wallace and Gillespie (eds.), *The Journal of Benjamin Moran*, vol. 2, p. 908, November 19, 1861.

55. Edward Chalfant, *Both Sides of the Ocean* (New York, 1982), p. 316.

56. PRO FO 198/21, p. 10, Lord Russell to Adams, November 28, 1861.

57. Henry Adams, *The Education of Henry Adams*, ed. Ernest Samuels (repr. Boston, 1973), p. 119.

58. Wallace and Gillespie (eds.), *The Journal of Benjamin Moran*, vol. 2, p. 913, November 27, 1861.

59. John Evan, *Atlantic Impact* (London, 1952), pp. 83–84. Karl Marx was scathing about Seward. His article for *Die Presse* on November 28 claimed, "We regard this latest operation of Mr. Seward as a characteristic act of tactlessness by self-conscious weakness simulating strength. If the naval incident hastens Seward's removal from the Washington Cabinet, the United States will have no reason to record it as an 'untoward event' in the annals of its Civil War."

60. MHS, Adams MSS, Diary of Charles Francis Adams, vol. 76, November 27, 1861.

61. Ibid., November 29, 1861.

62. *The Times*, November 29, 1861.

63. James Chambers, *Palmerston: The People's Darling* (London, 2004), p. 487, Palmerston to the Queen, December 5, 1861.

Chapter 8: The Lion Roars Back

1. William Howard Russell, *My Diary North and South*, ed. Eugene H. Berwanger (New York, 1988), p. 326, November 16, 1861. Russell made a mistake and called Macfarland, McClernand.

2. *BDOFA*, part I, ser. C, vol. 5, pp. 361–62, Lord Lyons to Lord Russell, November 19, 1861.

3. *New York Times*, November 18, 1861; *Sunday Transcript*, November 17, 1861.

4. For example, Seward's son Frederick, who was assistant secretary of state, wrote to the U.S. consul in Havana on November 22: "It gives the Department pleasure to acknowledge the great importance of the service which has been rendered by Captain Wilkes to his country." D. P. Crook, *The North, the South, and the Powers, 1861–1865* (New York, 1974), p. 115.

5. Charles Wilkes was the great-nephew of "Wilkes and Liberty" John Wilkes, the cheery eighteenth-century rogue who, in spite of himself, became a martyr and hero for political radicals opposing George III.

6. Allan Nevins, *The War for the Union*, 4 vols.; vol. 1: *The Improvised War 1861–1862* (New York, 1959), p. 388.

7. Russell, *My Diary North and South*, p. 327, November 19, 1861.

8. *The Times*, December 3, 1861.

9. B. J. Lossing, *A Centennial Edition of the History of the United States* (Chicago, 1876), p. 587.

10. Howard K. Beale (ed.), *The Diary of Edward Bates* (Washington, D.C., 1933), p. 202, November 19, 1861.

11. Stephen W. Sears, *The Civil War Papers of George B. McClellan: Selected Correspondence, 1860–1865* (New York, 1989), p. 136, McClellan to Mary Ellen, November 17, 1861.

12. PRO 30/22/35, ff. 317–23, Lyons to Russell, November 22, 1861.

13. Although the South was collectively holding its breath, in South Carolina a lonely General Robert E. Lee sent a little bouquet of violets to his daughter, and the following advice to his wife: "You must not build your hopes on peace on account of the United States going into a war with England. . . . Her rulers are not entirely mad, and if they find England is in earnest . . . they will adopt [peace]. We must make up our minds to fight our battles and win our independence alone. No one will help us." Robert E. Lee, *Recollections and Letters* (New York, repr. 2004), pp. 51–52.

14. Anthony Trollope, *North America* (repr. London, 1968), p. 138.

15. PRO FO 519/178, Lord Clarendon to Lord Cowley, November 29, 1861, quoted in Crook, *The North, the South, and the Powers*, p. 131.

16. As the Duke of Argyll wrote from France: "If such an act as that committed by the *San Jacinto* be allowed, I see nothing which would prevent any European Government seizing on board of our ships any refugees from their revolted provinces, who might be coming to England (as many do) to excite popular sympathy with their cause." *George Douglas, Eighth Duke of Argyll (1823–1900): Autobiography and Memoirs*, ed. the Dowager Duchess of Argyll, 2 vols. (London, 1906), p. 180, Duke of Argyll to Gladstone, December 7, 1861.

17. John Morely, *The Life of William Ewart Gladstone: 1809–1872*, 2 vols. (London, 1908), vol. 2, pp. 73–74, Gladstone to Argyll, December 3, 1861.

18. Sir Theodore Martin, *The Life of his Royal Highness the Prince Consort*, vol. 5 (New York, 1880), p. 349. Prince Albert continued: "We are therefore glad to believe that upon a full consideration of the circumstances, and of the undoubted breach of international law committed, they would spontaneously offer such redress as alone could satisfy this country, viz. the restoration of the unfortunate passengers and a suitable apology."

19. "I think now the American Government," he wrote, "under the inspiration of Seward will refuse us redress. The prospect is melancholy, but it is an obligation of honour which we cannot escape." PRO, Cowley MSS, FO 519/199, Russell to Lord Cowley, December 7, 1861.

20. Brian Jenkins, *Britain and the War for the Union*, 2 vols. (Montreal, 1974, 1980), vol. 1, p. 212.

21. Nancy Mitford (ed.), *The Stanleys of Alderley* (London, 1968), p. 270, Lord Stanley to Lady Stanley, December 2, 1861.

22. For some reason, he has generally been misidentified as Seymour Conway, although W. H. Russell refers to him properly as Conway Seymour.

23. G. P. Gooch (ed.), *The Later Correspondence of Lord John Russell, 1840–1878*, 2 vols. (London, 1925), vol. 2, p. 321, Lord Russell to Lord Clarendon, December 6, 1861. In fact, Lord Clarendon thought that Russell was generally far too namby-pamby with Seward. "I don't like the low tone taken by Johnny," he told the Duchess of Manchester; "he is right not to be quarrelsome but humility is not the way to keep vulgarity & swagger in order & there is not a despatch from that beast Seward that does not contain some menace to us."

A. L. Kennedy (ed.), *My Dear Duchess: Social and Political Letters to the Duchess of Manchester, 1858–1869* (London, 1956), p. 208, Clarendon to Duchess of Manchester, December 25, 1862.

24. Desmond McCarthy, *Lady John Russell*, p. 260, Lady John to Lady Dumferline, December 13, 1861.

25. *Letters of Sir George Cornewall Lewis*, ed. G. F. Lewis (London, 1870), pp. 405–6, Lewis to Twistleton, December 5, 1861.

26. The purchases were actually a coincidence. At the start of the war, the United States had 3 million pounds of saltpeter in reserve, which was all that had been left over from the Mexican–American War. The U.S. Navy commissioned Lammot Du Pont to replenish the country's supply before the *Trent* incident took place. It just so happened that he began loading his prodigious cargo on November 28, the day after England received news of the seizure. Once the ban was in effect, Charles Francis Adams advised Du Pont to offload the saltpeter surreptitiously in limited amounts in order to avoid flooding the market.

27. Regis Courtmanche, *No Need of Glory: The British Navy in American Waters* (Annapolis, Md., 1977), p. 59.

28. Mitford (ed.), *The Stanleys of Alderley*, p. 271, Lord Stanley to Lady Stanley, December 4, 1861.

29. Ibid., p. 271, Lord Stanley to Lady Stanley, December 6, 1861.

30. Somerset RO, Somerset MSS, d/RA/A/2a/34/7/1, Admiral Milne to Duke of Somerset, January 24, 1861. Milne also feared the loss of the West Indies as a possible result of the war: "The defence our West India Islands, also Brunswick, Nova Scotia, Newfoundland, and the St. Lawrence in spring, causes me much anxiety, but in so far as the force at my disposal will admit I will do all I can to defend them from aggression, but your Grace and the members of the Board must be aware the large naval force which these defensives will require, and that the efficiency of our ships will in a great measure depend on the supply of coal at the various stations." December 22, 1861.

31. Kenneth Bourne, "British Preparations for War with the North, 1861–1862," *English Historical Review*, 76/301 (Oct. 1961), pp. 600–632, at p. 609.

32. Some pessimists within the War Office feared that victory would be impossible without a deus ex machina–like intervention such as General MacClellan refusing to part with any troops until spring, Confederate activity tying down the majority of Federal troops, a cold winter inhibiting deployment, or New England states such as Maine turning against the Union.

33. *Army Historical Research*, vol. 19, pp. 112–14, Lieutenant Colonel G. J. Wolseley to Major Biddulph, December 12, 1861.

34. G. H. Warren, *Fountain of Discontent: The Trent Affair and Freedom of the Seas* (Boston, 1981), p. 130.

35. Mitford (ed.), *The Stanleys of Alderley*, p. 274, Lord Stanley to Lady Stanley, December 20, 1861.

36. Bourne, "British Preparations for War with the North, 1861–1862," p. 616.

37. Owen Ashmore (ed.), "The Diary of James Garnett of Low Moor, Clitheroe, 1858–65," vol. 2: "The American Civil War and the Cotton Famine, 1861–65," *Transactions of the Historic Society of Lancashire and Cheshire for the Year 1971*, 123 (1972), pp. 105–43, at p. 114, December 3, 1861.

38. MHS, Adams MSS, Diary of Charles Francis Adams, vol. 9, December 11, 1861.

39. W. C. Ford (ed.), *A Cycle of Adams Letters, 1861–1865*, 2 vols. (Boston, 1920), vol. 1, pp. 75–77, Henry Adams to Charles Francis Adams, Jr., November 30, 1861. Although Bright claimed to have a poor opinion of Lord Lyons, whom he had met once, when he had the opportunity to speak with him properly, he decided that Lyons was, "a sensible man, calm of temper and serious." R.A.J. Walling (ed.), *The Diaries of John Bright* (New York, 1931), p. 407.

40. T. Wemyss Reid, *Life of the Right Honorable William Edward Forster* (London, 1888), p. 344, Forster to his wife, December 4, 1861.

41. *Spectator*, December 7, 1861. Bright was fortunate that no one knew or remembered how he had warmly greeted Senator Slidell when the latter visited England a few years before. Then, he wrote in his diary: "Thro' the Park with Cobden. With him afterwards to dine at Fenton's Hotel with Mr. Brown, M.P. Among those present was Mr. Slidell, American Senator, who appeared to be a sensible man with more of the Englishman than American in his manners." Walling (ed.), *The Diaries of John Bright*, p. 151.

42. Deborah Logan (ed.), *The Collected Letters of Harriet Martineau*, 5 vols. (London 2007), vol. 4, p. 312, Martineau to Henry Reeve, December 4, 1861.

43. Sarah Agnes Wallace and Frances Elma Gillespie (eds.), *The Journal of Benjamin Moran, 1857–1865*, 2 vols. (Chicago, 1948, 1949), vol. 2, p. 922, December 12, 1861.

44. Warren, *Fountain of Discontent*, p. 142.

45. Wallace and Gillespie (eds.), *The Journal of Benjamin Moran*, vol. 2, p. 923, December 14, 1861.

46. "I am here quietly waiting the developments of events over which I have no control," Adams complained to Motley, the minister to Austria, "and in which I had no participation." Edward Chalfant, *Both Sides of the Ocean* (New York, 1982), p. 346.

47. Weed had assumed that Seward's trip to London in 1859 had been a success. Instead, he discovered that "every idle word he spoke here, in society, is treasured up and a bad meaning given to it. For example, he made enemies of a Noble Household for laughing at the enormous sums of money paid for Paintings. At another Dinner Table he gave offense by insisting that English Books were absurdly expensive, and that American re-productions were just as good, etc etc etc." Such boorish behavior would not have won Seward friends anywhere. In the first instance, he betrayed himself to be a philistine, and in the second, unscrupulous, since the American reproductions were cheap only because they were printed in defiance of copyright, thus depriving English authors of their royalties.

48. University of Rochester, Rochester, N.Y., Rush Rees Library, Seward MSS, Mission Abroad, 1861–1862 [microform]; a selection of letters from Archbishop Hughes, Bishop McIlvaine, W. H. Seward, and Thurlow Weed; Weed to Seward, December 18, 1861.

49. *The Times*, December 6, 1861.

50. University of Rochester, Rochester, N.Y., Rush Rees Library, Seward MSS, Weed to Seward, December 10, 1861.

51. "I am placed in a predicament almost as awkward as if I had not been commissioned here at all." OR, ser. 2, vol. 2, p. 1123, Adams to Seward, December 11, 1861. Warren, *Fountain of Discontent*, p. 164.

52. Ibid., p. 152.

53. T. C. Pease and J. Randall (eds.), *The Diary of Orville H. Browning, 1850–1881* (Springfield, Ill., 1925–31), December 10, 1861, p. 50.

54. Beverley Wilson Palmer (ed.), *The Selected Letters of Charles Sumner,* 2 vols. (Boston, 1990), vol. 1, p. 82, Sumner to Duchess of Argyll, November 18, 1861.

55. Ibid., pp. 88–89, Charles Sumner to Francis Lieber, December 24, 1861.

56. Jay Sexton, *Debtor Diplomacy* (Oxford, 2005), p. 96.

57. Columbia University, Blackwell MSS, Blackwell to Bodichon, December 30, 1861.

58. Frederick W. Seward (ed.), *Seward at Washington* (New York, 1891), p. 32.

59. Pease and Randall (eds.), *The Diary of Orville H. Browning, 1850–1881*, p. 51, December 15, 1861.

60. Russell, *My Diary North and South*, p. 331, December 16, 1861.

61. Martin Crawford (ed.), *William Howard Russell's Civil War: Private Diary and Letters, 1861–1862* (Athens, Ga., 1992), p. 207, Russell to John T. Delane, December 20, 1861.

62. The mood in the Senate was no different. Senator Orville Browning, for example, was adamantly against any kind of settlement. "We were clearly right in what we did," he insisted. England could send as many troops as she liked. "We are determined, at all hazards, to hold on to the prisoners. . . ." Pease and Randall (eds.), *The Diary of Orville H. Browning*, p. 50, fn.

63. The United States did not have a naval plan against Britain. Admiral Milne, on the other hand, had already put his fleet on alert. His instructions from London were to end the blockade of the Southern ports (without directly cooperating with the Confederacy). How he achieved this was to be his own affair. Regis Courtemanche, *No Need of Glory: The British Navy in American Waters* (Annapolis, Md., 1977), p. 59, Admiral Milne to Sir Frederick Grey, December 1861. Milne's strategy depended on a three-pronged attack. One force, under Commodore Dunlop, would sail from Veracruz and clear the Federal navy from the Gulf. The larger, Milne's, would attack the U.S. blockading fleet and then proceed up the coast to the Northeast, where it would establish a blockade of the major Northern ports. Milne would be able to count on reinforcements, a sufficient number of coaling vessels, and a working dockyard in Bermuda. He thought that his plan had, in the short term, a good chance of success. A mere three months later, however, after the launch of USS *Monitor*, he felt that the advantage had started to turn in favor of the North and he looked back to the *Trent* affair as Britain's most favorable moment.

64. Crawford (ed.), *William Howard Russell's Civil War*, p. 207, Russell to John T. Delane, December 20, 1861.

65. Michael Burlingame, *Abraham Lincoln*, 2 vols. (Baltimore, 2008), vol. 2, p. 224.

66. Palmer (ed.), *Selected Letters of Charles Sumner*, vol. 2, p. 87, Sumner to Bright, December 23, 1861. "Are Mr. Mason and Mr. Slidell so irresistibly eloquent that we must not run the danger of hearing them speak?" asked the Duchess

of Argyll in one of her letters to Sumner. MHS, Argyll Letters, p. 93, Duchess of Argyll to Charles Sumner, December 8, 1861.

67. James J. Barnes and Patience P. Barnes (eds.), *Private and Confidential: Letters from British Ministers in Washington to the Foreign Secretaries* (Selinsgrove, Pa., 1993), p. 273, Lyons to Russell, December 23, 1861.

68. Palmer (ed.), *Selected Letters of Charles Sumner*, vol. 1, pp. 88–89, Charles Sumner to Francis Lieber, December 24, 1861.

69. Ibid. Opinion remains divided on the issue. At one extreme are those who believe that the North would have crushed the Royal Navy, destroyed "the façade of British military preeminence," and rocked "the foundations of British economic primacy"; at the other are those who invisage humiliation for the North and swift independence for the South. The strength of these wildly divergent arguments depends, in part, on how long the war might have continued. Nevertheless, the evidence does suggest its own story, one in which all sides come out the worse for wear—except for the South. See, e.g., Russell F. Weigley, *A Great Civil War* (Bloomington, Ind., 2000), p. 81; Andrew Wellard, "After the *Trent*, or Third Time Lucky?," *Crossfire*, 62 (April 2000).

70. Beale (ed.), *The Diary of Edward Bates*, p. 216. Meanwhile, in England, people were beginning to worry that her naval superiority was not nearly superior enough. On the same day as the U.S. cabinet discussions, *The Times* warned that the North had extraordinary maritime resources. Furthermore, "Our adversaries will lose not a moment after the declaration of war in pressing forward the construction and equipment of cruisers and it must be expected that many of these vessels will, as in the last war, elude the blockade and prowl about the ocean in quest of prey. . . . It is quite possible that while England is ruling undisputed mistress of the waves a Yankee frigate may appear some fine morning off one of our ports and inflict no slight damage upon us."

71. James M. McPherson, *Battle Cry of Freedom* (London, 1988), p. 444. The result of the crisis was the Legal Tender Act of February 1862, which—inter alia—created a national paper currency, unleashed the power of government bonds, and provided the treasury with the money to pay its bills.

72. The way Seward framed the discussion, the *Trent* was really a continuation of the old impressment argument—the one that had led to war in 1812. Then it was over Britain stopping American ships and removing British deserters. Now, alleged Seward, the United States had inadvertently performed a similar violation that he was delighted to rectify, and in so doing, establish once and for all a fifty-year-old American principle. It was complete legal nonsense. The *Trent* had nothing to do with impressment. But the argument sounded stirring and patriotic, and was guaranteed to go down well with the public. Seward threw in a couple of other arguments for good measure, about ambassadors and dispatches being fair game on the high seas, and other such dubious nonsense.

73. David H. Donald, *Lincoln* (New York, 1995), p. 323.

74. Russell, *My Diary North and South*, p. 592, December 26, 1861.

75. Many years later, Trollope wrote in his autobiography: "I was at Washington at the time, and it was known there that the contest among the leading Northerners was very sharp on the matter. Mr. Sumner and Mr. Seward were, under Mr. Lincoln, the two chiefs of the party. It was understood that Mr.

Sumner was opposed to the rendition of the men, and Mr. Seward in favour of it. . . . I dined with Mr. Seward on the day of the decision, meeting Mr. Sumner at his house, and was told as I left the dining room what the decision had been." Anthony Trollope, *An Autobiography*, ed. Michael Sadleir (New York, 1923), p. 166.

76. Doris Kearns Goodwin, *Team of Rivals* (New York, 2005), p. 400. See Logan (ed.), *Collected Letters of Harriet Martineau*, vol. 4, passim, for Martineau's references to the plans and the advice.

77. Pease and Randall (eds.), *The Diary of Orville H. Browning*, December 27, 1861, p. 519.

78. Barnes and Barnes (eds.), *Private and Confidential*, p. 274, Lyons to Russell, December 31, 1861.

79. Edward L. Pierce (ed.), *Memoir of Charles Sumner*, 4 vols. (Boston, 1894), vol. 4: *1860–1870*, p. 59.

80. Warren, *Fountain of Discontent*, p. 20.

81. David H. Donald, *Charles Sumner and the Rights of Man, 1862* (New York, 1970), pp. 43–44.

82. Adam Gurowski, *Diary from March 4, 1861 to November 12, 1862* (Boston, 1862), p. 165.

Chapter 9: The War Moves to England

1. *Transactions of the Historic Society of Lancashire and Cheshire*, John Ward Diary, 171 Cont A, January 1, 1862.

2. Seward countered that he had been on tenterhooks himself, until they convened on Christmas Day. "Remember, that in a Council like ours, there are some strong wills to be reconciled." But Weed was not satisfied. The legation had been the last to know of the commissioners' release; even the clerks in the City were better informed. "I do not see how I could have prevented the difficulties which attended the delay and suspense in the *Trent* affair. The telegraph outstrips the mails—and I cannot send despatches or receive them by telegraph," rejoined Seward. Weed would not back down, insisting that Seward should have at least written privately to Adams, rather than leaving him in complete suspense. Margaret K. Toth (ed.), *Mission Abroad, 1861–1862* (Rochester, N.Y., 1954), Seward to Weed, January 22, January 30, and March 7, 1862.

3. Sarah Agnes Wallace and Frances Elma Gillespie (eds.), *The Journal of Benjamin Moran, 1857–1865*, 2 vols. (Chicago, 1948, 1949), vol. 2, p. 940, January 8 and 9, 1862.

4. *Letters of Lord St. Maur and Lord Edward St. Maur* (London, 1888), p. 245, Duke of Somerset to Lord Edward St. Maur, January 12, 1862.

5. Nancy Mitford (ed.), *The Stanleys of Alderley* (London, 1968), p. 281, Jonny Stanley to Maude Stanley, February 19, 1862.

6. Wellcome Library, RAMC.75, f. 2107, Sir Anthony Jackson, January 1862.

7. *Illustrated London News*, January 11, 1862. Later, when the extent of American anger became clear, it defended Britain's response: "And if the British people misinterpreted the sentiments of the Americans with regard either to slavery or secession, the Americans very palpably misinterpreted those of the British people and Government in the affair of the *Trent*." April 19, 1862.

8. Charles Francis Adams, Jr., "The Trent Affair: An Historical Retrospect," *Massachusetts Historical Society Proceedings*, 45 (1912), p. 529.

9. Toth (ed.), *Mission Abroad*, p. 236, Hughes to Seward, January 11, 1862.

10. MHS, Adams MSS, Diary of Charles Francis Adams, January 15, 1862.

11. Edward Chalfant, *Better in Darkness* (New York, 1994), p. 21.

12. Ibid., p. 25.

13. Wallace and Gillespie (eds.), *The Journal of Benjamin Moran*, vol. 2, p. 940, January 10, 1862.

14. Desmond McCarthy, *Lady John Russell*, p. 260, Lady John Russell to Lady Dumferline, December 13, 1861.

15. *Letters of Lord St. Maur and Lord Edward St. Maur*, p. 245, Duke of Somerset to Lord Edward St. Maur, January 12, 1862.

16. MHS, Adams MSS, Diary of Charles Francis Adams, April 19, 1862. His diary for just one week in April, for example, shows that he may have felt lonely, but he was not alone. He went to dinner at Lord Lansdowne's on April 1: "The dinner was pleasant without being animated." From there he went to a glittering reception at Stafford House. The next day he went to a dinner at the Duchess of Somerset's. On the third, he went to a reception of the president of the Royal Society at Burlington House. On April 5, Mrs. Adams had her first reception for Americans in London, with about thirty guests. On the seventh, he had dinner with the Duke and Duchess of Northumberland, with "Lord and Lady Macclesfield, Lord Ellenborough, Lord and Lady Colville, Lord and Lady Colchester and Mr. and Mrs. Spencer Walpole, and one or two others."

17. David H. Donald, *Lincoln* (New York, 1995), p. 329.

18. Anthony Trollope, *North America* (repr. London, 1968), pp. 139–40.

19. T. C. Pease and J. Randall (eds.), *The Diary of Orville H. Browning, 1850–1881* (Springfield, Ill., 1925–31), p. 520, December 28, 1861. Aware that people were whispering behind his back, in January Seward tried to rouse public support by publishing all of the previous year's correspondence between the State Department and the various legations. He made sure to include the originals of letters that had been toned down. His opponents replied by publishing a pamphlet entitled "A Review of Mr. Seward's Diplomacy," which exposed his considerable blunders. Jay Monaghan, *Diplomat in Carpet Slippers* (New York, 1945), p. 212.

20. Pease and Randall (eds.), *The Diary of Orville H. Browning*, January 25, 1861, p. 527.

21. BL Add. MS 415670, f. 219, Herbert to mother, January 14, 1862.

22. James M. McPherson, *Battle Cry of Freedom* (London, 1988), p. 372.

23. Martin Crawford (ed.), *William Howard Russell's Civil War: Private Diary and Letters, 1861–1862* (Athens, Ga., 1992), pp. 218–19, Russell to Delane, January 16, 1862.

24. *Illustrated London News*, February 22, 1862.

25. Ibid., March 22, 1862.

26. BL Add. MS 415670, f. 221, Herbert to mother, February 4, 1862.

27. Charles F. Johnson, *The Long Roll* (repr. Shepherdstown, W.V., 1986), p. 93.

28. *Illustrated London News*, March 22, 1862.

29. There were some minor incidents in January and February but Lyons brushed them off. Not serious, but annoying, was Seward's cheeky offer to let

British troops travel through Maine to Canada. It was actually a case of lost luggage, but Seward used the incident to make it appear as though he were graciously allowing the British Army to disembark in the United States on their way to invade her from Canada.

30. West Sussex RO, Lyons MSS, box 300, Lord Lyons to Augusta Mary Minna Lyons, January 31 and February 7, 1862.

31. PRO 30/22/36, f. 27–28, Lyons to Russell, February 1, 1862.

32. Edward Dicey, *Spectator of America*, ed. Herbert Mitgang (Athens, Ga., 1971), pp. 90–92.

33. John B. Jones, *A Rebel War Clerk's Diary at the Confederate States Capital*, ed. Earl Schenck Miers (Urbana, Ill., 1958), p. 63, January 1, 1862.

34. C. Vann Woodward (ed.), *Mary Chesnut's Civil War* (New Haven, 1981), p. 286, February 11, 1862.

35. Eli N. Evans, *Judah P. Benjamin* (New York, 1988), p. 146.

36. Crawford (ed.), *William Howard Russell's Civil War*, p. 219, Russell to Delane, January 16, 1862.

37. *Living Age*, 69/3 (Oct.–Dec. 1863), p. 189.

38. Burton J. Hendrick, *Statesmen of the Lost Cause* (New York, 1939), p. 235.

39. When Slidell was a boy, living in the First Ward, his best friend was Charles Wilkes. The friendship was broken when they were teenagers, over the affections of a local girl. They had not seen each other for many years when Slidell became Wilkes's unwilling guest on board the *San Jacinto*.

40. Woodward (ed.), *Mary Chesnut's Civil War*, p. 170, September 28, 1861.

41. Wallace and Gillespie (eds.), *The Journal of Benjamin Moran*, vol. 2, p. 1212, September 22, 1863.

42. Crawford (ed.), *William Howard Russell's Private Diary and Letters*, p. 61, May 25, 1861.

43. William Howard Russell, *My Diary North and South*, ed. Eugene H. Berwanger (New York, 1988), p. 164, May 25, 1861. Slidell's experience of foreign diplomacy was limited to his eighteen-month stint in Mexico, where he served as the American minister, 1845–46.

44. *The Times*, December 10, 1861.

45. Francis W. Dawson, *Reminiscences of Confederate Service, 1861–1865*, ed. Bell I. Wiley (Baton Rouge, La., 1980), p. 182, Dawson to mother, February 20, 1862.

46. ORN, ser. 2, vol. 3, encl. no. 3, p. 332, Mason to Hunter, February 7, 1862.

47. Stephen Z. Starr, *Colonel Grenfell's Wars* (Baton Rouge, La., 1971), p. 40.

48. Ibid.

49. E. D. Adams, *Great Britain and the American Civil War*, 2 vols. in 1 (New York, 1958), vol. 1, p. 243.

50. Ibid., p. 263.

51. ORN, ser. 2, vol. 3, p. 343, Mason to Hunter, February 22, 1862.

52. Adams, *Great Britain and the American Civil War*, p. 243.

53. Ibid., p. 261, and Brian Jenkins, *Britain and the War for the Union*, 2 vols. (Montreal, 1974, 1980), vol. 1, p. 253. The blockade issue was further muddied by Northern plans to block up Charleston Harbor with a "stone fleet"—that is, sinking wrecks to make passage impossible—which was considered in England to be shortsighted and inhumane.

54. Toth (ed.), *Mission Abroad*, p. 386, Weed to Seward, February 18, 1862.

55. Seward's continued silence was a gift to the South. *The Economist*, for example, pronounced, "It is in the independence of the South, and not in her defeat, that we can alone look with confidence for the early amelioration and the ultimate extinction of the slavery we abhor."

56. Citizenship was not conferred on free blacks until 1866. However, the legation began quietly giving out passports in 1862.

57. MHS, Adams MSS, Diary of Charles Francis Adams, January 25, 1862. Ironically, on March 6 the New York State Chamber of Commerce passed a resolution thanking John Bright for his advocacy of the "principles of constitutional liberty and international justice for which the American people were contending."

58. Devon RO, 2065m/c1/29, J. W. Buller, MP, to Georgiana, March 14, 1862.

59. Toth (ed.), *Mission Abroad*, p. 400, Weed to Seward, February 20, 1862.

60. Charles Vandersee, "Henry Adams Behind the Scenes: Civil War Letters to Frederick W. Seward," *Bulletin of the New York Public Library*, 71/4 (1967), p. 249.

61. MPUS, pp. 22–23, n. 112, Adams to Seward, February 7, 1862.

62. Stephen B. Oates, "Henry Hotze: Confederate Agent Abroad," *The Historian*, 27 (1965), p. 134.

63. Ibid., p. 135.

64. ORN, ser. 2, vol. 3, p. 347, Hotze to Hunter, February 23, 1862.

65. Wallace and Gillespie (eds.), *Diary of Benjamin Moran*, vol. 2, p. 961, March 6, 1862.

66. Roundell Palmer, *Memorials*, 2 vols. (London, 1894, repr. 2003), vol. 1, p. 404.

67. Toth (ed.), *Mission Abroad*, p. 463, Weed to Seward, March 8, 1862.

68. MHS, Adams MSS, Diary of Charles Francis Adams, March 8, 1862.

69. ORN, ser. 2, vol. 3, p. 359, Mason to Hunter, March 11, 1862.

Chapter 10: The First Blow Against Slavery

1. John Stuart Mill, *The Contest in America*, repr. from *Fraser's Magazine*, February 1862 (Boston, 1863). The Adams family met John Stuart Mill at a dinner given by the Argylls. Years later, Henry Adams sheepishly admitted that he drank too much wine that night, and "after dinner engaged in instructing John Stuart Mill on the peculiar merits of an American protective system. . . . Mr. Mill took no apparent pleasure in the dispute." Henry Adams, *The Education of Henry Adams*, ed. Ernest Samuels (repr. Boston, 1973), p. 126.

2. Philip Van Doren Stern, *When the Guns Roared: World Aspects of the American Civil War* (New York, 1965), p. 112.

3. W. D. Jones, "Blyden, Gladstone and the War," *Journal of Negro History*, 49 (1964), p. 58, fn.

4. *George Douglas, Eighth Duke of Argyll (1823–1900): Autobiography and Memoirs*, ed. the Dowager Duchess of Argyll, 2 vols. (London, 1906), vol. 2, p. 190, May 13, 1862.

5. Jones, "Blyden, Gladstone and the War," p. 58. Blyden had recently returned from a diplomatic mission to the United States where he was subjected to the usual treatment meted out to free blacks, such as being denied the right to

ride on public busses or eat in white-owned restaurants. He was particularly upset at being denied entry to the House of Representatives. There was no such bar to the Houses of Parliament, which surprised some Northerners. Benjamin Moran laughed at Charles Wilson's annoyance at having to sit beside "the negro representative from Hayti." On February 6, he wrote in his diary: "From what I have been told the black exhibited a good deal better manners than did my fellow secretary. For all his 'black republicanism,' he clearly indicated by his uneasiness a decided antipathy to 'the nigger'."

6. MHS, Adams MSS, Diary of Charles Francis Adams, April 16, 1862. Adams was convinced that Lord Shaftesbury was against the North, and was using his influence with the antislavery societies. However, Thurlow Weed became acquainted with Shaftesbury and realized that the earl, like so many others, had been alienated by the North's willingness to continue slavery.

7. Sarah Agnes Wallace and Frances Elma Gillespie (eds.), *The Journal of Benjamin Moran, 1857–1865*, 2 vols. (Chicago 1948, 1949), vol. 2, p. 979, April 16, 1862.

8. David Hepburn Milton, *Lincoln's Spymaster: Thomas Haines Dudley and the Liverpool Network* (Mechanicsburg, Pa., 2003), pp. 5–7.

9. Wallace and Gillespie (eds.), *The Journal of Benjamin Moran*, vol. 2, pp. 832–33, June 24, 1861.

10. "You may rest assured that no proper effort will be wanting on my part to report to you all that can be learned of the doings of rebel agents here," Consul Morse promised. NARA, T. 168, roll 30, vol. 30, desp.1, Morse to Seward, January 30, 1862.

11. Milton, *Lincoln's Spymaster*, p. 33.

12. F. L. Owsley, *The CSS Florida* (Philidelphia, 1965; repr. Tuscaloosa, Ala., 1987), p. 22.

13. He definitely could not afford marine insurance. In spite of Weed's conviction that Lloyds was making a handsome profit out of secretly providing insurance to blockade runners, Huse's experience was that the terms were so outrageous as to be prohibitive. ORN, ser. 4, vol. 1, p. 127, Caleb Huse to Major Gorgas, March 15, 1862.

14. BL Add. MS 38951, ff. 53–55, Lord Hammond to Austen Henry Layard, April 20, 1862.

15. See, for example, MHS, Adams MSS, Diary of Charles Francis Adams, May 9, 1862.

16. PRO FO5/818, Russell to Lyons, April 17, 1862.

17. Napoleon then said the complete opposite to William Dayton, the U.S. minister: "Mr. Adams tells me," reported Benjamin Moran on April 17, "that Louis Napoleon in a personal interview with Mr. Dayton expressed his regret at the precipitate recognition of the rebels as belligerents by France and Gt. B., and stated that it was England's work. He is now willing to withdraw it if Gt. B. will also."

18. Louis Martin Sears, "A Confederate Diplomat at the Court of Napoleon III," *American Historical Review*, 26/2 (Jan. 1921), pp. 255–81, Slidell to Mason, April 12, 1862.

19. NARA, T. 168, roll 30, d. 1, Morse to Seward, April 12, 1862.

20. Wallace and Gillespie (eds.), *The Journal of Benjamin Moran*, vol. 2, p. 969, March 22, 1862.

21. W. C. Ford, *A Cycle of Adams Letters, 1861–1865*, 2 vols. (Boston, 1920), vol. 1, p. 133, Henry Adams to Charles Francis Adams, Jr., April 11, 1862.

22. Adams, *The Education of Henry Adams*, p. 134.

23. ORN, ser. 2, vol. 2, p. 183, Bulloch to Mallory, April 11, 1862.

24. Wallace and Gillespie (eds.), *The Journal of Benjamin Moran*, vol. 2, p. 978, April 14, 1862.

25. ORN, ser. I, vol. 1, pp. 745–49, Captain Pegram to Mallory, March 10, 1862.

26. Francis W. Dawson, *Reminiscences of Confederate Service, 1861–1865*, ed. Bell I. Wiley (Baton Rouge, La., 1980), p. 32.

27. Duke University, Francis Dawson MSS, Dawson to mother, May 16, 1862.

28. James J. Barnes and Patience P. Barnes (eds.), *The American Civil War Through British Eyes*, vol. 1 (Kent, Ohio, 2003), pp. 313–14, Lyons to Russell, March 16, 1861.

29. It is true that wooden ships were defenseless against those made of iron. However, D. P. Crook quotes the *Manchester Guardian* (April 3, 1862), one of the few English newspapers to maintain a sense of perspective about the news: "There may be a certain truth in saying that our whole navy consists of but two men of war [*Warrior* and *Black Prince*]; but it is to be observed that, in the same sense, the French have but one, the Americans have only a gunboat, and no other nation has any navy at all." Crook, *The North, the South, and the Powers, 1861–1865* (New York, 1974), p. 188. In reality the *Monitor* and the *Warrior* could never have engaged each other because the former could only sail in calm water and the latter could only maneuver in the open sea.

30. John Black Atkins, *The Life of Sir William Howard Russell*, 2 vols. (London, 1911), vol. 2, p. 93.

31. Martin Crawford (ed.), *William Howard Russell's Civil War: Private Diary and Letters* (Athens, Ga., 1992), p. 231, Russell to Mowbray Morris, March 15, 1862.

32. Edward Dicey, *Spectator of America*, ed. Herbert Mitgang (Athens, Ga., 1971), p. 149.

33. Lawley's early life is described in Brian Jenkins, "Frank Lawley and the Confederacy," *Civil War History*, 23 (March 1977), and William Stanley Hoole, *Lawley Covers the Confederacy* (Tuscaloosa, Ala., 1964).

34. Jenkins, "Frank Lawley and the Confederacy," p. 148.

35. Julia Miele Rodas, "More Than a Civil (War) Friendship: Anthony Trollope and Frank Lawley," *Princeton University Library Chronicle*, 60/1 (1998), p. 42, Lawley to mother, February 2, 1862.

36. Crawford (ed.), *William Howard Russell's Civil War*, p. 230.

37. Alan Hankinson, *Man of Wars: William Howard Russell of "The Times," 1820–1907* (London, 1982), p. 180.

38. William Watson, *Life in the Confederate Army: Being the Observations and Experiences of an Alien in the South During the Civil War* (London, 1887; repr. Baton Rouge, La., 1995), p. 285.

39. Atkins, *The Life of Sir William Howard Russell*, vol. 2, p. 105, March 24, 1862.

40. Ilana Miller, *Reports from America* (Stroud, 2001), p. 212.

41. Crawford (ed.), *William Howard Russell's Civil War*, p. 235, Russell to Stanton, April 2, 1862.

42. Allan Nevins, *The War for the Union,* 4 vols.; vol. 2: *War Becomes Revolution, 1862–1863* (New York, 1960), p. 3.

43. William Howard Russell, *My Diary North and South*, ed. Eugene H. Berwanger (New York, 1988), p. 340.

44. Hankinson, *Man of Wars*, p. 181.

45. A. Taylor-Milne, "The Lyons-Seward Treaty of 1862," *American Historical Review*, 38/3, pp. 511–25.

46. The small U.S. fleet known as the Africa squadron had been patrolling the west coast of Africa since 1860; the largest fleet was the British Preventive Squadron, which had six ships.

47. James J. Barnes and Patience P. Barnes, *Private and Confidential: Letters from British Ministers in Washington to the Foreign Secretaries* (Selinsgrove, Pa., 1993), p. 280. The source for the footnote on this page is the same.

48. University of Rochester, Fanny Seward Diary, ff. 21–29, March 22, 1862.

49. Dicey, *Spectator of America*, p. 58.

50. Lincoln had calculated that paying owners compensation for all the slaves in the Northern states would cost the equivalent of eighty-seven days of warfare.

51. *The Reminiscences of Carl Schurz*, ed. Carl Schurz, Frederic Bancroft, and William Archibald Dunning, 3 vols. (Garden City, N.Y., 1917), vol. 2, p. 304.

52. Taylor-Milne, "The Lyons-Seward Treaty of 1862."

53. PRO 30/22/36, ff. 63–66, Lyons to Russell, April 8, 1862.

Chapter 11: Five Miles from Richmond

1. Nathaniel Cheairs Hughes, Jr. (ed.), *Sir Henry Morton Stanley, Confederate* (Baton Rouge, La., 2000), p. 129.

2. Ibid., pp. 123, 124.

3. Ibid., p. 126. Eighteen-year-old Henry D. Parker survived but was discharged from the army on April 10.

4. Stanley P. Hirshon, *The White Tecumseh* (New York, 1997), p. 120.

5. Grant was in fact named Hiram Ulysses Grant, but a mistake in his application to West Point resulted in his being known as Ulysses S. Grant.

6. Peter Batty and Peter Parish, *The Divided Union* (London, 1987), p. 80.

7. Hughes (ed.), *Sir Henry Morton Stanley*, p. 136.

8. Edward Dicey, *Spectator of America*, ed. Herbert Mitgang (Athens, Ga., 1971), p. 208.

9. Dawson's propensity for romantic flights of fancy helped him to survive his transition to life as a junior officer in the navy. There was nothing knightly about the first time he tried to climb into bed: "Like one of the heroes of my favorite Marryatt [sic], I signalized my entrance into the hammock on one side by pitching out on my head on the other side." Francis W. Dawson, *Reminiscences of Confederate Service, 1861–1865*, ed. Bell I. Wiley (Baton Rouge, La., 1980), pp. 40–42.

10. Lord Lyons was annoyed by Mercier's visit. It was his firm belief that they should respect the Northern embargo and refrain from any direct communi-

cation with the South. He also feared that it would give the impression of a crack in the Anglo-French accord. For that reason alone, Seward was not averse to Mercier's solo mission.

11. Robert Douthat Meade, *Judah P. Benjamin: Confederate Statesman* (Baton Rouge, La., 2001), p. 254.

12. James J. Barnes and Patience P. Barnes (eds.), *The American Civil War Through British Eyes*, vol. 2 (Kent, Ohio, 2005), p. 26, Lord Lyons to Lord Russell, April 28, 1862.

13. C. Vann Woodward (ed.), *Mary Chesnut's Civil War* (New Haven, 1981), p. 330, April 27, 1862.

14. Hudson Strode, *Jefferson Davis: Confederate President*, 3 vols. (New York, 1959), vol. 2, p. 246.

15. See Ella Lonn, *Foreigners in the Confederacy* (Chapel Hill, N.C., repr. 2001), pp. 113–15, for a discussion of the European Brigade. There were 2,500 Frenchmen, 800 Spaniards, 500 Italians, 400 Germans, Dutch, and Scandinavians, and 500 Swiss, Belgians, English, Slavonians, and others.

16. Virgil Carrington Jones makes clear that by April 30, New Orleans was relatively calm. "Truly the backbone of the rebellion is broken," reported Admiral Porter. Jones, *The Civil War at Sea*, 3 vols. (New York, 1961), vol. 2, p. 138.

17. Robert S. Holzman, "Ben Butler in the Civil War," *New England Quarterly*, 30/3 (Sept. 1957), pp. 330–45, at p. 335.

18. PRO FO5/848, ff. 403–10, Consul Coppel to Lord Russell, May 9, 1862.

19. Holtzman, "Ben Butler in the Civil War," p. 334.

20. The British consul tried to protect the 105 British members of Company B. When Butler learned that 39 of them had sent their uniforms and weapons to friends in the Confederate army, he ordered the entire company to appear before him in full kit, or face either expulsion or imprisonment. Two men, according to a petition from the British residents, Samuel Nelson and J. Turner Roe, were arbitrarily arrested and sent "to work as common laborers on the forts which is tantamount to a death sentence given the weather, conditions etc." They requested a British warship for protection. PRO FO5/848, ff. 433–39, Petition on behalf of British Residents of New Orleans, June 11, 1861.

21. PRO FO5/830, ff. 346–48, Lord Lyons to Lord Russell, May 30, 1862.

22. Seward dispatched a trusted representative to New Orleans to examine each claim of judicial abuse. It came as no surprise to Butler's critics when every one of his cases was overturned.

23. William Watson, *Life in the Confederate Army: Being the Observations and Experiences of an Alien in the South During the Civil War* (London, 1887; repr. Baton Rouge, La., 1995), p. 371.

24. James M. McPherson, *Battle Cry of Freedom* (London, 1988), p. 416.

25. Watson, *Life in the Confederate Army*, p. 361.

26. "The Journal of Robert Neve," private collection, p. 40.

27. Shelby Foote, *The Civil War*, 3 vols. (New York, 1986), vol. 1, p. 385.

28. Halleck proclaimed a blanket ban on all journalists and noncombatants on May 13, on the grounds that Confederate spies were among them.

29. *Illustrated London News*, April 26, 1862.

30. Ibid., June 14, 1862.

31. E. B. Long, with Barbara Lond, *The Civil War Day by Day: An Almanac, 1861–1865* (New York, 1971; repr. New York, 1985), p. 726.

32. *Illustrated London News*, July 19, 1862.

33. Ibid., July 26, 1862.

34. Camp Douglas was originally a training camp for volunteers; after the capture of Fort Donelson in February, the temporary barracks had been converted to hold enlisted prisoners of war; officers were sent to a separate prison. There, Stanley shared a straw pallet with W. H. Wilkes, a Southern nephew of the notorious Charles Wilkes.

35. Hughes, *Sir Henry Morton Stanley*, p. 141.

36. Ibid., p. 146.

37. PRO FO115/300, ff. 151–52, Lyons to Russell, May 5, 1862.

38. See, e.g., OR, ser. 2, vol. 4, S. 117, William Hoffman to Edwin Stanton, June 28, 1862.

39. Hughes (ed.), *Sir Henry Morton Stanley*, p. 148. Hughes notes that George Levy, the author of the most comprehensive study of Camp Douglas, has serious doubts about Stanley's account. However, there is sufficient evidence to accept that he was there, and did join the 1st Illinois Light Artillery.

40. OR, ser. 1, vol. 10/1, p. 73, Report of Col. John F. De Courcy, June 20, 1862.

41. Hugh Dubrulle, "A Military Legacy of the Civil War: The British Inheritance," *Civil War History* (June 2003), pp. 153–80. The military observers were genuinely impressed, however. Sir George Seymour wrote to Lord Russell on May 9, 1862: "I have just seen a letter from an English officer (a man who has seen a great deal of service) who has been taking a look at the Federal army. A finer one—or one better provided with all things necessary he never—he says—saw—and he adds . . . 'that it would require a force of 100,000 men to keep them out of Canada.' Meanwhile he says that he does not trace much hostile feeling towards us, and that he has met with a great deal of civility from the Federal Officers." PRO 33/22/39, f. 163.

42. Richard Taylor, *Destruction and Reconstruction* (1879, repr. New York, 1992), p. 21.

43. He claimed to be the son of Brigadier Sir Charles Wyndham of the 5th Light Cavalry, and a Frenchwoman named Zoë Vauthrin. His mother allegedly gave birth to him in the middle of the English Channel, on board the *Arab*. But there was no HMS *Arab* in commission in 1833, nor did the Royal Navy have a Captain Charles Wyndham. Nor was he the son, illegitimate or otherwise, of Lord Leconsfield, although there was a Captain Charles Wyndham, killed in action at Jagdalak on October 29, 1841.

44. Edward G. Longacre, *Jersey Cavaliers* (Hightstown, N.J., 1992), p. 47.

45. Taylor, *Destruction and Reconstruction*, p. 53.

46. Ruth Scarborough, *Siren of the South* (Macon, 1997), p. 53. This same Henry Kyd Douglas has been accused of being the man responsible for Robert E. Lee's Antietam battle plans falling into Federal hands. Wilbur D. Jones, "Who Lost the Lost Order?," *Civil War Regiments: A Journal of the American Civil War*, 5/3 (1997).

47. Mary Sophia Hill, *A British Subject's Recollections of the Confederacy* (Baltimore, 1875), pp. 19, 20.

48. Wyndham's lieutenant colonel reported: "All the officers, as far as I could see, behaved bravely in trying to rally their men, but to no avail. They retreated without order and in the greatest confusion—for the most part panic-stricken." OR, ser. 1, vol. 15/1, p. 680.

49. Longacre, *Jersey Cavaliers*, p. 92.

50. Douglas Southall Freeman, *Lee's Lieutenants*, 3 vols. (repr. New York, 1970), vol. 1, p. 432.

51. James I. Robertson, Jr., *Stonewall Jackson* (New York, 1997), p. 429.

52. Ibid., p. 449.

53. Wilmer Jones, *Generals in Blue and Gray* (New York, 2006), p. 80.

54. PRO 30/22/36, ff. 87–90, Lyons to Russell, May 6, 1862. "So strongly have I been impressed with the necessity of being at the seat of Government, that with the exception of the two months . . . attendance upon the Prince of Wales, I have been only four nights absent from Washington," he wrote apologetically.

55. West Sussex RO, Lyons MSS, box 300, Lord Lyons to Augusta Lyons, May 6, 1862.

56. When Lyons called on Seward to say goodbye, Lyons reassured him that it would be far better for him to spend his holiday in England than at an American resort, cut off from both capitals. Seward agreed, reported Lyons. "There was, [Seward] was happy to say, no difficult question pending between the two governments." PRO FO 5/831, ff. 171–74, Lyons to Russell, June 9, 1862.

57. The legation often acted as a missing persons bureau. Instructions like this one to the consulate in New York were not uncommon: "to insert in the New York Herald and New York Tribune the following advertisement: 'Ashley Norton Jones, otherwise called George Temple, who is believed to be serving in the United States Army, is earnestly entreated, for the sake of his afflicted parents to communicate at once with the Reverend Rush Buel, 44 William Street, Providence, RI. His parents will consult his wishes on all matters. Officers or comrades are requested to call his attention to this notice'. Notice should appear every alternative day for a month."

58. Bayly Ellen Marks and Mark Norton Schatz, *Between North and South: A Maryland Journalist Views the Civil War. The Narrative of William Wilkins Glenn, 1861–1869* (Cranbury, N.J., 1976), pp. 64–65, June 15, 1862.

59. Just before he left, on June 13, Lyons informed the Foreign Office that Congress had voted to recognize the Republics of Haiti and Liberia. Previous administrations had declined because "those Republics are governed by men of Negro descent."

60. Lord Newton (ed.), *Lord Lyons: A Record of British Diplomacy*, 2 vols. (London, 1914), vol. 1, pp. 85–86, Lyons to Russell, May 16, 1862.

61. *Letters of Lord St. Maur and Lord Edward St. Maur* (London, 1888), p. 251, Lord Edward St. Maur to Duke of Somerset, June 9, 1862; p. 254, to Duchess of Somerset, June 19, 1862.

62. Ibid., p. 260. It became a Southern myth that Lord Edward St. Maur "fought" alongside General Longstreet in the Seven Days' Battles. By the same token, Lord Edward returned home believing that Southern Anglophobia was a Northern myth.

63. Cueto had arrived in America at around the same time that W. H. Russell gave

up trying to follow the Army of the Potomac. Put off by Russell's tangle with officialdom, Cueto decided he would work as a free agent, traveling without passes or letters to wherever the action seemed most exciting. He did not get very far. A Yankee civilian remembered meeting him while they were both imprisoned in Castle Godwin. "Soon after I learned . . . that Cueto had died of typhoid fever in New York City." George Washington Frosst, *A South Berwick Yankee Behind Confederate Lines (Part II)*. Cueto was in a Confederate prison in North Carolina for eight months before he was able to smuggle out a letter to Consul Bunch in late November 1862. The consul immediately sent a letter of protest to Judah P. Benjamin, who ordered an investigation into Cueto's arrest.

64. But when Major George Longley started a fight with a Federal officer while traveling on a Northern train, and was arrested for breaching the peace, *The Times* awarded him ample space to complain about his treatment. William Stuart, secretary of the legation, was much less sympathetic. He refused to protest on Longley's behalf, saying that he had failed to mention, "as stated in Mr. Bernal's dispatch . . . that you had remarked to Colonel Massey, that you believed the South to be in the right . . . which must have given just grounds to a Federal Officer with whom you were unacquainted." PRO FO115/340, f. 36, Stuart to Major Longley, September 28, 1862.

65. Catherine Cooper Hopley, *Life in the South from the Commencement of the War by a Blockaded British Subject* (London, 1863, repr. New York, 1971), p. 348.

66. Strode, *Jefferson Davis*, vol. 2, p. 260.

67. Dawson, *Reminiscences*, p. 49.

68. Ibid., p. 51.

69. James M. Morgan, *Recollections of a Rebel Reefer* (Boston, 1917), pp. 226–27.

70. Devon RO, 867B/Z36, entr. 14, July 5, 1862, unknown writer.

Chapter 12: The South Is Rising

1. William Watson, *Life in the Confederate Army: Being the Observations and Experiences of an Alien in the South During the Civil War* (London, 1887; repr. Baton Rouge, La., 1995), p. 398.

2. Ibid., p. 407.

3. Ibid., p. 413.

4. W. C. Ford (ed.), *A Cycle of Adams Letters, 1861–1865*, 2 vols. (Boston, 1920), vol. 1, p. 146, Henry Adams to Charles Francis Adams, Jr., May 16, 1862.

5. Ibid., p. 145.

6. Ibid., p. 137, Charles Francis Adams to Charles Francis Adams, Jr., April 17, 1862.

7. Sarah Agnes Wallace and Frances Elma Gillespie (eds.), *The Journal of Benjamin Moran*, 2 vols. (Chicago, 1948, 1949), vol. 2, p. 996, May 6, 1862.

8. Ford (ed.), *A Cycle of Adams Letters*, vol. 1, p. 145, Henry Adams to Charles Francis Adams, Jr., May 16, 1862.

9. Ibid., p. 141, Henry Adams to Charles Francis Adams, Jr., May 8, 1862.

10. Countess of Stafford (ed.), *Leaves from the Diary of Henry Greville*, vol. 4 (London, 1905), p. 46, May 10, 1862.

11. John Black Atkins, *The Life of Sir William Howard Russell*, 2 vols. (London, 1911), vol. 2, p. 173.

12. Ford (ed.), *A Cycle of Adams Letters*, vol. 1, p. 142, Henry Adams to Charles Francis Adams, Jr., May 8, 1862.

13. MHS, Adams MSS, Diary of Charles Francis Adams, May 19, 1862.

14. *Illustrated London News*, June 14, 1862.

15. H. F. Bell, *Palmerston*, 2 vols. (London, 1936), vol. 2, p. 317.

16. Edward Chalfant, *Better in Darkness* (New York, 1994), p. 39.

17. MHS, Adams MSS, Diary of Charles Francis Adams, June 12, 1862.

18. Ibid., July 12, 1862.

19. F. L. Owsley, *King Cotton Diplomacy* (2nd ed., Chicago, 1959), p. 145.

20. Norman Longmate, *Hungry Mills: The Story of the Lancashire Cotton Famine, 1861–5* (London, 1978), p. 95.

21. D. P. Crook, *The North, the South, and the Powers, 1861–1865* (New York, 1974), p. 198.

22. The problem for the North and the South was that the cotton famine had been brought on by a complicated set of circumstances. The distress suffered by the workers was real, but the "famine" was a combination of overproduction during the previous three years, a surplus of some grades of cotton, and a dearth of other grades. As Howard Jones writes, "The initial surplus led to reduced work time, and its eventual depletion extended the layoffs." Jones, *Blue and Gray Diplomacy* (Chapel Hill, N.C., 2009), p. 227. Also, in the first year of the war, the cotton glut in England was so great that Northern textile mills were actually able to buy surplus British stock and ship it over.

23. Robert Douthat Meade, *Judah P. Benjamin: Confederate Statesman* (Baton Rouge, La., 2001), p. 248.

24. ORN, ser. 2, vol. 3, pp. 402–4, James Spence to James Mason, April 28, 1862.

25. Virginia Mason, *The Public Life and Diplomatic Correspondence of James M. Mason* (New York, 1906), pp. 271–72, Dispatch 9, Mason to Benjamin, May 2, 1862.

26. Trinity College Library, Cambridge, Houghton MS CB36/2[3], Henry Bright to Lord Houghton, July 22, 1862.

27. Library of Congress, Hotze Papers, Private Letter Book, Hotze to John George Witt, August 11, 1864.

28. For example, as Dudley Mann wrote excitedly to Judah P. Benjamin on September 15, 1862, after *Blackwood's* published a long article about Jefferson Davis, written by the Hon. Robert Bourke: "Blackwood stands in the same relation to the British periodical press as the *Times* does to the British newspaper press. They are wonderfully influential in molding European opinion; for their power is not confined to Great Britain." ORN, ser. 2, vol. 3, pp. 528–29.

29. OR, ser. 4, vol. 2, pp. 23–25, Edwin De Leon to Judah P. Benjamin, July 30, 1862.

30. Hotze's competitor was a shabby little rag called the *London American*, edited by the eccentric George Francis Train. By coincidence, its offices were one door down, separated from the *Index* by a tobacconist's. The *Liverpool Mail* once described Train as "our extremely fast Yankee cousin, famous for making galloping speeches, for writing galloping books, and galloping himself around the world" (February 4, 1860).

31. Ford (ed.), *A Cycle of Adams Letters*, vol. 1, p. 153, Henry Adams to Charles Francis Adams, Jr., June 6, 1862.

32. ORN, ser. 2, vol. 3, p. 326, Henry Hotze to Robert Mercer Hunter, February 1, 1862.

33. Thurlow Weed, Harriet A. Weed, and Thurlow Weed Barnes, *Life of Thurlow Weed*, 2 vols. (Boston, 1884), vol. 2, p. 416, Weed to New York Common Council, July 1, 1862.

34. Edward Dicey, *Spectator of America*, ed. Herbert Mitgang (Athens, Ga., 1971), p. 144.

35. For example, on April 19, 1862, the *Illustrated London News* asked why it was that Americans were so sensitive about British criticism—and why the English had such a knack for provoking them with "ill-timed and unfair comment." "The explanation," it decided, "is to be found in their mutual ignorance of each other's feelings and modes of thought. America does not understand England, and England does not understand America."

36. "I am disturbed by the state of feeling which is growing up between our two countries," he continued. "It matters not how averse your government or ours may be to war, your people have become so inflamed against us by the daily ministrations of the press that no government will be strong enough to control their resentment." National Library of Scotland, Tweeddale Mun./Yester MSS, (0439)MS14467, ff. 40–43, John Bigelow to Lord Russell, August 2, 1862.

37. For example, on August 8, Secretary of War Stanton announced that citizens eligible for the draft (which called for 300,000 new soldiers) were forbidden to travel abroad. That day, the British legation sent a report that hundreds of British travelers were being hauled off trains and arrested at quaysides on the grounds of being "draft evaders." Among the Britons forcibly removed from a Baltimore train was a Mr. Drury, the legation's diplomatic messenger. PRO 30/36/1, desp. 150, William Stuart to Lord Russell, August 14, 1862. *Letters of Lord St. Maur and Lord Edward St. Maur* (London, 1888), p. 250, n.d, *c.* 1862.

38. Countess of Stafford (ed.), *Leaves from the Diary of Henry Greville*, vol. 4, p. 55.

39. E. D. Adams, *Great Britain and the American Civil War*, 2 vols. (New York, 1958), vol. 1, p. 305–57.

40. Brian Jenkins, *Britain and the War for the Union*, 2 vols. (Montreal, 1974, 1980), vol. 2, p. 88.

41. R.S.M. Blackett, *Divided Hearts*, p. 173.

42. E. D. Adams, *Great Britain and the American Civil War*, vol. 2, p. 20, Lyons to Stuart, July 5, 1862.

43. "I know it will be said that this is giving them the means and money for a prolongation of the contest," admitted the duke. "But its effect in this way would be comparatively small, whilst it would greatly tend to dissipate the danger which is really a growing one." MHS, Argyll Letters, p. 99, Argyll to Sumner, July 12, 1862.

44. However, Zebina Eastman obtained circumstantial evidence in November that Lindsay's firm purchased the *Calypso* for blockade running. NARA, M. T-185, roll 7, vol. 7, Eastman to Seward, November 20, 1862.

45. Ford (ed.), *A Cycle of Adams Letters*, vol. 1, p. 163, Henry Adams to Charles Francis Adams, Jr., July 4, 1862.

46. Howard Jones, *Union in Peril: The Crisis over British Intervention in the Civil War*, p. 127.

47. Adams, *Great Britain and the American Civil War*, vol. 2, p. 20, Lyons to Stuart, July 5, 1862.

48. *MPUS*, p. 133, Adams to Seward, July 11, 1862.

49. Crook, *The North, the South, and the Powers*, p. 214.

50. West Sussex RO, Lyons MSS, box 300, Lyons to sister, July 19, 1862. "I had a long talk with Lord Palmerston. I had also a sufficiently long conversation with Lord Derby at his own home."

51. Wallace and Gillespie (eds.), *The Journal of Benjamin Moran*, vol. 2, p. 1037, July 17, 1862.

52. MHS, Adams MSS, Diary of Charles Francis Adams, July 17, 1862.

53. Jones, *Union in Peril*, p. 133.

54. Jenkins, *Britain and the War for the Union*, vol. 2, p. 100.

55. Ford (ed.), *A Cycle of Adams Letters*, vol. 1, p. 167, Henry Adams to Charles Francis Adams, Jr., July 19, 1862.

56. OR, ser. 4, vol. 2, pp. 23–25, Edwin De Leon to Judah P. Benjamin, July 30, 1862.

57. Wallace and Gillespie (eds.), *The Journal of Benjamin Moran*, vol. 2, p. 1044, July 19, 1862.

58. Confederate propaganda had been so successful that the great humanitarian and social reformer Lord Shaftesbury was firmly pro-South on *moral grounds*. He told John Slidell that he "viewed it as a struggle, on the one hand, for independence and self-government, on the other, for empire, political power, and material interests." ORN, ser. 2, vol. 3, pp. 546–48, Slidell to Benjamin, September 29, 1862. Edwin De Leon claimed, "With the tide of public opinion running so strong in England that even Lord Shaftesbury and Exeter Hall now abandon their Yankee sympathies as untrue. . . ." OR, ser. 4, vol. 2, S. 128, De Leon to Benjamin, September 30, 1862.

59. *MPUS*, p. 160, Adams to Seward, July 17, 1862.

60. Quoted in Crook, *The North, the South, and the Powers*, p. 219.

61. The reality of the situation, however, was much more complicated than Moran or Dudley allowed. The U.S. consul in Dundee was probably closer to the mark when he wrote that it was more of a matter of who got to whom first. "I have reason to believe," he told Seward on June 17, "that there are officials in HM govt that could be very easily induced to take service in the ranks of the U States or the so-called Confederate States quite indifferently." NARA, M.T-200, roll 3, vol. 3, U.S. Consuls in Dundee, Consul J. B. Holderby to Seward, June 17, 1862.

62. On May 1, 1862, Lord Russell told Lord Lyons that "separation would be best for the North as well as for the South . . . for the future welfare of the free, and for the future emancipation of the slave." PRO FO/5/189.

63. Philip Guedalla, *Gladstone and Palmerston, Being the Correspondence of Lord Palmerston and Mr. Gladstone, 1851–1865* (London, 1928), pp. 230–31.

64. ORN, ser. 2, vol. 3, pp. 505–58, Hotze to Benjamin, August 6, 1862.

65. *George Douglas, Eighth Duke of Argyll (1823–1900): Autobiography and Memoirs*, ed. the Dowager Duchess of Argyll, 2 vols. (London, 1906), vol. 2, p. 193, Argyll to Gladstone, September 2, 1862.

66. David F. Krein, *The Last Palmerston Government* (Ames, Iowa, 1978), p. 65.

67. Jenkins, *Britain and the War for the Union*, vol. 2, p. 112.

68. Krein, *The Last Palmerston Government*, p. 66.

69. *New York Times*, August 13, 1862.

70. T. C. Pease and J. Randall (eds.), *The Diary of Orville H. Browning, 1850–1881* (Springfield, Ill., 1925–31), p. 562, July 24, 1862.

71. Charles P. Cullop, "An Unequal Duel: Union Recruiting in Ireland, 1863–1864," *Civil War History*, 13 (1967), p. 104.

72. Adams, *Great Britain and the American Civil War*, vol. 2, p. 34, fn.

73. *Letters of Lord St. Maur and Lord Edward St. Maur*, p. 250, n.d.

74. David H. Donald, *Lincoln* (New York, 1995), p. 366.

75. "The Journal of Robert Neve," private collection, p. 53.

76. Robert L. Kincaid, *The Wilderness Road* (Middlesboro, Ky., 1966), p. 246.

77. Brian Holden Reid, *Robert E. Lee* (London, 2005), p. 106.

78. John B. Jones, *A Rebel War Clerk's Diary at the Confederate States Capital*, ed. Earl Schenck Miers (Urbana, Ill., 1958), pp. 95–96, 27, August 28, 1862.

79. Ford (ed.), *A Cycle of Adams Letters*, vol. 1, p. 177, Charles Francis Adams, Jr., to Adams, August 27, 1862.

80. Edward G. Longacre, *Jersey Cavaliers* (Hightstown, N.J., 1992), p. 100.

81. Captain W. D. L'Estrange, *Under Fourteen Flags: The Remarkable True Story of a Victorian Soldier of Fortune* (Newton Stewart, Wigtownshire, 1999), p. 80.

82. George Templeton Strong, *Diary of the Civil War, 1860–1865*, ed. Allan Nevins (New York, 1962), p. 252, September 4, 1862.

Chapter 13: Is Blood Thicker Than Water?

1. Henry Adams, *The Education of Henry Adams*, ed. Ernest Samuels (repr. Boston, 1975), p. 128.

2. Sarah Agnes Wallace and Frances Elma Gillespie (eds.), *The Journal of Benjamin Moran, 1857–1865*, 2 vols. (Chicago, 1948, 1949), vol. 2, p. 1068, September 9, 1862.

3. Ibid., p. 1058, August 22, 1862.

4. Adams, *The Education of Henry Adams*, p. 129.

5. On September 2, the British ambassador in Paris, Lord Cowley, had heard that opinion in the cabinet was tilting "in favor of mediation in America," and that if the emperor were to announce publicly what he was saying in private to the Confederates, England would probably go along with him. David F. Krein, *The Last Palmerston Government* (Ames, Iowa, 1978), p. 66.

6. *MPUS*, p. 184, Charles Francis Adams to William Henry Seward, September 4, 1862.

7. ORN, ser. 2, vol. 3, p. 524, Ambrose Dudley Mann to Judah P. Benjamin, September 5, 1862.

8. Sir Spencer Walpole, *Life of Lord John Russell*, 2 vols. (New York, 1968), vol. 2, p. 349, Russell to Palmerston, September 17, 1862.

9. ORN, ser. 2, vol. 3, pp. 535–36, Hotze to Benjamin, September 26, 1862.

10. Ibid., pp. 546–48, Slidell to Benjamin, September 29, 1862.

11. The Confederates in Europe were helped by recent reports in the European press that showed Lincoln in a poor light as far as abolition was concerned. One referred to Lincoln's meeting on August 14 with a delegation of freedmen. The president had been frank about his fears for them, saying it would

be best for everyone if the black population emigrated somewhere else, perhaps Central America. David H. Donald points out that, despite the message, the fact of the meeting was momentous—African Americans had always been barred from the White House. Donald, *Lincoln* (New York, 1995), p. 368.

12. In London, William Gregory naively asked the Southern commissioners whether the Confederacy could not devise an education program for the slaves so that they might eventually earn enough money to buy their own freedom. He was offered many reasons why this was absolutely impossible. Brian Jenkins, *Sir William Gregory of Coole: A Biography* (Gerrards Cross, 1986), p. 154. The American consul in Bristol reported that Yancey had been flagrant in his promises, telling one author of a pro-Confederate article that Richmond had given him "full powers to pledge gradual emancipation to the governments of Europe on condition of their guaranteeing the independence of the Confederate States." NARA, M. T-185, roll 7, vol. 7, Zebina Eastman to William Henry Seward, October 20, 1862.

13. University of Southampton, Hartley Library, Palmerston MSS, GC/AR/25/1, Argyll to Palmerston, September 2, 1862.

14. PRO 30/22/14D, Palmerston to Russell, September 22, 1862.

15. Philip Guedalla (ed.), *Gladstone and Palmerston, Being the Correspondence of Lord Palmerston and Mr. Gladstone, 1851–1865* (London, 1928), p. 232, Palmerston to Gladstone, September 24, 1862.

16. Thomas Nelson Page, *Lee, Man and Soldier* (New York, 1911), p. 219, Lee to Davis, September 8, 1862.

17. William Mark McKnight, *Blue Bonnets o'er the Border: The 79th New York Cameron Highlanders* (Shippensburg, Pa., 1998), p. 72.

18. Shelby Foote, *The Civil War*, 3 vols. (New York, 1986), vol. 1, pp. 664–65.

19. Wilbur D. Jones, *Giants in the Cornfield* (Shippensburg, Pa., 1997), p. 292.

20. Russell Weigley, *A Great Civil War* (Bloomington, Ind., 2000), p. 148.

21. OR, ser. 1, vol. 19/2, p. 218, McClellan to President, September 13, 1861.

22. Robert Underwood Johnson and Clarence Clough Buel (eds.), *Battles and Leaders of the Civil War*, 4 vols. (Secaucus, N.J., 1985), vol. 2, p. 660.

23. Ibid., pp. 660–61.

24. Captain W. D. L'Estrange, *Under Fourteen Flags, Being the Life and Adventures of Brigadier-General MacIver* (Newton Stewart, Wigtonshire, 1999), p. 83.

25. Charles Augustus Fuller, *Personal Recollections of the War* (Fairford, repr. 2010), p. 40.

26. James M. McPherson, *Crossroads of Freedom: Antietam* (Oxford, 2004), p. 127.

27. David L. Thompson, "With Burnside at Antietam," in Johnson and Buel (eds.), *Battles and Leaders of the Civil War*, vol. 2, p. 556.

28. Matthew J. Graham, *The Ninth Regiment New York Volunteers* (Lancaster, Ohio, 1997), p. 303.

29. James M. McPherson (ed.), *Battle Chronicles of the Civil War*, 6 vols. (Lakeville, Conn., 1989), vol. 2, p. 252.

30. New-York Historical Society, *Narrative of Ebenezer Wells* (c. 1881).

31. James M. McPherson, *Battle Cry of Freedom* (London, 1988), p. 544.

32. Devonshire MSS, Chatsworth, ser. 2 (340.180), Lord Hartington to Duke of Devonshire, September 29, 1862.

33. Ibid.

34. Ibid.

35. Donald, *Lincoln*, p. 375.

36. Frederick Bancroft, *The Life of William H. Seward*, 2 vols. (Gloucester, Mass., 1967), vol. 2, p. 338.

37. Francis W. Dawson, *Reminiscences of Confederate Service, 1861–1865*, ed. Bell I. Wiley (Baton Rouge, La., 1980), p. 66.

38. Ibid., p. 193, Dawson to mother, April 23, 1863.

39. Ibid., p. 56.

40. S. Frank Logan, "Francis W. Dawson, 1840–1889: South Carolina Editor," MA thesis, Duke University, 1947, p. 27.

41. Dawson, *Reminiscences*, p. 69.

42. Ibid., p. 190, Dawson to mother, November 22, 1862.

43. Wolseley was not the only British soldier to request a leave of absence in order to observe the war. Captain Edward Osborne Hewett, RE, also traveled around the North during October and November 1862. He wrote a report for the army that is now lost. See R. A. Preston, "A Letter from a British Military Observer of the American Civil War," *Military Affairs*, 16 (1952), pp. 49–60.

44. James A. Rawley (ed.), *The American Civil War: An English View* (Mechanicsburg, Pa., 2002), p. xiii.

45. Brian Jenkins, "Frank Lawley and the Confederacy," *Civil War History* (March 1977), p. 149.

46. William Stanley Hoole, *Lawley Covers the Confederacy* (Tuscaloosa, Ala., 1964), p. 15.

47. Ibid., pp. 20–21, *The Times*, November 4, 1862.

48. PRO FO5.909, ff. 36–37, n. 5, Moore to Russell, January 11, 1863.

49. Anon. (Wolseley), "A Month's Visit to the Confederate Headquarters," *Blackwood's Magazine*, 93 (Jan. 1863), p. 17.

50. Captain Hewett wrote of Northern officers: "At the end of a day's march the officers look out for themselves; never see that their men are properly and completely encamped, or fed, much less that the poor horses are fed or looked after; that the men's arms, accoutrements, or artillery or cavalry harness is cleaned or repaired, or in fact anything at all till the general order to fall in for the next day's march." Preston, "A Letter from a British Observer," p. 53. William Howard Russell had previously noticed that the social hierarchy of the South was replicated in the Confederate army, which shored up the chain of command between officers and men.

51. Wolseley was surprised and amused by the ever-present immediacy of the Revolutionary War. Wherever an Englishman wanders, he wrote, "his fellow-passengers in railway carriages or stages will invariably begin talking to him about Smiths, Browns, and Tomkinses in the same strain that we are accustomed to hear allusions made to the Pitts and to Marlborough or Wellington . . . If this war has no other result, therefore, it will at least afford American historians something to write about, and save them from the puerility of detailing skirmishes in the backwoods or on the highlands of Mexico, as if they were so many battles of Waterloo or Solferino." Anon. (Wolseley), "A Month's Visit to the Confederate Headquarters," p. 16.

52. Ibid., p. 14.

53. Ibid., p. 18.

54. Hoole, *Lawley*, pp. 31–32, *The Times*, December 30, 1862.

55. G.F.R. Henderson, *Stonewall Jackson and the American Civil War* (1898; repr. Cambridge, Mass., 1988), p. 554, fn.

56. Anon. (Wolseley), "A Month's Visit to the Confederate Headquarters," p. 21.

57. *The Times*, December 30, 1862.

58. If Wolseley had seen them in action, he might have revised his opinion. Another English observer thought that neither side was particularly adept at traditional cavalry engagements. "They approach one another with considerable boldness, until they get to within about forty yards, and then, at the very moment when a dash is necessary, and the sword alone should be used, they hesitate, halt, and commence a desultory fire with carbines and revolvers.... Stuart's cavalry can hardly be called cavalry in the European sense of the word." Quoted in Jay Luvaas, *The Military Legacy of the Civil War* (Lawrence, Kan., 1988), p. 21. On the other hand, both sides learned how to use their cavalry as effective scouts.

59. Heros von Borcke had arrived in the Confederacy in early May, via a blockade runner named the *Hero*. He was a tall, strapping German with a shock of blond hair and an unintelligible accent. He had decided to volunteer out of boredom with garrison duty, or, according to another version, to annoy his father. He was close in age to Stuart, and they became friends immediately. Borcke wrote his own highly colored reminiscences of his Confederate career. Nevertheless, his wounds were real and a bullet remained permanently lodged in his lung. After his return to the ancestral castle, Borcke occasionally flew the Confederate flag from the turrets.

60. William Stanley Hoole, *Vizetelly Covers the Confederacy* (Tuscaloosa, Ala., 1957), pp. 58–59.

61. Ibid., pp. 555–56, quoted from Heros von Borcke, "Memoirs of the Confederate War for Independence," *Blackwood's Magazine*, 99 (Jan.–June 1866), p. 90.

62. Anon. (Wolseley), "A Month's Visit to the Confederate Headquarters," p. 24.

63. Ibid., pp. 24–25, 29.

Chapter 14: A Fateful Decision

1. Sarah Agnes Wallace and Frances Elma Gillespie (eds.), *The Journal of Benjamin Moran, 1857–1865*, 2 vols. (Chicago, 1948, 1949), vol. 2, p. 1076, September 30, 1862.

2. Duncan Andrew Campbell, *English Public Opinion and the American Civil War* (Woodbridge, 2003), p. 103.

3. Countess of Stafford (ed.), *Leaves from the Diary of Henry Greville*, vol. 4 (London, 1905), p. 73, September 29, 1862.

4. Clare Taylor, *British and American Abolitionists: An Episode in Transatlantic Understanding* (Edinburgh, 1974), p. 491, George Thompson to William Lloyd Garrison, December 25, 1862.

5. Howard Jones, *Blue and Gray Diplomacy* (Chapel Hill, N.C., 2009), p. 232.

6. He added: "Lincoln has a certain moral dignity, but is intellectually inferior, &

as men do not generally measure others correctly who are above their own caliber, he has chosen for his instruments mediocre men. . . . I know the men at the head of affairs on both sides, & I should say that in energy of will, in comprehensiveness of view, in habits & power of command, & in knowledge of economical & fiscal questions, Jefferson Davis is more than equal to Lincoln & all his Cabinet." Elizabeth Hoon Cawley (ed.), *The American Diaries of Richard Cobden* (Princeton, 1952), p. 75, Cobden to Bright, October 7, 1862.

7. *The Times*, October 7, 1862. Even Liberal newspapers were shocked. The *Morning Advertiser* remarked on October 6: "We can give no credit to President Lincoln . . . the motive was not any abhorrence of Slavery in itself, but a sordid, selfish motive, nor can we approve the means to which he is prepared to resort." For Britain, the atrocities committed in the Indian Mutiny were still fresh memories. The suggestion that Lincoln was trying to engineer similar mayhem and bloodshed in the South was enough to stir the public against him.

8. E. D. Adams, *Great Britain and the American Civil War*, 2 vols. (New York, 1958), vol. 2, p. 44. For an in-depth discussion of the "intervention crisis," the following sources are indispensible: Robert Huhn Jones, "Anglo-American Relations, 1861–1865, Reconsidered," *Mid-America: An Historical Review*, 45 (Jan. 1963), pp. 36–49; Martin P. Claussen, "Peace Factors in Anglo-American Relations, 1861–5," *Mississippi Valley Historical Review*, 26/4 (March 1940), pp. 511–22; Henry Adams, "Why Did Not England Recognize the Confederacy?," *Massachusetts Historical Society Proceedings*, 66 (1972), pp. 204–22; Davis D. Joyce, "Pro-Confederate Sympathy in the British Parliament," *Social Science* (April 1969), pp. 95–100; Kinley J. Brauer, "British Mediation and the American Civil War: A Reconsideration," *Journal of Southern History*, 38/1 (Feb. 1972), pp. 49–64; Frank J. Merli and Theodore A. Wilson, "The British Cabinet and the Confederacy: Autumn, 1862," *Maryland Historical Society* (Fall 1967), pp. 239–62; Robert L. Reid (ed.), "William E. Gladstone's 'Insincere Neutrality' During the Civil War," *Civil War History*, 15/4 (1969), pp. 293–307; Howard Jones, *Union in Peril: The Crisis over British Intervention in the Civil War* (Chapel Hill, N.C., 1992); Brian Jenkins, *Britain and the War for the Union*, 2 vols. (Montreal, 1974, 1980); and Charles M. Hubbard, *The Burden of Confederate Diplomacy* (Knoxville, Tenn., 1998).

9. Adams, *Great Britain and the American Civil War*, vol. 2, p. 45, Russell to Palmerston, October 2, 1862.

10. Roy Jenkins, *Gladstone* (London, 1995), p. 472.

11. *George Douglas, Eighth Duke of Argyll (1823–1900): Autobiography and Memoirs*, ed. the Dowager Duchess of Argyll, 2 vols. (London, 1906), vol. 2, p. 195, Argyll to Gladstone, September 2, 1862.

12. Jenkins, *Gladstone*, pp. 472, 466.

13. ORN, ser. 2, vol. 3, pp. 549–51, Ambrose Dudley Mann to Judah P. Benjamin, October 7, 1862.

14. John Morely, *The Life of William Ewart Gladstone: 1809–1872*, 2 vols. (London, 1903), vol. 2, p. 536, and Henry Steele Commager (ed.), *The Civil War Archive* (New York, 2000), pp. 362–63.

15. *Harper's Magazine*, vol. 54, 1877, p. 111.

16. MHS, Adams MSS, Diary of Charles Francis Adams, October 5, 1862.

17. D. P. Crook, *The North, the South, and the Powers, 1861–1865* (New York, 1974), p. 266, November 8, 1862.

18. The literature on the cabinet discussions during October and November is voluminous. See E. D. Adams, *Great Britain and the American Civil War*, vol. 2, p. 52, for a discussion on the memoranda wars.

19. Henry Adams, *The Education of Henry Adams*, ed. Ernest Samuels (repr. Boston, 1973), pp. 183–84.

20. Adams, *Great Britain and the American Civil War*, vol. 2, p. 54, Clarendon to Russell, October 19, 1862.

21. ORN, ser. 2, vol. 3, pp. 560–61, Slidell to Benjamin, October 20, 1862.

22. Virginia Mason, *The Public Life and Diplomatic Correspondence of James M. Mason* (New York, 1906), pp. 371–72, Mason to wife, January 18, 1862.

23. ORN, ser. 2, vol. 3, pp. 565–67, Hotze to Benjamin, October 24, 1862.

24. Adams, *Great Britain and the American Civil War*, vol. 2, p. 56. In his memorandum, written on October 25, 1862, Gladstone insisted, somewhat improbably, that the Americans would not be able to resist "a general opinion on the part of civilized Europe that this horrible war ought to cease."

25. MHS, Adams MSS, Diary of Charles Francis Adams, October 23, 1862.

26. Adams, *Great Britain and the American Civil War*, vol. 2, p. 56, Russell to Palmerston, October 24, 1862.

27. West Sussex RO, Lyons MSS, box 300, Lord Lyons to sister, October 24, 1862.

28. ORN, ser. 2, vol. 3, pp. 542–78, Slidell to Benjamin, October 28, 1862.

29. G. P. Gooch (ed.), *The Later Correspondence of Lord John Russell, 1840–1878*, 2 vols. (London, 1925), vol. 2, p. 331, Russell to Grey, October 28, 1862.

30. Sir Herbert Maxwell, *Clarendon*, 2 vols. (London, 1913), vol. 2, p. 265, Clarendon to Lewis, October 25, 1862.

31. PRO 30/22/36, ff. 281–89, Lyons to Russell, November 11, 1862.

32. Jones, *Union in Peril*, p. 203.

33. Gooch (ed.), *The Later Correspondence of Lord John Russell*, vol. 2, p. 333, Palmerston to Russell, November 2, 1862.

34. ORN, ser. 2, vol. 3, p. 603, Hotze to Benjamin, November 7, 1862.

35. Deborah Logan (ed.), *The Collected Letters of Harriet Martineau*, 5 vols. (London, 2007), vol. 4, p. 365, September 17, 1862.

36. Wallace and Gillespie (eds.), *The Journal of Benjamin Moran*, vol. 2, p. 1088, November 11, 1862.

37. Sir Herbert Maxwell, *Clarendon*, vol. 2, p. 268, Lewis to Clarendon, November 11, 1862.

38. Howard Jones, *Union in Peril*, p. 217.

39. Morely, *The Life of William Ewart Gladstone,* vol. 2, p. 85, Gladstone to wife, November 13, 1862.

40. ORN, ser. 2, vol. 3, pp. 610–12, Hotze to Benjamin, November 22, 1862.

41. Quoted in Jones, *Union in Peril*, p. 223.

42. For example, Keele University, Sneyd MS, S[rs/hwv]/274, Henry William Vincent to Ralph Sneyd, November 17, 1862,.

43. ORN, ser. 2, vol. 3, p. 618, Mason to Benjamin, December 11, 1862.

PART II: FIRE ALL AROUND THEM

Chapter 15: Bloodbath at Fredericksburg

1. Sarah Agnes Wallace and Frances Elma Gillespie (eds.), *The Journal of Benjamin Moran*, 2 vols. (Chicago, 1948, 1949), vol. 2, p. 1092, November 19, 1862.

2. *The Reminiscences of Carl Schurz*, ed. Carl Schurz, Frederick Bancroft, and William Archibald Dunning, 3 vols. (Garden City, N.Y., 1917), vol. 2, p. 246.

3. Duke University, Malet family MSS, Kennedy to Malet, September 15, 1862.

4. Calvin D. Davis, "A British Diplomat and the American Civil War: Edward Malet in the United States," *South Atlantic Quarterly*, 77/2 (1978), pp. 160–61. In his memoir, Malet wrote that he always regretted obtaining his first post through his father's influence. "For many years it did me harm," he wrote. "The grade above mine was that of paid attaché, and ten of my juniors were passed to that rank over my head on the ground that I had been appointed when I ought to have been still in the schoolroom." E. Malet, *Shifting Scenes* (London, 1901), p. 18.

5. Davis, "A British Diplomat and the American Civil War," p. 171.

6. Duke University, Malet family MSS, Malet to Lady Malet, February 10, 1862.

7. Ibid., Malet to Lady Malet, December 2, 1862.

8. *The Civil War Papers of George B. McClellan: Selected Correspondence, 1860–1865*, ed. Stephen W. Sears (Cambridge, Mass., 1992), p. 517, McClellan to Lincoln, November 2, 1862.

9. Richard Wheeler, *Voices of the Civil War* (New York, 1990), p. 203.

10. The 12,000-strong corps was principally made up of German immigrants, and most of its commanders were foreign-born. A hero to many German Americans on account of his military leadership of the Baden revolutionaries in the 1848 revolution against Prussia, Sigel seemed to attract bad luck in the Civil War. At the Second Battle of Bull Run in August, his soldiers were mangled by the Confederates, resulting in the loss of 2,000 men. Since then, the XI corps had been designated the Reserve Grand Division. Some of the German volunteers' English did not run much further than the corps' slogan: "I fights mit Sigel."

11. NARA, CB MID64, roll 66, Sir Percy Wyndham to General Heintzelman, December 3, 1862.

12. BL Add. MS 41567, f. 240, Herbert to mother, January 3, 1863.

13. Hugh Dubrulle, "Fear of Americanization and the Emergence of an Anglo-Saxon Confederacy," *Albion: A Quarterly Journal Concerned with British Studies*, 33/4 (Winter 2001), pp. 583–613, at p. 604, Lieutenant Colonel Henry Malet to Layard, December 27, 1862, BL Add. MS 39104, Layard Papers.

14. BL Add. MS 41567, ff. 236–37, Herbert to brother Jack, November 26, 1862.

15. Ibid.

16. BL Add. MS 41567, ff. 238–39, Herbert to brother Jack, December 16, 1862.

17. William Mark McNight, *Blue Bonnets o'er the Border: The 79th New York Cameron Highlanders* (Shippensburg, Pa., 1998), p. 83.

18. Francis W. Dawson, *Reminiscences of Confederate Service, 1861–1865*, ed. Bell I. Wiley (Baton Rouge, La., 1980), p. 83.

19. Shelby Foote, *The Civil War*, 3 vols. (New York, 1986), vol. 2, p. 22.

20. Wheeler, *Voices of the Civil War*, p. 206.

21. Heros von Borcke, "Memoirs of the Confederate War for Independence," *Blackwood's Magazine*, 99 (Jan.–June 1866), p. 193.

22. After Wynne and Phillips came Colonel Bramston, followed by Captain Bushby, who "had just run the blockade into Charleston, after an exciting chase by the Federal cruisers, and could only spare a few days to look at our army. . . ." Bushby presented General Lee with a saddle and Stonewall Jackson with a breech-loading carbine. Borcke, "Memoirs," p. 463.

23. Ibid, p. 194.

24. Mary Sophia Hill, *A British Subject's Recollections of the Confederacy* (Baltimore, 1875), p. 31.

25. Foote, *The Civil War*, vol. 2, p. 26.

26. Borcke, "Memoirs," p. 196.

27. Nearly three decades later, a young British military historian and disciple of Viscount Wolseley summarized Burnside's mistakes: "Firstly, he underrated his antagonist; secondly, he neglected to reconnoiter as far as was within his power; thirdly, in preference to a line of operations which was feasible and safe, he selected one which . . . might possibly lead to terrible disaster." G.F.R. Henderson, *The Campaign of Fredericksburg* (London, 1886, privately repr. 1984), p. 36.

28. Mr. Goolrick, the British vice-consul (who was actually an American citizen), was also among the captives. He had long been an embarrassment to Lord Lyons, providing ample fodder to Northern newspapers who claimed that every British official was rabidly pro-South. Lyons took advantage of his arrest to close the vice-consulate permanently.

29. William Stanley Hoole, *Lawley Covers the Confederacy* (Tuscaloosa, Ala., 1964), p. 39.

30. Robert Underwood Johnson and Clarence Clough Buel (eds.), *Battles and Leaders of the Civil War*, 4 vols. (Secaucus, N.J., 1985), vol. 3, p. 116.

31. Ibid., p. 127.

32. New-York Historical Society, *Narrative of Ebenezer Wells* (*c.* 1881), December 11, 1862.

33. Henderson, *The Campaign of Fredericksburg*, p. 73.

34. *Illustrated London News*, January 31, 1863.

35. Brian Holden Reid, *Robert E. Lee* (London, 2005), p. 144.

36. Chicago Historical Society, George W. Hart MSS, George Hart to mother, January 12, 1863.

37. Hoole, *Lawley*, p. 40.

38. Johnson and Buel (eds.), *Battles and Leaders of the Civil War*, vol. 3, p. 116.

39. James A. Rawley (ed.), *The American Civil War: An English View* (Mechanicsburg, Pa., 2002), p. 158.

40. Hill, *A British Subject's Recollections of the Confederacy*, p. 30.

41. von Borcke, "Memoirs," p. 451. The quotation in the footnote on this page is from Stuart to G.W.C. Lee, December 18, 1862, quoted in *The Letters of General J.E.B. Stuart*, ed. Adele H. Mitchell (n.p.: Stuart-Mosby Historical Society, 1990), pp. 284–85.

42. *The Times*, January 23, 1863.

43. R. A. Preston, "Letter from a British Military Observer of the American Civil War," *Military Affairs*, 16 (1952), p. 55.

44. Quoted in Margaret Leach, *Reveille in Washington* (Alexandria, Va., 1962; repr. 1980), p. 276.

45. In contrast to the British Army, assistant surgeons in the Northern army were ranked as lieutenants and generally afforded much greater respect. "The social position of the medical, as compared with the combatant officers, is decidedly good, much better than in our own army," Mayo explained to British readers in an essay about his experiences. It did not provoke comment that "any person with decent prospects of success in civil practice should ever think of entering it." Francis Galton (ed.), *Vacation Tourists, 1862–1863* (London, 1864), p. 376.

46. Ibid., p. 384.

47. Duke University, Malet family MSS, Malet to father, December 16, 1862.

48. Michael Burlingame, *Abraham Lincoln*, 2 vols. (Baltimore, 2008), vol. 2, p. 446.

49. George Templeton Strong, *Diary of the Civil War, 1860–1865*, ed. Allan Nevins (New York, 1962), p. 282, December 18, 1862.

50. Ibid., p. 282, December 21, 1862.

51. William H. Seward (ed.), *Seward at Washington* (New York, 1891), p. 487, Seward to wife, December 28, 1860.

52. *Diary of Gideon Welles*, 3 vols. (Boston, 1911), vol. 1, p. 133, September 16, 1862.

53. *MPUS*, p. 160, Adams to Seward, July 31, 1862.

54. MHS, Adams MSS, Diary of Charles Francis Adams, December 22, 1862.

55. PRO 30/22/36, ff. 320–23, Lyons to Russell, December 12, 1862.

56. *PRFA* (1862), p. 124, Seward to Adams, July 5, 1862.

57. Frederick J. Blue, *Salmon P. Chase: A Life in Politics* (Kent, Ohio, 1987), p. 191.

58. John M. Taylor, *William Henry Seward: Lincoln's Right Hand* (New York, 1991), p. 208.

59. David H. Donald, *Charles Sumner and the Rights of Man* (New York, 1970), p. 90.

60. Burlingame, *Abraham Lincoln*, vol. 2., p. 453.

61. PRO 30/22/36, ff. 327–30, Lyons to Russell, December 22, 1862.

62. James J. Barnes and Patience P. Barnes (eds.), *The American Civil War Through British Eyes*, vol. 2 (Kent, Ohio, 2005), p. 282, Lyons to Russell, December 26, 1862.

63. *Rebellion Record: A Diary of American Events*, ed. Frank Moore, 12 vols. (New York, 1863), vol. 6, p. 299.

64. Devonshire MSS, Chatsworth, 2nd series (340.1831), Lord Hartington to Duke of Devonshire, December 18, 1862.

65. Ibid., Lord Hartington to Duke of Devonshire, December 25, 1862.

66. Ibid., Lord Hartington to Duke of Devonshire, September 29, 1862.

67. Ibid., Lord Hartington to Duke of Devonshire, October 17, 1862.

68. Ibid., Lord Hartington to Duke of Devonshire, December 28, 1862.

69. William Watson was in Baton Rouge, where slaves vastly outnumbered the white population. He watched his friends confront the possibility by speaking directly to their slaves. There seemed to be little desire to leave. "If we run

away, and go to New Orleans, like dem crazy niggers, where is we?" asked one slave wisely. "If so be we are to get free, we get it anyhow." William Watson, *Life in the Confederacy: Being the Observations and Experiences of an Alien in the South During the Civil War* (London, 1887; repr. Baton Rouge, La., 1995), p. 430.

70. Borcke, "Memoirs," p. 458.

71. Devonshire MSS, Chatsworth, 2nd series (340.1831), Lord Hartington to Duke of Devonshire, December 28, 1862.

Chapter 16: The Missing Key to Victory

1. Charles Herbert Mayo, *Genealogical History of the Mayo and Elton Family* (privately printed, 1882), p. 230.

2. Doris Kearns Goodwin, *Team of Rivals* (New York, 2005), p. 498.

3. James McPherson, *Tried by War* (New York, 2009), p. 149.

4. Winston Groom, *Vicksburg, 1863* (New York, 2009), p. 132. It is important to note, however, that James McPherson does not believe that Lincoln ever said those words; he concludes that the conversation was fabricated by Admiral David Dixon Porter. Even so, Lincoln himself would have agreed with them. McPherson, *This Mighty Scourge: Perspectives on the Civil War* (Oxford, 2007), p. 131.

5. *Memoirs of General William T. Sherman* (New York, 1876), p. 291.

6. Robert Underwood Johnson and Clarence Clough Buel (eds.), *Battles and Leaders of the Civil War,* 4 vols. (Secaucus, N.J., 1985), vol. 3, p. 467.

7. Ibid., p. 468.

8. Sherman wrote in his memoirs: "One brigade (De Courcey's) of Morgan's troops crossed the bayou safely, but took to cover behind the bank, and could not be moved forward. Frank Blair's brigade, of Steele's division, in support, also crossed the bayou, passed over the space of level ground to the foot of the hills: but, being unsupported by Morgan, meeting a very severe cross-fire of artillery, was staggered and gradually fell back. . . . I have always felt that it was due to the failure of General G. W. Morgan to obey his orders, or to fulfill his promise made in person. Had he used with skill and boldness one of his brigades, in addition to that of Blair's, he could have made a lodgment on the bluff, which would have opened the door for our whole force to follow." *Memoirs,* pp. 291–92.

9. He continued: "After capture, which was near night, we were marched through a drenching rain to Vicksburg, a distance of eleven miles, hungry and without blankets and were corralled in an old foundry where we laid on the cold wet ground for rest." Personal Papers of Major Milton Mills—16th OVI, letter from Benjamin Heckert, description of Battle of Chickasaw Bayou, December 21, 1904, doc. B028–01: http://www.mkwe.com/ohio/pages/B028–01 .htm.

10. OR, ser. 1, vol, 17/1, p. 650, December 29, 1862.

11. Owen Johnson Hopkins, *Under the Flag of the Nation: Diaries and Letters of a Yankee Volunteer* (Columbus, Ohio, 1961), p. 46. See also the diary of Sergeant Asa E. Sample of 54th Indiana Infantry, who recorded his part in the Chickasaw assault: "About this time the rebel batteries opened with canister shot and shell, replied to by our cannon in the rear. The ground before us was completely ob-

structed by fallen timber for near forty rods (660 feet). Over this we had to pass. Just now General DeCourcey gave the command 'advance the 54th and 22nd Kentucky about 50 yards!!' The fallen trees completely mingled the companies of both regiments but onward we went, whiz, boom, boom, went the shells above us, now lying down to evade that bursting burst, now advancing and many falling." http://www.hoosiersoldiers.com/54THINDIANA/1YEAR/DIARIES/SAMPLE/DIARY-DECEMBER-1862.htm

12. Allan Nevins, *The War for the Union*, 4 vols.; vol. 2: *War Becomes Revolution, 1862–1863* (New York, 1960), p. 386.

13. OR, ser. 1, vol. 17/1, S. 24, pp. 721–24, no. 4, Report by Brigadier General George Morgan, 13th Army Corps.

14. Ibid.

15. William L. Shea and Terrence J. Winschel, *Vicksburg Is the Key* (Lincoln, Nebr., 2003), p. 60.

16. Stanley Hirshson, *The White Tecumseh* (New York, 1997), p. 145.

17. John Y. Simon (ed.), *The Papers of Ulysses S. Grant*, 24 vols. (Carbondale, Ill., 2000), vol. 7, pp. 50–55. After the war, Grant denied that he was anti-Semitic and, to make amends, attended the dedication of the Adas Israel Congregation in Washington, D.C.

18. William Stanley Hoole, *Lawley Covers the Confederacy* (Tuscaloosa, Ala., 1964), p. 44.

19. OR, ser. 1, vol. 5, S. 5, p. 504. On February 8, General Smith ended his report on a skirmish around Fairfax Court House by saying, "Captain Currie, as usual, was everywhere to direct and make successful the expedition."

20. New York State Library, Edwin Morgan MSS, box 19, f. 11, Currie to Governor Morgan, March 2, 1863.

21. William Watson, *Life in the Confederacy: Being the Observations and Experiences of an Alien in the South During the Civil War* (London, 1887; repr. Baton Rouge, La., 1995), p. 440.

22. Bruce Catton, *Never Call Retreat* (London, 2001), p. 74.

23. New York State Library, Edwin Morgan MSS, box 19, f. 11, Currie to Governor Morgan, March 2, 1863.

24. OR, ser. 1, vol. 15, S. 21, p. 250, Telegram from L.D.H. Currie, February 26, 1863.

25. Once Banks had filled all the outposts and boosted the garrisons, his effective fighting force was less than half his 32,000-man army. At first he thought that a run up the Mississippi River was still possible with just 12,000 men. Catton, *Never Call Retreat*, p. 76.

26. Mary Sophia Hill, *A British Subject's Recollections of the Confederacy* (Baltimore, 1875), p. 28.

27. Ibid.

28. Raphael Semmes, *Service Afloat: A Personal Memoir of My Cruises and Services* (1868, repr. Baltimore, 1987), p. 402.

29. Charles Grayson Summersell, *CSS Alabama* (Tuscaloosa, Ala., 1985), p. 13.

30. Semmes, *Service Afloat*, p. 405.

31. The officers either knew or were related to one another to a remarkable degree. Fifth Lieutenant Irvine Bulloch, for example, was James Bulloch's younger

half-brother; midshipman Edward Maffit Anderson, was the son of Edward Charles Anderson who had directed the Confederate navy's purchasing operations so ably in 1861; and midshipman Eugene Anderson Maffit was his cousin.

32. Semmes, *Service Afloat*, p. 427.

33. Raimondo Luraghi, *A History of the Confederate Navy* (Annapolis, Md., 1996), p. 227.

34. In truth, USS *Hatteras* was not such a formidable opponent after all, being little more than a refitted passenger ship with about half the *Alabama*'s firepower. Charles Grayson Summersell, *The Journal of George Townley Fullam* (Tuscaloosa, Ala., 1973), p. 72.

35. Semmes, *Service Afloat*, p. 543.

36. Norman C. Delaney, *John McIntosh Kell of the Raider Alabama* (Tuscaloosa, Ala., 1973), p. 143.

37. Douglas Maynard, "Civil War 'Care': The Mission of the George Griswold," *New England Quarterly*, 34/3 (1961), p. 300.

38. Ibid., p. 303.

39. David Herbert Donald, *Charles Sumner and the Rights of Man* (New York, 1970), p. 109.

40. PRO 30/22/37, ff. 29–30, Lyons to Russell, February 24, 1863.

41. Beverly Wilson Palmer (ed.), *The Selected Letters of Charles Sumner*, 2 vols. (Boston, 1990), vol. 1, p. 148, Sumner to John Bright, March 16, 1863.

42. Brian Jenkins, *Britain and the War for the Union*, 2 vols. (Montreal, 1974, 1980), vol. 2, p. 185. Modern, low-cost, British-built and -owned steamships were monopolizing the Atlantic trade because their American competitors were old-fashioned sailboats.

43. *New York Times*, November 21, 1862.

Chapter 17: "The Tinsel Has Worn Off"

1. *Speeches, Arguments, Addresses, and Letters of Clement L. Vallandigham* (New York, 1864), p. 430.

2. BL Add. MS 415670, f. 245, Herbert to mother, March 10, 1863. The source for the footnote on this page is Francis Galton (ed.), *Vacation Tourists, 1862–1863* (London, 1864), p. 398.

3. Charles Herbert Mayo, *Genealogical History of the Mayo and Elton Family* (privately printed, 1882), p. 230.

4. Wendy Trewin, *All on Stage: Charles Wyndham and the Alberys* (London, 1980), p. 8.

5. Ibid., p. 11. This says his father encouraged him. But Wyndham himself says the family opposed the move and refused to support him financially. Thomas E. Pemberton, *Sir Charles Wyndham: A Biography* (London, 1904), pp. 8, 33.

6. Trewin, *All on Stage*, p. 18.

7. http://oha.alexandriava.gov/fortward/special-sections/voices/, testimony of William Wallace, 3rd Wisconsin Volunteer Infantry.

8. W. C. Ford (ed.), *A Cycle of Adams Letters, 1861–1865*, 2 vols. (Boston, 1920), vol. 1, p. 206, Charles Francis Adams, Jr., to mother, December 21, 1862.

9. Wyndham was always a favorite with the press, and his side was taken by *Dawson's Daily Times and Union*, a popular Indiana newspaper, which declared

that the resignation had been a matter of principle since he held Colonel Butler in such low esteem.

10. NARA, CB MID64, roll 66, Report by General Heintzelman, January 20, 1863.
11. BL Add. MS 415670, ff. 242–43, Herbert to Jack, January 28, 1863.
12. New-York Historical Society, *Narrative of Ebenezer Wells* (c. 1881), January 1863.
13. BL Add. MS 415670, ff. 242–43, Herbert to Jack, January 28, 1863.
14. Ford (ed.), *A Cycle of Adams Letters*, vol. 1, p. 250, Charles Francis Adams, Jr., to Henry Adams, January 30, 1863.
15. Ibid., p. 264, Charles Francis Adams, Jr., to Charles Francis Adams, March 8, 1863.
16. Galton (ed.), *Vacation Tourists*, p. 401.
17. Robert Underwood Johnson and Clarence Clough Buel (eds.), *Battles and Leaders of the Civil War*, 3 vols. (Secaucus, N.J., 1985), vol. 3, p. 150.
18. Ibid.
19. *The Memoirs of Colonel John S. Mosby*, ed. Charles W. Russell (Boston, 1917), p. 175.
20. Jeffry D. Wert, *Mosby's Rangers* (New York, 1990), p. 48.
21. Duke University, Malet family MSS, Malet to father, January 19, 1863.
22. Henry Vane, *Affair of State* (London, 2004), p. 62.
23. Devonshire MSS, Chatsworth, 2nd series (340.184), Hartington to 7th Duke, January 21, 1863.
24. University of Georgia Libraries, Athens, Ga., mss 340, A. Trevor-Batyre, "A Noble Englishman, Being Chapters in the Life of Henry Wemyss Feilden," p. 6.
25. Their romanticized portrayal of the Confederacy inspired fiction writers to develop the theme. In 1862 the pulp writer William Stephens Hayward began his series about Captain George, a dashing English adventurer who travels to the South to fight for its cause. The popularity of the series prompted a host of imitations, all based in the South.
26. The Charleston Chamber of Commerce and the Society of St. George both held farewell dinners for Mr. Bunch.
27. South Carolina Historical Society, Feilden-Smythe MSS, Feilden to aunt, March 4, 1863.
28. Ibid.

Chapter 18: Faltering Steps of a Counterrevolution

1. *Illustrated London News*, May 16, 1863. Vizetelly sometimes shocked his Confederate friends by his casual attitude toward strict accuracy. See G. Moxley Sorrel, *Recollections of a Confederate Staff Officer* (Lincoln, Nebr., 1999), p. 205.
2. Francis Galton (ed.), *Vacation Tourists, 1862–1863* (London, 1864), p. 399.
3. Robert N. Rosen, *Confederate Charleston* (Columbia, SC, 1994), p. 99.
4. South Carolina Historical Society, Feilden-Smythe MSS, Feilden to Phil, April 16, 1863. *Illustrated London News*, May 16, 1863.
5. *Diary of Gideon Welles*, 3 vols. (Boston, 1911), vol. 1, p. 276, April 20, 1863.
6. Doris Kearns Goodwin, *Team of Rivals* (New York, 2005), p. 511. Albert E. H. Johnson, "Reminiscences of the Hon. Edwin M. Stanton," *Records of the Columbia Historical Society* (1910), p. 80.
7. NARA, T.168, roll 31, vol. 31, doc. 3, Morse to Seward, January 3, 1863.

8. Russell was pleased by his success but annoyed with his publishers. They had cut out 186 pages, he told the U.S. consul in Paris, John Bigelow. The book accurately reflected his feelings, except "I must own I felt more hurt than I can or cared well to say at being refused leave to go with McClellan, as I was most anxious to show it was not my fault that Bull Run No. 1 ended with a panic. . . . I believe in my heart, however, that I do not entertain the smallest unkindly feeling towards a single citizen of the United States." John Bigelow, *Retrospections of an Active Life, Part I, 1817–1863,* 5 vols. (New York, 1909), vol. 1, pp. 605–6, Russell to Bigelow, February 25, 1863.

9. Sarah Agnes Wallace and Frances Elma Gillespie (eds.), *The Journal of Benjamin Moran,* 2 vols. (Chicago, 1948, 1949), vol. 2, p. 1106, January 14, 1863.

10. Ibid., p. 1110, January 21, 1863.

11. NARA, T. 168, roll 31, vol. 31, doc. 3, Morse to Seward, January 3, 1863.

12. *Illustrated London News,* February 7, 1863.

13. Philip Van Doren Stern, *When the Guns Roared: World Aspects of the American Civil War* (New York, 1965), p. 177.

14. Wallace and Gillespie (eds.), *The Journal of Benjamin Moran,* vol. 2, p. 1108, January 16, 1863.

15. Henry Adams, *The Education of Henry Adams,* ed. Ernest Samuels (repr. Boston, 1973), pp. 142–43.

16. Wallace and Gillespie (eds.), *The Journal of Benjamin Moran,* vol. 2, p. 1121, February 14, 1863.

17. Outraged by the plight of two British subjects imprisoned for alleged desertion, the British consul in Philadelphia sent an unofficial protest to the State Department. William Seward thought that the letter had to be an exaggeration, at least he hoped so, but he was sufficiently disturbed to write to the secretary of war, Edwin Stanton: "The granite walls of the dungeons are represented to be wet with moisture, the stone floor damp and cold, the air impure and deathly, no bed or couches to lie upon and offensive vermin crawling in every direction. It is also represented that the prisoners are allowed no water with which to wash themselves or change of clothing and are on every side surrounded by filth and vermin." OR, ser. 2, vol. 5, p. 118, Seward to Stanton, January 27, 1863.

18. MHS, Adams MSS, Diary of Charles Francis Adams, February 9, 1863.

19. Ibid., February 11, 1863.

20. Ibid., February 25, 1863.

21. Ibid., February 28, 1863.

22. Wallace and Gillespie (eds.), *The Journal of Benjamin Moran,* vol. 2, p. 1136, March 18, 1863.

23. Virginia Mason (ed.), *The Public Life and Diplomatic Correspondence of James M. Mason* (New York, 1906), pp. 387–92.

24. Spencer, *The Confederate Navy in Europe* (Tuscaloosa, Ala., 1983), pp. 135–36, January 21 and January 20, 1863.

25. Ibid., p. 131.

26. James M. Morgan, *Recollections of a Rebel Reefer* (Boston, 1917), pp. 96–97.

27. James D. Bulloch, *The Secret Service of the Confederate States in Europe,* 2 vols. (New York, 1884), vol. 1, p. 272.

28. Ibid., p. 270.

29. Ibid., p. 273, February 3, 1863.

30. There appears to be a great deal of confusion over which Emile Erlanger—the father or son—Mathilda actually married. Charles M. Hubbard, *The Burden of Confederate Diplomacy* (Knoxville, Tenn., 1998), p. 207, says the father, which the family website confirms: http://www.hydethomson.com/familytree/default.htm

31. Judith Fenner Gentry, "A Confederate Success in Europe: The Erlanger Loan," *Journal of Southern History* (1970), pp. 158–88. Spence always claimed that Erlanger took advantage of the Confederacy but subsequent studies have showed that the terms of the loan were comparable to, if not more favorable than, those offered to other governments with more grounds for legitimacy.

32. H. B. Wilson was a Canadian who had worked in the shipping industry. He did not arouse the Confederates' suspicion and, within a few weeks of introducing himself, had become a regular at their meetings and dinners. His success opened the doors to other U.S. agents.

33. ORN, ser. 1, vol. 13, p. 640, January 9, 1863. Excerpts of these reports were distributed to the navy, for example: "Liverpool. January 10 1863: The steamer *Pet* has just cleared and will go to sea this day. . . . The steamer *Banshee* has gone to-day on a trial trip. . . . It will not be very many days before she leaves for the South. . . . The *Peterhoff* went to sea yesterday. I herewith forward an invoice of her cargo, also an invoice and description of the *Sterlingshire*, a sailing bark in the Confederate service. From all I can learn the two steamers may attempt to get into Charleston. They are new, or nearly so, and would make good transport ships."

34. Frances Leigh Williams, *Matthew Fonatine Maury* (Piscataway, N.J., 1963), p. 403.

35. NARA, T.168, roll 31, vol. 31, doc.29, Morse to Seward, February 20, 1863.

36. Bulloch, *The Secret Service of the Confederate States in Europe*, vol. 1, p. 395, February 3, 1863.

37. ORN, ser. 2, vol. 3, pp. 712–16, Mason to Benjamin, March 19, 1863.

38. Stephen Wise, *Lifeline of the Confederacy: Blockade Running During the Civil War* (Columbia, S.C., 1988), p. 94.

39. Van Doren Stern, *When the Guns Roared*, p. 194.

40. Hubbard, *The Burden of Confederate Diplomacy*, pp. 132–33.

41. E. D. Adams, *Great Britain and the American Civil War*, 2 vols. in 1 (New York, 1958), vol. 2, p. 130.

42. Beverly Wilson Palmer (ed.), *Selected Letters of Charles Sumner*, 2 vols. (Boston, 1990), vol. 1, p. 154, Sumner to John Bright, April 7, 1863.

43. Lord Newton (ed.), *Lord Lyons: A Record of British Diplomacy*, 2 vols. (London, 1914), vol. 1, pp. 99–100, Russell to Lyons, March 28, 1863.

44. Adams, *Great Britain and the American Civil War*, vol. 2, p. 131.

45. NARA, T. 168, roll 31, vol. 31, doc. 41, Morse to Seward, March 27, 1863.

46. Adams, *Great Britain and the American Civil War*, vol. 2, p. 134.

47. Brooks Adams, "The Seizure of the Laird Rams," *Proceedings of the Massachusetts Historical Society*, 45 (1911–12), p. 248.

48. "We have had—I have had—some Experience of what any attempt of that sort may be expected to lead to," Palmerston told the House. He was referring to

the collapse of his previous premiership in 1859, when MPs punished him for truckling to French demands to curb the freedoms of political refugees living in Britain. Spencer, *The Confederate Navy in Europe*, p. 99.

49. MHS, Adams MSS, Diary of Charles Francis Adams, March 28, 1863.
50. Morgan, *Recollections of a Rebel Reefer*, p. 114.
51. Frank J. Merli, *Great Britain and the Confederate Navy* (Bloomington, Ind., 1965), p. 129.
52. The officer from the *Galatea* was singing the "Bonnie Blue Flag," which went: "Hurrah! Hurrah! For Southern rights hurrah! Hurrah for the Bonnie Blue Flag. . . . " *BDOFA*, ser. 1, vol. 6, doc. 193, pp. 146–47, Commodore Dunlop to Admiral Milne, February 7, 1863. In the Caribbean there was also an incident involving HMS *Greyhound*, when her band played "Dixie's Land" within earshot of a U.S. naval vessel. Commander Hickley immediately raced over to the players and made them follow up with "My Country, 'Tis of Thee," but the damage was already done.
53. "Here we are amongst the rebels enjoying ourselves very much," wrote Henry Gawne to his mother, a week after arriving at the port. "Everyone here is very hospitable. As much hunting as ever you please and of all descriptions, deer, foxes etc. Several of our officers are away now for four days in the Country hunting. I went out riding last Friday with a Col Browne of the Artillery." Buckinghamshire RO, Gawne MSS, D115/20 (1), Henry Gawne to Edward Moore Gawne and mother, January 6, 1863.
54. Regis Courtemanche, *No Need of Glory: The British Navy in American Waters* (Annapolis, Md., 1977), p. 117.
55. Newton (ed.), *Lord Lyons*, vol. 1, p. 100, Lord Russell to Lord Lyons, March 28, 1863.
56. PRO 30/22/37, f. 43, Lyons to Russell, April 13, 1863.
57. PRO 30/22/37, ff. 57–60, Lyons to Russell, May 5, 1863.
58. Adams, *Britain and the American Civil War*, vol. 2, p. 140.

Chapter 19: Prophecies of Blood and Suffering

1. *The Private Journal of Georgiana Gholson Walker*, ed. Dwight Franklin Henderson, Confederate Centennial Studies, 25 (Tuscaloosa, Ala., 1963), p. 13.
2. Kenneth Blume, "The Mid-Atlantic Arena: The United States, the Confederacy, and the British West Indies, 1861–1865," Ph.D thesis, SUNY Binghamton, 1984, p. 257.
3. James M. Morgan, *Recollections of a Rebel Reefer* (Boston, 1917), pp. 103–5.
4. PRO FO115/361, f. 3, Stanton to Seward, May 15, 1863. Montreal, where Abinger was stationed, was teeming with Confederate refugees, which further solidified his pro-Southern stand. On his return to Montreal, he married Helen Magruder, the daughter and niece of renowned Confederates.
5. George Alfred Lawrence, *Border and Bastille* (New York, 1864), p. 190.
6. James H. Wilkins (ed.), *The Great Diamond Hoax and Other Stirring Episodes in the Life of Asbury Harpending* (San Francisco, 1915), pp. 66, 74–76.
7. Ibid.
8. PRO FO5/1280, Consul Booker to Russell, June 29, 1863.
9. PRO FO5/1280, Scholefield to Austen M. Layard, May 1, 1863.

10. "Bright-Sumner Letters, 1861–1872," *Proceedings of the Massachusetts Historical Society*, 46 (1912), pp. 120–22, John Bright to Sumner, June 27, 1863.

11. "John Wilkes Booth: An Interview with the Press with Sir Charles Wyndham," *New York Herald*, quoted in Gordon Samples, *Lust for Fame* (New York, 1998), p. 113.

12. James J. Barnes and Patience P. Barnes (eds.), *Private and Confidential: Letters from British in Washington to Foreign Secretaries* (Selinsgrove, Pa., 1993), p. 320, Lyons to Russell, April 13, 1863, and p. 322, May 5, 1863. The most controversial revelation in the Blue Book was Lord Lyons's private meeting with New York Democrats in November 1862. The Republican administration put the worst possible interpretation on it, even though Lyons was not doing anything wrong or unusual for a diplomat by talking to the opposition party. "The Despatches of Lord Lyons prove how difficult it is to become familiar with the public spirit in this country, even for a cautious, discreet diplomat and an Englishman," wrote Adam Gurowski. "I am at a loss to understand why Earl Russell divulged the above mentioned correspondence, thus putting Lord Lyons into a false and unpleasant position with the party in power." *Diary from November 18, 1862–October 18, 1863* (New York, 1864), p. 182.

13. *Diary of Gideon Welles*, 3 vols. (Boston, 1911), vol. 2, p. 250, April 1, 1863. It was no help to Lyons that Welles vehemently opposed Seward on the letters of marque question. His chief objection stemmed from the fact that it would remain the purview of the State Department rather than his own.

14. Sumner calmed down a little, but remained adamant that the *Peterhoff*'s mails should have been dealt with by the prize court. Ironically, when the British cabinet had a chance to consider the *Peterhoff* affair rationally, it too reached the same conclusion. The Lord Chancellor asked: "What will be most [helpful] for our interest as a future belligerent?" The answer, obviously, was the right to seize the enemy's letters from neutral ships.

15. PRO 30/22/37, Frf. 42–43, Lyons to Russell, April 7, 1863.

16. PRO FO115/394, f. 35, B. Lowry to Lyons, May 28, 1863.

17. *Richmond Enquirer*, October 3, 1863.

18. Emory University, Gregory MSS, Lawley to Gregory, March 26, 1863.

19. Ibid.

20. BL Add. MS 41567, ff. 246–47, George Henry Herbert to mother, March 31, 1863.

21. Matthew John Graham, *The Ninth Regiment New York Volunteers* (Lancaster, Ohio, 1997), p. 420.

22. Bruce Catton, *The Civil War* (New York, 2004), p. 130.

Chapter 20: The Key Is in the Lock

1. Bernard Price, *Sussex: People, Places, Things* (London, 1975), p. 149.

2. Robert Underwood Johnson and Clarence Clough Buel (eds.), *Battles and Leaders of the Civil War*, 4 vols. (Secaucus, N.J., 1985), vol. 3, p. 161.

3. *The Times*, June 11, 1863.

4. William C. Davis (ed.), *The Civil War: A Historical Account of America's War of Secession* (New York, 1996), p. 114.

5. Jeffry D. Wert, *The Sword of Lincoln* (New York, 2006), p. 246.

6. Henry Hore identified the raiders as belonging to Mosby's Raiders, and, while there is no reason to doubt his word, it is worth noting that Mosby was at Warrenton Junction, Virginia, on May 3. See Jeffry D. Wert, *Mosby's Rangers* (New York, 1990), pp. 57–58.

7. Price, *Sussex*, p. 150.

8. Geoffrey C. Ward, Ric Burns, and Ken Burns, *The Civil War* (New York, 1990), p. 210.

9. W. C. Ford (ed.), *A Cycle of Adams Letters, 1861–1865*, 2 vols. (Boston, 1920), vol. 1, p. 294, Charles Francis Adams, Jr., to Charles Francis Adams, May 8, 1863.

10. Hore returned to England after the war. He joined the Capital and Counties Bank in Chichester, eventually rising to bank manager. He died in 1887. Price, *Sussex*, p. 145.

11. David Saville Muzzey, *The United States of America: Through the Civil War* (New York, 1931), p. 575.

12. Allan Nevins, *The War for the Union*, 4 vols.; vol. 2: *War Becomes Revolution, 1862–1863* (New York, 1960), p. 453.

13. *The Times*, June 16, 1863.

14. Winston S. Churchill, *The American Civil War* (New York, 1985), p. 100

15. Ian F. W. Beckett, *The War Correspondents: The American Civil War* (London, 1997), p. 102.

16. *Illustrated London News*, August 8, 1863.

17. Ibid., August 29, 1863.

18. William L. Shea and Terrence J. Winschel, *Vicksburg Is the Key* (Lincoln, Nebr., 2003), p. 151.

19. *Illustrated London News*, August 29, 1863.

20. Philip Tucker, "Confederate Secret Agent in Ireland: Father John B. Bannon and His Irish Mission, 1863–1864," *Journal of Confederate History*, 5 (1990), p. 55.

21. Francis Galton (ed.), *Vacation Tourists, 1862–1863* (London, 1864), p. 412.

22. Ibid., p. 410.

23. PRO FO 115/394, ff. 305–7, Mayo to Lyons, June 26, 1863.

24. James G. Hollandsorth, *Pretense of Glory* (Baton Rouge, La., 1998), p. 120.

25. Huguenot Historical Society, LeFevre/DuBois/Eltin Family Papers/ NYUL58T-320–0057, Assistant Surgeon S. E. Hasbrouck to Sol, 133rd New York Volunteers, June 16, 1863.

26. Arthur J. L. Fremantle, *Three Months in the Southern States* (Lincoln, Nebr., 1991), p. 120.

27. Ibid., p. 7.

28. Raphael Semmes, *Service Afloat: A Personal Memoir of My Cruises and Services* (1868; repr. Baltimore, 1987), p. 314.

29. Fremantle, *Three Months in the Southern States*, p. 108.

30. Ibid., p. 117.

31. Frank L. Klement, *The Limits of Dissent* (New York, 1998), p. 168.

32. The details of Colonel Grenfell's life are taken from Stephen Z. Starr, *Colonel Grenfell's Wars* (Baton Rouge, La., 1971), a brilliant piece of detective work on an extremely elusive figure.

33. Fremantle, *Three Months in the Southern States*, p. 149.

34. Ibid., pp. 149–50.

35. Ibid., p. 164.
36. Ibid., p. 180.

Chapter 21: The Eve of Battle

1. Henry Vane, *Affair of State* (London, 2004), p. 65.
2. Patrick Jackson, *The Last of the Whigs: A Political Biography of Lord Hartington, Later 8th Duke of Devonshire* (London, 1994), p. 33.
3. "Bow down ye ignoble hard-working members!," the Earl of Kimberley wrote sarcastically in his diary, who thought the position should have gone to him. *Journal of John Wodehouse, First Earl of Kimberley* (Cambridge, 1997), April 20, 1863. When Lawley heard the news of Hartington's promotion he sent him the official report on the U.S. attack on Charleston on April 7. "A printed copy of it was handed to me as a favour, and I was told that I might make any use of it in Europe which I tried, short of its publication."
4. Frances Leigh Williams, *Matthew Fontaine Maury* (Piscataway, N.J., 1963), p. 409. Maury learned of his son's disappearance on April 8, 1863.
5. Merseyside Maritime Museum, Fraser, Trenholm MSS, B/FT box 1/7, Bulloch to Prioleau, April 20, 1863.
6. MHS, Adams MSS, Diary of Charles Francis Adams, April 7, 1863.
7. Martin Duberman, *Charles Francis Adams*, p. 305.
8. W. C. Ford (ed.), *A Cycle of Adams Letters, 1861–1865*, 2 vols. (Boston, 1920), vol. 1, p. 275, Henry Adams to Charles Francis Adams, Jr., April 23, 1863.
9. The inscription on the plaque reads: "Presented by English gentlemen, as a tribute of admiration for the soldier and patriot, Thomas J. Jackson, and gratefully accepted by Virginia in the name of the Southern people. Done A. D. 1875, in the hundredth year of the commonwealth. 'Look! There is Jackson, Standing like a Stone-Wall.'" The Beresford Hope quotation is from his *The Results of the American Disruption* (London, 1862), p. 44.
10. Charles P. Cullop, "English Reaction to Stonewall Jackson's Death," *West Virginia History*, 29/1 (Oct. 1967), pp. 1–5.
11. James M. Morgan, *Recollections of a Rebel Reefer* (Boston, 1917), p. 126.
12. Library of Congress, Mason Papers, James Spence to Mason, June 16, 1863.
13. *Harriet Martineau: Selected Letters*, ed. Valerie Sanders (Oxford, 1990), p. 201, Martineau to Henry Bright, May 3, 1863.
14. Brian Jenkins, *Britain and the War for the Union*, 2 vols. (Montreal, 1974, 1980), vol. 2, p. 50.
15. Joyce Miank Lierley (ed.), *Affectionately Yours: Three English Immigrants, the American Civil War and a Michigan Family Saga* (Omaha, Nebr., 1998), p.166, Mary Ann Rutter to brother, September 24, 1863.
16. John Bailey (ed.), *Diary of Lady Frederick Cavendish*, 2 vols. (New York, 1927), vol. 1, p. 161. The future Lady Frederick was also Gladstone's niece, which no doubt played a role in her early political education.
17. Wilbur Devereux Jones, "The Confederate Rams at Birkenhead," *Confederate Centennial Studies*, 19 (Wilmington, N.C., 2000), p. 47.
18. Sarah Agnes Wallace and Frances Elma Gillespie (eds.), *The Journal of Benjamin Moran, 1857–1865*, 2 vols. (Chicago, 1948, 1949), vol. 2, p. 1178, June 27, 1863.

19. F. L. Owsley, *King Cotton Diplomacy* (2nd ed., Chicago, 1959), p. 450.

20. Ibid., p. 461.

21. Herman Ausubel, *John Bright: Victorian Reformer* (New York, 1966), p. 136.

22. Ibid.

23. Henry Adams, *The Education of Henry Adams*, ed. Ernest Samuels (repr. Boston, 1973), p. 187.

24. Emory M. Thomas, *Bold Dragoon: The Life of J.E.B. Stuart* (Norman, Okla., 1999), p. 226.

25. Devonshire MSS, Chatsworth, 2nd series (340.195), Lawley to Hartington, June 14, 1863.

26. Edward G. Longacre, *Jersey Cavaliers* (Hightstown, N.J., 1992), p. 144.

27. OR, ser. 1, vol. 27/1, doc. 39, p. 966, June 10, 1863.

28. OR, ser. 1, vol. 27/1, doc. 43, p. 1054, June 10, 1863.

29. Ford (ed.), *A Cycle of Adams Letters*, vol. 2, p. 32, Charles Francis Adams, Jr., to Henry Adams, June 14, 1863.

30. Thomas, *Bold Dragoon*, p. 226.

31. British Library of Political and Economic Science, LSE, Farr MSS, GB 0097 Farr/vol. 10, Add. 2, ff. 5–25.

32. PRO FO282/10/d.211, ff. 104–11, Archibald to Lyons, July 8, 1863.

33. PRO FO 114/402, f. 1038, Lyons to Revd. W. E. Hoskins, December 3, 1863. Lyons also passed on two letters from his brother officers, testimonials to how bravely Hoskins fought and died.

34. PRO FOI 15/394, f. 100, Miss Hodges to Lord Lyons, June 8, 1863. Many years later, Hoskins's family erected a gravestone on his burial plot.

35. West Sussex RO, Lyons MSS, box 301, Lyons to sister, June 16, 1863.

Chapter 22: Crossroads at Gettysburg

1. Devonshire MSS, Chatsworth, 2nd series (340.195), Lawley to Hartington, June 14, 1863.

2. Arthur J. L. Fremantle, *Three Months in the Southern States* (Lincoln, Nebr., 1991), p. 220. The quotation in the first footnote on this page is from p. 191.

3. Ibid., p. 208.

4. Ibid., p. 211.

5. According to William Torens, Davies was sent to the 7th Tennessee Infantry first, from August 1863 to November 1864, and then became a lieutenant and AAIG to Heth on November 30, 1864.

6. Fremantle, *Three Months in the Southern States*, p. 211.

7. Justus Scheibert wrote eloquently about such damaged terrain: "Only grunting swine wandered around on level ground, often rooting at the shallow graves and gnawing on bodies which stared with distorted horrible expressions at persons who rode by." Justus Scheibert, *Seven Months in the Rebel States During the North American War, 1863*, trans. Joseph C. Hayes, ed. William Stanley Hoole (Tuscaloosa, Ala., 2009), p. 33.

8. W. C. Ford (ed.), *A Cycle of Adams Letters, 1861–1865*, 2 vols. (Boston, 1920), vol. 2, pp. 36–37, Charles Francis Adams, Jr., to Henry Adams, June 19, 1863.

9. Emory M. Thomas, *Bold Dragoon: The Life of J.E.B. Stuart* (Norman, Okla., 1999), p. 241.

10. Francis W. Dawson, *Reminiscences of Confederate Service, 1861–1865*, ed. Bell I. Wiley (Baton Rouge, La., 1980), p. 91.

11. Morris to Lawley, June 25, 1863, quoted in Brian Jenkins, "Frank Lawley and the Confederacy," *Civil War History*, 23 (March 1997).

12. Fremantle, *Three Months in the Southern States*, p. 177.

13. Fitzgerald Ross, *Cities and Camps of the Confederate States*, ed. Richard Barksdale Harwell (Champaign, Ill., 1997), p. 42.

14. Historians have since exonerated Ewell. He had less than an hour to get his troops into line and charge the ridge before Federal defenders received thousands of reinforcements. James M. McPherson (ed.), *Battle Chronicles of the Civil War*, 6 vols. (Lakeville, Conn., 1989), vol. 3, p. 69. But when Francis Lawley wrote his report of the day's fighting he repeated without examination the accusation that Ewell had lost the battle through his bungling.

15. Ross, *Cities and Camps*, p. 48.

16. Joseph E. Persico, *My Enemy, My Brother: Men and Days of Gettysburg* (New York, 1988), p. 135.

17. *The Times*, August 18, 1863.

18. Fremantle, *Three Months in the Southern States*, p. 260.

19. *The Times*, August 18, 1863.

20. Susannah Ural Bruce, *The Harp and the Eagle* (New York, 2006), p. 163.

21. Jeffry D. Wert, *The Sword of Lincoln* (New York, 2006), p. 294.

22. "Rebel Without a Cause—From Shakespeare Country," *Crossfire: The Magazine of the American Civil War Round Table*, 48 (April 1993).

23. Dawson, *Reminiscences*, p. 95.

24. Fremantle, *Three Months in the Southern States*, p. 190.

25. Dawson, *Reminiscences*, p. 96.

26. Charles Francis Adams, Jr., *Charles Francis Adams, 1835–1915: An Autobiography with a Memorial Address* (New York, 1916), p. 151.

27. Somewhere in the stream was Lieutenant Colonel George T. Gordon of the 34th North Carolina Infantry. He had arrived in the South six months earlier, a fugitive from British and Canadian justice. An accomplished fraud, he tricked the authorities into awarding him the rank of major. To his surprise, the war exposed a hitherto completely hidden layer of decency. Promotions followed and by Gettysburg he was a brigade commander. After the war, however, he returned to his old ways.

28. Fremantle, *Three Months in the Southern States*, p. 267.

29. Dawson, *Reminiscences*, p. 96.

30. Edward Porter Alexander, *Fighting for the Confederacy: The Personal Recollections of General Edward Porter Alexander*, ed. Gary Gallagher (Chapel Hill, N.C., 1989), p. 266.

31. Adams, *Charles Francis Adams, 1835–1915: An Autobiography*, p. 151.

32. John B. Jones, *A Rebel War Clerk's Diary at the Confederate States Capital*, ed. Earl Schenck Miers (Urbana, Ill., 1958), p. 286.

33. Alexander, *Fighting for the Confederacy*, p. 268.

34. Fremantle, *Three Months in the Southern States*, p. 274.

35. James Longstreet, *From Manassas to Appomattox* (New York, 2004), p. 361. Longstreet added: "It is simply out of the question for a lesser force to march

over broad, open fields and carry a fortified front occupied by a great force of seasoned troops." Longstreet was stung by the criticisms of his own actions at Gettysburg and energetically defended himself against charges that ranged from treason to arrogance.

36. William Stanley Hoole, *Lawley Covers the Confederacy* (Tuscaloosa, Ala., 1964), p. 63.

37. *The Times*, August 18, 1863.

Chapter 23: Pressure Rising

1. Hansard, 3rd ser., vol. 171, cols. 1827–28, June 3, 1863, John Bright.

2. Henry Adams, *The Education of Henry Adams*, ed. Ernest Samuels (repr. Boston, 1973), p. 187.

3. F. L. Owsley, *King Cotton Diplomacy* (2nd ed., Chicago, 1959), p. 461.

4. E. D. Adams, *Great Britain and the American Civil War*, 2 vols. in 1 (New York, 1958), vol. 2, p. 172.

5. Ibid., p. 173.

6. ORN, ser. 2, vol. 3, no. 25, pp. 839–40, Hotze to Benjamin, July 11, 1863.

7. Sarah Agnes Wallace and Frances Elma Gillespie (eds.), *The Journal of Benjamin Moran, 1857–1865,* 2 vols. (Chicago, 1948, 1949), vol. 2, p. 1183, July 14, 1863.

8. Francis Galton (ed.), *Vacation Tourists, 1862–1863* (London, 1864), p. 412.

9. New-York Historical Society, *Narrative of Ebenezer Wells* (c. 1881).

10. William L. Shea and Terrence J. Winschel, *Vicksburg Is the Key* (Lincoln, Nebr., 2003), p. 185.

11. Sheffield Archives, WHM 461 (24), Hampson to Lord Wharncliffe, January 17, 1865.

12. PRO FO115/395, f. 60, Mayo to Lyons, July 24, 1863.

13. Adams, *Great Britain and the American Civil War*, vol. 2, p. 179.

14. *Historical Collection, Michigan Pioneer and Historical Society*, vol. 29 (Lansing, Mich., 1900), p. 604.

15. ORN, ser. 2, vol. 3, no. 26, pp. 849–51, Hotze to Benjamin, July 23, 1863.

16. W. C. Ford (ed.), *A Cycle of Adams Letters, 1861–1865*, 2 vols. (Boston, 1920), vol. 2, p. 59, Henry Adams to Charles Francis Adams, Jr., July 23, 1863; *Economist*, August 1, 1863, quoted in Hugh Brogan, "America and Walter Bagehot," *Journal of American Studies*, 11/3 (Dec. 1977), p. 340.

17. Charles Vandersee, "Henry Adams Behind the Scenes: Civil War Letters to Frederick W. Seward," 71/4 (1967), p. 259.

18. Adams, *The Education of Henry Adams*, pp. 204–55.

19. Ford (ed.), *A Cycle of Adams Letters*, vol. 2, p. 32, Henry Adams to Charles Francis Adams, Jr., July 23, 1863.

20. Ibid., p. 54, Charles Adams to Charles Francis Adams, Jr., July 24, 1863.

21. Norman Longmate, *The Hungry Mills: The Story of the Lancashire Cotton Famine, 1861–5* (London, 1978), p. 205.

22. Lance Davis and Stanley L. Engerman, *Naval Blockades in Peace and War* (Cambridge, 2006), pp. 128–29.

23. Wallace and Gillespie (eds.), *The Journal of Benjamin Moran*, vol. 2, p. 1188, July 27, 1863.

24. Allan Nevins, *The War for the Union*, 4 vols.; vol. 2: *War Becomes Revolution, 1862–1863* (New York, 1960), p. 120.

25. Susannah Ural Bruce, *The Harp and the Eagle* (New York, 2006), p. 177.

26. Edward Robb Ellis, *The Epic of New York City* (New York, 2005), p. 298.

27. Sarah Forbes Hughes (ed.), *Letters and Recollections of John Murray Forbes*, 2 vols. (New York, 1900), vol. 2, p. 49.

28. Arthur J. L. Fremantle, *Three Months in the Southern States* (Lincoln, Nebr., 1991), p. 300.

29. Ellis, *The Epic of New York City*, p. 305.

30. The description of the draft riots is largely taken from the following sources: Ellis, *The Epic of New York City*; Joel Tyler Hedley, *The Great Riots of New York, 1712–1873* (New York, 1873); David Barnes, *The Draft Riots of New York, July, 1863: The Metropolitan Police; Their Service During Riot Week* (New York, 1863); Edwin G. Burrows and Mike Wallace, *Gotham* (New York, 1999), pp. 888–99.

31. James M. McPherson, *Battle Cry of Freedom* (London, 1988), p. 610. The Gatling gun had been patented in 1862.

32. George Templeton Strong, *Diary of the Civil War, 1860–1865*, ed. Allan Nevins (New York, 1962), p. 339, July 15, 1863.

33. Fremantle, *Three Months in the Southern States*, p. 303.

34. Iver Bernstein, *The New York City Draft Riots* (Oxford, 1990), p. 17.

35. George Rowell, "Acting Assistant Surgeon," *Nineteenth Century Theatre Research*, 12 (1984), p. 33.

36. Strong, *Diary of the Civil War*, p. 341, July 17, 1863.

37. Ellis, *The Epic of New York*, p. 315.

38. PRO FO282/8, ff. 325–28, Archibald to Russell, July 18, 1863.

39. PRO FO282/10, ff. 126–27, d. 238, Archibald to Lyons, July 20, 1863.

40. Doris Kearns Goodwin, *Team of Rivals* (New York, 2005), p. 536.

41. Northumberland RO, 2179/1, C. A. Race to Father, July 24, 1863. Another lost soul in the Federal army was thirty-four-year-old Theodore Lee. Unhappy at home and beset by financial problems, he had fled England because "I wanted a radical change. . . . I needed a change to prevent both mind and body being comfortably boxed up at the expense of my friends." Joining the Federal army as a substitute had seemed his only option. So far his life was tolerable, he wrote to his brother and sister in England, except that "the mosquitoes and bugs are terrible at night." Leicestershire RO, D3796/6, Theodore Lee to his brother and sister, August 16, 1863.

42. British Library of Political and Economic Science, LSE, Farr MSS, Add. 2, J. G. Kennedy to William Farr, August 9, 1863. Sometimes, the case was reversed and the legation was pitted between a penitent son and his furious family. Charles Race, an English sergeant stationed at Fort Monroe, needed all his courage to inform his father that he was still alive: "With feelings of sorrow which it is utterly impossible for me to describe, I take my pen in a trembling hand to write and let you know where I am," he wrote on July 24, 1863. "I went as you are aware to London and, after passing a few miserable days there, a burning sense of shame at the idea of looking anybody in the face again combined, I now think with a kind of insanity, I formed the idea of

coming to America. . . . I left England whether ever to see you again or not, God only knows."

43. PRO FO115/395, f. 73, Belshaw to Lyons, August 14, 1863.
44. *Diary of Gideon Welles*, 3 vols. (Boston 1911), vol. 1, pp. 409–10, August 21, 1863.
45. University of Rochester, Rochester, N.Y., Rush Rhees Library, Seward MSS, Lyons to Seward, July 20, 1863.
46. PRO FO5/892, ff. 17–24, Lyons to Russell, August 3, 1863.
47. PRO 30/22/37, ff. 133–36, Lyons to Russell, August 7, 1863.
48. PRO 30/22/37, ff. 143–46, Lyons to Russell, August 14, 1863.
49. PRO 30/22/37, ff. 147–59, Lyons to Russell, September 2, 1863.
50. PRO 30/22/22, ff. 255–57, Palmerston to Russell, September 14, 1864.
51. C. Vann Woodward (ed.), *Mary Chesnut's Civil War* (New Haven, 1981), p. 664.
52. Justus Scheibert, *Seven Months in the Confederate States During the North American War, 1863*, trans. Joseph C. Hayes, ed. William Stanley Hoole (Tuscaloosa, Ala., 2009), pp. 132, 140.
53. PRO FO5/907, ff. 179–88, Stuart to Russell, August 15, 1863.
54. *Cornhill Magazine*, 10 (1864), pp. 99–110.
55. Fitzgerald Ross, *Cities and Camps of the Confederate States*, ed. Richard Barksdale Harwell (Champaign, Ill., 1997), p. 107.
56. Merseyside Maritime Museum, Fraser, Trenholm MSS, B/FT box 1/107, Thomas Prioleau to Charles K. Prioleau, September 9, 1863. The comment by Lawley in the footnote on this page is taken from Alan Hankinson, *Man of Wars: William Howard Russell of "The Times," 1820–1907* (London, 1982), p. 182.

Chapter 24: Devouring the Young

1. North Carolina State Archives, Private Collections, PC 1226, Rose O'Neal Greenhow MSS, London Diary, p. 3.
2. *The Private Journal of Georgiana Gholson Walker*, ed. Dwight Franklin Henderson, *Confederate Centennial Studies*, 25 (Tuscaloosa, Ala., 1963), p. 53.
3. Ann Blackman, *Wild Rose: Rose O'Neale Greenhow, Civil War Spy* (New York, 2005), p. 267.
4. Warren F. Spencer, *The Confederate Navy in Europe* (Tuscaloosa, Ala., 1983), pp. 144–76. In addition to Spencer, the other invaluable works on this subject are *King Cotton Diplomacy* by Frank Owsley (2nd ed., Chicago, 1959) and *Great Britain and the Confederate Navy* by Frank J. Merli (Bloomington, Ind., 1965).
5. David Hepburn Milton, *Lincoln's Spymaster: Thomas Haines Dudley and the Liverpool Network* (Mechanicsburg, Pa., 2003), p. 107.
6. *Diary of Gideon Welles*, 3 vols. (Boston, 1911), vol. 1, pp. 428, 437.
7. MHS, Adams MSS, Diary of Charles Francis Adams, August 28, 1863.
8. *PRFA*, 1 (1864), p.367, Adams to Russell, September 5, 1863.
9. MHS, June 1914. "Argyll Letters, 1861–1865," pp. 66–107, Duchess of Argyll to Sumner, July 23, 1863, p. 81.
10. "Letters of Richard Cobden to Charles Sumner," *American Historical Review*, 2 (1897), p. 312, Cobden to Sumner, August 7, 1863. Cobden continued: "Had England joined France they would have been followed by probably every

other State of Europe, with the exception of Russia. This is what the Confederate agents have been seeking to accomplish. They have pressed recognition on England and France with persistent energy from the first."

11. PRO 30/22/22, f. 243, Palmerston to Russell, September 4, 1863. In fact, he expected them to lose the case: "I think you are right in detaining the iron clads now building in the Mersey and the Clyde, though the result may be that we shall be obliged to set them free—There can be no doubt that ships coated with iron must be intended for warlike purposes, but to justify seizure we must, I conceive, be able to prove that they are intended for the use of the Confederates and to be employed against the Federal government, and this may not be easy as it will be to lay hold of them."

12. Brian Jenkins, *Britain and the War for Union*, 2 vols. (Montreal, 1974, 1980), vol. 2, p. 290.

13. Somerset RO, Somerset MSS, d/RA/A/2a/39/11, Palmerston to Somerset, September 13, 1863. Palmerston continued: "If we get these ships they will tend to give us moral as well as maritime strength." On October 2, Palmerston was ruminating on the theme of war with the United States: "We shall be pretty well off, I see, by next summer, with an addition for 1865; and there seems no good reason to expect a rupture with France within that period though it would be hazardous to say as much of our relations with the United States."

14. Detective Officer William Cozens filed the following report: "On Sunday the 13th instant, 95 men of the crew of the Florida arrived here by Railway from Cardiff the greater portion of them are natives of Ireland and some from various parts of Great Britain, the rest are composed of Germans, Dutchmen and a few Americans." PRO HO45/7261/122.

15. *BDOFA*, Part 1, ser. C, vol. 6, p. 184, Adams to Russell, September 16, 1863.

16. D. P. Crook, *The North, the South, and the Powers, 1861–1865* (New York, 1974), p. 326, *PRFA*, 1 (1864), p. 384, Russell to Adams, September 25, 1863.

17. W. C. Ford (ed.), *A Cycle of Adams Letters, 1861–1865*, 2 vols. (Boston 1920), vol. 2, p. 82, Henry Adams to Charles Francis Adams, Jr., September 16, 1863.

18. *Diary of Gideon Welles*, vol. 1, p. 435, September 17, 1863.

19. PRO 30/22/37, ff. 227–30, Lyons to Russell, November 6, 1863.

20. PRO 30/22/37, ff. 213–16, Lyons to Russell, October 23, 1863.

21. For a fuller discussion of Sumner's motives and the reaction to his speech, see David Herbert Donald, *Charles Sumner and the Rights of Man* (New York, 1970), pp. 126–37.

22. Beverly Wilson Palmer (ed.), *The Selected Letters of Charles Sumner*, 2 vols. (Boston, 1990), vol. 2, pp. 197–98, Sumner to Bright, October 6, 1863.

23. Quoted in Sarah Agnes Wallace and Frances Elma Gillespie (eds.), *The Journal of Benjamin Moran, 1857–1865*, 2 vols. (Chicago, 1948, 1949), vol. 2, p. 1220, October 8, 1863.

24. Edward Chalfant, *Better in Darkness* (New York, 1994), p. 69.

25. MHS, Adams MSS, *Diary of Charles Francis Adams*, October 24, 1863.

26. Wallace and Gillespie (eds.), *The Journal of Benjamin Moran*, vol. 2, p. 1212, September 22, 1863.

27. Benjamin did not have a clear idea, when he sent the dispatch on August 4, of

what Mason's departure would achieve, beyond pinning his hopes on the French to break clear of their alliance with Britain. Charles Hubbard, *The Burden of Confederate Diplomacy* (Knoxville, Tenn., 1998), p. 149.

28. North Carolina State Archives, Private Collections, PC 1226 Rose O'Neal Greenhow Papers, London Diary, p. 35.

29. Blackman, *Wild Rose,* p. 271.

30. PRO 30/22/26, Argyll to Russell, October 17, 1863.

31. Philip Guedalla (ed.), *Gladstone and Palmerston, Being the Correspondence of Lord Palmerston with Mr. Gladstone, 1851–1865* (London, 1928), pp. 264–66, Palmerston to Gladstone, October 9, 1863; Gladstone to Palmerston, October 8, 1863.

32. *BDOFA*, part 1, ser. C, vol. 6, doc. 348, Captain Inglefield to Lord Paget, November 1, 1863; Inglefield to Vice-Admiral Grey, October 25, 1863.

33. James M. Morgan, *Recollections of a Rebel Reefer* (Boston, 1917), p. 164.

34. University of Rochester, Rochester, N.Y., Rush Rhees Library, A.W39 Thurlow Weed MSS, Currie to Weed, September 15, 1863.

35. Some of James Horrocks's letters were deposited in the Lancashire Record Office in Preston; the rest are in the Blackburn Museum. In 1982, the curator of the Blackburn Museum, A. S. Lewis, collated the two collections and published them under the title *My Dear Parents*. The combination of Lewis's scholarship and Horrocks's engaging style makes the book one of the most important eyewitness accounts of Civil War life by an English volunteer. Horrocks's father owned a cotton mill and had suffered hard during the cotton famine. Horrocks was forced to abandon his studies at the Wesleyan teachers' training college in London and return home to Bolton. The pregnancy of Martha Jane Hammer had added another financial burden. She successfully sued him for financial support. He ran away to America rather than submit to the court, leaving his family with the embarrassment of the unpaid support.

36. A. S. Lewis (ed.), *My Dear Parents* (New York, 1982), p. 23, Horrocks to parents, September 5, 1863.

37. Ibid.

38. Daniel B. Lucas, *Memoir of John Yates Beall* (Montreal, 1865), p. 265.

39. W. W. Baker, "Memoirs of Service" (property of Mr. Jack Beall), p. 21.

40. Jeffry D. Wert, *Mosby's Rangers* (New York, 1990), p. 98.

41. Jeffry D. Wert, *The Sword of Lincoln* (New York, 2006), p. 313.

42. Frank E. Vandiver (ed.), *The Civil War Diary of Josiah Gorgas* (Tuscaloosa, Ala., 1947), p. 55.

43. Sam Watkins, *Company Aytch* (New York, 1999), p. 74.

Chapter 25: River of Death

1. Robert L. Kincaid, *The Wilderness Road* (Middlesboro, Ky., 1966), pp. 268–69.

2. Ibid., pp. 263–65.

3. OR, ser. 1, vol. 30, doc. 52, p. 435, De Courcy to Brigadier General Potter, September 7, 1863.

4. William Marvel, *Burnside* (Chapel Hill, N.C., 1991), p. 278. For example, De Courcy wrote to Brigadier General Potter on September 7, 1863: "My sick are

filling the houses in my rear, and I have no surgeons or medicines to leave with them. Dr. Wilson can inform you that I foretold this and some of the other disasters which must take place on this line of operations unless commissary, quartermaster's, and medical departments work in a different fashion from what they are now doing." OR, ser. 1, vol. 30, doc. 52, p. 435.

5. Kincaid, *The Wilderness Road,* p. 271.

6. Ibid.

7. Ibid.

8. Frank E. Vandiver (ed.), *The Civil War Diary of Josiah Gorgas* (Tuscaloosa, Ala., 1947), p. 62, September 17, 1863.

9. NARA, M552, roll 26, Compiled Military Service Record, De Courcy to Colonel Richmond, September 18, 1863.

10. http://www.mkwe.com/ohio/pages/linn-03.htm, 16th Ohio Volunteers, Diary and Letters of Thomas Buchannan Linn, September 21, 1863.

11. NARA, RG9, Loring to Burnside, September 18, 1863.

12. OR, ser. 1, vol. 30/3, doc. 52, p. 943, General Field Orders No. 15.

13. Hudson Strode, *Jefferson Davis: Confederate President,* 3 vols. (New York, 1959), vol. 2, p. 475.

14. Francis W. Dawson, *Reminiscences of Confederate Service, 1861–1865,* ed. Bell I. Wiley (Baton Rouge, La., 1980), p. 100.

15. Mary Boykin Chesnut, *A Diary from Dixie,* ed. Isabella D. Martin and Myrta Lockett Avary (New York, 1906), p. 241.

16. Brian Holden Reid, *The American Civil War,* p. 132.

17. Sam Watkins, *Company Aytch* (New York, 1999), p. 88.

18. Ibid., p. 89.

19. *Illustrated London News,* December 26, 1863.

20. Dawson, *Reminiscences,* p. 102.

21. Edward Porter Alexander, *Fighting for the Confederacy: The Personal Recollections of General Edward Porter Alexander,* ed. Gary Gallagher (Chapel Hill, N.C., 1989), p. 301. Vizetelly's brother claimed that he offered to deliver a message for Longstreet during the battle, since all the other couriers had been picked off by Federal sharpshooters. "Upon his return to the General's headquarters, Longstreet commissioned him an 'honorary captain' in the Confederate States Army." William Stanley Hoole, p. 104. It is possible that Vizetelly delivered messages, but not during a battle that he missed.

22. Dawson, *Reminiscences,* p. 102.

23. Emory University, Gregory MSS, Lawley to Gregory, September 16, 1863.

24. Julia Miele Rodas, "More Than a Civil (War) Friendship: Anthony Trollope and Frank Lawley," *Princeton University Library Chronicle,* 60/1 (1998), pp. 39–60, at p. 48, Morris to Lawley, September 24, 1863.

25. Emory University, Gregory MSS, box 24, Lawley to Gregory, September 16, 1863.

26. Doris Kearns Goodwin, *Team of Rivals* (New York, 2005), p. 556.

27. Michael Burlingame and John R. Turner Ettlinger (eds.), *Inside Lincoln's White House: The Complete War Diary of John Hay* (Carbondale, Ill., 1997), p. 84, September 11, 1863.

28. Frederic William Maitland, *Life and Letters of Leslie Stephen* (New York, 1906), p. 119.

29. It should be noted that Seward already suspected that the ships had been detained. Leslie Stephen dismissed Seward as a lightweight after he confused John Stuart Mill with Richard Monckton Milnes. Yet Seward was not so different than the MP who remarked to an American visitor that Lee would presumably follow up his Gettysburg victory by taking Washington and New Orleans, since "New Orleans is about 100 miles from Washington, I think?" J. G. Randall, *Lincoln the President*, 4 vols.; vol. 3: *Midstream* (New York, 1953), p. 317.

30. Maitland, *Life and Letters of Leslie Stephen*, p. 122.

31. *An Englishman in the American Civil War: The Diaries of Henry Yates Thompson, 1863*, ed. Sir Christopher Chancellor (New York, 1971), p. 86.

32. Ibid., p. 98.

33. Randall, *Lincoln the President*, p. 370.

34. James J. Barnes and Patience P. Barnes (eds.), *Private and Confidential: Letters from British Ministers in Washington to the Foreign Secretaries* (Selinsgrove, Pa., 1993), p. 335.

35. Philip Van Doren Stern, *When the Guns Roared: World Aspects of the American Civil War* (New York, 1965), p. 234.

36. "I never was in such a town or place in all my life," Milne wrote admiringly. He believed that below the surface of hostility was a deep bond between the two countries that it was his duty to nurture. Somerset RO, Somerset MSS, D/RA/A/2a/34/32, Milne to Somerset, October 18, 1863.

37. Ibid.

38. *New York Albion*, October 17, 1863.

39. PRO 30/22/37, ff. 203–7, Lyons to Russell, October 16, 1863.

40. PRO 30/22/37, ff. 219–26, Lyons to Russell, October 26, 1863.

41. PRO 30/22/37, ff. 203–7, Lyons to Russell, October 16, 1863.

42. PRO FO5/895, ff. 69–71, d. 758, Lyons to Russell, October 23, 1863.

43. Eugene H. Berwanger, *The British Foreign Service and the American Civil War* (Lexington, Ky., 1994), p. 119.

44. William Watson, *The Civil War Adventures of a Blockade Runner* (College Station, Tex., 2001), pp. 50, 56.

45. PRO FO5/909, ff. 361–62, Lynn to Magruder, October 3, 1863.

46. Watson, *The Civil War Adventures of a Blockade Runner,* pp. 50, 58.

47. PRO FO5/896, f. 40, Lyons to Russell, November 6, 1863. "My Lord, I have much to say regarding the barbarous manner in which British subjects are treated in the Southern Confederacy," wrote Mr. McIntyre from Alabama on October 3, 1863. His friend James Maloney applied for a British passport in 1861 and started for home. The provost marshal arrested him anyway and sent him to General Bragg's army, sneering at "his dammed English protection." "I do not know whether your Lordship is acquainted with these facts or not. But if you are . . . it is very strange that something cannot be done to secure for British Subjects that protection which they seek." In January 1864, the legation had to return the Southern consuls' pay receipts to London, explaining that Lord Lyons "has no means of sending these letters to their destina-

tion, nor does he know whether the Consular officers to whom they are addressed are still at their posts." The source for the quotation in the footnote on this page is PRO FO5/948, f. 57, Lyons to Russell, April 19, 1864.

48. Berwanger, *The British Foreign Service and the American Civil War*, p. 104.

Chapter 26: Can the Nation Endure?

1. PRO FO5/908, ff. 115–17, no. 30, Cridland to Russell, November 14, 1863.
2. Fitzgerald Ross, *Cities and Camps of the Confederate States*, ed. Richard Barksdale Harwell (Champaign, Ill., 1997), p. 140.
3. *The Times,* December 1, 1863.
4. Ross, *Cities and Camps*, p. 143.
5. John G. Nicolay and John Hay (eds.), *Complete Works of Lincoln*, vol. 9 (New York, 1907), p. 26, Lincoln to Grant, July 13, 1863.
6. "The Journal of Robert Neve," private collection, p. 140.
7. Ibid., p. 143.
8. Francis W. Dawson, *Reminiscences of Confederate Service, 1861–1865*, ed. Bell I. Wiley (Baton Rouge, La., 1980), p. 105.
9. Jeffrey Wert, *General James Longstreet: The Confederacy's Most Controversial Soldier* (New York, 1993), p. 341.
10. Dawson, *Reminiscences,* p. 109.
11. *The Times*, December 15, 1863.
12. Bruce Catton, *Never Call Retreat* (London, 2001), p. 273.
13. *Decatur Daily News*, March 20, 1879.
14. David Donald provides the following footnote in his edition of Salmon P. Chase's diary: "Henry Charles De Ahna wrote the President his version of these events on January 31, 1864: 'As Your Excellency probably recollects, it was brought to the knowledge of the Government several months ago, that through a singular mistake in a name, I found myself approached by an agent of the Rebel government and an offer of $50,000 was made to me, if I would undertake to enter into a negotiation with Col. Percy Wyndham and by offering him in the name of the Rebel Government the sum of 100,000 Dollars, would succeed in persuading the said Percy Wyndham to allow himself to be taken prisoner with his whole Cavalry Brigade.' De Ahna told his story to V. Hogan, 'who was then well known as Secretary Chase's Detective,' and he also had an interview with Chase himself, but he claimed that Chase failed properly to investigate the matter." *Inside Lincoln's Cabinet: The Civil War Diaries of Salmon P. Chase*, ed. David Donald (New York, 1954), p. 316.
15. PRO FO 115/400, f. 247, Lyons to John Livingston, November 3, 1863.
16. Nicolay and Hay (eds.), *Complete Works of Abraham Lincoln*, vol. 9, p. 204, Lincoln to Meade, November 9, 1863; Lincoln to Burnside, November 8, 1863.
17. Ibid., p. 154, Lincoln to Rosecrans, October 4, 1863.
18. Sarah Forbes Hughes (ed.), *Letters and Recollections of John Murray Forbes*, 2 vols. (New York, 1990), vol. 2, p. 74, Forbes to Lincoln, September 8, 1863.
19. Michael Burlingame, *Abraham Lincoln*, 2 vols. (Baltimore, 2008), vol. 2, p. 573; Ronald White, Jr., *Lincoln* (New York, 2009), p. 604.
20. David H. Donald, *Lincoln* (New York, 1995), p. 465.
21. *The Times*, December 4, 1863.

22. Michael Burlingame and R. Turner Ettlinger (eds.), *Inside Lincoln's White House: The Complete War Diary of John Hay* (Carbondale, Ill., 1997), pp. 112–13, November 18–19, 1863.

23. Burlingame, *Abraham Lincoln*, vol. 2, p. 576.

24. Nicolay and Hay (eds.), *Complete Works of Abraham Lincoln*, vol. 9, pp. 209–10.

25. *An Englishman in the American Civil War: The Diaries of Henry Yates Thompson, 1863*, ed. Sir Christopher Chancellor (New York, 1971), pp. 141–42.

26. Sam Watkins, *Company Aytch* (New York, 1999), p. 91.

27. *An Englishman in the American Civil War*, p. 152.

28. "The Journal of Robert Neve," p. 158.

29. *An Englishman in the American Civil War*, p. 153.

30. Cleburne realized that he had a volunteer of exceptional quality the moment Byrne presented himself at his headquarters. Cleburne requested a commission for him on November 8, writing: "This young gentleman is eminently deserving. He left England to volunteer his services in our cause. He has been on my staff. I have found him a brave and gallant officer, highly intelligent, and devoted to our cause. I am the more anxious he should be appointed, because he sacrificed the opportunity of being commissioned in the British Service. He passed the examination required to entitle him to be placed on the list of possible appointees, before he left England, which he did upon a limited leave of absence. His leave has now expired, and, as he understands, he had forfeited his chance of being subjected in that service." Irving A. Buck, *Cleburne and His Command* (Wilmington, N.Y., 1995), p. 27.

31. "The Journal of Robert Neve," p. 161.

32. Watkins, *Company Aytch*, p. 95.

33. *An Englishman in the American Civil War*, pp. 166–67.

34. Ibid., p. 18.

35. George Templeton Strong, *Diary of the Civil War, 1860–1865*, ed. Allan Nevins (New York, 1962), p. 375, November 27, 1863.

36. R. W. McFarland, *The Surrender of Cumberland Gap* (Columbus, Ohio, 1898), p. 29.

37. For a complete description of the 16th Ohio Volunteer Infantry, and De Courcy's career as its colonel, along with scanned documents, muster rolls, and much more, see http://www.mkwe.com/home.htm.

38. Ten years later, De Courcy's cousin died. Thus, *Kind Hearts and Coronets* style, though De Courcy was the fourth child of a second son, he became the 31st Baron Kingsale, Ireland's premier barony.

39. Jeffry D. Wert, *The Sword of Lincoln* (New York, 2006), p. 321.

40. British Library of Political and Economic Science, LSE, GB 0097, Farr MSS, vol. 10, Henry Ezechiel to Mr. Murray, January 6, 1864.

41. Jones, *A Rebel War Clerk's Diary*, p. 306, November 12, 1863.

PART III: IF ONLY WE ARE SPARED

Chapter 27: Buckling Under Pressure

1. W. C. Ford (ed.), *A Cycle of Adams Letters, 1861–1865*, 2 vols. (Boston, 1920), vol. 2, p. 106, Henry Adams to Charles Francis Adams, Jr., November 27, 1863.

2. ORN, ser. 2, vol. 2, p. 514, Stephen Mallory to Bulloch, October 22, 1863.

3. Fitzgerald Ross, *Cities and Camps of the Confederate States*, ed. Richard Barksdale Harwell (Champaign, Ill., 1997), p. 172.

4. Stephen Z. Starr, *Colonel Grenfell's Wars* (Baton Rouge, La., 1971), pp. 106–7, Ross, *Cities and Camps*, pp. 172–73.

5. C. Vann Woodward (ed.), *Mary Chesnut's Civil War* (New Haven, 1981), p. 337, January 12, 1864.

6. *Illustrated London News*, April 2, 1863, p. 313.

7. Raphael Semmes, *My Adventures Afloat: A Personal Memoir of My Cruises and Services* (1868; repr. Baltimore, 1987), p. 629.

8. They were Baron Maximilian von Meulnier of Bremen and Julius Schroeder of Hanover.

9. Norman C. Delaney, *John McIntosh Kell of the Raider Alabama* (Tuscaloosa, Ala., 1973), p. 153.

10. Charles Francis Adams made the first claim for redress against the *Alabama*, "for the national and private injuries sustained by the proceedings of this vessel," on November 20, 1862. Russell replied on December 19, categorically stating that "Britain cannot be held responsible . . . for these irregular proceedings of British subjects," and to claim otherwise would be as reasonable as the British government suing the American "for the injuries done to the property of British subjects by the *Alabama* . . . on the ground that the United States claim authority . . . over the Confederate States, by whom that vessel was commissioned." *PRFA*, 1 (1864), p. 35, Russell to Charles Francis Adams, December 22, 1862.

11. PRO FO282/7 (2), Consul Archibald to Lord Lyons, April 9, 1863.

12. PRO HO45/7261/216, Colonial Office to Home Office, February 10, 1864. Final estimates for Irish-American recruitment throughout the war hover around 140,000 in the Federal army, and between 20,000 and 40,000 in the Confederate. Of the sixteen stowaways on the *Kearsarge*, five were tried in April 1864 for violating the Foreign Enlistment Act. They pleaded guilty to the charge and were released on their own cognizance. By then, Adams thought the government was pursuing the case in order to appear evenhanded in its battle to shut down Confederate operations.

13. Charles P. Cullop, "An Unequal Duel: Union Recruiting in Ireland, 1863–1864," *Civil War History*, 13 (1967), p. 108.

14. James D. Bulloch, *The Secret Service of the Confederate States in Europe*, 2 vols. (New York, 1886), vol. 1, p. 444.

15. Duke University, Special Collections Library, Rose O'Neal Greenhow Papers, Greenhow to Alexander Boteler, December 10, 1863.

16. The captured blockade runner is incorrectly identified as the *Ceres* in William C. Davis (ed.), *Secret History of Confederate Diplomacy Abroad* (Lawrence, Kan., 2005), p. xxii.

17. Ann Blackman, *Wild Rose: Rose O'Neal Greenhow, Civil War Spy* (New York, 2005), p. 275.

18. Ibid.

19. Lynda L. Crist, Kenneth H. Williams, and Peggy L. Dillard (eds.), *The Papers of Jefferson Davis*, vol. 10 (Baton Rouge, La., 1999), p. 143.

20. Bayly Ellen Marks and Mark Naton Schatz (eds.), *Between North and South: A Maryland Journalist Views the Civil War; The Narrative of William Wilkins Glenn, 1861–1869* (Cranbury, N.J., 1976), p. 123, February 1864.

21. North Carolina State Archives, Private Collections, PC1226, Rose O'Neal Greenhow Papers, London Diary, p. 48.

22. *The Private Journal of Georgiana Gholson Walker*, ed. Dwight Franklin Henderson, Confederate Centennial Studies, 25 (Tuscaloosa, Ala., 1963), p. 74, March 8, 1864.

23. North Carolina State Archives, Greenhow diary, p. 53.

24. Bulloch, *The Secret Service of The Confederate States of America*, p. 296.

25. Ibid.

26. Stanley Lebergott, "Through the Blockade: The Profitability and Extent of Cotton Smuggling, 1861–1865," *Journal of Economic History*, 41 (Dec. 1981), p. 876.

27. ORN, ser. 2, vol. 3, pp. 981–85, Hotze to Benjamin, December 26, 1863.

28. R.J.M. Blackett, *Divided Hearts: Britain and the American Civil War* (Baton Rouge, La., 2001), p. 190.

29. *Index*, January 14, 1863.

30. ORN, ser. 2, vol. 3, pp. 1007–9, Mason to Benjamin, January 25, 1864. For example, Lady Wharncliffe wrote on January 30, 1864: "To think that having started [the war in 1861 with our friends] here drawn with indignation at the conduct of the Confederates, and that now one should be wishing for their success, slave owners as they are! . . . However I am convinced that somehow the knell of slavery is rung." Durham University, Grey MSS, GRE/G17/21/18–19, Georgiana Elizabeth, Lady Wharncliffe, to Miss Elizabeth Copley.

31. Benjamin to Spence, January 11, 1864, quoted in John Bigelow, "The Confederate Diplomatists and Their Shirt of Nessus," *Century Magazine*, 20 (1891), p. 122.

32. MPUS, *Papers Relating to Foreign Affairs*, 1 (1864), p. 44.

33. Sarah Agnes Wallace and Frances Elma Gillespie (eds.), *The Journal of Benjamin Moran, 1857–1865*, 2 vols. (Chicago, 1948, 1949), vol. 2, p. 1263, February 11, 1863.

34. Wilbur Devereux Jones, *The Confederate Rams at Birkenhead*, Confederate Centennial Studies, 19 (Wilmington, N.C., 2000), p. 107.

35. W. G. Wiebe, Mary S. Miller, and Anne P. Robson, *Benjamin Disraeli Letters: 1860–1864* (Toronto, 2009), p. 314.

36. Ford (ed.), *A Cycle of Adams Letters*, vol. 2, pp. 118–19, Charles Francis Adams, Jr., to Charles Francis Adams, January 16, 1864.

37. Wallace and Gillespie (eds.), *The Journal of Benjamin Moran*, vol. 2, p. 1264, February 16, 1864, and February 17, 1864.

38. Ibid., p. 1266, February 20, 1864.

39. Ibid., p. 1269, March 1, 1864.

40. Edward Chase Kirkland, *Charles Francis Adams Jr.* (Cambridge, Mass., 1965), p. 28.

41. Wallace and Gillespie (eds.), *The Journal of Benjamin Moran*, vol. 2, p. 1274, March 12, 1863.

42. ORN, ser. 2, vol. 3, pp. 874–81, Hotze to Benjamin, August 27, 1863.

43. The book was far superior to the novelist George Alfred Lawrence's self-pitying account of his capture and imprisonment, called *Border and Bastille*. It was also much more effective as a piece of pro-Confederate propaganda than a work such as *The South as It Is*, by the Rev. T. D. Ozanne, who had spent twenty-one years in the South and could not understand why it should be made to suffer all because of "one social evil."

44. Hugh Dubrulle, "Fear of Americanization and the Emergence of an Anglo-Saxon Confederacy," *Albion: A Quarterly Journal Concerned with British Studies*, 33/4 (Winter 2001), pp. 583–613, at p. 594.

45. Brian Jenkins, "Frank Lawley and the Confederacy," *Civil War History*, 23 (March 1977), p. 158.

46. Ibid.

47. ORN, ser. 2, vol. 3, pp. 1046–47, Slidell to Benjamin, March 5, 1864.

48. Jenkins, "Frank Lawley and the Confederacy," p. 158.

49. Quoted in Edward Chalfant, *Better in Darkness* (New York, 1996), p. 75.

50. North Carolina State Archives, Greenhow diary, p. 65.

Chapter 28: A Great Slaughter

1. A head count in the South at the end of 1863 revealed that only 277,000 soldiers remained after three years. President Davis did not dare allow such alarming information to reach the public. The North, on the other hand, had 611,000 men in arms.

2. John Bierman, *Napoleon III and His Carnival Empire* (New York, 1988), p. 234.

3. Thomas Edgar Pemberton, *Sir Charles Wyndham: A Biography* (London, 1904), p. 27; "Britons in the Civil War: Sir Charles Wyndham," *Crossfire*, 37 (Nov. 1990).

4. OR, ser. 1, vol. 34/1, p. 219, Report of Admiral Porter, June 13, 1864. "I trust some future historian will treat this matter as it deserves to be treated," he declared, "because it is a subject in which the whole country should feel an interest."

5. Although Dahlgren's massacre plan could have been a forgery, the South believed that the papers were authentic.

6. Duane Schultz, *The Dahlgren Affair* (New York, 1998), p. 157. Two weeks before Colonel Dahlgren made his doomed ride toward Richmond, the Confederate Congress had secretly approved a bill on February 15 to transfer $5 million to a Secret Service fund. The bill also authorized the use of covert warfare against the North. The government had finally accepted that Lee could not win the war by himself.

7. Ibid., p. 181.

8. Mabel Clare Weaks, "Colonel George St. Leger Grenfell," *Filson Club History Quarterly*, 34 (1960), p. 11.

9. Stephen Z. Starr, *Colonel Grenfell's Wars* (Baton Rouge, La., 1971), p. 125.

10. Frank Moore (ed.), *Rebellion Record*, ser. 1, 53 vols., vol. 8 (New York, 1883), p. 515, Burton N. Harrison to Lord Lyons, April 6, 1864.

11. Oscar A. Kinchen, *Confederate Operations in Canada* (Hanover, Mass., 1970), p. 36.

12. John Jones passed a pleasant two days in February 1863, working out possible

permutations of a three-way partition between the states; John B. Jones, *A Rebel War Clerk's Diary at the Confederate States Capital*, ed. Earl Schenck Miers (Urbane, Ill., 1958), p. 165.

13. James Morton Callahan, *The Diplomatic History of the Confederacy* (Baltimore, 1901), p. 225.

14. Hudson Strode, *Jefferson Davis: Confederate President*, 3 vols. (New York, 1959), vol. 3, p. 35.

15. "There is no doubt he has got the best military head of any man in this Confederacy, and if he only gets a chance he will make his mark on the enemy this Spring and Summer," Feilden had written enthusiastically. South Carolina Historical Society, Feilden-Smythe MSS (3), Feilden to Julia McCord, April 20, 1864.

16. Ibid., (10), Feilden to Julia McCord, April 20, 1864.

17. Ibid., (6), Feilden to Julia McCord, April 30, 1864.

18. E. Milby Burton, *The Siege of Charleston* (Columbia, S.C., 1982), p. 283.

19. PRO FO5/896, f. 23, Lyons to Russell, November 3, 1863; the reference for the quotation in the footnote is PRO FO 5/896, f. 33, Lyons to Russell, November 3, 1863.

20. PRO FO 5/948/274, f. 63, Lyons to Russell, April 19, 1864; James J. Barnes and Patience P. Barnes (eds.), *The American Civil War Through British Eyes*, vol. 3 (Kent, Ohio, 2005), p. 178.

21. *New York Times*, February 2, 1864.

22. West Sussex RO, Lyons MSS, box 301, Lyons to sister, December 26, 1863; PRO 30/22/37, f. 63, Lyons to Russell, December 24, 1863.

23. PRO 30/22/38, ff. 46–49, Lyons to Russell, May 17, 1864.

24. British Library of Political and Economic Science, LSE, Farr MSS, ADD 2, unknown writer to Captain Hatch, February 19, 1864.

25. Duke University, Malet family MSS, Malet to mother, January 4, 1863.

26. Edmund Hammond, the permanent undersecretary of state for foreign affairs, had a low opinion of young men who wanted to have a personal life outside the Foreign Office: "The labour required of the Foreign Office Clerks is great, the attendance long, and the hours late and uncertain. . . ." *Reports from Commissioners*, 20 vols., vol. 5 (London, 1856), p. 67, Hammond to Horace Mann, June 25, 1855.

27. PRO FO5/949, f. 5, d. 289, Lyons to Russell, May 3, 1864.

28. PRO FO282/10, f. 294, Archibald to Lyons, January 30, 1863.

29. Bright-Sumner Letters, 1861–1872, *Proceedings of the Massachusetts Historical Society*, 46 (1912), pp. 93–165, at p. 125, Bright to Sumner, December 15, 1863. Thomas Smelt, the father of young Stephen, wrote to Lincoln on March 6, imploring him to release his son, who had been drugged and drafted into the army. The humble clerk struggled to express himself: "I also appeal to you as a Father and man of honour that you take all these circumstances into your consideration, and for the sake of his family, you be graciously pleased to grant this my prayer," he begged. By the time Mr. Smelt's letter had passed from Lincoln's desk to the adjutant general's office, and from there into the hands of the War Department clerks, Stephen had been wounded and captured by the Confederates. Stephen Smelt was a prisoner of war in Ander-

sonville, the prison with the highest death toll in the South, and he was beyond the reach of his father or the indifferent Northern authorities. NARA RG 94/SKM 06, Thomas Smelt to Lincoln, March 6, 1864.

30. PRO FO 5/898, f. 66, Lyons to Russell, December 7, 1863.

31. The Foreign Office could not, officially, applaud a solution that forced British subjects to pledge their allegiance to a foreign country, but there was relief in London that a hideous injustice against conscripted Britons in the Southern armies had been resolved.

32. Warwickshire RO, CR114A/533/23 (1), Seymour MSS, General Wistar to General Dix, April 15, 1864.

33. A. S. Lewis (ed.), *My Dear Parents*, p. 67.

34. James Pendlebury MSS, private collection, p. 1.

35. James Pendlebury MSS, p. 2.

36. PRO FO5/1287, d.189, Francis Lousada to Lord Lyons, March 11, 1864, and passim.

37. Fitzgerald Ross, *Cities and Camps of the Confederate States*, ed. Richard Barksdale Harwell (Champaign, Ill., 1997), p. 219.

38. Frances Elizabeth Owen Monck, *My Canadian Leaves: Diary of a Visit to Canada, 1865–6* (London, 1891), p. 127.

39. *Journal of John Wodehouse, First Earl of Kimberley* (Cambridge, 1997), p. 75.

40. R.A.J. Walling (ed.), *The Diaries of John Bright* (New York, 1931), p. 271.

41. Edward Lyulph Stanley, Fourth Baron Stanley of Alderley, letters from America, Royal Commonwealth Society Library, Cambridge, Stanley to Lady Stanley, April 17, 1864.

42. Ibid., April 27, 1864.

43. W. C. Ford (ed.), *A Cycle of Adams Letters, 1861–1865*, 2 vols. (Boston, 1920), vol. 2, p. 128, Charles Francis Adams, Jr., to Charles Francis Adams, May 1, 1864.

44. OR, ser. 1, vol. 32/3, p. 246, Grant to Sherman, April 3, 1864.

45. Lewis (ed.), *My Dear Parents*, p. 77, Horrocks to parents, May 8, 1864.

46. Ibid.

47. Ibid., p. 78.

48. James Pendlebury MSS, pp. 4–5.

49. Shelby Foote, *The Civil War*, 3 vols. (New York, 1986), vol. 3, p. 170.

50. Francis W. Dawson, *Reminiscences of Confederate Service, 1861–1865*, ed. Bell I. Wiley (Baton Rouge, La., 1980), p. 197, Dawson to mother, June 1, 1864.

51. Jeffry D. Wert, *General James Longstreet: The Confederacy's Most Controversial Soldier* (New York, 1993), p. 385.

52. New-York Historical Society, *Narrative of Ebenezer Wells* (c. 1881), May 5, 1864.

53. Dawson, *Reminiscences*, p. 197, Dawson to mother, June 1, 1864, and p. 115.

54. Grant was annoyed by the halfhearted performance from his tired army, but, wrote a British military historian in the 1930s, "it is sometimes difficult to decide where driving force deteriorates into mere pigheadedness and refusal to face unpalatable facts." Alfred H. Burne, *Lee, Grant, and Sherman* (repr. Lawrence, Kan., 2000), p. 24.

55. New-York Historical Society, *Narrative of Ebenezer Wells*, May 10, 1864.

56. Horace Porter, *Campaigning with Grant* (New York, 1906), p. 110.

57. Lewis (ed.), *My Dear Parents*, p. 85, Horrocks to father, May 31, 1864.

58. Ford (ed.), *A Cycle of Adams Letters*, vol. 2, p. 131, Charles Francis Adams, Jr., to Charles Francis Adams, May 29, 1864.

Chapter 29: "Defiance to Her Enemies"

1. Transactions of the Historical Society of Lancashire and Cheshire, John Ward Diary, pp. 178–79.
2. *The Times,* May 27, 1864. *Les Misérables* had been published in New York to great acclaim in 1862.
3. Francis W. Dawson, *Reminiscences of Confederate Service, 1861–1865*, ed. Bell I. Wiley (Baton Rouge, La., 1980), p. 130.
4. Merseyside Maritime Museum, Fraser, Trenholm MSS, B/FT, box 81, p. 298, Prioleau to Henry Wise, May 17, 1864.
5. Samuel Bernard Thompson, *Confederate Purchasing Operations Abroad* (Gloucester, Mass., 1973), p. 40.
6. James M. Morgan, *Recollections of a Rebel Reefer* (Boston, 1917), p. 180.
7. Ibid., p. 182.
8. Ibid.
9. Warren F. Spencer, *The Confederate Navy in Europe* (Tuscaloosa, Ala., 1983), p. 194. The blockade-running business had remained an exclusive club of a small number of shipping firms. The most accurate calculation to date lists only 111 British-owned ships between 1861 and 1865.
10. Library of Congress, Mason Papers, Lindsay to Mason, May 10, 1864.
11. Ibid., Tremlett to Mason, June 2, 1864.
12. Ibid., Maury Papers, Tremlett to Maury, June 1, 1864.
13. ORN, ser. 2, vol. 3, p. 1144, Mason to Benjamin, June 9, 1864.
14. The name Cold Harbor came from the local tavern, which offered beds for the night but not hot meals.
15. Frederick W. Seward (ed.), *Seward at Washington* (New York, 1891), p. 223.
16. Ernest Samuels (ed.), *Henry Adams: Selected Letters* (Cambridge, Mass., 1988), p. 68, Henry Adams to Charles Francis Adams, Jr., June 10, 1864.
17. Norman C. Delaney, *John McIntosh Kell of the Raider Alabama* (Tuscaloosa, Ala., 1973), p. 157.
18. Raphael Semmes, *Service Afloat: A Personal Memoir of My Cruises and Services* (1868; repr. Baltimore, 1987), p. 750.
19. John Morris Ellicott, *The Life of John Ancrum Winslow* (New York, 1905), p. 179.
20. Frederick Milnes Edge, *An Englishman's View of the Battle Between the Alabama and the Kearsarge* (New York, 1864), pp. 27–28, D. H. Llewellyn to Travers, June 14, 1864.
21. Robert Underwood Johnson and Clarence Clough Buel (eds.), *Battles and Leaders of the Civil War*, 4 vols. (Secaucus, N.J., 1985), vol. 4, p. 607.
22. Ellicott, *The Life of John Ancrum Winslow*, p. 193.
23. Charles Grayson Summersell, *CSS Alabama* (Tuscaloosa, Ala., 1985), p. 77.
24. Ibid., p. 78.
25. Edge, *An Englishman's View of the Battle Between the Alabama and the Kearsarge*, p. 28.

26. · A week after Llewellyn's death, the doctors and students at his alma mater, Charing Cross Medical School, voted to open a subscription fund in memory of his sacrifice. The public subscription was especially popular with doctors in the Indian Army. Enough money was raised to found the Llewellyn Scholarship Prize, and two memorials, one at Charing Cross Hospital and the other at his parish church, Easton, in Wiltshire. The marble plaque at Charing Cross paid tribute to Llewellyn's bravery and sacrifice under fire: IN MEMORY OF DAVID HERBERT LLEWELLYN, FORMERLY A STUDENT OF THIS HOSPITAL AND AFTERWARDS SURGEON TO THE CONFEDERATE STATES WAR STEAMER ALABAMA. AFTER HER ACTION WITH THE FEDERAL STEAMER "KEARSARGE" OFF CHERBOURG, THOUGH ENTREATED BY THE WOUNDED TO JOIN THEM IN THEIR BOAT, HE REFUSED TO PERIL THEIR SAFETY BY SO DOING, AND WENT DOWN WITH THE SINKING VESSEL, ON 19TH JUNE 1864 IN THE 26TH YEAR OF HIS AGE. THIS TABLET HAS BEEN ERECTED AND A SCHOLARSHIP FOUNDED IN HIS NAME BY HIS FELLOW STUDENTS, AND OTHERS IN ENGLAND AND INDIA TO COMMEMORATE HIS SELF-SACRIFICING COURAGE AND DEVOTION.

27. NARA, M.T-185, roll 8, vol. 8, U.S. Consuls in Bristol, Consul Eastman to Seward, June 23, 1864.

28. Somerset RO, Somerset MSS, d/RA/A/2a/40/10, Palmerston to Somerset, June 21, 1864.

29. W. C. Ford (ed.), *A Cycle of Adams Letters: 1861–1865*, 2 vols. (Boston, 1920), vol. 2, p. 158, Henry Adams to Charles Francis Adams, Jr., June 24, 1864.

30. See Beth Archer Brombert, *Édouard Manet* (Chicago, 1997), pp. 159–60, for the reasons why, contrary to popular belief, Manet did not witness the battle. The quotation in the footnote on this page is from W. S. Hoole, *Confederate Foreign Agent: The European Diary of Edward C. Anderson* (Tuscaloosa, Ala., 1976), July 17, 1864.

31. Brian Jenkins, *Britain and the War for the Union*, 2 vols. (Montreal, 1974, 1980), vol. 2, p. 333.

32. A week later, one of the *Phaeton's* lieutenants was kidnapped and crimped while on shore leave. Consul Bernal eventually rescued him from trench duty outside Baltimore.

33. New-York Historical Society, *Narrative of Ebenezer Wells* (c. 1881), June 9, 1864.

34. OR, ser. 1, vol. 36/4, soc. 64, p. 138, Canby to Major General A. J. Smith.

35. Thomas E. Pemberton, *Sir Charles Wyndham: A Biography* (London, 1904), p. 21.

36. James G. Hollandsworth, Jr., *Pretense of Glory* (Baton Rouge, La., 1998), p. 211.

37. Edward Lyulph Stanley, 4th Baron Stanley of Alderley, letters from America, Royal Commonwealth Society Library, Cambridge, Stanley to Blanche, May 21, 1864.

38. Ibid., Stanley to Kate, June 9, 1864. When Stanley visited General Banks at his office on June 3, the general showed no embarrassment over his recent demotion, though he admitted his frustration with the slow pace of change for former slaves. His main source of pride was the number of negroes entering the army. The Louisiana Native Guards who fought at Port Hudson had been the first black regiment officially mustered into the army. Since then another thirty

black regiments had been formed, with at least 18,000 black recruits, and more were coming.

39. Ibid., Stanley to Blanche, May 12, 1864.

40. Mary Sophia Hill, *A British Subject's Recollections of the Confederacy* (Baltimore, 1875), p. 90.

41. Ibid., p. 62. The source for the footnote is PRO FO5/906, ff.104–7, d. 2, Coppell to Lord Russell, May 20, 1864.

42. Hill, *A British Subject's Recollections of the Confederacy*, p. 63.

43. Belle Boyd, *Belle Boyd in Camp and Prison* (New York, 1865; repr. Baton Rouge, La., 1998), p. 197.

44. Ruth Scarborough, *Siren of the South* (Macon, Ga., 1997), p. 157.

45. Boyd, *Belle Boyd in Camp and Prison*, pp. 200–203.

46. Stephen Z. Starr, *Colonel Grenfell's Wars* (Baton Rouge, La., 1971), p. 126.

Chapter 30: "Can We Hold Out?"

1. University College of North Wales, Bangor, Evans MSS 2854, ff. 63–69, *c.* June 1864.

2. PRO FO5/1258, n. 73 enc. 2, Mary Sophia Hill to Lyons, June 17, 1864.

3. PRO FO5/1258, n. 73 enc. 1, Coppell to Lyons, July 1, 1864.

4. E. Milby Burton, *The Siege of Charleston* (Columbia, S.C., 1982), p. 285.

5. Just fifteen blockade runners had been able to get out in May, but Feilden was able to put a few cotton bales on one of them for his own account. "All my English friends in the Blockade runners came to me for assistance and it was no great return if a bale of cotton was now and again taken out for me," Feilden wrote later. South Carolina Historical Society, Feilden-Smythe MSS, (11), Feilden to Julia, May 23, 1864.

6. Ibid., (12), Feilden to Julia McCord, May 28, 1864.

7. Ibid., (14), Feilden to Julia McCord, June 18, 1864.

8. Ibid., (16), Feilden to Julia McCord, June 30, 1864.

9. Jubal A. Early, *The Campaigns of Gen. Robert E. Lee: An Address by Lieut. General Jubal A. Early, Before Washington and Lee University, January 19th, 1872* (Baltimore, 1872), p. 42

10. Brian Holden Reid, *Robert E. Lee* (London, 2005), p. 219.

11. W. C. Ford (ed.), *A Cycle of Adams Letters, 1861–1865,* 2 vols. (Boston, 1920), vol. 2, p. 154, Charles Francis Adams, Jr., to Charles Francis Adams, June 19, 1864.

12. James Pendlebury MSS, private collection, p. 7.

13. Francis W. Dawson, *Reminiscences of Confederate Service, 1861–1865,* ed. Bell I. Wiley (Baton Rouge, La., 1980), pp. 195–96, Dawson to Mother, June 1, 1864. His letters occasionally assumed a finality in their tone: "I feel how much I have sinned against your tender care and loving kindness!" he wrote. "Forgive me, my dear Parents, every unkind word and harsh thought."

14. *Illustrated London News*, August 6, 1864.

15. Edward Porter Alexander, *Military Memoirs of a Confederate* (New York, 1907), p. 564.

16. OR, ser. 1, vol. 40/2, doc. 81, order from Secretary of War, June 25, 1864.

17. Augustus Charles Hobart-Hampden, *Hobart Pasha* (New York, 1915), p. 176.

18. Ibid., pp. 180–81.

19. A. S. Lewis (ed.), *My Dear Parents* (New York, 1982), p. 92.
20. University College of North Wales, Bangor, Evans MSS 2854, ff. 74–75, July 4, 1864.
21. PRO 30/22/38, f. 71, Lyons to Russell, July 15, 1864.
22. West Sussex RO, Lyons MSS, box 302, Lord Lyons to Augusta, July 13 and 15, 1864.
23. Ibid., Lyons to Augusta, June 2, 1864.
24. University College of North Wales, Bangor, Evans MSS 2854, f. 82, July 21, 1864.
25. Mark E. Neely, *The Fate of Liberty: Abraham Lincoln and Civil Liberties* (New York, 1991), pp. 110–11.
26. PRO 30/22/38, f. 74, Lyons to Lord Russell, July 22, 1864.
27. Doris Kearns Goodwin, *Team of Rivals* (New York, 2005), p. 646.
28. Ford (ed.), *A Cycle of Adams Letters*, vol. 2, pp. 168–69, Charles Francis Adams, Jr., to Henry Adams, July 27, 1864; Charles Francis Adams, Jr., to Henry Adams, July 22, 1864.
29. OR, ser. 1, vol. 40/3, doc. 82, p. 489, General Birney to Foster, July 26, 1864.
30. PRO FO/1281, Memorial of Edward Sewell; Private Sewell of the 93rd New York Volunteers was recovering from dysentery in a military hospital when he had heard from other patients "that we were likely to have liberty to go to New York to vote for the President. . . . I at once conceived the notion of escaping and gave my name and represented my state to be New York. On the fifth passes were given to us, and on the sixth I and many others went to New York by Railway. I arrived at New York on the seventh. I immediately went to the house of a friend named Eiglaugh. I told him my story and arranged with him, to obtain me a Berth on board a steamer for England."
31. Howard Westwood, *Black Troops, White Commanders, and Freedmen During the Civil War* (Carbondale Ill., 1992), p. 32; Gabor S. Boritt, *Lincoln's Generals* (New York, 1995), p. 147.
32. Alexander, *Military Memoirs*, p. 569.
33. Ulysses S. Grant, *Personal Memoirs of Ulysses S. Grant* (New York, 2003), p. 505.
34. *The Times*, August 23, 1864.
35. Frederick W. Seward (ed.), *Seward at Washington* (New York, 1891), p. 238, Seward to Frances, August 5, 1864.
36. Grant, *Memoirs*, p. 506.
37. Adam Badeau, *Military History of Ulysses S. Grant,* 3 vols. (New York, 1885), vol. 2, p. 502.
38. Richard Bache Irwin, *History of the Nineteenth Army Corps* (New York, 1892), p. 442.
39. Dawson, *Reminiscences*, p. 123.
40. Ibid., p. 201, Dawson to mother, August 7, 1864.
41. Ford (ed.), *A Cycle of Adams Letters*, vol. 2, p. 181, Charles Francis Adams, Jr., to Henry Adams, August 13, 1864.
42. Lewis (ed.), *My Dear Parents,* p. 92.
43. Timothy Holmes (ed.), *David Livingstone: Letters and Documents, 1861–1872* (London, 1990), pp. 85, 73, Livingstone to James Young, February 19, 1862,

Livingstone to James Young, *c.* July–August 1863. The source for the footnote is George Seaver, *David Livingstone: His Life and Letters* (London, 1957), p. 453.

44. William Garden Blaikie, *Personal Life of David Livingstone*, p. 339.

45. Holmes (ed.), *David Livingstone: Letters and Documents*, p. 96; David Livingstone to Charles Livingstone, September 2, 1864.

46. *The Times*, September 20, 1864.

47. Frank E. Vandiver (ed.), *The Civil War Diary of Josiah Gorgas* (Tuscaloosa, Ala., 1947), p. 132, August 8, 1864.

48. *The Times*, September 24, 1864.

49. Vandiver (ed.), *The Civil War Diary of Josiah Gorgas*, p. 137, August 29, 1864.

Chapter 31: The Crisis Comes

1. James M. McPherson, *Battle Cry of Freedom* (London, 1988), p. 751.

2. OR ser. 1, vol. 35/2, doc. 66, p. 615, Feilden to Gorgas, August 20, 1864.

3. South Carolina Historical Society, Feilden-Smythe MSS (22), Feilden to Julia McCord, September 1, 1864.

4. Ibid., (20), Feilden to Julia McCord, August 26, 1864.

5. John B. Jones, *A Rebel War Clerk's Diary at the Confederate States Capital*, ed. Earl Schenck Miers (Urbana, Ill., 1958), p. 414, August 25, 1864.

6. Philip Van Doren Stern, *When the Guns Roared: World Aspects of the American Civil War* (New York, 1965), pp. 314–15.

7. ORN, ser. 2, vol. 3, p. 1202, Benjamin to Colin McRae, September 6, 1864.

8. John Bierman, *Dark Safari: The Life Behind the Legend of Henry Morton Stanley* (New York, 1990), p. 38. See also Nathaniel Cheairs Hughes, Jr. (ed.), *Sir Henry Morton Stanley, Confederate* (Baton Rouge, La., 2000), pp. 150–54.

9. July 12, 1864, and August 6, 1864; quoted in James McPherson, *Tried by War* (New York, 2009), pp. 231–32.

10. PRO 30/22/38, ff. 91–94, Lyons to Russell, August 15, 1864, and f. 95, August 23, 1864.

11. ORN, ser. 2, vol. 3, p. 1032, Benjamin to Slidell, February 19, 1864. The Knights of the Golden Circle also boasted Harpending and Rubery—the California raiders—as members. Other members included Jesse James, John Wilkes Booth, and the rampaging Quantrill's Raiders in Missouri. The secretive order answered only to itself, but its aims included an independent South, the protection of slavery, and the acquisition of territory from Mexico.

12. OR, ser. 4, vol. 3, pp. 585–86, Clay to Benjamin, August 11, 1864.

13. The Confederates had initiated the contact; it was the idea of Confederate gadfly and sometime agent George N. Sanders, whose dreams and schemes were forever ending in disaster. However, his powers of persuasion were legendary and—to the other Confederates' dismay—Sanders had no sooner arrived in Canada when he latched on to Clay and Holcombe and brought them completely under his sway. He played them like puppets, thoroughly enjoying his power to script the occasion. "In my long life I have known no counterpart to this man," recorded an observer. "He was a constant menace to the interests for which the commissioners were responsible." Adam Mayers, *Dixie and the Dominion: Canada, the Confederacy, and the War for the Union* (Toronto, 2003), p. 65.

14. Michael Burlingame, *Abraham Lincoln*, 2 vols. (Baltimore, 2008), vol. 2, pp. 669–70.

15. George Templeton Strong, *Diary of the Civil War, 1860–1865*, ed. Allan Nevins (New York, 1962), p. 474, August 19, 1864.

16. W. C. Ford (ed.), *A Cycle of Adams Letters, 1861–1865*, 2 vols. (Boston, 1920), vol. 2, p. 182, Charles Francis Adams, Jr., to Charles Francis Adams, August 20, 1864.

17. David Herbert Donald, *Lincoln* (New York, 1995), p. 529.

18. George Congdon Gorham, *Life and Public Services of Edwin M Stanton*, 2 vols. (New York, 1899), vol. 2, p. 149.

19. Doris Kearns Goodwin, *Team of Rivals* (New York, 2005), p. 648.

20. Library of Congress, Papers of Abraham Lincoln, "Blind Memorandum," August 23, 1864.

21. PRO 30/22/38, ff. 95–97, Lyons to Russell, August 23, 1864.

22. PRO 30/22/38, ff. 85–90, Lyons to Russell, August 9, 1864.

23. PRO FO5/1258, n. 73, Mary S. Hill to Lord Lyons, August 20, 1864.

24. *Widow of Andrew Cunningham, late a British subject: Correspondence between the State department and the British legation, relative to the claim of the widow of the late Andrew Cunningham, a British subject, improperly enlisted into the military service of the United States, March 5, 1866* (39th Congress, Hse Rep., 1866). Seward promised Lyons that Cunningham's widow would receive his bounty and army pay without delay. But the War Department ignored his repeated requests.

25. *BDOFA*, part 1, ser. C, vol. 6, p. 313, Monck to Cardwell, September 26, 1864.

26. Fitzgerald Ross, *Cities and Camps of the Confederate States*, ed. Richard Barksdale Harwell (Champaign, Ill., 1997), p. 228.

27. Duane Schultz, *The Dahlgren Affair* (New York, 1998), p. 209.

28. Mabel Clare Weaks, "Colonel George St. Leger Grenfell," *Filson Club History Quarterly*, 34 (1960), p. 11, Grenfell to Mary, July 18, 1864.

29. K. W. Wheeler, *For the Union: Ohio Leaders in the Civil War* (Columbus, Ohio, 1968), p. 50.

30. The "Northwest" encompassed Illinois, Wisconsin, Indiana, Michigan, and Iowa, states that not only felt little cultural or political affinity with New England, but also felt unfairly targeted by the tax system. The Knights of the Golden Circle had changed its name first to the Order of the American Knights, and then in 1864 to Sons of Liberty. Its membership remains impossible to determine, but at its height may have been as many as 300,000. The sons claimed to have a membership closer to a million.

31. ORN, ser. 1, vol. 3, p. 714, Thompson to Benjamin, December 3, 1864.

32. William Tidwell, *April '65: Confederate Covert Action in the American Civil War* (Kent, Ohio, 1995), p. 130.

33. Weaks, "Colonel George St Leger Grenfell," p. 10, Grenfell to "Hunter," July 31, 1864.

34. John W. Headley, *Confederate Operations in Canada and New York* (New York, 1906), p. 225.

35. Oscar A. Kinchen, *Confederate Operations in Canada*, p. 58.

36. Stephen Z. Starr, *Colonel Grenfell's Wars* (Baton Rouge, La., 1971), p. 172.

37. James Horan, *Confederate Agent: A Discovery in History* (New York, 1954), p. 129.

38. D. Alexander Brown, "The Northwest Conspiracy," *Civil War Times Illustrated*, 10 (May 1971), p. 16.

39. Weaks, "Colonel George St. Leger Grenfell," p. 11, Grenfell to William Maynard, August 31, 1864.

40. ORN, ser. 1, vol. 3, p. 714, Thompson to Benjamin, December 3, 1864.

Chapter 32: The Tyranny of Hope

1. ORN, ser. 2, vol. 3, pp. 1162–63, Hotze to Benjamin, July 4, 1864.

2. W. C. Ford (ed.), *A Cycle of Adams Letters, 1861–1865*, 2 vols. (Boston, 1920), vol. 2, p. 165. Henry Adams to Charles Francis Adams, Jr., July 8, 1864. Edward Chalfant, *Better in Darkness* (New York, 1991), p. 79.

3. On June 28, 1864, Rose recorded the following conversation in her diary: "Called upon Lady Chesterfield. Lady Derby was there, Marchioness of Ailesbury also came in. Much talk upon politics. . . . I asked, 'Will ministers go out?' Answer, 'No.' The radicals have promised to support the Gov. in their peace policy and there will be a division of 25 or 30 in support. Lady C: 'I don't believe they can have such a majority, not more than five or 6.' In that case it will be a defeat. Then they will dissolve Parliament and go to the country. They love office too well to go out. Lady C: 'They will be hard pressed.' Lady A: 'Yes but you will see, they will manage it.' The discussion is put off for Monday. Lord Derby will man it in the House of Lords. Mr. Disraeli in the Commons." North Carolina State Archives, Private Collections, PC 1226, Rose O'Neal Greenhow Papers, London Diary, p. 103

4. MHS, Adams MSS, *Diary of Charles Francis Adams*, July 8, 1864.

5. Greenhow, London Diary, p. 111, July 8, 1864.

6. William Flavelle Monypenny, *Life of Benjamin Disraeli, Earl of Beaconsfield*, vol. 3 (London, 1916), p. 405.

7. Mary Ellison, *Support for Secession* (Chicago, 1972), p. 153.

8. Greenhow, London Diary, p. 119, July 21–24, 1864.

9. *The Times*, July 26, 1864.

10. *PRFA*, 1/2, (1864), p. 229, Adams to Seward, July 28, 1864.

11. Ibid., p. 223, Adams to Seward, July 21, 1864.

12. Ibid., p. 250, Adams to Seward, July 29, 1864.

13. Greenhow, London Diary, p. 115, July 14, 1864.

14. Ibid., p. 123, August 7, 1864.

15. Diane Fontaine Corbin, *A Life of Matthew Fontaine Maury* (London, 1880), p. 223.

16. Greenhow, London Diary, p. 122, August 1, 1864. *The Private Journal of Georgiana Gholson Walker*, ed. Dwight Franklin Henderson, Confederate Centennial Studies, 25 (Tuscaloosa, Ala., 1963), p. 94, May 16, 1864. Rose procured the best ophthalmologist in London for Georgiana's child, who pronounced the condition to be incurable.

17. ORN, ser. 2, vol. 3, p. 1184, Mason to Benjamin, August 4, 1864.

18. MHS, Adams MSS, Diary of Charles Francis Adams, August 1, 1864.

19. *The Letters of Henry Adams*, vol. 1, p. 441, Henry Adams to Charles Francis Adams, Jr., July 1, 1864.

20. MHS, Adams MSS, Diary of Charles Francis Adams, July 30, 1864.

21. Greenhow, London Diary, p. 123, August 7, 1864.

22. Ibid., p. 128, August 10, 1864.

23. ORN, ser. 2, vol. 3, p. 1143, Hotze to Benjamin, June 3, 1864.

24. Library of Congress, Hotze Papers, private letterbook, Hotze to Witt, June 18, 1864.

25. *Punch*, August 6, 1864.

26. Andrew Ross, *David Livingstone: Mission and Empire* (London, 2002), p. 190.

27. Timothy Holmes, ed., *David Livingstone, Letters and Documents, 1861–1872* (London, 1990), p. 100, Livingstone to W. C. Oswell, October 21, 1864.

28. Sarah Agnes Wallace and Frances Elma Gillespie (eds.), *The Journal of Benjamin Moran*, vol. 2, p. 1327, September 16, 1864.

29. Ibid., p. 1329, September 22, 1864.

30. NARA, M. T. 185, roll 8, vol. 8, Consul Eastman to Seward, August 24, 1864.

31. *PRFA*, 1/2, (1864), p. 313, Charles Francis Adams to Seward, September 29, 1864.

32. The Duchess of Sutherland's antislavery petition of 1852, "The Affectionate and Christian Address of Many Thousands of Women of Great Britain and Ireland to Their Sisters, the Women of the United States of America," was signed by more than 500,000 British women. It caused considerable offense in both the North and the South. But at least that petition was addressed to the citizens of the United States. Kershaw's intention to present the petition to the Northern government was both preposterous and presumptuous.

33. Library of Congress, Hotze Papers, private letterbook, Hotze to Benjamin, September 2, 1864.

34. Belle Boyd, *Belle Boyd in Camp and Prison* (New York, 1965; repr. Baton Rouge, La., 1998), p. 206.

35. Ibid., p. 208; Wallace and Gillespie (eds.), *The Journal of Benjamin Moran*, vol. 2, p. 1317, August 25, 1864.

36. MHS, Adams MSS, Diary of Charles Francis Adams, September 5, 1864.

37. *Army and Navy Gazette*, September 3, 1864. Not everyone doubted the news. Northern supporters in Perth, Scotland, celebrated Sherman's victory by flying the American flag and firing the town cannon.

38. ORN, ser. 2, vol. 3, p. 1219, Slidell to Benjamin, September 29, 1864.

39. Ibid., p. 1209, Hotze to Benjamin, September 17, 1864.

40. *The Private Journal of Georgiana Gholson Walker*, p. 112.

Chapter 33: "Come Retribution"

1. Duke University, Malet family MSS, Malet to mother, August 30, 1864, and September 29, 1864.

2. Brian Jenkins, *Britain and the War for the Union*, 2 vols. (Montreal, 1974, 1980), vol. 2, p. 369.

3. Robin Winks, *Canada and the United States: The Civil War Years* (Lanham, Md., 1988), pp. 143–47. Monck had telegraphed Lord Lyons, who immediately sent a message to Seward, alerting him to the plot. Meanwhile Monck ordered the Welland Canal between Lake Erie and Lake Ontario to be watched for suspicious steamboats. General Cox in Ohio informed Edwin Stanton on November 15 that "the Rebels who left Windsor to join the raid are returning,

saying that the plans are frustrated for the present, and will have to be postponed for a time." OR, ser. 3, vol. 3, p. 1043, Cox to Stanton, November 15, 1863.

4. Madeline House, Graham Storey, and Kathleen Tillotson (eds.), *The Letters of Charles Dickens*, 3 vols. (New York, 1974), vol. 3, p. 207, Dickens to John Forster, April 24, 1842.

5. Bradley A. Rodgers, *Guardian of the Great Lakes* (Ann Arbor, Mich., 1996), p. 84.

6. Charles Frohman, *Rebels on Lake Erie* (Columbus, Ohio, 1975), p. 98.

7. Oscar A. Kinchen, *Confederate Operations in Canada* (Hanover, Mass., 1970), p. 105.

8. Frohman, *Rebels on Lake Erie*, p. 73.

9. John W. Headley, *Confederate Operations in Canada and New York* (Kent, Ohio, 1906), p. 252.

10. Daniel B. Lucas, *Memoir of John Yates Beall* (Montreal, 1865), p. 32.

11. Frohman, *Rebels on Lake Erie*, p. 93.

12. Ibid., p. 80.

13. Frances Elizabeth Owen Monck, *My Canadian Leaves: Diary of a Visit to Canada, 1865–6* (London, 1891), p. 122.

14. Ibid., p. 137.

15. Ibid., p. 148, October 4, 1864.

16. Ibid., p. 170.

17. Ann Blackman, *Wild Rose: Rose O'Neal Greenhow, Civil War Spy* (New York, 2005), pp. 298–99.

18. Thomas E. Taylor, *Running the Blockade* (Annapolis, Md., repr. 1995), p. 123.

19. Blackman, *Wild Rose*, p. 300.

20. *The Times*, November 15, 1864.

21. South Carolina Historical Society, Feilden-Smythe MSS, Beauregard to Feilden, September 5, 1864.

22. James M. Morgan, *Recollections of a Rebel Reefer* (Boston, 1917), pp. 197–98.

23. South Carolina Historical Society, Feilden-Smythe MSS, Feilden to Julia McCord, September 27, 1864.

24. Ibid., Feilden to Julia McCord, September 25, 1864.

25. The wine, for example, was coming from Bermuda, and the ring was being made from the last of his gold sovereigns. Ibid., Feilden to Julia McCord, September 27, 1864.

26. South Carolina Historical Society, Feilden-Smythe MSS, Jordan to Hardee, October 12, 1864.

27. *The Times*, November 5, 1864.

28. Frank E. Vandiver (ed.), *The Civil War Diary of Josiah Gorgas* (Tuscaloosa, Ala., 1947), p. 145, October 6, 1864.

29. *Illustrated London News*, January 21, 1865.

30. Ibid., October 22, 1864, p. 407.

31. John B. Jones, *A Rebel War Clerk's Diary at the Confederate States Capital*, ed. Earl Schenck Miers (Urbana, Ill., 1958), p. 433, October 10, 1864.

32. Mary Sophia Hill, *A British Subject's Recollections of the Confederacy* (Baltimore, 1875), p. 66.

33. PRO FO5/1285, n. 78, Burnley to Russell, September 26, 1864.

34. Jones, *A Rebel War Clerk's Diary*, p. 433, October 4, 1864.

35. Hill, *A British Subject's Recollections*, p. 40.

36. Francis W. Dawson, *Reminiscences of Confederate Service, 1861–1865*, ed. Bell I. Wiley (Baton Rouge, La., 1980), p. 125.

37. Ibid., pp. 201–2, Dawson to mother, October 13, 1864.

38. W. C. Ford, *A Cycle of Adams Letters, 1861–1865*, 2 vols. (Boston, 1920), vol. 2, pp. 194–96, September 18, 1864. Charles Francis Adams, Jr., was vastly overstating the condition of the 5th Massachusetts Colored Cavalry, an elite black regiment that included Charles Douglass, the son of the abolition campaigner Frederick Douglass; and Joshua Laurence, father of the poet Paul Laurence Dunbar, whose work was set to music by Samuel Coleridge-Taylor.

39. Ernest Duvergier de Hauranne, *Eight Months in America: Letters and Travel Notes*, 2 vols. (Chicago, 1974), vol. 1, p. 32, June 20, 1864.

40. A. S. Lewis (ed.), *My Dear Parents* (New York, 1982), p. 107, Horrocks to parents, November 19, 1864.

41. James McPherson (ed.), *Atlas of the Civil War* (Philadelphia, 2005), p. 190.

42. Gary W. Gallagher (ed.), *The Shenandoah Valley Campaign of 1864* (Chapel Hill, N.C., 2006), p. 212.

43. Quoted in Horace Greeley, *The American Conflict: A History of the Great Rebellion*, 2 vols. (London, 1867), vol. 2, p. 611.

Chapter 34: "War Is Cruelty"

1. *The Private Journal of Georgiana Gholson Walker*, ed. Dwight Franklin Henderson, Confederate Centennial Studies, 25 (Tuscaloosa, Ala., 1963), p. 113, October 11, 1864.

2. William Tidwell lists five separate Confederate "cells" operating in Canada: in Toronto, under Jacob Thompson; in Hamilton, under Cassius F. Lee; in St. Catherine's, under Clement Clay; in Windsor, under Steele; and in Montreal, under Patrick Charles Martin and George N. Sanders. *April '65: Confederate Covert Action in the American Civil War* (Kent, Ohio, 1995), p. 135.

3. John W. Headley, *Confederate Operations in Canada and New York* (New York, 1906), p. 265.

4. Mabel Clare Weaks, "Colonel George St. Leger Grenfell," *Filson Club History Quarterly*, 34 (1960), p. 12, Grenfell to Mary, October 11, 1864. Stephen Z. Starr says it is only speculation that Grenfell was Hines's deputy, although well-founded speculation. *Colonel Grenfell's Wars* (Baton Rouge, La., 1971), p. 183.

5. Stephen Starr writes, "There is unfortunately no way of discovering what thoughts passed through his mind as he sat quietly in his hotel room in the dreary hours of a November night." Ibid., p. 203.

6. Duke University, Malet family MSS, Sheffield to Malet, November 11, 1864.

7. PRO 30/22/38, f.120, Lyons to Russell, October 28, 1864.

8. Bulloch's successful manipulation of the legal system made it appear as though there was a vast conspiracy by the British to help the Confederacy. Dudley reported to Seward on November 15 that the owners of the *Laurel* and the *Sea King* were British. They both sailed under the British flag and the

sailors were British. "The armament, shot, shell, guns, powder, and everything down to the coal in the hold are English, all the produce and manufacture of Great Britain. Even the bounty money paid for enlisting the men was English sovereigns and the wages English coin, pounds, shillings and pence. It seems to me that nothing is wanting to stamp this as an English transaction from beginning to end. . . ." NARA M. 141, roll t-29, d. 386.

9. ORN, ser. 2, vol. 2, p. 731, Bulloch to Whittle, October 6, 1864.

10. Tom Chaffin, *Sea of Gray* (New York, 2006), pp. 58–64.

11. Chester G. Hearn, *Gray Raiders of the Sea: How Eight Confederate Warships Destroyed the Union's High Seas Commerce* (Camden, Me., 1992), p. 152. The American merchant marine had shipped over 5 million tons before the war. The latest statistics point to a decline of 4 million tons.

12. The ship and her crew had been continuously at sea since sneaking out of Brest on February 10, 1864. Yet the flight from the U.S. flag meant that in eight months the *Florida* had only managed to capture thirteen prizes. Short of coal, and worried that his bored crew might mutiny unless given their shore leave, Captain Charles Morris (Maffitt's replacement) had sailed into Bahia, Brazil, where he was pounced upon by the waiting USS *Wachusett*.

13. ORN, ser. 2, vol. 2, p. 736, Bulloch to Stephen Mallory, October 20, 1864. R. I. Lester, *Confederate Finance and Purchasing in Great Britain* (Charlottesville, Va., 1975), pp. 190–91.

14. Virginia Historical Society, Raphael Semmes MSS, MSS1Se535a/53–65, Maury to Tremlett, October 23, 1864.

15. Virginia Mason, *The Public Life and Diplomatic Correspondence of James M. Mason* (New York, 1906), p. 514.

16. John Bennett, "The Confederate Bazaar at Liverpool," *Crossfire: The Magazine of the American Civil War Round Table,* 61 (Dec. 1999).

17. David Hepburn Milton, *Lincoln's Spymaster: Thomas Haines Dudley and the Liverpool Network* (Mechanicsburg, Pa., 2003), p. 121.

18. Sarah Agnes Wallace and Frances Elma Gillespie (eds.), *The Journal of Benjamin Moran, 1857–1865,* 2 vols. (Chicago, 1948, 1949), vol. 2, pp. 1346–47, November 7–8, 1864.

19. Sheffield Archives, WHM 460a/47, Spence to Wharncliffe, November 2, 1864. C. Vann Woodward, *Mary Chesnut's Civil War* (New Haven, 1981), p. 664, Varina Davis to Mary Chesnut, October 8, 1864. The source for the quotation in the first footnote on this page is Sheffield WHM 460a/46, Spence to Wharncliffe, October 31, 1864.

20. Sheffield, WHM 460a/51, Wharncliffe to Adams, November 9, 1864.

21. Library of Congress, Hotze Papers, private letterbook, Hotze to Gregg, October 8, 1864. The journal was moving from its two rooms in Bouverie Street to more spacious premises at 291 Strand, and Hotze could not afford any decrease in the circulation. Yet he must have seen the increasing references in the press to the South as a slave state. On the same day as his reproof to Gregg, a writer in the *Dumfries Standard* declared that he hoped "the day is not far distant when a deep sense of shame shall be felt in this country for even the partial and temporary sympathy manifested for the pro-slavery States of

America." Loraine Peters, "The Impact of the American Civil War on the Local Communities of Scotland," *Civil War History*, 49 (2003).

22. The *Index* was printing 2,250 copies a week—an impressive circulation considering that John Bright's *Morning Star* circulation was only 5,000.

23. Angus Hawkins, *The Forgotten Prime Minister*, vol. 2 (Oxford, 2008), p. 291.

24. SRO, Somerset MSS, d/RA/A/2a/40/13, Palmerston to Duke of Somerset, September 6, 1864.

25. Scott Thomas Cairns, "Lord Lyons and Anglo-American Diplomacy During the American Civil War," Ph.D thesis, London School of Economics, 2004, p. 348, Palmerston to de Grey, September 11, 1864.

26. Somerset RO, Somerset MSS, d/RA/A/2a/40/16, Palmerston to Duke of Somerset, November 30, 1864.

27. MHS, Adams MSS, Diary of Charles Francis Adams, November 21, 1864. While writing about his fears of a Democratic victory, he revealed an ugly prejudice against the Democratic financier Augustus Belmont, whom he slated as "the German Jew agent of the foreign stockbrokers, the Rothschilds."

28. Russell thought he was giving more than they deserved when he wrote: "Of the causes of the rupture Her Majesty's Government have never presumed to judge. . . . Such a Neutrality Her Majesty has faithfully maintained and will continue to maintain." *A Compilation of the Messages and Papers of the Confederacy, Including the Diplomatic Correspondence, 1861–1865*, 2 vols. (Nashville, 1905), vol. 2, p. 687, Russell to Commissioners, November 25, 1864.

29. E. D. Adams, *Great Britain and the American Civil War*, 2 vols. in 1 (New York, 1958), vol. 2, p. 243. Slidell visited the French Foreign Ministry, thinking that the foreign minister wished to discuss the manifesto. Instead, he received an official complaint regarding the forced enlistment of French subjects into the Confederate army. The minister refused to show any interest in the capture of CSS *Florida* in neutral waters, or in any other U.S. infringements dangled before him by Slidell.

30. Ernest Samuels (ed.), *Henry Adams: Selected Letters* (Cambridge, Mass., 1985), p. 71, Adams to Charles Francis Adams, Jr., November 25, 1864.

31. Wallace and Gillespie (eds.), *The Journal of Benjamin Moran*, vol. 2, p. 1354, December 1, 1864, and November 30, 1864.

32. W. C. Ford (ed.), *A Cycle of Adams Letters, 1861–1865*, 2 vols. (Boston, 1920), vol. 2, p. 223, Charles Francis Adams, Jr., to Henry Adams, November 14, 1864.

33. The system for exchanging prisoners had worked according to a strict hierarchy: 1 general = 46 privates; 1 major general = 40 privates; 1 brigadier general = 20 privates; 1 colonel = 15 privates; 1 lieutenant colonel = 10 privates; 1 major = 8 privates; 1 captain = 6 privates; 1 lieutenant = 4 privates; 1 noncommissioned officer = 2 privates.

34. William Elsey Connelley, *A Standard History of Kansas and Kansans*, 5 vols. (New York, 1918), vol. 5, p. 2473.

35. James Pendlebury MSS, private collection.

36. Arnold Haultain (ed.), *Reminiscences by Goldwin Smith* (New York, 1910), p. 336.

37. Goldwin Smith wrote, for example: "Does the Bible Sanction American Slavery?" (1863), as well as his "Letter to a Whig Member of the Southern Independence Association" (1864).

38. Haultain (ed.), *Reminiscences by Goldwin Smith*, p. 353.

39. Robin Winks, *Canada and the United States: The Civil War Years* (Lanham, Md., 1988), p. 305.

40. Michael Burlingame, *Abraham Lincoln*, 2 vols. (New York, 2008), vol. 2, p. 740.

41. *PFRA*, 2/2 (1864), p. 760, Seward to Lyons, November 3, 1864.

42. Frederick W. Seward (ed.), *Seward at Washington* (New York, 1891), p. 250.

43. William Cooper, *Jefferson Davis, American* (New York, 2000), p. 539.

44. Bell I. Wiley, *Confederate Women* (New York, 1975), p. 109.

45. John B. Jones, *A Rebel War Clerk's Diary at the Confederate States Capital*, ed. Earl Schenck Miers (Urbane, Ill., 1958), p. 447, November 9, 1864.

46. A. S. Lewis (ed.), *My Dear Parents* (New York, 1982), p. 108.

47. Francis W. Dawson, *Reminiscences of Confederate Service, 1861–1865*, ed. Bell I. Wiley (Baton Rouge, La., 1980), p. 204, Dawson to mother, November 25, 1864.

48. Ibid., pp. 132–33.

49. Jones, *A Rebel War Clerk's Diary*, p. 456, December 5, 1864.

50. Dawson, *Reminiscences,* p. 205, Dawson to mother, November 25, 1864.

51. Mark Grimsley, *The Hard Hand of War* (Cambridge, 1995), p. 188. In popular myth, thousands of families were driven out into the desolate countryside at the point of the bayonet. In reality, 1,644 people, including 860 children, were put on trains to nearby towns.

52. Archibald McCowan, "Five Months in a Rebel Prison, 1 October 1864 to 1 March 1865," *Victorian Periodical Review* (1993).

Chapter 35: "The British Mark on Every Battle-field"

1. Oscar A. Kinchen, *Confederate Operations in Canada* (Hanover, Mass., 1970), p. 117.

2. ORN, ser. 1, vol. 3, p. 718, Thompson to Benjamin, December 3, 1864.

3. Frederick Job Shepard, *The Johnson's Island Plot: An Historical Narrative of the Conspiracy of the Confederates . . .* , ed. Frank H. Severance (Buffalo, 1906; repr. Ithaca, N.Y., 2007), p. 45.

4. John W. Headley, *Confederate Operations in Canada and New York* (New York, 1906), p. 271.

5. Ibid., p. 272.

6. *New York Times*, November 26, 1864.

7. Edward O. Cunningham, "In Violation of the Laws of War," *Journal of the Louisiana Historical Association*, 18/2 (Spring 1977), pp. 189–201.

8. *New York Times*, November 27, 1864.

9. George Templeton Strong, *Diary of the Civil War, 1860–1865*, ed. Allan Nevins (New York, 1962), p. 522, November 29, 1864.

10. *Papers Relating to Foreign Affairs*, 2 (1864), p. 370, Seward to Lyons, December 4, 1864.

11. Joseph Burnley, the new legation secretary, complained that once Lyons fell ill it became next to impossible to get him to write his letters. An unofficial count by Lord Lyons's biographer revealed a grand total of 8,236 letters writ-

ten by Lyons since 1861. It was no wonder that he could not face another dispatch.

12. *Papers Relating to Foreign Affairs*, 1 (1864), p. 370, Seward to Adams, December 5, 1864.

13. PRO FO881/1334, p. 72, Monck to Burnley, December 14, 1864.

14. Headley, *Confederate Operations*, p. 309.

15. W. C. Ford (ed.), *A Cycle of Adams Letters, 1861–1865*, 2 vols. (Boston, 1920), vol. 2, p. 238, Charles Francis Adams, Jr., to Henry Adams, December 25, 1864.

16. Sumner's bill to forbid segregation on Washington's streetcars died in the House through lack of support.

17. "Letters of Goldwin Smith to Eliot Norton," *Proceedings of the Massachusetts Historical Society*, 49 (1916), p. 115, Goldwin Smith to Norton, December 29, 1864.

18. Kinchen, *Confederate Operations in Canada*, p. 177; ORN, ser. 1, vol. 3, p. 930, Thompson to Benjamin, December 3, 1864.

19. William Tidwell, James Hall, and David Winfred Gaddy, *Come Retribution: The Confederate Secret Service and the Assassination of Lincoln* (Ann Arbor, Mich., 1988), p. 203.

20. Cleburne concluded: "It is said slavery is all we are fighting for, and if we give it up we give up all. Even if this were true, which we deny, slavery is not all our enemies are fighting for. It is merely the pretense to establish sectional superiority and a more centralized form of government, and to deprive us of our rights and liberties. We have now briefly proposed a plan which we believe will save our country. It may be imperfect, but in all human probability it would give us our independence. . . . Negroes will require much training; training will require time, and there is danger that this concession to common sense may come too late." OR, ser. 1, vol. 52/2, p. 592, Cleburne to Johnston, January 2, 1864.

21. OR, ser. 1, vol. 39/3, p. 162, Sherman to Grant, October 9, 1864; OR, ser. 1, vol. 39/3, p. 377, Sherman to Thomas, October 20, 1864.

22. Frank E. Vandiver (ed.), *The Civil War Diary of General Josiah Gorgas* (Tuscaloosa, Ala., 1947), p. 157, December 20, 1864.

23. Thomas Taylor, *Running the Blockade* (Annapolis, Md., repr. 1995), p. 140.

24. *The Times,* February 7, 1865.

25. Taylor, *Running the Blockade*, p. 141.

26. John B. Jones, *A Rebel War Clerk's Diary at the Confederate States Capital*, ed. Earl Schenck Miers (Urbane, Ill., 1958), p. 467, December 27, 1864.

27. ORN, ser 2, vol. 3, pp. 1253–56, Benjamin to Mason and Slidell, December 27, 1864.

28. Craig A. Bauer, "The Last Effort: The Secret Mission of the Confederate Diplomat, Duncan F. Kenner," *Louisiana History*, 22 (1981).

29. *The Times*, March 8, 1865.

30. South Carolina Historical Society, Feilden-Smythe MSS, Feilden to Julia Feilden, December 21, 1865.

31. "It does seem strange," he wrote on January 4, 1865, in a letter to William Porcher Miles, the chairman of the House Military Affairs Committee. He had served three different generals and been recommended for promotion on three separate occasions, without success. "I expect I know more of the locali-

ties and the organization of the troops than any other AA general in the office." NARA, Feilden military records, Feilden to Porcher Miles, January 4, 1865.

32. South Carolina Historical Society, Feilden-Smythe MSS, Feilden to Julia Feilden, January 5, 1865.

33. James Ford Rhodes, "Who Burned Columbia?," *Proceedings of the Massachusetts Historical Society*, 35 (1901), p. 268.

34. South Carolina Historical Society, Feilden-Smythe MSS, Feilden to Julia Feilden, January 5, 1865.

35. The Hon. Maurice Berkeley Portman, third son of Viscount Portman, and an old friend of Lord Wharncliffe's, had recently arrived from Canada to serve under General Wade Hampton. He told Wharncliffe that the wife of one acquaintance had allegedly been bayoneted to the wall and her house set on fire, another had been "violated," and a third stripped and forced to dance for the soldiers. Sheffield Archives, WHM 461 (18), identified by the author as Maurice B. Portman, January 10, 1865. Portman's judgment of the situation was utterly absurd. Despite having witnessed the first battle for Fort Fisher, and visited Lee's headquarters in Petersburg, he still wrote as though the South was going to win.

36. Jones, *A Rebel War Clerk's Diary*, p. 485, January 23, 1865.

37. Bauer, "The Last Effort," p. 80.

38. National Archives of Canada, Burley, Extradition MSS, Sec. C-1, RG 13, vol. 987, Robert Harrison to John Macdonald, February 4, 1865.

39. Stephen Z. Starr, *Colonel Grenfell's Wars* (Baton Rouge, La., 1971), p. 210.

40. See ibid., p. 212, and PRO FO, 5/1155, on the Grenfell correspondence.

41. Starr, *Colonel Grenfell's Wars*, p. 212.

42. Buckinghamshire, D11/1/3.c, memorandum by Joseph Wheeler.

43. *Diary of Gideon Welles*, 3 vols. (Boston, 1911), vol. 2, p. 229, January 21, 1865. The source for the footnote is OR, ser. 1, vol. 46, 3, p. 38, Grant to Seward, March 19, 1864.

44. "Bright-Sumner Letters," *Proceedings of the Massachusetts Historical Society*, 46 (1913), p. 132, Bright to Sumner, January 26, 1865.

45. Bauer, "The Last Effort," p. 86.

Chapter 36: "Richmond Tomorrow"

1. West Sussex RO, Lyons MSS, box 299, Malet to Lyons, February 24, 1865.

2. PRO 30/22/38, Lyons to Russell, December 27, 1864.

3. Arthur Irwin Dasent, *John Thadeus Delane, Editor of "The Times,"* 2 vols. (London, 1908), vol. 2, p. 135, Delane to Dasent, December 25, 1864; p. 136, Delane to Dasent, December 26, 1864.

4. Sheffield, WHM461/6, Spence to Wharncliffe, January 5, 1865.

5. The controversy rescued the year-old London branch from its torpid existence. New York Public Library, U.S. Sanitary Commission MSS, Box 339/120, C.S.P. Bowles to E. C. Fisher, January 2, 1865.

6. W. C. Ford (ed.), *A Cycle of Adams Letters, 1861–1865,* 2 vols. (Boston, 1920), vol. 2, p. 244, Charles Francis Adams, Jr., to Abigail Adams, January 8, 1865.

7. A recent traveler to America suggested to Wharncliffe that they donate the money to the U.S. Sanitary Commission. "I witnessed there on many and

various occasions the untiring efforts of this Commission who took care of the sick, wounded and PRISONERS on each side," the correspondent asserted. Sheffield Archives, WHM461/15, Bower Wood to Wharncliffe, January 3, 1865. The sources for the quotations in the footnote are Sheffield Archives, WHM461/16, PC Joseph Taylor to Wharncliffe, January 5, 1865, and Sheffield Archives, WHM461/24, Captain Hampson, late 13th Louisiana Regiment, to Wharncliffe, January 17, 1865.

8. Timothy Holmes (ed.), *David Livingstone: Letters and Documents, 1861–1872* (London, 1990), p. 102, Livingstone to James Young, January 4, 1865.

9. NARA RG94/skm/414, Smelt to Lincoln, March 17, 1865. Smelt stated that he had written twelve months previously to get his son discharged on grounds of youth and inability; "I have today a letter from him, he having been exchanged [from a Confederate prison] and is now at Annapolis—He was wounded in 3 places . . . and lay for two days uncared for on the field of battle, yet singular to relate—lives!" (see also Chapter 28, n. 29).

10. Sheffield Archives, WHM461/23, Spence to Wharncliffe, January 16, 1865.

11. Not even the knowledge that every dispatch since July 1863 had been lost or captured diminished Bulloch's belief that seapower could save the South. ORN, ser. 2, vol. 2, p. 787, Bulloch to Mallory, December 24, 1864.

12. Ibid., Bulloch to Low, January 8, 1865.

13. "If you approve this suggestion, you will please give me the earliest possible intimation of your views," he wrote to Mallory. ORN, ser. 1, vol. 3, p. 722, Bulloch to Mallory, January 10, 1865.

14. Library of Congress, Hotze MSS, private letterbook, Hotze to Bulloch, January 25, 1865.

15. Two British officers were allowed on board. They were amazed that such a large ship could be managed by so small a crew. The governor of Australia was perplexed by the *Shenandoah*'s arrival and unsure whether to apply the usual belligerent rules or act on his own initiative. He decided to be safe and ordered her departure after recoaling and carrying out emergency repairs.

16. "Diary of John R. Thompson," *Confederate Veteran*, 37 (1929), p. 99, January 27, 1865.

17. Sheffield Archives, WHM461/25, Collie to Wharncliffe, January 23, 1864.

18. ORN, ser. 1, vol. 3, p. 736, Bulloch to Mallory, February 11, 1865.

19. ORN, ser. 2, vol. 3, p. 1260, Mason to Benjamin, c. February 1865.

20. *Economist*, February 5, 1865.

21. Stephen Wise, *Lifeline of the Confederacy: Blockade Running During the Civil War* (Columbia, S.C., 1988), p. 266, and David Surdam, *Northern Naval Superiority and the Economics of the American Blockade* (Columbia, S.C., 2001), p. 87.

22. Lance Davis and Stanley L. Engerman, *Naval Blockades in Peace and War* (Cambridge, 2006), p. 154.

23. See, e.g., Surdam, *Northern Naval Supremacy*, pp. 207–9.

24. Sarah Agnes Wallace and Frances Elma Gillespie (eds.), *The Journal of Benjamin Moran 1857–1865*, 2 vols. (Chicago, Ill., 1948, 1949), vol. 2, pp. 1371, 1373, 1382, February 1, 1865, February 6, 1865, and February 23, 1865.

25. ORN, ser. 2, vol. 3, p. 1260, Mason to Benjamin, c. February 1865.

26. *PRFA*, part 1 (1866), p. 131, Adams to Seward, February 9, 1865.

27. MHS, Adams MSS, Diary of Charles Francis Adams, December 28, 1864.

28. G. P. Gooch (ed.), *The Later Correspondence of Lord John Russell, 1840–1878*, 2 vols. (London, 1925), vol. 2, p. 336, February 7, 1865. As late as January 15, Palmerston was still arguing with the Duke of Somerset that Quebec, Montreal, Halifax, and Bermuda must all be fortified. "The warnings of eventual hostility on the part of the United States are not to be disregarded, and the Irish Fenians in North America would give us trouble in Ireland if we had war with America."

29. Kenneth Bourne, *Britain and the Balance of Power* (Berkeley, 1967), p. 271. The source for the footnote is Somerset RO, Somerset MSS, d/RA/A/2a/270/13, Donald McKay to Rear Admiral Robinson, February 14, 1864.

30. Dean Mahin, *One War at a Time* (Dulles, Va., 1999), p. 226.

31. Scott Thomas Cairns, "Lord Lyons and Anglo-American Diplomacy During the American Civil War," Ph.D. thesis, London School of Economics, 2004, p. 362, Journal of Queen Victoria, March 10, 1865.

32. *PRFA*, part 1 (1866), pp. 69–71, Adams to Seward, December 30, 1864.

33. Ibid., p.176, Russell to Mason, Slidell, and Mann, February 13, 1865. Brian Jenkins, *Britain and the War for the Union*, 2 vols. (Montreal, 1974, 1980), vol. 2, p. 366. The Queen thought it was somewhat undignified to ask for Seward's help in delivering the letter. But Russell replied that if the only reason against sending the letter was "because we do not like to be thought afraid," he was prepared to suffer that consequence "for the humanity of the country."

34. MHS, Adams MSS, Diary of Charles Francis Adams, February 14, 1865, and *PRFA*, part 1 (1866), p. 165, Adams to Seward, February 16, 1865.

35. Ibid., p.183, Adams to Seward, February 23, 1865.

36. The situation in France also worried Adams after hearing in confidence from General McClellan's former military adviser the Prince de Joinville that the emperor was building a large fleet at Cherbourg which he would be prepared to employ on behalf of the Confederates if Seward showed the slightest inclination to meddle in Mexico.

37. Fitzgerald Ross, *Cities and Camps of the Confederate States*, ed. Richard Barksdale Harwell (Champaign, Ill., 1997), p. xix, Ross to Blackwood, March 24, 1865.

38. Library of Congress digital online MSS, Lincoln MS, Belle Boyd to Lincoln, January 24, 1864. Sala had a robust view of sex and extramarital relations and Belle was not in a position to dictate their relationship. Sala's contribution to the development of Victorian pornography is well documented, not least his co-authorship of the underground magazine the *Pearl*. After helping Belle, Sala became the ghostwriter for Lieutenant Colonel Heros von Borcke, Jeb Stuart's staff officer, who published his memoir in 1866.

39. See Louis A. Sigaud, *Belle Boyd—Confederate Spy* (Richmond, Va., 1944), pp. 185–87. Sigaud ponders the various rumors and half-truths concerning Hardinge and Grace.

40. "We all agree, however," wrote Slidell, "that the letter of the Secretary for Foreign Affairs is extremely insolent and offensive." ORN, ser. 2, vol. 3, p. 1263, Slidell to Benjamin, February 24, 1864. Shortly after Kenner's arrival in France, another emissary arrived: the French volunteer in the Confederate army Prince Camille de Polignac, who reached Paris on March 21, 1865, hoping to persuade the emperor that giving aid to the Confederacy would be ben-

eficial to his long-term plans for Mexico. "When I left the country on what I expected to be a six month's absence, I was unaware of the hopeless conditions of the affairs in the east," he wrote subsequently. Jeff Kinaird, *Lafayette of the South* (College Station, Tex., 2001), p. 184.

41. "The rumors lately prevalent coming from the South . . . [have] attracted much attention in England," Mason wrote to Benjamin. "Many enquiries have been made of me by our well-wishers whether I thought it would be done. It is considered by them with much favor as a measure . . . whilst in their opinion it would be a first step toward emancipation." Mason reassured Benjamin that he had disabused them of the idea. ORN, ser. 2, vol. 3, p. 1258, Mason to Benjamin, January 21, 1865.

42. Robert W. Young, *Senator James Murray Mason* (Knoxville, Tenn., 1998), p. 180.

43. Craig A. Bauer, "The Last Effort: The Secret Mission of the Confederate Diplomat, Duncan F. Kenner," *Louisiana History*, 22 (1981), pp. 67–95.

44. *A Compilation of the Messages and Papers of the Confederacy*, 2 vols. (Nashville, 1905), vol. 2, p. 717, Mason to Benjamin, March 26, 1865.

45. "Diary of John R. Thompson," p. 99.

46. Wallace and Gillespie (eds.), *Journal of Benjamin Moran*, vol. 2, p. 1393, March 14, 1865.

47. Sheffield Archives, WHM 461 (31), Hill to Wharncliffe, February 17, 1865.

48. PRO FO5/128, Hill to Russell, February 18, 1865.

49. PRO FO 83/2223, Roundell Palmer to Russell, March 18, 1865.

50. PRO FO5/1101, ff. 23–25, Robert Dalglish to Mr. Layard, February 24, 1865.

51. PRO FO 5/1101, ff. 53–56, Robert Burley to Russell, March 25, 1865.

52. *Lord Lyons: A Record of British Diplomacy*, 2 vols. (London, 1914), vol. 1, pp. 139–41.

53. PRO FO5/1009, d. 112, Russell to Bruce, March 24, 1865.

54. PRO FO5/1009, d. 112, Lord Russell to Sir Frederick Bruce, March 24, 1865.

55. Wallace and Gillespie (eds.), *The Journal of Benjamin Moran*, vol. 2, p. 1398, March 24, 1865.

56. Ford (ed.), *A Cycle of Adams Letters*, vol. 2, p. 258, Charles Francis Adams to Charles Francis Adams, Jr., March 24, 1865.

57. Ibid., p. 259, Charles Francis Adams to Charles Francis Adams, Jr., March 24, 1865.

Chapter 37: Fire, Fire

1. South Carolina Historical Society, Feilden-Smythe MSS (41), Feilden to Julia, February 14, 1865.

2. E. Milby Burton, *The Siege of Charleston* (Columbia, S.C., 1982), p. 321.

3. Walker defended himself to the Foreign Office: "I have endeavoured, as I had done previously, to perform my consular duties with the utmost strictness and impartiality." PRO FO5/1015, f. 287, Pinckney Walker to Mr. Burnley, February 20, 1865.

4. South Carolina Historical Society, Feilden-Smythe MSS (40), Feilden to Julia, February 28, 1865.

5. Nathaniel Cheairs Hughes, Jr., *Bentonville: The Final Battle of Sherman and Johnston* (Chapel Hill, N.C., 2006), p. 32.

6. Nelson D. Lankford, *An Irishman in Dixie* (Columbia, S.C., 1988), p. 25.

7. Ibid., p. 32, March 4, 1865.

8. Ibid., p. 39, March 9, 1865.

9. Ibid., p. 42, March 10, 1865. Mrs. Brown, according to Lankford, was one of the couriers who carried messages between Richmond and the Confederates in Canada.

10. Ibid., p. 48, March 13, 1865.

11. John B. Jones, *A Rebel War Clerk's Diary at the Confederate States Capital*, ed. Earl Schenk Miers (Urbana, Ill., 1958), p. 517, March 14, 1865.

12. Conolly whiled away the time before dinner visiting other camps. At General Heath's, he was surprised to meet Captain Sydney Herbert Davis, the British volunteer who had come to the Confederacy in 1863.

13. At his hotel, Conolly bumped into the Hon. Maurice Berkeley Portman, whose own optimism about the war had been shaken by an encounter with Sheridan's bummers.

14. Jones, *A Rebel War Clerk's Diary*, p. 520, March 19, 1865.

15. South Carolina Historical Society, Feilden-Smythe MSS (45), Feilden to Julia, March 13, 1865.

16. Ibid., (46), Feilden to Julia, March 25, 1865.

17. The Saundersons of Saunderson Castle, County Cavan, were an old Anglo-Irish family with a large fortune to spend. Twenty-four-year-old Welly was the youngest of five brothers, three of whom belonged to the same regiment. "The trio were not without notoriety and were generally known as Rats No. 1, No. 2 and No. 3," wrote a historian of the family: "They were always doing something dangerous." Conolly was deeply impressed when Welly told him that he had even sold his commission in order to fight with Lee, unaware that the British Army officer had something to prove. Welly was desperately in love with Lady Rachel Clonmell, but her father thought he was a wastrel and had refused him permission to set foot in the house, let alone propose marriage. A. Lucas, *Colonel Saunderson: A Memoir* (London, 1908), p. 14. I am indebted to Derek Mayhew for this information.

18. James M. Morgan, *Recollections of a Rebel Reefer* (Boston, 1917), p. 232.

19. Southern Historical Society Papers, vol. 4 (Richmond, Va., 1877), ed. Revd. J. W. Jones, p. 22, fn.

20. Virginia Historical Society, Diary of Llewellyn Saunderson, MSS5:1Sa877:1, March 31, 1865.

21. Francis Dawson, *Reminiscences of Confederate Service 1861–1865,* ed. Bell I. Wiley (Baton Rouge, La., 1980) pp. 142–43.

22. Virginia Historical Society, Diary of Llewellyn Saunderson, April 1, 1865.

23. *The Times*, April 25, 1865.

24. Jones, *A Rebel War Clerk's Diary*, p. 528, April 2, 1865.

25. *The Times,* April 25, 1865.

26. Edward M. Boykin, *The Falling Flag: Evacuation of Richmond* (New York, 1874), pp. 12–13.

27. Sallie A. Brock, *Richmond During the War: Four Years of Personal Recollections* (repr. Lincoln, Nebr., 1996), p. 367.

28. W. C. Ford (ed.), *A Cycle of Adams Letters* (Boston, 1920), vol. 2, p. 263, Charles Francis Adams, Jr., to Charles Francis Adams, April 10, 1865.

29. Lincoln and Grant had some memorable conversations during the president's stay on the *River Queen*. Grant asked Lincoln about the *Trent* affair. Lincoln answered, "Yes, Seward studied up all the works ever written on international law, and came to cabinet meetings loaded to the muzzle with the subject. We gave due consideration to the case, but at that critical period of the war it was soon decided to deliver up the prisoners. It was a pretty bitter pill to swallow, but I contented myself with believing that England's triumph in the matter would be short-lived, and that after ending our war successfully we would be so powerful that we could call her to account for all the embarrassment she had inflicted upon us." Doris Kearns Goodwin, *Team of Rivals* (New York, 2005), p. 711.

30. A. S. Lewis (ed.), *My Dear Parents* (New York, 1982), p. 131, Horrocks to brother Joseph, April 8, 1865.

Chapter 38: "A True-Born King of Men"

1. *Illustrated London News*, May 20, 1865.
2. Michael Burlingame, *Abraham Lincoln*, 2 vols. (Baltimore, 2008), vol. 2, p. 793.
3. John Hay and John G. Nicolay (eds.), *Abraham Lincoln: Complete Works*, 2 vols. (New York, 1922), vol. 2, p. 669, Lincoln to Grant, April 6, 1865.
4. Ulysses S. Grant, *Personal Memoirs of Ulysses S. Grant* (New York, 2003), p. 593.
5. *The Times*, April 25, 1865.
6. Brian Holden Reid, *Robert E. Lee* (London, 2005), p. 237.
7. Virginia Historical Society, Diary of Llewellyn Saunderson, MSS5:1Sa877:1, April 6, 1865.
8. PRO FO115/448, f. 402, Henry O'Brien to Sir Frederick Bruce, June 14, 1865.
9. Francis Lawley, "The Last Six Days of Secessia," *Fortnightly Review*, 2 (June 1865), pp. 1–10, at p. 7.
10. General Fitz Lee had taken a liking to Welly—because he behaved "admirably under fire" and "was bold, bright, and witty of course." Fitzhugh Lee, *General Lee* (New York, 1925), p. 387.
11. Burke Davis, *To Appomattox: Nine April Days, 1865* (New York, 1959), p. 282.
12. Virginia Historical Society, Diary of Llewellyn Saunderson, April 8, 1865.
13. James Ford Rhodes, *History of the Civil War, 1861–1865* (New York, 1917), p. 434.
14. Frederick Maurice (ed.), *An Aide de Camp of Robert E. Lee* (New York, 1927), p. 273.
15. Grant, *Memoirs*, p. 629.
16. Lawley, "The Last Six Days of Secessia," p. 9.
17. Jay Winik, *April 1865* (New York, 2001), p. 197.
18. Duke University, Francis Dawson MSS, no. 27, Dawson to mother, April 7, 1865; Francis W. Dawson, *Reminiscences of Confederate Service, 1861–1865*, ed. Bell I. Wiley (Baton Rouge, La., 1980), p. 146.
19. South Carolina Historical Society, Feilden-Smythe MSS, 47, Feilden to Julia, April 6, 1865.
20. With the exception of Judah Benjamin, no one thought that this was even a remote possibility.

21. Frederick W. Seward (ed.), *Seward at Washington* (New York, 1891), p. 270.

22. Charles A. Dana, *Recollections of the Civil War* (New York, 1913), p. 274.

23. *Diary of Gideon Welles*, 3 vols. (Boston, 1911), vol. 2, p. 284, April 14, 1865.

24. Burlingame, *Abraham Lincoln*, vol. 2, p. 806.

25. Ibid., p. 814.

26. Seward, ed., *Seward at Washington*, p. 278.

27. I am indebted to Derek Mayhew for supplying me with this information about his ancestor. Source for the footnote is *Southern Historical Society Papers*, vol. 4 (Richmond, Va., 1877), ed. Rev. J. W. Jones, p. 22. Conolly's return to Ireland was reported in the *Donegal Advertiser*, which noted acidly: "Here again, we have him impressing upon the Donegal electors how much better it was for him to go to America than to stay like ordinary members and attend to the dull routine of his parliamentary duties." NARA, Dispatches, U.S. Consuls in Sheffield, Consul Abbot to Seward, May 15, 1865.

28. South Carolina Historical Society, Feilden-Smythe MSS, 48, Feilden to Julia, May 4, 1865.

29. Keith Robbins, *John Bright* (London, 1978), p. 175.

30. MHS, Adams MSS, Diary of Charles Francis Adams, April 26, 1865.

31. Alan Hankinson, *Man of Wars: William Howard Russell of "The Times,"* *1820–1907* (London, 1982), p. 182.

32. George S. Wykoff, "Charles Mackay: England's Forgotten Civil War Correspondent," *South Atlantic Quarterly*, 26 (1927), pp. 59–60.

33. *Economist*, April 29, 1865.

34. Oscar Maurer, "Punch on Slavery and the Civil War," *Victorian Studies* (Sept. 1957), pp. 4–28.

35. Sarah Agnes Wallace and Frances Elma Gillespie (eds.), *The Journal of Benjamin Moran, 1857–1865*, 2 vols. (Chicago, 1948, 1949), vol. 2, p. 1419, April 30, 1865.

36. NARA, M.T-185, roll 8, vol. 8, Consul Zebina Eastman to Mr. Hunter, Acting Secretary of State, May 8, 1865; Liverpool RO, Durning-Holt MSS, Diary of Emma Holt, 902 Dur 1/4, May 8, 1865.

37. Virginia Mason, *The Public Life and Diplomatic Correspondence of James M. Mason* (New York, 1906), p. 562.

38. Library of Congress, Mason MSS, private letterbook, Mason to Wood, April 21, 1865.

39. Louis Martin Sears, "A Confederate Diplomat at the Court of Napoleon III," *American Historical Review*, 26, 2 (Jan. 1921), p. 278, Slidell to Mason, April 26, 1865.

40. Robert Underwood Johnson and Clarence Clough Buel (eds.), *Battles and Leaders of the Civil War*, 4 vols. (Secaucus, N.J., 1985), vol. 3, p. 764.

41. James M. Morgan, *Recollections of a Rebel Reefer* (Boston, 1917), p. 238.

42. Frank E. Vandiver (ed.), *The Civil War Diary of General Josiah Gorgas* (Tuscaloosa, Ala., 1947), p. 184, May 4, 1864.

43. The money was taken from Davis when he was captured. A typical rate on the Inman line between New York and London was £5 per adult.

44. ORN, ser. 1, vol. 16, p. 333, report of Commander Reynolds, May 16, 1865.

45. James J. Barnes and Patricia P. Barnes (eds.), *The American Civil War Through British Eyes,* vol. 3 (Kent, Ohio, 2005), p. 302, Bruce to Russell, May 16, 1865.

46. William Watson, *The Adventures of a Blockade Runner* (College Station, Tex., 2001), p. 823.

47. Margaret Leach, *Reveille in Washington* (Alexandria, Va., 1962, repr. 1980), p. 379.

48. News and letters were trickling in from the South. Consul Arthur Lynn was finally rescued from his Crusoe-like existence in Galveston. He had continued to send his dispatches, never knowing if they had reached their destination. Miraculously, a few did eventually arrive. The Foreign Office, on the other hand, had written him off as lost until further notice more than a year earlier. Lynn now learned that his sister had been trying to contact him for the past eighteen months with questions arising from their late father's estate. PRO FO5/976, draft, Foreign Office to Messrs. Brown and Dunlop, Glasgow, Solicitors, January 4, 1865.

49. Edward Waldo Emerson, *The Early Years of the Saturday Club* (New York, 1918), p. 405.

50. PRO 30/22/38, ff. 186–89, Bruce to Russell, April 20, 1865.

51. PRO 30/22/38, ff. 198–99, Bruce to Russell, April 27, 1865.

52. James J. Barnes and Patience P. Barnes (eds.), *Private and Confidential: Letters from British Ministers to the Foreign Secretaries* (Selinsgrove, Pa., 1993), p. 362, Bruce to Russell, May 22, 1865.

53. South Carolina Historical Society, Feilden-Smythe MSS (49), Feilden to Julia, May 30, 1865.

54. Columbia University, Blackwell MSS, Elizabeth Blackwell to Barbara Bodichon, May 25, 1865.

Epilogue

1. The second largest army, the Prussian, was roughly half the size at 484,000; the French had about 343,000; and the British Army no more than 220,000 regulars plus 370,000 volunteer and militia soldiers.

2. Allan Nevins, *The War for the Union,* 4 vols., vol. 4: *The Organized War to Victory, 1864–1865* (New York, 1971), pp. 367–68.

3. Craig L. Symonds and William J. Clipson, *The Naval Institute Historical Atlas of the U.S. Navy* (Annapolis, Md., 1995), p. 105.

4. The reopening of communications with the South meant release for the many families in Britain held fast in the agony of limbo. Joseph Burnley received definite proof of Frederick Farr's death. He also began fresh inquiries about Robert Livingstone and Stephen Smelt, the Manchester boy who had run away with his best friend in 1863. Nothing was forthcoming with regards to Robert; Livingstone had been so optimistic that he had visited the American legation on March 11 to make sure Charles Francis Adams had not forgotten his son. But there was positive news in Stephen's case. Burnley learned that the boy had been wounded at the Battle of Olustee and captured by the Confederates. The Federal authorities thought he was still alive. Mr. Smelt, Stephen's father, learned that his son had been found but was not coming

home after all. Stephen had discovered a taste for army life. "I have the honor to state that I have no desire to leave the U.S. service as I wish to serve out my term of enlistment and become a citizen of the U.S. since I joined from a Prisoner of War my health was never better, as the surgeon's certificate will show." NARA, Stephen Smelt, in camp in Raleigh, N.C., July 9, 1865, to Lieutenant J. O'Connel, Adjutant, 47th New York State Volunteers. I am grateful to Mike Musick for bringing these letters to my attention.

5. Drew Gilpin Faust, *This Republic of Suffering* (Cambridge, Mass., 2008), pp. 211–13.

6. Colonel Currie had married an American woman in 1864, Harriet Caroll Jackson, a granddaughter of one of the signers of the Declaration of Independence. After the war he became a special agent for the Post Office, overseeing the delivery of diplomatic mail en route between San Francisco and Hong Kong. On his retirement, the couple moved to Britain to live on the Isle of Wight.

7. A. S. Lewis (ed.), *My Dear Parents* (New York, 1982), pp. 159, 169.

8. *Isle of Man Examiner*, October 2, 1897.

9. The total cost of the war could have bought the freedom of every slave, given each one 40 acres and a mule, and provided a bounty for a hundred years of lost earnings. See E. B. Long with Barbara Long, *The Civil War Day by Day: An Almanac, 1861–1865* (New York, 1971; repr. New York, 1985), appendix.

10. Frances Leigh, *Ten Years on a Gerogia Plantation Since the War* (London, 1883), pp. 52–53.

11. The consular records show that there were 352 British residents still living in Charleston in May 1865. Some of them were blockade runners who had no means of getting home.

12. South Carolina Historical Society, Feilden-Smythe MSS, Trevor-Battye MSS, n.d.

13. Robert Summers, *The Fall and Redemption of Dr. Samuel A. Mudd* (n.p., 2008), p. 56.

14. Sir Frederick Bruce was relieved that the amnesty included the discharge of all military prisoners still awaiting trial. But there was a catch for foreign prisoners of war. Henry O'Brien sent a plaintive letter to the legation, asking for help because he did not want to swear allegiance to the United States, since "by doing so I expatriate myself. . . . I am aware that I did wrong in joining a foreign army without Her Majesty's Licences and consequently have born humiliation and insult without any hope of redress, but now as the war is over and all the prisoners of war being released and as I only ask to be allowed to leave the U.S., I hope you will at least obtain for me some decision by the Washington Military Authorities." PRO FO115/448, f. 402, Henry O'Brien to legation, June 14, 1865.

15. Lonnie A. Burnett, *Henry Hotze, Confederate Propagandist* (Tuscaloosa, Ala., 2008), p. 30.

16. *New York Times*, June 26, 1878.

17. James T. Hubbell and James Geary (eds.), *Biographical Dictionary of the Union* (Westport, Conn., 1995), p. 360.

18. Jay Luvaas, *The Military Legacy of the Civil War* (Lawrence, Kans., 1988), p. 122.

19. *Letters of Queen Victoria*, ed. George E. Buckle, 3 vols. (London, 1930–32), vol. 1, p. 594, Lord Clarendon to Queen Victoria, May 1, 1869.

20. Bancroft was so gratuitously rude about Lord Palmerston, who had been dead for less than four months, that an official protest was lodged by the Foreign Office with the American legation: "Lincoln took to heart the eternal truths of liberty . . . Palmerston did nothing that will endure; Lincoln finished a work which all time cannot overthrow. . . . Palmerston . . . was attended by the British aristocracy to his grave, which, after a few years, will hardly be noticed. . . . Lincoln [will] . . . be remembered through all time by his countrymen, and by all the peoples of the world."

21. MHS, Argyll Letters, p. 86, Duchess of Argyll to Charles Sumner, July 4, 1865.

22. The easiest route to winning Seward's trust was to behave toward him as if he were still the most powerful politician in Washington. "He is vain," wrote the British minister, Frederick Bruce, on May 2; "to show deference to his judgment . . . is a species of subtle flattery which is not without weight." James J. Barnes and Patience P. Barnes (eds.), *Private and Confidential: Letters from British Ministers to the Foreign Secretaries* (Selinsgrove, Pa., 1993), p. 378.

23. *PRFA*, I (1868), p. 83, Charles Francis Adams to Seward, May 2, 1867.

24. The Dominion of Canada was a semiautonomous state under the sovereignty of the Crown. In theory, its parliament was answerable to the Imperial Parliament in London, but in practice the Canadians were left to govern their internal affairs, though not their external relationships with foreign countries, including America.

25. MHS, Adams MSS, Diary of Charles Francis Adams, April 25, 1867.

26. *Correspondence Concerning Claims Against Great Britain,* vol. 3 (Washington, 1869), p. 674, Seward to Adams, May 2, 1867.

27. Wendell Phillips Garrison and Francis Jackson Garrison, *William Lloyd Garrison, 1805–1879: The Story of His Life,* 4 vols. (New York, 1889), vol. 4, pp. 205–9.

28. Lord Russell, quoted in ibid., p. 210.

29. *Correspondence Concerning Claims Against Great Britain*, vol. 3, p. 683, Seward to Adams, November 16, 1867.

30. *Letters of Henry Adams*, ed. Jacob Clavner Levenson (Cambridge, Mass., 1988), vol. 1, p. 498, Henry Adams to Charles Francis Adams, Jr., July 14, 1865. He remained the same stiff and isolated figure who had arrived in 1861. "I am continually puzzled to know how we get along together," complained his son Henry. "I find the Chief rather harder, less a creature of our time than ever. It pains me absolutely . . . to see him so separate from the human race. I crave for what is new. . . . He cares nothing for it, and a new discovery in physics or in chemistry, or a new development in geology never seems to touch any chord in him."

31. Martin Duberman, *Charles Francis Adams* (New York, 1961), pp. 330–31.

32. Frederick W. Seward (ed.), *Seward at Washington* (New York, 1891), p. 538.

33. Henry Adams, *The Education of Henry Adams,* ed. Ernest Samuels (repr. Boston, 1973), p. 246.

34. New York *Nation*, 3 (1866), p. 234.

35. Calculations based on http://www.measuringworth.com.

36. Doris Kearns Goodwin, *Team of Rivals* (New York, 2005), p. 711.

37. Maureen Robson, "The *Alabama* Claims and the Anglo-American Reconciliation," *Canadian Historical Review*, 42/1 (1961), p. 22.

38. Baxter, "June Meeting: The British High Commissioners at Washington in 1871," p. 350.

39. Mary Sophia Hill, *A British Subject's Recollections of the Confederacy* (Baltimore, 1975), p. 66.

40. Richard Shannon, *Gladstone: Heroic Minister, 1865–1898* (London, 1999), p. 114.

41. *Bruce Herald*, March 28, 1873.

42. Ulysses S. Grant, *Personal Memoirs of Ulysses S. Grant* (New York, 2003), p. 640.

43. William Michael Rossetti, "English Opinion on the American War," *Atlantic Monthly*, 17 (Feb. 1866), p. 129.

44. Ella Lonn's magisterial studies of foreign volunteers (published between 1940 and 1951) shed much-needed light on their numbers, but placing the volunteers alongside the other aspects of Britain's role in the war was outside the scope of her work.

45. An essential reading list for the Civil War and Anglo-American diplomacy would include: Ephraim D. Adams, H. C. Allen, Richard J. M. Blackett, Kinley Brauer, Duncan Andrew Campbell, Adrian Cook, D. P. Crook, Hugh Dubrulle, Norman B. Ferris, Charles M. Hubbard, Brian Jenkins, Howard Jones, Dean B. Mahin, Robert E. May, Frank Merli, Philip Myers, Frank Owsley, Jay Sexton, Warren F. Spencer, Brian Holden Reid, Philip Van Doren Stern, and Robin Winks.

46. Gladstone, for example, later blamed his support for the South on his inability to see the issue in its entirety: "That my opinion was founded upon a false estimate of the facts was the very least part of my fault. I did not perceive the gross impropriety of such an utterance from a cabinet minister, of a power allied in blood and language, and bound to loyal neutrality; the case being further exaggerated by the fact that we already, so to speak, under indictment before the world for not (as was alleged) having strictly enforced the laws of neutrality in the matter of the cruiser. My offence . . . illustrates vividly . . . an incapacity of viewing subjects all round, in their extraneous as well as in their internal properties." John Morley, *The Life of William Ewart Gladstone, 1809–1872*, 2 vols. (London, 1908), vol. 2, p. 82.

47. Rossetti, "English Opinion on the American War," p. 149.

Glossary

adjutant—A staff officer assigned to handle administrative duties for a commanding officer.

battery—A Union artillery battery had six cannons with more than one hundred men, Confederate batteries usually had four; a position where cannons were mounted.

blockade runner—A swift vessel used by the Confederates to evade the Federal naval blockade of Southern ports; the captain of a blockade runner.

bombproof—A shelter from artillery attack, often built with timber and packed earth.

bounty—A cash bonus paid to entice men into the army.

breastwork—A chest-high barricade built to shield defenders from enemy fire.

canister—A tin can containing twenty-seven iron balls packed in sawdust; when fired from a cannon, the can ripped open and showered the balls at the enemy.

contraband—A term popularized by General Benjamin Butler in 1861 for fugitive slaves who crossed into Northern territory.

corduroy road—A road constructed with logs, often in otherwise impassable muddy areas.

crimping—The forced enlistment of soldiers or sailors by trickery or coercion.

division—A force of approximately 12,000 soldiers in three or four brigades. A brigade generally consisted of four to six regiments. A regiment was composed of about a thousand officers and men divided into ten companies.

drill—Formal training received by a recruit, including how to march in formation.

gunboat—A vessel designed to carry one or more guns, usually used in shallow water or on rivers.

hardtack—A flour-and-water wafer, usually three inches square; cheap and durable, it was a staple of military campaigns.

housewife—A sewing kit that also contained toiletries and personal items.

howitzer—A short-barreled artillery piece designed to propel projectiles at relatively high trajectories.

ironclad—A warship clad with iron or steel plates to protect it from explosive or incendiary shells.

mess—A group of soldiers who cooked and ate together; the place where food was prepared and eaten.

minié ball—A conical bullet whose hollow base expanded when fired, forcing its sides into the rifling and making it spin, assuring greater accuracy.

monitor—A class of Federal ironclad warships with revolving gun turrets, named after the design of USS *Monitor,* launched in 1862.

mortar—Heavy artillery designed to fire projectiles, usually balls, with a high angle of fire into enemy positions. Mostly used in siege, garrison, and coastal warfare.

musket—A muzzle-loading shoulder gun with a long barrel.

parole—The pledge of a soldier released from captivity not to take up arms until formally exchanged for an enemy POW of equal rank.

Parrott gun—A muzzle-loading rifled artillery weapon patented by West Point graduate and former U.S. Army officer Robert Parrott in 1861.

percussion cap—A small copper cylinder containing shock-sensitive explosive; the cap was placed over the hollow metal "nipple" at the rear of a gun barrel. Pulling the trigger released the hammer, which struck and ignited the cap. The flame passed through the nipple to ignite the main powder charge. Caps enabled muzzle-loading guns to fire reliably in any weather.

picket—Soldiers on guard to protect a larger military unit from enemy attack.

pontoon bridge—A portable bridge supported by floating pontoons.

provost guard—Soldiers acting as military police under the authority of a provost marshal.

quartermaster—An officer in charge of procuring food, equipment, and clothing for troops.

ram—A ship built with an iron prow designed to pierce and sink enemy vessels.

rifle pit—A shallow trench dug to protect soldiers from enemy fire while shooting weapons.

round shot—A solid spherical projectile fired from artillery; also called *solid shot* or *cannonball.*

shrapnel—A hollow cast-iron projectile filled with metal balls packed around an explosive charge, designed to explode in midair, showering the enemy with smaller projectiles.

smoothbore—A firearm or cannon with an unrifled barrel.

solid shot—A solid projectile with no explosive, designed to be used against cavalry, buildings, or troops in a column.

Springfield rifle—An American-made rifle, the most prevalent in the war. The second most popular was the Enfield, which was manufactured in England and exported by the hundreds of thousands. Both were single-shot muzzle-loading rifles with an accuracy that was excellent at 300 yards and passable at 500. Compared to the maximum range of 200 yards for a Napoleonic-era rifle, Civil War rifles were killing machines.

sutler—A merchant licensed to sell provisions to troops in an army camp or on the field.

torpedo—A stationary underwater mine that exploded upon contact with a ship. Some torpedoes could be detonated electronically from the shore.

Zouaves—Northern or Confederate regiments that modeled themselves on the original elite North African corps in the French army, distinguished by their colorful uniforms.

Index

Page numbers in *italics* refer to illustrations and maps.

British-American relations (*cont'd*):
provoke war between the North and
Britain, 650–51, 698–99; Confederate
violation of British neutrality in
Canada, 595, 650–51, 698–702, 711,
716–19, 721, 740–41; cotton and, 64,
68–69, 78–79, 85, 92, 140, 149, 161–62,
199, 218, 273–74, 277–78, 327–28,
411–12; debate on Civil War, 279–80;
effect of Bull Run on British
sympathies, 139–41; and the
emergence of Prussia, 793; Europe
and, *see* Europe and the Civil War;
expulsion of British Consuls from
Confederacy, 547; following
Lincoln's assassination, 773–77;
growing British support for the
North (1863), 393–97; Hartington
and, 458; imperative to stay out of
America's troubles, 61–62, 89, 91–92,
324–25; *see also* recognition of the
South; Jacob Thompson's mission to
create a crisis in, 596–97; Johnson-
Clarendon Treaty, 801; language
divide, 26; *Leicester Guardian* on
British emotional response to war,
836n38; letters of marque, 375; Lord
Russell and, 91–94; Mason and, 525;
mediation, *see* mediation; Milne and,
546–47; Morrill Tariff and, 68, 164;
Northern hostility to Britain, 27–28,
115–16, 118, 152, 276–77, 308, 721–22,
745–46, 796–97; Palmerston's caution
concerning British officers in the
field, 257; the Peace Address, 673–74;
post-*Alabama* claims settlement,
805–6; preparations for military
threat from America, 707, 740,
908n28; under President Grant, 801,
805; under President Johnson, 781,
794, 800; *see also Alabama* claims
controversy; and Prince of Wales'
visit to America (1860), 54–57, 59–60,
819n41; prospect of war, 180–97; and
the rams, 518–23, 525–28; recognition
issue, *see* recognition of the South;
revolution in spring 1865 in British

attitudes, 744–45, 746; "roar of the
British Lion," 180–89, 208; Roebuck,
284, 458, 460, 463, 465, 466, 491–94;
Rossetti's claims on the Civil War
and, 805; secession and the anti-
slavery cause, 281–82; Seward and
Anglo-American relations, 40–46,
58–59, 66, 69–70, 77, 99, 102–4,
158–61, 163–64, 187, 330, 375–76, 465,
511, 547, 586–87, 721, 740, 745–46,
804, 840n47, 844n19; *see also Alabama*
claims controversy; ship building and
the American question, 406–9;
slavery and, 27, 69, 92, 93–94, 140,
214–15, 219n, 239, 281–82, 294–95,
462, 726; Southern propaganda and,
215–16, 274–75, 460–61, 500–501, 596,
734–35, 864–55n58; Southern
questioning of England's sympathies,
208; Southern rage against Britain,
208; Southern resentment towards
Britain, 557; Southern support swing
following Jackson's death, 458–63;
Sumner's Cooper Union speech
against Britain, 522–24; treatment of
British residents in the South, 549;
and the *Trent* affair, 172–74, 175–98,
201, 276, 842n72, 843n7; and
Trollope's *Domestic Manners of the
Americans,* 28–29, 148–49; troops sent
to America and Canada, 184–86, 189,
200–201; and the War of 1812, 19–20,
178; Weed and, 276; William Russell's
intervention thoughts in *The Times*
(1861), 835–36n33; and the "Woman
Order," 272

British and Foreign Anti-Slavery
Society, 221, 397
British army, 913n1
British Columbia, 51
British Friend, 47
British Guard, 250, 850n20
British Jackson Monumental Fund, 458
British legation, Washington, 3, 7, 12,
600, 639, 852n57; appointment of
Bruce to replace Lyons, 745–46;
Ministers, *see* Bruce, Sir Frederick;

PHOTO: BIBI BASCH

AMANDA FOREMAN is a Visiting Research Fellow at Queen Mary, University of London. She won the Whitbread Prize for *Georgiana: Duchess of Devonshire,* which was adapted for the screen as *The Duchess.* Educated as an undergraduate at Sarah Lawrence College and with master's and doctorate degrees in history from Oxford University, she is now married with five children and lives in New York.